REFORMED
DOGMATICS

Herman Bavinck (1854–1921)
Graphite Sketch by Erik G. Lubbers

REFORMED DOGMATICS

VOLUME 2: GOD AND CREATION

HERMAN BAVINCK

JOHN BOLT, GENERAL EDITOR
JOHN VRIEND, TRANSLATOR

B

Baker Academic

Grand Rapids, Michigan

© 2004 by the Dutch Reformed Translation Society
P.O. Box 7083, Grand Rapids, MI 49510

Published by Baker Academic
a division of Baker Publishing Group
P.O. Box 6287, Grand Rapids, MI 49516-6287
www.bakeracademic.com

Fourth printing, November 2009

Printed in the United States of America

Library of Congress Cataloging-in-Publication Data
Bavinck, Herman, 1854–1921.
    [Gereformeerde dogmatiek. English]
    Reformed dogmatics / Herman Bavinck ; John Bolt, general editor ; John Vriend, translator.
        p.   cm.
    Contents: v. 1. Prolegomena ; v. 2. God and creation
    Includes bibliographical references and indexes.
    ISBN 0-8010-2632-6 (cloth : v. 1)
    ISBN 0-8010-2655-5 (cloth ; v. 2)
    1. Christelijke Gereformeerde Kerk (Netherlands)—Doctrines. 2. Reformed Church—Doctrines. 3. Theology, Doctrinal. I. Bolt, John, 1947– II. Vriend, John, d. 2002. III. Title.
BX9474.3.B38 2003
230′.42—dc21   2003001037

To the Memory of
M. Eugene Osterhaven
1915–2004

CONTENTS

Dutch Reformed Translation Society

"The Heritage of the Ages for Today"
P.O. Box 7083
Grand Rapids, MI 49510

Board of Directors

Rev. Dr. Joel Beeke
president and professor of systematic theology and homiletics
Puritan Reformed Theological Seminary
Grand Rapids, Michigan

Rev. Dr. Gerald M. Bilkes
pastor, Free Reformed Church
Grand Rapids, Michigan

Dr. John Bolt
professor of systematic theology
Calvin Theological Seminary
Grand Rapids, Michigan

Dr. Arthur F. De Boer
retired surgeon
Grand Haven, Michigan

Dr. James A. De Jong
president and professor of historical theology, emeritus
Calvin Theological Seminary
Grand Rapids, Michigan

Rev. David Engelsma
professor of theology
Protestant Reformed Seminary
Grandville, Michigan

Dr. I. John Hesselink
Albertus C. Van Raalte Professor of Systematic Theology, emeritus
Western Theological Seminary
Holland, Michigan

James R. Kinney
director of Baker Academic
Baker Publishing Group
Grand Rapids, Michigan

Dr. Nelson Kloosterman
professor of ethics and New Testament studies
Mid-America Reformed Seminary
Dyer, Indiana

Dr. Richard A. Muller
P. J. Zondervan Professor of Doctoral Studies
Calvin Theological Seminary
Grand Rapids, Michigan

Dr. Adriaan Neele
professor and academic dean
Institut Farel
Dorval, Quebec

† Dr. M. Eugene Osterhaven
Albertus C. Van Raalte Professor of Systematic Theology, emeritus
Western Theological Seminary
Holland, Michigan

Henry I. Witte
president, Witte Travel
consul of the government of the Netherlands
Grand Rapids, Michigan

† Deceased

PREFACE

The Dutch Reformed Translation Society (DRTS) was formed in 1994 by a group of businesspeople and professionals, pastors, and seminary professors, representing six different Reformed denominations, to sponsor the translation and facilitate the publication in English of classic Reformed theological and religious literature published in the Dutch language. It is incorporated as a nonprofit corporation in the State of Michigan and governed by a board of directors.

Believing that the Dutch Reformed tradition has many valuable works that deserve wider distribution than the limited accessibility the Dutch language allows, society members seek to spread and strengthen the Reformed faith. The first project of the DRTS is the definitive translation of Herman Bavinck's complete four-volume *Gereformeerde Dogmatiek* (*Reformed Dogmatics*). The society invites those who share its commitment to, and vision for, spreading the Reformed faith to write for additional information.

EDITOR'S
INTRODUCTION

With the publication of this second full volume of Herman Bavinck's *Reformed Dogmatics*, the Dutch Reformed Translation Society has completed half of its decade-long project to publish the complete English translation from Dutch of Bavinck's classic four-volume work. In addition to the first volume on Prolegomena, published a year ago, two half-volume works, one on the eschatology section[1] and the other on the creation section,[2] have been published. In chapters 8–14 this present volume contains the entirety of the creation volume (from *Gereformeerde Dogmatiek,* vol. 2, part 5, §§33–39 [##250–306], "Over de Wereld in haar Oorspronkelijke Staat" [Concerning the World in Its Original State]). The first seven chapters are a new translation of part 4, §§23–32 [##161–249], "God," from *Gereformeerde Dogmatiek,* volume 2. This material had been available in an English translation by William Hendriksen.[3] Hendriksen's translation provided helpful outlines and summaries but did not include any footnotes or bibliographic material. The present edition contains all the footnotes, has been rearranged with new headings and subheadings, and introduces each chapter with a précis prepared by the editor. For ease of reference, the subparagraph numbers used by Bavinck have been retained in this volume. Later in this introduction we will briefly consider the contemporary relevance of both the section on the doctrine of God and the section on creation, but first we provide a few words about the author of *Reformed Dogmatics.* Who was Herman Bavinck, and why is this work of theology so important?

1. Herman Bavinck, *The Last Things: Hope for This World and the Next,* ed. John Bolt and trans. John Vriend (Grand Rapids: Baker, 1996). This volume presented the second half of volume 4 of the *Gereformeerde Dogmatiek.*
    2. Herman Bavinck, *In the Beginning: Foundations of Creation Theology,* ed. John Bolt and trans. John Vriend (Grand Rapids: Baker, 1999). This volume presented the second half of volume 2 of the *Gereformeerde Dogmatiek.*
    3. Herman Bavinck, *The Doctrine of God,* trans. W. Hendriksen (Grand Rapids: Eerdmans, 1951; reprinted, Grand Rapids: Baker, 1979).

11

Herman Bavinck's *Gereformeerde Dogmatiek*, first published a century ago, represents the concluding high point of some four centuries of remarkably productive Dutch Reformed theological reflection. From Bavinck's numerous citations of key Dutch Reformed theologians such as Voetius, de Moor, Vitringa, van Mastricht, Witsius, and Walaeus as well as the important Leiden *Synopsis purioris theologiae*,[4] it is clear he knew that tradition well and claimed it as his own. At the same time Bavinck was not simply a chronicler of his own church's past teaching. He seriously engaged other theological traditions, notably the Roman Catholic and the modern liberal Protestant ones; effectively mined the church fathers and great medieval thinkers; and placed his own distinct neo-Calvinist stamp on the *Reformed Dogmatics*.

KAMPEN AND LEIDEN

To understand the distinct Bavinck flavor a brief historical orientation is necessary. Herman Bavinck was born on December 13, 1854. His father was an influential minister in the Dutch Christian Reformed Church (Christelijke Gereformeerde Kerk) that had seceded from the National Reformed Church in the Netherlands twenty years earlier.[5] The secession of 1834 was in the first place a protest against the state control of the Dutch Reformed Church; it also tapped into a long and rich tradition of ecclesiastical dissent on matters of doctrine, liturgy, and spirituality as well as polity. In particular, mention needs to be made here of the Dutch equivalent to English Puritanism, the so-called Second Reformation (*Nadere Reformatie*),[6] the influential seventeenth- and early-eighteenth-century movement of experiential Reformed theology and spirituality,[7] as well as an early-nineteenth-century international, aristocratic, evangelical revival movement known as the *Réveil*.[8] Bavinck's church, his fam-

4. The Leiden *Synopsis,* first published in 1625, is a large manual of Reformed doctrine as it was defined by the Synod of Dort. Well into the twentieth century it served as a standard reference textbook for the study of Reformed theology. (It is even cited by Karl Barth in his *Church Dogmatics.*) As an original-source reference work of classic Dutch Reformed theology, it is comparable to Heinrich Heppe's nineteenth-century, more broadly continental anthology *Reformed Dogmatics: Set Out and Illustrated from the Sources,* rev. and ed. Ernst Bizer, trans. G. T. Thomson (London: Allen & Unwin, 1950; reprinted, Grand Rapids: Baker, 1978). While serving as the minister of a Christian Reformed church in Franeker, Friesland, Bavinck edited the sixth and final edition of this handbook, which was published in 1881.

5. For a brief description of the background and character of the Secession church, see James D. Bratt, *Dutch Calvinism in Modern America* (Grand Rapids: Eerdmans, 1984), ch. 1: "Secession and Its Tangents."

6. See Joel R. Beeke, "The Dutch Second Reformation (*Nadere Reformatie*)," *Calvin Theological Journal* 28 (1993): 298–327.

7. The crowning theological achievement of the *Nadere Reformatie* is the devout and theologically rich work of Wilhelmus à Brakel, *Redelijke Godsdienst,* first published in 1700 and frequently thereafter (including twenty Dutch editions in the eighteenth century alone!). This work is now available in English translation (ET): *The Christian's Reasonable Service,* trans. Bartel Elshout, 4 vols. (Ligonier, Pa.: Soli Deo Gloria, 1992–95).

8. The standard work on the *Réveil* is M. Elizabeth Kluit, *Het Protestantse Réveil in Nederland en Daarbuiten, 1815–1865* (Amsterdam: Paris, 1970). Bratt also gives a brief summary in *Dutch Calvinism in Modern America,* 10–13.

ily, and his own spirituality were thus definitively shaped by strong patterns of deep pietistic Reformed spirituality. Though the earlier phases of Dutch pietism affirmed orthodox Reformed theology and were also nonseparatist in their ecclesiology, by the mid-nineteenth century the Seceder group had become significantly separatist and sectarian in outlook.[9]

The second major influence on Bavinck's thought comes from the period of his theological training at the University of Leiden. The Christian Reformed Church had its own theological seminary, the Kampen Theological School, established in 1854. Bavinck, after studying at Kampen for one year (1873–74), indicated his desire to study with the University of Leiden's theological faculty, renowned for its aggressively modernist, "scientific" approach to theology.[10] His church community, including his parents, was stunned by this decision, which Bavinck explained as a desire "to become acquainted with the modern theology firsthand" and to receive "a more scientific training than the Theological School is presently able to provide."[11] The Leiden experience gave rise to what Bavinck perceived as the tension in his life between his commitment to orthodox theology and spirituality and his desire to understand and appreciate what he could about the modern world, including its worldview and culture. A telling and poignant entry in his personal journal at the beginning of his study period at Leiden (September 23, 1874) indicates his concern about being faithful to the faith he had publicly professed in the Christian Reformed church of Zwolle in March of that same year: "Will I remain standing [in the faith]? God grant it."[12] Upon completion of his doctoral work at Leiden in 1880, Bavinck candidly acknowledged the spiritual impoverishment that Leiden had cost him: "Leiden has benefited me in many ways: I hope always to acknowledge that gratefully. But it has also greatly impoverished me, robbed me, not only of much ballast (for which I am happy), but also of much that I recently, especially when I preach, recognize as vital for my own spiritual life."[13]

9. Bavinck himself called attention to this in his Kampen rectoral oration of 1888, when he complained that the Seceder emigration to America was a spiritual withdrawal and abandonment of "the Fatherland as lost to unbelief" ("The Catholicity of Christianity and the Church," trans. John Bolt, *Calvin Theological Journal* 27 [1992]: 246). Recent historical scholarship, however, suggests that this note of separatism and cultural alienation must not be exaggerated. Though clearly a marginalized community in the Netherlands, the Seceders were not indifferent to educational, social, and political responsibilities. See John Bolt, "Nineteenth- and Twentieth-Century Dutch Reformed Church and Theology: A Review Article," *Calvin Theological Journal* 28 (1993): 434–42.

10. For an overview of the major schools of Dutch Reformed theology in the nineteenth century, see James Hutton MacKay, *Religious Thought in Holland during the Nineteenth Century* (London: Hodder & Stoughton, 1911). For more detailed discussion of the "modernist" school, see K. H. Roessingh, *De Moderne Theologie in Nederland: Hare Voorbereiding en Eerste Periode* (Groningen: Van der Kamp, 1915); Eldred C. Vanderlaan, *Protestant Modernism in Holland* (London and New York: Oxford University Press, 1924).

11. R. H. Bremmer, *Herman Bavinck en Zijn Tijdgenoten* (Kampen: Kok, 1966), 20; cf. V. Hepp, *Dr. Herman Bavinck* (Amsterdam: W. Ten Have, 1921), 30.

12. Bremmer, *Herman Bavinck en Zijn Tijdgenoten,* 19.

13. Hepp, *Dr. Herman Bavinck,* 84.

It is thus not unfair to characterize Bavinck as a man between two worlds. One of his contemporaries once described Bavinck as "a Secession preacher and a representative of modern culture," concluding: "That was a striking characteristic. In that duality is found Bavinck's significance. That duality is also a reflection of the tension—at times crisis—in Bavinck's life. In many respects it is a simple matter to be a preacher in the Secession Church, and, in a certain sense, it is also not that difficult to be a modern person. But in no way is it a simple matter to be the one as well as the other."[14] However, it is not necessary to rely only on the testimony of others. Bavinck clearly summarizes this tension in his own thought through an essay on the great nineteenth-century liberal Protestant theologian Albrecht Ritschl:

> Therefore, whereas salvation in Christ was formerly considered primarily a means to separate man from sin and the world, to prepare him for heavenly blessedness and to cause him to enjoy undisturbed fellowship with God there, Ritschl posits the very opposite relationship: the purpose of salvation is precisely to enable a person, once he is freed from the oppressive feeling of sin and lives in the awareness of being a child of God, to exercise his earthly vocation and fulfill his moral purpose in this world. The antithesis, therefore, is fairly sharp: on the one side, a Christian life that considers the highest goal, now and hereafter, to be the contemplation of God and fellowship with him, and for that reason (always being more or less hostile to the riches of an earthly life) is in danger of falling into monasticism and asceticism, pietism and mysticism; but on the side of Ritschl, a Christian life that considers its highest goal to be the kingdom of God, that is, the moral obligation of mankind, and for that reason (always being more or less adverse to the withdrawal into solitude and quiet communion with God), is in danger of degenerating into a cold Pelagianism and an unfeeling moralism. *Personally, I do not yet see any way of combining the two points of view, but I do know that there is much that is excellent in both, and that both contain undeniable truth.*[15]

A certain tension in Bavinck's thought between the claims of modernity—particularly its this-worldly, scientific orientation—and Reformed pietist orthodoxy's tendency to stand aloof from modern culture continues to play a role even in his mature theology expressed in the *Reformed Dogmatics*. In his

---

14. Cited by Jan Veenhof, *Revelatie en Inspiratie* (Amsterdam: Buijten & Schipperheijn, 1968), 108. The contemporary cited is the Reformed jurist A. Anema, who was a colleague of Bavinck at the Free University of Amsterdam. A similar assessment of Bavinck as a man between two poles is given by F. H. von Meyenfeldt, "Prof. Dr. Herman Bavinck: 1854–1954, 'Christus en de Cultuur,'" *Polemios* 9 (October 15, 1954); and G. W. Brillenburg-Wurth, "Bavincks Levenstrijd," *Gereformeerde Weekblad* 10.25 (December 17, 1954).

15. H. Bavinck, "De Theologie van Albrecht Ritschl," *Theologische Studiën* 6 (1888): 397; cited by Veenhof, *Revelatie en Inspiratie*, 346–47, emphasis added by Veenhof. Kenneth Kirk contends that this tension, which he characterizes as one between "rigorism" and "humanism," is a fundamental conflict in the history of Christian ethics from the outset. See K. Kirk, *The Vision of God* (London: Longmans, Green, 1931), 7–8.

eschatology Bavinck in a highly nuanced way still continues to speak favorably of certain emphases in a Ritschlian this-worldly perspective.[16]

In the section on the doctrine of creation in this volume (chs. 8–14) we see the tension repeatedly in Bavinck's relentless efforts to understand and, where he finds appropriate, to affirm, correct, or repudiate modern scientific claims in light of scriptural and Christian teaching.[17] Bavinck takes modern philosophy (Kant, Schelling, Hegel), Darwin, and the claims of geological and biological science seriously but never uncritically. His willingness as a theologian to engage modern thought and science seriously is a hallmark of his exemplary work. Though Bavinck's theological framework remains a valuable guide for contemporary readers, many of the specific scientific issues he addresses in this volume are dated by his late-nineteenth-century context. As Bavinck's own work illustrates so well, today's Reformed theologians and scientists learn from his example not by repristination but by fresh address to new and contemporary challenges.

GRACE AND NATURE

It is therefore too simple merely to characterize Bavinck as a man trapped between two apparently incommensurate tugs at his soul, that of other-worldly pietism and this-worldly modernism. His heart and mind sought a trinitarian synthesis of Christianity and culture, a Christian worldview that incorporated what was best and true in both pietism and modernism, while above all honoring the theological and confessional richness of the Reformed tradition dating from Calvin. After commenting on the breakdown of the great medieval synthesis and the need for contemporary Christians to acquiesce in that breakdown, Bavinck expressed his hope for a new and better synthesis: "In this situation, the hope is not unfounded that a synthesis is possible between Christianity and culture, however antagonistic they may presently stand over against each other. If God has truly come to us in Christ, and is, in this age too, the Preserver and Ruler of all things, such a synthesis is not only possible but also necessary and shall surely be effected in its own time."[18] Bavinck found the vehicle for such an attempted synthesis in the trinitarian worldview of Dutch neo-Calvinism and became, along with neo-Calvinism's visionary pioneer Abraham Kuyper,[19] one of its chief and most respected spokesmen as well as its premier theologian.

16. Herman Bavinck, *The Last Things*, 161 (*Reformed Dogmatics*, IV, #578). According to Bavinck, Ritschl's this-worldliness "stands for an important truth" over against what he calls the "abstract supernaturalism of the Greek Orthodox and Roman Catholic Church."

17. Herman Bavinck, *In the Beginning*, passim (*Reformed Dogmatics*, below, pp. 407–619 [##250–306]).

18. H. Bavinck, *Het Christendom*, Groote Godsdiensten 2.7 (Baarn: Hollandia, 1912), 60.

19. For a brief overview, see J. Bratt, *Dutch Calvinism in Modern America*, ch. 2: "Abraham Kuyper and Neo-Calvinism."

Unlike Bavinck, Abraham Kuyper grew up in the National Reformed Church of the Netherlands in a congenially moderate-modernist context. Kuyper's student years, also at Leiden, confirmed him in his modernist orientation until a series of experiences, especially during his years as a parish minister, brought about a dramatic conversion to Reformed, Calvinist orthodoxy.[20] From that time Kuyper became a vigorous opponent of the modern spirit in church and society[21]—which he characterized by the siren call of the French Revolution, "Ni Dieu! Ni maitre!"[22]—seeking every avenue to oppose it with an alternative worldview, or as he called it, the "life-system" of Calvinism:

> From the first, therefore, I have always said to myself, "If the battle is to be fought with honor and with a hope of victory, then principle must be arrayed against principle; then it must be felt that in Modernism the vast energy of an all-embracing life-system assails us, then also it must be understood that we have to take our stand in a life-system of equally comprehensive and far-reaching power. . . . When thus taken, I found and confessed and I still hold, that this manifestation of the Christian principle is given us in Calvinism. In Calvinism my heart has found rest. From Calvinism have I drawn the inspiration firmly and resolutely to take my stand in the thick of this great conflict of principles.["][23]

Kuyper's aggressive, this-worldly form of Calvinism was rooted in a trinitarian theological vision. The "dominating principle" of Calvinism, he contended, "was not soteriologically, justification by faith, but in the widest sense cosmologically, the Sovereignty of the Triune God over the whole Cosmos, in all its spheres and kingdoms, visible and invisible."[24]

For Kuyper, this fundamental principle of divine sovereignty led to four important derivatory and related doctrines or principles: common grace, antithesis, sphere sovereignty, and the distinction between the church as institute and the church as organism. The doctrine of common grace[25] is based on the

20. Kuyper chronicles these experiences in a revealing autobiographical work entitled *Confidentie* (Amsterdam: Höveker, 1873). A rich portrait of the young Abraham Kuyper is given by G. Puchinger, *Abraham Kuyper: De Jonge Kuyper (1837–1867)* (Franeker: T. Wever, 1987). See also the somewhat hagiographic biography by Frank Vandenberg, *Abraham Kuyper* (Grand Rapids: Eerdmans, 1960); and the more theologically and historically substantive one by Louis Praamsma, *Let Christ Be King: Reflection on the Times and Life of Abraham Kuyper* (Jordan Station, Ont.: Paideia, 1985). Brief accounts can also be found in Benjamin B. Warfield's introduction to A. Kuyper, *Encyclopedia of Sacred Theology: Its Principles*, trans. J. H. De Vries (New York: Charles Scribner's, 1898); and in the translator's biographical note in A. Kuyper, *To Be Near to God*, trans. J. H. De Vries (Grand Rapids: Eerdmans, 1925).

21. See especially his famous address, *Het Modernisme, een Fata Morgana op Christelijke Gebied* (Amsterdam: De Hoogh, 1871). On page 52 of this work he acknowledges that he, too, once dreamed the dreams of modernism. This important essay is now available in J. Bratt, ed., *Abraham Kuyper: A Centennial Reader* (Grand Rapids: Eerdmans, 1998), 87–124.

22. A. Kuyper, *Lectures on Calvinism* (Grand Rapids: Eerdmans, 1931), 10.

23. Ibid., 11–12.

24. Ibid., 79.

25. Kuyper's own position is developed in his *De Gemeene Gratie*, 3 vols. (Amsterdam and Pretoria: Höveker & Wormser, 1902). A thorough examination of Kuyper's views can be found in S. U. Zuidema,

conviction that prior to, and to a certain extent independent of, the particular sovereignty of divine grace in redemption, there is a universal divine sovereignty in creation and providence, restraining the effects of sin and bestowing general gifts on all people, thus making human society and culture possible even among the unredeemed. Cultural life is rooted in creation and common grace and thus has a life of its own apart from the church.

This same insight is expressed more directly via the notion of sphere sovereignty. Kuyper was opposed to all Anabaptist and ascetic Christian versions of world-flight but was also equally opposed to the medieval Roman Catholic synthesis of culture and church. The various spheres of human activity—family, education, business, science, art—do not derive their raison d'être and the shape of their life from redemption or from the church, but from the law of God the Creator. They are thus relatively autonomous—also from the interference of the state—and are directly responsible to God.[26] In this regard Kuyper clearly distinguished two different understandings of the church—the church as institute gathered around the Word and sacraments, and the church as organism diversely spread out in the manifold vocations of life. It is not explicitly as members of the institutional church but as members of the body of Christ, organized in Christian communal activity (schools, political parties, labor unions, institutions of mercy), that believers live out their earthly vocations. Though aggressively this-worldly, Kuyper was an avowed and articulate opponent of the *volkskerk* tradition, which tended to merge national sociocultural identity with that of a theocratic church ideal.[27]

To state this differently: Kuyper's emphasis on common grace—used polemically to motivate pious, orthodox Dutch Reformed Christians to Christian social, political, and cultural activity—must never be seen in isolation from his equally strong emphasis on its spiritual antithesis. The regenerating work of the Holy Spirit breaks humanity in two and creates, according to Kuyper, "two kinds of consciousness, that of the regenerate and the unregenerate; and these two cannot be identical." Furthermore, these "two kinds of people" will develop "two kinds of science." The conflict in the scientific enterprise is not

---

"Common Grace and Christian Action in Abraham Kuyper," in *Communication and Confrontation* (Toronto: Wedge, 1971), 52–105. Cf. J. Ridderbos, *De Theologische Cultuurbeschouwing van Abraham Kuyper* (Kampen: Kok, 1947). The doctrine of common grace has been much debated among conservative Dutch Reformed folk in the Netherlands and the United States, tragically leading to church divisions. For an overview of the doctrine in the Reformed tradition, see H. Kuiper, *Calvin on Common Grace* (Goes: Oostebaan & Le Cointre, 1928).

26. "In this independent character a special *higher authority* is of necessity involved and this highest authority we intentionally call *sovereignty in the individual social sphere*, in order that it may be sharply and decidedly expressed that these different developments of social life have *nothing above themselves but God*, and that the state cannot intrude here, and has nothing to command in their domain" (*Lectures on Calvinism*, 91).

27. On Kuyper's ecclesiology, see H. Zwaanstra, "Abraham Kuyper's Conception of the Church," *Calvin Theological Journal* 9 (1974): 149–81; on his attitude to the *volkskerk* tradition, see H. J. Langman, *Kuyper en de Volkskerk* (Kampen: Kok, 1950).

between science and faith but between "two scientific systems, . . . each having its own faith."[28]

Here in this trinitarian, world-affirming, but nonetheless resolutely anti-thetical Calvinism, Bavinck found the resources to bring some unity to his thought.[29] "The thoughtful person," he notes, "places the doctrine of the trinity in the very center of the full-orbed life of nature and mankind. . . . The mind of the Christian is not satisfied until every form of existence has been referred to the triune God and until the confession of the trinity has received the place of prominence in our thought and life."[30] Repeatedly in his writings Bavinck defines the essence of the Christian religion in a trinitarian, creation-affirming way. A typical formulation: "The essence of the Christian religion consists in this, that the creation of the Father, devastated by sin, is restored in the death of the Son of God, and re-created by the Holy Spirit into a kingdom of God."[31] Put more simply, the fundamental theme that shapes Bavinck's entire theology is the trinitarian idea that grace restores nature.[32]

The evidence for "grace restores nature" being the fundamental defining and shaping theme of Bavinck's theology is not hard to find. In an important address on common grace, given in 1888 at the Kampen Theological School, Bavinck sought to impress on his Christian Reformed audience the importance of Christian sociocultural activity. He appealed to the doctrine of creation, insisting that its diversity is not removed by redemption but cleansed. "Grace does not remain outside or above or beside nature but rather permeates and wholly renews it. And thus nature, reborn by grace, will be brought to its highest revelation. That situation will again return in which we serve God freely and happily, without compulsion or fear, simply out of love, and in harmony with our true nature. That is the genuine *religio naturalis*." In other words: "Christianity does not introduce a single substantial foreign element into the creation. It creates no new cosmos but rather makes the cosmos new. It restores what was corrupted by sin. It atones the guilty and cures what is sick; the wounded it heals."[33]

---

28. A. Kuyper, *Lectures on Calvinism*, 133; cf. *Encyclopedia of Sacred Theology*, 150–82. A helpful discussion of Kuyper's view of science is given by Del Ratzsch, "Abraham Kuyper's Philosophy of Science," *Calvin Theological Journal* 27 (1992): 277–303.

29. The relation between Bavinck and Kuyper, including differences as well as commonalities, is discussed in greater detail in John Bolt, "The Imitation of Christ Theme in the Cultural-Ethical Ideal of Herman Bavinck" (Ph.D. diss., University of St. Michael's College, Toronto, Ontario, 1982), especially ch. 3: "Herman Bavinck as a Neo-Calvinist Thinker."

30. H. Bavinck, *The Doctrine of God*, trans. W. Hendriksen (Grand Rapids: Eerdmans, 1951), 329; see below, pp. 329–34 (#231).

31. H. Bavinck, *Reformed Dogmatics*, I, 112 (#35).

32. This is the conclusion of Veenhof, *Revelatie en Inspiratie*, 346; and Eugene Heideman, *The Relation of Revelation and Reason in E. Brunner and H. Bavinck* (Assen: Van Gorcum, 1959), 191, 195. See Bavinck, *The Last Things*, 200 n. 4 (*Reformed Dogmatics*, IV, #572).

33. H. Bavinck, "Common Grace," trans. Raymond Van Leeuwen, *Calvin Theological Journal* 24 (1989): 59–60, 61.

CREATION: IN THE BEGINNING

The creation section of this volume (chs. 8–14) illustrates well these distinctive characteristics of Bavinck's thought. The fundamental theme that grace does not undo nature but restores and heals means that Bavinck's doctrine of creation must be a key starting place for understanding his theology. It is thus no surprise that Bavinck begins by telling us that the doctrine of creation is the starting point and distinguishing characteristic of true religion. Creation is the formulation of human dependence on a God who is distinct from the creature but who nonetheless in a loving, fatherly way preserves it. Creation is a distinct emphasis of the Reformed tradition according to Bavinck, a way of affirming that God's will is its origin and God's glory its goal. In the opening chapter Bavinck demonstrates his full awareness of ancient and contemporary alternatives to creation—of a popular as well as philosophical nature—and insists that it is through revelation alone that we can confidently repudiate emanationist and pantheist worldviews. What Bavinck says here sounds remarkably current and relevant for today's many forms of New Age spirituality.

Remarkably relevant too is Bavinck's careful, biblically circumspect discussion, in the ninth chapter, of angels and the spiritual world. Materialist denials of the spiritual world of angels and demons destroy religion itself, he contends, because religion depends on the supernatural, upon miracle and revelation. Bavinck's strong emphasis on this world as the theater of God's glory and thus on the importance of Christian cultural activity does not lead to the dualophobia of some later neo-Calvinists who stoutly resist all "dualism" (such as body/soul) in fear that they diminish and devalue the creational and material in favor of the spiritual.[34] Bavinck insists upon a clear distinction between the spiritual and the material world, though he also insists that they must never be separated in Christian thought.

Balance also characterizes Bavinck's treatment of origins and the relation between science and the Genesis accounts of creation. All religions, he notes, have "creation" stories, but the biblical account is strikingly different in its orientation: Theogonic myths have no place in the Genesis accounts, and the Bible simply assumes the existence of one God. Though Genesis does not give a precise scientific explanation of origins—the earth is the *spiritual* rather than the astronomical center of the universe—it is important, according to Bavinck, to insist on the historical rather than merely mythical or visionary character of its creation account. An original unity of the human race and its historical fall into sin are essential to the biblical narrative and worldview. Creation is thus more than just a debate about the age of the earth and the evolutionary origins of humanity, important as these questions are. The solidarity of the human race, original sin, the atonement in Christ, the universality of the kingdom of God, and our responsibility to love our neighbor—all are grounded in a key

---

34. For an example, offered in critique of this tendency, see John M. Frame, *The Doctrine of the Knowledge of God* (Phillipsburg, N.J.: Presbyterian & Reformed, 1987), 235–36.

dimension of the doctrine of creation, the unity of the human race created in God's own image. Creation thus is the presupposition of all religion and morality. It is especially in the fifth part of this volume, on the image of God, that Bavinck's characteristic understanding of the relation between nature and grace, discussed above, comes clearly into view.

That a present-day emphasis on creation does not imply a devaluation of the future life of eternal glory is clear from Bavinck's discussion of human destiny. The final state of glory for humanity, given in Christ, the Second Adam, is far greater than the original state of integrity of humanity. Here again, Bavinck displays no fear of "dualism" but insists that the original creation perfection was only a preparation for the final glory, where God will be all in all and impart his glory to his creatures. In the confidence of that hope the Christian believer trusts in the heavenly Father's care and preservation of his creation, a believing hope that provides unspeakable comfort and consolation in the midst of this vale of tears. Here the pastoral purpose of good creation theology becomes clear; our heavenly Father is Almighty God, the Creator of heaven and earth, who turns all things to our good.

THE CREATOR IS THE TRIUNE GOD

Bavinck's balanced doctrine of creation is self-consciously rooted in his trinitarian doctrine of God. He begins the chapter (8) on creation with the following direct linkage: "The realization of the counsel of God begins with creation. Creation is the initial act and foundation of all divine revelation and therefore the foundation of all religious and ethical life as well." A biblical doctrine of God sees his counsel or decree as the link that connects God and the world. As the first of God's external acts, creation is vitally important; subsequent acts of God must be seen in the light of creation. Thus, redemptive grace does not diminish or elevate or divinize creation but *restores* it. As the same time, as the expression of God's decree, creation is not necessary but is contingent and dependent on God. God is self-sufficient; he does not need creation, and thus the error of pantheism is avoided as well as that of Deism.

Creation out of nothing is the work of the triune God. Bavinck's understanding of creation is inseparable from his strongly trinitarian theology, and the doctrines of God and creation taken together provide a response to two important contemporary challenges to theism: emanationism and deistic secularism. The latter is the fruit of Enlightenment thought after Immanuel Kant and Isaac Newton, in which there is no room for God's immanence in the physical cosmos. The universe is seen as a well-oiled machine, a wound-up clock that runs on its own mechanism and immanent laws. In this scientific materialism God is made mundane, and an Arian view of Christ follows; he can only be a creature, a human who is extraordinary but most definitely not divine. Enlightenment rationality is cold comfort for flesh-and-blood people;

a nude physical universe, without spiritual clothing, cannot satisfy the longings of the human heart either in its joys or its sorrows.

As we begin the third millennium anno Domini, our Western world is awash with a new spirituality that is the exact opposite of the Enlightenment; the cosmos is once again regarded as enchanted.[35] Here the doctrine of creation ex nihilo and a contingent universe is replaced with a doctrine of emanation from the divine. Now the universe is deified; it is overflowing with divine "stuff." Jesus can now be considered divine, but so is everyone else; in fact, so is every*thing* else. By contrast, Christian theology posits a twofold communication in God—the generation (emanation) of the Son as an inner trinitarian reality, and the creation of the world ex nihilo. According to Bavinck, the reality of creation, even its very possibility, depends on God being triune. "Without generation, creation would not be possible. If, in an absolute sense, God could not communicate himself to the Son, he would be even less able, in a relative sense, to communicate himself to his creature. If God were not triune, creation would not be possible."[36]

A few more examples of Bavinck's contemporary relevance, also in relation to his doctrine of creation, can be found in the doctrine of God in the first half of this volume. In chapter 2 Bavinck's treatment of the cosmological and teleological arguments for the existence of God parallels recent discussions on evolution and "intelligent design."[37] The discussion of God's names (ch. 3) is a solid though indirect response to recent efforts by some feminist theologians to invoke feminine names for God. Bavinck argues convincingly that only God can name himself and that this naming is restricted by biblical revelation, which cannot be accommodated to fashionable currents of contemporary ideology and arbitrarily changed. Bavinck also provides clear, understandable biblical guidance on current discussions in theology about divine aseity, eternity, personality, and simplicity (in ch. 4). Bavinck strongly opposes all notions of divine temporality and mutability: "The idea of becoming predicated of the divine being is of no help whatever in theology."[38] To deny immutability is to "rob God of his divine nature and religion of its firm foundation and assured comfort."

The same concern about "religion's firm foundation" and "assured comfort" for believers also applies to Bavinck's treatment of God's omniscience, foreknowledge, middle knowledge (ch. 5), as well as the chapter (14) on providence. Those who have been confused by some of the claims of so-called open theism, which denies God's omniscience and foreknowledge of future contingent events, will find here solid biblical-theological analysis and sure-footed pastoral guidance.

---

35. See James A. Herrick, *The Making of the New Spirituality: The Eclipse of the Western Religious Tradition* (Downers Grove, Ill.: InterVarsity, 2003).

36. See below, p. 420 (#254) [= *In the Beginning*, p. 39].

37. For an overview of the debate and literature, see Thomas Woodward, *Doubts about Darwin: A History of Intelligent Design* (Grand Rapids: Baker, 2003).

38. See below, p. 158 (#193).

In sum, Bavinck's *Reformed Dogmatics,* of which this volume is a truly representative sample, is biblically and confessionally faithful, pastorally sensitive, challenging, and still relevant. Bavinck's life and thought reflect a serious effort to be pious, orthodox, and thoroughly contemporary. To pietists fearful of the modern world, on the one hand, and to critics of orthodoxy skeptical about its continuing relevance, on the other, Bavinck's example suggests a model answer: an engaging trinitarian vision of Christian discipleship in God's world.

In conclusion, a few words are needed about the editing decisions that govern this translated volume, which is based on the second, expanded edition of the *Gereformeerde Dogmatiek.*[39] The fourteen chapters of this volume correspond to seventeen in the original (called "paragraphs" in the Dutch edition). All chapters correspond to the Dutch units except for chapter 2, "The Knowledge of God," which combines units 24 and 25 in the original; and chapter 3, "The Names of God," which combines units 26–28 in the original. In addition, the headings subdividing each chapter are new. These, along with the chapter synopses, which are also not in the original, have been supplied by the editor. Bavinck's original footnotes have all been retained and brought up to contemporary bibliographic standards. Additional notes added by the editor are clearly marked. Works from the nineteenth century to the present are noted usually with full bibliographic information given in the first note of each chapter and with subsequent references abbreviated. Classic works produced prior to the nineteenth century (the church fathers, Aquinas's *Summa,* Calvin's *Institutes,* post-Reformation Protestant and Catholic works), for which there are often numerous editions, are cited only by author, title, and standard notation of sections. More complete information for originals or accessible editions is given in the bibliography appended at the end of this volume. Where English translations (ET) of foreign titles were available and could be consulted, they have been used rather than the original. Unless indicated in the note by direct reference to a specific translation, renderings of Latin, Greek, German, and French material are those of the translator, working from Bavinck's original text. References in the notes and bibliography that are incomplete or could not be confirmed are marked with an asterisk (*). To facilitate comparison with the Dutch original, this English edition retains the subparagraph numbers (##161–306 in square brackets in the text) used in the second and subsequent Dutch editions. Cross-references to volumes 1 and 2 of *Gereformeerde Dogmatiek* cite the page numbers of the already released *Reformed Dogmatics,* volume 1: *Prolegomena,* and of the present volume. Subparagraph numbers (marked with #) accompany these references to facilitate cross-reference to the Dutch editions. Cross-references to volumes 3 and 4 of *Gereformeerde Dogmatiek* cite only the subparagraph number (marked with #).

39. The four volumes of the first edition of *Gereformeerde Dogmatiek* were published in the years 1895 through 1901. The second revised and expanded edition appeared between 1906 and 1911; the third edition, unaltered from the second, in 1918; the fourth, unaltered except for different pagination, in 1928.

On January 24, 2004, while this volume was in production, Dr. M. Eugene Osterhaven (emeritus Albertus C. Van Raalte Professor of Systematic Theology at Western Theological Seminary, Holland, Michigan) went to be with his Lord and ours. Gene was one of the founders of the Dutch Reformed Translation Society, our colleague on the board, a dear friend, trusted advisor, and beloved brother in Christ. We thank God for his service to Christ's church and kingdom, service of which we were richly blessed beneficiaries. We shall miss him deeply and in gratitude dedicate this volume to his memory.

PART I

KNOWING
GOD

1

THE INCOMPREHENSIBILITY
OF GOD

The knowledge of God is the central, core dogma, the exclusive content of theology. From the start of its labors dogmatic theology is shrouded in mystery; it stands before God the incomprehensible One. This knowledge leads to adoration and worship; to know God is to live. Knowing God is possible for us because God is personal, exalted above the earth and yet in fellowship with human beings on earth.

God's special relationship with his people Israel, with Zion as his dwelling place, suggests not confinement or limitation but election. Israel's religion did not evolve from henotheism to ethical monotheism but is rooted in the divine call of Abraham/Israel and God's initiative in establishing a covenant with Israel. Though the Old Testament refers to "other gods," it never takes their reality seriously. Israel's God is God alone, the Lord of heaven and earth. He is the Creator of heaven and earth, who manifests himself in various ways to specific people at particular times. This revelation is never exhaustive of God's being but partial and preparatory to the supreme and permanent revelation in Jesus Christ. This personal God is the high and lofty One, who inhabits eternity and also is with those who are of a contrite and humble spirit. His fullness dwells bodily in Christ, who emptied himself and took on the form of a servant. He also resides in the church as his temple. God is both personal and absolute.

Unity of God's personality and absoluteness is not maintained outside the revelation given in Scripture. Philosophers, notably in the Platonist tradition, see God (the Good) as the distant One, the unknowable One, transcending even Being itself. In Plotinus only negative theology remains; we can only say what God is not. Gnosticism went even further, considering God as absolutely unknowable and ineffable, the eternal silent abyss.

Christian theology agrees that human knowledge of God is not exhaustive: we cannot know God in his essence. Since no description or naming of God can be adequate, human language struggles even to say what God is not. This incomprehensibility of God's essence was most vigorously affirmed by Pseudo-Dionysius and John Scotus Erigena, for whom God transcends even being and knowing itself. Scholastic theology was more cautious and positive but affirmed

27

God's essential unknowability. Thomas Aquinas distinguished the immediate vision of God, knowledge by faith, from knowledge by reason. The former is ordinarily reserved for heaven; on earth all knowledge is mediate. God is knowable only in his works, notably in the perfections of his creatures.

Though not necessarily following Luther's "hidden God," Reformed theology in its aversion to all idolatry has insisted that God infinitely surpasses our understanding, imagination, and language. As the Reformation tradition's consciousness of divine incomprehensibility waned, philosophers, notably Kant, reaffirmed it. The three transcendental ideas—the soul, the world, and God—cannot be objectively demonstrated; they can only be postulated as the necessary conditions for knowledge. That they are "known" by practical reason does not add to our volume of real, meaning scientific, knowledge. With the exception of Hegel, the doctrine of divine unknowability has penetrated modern consciousness. All predicates about God are seen to be statements about humanity writ large. God is a human projection (Feuerbach); religion is the deification of humanity itself.

For others, this sort of atheism has also claimed too much. Human limitations and the finiteness of human knowledge should lead us to abstain from such judgments. Knowledge is limited to the observable (positivism), and beyond that we confess our ignorance (agnosticism). Metaphysics was distrusted and speculation eschewed. This agnosticism, of course, means the death of theology, though theologians did attempt various rescue missions.

Agnosticism does have weighty arguments on its side. As humans we are limited in our finiteness. Modern thought, however, goes further and argues that divine absoluteness and personality are forever incompatible. To conceive of God in personal terms is to make him finite. For God to relate to us, he must be somehow limited. Consequently, all that is reasonably left is some version of an impersonal moral world order.

Now, Christian theology has always acknowledged the tension between our view of God as personal and absolute. We are limited to the knowledge obtained by sense perception; we affirm the unsearchable majesty and sovereign highness of God. But though God is thus beyond our full comprehension and description, we do confess to having the knowledge of God. This knowledge is analogical and the gift of revelation. We know God through his works and in his relation to us, his creatures. This truth is beyond our comprehension; it is a mystery but not self-contradictory. Rather, it reflects the classic distinction Christian theology has always made between negative (apophatic) and positive (cataphatic) theology.

If we cannot speak of God analogically, then we cannot speak of him at all. If God cannot be known, neither can he be felt or experienced in any way. All religion is then empty. But modern philosophical agnosticism makes the same error as ancient Gnosticism. By reducing God to "inexpressible depth" and "eternal silence," they make the universe godless, in the most absolute sense of the word. What it all comes down to is whether God has willed and found a

*way to reveal himself in the domain of creatures. This, the Christian church
and Christian theology affirm, has indeed occurred. Thanks to revelation,
we have true knowledge of God, knowledge that is relative and finite rather
than comprehensive. Incomprehensibility does not imply agnosticism but an
ingredient of the Christian claim to have received by revelation a specific,
limited, yet well-defined and true knowledge of God. In the words of Basil,
"The knowledge of God consists in the perception of his incomprehensibility."*

BEFORE THE DIVINE MYSTERY

[161] Mystery is the lifeblood of dogmatics. To be sure, the term "mystery"
(μυστηριον) in Scripture does not mean an abstract supernatural truth in the
Roman Catholic sense. Yet Scripture is equally far removed from the idea that
believers can grasp the revealed mysteries in a scientific sense.[1] In truth, the
knowledge that God has revealed of himself in nature and Scripture far surpasses
human imagination and understanding. In that sense it is all mystery with
which the science of dogmatics is concerned, for it does not deal with finite
creatures, but from beginning to end looks past all creatures and focuses on the
eternal and infinite One himself. From the very start of its labors, it faces the
incomprehensible One. From him it derives its inception, for from him are all
things. But also in the remaining loci, when it turns its attention to creatures,
it views them only in relation to God as they exist from him and through him
and for him [Rom. 11:36]. So then, the knowledge of God is the only dogma,
the exclusive content, of the entire field of dogmatics. All the doctrines treated
in dogmatics—whether they concern the universe, humanity, Christ, and so
forth—are but the explication of the one central dogma of the knowledge of
God. All things are considered in light of God, subsumed under him, traced
back to him as the starting point. Dogmatics is always called upon to ponder
and describe God and God alone, whose glory is in creation and re-creation,
in nature and grace, in the world and in the church. It is the knowledge of
him alone that dogmatics must put on display.

By pursuing this aim, dogmatics does not become a dry and academic
exercise, without practical usefulness for life. The more it reflects on God, the
knowledge of whom is its only content, the more it will be moved to adoration and worship. Only if it never forgets to think and speak about matters
rather than about mere *words*, only if it remains a theology of facts and does not
degenerate into a theology of rhetoric, only then is dogmatics as the scientific
description of the knowledge of God also superlatively fruitful for life. The
knowledge of God-in-Christ, after all, is life itself (Ps. 89:16; Isa. 11:9; Jer.
31:34; John 17:3). For that reason Augustine desired to know nothing other
and more than God and himself. "I desire to know God and the soul. Nothing
more? No: nothing at all." For that reason, too, Calvin began his *Institutes* with
the knowledge of God and the knowledge of ourselves, and for that reason

---

1. Cf. H. Bavinck, *Reformed Dogmatics,* I, 618 (#159).

the Genevan catechism, answering the first question, "What is the chief end of human life?" stated, "That human beings may know the God by whom they were created."[2]

But the moment we dare to speak about God the question arises: How can we? We are human and he is the Lord our God. Between him and us there seems to be no such kinship or communion as would enable us to name him truthfully. The distance between God and us is the gulf between the Infinite and the finite, between eternity and time, between being and becoming, between the All and the nothing. However little we know of God, even the faintest notion implies that he is a being who is infinitely exalted above every creature. While Holy Scripture affirms this truth in the strongest terms, it nevertheless sets forth a doctrine of God that fully upholds his knowability. Scripture, one must remember, never makes any attempt to prove the existence of God, but simply presupposes it. Moreover, in this connection it consistently assumes that human beings have an ineradicable sense of that existence and a certain knowledge of God's being. This knowledge does not arise from their own investigation and reflection, but is due to the fact that God on his part revealed himself to us in nature and history, in prophecy and miracle, by ordinary and by extraordinary means. In Scripture, therefore, the knowability of God is never in doubt even for a moment. The fool may say in his heart, "There is no God," but those who open their eyes perceive from all directions the witness of his existence, of his eternal power and deity (Isa. 40:26; Acts 14:17; Rom. 1:19–20). The purpose of God's revelation, according to Scripture, is precisely that human beings may know God and so receive eternal life (John 17:3; 20:31).

Thanks to that revelation, it is certain, first of all, that God is a person, a conscious and freely willing being, not confined to the world but exalted high above it. The pantheistic understanding that equates God and the world is absolutely foreign to Scripture. This personality of God is so prominent everywhere that the question may arise whether by it his oneness, spirituality, and infinity are not being shortchanged. Some texts convey the impression that God is a being who, though greater and more powerful than human beings, is nevertheless confined to certain localities and restricted in his presence and activity by the boundaries of country and people. Not only does Scripture ascribe to God—as we will see later—an array of human organs and attributes; but also it even says that he walked in the garden (Gen. 3:8), came down to see Babel's construction of a tower (Gen. 11:5, 7), appeared to Jacob at Bethel (Gen. 28:10ff.), gave his law on Mount Sinai (Exod. 19ff.), dwelt between the cherubim on Zion in Jerusalem (1 Sam. 4:4; 1 Kings 8:7, 10–11). Scripture also therefore calls him the God of Abraham, Isaac, and Jacob, the king of Zion, the God of the Hebrews, the God of Israel, and so on. Many modern

2. Cf. Westminster Catechism, Q & A 1, in *Creeds of Christendom*, ed. P. Schaff and rev. D. S. Schaff, 6th ed. (New York: Harper & Row, 1931; reprinted, Grand Rapids: Baker, 1990). Ed. note: Bavinck refers to E. F. Karl Müller, *Die Bekenntnisschriften der reformierten Kirche* (Leipzig: A. Deichert, 1903), 612.

theologians have inferred from these expressions that Israel's most ancient religion was polydaemonism, that YHWH, taken over from the Kenites, was originally a mountain god, a fire god, or a thunder god, and that after the conquest of Canaan he gradually became the God of Israel's land and people, and that this henotheism only became absolute monotheism as a result of the ethical conception of his essence in the works of the prophets.[3]

This evolutionistic representation, however, fails to do justice to the facts of Scripture and is incompatible with a number of elements that, according to the witness of Scripture, are integral to the doctrine of God. A few remarks will make this clear. The creation of Adam and Eve (Gen. 2:7, 21), like YHWH's walking in the garden (Gen. 3:8), are recounted graphically but are represented as being the activity of the same God who made the entire universe (Gen. 2:4b). YHWH's appearance at the building of the tower of Babel (Gen. 11:5, 7) is introduced by saying that he descended, that is, came down from heaven, which is therefore viewed as his real dwelling place. In Genesis 28:11ff., a pericope that in modern works on Israel's religious history is considered a locus classicus (also cf. Josh. 24:26ff.; Judg. 6:20ff.; 1 Sam. 6:14), not the stone but heaven is YHWH's dwelling place; in verses 12 and 13, the LORD introduces himself as the God of Abraham and Isaac, promises to Jacob the land of Canaan and innumerable descendants, and guarantees that he will protect him wherever he may go (vv. 13–15). The idea of a "stone deity" is wholly absent here; the stone is merely a memorial of the marvelous event that occurred there. The localization of YHWH on Mount Sinai (Exod. 3:1, 5, 18; Judg. 5:5; 1 Kings 19:8) occurs just as much in writings that, according to modern criticism, are of later origin and definitely monotheistic (Deut. 33:2; Hab. 3:3; Ps. 68:8). True, YHWH revealed himself on Mount Sinai, but he does not reside there in the sense that he was confined to it. On the contrary, he came down from heaven upon Mount Sinai (Exod. 19:18, 20). In the same way, Scripture speaks of an intimate relationship between YHWH and the land and people of Israel but does this not only in records from an older period (Gen. 4:4; Judg. 11:24; 1 Sam. 26:19; 2 Sam. 15:8; 2 Kings 3:27; 5:17) but also in witnesses that, according to many critics, date from the monotheistic period (Deut. 4:29; Amos 1:2; Isa. 8:18; Jer. 2:7; 12:14; 16:13; Ezek. 10:18ff.; 11:23; 43:1ff.; Jon. 1:3; Ruth 1:16; cf. John 4:19). YHWH is the God of Israel by virtue of his election and covenant. Accordingly, in an unclean pagan country he cannot be worshiped in the proper, prescribed manner, as also the prophets testify (Hos. 9:3–6; Amos 7:17; etc.), but that is very different from saying that outside of Canaan he cannot be present and active. On the contrary: he accompanies Jacob wherever he travels (Gen. 28:15), is with Joseph in Egypt (Gen. 39:2), raises up the widow's son by the prophet Elijah in Zarephath (1 Kings 17:10ff.), is recognized by Naaman as the God of the whole earth (2 Kings 5:17ff.).

3. Cf. Karl Marti, *Geschichte der israelitischen Religion*, 3d ed. (Strassburg: F. Bull, 1897), 22ff.

GOD AND THE GODS

As a result of this close relationship between God and Israel in the Old Testament dispensation, many texts do not pronounce themselves, so to speak, on the question whether the gods of other peoples are in any way real. In the first commandment the Lord himself says: "You shall have no other gods before me" (Exod. 20:3), and elsewhere we are told that the Lord is greater than all other gods (Exod. 15:11; 18:11). In Judges 11:24 Jephthah speaks as if Chemosh, Moab's god, really existed, and in 1 Samuel 26:19 David talks as if banishment from the heritage of the Lord amounted to the worship of other gods. But viewed in their context none of these passages conveys the kind of henotheism many [scholars] attempt to infer from them. This is evident from the fact that next to the first commandment (Exod. 20:3), there is the fourth (Exod. 20:10), which ascribes the creation of heaven and earth to YHWH and by implication confesses the clearest monotheism. Also, according to the Yahwist, the Lord is the God of heaven and earth, the God of all humanity (Gen. 6:5–7; 8:21; 9:19; 18:1ff., 25; etc.). In Genesis 24:3, 7 he is called the God of heaven and earth, and in Exodus 19:5 the whole earth is his. In the text cited above [Judg. 11:24], Jephthah accommodates himself to the person to whom he is speaking, and in 1 Samuel 26:19 David says nothing but what we find everywhere in the Old Testament, namely, that in this dispensation God has a special relationship to Israel's land and people. In the writings which, also according to modern critics, are of a later date and hold to a definite monotheism, the same expressions occur that we find in more ancient books: the Lord is God of gods and superior to all gods (Deut. 3:24; 4:7; 10:17; 29:26; 32:12, 16; 1 Kings 8:23; 2 Chron. 28:23; Jer. 22:9; Ps. 95:3; 97:9; etc.; cf. 1 Cor. 8:5ff.; 10:20).

The distinction between a higher and a lower deity in the Old Testament—a distinction already advocated by Gnosticism—therefore does violence to the facts and, when employed as a standard for source criticism, leads to boundless arbitrariness and hopeless confusion. There of course is a difference between the religion of the people, which often consisted of image worship and idolatry, and the religion that the Lord required both in his law and through the prophets of Israel, and in connection with this a difference between a history of the religion of Israel and a theology of the Old Testament (*historia revelationis*). Neither can it be denied that different authors in the Old Testament highlight different attributes of the divine being. But the sources by no means warrant the evolutionistic view, according to which the religion of Israel developed from polydaemonism, via henotheism, into absolute monotheism. On the contrary: throughout the whole Old Testament and in all its authors, the doctrine of God comprises, albeit in varying degrees, the following elements:

1. God is a personal being, self-existent, with a life, consciousness, and will of his own, not confined to nature but exalted high above it, the Creator of heaven and earth.

2. This God can appear and manifest himself in certain specific places, at certain specific times, to specific persons: to the patriarchs, to Moses and the prophets; in the garden of Eden, at Babel's construction of a tower, at Bethel, on Mount Sinai, in Canaan, at Jerusalem, on Mount Zion, and so forth.

3. Throughout the whole Old Testament, not only in the preprophetic but also in the prophetic era, this revelation is preparatory in character. It occurs in signs, dreams, and visions, by means of the lot, the Urim and Thummim, by angels and by the *malakh* YHWH [angel of the LORD]. It usually occurs at certain specific moments, then ceases and becomes history. It is therefore more or less external, stays outside of and above the persons in question, is more a revelation to than in people, and indicates by this peculiar feature that it serves to announce and prepare for the supreme and permanent revelation of God in the person of Christ and his ongoing indwelling in the church.

4. The revelation of God in the Old Testament, accordingly, does not exhaustively coincide with his being. It does indeed furnish true and reliable knowledge of God, but not a knowledge that exhaustively corresponds to his being. The stone at Bethel, the pillar of cloud and the pillar of fire in the wilderness, the thunder on Mount Sinai, the cloud in the tabernacle, the ark of the covenant (etc.) are signs and pledges of his presence, but do not encompass and confine him. Moses, with whom God spoke as with a friend, only saw God after he had passed by him (Exod. 33:23). One cannot see God and live (Exod. 33:20; Lev. 16:2). He is without form (Deut. 4:12, 15). One cannot make an image of him (Exod. 20:4). He dwells in darkness: clouds and darkness are the sign of his presence (Exod. 20:21; Deut. 4:11; 5:22; 1 Kings 8:12; 2 Chron. 6:1).

5. The same God who in his revelation limits himself, as it were, to certain specific places, times, and persons is at the same time infinitely exalted above the whole realm of nature and every creature. Even in the parts of Scripture that stress this temporal and local manifestation, the sense of his sublimity and omnipotence is not lacking. The Lord who walks in his garden is the Creator of heaven and earth. The God who appears to Jacob is in control of the future. Although the God of Israel dwells in the midst of his people in the house that Solomon built for him, he cannot even be contained by the heavens (1 Kings 8:27). He manifests himself in nature and sympathizes, as it were, with his people, but he is simultaneously the incomprehensible One (Job 26:14; 36:26; 37:5), the incomparable One (Isa. 40:18, 25; 46:5), the one who is infinitely exalted above time and space and every creature (Isa. 40:12ff.; 41:4;

44:6; 48:12), the one true God (Exod 20:3, 11; Deut. 4:35, 39; 32:19; 1 Sam. 2:2; Isa. 44:8). Although he reveals himself in his names, no name is adequate to the purpose. He is nameless; his name is a name of wonder (Gen. 32:29; Judg. 13:18; Prov. 30:4). Neither the hidden ground, the depths [חֵקֶר] of God, nor the boundaries, the extreme limit, the very essence [תַּכְלִית] of the Almighty, is attainable (Job 11:7; Sirach 43:31–32). In a word, throughout the Old Testament these two elements occur hand in hand: God is with those who are of a contrite and humble spirit, and nevertheless is the high and lofty One who inhabits eternity (Isa. 57:15).

6. In the New Testament we encounter the same combination. God dwells in inaccessible light. No one has seen him or can see him (John 1:18; 6:46; 1 Tim. 6:16). He is above all change (James 1:17), time (Rev. 1:8; 22:13), space (Acts 17:27–28), and creatures (Acts 17:24). No one knows him except the Son and the Spirit (Matt. 11:27; 1 Cor. 2:11). But God has caused his fullness to dwell in Christ bodily (Col. 2:9), resides in the church as in his temple (1 Cor. 3:16), and makes his home in those who love Jesus and keep his Word (John 14:23). Or to put it in modern theological language, in Scripture the personality and the absoluteness of God go hand in hand.

[162] The moment we step outside the domain of this special revelation in Scripture, we find that in all religious and philosophical systems the unity of the personality and absoluteness of God is broken. Generally speaking, pagans identify themselves religiously by the fact that, knowing God, they do not glorify him as God but exchange his glory for creaturely images [Rom. 1:21–23]. Then, sooner or later, a philosophical view reacts against this disposition and emphasizes God's absoluteness while denying his personality. Among Brahmans, God is the Unknowable One without either names or attributes, who is known only by those who do not know.[4] The Qur'an frequently describes Allah in very anthropomorphic language. Among Muhammad's followers, however, many arose who interpreted this language spiritually and even refused to ascribe any attributes to God.[5] Greek philosophy also frequently taught this unknowability with regard to God. According to a famous tale, the philosopher Simonides, responding to the question, Who is God? put to him by the tyrant Hiero, kept on asking for more and more time to frame

4. S. Hoekstra, *Wijsgerige Godsdienstleer*, 2 vols. (Amsterdam: Van Kampen, 1894–95), II, 2; Eduard von Hartmann, *Religionsphilosophie*, 2d ed., 2 vols. (Bad Sachsa im Harz: Hermann Haacke, 1907), I, 278; Pierre Daniel Chantepie de la Saussaye, *Lehrbuch der Religionsgeschichte*, 3d ed., 2 vols. (Tübingen: J. C. B. Mohr [Paul Siebeck], 1905), II, 49ff.; Paul Wurm, *Handbuch der Religionsgeschichte* (Calwer Verlagsverein; Stuttgart: Verlag der Vereinsbuchhandlung, 1904).

5. R. P. A. Dozy, *Het Islamisme* (Haarlem: A. C. Kruseman, 1836), 131ff.; M. Houtsma, *De Strijd over het Dogma in den Islam tot op el-Ash'ari* (Leiden: S. C. van Doesburgh, 1875), 120ff.; P. de la Saussaye, *Lehrbuch der Religionsgeschichte*, 3d ed., II, 510.

an answer.[6] According to Diogenes, Protagoras's book *On the Gods* began as follows: "With regard to the gods I do not have the ability to know whether they exist or not. For there are many things that prevent a person from knowing; for example, the obscurity of the subject and the brevity of human life."[7] Carneades of Cyrene not only sharply criticized belief in the gods but denied the possibility of forming an idea of God. Plato rejected all anthropomorphic and anthropopathic representations of the deity and stated in *Timaeus* §34: "Now to discover the Maker and Father of this universe is an enormous job, and, having discovered him, to tell everyone about him is impossible."[8]

Similarly in *The Republic* VI, 19, he states that the deity or idea of the good transcends not only all that exists but even "Being itself." Philo combined this Platonic philosophy with the teaching of the Old Testament and found the same idea expressed in the name YHWH. Not only is God free from all the imperfections present in finite, changeable, and dependent creatures, but also far exceeds their perfections. He is better than virtue, knowledge, and beauty; purer than oneness, more blessed than bliss itself. Actually, he is without any attributes or qualities and without names and therefore cannot be understood or described. He is unknowable in his very being. We can know *that* he is, not *what* he is. Only "being" can truly be ascribed to him; the name YHWH alone describes his being.[9]

Plotinus is the most radical of all. Plato still ascribed many attributes to God. Philo complements his negative theology with a positive one in which he describes God as a personal, omnipotent, and perfect being. But according to Plotinus nothing can be said of God that is not negative. God is absolutely one—above all plurality—and therefore not describable in terms of thought or the good, not even in terms of being, for all these determinations still imply a certain plurality. As pure unity, God is indeed the cause of thought, being, and the good, but he himself is distinct from them and transcends them. He is unbounded, infinite, without form, and so altogether different from every creature that not even activity, life, thought, consciousness, or being can be ascribed to him. He is inapprehensible by our thought and language. We cannot say what he is, only what he is not. Even the terms "the One" and "the Good," which Plotinus usually employs, do not describe his essence but only his relation to his creatures, and only denote his absolute causality.[10]

Gnosticism made the gulf between God and his creatures even greater. It posited an absolute separation between the supreme God and the world. In nature, in Israel, and in Christianity there was no real revelation of God, only of

6. Cicero, *On the Nature of the Gods*, I, 22.

7. H. Ritter and Ludwig Preller, *Historia philosophiae graecae* (Gothae: I. A. Perthes, 1888), 183.

8. E. Zeller, *Die Philosophie der Griechen*, 4th ed., 3 vols. (Leipzig: O. R. Reisland, 1879), II, 928ff.

9. E. Zeller, *Die Philosophie der Griechen*, 3d ed., 5 vols. (Leipzig: Fues's Verlag [L. W. Reisland], 1895), V, 353ff.; A. F. Dähne, *Geschichtliche Darstellung der jüdisch-alexandrinischen Religionsphilosophie* (Halle: Buchhandlung des Waisenhauses, 1834), I, 114ff.; Emil Schürer, *A History of the Jewish People in the Time of Jesus Christ*, 2d ed., 5 vols. (1890; reprinted, Edinburgh: T. & T. Clark, 1987), III.2, 880ff.

10. E. Zeller, *Die Philosophie*, 3d ed., 476–96.

aeons. Hence, there was no natural theology—either innate or acquired—nor a revealed theology. For a creature, the supreme God is absolutely unknowable and inaccessible. He is an "unknowable abyss, ineffable, eternal silence."[11]

DIVINE INCOMPREHENSIBILITY IN CHRISTIAN THEOLOGY

This theory of the incomprehensibility of God and of the unknowability of his essence also became the starting point and fundamental idea of Christian theology. Neither in creation nor in re-creation does God reveal himself exhaustively. He cannot fully impart himself to creatures. For that to be possible they themselves would have to be divine. There is, therefore, no exhaustive knowledge of God. There is no name that makes his essence known to us. There is no concept that fully encompasses him. There is no description that fully defines him. That which lies behind revelation is completely unknowable. We cannot approach it either by our thought, our imagination, or our language. The letter of Barnabas already poses the question: "If the Son of God had not become incarnate, then how could human beings have beheld him and lived?" Justin Martyr calls God inexpressible, immobile, nameless. Even words like "Father," "God," and "Lord" are not real names but "appellations derived from [his] beneficence and works." God cannot appear, go about, or be seen; whenever such things are ascribed to God, they refer to the Son, his emissary. Also in Irenaeus, one encounters the antithesis—very common in his time, yet mistaken, and partly gnostic—between the Father who is hidden, invisible, and unknowable, and the Son who has revealed him. In the work of Clement of Alexandria, God is "pure oneness." If we eliminate from our thoughts all that is creaturely, we do not apprehend what he is, but only what he is not. Neither form, movement, location, number, properties, nor names, and so on, can be attributed to him. If we nevertheless call him "one," "good," "Father," "Creator," "Lord," and so forth, we do not thereby express his true essence but only his power. He even transcends oneness. In a word, as Athanasius puts it, he "transcends all being and human comprehension."[12] So also speak Origen, Eusebius, and many other theologians of the early centuries.[13]

11. Irenaeus, *Against Heresies*, I, 11, 24.

12. *Epistle of Barnabas*, ch. 5; Justin Martyr, *Apology*, I, 61; II, 6; idem, *Dialogue with Trypho*, 127; Irenaeus, *Against Heresies*, IV, 20; Clement of Alexandria, *Stromateis*, V, 11–12; idem, *Paedagogus*, I, 8; Athanasus, *Against the Nations*, 2.

13. Origen, *On First Principles*, I, 1, 5ff.; idem, *Against Celsus*, VI, 65; Eusebius, *Praep. evang.*, V, 1; Theophilus, *To Autolycus*, I, 3; Tatian, *Oratio ad Graecos* (Leipzig: J. C. Heinrichs, 1888), 5; Minucius Felix, *The Octavius of Marcus Minucius Felix*, trans. G. W. Clarke (New York: Newman Press, 1974); Novatianus, *Novatiani Romanae urbis Presbytery de trinitate liber* (Cambridge: Cambridge University Press, 1909), 2; Cyprian, *On the Vanity of Idols*, 5; Lactantius, *Divine Institutes*, I, 6. Cf. W. Münscher, *Lehrbuch des christlichen Dogmengeschichte*, ed. D. von Coelln, 3d ed., 2 vols. in 3 (Cassel: J. C. Drieger, 1832–38), I, 132ff.; K. R. Hagenbach, *A Textbook of the History of Doctrines*, trans. C. W. Buch, 6th rev. ed., 2 vols. (New York: Sheldon, 1869), §37; J. Schwane, *Dogmengeschichte*, 4 vols. (Freiburg i.B.: Herder, 1882–95), I², 72ff.

We encounter the same idea in Augustine and John of Damascus. In his description of God Augustine proceeds from the concept of "being." He is the One who is, as the name YHWH indicates. This is his true name, the name that indicates what he is in himself; all other names indicate what he is toward us (*Serm.* 6 n. 4; *Serm.* 7 n. 7). Therefore, when we want to say what he is, we are only saying what, by comparison with all finite beings, he is not. He is "inexpressible. It is easier for us to say what he is not than what he is." He is not earth, sea, heaven, angel, and so on, nothing creaturely. All we can say is what he is not (*Enarr.,* in Ps. 85 n. 12; *De doctr. chr.,* I, 6; *De ord.,* II, 47). "By thinking we try to reach a nature than which nothing is better or more sublime" (*De doctr. chr.,* I, 7). But he cannot be conceived as he is, for he transcends all that is physical, changeable, and the result of process (*Tr. Act.* 23 in *Ev. John.* n. 9). "Who is there whose conception of God truly corresponds to how he is?" (*Isa.* VI, 29). He is incomprehensible and has to be so, "for if you comprehend him it is not God you comprehend" (*Serm.* 117 n. 5). If, then, we finally want to say what we think of him, we struggle with language. "For what is thought of God is truer than what is said, and his being is truer than what is thought" (*De trin.,* VII, 4). If we nevertheless insist on saying something about him, our language is not "adequate" but only serves to enable us to say something, and to think of a being who surpasses all else (*De doctr. chr.,* I, 6).

"Just as no intellect is able properly to conceive of God, so no definition is able properly to define or describe him" (*De cogn. verae vitae,* 7). "God is known better by not knowing" (*De ord.,* II, 44). John of Damascus similarly avers that God is the "ineffable and incomprehensible divine being." We speak of God in our own way and know what God has revealed of himself, but the nature of God's being and the manner of his existence in all creatures we do not know. That God is, is clear, but "what he is in essence and nature is altogether incomprehensible and unknowable." When we say God is unborn, immutable, without beginning, and so on, we are only saying what he is not. To state positively what he is, is impossible. He is no part of all existing things, not because he does not exist, but because he transcends "all beings and even being itself." What we say positively concerning God does not refer to his nature but to "the things regarding his nature."[14]

[163] This unknowability of God's essence was even more vigorously affirmed by Pseudo-Dionysius (to whom John of Damascus already appeals) and by John Scotus Erigena. According to the Areopagite, there is no concept, expression, or word that directly expresses God's essence. Accordingly, God is described with unusual, metaphorical terms. He is "infinity beyond being," "oneness that is beyond intelligence," "the inscrutable One out of the reach of every rational process." "Nor can any words come up to the inexpressible Good, this One, this Source of all unity, this supraexistent Being. Mind beyond mind, word beyond speech, it is gathered up by no discourse, by no intuition, by no

14. John of Damascus, *The Orthodox Faith,* I, 1, 2, 4, 9.

name. It is and it is as no other being is. Cause of all existence, and therefore itself transcending all existence; it alone could give an authoritative account of what really is."[15] We can neither describe nor think this one, unknown Being, who transcends the entire realm of existent being, who is above every name, word, and intellect, and all that is finite. It is only because he is the cause and origin of all things that we, like Scripture, can name him in terms of his effects. Hence, on the one hand, he is "nameless" (anonymous), and on the other, he "has many names." But even the positive names we assign to God by virtue of his works do not reveal God's essence to us, for they fit him in a totally different and infinitely more perfect way than they do creatures. Consequently, negative theology is more excellent than positive theology: it makes God known to us as transcending all creatures. Nevertheless, even negative theology fails to furnish us any knowledge of God's being, for in the final analysis God surpasses both all negation and all affirmation, all assertion and all denial.[16]

We find precisely the same line of thought in the work of Erigena: God transcends all that is creaturely, even being and knowing. We only know *that* he is, not *who* he is. What we predicate of him is only true of him figuratively; in reality he is altogether different. Affirmative theology is unreal, metaphorical. It is surpassed by negative theology. "For God is more truthfully said not to be any of those things that are claimed of him than he is said to be. He is better known by not being known; ignorance of him is true wisdom." Predicates of him, accordingly, are best augmented with the words *super* (above) and *plusquam* (beyond). He is above and beyond "essence," "truth," and "wisdom." Indeed, he so far surpasses everything creaturely that he can be fairly described with the word "nothingness" *(nihilum)*.[17]

Now, scholasticism at several points expressed itself more cautiously, and especially attached greater value to positive theology than did Pseudo-Dionysius and Erigena. Nevertheless, it fully affirmed the theory that God's being as such is unknowable by humans. Anselm says that God's names only describe him "by likeness" *(per similitudinem)*, that the relative attributes of his being cannot be predicated, and the absolute only in a quidditative, not in a qualitative sense.[18] According to Albert the Great, God transcends all being and thought. He cannot be reached by human thought: "He can be touched but not grasped

15. Pseudo-Dionysius, *The Divine Names* I, 1 (588B), in *Pseudo-Dionysius: The Complete Works*, trans. Colin Luibheid, Classics of Western Spirituality (New York and Mahwah, N.J.: Paulist, 1987), 49–50. Ed. note: For clarity and accuracy, Bavinck's loose paraphrasing of this passage in Pseudo-Dionysius has been changed to the full citation from I.1 of *The Divine Names*.

16. Pseudo-Dionysius, *The Divine Names and Mystical Theology*, trans. John D. Jones (Milwaukee: Marquette University Press, 1980), c. 1 §1ff., §2; c. 5.

17. Erigena, *The Divine Nature*, I, 7ff.; II, 23ff.; III, 19ff.; A. Stöckl, *Geschichte der Philosophie des Mittelalters*, 3 vols. (Mainz: Kirchheim, 1864–66), I, 45ff.; F. C. Baur, *Die christlichen Lehre von der Dreieinigkeit und Menschwerdung Gottes*, 3 vols. (Tübingen: C. F. Oslander, 1841–43), II, 274; J. I. Doedes, *Inleiding tot de Leer von God* (Utrecht: Kemink, 1876), 133ff.

18. Anselm, *Monologion*, c. 15–17, 63.

by our comprehension." There is no name that gives expression to his essence. He is incomprehensible and inexpressible.[19]

Thomas Aquinas differentiates between three kinds of knowledge of God: the immediate vision of God (in terms of his essence), knowledge by faith, and knowledge by natural reason. The first far surpasses natural human knowledge and can only be attained by supernatural grace. It is reserved for heaven, only rarely granted to a person here on earth, and in any case never renders possible the comprehension of God. On earth the knowledge of God is mediate. We cannot know God as he is in himself, but only "as the first and most eminent cause of all things." We can only deduce the cause from the effects. The same is true of the knowledge we receive of God from his special revelation through faith. We learn to know him more fully "the more and the more excellent of his effects are shown to us." But even this faith-knowledge does not give us a knowledge of God *per essentiam* (in terms of his essence). There is no knowledge of God's essence, his "whatness," in terms of its uniqueness; we only know his disposition toward his creatures. There is no name that fully expresses his essence. It far surpasses that which we can know and say concerning God. Although positive names may designate God's essence, they do so most imperfectly, just as the creatures, from which the names are derived, imperfectly represent him. God is knowable only "insofar as he is represented in the perfections of his creatures."[20]

In the subsequent development of scholasticism, however, this truth of the incomprehensibility of God was pushed into the background. The doctrine of God became increasingly elaborate. God's existence, names, essence, persons, and attributes were so minutely and precisely developed that no room was left for his incomprehensibility. It became an ordinary attribute alongside the others, and was given equally elaborate and dialectical treatment. Against Thomas, Duns Scotus asserted that there was indeed a quidditative, albeit imperfect, knowledge of God.[21] Nominalism already registered its protests against Scotus's position and became more or less skeptical. Durandus wrote that there was no such thing as an "abstract knowledge" of the divine essence. And Occam declared: "Neither the divine essence, nor divine quiddity, nor anything that pertains to the nature of God, nor anything that is truly God, can be known by us here so that there is nothing else that comes to us from God in the way of an object."[22]

Mysticism sought to obtain a knowledge of God other than that which is garnered in the way of dialectics. Toward the end of the Middle Ages, Nicholas of Cusa, in his work *On Learned Ignorance*, asserted that no truth could be obtained by reason but only by faith—faith conceived mystically as a new organ in humans. After the Reformation, Roman Catholic theology returned

19. According to A. Stöckl, *Philosophie des Mittelalters*, II, 370.
20. T. Aquinas, *Summa theol.*, I, qu. 12, 13.
21. Duns Scotus, *Sentences*, I, dist. 3, qu. 2.
22. According to A. Stöckl, *Philosophie des Mittelalters*, II, 1009.

to scholasticism and again adopted the doctrine of the unknowability of God's essence in the way Thomas understood it.[23] At the Lateran Council, convened by Pope Innocent III, this doctrine was even ecclesiastically defined and proclaimed: "God is ineffable."

The theology of the Reformation did not modify this view. In his work "The Bondage of the Will," Luther differentiates between the "hidden" and the "revealed" God, between God himself and the Word of God. In later years he gradually confined himself more to the latter, namely, to God as he has revealed himself in Christ: "That which is above us does not concern us." Yet, to him, the fullness of God's being was not exhaustively revealed in Christ either; on the contrary, there remained in God a dark and hidden background: "God as he is in his own nature and majesty, God in his absoluteness." And he, according to Luther, is "plainly unknowable, incomprehensible, and inaccessible."[24] Later Lutheran theologians, though they did not make such a sharp distinction between God's essence and his revelation, nevertheless all affirmed that there is no possibility of adequately naming and defining God.[25]

The Reformed concurred. Their profound aversion to all forms of idol worship made them everywhere distinguish sharply between that which is of God and that which is creaturely. More than any other theology they took seriously the proposition that "the finite cannot contain the infinite." Zwingli wrote: "*Of ourselves*[26] we know no more about the nature of God than beetles know about the nature of humans."[27] Calvin writes that we are toying with idle speculations when we pose the question: What is God? For us it is enough to inquire: "What is his nature and what is consistent with his nature?"[28] Later theologians spoke of the nonknowability of God's being in even stronger terms. Inasmuch as the finite cannot contain the infinite, all God's names serve not to make God's essence known to us but—in accordance with our understanding—to describe to some extent that of God which we need to know. The statements: "God cannot be defined," "God has no name," and "The finite cannot contain the infinite" recur in all [Reformed] theologians. They unanimously affirm that God infinitely surpasses

23. Cf., e.g., Franciscus Sylvius, *Commentarii in totam primam partem S. Thomae Aquinatis*, 4th ed., 4 vols. (Antwerp, 1693), I, 96ff. Ed. note: An English edition of 1726 (Venice: Typographia Balleoniana) is also available in microform (Pius XII Memorial Library, St. Louis University, St. Louis, Mo.). C. R. Billuart, *Cursus theologiae*, 9 vols. (1769–70), I, 228ff.; D. Petavius, *Theol. dogm.*, I, ch. 5; VIII, c. 6; G. Jansen, *Praelect. theol.*, II, 78ff.; *Theologia Wirceburgensi* (ed. Paris, 1880), II, 73ff.; C. Pesch, *Praelect. dogm.* (1895), II, 46ff.

24. J. Köstlin, *The Theology of Luther in Its Historical Development and Inner Harmony*, trans. Charles E. Hay, 2 vols. (Philadelphia: Lutheran Publication Society, 1897), I, 99ff., 428ff.

25. J. Gerhard, *Loci. theol.* II, c. 5; cf. Heinrich F. F. Schmid, *Die Dogmatik der evangelische-lutherischen Kirche*, 9th ed. (Gütersloh: Gütersloher Verlagshaus Mohn, 1979), §17; K. Bretschneider, *Handbuch der Dogmatik* (Leipzig: J. A. Barth, 1838), I, 443.

26. These italicized words must not be omitted as, for example, Hoekstra does in *Wijsgerige Godsdienstleer*, II, 14.

27. U. Zwingli, *Opera*, III, 157.

28. J. Calvin, *Institutes*, I.ii.2; I.v.9; *Commentary*, on Rom. 1:19.

our understanding, imagination, and language. Polanus, for example, states that the attributes ascribed to God in Scripture do not explain his nature and being. These attributes show us what is not God's nature and character rather than what is. "Whatever is said of God is not God, for God is ineffable. No divine attributes sufficiently explicate God's essence or nature, for it is infinite. That which is finite, moreover, cannot fittingly and fully enough explicate the infinite."[29]

However, in Reformed theology, too, the significance of God's incomprehensibility was increasingly lost from view. While it was still taught, it existed in the abstract and exerted no influence. The form in which the doctrine of God was treated soon became almost completely unchangeable. Other groups even did much worse. Socinianism did not even entertain the question of God's knowability. It had not the slightest interest in the knowledge of God's being. Knowing God was virtually tantamount to knowing him as the absolute Lord.[30] In his *Book about God and His Attributes* (1656), [Johann] Crell did indeed prove God's existence with an array of arguments but refrained from dealing with all questions relating to God's being, knowability, and so forth. Conrad Vorstius wrote *Treatise on God, or On the Nature and Attributes of God* (1610), in which he lapsed into the same Socinian errors.[31] The Remonstrants likewise felt no need to discuss metaphysical issues but warned against vain speculation and insisted on simplicity. According to them, the only thing that is strictly necessary to know is the will of God. The worship of God is much more necessary than the knowledge of God.[32] Rationalism considered itself sure of God's existence and attached but little value to knowledge of his being. It is as if people had lost all sense of the majesty and grandeur of God. Disregarding all so-called metaphysical questions, people rushed on to the will of God in order to know and to do it. Eternal life, they maintained, does not consist in knowing God but in doing his will. Bretschneider totally dismisses as superfluous the question whether God can be defined.[33]

PHILOSOPHICAL AGNOSTICISM

[164] But when this truth of the incomprehensibility of God had been almost totally forgotten by theology, philosophy rose up to remind us of it. Rationalism, armed with its proofs for God's existence and its theory concerning God's attributes, saw itself as standing upon a solid scientific foundation. But Kant, though with his doctrine of God, virtue, and im-

---

29. A. Polanus, *Synt. theol.*, II, 6, 137. Cf. J. Zanchi(us), *De natura Dei, seu de divinis attributis*, in *Op. theol.*, II, col. 9–10; A. Hyperius, *Meth. theol.* (1574), 83–84; Z. Ursinus, *Tract. theol.* (1584), 35, 36, 39; *Synopsis purioris theologiae*, VI, 2; S. Maresius, *Syst. theol.*, 48; J. Alsted, *Theol. schol. did.*, 56ff.; B. de Moor, *Comm. in Marckii Comp.*, I, 505ff.

30. O. Fock, *Der Socianismus* (Kiel: C. Schröder, 1847), 414–16.

31. Cf. *Acta Syn. Dort*, session, 149ff.

32. Episcopius, *Inst. theol.* IV, 2, ch. 1; Limborch, *Theol. chr.*, II, 1.

33. Bretschneider, *Dogmatik*, I⁴, 443; idem, *Systematische Entwicklung aller in der Dogmatik* (Leipzig: J. A. Baith, 1841), 341.

mortality he was still completely caught up in rationalism and moralism, nevertheless brought about an enormous change in the foundation on which this knowledge rested. Just as sensibility a priori brings with it the forms of space and time and the intellect a priori brings with it the categories, so also reason contains a priori synthetic principles and rules—especially the principle that it advances from the conditioned to the unconditioned.[34] The result is three transcendental ideas: the soul, the world, and God. However, these three ideas cannot be objectively demonstrated, only subjectively deduced from the nature of reason itself. We cannot perceive the object of these ideas; therefore, we cannot gain any scientific knowledge about them. In a scientific sense they are paralogisms, antinomies, ideals; our knowledge, however, is restricted to the sphere of experience.

These ideas, therefore, do not expand our knowledge but only regulate it. They introduce unity into our concepts and prompt us to view everything *as if* God, the soul, and the world existed. Science can neither prove nor deny the reality of these ideas. Psychology, cosmology (teleology), and theology, accordingly, are not sciences. The critique of pure reason winds up with a negative result. Practical reason, however, does allow us to accept the reality of these ideas. And Kant admittedly ascribes to God intellect, will, and other attributes, yet his real being remains hidden. Practical reason knows that these three ideas possess objective reality but no more than that. It does not add to the volume of our scientific knowledge. Speculative reason cannot do anything with these ideas except to let them regulate and purify our knowledge, and uses the idea of God to combat and avert anthropomorphism as a source of superstition and fanaticism. When intellect and will are attributed to God, it is merely a "practical" knowledge of God; it is in no sense a speculative one. For a person to abstract the anthropomorphic elements from it is to be left with no more than the word. The concept of God does not belong in metaphysics (which is nonexistent) but in ethics.[35]

Initially J. G. Fichte completely shared Kant's point of view. In his *Attempt at a Critique of All Revelation,* he allows belief in God on the postulates of reason and also ascribes to God certain definite qualities, like holiness, blessedness, omnipotence, justice, omniscience, and eternity. However, these alone do not furnish us with a definite understanding of God and a knowledge of his being per se. Even if they did, this still would not foster pure morality, but only damage it. Religion always pictures God anthropomorphically, in time and space, and even physically and does no harm by this as long as it does not conflict with morality and as long as this graphic representation is not held to be objectively valid. It must all be viewed as accommodation to our subjective need. Only

34. I. Kant, *Critique of Pure Reason*, trans. Norman Kemp Smith (1929; reprinted, New York: St. Martin's Press, 1965), 258ff.

35. I. Kant, *Critique of Practical Reason*, trans. Mary Gregor (Cambridge: Cambridge University Press, 1997), 103ff.

such a revelation can be of divine origin that presents an anthropomorphized God as being not objectively but only subjectively valid.[36]

Also Schleiermacher, though diverging in many respects from Kant and Fichte and aligning himself more closely with Spinoza, agreed with the former in the doctrine of the unknowability of God. While the idea of the unity of being and thought, of the real and the ideal, that is, the idea of God, is the assumption of all our knowledge, the ground of our thinking, this idea cannot be captured in thought and remains hidden "behind an [epistemological] curtain." The moment we try to bring the Absolute closer to us, it is finitized in our thinking and we begin to speak in images.[37] In a word, the Absolute is not accessible to human knowledge. In his *Christian Faith,* Schleiermacher proposed the same ideas, though in a more religious and less elaborate form. God is the "whence" of our existence; and as such an absolute causality, he cannot be the object of our knowing but only the content of the feeling of absolute dependence.[38]

Since then the doctrine of the unknowability of God has progressively penetrated modern consciousness. Hegel, to be sure, had another position. While acknowledging that a religious representation was inadequate and suited only for the masses, he nevertheless believed that philosophy was able to strip this representation of its sense-related form and raise it to a "fully adequate" concept. Reason, in his opinion, raises itself step by step through several stages to the level of absolute knowledge, then looks at truth face to face and knows its essence to be Reason, Thought, the Idea itself. Philosophy, the pure science, specifically logic, is the description of God's being as such. It understands the Absolute in its appropriate correspondent form as thought—in the form of a concept.[39] Along these Hegelian lines, by purifying and deepening the concepts, many thinkers[40] (e.g., Strauss, Biedermann, Ed. von Hartmann, Scholten) attempted to get even closer to transcendent reality. But in the case of others, Hegel's philosophy led to a totally different outcome. They made the claim that a sense-related representation could never be overcome in the idea of God and therefore ended up in atheism. Feuerbach said that the personal God was nothing other than the essence of humans themselves, and theology nothing but anthropology.

---

36. J. G. Fichte, *Attempt at a Critique of All Revelation,* trans. Garrett Green (Cambridge and New York: Cambridge University Press, 1978), 152ff.

37. F. Schleiermacher, *Dialektik* (Berlin: G. Reimer, 1839), 60ff.

38. F. Schleiermacher, *The Christian Faith* (Edinburgh: T. & T. Clark, 1989), §4, 4.

39. G. W. F. Hegel, *Wissenschaft der Logik,* in *Sämtliche Werke* (Stuttgart: Fr. Frommans, 1949–59 [1837]), IV, 43 [*Werke,* III, 33]. Ed. note: Where possible, references to Hegel's writings will be cited from the modern Stuttgart edition or a published English translation. The title of Hegel's work and Bavinck's original citation from Hegel's *Werke* will be given in square brackets.

40. D. F. Strauss, *Die christliche Glaubenslehre,* 2 vols. (Tübingen: C. F. Osiander, 1840–41), I, 523ff., 547ff., 609ff.; A. E. Biedermann, *Christliche Dogmatik* (Zürich: Fussli, 1869), II, 516ff.; E. von Hartmann, *Philosophie des Unbewussten,* 11th ed. (Leipzig: H. Haacke, 1904), 155ff., 175ff.; idem, *Religionsphilosophie* (Bad Sachsa im Harz: Hermann Haacke, 1907), 608ff.; J. H. Scholten, *Dogmatices christianae initia,* 2d ed. (Lyons: P. Engels, 1858), 109ff.; idem, *De Leer der Hervormde Kerk in Hare Grondbeginselen,* 2d ed., 2 vols. (Leyden: P. Engels, 1850–51), 199–200.

All that is predicated of God is derived from the sphere of humanity, not only personality but all attributes and names. Religion is the deification of humanity itself. Humans cannot rise above their own essence, and God therefore is, and always remains, a sense-related human being, not only in Christian dogmatics but also in philosophy.[41] Many, agreeing with Feuerbach, discarded the whole idea of God along with its anthropomorphic representation.[42]

Others, however, viewed this atheism as too radical. Considering the limited character of the human faculty of knowledge, which always remains confined to the sphere of the finite, these thinkers believed that we should limit ourselves to that which is given by observation (positivism), abstain from making any pronouncements on the existence and character of the supersensuous (abstentionism), and with reference to the latter, therefore, confess our absolute ignorance (agnosticism). In France, Auguste Comte limited the task of science to the observation and explanation of phenomena and hence excluded theology from the domain of the sciences.[43] In England it was especially Herbert Spencer who, armed with an array of arguments, combated the idea of the knowability of God.[44] And in Germany, sated with Hegel's panlogism, people returned to Kant's critical philosophy. Thus in the latter half of the nineteenth century agnosticism virtually reigned supreme. People distrusted all metaphysics and had an aversion to speculation. Only that which was concrete was considered trustworthy and belonged to the domain of the exact sciences.

Theology has so far fallen victim to the dread of this agnosticism that it hardly any longer dares to speak of a knowledge of God. It tries as much as possible to exclude all metaphysics (although of late we can see some reaction to this trend) and to restrict itself to the realm of the religious. It has become ashamed of its own name and has allowed itself to be rebaptized into a science of religion. For although agnosticism is in fact the death of theology, many theologians have nevertheless maintained it in another form. Kant regained by practical reason what he had lost by theoretical reason. Spencer left room for a religious veneration of the Unknowable. Even before him Sir William Hamilton and Dr. Henry Longueville Mansel had maintained that inasmuch as our thinking is always bound by space, time, distinction, and antithesis (etc.), it can never penetrate to the Absolute, though on religious grounds we

41. L. Feuerbach, *The Essence of Christianity*, trans. G. Eliot (New York: Harper Torchbook, Harper & Row, 1957 [1854]).

42. L. Büchner, *Kraft und Stoff* (Frankfurt a.M.: Meidinger Sohn, 1858), 392. Ed. note: This work is translated into English as *Force and Matter* from the 15th German edition, 4th ed. (New York: P. Eckler, 1891); idem, *Der Gottesbegriff und dessen Bedeutung in der Gegenwart*, 2d ed. (Leipzig: Th. Thomas, 1874); E. Haeckel, *The History of Creation*, trans. and rev. E. R. Lankester, 2 vols. (New York: Appleton, 1883), 30ff.; idem, *The Riddle of the Universe*, trans. Joseph McCabe (New York: Harper & Brothers, 1900), 319ff.; D. F. Strauss, *The Old Faith and the New*, trans. Mathilde Blind (New York: Holt, 1873), 155ff.; F. Nietzsche, *On the Genealogy of Morals*, trans. Douglas Smith (New York: Oxford University Press, 1998), 80; B. Carneri, *Der moderne Mensch: Versuche über Lebensführung* (Leipzig: Kröner, 1901), 73.

43. Cf. H. Bavinck, *Reformed Dogmatics*, I, 220 (#66).

44. H. Spencer, *First Principles*, 5th ed. (London: Williams & Norgate, 1887), 68–97.

must continue to affirm the idea of God as a personal being.[45] Neo-Kantians in Germany arrived at a similar dualism. While thinking at its best may lead us to the idea of the Absolute, in religion we cannot be satisfied with that notion. Here we need a God who is like us, whom we may picture as a person, and who cares for his children like a father. True, such a religious view is always vulnerable to criticism on the part of science. It is not the highest and the most truthful, but we cannot do better.[46] In the same way others have searched for compensation in humanism, moral idealism, the formation of ideals, spiritism, theosophy, Buddhism, etc., in exchange for what science had stolen from them in Christian theology.

[165] The grounds on which this agnosticism bases itself are very weighty. In the first place, it can marshal the argument which from antiquity has been advanced against all possibility of knowledge by sophists and skeptics, namely, that all human knowledge is subjective and relative. Nothing in the universe stands by itself: object and subject are interdependent. Things and their properties only come into being as they are when they come to stand in some relation to someone's perception. A thing only becomes something as a result of its relation to the senses of a subject. We can therefore never say what a thing essentially is aside from our observation of that thing. We can only say that at a given moment something appears to us to be such and such. "Man is the measure of all things." Although this argument is weighty, it proves too much. If it were valid it would not only render impossible the knowledge of God but all knowledge of the human race and the world. We have already discussed this idealism in the previous volume,[47] moreover, and can therefore be excused from further dealing with it here.

But agnosticism has at its disposal a number of grounds that are especially directed against the knowability of God. To be sure, philosophy and theology were at all times, as we saw above, persuaded of the inadequate character of our knowledge of God. Negative predicates only tell us what God is not and positive predicates apply to him in a way that is very different from the way they apply to creatures. The limited, finite, and anthropomorphic character of our knowledge of God was recognized by all. But in modern times the nonattainability of knowledge of God has been argued on the basis of other, more radical, grounds. Subjectively, scholars have pointed out the limited character

---

45. W. Hamilton, "On the Philosophy of the Unconditioned," *Edinburgh Review* (October 1829); H. Mansel, *The Limits of Religious Thought* (Oxford: J. Wright, 1858); I. Dorner, *Jahrbücher für deutsche Theologie*, 6 (1861): 320ff., 347ff.; C. Hodge, *Systematic Theology*, 3 vols. (New York: Charles Scribner's Sons, 1988), I, 346ff.

46. R. A. Lipsius, *Lehrbuch der evangelisch-protestantischen Dogmatik* (Braunschweig: C. A. Schwetsche, 1893), §§229ff., 243ff.; A. Ritschl, *Theologie und Metaphysik* (Bonn: A. Marcus, 1886), 8ff. (ed. note: Bavinck, likely in error, cites an unknown title *Metaphysik und Religion*); idem, *Die christliche Lehre von der Rechtfertigung und Versöhnung*, 4th ed., 3 vols. (Bonn: A. Marcus, 1895–1903), III, 211ff.; L. W. E. Rauwenhoff, *Wijsbegeerte van de Godsdienst* (Leiden: Brill & van Doesburgh, 1887), 611ff.; S. Hoekstra, *Wijsgerige Godsdienstleer*, II, 11ff.

47. See H. Bavinck, *Reformed Dogmatics*, I, 214 (#64).

of the human faculty of knowledge; and, objectively, they have pointed out the self-contradiction to which every God-concept is subject. Kant did the former; Fichte the latter. Kant examined the human faculty of cognition and came to the conclusion that the forms of perception and the categories of the intellect came along with the subject and had validity in the world of phenomena, but made impossible for us any knowledge of the noumena. The transcendent ideas of God, the world, and the soul do regulate our conduct, and a moral person can only act as if, corresponding to these three ideas, there is an objective reality, but none of this is demonstrable.

At this point Fichte weighed in with the further objection that absoluteness and personality are forever incompatible. Spinoza had already made the point that all determination is negation and, therefore, that the more determined and concrete a thing becomes, the more finite and limited it is. By that process, certainly, it ceases to be what other things are: when a given thing is white, it can no longer be red or black. God, accordingly, cannot be something determinate alongside and distinct from creatures, but is the substance of all creatures, the one infinite being, so that everything that exists, exists in him.[48] Now this philosophical premise was applied by Fichte to the concept of personality. Personality and consciousness are things we have found in ourselves and therefore cannot be conceived without limitation and finiteness. The moment we apply them to God, we make him a finite, limited, human being. The only thing religion really needs, accordingly, is the moral world order. That is all. The idea of a particular personal existence of God is not necessary for religion and also indemonstrable, even impossible and self-contradictory.[49] Those who desire such a God are still in the power of eudaemonism. This argument then became widespread and returns with great frequency.[50]

At bottom this antithesis between absoluteness and personality is none other than that which in Christian theology was always felt and expressed in negative and positive (apophatic and cataphatic) theology. However much the proofs against the knowability of God are each time presented in a different form, in fact they are always the same and consistently come down to the following. Human beings are bound to sense perception and always derive the

48. B. Spinoza, *Epist.* 50; *Ethics,* I, prop. 14, 15.

49. J. G. Fichte, "Über den Grund unseres Glaubens an eine göttliche Weltregierung," in *Gesamtausgabe,* by J. G. Fichte, 15 vols. (Stuttgart: Bad Cannstatt, 1977), V, 318–57; cf. Kuno Fischer, *Geschichte der neueren Philosophie,* 2d ed., 11 vols. (Heidelberg: Winter, 1924), V, 628ff.

50. Cf. Schelling in his first period, "Vom Ich als Princip der Philosophie," in *Ausgewählte Werke,* by F. W. J. Schelling (Darmstadt: Wissenschaftliche Buchgesellschaft, 1967–68), I, 8 [*Werke,* I, 1, 200]. Hegel, *Wissenschaft der Logik,* vol. II, sect. 2, 1, B: "Der mechanische Process," in *Sämtliche Werke,* by G. W. F. Hegel, 22 vols. (Stuttgart: Fr. Frommans Verlag, 1949–58), V, 184ff. Ed. note: Bavinck's references to Schelling that are to works incorporated into the new unrevised but abridged and repaginated *Ausgewählte Werke* (Darmstadt: Wissenschafliche Buchgesellschaft, 1968) will be cited with the full title of the work as well as Bavinck's original reference. Since this is not a complete edition of Schelling's original *Sämmtliche Werke* (Stuttgart and Augsburg: J. G. Cotta'scher, 1856–61), writings not included in the new edition will be cited as *Werke,* using Bavinck's original reference. F. Schleiermacher, *Speeches on Religion;* A. Schopenhauer, *Parerga und Paralipo-*

material of thought from the visible world. They do not see the spiritual and cannot elevate themselves to the world of invisible things, inasmuch as they always remain bound to space and time. Also, their thinking is material and finite and limited. Just as the eagle is confined to the atmosphere (Hamilton) and fish to the water of a pond (Lange), so our thinking always moves within the sphere of that which is finite. In addition, thought by virtue of its nature presupposes a distinction between subject and object; and since these are opposed to each other and limit each other, neither of them can be absolute. Hamilton therefore said, "To think is to condition," and Mansel expressed the same thing by saying, "Distinction is necessarily limitation." Knowledge of the absolute, accordingly, is a contradiction in terms. It indicates that one has knowledge of something that is "absolute," that is, detached, without relation, and is at the same time related to a knowing subject because it is known. Now if this is the structure of thought and we still want to think (about) and know God, we invariably either lower the Absolute to the level of the finite and make God into a personal, limited, humanlike being; or attempt to transcend all the limitations of space and time, strip our idea of God of all likeness to a finite creature, and end up with an empty abstract idea devoid of value for religion. Indeed, even the idea slips away: under the sway of our thinking the Absolute has been reduced to nothing. Absoluteness and personality, infinity and causality, immutability and communicability, absolute transcendence and likeness to the creature—all these pairs seem irreconcilable in the concept of God. We are caught up in an insoluble antinomy. It is as if we are only left with the choice between gross realism and vacuous idealism, between a God who is nothing but an enlarged version of a human person and a cold abstraction that freezes and destroys the religion of the heart.

THE MYSTERY OF AN ABSOLUTE, PERSONAL GOD

[166] To a considerable extent we can assent to and wholeheartedly affirm this doctrine of the unknowability of God. Scripture and the church emphatically assert the unsearchable majesty and sovereign highness of God. There is no knowledge of God as he is in himself. We are human and he is the Lord our God. There is no name that fully expresses his being, no definition that captures him. He infinitely transcends our picture of him, our ideas of him, our language concerning him. He is not comparable to any creature. All the nations are accounted by him as less than nothing and vanity. "God has no name. He cannot be defined." He can be apprehended; he cannot be comprehended. There is some knowledge (γνωσις) but no thorough grasp (καταληψις) of God. This

mena I, in *Sämmtliche Werke*, vol. 5 (Leipzig: F. V. Brockhaus, 1919), 123ff.; E. von Hartmann, *Philosophie des Unbewussten*, 11th ed. (Leipzig: H. Haacke, 1904) II, 175ff.; idem, *Religionsphilosophie*, 2d ed., 2 vols. (Bad Sachsa im Harz: Hermann Haacke, 1907), II, 145–63; idem, *Lotzes Philosophie* (Leipzig: W. Friedrich, 1888), 168ff.; D. F. Strauss, *Christliche Glaubenslehre*, I, 502; A. Biedermann, *Dogmatik*, II, 457–72, 537–47; A. Drews, *Die Religion als Selbstbewusstsein Gottes* (Jena and Leipzig: E. Diederichs, 1906), 324ff.

is how the case is put throughout Scripture and all of theology. And when a shallow rationalism considered a fully adequate knowledge of God a possibility, Christian theology always opposed the idea in the strongest terms.

According to Socrates Scholasticus, Eunominus, a follower of Arius, is said to have taught that he knew God equally well as himself.[51] God's being, according to him, consisted solely in his "uncreatedness" (ἀγεννησια), and this idea gave him a clear, distinct, and fully adequate concept of the divine being. God's knowledge of himself was not any more adequate, and a human knowledge of God was not any less adequate, than was expressed in this predicate. Centuries later Spinoza declared he had just as clear an idea of God as he did of a triangle, though he did not mean to say he knew God totally.[52] And in the nineteenth century Hegel taught that in conceptual philosophy the Absolute achieved full self-consciousness and was therefore fully and adequately known by the philosopher; and that our God-consciousness is nothing other than God's self-consciousness. God exists to the extent he is known by us, that is, to the extent he knows himself in us. This rationalism has most energetically been opposed and repudiated in the Christian church.[53]

Involved here is a matter of profound religious importance, to which Augustine gave expression as follows: "We are speaking of God. Is it any wonder if you do not comprehend? *For if you comprehend, it is not God you comprehend.* Let it be a pious confession of ignorance rather than a rash profession of knowledge. To attain some slight knowledge of God is a great blessing; to comprehend him, however, is totally impossible."[54] God is the sole object of all our love, precisely because he is the infinite and incomprehensible One. Although Scripture and the church, thus as it were, accept the premises of agnosticism and are even more deeply convinced of human limitations and the incomparable grandeur of God than Kant and Spencer, they draw from these realities a very different conclusion. Hilary put it as follows: "The perfection of learning is to know God in such a way that, though you realize he is not unknowable, yet you know him as indescribable."[55] The knowledge we have of God is altogether unique. This knowledge may be called positive insofar as by it we recognize a being infinite and distinct from all finite creatures. On the other hand, it is negative because we cannot ascribe a single predicate to God as we conceive that predicate in relation to creatures. It is therefore an *analogical* knowledge: a knowledge of a being who is unknowable in himself, yet able to make something of himself known in the being he created.

51. Socrates Scholasticus, *The Ecclesiastical History of Socrates* (London: S. Bagster, 1844; H. Bonn, 1853), IV, 7.

52. B. Spinoza, *Epist.* 60.

53. Basil, *Hexaemeron*, hom. 1; Gregory of Nazianzus, *Orat.* 28; cf. J. Schwane, *Dogmengeschichte*, II², 27ff.

54. Augustine, *Lectures on the Gospel of John*, tract. 38, *NPNF (1)*, VII, 217–21.

55. Hilary of Poitiers, *De trinitate*, II, 7.

Here, indeed, lies something of an antinomy. Rather, agnosticism, suffering from a confusion of concepts, sees here an irresolvable contradiction in what Christian theology regards as an adorable mystery. It is completely incomprehensible to us how God can reveal himself and to some extent make himself known in created beings: eternity in time, immensity in space, infinity in the finite, immutability in change, being in becoming, the all, as it were, in that which is nothing. This mystery cannot be comprehended; it can only be gratefully acknowledged. But mystery and self-contradiction are not synonymous. Pantheistic philosophy has turned the one, mystery, into the other, self-contradiction. When it equates the absolute with the indefinite and calls all determination a limitation and negation, it is guilty of confusing concepts. There is a world of difference between infinite and endless, between omnipotent and the sum of all power, between eternity and the sum of all moments of time, and so forth, and in the same way between the Absolute and the indefinite, the unbounded, the boundless. Pantheism begins by injecting its own God-concept into these words and so finds it easy to accuse theism of being inconsistent with them. To say that God is the infinite One and can and does nevertheless reveal himself in finite creatures, though this belief is a recognition of an incomprehensible mystery—the miracle of creation, after all—is by no means the admission of a palpable absurdity. The finite cannot diminish the infinity of God if it is only grounded in God's Absolute being.

Similarly, our knowledge does not limit God because (1) it is grounded in him, (2) can only exist through him, and (3) especially has as its object and content God as the infinite One. Furthermore, if absoluteness precludes all limitation, and all determination is negation, it is not only not permissible to speak of God as personality, but it is equally wrong still to call him the Absolute, unity, the good, essential being, substance (etc.). Pantheism suffers from the illusion that it has completed its God-concept if only the ideas of personality and self-consciousness are removed from it as contradictory elements. And the theistic philosophers of the first half of the nineteenth century (for example, I. H. Fichte, Carus, Steffens, Weisse, Ulrici, et al.), driven by reaction, became all too attached to this concept of personality, thinking that in the concept of absolute personality they possessed a fully adequate description of the divine being. Indeed, many pertinent remarks have been made in criticism of pantheism to prove that personality is not inconsistent with the absolute being of God. As long as absoluteness is not equated with boundlessness, with infinite extension in all directions, it is hard to see how personality would be incompatible with it. Rightly considered, all it means is that God's self-consciousness is equally deep and rich, equally infinite, as his being. Granted, while in our (human) case personality may arise and awaken over against that which is a nonself, it does not originate there, but has roots and a content of its own in human nature. In the case of God personality is and can therefore be the eternal synthesis of himself with himself, infinite self-knowledge and self-determination, and therefore not dependent on a nonself.[56]

Still we have to grant the truth of what the older Fichte said, namely, that personality is a concept borrowed from the human realm and hence, when applied to God, always to some extent falls short. The concept of personality, when applied to God, is not fully adequate and in principle no better than all other anthropomorphisms we use with reference to God. The Christian church and Christian theology, it must be remembered, never used the word "personality" to describe God's being; and in respect of the three modes of subsistence in that being, they only spoke of persons reluctantly and for lack of a better term. At the same time this situation makes clear that pantheism has not gained anything when it points out the incongruity of this concept. The antithesis between absoluteness and personality is identical with that between negative and positive theology. Even if the word "personality" is inappropriate, this does not settle anything: the same question is bound to surface again and again. If all determination is negation, then God may not be called the One, the Existent One, or the Absolute either. In that case all thought and speech about God is prohibited. If as humans we may not speak of God in a human and analogical manner, we have no choice but to be silent. To think and speak divinely of God is beyond us. But then all religion implodes. If God cannot be known, neither can he be felt and, in that feeling, enjoyed. Feeling is as finite as the intellect and finitizes and humanizes God in the same way. No possibility then exists either of God revealing himself objectively in his creatures or of us subjectively perceiving him by any organ. All religion, then, is sacrilege and all theology blasphemy.

Given this outcome, the question concerning God's knowability has been reduced to another question, namely, whether God has willed and found a way to reveal himself in the domain of creatures. For Kant is perfectly correct when he says that our knowledge does not extend farther than our experience.[57] If God has not revealed himself, then neither is there any knowledge of him. But if he has revealed himself there is something, however little, that can be perceived by us and so lead to knowledge. Then, however, it is also self-evident that the denial of the knowability of God coincides completely with the denial that God has revealed himself in the works of his hands.

Agnosticism, in fact, relapses into the error of ancient Gnosticism. God is mere "inexpressible depth" and "eternal silence." There is no communion or kinship between him and his creatures. The universe is, then, in the most absolute sense of the word, godless. There is not a trace of him to be found in the whole world. The world, then, is the product of an inferior God, a demiurge, or of chance. Humanity has not been created in God's image but is simply a product of nature and without God in the world. No religion or

---

56. I. H. Fichte, *Die Idee der Persönlichkeit und der individuellen Fortdauer* (Leipzig: Dyk, 1855).

57. I. Kant., *Critique of Pure Reason*, 432ff.

theology is possible on the basis of either creation or re-creation. God and the world are absolutely separate.

Worse, agnosticism cannot escape the implication that God *cannot* reveal himself. It confines him to himself, makes him into an unknown invisible power who has neither consciousness nor will, who can in no way communicate himself, who is eternal silence. And, just as in Manichaeism, the world is elevated to the status of a power alongside and over against God, a power incapable of in any way giving him access to itself and completely unfit to radiate even a particle of his glory. Agnosticism thus actually ends in atheism, of which it is merely the nineteenth-century form and name. Still, as a rule agnosticism does not go that far and still maintains the existence of the Unknowable. As soon as it adopts this position, however, it is caught up in an intolerable self-contradiction. Augustine already commented that the proposition that we know nothing of God already presupposes a lot of knowledge of God and therefore that what we have here is a contradiction in terms. For when we call God "inexpressible," we are at the same time saying a lot about him, so that in fact he is not "inexpressible." "For it is no small amount of knowledge . . . if before we know what God is we already know what he is not." Not-knowing is itself extensive and positive: it amounts to "no small beginning of the knowledge of God."[58] It is already quite significant to know that God is in no way creaturely. The same is true with reference to the agnostics. Spencer, for example, asserts that we are under pressure from our own thinking to assume the existence of an absolute being as ground of the universe, though on account of our finiteness and limitedness we cannot form any concept of such a being. But if we are so finite and limited, what is it that prompts us to conceive the idea of an absolute Being and to assume its existence? And if we are really forced to assume the existence of such an absolute Being, why should knowledge of that Being be totally impossible?

There is a big difference, certainly, between having an absolute knowledge and having a relative knowledge of such an absolute Being. Given the finiteness of human beings, the former is never an option. If Eunomius were correct in saying that either we know God's being or else we do not know God at all, then human beings could not possess true knowledge of finite things either. What we know of God we know only of his revelation and therefore only as much as he is pleased to make known to us concerning himself and as much as finite humans can absorb. Knowledge of God, accordingly, can be true and pure, but it is always most relative and does not include but excludes comprehension. Basil was right in telling Eunomius that "the knowledge of God consists in the perception of his incomprehensibility."[59] But this insight itself already constitutes substantial knowledge. For that reason not a single agnostic is prepared in the end to restrict himself or herself to saying that the matter is unclear *(non liquet)*. Spencer, for example, keeps saying that we do

58. Augustine, *On Christian Doctrine*, I, 6; idem, *The Trinity*, VIII, 2; idem, *Epistle ad Consent.*
59. Basil, according to O. Bardenhewer, *Patrologie* (Freiburg i.B.: Herder, 1894), 260. Ed. note: ET: *Patrology* (St. Louis: Herder, 1908).

not know the Absolute; at the same time he has an idea of it, demonstrates its existence, and assigns an array of properties to it. He asserts that it is not a negative but a positive concept; that it is the cause of everything; that it is a power mostly analogous to our will, infinite, eternal, omnipresent (etc.). This certainly is no longer agnosticism, but a very specific kind of knowledge and a rather well-defined God-concept. Agnosticism, inherently untenable and afraid of atheism, serves in the end to justify a pantheistic God-concept.

2

THE KNOWLEDGE OF GOD

All knowledge of God rests on revelation. Though we can never know God in the full richness of his being, he is known to all people through his revelation in creation, the theater of his glory. The world is never godless. In the end there are no atheists; there is only argument about the nature of God. The recognition is universal of a power greater than human beings themselves, to whom they owe piety.

Atheistic naturalism and similar forms of thought are philosophical rather than religious trends and owe their existence to criticism of the religious views of others. They never arise spontaneously or give rise to communities of believers existing over time. Even philosophers acknowledge this when they grant religious representations as necessary for people who are incapable of rising to the heights of pure conceptuality. Belief in a personal God is both natural and normal; it arises in human consciousness spontaneously and universally. Unbelief requires enormous effort. There is no proof available to it.

Explanations for this universal religious impulse vary. Greek philosophy spoke of universal ideas, though, strictly speaking, it was Cicero who first developed the notion of "innate ideas" or "inborn principles of the virtues," implanted in the soul by God. In modern philosophy, the trajectory of thought beginning with Descartes, while judging all knowledge to be triggered by the senses, did consider it finally to arise from the inner mental capacity for representation. Kant modified this with his teaching about innate forms of perception, categories of mind, and forms of reason. Idealism extended this by considering all knowledge, indeed all being itself, to arise out of the thinking process.

The notion of innate ideas was criticized by empiricists such as Locke and Hobbes, who insisted that all knowledge stems from sense perception. "There is nothing in the mind which was not previously in the senses." Christian theology did assume that some natural truth was universally known apart from special revelation, but it rejected the notion of innate ideas. It is in

Ed. note: This chapter was originally two major sections (§24 and §25) in the *Gereformeerde Dogmatiek*. Both sections were entitled "The Knowledge of God" with the respective subtitles *Cognita Dei insita* and *Cognita Dei acquisita*. These terms have been translated as "The Implanted Knowledge of God" and "The Acquired Knowledge of God" and serve as two of the major divisions in this single chapter.

mysticism that some, such as Bonaventure, taught a knowledge of God that is immediate, apart from the senses. Yet, even then, Bonaventure placed limits on this knowledge; it was a gift of grace and thus not a strictly innate idea. All we can say is that as created beings we have a God-given disposition or capacity to know him.

It is this capacity that Calvin called a sensus divinitatis *and a* semen religionis. *The Reformed confessions and theologians consistently affirmed a "natural theology" of this sort while at the same time rejecting the notion of "innate ideas." The danger of this theory is twofold: rationalism and mysticism. If human beings at birth came fully endowed with clear and distinct knowledge of God, being, or all ideas, they would be completely autonomous and self-sufficient, needing neither God, the world, nor revelation. The logical conclusion of this kind of thinking is idealism, which considers reality itself to be a creation of immanent human thought processes.*

The sentiments of rationalists and mystics are thus pantheistic, confusing God and the order of being with the human order of knowing. We do not know God immediately; all our knowledge of God is obtained indirectly and bears an analogical character. Like all knowledge, knowledge of God is mediated to us through our senses, through speech and symbol, mediated to us by parents and others. If this were not the case, we would have no way of accounting for the great diversity of representations of God. If knowledge of God, of the moral order, of the beautiful—if these were all innate, they would be universally identical and acknowledged as such. Nothing is farther from the truth.

At the same time we must speak of "implanted knowledge of God" in some sense. This means simply that, as in the case of language, human beings possess both the capacity and the inclination to arrive at some firm, certain, and unfailing knowledge of God. We gain this knowledge in the normal course of human development and in the environment in which God gives us the gift of life. From the entire realm of nature, both exterior and interior to us humans, we receive impressions and gain perceptions that foster in us the sense of God. It is God himself who does not leave us without witness.

It is important, however, to make some distinction between implanted and acquired knowledge of God. In the former God's revelation acts upon human consciousness, creating impressions and intuitions. In the case of the acquired knowledge of God, human beings reflect upon that revelation of God and seek by reasoning and proof to rise above impressions and intuitions to clearer ideas. This is the natural human desire to explain the how *and* why *of our knowledge. This distinction must not be restricted to so-called natural theology in opposition to revealed theology. God reveals himself to us in his handiwork of creation, but even Christian believers depend on Scripture and the illumination of the Holy Spirit to truly know God the Creator. We are indebted to Scripture for both implanted and acquired knowledge.*

This insight helps us to consider aright the so-called proofs for God's existence, neither overestimating nor disdaining them. Christian theology accepts the support given to its convictions about God by pagan philosophy but judges these proofs within the doctrine of faith, not as preambles to it. Christian conviction about what can be known about God apart from special revelation is a valid natural theology. However, when this natural theology stands on its own and in a self-sufficient and rationalistic fashion sets aside the need for special revelation, it is an invalid and impious activity. Under the critique of modern thought, notably Kant and Darwin, the ontological and teleological proofs have had a difficult time. The moral argument continues to have some persuasiveness in certain circles.

The cosmological argument attempts to deduce the existence of a cause from the demonstrable existence of an effect. This argument has some validity but fails to tell us anything about the character and nature of the cosmic cause. All we have is a self-existent, first, and absolute World-cause. The teleological argument, proceeding from the world's order and beauty, takes us one step further to an intelligent cause that must be conscious. However, we still do not know whether this means one intelligent Being or several working in harmony. We are still not nearly at a knowledge of the God of Scripture.

The ontological argument, in its various forms, attempts to infer existence from thought. Our common sense recognizes that this argument is not true when it comes to creatures. Nonexistent beings can be conceived. With God matters are slightly different. Though we cannot convincingly demonstrate the reality of God from our ideas about God, it is true that whenever we do think about God we necessarily think of God existing. The benefit of this argument is that human beings are confronted with the choice of either trusting this necessary witness of their consciousness or else despairing of their own consciousness.

The moral argument infers the existence of a supreme and sovereign Lawgiver from moral phenomena such as human conscience, fear of death and judgment, repentance, and reward and punishment. While these phenomena are powerful witness to the enduring moral nature of even fallen humanity, they are less than a proof for the existence of a righteous and holy God. The same is true for the argument that proceeds from the universal reality of religion. This fact bears powerful witness to the existence, revelation, and knowability of God but cannot as such disprove the claim that it reflects a universal pathology of the human mind, a passing fancy or delusion. Finally, arguments based on the purposefulness of history presuppose what they claim to demonstrate. History is susceptible to different interpretations that are, in the final analysis, a matter of faith, not proof. The heart rather than the intellect is the final arbiter.

That must also be our judgment concerning these "proofs" in general. Even the term "proofs" is infelicitous. The cosmological, teleological, and moral testimony to God is not a matter of logical, mathematical proof but belongs to the category of moral and religious truth.

The proofs may augment and strengthen our faith, but they do not serve as its grounds. They are, rather, the consequences, the products of faith's *observation of the world. The proofs do not induce faith, and objections against them do not wreck it. They are, instead, testimonies by which God is able to strengthen already-given faith.*

THE PROBLEM OF ATHEISM

[167] Just as we saw in the case of religion,[1] so now it is also apparent that the knowledge of God can have its origin only in revelation. Naturally, if God does not become manifest in his creatures, no knowledge of him is even possible. But if he does display his perfections in the world of creatures, his knowability can no longer be disputed. Of course, in saying this, we have not defined the character and extent of that knowledge. All who teach the knowability of God readily agree that this knowledge is entirely unique *(sui generis)* and of a very limited scope. For though God to some extent becomes manifest in his creatures, there remains in him an infinite fullness of power and life that is not revealed. His knowledge and power are not confined to the world nor exhaustively displayed there. It is not even possible for him to fully reveal himself to and in his creature, inasmuch as the finite cannot grasp the infinite. "No one knows the Father except the Son" (Matt. 11:27; cf. Deut. 29:29). Furthermore, that which God reveals of himself in and through his creatures is already so rich and profound that it can never be fully known by any human being. In so many respects we do not even understand the world of created things and are at every moment confronted in all directions by enigmas and mysteries. How then should we be able to understand God's revelation in all its riches and depths? But in saying this we are certainly not nullifying God's knowability. God's incomprehensibility, so far from canceling out God's knowability, rather presupposes and affirms it. The riches of God's being—riches that surpass all knowledge—are in fact a necessary and significant component of our knowledge of God. The fact remains that God makes himself known to us in the manner and measure in which he reveals himself in his creatures.

Now the fact that the world is the theater of God's self-revelation can hardly be denied. In the first place, Scripture at no time leaves us in doubt about this. It does not erect an altar to the unknown God but proclaims the God who made the world (Acts 17:23–24); whose power and deity can be clearly perceived by the human mind in the things that have been made (Rom. 1:19–20); who above all created humanity in his image and likeness (Gen. 1:26), as his offspring who live and move in him (Acts 17:28). He has spoken to them by prophets and apostles, above all by his Son himself (Heb. 1:1), and now continually reveals himself to and in them (Matt. 16:17; John 14:22–23; etc.). According to Scripture the whole universe is a creation and hence also a revelation of God.

In an absolute sense, therefore, nothing is atheistic. And this witness of Scripture is confirmed on every side. There is no atheistic world. There are no

---

1. Cf. H. Bavinck, *Reformed Dogmatics*, I, 276 (#81).

atheistic peoples. Nor are there atheistic persons. The world cannot be atheistically conceived since in that case it could not be the work of God but would have to be the creation of an anti-god. Now the dualism that has recurrently surfaced in religion and philosophy has on occasion viewed matter as a demonic principle, but with reference to the universe it has nevertheless consistently recognized a combination of idea and matter, a conflict between light and darkness. There is nobody able, absolutely and with logical consistency, to deny God's knowability and hence his revelation. Agnosticism itself is proof of this point: like skepticism, it cannot maintain itself except with the aid of what it opposes. And precisely because the world cannot be conceived as godless, there are no atheistic and areligious peoples. True, the opposite has been claimed by Socinus, Locke, and many people in modern times, for example, Büchner, Darwin (et al.).[2] But their opinion has been sufficiently refuted and has now been almost universally abandoned.[3] Cicero's well-known statement to the effect that "there is no people so barbarous as not to believe in the gods" has been confirmed for centuries. This fact is of great significance. The belief that all humans share by virtue of their nature cannot be false. "Time obliterates the inventions of the imagination, but confirms the judgments of nature."[4]

Thus, in the end, there are no atheistic persons. There is disagreement not so much about the existence as about the nature of God. Admittedly, there exists a practical atheism, life without God in the world (Ps. 14:1; 53:2; Eph. 2:12). But a conscious theoretical atheism in an absolute sense, if it ever occurs, is rare. The word "atheism" has, however, often been used in a relative sense, not as the denial of any kind of deity, but as the denial of a certain specific deity. The Greeks charged Socrates with atheism.[5] Cicero counted Protagoras and Prodicus as atheists since they denied the existence of the national gods.[6] For the same reason Christians were frequently accused of atheism by pagans.[7] And Christians in turn applied the word to those who rejected the God of revelation. Roman Catholics sometimes counted Luther, Melanchthon, and Calvin as atheists, and Voetius, employing it in a broad sense, applied it also

2. F. Socinus, *Tract. theol.*, ch. 2; "*De auctor script.*," ch. 2; J. Locke, *Essay on Human Understanding*, I, 4, 8; L. Büchner, *Force and Matter*, trans. from 15th German ed., 4th ed. (New York: P. Eckler, 1891); C. Darwin, *The Descent of Man*, 2d ed. (New York: D. Appleton, 1903), 95ff.

3. B. de Moor, *Comm. in Marckii Comp.*, I, 57; C. Vitringa, *Comm.*, I, 16; O. Peschel, *Abhandlungen zur Erd- and Völkerkunde*, 5th ed. (Leipzig: Duncker & Humboldt, 1878), 260; F. Ratzel, *Völkerkunde*, 3 vols. (Leipzig: Bibliographisches Institut, 1885–90), I, 30ff.; ed. note: ET: *The History of Mankind*, trans. A. J. Ruther, 3 vols. (New York: Macmillan, 1896–98); C. P. Tiele, *Geschiedenis van de Godsdienst* (Amsterdam: P. N. van Kampen & Zoon, 1876), 8; R. Flint, *Anti-theistic Theories*, 3d ed. (Edinburgh and London: W. Blackwood and Sons, 1885), 250, 289, 519, 532; G. Tr. Ladd, *The Philosophy of Religion*, 2 vols. (New York: Scribner, 1905), I, 120ff.; O. Zöckler, *Das Kreuz Christi* (Gütersloh: C. Bertelsmann, 1875), 117ff.

4. Cicero, *On the Nature of the Gods*, I, 17; II, 2.

5. Xenophon, *Memorabilia*, I, 1.

6. Cicero, *On the Nature of the Gods*, I, 42.

7. J. C. Suicerus, *Thesaurus ecclesiasticus*, s.v. "θεος"; Harnack, *Der Vorwurf des Atheismus in den drei ersten Jahrhundert* (Leipzig: J. C. Hinrichs, 1905).

to Descartes.[8] In modern times J. G. Fichte was openly charged with atheism because he equated the moral world order itself with God. And still today the term "atheist" is sometimes given to those who know no other power than "matter," like Feuerbach, Strauss, Büchner, Haeckel, Czelbe, and Dühring.[9] Indeed, when materialists recognize nothing but matter and the changing processes of matter, they *are* atheists and make no bones about wanting to be so considered.

But this almost never happens. Taken in an absolute sense, as the denial of an absolute power, atheism is almost unthinkable. In the final analysis, all people again recognize a power that they venerate as God. Just as the Christian believer calls others to reverence his or her God, so Strauss demands a like piety toward his universe.[10] Atheism and materialism again and again changed into pantheism[11] for the obvious reason that humans cannot resist the recognition of a Supreme Power. At the very moment they deny the true God, they fashion for themselves a false God. Religion is too deeply rooted in human nature, and God's revelation speaks too clear a language for them to resist this tendency. Even when in certain periods the tides of religious indifferentism and skepticism run deep and wide, as, for example, in the age of Pericles, Emperor Augustus, the Renaissance, and our own time as well, religion nevertheless always again rises to the surface. People tend rather to adopt the crudest superstition than to stick in the long run with cold and naked unbelief. But we can state it even more strongly. Not only does atheism in the absolute sense hardly ever occur, but it also is rare even in the sense that it would deny the existence of a personal God who has a claim on our adoration.

Undoubtedly, naturalism, hylozoism, and pantheism are repeatedly occurring intellectual trends. But they are philosophical rather than religious trends. They never arise spontaneously but owe their existence to criticism of the religious views of others. They are not grounded in dogma but in criticism, and therefore always serve but for a time and in a limited circle. A nation, a society, a denomination or congregation of this kind of naturalists and pantheists is inconceivable and cannot exist. Pantheists themselves acknowledge this when they say that graphic religious representations are necessary for ordinary people and that only philosophers can raise themselves to the level of pure conceptuality. Belief in a personal God, accordingly, is both natural and normal; it arises in human consciousness spontaneously and universally. But atheism, even the denial of the existence of a personal God, is

8. J. Buddeus, *Theses theologicae de atheismo et superstitione*, ed. J. Lulofs (1747), 116; on Voetius, see A. C. Duker, *G. Voetius*, 4 vols. (Leiden: Brill, 1897–1915), II, 151ff.

9. Cf. A. Drews, *Die deutsche Spekulation seit Kant*, 2 vols. (Berlin: P. Maetes, 1893), II, 235ff.

10. D. F. Strauss, *The Old Faith and the New*, trans. Mathilde Blind (New York: Holt, 1873), 141ff.

11. L. Büchner, *Force and Matter*, 370ff.; E. Haeckel, *Naturale Schöpfungsgeschichte* (Berlin: G. Reimer, 1889), 20, 32, 64; ed. note: ET: *The History of Creation*, trans. E. R. Lankester, 2 vols. (New York: D. Appleton, 1883); idem, *Der Monismus als Band zwischen Religion und Wissenschaft*, 6th ed. (Bonn: Emil Strauss, 1893); idem, *The Riddle of the Universe*, trans. Joseph McCabe (New York: Harper & Brothers, 1900), 288ff.

the exception. It is philosophy, not religion. There is truth in Schopenhauer's stinging statement: "An impersonal God is no God at all. It is no more than a misused word, a misconception, a contradiction in terms, a shibboleth for professors of philosophy who, after having had to abandon the thing itself, sneak through with the word."[12] It therefore requires a certain effort not to believe in a personal God: "No one disbelieves the existence of God except the person to whom God's existence is not convenient." There are no atheists so thoroughly sure of their unbelief as to be willing to die a martyr's death for it. Since atheism is abnormal and unnatural, based not on intuitions but on inferential proofs and fallible reasoning, it is never sure of its causes. The arguments for the existence of God may be weak, but in any case they are stronger than those advanced for its denial. It is even impossible to prove that there is no God. To accomplish that feat a person would have to be omniscient and omnipresent, that is, to be God![13]

THE IMPLANTED KNOWLEDGE OF GOD

[168] The natural, universal, and necessary character of religion and the knowledge of God already in ancient times led to the idea that it was increated in humans and innate by nature. It is simply a fact, certainly, that all persons from their earliest youth are conscious of a psychic, spiritual, invisible world as well as of a physical one. Though truth and falsehood, good and evil, right and wrong, and beauty and ugliness are not quantifiable entities and cannot be perceived by the five senses, they *are* things the reality of which is much more firmly fixed in our consciousness than that of matter and force. Materialism may only take into consideration gravity, temperature, and electricity, but faith, hope, and love, which are very different forces, have nevertheless governed humankind and kept it from sinking into bestiality. Augustine was right when he wrote that the truth of spiritual things is actually much more certain than that of visible things. "Nothing can be more absurd than to say that the objects we see with our eyes have being while the things we discern with our intellect do not, since only a fool would doubt the fact that the intellect is

---

12. A. Schopenhauer, *Parerga und Paralipomena*, 2 vols. (Leipzig: P. Reclam, 1895), I, 123; cf. idem, *Die Welt als Wille und Vorstellung*, 6th ed., 2 vols. (Leipzig: Brockhaus, 1887), II, 398, 406, 739; ed. note: ET: *Parerga and Paralipomena*, trans. E. F. J. Payne, 2 vols. (Oxford: Clarendon Press, 1974); and *The World as Will and Representation*, trans. E. F. J. Payne (New York: Dover Publications, 1966).

13. G. Voetius, "De atheismo," *Select. disp.*, I, 114–225; G. J. Vossius, "De origine ac progressu idololatriae," *Opera omnia*, I, ch. 3; Leydecker, *Fax veritas*, III, controv. 3; F. Turretin, *Institutes of Elenctic Theology*, trans. G. M. Giger, ed. J. T. Dennison, 3 vols. (Phillipsburg, N.J.: Presbyterian and Reformed, 1992), III, qu. 2.; S. Maresius, *Syst. theol.* (1673), 44; Buddeus, *Theses theol. de atheismo et superstitione*; C. Hodge, *Systematic Theology*, 3 vols. (New York: Charles Scribner's Sons, 1888), I, 198, 242; R. Flint, *Anti-theistic Theories*, lecture 1; S. Hoekstra, *Das Christens Godsvrucht* (Amsterdam: Gebroders Kraay, 1866), 6; J. I. Doedes, *Inleiding tot de Leer van God* (Utrecht: Kemink, 1870), 57ff.; J. B. Heinrich and C. Gutberlet, *Dogmatische Theologie*, 2d ed., 10 vols. (Mainz: Kirchheim, 1881–1900), III, 23ff.; P. B. Adlhoch, "Zur wissenschaftlichen Erklärung des Atheismos," *Philosophisches Jahrbuch* 18/3–4 (1905); A. Sabatier, *Outlines of a Philosophy of Religion*, trans. T. A. Seed (New York: James Pott, 1902), 66ff.

of incomparably higher rank than the eyes."[14] The truths of mathematics and logic and the principles of ethics, jurisprudence, and religion are indubitably established for everyone. Their natural, universal, and necessary character cannot be denied by anyone. As "innate ideas" they seem to be congenitally a part of human nature.

Innate Ideas in Philosophy

The theory of innate ideas has its roots in Greek philosophy. The question how in the world humans could possibly gain knowledge was an enormous problem to this philosophy. Certainly two possibilities exist: *either* we already know something and hence cannot learn it anymore, *or* we do not know anything—but then the question is: how is it that we strive to learn it?[15] Plato solved this problem with his theory of recollection. Before the soul was joined to the body, it had witnessed the ideas in all their beauty and stored away their images deep in its memory. He demonstrated this especially with respect to mathematics, which we are able to construct totally from within our mind without the aid of observation. For the rest he believed that all learning presupposes the preexistence of the soul.[16] Aristotle, while he regarded sense perception as the road to knowledge, nevertheless judged that inherent in reason as such there are a number of very general principles that are axiomatic, underlie all arguments, and are acknowledged by everyone.[17] The Stoics spoke of "common" or "natural" ideas, "implanted preconceptions," that is, concepts that everyone derives from sense perception by virtue of the structure of human thinking.[18]

The theory of innate ideas, strictly speaking, is not yet present in any of these philosophers. Plato does not limit recollection to a few innate ideas but extends it to all knowledge; and Aristotle and others as well, though they speak of universal principles, expressly teach that these principles are not ideas supplied at birth but specifically discovered by observation and reflection. This, however, occurs in a way such that every normal person has to find them.

The theory of innate ideas, again strictly speaking, occurs for the first time in Cicero. He speaks of "notions impressed on the mind," "implanted or innate thoughts," and assumes the existence of a knowledge of an array of truths prior to all experience and observation. According to him, there are "inborn principles of the virtues," "faint notions of the greatest things," which nature

---

14. Augustine, *The Imortality of the Soul*, 10 n. 17; idem, *City of God*, xix, 18.

15. E. Zeller, *Die Philosophie der Griechen*, 4th ed., 3 vols. in 5 (Leipzig: Fues's Verlag, 1875–81), I, 996; II, 823; III, 189. Ed. note: The final reference (III, 189) might be to the first edition rather than the fourth edition. Bavinck marked the first two references clearly as I[4] and II[4] while the third reference included no edition marker. The same is true of the references in nn. 16–18. The reference in n. 15 is clearly marked as the fourth edition.

16. Ibid., II,[4] 639, 643f., 829.

17. Ibid., III, 188ff.

18. Ibid., IV, 74ff., 389ff.

implanted in the soul "without prior instruction," an innate knowledge of God. "By nature we believe the gods exist."[19]

In modern philosophy the theory of innate ideas was advanced by Descartes, who was also the first to use that term and idea, therefore, in an—up until that time—quite unusual sense. In Descartes's thinking, this theory followed from the dualism he posited between soul and body. Intellectual knowledge, he said, cannot be derived from sense perception; the latter merely supplies the "occasion" in connection with which our mind, "by its own innate ability," forms the mental representations and concepts. Knowledge proceeds from a principle of its own, that is, from innate ideas. Paramount among these innate ideas is that of God, which is, as it were, "the author's stamp upon his work." But by the "innateness" of these ideas he means that the soul by nature possesses the power, the capacity, the disposition to produce them out of itself. Hence, the ideas are not actually but potentially present in our mind.[20]

According to Leibniz, as well, necessary and universal truths—such as substance, duration, change, causation, the axioms of mathematics, and especially the idea of God—do not come to us from without but originate in ourselves. Altogether these truths constitute the natural light of reason. But the innate character of these truths was explained at greater length and more clearly by Leibniz than by Descartes. The latter merely taught that those ideas were potentially present in our mind. Leibniz, however, maintains that they are "virtually" innate, "in the sense in which inclinations, dispositions, attitudes, or natural energies," unlike actions, are innate. The human mind not only has the capacity to know them, for if that were the case all knowledge could be called innate, but also is itself the source of these truths "that it can produce from within its own depths." The ideas, as they lie in the human mind, are thus, as it were, "preformed." And this is possible because there is a capacity for mental representation and reflection aside from consciousness. They become conscious when sense perception triggers the process. It actualizes in the mind the ideas that are virtually present in it.[21]

Malebranche similarly thought that in the case of humans the acquisition of knowledge could be explained only on the assumption that we see the ideas in God and hence that God, as universal and infinite being, is immediately present in our intellect. Following this line of thought, the ontologism of Gioberti, Gratry, and Ubaghs (et al.) taught that the human mind can see God directly as absolute being and therefore that there exists in humans an intuitive knowledge of God.[22]

19. Cicero, *Tusc.*, I, 16, 36; III, 1, 2; *De finibus*, V, 21, 59; *The Nature of the Gods*, I, 1, 2; cf. E. Zeller, *Philosophie der Griechen*, IV, 659ff.

20. R. Descartes, *Notae*, 185; *Third Meditations*, 24; *Object. et réponse*, 102; cf. F. O. Rose, *Die Lehre von den eingeborenen Ideen bei Descartes und Locke* (Bern: C. Sturzenegger, 1901).

21. Cf. C. B. Spruyt, *Proeve van eene Geschiedenis der Aangeboren Begrippen* (Leiden: Brill, 1879), 114; A. Stöckl, *Geschichte der neuern Philosophie*, 2 vols. (Mainz: F. Kirchheim, 1883), I, 426.

22. A. Stöckl, *Geschichte der neuern Philosophie*, II, 568ff., 620ff.; J. Heinrich and C. Gutberlet, *Dogmatische Theologie*, III, 119ff.

This theory of innate ideas was significantly modified by Kant. Following Wolff's terminology he spoke of a priori and a posteriori knowledge, and while he did not teach the notion of innate ideas, he did favor the idea of innate forms, that is, forms of perception (i.e., space and time), forms of the mind (i.e., the categories), and forms of reason (i.e., the ideas of God, virtue, and immortality). The idealism of Fichte and Hegel took this theory to such extreme lengths that they constructed not only the knowledge of necessary and universal truths, but all knowledge, indeed all being, the entire material world, out of the thinking process.

The grounds on which this theory of innate ideas rests are the following: Learning, the ability to learn, presupposes some kind of antecedent knowledge. Reasoning and proofs are based on principles that are axiomatically, a priori, certain. Experience merely furnishes "opinions," contingent truths. Universal and necessary truths can only originate in the human mind. The fact that such universal and necessary truths exist is established by universal agreement. And especially the opposition between soul and body is of such a nature that mental representations and concepts cannot have their origin in sense perception. They must be explained either in terms of the human mind or of the Spirit of God, in whom humans view all ideas.

On the other hand, the theory of innate ideas was opposed by Socinianism, which rejected natural religion, and above all by Locke, Hobbes, and others.[23] Their arguments rest on the following considerations: The theory of innate ideas is completely superfluous inasmuch as the origination of these ideas can very well be explained in another way. History teaches that there is not a single representation and concept that is the same to the mind of all humans and peoples. Not even innate moral principles exist. The greatest possible divergence of opinion exists with respect to good and evil. And the concept of God is so far from being innate that we know even of atheistic persons and peoples. Children and mentally handicapped or insane persons have no inkling of such innate concepts. In the case of humans, all knowledge stems from sense perception. "There is nothing in the mind that was not previously in the senses." In the eighteenth century this criticism of the theory of innate ideas became quite popular in England and France, and a century later the rising tide of materialism adopted it as well. Herbert Spencer, however, brought about a significant change in this rejection of innate ideas. His theory of evolution seemed to enable him to point out a way in which the ancient conflict between empiricism and nativism could be resolved. The law of evolution, certainly, also had to be applied to the human mind. This mind, he said, did not come into existence all at once, nor was it endowed from the beginning with an immutable set of capabilities, but gradually became what it is now. With a view to these very earliest beginnings, therefore, empiricism was correct and

23. O. Fock, *Der Socianismus* (Kiel: C. Schröder, 1847), 307ff.; S. Episcopius, *Inst. theol.*, I, 3; J. Locke, *Essay*, I, ch. 2; T. Hobbes, *On the Citizen*, 14 n. 19.

the human mind was a blank. But the experience of countless generations had gradually so shaped that mind that it can now be deemed to possess an array of forms and ideas by which it is naturally adapted to its entire environment. And that is the truth of nativism.[24]

Innate Ideas in Christian Theology

[169] It is important for us to know the attitude that Christian theology has assumed to this theory of innate ideas. Professor Spruyt found it strange that the scholastics, with rare unanimity, pronounced themselves opposed to this theory, and suspected the presence of a theological reason for this, but could not state it.[25] This is indeed the case and will become clear later. Although Christian theology universally assumed that there were truths known by nature and not by revelation, truths obtained spontaneously, as it were, and not by intentional study and reflection, it nevertheless firmly rejected the theory of innate ideas. It is true that in later times[26] the proponents of this theory (Thomasius, Staudenmaier, Kuhn, and Klee, for example), and ontologists (Malebranche, Gioberti, Ubaghs, et al.) appealed to some of the church fathers, but were mistaken about this. Justin Martyr, to be sure, refers to the idea of God as "humanity's innate opinion concerning a matter that is hard to explain" but does not tell us what he means by "innate" (ἔμφυτος).[27] Irenaeus, writing against the Gnostics, does assert that the world has been created by God, reveals him, and makes him known, but he does not say a word about innate knowledge.[28] Clement of Alexandria also affirms that the Father and Creator of all things is known by all "by nature and apart from any instruction," but he himself repeatedly states that this knowledge is obtained by the contemplation of God's works.[29]

Tertullian strongly emphasizes the natural knowledge of God: In danger and distress all humans—despite their worship of false gods—invoke the one true God. And they learned this, not from Moses and the prophets, but from their own soul. "For from the beginning an inner knowledge of God has been an endowment of the soul." The soul is the same among all peoples and by natural instinct Christian. By this Tertullian only means that some truths, such as the existence and unity of God, are known by nature and not just by special revelation: "For certain things are even known by nature. The immortality of the

---

24. C. Darwin, *Descent of Man*, chs. 3–4; Spencer, according to Spruyt, *Proeve*, 342; L. Büchner, *Force and Matter*, 344ff.

25. Cf. H. Bavinck, *Reformed Dogmatics*, I, 224 (#67). Ed. note: The reference is to C. B. Spruyt, *Proeve van eene Geschiedenis van de Leer der Aangeboren Begrippen* (Leiden: Brill, 1879).

26. G. Thomasius, *Theol. Dogm.*, I, 4; F. Staudenmaier, *Die christlich. Dogmatik* (Freiburg in Breisgau: Herder, 1844), II, 57ff.; J. Kuhn, *Die christliche Lehre von der gottlichen Gnade* (Tübingen: H. Laupp'sche Buchhandlung, 1868), 542ff.; H. Klee, *Katholische Dogmatik*, 2d ed., 3 vols. (Mainz: Kirchheim, 1839–41), II, 1–4.

27. Justin Martyr, *Apology*, II, 6.

28. Irenaeus, *Against Heresies*, II, 1ff.

29. Clement of Alexander, *Stromata*, V, 13, 14.

soul, for example, is known by a majority, our God by everyone."[30] Somewhat
more legitimate is the appeal to Augustine, who in many respects was influenced by Plato, as he himself acknowledges.[31] He indeed attaches much more
value to thought than to sense perception. The senses only perceive transient
objects, whereas reason, though distinct in every person, perceives and knows
universal, necessary, unchanging truths. This can only be explained in light
of the fact that each person's individual reason sees these universal truths in
the one universal Reason, the one unchanging Truth, which is God himself.
Along the same line Augustine repeatedly states that, just as we see material
objects by the light of the sun, so we contemplate the intelligible truths in the
light of God (*De civ.,* VIII, 7; *De trin.,* XII, 15). He is closer to us and easier
to find than creatures *(De Gen. ad litt.,* V, 16). He is "the truth presiding over
all things" *(Conf.,* X, 41). He even says that "the God and Lord of all things
directs the minds of humans without the intervention of nature" *(De musica,*
VI, 1). From this material it is clear that Augustine considers it much better
and easier to reach God by the contemplation of eternal truths than by the
observation of the external world of nature. It would be wrong for us to infer
from this, however, that [according to Augustine] the soul has the capacity
to contemplate God directly and immediately here on earth and thus to arrive at the knowledge of eternal truths. For elsewhere he clearly states that
"the vision of God" is reserved for heaven *(De trin.,* II, 17); that on earth we
are granted a "twilight knowledge" *(De Gen. ad litt.,* IV, 32); that the eternal
truths recognized by humans are distinct from God, who is the personified
Truth *(De lib. arb.,* II, 13; *Solil.,* I, 5); that from the contemplation of nature,
the knowledge of reason and its laws, humans advance to knowledge of God
(Conf., VII, 10; *De lib. arb.,* II, chs. 3–13).[32]

Mysticism, however, gaining powerful support from Augustine, taught that
in addition to "the eye of the flesh" and "the eye of reason," humans had originally received "the eye of contemplation," which, healed by grace, is at times
able to see God on earth already and will do so perfectly in glory.[33]

Bonaventure, accordingly, opposes the proposition that "all knowledge
derives from the senses": the soul knows God and itself without the aid of the
senses.[34] Mysticism, in the work of Bonaventure, though disagreeing on this
point with Thomas, nevertheless remains within clear boundaries. "Although
God is present, nevertheless, on account of the blindness and darkness enshroud-

30. Tertullian, *Against Marcion,* 10; idem, *Apology,* 17; idem, *On the Resurrection of the Flesh,* 3.

31. Augustine, *De beata vita: Happiness, a Study,* trans. F. E. Tourscher (Philadelphia: Peder Reilly,
1937), 4.

32. Cf. J. Kleutgen, *Philosophie der Vorzeit,* 2d ed., 5 vols. (Münster: Theisung, 1867–74), I, 756ff.;
J. Schwane, *Dogmengeschichte,* 4 vols. (Freiburg i.B.: Herder, 1882–95), II², 54–67; T. Gangauf, *Des heiligen
Augustinus speculative Lehre von Gott dem Dreieinigen* (Augsburg: Schmidt, 1883), 137ff.; C. B. Spruyt,
Proeve, 43–57; J. Heinrich and Gutberlet, *Dogmatische Theologie,* III, 81ff.

33. Bonaventure, *Breviloquium,* II, 12.

34. Bonaventure, *Sent.,* II, dist. 39, art.1, qu. 2.

ing our intellect, we know him as one absent." The vision of God is given to some—like the apostle Paul—but, as a gift of grace, it is not given to all. And though the knowledge of first principles is called "innate" in Bonaventure, he adds: "Because that light is enough for the purpose of my knowing these things upon receiving the forms (aside from any superadded persuasion) on account of their own internal evidence. . . . For I possess the natural light, which is sufficient for the purpose of knowing that parents should be honored and that one must not hurt one's neighbors, yet I do not have impressed upon me by nature the form of a father or the form of a neighbor."[35] Hence, though Bonaventure also assumes that there are truths we do not obtain by sense perception but by interior contemplation and communion with God, even he does not believe in innate ideas in the strict sense of the term.[36] Scholasticism in its entirety rejected the theory of innate ideas. By contrast, it taught that the essence of things is the real object of intellectual knowledge. All knowledge begins with sense perception. But when things have been so perceived, the intellect has the capacity to abstract from them that which is common and, first of all, the so-called innate ideas. These ideas, therefore, do not come ready-made with the intellect but, in keeping with its nature, are abstracted from the observation of *sensory* things. This is also true of the idea of God. God is not the substance but the *cause* of things. Accordingly, his existence and perfections can to a certain extent be known by perception and reflection from his works. We can speak of innate knowledge only in the sense that there has been created in our understanding a natural disposition *(habitus)* to proceed from the finite to the infinite, from the particular to the universal.[37] The ontologism of Gioberti and Ubaghs was condemned at Rome on September 18, 1861, and September 21, 1866, respectively.

In Lutheran theology the wholesome and true element inherent in the theory of innate ideas could not come into its own. Natural theology, both "implanted" and "acquired," was not well received there. By virtue of Luther's rejection of the scholastic doctrine that "what pertains to nature has remained unimpaired," Luther allowed himself to be driven to an opposite extreme. According to him, the image of God in humanity was totally lost. "Apart from the Holy Spirit [human] reason is simply devoid of the knowledge of God. When it comes to divine matters, humans are totally in the dark." Actually, what is still left to humans is only a "passive capacity," the capacity to be saved. For the rest their understanding, will, and affections are limited to "civil affairs." In spiritual things they are completely blind and dead. Luther does indeed

35. Bonaventure, *Sent.*, II, dist. 10, art. 1, qu. 1; dist. 23, art. 2, qu. 3; dist. 39, art.1, qu. 2.

36. Cf. the Freiburg edition of the *Breviloquium* (1881), 79ff., 148ff.; J. Schwane, *Dogmengeschichte*, III, 111ff.; *G. Sanseverino, *Philosophie der christlichen Neoplatonisme*, III, art. 41.

37. Cf. H. Bavinck, *Reformed Dogmatics*, I, 223 (#67); T. Aquinas, *Summa theol.*, I, qu. 2, art. 1; idem, *Summa contra gentiles*, I, 10, 11; *Theologia Wirceburgensi*, III, 5ff.; C. Pesch, *Theol. dogm.*, II, 10–13; J. Kleutgen, *Philosophie der Vorzeit*, I, 67ff., 587ff.; H. Denzinger, *Vier Bücher von der religiösen Erkenntnis*, 2 vols. (1856; Frankfurt a.M.: Minerva; Würzburg: Stahel, 1967), II, 28ff.

recognize that God still reveals himself in his works, that creation is a mode of revelation, God's "mask"; but humans no longer know him through this means. Luther sometimes even goes to the extreme of calling sin "the essence" of humans and humans "nothing but sin"—expressions that we certainly must not press unfairly, but which are still telling for his view of the innate and acquired knowledge of God.[38]

The same negative position is expressed in the Lutheran symbols and propagated by certain Lutheran theologians, like Flacius and Chemnitz, who reject all "natural knowledge of God."[39] Soon, however, this one-sided position was abandoned. Luther himself at times spoke a different language, seeing and extolling nature as a work of God. Melanchthon, for that matter, taught both an "innate" and an "acquired" knowledge of God. Vestiges of God are found in all his works. These would be insufficient "if the mind did not have implanted in it a certain knowledge or preconception of God."[40] Later theologians followed this example: Gerhard, Quenstedt, Hollaz, Calovius, Buddeus, and others treated "natural theology" and expressly defended it against the Socinians.[41] Some theologians (Jaeger et al.) even systematized natural theology and accorded it a separate place in dogmatics. These theologians variously defined the implanted knowledge of God *(cognitio Dei insita)* as "an ability" *(facultus)* or "disposition" *(habitus)* or "characteristic tendency" or "perfection" or "inborn light on the order of a natural disposition."

They all agreed, however, that it did not consist in an "impressed form" present in humans prior to any use of reason.[42] They therefore rejected Descartes's theory of innate ideas as well as the mystical doctrine of the "inner light" and contemplation. Instead, "implanted theology" was viewed as a natural fitness and inclination implanted in the human mind, enabling it to attain to knowledge of God "apart from any discursive thought and reasoning of the mind," and to back up this knowledge with an incontrovertibly certain testimony. "Prior to any sense perception there is nothing in the mind in the nature of an ideal representation of things, yet something in the nature of habitual knowledge."[43]

Natural Theology

Reformed theologians from the very beginning adopted a friendlier posture toward natural theology. Calvin made a distinction between general and special

---

38. J. Köstlin, *The Theology of Luther*, trans. Charles E. Hay, 2 vols. (Philadelphia: Lutheran Publication Society, 1897), II, 344ff., 455ff.

39. J. T. Müller, *Die symbolischer Bücher der evangelisch-lutherischen Kirche*, 5th ed. (Gütersloh: Bertelsmann, 1882), 522, 585, 589, 594; O. Zöckler, *Theologia naturalis* (Frankfurt a.M.: Heyder & Zimmer, 1860), 64.

40. O. Zöckler, *Theologia naturalis*, 60ff.; *Corpus reformatorum*, XIII, 137ff.

41. J. Gerhard, *Loci theol., prooemium*, 517; loc. II, c. 4; J. Quenstadt, *Theologia*, did. pol., I, 250ff.; D. Hollaz, *Examen. theol.*, 187ff.; A. Calovius, *Isag. ad SS. theol.*, 4; J. Buddeus, *De atheismo* (1767), 225ff.

42. D. Hollaz, *Examen*, 189; J. Quenstedt, *Theologia*, 253; Calovius, *Isag.*, 77.

43. D. Hollaz, *Examen*, 187ff.; J. Quenstedt, *Theologia*, I, 250ff.

grace and explained all the good still left also in sinful humans in terms of the former.[44] He specifically believed that an "awareness of divinity" *(sensus divinitatis)* was present within the human mind "by natural instinct." "God himself implanted in all humans an understanding of his divine majesty, persistently renewing its memory and constantly instilling fresh drops" *(Inst.* I.iii.1). Another name he gives to this awareness is "the seed of religion" *(semen religionis),* which explains the universality of religion (ibid.). The conviction that there is a God is "naturally inborn." It can never be eradicated (I.iii.3). "But barely one in a hundred can be found who nourishes in his own heart what he has conceived and not even one in whom it matures" (I.iv.1). Added to "this seed of religion" comes the revelation of God in his works; hence, now "people cannot open their eyes without being compelled to see him" (I.v.1). "There is no spot in the universe in which you cannot discern at least some sparks of his glory" (I.v.1). First of all, as microcosm, a human being as such is an excellent workshop for the innumerable works of God (I.v.3–4), but this is also true of the entire realm of nature, which, speaking reverently, we may even call God.[45]

All the Reformed symbols and theologians say the same. Ursinus writes that God reveals himself to humans "not only by notions about themselves impressed upon their mind, but also by way of all created things displayed as so many mirrors and documents of his divinity." And among the inborn items of knowledge he also counts the awareness that there is a God, as the universality of religion attests. Zanchius, rejecting both Plato and Aristotle [on this point], joins the Stoics and Cicero in teaching that "the ideas common to us all are inborn, not furnished by experience"; that children are immediately aware that three is more than two and that good and evil differ (etc.). According to Polanus, "right understanding consists in true knowledge of the will and works of God as also of the divine order and judgment inscribed upon the human mind by God," the author of which [knowledge] is the Logos, whose forms and norms constitute the natural principles, and which is expanded by the study of God's works.[46] Nevertheless, despite this vigorous defense of natural theology, Descartes's theory of innate ideas was resolutely rejected by Voetius. He charges Descartes especially with three errors: (a) that he falsifies the word "idea" by changing its meaning; (b) that he fails to state clearly what we are to understand by that "innate idea of God" (whether it belongs to "implanted" or "acquired" theology; whether it is an ability *[facultas]* or an

---

44. Cf. H. Bavinck, "Common Grace," trans. R. Van Leeuwen, *Calvin Theological Journal* 24 (1989): 50–55.

45. J. Calvin, *Institutes,* I.i–v; cf. II.ii.18; idem, *Commentary,* on Ps. 8; Ps. 19; Acts 17; 27; 28; Rom. 1:19; Heb. 11:3.

46. Z. Ursinus, *Tract. theol.* (1584), 35, 39; J. Zanchi(us), *Op. theol.,* III, 636ff.; A. Polanus, *Syn. theol.,* 325ff.; cf. P. M. Vermigli, *Loci comm.,* 2ff.; S. Maresius, *Syst. theol.,* 41; H. Alting, *Theol. elenctica* (1654), 2ff.; M. Leydekker, *Fax verit.,* loc. 3, contr. 1; J. H. Alsted, *Theol. polem.* (1629), 185–87; F. Turretin, *Institutes of Elenctic Theology,* I, qu. 3, n. 2; B. de Moor, *Comm. in Marckii Comp.,* I, 41.

act *[actus]*, a "real" or "intentional" entity, etc.), and (c) that he discounts the value and certainty of the knowledge that comes to us by the senses. Voetius then proceeds to offer a clear statement of the sense in which he would have us understand the term "implanted theology" *(theologia insita)*. It is "a capacity or power or aptitude belonging to the rational faculties; or a natural light in the sense that the intellect is able to grasp the truth of principles apart from any effort, previous study, or reasoning; and by compelling assumptions (such as a knowledge of limits) the intellect in fact so comprehends it, tending as it is toward the sense of truth and assent to it from a kind of natural necessity and by the force of its own inherent weight." All this in the same manner in which by virtue of a natural inclination the will pursues the good and the eye looks at the light and things that are visible. The familiar saying, "There is nothing in the intellect that was not previously in the senses," accordingly, is recognized as true in the sense that in some fashion, as direct object or as product, or as component, or by way of contrast, the world around us is necessary to bring us to conscious knowledge.[47]

OBJECTIONS TO INNATE IDEAS

[170] From all that has been said above, the reason why Christian theology so unanimously rejected the theory of innate ideas becomes clear: it is the fear of rationalism and of mysticism. If human beings at birth came fully endowed with a clear and distinct knowledge, either of all ideas (Plato) or of God (Descartes) or of being (Gioberti), they would become independent of the world. They would be able to produce pure knowledge from within their own minds and so be self-sufficient. They could dispense with the revelation God had given in his Word. They could more efficiently find perfect knowledge in their own minds than in nature or Scripture. Furthermore, the theory of innate ideas creates an unbridgeable chasm between mind and matter, soul and body. The visible world, consequently, would no longer be a creation and revelation of God, an embodiment of divine thoughts. From it no eternal truths or intellectual knowledge could be deduced. Humans could only arrive at these by way of self-reflection and recollection as they isolated themselves from the world and retreated into themselves.

And this indeed describes the ever-threatening danger of the theory of innate ideas. In Neoplatonism and subsequently in the Christian (especially the Catholic) church, Plato's dualism led to a kind of mysticism that initially at least, in the earlier stages of meditation, still used God's revelation in nature and Scripture, but which, having reached the higher stage of contemplation, could dispense with external aids and was content with the internal word, the spiritual light, the vision of God, and communion with God in the innermost recesses of the soul. And the dualism of Descartes linked with his theory of the innate idea of God, again introduced in modern philosophy, has led first Leibniz

---

47. G. Voetius, *Select. disp.*, I, 141; V, 477ff., 516, 525.

and Wolff and later Kant, Fichte, and Hegel to a rationalism that constructs the entire universe of being itself from the immanent thought-processes of the human mind. Now it is as clear as day that Scripture wants no part of this human autarchy (self-sufficiency) and of such contempt for the body and the material universe. It teaches that humans are image-bearers of God in soul and body, and that by their body they are akin to, and connected with, the whole visible world. But these bonds are not the chains of slaves. On the contrary: the world in which humans have been placed leads them not away from God but to God. It is a creation of God, a mirror of his perfections, a manifestation of his ideas. And, in the splendid language of Calvin, "there is no spot in the universe in which you cannot discern at least some sparks of his glory."[48] Seeing that Christian theology understood this, it unanimously rejected the theory of innate ideas.

Added to this were the objections derived from psychology and history lodged against this theory among others by Locke. Empiricism, in its polemic against mysticism and rationalism, defended a precious truth. These schools of thought were well intended when they maintained that the essence or idea of things could not be grasped through sense perception but apprehended only in God (Malebranche), in the soul by recollection (Plato), or by thought processes from the human mind (Descartes, Hegel). God is indeed the light of human souls. In his light we see light. The Logos enlightens every person coming into the world. Yet it is true that on earth we do not see face to face; we walk by faith; we see in a mirror dimly. We come to the knowledge of God only by contemplating God's revelation in nature and Scripture (Rom. 1:19; 1 Cor. 13:12; 2 Cor. 3:18). On earth we cannot obtain a direct, immediate knowledge of God and his thoughts but only a mediate knowledge "through and in a mirror." The sentiments of mystics, rationalists, and ontologists, accordingly, are not theistic but pantheistic. They confuse the light of reason with the light of God, the universal truths in us with the ideas in the mind of God, our "logos" with "the Logos of God," the order of being with the order of our knowing. In the order of being, God is undoubtedly first. He is the Creator and Sustainer of all things; also, his thinking and knowing is antecedent to the existence of things. It is not the case that God knows the world because and after it exists, but the world exists because God thought it and called it into being by an act of his will.

This does not mean that our knowing follows the same course and has to be identical with the order of being, hence, that we must first of all know God from and through his idea within us and only then come to know the world. For we are creatures and exist on the level of creatureliness. We get to know things because they exist and after they come into existence, and in our perception and thought we advance from the visible to the invisible, from the world to God. Should ontologism deem itself to be strong over against the

48. J. Calvin, *Institutes*, I.v.1.

idealism that considers the objective reality of things incapable of existing or of being known, it is abandoning itself to an illusion. For ontologism itself on its position can only maintain the objectivity of that reality by equating the idea of God within us with the being of God, the logos of God within us with the Logos of God, and thereby lapse into the error of pantheism. And against this view Christian theology posited the doctrine of Scripture, so that since we cannot know God's being as such, all our knowledge of God is obtained indirectly and bears an analogical character. In fact, no one ever arrives at the knowledge of first principles or the idea of God apart from the universe. A baby, born without consciousness, gradually receives an array of impressions and ideas from the environment in which it is raised. With the first humans this may, in the nature of the case, have been different. But all who were born later were brought to a conscious and clear knowledge both of visible and invisible things by their parents and the environment in which they grew up, not by personal initiative and reflection. For that reason there is no knowledge of the invisible world except by way of the symbols of that which is visible. Those who lack one of the senses have no conception of the phenomena that correspond to that organ of sense perception. A blind person does not know what light is and therefore does not know either what it means to say that God is light except by negation and contrast.

This also explains the potential for disagreement among persons and peoples in matters of justice and morality, of religion and art. This would be inexplicable if ideas as such were innate and were directly implanted in our mind by God himself. Now we see, however, that, though all people possess a capacity for speech, they still speak very different languages; that, though all have an idea of God, they clothe that idea in a wide array of representations; that there are people who say in their heart that there is no God; that, though the difference between good and evil is known everywhere, the content of these two categories is defined in very divergent ways; that human opinions on right and wrong, on beauty and ugliness, differ radically. In a word, there is not a single ethical truth that is recognized "everywhere, always, and by all." Strictly speaking, *natural theology* never existed any more than "natural rights" and "natural morality."

INNATE DISPOSITION

[171] With this, however, we have only highlighted one side of the truth. There is another side, one that is no less important. It cannot be denied, after all, that for us to see we need both the light of the sun (objectively) and our eyes (subjectively). That humans learn and obtain knowledge from their environment is a fact; but it assumes that they come equipped with an ability, an aptitude, and a disposition to learn. Language is taught us by the people among whom we are born, but it presupposes in everyone a disposition to speak. This is how it is in all spheres of life: in religion, art, morality, jurisprudence, science, and so

on. The "seeds of the sciences" are naturally inherent in humans. Every science is grounded in general, self-evident principles. All knowledge rests in faith. All proof, finally, presupposes "a principle of demonstration." There are logical, mathematical, philosophical, ethical, and, similarly, religious and theological principles that, though they are very general and abstract, are nevertheless accepted by all persons and in all ages and bear the stamp of naturalness and necessity. The laws of thought are the same for all; the theory of numbers is everywhere the same; the difference between good and evil is known by all. Similarly, there is no people without religion and knowledge of God. This is explicable only on the assumption of self-evident principles, ideas common to all, "eternal verities," which have been instilled in the human mind by nature. In religion, whether we want to or not, we always have to go back to a "seed of religion," a "sense of divinity," a "divine instinct," an "innate knowledge." Scripture itself sets an example in this. While it binds us as powerfully as possible to God's objective revelation in nature and grace, it at the same time attests that humanity is God's image and offspring, that humans possess in their minds a capacity to see God in his works and have the requirement of the law written in their heart (Gen. 1:26; Acts 17:27; Rom. 1:19; 2:15).

Everything depends, in this connection, on a correct understanding of this original character of the "common ideas." They have been variously described as "implanted," "inborn," "increated," and so on. No one employs these words in a literal sense. Upon reflecting on these expressions, almost all theologians quickly explain that they do not mean that these "innate ideas" come ready-made at birth and are present in the human mind as "impressed forms." In that sense, therefore, there are no innate ideas. God in no respect causes humans to enter the world as adults but lets them be born as helpless infants in need of care. And those infants would die if they were not fed and cared for by their environment. Yet, concealed in those children is the full-grown adult of the future. And this is true intellectually, ethically, and religiously as well.

"Implanted knowledge of God" does not mean that all people are immediately endowed by God himself with sufficient knowledge so as to be able to dispense with revelation. The term does not say that we are able, all by ourselves, to deduce conscious, clear, and valid knowledge of God from the contents of our own minds. What it does say is that we possess both the *capacity* (aptitude, faculty) and the *inclination* (*habitus,* disposition) to arrive at some firm, certain, and unfailing knowledge of God. Human beings gain this knowledge in the normal course of development and in the environment in which God gave them the gift of life. It arises spontaneously and without coercion, without scientific argumentation and proof. The words "implanted," "natural," and "innate," accordingly, are not meant to convey the "wherewithal" with which a person is born but merely to indicate that knowledge of God arises naturally, aside from any scientific input, from the human mind. They are not to be viewed as being opposed to the doctrine that humans are born as blank sheets of paper, without any specific material content in their mind. Rather, they are opposed to the view that humans are first brought to knowledge of God externally—by a specific revelation, a scientific proof, artificially, so to speak, by some form of coercion. This is how Christian theology has always intended these expressions. They are therefore interchangeable with such terms as "without instruction," "by nature," "an implanted power," "without previous study," "apart from laborious reasoning." The knowledge of God is said to be innate in us insofar as, through principles inborn in us, we can readily perceive that God exists.[49]

Locke is therefore wrong in commenting that if by the term "innate ideas" we only meant a capacity for knowledge, then all knowledge could be called "innate." For the knowledge of God is called "implanted" or "innate" inasmuch as every human being, in the normal course of his or her development, *must* come to it. Just as people, upon opening their eyes, automatically see the sun and by its light discern objects, so by their very nature—the moment they hear that there is a God and a difference between good and evil—they must assent to these statements. They cannot do otherwise. They accept these truths without any compulsion or proof, because they are self-evident. For that reason the knowledge of God is called "innate" and talk of an innate potency or faculty was found unsatisfactory. On the one hand, over against the theory of innate ideas, it expresses that humans are not born fully equipped with a ready-made knowledge of God, but obtain it mediately, by the interior impact of revelation upon their consciousness. On the other hand, vis-à-vis empiricism it indicates that this revelation of God speaks so loudly and forcefully and meets with such resonance in everyone's heart that it can be called uniquely appropriate to, and increated in, humans. In speaking this language theology does full justice not only to Scripture but also to psychology and history. There is a revelation of God in all his works, not only outside of, but especially within humans. Humanity itself constitutes the primary part of the nature from which God is known. From that entire realm of nature, both that which is exterior and that which is interior to us humans, we receive impressions and gain perceptions which, prior to all reasoning and proof, foster in our mind the sense of a Supreme Being. It is God himself who does not leave any person without a witness [cf. Acts 14:17].

THE ACQUIRED KNOWLEDGE OF GOD

[172] While "implanted knowledge of God" and "acquired knowledge of God" may not be opposites, there is nevertheless a distinction between the two. Frequently this distinction is construed to mean that the former denotes the knowledge of God with which persons are born and which arises from their own being, and the latter that which comes to humans from without by observation and serves to augment and expand the former. This construal,

49. Thomas, according to J. Kleutgen, *Philosophie der Vorzeit*, I, 348.

however, does not describe the difference accurately. For, strictly speaking, no knowledge, either of God or of the world, is innate. All knowledge enters the human mind from without. Innate only is the capacity for knowledge; but this innate capacity is only activated by the action and impact of the world within and around us. While the "seed of religion" is indeed inherent in humans, it takes the whole field of human life to make it germinate and grow. Just as humans, though they have eyes from the moment of birth, do not see objects except by the light of the sun, so believers first see God in all the works of his hands. In the previous chapter we learned, moreover, that Christian theology never took the "innateness" and "increatedness" of our knowledge of God to mean that humans bring along with them a certain conscious knowledge of God from the moment of birth. It only used that language to indicate that a knowledge of God never needs to be instilled in people by coercion or violence, nor by logical argumentation or compelling proofs, but belongs to humans by their very nature and arises spontaneously and automatically. Humans in the course of a normal development arrive at a certain knowledge of God without compulsion or effort. Accordingly, the innate knowledge of God is not opposed to the acquired knowledge of God, for in a broader sense also the former can be called acquired. In fact, God's revelation precedes both, for God does not leave himself without a witness. With his eternal power and deity he exerts revelatory pressure upon humans both from without and from within. God confronts humans in the realm of nature as well as in the realm of humankind, in heart and conscience, both in adversity and in prosperity. And humans, having been created in the divine image, were gifted with the capacity to receive the impressions of this revelation and thereby to acquire some sense and knowledge of the Eternal Being. The innate knowledge of God, the moment it becomes cognition and hence not only cognitive ability but also cognitive action, never originated apart from the working of God's revelation from within and without, and is to that extent therefore acquired.

For these reasons the distinction between innate and acquired knowledge of God was usually defined differently in the past. It consisted in the following two things: (1) Innate knowledge of God is acquired spontaneously, without effort or coercion, whereas the acquired knowledge of God is achieved by reasoning and argument, reflection and demonstration along the lines of causality, eminence, and negation. The former was noetic (apprehended by the intellect), the latter dianoetic (the result of discursive thinking). (2) From this arises the further distinction that whereas the former consists only in principles and is universal and necessary, the latter is more detailed and elaborated, furnishes more concrete proposition, and is therefore subject to all sorts of doubt and criticism. Almost everyone accepts as an established fact that God exists. The proofs for the existence of God, however, have been developed by the human mind and therefore have in turn been both disdained and highly valued.[50]

---

50. B. de Moor, *Comm. in Marckii Comp.*, I, 41, 44.

With that the distinction between the two has been correctly described. The difference is not that innate knowledge of God has its source in humans while acquired knowledge of God arises from the world. Even the moral proof is the product of the moral consciousness inherent in humans. In both cases it is the same complete revelation of God that introduces the knowledge of God into our consciousness. But in the case of the innate knowledge of God, that revelation acts upon the human consciousness, creating impressions and intuitions. In the case of the acquired knowledge of God, human beings reflect upon that revelation of God. Their minds go to work, thought processes are set in motion, and with clear heads they seek by reasoning and proof to rise from the observation of creatures to [the reality of] God. The fact is, humans are not content with impressions and intuitions in any area of knowledge. Mere consciousness of a thing is not enough for them. It is not sufficient for them to know: they want to know they know. They desire to explain the *how* and the *why* of their knowledge. Common everyday empirical knowledge is always driven to achieve true, scientific, knowledge. That is also why faith aspires to become theology, and the innate knowledge of God seeks to complete itself in the acquired knowledge of God.

The division between innate and acquired knowledge of God is usually applied only to "natural theology," which is then distinguished from, and often set in opposition to, "revealed theology." Earlier already we have taken pains to criticize this view at some length.[51] There is no such thing as a separate natural theology that could be obtained apart from any revelation solely on the basis of a reflective consideration of the universe. The knowledge of God that is gathered up in so-called natural theology is not the product of human reason.

Rather, natural theology presupposes, first of all, that *God* reveals himself in his handiwork. It is not humans who seek God but God who seeks humans, also by means of his works in nature. That being the case, it further presupposes that it is not humans who, by the natural light of reason, understand and know this revelation of God. Although all pagan religions are positive [concrete], what is needed on the human side is a mind that has been sanctified and eyes that have been opened in order to be able to see God, the true and living God, in his creatures. And even this is not enough. Even Christian believers would not be able to understand God's revelation in nature and reproduce it accurately had not God himself described in his Word how he revealed himself and what he revealed of himself in the universe as a whole. The natural knowledge of God is incorporated and set forth at length in Scripture itself. Accordingly, Christians follow a completely mistaken method when, in treating natural theology, they, as it were, divest themselves of God's special revelation in Scripture and the illumination of the Holy Spirit, discuss it apart from any Christian presuppositions, and then move on to special revelation.

---

51. Cf. H. Bavinck, *Reformed Dogmatics*, I, 302–22 (##85–89: "General Revelation").

Even when Christians do theology, from the very beginning they stand with both feet on the foundation of special revelation. They are Christ-believers not only in the doctrine of Christ but equally in the doctrine of God. Standing on this foundation, they look around themselves, and armed with the spectacles of Holy Scripture, they see in all the world a revelation of the same God they know and confess in Christ as their Father in heaven. Then, however, we cannot interpret the innate and acquired knowledge of God as the knowledge we derive from creation apart from special revelation. From our earliest youth God's special revelation in Christ has exerted its influence on us all. We have been born in the covenant of grace, hence as Christians. All sorts of Christian influences have produced the knowledge of God we now possess. These influences have affected us much more than the impact God's revelation in nature had on us, and in the light of that *special* revelation we have all learned to view nature and the world around us. We are all indebted to God's *special* revelation in his Word for the knowledge of God we have derived from nature. If we had not heard God speaking to us in the works of grace and by that means also discerned his voice speaking to us in the works of nature, we would all be like pagans, for whom nature speaks in a cacophony of confusing tongues. Now, however, that revelation of God in nature also is most precious. Now, whether God speaks to us in the realm of nature or in that of grace, in creation or in re-creation, through the Logos or in Christ, in the Spirit of God or in the Spirit of Christ, it is always the same God we hear speaking to us. Nature and grace are not opposites: we have one God from whom, through whom, and to whom both exist.

This applies both to innate and to acquired knowledge of God as well; we are indebted to Scripture for both. It is true that Scripture makes no attempt to prove the existence of God.[52] It proceeds from it and assumes that humans know and acknowledge God. It does not regard humans as having fallen so deep that in order to believe they need prior proof of God's existence. For they are God's image bearers, God's offspring, and endowed with a mind (νους) to discern God's eternal power and deity in the work of creation. Scripture views the denial of God's existence as a sign of folly, of profound moral degradation (Ps. 14:2). People guilty of this are exceptions, not the rule. As a rule, Scripture counts on people who freely and instinctively acknowledge the existence of God. It appeals to the rational and moral consciousness, not to the reasoning intellect. It does not analyze and argue, but shows us God in all the works of his hands. But *that* it does, abundantly and emphatically. "Heaven and earth and all creatures, leaf and blade, rain and drought, fruitful and lean years, food and drink, health and sickness, prosperity and poverty, all things, in fact"[53] speak to believers of God. There is no particle of the world in which his power

---

52. A. B. Davidson, *The Theology of the Old Testament,* ed. S. D. F. Salmond (Edinburgh: T. & T. Clark, 1904), 73ff.

53. Cf. Heidelberg Catechism, Lord's Day 10, Q. & A. 27.

and deity do not come through. Humans are referred to heaven and earth, birds and ants, the lilies of the field and other flowers, so that they may see and recognize God in them. "Lift up your eyes on high and see: Who created these?" (Isa. 40:26). Scripture does not reason in the abstract. It does not make God the conclusion of a syllogism, leaving it to us to ask whether we think the argument compelling or not. Instead, it speaks with authority. Theologically and religiously, it proceeds from God as its starting point. It exhibits God's perfections in his works and demands that we shall recognize him. "The ox knows its owner, and the ass its master's crib, but Israel does not know, my people do not understand" (Isa. 1:3). It never for a minute doubts that God reveals himself in his creatures and never leaves anyone without a witness (Acts 14:17; Rom. 1:19).

Thus, appealing to the whole created world as a witness to, and revelation of, God, Scripture contains germinally all that was later elaborated and dialectically unfolded in the proofs. There is truth in C. I. Nitzsch's comment[54] that Scripture gives us a beginning and analogy of the etiological [cosmological] proof in Romans 1:20, of the teleological proof in Psalm 8 and Acts 14:17, of the moral proof in Romans 2:14, and of the ontological proof in Acts 17:24 and Romans 1:19, 32. To this collection we can further add that Scripture, in a remarkable text, reasons from the being of humans to the being of God. The wicked think God does not and cannot see them, so the poet asks: "He who planted the ear, does he not hear? He who formed the eye, does he not see?" (Ps. 94:9; cf. Exod. 4:11). The poet here proceeds from the idea that God made humans in his likeness and therefore that capacities present in humans must also be present in God, just as Paul infers from the fact that we are God's offspring that the deity cannot be like gold or silver or stone (Acts 17:29).

Now when Scripture speaks in this fashion, not in the language of logic but in the language of witness, not appealing to the reasoning intellect but to the human heart and conscience, to the entire rational and moral consciousness of humans, it is never without power and influence. Also, in this respect it "is living and active, sharper than any two-edged sword, piercing until it divides soul from spirit, joints from marrow, . . . to judge the thoughts and intentions of the heart" (Heb. 4:12 NRSV). Also, without logical argument and philosophical argumentation, Scripture is powerful in its witness because it is the word of God and finds resonance in the rational and moral nature of every human being. It is God himself who does not leave himself without a witness to anyone. And it is humans themselves who, having been created in God's image, are compelled to listen to this witness and assent to it despite themselves. In this light we should also consider the so-called proofs for the existence of God. That will prevent us both from overestimating and from disdaining these proofs.

---

54. C. I. Nitzsch, *System of Christian Doctrine* (Edinburgh: T. & T. Clark, 1849), 142.

PROOFS FOR GOD'S EXISTENCE

[173] Even in the ancient philosophers (Anaxagoras, Socrates, Plato, Aristotle, Plutarch, Seneca, and Cicero) we already encounter the proofs advanced for the existence of God. From the beauty, harmony, motion, purpose, and design of the world, from reason and innate awareness, from the importance of religion for the state and for society, and from the consensus of opinion among the peoples of the earth, these thinkers inferred the existence of a self-conscious rational divine being.[55] Christian theology adopted all these proofs, taking particular pleasure in treating them. Augustine even added the argument from the existence of universals.[56] It did not disdain the support offered to it by pagan philosophy, and while it rejected the dualism of Gnosticism and Manicheism, it did see nature as a work of God. Now this posture of Christian theology is all the more remarkable inasmuch as Christianity to a certain extent assumed a hostile attitude to the cosmos and stressed above all else the salvation of humanity. But despite the asceticism that made its way into the Christian church, nature was and remained for Christian theology a creation by the same God who had revealed himself in Christ as Re-creator and Savior. It even soon began to overestimate the value and force of these proofs. True, some church fathers declared that pagans never arrived at a pure natural religion and that the way of these proofs is very difficult for sinners.[57] But little by little the proofs lost their religious character. They were severed from all moral conditions. The acquired knowledge of God was detached from, and assigned a place next to, the innate knowledge of God. And Christian theology became increasingly convinced that the truths of natural religion were demonstrable in the same way as those of mathematics or logic. They were not really "articles of faith" but "preambles to the articles of faith."[58] The ontological argument of Anselm's *Proslogium,* taken over by a few theologians like Hales and Bonaventure, was in fact rejected by most of them, because, they said, it is only by way of creatures that we can arrive at the existence of God.[59] But, for the rest, the proofs were highly valued, and much care was bestowed on them. In natural theology, according to the general view, one stood on a rational scientific foundation prior to and apart from faith.[60] And to this day Rome and Roman Catholic theology still maintain the same rationalistic position.[61]

55. E. Zeller, *Philosophie der Griechen,* I[4], 885ff.; II[4], 771ff.; III[3], 357ff.; IV[3], 133ff.

56. Augustine, *Bondage of the Will,* II, 3–15; W. Münscher, *Lehrbuch des christlichen Dogmengeschichte,* ed. D. von Coelln, 3d ed., 2 vols. in 3 (Cassel: K. C. Drieger, 1832–38), I, 125–29.

57. Athanasius, *Against the Nations,* 35ff.

58. T. Aquinas, *Summa theol.,* I, qu. 2, art. 2; idem, *Summa contra gentiles,* I, 10–13.

59. T. Aquinas, *Summa contra gentiles,* I, 10–12.

60. J. Schwane, *Dogmengeschichte,* III, 107ff.

61. D. Petavius, *Theol. dogm.,* I, ch. 2; F. Sylvius, *Commentarii in totam primam partem S. Thomae Aquinatis,* 4th ed., 4 vols. (Venetiis: Typographia Balleoniana, 1693), I, 22–26; *Theologia Wirceburgensis* (1880), III, 1–20; G. Perrone, *Prael. theol.,* II, 3–41; J. Kleutgen, *Philosophie der Vorzeit,* I[3], 673ff.; II[2], 668ff.; J. Schwetz, *Theologia fundamentalis seu generalis* (Vienna: Congregationis Mechitharisticae, 1867),

The Vatican declared that God can be known with certainty from creation by the natural light of reason.[62]

Now the Reformation indeed adopted this natural theology along with its proofs but, instead of treating it prior to the doctrine of faith, incorporated it in the doctrine of faith. Calvin, taking as his starting point "the seed of religion," saw incontrovertible signs and testimonies of God's majesty in "every particle of the universe": in the starry heavens, in the human body, in the soul, in the preservation of all things (etc.); but, having said this, he immediately reminds us that this "seed of religion," though ineradicably implanted in all humans, can be choked and cannot bear good fruit. Humans, having lost the capacity to see God, need the eye of faith.[63] In other Reformed theologians we see natural theology occupying the same place.[64]

Soon, however, Protestant theology started taking the road of rationalism. Whereas natural theology was initially an account, in the light of Scripture, of what Christians can know concerning God from creation, it soon became an exposition of what nonbelieving rational persons could learn from nature by the power of their own reasoning. In other words, natural theology became rational theology. Descartes considered the innate idea [of God] irrefutable proof for the existence of God. Voetius still discerned the difference between this rationalistic argumentation and the Reformed doctrine of natural theology,[65] but later theologians progressively lost sight of it.[66] Rationalism everywhere made its triumphal entry. Natural theology became the real, the scientific and demonstrable theology by which revealed theology was increasingly marginalized and driven from the field. The proofs were divided into classes and elaborately developed. Metaphysical proofs were subdivided into proofs based on the motion, causality, and accidental character of the universe; physical proofs on the harmony, order, and purpose of the universe, and in particular on the sun, moon, stars, fire, light, earth, water, animals, plants, humans, souls, ears, eyes, hands, instincts, and so on; historical proofs on "universal consent," society, the arts and sciences, revelation, prophecy, and miracles; moral proofs on conscience, freedom, morality, judgment, reward and punishment, and finally also mathematical proofs.[67]

I, §§4–8; C. Pesch, *Prael. dogm.*, II, 1–20; F. Hettinger, *Apologie des Christenthums*, 3 vols. (Freiburg i.B. and St. Louis: Herder, 1895–96), I', 103ff.; G. Jansen, *Prael. theol.*, I, 39–51.

62. Cf. H. Bavinck, *Reformed Dogmatics*, I, 302 (#85).

63. J. Calvin, *Institutes*, I.iv.1; I.v.1–10, 11–15.

64. Z. Ursinus, *Tract. theol.* (1584), 37–44; P. M. Vermigli, *Loci*, 2ff.; Musculus, *Loci*, 2ff.; A. Polanus, *Syn. theol.*, II, 4; cf. A. Schweizer, *Die Glaubenslehre der evangelisch-reformirten Kirche*, 2 vols. (Zürich: Orell, Füssli, 1844–47), I, 156ff.

65. G. Voetius, *Select disp.*, V, 445–525; cf. I, 167ff.

66. J. Alsted, *Theologia naturalis* (1623); P. van Mastricht, *Theol.*, II, 2; Johannes à Marck, *Het Merch der christene Gotgeleerheit* (Rotterdam: Nicolaas en Paulus Topyn, 1741), I, 1, 14; F. Turretin, *Institutes of Elenctic Theology*, III, qu. 1.

67. J. Buddeus, *De atheismo et superstitione*, ed. Lulofs (1767), 224–318; and additional literature in C. Vitringa, *Comm.*; and in J. Walch, *Bibl. theol. sel.*, I, 676; J. Doedes, *Inleiding to de Leer van God*, 200–217.

This self-sufficiency of natural theology lasted until Kant, who subjected the proofs to rigorous criticism, arguing that theoretical reason had to end with a *non liquet* (it is not clear). But then he again attempted to establish the existence of God as a postulate of practical reason.[68] Since then the proofs have been discredited in the works of numerous philosophers and theologians. Jacobi even considered it impossible to prove God's existence, since God would then be a conclusion dependent on the grounds used in an argument.[69] Others, though seeing the fallacy of this reasoning, still had very little, if any, use for these proofs for God's existence, called them unnecessary for believers and unprofitable for unbelievers, and concluded that they should be eliminated from dogmatics.[70] But, however great the number of these critics may be, their attempt to relieve the doctrine of God in theology and philosophy from the burden of these proofs has had only little success. They themselves discuss them all—sometimes at great length—if only to prove their lack of cogency. On and on, in steady procession, philosophers and theologians continue to treat the proofs for God's existence painstakingly and at length.

There is, however, substantial disagreement about the form in which the proofs should be presented, the force they collectively or individually possess, and the result to which they lead. In the philosophy of Hegel the proofs had much greater significance than they did in Kant. Hegel rated them highly as God's self-demonstration in the human mind, and therefore attached great value especially to the ontological proof.[71] In the form given to it by Anselm and Descartes, this ontological argument has been virtually universally abandoned. Many thinkers, however, have attempted to further develop it along the lines of Plato, Augustine, and Thomas and to maintain it as a proof arising from the ideas and norms of the human mind.[72] In the nature of the case the cosmological argument is presented in very different forms, for it has been rightly said that if the existence of God can be proved from the existence of the universe, every piece of straw can serve the purpose.[73] Also, on the force

68. See H. Bavinck, *Reformed Dogmatics*, I, 535 (#141).

69. F. H. Jacobi, *Von den gottliche Dingen*, in *Werke*, 8 vols. (Leipzig: Gerhard Fleischer, 1812–25), III, 368, 567.

70. F. V. Reinhard, *Grundriss der Dogmatik* (Munich: Seidel, 1802), §30; F. Schleiermacher, *The Christian Faith* (Edinburgh: T. & T. Clark, 1989), II, §33; A. Twesten, *Vorlesungen über die Dogmatik*, 2d ed., 2 vols. (Hamburg: F. Perthes, 1829–37), II, 19; J. C. K. von Hoffmann, *Der Schriftbeweis*, 3 vols. (Nördlingen: Beck, 1857–60), I², 62; J. T. Beck, *Vorlesungen über christliche Glaubenslehre*, 2 vols. (Gütersloh: C. Bertelsmann, 1886–87); F. H. R. Frank, *System der christlichen Wahrheit*, 2 vols. (Erlangen: A. Deichert, 1878–80), I², 62; F. Philippi, *Kirchliche Glaubenslehre*, 6 vols. (Gütersloh: C. Bertelsmann, 1902), II, 1–17; E. Böhl, *Dogmatik* (Amsterdam: Scheffer, 1887), 16ff.; A. von Oettingen, *Lutherische Dogmatik*, 2 vols. (Munich: C. H. Beck, 1897–1902), II, 30ff.; J. Bovon, *Dogmatique chrétienne*, 2 vols. (Lausanne: Georges Bridel, 1895–96), I, 216; L. W. E. Rauwenhoff, *Wijsbegeerte van den Godsdienst* (Leiden: Brill & Van Doesburgh, 1887), 499ff.

71. G. W. F. Hegel, "Über die Beweise vom Dasein Gottes," in *Werke*, 4th ed. (Frankfurt a.M.: Suhrkamp, 1999–2000), XII, 169ff., 291ff.

72. James Orr, *The Christian View of God and the World* (New York: Randolph, 1893), 124–27, 479. Orr also appeals to Pfleiderer, Green, Harris, etc.

73. Vanini, cited by A. von Oettingen, *Lutherische Dogmatik*, II, 31.

of this proof opinions are widely divergent. According to some, it does not lead to an absolute cause;[74] according to others, it only proves the existence of an absolute "world-ground"[75] without shedding any light on the nature of it;[76] and still others claim it indirectly or directly attests to the existence of a personal God.[77]

Under pressure from Darwinism's denial of all purpose, the teleological argument often backs away as proof from the order and purpose of the universe, but, in the opinion of many, it gains renewed force when as an argument from design it is grounded in the evolutionary process itself, a process that can be observed in the world as it gradually brings about the existence of life, the human mind, science and art, religion and morality, and so evidences striving, a will, a purpose.[78] The moral argument, which is also presented in a variety of forms, has gained great significance especially as a result of the work of Kant. At present it is framed especially in the following form: from the autonomy of mind vis-à-vis nature—an autonomy that is manifest throughout human culture, particularly in the moral consciousness and life of humans—proceeds the existence either of a moral world order[79] or of a personal God.[80] The argument from universal consent, finally, is maintained either in the old form or modified in the sense that it derives its primary force from the religious nature of humankind, which has been established beyond all doubt by historical, psychological, and philosophical research and—provided it is not an illusion—postulates the existence, revelation, and knowability of God.[81] In the works of numerous thinkers these proofs end with the conclusion that materialism and pantheism (naturalism and idealism) are powerless to solve

74. A. B. Bruce, *Apologetics* (Edinburgh: T. & T. Clark, 1892), 149.

75. A. E. Biedermann, *Christliche Dogmatik* (Zürich: Fussli, 1869), §§645ff.; cf. E. von Hartmann, *Religionsphilosophie*, 2d ed., 2 vols. (Bad Sachsa im Harz: Hermann Haacke, 1907), II, 114ff.; F. Paulsen, *Einleitung in die Philosophie* (Berlin: Hertz, 1892), 239ff.

76. H. Spencer, *First Principles,* 51–123, esp. 87–97; C. B. Spruyt, "Iets over den Oorspron en het Wezen van den Godsdienst," *De Gids* 50 (April 1886); *Molenaar, *Bijblad van de Hervorm* (May 21, 1885).

77. I. Dorner, *A System of Christian Doctrine,* trans. Alfred Cave and J. S. Banks, rev. ed., 4 vols. (Edinburgh: T. & T. Clark, 1888), I, 248; K. F. A. Kahnis, *Die lutherische Dogmatik,* 3 vols. (Leipzig: Dörffling & Franke, 1861–68), I², 122; J. Doederlein, "Was fehlt dem ontologischen Beweis?" *Zeitschrift für Philosophie und philosophischen Kritik* 88/1 (1886): 52; James Orr, *Christian View,* 116.

78. James Martineau, *A Study of Religion,* 2 vols. (Oxford: Clarendon; New York: Macmillan, 1888), I, 270–333; J. Orr, *Christian View,* 117ff.; Robert Flint, *Theism: Being the Baird Lecture for 1876* (Edinburgh and London: W. Blackwood, 1883); James Houghton Kennedy, *Gottesglaube und moderne Weltanschauung* (Berlin: H. Reuthers, 1893); J. H. A. Ebrard, *Apologetics,* trans. W. Stuart and John MacPherson, 2d ed., 3 vols. (Edinburgh: T. & T. Clark, 1886–87), I, 235ff.; Paul Janet, *Les causes finales,* 2d ed. (Paris: G. Bailliére et Cie, 1882).

79. L. Rauwenhoff, *Wijsbegeerte von de Godsdienstleer,* 321ff.

80. A. Ritschl, *Theologie und Metaphysik* (Bonn: A. Marcus, 1886), 8ff.; idem, *Rechtfertigung und Versuchung,* III³, 200; J. Kaftan, *Truth of the Christian Religion,* trans. George Ferries, 2 vols. (Edinburgh: T. & T. Clark, 1894), II, 76ff.; J. Köstlin, "Die Beweise für das Dasein Gottes," *Theologische Studien und Kritiken* 48 (1875): 601–55; 49 (1876): 7–80.

81. J. Orr, *Christian View,* 134–37; Samuel Harris, *The Philosophic Basis of Theism* (New York: C. Scribner's Sons, 1893), 345–65.

the problem of existence and that this entire universe, in its origin, nature, and destiny, can be explained only on a theistic position.[82]

[174] The classification of proofs need not detain us very long. For although it differs terminologically and in form, it usually comes down to the same things. Two of the proofs (the cosmological and the teleological argument) respectively deduce the existence of God from the world's origin and purpose. Two others are based, respectively, on the rational and the moral nature of humans (the ontological and the moral argument). And the remaining two are based especially on history and deduce the existence of God, respectively, from the universal consent and history of humankind (the argument from consensus and the historical-theological argument).[83]

The Cosmological Argument

The cosmological proof occurs in different forms. From motion it deduces a "primary unmoved mover" (Aristotle). From the mutable it infers the immutable (John of Damascus). From the relative, it reasons back to the absolutely perfect (Boethius, Anselm). From a series of causes which cannot be infinite, it argues for a "first efficient cause" (Thomas). From the contingent existence of the world it moves to a necessary being; from dependent existence to self-existence (Richard of St. Victor); from the existence of the relative to the existence of the absolute (Spinoza, Hegel, Hartmann, Scholten); from the relative interdependence of all creatures to the absolute dependence of all creatures upon a higher divine power (Lotze), and so forth. In all these forms, however, the cosmological argument comes down to the same thing. It deduces the existence of a cause from the demonstrable existence of an effect. Now by itself this conclusion is perfectly legitimate, the criticism of Hume and Kant notwithstanding. If we may no longer apply the law of causality, all science is impossible. But the cosmological proof proceeds from certain assumptions that are not self-evident and certain to everyone. It assumes not only that all particular objects in the world are contingent, finite, relative, and imperfect, but that the same is true of the entire universe. It assumes that an infinite chain of causes is inconceivable, and that the law of causality also applies to the universe as a whole.

Now the cosmological proof has evidential force only if all these assumptions are correct. It rightly concludes that, like all things individually, so also the world as a whole, as comprising all these things, must have a cause. But that is as far as it takes us. It does not say anything about the character and nature of that cause. Anyone concluding that the world must have a cause, which must itself in turn also have a cause, has done justice to the logical force of this argu-

82. A. Bruce, *Apologetics*, 159ff.; R. Flint, *Antitheistic Theories: Being the Baird Lectures for 1877* (Edinburgh and London: W. Blackwood, 1879); J. McCosh, *The Method of Divine Government* (New York: R. Carter, 1860); Samuel Harris, *God the Creator and Lord of All*, 2 vols. (Edinburgh: T. & T. Clark, 1897); J. Morris, *A New Natural Theology: Based on the Doctrine of Evolution* (London: Rivington, Percival, 1896).

83. A. von Oettingen, *Lutherische Dogmatik*, II, 43–44.

ment. That this cause is infinite, absolute, and perfect does not follow directly from the cosmological argument but has its source in other considerations. Now an infinite series of causes is in fact inconceivable and impossible. No one accepts such an infinite series. All recognize the existence of an absolute ground, a primary being, whether it is called God, or the Absolute, substance or Power, Matter or Will. Now if this supposition is correct—as everyone in fact admits—the cosmological argument takes us to an important conclusion, namely, to a self-existent, hence infinite, eternal, and absolute Cause of the world. But whether this cause is transcendent or merely immanent, personal or impersonal, conscious or unconscious, has not in any way been settled by the argument.

Now, many thinkers have tried to infer something more from the cosmological argument, whether by way of direct or indirect inference. Some have tried to do this by direct inference, arguing that an effect cannot contain more than cause, and that one may therefore infer from the existence of personal, conscious, and free beings, plus that of ideas in the world, the existence of a personal, conscious, and free Being who is simultaneously the supreme Idea, absolute Reason. This logic does not hold, however, because it arbitrarily conceives the cause-and-effect nexus as an emanation and, when applied to God, would also require that he be material, physical, even impure and unholy. Others, therefore, taking an indirect route, argue that an infinite and absolute Cause, an entity that exists of, in, and by itself, has to be Spirit or Person. Against this position we must object that the cosmological argument does not yield any information about the inner nature of such a first cause, that we have no right again to apply the law of causality to such a first cause, and that we therefore cannot say anything specific about it. So we are left with the conclusion that—granting the impossibility of an infinite series of causes—the cosmological argument at best yields a self-existent, first, and absolute World-cause.

The Teleological Argument

The teleological argument, proceeding from the order and beauty, the harmony and purpose observable in the world either in its entirety or in particular creatures (the stars, elements, earth, humans, animals, plants, the hand, the eye, etc.), infers the existence of an intelligent cause. Although the teleological argument never fails to impress people and was mentioned with respect by Kant, it has nevertheless, especially of late, encountered numerous objections.

First of all, materialism asserts that there is no purpose in things, and the teleological interpretation of nature must give way to the mechanical one.[84] Pantheism, moreover, affirms that the presence of order and purpose in the universe gives us absolutely no warrant to posit the existence of a conscious, intelligent cause since, both in the case of the individual human and that

---

84. E. Haeckel, *Naturliche Schöpfungsgeschichte*, 16; idem, *The Riddle of the Universe*, 258ff.; L. Büchner, *Force and Matter*, 214ff.; F. Lange, *Geschichte des Materialismus* (Leipzig: Gaedeken, 1882), 270ff.; Went, "Ondoelmatigheid in de levende natuur," *De Gids* 70 (1906): 77–99.

of the world as a whole, the unconscious functions with more wisdom and certainty than conscious reflection and deliberate calculation.[85] Finally, Kant raised the objection that this argument at most leads to a World-shaper, not to a World-creator.[86]

Now these objections can be answered with a fairly large array of counterconsiderations. Scripture, for one thing, everywhere recognizes purpose in creation (Gen. 1; Prov. 8; 1 Cor. 3:21–23; Rom. 8:28; etc.). The teleological worldview is held by almost all philosophers (Anaxagoras, Socrates, Plato, Aristotle, et al.). Despite the misuse to which it has been subjected, especially in the eighteenth century, it continues to urge itself upon every person. Purpose is discernible both in particular phenomena, such as climate, seasons, water temperature, the fertilization of plants, the blood-circulation, organisms, the hand, the eye (etc.), and in the universe as a whole. All atoms obey one single law. Everything is based on thought, which can be understood by humans. The universe can no more be interpreted by chance than Homer's *Iliad* by an arbitrary throw of the letters of the alphabet. And even the fact that often we cannot show a purpose proves that, when we observe it, we do so rightly.

In recent years, accordingly, many practitioners of the natural sciences have returned to vitalism and even to teleology. The Darwinism doctrine of descent was initially characterized by the attempt to everywhere substitute the cause for the purpose, but rather brought to light the indispensability of the teleological view. The theory of natural selection, after all, aimed at explaining the functionality of things. Matter, force, and motion are obviously not enough: there also has to be direction, and direction is inconceivable without purpose. Accordingly, in recent years G. Wolff, H. Driesch, J. Reinke, and earlier already Fechner and K. E. von Baer, and many others have recognized the good right of teleology to play a role alongside causality. Teleology and causality certainly do not exclude each other. Anyone positing a goal will then apply the means needed to reach that goal. There is even ample room within a teleological worldview for mechanical causality. The latter only exceeds its power and competence when it seeks to explain all phenomena in the world, from matter and metabolism—also the conscious and the mental.[87] Now if the presence of order and purpose were an established fact for everyone and in our day did not need such vigorous and detailed demonstration, the teleological proof would in fact give us the right to infer from the beauty and harmony of the world the existence of a conscious being, for there is no such thing as an unconscious purpose. Von Hartmann indeed has tried to prove the opposite,

---

85. E. von Hartmann, *Philosophie des Unbewusste*, 11th ed. (Leipzig: H. Haacke, 1907), passim.

86. I. Kant, *Critique of Pure Reason*, trans. Norman Kemp Smith (New York: St. Martin's Press, 1965), 522ff.

87. C. Gutberlet, "Teleologie und Causalität," *Philosophisches Jahrbuch* 13/4 (1900); 14/1 (1901); cf. O. Liebmann, *Zur Analysis der Wirklichkeit*, 3d ed. (Strassburg: K. J. Trübner, 1900), 391; idem, *Gedanken und Thatsachen*, 2 vols. (Strassburg: K. J. Trübner, 1882–99), II, 140ff.; R. Eisler, *Kritische Einführung in die Philosophie* (Berlin: E. S. Mittler, 1905), 182ff.

but his arguments for the purposive activity of the unconscious lack cogency, since for a creature in general to act with an intentional goal in mind is one thing and the discernment of a purpose in an unconscious act is another. Instinct indeed operates unconsciously; nevertheless, in the unconscious act of that instinct there may be a discernible purpose that points back to a being who consciously produced the instinct. If there is a purpose in the world, it must be preconceived. It may be true that even then the teleological proof may take us no further than to a World-shaper; such a proof would still be of no little significance. Even if this proof did not specifically lead us to one intelligent Being, but left open the possibility of the existence of many divine beings who jointly produced the world, the teleological argument would still not be devoid of all value. Intelligence would then be required as a component in the first cause(s) by the way the world was structured, and this proof would have furnished what it could. Only, having arrived at one or more World-shapers by this route, one would face the difficult question how a being that had not created matter could nevertheless give form and shape to it, or the question how more than one being could be the first cause of the universe. Logically, these objections may still have some value; practically, however, they no longer have any meaning to our mind. Everything here depends on the presence of purpose in the world. Once that is established, the existence and consciousness of a Supreme Being are implied.[88]

The Ontological Argument

[175] The ontological argument occurs in three distinct forms. (1) From the general ideas and norms present in the human mind, that is, from that reason which transcends our individual reason and that of the entire world, it deduces the existence of absolute Reason, the sum total of all those ideas and norms, absolute truth, goodness, and beauty, that is, God (Plato, Augustine, Boethius, Anselm in his *Monologium*). (2) Or it proceeds from the necessity of thinking the highest absolute idea, that is, of the idea of God, and concludes from it the actual existence of that idea, since otherwise it would not be the absolute or greatest idea, inasmuch as an idea that simultaneously exists in reality is greater and higher than one that does not really exist (Anselm in his *Proslogium*). (3) Or it regards the innateness of the idea of God as a fact that can in no way be explained except by the existence of the God who implanted this idea in the human mind (Descartes).

The forms differ but the proof is one and the same, inasmuch as it infers existence from thought. Now in respect to creatures, as everyone recognizes, this does not hold water. They are contingent; without any logical contradiction they can be conceived as nonexistent. Existence in thought and existence in reality are distinct categories, two totally different things. From the existence of a thing in thought, say a winged horse, it absolutely does not follow that this

---

88. J. Mayer, *Der teleologische Gottesbeweis und der Darwinismus* (Mainz: I. Kirchheim, 1901).

thing exists in reality as well. Existence in reality is not a product of existence in thought. No one, accordingly, meant to claim this in using the ontological argument. The question is whether, with reference to the idea of God, it is not legitimate to derive existence in reality from existence in thought. The answer is first of all, *yes,* but under one condition: namely, *if* God exists. *If* God exists, he exists necessarily: essence and existence coincide in him. But this condition is precisely what has to be demonstrated. It has to be proved that God exists.[89]

Second, the answer has to be *no:* from *our* thinking, even our *necessary* thinking of the idea of God, we may not infer the existence of God, since God's existence of course is not and cannot be a product of our thinking the idea of God. The world of ideas and norms, including the idea of God, cannot be identified with God but is something in us. Hence, the existence of God is not an automatic given, implied in those ideas. At most one can reason from the presence of those ideas in us to the existence of God, but then that is actually not the ontological but a cosmological argument. But the existence in us of the idea of God, however necessary this may be, never includes, nor can ever as such include, the existence of God. The ontological proof is therefore not a real proof. It only implies the following: (1) that the universe of ideas and norms and hence also the idea of God is not arbitrarily but necessarily present in our thinking; and (2) that the moment we think of that universe of ideas and norms, especially the idea of God, we think and must think of it as really existing. The necessity of thinking the idea of God carries with it the necessity of thinking of that idea as really existing. But that is as far as it goes. We remain in the sphere of thought. It does not carry us from the realm of thought into that of being. This it would do only if from the presence of those ideas in us—not from those ideas as such—we might deduce a being who created those ideas in us, and he himself were the Supreme Idea; but then, as we noted above, we would have a cosmological, not an ontological, proof.[90] The value of this argument, accordingly, consists rather in the fact that it demonstrates the necessity with which humans think the idea of God and think him as existing, and so confronts them with the choice of either trusting this necessary witness of their consciousness or else despairing of their own consciousness.

The Moral Argument

The moral argument, noting the moral phenomena occurring in the life of humankind—conscience, moral responsibility, repentance, reward and punishment, virtue and happiness, the fear of death and judgment, the triumph of the good, and so forth—infers from them the existence of a moral being who

89. F. W. J. Schelling, *Werke,* 13 vols. (Munich: C. H. Beck, 1979–97), II, 3, 159.
90. G. Runze, *Der ontologischen Gottesbeweis* (Halle: C. E. M. Pfeffer, 1882); *Körber, *Das ontologischen Argument* (Bamberg, 1884); O. Bensow, *Über die Möglichkeit eines ontologischen Beweises für das Dasein Gottes* (Rostock: Adler's Erben, 1898).

created and maintains that moral world order. Some thinkers, in this connection, highlight the human conscience, whose voice is heard in everyone, the moral law to which all humans know themselves bound, and thus arrive at a supreme and sovereign Lawgiver. Others, noting especially the disproportion between virtue and happiness, between sin and punishment, postulate from it a being who will bring about true correspondence between them in the hereafter. Also, viewing the entire moral world order in its connection with, and supremacy over, the natural order, infer from that fact the existence of a being who created the moral order and placed it over the natural order. Always, however, this argument is based on the ethical phenomena present in the human world and so arrives at God as the supreme moral being.

Objections have also been raised against this proof. First of all, the advocates of the theory of evolution object that the moral life of humans, like their conscious life, does not constitute an established and independent order but one that only gradually originated by a process and therefore manifests itself in various ways in different places. The moral consciousness of humans, we are told, is not something absolutely new but consists in a development of tendencies that, in a more primitive form, occur also in the animal world. If animals only had greater powers of intellect, then, as they formed societies, they would have developed the same or similar moral ideas and feelings as humans have, for the actions that arise from social instincts are bound to harvest approval and praise in a society, whereas self-centered conduct of course encounters disapproval and punishment. Then, in the human consciousness, the motive for an act is gradually abstracted from the act itself and viewed as either good or bad. Morality, accordingly, is a product of society, and humans, also as moral agents, are the product of circumstances.[91]

Against this moral argument—second—Fichte and after him all the proponents of an independent ethics try to demonstrate that the moral consciousness present in humans does not warrant the inference of a personal God but only of a moral world order, that is, a world order in which there is room for the good, a chance for virtue to maintain itself and to secure the victory for itself.[92]

Third, there is the obvious objection that often there is little evidence of the power of the good and of a moral world order. Virtue is not always rewarded and evil is not always punished. The wicked often even enjoy prosperity and peace, while the righteous are persecuted and oppressed; and nature seems so totally indifferent to issues of good and evil that with its disasters and catastrophes it time and again strikes those who cannot possibly be other than innocent.

Finally, even if there is something like a moral world order, no one can show the connection between it and the natural order. It cannot possibly be proved that the former will one day triumph over the latter. And, according to some,

91. Cf. C. Darwin, *The Descent of Man*, 2d ed. (New York: D. Appleton & Co., 1903), chs. 3–5.

92. J. Fichte, "Über den Grund unseres Glaubens an eine göttliche Weltregierung" (1798; reprinted in *Complete Works of J. G. Fichte*, vol. 5: *Works 1798–1799*, ed. R. Lauth et al. [Stuttgart: Frommann-Holzoog, 1977]); cf. K. Fischer, *Geschichte der neuern Philosophie*, 11 vols. (Heidelberg: Winter, 1924), V, 625; C. Coignet, *La morale indépendant* (Paris: G. Bailliére, 1869).

there is even much to be said in favor of the position that the two orders exist independently, side by side, and refer back to two distinct agencies. Polytheism, it is said, contains a truth that cannot come into its own in monotheism.[93]

These objections can undoubtedly all be refuted on good grounds. The theory of evolution has until now proved unable to explain the origin and essence of the human moral consciousness and in attempting to do so always confuses the good with the pleasant and the useful. The idea of a moral world order apart from a personal, righteous, and holy God cannot be clearly conceived and ends with the apotheosis of the abstract power of goodness. The disproportion between virtue and happiness in this life certainly presents a serious objection to the supremacy of a moral world order but does not make it either unreal or impossible. And the return to polytheism looks too much like a desperate strategy to be taken seriously as a solution.

But the objections raised do make very clear that also the moral argument for God's existence cannot, strictly speaking, lay claim to the name of "proof." Hence, if in the case of Kant and others after him this argument has received such a warm reception that the other proofs have been completely overshadowed by it, this is due not to its logical cogency but to the irresistible witness of humanity's moral consciousness. Even though in the world around us there frequently is ever so little discernible evidence of a moral order, still in their conscience people willy-nilly feel just as much bound to such an order as in their intellect and rationality they know themselves controlled by the laws of thought. Logically, this moral order, which asserts itself in everyone's conscience, may not be able to drive people to the recognition of the existence of God. It nevertheless remains a powerful witness to the effect that in this world the brute force of nature will not have the last word. Even though the entire world should rise up in opposition and the intellect should lodge ever so many objections to this order, humans will continue to assert themselves as moral agents; they will persevere in their belief in the existence and supremacy of the moral world order, and this conviction will instinctively lead them to the recognition of a righteous and holy God, who rules supreme over all things.[94]

The Argument from Universal Consent

[176] Of similar force is the argument from universal consent. Already rated highly by Cicero, in modern times it has been greatly reinforced by the

---

93. Cf. William James, *The Varieties of Religious Experience* (New York: Modern Library, 1902), 515–16.

94. E. Katzer, "Der moralische Gottesbeweis nach Kant und Herbart," *Jahrbuch für protestantische Theologie* 4 (1878): 482–532, 635–89. Discussion about the cosmic moral order can be found, inter alia, in E. Zeller, *Vorträge und Abhandlungen geschichtlichen Inhalts*, 3 vols. (Leipzig: Fues [L. W. Reisland], 1865–84), III, 189ff.; M. Carrière, *De Zedelijke Wereldorde* (Leipzig: F. A. Brockhaus, 1880); E. von Hartmann, *Das sittlichen Bewusstsein* (Leipzig: W. Friedrich, 1886), 570ff.; P. Christ, *Die sittliche Weltordnung* (Leipzig: E. J. Brill, 1894); F. Traub, *Die sittliche Weltordnung* (Freiburg: Akademische Verlagsbuchhandlung von J. C. B. Mohr [Paul Siebeck], 1892); A. B. Bruce, *The Moral Order of the World in Ancient and Modern Thought* (London: Hodder & Stoughton, 1900); A. B. Pierson, "Over Ethika," *De Gids* 59 (November 1895): 245–63.

study of religions. Although [in the past] some scholars have demurred, all
scientists of religion now agree that there are no peoples without religion and
hence that religion is the common possession of all humankind. Historical
research into the origin of religion has ended with the acknowledgment that
[recorded] history nowhere takes us so far back that we encounter people
without religion. Everywhere, even in the most ancient times, humans are
religious beings; and by the historical route the question concerning the origin
of religion is unanswerable. The psychological study of religion, which replaces
or augments historical research, always again leads to the result that religion
has not originated and cannot have accidentally originated from a combination of nonreligious elements, but is rooted in the essence of human nature
itself. Some philosophers of religion find themselves compelled, willy-nilly, to
assume a "seed of religion, indeed to recognize a creation of humans in God's
image." And inasmuch as history and psychology can only introduce us to
phenomena in the domain of religion and cannot pronounce on their validity
and value, there has recently reawakened in the minds of many people a need
for a metaphysics of religion that attempts to establish the objective validity
of this important phenomenon and can only do this if it rises to belief in the
existence, revelation, and knowability of God.

Against this "universal consent" argument one can, of course, always raise
the objection that, nonetheless, religion constitutes a chapter in the pathology
of the human mind. Those who prefer to consider religion a passing fancy or
delusion that, like other such errors, will in time be driven out by scientific
enlightenment cannot be compelled by a syllogism to abandon this view. Still
this universal consent remains a fact of great importance, for from it we learn
that religion is not an individual or particularistic but a universal phenomenon
rooted in human nature itself. If human nature cannot be trusted at this point
of universal consent, it loses its credibility in every respect. And therefore, even
though the argument lacks logical cogency, in making the choice between illusion or reality, our decision cannot be doubtful.

The Historical-Theological Argument

Joining this witness, finally, is the so-called historical-theological argument.
One can base this argument either on the facts that historians unearth or on
the idea from which, consciously or unconsciously, their view and study of
history proceed. In the first case, scholars appeal to the ongoing development
that can be discerned in human culture and civilization, human science and
art, and in humanity's schools and societies. They then conclude that there is
momentum in history, that an idea and a plan are being realized, that a goal
is being pursued. All of this, they say, points back to a wise and omnipotent
World Ruler. It cannot be denied, however, that weighty arguments can be
advanced against all these reasonings, arguments so strong they could easily
shake one's faith in God's providence if it had no other foundations to rest
on. History confronts us at every moment with insoluble riddles. We get no

answers to the "why?" that comes out of our mouth at every turn. The "real" so rarely coincides with the "rational" that both pessimism and optimism can appeal to history for its positions. Even when we acknowledge that there has been progress in intellectual development and material culture, we face vast differences of opinion when it comes to the question whether the human race is making religious and moral progress, and there is no statistical science that can settle it.

It is therefore all the more remarkable that all students of history proceed—often without being conscious of it—from the assumption that there is in it a plan and guidance, development and purpose. It was also for this reason that the theory of evolution was so warmly received. As belief in God's providence eroded, this theory nevertheless seemed to furnish grounds for hope of a better future. The idea of progress, though not self-evidently inherent in that of evolution—for even death and dissolution are evolutionary processes—is readily associated and often unconsciously equated with it. Historians for that reason furnish proof that in their view of history they cannot do without the idea of guidance, plan, and purpose. There is, to be sure, much disagreement about the character of this guidance and about the content of that plan and purpose. But whether people favor a Christian or a humanistic, a positivistic or a historical-materialistic view of history, they always proceed from the belief that history is not a product of fate or chance but guided by a firm hand toward a definite goal. The human mind is restless until at the end of world history it finds some satisfaction, if not in a kingdom of God, then in a kingdom of humanity, or in a socialistic welfare state, or if necessary in Nietzsche's "eternal recurrence of all things." Logical arguments cannot prove such a belief. Those who prefer to believe that the world only deserves to be destroyed cannot be convinced of the contrary by any intellectual argumentation. But it is noteworthy that belief in guidance and purpose in history is ineradicably implanted in the human heart and an indispensable component in the philosophy of history. Now if this is the case, we again face here the dilemma: illusion or reality? and thus, in principle, the choice between atheism and theism. And in making that choice it is not the intellect but the heart that clinches it.

THE PROOFS: AN APPRAISAL

[177] It is regrettable that in theology these arguments for the existence of God are called "proofs." Not, however, for the reason cited by Jacobi: Although the verb "to prove" means to infer one proposition from another, proving the existence of God is not for that reason a contradiction in terms. Dependence in a syllogism is something very different from dependence in reality. A "ground of knowledge" is far from being a "ground of existence." Although in a syllogism the existence of God may be the *conclusion*—just as, generally speaking, one may infer the existence of a worker from the existence of a piece of work—that

existence in reality is still in fact the *origin* and *ground* of the existence of all things; indeed, it is even posited as such in the conclusion.

But the term "proofs" for these arguments is infelicitous. The reason is that the term transfers the arguments to a category in which they do not belong, the category, that is, of logical, mathematical, exact, compelling arguments, and thereby deprives them of their ethical and religious character. Now it appears as if belief in the existence of God is based on these proofs and has no foundation apart from them. And surely it would be "a wretched faith that first had to prove God's existence before it prayed to him."[95] The contrary, rather, is the case. There is not a single thing whose existence is certain to us only on the basis of proofs. We are fully convinced—prior to any argumentation—of our own existence, the existence of the world around us, the laws of logic and morality, simply as a result of the indelible impressions all these things make on our consciousness. We accept that existence—without constraint or coercion—spontaneously and instinctively. And the same is true of God's existence. The so-called proofs may introduce greater distinctness and lucidity, but they are by no means the final grounds on which our certainty regarding God's existence is ultimately based. This certainty is solely determined by faith, that is, the spontaneity with which our consciousness bears witness to the existence of God that urges itself upon us from all directions. The proofs, as proofs, are not the grounds but rather the products of faith.

The situation is this: Faith attempts to give an account of the religious impressions and feelings that we humans receive and carry with us in our soul. That faith also exerts its influence on the intellect, which in turn seeks little by little to introduce some order in that chaos of impressions and notions. It classifies them and reduces them to a few categories. Impressions come to us from the world of ideas (the ontological argument); from the world of finite, contingent, and mutable things (the cosmological arguments); from the world of beauty and harmonious design (the teleological argument); from that of moral order (the moral argument); from the speech and history of all humankind (the universal consent and the historical argument). However, although these impressions may be so classified, no one should ever think that these six proofs are the sole, isolated testimonies God sends us. On the contrary: to the believer all things speak of God; the whole universe is the mirror of his perfections. There is not an atom of the universe in which his everlasting power and deity are not clearly seen. Both from within and from without, God's witness speaks to us. God does not leave himself without a witness, either in nature or history, in heart or conscience, in life or lot. This witness of God is so powerful, accordingly, that almost no one denies its reality. All humans and peoples have heard something of the voice of the Lord. The consent of all peoples is confirmation of the fact that God does not leave himself without a witness; it is humanity's response to the voice of God.

---

95. K. F. A. Kahnis, *Die lutherische Dogmatik*, 3 vols. (Leipzig: Dörffling & Franke, 1861–68), I, 128.

Now these testimonies that come from God and are addressed to humans throughout the world are ordered and arranged in the proofs. The syllogistic form in which they are cast does not give them greater power. Though weak as proofs, they are strong as testimonies. They are not arguments that strike the mind of unbelievers with compelling force, but "signs and testimonies" that never fail to make an impression on everyone's mind. Analyzed, isolated, detached from each other and put side by side, they can be attacked at every point of the argument and hold back the act of believing, which occurs spontaneously. But conceived as testimonies, and proclaimed as the revelation of the God of whose existence every human is by nature—and prior to any reasoning or study—assured in the very depths of his or her soul, they are of no small value. For though, so presented, they will encounter objections and reservations, they will not be nullified by such encounters. Just as no one believes in God's love because all things reveal that love, but despite everything that produces doubt, so everyone is also convinced in advance of God's existence. The proofs do not induce faith and the objections do not wreck it. In every sphere of life it is the case that upon reflection we are assailed by difficulties. No one, however, will for that reason throw overboard as so much foolishness the moral law, the laws of logic, religion, art, and science, solely because his or her mind is not able to explain all the phenomena it recognizes and to defend them against all objections. Yet, with regard to existence, reflection produces not certainty but clarity. To believers, the so-called proofs for the existence of God account for their own religious and ethical consciousness. They furnish them the weapons with which their opponents, who in any case are not better armed than they, can be repulsed. For Christians these proofs signify that it is one and the same God who manifests himself in nature and in grace, therefore that creation and re-creation, the realm of nature and the world of ethics, do not exist side by side in Manichaean and dualistic fashion, but constitute one cosmos: the perfections of God that shine out in the world are the same as those which sparkle in the kingdom of God. Collectively, the testimonies that God sends to us in the world and are condensed in the so-called proofs are nothing other than a revelation of the name of the Lord by means of which he makes himself known to his creatures and gives us the right to address him. Together they make him known to us as the divine being who must be conceived by us as necessary and necessarily as existing; who is the sole, first, and absolute Cause of all creatures; who consciously and purposefully governs all things, and who above all reveals himself as the Holy One in the conscience of everyone who believes.

PART II

THE LIVING, ACTING GOD

3

THE NAMES OF GOD

*In Scripture God's name is his self-revelation. Only God can name himself;
his name is identical with the perfections he exhibits in and to the world.
He makes himself known to his people by his proper names; to Israel as
YHWH, to the Christian church as Father. God's revealed names do not reveal
his being as such but his accommodation to human language. Scripture is
accommodated language; it is anthropomorphic through and through. God
himself is described in human terms via human faculties, body parts, emotions,
sensations, and actions. In Scripture all creation, the theater of God's glory, is
mined for the description of the knowledge of God. God is immanent in all
creation. Therefore, Christian theology opposes all dualisms, including those of
modernity, that empty created reality of God, for then theology could not speak
of God at all.*

*We rightly use anthropomorphic language because God accommodated
himself to creatures by revealing his name in and through creatures. We
cannot see God himself; we can only see him in his works and name him in
accordance with his self-revelation in his works. To deny this is to deny the
possibility of knowing God at all. Some philosophers (Plato, Hegel) have tried
to get around this by rejecting concrete representations of God in favor of
abstractions such as the Absolute, the One, Life, or Reason. But, since these too
are anthropomorphisms, they fail to solve the problem.*

*Of course, all our knowledge of God is ectypal or derived from Scripture.
Only God's self-knowledge is adequate, underived, or archetypal. Yet our finite,
inadequate knowledge is still true, pure, and sufficient. Ectypal knowledge
must not be seen as merely symbolic, a product of poetic imagination. God then
becomes mere projection and religion mere subjective art. Christian theology
teaches the opposite. We are God's creation; he is not ours. While our knowledge
of him is accommodated and limited, it is no less real, true, and trustworthy.
As God reveals himself, so he truly is. His revealed attributes truly reveal his
nature.*

Ed. note: This chapter was originally three major sections (§§26–28) in the *Gereformeerde Dogmatiek*. They
have been combined here because of their shared subject matter, the names of God. The three divisions
are now marked by the subheadings "Biblical Names for God," "Classifying God's Names," and "God's
Proper Names."

Scripture provides us with a variety of divine names, and theologians have suggested distinctions among them. The name YHWH, for example, points to the very being of God, the "One who is." Philosophers came to speak of the Supreme Being or Nature and of the divine essence as Infinite Being or even Intelligent Being. Spinoza, for example, viewed God "as the unique, infinite, necessarily existing substance. . . . The absolute and immanent first cause." This sort of theistic speculation easily deteriorated into pantheism.

In reaction to this rather cold, impersonal, rationalistic view of God, much nineteenth-century theology turned away from metaphysics and reduced religion to morality (e.g., Ritschl). God was the Father, the fountain of goodness and love; he is not Absolute Being but Love. There is much of value in this response, but it too is one-sided. The challenge of theology is to do justice to all the attributes of God revealed in Scripture.

It is this conviction that lies behind the teaching of Christian theology that God is "simple," that is, free from composition. God is identical with each of his attributes; he is what he possesses. In God "to be" is the same as to be wise, to be good, or to be powerful. All God's attributes are identical with his essence. In all his attributes he is pure being, absolute reality. We cannot refrain from speaking of God's being, and in the description of God's essence Christian theology places his aseity in the foreground as the primary attribute traditionally associated with the name YHWH. God is the One who exists of and through himself, the perfect being who is absolute in wisdom and goodness, righteousness and holiness, power and blessedness.

Though we cannot make distinctions between God's essence and his attributes, it is permissible to make distinctions among the attributes. Each attribute expresses something special about God. God himself reveals his many perfections to us; we name him with the names Scripture itself provides. No one perfection fully expresses God's being. In the past, theologians have distinguished three ways of obtaining the names of God, in the way of negation, or of eminence, or of causality, in relation to creatures.

Among Reformed theologians the distinction between incommunicable and communicable properties became the favored distinction. In the former were included oneness, simplicity, immutability, eternity; the second group was usually divided further into attributes of intellect (knowledge, wisdom, veracity), will (goodness, righteousness, holiness), and power. Nonetheless, the negations ("God is not . . .") must not be seen as wholly incommunicable, because then they would be unknowable and unnameable. All that we can say about God must be based on his self-revelation. Our knowledge of God is not, in fact cannot be, exhaustive; it is analogical and ectypal. But it is true knowledge, and because God's attributes are identical with his being, we can speak truly about God as he really is. Since in his perfections God is both absolutely superior to us and in fellowship with his creatures, each of his attributes can be said, in different senses, to be both incommunicable and communicable. Thus we distinguish attributes that accent transcendence

from those that accent immanence. Reformed theology uses the terms
"incommunicable" and "communicable" here to underscore the strong
opposition of Christian theism to the error both of pantheism and of deism.

Holy Scripture not only describes God's perfections but also reveals to us
God's personal names. The simplest name for God in the Old Testament is El
(Elohim, El Shaddai). This name emphasizes God's power and might; he is
high and strong. As the God of grace, Scripture reveals God to us as YHWH *(the*
LORD). YHWH *is the covenant God of promise, the faithful one who saves his*
people. YHWH *is the highest revelation of God in the Old Testament;* YHWH *is*
God's real name. The New Testament retains these names, notably following
the LXX in translating YHWH *as Kyrios (Lord). The one new name, added by*
our Lord Jesus Christ, is the personal name "Father," indicating God's special
familial relationship with his people. "Father" is thus the supreme revelation of
God, and since the Father is made known to us by Jesus through the Spirit, the
full, abundant revelation of God's name is trinitarian: Father, Son, and Holy
Spirit.

BIBLICAL NAMES FOR GOD

[178] All we can learn about God from his revelation is designated his Name
in Scripture. The original meaning of the Hebrew word שֵׁם (name) is probably "sign," "distinguishing mark," just as the Greek ὄνομα and the Latin
nomen are derived from the stem *gno* and hence indicate the characteristic
feature by which a thing is known, a distinguishing mark. A name is a sign of
the person bearing it, a designation referring to some characteristic in which
a person reveals himself or herself and becomes knowable. There is a connection between a name and its bearer, and that connection, so far from being
arbitrary, is rooted in that bearer. Even among us [moderns], now that names
have for the most part become mere sounds without meaning, that connection
is still felt. A name is something personal and very different from a number
or a member of a species. It always feels more or less unpleasant when others
misspell or garble our name: it stands for our honor, our worth, our person
and individuality. But that linkage was much more vital in earlier times when
names still had a transparent meaning and actually revealed the identity of a
person or thing.

This is also how it is in Scripture. Adam had to name the animals in accordance with their nature (Gen. 2:19–20). Scripture spells out the meaning
of many names as well as the reason for them. Examples: Eve (Gen. 3:20),
Cain (4:1), Seth (4:25), Noah (5:29), Babel (11:9), Ishmael (16:11), Esau
and Jacob (25:25–26), Moses (Exod. 2:10), Jesus (Matt. 1:21), and so on.
Repeatedly a name is changed or a surname is added when a person acts in
another capacity: Abraham (Gen. 17:5), Sarah (17:15), Israel (32:28), Joshua
(Num. 13:16), Jedidiah (2 Sam. 12:25), Mara (Ruth 1:20), Peter (Mark 3:16),
and so on. Following his ascension Christ received a name that is above every

name (Phil. 2:9; Heb. 1:4), and in the new Jerusalem a new name is given to believers (Rev. 2:17; 3:12; 22:4).

The same is true of God's name. There is an intimate link between God and his name. According to Scripture, this link too is not accidental or arbitrary but forged by God himself. We do not name God; he names himself. In the foreground here is the name as a revelation on the part of God, in an active and objective sense, as revealed name. In this case God's name is identical with the attributes or perfections that he exhibits in and to the world: his glory (Ps. 8:1; 72:19), honor (Lev. 18:21; Ps. 86:10–11; 102:16), his redeeming power (Exod. 15:3; Isa. 47:4); his service (Isa. 56:6; Jer. 23:27); his holiness (1 Chron. 16:10; Ps. 105:3). The name is God himself as he reveals himself in one relationship or another (Lev. 24:11, 16; Deut. 28:58). That name, being a revelation of God, is great (Ezek. 36:23), holy (Ezek. 36:20), awesome (Ps. 111:9), a high refuge (Ps. 20:1),[1] a strong tower (Prov. 18:10). By proper names, particularly by the name YHWH, God made himself known to Israel. He revealed himself to Israel by the angel in whom the Lord's name was present (Exod. 23:20). And by him he put his name on the children of Israel (Num. 6:27), caused his name to be remembered (Exod. 20:24), put his name among them and made it to dwell there (Deut. 12:5; 14:23), especially in the temple that was built for his name (2 Sam. 7:13). Now his name lives in that temple (2 Chron. 20:9; 33:4). By that name he saves (Ps. 54:1), and on account of that name he cannot abandon Israel (1 Sam. 12:22; Isa. 48:9, 11; Ps. 23:3; 31:3; 143:11–12). Israel, accordingly, may not blaspheme and desecrate that name, or use it in vain (Exod. 20:7; Lev. 18:21; 19:12; 24:11). On the contrary: that name must be invoked, passed on in story, magnified, known, feared, exalted, expected, sought out, sanctified (Gen. 4:26; 12:8; Exod. 9:16; Deut. 28:58; 1 Kings 8:33; Ps. 5:12; 34:3; 52:9; 83:17; 122:4; Isa. 26:8; Matt. 6:9; John 12:28; etc.).

In the New Testament God's name acquires an even richer and deeper meaning. For the Logos, who was in the beginning with God and is in the bosom of the Father, has made him known (John 1:18) and revealed his name (John 17:6, 26). Since no one knows the Father except the Son, only those to whom the Son reveals the Father gain knowledge of God (Matt. 11:27). Those who confess the Son have the Father also (1 John 2:23). Those who have seen him have seen the Father (John 14:9). The name of Jesus Christ, accordingly, guarantees the truth of our knowledge of God and all the associated benefits. He is called Jesus because he saves his people (Matt. 1:21) and is the only name given under heaven by which we must be saved (Acts 4:12). By his name miracles are performed (Acts 4:7); by it we receive forgiveness (Acts 2:38), the right to become God's children (John 1:12), and eternal life (1 John 5:13). Where two or three people are gathered in his name, he is in their midst (Matt.

---

1. Ed. note: For Ps. 20:2 (MT), Bavinck uses the Dutch *Statenvertaling,* "een hoog Vertrek," which we have translated as "a high refuge." The Hebrew verb root used is שָׂגַב = to "set (securely) on high" (F. Brown, S. R. Driver, and C. A. Briggs, *A Hebrew and English Lexicon of the Old Testament* [Oxford: Clarendon, n.d.], 960). Most contemporary translations provide the dynamic equivalent: "protect you," "defend you," etc.

18:20). Those who pray in his name are heard (John 14:13), and those who call on the name of the Lord are saved (Acts 2:21). All salvation for humanity is comprehended within the name of the Father, the Son, and the Holy Spirit. Being baptized in that name is a sign and seal of fellowship with God. And an even richer revelation awaits believers in the new Jerusalem (Rev. 3:12), when his name will be inscribed upon everyone's forehead (Rev. 22:4).

The name of God in Scripture does not describe God as he exists within himself but God in his revelation and multiple relations to his creatures. This name, however, is not arbitrary: God reveals himself in the way he does because he is who he is. Summed up in his name, therefore, is his honor, his fame, his excellencies, his entire revelation, his very being. Upon those to whom it is revealed, therefore, the name confers special privileges and imposes unique obligations. The name of God implies that, having revealed himself in it, God expects to be called by it. The "divulged" name becomes the name "called upon." In Scripture, "to be" and "to be called" are two sides of the same thing. God is what he calls himself and calls himself what he is. What God reveals of himself is expressed and conveyed in specific names. To his creatures he grants the privilege of naming and addressing him on the basis of, and in keeping with, his revelation. The *one* name of God, which is inclusive of his entire revelation both in nature and in grace, is divisible for us in a great many names. Only in that way do we obtain a full view of the riches of his revelation and the profound meaning of his name. We call him and indeed may call him by all that has become known of his being in creation and re-creation. But all those names, as designations of God, impose on us the obligation to consecrate and glorify them. It is the one name, the full revelation and to that extent the very being of God himself, with which we are dealing in all those names. By his name God puts himself in a certain relation to us, and the relation we assume to him must be congruent with it.

Accommodation and Anthropomorphism

Accordingly, [as stated above] the names by which we call and address God are not arbitrary: they were not conceived by us at our own pleasure. It is God himself who deliberately and freely, both in nature and in grace, reveals himself, who gives us the right to name him on the basis of his self-revelation, and who in his Word has made his own names known to us on that same basis. Now all these names without distinction are characterized by the fact that they have been derived from revelation. Not a single one of them describes God's being as such. The revealed name is the foundation of all the names by which we address him. And inasmuch as the revelation of God in nature and in Scripture is specifically addressed to humanity, it is a human language in which God speaks to us of himself. For that reason the words he employs are human words; for the same reason he manifests himself in human forms. From this it follows that Scripture does not just contain a few scattered anthropomorphisms but is anthropomorphic through and through. From the first page to the last it wit-

nesses to God's coming to, and searching for, humanity. The whole revelation
of God is concentrated in the Logos, who became "flesh" and is, as it were, one
single act of self-humanization, the incarnation of God. If God were to speak
to us in a divine language, not a creature would understand him. But what
spells out his grace is the fact that from the moment of creation God stoops
down to his creatures, speaking and appearing to them in human fashion.
This is why all the names by which God calls himself and allows us to call him
are derived from earthly and human relations. In Scripture, accordingly, he is
called El, the strong One; El Shaddai, the mighty One; YHWH, the One who
is there; he is called Father, Son, Spirit, good, merciful, gracious, just, holy
(etc.); all of them are expressions that first of all apply to creatures and are then
transferred to God by way of eminence. Even the so-called incommunicable
attributes of God, such as immutability, independence, simplicity, eternity,
and omnipresence, are presented in Scripture in forms and expressions derived
from the finite world and are therefore stated negatively. Eternity cannot be
defined except as a negation of time. Scripture never even attempts to describe
these perfections of God positively in terms of their own essence and apart
from any relation to the finite.

But anthropomorphism in Scripture is even much more extensive. All that
pertains to humans and even to creatures in general is also attributed to God,
especially "human faculties, body parts, sensations, affections, actions, things
pertaining to and connected with humanity." God is said to have a soul (Lev.
26:11) and a Spirit (Gen. 1:2; Matt. 12:28; etc.). Though there is never any
reference to God's body, in Christ God also assumed a real body (John 1:14;
Col. 1:18), and the church is called the body of Christ (Eph. 1:22). Yet all
the physical organs are attributed to God. There is mention of his face (Exod.
33:20, 23; Isa. 63:9; Ps. 16:11; Matt. 18:10; Rev. 22:4), his eyes (Ps. 11:4;
Heb. 4:13), his eyelids (Ps. 11:4), the apple of his eye (Deut. 32:10; Ps. 17:8;
Zech. 2:8), his ears (Ps. 55:3), his nose (Deut. 33:10), his mouth (Deut. 8:3);
his lips (Job 11:5), his tongue (Isa. 30:27), his neck (Jer. 18:17), his arm (Exod.
15:16), his hand (Num. 11:23), his right hand (Exod. 15:12); his finger (Exod.
8:19), his heart (Gen. 6:6), his intestines (Isa. 63:15; Jer. 31:20; Luke 1:78);
his bosom (Ps. 74:11; John 1:18), his feet (Isa. 66:1).

Every human emotion, furthermore, is also present in God: rejoicing (Isa.
62:5; 65:19); sorrow (Ps. 78:40; Isa. 63:10); grief (Ps. 95:10); provocation (Jer.
7:18–19); fear (Deut. 32:27); love in all its variations such as mercy, compassion, grace, long-suffering, and so on; also zeal and jealousy (Deut. 32:21);
repentance (Gen. 6:6); hatred (Deut. 16:22); wrath (Ps. 2:5); and vengeance
(Deut. 32:35).

All human actions, moreover, are attributed to God: investigating (Gen.
18:21), searching minds (Ps. 7:9), knowing (Gen. 3:5), intending (Gen. 50:20),
forgetting (1 Sam. 1:11), remembering (Gen. 8:1; Exod. 2:24), speaking (Gen.
2:16), calling (Rom. 4:17), commanding (Isa. 5:6), rebuking (Ps. 18:15; 104:7),
answering (Ps. 3:4), witnessing (Mal. 2:14), resting (Gen. 2:2), working (John

5:17), seeing (Gen. 1:10), hearing (Exod. 2:24), smelling (Gen. 8:21), testing (Ps. 11:4–5), sitting (Ps. 9:7), arising (Ps. 68:1), going (Exod. 34:9), coming (Exod. 25:22), walking (Lev. 26:12), going down (Gen. 11:5), meeting (Exod. 3:18), visiting (Gen. 21:1), passing (Exod. 12:13), abandoning (Judg. 6:13), writing (Exod. 34:1), sealing (John 6:27), engraving (Isa. 49:16), striking (Isa. 11:4), chastising (Deut. 8:5), working (John 5:17), binding up (Ps. 147:3), healing (Ps. 103:3; Deut. 32:39), killing and making alive (Deut. 32:39), wiping away (Isa. 25:8), wiping out (2 Kings 21:13), washing (Ps. 51:2), cleansing (Ps. 51:2), anointing (Ps. 2:2), adorning (Ezek. 16:11), clothing (Ps. 132:16), crowning (Ps. 8:5), girding (Ps. 18:32), destroying (Gen. 6:7; Lev. 26:31), killing (Gen. 38:7), inflicting (Gen. 12:17), judging (Ps. 58:11), condemning (Job 10:2), and so forth.

In addition, God is also very frequently described with names that denote a certain occupation, office, position, or relationship among people. He is a bridegroom (Isa. 61:10), a man (Isa. 54:5–6), a father (Deut. 32:6), a judge, king, a lawgiver (Isa. 33:22), a warrior (Exod. 15:3), a mighty hero (Ps. 78:65–66; Zeph. 3:17), an architect and builder (Heb. 11:10), a gardener (John 15:1), a shepherd (Ps. 23:1), a physician (Exod. 15:26), and so on. In connection with these occupational descriptions there is mention of his seat, throne, footstool, rod, scepter, weapons, bow, arrow, shield, chariot, banner, book, seal, treasure, inheritance, and so on. Then, to express what God means to his own, all sorts of expressions are even derived from the organic and inorganic creation. He is compared to a lion (Isa. 31:4), an eagle (Deut. 32:11), a lamb (Isa. 53:7), a hen (Matt. 23:37), the sun (Ps. 84:11), the morning star (Rev. 22:16), a light (Ps. 27:1), a lamp (Rev. 21:23), a fire (Heb. 12:29), a spring or fountain (Ps. 36:9; Jer. 2:13), food, bread, drink, water, ointment (Isa. 55:1; John 4:10: 6:35, 55), a rock (Deut. 32:4), a refuge (Ps. 119:114), a tower (Prov. 18:10), a stronghold (Ps. 9:9), a shadow (Ps. 91:1; 121:5), a shield (Ps. 84:11), a road (John 14:6), a temple (Rev. 21:22), and so on.[2]

[179] The entire creation, all of nature with all its [diverse] kingdoms, but especially the human world, is mined in Scripture for the description of the knowledge of God. Almost no limit is set to the use of anthropomorphic language. All creatures, animate and inanimate, organic and inorganic, furnish names with which to somewhat bring home to us the greatness of God. Although nameless within himself, in his revelation God possesses many names. "All things can be said of God," writes Augustine, "but nothing can be said worthily of him. Nothing is more widespread than this poverty [of expression]. You are looking for a fitting name for him? You will not find it. You try to speak of him in some way? You find that he is everything." And to clarify why so many names can be applied to God, Augustine uses a striking illustration. Our body, he says, has many needs: light and air, food and drink, shelter and clothing, and so on. Now all these things are very different and exist side by

2. Cf., also S. Glassius, *Philologiae sacrae*, 6th ed. (Francofurti & Lipsiae: Fleischer, 1691), 1116–81.

side in the various parts of creation. Now also our spirit has many and various needs, but what provides for these needs is not multiform but always the one selfsame divine being.

> On earth, a fountain is one thing, light another. When you are thirsty, you look for a fountain, and to get to the fountain you look for light; and if there is no daylight, you light a lamp to get to the fountain. But he is both a fountain and a light: to the thirsty he is a fountain, to the blind a light. Let [your] eyes be opened to see the light; let the lips of [your] heart be opened to drink of the fountain. That which you drink, you see and hear. God becomes everything to you, for he is the whole of the things you love. If you attend to visible things, well, God is neither bread nor is he water, nor light, nor a garment, nor a house. For all these things are visible, individual, and separate. What bread is, water is not; what a garment is, a house is not; and what these things are, God is not, for they are visible things. God is all of these things to you: if you are hungry, he is bread to you; if you are thirsty, he is water to you; if you live in darkness, he is light to you, for he remains incorruptible. If you are naked, he is a garment of immortality to you when this corruptible shall put on incorruption and this mortal shall put on immortality.[3]

Pseudo-Dionysius, thinking along the same lines, states that God is both "nameless and yet has the names of everything that is." He is both "all that exists" and "nothing of all that exists."[4] In Thomas we read: "God, being himself simply and universally perfect, has preexisting in himself the perfections of all his creatures."[5] Bonaventure says it even better:

> In order that we may be able to extol and glorify God, and in order that we may advance to the knowledge of God, we must transfer to the divine that which pertains to the creature. Now the ground or purpose of this transference is twofold. In the first place, it is necessary with a view to the glory of God; in the second place, with a view to the guidance of our intellect. God's glory requires this transference. For, since God is greatly to be praised, lest he should ever lack praise because of the scarcity of words, Holy Scripture has taught us that the names of creatures—indefinite in number—should be transferred to God, in order that just as every *creature* glorifies God, so also every *name* that is ascribed to creatures might glorify him, and in order that he who is so glorious that not one single name can do justice to him—for he surpasses, as it were, every name—might be glorified by all the names. This transference is also necessary with a view to the guidance of our intellect. For, since we arrive at knowledge of the Creator through the creature, and especially in view of the fact that nearly all creatures possess certain noble characteristics that furnish a source for our understanding of God—for example, the lion possesses fortitude;

3. Augustine, *Lectures on the Gospel of John*, tract. 13.5 (on John 3:22–29).
4. Pseudo-Dionysius, *The Divine Names*, I, §§6–7.
5. T. Aquinas, *Summa theol.*, I, qu. 13, art. 2.

the lamb, meekness; the rock, solidity; the serpent, prudence, and so on—hence it is fitting that many names be transferred to God.[6]

Calvin concurs with this when he writes: "There is not an atom of the world in which one cannot discern at least some bright sparks of his glory." God is immanent in the whole of creation. The pure of heart see God everywhere. Everything is brimful of God. "I confess, of course, that it can be said reverently—provided it proceeds from a reverent mind—that nature is God."[7]

But not all creatures are of equal rank: there is a hierarchy in the realm of creatures. The position and rank that creatures occupy is determined by their kinship with God. All creatures express some aspect of God's being, but of all of them human beings are at the top. They alone have the honor of being called "image, son, child of God." They alone are called God's offspring. Most of the names of God, particularly the most sublime ones, derive from the existence of humans. However, humans should never be detached from the realm of nature; neither may any creature or any part of the universe ever be put on a par with, or in opposition to, God. Nothing exists outside of or apart from God. This truth, it must be said, has over and over been violated: Plato's dualism, Neoplatonism, Gnosticism, Manichaeism—they all put a limit to God's revelation and posited a material substance hostile to God over against him. And in all sorts of ways these dualisms have for centuries impacted theology. The same dualistic principle is at work when in modern times, under the influence of Kant and Jacobi, the revelation of God is restricted to the sphere of religion and ethics, when only the religious and ethical content of Scripture is recognized, when the seat of religion is found only in the heart or the conscience, in the emotions or the will. In this way nature with its elements and forces, human life in society and politics, the arts and sciences, are assigned a place outside the sphere of God's revelation. They are considered neutral areas existing apart from God. Then, of course, a proper appreciation of the Old Testament and a very large part of the New Testament is no longer possible. Nature and the world no longer have anything to say to believers. Revelation, which comes to us in the Word of God, loses all influence in public life. Religion, now confined to the inner recesses of the heart and the privacy of one's home, forfeits all claim to respect. Dogmatics, specifically the doctrine of God, shrinks by the day, and theology is no longer able to maintain its place. Theology is no longer able to speak of God because it no longer speaks from him and through him. It no longer has any names with which to name God. God becomes the great Unknown; the world first becomes a domain without God (ἄθεος), then a domain that is anti-God (ἀντίθεος).

6. Bonaventure, *Sent.*, I, dist. 34, art. 1, qu. 4.
7. J. Calvin, *Institutes*, I.v.1, 5.

Naming the Nameless

Now the names by which God calls himself in his revelation present a peculiar intellectual difficulty. In an earlier chapter we learned that God is incomprehensible and far superior to all finite creatures. In his names, however, he descends to the level of the finite and becomes like his creatures. What we encounter here is an antinomy that seems insoluble. On the one hand, God is without a name; on the other, he possesses many names. After first banishing all anthropomorphism, we are now reintroducing it. What right have we to apply these names to God? On what grounds do we ascribe them to God, who is infinitely superior to all his creatures and cannot be contained by the finite?

The reason can only be this: the whole creation, though as creature it is infinitely far removed from God, is still God's handiwork and related to him. The world is not an independent entity on a par with, and antithetically related to, God. It is not a second God, but totally God's work, both in its "isness" and its "whatness." From the very beginning it was designed to reveal God. The entire people of Israel were designed to make known God's excellencies in its laws and institutions, its offices and ministries, its character and mores. And Christ's humanity was equipped by the Holy Spirit to make known to people the Father and his name. The circle of the apostles, with its diversity of education, preparation, gifts, and calling, was designated to tell the world the "mighty acts of God." Here lies the reason why we can and may speak of God in creaturely language. We have the right to use anthropomorphic language because God himself came down to the level of his creatures and revealed his name in and through his creatures. Accordingly, as we saw above, the use of anthropomorphism is absolutely not confined to an occasioned expression like personality. In fact, we cannot speak of God in any other way. For we do not see God himself; we can see him only in his works and name him in accordance with his self-revelation in his works. But that is not all. On earth at least we cannot see God face to face. If God nevertheless wants us to know him, he has to come down to our level and accommodate himself to our limited, finite, human consciousness and speak to us in human language. Those, therefore, who contest our right to use anthropomorphisms, thereby in principle deny the possibility that God in fact reveals himself in his creatures, are logically bound to proceed to the denial of the creation, and are finally left with nothing more than an eternal dualism between God and the world, the infinite and the finite. For if our calling God by anthropomorphic names implies a finitization of God, this applies to a much greater extent to God's self-revelation in creation. As the infinite One, God is then powerless to produce another form of being outside of his own being. The world is in no way a revelation of God but solely an act of divine self-concealment. Humanity, then, is God's polar opposite and not related to him in the way of kinship. And God is an eternal abyss (βυθος), a nameless silence (σιγη), to himself as well as to us humans. Naturally, no knowledge of God is any longer possible either. If anthropomorphic, creaturely names violate God's being, we cannot and may not call him by any name and have to be totally silent. For then any name by which we might wish to refer to him is an act of defamation, an assault on God's majesty, blasphemy.[8]

Some philosophers have attempted to escape this obvious consequence by distinguishing between a concrete representation and an abstract concept. Plato already started it, Neoplatonism and Gnosticism continued the process, and Hegel reintroduced the distinction. But it makes no difference. Even the most advanced speculation and the most searching philosophy still has to think and speak about God. Though they throw out all concrete representations and only retain pure and abstract concepts, they will never transcend the necessity of thinking and speaking in human, creaturely terms or come closer to the infinite One himself. Even the most abstract names—such as existence, substance, the Absolute, the One, the Spirit, Reason—are and remain anthropomorphisms. As humans we have only two alternatives: either absolute silence or human thought and speech about God; either agnosticism (i.e., theoretical atheism) or anthropomorphism. Philosophy, accordingly, has always again returned to anthropomorphism; if it had not, it would of course also have ended up with a negative criticism. Plato, Philo, Plotinus, Pseudo-Dionysius, John of Damascus, and Erigena all again in the end assigned an array of names to God. Positive (kataphatic) theology built up what negative (apophatic) theology had broken down. Spinoza's "substance" was adorned with countless attributes and modes. In Hegel's philosophy God nevertheless again became "life," "mind," "thought," "reason," "subject." Rauwenhoff trots out the imagination where the intellect had to quit.[9] Numerous philosophers, therefore, defend the good right of anthropomorphism.[10] And, of course, also Christian theology has always made this judgment. In it God "treads the path of his human children (דֶּרֶךְ בְּנֵי אָדָם)," as the Jews express it. "God's words and actions are incomprehensible. We could in no way understand them had not Holy Scripture, in speaking of God, used such expressions as arise from human affairs. Hence, with a view to our feeble minds, it pleased the Holy Spirit, the author of Scripture, to stammer in our fashion and to deal with us—in a way more persuasive and lowly than is fitting for so great a Majesty—by images and words."[11]

[180] So the propriety of these names may be considered well established, but what is their value? What, and what kind of, knowledge do they furnish

8. See above, pp. 47–52 (#166).

9. L. W. E. Rauwenhoff, *Wijsbegeerte von den Godsdienst* (Leiden: Brill & van Doeburgh, 1887), 611ff.

10. I. Kant, *Critique of Judgment*, trans. J. H. Bernard (New York and London: Hafner Publishing, 1968 [1951]), 336–38 (§91); F. Jacobi, *Gesammelte Werke*, 8 vols. (Leipzig: Gerhard Fleischer, 1812–25), III; F. Paulsen, *Einleitung in die Philosophie* (Berlin: Hertz, 1892), 262ff.; E. von Hartmann, *Philosophie des Unbewussten*, 9th ed., 2 vols. (Berlin: C. Duncker, 1882).

11. Flacius in S. Glassius, *Philologiae sacrae* (Jena: Steinmann, 1668), 116; Luther in G. F. Oehler, *Theology of the Old Testament*, trans. Ellen D. Smith and Sophia Taylor (Edinburgh: T. & T. Clark, 1892–93), 162.

us concerning God? The idea that this knowledge is fully adequate for the subject is, of course, absurd. It is in every respect finite and limited, but not for that reason impure or untrue. Fully adequate [exhaustive] knowledge is something of which we possess very little. Everywhere and in every area of life we finally run into mystery. The inner being of things, the thing as such, escapes our perception. We observe phenomena and from them infer the essence of things; we learn to know stable properties and from them we deduce the substance, but this substance itself lies behind the phenomenon and as such is unknown to us. Physics assumes the existence of atoms or electrons or energies as the final components of the material world, but does not have even a smidgen of empirical knowledge of them. Only the most simple things can be defined. As soon as things are of a somewhat higher order, they can no longer be completely captured in a concept. This is already true of the visible world, but it is even more applicable in the world of invisible things. Human beings are corporeal, sense-oriented beings. All their knowledge originates in, and arises from, sense perception. Our thinking is bound up with our senses, just as our soul is with our body. We never perceive spiritual realities directly but only by the medium of material things. We see all things "dimly." Not only God but also the soul and the entire spiritual world only become known to us through the medium of the world of the senses. This is why we refer to all spiritual matters with names that have their primary reference in the visible world. We denominate the human soul in terms of physical phenomena. To bring home to ourselves and to others the activities of the soul—such as knowing, thinking, understanding, judging, deciding, feeling, and so on—we resort to words that originally referred to a physical act. Hence, all our talk of invisible things is metaphorical, figurative, poetic. "For the things that are known are beyond all naming, for the principal name of things known and immaterial is 'nothing.'"[12] But this does not mean that what we say is untrue and incorrect. On the contrary, real poetry is truth, for it is based on the resemblance, similarity, and kinship that exist between different groups of phenomena. All language, all metaphors and similes, all symbolism[13] are based on and presuppose this penetration of the visible by the invisible world. If speaking figuratively were untrue, all our thought and knowledge would be an illusion and speech itself impossible.

The same is true in religion and theology. There is no fully adequate knowledge of God. We cannot name him as he is within himself. All his names are derived from the world of creatures. But this does not make them untrue, a product of human imagination. Just as there is resemblance between various parts of the world, making comparison between them a possibility, so also there is kinship between God and his creatures, a kinship that warrants the use of

12. Gregory of Nazianzus, *Oration* 45.

13. W. Menzel, *Christliche Symbolik*, 2 vols. (Regensburg: Manz, 1855); O. Zöckler, *Theologia naturalis* (Frankfurt a.M.: Heyder & Zimmer, 1860); F. Bettex, *Das Lied der Schöpfung*, 5th ed. (Stuttgart: J. F. Steinkopf, 1906).

creaturely language in speaking of him. Furthermore, though temporally the natural is prior to the spiritual, logically and ideally the spiritual precedes the natural. The natural could never guide us to the spiritual if it had not itself proceeded from the spiritual. Plato viewed the world as the realization of ideas. And Scripture teaches that all things have been made by the Logos and not from the things that do appear (John 1:3; Heb. 11:3). It is God himself who made all things, including the material world, subservient to the manifestation of his perfections. He could do this, since he is the omnipotent Creator and has total control also over matter. Hence, while it is true that we call God by names derived from the world of creatures, these names were first increated in those creatures by God himself. It is true: we first apply to creatures the names by which we speak of God because we know them before we know God. But materially they first apply to God and then to creatures. All perfections are first in God, then in creatures. He possesses them because they belong to his essence; we possess them only by participation. Just as the temple was built according to the pattern (τυπος) shown to Moses on the mountain (Heb. 8:5), so every creature is first conceived in eternity and then created in time. All fatherhood (πατρια) in heaven and on earth is named after the Father (πατηρ), who created all things (Eph. 3:15; cf. Matt. 23:9).[14]

Archetypal and Ectypal Knowledge of God

In Scripture all heavenly things are portrayed to us in earthly shades and colors. God himself comes to us through his whole creation and, in Christ's human nature, pitched his tent among us. This human nature, certainly, was not a fully adequate organ for his deity; in fact, his glory was even concealed by it. Still the fullness of the deity dwelt in Christ bodily: those who saw him saw the Father. It is not contradictory, therefore, to say that a knowledge that is inadequate, finite, and limited is at the same time true, pure, and sufficient. God reveals himself in his works, and according to that revelation we name him. He permits us to speak of him in language that is weak and human because he himself displayed his perfections to us in his creatures. Hence, in actual fact, it is not we who name God. Where would we get the ability and the right to do that? It is God himself who, through nature and Scripture, has put his splendid names in our mouth. According to an old distinction, the names of God are not the product of "reasoning reason" *(ratio ratiocinans),* subjective human rationality, but of "reasoned reason" *(ratio ratiocinata),* objective reason in revelation. God's self-consciousness is archetypal; our knowledge of God, drawn from his Word, is ectypal.

Now this describes the nature of the knowledge of God that is consistently characteristic for creatures. By it we avoid two extremes. On the one hand, there are those who consider an essential, quidditative, adequate knowledge of God a possibility, either by mystical contemplation (Plotinus, Malebranche,

---

14. John of Damascus, *The Orthodox Faith,* I, 9; T. Aquinas, *Summa theol.,* I, qu. 3, art. 2; I, qu. 13, arts. 3 and 6; Bonaventure, *Sent.,* I, dist. 22, art. 1, qu. 3; J. Zanchi(us), *Op. theol.,* II, col. 11–14.

the ontologists, and Catholic theologians who teach a vision of God in terms of his essence in the state of glory), or by logical thought (Eunomius, Scotus, Spinoza, Hegel). Against all such the saying remains true that "no one has ever seen God, except the Son, who, being in the bosom of the Father, made him known" [John 1:18]. Moses did not see God's glory until after it had passed by him. The prophets only saw God in visions. Both in creation outside of us and in the life of our own soul, that which is created ever stands between God and our consciousness: innate ideas do not exist. We see in a mirror dimly and walk by faith. Absolute, fully adequate knowledge of God is therefore impossible. Converting the representation into the concept, the language of the imagination into that of cerebration, positive into negative theology, Semitic-concrete language into Japhetic-abstract language, always results in the total loss of the knowledge of God.

On the other hand, the name "ectypal theology" also implies the rejection of the view of those who, though regarding the use of creaturely names unavoidable in referring to God's being, see in them nothing more than symbols, products of the poetic imagination. In a sense even John of Damascus and Pseudo-Dionysius belong to this category.[15] For they claim that all those names merely make God known as the cause of all things; for example, the name "wisdom" ascribed to God means no more than that he is the cause of all wisdom. But Thomas, rejecting this view, already correctly countered that in that case God could equally well be called "gold," "silver," "sun," "moon," "body," and so on, since he is certainly the cause of these creations; furthermore, [he argued] that all of us mean something different and more when we say "God is good" than when we say "God is the cause of goodness." Not all of God's perfections are revealed in all of his creatures, nor can they be seen alike in all.[16] Later, however, this opinion was again revived, especially by Schleiermacher. God, it was said, is absolute causality and nothing more. His so-called attributes are subjective designations on our part. Theology can be called neither ectypal nor analogical but should be considered symbolic.[17] In this view religious representations are the products of the poetic imagination, ideals to be assessed aesthetically (Rauwenhoff, Pierson, F. A. Lange, et al.). Of late one can observe in certain modernist circles a tendency to persist in using biblical and ecclesiastical terms [merely] as symbols of higher spiritual truths.

15. John of Damascus, *The Orthodox Faith*, I, 12; Pseudo-Dionysius, *The Divine Names*, ch. 1; cf. Moses Maimonides, *Moreh nebukhim* (Warsaw: Goldman, 1872), I, 58; Cusanus (Nicholas of Cusa), *Of Learned Ignorance*, trans. Fr. German Heron (New Haven: Yale University Press, 1954), I, 53ff.

16. T. Aquinas, *Summa theol.*, I, qu. 13, art. 2; J. Zanchi(us), *Op. theol.*, II, col. 11–13.

17. F. Schleiermacher, *On Religion: Speeches to Its Cultured Despisers* (Cambridge and New York: Cambridge University Press, 1996); K. G. Bretschneider, *Handbuch der Dogmatik* (Leipzig: Barth, 1838), I⁴, 477; F. Paulsen, *Einleitung in die Philosophie*, 263; R. Eisler, *Kritische Einführung in die Philosophie* (Berlin: E. S. Mittler, 1905), 437; Wundt, in Edmund König, *W. Wundt: Seine Philosophie und Psychologie* (Stuttgart: F. Frommann, 1901), 188; A. Sabatier, as discussed in H. Bavinck, *Reformed Dogmatics*, I, 551 (#144), 558–59 (#146); Friedrich Niebergall, "Die religiöse Phantasie und die Verkündigung an unsere Zeit," *Zeitschrift für Theologie und Kirche* 16 (1906) 251–85.

This view of the character of theology, however, is not tenable. The term "symbolic" can indeed be applied to the theology whose object is to explain the sacred symbols that occur in Scripture and in the church. Vitringa, to cite one example, calls this branch of theology "theologia symbolica" (1726).[18] But a symbol is always a sensible object or action to denote a spiritual truth, while theology as such has to do not with such symbols but with spiritual realities. When consciousness, will, holiness, and so forth are ascribed to God, no one takes this in a "symbolic" sense. Not a single religious person views such representations as products of his or her own imagination, while everyone readily acknowledges this in the case of works of art. On the contrary: religious persons view such religious representations as being objectively true, and their religion languishes and dies the moment they begin to doubt this fact. If, accordingly, they were products of the imagination, their objective truth could not be maintained. In that case they may still have some aesthetic value, but religiously and ethically they have lost their value. Religion can no more be converted into art than into philosophy. Attempts to still maintain these representations as symbols always end in disappointment. Those who, like Hegel, make a sharp distinction between representations and concepts are no longer satisfied with these representations. They always attempt to arrive at pure concepts and, as a result, later want to return to religious representations understood as symbols. This "symbolic" character of theology turns the names of God into a reflex of one's own inner life, deprives them of all objective reality, and looks for their ground in ever-changing subjective reason. Humanity then becomes the standard of religion: as humans are, so is their God.

Scripture takes a different position. It teaches, first of all, that God is the Creator of heaven and earth. The things we perceive "were not made out of what is visible" (Heb. 11:3) but existed and exist eternally as ideas in the mind of God. They, therefore, derive their origin from God, are to a greater or lesser extent related to him, and so also have the capacity to display his perfections before the eyes of his creatures. Because the universe is God's creation, it is also his revelation and self-manifestation. There is not an atom of the world that does not reflect his deity.

Second, Scripture teaches us that among all those creatures human beings occupy a unique position. Whereas creatures in general display only vestiges of God's perfections, humans are his image and likeness. From this fact flows our right to call God by names that are derived from the realm of creatures, particularly that of humanity. We know God because we are known by him: "I understand because I am understood" (von Baader). We have the right to anthropomorphize God because he himself theomorphized when he created humans (Jacobi).

---

18. Cf. also J. d'Outrein, *Proef-stukken van heilige Sinne-beelden* (Amsterdam: G. Borstius, 1700); V. Schultze, "Sinnebilder," *PRE³*, XVIII, 388–95.

Third, despite all the foregoing, Scripture continually confronts us with God's absolute transcendence over all creatures. Implied in creation is both God's transcendence and God's immanence, the essential difference as well as the close kinship between God and his creatures. He lives in a high and holy place, yes, but also with those who are contrite and lowly in spirit—that is the theme which comes to our ears from every page of Scripture [Isa. 57:15].[19]

For these reasons theology must be called ectypal or analogical, not symbolic. Implied in this is the following:

1. All our knowledge of God is from and through God, grounded in his revelation, that is, in objective reason.
2. In order to convey the knowledge of him to his creatures, God has to come down to the level of his creatures and accommodate himself to their powers of comprehension.
3. The possibility of this condescension cannot be denied since it is given with creation, that is, with the existence of finite being.
4. Our knowledge of God is always only analogical in character, that is, shaped by analogy to what can be discerned of God in his creatures, having as its object not God himself in his knowable essence, but God in his revelation, his relation to us, in the things that pertain to his nature,[20] in his habitual disposition to his creatures.[21] Accordingly, this knowledge is only a finite image, a faint likeness and creaturely impression of the perfect knowledge that God has of himself.
5. Finally, our knowledge of God is nevertheless true, pure, and trust-worthy because it has for its foundation God's self-consciousness, its archetype, and his self-revelation in the cosmos.

CLASSIFYING GOD'S NAMES

[181] While Scripture calls God by many names, it never proceeds from an abstract concept of God, nor does it ever highlight one attribute of God at the expense of others. Granted, sometimes one and then another attribute comes to the fore, but perfect harmony exists among them all. It is the intent of Scripture to let all of God's perfections come equally into their own. Just as the person of Christ does not represent a one-sided character or tempera-ment, yet is fully alive and real as a person, so also God in his revelation always unfolds all his perfections as a harmonious whole. Nowhere do we encounter God's being in the abstract. The Hebrew word תּוּשִׁיָּה, from the root יָשָׁה (to exist, to be; Arabic III: to help, to raise up), denotes that which lasts, gives advantage, concretely especially true wisdom and happiness (Job 5:12; 6:13; 12:16; 26:3 [30:22]; Prov. 2:7; 3:21; 8:14; and further only Isa. 28:29; Mic.

19. See above, pp. 33–34 (#161).
20. John of Damascus, *The Orthodox Faith*, I, 4.
21. T. Aquinas, *Summa theol.*, I, qu. 12, art. 12.

6:9), but in none of these places does it stand for God's being.[22] Neither do the New Testament words "deity" (θεοτης, Col. 2:9; θειοτης, Rom. 1:20), "form of God" (μορφη θεου, Phil. 2:6), "the divine nature" (θεια φυσις, 2 Pet. 1:4; cf. Gal. 4:8) prove that the reference there is to the being or nature of God in distinction from his attributes, as Polanus insists.[23] God's being is revealed to us in his revelation, that is, in his names. The names of God are designations of his excellences, mighty deeds, praises (ἀρεται, 1 Pet. 2:9), a word usage that ties in with Isaiah 42:8, 12; 43:21; and 63:7, where the Hebrew תְּהִלָּה (praise, honor) is rendered in the LXX as ἀρετη (cf. Hab. 3:3; Zech. 6:13). The church's calling is to proclaim God's "virtues," that is, to honor him for the glory (δοξα) manifested in all his works. Scripture knows nothing of God's being aside from his attributes.

Not implied in Scripture's teaching concerning God's being, of course, is the idea that with reference to God it would not be permissible to speak of his nature. On the contrary, Scripture itself leads the way in using this language. Moreover, with a view to pantheism, which equates the being of God with that of the universe, it is even supremely important to stress the fact that God has a nature of his own, that he is an independent being, whose essence is distinct from that of the universe. One must, however, keep in mind that Scripture knows nothing of a divine essence that can be discovered and known by the powers of the human intellect apart from revelation. It posits no split, much less a contrast, between God's ontological existence and his "economic" self-revelation. As God reveals himself, so is he; in his names he himself becomes knowable to us. Though he is indeed infinitely superior to all his creatures—so that we can possess only an analogical knowledge of him not an exhaustive (adequate) knowledge—yet his several attributes, attributes that come through in his revelation, bring to our mind, each time from a special perspective, the fullness of his being.

In the early centuries Christian theologians were well aware of this fact. The "names of God" included everything they had to say about God. Not only the proper names but also—to use a later terminology—the "attributes," and even the persons in the divine being fell under that heading, while the attributes were immediately incorporated in the idea of God.[24] Though Augustine does speak of God's "essence," he means by it the fullness of God's being and immediately includes in it all God's attributes (simplicity, eternity, goodness, wisdom, etc.). Also his *Confessions* often speak of God in this way without any attempt to distinguish between God's being and attributes or to classify the attributes.[25] Also

22. C. F. Keil and F. Delitzsch, *Commentary on the Old Testament*, 10 vols. (reprinted, Grand Rapids: Eerdmans, 1975), 4:100 (on Job 5:12).

23. A. Polanus, *Syn. theol.*, 135.

24. E.g., in Irenaeus, *Against Heresies*, I, 14; II, 13, 35.

25. Lateran Council in H. Denzinger, *Enchiridion symbolarum*, #355; First Vatican Council, *De fide*, ch. 1; Augsburg Confession, art. 1; Gallican Confession, art. 1; Scots Confession, art. 1; Westminster Confession, ch. 2.

in later years several theologians still refrained from discussing these distinctions and treated the attributes without first speaking about God's nature.[26]

Names of Being

Soon, however, certain distinctions were introduced. These distinctions arose from consideration of the following questions: Which attribute of God at once differentiates him from all creatures? What in fact is the predominant idea in thinking of his essence? And, therefore, from which base should one proceed in the doctrine of God? In this connection theologians recognized, to be sure, that each distinct attribute constituted God's being itself. Still, they wondered whether among all these attributes there was not one that most fundamentally described God's very being and hence from which the other attributes could, so to speak, be derived. Now Platonic philosophy had already identified that predominant idea as "being," and Philo had connected it with the name YHWH, the only name that denoted, not an effect or a power, but God's being itself, and therefore often called God "he who is" or "that which is" (ὁ ὤν or τὸ ὄν).[27] This description of God's being was then taken over by Christian theology. Irenaeus repeatedly describes God as "absolutely simple" and even calls him "incomprehensible" and "not reducible to matter," yet against Gnosticism he stresses especially that God is the Creator of all things and revealed himself in his works.[28] In Origen, Athanasius, John of Damascus, and others, on the other hand, God is the One, he who is, even the One who transcends all being, who is being itself and the source of his own being.[29] And, following Philo, they inferred all this from, or connected it with, the name YHWH in the Old Testament.

In the West these definitions were taken over. Augustine variously describes God as "supreme being," "the supreme good, truth, beauty," and so forth. God is a substance, for that which has no substance does not exist. But since the word "substance" is often used in contrast with the term "accidents" (which inhere in the substance and of which the substance is the bearer), Augustine, when speaking of God, prefers to use the word "essence," which the Greeks call οὐσία and for which also the term *natura* is used.[30] For in the case of God, says Augustine, there is no distinction between substance and accidents; his being is not the bearer of attributes, but his attributes are identical with

26. T. Aquinas, *Summa theol.*, I, qu. 3ff.; Z. Ursinus, *Tract. theol.*, 46–70.

27. Eduard Zeller, *Die Philosophie der Griechen*, 3d ed., 5 vols. (Leipzig: O. R. Reisland [L. W. Reisland, 1895]), V, 356.

28. Irenaeus, *Against Heresies*, II, 1, 13, 28; IV, 11; cf. A. von Harnack, *History of Dogma*, trans. N. Buchanan, J. Miller, E. B. Speirs, and W. McGilchrist, and ed. A. B. Bruce, 7 vols. (London: Williams & Norgate, 1896–99), II, 204ff.

29. Origen, *On First Principles*, I, 1, v; *Against Celsus*, VI, 64; Athanasius, *Council of Nicaea*, 11, 76; John of Damascus, *The Orthodox Faith*, I, 2, 4, 9; cf. A. von Harnack, *History of Dogma*, III, 244; J. Schwane, *Dogmengeschichte*, 4 vols. (Freiburg i.B.: Herder, 1882–95), I², 32; II², 35; F. Kattenbusch, *Lehrbuch der vergleichenden Confessionskunde* (Freiburg i.B.: J. C. B. Mohr [Paul Siebeck], 1892), I, 310ff.

30. Augustine, *The Trinity*, V, 2; VII, 5ff.; idem, *City of God*, XII, 2; idem, *On Christian Doctrine*, I, 6.

his being. God is the highest, best, most beautiful, and most perfect being, "than which nothing better can be or be thought." He is "God, above whom there is nothing, outside of whom there is nothing, apart from whom there is nothing: supreme life, supreme truth, supreme blessedness, supreme wisdom, supreme being."[31] And Augustine, too, appeals to the name YHWH to justify this description of God.[32] We find the same description again later in Hilary, Pseudo-Dionysius (who, however, elsewhere proceeds from the idea of the good, which according to him is even broader in scope than that of essence), Anselm, Lombard, Thomas, Bonaventure, and many others.[33] Roman Catholic theologians, in their treatment of the doctrine of God, usually proceed from the same description of God's being.

Yet there were, and still are today, those who give first place to another attribute of God. Some regard "infinity" rather than "absolute being" or "aseity" central in the idea of God and therefore prefer to describe God as an "infinite being." One of these theologians is Duns Scotus, who asserted that "essence" can be equally and univocally attributed to God and to creatures but that the mark of distinction between God and creatures is that the former is an infinite being and the latter are finite.[34] Thus, whereas all of these theologians proceed from the idea of absolute being and regard as the predominant concept some incommunicable attribute (aseity, infinity, or eternity),[35] others prefer to put more emphasis on the intellectual nature of God and hence proceed rather from the idea of personality than from that of absoluteness. Accordingly, they describe God's essence as that of an "intelligent being" and differ among themselves in that some view radical knowing (in other words, spirituality), and others view actual knowledge, as the constitutive principle of the divine essence.[36]

[182] The Reformation did little to change these views. People simply aligned themselves with one or the other. Reformed theologians, at least initially, mostly adopted the definitions of Augustine and Thomas. They proceeded from the idea of "aseity" or that of "independence" and hence described God as an "independent being."[37] In addition, we encounter de-

31. Augustine, *On Free Will*, II, 6; idem, *On Christian Doctrine*, I, 7; idem, *City of God*, XII, 8; idem, *Soliloquies*, I, 1.

32. Augustine, *The Trinity*, V, 2; VII, 5; idem, *On Christian Doctrine*, I, 32.

33. Hilary, *The Trinity*, I, 1ff.; Pseudo-Dionysius, *The Divine Names*, 1, §6; cf. 4, §1 and 5, §1; Anselm, *Monologion*, ch. 28; idem, *Proslogion*, ch. 17ff.; P. Lombard, *Sent.*, I, dist. 8; T. Aquinas, *Summa theol.*, I, qu. 2, art. 3; I, qu. 3; idem, *Summa contra Gentiles*, I, 16ff.; Bonaventure, *Breviloquium*, I, 2; idem, *Sent.* I, dist. 8; D. Petavius, "De Deo," in *Theol. dogm.*, I, ch. 6; G. Perrone, *Prael. theol.*, II, 81–90; C. Pesch, *Prael. dogm.*, II, 46–70; G. Jansen, *Prael. theol.*, II, 26–46.

34. Duns Scotus, *Sent.*, I, dist. 3, qu. 1; I, dist. 8, qu. 3.

35. According to C. M. Schneider, in J. Heinrich and C. Gutberlet, *Dogmatische Theologie*, 2d ed., 10 vols. (Mainz: Kirchheim, 1881–1900), III, 325.

36. Cf. J. Heinrich, *Dogmatische Theologie*, III, 325; G. Perrone, *Prael. theol.*, II, 82; J. Kleutgen, *Die Theologie der Vorzeit*, 2d ed., 5 vols. (Münster: Theissing, 1867–74), 229.

37. U. Zwingli, *Opera*, III, 155ff.; IV, 81ff.; A. Hyperius, *Meth. theol.*, 87; P. M. Vermigli, *Loci communes*, 39; A. Polanus, *Syn. theol.*, II, c. 5; J. Zanchi(us), *Op. theol.*, II, 49ff.; Z. Ursinus, *Tract. theol.* (1584), 46ff.

scriptions of God as "the uncreated Spirit," "the most simple Spirit," "the self-existent Spirit," to which at times was added the trinitarian formula: "one in essence, threefold in persons."[38] Lutherans followed the definitions "infinite spiritual essence," "spiritual self-subsistent being," "the independent Spirit."[39]

Socinianism, on the other hand, took another position. Disregarding all metaphysical questions, it put all emphasis on the will of God. The knowledge of God is tantamount to the knowledge of his will. Religion loses all its mysticism and exhausts itself in worship. God is increasingly distant from the world and humankind. This trend is continued in Remonstrantism, rationalism, and British Deism.

From the ranks of philosophy a reaction again set in against this cold, moralistic concept of God. Spinoza was one who returned to the idea of essence, viewed God "as the unique, infinite, necessarily existing substance," "the absolute and infinite being," "the absolute and immanent first cause," and spoke again of a love of God, "the intellectual love of God," which is the source of supreme bliss.[40] Rationalism and Deism indeed continued to be dominant even after Spinoza, but around the middle of the eighteenth century people grew increasingly weary of this. The great minds, Goethe, Lessing, and Herder, felt attracted to Spinoza, and soon pantheism made its triumphal entry in philosophy. Kant had already undermined the foundations of rationalism, although he continued to call himself a Deist.[41] Fichte undertook the battle against the concepts of "God and immortality," viewing them as products of eudaemonism. In his extreme moralism he equated God with the pure Ego, the moral world order. God, he contended, was neither essence nor substance but absolute action or activity.[42] Later he retreated somewhat from this position and aligned himself more closely with Spinoza.[43] Schleiermacher displayed even greater resemblance to Spinoza. God and the universe are correlates: God is "the whence of our receptive and self-active existence."[44] Schelling distinguished himself from these two by the fact that he not only took account of

38. H. Heppe, *Die Dogmatik der evangelisch-reformierten Kirche* (Elberseld: R. L. Friedrich, 1861), 35ff.; A. Schweizer, *Die Glaubenslehre der evangelisch-reformirten Kirche*, 2 vols. (Zürich: Orell, Füssli, 1844–47), I, 244.

39. H. Schmid, *The Doctrinal Theology of the Evangelical Lutheran Church*, trans. Charles A. Hay and Henry Jacobs, 5th ed. (Philadelphia: United Lutheran Publication, 1899), 111–17; K. Hase, *Hutterus redivivus* (Helsingfors: A. W. Gröndahl, 1846), §54.

40. B. Spinoza, *Ethics*, I, prop. 7ff.; V, prop. 15ff.

41. A. Drews, *Die deutsche Spekulation seit Kant*, 2 vols. (Berlin: P. Maeter, 1893), I, 104.

42. According to J. G. Fichte's *Science of Knowledge* (Cambridge: Cambridge University Press, 1982); idem, "Über den Grund unseres Glaubens an eine göttliche Weltregierung," in *Philosophisches Journal einer Gesellschaft Teutscher Gelehrten*, Erstes Heft (Jena and Leipzig: Gabler 1798); idem, *Appellation an das Publikum* (Leipzig: Reclam, 1799).

43. J. G. Fichte, *Anweisung zum seligen Leben oder Religionslehre* (1806); ET: "The Doctrine of Religion," in *Popular Works*, trans. William Smith (London: Trübner & Co., 1873).

44. F. Schleiermacher, *Dialektik* (Berlin: G. Reimer, 1839), 162; idem, *The Christian Faith*, 16ff.

spiritual reality, that is, of religion and morality, but also of objective nature. It was his aim to lift natural science from the deplorable condition into which it had fallen. He therefore combined the two, nature and spirit: nature is visible spirit, spirit invisible nature. In both he saw an ongoing organic revelation of the Absolute, which transcends all opposites and is one, simple, and eternal, without predicates, a union of the infinite and the finite, of God and the universe, the One and All.[45] Hegel finally converted this system into a form of logical idealism. Nature and history are a logically necessary self-unfolding of the Idea. Everything is rational; everything is embodied thought. Reason, therefore, is absolute substance, God himself. For God is nothing other than the one, living World-idea in process of becoming self-conscious. Hence, in Hegel God is indeed Reason, Thought, Mind, Subject, but not in the sense that he had a life of his own prior to and apart from the world. "Without the world God is not God"; the world, therefore, is an essential component in the life of God.[46]

But this form of pantheism also did not remain unchallenged. An entire series of theistic philosophers rose up to demonstrate the untenability of pantheism and to defend the rights of theism. They majored in the idea of absolute personality, connected it with the idea of becoming, and thus introduced in God a theogonic process, either in a unitarian (Jacobi, Herbart, Drobish, Rothe, Lotze, Ulrici, Carrière, et al.) or a trinitarian sense (Baader, Schelling, I. H. Fichte, Weisse, Dorner, et al.).

Personal, Moral Names

But this theistic speculation too passed from the scene. The separation of theology and philosophy, religion and metaphysics, became the new watchword. Science *(Wissenschaft),* for one, increasingly withdrew from the domain of religion and theology, and became exact and positive. Religion, on the other hand, increasingly sought to free itself from science and to banish all metaphysics and philosophy. For the doctrine of God this meant that the essence of God was exclusively identified with ethical goodness. The Groninger theology, in speaking of God, highlighted his fatherhood and love.[47] Whereas Scholten proceeded from God's absolute sovereignty,[48] the so-called ethical modernists resisted his speculative intellectualism and monistic determinism and viewed God as Father, as the moral ideal, the power of the good and of holiness.[49]

45. A. Drews, *Die deutsche Spekulation,* I, 201ff.
46. A. Drews, *Die deutsche Spekulation,* I, 229ff.
47. Hofstede de Groot, *De Groninger Godgeleerden* (Groningen: A. L. Scholtens, 1855), 155ff.
48. J. H. Scholten, *De Leer der Hervormde Kerk,* 2 vols. (Leiden: P. Engels, 1850–51), II.
49. S. Hoekstra, *Des Christens Godsvrucht* (Amsterdam: Gebroders Kraay, 1866), 103ff.; idem, *Bronnen en Grondslagen van het Godsdienstig Geloof* (Amsterdam: P. N. van Kampen, 1864), 265ff.; I. Hooykaas, *God in de Geschiedenis* (Schiedam: Van Dijk, 1870); I. Hooykaas, J. H. Herderscheê, H. Oort, A. G. van Hamel, *Godsdienst volgens der ethische Richting onder de Modernen* ('s Hertogenbosch: G. H. van der Schuyt, 1876). Ed. note: See further on ethical modernism, H. Bavinck, *Reformed Dogmatics,* I, 540 (#142), 555 (#146).

Similarly, in Germany the neo-Kantianism of Ritschl arose to challenge the speculative theology of the mediating schools *(Vermittelungstheologie)*.[50] Ritschl denied that religion is a legal relationship. He pointed out that according to Duns Scotus, Socinianism, and Arminianism, God is the unrestricted Potentate who, though humans have no rights before him, nevertheless treats them with fairness. In their theory "arbitrariness," "absolute dominion," is God's essence and the law of the universe. God can do one thing as well as another. The relationship between God and humans is a private-law arrangement illustrated by the slaveholder who treats his slaves fairly.[51]

As Ritschl sees it, according to orthodox Protestants God's relation to the world is governed by justice. If humans observe God's law, they are entitled to eternal life; otherwise they deserve punishment. This theory is based on public law. It is derived from the Old Testament, particularly from Pharisaism, was taken over by Paul, and thus entered the Christian church.[52] Both conceptions, however, are mistaken [says Ritschl]. Law and religion are treated as opposites. Theologians must not introduce a dualism between God's justice and his grace. We must abandon the entire abstract, Areopagite concept of God, the idea that envisions God in negative transcendence above the world and does not accept the existence of fellowship between God and humanity.[53] Religion consists in a moral relation, and Christianity is "the completely spiritual and absolutely moral religion."[54] God's relation to us is neither that of master to his servant nor that of a government to its subjects, but that of a father to his child. Its model is the family.[55] Accordingly, God must be conceived as Love; no other concept compares with it.[56] A Christian dogmatician, therefore, should not—following a synthetic method—begin with an array of metaphysical abstractions about God as the Absolute,[57] nor with a so-called natural theology, which does not exist,[58] nor even with the concept of personality or the attribute of holiness.[59] No: the theologian's task is to proceed from the concept of

50. Ed. note: For further discussion of the "mediating theology" *(Vermittelungstheologie),* see H. Bavinck, *Reformed Dogmatics,* I, 127 (#39), 171 (#53), 290–92 (#83), 372 (#102), 436 (#115), 471–72 (#123), 519–20 (#135).

51. A. Ritschl, *Die christliche Lehre von der Rechtfertigung und Versöhnung,* 2d ed., 3 vols. (Bonn: A. Marcus, 1882–83), III, 223–29.

52. Ibid., III², 229–45. Also see the literature on the doctrine of God that A. Ritschl provides in "Geschichtliche Studien zur Lehre von Gott," *Jahrbücher für deutsche Theologie* 10 (1865) and 13 (1868), literature that is also provided in his *Gesammelte Aufsätze, Neue Folge* (Freiburg, i.B.: J. C. B. Mohr, 1896).

53. Ibid., 253.

54. Ibid., 8.

55. Ibid., 90.

56. Ibid., 255.

57. A. Ritschl, *Theologie und Metaphysik* (Bonn: A. Marcus, 1881), 12ff.; idem, *Rechtfertigung und Versöhnung,* III², 2–8, 32.

58. Idem, *Rechtfertigung und Versöhnung,* III², 200ff.; *Theologie und Metaphysik,* 8ff.

59. Idem, *Rechtfertigung und Versöhnung,* III², 255.

love and to try to infer everything (creation, providence, reconciliation, justification) from that concept.[60]

Many theologians heartily endorsed this criticism of the earlier treatment of the doctrine of God and in their description of God's essence proceeded, with Ritschl, from the concept of love. Reischle, applying Ritschl's method consistently, even believed he should proceed, not from love, but from the kingdom of God, in order to infer from it the idea that God is love and that he is personal.[61] Furthermore, even outside the circle of his own immediate friends and followers, Ritschl found acceptance in that some, such as Cremer and von Oettingen, rejected the concept of the Absolute as irreligious.[62] By contrast, other members of the school of Ritschl regarded this concept indispensable in the doctrine of God. Kaftan, for example, is of the opinion that Ritschl's problem with the word "absolute," namely, that it originally means "detached from," is unfounded, because the meaning of words is determined by usage. He therefore retains the concept as the form that must later be filled with the content of the Christian view of God, which gives prominence to the concept of God as "supramundane, personal Spirit."[63] Although Kaftan began with sharp criticism of the traditional dogmatic treatment of the doctrine of God and considered the two elements—the absoluteness of being and the personality of God—incompatible,[64] in the end he faces the same difficulty and fails to offer an alternative solution. The same is true of Wobbermin, who also retains the concept of absoluteness and believes he has found a synthesis in the definition that God is "the archetype and unitary totality of spiritual-personal life."[65]

Thus theology, today as much as in the past, continues to struggle with the difficulty of offering a somewhat satisfactory description of God's essence. God is alternately described as "that which has being," "absolute being," "absolute substance"; or as "Sovereign," "the Lord," "the Supreme Being"; or as "infinite Spirit," "absolute causality," "absolute personality"; or as the "Father," "love," "the personal almighty will of love," "goodness," and so forth. To proceed from the unity and harmony of all God's attributes and to persist in this to the end is difficult. We always especially face the problem of doing equal justice to the absoluteness and the personality of God, the incommunicable and the communicable attributes, God's absolute superiority over, and his communion with, the world. Added to this is the complication that every human being is limited and readily stresses one attribute of God at the expense of another. Jansen saw

---

60. Ibid.; cf. J. Kaftan, *Das Wesen der christlichen Religion* (Basel: C. Detloff, 1888), 383; W. Herrmann, *Die Religion im Verhältnis zum Welterkennen und zur Sittlichkeit* (Halle: M. Niemeyer, 1879), 121ff.; J. Gottschick, *Die Kirchlichkeit der sogenannte kirchliche Theologie* (Freiburg i.B: J. C. B. Mohr, 1890), 152ff.

61. J. Kaftan, *Zur Dogmatik* (Tübingen: Mohr [Paul Siebeck], 1904), 44.

62. H. Cremer, *Die christlichen Lehre von den Eigenschaften Gottes* (Gütersloh: C. Bertelsmann, 1897), 7; A. von Oettingen, *Lutherische Dogmatik*, 2 vols. (Munich: C. H. Beck, 1897–1902), II, 83.

63. J. Kaftan, *Dogmatik*, 2d ed. (Tübingen: Mohr, 1897), §§16–17.

64. J. Kaftan, *Dogmatik²*, 136, 150.

65. G. Wobbermin, *Der christlichen Gottesglaube* (Berlin: Alexander Duncker, 1902), 92.

especially God's veracity, Francis de Sales his love, Vincent his goodness, St. Cyran his omnipotence.[66] Still, it remains the calling of theology, following the example of Scripture, to honor equally all the attributes of God.

DIVINE SIMPLICITY; ESSENCE AND ATTRIBUTES

[183] Now Christian theology has always been more or less conscious of this calling. On the whole, its teaching has been that God is "simple," that is, sublimely free from all composition, and that therefore one cannot make any real [i.e., ontological] distinction between his being and his attributes. Each attribute is identical with God's being: he *is* what he *possesses*. In speaking of creatures we make all sorts of distinctions between what they are and what they have. A person, for example, is still human even though he or she has lost the image of God and has become a sinner. But in God all his attributes are identical with his being. God is light through and through; he is all mind, all wisdom, all logos, all spirit, and so forth.[67] In God "to be is the same as to be wise, which is the same as to be good, which is the same as to be powerful. One and the same thing is stated whether it be said that God is eternal or immortal or good or just." Whatever God is, he is that completely and simultaneously. "God has no properties but is pure essence. God's properties are really the same as his essence: they neither differ from his essence nor do they differ materially from each other."[68]

This doctrine of God's simplicity was the means by which Christian theology was kept from the danger of splitting God's attributes from his essence and of making them more or less independent from, and opposed to, his essence. In a sense polytheism represents this error insofar as it personifies and deifies the various forces operative in creation. But in philosophy and theology this error occurs as well. Plato, positing the ideas as archetypes of existing things, ascribed to them an independent existence alongside God. While Gnosticism described God as the Unknowable and Inexpressible, it made the Platonic ideas into aeons that emanated from God and distanced themselves from him in a descending series. Called "idea," "mind," "reason" (logos), "life," "wisdom," they were nothing but the personified attributes of God, which emanated from him and were represented as divine beings.[69] Also Philo, reflecting Plato's influence, often represented the divine energies—especially his goodness, power, and rationality (logos)—as hypostases (substances).[70] Jewish theology assumed the existence of various hypostases (e.g., *metatron, memra, sheki-*

66. H. P. G. Quack, "Port Royal par Sainte-Beuve," *De Gids* 36 (December 1872).

67. Irenaeus, *Against Heresies*, II, 28; IV, 11.

68. Augustine, *The Trinity*, VI, 7; John of Damascus, *The Orthodox Faith*, I, 9; T. Aquinas, *Summa theol.*, I, qu. 2, art. 3; H. Heppe, *Dogmatik der evangelisch-reformierten Kirche*, 42, 51–53; H. F. F. Schmid, *Doctrinal Theology of the Evangelical Lutheran Church*, 122.

69. Irenaeus, *Against Heresies*, I, 11, 24.

70. Eduard Zeller, *Die Philosophie der Griechen*, 3d ed., 5 vols. (Leipzig: Fues's Verlag [L. W. Reisland], 1895), V, 358ff.

nah, ruach, bath-kal)[71] and in the Kabbalah the ten *sefiroth* (attributes) of God are described as emanations from the divine being.[72] Even in later periods this gnostic and kabbalistic philosophy still exerted great influence. Arianism was still tinctured by Gnosticism insofar as it assumed a kind of gradation among the divine persons. The moment monotheism is no longer supported by belief in the Trinity, it risks losing its purity, being threatened by pantheism or monism, on the one hand, and by polytheism or pluralism, on the other. In modern times not only do many people practically put the state, science, art, industry, fortune, and fate as so many independent powers on a level with God and venerate them in the place of God, but also even polytheistic sympathies are sometimes voiced with great candor as well.[73]

Even Christian theologians sometimes fail to observe the necessary caution in determining the relation between God's essence and his attributes. In the Middle Ages, for example, Gilbert Porretan made a distinction between God's essence or nature (divinity) and God himself. Divinity, he claimed, is the form by virtue of which God is God, but not itself God. "God exists by virtue of divinity, but divinity as such is not God."[74] Duns Scotus indeed denied that there is a real [ontological] difference *(distinctio realis)* between [God's] being and his attributes, but nevertheless maintained—with an appeal to Augustine and John of Damascus—that the attributes of God can be formally distinguished from God's being and each other.[75] Socinianism spoke of "accidents" [incidental properties] in God and held that a different view and description of the attributes were necessary.[76] In recent times many have even gone further, assuming an objective difference in God at the expense of his simplicity and immutability.[77] Doedes, continuing along this line, first treated those characteristics that are given with the idea of deity, such as oneness, incommunicability, incomparability, incomprehensibility, independence (etc.), and subsequently those characteristics that additionally apply to the divine being and are only five in number: omnipotence, wisdom, goodness, love, and holiness.[78] Under the rubric of God's essence F. A. B. Nitzsch similarly first discusses

71. F. W. Weber, *System der altsynagogalen palästinischen Theologie* (Leipzig: Dörffling & Franke, 1880), 172.

72. F. Ueberweg, *Geschichte der Philosophie*, ed. Max Heinze, 9th ed., 4 vols. (Berlin: E. S. Mittler & Sohn, 1901–5), II, 261; Wunsche, "Kabbala," *PRE*[3], IX, 670–89.

73. Cf. above, pp. 84–87 (#175).

74. Cf. D. Petavius, "De Deo," in *Theol. dogm.*, I, ch. 8.

75. Duns Scotus, *Sent.*, I, dist. 8, qu. 4, nn. 17ff.

76. O. Fock, *Der Socianismus* (Kiel: C. Schröder, 1847), 427.

77. R. Rothe, *Theologische Ethik*, 2d rev. ed., 5 vols. (Wittenberg: Zimmerman, 1867–71), §38; H. Martensen, *Christian Dogmatics*, trans. William Urwick (Edinburgh: T. & T. Clark, 1871), §85; A. F. C. Vilmar, *Dogmatik*, 2 vols. (Gütersloh: C. Bertelsmann, 1874), I, 190ff.; I. Dorner, *A System of Christian Doctrine*, trans. A. Cave and J. Banks, rev. ed., 3 vols. (Edinburgh: T. & T. Clark, 1888–91), I, 194ff.; G. Thomasius, *Christi Person und Werk*, 3d ed., 2 vols. (A. Deichert, 1886–88), I, 34ff.; W. Schmidt, *Christliche Dogmatik*, II, 102ff.; C. Hodge, *Systematic Theology*, 3 vols. (New York: Charles Scribner's Sons, 1888), I, 371ff.; J. J. van Oosterzee, *Christian Dogmatics*, trans. J. Watson and M. Evans, 2 vols. (New York: Scribner, Armstrong, 1874), §47.

78. J. I. Doedes, *Inleiding tot de Leer van God* (Utrecht: Kemink, 1870), 200ff.

certain "fundamental qualifications of the divine nature," which subsequently form the substratum for the attributes treated after the doctrine of creation.[79] C. Pesch also calls the attributes "qualities *superadded* to the divine substance."[80]

Personal Absolute Being

Given such a view, one cannot do justice to the Christian idea that *all* God's attributes are identical with his essence. One cannot make a distinction between determinations that are given with the idea of God, and others that have been added. For one thing, the above theologians to such an extent disagree among themselves that the one attributes to the essence what the other discusses among the [secondary] attributes and vice versa. But there is still another reason for taking exception to this distinction: it results in an impoverished, not an enriched, understanding of God, inasmuch as it gives the impression that the attributes, such as the love of God, are not in the same absolute sense present in God as, for example, his infinity, or had accrued to God from without as a result of creation. However, this view impairs the absoluteness of God in all his attributes and has, accordingly, been prudently avoided by Christian theology specifically in its doctrine of the simplicity of God. Frequently, it is true, the impression has been given[81] that theology, proceeding from the description of God as the Supreme Being, has gone down the same path as philosophy, which views God as the Absolute and confines itself to this abstraction. But between these two terms there is a large distinction that must not be overlooked.

When the church fathers, in their attempt to determine the nature of God's being, started with the name YHWH and described him as "Being," they had in mind not God's being apart from his attributes, but the total fullness of God's being as it exists and is revealed in his attributes. Hence, the being ascribed to God was not an abstraction but a living, infinitely rich, and concrete Being, a Supreme Being at once identical with supreme life, supreme truth, supreme wisdom, supreme love (etc.), as Augustine repeatedly said, and hence "an ocean of boundless being."[82] The description of God as "being" was used to indicate that he is the sum total of all reality. It certainly did not mean that he is abstract "being," being without content, "the Absolute" in the philosophical sense of the word. Although that term perhaps arose under the influence of philosophy, it still has a very different meaning than when philosophy speaks of God

79. F. Nitzsch, *Lehrbuch der evangelischen Dogmatik*, 3d ed. (Tübingen: J. C. B. Mohr, 1902), 351ff., 396ff.

80. C. Pesch, *Prael. dogm.*, II, 72. Most extreme is William James, who distinguishes between metaphysical and ethical attributes and considers the former as worthless; W. James, *The Varieties of Religious Experience*, Modern Library (1902; reprinted, New York: Random House, n.d.), 435–37.

81. F. C. Baur, *Die christliche Lehre von der Dreieinigkeit*, 3 vols. (Tübingen: C. F. Oslander, 1841–43), II, 644; A. Ritschl, in his studies on the doctrine of God, *Jahrbücher für deutsche Theologie* 10 (1865) and 13 (1868); ed. note: see above, p. 116 n. 52; J. Kaftan, *Dogmatik*, §14.

82. Gregory of Nazianzus, *Oration* 38; John of Damascus, *The Orthodox Faith*, I, 9.

as Absolute Being. Philosophy, after all, obtains this concept by abstraction. When philosophy strips from existing things all that is unique in each existing thing, what is left in the end is nothing but "being," "isness," the bare existence that they all have in common. Furthermore, that bare existence must even in each case be understood in a different sense. Bodies exist in a different way than spirits; substances have existence in another way than accidents; thoughts exist differently than objects; and that which is possible differs in its mode of existing from that which is real. Still, they all have in common the most general concept of being or existence. It is immediately clear, however, that this concept, obtained as it is in the way of progressive abstraction, is nothing other and nothing more than a concept. It is absolutely devoid of content and vacuous, and has no objective and independent reality whatever. On the other hand, when theology speaks of God as "essence," it did not obtain this concept by abstraction but by the opposite process of addition, that is, by attributing to God in an absolute sense all the perfections that occur in creatures and therefore by thinking of him as absolute reality, the sum total of all being, the "purest and simplest actuality." Accordingly, the being that is ascribed to God in theology is at the same time the richest, most perfect, most intensive, most determinate and concrete, absolute and simple Being.[83]

[184] Hence, when Christian theology threw out the distinction between God's essence and attributes, this was not done to deny that God has "being," nor to forbid the use of the word "being" in the doctrine of God. On the contrary, it did this to hold at bay from God all that is nonreal and to express as strongly as possible that in all his attributes he is pure being, absolute reality. And there is still another reason why the word "being" cannot be dispensed with in the doctrine of God. In the doctrine of the Trinity we need it to get somewhat of a handle on the distinction between God's nature and the modes of its subsistence. But even aside from that matter, in the doctrine of God's attributes we cannot refrain from speaking of his "being." For precisely because God is pure being—the absolute, perfect, unique, and simple being—we cannot give a definition of him. There is no genus to which he belongs as a member, and there are no specific marks of distinction whereby we can distinguish him from other beings in this genus. Even the being he has, so to speak, in common with all creatures does not pertain to him in the same sense as it does to them (univocally), but only analogically and proportionally. Yet name him we must; in religion as well as in theology we need a description to refer to him and to distinguish him from all that is not God. But here we face the problem that God, on the one hand, has no name (is anonymous) and, on the other hand, has many names (is polyonymous). We need not bother ourselves about the question whether God has still more attributes than those that he has revealed in creation and re-creation. Spinoza wrote that the greater the reality present in a given substance, the more attributes it possesses, and that as infinite substance

83. Cf. J. Heinrich, *Dogmatische Theologie*, III³, 339ff.

God also possesses an infinite number of attributes,[84] though we know only two: extension and thought. And, according to Reinhard, it is highly probable that God "might possess a multitude of attributes of which we have no conception, seeing that it is altogether impossible for infinite perfection to unite with himself all resemblances into such limited creatures as we are."[85] However this may be, the number of attributes he has revealed of himself is so great that one cannot possibly sum them up completely. So we must either totally refrain from any description whatever or else make a selection from among them.

The outcome of this selection differs greatly in various schools of theology.[86] We need not discuss all the descriptions given of God, but a couple of them do merit our attention because in recent times they have found so much acceptance. Theistic philosophers preferred to proceed from the "personality" of God, which they regarded as the correct designation of God's being. With a view to warding off the pantheistic concept of God, they were indeed right; but in every other setting it is nevertheless inadvisable to take this line in describing the divine being. For in the first place, the word "person" is already being used in a specific and unique sense in the doctrine of the Trinity. Second, using the word "personality" in reference to God's being can easily lead to our viewing God as "unipersonal" and to our failing to do justice to his "tripersonality," as the doctrine of the Trinity makes it known. Third, in the modern, abstract, and formal concept of personality, there is as yet nothing that distinguishes God as such from us humans.[87] Questionable, too, is the practice proceeding from the idea of love in describing God's being. For love as such already presupposes personality, consciousness, and will; it most certainly constitutes God's essence, but not in a different sense than that in which all God's attributes constitute God's essence; and it exposes us to the danger of regarding other attributes of God, such as righteousness and holiness, as less real.[88]

Christian theology has sought to avoid this one-sidedness in its description of God's essence by placing his aseity in the foreground. And, indeed, absoluteness cannot be dispensed within that description since in this connection everything depends on describing God as God and on distinguishing him from all that is not God.[89] But that absoluteness, as stated above, must be understood correctly. It is not correct to say that absoluteness is a philosophical and not a religious concept and therefore does not belong in theology. There is just as much to be said for the thesis that the word "absolute," when also

84. B. Spinoza, *Ethics*, I, prop. 9, 11.

85. F. V. Reinhard, *Grundriss der Dogmatik* (Munich: Seidel, 1802), 100; cf. L. Meijer, *Verhandelingen over de Goddelijke Eigenschappen*, 4 vols. (Groningen: Jacob Bolt, 1783), I, 186ff.

86. See H. Bavinck, *Reformed Dogmatics*, I, 287–95 (#83).

87. F. A. B. Nitzsch, *Evangelische Dogmatik*, 354; A. von Oettingen, *Lutherische Dogmatik*, II, 100.

88. F. Nitzsch, *Evangelische Dogmatik*, 352ff.

89. F. H. R. Frank, *System der christlichen Wahrheit*, 2 vols. (Erlangen: A. Deichert, 1878–80), §10; J. Kaftan, *Dogmatik*, §16; F. Nitzch, *Evangelische Dogmatik*, 354; A. von Oettingen, *Lutherische Dogmatik*, II, 106.

used by philosophers, actually has a religious character.[90] For although there is disagreement over the validity of the arguments for the existence of God, that is, over the logical propriety of inferring the absolute from the relative, no human being allows himself or herself to be kept by this scientific uncertainty from accepting the existence of the absolute as the ground and cause of the existence of all things. The metaphysical or religious need of humans always asserts itself to some extent in this connection. For that reason religion and theology cannot dispense with the concept of the absolute either. What matters here, of course, is not primarily the word but the matter itself. For religion and theology God must always be God, distinct from and above all things, the Creator and Ruler of all that exists, on whom believers can rely in times of distress and death, or else God can no longer be God to them. As such God is the strictly independent and only absolute being. This is what the concept of absoluteness meant in the past. "Absoluteness" was not obtained by abstraction, deprived of all content, and the most general kind of being, but true, unique, infinitely full being, precisely because it was absolute, that is, independent being, belonging only to itself and self-existence. "Absolute is that which is not dependent on anything else."[91]

From ancient times Christian theology connected this view and description of God with the meaning of the name YHWH as that is given in Exodus 3:14. Now people can disagree on the question whether the concept of "absolute being" is implied in the name YHWH, and we will expressly revisit it in the following section. In any case it is certain that the unicity, his distinctness from, and his absolute superiority over, all creatures is highlighted throughout Scripture. However much he is able to descend to the level of creatures, specifically humans—represented as he is as walking in the garden, coming down to earth to see the city and tower of Babel (etc.)—nevertheless he is the Creator of heaven and earth. He speaks and things come to be; he commands and they stand forth. From everlasting to everlasting he is God, the First and the Last, from whom, through whom, and to whom are all things (Gen. 1:1ff.; Ps. 33:6, 9; 90:2; Isa. 41:4; 43:10–13; 44:6; 48:12; John 5:26; Acts 17:24ff.; Rom. 11:36; Eph. 4:6; Heb. 2:10; Rev. 1:4, 8; 4:8, 11; 10:6; 11:17; etc.).

Stated or implied in this biblical teaching is all that Christian theology intended to say with its description of God's essence as absolute being. God is the real, the true being, the fullness of being, the sum total of all reality and perfection, the totality of being, from which all other being owes its existence. He is an immeasurable and unbounded ocean of being; the absolute being who alone has being in himself. Now, this description of God's being deserves preference over that of personality, love, fatherhood, and so forth, because it encompasses all God's attributes in an absolute sense. In other words, by this description God is recognized and confirmed as God in all his perfections.

90. F. Nitzch, *Evangelische Dogmatik*, 356.
91. J. Alsted, *Encyclopaedia* (Herbornae Nassovorium, 1630), 596. Cf. Eisler, *Wörterbuch*, s.v. "absolutum."

These attributes cannot, of course, be logically developed from the concept of absolute being, for what God is and what his attributes are can only be known by us from his revelation in nature and Scripture. Yet all these attributes are only *divine* characteristics because they pertain to God in a unique and absolute sense. Hence, in that respect *aseity* may be called the primary attribute of God's being. We can even say—on the basis of God's revelation, not by means of a priori reasoning—that along with his aseity all those attributes have to be present in God that nature and Scripture make known to us. If God is God, the only, eternal, and absolute Being, this implies that he possesses all the perfections, a faint analogy of which can be discerned in his creatures. If God is the absolutely existing being, he is also absolute in wisdom and goodness, in righteousness and holiness, in power and blessedness. As One who exists of and through and unto himself, he is the fullness of being, the independent and supremely perfect Being.

Distinction of Attributes

[185] Although we cannot really make a distinction between God's essence and his attributes (seeing that each attribute constitutes that essence), it does not follow that distinctions among the attributes themselves are merely nominal and subjective without any basis in reality. This has to be stressed because many have drawn this false conclusion. Eunomius, following the example of Aetius before him, reasoned as follows: God is "simple," totally noncomposite; hence, the attributes we ascribe to him are identical with his being and can only differ among themselves in our minds, that is, subjectively. Furthermore, our knowledge of God has to be fully adequate or else it would be false. Now in the concept of *agennesia* (lit., "nonbegottenness") we have a fully adequate knowledge of the divine being. Consequently, all the other attributes—for example, goodness, wisdom, power—must in reality coincide with it, for all God's attributes are synonymous. And since *agennesia* constitutes God's essence, the Son, who was begotten by the Father, cannot be truly divine.[92]

In the Middle Ages Gilbert Porretan, bishop of Poitiers (d. 1159), in his teaching insisted on an ontological distinction between God's essence and persons, between deity and God, and perhaps also (though this is uncertain) between God's essence and his attributes and between the various attributes among themselves.[93] According to the nominalists, especially Occam, the attributes differed only in "subjective reason, connoting as they did different effects," that is, with a view to the relation between them and the several works of God. The idea of any one attribute, therefore, was implied in that of every other. In calling God "good" we at the same time thereby call him "just," "powerful," and so on.[94]

92. Eunomius, *The Apology*, in *Eunomius: The Extant Works*, trans. Richard Paul Vaggione (Oxford: Clarendon Press, 1987), 34–75.

93. A. Stöckl, *Philosophie des Mittelalters*, I, 272–88.

94. Ibid., II, 968.

Scotists thought it better to say that the attributes differed "not in objective or in subjective reason but formally."[95]

The Palamites of the fourteenth century were named after Gregory Palamas, archbishop of Thessalonica, who taught a kind of emanation theory and who represented the acts of God in creation, providence, and so on, as well as the attributes of omnipotence, goodness, wisdom, and so forth, as eternal emissions of light from the unknowable divine essence, emissions that were essentially distinct from the divine essence and had to be viewed as a kind of inferior deities. Also, in Arabic and Jewish philosophy one repeatedly encounters a purely subjective view of God's attributes.[96] Spinoza understood "by attribute what the intellect perceives of a substance as constituting its essence."[97] Depending on whether one focuses on the first or on the second part of this definition, one may either say that Spinoza viewed attributes as subjective construals of the intellect or as objective, existing properties of a substance.[98] Pantheism, which as a result of Spinoza's work found acceptance in philosophy, no longer has any room for the attributes of God. In pantheism God has no distinct being, no life of his own apart from the world. His attributes are identical with the laws of the universe.[99] Schleiermacher, accordingly, describes them in purely subjective terms as "something special in the way we relate the feeling of absolute dependence to God." Their origin lies in religious-poetic invention and are devoid of speculative content. They express neither God's essence (which is unknowable) nor his relations to the world, since this would imply that God sustained many different relations to the world. They are simply subjective ideas without any objective basis. Schleiermacher, therefore, did not deal with the doctrine of the attributes of God separately but interspersed it throughout his dogmatics.[100]

On the basis of God's revelation it is our obligation—against this view of the names of God—to hold onto the belief that, though every attribute is identical with the divine being, the attributes are nevertheless distinct. So Basil and Gregory of Nyssa taught in their writings against Eunomius. On the one hand, they maintained that the attributes did not differ in substance, since God is "simple" and transcends all composition, yet, on the other, they do not differ only in name. Avoiding both extremes, they judged that the names of God differ in thought, that in our mind we have different "ideas, thoughts, and considerations" of the same divine being. Therefore, with reference to the different attributes (such as goodness, wisdom, etc.), we do not just use different names but in that connection really entertain different ideas. No single name expresses God's being with full

95. D. Petavius, "De Deo," in *Theol. dogm.*, I, chs. 12–13; Heinrich, *Dogmatische Theologie*, III, 402.

96. A. Stöckl, *Philosophie des Mittelalters*, II, 18, 27, 60, 88, 268ff.; cf. D. Kaufmann, *Geschichte der Attributenlehre in der judischen Religionsphilosophie des Mittelalters von Saadja bis Maimuni* (Gotha: F. A. Perthes, 1877).

97. B. Spinoza, *Ethics*, I, def. 4.

98. R. Falckenberg, *Geschichte der neueren Philosophie*, 5th ed. (Leipzig: Veit, 1908), 90.

99. D. Strauss, *Glaubenslehre*, I, 613.

100. F. Schleiermacher, *The Christian Faith*, §50.

adequacy, but there are nevertheless many "names, properties, ideas, and fitting honors" by which "some characteristic of God becomes known to us." Gregory of Nyssa even spoke of the essence (οὐσία) of God as the "subject" and of "different qualities or properties" pertaining to that essence.[101] Accordingly, the ideas that we associate with the names of God are distinct from each other. It was therefore considered an error to use the names of God interchangeably or to confuse them. They could be considered by themselves. So, whereas God is certainly identical with the attributes of "divinity, goodness, wisdom, paternity, sonship," and so on, these attributes themselves are not interchangeable with each other. Hence, the one property is not so involved in another that we cannot conceive the one without the other. Each attribute expresses something special.[102]

Augustine even more vigorously asserts that every attribute is identical with God's essence and to that extent with every other attribute as well. "For whatever seems to be predicated with respect to qualities is to be understood with respect to substance or essence." Furthermore, "for God to *be* is the same as *to be strong* or *to be just* or *to be wise* (etc.)." Neither do the attributes differ among themselves. "That which is justice is also itself goodness, and that which is goodness is also itself blessedness. His greatness is the same as his wisdom, for he is not greater in size but in virtue, and his goodness is the same as his wisdom and his greatness, and his truth is the same as all of these; and with respect to him it is not one thing to be blessed and another to be great or wise, or true or to be good, or in general to be himself."[103] Indeed, he expressly states that these "predicates or qualities," when attributed to God, are really the passions *(affectiones)* of our own spirit.

> Whichever of these you affirm concerning God, not only is it wrong to suppose that one ascription refers to one thing and another to a very different thing, but also that anything is affirmed worthily, that is, adequately, because these ascriptions pertain to souls, which in a measure are filled with that Light and affected by it in accordance with their own qualities, just as when this visible light begins to shine upon physical objects. If it is withdrawn, all these objects have the same color; or rather, they have no color. But once it has been brought out and illumined these objects, then although this light is of one kind, nevertheless it suffuses the objects with a luster that varies in accordance with their different qualities. Consequently, these passions pertain to our own souls which are wondrously affected by that Light, which is not affected, and are formed by that which is not formed.[104]

Yet, however strong Augustine's assertions are here, he nevertheless fully maintains that all these predicates are rightly and truthfully used of God. God *is* all that he

101. *The Apology*, II, 42. Cf. F. Diekamp, *Die Gotteslehre des heiligen Gregor von Nyssa* (Münster: Aschendorff, 1896), I, 190.

102. D. Petavius, "De Deo," in *Theol. dogm.*, I, chs. 7–10; J. Schwane, *Dogmengeschichte*, II², 19–31; J. Heinrich, *Dogmatische Theologie*, III, 408.

103. Augustine, *The Trinity*, VI, 4, 6; XV, 5, 8.

104. Augustine, *Homily* 341, n. 8.

has and what is attributed to him in the names. In speaking of the "simplicity of God" it is not Augustine's intent to take anything away from God but, on the contrary, to conceive of God in the fullness of his being. With this in view he speaks of the "simple multiplicity" or the "manifold simplicity" present in God, and calls God's wisdom "simply manifold and uniformly multiform."[105]

In later times the distinction between reason reasoning *(ratio ratiocinans)* and the rational analysis of a thing *(ratio ratiocinata)* was employed in the search for a solution to the difficulty that presents itself in this connection. On the one hand, the diversity of the attributes could not in any way be allowed to impair the unity, simplicity, and immutability of God's being. Nor, on the other hand, could this be viewed as a subjective, arbitrary, and untrue human invention. It was therefore correctly said that this diversity is rooted in God's revelation itself. For it is not we who call God by these names. We do not invent them. On the contrary, if it depended on us, we would be silent about him, try to forget him, and disown all his names. We take no delight in the knowledge of his ways. We tend continually to oppose his names: his independence, sovereignty, righteousness, and love, and resist him in all his perfections. But it is God himself who reveals all his perfections and puts his names on our lips. It is he who gives himself these names and who, despite our opposition, maintains them. It is of little use to us to deny his righteousness: every day he demonstrates this quality in history. And so it is with *all* his attributes. He brings them out despite us. The final goal of all his ways is that his name will shine out in all his works and be written on everyone's forehead (Rev. 22:4). For that reason we have no choice but to name him with the many names his revelation furnishes us.

This diversity of attributes, moreover, does not clash with God's simplicity. For that simplicity does not describe God as an abstract and general kind of being; on the contrary, it speaks of him as the absolute fullness of life. It is for this very reason that God reveals himself to finite creatures by many names. The divine essence is so infinitely and profusely rich that no creature can grasp it all at once. Just as a child cannot picture the worth of a coin of great value but only gains some sense of it when it is counted out in a number of smaller coins, so we too cannot possibly form a picture of the infinite fullness of God's essence unless it is displayed to us now in one relationship, then in another, and now from one angle, then from another.[106] God remains eternally and immutably the same, but the relation in which he stands to his creatures and they to him varies. The light remains the same even though it breaks up into different colors (Augustine). Fire does not change whether it warms us, illumines us, or consumes us (Moses Maimonides). And grain remains grain even though, depending on the stage in which it comes to us, we call it seed, or food, or fruit (Basil). God is called by different names on account of the varying effects he produces in his creatures by his ever-constant being.

105. Augustine, *The Trinity*, VI, 4; idem, *City of God*, XII, 18.
106. Augustine, *Lectures on the Gospel of John*, tract. 13; P. Vermigli, *Loci comm.*, 39; B. de Moor, *Comm. in Marckii Comp.*, I, 582.

In this connection we must remember that God can act in so many different qualities and be called by so many different names, because there is kinship between him and his creatures. If this kinship did not exist, all the names would be untrue. But now there is in his creatures an analogy to what is present in God himself. The names do not merely denote God as the cause of things, but furnish, however feebly and inadequately, some inkling of the divine essence. So, referring to God by all these names, we indeed speak imperfectly, in finite terms, in limited human ways, yet not falsely. For though in God knowing and willing, righteousness and grace always constitute the one full being, yet in these many perfections God displays before our eyes that one rich being, as it were, consecutively and in juxtaposition. Although it is always the same being that confronts us in these names, each name by itself gives us a succinct statement of what that being truly is in its infinite fullness. In God holiness and mercy may be the same in essence, yet our understanding of these two attributes, formed from God's self-revelation, differs. There is no name capable of expressing God's being with full adequacy. Given that reality, many names serve to give us an impression of his all-transcending grandeur.[107]

Two or Three Ways

[186] As already stated above, in early times of the church all that could be thought and said of God was subsumed under his names. But the vast amount of material made it necessary to organize it. Some limitation occurred very soon because the term ("the names of God") came to be restricted to terms of address: God, Lord, and so on. Subsequently, the doctrine of the Trinity was soon treated separately, either before or after the attributes, and in a terminology all its own. Also, the attempt to give a description of God brought with it the necessity of putting one or another attribute (say, aseity or personality) in the foreground, and even of treating this attribute in a separate chapter under the heading of "The Divine Essence" before dealing with the remaining attributes. The division of this latter category, which then most readily suggested itself and is also the most ancient, was that of *negative* and *positive* attributes. For as soon as theologians began to reflect on the origin of the terms used, they noted that they had been obtained from the domain of creatures, either in the way of *negation* or of *eminence* and *causality*. We already encounter this classification or at least this two- or threefold method of learning to know God in the works of Philo and Plotinus.[108] In

---

107. In addition to the authors mentioned above, see John of Damascus, *The Orthodox Faith*, I, 10; T. Aquinas, *Summa theol.*, I, qu. 3, art. 3; I, qu. 13, art. 4; idem, *Summa contra gentiles*, I, 5; D. Petavius, "De Deo," in *Theol. dogm.*, I, chs. 7–13; C. Pesch, *Praelect dogm.*, II, 71–76; J. Zanchi(us), *Op. Theol.*, II, 49; A. Polanus, *Syn. theol.*, lib. 2, c. 7; G. Voetius, *Select. disp.*, I, 233; H. Heppe, *Dogmatik der evangelisch-reformierten Kirche*, 51–53; H. Schmid, *Die Dogmatik der evangelisch-lutherischen Kirche*, 9th ed. (Gütersloh: Gütersloher Verlagshaas Mohn, 1979), §18.

108. Cf. E. Zeller, *Philosophie der Griechen*, V³, 355, 483; M. Heinze, "Neoplatonismus," *PRE³*, XIII, 772ff.

the thinking of the church fathers God was both unknowable and knowable: unknowable in essence, yet knowable from revelation. On the one hand, they wrote, one can only say of God what he is *not;* on the other, in some defective and inadequate fashion, one can nevertheless predicate something *positive* about him. Pseudo-Dionysius, John of Damascus, and Erigena, proceeding from this idea, worked it into a formal division, a twofold theology, namely, "apophatic" and "kataphatic."[109] Pseudo-Dionysius describes the three ways explicitly when he says that we arrive at the knowledge of God "by way of the denial and the transcendence of all things and by way of the cause of all things."[110] And scholasticism, especially since Durandus de S. Porciano, began to speak of the three ways by which one attains to the knowledge of God: the way of negation, eminence, and causality. These three ways have been recognized in dogmatics right into modern times. Catholic, Lutheran, and Reformed theologians have all adopted them and sometimes treated them at great length. But they have also repeatedly been sharply criticized. Spinoza rejected the "way of eminence" by commenting that if a triangle could speak, it would say that "God is eminently triangular."[111] Kant held that the usefulness of the way of causality was confined to the sphere of the phenomena. Schleiermacher, disapproving of the way of negation and eminence, retained only the way of causality.[112] Still others have cast aside the entire method of attaining to God by one of these three ways and, by contrast, posited that we should not try to reach God from a position in the world but, conversely, descend to the world from a position in God.[113]

In response to all this, it should be recognized that the knowledge of God's attributes existed long before these three ways had been conceived, and hence that they were born much later from reflection on attributes already well known and described. Nor can it be denied that the way of eminence and the way of causality are actually one and may together be posited as the way of affirmation over against the way of negation. And finally, there is no doubt that the mode of knowing should not be confused with the mode of being. In reality God, not the creature, is primary. He is the archetype [the original]; the creature is the ectype [the likeness]. In

109. Pseudo-Dionysius, *The Divine Names and Mystical Theology*, I, 2, 4; John of Damascus, *The Orthodox Faith*, I, 2, 4; Erigena, *On the Divine Nature*, I, 78.

110. Pseudo-Dionysius, *On the Divine Names*, 7, §3.

111. B. Spinoza, *Epist.* 60, in *The Letters*, trans. Samuel Shirley (Indianapolis and Cambridge: Hackett, 1995), 290–91; cf. already in Xenophanes, according to E. Zeller, *Philosophie der Griechen*, I³, 490.

112. F. Schleiermacher, *The Christian Faith*, §§50–51.

113. On the three ways, see further A. Twesten, *Vorlesungen über die Dogmatik*, 2d ed., 2 vols. (Hamburg: F. Perthes, 1829–37), II, 30ff.; D. F. Strauss, *Glaubenslehre*, I, 536ff.; J. Bruch, *Lehre von den göttlichen Eigenschaften* (Hamburg: Friedrich Perthes, 1842), 83ff.; I. Dorner, *A System of Christian Doctrine*, I, 201ff.; J. Doedes, *Leer van God*, 208; F. Frank, *System der christlichen Wahrheit*, I², 228; A. Vilmar, *Dogmatik*, I, 190; J. Lange, *Christliche Dogmatik*, 3 vols. (Heidelberg: K. Winter, 1852), II, 42ff.; C. Hodge, *Systematic Theology*, I, 339; J. Wichelhaus, *Die Lehre der heiligen Schrift vom Worte Gottes* (Stuttgart: J. F. Steinkopf, 1892), 332ff.

him everything is original, absolute, and perfect; in creatures everything is derived, relative, and limited. God, therefore, is not really named after things present in creatures, but creatures are named after that which exists in an absolute sense in God.

On the other hand, it must not be overlooked that we have no knowledge of God other than from his revelation in the creaturely world. Since on earth we walk by faith and not by sight, we have only an analogous and proportional knowledge of God. Of God we have no direct but only an indirect kind of knowledge, a concept derived from the creaturely world. Though not exhaustive, it is not untrue, since all creatures are God's creatures and therefore display something of his perfections. Bearing this in mind, we can say that both of these ways can be taken with safety. Scripture, which is theological through and through and derives all things from God, over and over in its method of knowing nevertheless—or rather because of this—ascends to God from a position in the world (Isa. 40:26; Rom. 1:20). Precisely because everything comes from God, everything points back to God. All who think about him or want to speak about him derive—whether by way of affirmation or negation—the forms and images needed for that purpose from the world around them.

On the one hand, in speaking of God, we deny that the imperfections and limitations we find in creatures also exist in him; on the other, we ascribe to God in an absolute sense all the perfections we observe in creatures. But these two paths are not separated by a wide chasm. They do not even run parallel; neither can we take the one without taking the other. To reach our goal we consistently and simultaneously need both methods. At all times they are the two complementary components that go into the formation of the one pure knowledge of God. When, in the way of negation, we deny to God all creaturely imperfections, this assumes that we have a positive appreciation of God as the Absolute Being, even if we cannot put this awareness in so many words. The confession of his incomprehensibility is a proof of his knowability. And conversely, when in the way of affirmation we ascribe to God all the perfections found in created things, we always do this also by using the way of eminence. We only ascribe these perfections to him in a supereminent sense; that is, proceeding affirmatively, we simultaneously deny that those perfections are present in God in the same manner in which we find them present in his creatures. That is the reason we can say that all attributes are simultaneously ascribed and denied to him. Indeed, he is wise and good and holy and glorious—but not in the way his creatures are. Mysticism, which loved to speak of God in this way, said that God was above all wisdom, goodness, holiness, life, being, even above all divinity, not to deny that God was all these things, but to inculcate that he was all these things in a way that infinitely surpassed our comprehension. God is simultaneously panonymous (the possessor of all names) and anonymous (the possessor of no name). Those know him best who do not know him—who think he transcends the conceivable. The most brilliant light dwells in deepest darkness (Exod. 20:21). Pseudo-Dionysius, accordingly, calls God "the affirmation of all things and the negation of all things: the Cause beyond all affirmation and denial."[114]

CLASSIFYING GOD'S ATTRIBUTES

The division of the divine perfections into negative and positive attributes is closely connected with these two ways. It is of ancient origin, soon met with general acceptance, and actually underlies all other and later divisions. It can already be found in the works of Philo, Plotinus, and the church fathers, and was subsequently followed by John of Damascus, Anselm, Thomas, Petavius, and numerous others.[115] Among Roman Catholic theologians this division is the most common, while a number of Reformed and Lutheran theologians have adopted it as well. Occasionally other distinctions are also introduced. Augustine already commented that some names of God are used "properly," others "metaphorically," and still others "relatively."[116] The "negative names," accordingly, were again subdivided into those that are "purely negative" and those "relatively negative," while the "positive names" were subdivided into the "proper" and the "metaphorical."[117]

Along with this division into negative and positive attributes, still another one arose. Plato already taught that God is inherently good, whereas creatures are good by participation (μετοχη). This idea has borne abundant fruit in Christian theology, especially in the case of Augustine. Over against pantheism it was maintained that God's essence is incommunicable and that the soul was "no part" of God.[118] At the same time it was held that all God's creatures are related to God, and especially that human beings are his image and likeness. Between the Creator and the creature, it was said, there is analogy. This then led to the division between *communicable* and *incommunicable* attributes. Earlier these expressions were already employed in the doctrine of the Trinity. For, as it was put, God's essence or deity is communicable (communicated by the Father to the Son in the generation of the Son), but the persons and the personal properties (say, fatherhood) are incommunicable.[119] From there the two terms were also adopted in the doctrine of the divine attributes with

114. Pseudo-Dionysius, *The Divine Names and Mystical Theology*, ch. 2; cf. M. J. Scheeben, *Handbuch der katholischen Dogmatik*, 4 vols. (1873–1903; reprinted, Freiburg im Breisgau: Herder, 1933), I, 483; J. Heinrich, *Dogmatische Theologie*, III, 309.

115. John of Damascus, *On the Orthodox Faith*, I, 4, 9, 12; Anselm, *Monologion*, 15; idem, *Proslogion*, 5–6; T. Aquinas, *Summa theol.*, I, qu. 13, art. 2; D. Petavius, "De Deo," in *Theol. dogm.*, I, ch. 5; G. Perrone, *Prael. theol.*, II, 91; J. Heinrich, *Dogmatische Theologie*, III, 375.

116. Augustine, *Sermon* 38, "On Time."

117. T. Aquinas, *Summa theol.*, I, qu. 13, arts. 2–3.

118. Ibid., I, qu. 90, art. 1; J. Zanchi(us), *Op. theol.*, II, 53ff.

119. Pseudo-Dionysius, *On the Divine Names*, 2 §5; Bonaventure, *Breviloquium*, I, 4; idem, *Sent.*, I, dist. 27, p. 1, art. 1, qu. 3.

a view to maintaining both God's transcendence and his immanence.[120] This division was especially welcome among Reformed theologians, no doubt in part because it gave them a ready means with which to combat the Lutheran doctrine of ubiquity.[121] Yet everyone admits that the communicable attributes in an absolute sense—as they exist in God—are just as incommunicable as the others.[122] The Lutherans mostly favored another division, namely, that into "quiescent" and "operative," also called "indwelling" and "outgoing" attributes, employed in part in defense of the doctrine of the "communication of proper qualities" *(communication idiomatum)*.[123] Usually treated in the first group (the negative, incommunicable, metaphysical, quiescent) were the attributes of oneness, simplicity, independence, immutability, eternity, and omnipresence. The second group (positive, communicable, operative, personal) was usually again subdivided into attributes of intellect, will, and power.

In modern times many other divisions have been added to these old and common ones. Schleiermacher viewed the attributes merely as subjective ideas grounded only in reasoning and therefore divided them in terms of the relation in which, to our mind, God stands to the world, sin, and redemption. Thus, first there are the attributes that are integral to the human feeling of dependence, apart from any sense of the antithetical nature of sin: eternity, omnipresence, omnipotence, omniscience. Next come those that presuppose the consciousness of the antithetical nature of sin: holiness, righteousness. And finally there are attributes that are experienced when that antithesis has been overcome: love and wisdom. Related to this is the division of the attributes in terms of the relation in which God stands to the universe, specifically to the universe in general: infinity, eternity, omnipresence; to the ethical world: holiness, righteousness, grace, mercy; and to the ethical-physical world: wisdom, blessedness.[124]

Among those who derive the attributes of God totally from his relation to the universe is Dorner, who does this by relating the attributes of God to the arguments for God's existence, inferring a class of attributes from each of the arguments. The ontological argument, for example, makes us think of God as "the One who is" and suggests to us the idea of the absolute as possessing the attributes of unity, simplicity, and infinity. The cosmological argument, to give a second example, leads to God as the cause of all things, hence as the One who is himself absolute Life, and so forth.[125]

120. Anselm, *Monologion*, 15; T. Aquinas, *Summa theol.*, I, qu. 13, arts. 9–10.

121. G. Sohn(ius), *Opera*, I, 97; J. Zanchi(us), *Op. theol.*, II, 50; A. Polanus, *Syn. theol.*, II, 7, 14; P. van Mastricht, *Theologia*, II, 5, 12.

122. Cf. H. Heppe, *Dogmatik der evangelisch-reformierten Kirche*, 52ff.

123. H. Schmid, *Dogmatik der evangelisch-lutherischen Kirche*, 78.

124. J. Wegscheider, *Instit. theol.*, §60; J. Bruch, *Lehre von den göttlichen Eigenschaften*, 110ff.; J. Lange, *Dogmatik*, II, 61ff.; H. Martensen, *Christian Dogmatics*, §47; C. Luthardt, *Compendium der Dogmatik* (Leipzig: Dörffling & Franke, 1865), §29; R. Lipsius, *Dogmatik*, §298; A. Gretillat, *Exposé de théologie systématique*, 4 vols. (Paris: Fischbacher, 1885–92), III, 220; S. Hoekstra, *Wijsgerige Godsdienstwetenschap*, II, 92–99.

125. I. Dorner, *A System of Christian Doctrine*, I, 177ff.

Others think that we should preface the attributes we derive from God's relation to the world with others that describe God as he is within himself *(an sich)*, and treat them under the heading of "metaphysical" attributes, or as attributes of being, of the absolute, of absolute personality, of "the all-glorious Spirit who conditions all of life," and so on. The attributes that follow and describe God's relation to the world are again arranged in different ways: attributes of intellect and will (to which Hase adds that of feeling); or intellectual, ethical, and dynamic attributes; or physical and moral attributes, also known as psychological attributes or as the attributes of holy love. Some theologians add a third group that describe, as it were, the result of the divine being and life, and make God known in his blessedness and glory.[126] Still others refrain from actually classifying the attributes and only try to follow some kind of order in the treatment of these attributes.[127]

[187] All the above divisions seem to be very different and called by very different names. But materially they are not that far apart. Whether people speak of negative and positive, incommunicable and communicable, quiescent and operative, absolute and relative, metaphysical and psychological attributes, of attributes of the substance and subject apart from or in relation to the universe and humankind, actually they consistently refer to the same order in which the attributes are treated. Against all the above arrangements one can lodge virtually the same objections. They all appear to divide God's being into two halves. They all seem to treat first God's absoluteness, then his personality; first God's being as such, then God in relation to his creatures. They all seem to imply that the first group of terms is obtained apart from the creation, and the second from God's creatures, and that, consequently, there is no unity or concord among God's perfections.[128]

It is the incontrovertible teaching of Scripture, however, that in God's secret being he is unknowable and unnamable, and that all God's names presuppose his self-revelation, that is, his creation. Of God's being and life apart from creation we know nothing for the simple reason that we ourselves are creatures and therefore always bound to creation. In the past this was clearly understood and articulated with respect to the relative, metaphorical, and positive names of God. Relative terms, such as "Lord," "Creator," "Sustainer," "Savior," and so on, belong to God only on account of, and upon the com-

126. Cf. K. Bretschneider, *Handbuch der Dogmatik der evangelisch-lutherischen Kirche*, 4th ed., 2 vols. (Leipzig: Johann Ambrosius Barth, 1814–18), I, 480; K. Hase, *Lehrbuch der evangelischen Dogmatik* (Leipzig: Breitkopf & Härtel, 1838), 271; A. Biedermann, *Christliche Dogmatik*, II², 261; G. Thomasius, *Christi Person und Werk*, I, 14ff.; A. Vilmar, *Dogmatik*, I, 195; F. Philippi, *Kirchliche Glaubenslehre*, II, 23; F. Frank, *System der christlichen Wahrheit*, §§10ff., §§17ff.; F. A. B. Nitzsch, *Evangelische Dogmatik*, 351ff., 396ff.; W. Schmidt, *Christliche Dogmatik*, II, 121ff.; A. von Oettingen, *Lutherische Dogmatik*, II, 84ff.; T. Haering, *The Christian Faith*, trans. John Dickie and George Ferries, 2 vols. (London: Hodder & Stoughton, 1913), I, 405ff.; J. van Oosterzee, *Christian Dogmatics*, §47.

127. J. Schwetz, *Theologia dogmatica catholica*, 3 vols. (Vienna: Congregationis Mechitharisticae, 1869), I, 111; J. I. Doedes, *Leer van God*, 217.

128. F. Frank, *System der christlichen Wahrheit*, I, 228ff.

ing into being of, the creation. No one can be called "master" unless he has servants. Human beings, the servants of God, were created in time, so in time God became our Lord.[129] With respect to metaphorical names, to which also the anthropomorphisms belong, it is clear that they presuppose the creation. In the same way the positive names—such as "good," "holy," "wise"—have some meaning to our mind, because we observe examples (ectypes) of them in creatures.[130] But all these names, though relative, metaphorical, and positive, nevertheless definitely denote something in God that exists in him absolutely, "properly," and hence also "negatively," that is, in another sense than it exists in creatures. Augustine sought to demonstrate that, though God became Lord in time, his essence is nonetheless unchanging and all the change occurs in creatures alone. "Accordingly, that which is first said of God in time, and was not said of him before, is manifestly said of him relatively, yet not because of some accident in God, as though something happened to him, but plainly on account of some accident of that with reference to which God begins to be called something relative."[131]

The reverse is true of the second group of attributes, whether these are called negative, incommunicable, quiescent, absolute, or something else. For although they deny to God some quality that pertains to creatures, they are all in a sense also positive, communicable, transferable, and relative. If that were not the case, if they were totally incommunicable, they would also be totally unknowable and unnamable. The fact that we can think and name them is proof that in some way or other they have been revealed by God in his works. The negative terms, therefore, also have a positive content. Although we can learn to know God's eternity only by and in time, his omnipresence by and in space, his infinity and immutability by and in the midst of finite and changeable creatures, yet these attributes do furnish us some—and even important—knowledge of God. Even though we cannot understand eternity in a positive sense, it means a lot to know that God is exalted above all the conditions of time. By means of that knowledge we, as it were, continually correct our notions concerning God. We speak of him in human terms and attribute to him a range of human qualities, but as we are doing this we are ever acutely conscious of the fact that all these properties pertain to God in a sense quite different from that in which we find them in creatures.

The knowledge we have of God is correct because we know that it is not exhaustive—not false and untrue, but analogical and ectypal. But for that very reason it remains objectionable to so classify the attributes of God that, on the one hand, we end up with a group of perfections that are called negative,

---

129. Augustine, *The Trinity*, V, 16; cf. *De ordine* (*Divine Providence*), II, 7; T. Aquinas, *Summa theol.*, 1, qu. 13, art. 7; Anselm, *Monologion*, 15; P. Lombard, *Sent.*, I, dist. 30; Bonaventure, *Sent.*, I, dist. 30, art. 1; J. Zanchi(us), *Op. theol.*, II, 24–26; A. Polanus, *Syn. theol.*, 192.

130. T. Aquinas, *Summa theol.*, I, qu. 12, art. 12.

131. Augustine, *The Trinity*, V, 16.

incommunicable, quiescent, absolute, and metaphysical and view God "as such" apart from his relation to the universe and, on the other hand, with a group of perfections that are called positive, communicable, operative, relative, and psychological, and are derived from his relation to the universe. For all God's attributes are both absolute and relative. They are all absolute, yet only known first from his relation to his creatures. Conversely, we can only name God in terms of what is revealed of him in his creatures, but in so doing we are still naming him who is infinitely exalted above all his creatures. One can even say on good grounds that because the attributes are in reality identical with God's being and, in God, identical with each other as well, no classification will be found that is objectively based on the attributes themselves.

But since God can be called by many names, we still need to treat them in a certain order. Now when we summarize all that God has revealed of himself in his names, we find there are two groups that can be readily separated from the rest. On the one hand, there are those among them that were later singled out as the names of God and can be characterized as proper names of address. On the other, there are the unique attributes that pertain not to the divine being but to the three persons in that being. They come up in the doctrine of the Trinity and were referred to as properties (ἰδιώματα), notions, notional or personal properties, and relative attributes. Left between these two groups is a large space for the attributes that describe God's being and have received very different names in theology, such as characteristics (ἀξιώματα), values (ἄξιαι), thoughts, concepts, principles (ἐπιλογισμοι), qualities, virtues, properties, perfections, and so on.

Now, it is extremely difficult to introduce order into the treatment of the numerous attributes belonging to this last group. But in this connection we do receive guidance from the relation in which God stands to his creatures. For the entire universe is a revelation of God. There is no part of the universe in which something of his perfections does not shine forth. Yet among his creatures there are distinctions: not all of them proclaim all God's perfections, and not all these creatures proclaim them with the same clarity. There is order and gradation: all creatures display vestiges of God, but only human beings are God's image and likeness. Not only do humans have existence in common with the lower creation, and life and spirit with the higher creation, but in this community of the material and the spiritual world they are also uniquely related to God himself, created in true knowledge, holiness, and righteousness as prophets, priests, and kings. Thus God, the source of all being and archetypically related to humans, is himself all that which belongs to his creatures in the way of being, life, and spirit, in knowledge, holiness, and righteousness. In all creatures but especially in humanity there is something analogous to the divine being. But all the perfections found in creatures exist in God in a wholly unique and original way. Discernible in every one of God's perfections is both his absolute superiority over, and his kinship with, his creatures. Hence, in one sense each of his attributes is incommunicable and in another communicable.

Scripture, in this regard, leads the way and simultaneously maintains both God's transcendence over, and his orientation to, the world. And Christian theology follows this pattern when it successively treats God's negative and positive (incommunicable and communicable) attributes. Actually, with every positive attribute (which, as it were, makes known the content of God's being) we should have to show that it is at the same time negative, inasmuch as the categories of being, life, spirit, knowledge, righteousness, holiness (etc.) pertain to God in a different way than they do to created beings. That is, in God these perfections are independent, immutable, eternal, omnipresent, and simple. But this would result in continual repetition and render impossible a separate and urgently necessary treatment of these perfections. We must, therefore, treat the attributes consecutively, and an orderly discussion of all of them finally again ends up—be it under different names—with the old division. The difficulty inherent in this division is natural and therefore insurmountable. In the doctrine of God we have no choice but to hold onto both his transcendence over, and his kinship with, the world. If this is true, it matters less what words we use to describe the two groups of attributes, whether negative and positive, quiescent and operative, incommunicable and communicable, or some other combination.

The last combination (incommunicable and communicable), in use among the Reformed, has the advantage in that it safeguards Christian theism against both the error of pantheism and that of Deism. There is no objection, therefore, to speaking of incommunicable attributes, provided one consistently bears in mind that these perfections are in fact descriptions of the wholly unique, absolute, divine manner in which the other attributes—those of being, life, and spirit, of intellect and will, of love and righteousness, and so forth—exist in God. In the usual order, there are four such attributes: aseity, immutability, infinity (eternity and immensity), and oneness (numerical oneness, unity, and qualitative oneness, simplicity). To be distinguished from these incommunicable attributes are all those perfections that affirm something positively (though always analogically and proportionately) concerning the content of the divine being. A suitable and almost universally adopted division, derived from the image and likeness according to which humans have been created, is as follows. First, there are the attributes that reveal to us God as the Living One, as Spirit: his spirituality and invisibility. Second, there are the attributes that describe God as perfectly self-conscious: knowledge, wisdom, and veracity. Third, there are the attributes that refer to God's ethical nature: goodness, righteousness, and holiness. Fourth, there are the attributes in which God appears before us as Lord, king, and sovereign: his will, freedom, and omnipotence. Finally, there are the attributes that sum up and complete all the preceding ones and reveal God in his absolute blessedness: perfection, beatitude, and glory. This classification is related, on the one hand, to the knowledge of God that can be derived from the vestiges of God in all his creatures and summed up in the so-called proofs for his existence; and, on the other hand, it points forward to the image of God, which was imprinted on humans and in its full splendor again confronts us in the person of Christ. So there is no knowledge of God apart from his revelation in his creatures, hence always analogical and ectypical, but by that revelation we do have true and authentic knowledge of God's incomprehensible and adorable being!

GOD'S PROPER NAMES

[188] If we speak of God's names in distinction from his attributes and hence in a restricted sense, we understand by them the names by which we refer to or address God as an independent personal being. Such names for the divine being exist in every language. Although in himself God has no name, we have a need to refer to him, and for this we have no other means than a name. "For unless you know the name, your knowledge of things vanishes."[132]

Formerly, the Greek word for God (θεος) was believed to derive from τιθε-ναι, θεειν, θεασθαι,[133] but nowadays some philologists relate it to Zeus, Dios, Jupiter, Deus, Diana, Juno, Dio, Dieu. In that case it is identical with the Sanskrit *deva* (clear sky), derived from the stem *div,* to shine, glitter. Others again strongly oppose all etymological connection between the Greek and the Latin word and link the word θεος with the stem θες in θεσσασθαι, to desire, to call upon.[134] In many languages the words "heaven" and "God" are used interchangeably. The oldest Greek deity, Uranus, was almost certainly identical with the Sanskrit Varuna. The Tartar and Turkish word *Taengri* and the Chinese word *Thian* mean both heaven and God; and also in Scripture the words "heaven" and "God" are used interchangeably, for instance, in the expression "kingdom of heaven" or "kingdom of God." Another Greek name, δαιμων (derived from the verb δαιω), means God as the determiner of our lot. The word κυριος (derived from κυρος), on the other hand, is the mighty One, Lord, Owner, Ruler. Our word "God" is of uncertain origin. It has been linked to the word *good,* to the Avestan *khoda* (self-existent), to the Sanskrit *gudha,* or *gutha,* which is said to refer to God as "the hidden One." Other possibilities are the Indo-Germanic root *ghu* (Sanskrit *hû*), which means "to call upon" and is therefore said to refer to God as "the One called upon," or to a stem κοδω (κοσμος), which is said to mean "to order, to arrange," or to the Aryan *cuddhas* (pure, good). All these derivations, however, are uncertain. The name *Asura,* used among the East Indians, and *Ahura,* a Persian name, refer to God as the Living One.[135]

132. Isidore, in B. de Moor, *Comm. in Marckii Comp.,* I, 504.

133. J. C. Suicerus, *Thesaurus ecclesiasticus,* s.v. "θεος"; C. Vitringa, *Doctr. christ.,* I, 134.

134. H. Cremer, *Biblisch-theologisches Wörterbuch der neutestamentlichen Gräcität* (Gotha: F. A. Perthes, 1880), s.v. "θεος"; J. Köstlin, "Gott," *PRE*³, VI, 779ff.

135. Cf. F. Kluge, *Etymologisches Wörterbuch der deutschen Sprache* (Strassburg: K. J. Trübner, 1883), s.v. "Gott"; *Woordenboek der Nederlanse Taal,* V, 180; S. Hoekstra, *Wijsgerige Godsdienstwetenschap,* I, 309.

Scripture often uses the expression "God's name" in a very inclusive sense. The Jews, consequently, listed no fewer than seventy names;[136] and Christian theology initially included God's attributes in the category of his names as well. But gradually a distinction was made. Jerome already limited the divine names to the following ten: El, Elohim, Elohe, Sabaoth, Elyon, Asher Ehyeh, Adonai, Yah, YHWH, Shaddai, and many scholars followed his example.[137]

El, Elohim, El Shaddai

The simplest name used for God in Scripture and by the Semites generally is *El* (אֵל). There is disagreement about its derivation. Lagarde relates the word to the root *ʾly* (אלי) and the preposition *ʾel* (אֶל, to) and thinks the word describes God as the One who is the ultimate object of human desire. Though some scholars have taken over this derivation,[138] according to others it is just as improbable as the notion that *ʾel* is connected with *ʾēlâ* (אֵלָה), the sacred tree. According to most philologists the word derives from the stem *ʾûl* (אוּל), and means either the most prominent or primary Lord (Nöldeke) or the One who is strong and mighty (Gesenius).[139] The name *ʾElōah* (אֱלֹהַּ; pl. *ʾElōhîm,* אֱלֹהִים) is from the same root, *ʾûl* (אוּל), or from *ʾlh* (אלה, to dread) and hence points to God as the Strong One or as the object of dread. The singular, rarely used, is poetic (e.g., Ps. 18:31 [32 MT]; Job 3:4); the plural is the usual name for God. The plural, however, must not be interpreted as a plural of majesty, which is never used in Scripture of God, nor viewed as a reference to the Trinity, as was done by Lombard and many after him,[140] since it nearly always occurs with an adjective and verb in the singular.[141] Modern critics mostly regard it as a remnant of an earlier polytheism, but this explanation fails for the same reason as the earlier trinitarian one. Also, as has been shown by investigations outside of Israel, the word occurs there as the name of one single God.[142] It is therefore better to view it as a plural of abstraction (Ewald), or as a plural of quantity, which, as in the case of מִם and שָׁמַיִם, is used to refer to an unbounded entity (Oehler), or as an intensive plural that serves to express fullness of power (Delitzsch). A few times *ʾElōhîm* is con-

---

136. J. Eisenmenger, *Entdecktes Judenthum*, 2 vols. (Königsberg in Preussen, 1711), I, 455.

137. J. Alsted, *Theol. schol.*, 71; B. de Moor, *Comm. in Marckii Comp.*, I, 511.

138. E.g., F. Delitzsch, *Babel and Bible*, trans. T. J. McCormack and W. H. Carruth (Chicago: Open Court, 1903), 60ff.; Marie-Joseph Lagrange, *Études sur les religions sémitiques* (Paris: V. Lecoffre, 1903), 79.

139. Cf. C. Vitringa, *Doctr. christ.*, I, 32; B. de Moor, *Comm. in Marckii Comp.*, I, 515; H. Schultz, *Alttestamentliche Theologie*, 2d ed. (Göttingen: Vandenhoeck & Ruprecht, 1889), 508; R. Smend, *Lehrbuch der alttestamentlichen Religionsgeschichte* (Freiburg: J. C. B. Mohr, 1893), 26; K. Marti, *Geschichte der israelitischen Religion*, 3d ed., 25; M.-J. Lagrange, *Études*, 81.

140. P. Lombard, *Sent.*, I, dist. 2; J. Zanchi(us), *Op. theol.* I, 25; G. Voetius, *Select. disp.*, V, 27; C. Vitringa, *Doctr. christ.*, I, 209.

141. Cf. already in Augustine, *The Trinity*, II, 11; R. Bellarmine, "De Christo," *Controversiis*, 6; J. Calvin, *Institutes*, I.xiii.9; F. Gomarus, *Theses theol. disp.*, V; B. de Moor, *Comm. in Marckii Comp.*, I, 796.

142. M. Noordtzij, *Oostersche Lichtstralen over Westersche Schriftbeschouwing* (Kampen: J. H. Bos, 1897), 41ff.

structed with an adjective and/or a verb in the plural (Gen. 20:13; 28:13f.; 35:7; Exod. 32:4, 8; Josh. 24:19; 1 Sam. 4:8; 17:26; 2 Sam. 7:23; 1 Kings 12:28; Ps. 58:11 [12 MT]; 121:5; Job 35:10; Jer. 10:10). A similar plural occurs in the personal pronoun (Gen. 1:26; 3:22; 11:7; Isa. 6:8; 41:22), in *qĕdôšîm* (קְדוֹשִׁים, Prov. 9:10; Hos. 11:12 [12:1 MT]), in *'ōśîm* (עֹשִׂים, Job 35:10; Ps. 149:2; Isa. 54:5), in *bôr'îm* (בּוֹרְאִים, Eccles. 12:1), and in *'Ădōnāy* (אֲדֹנָי). All of these plural constructions denote God as the fullness of life and power. "The name Elohim describes the divine being in his original relation and constant causal relation to the universe. It is a designation of relationship, not of immediate inner being. In fact, it expresses the idea of absolute transcendence with respect to the entire universe."[143]

The name *'Elyôn* (עֶלְיוֹן; LXX: ὕψιστος) refers to God as the One who is exalted high above everything. The name is used by Melchizedek (Gen. 14:18), Balaam (Num. 24:16), and the king of Babylon (Isa. 14:14; cf. Mark 5:7; Luke 1:32, 35; Acts 16:17) and further occurs especially in poetry. *'Ēdōnāy* (אֲדֹנָי), used alternately with *hā-'ādôn* (הָאָדוֹן), which is further intensified in "Lord of lords" (אֲדֹנֵי אֲדֹנִים) or "Lord of all the earth" (אֲדוֹן כָּל־הָאָרֶץ), refers to God as the Ruler to whom all things are subject and to whom humans are related as servants (Gen. 18:27). In an earlier period the name Ba'al (בַּעַל) was used of God with the same meaning (Hos. 2:16 [18MT]), but later this use was discontinued because of its idolatrous connotations.[144] Now these names are not proper names in the restricted sense. They are used as well of idols, people (Gen. 33:10; Exod. 7:1; 4:16), and authorities (Exod. 12:12; 21:5–6; 22:7; Lev. 19:32; Num. 33:4; Judg. 5:8; 1 Sam. 2:25; Ps. 58:1 [2 MT]; 82:1) but are nevertheless the usual names by which God is called and addressed. They are, moreover, common Semitic names referring to God in his transcendence over all creatures. The Semites loved to call God "Lord" or "king." They felt deeply dependent on him, and as his servants they humbly bowed before him. They did not use these names to give expression to philosophical theories about God's essence but to give prominence to his relation to his creatures, especially to human beings.[145]

[189] Though high and exalted, this God also comes down from his transcendence to the level of his creatures. Not only does he reveal himself in general, through creation, to all peoples, but has made himself known in a special sense also to Israel. Now the first name by which God appears in his

143. J. T. Beck, *Vorlesungen über christliche Glaubenslehre*, 2 vols. (Gütersloh: C. Bertelsmann, 1886–87), II, 22; cf. further C. Vitringa, *Doctr. christ.*, I, 133; B. de Moor, *Comm. in Marckii Comp.*, I, 518; G. F. Oehler, *Theology of the Old Testament*, trans. Ellen D. Smith and Sophia Taylor (Edinburgh: T. & T. Clark, 1892–93), §36; H. Schultz, *Alttestamentliche Theologie*, 516; A. B. Davidson, *The Theology of the Old Testament*, ed. S. P. F. Salmond (Edinburgh: T. & T. Clark, 1904), 41, 99; R. Kittel, "Elohim," *PRE³*, V, 316–19; H. Zimmermann, *Elohim: Eine Studie zur israelitischen Religions und Litteraturgeschichte* (Berlin: Mayer & Müller, 1900).

144. J. Robertson, *Israel's oude godsdienst* (Culemborg: Blom en Oliverse, 1896), 200ff.; ed. note: Eng. edition: *The Early Religion of Israel*, 2d ed. (New York: Westminster Press [Thomas Wittaker], 1903).

145. W. Robertson Smith, *Die Religion der Semiten* (Freiburg: Mohr, 1899), 48.

special revelation is *Šadday* (שַׁדַּי) or *ʾEl Šadday* (אֵל שַׁדַּי). As such, God reveals himself to Abraham when he makes him a father of many peoples and seals his covenant with him by the rite of circumcision (Gen. 17:1). Accordingly, in the period of the patriarchs this name occurs repeatedly (Gen. 28:3; 35:11; 43:14; 48:3; 49:25; Exod. 6:3; Num. 24:4). It is further found in Job, in a number of psalms, and a few times in the prophets. The New Testament equivalent is the Lord Almighty (παντοκράτωρ, 2 Cor. 6:18; Rev. 4:8; etc.). The origin of this name has not yet been established with certainty. Nöldeke derived it from *Šad* (שַׁד), "Lord," and punctuated it as שַׁדַּי, but according to Genesis 43:14; 49:25; and Ezekiel 10:5, the name is undoubtedly an adjective. Formerly it was derived from שׁ (from אֲשֶׁר) and דִּי (sufficient) and translated as "the All-Sufficient One," or from שָׁדַד, meaning "to be strong, to destroy"; or also from שָׁדָה or אֲשָׁד, "to pour out," so designating God as "he who bountifully supplies all things."

Wherever the name appears, it highlights the idea of power and invincible strength; and Isaiah 13:6 connects it, be it only in a wordplay, with שָׁדַד, to destroy (cf. Joel 1:15). This name, accordingly, makes God known to us as the One who possesses all power, and can therefore overcome all resistance and make all things subservient to his will. Whereas "Elohim" is the God of creation and nature, "El Shaddai" is the God who makes all the powers of nature subject and subservient to the work of grace.[146] In this name God's deity (θειότης) and eternal power (ἀΐδιος δύναμις) is no longer an object of dread but a source of well-being and comfort. God gives himself to his people, and his invincible power is for them the guarantee of the fulfillment of his covenant promises. From this point on, therefore, he is over and over called the God of Abraham (Gen. 24:12), of Isaac (Gen. 28:13), of Jacob (Exod. 3:6), the God of the Fathers (Exod. 3:13, 15), the God of the Hebrews (Exod. 3:18), the God of Israel (Gen. 33:20), and in Isaiah the Holy One of Israel [Isa. 1:4; 5:19, 24; et al.]. God is the Exalted One, Creator of heaven and earth, the Almighty, but at the same time he stands in a special and most beneficent relation to his people.

YHWH

As the God of grace, however, he manifests himself especially in the name יהוה (YHWH). The Jews called it the preeminent name, the name that describes God's essence, God's proper name, the glorious, the four-letter name (the tetragrammaton), and concluded from Leviticus 24:16 and Exodus 3:15 (where they read the word for "forever" as the word for "to conceal it" [לְעַלֵּם]) that they were forbidden to pronounce it. Just when this idea arose among the Jews we do not know. But it is certain that the LXX already read *Adonai* here and

---

146. Commentary of the *Statenvertaling* on Gen 17:1. Ed. note: The *Statenvertaling* is the annotated Dutch Scripture translation officially sanctioned by the Synod of Dordrecht, 1618–19. J. Zanchi(us), *Op. theol.*, II, 43; C. Vitringa, *Doctr. christ.*, I, 132; B. de Moor, *Comm. in Marckii Comp.*, I, 522ff.; G. Oehler, *Theology of the Old Testament*, §37; F. Delitzsch, *Commentary*, on Gen. 17:1.

therefore translated it by κυριος. Subsequent translations followed this example and reproduced it by *Dominus* (Latin), *the Lord* (English), *der Herr* (German), HEERE (Dutch),[147] *l'Eternal* (French). Because of the Jewish dread of pronouncing this name, the original and correct pronunciation has been lost. The church fathers called it the forbidden (ἀπορρητον), the indescribable (ἀλεχτον), the unutterable (ἀφραστον) name, probably not because they themselves held it to be impermissible to say the name, but because the Jews were of that opinion and because the proper pronunciation of it had in fact been lost.[148]

In the Greek, the four letters were written ΙΙΙΙΙ or transliterated as Ἰαω or Ἰαη, as we learn from Diodorus Siculus and Origen. According to Jerome, the name was translated by *Jaho,* according to Philo Byblius by Ἰευω, and according to Clement of Alexandria, by Ἰαου. Theodoret relates that the Jewish pronunciation was Ἀϊα and the Samaritan, Ἰαβε. All this information probably refers back to an ancient pronunciation of *Yahweh.*[149] Appealing to Jewish tradition some scholars, Joachim of Floris in his *Evangelium Aeternum,* for example, pronounced the name *Yewe,* and indeed this vocalization can be found in Samuel B. Meir and was later still defended by Hottinger, Reland, and others.[150] The pronunciation of "Jehovah" is of recent origin. It found wide acceptance through the advocacy of the Franciscan Peter Galatinus, who, however, was opposed in this by many scholars, Genebrardus among them.[151] Later on, Drusius, Amama, Scaliger, Vriemoet, and others, maintained that the pronunciation "Jehovah" could not be correct, asserting that the vocalization had been derived from the word *Adonai.*[152] And in fact this vocalization is highly questionable. In the first place, the word YHWH is a *Qere perpetuum* in the Hebrew Bible, having at times the vowels of *Adonai* and at other times those of *Elohim.* Furthermore, the form *Yehōwāh* is un-Hebrew and inexplicable. Finally, this vocalization dates from a time when the notion that the name should never be pronounced had already been long entrenched in Jewish tradition.

If this vocalization is incorrect, the question arises how then we must explain the name. The assertion that it is of Egyptian origin (Voltaire, Schiller, Wegscheider, Heeren, Brugsch) is contradicted by Exodus 5:2 and is hardly ever still defended. Also, the opinion of Hartmann, Bohlen, Colenso, Dozy, and Land that it is of Canaanite or Phoenician origin and was adopted by the Israelites after their entry into Canaan has proved to be untenable and has been properly refuted.[153] Still, though on different grounds, the same claim has been repeated by Friedrich

147. Acts of Synod of Dort, session 12.

148. B. de Moor, *Comm. in Marckii Comp.,* I, 534; J. Buddeus, *Inst. theol. dogm.,* I, 188.

149. H. Schultz, *Alttestamentliche Theologie,* 4th ed., 523.

150. F. Delitzsch, *Neuer Comentar über die Genesis* (Leipzig: Dörffling & Franke, 1887), 546ff.

151. D. Petavius, "De Deo," in *Theol. dogm.,* VIII, ch. 9.

152. G. Voetius, *Select. disp.,* V, 55; C. Vitringa, *Doctr. christ.,* I, 130.

153. A. Kuenen, *De Godsdienst van Israël tot den Ondergang van den Joodschen Staat,* 2 vols., De Voornaamste Godsdiensten (Haarlem: Kruseman, 1869–70), I, 397–401; J. J. P. Valeton Jr., "De Israëlitische Godsnaam," *Theologische Studiën* 7 (1889): 173–221.

Delitzsch in his first lecture on *Babel und Bibel.* According to his reading of it, the name YHWH already occurs in two [compound] proper names found on clay tablets from the time of Hammurabi, *Ya-a³-ve-elu* and *Ya-u-um-ilu.* From this discovery he concludes that the name YHWH was originally of Canaanite origin, and that the tribe of Hammurabi brought it from Canaan to Babylonia.

There is great disagreement, however, over the correctness of this reading. Many scholars consider it definitely wrong or highly improbable. They interpret the first part of these "proper nouns" not as a noun but as a verb, so that it would mean "El protects me" or be the name of a Babylonian Yahu or Yau. Second, even if Delitzsch's reading were correct, it is an error to think that the name YHWH is originally of Canaanite origin, for the Semitic origin of the Canaanites and the emigration of the tribe of Hammurabi from Canaan to Babylon are unproved hypotheses, and we have found no trace in that ancient period of a Canaanite deity named YHWH. Third, though it is definitely not impossible that the name YHWH existed well before the time of Moses and was even known to Semites and Babylonians, it is nevertheless remarkable that, aside from the above two names of doubtful interpretation, all evidence for this is lacking. YHWH was definitely the God of Israel, not only according to Scripture (Judg. 5:3–4) but also according to the [Moabite] Mesha stone, which dates from the ninth century B.C. And finally, even if the name YHWH were the name of some Babylonian deity, the meaning of that name and the deity denoted by it would be totally different to Israel, for here YHWH is the God of Israel and at the same time the only God, the Creator of heaven and earth.[154]

Now, as to the etymology of the name, it is rather generally assumed that it refers back to the stem *hwh* (הוה) or *hyh* (היה), and there is disagreement only over the question whether it is the third person imperfect tense of Qal or of Hiphil (the pronunciation *Yaho* advocated by von Hartmann[155] merits no consideration).[156] The latter choice (Hiphil) is defended by Gesenius, Schrader, Lagarde, Schultz, Land, Kuenen,[157] actually only on the ground that in their view such a sublime concept of God as comes through in the Qal form is not yet conceivable in the time of Moses. According to them, the name YHWH does not mean "he who is," but "he who causes to be, who bestows life," the Creator. But Smend observes (correctly, in light of his position) that even this name is still much too sublime for that time, and also calls this explanation highly improbable because the Hiphil form of the verb הוה occurs nowhere.[158] Hence, the only remaining derivation is that given in Exodus 3.

154. H. H. Kuyper, *Evolutie of Revelatie* (Amsterdam: Höveker & Wormser, 1903), 95; Robertson, *Theology of the Old Testament,* 52; J. Orr, *The Problem of the Old Testament,* 221ff.

155. E. von Hartmann, *Religionsphilosophie,* 2 vols. (Bad Sachsa im Harz: Hermann Haacke, 1907), I, 370ff.

156. A. Kuenen, *Volksgodsdienst en Wereldgodsdienst* (Leiden: S. C. Van Doesburgh, 1882), 261ff.

157. A. Kuenen, *Godsdienst van Israel,* I, 275.

158. R. Smend, *Lehrbuch der alttestamentlichen Religionsgeschichte,* 21.

Yet even then there is still disagreement over the meaning of the name. The church fathers thought it referred to God's aseity. God is the One who *is,* an eternal immutable being, over against the factual nonbeing (οὐκ ὄν) of idols and the nonabsolute being (μη ὄν) of creatures. Other scholars, such as W. R. Smith and Smend, appealing to Exodus 3:12, take the name to be "he who will be *with you.*" Both of these interpretations are unacceptable, the latter because if it were correct the addition "with you" (עִמָּךְ) could not be absent, and the former because it has too philosophical a ring to it and lacks support in Exodus 3. In verses 13–15, after all, the meaning of the name is clearly indicated. In full it reads: אֶהְיֶה אֲשֶׁר אֶהְיֶה; by it the Lord says that he who now calls Moses and wants to save his people is the same [God] as he who appeared to their fathers. He is who he is, the same yesterday, today, and forever. This meaning is further explained in verse 15: YHWH—the God of your fathers, the God of Abraham, Isaac, and Jacob—sends Moses, and that is his name forever. God does not simply call himself "the One who is" and offer no explanation of his aseity, but states expressly what and how he is. Then how and what will he be? That is not something one can say in a word or describe in an additional phrase, but "he will be what he will be." That sums up everything. This addition is still general and indefinite, but for that reason also rich and full of deep meaning. He will be what he was for the patriarchs, what he is now and will remain: he will be everything to and for his people. It is not a new and strange God who comes to them by Moses, but the God of the fathers, the Unchangeable One, the Faithful One, the eternally Self-consistent One, who never leaves or forsakes his people but always again seeks out and saves his own. He is unchangeable in his grace, in his love, in his assistance, who will be what he is because he is always himself. So in Isaiah he calls himself: "I am he, the first and the last" (אֲנִי הוּא, 41:4; 43:10, 13, 25; 44:6; 48:12). And indeed, his aseity underlies this view of God, but it is not in the foreground nor directly expressed in the name.

From this explanation it is also clear whether and how far the name YHWH was already known before the time of Moses. Exodus 6:3 does not say that the name as such was communicated to Moses, but that the Lord had not been known to the fathers by that name. Accordingly, the name is found repeatedly before Exodus 6, occurs in numerous proper names (Jochebed, Ahijah, Abijah, 1 Chron. 2:24–25). It could not be a totally new and unfamiliar name since Moses, in order to get a hearing among his people, obviously could not come to them with a new name but had to act in the name of the God of the fathers (Exod. 3:12, 15). The intent of Exodus 6:3, therefore, has to be that now for the first time the Lord himself made known to Moses the meaning of this name. And the facts support this explanation. Not until Exodus 3 did the Lord himself give an explanation of this name; here he tells Moses how he wants people to understand it. Certainly it existed before this time, had already been used repeatedly by the Lord himself (Gen. 15:7; 28:13), and was current as a name of address (Gen. 14:22; 15:2, 8; 24:3; 28:16; 32:9). But nowhere do we find an explanation of it.

In the abstract it is very well possible that originally, in its derivation, the name YHWH meant something very different from what is stated in Exodus 3. Exodus 3 gives not the etymology of a word but the explanation of a name. Just as in his special revelation to Israel God had taken over an assortment of religious practices (circumcision, Sabbath, sacrifice, priesthood, etc.) and given them a special meaning, so he does here with this name. Aside from its provenance and original meaning the Lord states in Exodus 6 how and in what sense he is YHWH, the "I will be who I will be." From this point on the name YHWH is the description and guarantee of the fact that God is and remains the God of his people, unchanging in his grace and faithfulness. And that is something that could not have been disclosed before the time of Moses. A long time had to pass to prove that God is faithful and unchanging. A person's faithfulness can only be tested in the long run and especially in times of distress. So it was also in the case of Israel. Centuries had elapsed following the period of the patriarchs. Israel had been oppressed and had experienced great distress. Now God says: "I am who I am, YHWH, the unchangingly faithful One, the God of the fathers, your God even now and forever." At this point God injects a totally fresh meaning into an old name, one that could only now be understood by the people. And for that reason YHWH is Israel's God "from the land of Egypt" (Hos. 12:9; 13:4).

YHWH *Sabaoth*

[190] In the Old Testament the name YHWH is the highest revelation of God. No new names are added. YHWH is God's real name (Exod. 15:3; Ps. 83:18; Hos. 12:5; Isa. 42:8). This name is therefore never used for any god other than the God of Israel and never occurs in the construct state, in the plural, or with suffixes. Admittedly, the form of the name is repeatedly modified or heightened in meaning by some kind of addition. Abbreviation produced the forms יֶהוּ, יְהוֹ, יְהָ, יְ, used especially in combinations, and from this process arose the substantive יָהּ. This abbreviated form of the name occurs regularly in the exclamation "Hallelu-yah" (הַלְלוּ־יָהּ), and also independently (Exod. 15:2; Ps. 68:4 [5 MT]; 89:8 [9 MT]; 94:7, 12; 118:14; Isa. 12:2; 38:11), sometimes in connection with YHWH (Isa. 26:4). Also very common is the combination Adonai YHWH (e.g., Ezek. 22:12). The name YHWH receives added force when combined with Sabaoth יהוה צבאות (Ps. 69:6 [7 MT]; 84:1; Hag. 2:7–9); once as יהוה הצבאות (Amos 9:5), really an abbreviation of יהוה אלהי צבאות (1 Sam. 1:3; 4:4; Isa. 1:24) or יהוה אלהים צבאות (Ps. 80:4 [5 MT]; 84:8 [9 MT]). Because Sabaoth is linked with YHWH, which does not permit the construct state, and sometimes with Elohim in the absolute state, Origen, Jerome, and others concluded that Sabaoth was appositive. They were confirmed in this opinion by the fact that in the LXX, especially in 1 Samuel and Isaiah (cf. Rom. 9:29; James 5:4),

the word was left untranslated.[159] But this opinion is not well founded. In other places Sabaoth is rendered by "the Almighty" or by "Lord of powers," and the name of YHWH who *is* Sabaoth (armies, hosts) does not yield any sense.

It is hard to say, however, what precisely is meant by the word "Sabaoth." Some, associating it with the armies of Israel, think that the name "Lord of hosts" refers to God as the God of war. But most of the verses cited in support (such as 1 Sam. 1:3, 11; 4:4; 15:2; 17:45; 2 Sam. 5:10; 6:2, 18; 7:8, 26–27; 1 Kings 17:1; 18:15 LXX; 19:10, 14; 2 Kings 19:31; Ps. 24:10) prove nothing. Only three verses (1 Sam. 4:4; 17:45; 2 Sam. 6:2) offer some semblance of proof, and 2 Kings 19:31 rather conflicts with this notion. Furthermore, while the plural Sabaoth is indeed used with reference to the hosts of the *people* of Israel (Exod. 6:26; 7:4; 12:17, 41, 51; Num. 1:3; 2:3; 10:14; 33:1; Deut. 20:9), the *army* of Israel is always referred to with the singular (Judg. 8:6; 9:29; 2 Sam. 3:23; 8:16; 10:7; 17:25; 20:23; 1 Kings 1:25). Finally, all agree that in the prophets the name "Lord of hosts" no longer has the meaning of God of war, but they leave unanswered the question how and by what circumstances the meaning of the term was so profoundly changed. Others, appealing to such references as Deuteronomy 4:19; Psalm 33:6; Jeremiah 19:13; 33:22; Isaiah 34:4; 40:26; and Nehemiah 9:6, think the word "hosts" refers to the stars of heaven. Smend, expanding this view, thinks the reference includes the powers and elements of the entire cosmos (with an appeal to Gen. 2:1; Ps. 103:21; Isa. 34:1–2). Admittedly, Scripture repeatedly speaks of the stars as the hosts of heaven (Deut. 4:19) and of all creatures collectively as the host of heaven and earth (Gen. 2:1). But (1) in that case only the singular is used and never the plural; (2) the stars are indeed called "the host of heaven" but never "the army of God"; and (3) the term "host" is indeed used to refer to all creatures, but never to such an abstract notion as "the powers and elements of the cosmos."

The implausibility of these new explanations enhances the value of the old interpretation which, in reading "hosts," thought of angels. And this interpretation finds abundant support in Scripture. The name "Lord of hosts" is repeatedly used with reference to angels (1 Sam. 4:4; 2 Sam. 6:2; Isa. 37:16; Hos. 12:5–6; Ps. 80:1 [2 MT], 4f.; 89:5–8 [6–9 MT]) and the angels are frequently pictured as a "host" surrounding the throne of God (Gen. 28:12–13; 32:1–2; Josh. 5:14; 1 Kings 22:19; Job 1:6; Ps. 68:17 [18 MT]; 89:8 [9 MT]; 103:21; 148:2; Isa. 6:2). Although Scripture usually speaks of a host (sing.) of angels, this is not a problem because Scripture also repeatedly mentions many hosts of angels (Gen. 32:2; Deut. 33:2; Ps. 68:17; 148:2). This fits the meaning of the name, which has absolutely no warlike or martial character (this cannot even be inferred from 1 Sam. 4:4; 17:45; 2 Sam. 6:2), but everywhere expresses the glory of God as king (Deut. 33:2; 1 Kings 22:19; Ps. 24:10; Isa.

159. B. de Moor, *Comm. in Marckii Comp.*, I, 512.

6:2; 24:23; Zech. 1:14; 14:16). The angels belong to the glory (δοξα) of God or of Christ: they heighten and expand it (Matt. 25:31; Mark 8:38; 2 Thess. 1:7; Rev. 7:11). Throughout the Scriptures "YHWH Sabaoth" is the solemn royal name of God, full of majesty and glory. The name *Elohim* denotes God as Creator and Sustainer of all things; *El Shaddai* represents him as the mighty One who makes nature subservient to grace; *YHWH* describes him as the One who in his grace remains forever faithful; *YHWH Sabaoth* characterizes him as king in the fullness of his glory who, surrounded by regimented hosts of angels, governs throughout the world as the Almighty, and in his temple receives the honor and acclamation of all his creatures.[160]

[191] In the New Testament all these names have been retained. El and Elohim are rendered by God (θεος), Elyon is translated by "the Most High" (ὑψιστος θεος, Mark 5:7; Luke 1:32, 35, 76; 8:28; Acts 7:48; 16:17; Heb. 7:1; cf. Luke 2:14, "God in the highest," ἐν ὑψιστοις θεῳ). Also, the appellation of God as the "God of Abraham, Isaac, and Jacob" or as "the God of Israel" passes into the New Testament (Matt. 15:31; 22:32; Mark 12:26; Luke 1:68; 20:37; Acts 3:13; 7:32, 46; 22:14; 24:14; Heb. 11:16). As a rule, however, these appositions are replaced by the genitives "my," "your," "our," "your" (pl.), for in Christ God has become the God and Father of his people and of each of his children (Heb. 8:10; Rev. 7:12; 19:5; 21:3). The name YHWH is explicated a few times as "the Alpha and the Omega," "him who is and who was and who is to come," "the beginning and the end," "the first and the last" (Rev. 1:4, 8, 11 [KJV], 17; 2:8; 21:6; 22:13). For the rest, following the example of the LXX, which already read Adonai, the name YHWH is translated by Lord (Κυριος, derived from κυρος, strength). Lord, or Κυριος, makes God known as the Mighty One, the Lord, Owner, and Ruler who *legally* exercises power and authority (in distinction from the δεσποτης who *actually* exercises power), and in the NT Lord is variably used both of God and of Christ.[161] Also the combinations "YHWH Elohim" and "YHWH Elohim Sabaoth" are found again in the New Testament, as "Lord God" (Luke 1:16; Acts 7:37; 1 Pet. 3:15; Rev. 1:8; 22:5) and "Lord God Almighty" (Rev. 4:8; 11:17; 15:3; 16:7; 21:22), while in Romans 9:29 and James 5:4 "Sabaoth (hosts)" remains untranslated.

160. Cf. further concerning "JHWH Sabaoth," F. Delitzsch, "Die neue Mode der Herleitung des Gottes-namens," *Lutherische Zeitschrift* (1877). On Psalm 24:10, see E. Schrader, "Semitismus und Babylonismus," *Jahrbücher für protestantische Theologie* 1 (1875): 316–20; G. Oehler, *Theology of the Old Testament*, §195ff.; R. Smend, *Lehrbuch der alttestamentlichen Religionsgeschichte*, 185ff.; Eduard König, *Das Hauptproblem der altisraëlitischen Religionsgeschichte* (Leipzig: J. C. Hinrichs, 1884), 49ff.; A. Kuenen, *Godsdienst van Israël*, II, 46; B. Stade, *Geschichte des Volkes Israel*, 2 vols. (Berlin: Baumgärtel, 1887), I, 437; J. J. P. Valeton Jr., "De Israëlitische Godsnaam," 208ff.; E. Raubsch, "Zebaoth," *PRE²*, XVIII, 720; E. Riehm, *Handwörterbuch des biblischen Altertums für gebildete Bibelleser*, 2 vols. (Bielefield and Leipzig: Velhagen & Klasing, 1884), s.v. "Zebaoth"; Borchert, "Der Gottes Name Jahre Zebaoth," *Theoloische Studien und Kritiken* 68 (1896): 619–42.

161. S. Herner, *Die Anwendung des Wortes κυριος im Neuestestament* (Lund: E. Malström, 1903).

Father

One new name seems to have been added in the New Testament, the name Father (Πατηρ). Yet this name for the Deity also occurs in pagan religions[162] and is already used several times of God in the Old Testament (Deut. 32:6; Ps. 103:13; Isa. 63:16; 64:8; Jer. 3:4, 19; 31:9; Mal. 1:6; 2:10), just as Israel is also repeatedly called his Son (Exod. 4:22; Deut. 14:1; 32:19; Isa. 1:2; Jer. 31:20; Hos. 1:10; 11:1). The name "Father" expresses the special theocratic relation that God sustains to his people Israel. He has marvelously formed that people out of Abraham. In the more general sense of Origin and Creator the name "Father" is used in 1 Corinthians 8:6; Ephesians 3:14–15; Hebrews 12:9; and James 1:17 (cf. Luke 3:38; Acts 17:28). But above all the name expresses the ethical relation in which God, through Christ, now stands to all his children. The relation that existed in the Old Testament between God and Israel is the type and model of this. But now that relation has been deepened and expanded, made personal, ethical, individual.

The name "Father" is now the common name of God in the New Testament. The name YHWH is inadequately conveyed by Lord (κυριος) and is, as it were, supplemented by the name "Father." This name is the supreme revelation of God. God is not only the Creator, the Almighty, the Faithful One, the King and Lord; he is also the Father of his people. The theocratic kingdom known in Israel passes into a kingdom of the Father who is in heaven. Its subjects are at the same time children; its citizens are members of the family. Both law and love, the state and the family, are completely realized in the New Testament relation of God to his people. Here we find perfect kingship, for here is a king who is simultaneously a Father who does not subdue his subjects by force but who himself creates and preserves his subjects. As children, they are born of him; they bear his image; they are his family. According to the New Testament, this relation has been made possible by Christ, who is the true, only-begotten, and beloved Son of the Father. And believers obtain adoption as children and also become conscious of it by the agency of the Holy Spirit (John 3:5, 8; Rom. 8:15f.). God has most abundantly revealed himself in the name "Father, Son, and Holy Spirit." The fullness that from the beginning inhered in the name Elohim has gradually unfolded and become most fully and splendidly manifest in the trinitarian name of God.

---

162. W. Robertson Smith, *Die Religion der Semiten*, 27ff.

4

GOD'S INCOMMUNICABLE ATTRIBUTES

Scripture itself reveals the general attributes of God's nature before, and more clearly than, it reveals his trinitarian existence. God is independent, *all-sufficient in himself, and the only source of all existence and life.* YHWH *is the name that describes this essence and identity most clearly: "I will be what I will be." It is in this aseity of God, conceived not only as having being from himself but also as the fullness of being, that all other divine perfections are included.*

Immutability *is a natural implication of God's aseity. While everything changes, God is and remains the same. If God were not immutable, he would not be God. To God alone belongs true being, and that which truly* is *remains. Contrary to both Deism and pantheism God who* is *cannot change, for every change would diminish his being. This doctrine of God's immutability is important; the very distinction between Creator and creature hinges on the contrast between being and becoming. Our reliance on God depends on his immutability. Philosophic notions of absolute becoming have no place in Christian theology, nor should immutability be understood in static philosophic terms. The unchanging God is related to his creatures in manifold ways and participates in their lives. God is transcendent and immanent. Without losing himself he can give himself and, while absolutely maintaining his immutability, he can enter into an infinite number of relations to his creatures.*

When applied to time, God's immutability (or infinity) is called *eternity; when applied to space it is called* omnipresence. *Properly understood, infinity is not a philosophical notion obtained negatively by abstraction from finite things. God is positively infinite in his characteristic essence, absolutely perfect, infinite in an intensive, qualitative sense.*

God's *eternity, contrary to Deism, is qualitative and not merely quantitatively an infinite extension of time. Christian theology must also avoid the error of pantheism, which simply considers eternity as the substance or essence of time itself. Eternity excludes a beginning, an end, and succession of moments. God is unbegotten, incorruptible, and immutable. Time is the mode of existence of all finite creatures. God, on the other hand, is the eternal I AM, who is without beginning or end and not subject to measuring or counting in his duration. God's eternity, however, is not static or immobile but fullness of being, present and immanent in every moment of time. God pervades time and every moment of time with his eternity; he maintains a definite relation to time, entering into it with his eternity.*

Infinity in the sense of not being confined by space is synonymous with God's omnipresence. While heaven and earth cannot contain God, neither can he be excluded from space. Rather, he fills heaven and earth with his presence. This omnipresence includes God's being as well as his power. God is not "somewhere," yet he fills heaven and earth; he is uniquely a place of his own to himself. Here again, we need to remind ourselves that in each attribute we speak of God in human terms. God relates to space as the infinite One who, existing within himself, also fills to repletion every point of space and sustains it by his immensity.

The last of God's incommunicable attributes, his oneness, is differentiated into the unity of singularity and the unity of simplicity. God is numerically and quantitatively one, absolutely and exclusively. Evolutionist views of development from polytheism to monotheism in the Old Testament are untenable. Scripture is monotheistic from beginning to end. Polytheism fails to satisfy the human spirit; only confession about the one true God sustains religion, truth, and morality.

The unity of simplicity insists that God is not only truthful and righteous, loving and wise, but the truth, righteousness, love, and wisdom. On account of its absolute perfection, every attribute of God is identical with his essence. Though sometimes opposed on philosophical grounds, the doctrine of divine simplicity is of great importance for our understanding of God. If God is in any sense composite, then it is impossible to maintain the perfection of his oneness, independence, and immutability. Simplicity is not a philosophic abstraction but the end result of ascribing to God all the perfections of creatures to the ultimate divine degree. It is necessary as a way of affirming that God has a distinct and infinite life of his own within himself. Nor is simplicity inconsistent with the doctrine of the Trinity, for the term "simple" is not an antonym of "twofold" or "threefold" but of "composite." God is not composed of three persons, nor is each person composed of the being and personal attributes of that person, but the one uncompounded (simple) being of God exists in three persons.

[192] In the work of some theologians the locus of the Trinity precedes that of the attributes of God; and Frank even has serious objections to the reverse order.[1] If treating the attributes of God before the doctrine of the Trinity implied a desire to gradually proceed from "natural" to "revealed" theology, from a natural to the Christian concept of God, then this procedure would undoubtedly be objectionable. But this is by no means the case. In the doctrine of the

---

1. John of Damascus, *The Orthodox Faith*, I, 6ff.; P. Lombard, *Sent.*, I, dist. 2ff.; Bonaventure, *Breviloquium*, I, 2ff.; P. M. Vermigli, *Loci comm.*, 36ff.; F. H. R. Frank, *System der christlichen Wahrheit*, 2 vols. (Erlangen: A. Deichert, 1878–80), I, 151ff.; A. von Oettingen, *Lutherische Dogmatik* (Munich: C. H. Beck, 1897–1902), II, 243ff.

attributes of God the tradition includes the treatment of the divine nature as it is revealed to us in Scripture, is confessed by the Christian faith, and exists—as will be evident in the locus of the Trinity—in a threefold manner. In order for us to understand in the locus of the Trinity that Father, Son, and Spirit share in the same divine nature, it is necessary for us to know what that divine nature comprises and in what ways it differs from every created nature.

In this matter of order, too, Scripture is our model. In Scripture the nature of God is shown us earlier and more clearly than his trinitarian existence. The Trinity is not clearly revealed until we get to the New Testament. The names YHWH and Elohim precede those of Father, Son, and Spirit. The first thing Scripture teaches us concerning God is that he has a free, independent existence and life of his own that is distinct from all creatures. He has a being ("nature," "substance," "essence") of his own, not in distinction from his attributes, but coming to the fore and disclosing itself *in* all his perfections and attributes. He bears his own names—names that do not belong to any creature. Among these names that of YHWH stands supreme (Exod. 3:14–15). This name describes him as the One who is and will always be what he was, that is, who eternally remains the same in relation to his people. He is self-existent. He existed before all things, and all things exist only through him (Ps. 90:2; 1 Cor. 8:6; Rev. 4:11). In an absolute sense he is Lord (אָדוֹן, κυριος, δεσποτης), Lord of all the earth (Exod. 23:17; Deut. 10:17; Josh. 3:13). He is dependent on nothing, but everything depends on him (Rom. 11:36). He kills and makes alive; he forms the light and creates the darkness; he makes weal and creates woe (Deut. 32:39; Isa. 45:5–7; 54:16). He does according to his will with the host of heaven and the inhabitants of the earth (Dan. 4:35), so that people are in his hand as clay in the hands of a potter (Isa. 64:8; Jer. 18:1ff.; Rom. 9:21). His counsel and good pleasure is the ultimate ground of all that is and happens (Ps. 33:11; Prov. 19:21; Isa. 46:10; Matt. 11:26; Acts 2:23; 4:28; Eph. 1:5, 9, 11). Accordingly, he does all things for his own sake, for the sake of his name and praise (Deut. 32:27; Josh. 7:9; 1 Sam. 12:22; Ps. 25:11; 31:3; 79:9; 106:8; 109:21; 143:11; Prov. 16:4; Isa. 48:9; Jer. 14:7, 21; Ezek. 20:9, 14, 22, 44). Nor does he need anything, for he is all-sufficient (Job 22:2–3; Ps. 50:19ff.; Acts 17:25) and has life in himself (John 5:26). Thus he is the first and the last, the alpha and the omega, who is and who was and who is to come (Isa. 41:4; 44:6; 48:12; Rev. 1:8); absolutely independent, not only in his existence but consequently also in all his attributes and perfections, in all his decrees and deeds. He is independent in his intellect (Rom. 11:34–35), in his will (Dan. 4:35; Rom. 9:19; Eph. 1:5; Rev. 4:11), in his counsel (Ps. 33:11; Isa. 46:10), in his love (Hos. 14:4), in his power (Ps. 115:3), and so forth. Thus, being all-sufficient in himself and not receiving anything from outside of himself, he is, by contrast, the only source of all existence and life, of all light and love, the overflowing fountain of all good (Ps. 36:10; Acts 17:25).

INDEPENDENCE

Now this independence of God is more or less recognized by all humans. Pagans, to be sure, degrade the divine by drawing it down to the level of the creature and teach a theogony; however, behind and above their gods they often again assume the existence of a power to which everything is subject in an absolute sense. Many of them speak of nature, chance, fate, or fortune as a power superior to all else; and philosophers tend to speak of God as the Absolute. In Christian theology this attribute of God was called his independence (αὐτάρκεια), aseity, all-sufficiency, greatness. In the East, a number of terms were used: "(θεος ἀναρχος) God, without beginning or cause, unbegotten," and theologians preferably spoke of God as "(αὐτογεννητος) the self-generate, (αὐτο-φυης) self-begotten, (αὐτουσιος) self-existent, (αὐτοθεος) self-divine, (αὐτοφως) self-luminous, (αὐτοσοφια) self-wise, (αὐτοαρετη) self-virtuous, (αὐταγαθος) self-excellent, and so on."[2] All that God is, he is of himself. By virtue of himself he is goodness, holiness, wisdom, life, light, truth, and so on. As stated earlier, the church fathers usually followed Philo in grounding their description of God in the name YHWH. That was the name that described his essence par excellence. God was the Existent One. His whole identity was wrapped up in the name: "I will be what I will be." All God's other perfections are derived from this name. He is supreme *(summum)* in everything: supreme being *(esse),* supreme goodness *(bonum),* supreme truth *(verum),* supreme beauty *(pulchrum).* He is the perfect, highest, the most excellent being, "than whom nothing better can exist or be thought." All being is contained in him. He is a boundless ocean of being. "If you have said of God that he is good, great, blessed, wise or any other such quality, it is summed up in a single word: *he is (Est).* Indeed, for him to *be* is to be all these things. Even if you add a hundred such qualities, you have not gone outside the boundaries of his being. Having said them all, you have added nothing; having said none of them, you have subtracted nothing."[3] Scholasticism as a whole fell in line with this view,[4] also treating this attribute under the name of the "infinity" or "spiritual greatness" of God,[5] or under that of the "aseity" of God, meaning that as the "supreme substance," God is "what he is through or by his own self."[6] Later Roman Catholic theologians as a rule also proceeded from this aseity or independence.[7]

2. Cf. J. C. Suicerus, *Thesaurus ecclesiasticus,* s.v. "αὐταρκεια."

3. Bernard de Clairvaux, *De consideratione* (Utrecht: Nicolaus Ketelaer and Gerhardus Leempt, 1473), I, 5, ch. 6.

4. Anselm, *Monologion,* 6; P. Lombard, *Sent.,* I, dist. 8; T. Aquinas, *Summa theol.,* I, qu. 2, art. 3; I, qu. 13, art. 11; idem, *Summa contra gentiles,* I, 43.

5. T. Aquinas, *Summa theol.,* I, qu. 7; idem, *Summa contra gentiles,* I, 43.

6. Anselm, *Monologion,* 6.

7. Dionysius Petavius, "De Deo deique proprietabus," in *De theologicis dogmatibus,* I, ch. 6; *Theologia Wirceburgensi,* III, 38ff.; G. Perrone, *Prael. theol.,* II, 88–90; J. B. Heinrich, *Dogmatische Theologie,* III, 326; G. Jansen, *Prael. theol.,* II, 26ff. A. Straub, in several articles on "Die Aseität Gottes," *Philosophisches Jahrbuch* 16–17 (1903–4), properly distinguishes, speaking of the divine essence as basic metaphysical being (*ens metaphysicum*) and aseity as the first attribute of that being.

In this regard the Reformation introduced no change. Luther, too, on the basis of name YHWH, described God as the absolutely existent one and as pure being. Yet, refusing to dwell on abstract metaphysical descriptions, Luther swiftly passed from "the hidden God" *(Deus absconditus)* to the "God revealed in Christ" *(Deus revelatus in Christo)*.[8] Melanchthon in his *Loci* describes God as "spiritual essence." While Lutherans usually adopted this description, they often added the qualifying words "infinite," "subsisting of himself," or "independent."[9] Among the Reformed this perfection of God comes more emphatically to the fore, though the word "aseity" was soon exchanged for that of "independence." While aseity only expresses God's self-sufficiency in his existence, independence has a broader sense and implies that God is independent in everything: in his existence, in his perfections, in his decrees, and in his works. Accordingly, while in the past theologians mostly used the name YHWH as their starting point,[10] in later years God's independence occurs most often as the first of the incommunicable attributes.[11]

Now when God ascribes this aseity to himself in Scripture, he makes himself known as absolute being, as the one who *is* in an absolute sense. By this perfection he is at once essentially and absolutely distinct from all creatures. Creatures, after all, do not derive their existence from themselves but from others and so have nothing from themselves; both in their origin and hence in their further development and life, they are absolutely dependent. But as is evident from the word "aseity," God is exclusively from himself, not in the sense of being self-caused but being from eternity to eternity who he is, being not becoming. God is absolute being, the fullness of being, and therefore also eternally and absolutely independent in his existence, in his perfections, in all his works, the first and the last, the sole cause and final goal of all things. In this aseity of God, conceived not only as having being from himself but also as the fullness of being, all the other perfections are included. They are given with the aseity itself and are the rich and multifaceted development of it. Yet, whereas in the case of this perfection the immeasurable distinction between the Creator and creature stands out vividly and plainly, there is nevertheless a weak analogy in all creatures also of this perfection of God. Pantheism, indeed, cannot acknowledge this, but theism stands for the fact that a creature, though absolutely dependent, nevertheless also has a distinct existence of its own. And implanted in this existence there is "a drive toward self-preservation." Every creature, to the extent that it shares in existence, fears death,

8. J. Köstlin, *Luthers Theologie in ihrer geschichtilichen Entwicklung und ihrem inneren Zusammenhange,* 2d ed., 2 vols. (Stuttgart: J. F. Steinkopf, 1901), II, 302ff.

9. H. F. F. Schmid, *The Doctrinal Theology of the Evangelical Lutheran Church,* trans. Charles A. Hay and Henry Jacobs, 5th ed. (Philadelphia: United Lutheran Publication House, 1899), §17.

10. A. Hyperius, *Methodi theologiae moralis,* 87, 135; Georg Sohn, *Opera sacrae theologiae,* II, 48; III, 261; Amandus Polanus, *Syn. theol.,* 135.

11. Peter van Mastricht, *Theologia,* II, 3; J. H. Heidegger, *Corpus theologiae christianae,* III, 30; S. Maresius, *Systema theologicum* (Groningen: Aemilium Spinneker, 1673), 2, §17; Johannes á Marck, *Het Merch der christene Got-geleerheit* (Rotterdam: Nicolaas en Paulus Topyn, 1741), IV, §20; L. Meijer, *Verhandelingen over de goddelyke Wigenschappen,* 4 vols. (Groningen: Jacob Bolt, 1783), I, 39–110.

and even the tiniest atom offers resistance to all attempts at annihilating it. Again: it is a shadow of the independent, immutable being of our God.

IMMUTABILITY

[193] A natural implication of God's aseity is his immutability. At first blush this immutability seems to have little support in Scripture. For there God is seen as standing in the most vital association with the world. In the beginning he created heaven and earth and so moved from not creating to creating. And from that beginning he is, as it were, a coparticipant in the life of the world and especially of his people Israel. He comes and goes, reveals and conceals himself. He averts his face [in wrath] and turns it back to us in grace. He repents (Gen. 6:6; 1 Sam. 15:11; Amos 7:3, 6; Joel 2:13; Jon. 3:9; 4:2) and changes plans (Exod. 32:10–14; Jon. 3:10). He becomes angry (Num. 11:1, 10; Ps. 106:40; Zech. 10:3) and sets aside his anger (Deut. 13:17; 2 Chron. 12:12; 30:8; Jer. 18:8, 10; 26:3, 19; 36:3). His attitude toward the pious is one thing, his disposition to the ungodly another (Prov. 11:20; 12:22). With the pure he is pure; with the crooked he shows himself a shrewd opponent[12] (Ps. 18:26–27). In the fullness of time he even becomes human in Christ and proceeds to dwell in the church through the Holy Spirit. He rejects Israel and accepts the Gentiles. And in the life of the children of God there is a consistent alternation of feelings of guilt and the consciousness of forgiveness, of experiences of God's wrath and of his love, of his abandonment and his presence.

At the same time the Scriptures testify that amid all this alternation God is and remains the same. Everything changes, but he remains standing. He remains who he is (Ps. 102:26–28). He is YHWH, he who is and ever remains himself. He is the first and with the last he is still the same God (Isa. 41:4; 43:10; 46:4; 48:12). He is who he is (Deut. 32:39; cf. John 8:58; Heb. 13:8), the incorruptible who alone has immortality, and is always the same (Rom. 1:23; 1 Tim. 1:17; 6:16; Heb. 1:11–12). Unchangeable in his existence and being, he is so also in his thought and will, in all his plans and decisions. He is not a human that he should lie or repent. What he says, he will do (Num. 15:28; 1 Sam. 15:29). His gifts (charismata) and calling are irrevocable (Rom. 11:29). He does not reject his people (Rom. 11:1). He completes what he has begun (Ps. 138:8; Phil. 1:6). In a word, he, YHWH, does not change (Mal. 3:6). In him there is "no variation or shadow due to change" (James 1:17).

On this foundation Christian theology constructed its doctrine of divine immutability. Mythological theogony could not attain to this level, but philosophy frequently named and described God as the unique, eternal, immutable, unmoved, and self-consistent Ruler over all things.[13] From the presence of

12. Ed. note: This translation adds to the NIV ("shrewd") the notion of Bavinck's original *Statenvertaling: worstelaar* (wrestler).

13. Philolaus et al., according to E. Zeller, *Philosophie der Griechen*, 4th ed, I, 425, 488; II, 928. Ed. note: ET: *The Stoics, Epicureans, and Sceptics*, trans. Oswald J. Reichel (New York: Russell & Russell, 1962).

motion in the universe Aristotle inferred the existence of a "first mover," an "everlasting immovable being," who is one and eternal, necessary, immutable, free from all composition, devoid of potentiality, matter, change; and who is pure act, pure form, unadulterated essence, absolute form, "the very nature of a thing, primary substance."[14] Philo called God "unchangeable, self-consistent, invariable, steadfast, firm, fixed, unalterable."[15] And with this assessment Christian theology concurred. God, according to Irenaeus, is always the same, self-identical.[16] In Augustine, God's immutability flows directly from the fact that he is supreme and perfect being: "It is instinctual for every rational creature to think that there is an altogether unchangeable and incorruptible God."[17] This concept of an eternal and unchangeable being cannot be obtained by the senses, for all creatures, also humans themselves, are changeable; but within their souls humans see and find the immutable something that is better and greater than all the things that are subject to change.

If God were not immutable, he would not be God.[18] His name is "being," and this name is "an unalterable name." All that changes ceases to be what it was. But true being belongs to him who does not change. That which truly *is* remains. That which changes "was something and will be something but *is* not anything because it is mutable."[19] But God who *is* cannot change, for every change would diminish his being. Furthermore, God is as immutable in his knowing, willing, and decreeing as he is in his being. "The essence of God by which he is what he is, possesses nothing changeable, neither in eternity, nor in truthfulness, nor in will."[20] As he is, so he knows and wills—immutably. "For even as you totally are, so do you alone totally know, for you immutably are, and you know immutably, and you will immutably. Your essence knows and wills immutably, and your knowledge is and wills immutably, and your will is and knows immutably."[21] Neither creation, nor revelation, nor incarnation (affects, etc.) brought about any change in God. No new plan ever arose in God. In God there was always one single immutable will. "[In God the former purpose is not altered and obliterated by the subsequent and different purpose, but] by one and the same eternal and unchangeable will he effected regarding the things he created, both that formerly, so long as they were not, they should not be, and that subsequently, when they began to be, they should come into existence." In creatures the only change is from nonbeing to being, from good to evil.[22] The same idea comes back repeatedly in the scholastics

14. E. Zeller, *Philosophie der Griechen*, 4th ed., II, 359–65.

15. A. F. Dähne, *Geschichtliche Darstellung der jüdisch-alexandrinischen Religions-Philosophie*, 2 vols. (Halle: Verlag der Buchhandlung des Waisenhauses, 1834), I, 118.

16. Irenaeus, *Against Heresies*, IV, 11; Origen, *Contra Celsus*, I, 21; IV, 14.

17. Augustine, *Literal Meaning of Genesis*, VII, 11.

18. Idem, *On Grace and Free Will*, II, 6; idem, *On Christian Doctrine*, I, 9; idem, *Confessions*, VII, 4.

19. Idem, *The Trinity*, V, 2.

20. Ibid., IV.

21. Idem, *Confessions*, XIII, 16.

22. Idem, *De ordine*, II, 17; idem, *City of God*, XII, 17.

and Roman Catholic theologians[23] as well as in the works of Lutheran and Reformed theologians.[24]

This immutability of God, however, was frequently combated from the side of both Deism and pantheism. In the opinion of Epicurus the gods totally resemble excellent human beings, who make changes with respect to location, activity, and thought (etc.); and according to Heraclitus and later the Stoics, the deity as the immanent cause of the world was also caught up in its perpetual flux.[25] Opposition to God's immutability in Christian theology was of the same nature. On the one hand, there is the Pelagianism, Socinianism, Remonstrantism, and rationalism, which especially opposes the immutability of God's knowing and willing and makes the will of God dependent on—and hence change in accordance with—the conduct of humans. Especially Vorstius, in his work *On God and His Attributes,* criticized the immutability of God. He made a distinction between God's essence, which is simple and unchangeable, and God's will, which being free does not will everything eternally and does not always will the same thing.[26]

Much more serious even is the opposition to God's immutability from the side of pantheism. Common to all pantheistic criticism is that the idea of becoming is transferred to God, thus totally obliterating the boundary line between the Creator and the creature. The idea of God as "substance," as it occurs in Spinoza, proved to be an abstraction devoid of content. In order to breathe life into that concept, philosophy frequently substituted "becoming" for "being." In that connection it makes a big difference, naturally, whether or not this process—by which God himself comes into being—is conceived in unitarian or trinitarian terms and whether it is viewed as occurring immanently in the being of God or transitively in the world. Belonging in this category are, first of all, Gnosticism, but further also the theosophy of the Kabbalah, of Böhme, Schelling, Rothe, Hamberger, and others, having an aftereffect in the doctrine of *kenosis,* and finally the pantheistic philosophy of Fichte, Hegel, Schleiermacher, Schopenhauer, von Hartmann, and others. However variously it may be elaborated, the basic idea is the same: God *is* not, but *becomes.* In and of himself, in the initial moment, he is an "unknown oceanic depth (βυθος ἀγνωστος)," purely abstract potential being, unqualified nature, contentless idea, a dark brooding urge, a blind alogical will—in a word, a form of being that *is* nothing but can *become* anything. But from that mass of potential existence, in the form of a process, God gradually heaves himself into actuality. He is his

23. John of Damascus, *The Orthodox Faith,* I, 8; Thomas, *Summa theologia,* I, qu. 9; P. Lombard, *Sent.,* I, dist. 8, 3; Bonaventure, *Sent.,* I, dist. 8, art. 2, qu. 1–2; D. Petavius, "De Deo," in *Theol. dogm.,* III, chs. 1–2.

24. J. Gerhard, *Loci theol.,* II, c. 8, sect. 5; Jerome Zanchi(us), *Op. theol.,* II, 77–83; A. Polanus, *Syn. theol.,* II, c. 13; cf. Gallican Confession, art. 1; Belgic Confession, art. 1.

25. E. Zeller, *Philosophie der Griechen,* IV, 133ff., 430ff.

26. I. Dorner, *Gesammelte Schriften aus dem Gebiet der systematischen Theologie* (Berlin: W. Hertz, 1883), 278.

own Creator. He produces himself. Very gradually, either within himself or in the world, he matures into personality, self-consciousness, mind, spirit.

Under the influence of this philosophical idea of the Absolute becoming, also modern theology has repeatedly denied or delimited the immutability of God and with a passion favored calling God his own cause *(causa sui)*, a self-actualizing power.[27] As Luthardt puts it: "God is his own deed."[28] Others speak of "God's self-postulation."[29] In a special treatise Dorner, attempting to avoid both Deism and pantheism (acosmism), sought to reconcile God's immutability and his "aliveness."[30] He believes he can achieve this goal by locating God's immutability in the dimension of the ethical. Ethically, God is immutable and always self-consistent. He remains holy love. But for the rest, Dorner believes that as a result of the creation, the incarnation, and the atonement, a change has come about in God; that he stands in a reciprocal relation to humankind, that he only knows reality from his interaction with the world. This means that for God, too, there is a past, a present, and a future; that he becomes angry, justifies; and that in general his disposition corresponds to that of humans.[31] Many theologians on the doctrine of God also refrain from speaking about this important attribute but on the doctrine of creation, or the incarnation, or the kenosis only let their readers know that they accept mutability in God (Ebrard, Hofmann, Thomasius, von Oettingen, et al.).

Nevertheless, the doctrine of God's immutability is highly significant for religion. The difference between the Creator and the creature hinges on the contrast between being and becoming. All that is creaturely is in process of becoming. It is changeable, constantly striving, in search of rest and satisfaction, and finds this rest only in him who is pure being without becoming. This is why, in Scripture, God is so often called the Rock (Deut. 32:4, 15, 18, 30, 31, 37; 1 Sam. 2:2; 2 Sam. 22:3, 32; Ps. 19:14; 31:3; 62:2, 7; 73:26; etc.). We humans can rely on him; he does not change in his being, knowing, or willing. He eternally remains who he is. Every change is foreign to God. In him there is no change in time, for he is eternal; nor in location, for he is omnipresent; nor in essence, for he is pure being. Christian theology frequently

---

27. Richard Rothe, *Theologische Ethik*, 2d rev. ed., 5 vols. (Wittenberg: Zimmermann, 1867–71), §§16–38; H. L. Martensen, *Christian Dogmatics*, trans. W. Urwick (Edinburgh: T. & T. Clark, 1856), 94ff., 124ff.; cf. idem, *Christliche Ethik*, I, 90.

28. C. Luthardt, *Apologetische Vorträge über die Grundwahrheiten des Christenthums* (Leipzig: Dörffling & Franke, 1870), I, 45. Ed. note: ET: *Apologetic Lectures on the Truths of Christianity* (Edinburgh: T. & T. Clark, 1870). Cf. J. Müller, *Die christliche Lehre von der Sünde* (Breslau: J. Max & Co., 1849), 171ff.; Ed. note: ET: *The Christian Doctrine of Sin*, trans. W. Urwick, 5th ed., 2 vols. (Edinburgh: T. & T. Clark, 1868).

29. I. A. Dorner, *A System of Christian Doctrine*, trans. A. Cave and J. Banks, rev. ed., 4 vols. (Edinburgh: T. & T. Clark, 1888–91), I, 258–59; F. H. R. Frank, *System der christlichen Wahrheit*, I, 116.

30. I. A. Dorner, "Über die richtige Fassung des dogmatischen Begriffs der Unveränderlichkeit Gottes," in *Gesammelte Schriften* (1883), 188–377.

31. C. H. Weisse, *Philosophische Dogmatik oder Philosophie des Christentums*, 2 vols. (Leipzig: Hirzel, 1855–62), I, 573; F. A. B. Nitzsch, *Lehrbuch der evangelische Dogmatik*, 3d ed. (Tübingen: J. C. B. Mohr, 1902), 365.

also expressed this last point in the term "pure actuality" *(purus actua)*. Aristotle thus conceived God's being as the "primary form" (reality) without any change (δυναμις), as absolute actuality (ἐνεργεια). Scholasticism, accordingly, began to speak of God as "utterly pure and simple actuality" to indicate that he is perfect and absolute being without any capability *(potentia)* for nonbeing or for being different. Boethius states, for example, that God does not change in essence "because he is pure actuality."[32] For that reason, too, the expression *"causa sui"* (his own cause) was avoided with reference to God.

The idea of the absolute becoming was first clearly voiced by Heraclitus and subsequently recurs again and again in philosophy. Plotinus more than anyone else made use of this concept, applying it not only to matter but also to that which he held to be absolute being. He taught that God had brought forth his own being—that he was active before he existed.[33] Granted, Christian theology indeed spoke of God as "a being who exists of himself" and hence of his aseity. Lactantius, Synesius, and Jerome, moreover, used the expression *"causa sui"* (his own cause). Jerome wrote: "The God who always is does not have any other beginning; he is his own origin and the cause of his own substantiation, nor can any other thing be imagined to exist that stands on its own."[34] But this expression was always understood to mean that, while God existed of himself, he had not become or been brought forth by himself.[35]

Descartes later accorded primacy to the will of God over his intellect and made the essence of all things depend on that will; he indeed made God's existence the product of his own will. Said he: "God in truth preserves himself." God is his own cause and derives from himself—not in a negative but in a positive sense. "God is the efficient cause of his own existence." He derives his being "from the real immensity of his own power."[36] Hearing these things said by him, a few of his followers did adopt this expression *(causa sui)*, but Reformed theologians wanted the expressions ("his own cause," "self-derived existence") interpreted exclusively in a purely negative sense.[37] Being "one's own cause" in a positive sense is an impossibility because in that case the self same object is at one and the same time said to exist, insofar as it produces itself, and not to exist, insofar as it is being produced. Now it is not hard to understand why monistic philosophy should resort to this idea of absolute becoming in order to furnish at least a semblance of an interpretation of reality. But Herbart rightly

---

32. Boethius, *The Consolation of Philosophy*, III; T. Aquinas, *Summa theologiae*, I, qu. 3.

33. C. A. Thilo, *Kurze pragmatische Geschichte der neueren Philosophie* (Cöthen: O. Schulze, 1874), 352ff.

34. Jerome, *Commentary on Ephesians,* in Ronald E. Heine, *The Commentaries of Origen and Jerome on St. Paul's Epistle to the Ephesians* (New York: Oxford University Press, 2002), 156–59 (on Eph. 3:15).

35. H. Klee, *Katholische Dogmatik*, II, 43.

36. René Descartes, *Meditations on First Philosophy,* in *Descartes' Philosophical Writings*, selected and trans. Norman Kemp Smith (London: MacMillan, 1952), 228–31 ("Meditation III").

37. Frans Burmann, *Synopsis theologiae*, I, 15, 2; Leonardus Ryssen, *De oude rechtsinnige waerheyt verdonkert* (Middleburgh: Benedictus Smidt, 1764); Mastricht, *Theoretico-practica theologia*, II, c. 3, §22; Bernhard de Moor, *Comm. in Marckii Comp.*, I, 590ff.

subjected this idea to sharp criticism, and his adherents[38] have not without reason expressed their amazement at the fact that this idea should be so well received in speculative theology. Indeed, the idea of becoming predicated of the divine being is of no help whatever in theology. Not only does Scripture testify that in God there is no variation nor shadow due to change [James 1:17], but reflection on this matter also leads to the same conclusion. Becoming presupposes a cause, for there is no becoming without a cause. But being in an absolute sense no longer permits the inquiry concerning a cause. Absolute being is because it is. The idea of God itself implies immutability. Neither increase nor diminution is conceivable with respect to God. He cannot change for better or worse, for he is the absolute, the complete, the true being. Becoming is an attribute of creatures, a form of change in space and time. But God is who he is, eternally transcendent over space and time and far exalted above every creature. He rests within himself and is for that very reason the ultimate goal and resting place of all creatures, the Rock of their salvation, whose work is complete. Those who predicate any change whatsoever of God, whether with respect to his essence, knowledge, or will, diminish all his attributes: independence, simplicity, eternity, omniscience, and omnipotence. This robs God of his divine nature, and religion of its firm foundation and assured comfort.[39]

This immutability, however, should not be confused with monotonous sameness or rigid immobility. Scripture itself leads us in describing God in the most manifold relations to all his creatures. While immutable in himself, he nevertheless, as it were, lives the life of his creatures and participates in all their changing states. Scripture necessarily speaks of God in anthropomorphic language. Yet, however anthropomorphic its language, it at the same time prohibits us from positing any change in God himself. There is change around, about, and outside of him, and there is change in people's relations to him, but there is no change in God himself. In fact, God's incomprehensible greatness and, by implication, the glory of the Christian confession are precisely that God, though immutable in himself, can call mutable creatures into being. Though eternal in himself, God can nevertheless enter into time and, though immeasurable in himself, he can fill every cubic inch of space with his presence. In other words, though he himself is absolute being, God can give to transient beings a distinct existence of their own. In God's eternity there exists not a moment of time; in his immensity there is not a speck of space; in his being there is no sign of becoming. Conversely, it is God who posits the creature, eternity which posits time, immensity which posits space, being which posits becoming, immutability which posits change. There is nothing

38. C. A. Thilo, *Die Wissenschaftlichkeit der modernen speculativen Theologie in ihren Principien* (Leipzig: Fleischer, 1851), 25; O. Flügel, *Die spekulativ Theologie in der Gegenwart* (Cöthen: O. Schulze, 1888), 201; idem, *Die Probleme der Philosophie und ihre Lösungen* (Cöthen: O. Schulze, 1888), 10; F. A. Trendelenburg, *Logische Untersuchungen* (Hindelsheim: Gg. Olms, 1870), II, 440.

39. Chr. Pesch, "Ist Gott die Ursache seiner selbst?" *Theologische Zeitfragen* (Freiburg: Herder, 1900), 133–67.

intermediate between these two classes of categories: a deep chasm separates God's being from that of all creatures. It is a mark of God's greatness that he can condescend to the level of his creatures and that, though transcendent, he can dwell immanently in all created beings. Without losing himself, God can give himself, and, while absolutely maintaining his immutability, he can enter into an infinite number of relations to his creatures.

Various examples have been employed to illustrate this truth. The sun itself does not change, whether it scorches or warms, hurts or animates (Augustine). A coin remains a coin whether called a price or a pledge (idem). A pillar remains unchanged whether a person sees it on her right or on her left (Thomas). An artist does not change when he gives shape to his inner vision in words or in tone, in voice or in color, nor does a scholar when he puts down his ideas in a book. None of these comparisons is perfect, but they do suggest how a thing may change in its relations while remaining the same in essence. This is especially true of God since he, the immutable One, is himself the sole cause of all that changes. We should not picture God as putting himself in any relation to any creature of his as though it could even in any way exist without him. Rather, he himself puts all things in those relations to himself, which he eternally and immutably wills—precisely in the way in which and at the time at which these relations occur. There is absolutely no "before" or "after" in God; these words apply only to things that did not exist before, but do exist afterward.[40] It is God's immutable being itself that calls into being and onto the stage before him the mutable beings who possess an order and law that is uniquely their own.

INFINITY

[194] When applied to time, God's immutability is called eternity; when applied to space, it is called omnipresence. From time to time the two have been included under the umbrella term of "divine infinity." As such the term "infinity," however, is ambiguous. In the first place, it can be used negatively in the sense of "endless." A thing is called endless when in fact it has no end though conceivably it could have. In philosophy the term has often been applied to God in that sense. Neoplatonism, for example, viewed God in that sense as being without boundary and form, totally indeterminate, boundless, an overflowing fullness from which the universe emanated.[41] Similarly, the Kabbalah spoke of God as the boundless one (אֵין סוֹף), without limit and form, who in the ten sephiroth created intermediate forms between the infinite and the finite.[42] Later, Spinoza's philosophy won acceptance for this concept of God's infinity. Spinoza's "substance," that is, God, is not a being distinct from the world; rather, it is that which constitutes the basic stuff in

---

40. Augustine, *City of God*, XII, 17.
41. E. Zeller, *Philosophie der Griechen*, V, 485ff., 497.
42. Adolphe Franck, *The Kabbalah* (New York: Arno Press, 1973), 179.

creatures and hence is automatically infinite, absolutely undetermined being. All determination, accordingly, is negation, deprivation, a lack of existence. God, however, transcends all limitation and definition. He is nondetermined substance. Extension is one of his attributes.[43] In Hegel this concept of infinity again acquires another meaning because he conceives of Spinoza's substance, not as eternal and immutable being, but as absolute becoming. Hence, God was called infinite because he could become anything and everything, somewhat like "the infinite" (ἄπειρον) in Anaximander's system, which, though itself indeterminate, could produce all sorts of things.

The error of this view is that it takes the lowest common denominator the intellect can obtain from finite things by abstraction and equates this abstraction with the infinite. It was precisely the goal of the philosophy of identity to derive the particular from the general, the specific from the nonspecific, the finite from the infinite, by process thinking. God as such is infinite potentiality; he then becomes finite, personal, conscious, determinate in the creatures, which are his self-manifestation. But this view is untenable. Infinity is not a negative but a positive concept; it means, not that God has no distinct being of his own, but that he is not limited by anything finite and creaturely. Of course, such a denial of creaturely limitation can be variously construed. If one means that God cannot be confined by time, his infinity coincides with his eternity. If one means that God cannot be confined by space, then his infinity coincides with his omnipresence. This in fact is how God's infinity is often defined.[44] But infinity can also be construed in the sense that God is unlimited in his virtues, that in him every virtue is present in an absolute degree. In that case infinity amounts to perfection.[45] But then even this attribute of divine infinity has to be properly understood. This divine infinity is not an infinity of magnitude—in the sense in which people sometimes speak of the infinite or boundless dimensions of the spatial universe—for God is incorporeal and has no extension. Neither is it an infinity of number—as in mathematics we speak of something as being infinitesimally small or infinitely large—for this would conflict with God's oneness and simplicity. But it is an "infinity of essence." God is infinite in his characteristic essence, absolutely perfect, infinite in an intensive, qualitative, and positive sense. So understood, however, God's infinity is synonymous with perfection and does not have to be treated separately.

Eternity

Infinity in the sense of not being determined by time is the eternity of God. Scripture nowhere speaks of a beginning of or an end to God's existence. Though he is often most vividly pictured as entering into time, he still transcends it. He is the first and the last (Isa. 41:4; Rev. 1:8), who existed before the world

---

43. Spinoza, *Ethics*, I, prop. 8.
44. A. Polanus, *Syn. theol.*, II, c. 10–11; J. Zanchi(us), *Op. theol.*, II, 90.
45. T. Aquinas, *Summa theol.*, I, qu. 7.

was (Gen. 1:1; John 1:1; 17:5, 24) and who continues despite all change (Ps. 102:27–28). He is God from eternity to eternity (Ps. 90:2; 93:2). The number of his years is unsearchable (Job 36:26). A thousand years in his sight are as brief as yesterday is to our mind (Ps. 90:4; 2 Pet. 3:8). He is the everlasting God (Isa. 40:28; Rom. 16:26), who inhabits eternity (Isa. 57:15), lives forever and ever (Deut. 32:40; Rev. 10:6; 15:7), swears by his life (Num. 14:21, 28), is called "the living and enduring God" (1 Pet. 1:23), the immortal God (Rom. 1:23; 1 Tim. 6:16), who is and who was and who is to come (Exod. 3:14; Rev. 1:4, 8). Here too, to be sure, Scripture speaks of God in human fashion, and of eternity in the forms of time. At the same time it clearly indicates that God transcends time and cannot be measured or defined by the standards of time. The Deism of past and present, however, defines eternity as time infinitely extended in both directions. According to it, the difference between time and eternity is merely quantitative, not qualitative; gradual, not essential. The difference is not that eternity excludes the succession of moments but that it is without beginning and end. The past, present, and future exist not only for humans but also for and in God. So taught the Socinians[46] and many people after them.[47] Pantheism, on the other hand, similarly confused eternity and time. According to it, God and the world are related as "nature begetting" *(natura naturans)* and "nature begotten" *(natura naturata)*.[48] Eternity, says pantheism, is not essentially distinct from time but rather the "substance," the immanent cause of time, while time is the "mode," the "accident" of eternity, as waves are the incidental forms in which the ocean appears to us. God himself is pulled down into the stream of time and only comes to full relation in time.[49] Strauss voiced this view clearly: "Eternity and time relate to each other as substance and its accidents,"[50] while Schleiermacher cautiously defined God's eternity as "God's absolutely timeless causality, which conditions all that is temporal and even time itself."

Also, with respect to this perfection of God, Christian theology must avoid the errors of both Deism and pantheism. It is of course true that one distinction between eternity and time is that the latter has a beginning and an end (at least potentially) and the former does not. But this does not exhaust the

46. Faustus Socinus, *Praelectiones theologicae* (Racoviae: Sebastiani Sternacii, 1627), c. 8; J. Crell, *Liber deo ejusque attributis*, c. 18; *The Racovian Catechism*, trans. Thomas Rees (London, 1609; reprinted, London, 1818), qu. 60; O. Fock, *Der Socianismus*, 427ff.

47. F. V. Reinhard, *Grundriss der Dogmatik* (Munich: Seidel, 1802), 166; J. A. L. Wegscheider, *Institutiones theologiae christianae dogmaticae*, §63; I. Dorner, *A System of Christian Doctrine*, I, 145ff.; idem, *Gesammelte Schriften*, 322.

48. Spinoza, *Ethics*, I, prop. 29.

49. Spinoza, *Cogitata metaphysica*, I, c. 4; II, c. 1; ed. note: ET: *The Principles of Descartes' Philosophy*, trans. Halbert Hains Britan (Chicago: Open Court, 1974). G. Hegel, *Enzyklopädie der philosophischen Wissenschaften* (1830; reprinted, Hamburg: F. Meiner, 1959), §§257ff.; ed. note: ET: *Encyclopedia of the Philosophical Sciences*, trans. Steven A. Taubeneck (New York: Continuum, 1990); E. von Hartmann, *Philosophie des Unbewussten*, 11th ed., I, 281ff.; A. E. Biedermann, *Christliche Dogmatik*, II, 518ff.

50. D. E. Strauss, *Die christliche Glaubenslehre*, 2 vols. (Tübingen: C. F. Osiander, 1840–41), I, 562.

difference between them. The marks of the concept of eternity are three: it excludes a beginning, an end, and the succession of moments. God is unbegotten (ἀγέννητος) and incorruptible (ἄφθαρτος) but also immutable.[51] Between eternity and time there is a distinction not only in quantity and degree but also in quality and essence. Even though he thought he could conceive of motion in a world without any beginning, Aristotle already commented that though time is not synonymous with motion, it is most intimately connected with it, with "becoming," that is, with the transition from the potential to the actual. Augustine expressed this somewhat differently by saying that time exists only where the present becomes past and the future becomes present.

"What, then, is time? If no one asks me, I know; if I want to explain it to someone who asks me, I do not know. I can state with confidence, however, that this much I do know: if nothing passed away, there would be no past time; if there was nothing still on its way, there would be no future time; and if nothing existed, there would be no present time."[52] Time is not a separate substance, a real something, but a mode of existence. If there were no creatures, there would be no time. "Time began with the creature" is a truer statement than that which says, "The creature began with time."[53] On the other hand, time is also not merely a subjective form of observation either, as Kant thought.[54] Admittedly, there is an element of truth here, too, and Augustine reasoned that for humans to measure and compute time, a thinking mind is required—a mind that retains the past by recollection, exists in the present, and expects the future, and to that extent measures the times within itself.[55] But in saying this, Augustine did not imply that there would be no measurable and divisible movement of things if there were no thinking mind that counted and measured it. A distinction needs to be made, however, between extrinsic and intrinsic time. By extrinsic time we mean the standard by which we measure motion. In a sense this is accidental and arbitrary. We derive it from the motion of the heavenly bodies, which is constant and universally known (Gen. 1:14ff.). Time in this sense will one day cease (Rev. 10:6; 21:23ff.). But intrinsic time is something else. It is the mode of existence by virtue of which things have a past, present, and future as so many parts which, whatever the standard employed, can be measured and counted. Now whatever can be measured and counted is subject to measure and number and thus limited, for there always remains a measure and a number greater than that which was measured and numbered.

51. D. Petavius, "De Deo," in *Theol. dogm.*, III, ch. 3, §6.

52. Augustine, *Confessions*, XI, 14.

53. Idem, *Literal Meaning of Genesis*, V, 5; idem, *City of God*, XI, 6.

54. I. Kant, *Critique of Pure Reason*, trans. Norman Kemp Smith (New York: St. Martin's; Toronto: MacMillan, 1965 [1929]), 76 ("Time").

55. Augustine, *Confessions*, XI, 23–28; cf. the same idea, but developed and applied quite differently in Josiah Royce, *The Conception of Immortality* (London, 1906), 162ff.

Accordingly, the essential nature of time is not that either with respect to the earlier or the later it is finite or endless, but that it encompasses a succession of moments, that there is in it a period that is past, a period that is present, and a period that comes later. But from this it follows that time—intrinsic time—is the mode of existence that is characteristic of all created and finite beings. One who says "time" says motion, change, measurability, computability, limitation, finiteness, creature. Time is the duration of creaturely existence. "Time is the measure of motion in a movable object." Hence, there can be no time in God. From eternity to eternity he is who he is. There is in him "no variation or shadow due to change" [James 1:17]. God is not a process of becoming but an eternal being. He is without beginning and end, but also knows no earlier and later. He can neither be subjected to measuring or counting in his duration. A thousand years are to him as a day. He is the eternal I AM (John 8:58). God's eternity, accordingly, should be thought rather as an eternal present without past or future. "To God all things are present. Your today is eternity. Eternity itself is the substance of God, which has in it nothing that is changeable."[56] Concerning God's eternity Boethius stated that "God comprehends and at the same time possesses a complete fullness of endless life."[57] And Thomas described this eternity "as a complete and at the same time a full possession of endless life."[58] And so speak all the theologians, not only the Roman Catholic but the Lutheran and the Reformed as well.[59]

Nevertheless, God's eternity should not for that reason be conceived as an eternally static, immobile moment of time. On the contrary: it is identical with God's being and hence with his fullness of being. Not only is God eternal; he is his own eternity.[60] A true analogy of it is not the contentless existence of a person for whom, as a result of idleness or boredom, grief or fear, the minutes seem like hours and the days do not go but creep. The analogy lies rather in the abundant and exuberant life of the cheerful laborer, for whom time barely exists and days fly by. From this perspective there is truth in the assertion that in hell there is no eternity but only time, and that the more a creature resembles God and is his image, the more he or she will rise above the imperfections of time and approach eternity.[61] Hence, God's eternity does not stand, abstract and transcendent, above time, but is present and immanent in every moment of time. There is indeed an essential difference between eternity and time, but there is also an analogy and kinship between them so that the former can

56. Augustine, *Confessions*, XI, 10–13; *De vera religione*, c. 49.

57. Boethius, *The Consolation of Philosophy*, V.

58. T. Aquinas, *Summa theol.*, I, qu. 10, art. 1.

59. Tertullian, *Against Marcion*, I, 8; Gregory of Nyssa, *Against Eunomius*, *NPNF (2)*, V, 33ff., I; Gregory of Nazianzus, *Oratio in novam Dominicam*, 38, 11; Pseudo-Dionysius, *On the Divine Names*, c. 5, §4; Anselm, *Monologion*, c. 18–24; idem, *Proslogion*, c. 18; P. Lombard, *Sententiae*, I, dist. 8, 2; T. Aquinas, *Summa theol.*, I, qu.10; D. Petavius, "De Deo," in *Theol. dogm.*, III, chs. 3–6; J. Gerhard, *Loci thologici*, II, c. 8; J. Zanchi(us), *Op. theol.*, II, 73–77; H. Alting, *Theologia problematica*, loc. 3, probl. 20.

60. T. Aquinas, *Summa theol.*, I, qu.10, art. 2.

61. T. Aquinas, *Summa theol.*, I, qu.10, art. 3, ad. 3, arts. 4–5.

indwell and work in the latter. Time is a concomitant of created existence. It is not self-originated. Eternal time, a time without beginning, is not conceivable. God, the eternal One, is the only absolute cause of time. In and by itself time cannot exist or endure: it is a continuous becoming and must rest in immutable being. It is God who by his eternal power sustains time, both in its entirety and in each separate moment of it. God pervades time and every moment of time with his eternity. In every second throbs the heartbeat of eternity. Hence, God maintains a definite relation to time, entering into it with his eternity. Also, for him time is objective. In his eternal consciousness he knows time as a whole as well as the succession of all its moments. But this fact does not make him temporal, that is, subject to time, measure, or number. He remains eternal and inhabits eternity, but uses time with a view to manifesting his eternal thoughts and perfections. He makes time subservient to eternity and thus proves himself to be the King of the ages (1 Tim. 1:17).

Omnipresence

[195] Infinity in the sense of not being confined by space is synonymous with God's omnipresence. This attribute too is most vividly represented in Scripture. God is the creator, and all that exists is and remains his in an absolute sense. He is the Lord, the possessor of heaven and earth (Gen. 14:19, 22 KJV; Deut. 10:14), exalted above all creatures, also above all space. Heaven and earth cannot contain him, how much less an earthly temple (1 Kings 8:27; 2 Chron. 2:6; Isa. 66:1; Acts 7:48), but neither is he excluded from space. He fills heaven and earth [with his presence]. No one can hide from him. He is a God at hand no less than a God from afar (Jer. 23:23, 24; Ps. 139:7–10; Acts 17:27). In him we live and move and have our being (Acts 17:28). In the different places of his creation he is even present to a different degree and in a different manner. All of Scripture assumes that heaven, though also created, has in a special sense been God's dwelling and throne from the first moment of its existence (Deut. 26:15; 2 Sam. 22:7; 1 Kings 8:32; Ps. 11:4; 33:13; 115:3, 16; Isa. 63:15; Matt. 5:34; 6:9; John 14:2; Eph. 1:20; Heb. 1:3; Rev. 4:1ff.; etc.). But from there he also comes down to earth (Gen. 11:5, 7; 18:21; Exod. 3:8), walks in the garden (Gen. 3:8), appears repeatedly and at various locations (Gen. 12, 15, 18, 19, etc.), and comes down to his people especially on Mt. Sinai (Exod. 19:9, 11, 18, 20; Deut. 33:2; Judg. 5:4). Whereas he allowed the Gentiles to walk in their own ways (Acts 14:16), he dwells in a special way among his people Israel (Exod. 19:6; 25:8; Deut. 7:6; 14:2; 26:19; Jer. 11:4; Ezek. 11:20; 37:27), in the land Canaan (Judg. 11:24; 1 Sam. 26:19; 2 Sam. 14:16; 2 Kings 1:3, 16; 5:17), in Jerusalem (Exod. 20:24; Deut. 12:11; 14:23, etc.; 2 Kings 21:7; 1 Chron. 23:25; 2 Chron. 6:6; Ezra 1:3; 5:16; 7:15; Ps. 135:21; Isa. 24:23; Jer. 3:17; Joel 3:16, etc.; Matt. 5:34; Rev. 21:10); in the tabernacle and in the temple on Zion, which is called his house (Exod. 40:34–35; 1 Kings 8:10; 2 Kings 11:10, 13; 2 Chron. 5:14; Ps. 9:11; Isa. 8:18; Matt. 23:21), and above the ark between the cherubim (1 Sam. 4:4; 2 Sam. 6:2; 2 Kings 19:15; 1 Chron. 13:6; Ps. 80:1; 99:1; Isa.

37:16). Again and again, however, the prophets warn against a complacent and carnal trust in this dwelling of God in the midst of Israel (Isa. 48:1–2; Jer. 3:16; 7:4, 14; 27:16). For the Lord is far from the wicked (Ps. 11:5; 37:9f.; 50:16f.; 145:20) but the upright will behold his face (Ps. 11:7). He dwells with those who are of a contrite and humble spirit (Isa. 57:15; Ps. 51:17–19). When Israel forsakes him, he comes to them again in Christ, in whom the fullness of the deity dwells bodily (Col. 2:9). Through him and through the Spirit whom he sends, he dwells in the church as his temple (John 14:23; Rom. 8:9, 11; 1 Cor. 3:16; 6:19; Eph. 2:21; 3:17), until one day he will dwell with his people and be everything to everyone (1 Cor. 15:28; Rev. 21:3).

In polytheism, Gnosticism, and Manichaeism this omnipresence of God could not be acknowledged. But even in the Christian church there were many who, though willing to recognize the omnipresence of God's power, wanted nothing to do with the omnipresence of his being. The Anthropomorphites could not conceive of God without a definite form and location. In order to safeguard God from being commingled with material substance and the impurity of the world, some church fathers went so far in their opposition to the Stoics as to assert that God was "far removed as to being but as near as possible in power,"[62] that he dwelt in heaven as the human mind does in the head.[63] Yet in saying this these authors do not deny the essential presence of God in every place. Not until later was God's omnipresence definitely denied and opposed by Augustine Steuchus, bishop of Eugubium (d. 1550), in his commentary on Psalm 138, and also by Crell, who while accepting an "operative omnipresence," denied God's "essential omnipresence," restricting the latter to heaven.[64]

Remonstrantism expressed itself cautiously on this issue, described the question as one of little significance, and as in the case of God's eternity, tended to refrain from taking a definite stand.[65] Coccejus, too, was accused of limiting the omnipresence of God exclusively to "the most efficacious will of God by which he sustains and governs all things," a charge against which he defended himself in letters to Anslar and Alting.[66] The Cartesians asserted that God was omnipresent not by the extension of his being, but by a simple act of his mind or a powerful deed of his will, acts that were one with his being, and denied that the idea of "location" could be attributed to God.[67] Rationalism went even further, confining God's essential presence to heaven and separating it deistically from the world.[68] Deism arrived at this restriction of the omnipres-

---

62. Clement of Alexandria, *Stromateis*, II, c. 2.

63. Lactantius, *De opificio Dei* (Cologne: Quentell, 1506), c. 16; *The Divine Institutes*, VIII, 3.

64. J. Crell, *Liber de Deo ejusque attributis*, c. 27.

65. S. Episcopius, *Institutiones theologicae*, IV, 2, 13; P. Limborch, *Theologia christianae*, II, 6.

66. J. Coccejus, *Opera omnia theologica*, 12 vols. (Amsterdam, 1701–6); *Epistolae ad Hebraeos* (Leiden: J. Elsevier, 1659), 169, 170, 176.

67. F. Burmann, *Synopsis theologiae*, I, 26, 6; Chr. Wittichius, *Theologia pacifica* (Leiden, 1671), c. 14.

68. F. Reinhard, *Grundriss der Dogmatik*, 106, 120; J. Wegscheider, *Institutiones theologiae christianae dogmaticae*, §63.

ence of God out of fear of the pantheistic error of identifying God with the world and of polluting the divine being with the moral and material impurity of created things. And indeed, that fear is not unfounded. The Stoics already taught that the deity—like fire, ether, air, or breath—permeates all things, also those that are filthy and ugly.[69] Spinoza spoke of substance as corporeal, described God as an "extended thing," and taught a presence of God that coincides with the being of the world.[70] In Hegel God's omnipresence is identical with his absolute substantiality.[71] In line with this view is Schleiermacher's description of the omnipresence of God as "the absolutely spaceless causality of God, which conditions not only all that is spatial but space itself as well."[72] In the same way Biedermann writes that the pure "being-in-itself of God" is the very opposite of all spatiality and to that extent transcendent, but that as ground of the universe God is immanent in it, and that this Ground-of-being *(Grundzein)* is God's very own being.[73]

Here again, Christian theology avoided both Deism and pantheism. This is not surprising since Scripture clearly teaches that God transcends space and location and cannot be determined or confined by them (1 Kings 8:27; 2 Chron. 2:6; Jer. 23:24). Even where Scripture speaks in human terms and—with a view to giving us an image of God's being—as it were, infinitely enlarges space (Isa. 66:1; Ps. 139:7; Amos 9:2; Acts 17:24), the underlying idea is still that God transcends all spatial boundaries. Accordingly, just as there is an essential difference between eternity and time, so also between God's immensity and space. Aristotle defined space or location as "the immovable boundary of an enclosing entity."[74] This definition, however, proceeds from a conception of space that is too external in character. Space, to be sure, is the distance of a certain object from other fixed points. But if we were to imagine just one simple object, even then space and location would pertain to it on account of its relation to imaginary points we could assume in our mind. Hence space and location are attributes of all finite beings. It is implied as such in whatever is finite. Whatever is finite exists in space. Its limited character carries with it the concept of a "somewhere." It is always somewhere and not at the same time somewhere else. Regardless of all measurable distance from other points (extrinsic location), an intrinsic location is characteristic of all creatures, not excepting even spiritual beings. In another dispensation distances may be totally different from those we know here on earth, just as steam and electricity have already greatly altered our ideas of distance. Yet a limited and local existence will nevertheless always be characteristic for all creatures.

69. E. Zeller, *Philosophie der Griechen*, IV, 138.

70. B. Spinoza, *Ethics*, I, prop. 15; II, prop. 2; idem, *Cogitata metaphysica*, I, c. 3.

71. G. Hegel, *Vorlesungen über die Philosophie der Religion* (1832), in *Sämtliche Werke*, XV, 284 (*Werke*, XI, 268).

72. F. Schleiermacher, *The Christian Faith* (Edinburgh: T. & T. Clark, 1989), §53.

73. A. E. Biedermann, *Christliche Dogmatik*, §702; J. Scholten, *Dogmatices christianae initia*, 124.

74. Aristotle, *The Physics*, trans. Thomas Taylor (London: Robert Wilks, 1806), IV, c. 5.

Space, accordingly, is not a form of perception (Kant), but a mode of existence characteristic of all created beings. Even less true is the idea that space is a form of external perception, while time is a form of internal perception, so that the idea of space would apply only to the physical universe, and that of time only to the spiritual or intellectual world. On the contrary, both time and space are internal modes of existence characteristic of all finite beings. From this it follows, however, that neither space nor time can be predicated of God, the infinite One. He transcends all space and location. Philo and Plotinus already spoke along these lines,[75] and Christian theology likewise stated that God "contains all things and he alone is uncontained."[76] In his Manichaean days Augustine believed that, like a fine ether, God was spread throughout endless space in every direction.[77] But later he learned to see things differently. God transcends all space and location. He is not "somewhere," yet he fills heaven and earth. He is not spread throughout space, like light and air, but is present with his whole being in all places: "whole and entire in every place but confined to none."[78] There is no place or space that contains him; hence, instead of saying that he is in all things, it would be better to say that all things are in him. Yet this is not to be understood to mean that he is the space in which things are located, for he is not a place. Just as the soul in its entirety is present in the body as a whole and in every part of it, and just as one and the same truth is acknowledged everywhere, so also, by way of analogy, God is in all things and all things are in God.[79] And these thoughts of Augustine surface again later in the works of the scholastics.[80] Catholic and Protestant theologians have not added anything essentially new.[81]

Of course, neither space nor location can be predicated of God. Space is a form of existence characteristic of finite beings. Immensity pertains to God alone and not to any creature, not even to the human nature of Christ. Implied in it, first of all, is that God infinitely transcends all space and location. "God is uniquely a place of his own to himself."[82] "Within his very self he is wholly everywhere." In that sense it can be equally well said of God that he is nowhere and somewhere (Philo, Plotinus), for the idea of a specific location does not apply to him. The term *omnipresence*, however, does not in the first place express

75. E. Zeller, *Philosophie der Griechen*, V, 354, 483.

76. Pastor (Shepherd) of Hermas, II, *Commandment* 1; Irenaeus, *Against Heresies*, II, 1; IV, 19; Clement of Alexandria, *Stromateis*, VII, c. 7; Origen, *Contra Celsus*, VII, 34; Athanasius, *De decretis Nicaea*, c. 11; Gregory of Nazianzus, *Oratio*, 34; John of Damascus, *The Orthodox Faith*, I, 9.

77. Augustine, *Confessions*, VII, 1.

78. Idem, *Confessions*, VI, 3; idem, *City of God*, VII, 30.

79. Idem, *Expositions on the Psalms*, VIII, 342–50 (on Ps. 74).

80. Anselm, *Monologion*, c. 20–23; P. Lombard, *Sent.*, I, dist. 36–37; T. Aquinas, *Summa theol.*, I, qu. 8; idem, *Summa contra gentiles*, III, 68; Bonaventure, *Sent.*, I, dist. 37.

81. D. Petavius, "De Deo," in *Theol. dogm.*, III, chs. 7–10; J. Gerhard, *Loci theol.*, I, c. 8, sect. 8; A. Polanus, *Syn. theol.*, II, c. 12; J. Zanchi(us), *Op. theol.*, II, cols. 90–138.

82. Tertullian, *Against Praxeas*, c. 5; Theophilus, *To Autolycus*, II, 10; John of Damascus, *The Orthodox Faith*, I, 13.

this being of God within himself, but especially denotes the specific relation of God to the space that was created along with the world. Here, too, of course, we can only speak of God in creational terms. Scripture even refers to God's going, coming, walking, and coming down. It employs human language, the kind of language to which we too are bound. "To discover where he *is*, is hard; to discover where he is *not*, is even harder."[83] It is therefore a good thing in connection with each attribute to remind ourselves that we are speaking of God in human terms.[84] It is precisely the realization that God cannot be measured by time or space—even if this is purely negative—that keeps us from depriving God of his transcendence over all creatures. Again, in the negation lies a strong affirmation. God's relation to space cannot consist in the notion that he is in space and is enclosed by it, in the manner in which, in Greek mythology, Uranos and Chronos were powers over Zeus. For God is not a creature. "If he were confined to a particular place, he would not be God."[85] He is neither a body extended throughout space and "circumscriptively" present in space, nor is he a finite created spirit permanently bound to a specific location, and therefore "definedly" present in space. Nor can the relation be such that space is within him and bounded by him as the larger unbounded space, as some in the past conceived of God when they called him "the spatial container (τοπος) of the universe," and Weisse speaks of infinite space as being immanent in God.[86] For in the nature of the case, space is a mode of existence that is characteristic of finite creatures and not of God, the infinite One. But the relation of God to space is such that as the infinite One, existing within himself, God fills to repletion every point of space and sustains it by his immensity.

To be avoided here, certainly, is the pantheism that reduces God's being to the substance of things and thereby also makes the divine being spatial. Equally to be resisted, however, is the Deism that pictures God as omnipresent in power but not in essence and nature. Though God is essentially distinct from his creatures, he is not separate from them. For all parts of existence and every point of space require nothing less than the immensity of God for their existence. The deistic notion that God dwells in a specific place and from there governs all things by his omnipotence is at war with God's nature. Actually, it negates all his attributes, his simplicity, his immutability, and his independence; it reduces God to a human and renders creation independent. God is present in his creation, but not like a king in his realm or a captain aboard his ship. His activity is not a form of remote control. As Gregory the Great put it, he is present in all things: "By his being, presence, and power God is internally, presently, and powerfully present here and everywhere." His omnipresence is right at hand: in hell as well as in heaven, in the wicked as well as in the

83. Augustine, *The Magnitude of the Soul* (New York: Fathers of the Church, 1947), ch. 34.
84. Such as, e.g., R. Lipsius, *Lehrbuch der evangelisch-protestantischen Dogmatik*, §306; S. Hoekstra, *Wijsgerige godsdienstleer*, 2 vols. (Amsterdam: Van Kampen, 1894–95), II, 121, 128.
85. Augustine, *Expositions on the Psalms*, on Ps. 74.
86. C. Weisse, *Philosophische Dogmatik*, I, §§492ff.

devout, in places of impurity and darkness as well as in the palaces of light. Because his being, though omnipresent, differs from that of creatures, he is not polluted by that impurity. Anselm, accordingly, stated that it is better to say that God is present *side by side with* time and space than that he is present *in* time and space.[87]

Nevertheless, this does not alter the fact that in another sense God is present in his creatures in different ways. There is a difference between his physical and his ethical immanence. To suggest an analogy: people, too, may be physically very close to each other, yet miles apart in spirit and outlook (Matt. 24:40–41). The soul is present throughout the body and in all its parts, yet in each of them in a unique way, one way in the head and another in the heart, in the hands differently from in the feet.

"These things the one true God makes and does, but as *the same* God—that is, as he who is wholly everywhere, included in no space, bound by no chains, mutable in no part of his being, filling heaven and earth with omnipresent power, not with a needy nature. Therefore he governs all things in such a manner as to allow them to perform and exercise their own proper movements. For although they can be nothing without him, they are not what he is."[88] God's immanence is not an unconscious emanation but the conscious presence of his being in all creatures. For that reason that presence of God differs in accordance with the nature of those creatures. Certainly all creatures, even the tiniest and least significant, owe their origin and existence solely to God's power, to nothing less than the being of God himself. God dwells in all his creatures, but not in all alike.[89] All things are indeed "in him" *(in eo)* but not necessarily "with him" *(cum eo).*[90] God does not dwell on earth as he does in heaven, in animals as in humans, in the inanimate as in the animate creation, in the wicked as in the devout, in the church as he does in Christ. Creatures differ depending on the manner in which God indwells them. The nature of creatures is determined by their relation to God. Therefore, though all creatures reveal God, they do so in differing degrees and along different lines. "With the pure you show yourself pure; and with the wicked you show yourself perverse" (Ps. 18:26 NRSV). God dwells in all creatures through his being, but in no one other than Christ does the whole fullness of deity dwell bodily [Col. 2:9]. In Christ he dwells uniquely: by personal union. In created beings God dwells according to the measure of their being: in some in terms of nature, in others in terms of justice, in still others in terms of grace or of glory. There is endless diversity in order that all of them together might reveal the glory of God.

It is not much to our advantage to deny God's omnipresence. He makes it felt in our heart and conscience. He is not far from any of us. What alone separates us from him is sin. It does not distance us from God locally but

---

87. Anselm, *Monologion*, c. 22.
88. Augustine, *City of God*, VII, 30.
89. Augustine, *Epist.*, 187, c. 5, n. 16; Bonaventure, *Sent.*, I, dist. 37, pt. 1, art. 3, qu. 1–2.
90. P. Lombard, *Sent.*, I, dist. 37.

spiritually (Isa. 59:2). To abandon God, to flee from him, as Cain did, is not a matter of local separation but of spiritual incompatibility. "It is not by location but by incongruity that a person is far from God."[91] Conversely, going to God and seeking his face does not consist in making a pilgrimage but in self-abasement and repentance. Those who seek him, find him—not far away, but in their immediate presence. For in him we live and move and have our being. "To draw near to him is to become like him; to move away from him is to become unlike him."[92]

> Do not think, then, that God is present in certain places. With you he is such as you have been. What is the sort of person which you have been? He is good, if you have been good; and he seems evil to you if you have been evil; a helper if you have been good, an avenger if you have been bad. There you have a judge in your own heart. When you want to do something bad, you withdraw from the public and hide in your house where no enemy may see you; from those parts of the house that are open and visible you remove yourself to go into your own private room. But even here in your private chamber you fear guilt from some other direction, so you withdraw into your heart and there you meditate. But he is even more deeply inward than your heart. Hence, no matter where you flee, he is there. You would flee from yourself, would you? Will you not follow yourself wherever you flee? But since there is One even more deeply inward than yourself, there is no place where you may flee from an angered God except to a God who is pacified. There is absolutely no place for you to flee to. Do you want to flee from him? Rather flee to him.[93]

UNITY

[196] The last of the incommunicable attributes is God's oneness, differentiated into the unity of singularity and the unity of simplicity. By the first we mean that there is but one divine being, that in virtue of the nature of that being God cannot be more than one being and, consequently, that all other beings exist only from him, through him, and to him. Hence, this attribute teaches God's absolute oneness and uniqueness, his exclusive numerical oneness, in distinction from his simplicity, which denotes his inner or qualitative oneness. Scripture continually and emphatically proclaims this attribute and maintains it over against all polytheism. All agree that this is true of the New Testament and the later writings of the Old Testament. Many critics believe, however, that monotheism does not yet occur in the earlier parts of the Old Testament, and that especially as a result of the witness and activity of the prophets, it gradually developed from the earlier polytheism that was generally dominant also in Israel. But against this view so many objections are being raised that its untenability is becoming increasingly more apparent. It is clear that the

91. Augustine, *Expositions on the Psalms*, on Ps. 94.
92. Ibid., on Ps. 34.
93. Ibid., on Ps. 74.

prophets were not at all conscious of bringing to their people a new religion in the form of an ethical monotheism. On the contrary, they view themselves as standing on the same foundation as the people of Israel, the foundation of YHWH's election and covenant. They regard idolatry as apostasy, infidelity, and a breach of the covenant, and call the people back to the religion of YHWH, which they have willfully forsaken.

Furthermore, no one can tell us what Israel's actual religion was before the ethical monotheism of the prophets gained acceptance. Critics speak of animism, fetishism, totemism, ancestor worship, and polydaemonism, and are especially at a loss when it comes to the character of YHWH. According to one, he was a fire god akin to Molech; according to another, he was a storm god from Mt. Sinai; according to a third, a tribal deity who had already acquired certain ethical traits. And with respect to his origin, there is an even broader array of answers. Canaan and Phoenicia, Arabia and Syria, Babylon and Egypt have all had their turn as being *the* answer. However, quite apart from these divergent beliefs concerning Israel's earlier religious state, if under the influence of the prophets, polytheism developed into ethical monotheism, the manner in which this occurred should certainly be made somewhat clear. At this point, however, a new difficulty presents itself. The evolutionistic viewpoint, which underlies the position of the critics, naturally precludes the idea that ethical monotheism made its appearance as something entirely new, as an invention of the prophets. The principle at work here demands that the ethical monotheism of the prophets must have existed, at least in a primitive form, long before the time of the prophets.

So now the critics face a dilemma: They can refrain from providing further explanation [as to the rise of ethical monotheism], continue to be stumped by the sudden appearance of ethical monotheism in the writings of the prophets, hide behind the currently popular notion of "the mystery of personality," and join Wellhausen in saying: "Even if we were able to trace the development of Israel's religion more accurately, this would fundamentally explain very little. Why, for example, did not Chemosh of the Moabites become the God of righteousness and the Creator of heaven and earth? No one can give a satisfactory answer to that question."[94] In fact, the promise and prospect of a satisfactory answer had been repeatedly held out as a result of the new critical method. Many others, accordingly, regarding this position unacceptable, resorted to the second alternative: they are prepared to concede that monotheism existed long before the prophets—in the time of Abraham and in the case of Moses. They explain this in light of the influence of the religions surrounding Israel, in light of the "tendencies converging toward monarchy in the world of the gods," tendencies that can already be discerned in Syria, Palestine, and Canaan,

---

94. J. Wellhausen, *Die christliche Religion: Mit Einschluss der israelitisch-judischen Religion*, I, IV, 1, 15, in *Die Kultur der Gegenwart*, ed. Paul Hinneberg, 24 vols. (Berlin and Leipzig: B. G. Teubner, 1905–23). Cf. Nödelke, who would rather admit that "Israel was to him an enigma than explain this phenomenon by accepting a revelation" (in H. H. Kuyper, *Evolutie of revelatie* [Amsterdam: Höveker & Wormser, 1905], 67).

at least among the "intellectual elite," or in light of the "monotheizing ideas" that penetrated Canaan from Babylonia and perhaps also from Egypt.[95] So, by way of a history-of-religions approach, the theory arises that from very ancient times polytheism rested on a more or less conscious monotheism, somewhat analogously to the way in which, according to Haeckel, the origin of life needs no explanation because it is nothing new, but something in principle inherent already in the inorganic world and in fact in all atoms.

Thus scholars shift from one extreme position to another. Nevertheless, the latter view has an advantage over the former: it is not compelled by a principle—by a preconceived idea of development—either to deny the presence of monotheism in the earlier parts of the Old Testament or for that reason to shift it to a much later time. Indeed, Scripture is monotheistic—not only in its later, but also in its earlier parts. Though YHWH's interaction with humans is described in very dramatic, graphic, and anthropomorphic language, YHWH is nevertheless the Creator of heaven and earth, the Maker of humankind, the Judge of all the earth. He destroys the human race in the flood, is present and active in all parts of the world, divides humankind over the earth, and by calling Abraham prepares for his election of Israel.[96] Even though there is certainly a kind of progression in revelation and development in its ideas, the entire Old Testament, with its teaching of the unity of the world and of the human race, the election of, and covenant with, Israel, and its teaching of the religion and morality described in the law, is based from beginning to end on the oneness of God. YHWH is the Creator of the world (Gen. 1 and 2), the Owner and Judge of the whole earth (Gen. 14:19, 22; 18:25), the only Lord (Deut. 6:4), who will tolerate no other gods before him (Exod. 20:3). Besides him there is no other god (Deut. 4:35; 32:39; Ps. 18:31; 83:18; Isa. 43:10; 44:6; 45:5ff.; etc.), and the gods of the Gentiles are idols, nongods, dead gods, lies and deception, not Elohim but *elilim* [worthless gods] (Deut. 32:21; Ps. 96:5–6; Isa. 41:29; 44:9, 20; Jer. 2:5, 11; 10:15; 16:19; 51:17–18; Dan. 5:23; Hab. 2:18–19; etc.) and insofar as real powers are worshiped as idols, they are considered demonic (Ps. 106:37; 1 Cor. 10:20). In the New Testament this singularity of God becomes even clearer in the person of Christ (John 17:3; Acts 17:24; Rom. 3:30; 1 Cor. 8:5–6; Eph. 4:5–6; 1 Tim. 2:5).

With this confession of the only true God the Christian church made its debut in the Gentile world. Though in that world official religion had in many cases become a target of ridicule for the intellectual elite, polytheism was still enormously influential in the political and social life of the people and continued to be so also in the worldview of those who took a philosophical position or sought to elevate themselves above popular religion by adopting

95. Cf. F. Delitzsch, *Babel and Bibel*, trans. T. J. McCormack and W. H. Carruth (Chicago: Open Court, 1903), ch. 1; and Bruno Baentsch, *Altorientalischer und israelitischer Monotheismus* (Tübingen: J. C. B. Mohr, 1906), reviewed by W. Nowack, *Theologische Rundschau* (December 1906): 449–59.

96. See H. Bavinck, *Reformed Dogmatics*, I, 84–86 (#23); also James Orr, *The Problem of the Old Testament* (London: James Nisbet, 1905), 40ff., 125ff.

some kind of religious syncretism. Hence, from the very beginning the Christian church saw itself involved in a serious conflict, and in waging this battle its spokesmen employed not only defensive but also offensive means. Feeling strong in their confessional position, Christian thinkers proved the uniqueness of God not only by appealing to Scripture but also by deriving arguments for the truth they proclaimed from every domain of human knowledge. They appealed to the witness of the human soul, to pronouncements made by many Gentile philosophers and poets, to the unity of the world and the human race, to the unitary nature of truth and morality, to the nature of the divine being, which tolerates no equals. And along with polytheism they attacked all things directly or indirectly connected with it: demonism and superstition, mantic and magic, the deification of humans and emperor worship, the theaters and the games.[97] In this mighty, centuries-long struggle polytheism was overcome and deprived both religiously and scientifically of all its power. However, this does not alter the fact that polytheistic ideas and practices survived in various forms, repeatedly found fresh acceptance, and especially in modern times powerfully reasserted themselves. When the confession of the one true God weakens and is denied, and the unity sought in pantheism eventually satisfies neither the intellect nor the heart, the unity of the world and of humankind, of religion, morality, and truth can no longer be maintained. Nature and history fall apart in fragments, and along with consciously or unconsciously fostered polytheistic tendencies, every form of superstition and idolatry makes a comeback. Modernity offers abundant proof for this state of affairs, and for that reason the confession of the oneness of God is of even greater significance today than it was in earlier times.[98]

SIMPLICITY

[197] The oneness of God does not only consist in a unity of singularity, however, but also in a unity of simplicity. The fact of the matter is that Scripture, to denote the fullness of the life of God, uses not only adjectives but also substantives: it tells us not only that God is truthful, righteous, living, illuminating, loving, and wise, but also that he is the truth, righteousness, life, light, love, and wisdom (Jer. 10:10; 23:6; John 1:4–5, 9; 14:6; 1 Cor. 1:30; 1 John 1:5; 4:8). Hence, on account of its absolute perfection, every attribute of God is identical with his essence.

---

97. J. Schwane, *Dogmengeschichte*, 4 vols. (Freiburg i.B.: Herder, 1882–95), I², 67ff.; A. von Harnack, *Mission and Expansion of Christianity in the First 300 Years* (New York: Harper, 1962), 125–46, 206–18, 234–39, 290–311.

98. Cf. on the unity of God: T. Aquinas, *Summa theol.*, I, qu. 11; idem, *Summa contra gentiles*, I, c. 42; D. Petavius, "De Deo," in *Theol. dogm.*, I, chs. 3–4; II, c. 8; M. J. Scheeben, *Handbuch der katholischen Dogmatik*, 4 vols. (1873–1903; reprinted, Freiburg i.B.: Herder, 1933), I, 576ff.; J. Heinrich and C. Gutberlet, *Dogmatische Theologie*, III, 269ff.; J. Gerhard, *Loci theol.*, II, c. 6; F. Turretin, *Institutes of Elenctic Theology*, III, qu. 3; O. Zöckler, "Polytheismus," *PRE³*, XV, 538ff.

Theology later taught this doctrine of Scripture under the term "the simplicity of God." Irenaeus calls God "all thought, all perception, all eye, all hearing, the one fountain of all good things."[99] Over against Eunomius the three Cappadocians were forced especially to defend the correctness of the different divine names and attributes, but Augustine again and again reverted to the simplicity of God. God, said he, is pure essence without accidents. Compared to him, all created being is nonbeing.[100] In the realm of creatures there are differences between existing, living, knowing, and willing; there are differences of degree among them. There are creatures that only exist; other creatures that also live; still others that also think. But in God everything is one. God is everything he possesses. He is his own wisdom, his own life; being and living coincide in him.[101] After Augustine we find this teaching in John of Damascus,[102] in the works of the scholastics,[103] and further in the thought of all Roman Catholic, Lutheran, and Reformed theologians.[104]

Others, however, firmly rejected and criticized the doctrine of the simplicity of God. Eunomius, who did in fact teach the absolute simplicity of God, concluded from it that all the divine names were merely sounds, and that the divine being coincided with his "nonbegottenness" (ἀγεννησία). This one attribute, he believed, made all the others superfluous and useless.[105] The Anthropomorphites of earlier and later date rejected the simplicity of God inasmuch as they ascribed a body to God. Arabian philosophers held to the simplicity of God but used it as a means of opposing the Christian doctrine of the Trinity, since according to them the three persons were simply "names added to the substance."[106] Duns Scotus, who for that matter expressly taught the doctrine of God's simplicity,[107] came into conflict with it insofar as he assumed that the attributes are formally distinct from each other as well as from the divine essence.[108] Nominalism, being

99. Irenaeus, *Against Heresies*, I, 12; II, 13, 28; IV, 4; Clement of Alexandria, *Stromateis*, V, 12; Origen, *On First Principles*, I, 1, 6; Athanasius, *De decr. Nic. Syn.*, c. 22; *Against the Arians*, II, 38.

100. Augustine, *The Trinity*, V, 4; VII, 5; idem, *Confessions*, VII, 11; XI, 4.

101. Augustine, *City of God*, VIII, 6; X, 10; idem, *The Trinity*, XV, 5; T. Gangauf, *Des heiligen Augustinus speculativ Lehre von Gott dem Dreieinigen* (Augsburg: Schmidt, 1883), 147–57.

102. John of Damascus, *The Orthodox Faith*, I, 9.

103. Anselm, *Monologion*, c. 15; P. Lombard, *Sent.*, I, dist. 8, nn. 4–9; T. Aquinas, *Summa theol.*, I, qu. 3; idem, *Summa contra gentiles*, I, 16ff.; Bonaventure, *Sent.*, I, dist. 8, art. 3.

104. D. Petavius, "De Deo," in *Theol. dogm.*, II, chs. 1–8; *Theologia Wirceburgensi*, III, 64; G. Perrone, *Prael. theol.*, II, 92ff.; J. Heinrich and C. Gutberlet, *Dogmatische Theologie*, III, 417; G. Jansen, *Theologia dogmatica specialis*, II, 60ff.; J. Kleutgen, *Die Theologie der Vorzeit*, I, 183ff.; *Philosophie der Vorzeit*, II, 183ff.; J. Gerhard, *Loci theol.*, II, c. 8, sect. 3; J. W. Baier, *Compendium theologiae positivae*, I, 1, 9; J. Buddeus, *Institutiones theologiae moralis*, II, 1, 17; A. Hyperius, *Methodi theologiae*, 88–89; J. Zanchi(us), *Op. theol.*, II, 63–73; A. Polanus, *Syn. theol.*, II, 8; J. Trigland, *Antapologia* (Amsterdam: Joannam Janssonium et al., 1664), c. 4; G. Voetius, *Select. disp.*, I, 226–46; H. Alting, *Theologia elenctica nova*, 119ff.; B. de Moor, *Comm. in Marckii Comp.*, I, 604–18; L. Meijer, *Verhandelingen over de goddelyke Wigenschappen*, IV, 517–52.

105. J. Schwane, *Dogmengeschichte*, II², 21.

106. A. Stöckl, *Geschichte der Philosophie des Mittelalters*, II, 89.

107. Duns Scotus, *Sent.*, I, dist. 8, qu.1–2.

108. Ibid., qu. 4.

even much more radical, held that there were realistic distinctions between the attributes among themselves. In the period of the Reformation this view was adopted by the Socinians. In the interest of assuring the independence of humans, they arrived at the idea of finitizing the divine being and as a result were at a loss to know what to do with God's simplicity. Socinus questioned whether Scripture permits us to ascribe simplicity to God. The Catechism of Rakow totally omits this attribute. Schlichting, Volkelius (et al.) denied that the attributes coincide with God's being and asserted that a fullness of attributes is not inconsistent with his oneness.[109] Vorstius, agreeing with this view and basing himself especially on the doctrine of the Trinity, stated that with reference to the divine being we must distinguish between matter and form, essence and attributes, *genus* and *differentiae*. Scripture, accordingly, reports that God swore "by his soul" (Jer. 51:14 MT) and that the Spirit is "within him" (1 Cor. 2:11). There is a difference, said Vorstius, between knowing and willing, between the subject that lives and the life by which the subject lives.[110]

The Remonstrants were of the same opinion. In the second chapter of their Confession they said that Scripture does not contain a single syllable about the simplicity of God, that it is a purely metaphysical doctrine and not at all necessary for Christians to believe. They especially raised the objection that the idea of the simplicity of God is incompatible with the freedom of his will and the changing character of his disposition. While Episcopius still listed the simplicity of God among the attributes and believed that the "relations, volitions, and free decrees" could be harmonized with it,[111] Limborch no longer mentioned it. In rationalistic works it was either completely relegated to the background or left undiscussed altogether.[112] Bretschneider writes that Scripture knows nothing of these philosophical subtleties.

Nor was pantheism able to recognize or appreciate the doctrine of God's simplicity. It equated God with the world, while Spinoza, one of its exponents, even attributed to God the attribute of extension. Thus the attribute of God's simplicity almost totally disappeared from modern theology. Its significance is no longer understood, and sometimes it is vigorously opposed. Schleiermacher refused to put the simplicity of God on a par with the other attributes, regarding it only as "the unseparated and inseparable mutual inherence of all divine attributes and activities."[113] In the works of Lange, Kahnis, Philippi, Ebrard, Lipsius, Biedermann, F. A. B. Nitzsch, Kaftan, von Oettingen, Haering, van Oosterzee (et al.), this attribute no longer occurs. Others vigorously oppose it,

---

109. J. Hoornbeek, *Socianismus confutatus*, 3 vols. (Utrecht, 1650–64), I, 368–69.

110. J. Trigland, *Kerkelycke Geschiedenissen* (Leyden: Andriae Wyngaerden, 1650), IV, 576, 585ff.; Schweizer, *Theol. Jahrb.* 15 (1856): 435ff.; 16 (1857): 153ff.; I. Dorner, *Gesammelte Schriften* (1883), 278ff.

111. S. Episcopius, *Institutiones theologicae*, IV, sect. 2, c. 7.

112. J. Wegschneider, *Institutiones theologiae christianae dogmaticae*, §61; F. Reinhard, *Grundriss der Dogmatik*, §33; K. G. Bretschneider, *Handbuch der Dogmatik*, 4th ed., I, 486.

113. F. Schleiermacher, *The Christian Faith*, §56.

especially on the following two grounds: it is a metaphysical abstraction and inconsistent with the doctrine of the Trinity.[114]

This simplicity is of great importance, nevertheless, for our understanding of God. It is not only taught in Scripture (where God is called "light," "life," and "love") but also automatically follows from the idea of God and is necessarily implied in the other attributes. Simplicity here is the antonym of "compounded." If God is composed of parts, like a body, or composed of *genus* (class) and *differentiae* (attributes of differing species belonging to the same *genus*), substance and accidents, matter and form, potentiality and actuality, essence and existence, then his perfection, oneness, independence, and immutability cannot be maintained. On that basis he is not the highest love, for then there is in him a subject who loves—which is one thing—as well as a love by which he loves—which is another. The same dualism would apply to all the other attributes. In that case God is not the One "than whom nothing better can be thought." Instead, God is uniquely his own, having nothing above him. Accordingly, he is completely identical with the attributes of wisdom, grace, and love, and so on. He is absolutely perfect, the One "than whom nothing higher can be thought."[115]

In the case of creatures all this is very different. In their case there is a difference between existing, being, living, knowing, willing, acting, and so on. "All that is compounded is created." No creature can be completely simple, for every creature is finite. God, however, is infinite and all that is in him is infinite. All his attributes are divine, hence infinite and one with his being. For that reason he is and can only be all-sufficient, fully blessed, and glorious within himself.[116] From this alone it is already evident that the simplicity of God is absolutely not a metaphysical abstraction. It is essentially distinct from the philosophical idea of absolute being, the One, the only One, the Absolute, or substance, terms by which Xenophanes, Plato, Philo, Plotinus, and later Spinoza and Hegel designated God. It is not found by abstraction, that is, by eliminating all the contrast and distinctions that characterize creatures and describing him as the being who transcends all such contrasts. On the contrary: God's simplicity is the end result of ascribing to God all the perfections of creatures to the ultimate divine degree. By describing God as "utterly simple essence," we state that he is the perfect and infinite fullness of being, an "unbounded ocean of being." Far from fostering pantheism, as Bauer thinks,[117] this doctrine of the "utterly

---

114. A. Vilmar, *Dogmatik*, I, 208ff.; I. Dorner, *A System of Christian Doctrine*, I, 234ff.; idem, *Gesammelte Schriften*, 305; F. Frank, *System der christlichen Wahrheit*, 2d ed., I, 124; A. Ritschl, *Theologie und Metaphysik*, 12ff.; idem, *Rechtfertigung und Versuchung*, 2d ed., III, 2ff.; idem, *Jahrbücher für deutsche Theologie* 10 (1865): 275ff.; 13 (1868): 67ff., 251ff.; J. Doedes, *De Nederlandsche geloofsbelijdenis en de Heidelbergsche catechismus*, 9; A. Schweizer, *Christliche Glaubenslehre*, I, 256–59; W. G. T. Shedd, *Dogmatic Theology*, 3d ed., 3 vols. (New York: Scribner, 1891–94), I, 338; A. Kuyper, *Ex ungue leonem* (Amsterdam: Kruyt, 1882).

115. Augustine, *The Trinity*, V, 10; VI, 1; Hugo of St. Victor, *The Trinity*, I, 12.

116. D. Petavius, "De Deo," in *Theol. dogm.*, II, ch. 2.

117. F. C. Baur, *Die christliche Lehre von den Dreieinigen Gottes*, II, 635.

simple essence of God" is diametrically opposed to it. For in pantheism God has no existence and life of his own apart from the world. In the thought of Hegel, for example, the Absolute, pure Being, Thought, Idea, does not exist before the creation of the world, but is only logically and potentially prior to the world. All the qualifications of the Absolute are devoid of content—nothing but abstract logical categories.[118]

In describing God as "utterly simple essence," however, Christian theology above all maintains that God has a distinct and infinite life of his own within himself, even though it is true that we can only describe that divine being with creaturely names. Pantheistic philosophy's Absolute, Supreme Being, Substance—favorite names used for the divine being in this philosophy—are the result of abstraction. All qualifiers have been stripped from things until nothing is left but the lowest common denominator: pure being, unqualified existence. This "being" is indeed an abstraction, a concept for which there is no corresponding reality and which may not be further defined. Every further qualification would finitize it, make it into something particular, and hence destroy its generality. "All determination is negation." But the being ascribed to God in theology is a unique, particular being distinct from that of the world. It describes God not as a being with which we cannot make any association other than that it is, but as someone who is all being, the absolute fullness of being. This simplicity of being does not exclude the many names ascribed to him, as Eunomius thought, but demands them. God is so abundantly rich that we can gain some idea of his richness only by the availability of many names. Every name refers to the same full divine being, but each time from a particular angle, the angle from which it reveals itself to us in his works. God is therefore simple in his multiplicity and manifold in his simplicity (Augustine). Hence, every qualification, every name, used with reference to God, so far from being a negation, is an enrichment of our knowledge of his being. "The divine essence is self-determined and is distinct from everything else in that nothing can be added to it."[119] Nor, taken in this sense, is this simplicity of God inconsistent with the doctrine of the Trinity, for the term "simple" is not used here as an antonym of "twofold" or "threefold" but of "composite." Now, the divine being is not composed of three persons, nor is each person composed of the being and personal attributes of that person, but the one uncompounded (simple) being exists in three persons. Every person or personal attribute is not distinguishable in respect of essence but only in respect of reason. Every personal attribute is indeed a "real relation" but adds nothing real to the essence. The personal attributes "do not make up but only distinguish [the persons]."[120]

118. A. Drews, *Die deutsche Spekulation seit Kant*, I, 249.
119. T. Aquinas, *Sent.*, I, dist. 8, qu. 4, art. 1, ad. 1; J. Kleutgen, *Theologie der Vorzeit*, 2d ed., I, 204ff.
120. D. Petavius, "De Deo," in *Theol. dogm.*, II, chs. 3–4; Zanchi(us), *Op. theol.*, II, 68–69.

5

GOD'S COMMUNICABLE ATTRIBUTES

That God is Spirit is the presupposition of the Old Testament and explicitly taught in the New Testament. Despite efforts by theosophists, pantheists, Socinians, and certain philosophers to ascribe a body to God, the Christian church and Christian theology have steadfastly maintained God's spirituality. The term is used to mean that God is a unique substance, distinct from the universe, immaterial, imperceptible to the human senses, without composition or extension. Though there are analogues with the human spirit, even the soul eludes our observation.

Implied in God's spirituality is his invisibility. What then does Scripture mean when it speaks of "seeing God"? For the church fathers God could make himself visible, though some continued to deny a vision of God with respect to his essence. This changed with the influence of Neoplatonism, particularly as mediated through the mystical writings of Pseudo-Dionysius. Now it was believed that the soul, elevated by supernatural grace, could be divinized and have a clear essential vision of God.

Most Reformed theologians were more modest, rejecting the idea altogether or brushing aside these speculations of scholasticism. Every vision of God is an act of divine condescension, not a deification of humanity. The beatific vision is one that only is possible for a finite and limited human nature.

Scripture presupposes God's consciousness and knowledge, speaking figuratively of this as "light." Nothing is outside the scope of God's knowledge. Pantheistic thought, however, denies this when, as in Eduard von Hartmann, it conceives of the Unconscious as the unity of all things. The Absolute is then incapable of consciousness. In critique, anyone who argues for a teleological worldview must have a self-conscious and intelligent God. Thus, observing purpose in the world leads to acknowledging a divine, intelligent Being. Unlike finite human consciousness, divine self-consciousness has no limitation. The content of God's self knowledge is no less than his being; being and knowing coincide in God.

God's self-consciousness differs but is inseparable from his world-consciousness. Out of the infinite fullness of his own ideas God created the world to best reveal his perfections in his creatures. God's archetypal perfections are revealed ectypically in the universe. Thus, while God's knowledge and world-consciousness are communicable to humanity, they still differ qualitatively from human knowledge of the world. God's knowledge is comprehensive, excluding nothing from its scope. Unlike human knowledge, God's is not based on observation; it is undivided, simple, unchangeable, eternal. All things are eternally present to him.

Strictly speaking, it is a mistake to speak of divine foreknowledge; there is only one knowledge of God. For many this divine omniscience is irreconcilable with human free will. Attempts to square omniscience and free will take one of two forms: God only knows what free human agents will do (Origen), or God knows because it will necessarily happen because he has decreed it (Augustine). In the latter case, we affirm both free will and omniscience as an article of faith without professing fully to understand it.

After the Reformation a new notion of "middle knowledge" gained ascendancy, a divine knowledge of contingent events logically antecedent to God's decrees. Promoted by Molina and Suárez, among others, it gained acceptance among Roman Catholic Jesuit theologians but was rejected by Reformed thinkers. The theory of middle knowledge attempts to harmonize the Pelagian notion of an indifferent free will with God's omniscience and thus is incompatible with a decree of God. God is seen to derive his knowledge of free human actions not from his own being but from the will of creatures and thus becomes dependent on the world for his own knowledge. Creatures gain independence, and God becomes the chief executive of a world in which he is the slave of his subordinates.

While Scripture teaches conditional connections between events it never denies divine determination in those cases. In fact, the theory of middle knowledge cannot bring freedom of an indifferent human will into harmony with any notion of divine foreknowledge. The solution cannot be found in "indifference" but in "rational delight." In keeping with their divinely known and ordained nature, contingent events and free actions are links in the order of causes that, little by little, are revealed to us in the history of the world.

Viewed from another angle, God's knowledge is called "wisdom." While knowledge suggests a discursive, theoretical Greek model, wisdom is more Oriental, contemplative, intuitive, practical, goal-oriented. This Oriental characteristic is found to a high degree in Israel but now as the handmaiden of revelation. True wisdom is rooted in the fear of the Lord and consists in the moral discipline of conforming to God's law. Both the constitution of the world and revelation to Israel are attributed to God's wisdom. In the New Testament this Wisdom is identified as the Word.

Philo, and after him Augustine, linked this cluster of terms to Plato's Ideas, though with modification. The Ideas are not autonomous powers but subject to God's will. In modern philosophy ideas no longer refer to the pattern in the divine mind but to concepts, to the product of pure thought itself. Yet fragments of the former usage remain especially in the realm of art, where reference is made to paradigmatic patterns, to ideal forms. God can thus also be viewed as

*an artist in his creating though his ideas are not outside of him but original,
coming from his very being. It is for this reason that sin has no "being" of its
own; it is privation of being.*

*God is also true and trustworthy; he can be counted on. Truth is a matter
of veracity and genuineness, of logical consistency, and ethical correspondence
between a person's being and self-revelation. God is true in all senses. He is the
only God, and he cannot lie or be in error. He is truth in its absolute fullness,
the source and ground of all truth, all reality. He is the light by which alone we
can know truth.*

*The first of God's moral attributes is his goodness. This is not to be
understood in a relative or utilitarian sense but absolutely. God's goodness is
perfection, the sum of all goodness. God is also the supreme good of all creatures,
the object of every creature's desire. As the overflowing fountain of all good,
God's goodness is manifested to his creatures as steadfast love, as mercy, as
forbearance, and most wonderfully as grace. The doctrine of grace as voluntary,
unmerited favor shown by God to sinners, was first developed in the Christian
church by Augustine. When God's goodness conveys not only benefits but God
himself, it appears as love. Portrayed as covenantal, marital love in the Old
Testament, it is supremely revealed as ἀγαπη in the New Testament, the love the
Father gives to and through the Son.*

*God is holy as well as good, morally perfect. People and things only become
sanctified in relation to God by being chosen and set apart. Because YHWH is
holy, he wants a holy people for himself, a holy priesthood, a holy dwelling.
When his people are unfaithful, it is God's holiness that incites him to mete
out punishment. The holiness by which YHWH put himself in a special relation
to Israel and which totally claims Israel for the service of YHWH is finally
supremely manifest in that in Christ God gives himself to the church, which he
redeems and cleanses from all its iniquities.*

*Closely related to holiness is God's righteousness, by which he equitably
and justly vindicates the righteous and condemns the wicked. God's wrath is
terrible and must be taken seriously. Still, in Scripture, while God's retributive
justice is real, his remunerative justice is far more prominent. God vindicates
the righteous and raises them to positions of honor and well-being. This is the
pattern for earthly justice as well—for kings, judges, and every Israelite. YHWH
is the true judge, and the manifestation of his righteousness is simultaneously
the manifestation of his grace.*

*In dogmatics the term "righteousness" has a broader meaning as the sum of
all divine virtue. The advantage of this use is to afford opportunity to defend
God's justice against assailants such as the Gnostics, Marcion, and modern
theologians who only see God as love. God is not under external obligation,
but his righteousness and justice do rest on a moral foundation. God acts
covenantally with creation and in grace with his people; he binds himself by his
holiness and grace.*

The attributes that belong to God's sovereignty are ultimately grounded in his will as Creator and Lord of all. Contrary to attempts by rationalistic philosophers, nothing can be considered beyond it. Existence cannot be derived from absolute thought without a will, but a primary will without intellect is blind, a dark force of nature. If the will is as primary as striving, no rest or blessedness is possible for creatures except by annihilation of the will, the loss of the soul.

This is not the teaching of Scripture or Christian theology. Instead, true blessedness raises the soul to the highest level of love. There is a will in God; his absolute self-love is self-willing, not as produced but as eternal will of delight. God eternally loves himself with divine love and is completely blessed within himself. This necessary will is to be distinguished from God's free will toward his creatures, which is the final ground of all things created.

Proceeding from God's absolute freedom, many theologians began to think along the lines of medieval nominalism (Duns Scotus). From God's absolute free will Scotus also inferred human freedom of will as absolutely as possible. The will is the seat of blessedness, the second table of the law could have been different, the Logos could have assumed a nature other than human, and the incarnation would probably have occurred apart from sin. God could have redeemed humanity some other way, even apart from Christ's merits. This nominalist position severs God's will from his nature and perfections and results in complete arbitrariness.

Christian theology, in its doctrine of God, takes its point of departure in God's nature, not his will. The existence of things depends on God's will, but their nature or essence depends on his mind. God creates and preserves the world by the Logos; he does not act arbitrarily or accidentally but with supreme wisdom. We may search for God's motives and reasons but must also acknowledge the limits of human knowing. Against both pantheism and Deism, Christian theology maintains that the world was brought into being by an act of God's free and sovereign will, and that God had his own wise reasons for his will. God's freedom is that of a wise, just, holy, and merciful God. His will is one with his being, his wisdom, goodness, and all his other perfections. God's sovereignty is one of unlimited power, but not of blind fate, incalculable choice, or dark force of nature. Rather, it is the will of an almighty God and gracious father.

God is father to all his creatures but not in the same way. In our world there is one thing that creates a special difficulty for the doctrine of God's will, and that is the problem of evil, both ethical and physical. Though evil is under God's control, it cannot be the object of his will as is the good. A distinction must be make between God's revealed will and his hidden purpose or decretive will. That the actual will of God is the will of his good pleasure, that this will is identical with God's being and efficacious, is most consistently taught in Reformed theology. God's hidden and revealed will are not incompatible; his decree is his ultimate will, and his revealed will indicates what he wills that we do. The revealed will is the way the hidden will is brought to realization. Those who deny God's revealed will fail to take sin seriously; denying the hidden will undermines faith in God's sovereignty. In the former case, the spiritual risk is shallow optimism; in the latter, dark cynicism. In faith and hope, Christian theism confidently affirms both.

God is omnipotent in his sovereignty. Names such as El, Elohim, El Shaddai, and Adonai indicate his power: he is the mighty king and lord over all. All his works proclaim his omnipotence. Nominalism claimed God could do anything, and the Platonist tradition claimed that the real world is the only possible world. Scripture and Christian orthodoxy, by contrast, while stating that God cannot deny himself, and that his will and being coincide, also insist that the possible is greater than that which exists. What the Reformed tradition denied was a notion of "absolute power" that was not bound to God's own nature. God's existence is not exhausted by the existence of the world; so too his omnipotence infinitely transcends even the boundless power manifested in the world.

God is the sum total of all his perfections, the One than whom no greater, higher, or better can exist either in thought or reality. God, in other words, fully answers to the idea of God. He also has perfect knowledge of himself and has instilled in our hearts an impression of himself. Every attribute of God is precious to believers.

GOD'S SPIRITUAL NATURE

[198] The simplicity of God, which came last in the discussion of God's incommunicable attributes, leads very naturally (since all that is corporeal is composite) to the treatment of God's spiritual nature. Scripture, to be sure, always speaks of God in human fashion, and ascribes to him an array of physical organs and activity, but even in this connection it observes a certain limit. Of the human body's internal organs only the heart and the "intestines" are attributed to him, never organs of food intake, digestion, and reproduction. Sight, hearing, and smell are ascribed to him, not taste and touch. Nowhere is a body assigned to him. Although the Old Testament also at no point explicitly states that God is Spirit, yet this view is basic to its entire description of God. God is YHWH, who comes down to his people and reveals himself in human fashion, but from the outset he is also Elohim, who is far above all that is creatural. He is self-existent (Exod. 3:13–14; Isa. 41:4; 44:6), eternal (Deut. 32:40; Ps. 90:1ff.; 102:27), omnipresent (Deut. 10:14; Ps. 139:1ff.; Jer. 23:23–24), incomparable (Isa. 40:18, 25; 46:5; Ps. 89:7, 9), invisible (Exod. 33:20, 23), "unpicturable" (Exod. 20:4; Deut. 5:8) since he is without form (Deut. 4:12, 15). God and humans relate to one another as "spirit" and "flesh" (Isa. 31:3). Although he frequently reveals himself in theophanies, dreams, and visions and to that extent makes himself visible (Gen. 32:30; Exod. 24:10; 33:11; Num. 12:8; Deut. 5:24; Judg. 13:22; 1 Kings 22:19; Isa. 6:1), it is nevertheless by

his Spirit that he is present in his creation and creates and sustains all things (Ps. 139:7; Gen. 2:7; Job 33:4; Ps. 33:6; 104:30; etc.).[1]

In the New Testament, however, the spiritual nature of God stands out more clearly. Not only do we learn from this that God is eternal (Rom. 16:26; 1 Tim. 6:16; 1 Pet. 1:23; Rev. 1:8; 10:6; 15:7) and omnipresent (Acts 17:27–28; Rom. 1:22–23), but it is also stated directly by Jesus when he calls God "spirit" (πνευμα) and therefore demands that we worship God in spirit and in truth (John 4:24). And while the apostles do not literally repeat this statement, they themselves have the same understanding of God's nature when they call him "invisible" (John 1:18; cf. 6:46; Rom. 1:20; Col. 1:15; 1 Tim. 1:17; 6:16; 1 John 4:12, 20), a view that is not inconsistent with the promise of the vision of God in the state of glory (Job 19:26; Ps. 17:15; Matt. 5:8; 1 Cor. 13:12; 1 John 3:2; Rev. 22:4).

Corporeality and Anthropomorphism

Pagans tend to misconstrue and deny this spiritual nature of God (Rom. 1:23). Even philosophy has not been able to divest itself from sensuous notions of God.[2] Materialism considers material atoms to be the final ground of being. Deism finitizes God, making him essentially similar to humans. Epicurus pictures the gods as a company of reasoning philosophers, with fine ethereal bodies and distinct in gender.[3] But pantheism also fails to do justice to the spiritual nature of God. According to Heraclitus and the Stoics, the first cause must be conceived as material and physical. At the same time God is the primal power, which in the course of time brings forth all things and also again reabsorbs them into himself.[4] Now all these schools of thought continued to exert influence also in the Christian church and do so to this day. The realistic, eschatological theories that were widely current during the latter half of the second century were not far removed from the notion that, in a certain sense, God is corporeal. It is not altogether certain that Tertullian ascribed a material body to God. He does say: "Who will deny that God has a body, even though God is spirit? For spirit has its own unique kind of body and form."[5] But he seems to use the term "body" in the sense of "substance" when he says: "Everything that exists is corporeal in a unique sense (sui generis); nothing is incorporeal except that which does not exist," and elsewhere he speaks of the soul in equally realistic terms.[6] Nevertheless, this identification of "body" and "substance" is significant; it proves that Tertullian could conceive of substance only as corporeal. And elsewhere, accordingly,

1. G. F. Oehler, *Theology of the Old Testament*, trans. Ellen D. Smith and Sophia Taylor (Edinburgh: T. & T. Clark, 1892–93), §46; H. Schultz, *Alttestamentliche Theologie*, 4th ed., 2 vols. (Göttingen: Vandenhoeck & Ruprecht, 1889), 496–504; A. B. Davidson, *The Theology of the Old Testament*, edited from the author's manuscripts by S. D. F. Salmond (New York: Charles Scribner's, 1904), 106ff.

2. K. F. Nösgen, *Der heilige Geist sein Wesen* (Berlin: Trowitzsch & Sohn, 1905), 10ff.

3. E. Zeller, *Die Philosophie der Griechen*, 3d ed., 5 vols. (Leipzig: Fues's Verlag [L. W. Reisland], 1895), IV, 433.

4. Zeller, *Philosophie der Griechen*, IV³, 133–46.

5. Tertullian, *Against Praxeas*, 7.

6. Tertullian, *On the Resurrection of the Flesh*, 11; idem, *A Treatise on the Soul*, 6.

he affirms that God is no more free of affects than humans, although in him they are present in perfection. He even goes so far as to say that he conceives the "hands" and "eyes" that Scripture ascribes to God, not in a spiritual but in a literal sense, though again in perfection.[7] Tertullian can therefore be called the father of biblical realism. The spiritualizing tendency of the Alexandrian school, a result of its allegorical method of exegesis, drove many in the direction of anthropomorphism. According to Origen, Melito, bishop of Sardis, ascribed a body to God, but we cannot tell to what extent this report is true.[8] In the fourth century Audius and his followers, as also many Egyptian monks, taught a similar anthropomorphism, against which especially the treatise *Contra anthromorphitas,* a work attributed to Cyril, was directed.

In later years, this ascription of a human form to God recurred in Socinianism. Here God is exclusively represented as a Lord who has power over us. No mention is made of the simplicity, infinity, independence, and spirituality of his nature.[9] Crell maintained that the word "spirit," when applied to God, an angel, or the soul, was not used equivocally and analogically, but univocally.[10] And Vorstius, echoing Tertullian, asserted that "we must attribute to God a real body, if by body we mean a real and solid substance."[11] Theosophy as well teaches that God, in some sense, definitely has a body and therefore that humans are also physically created after God's image. In the Kabbalah, the ten *sefiroth,* that is, the attributes or modes in which God reveals himself, are collectively called Adam Qadmon, that is, the first heavenly human being, inasmuch as the human form is the highest and most perfect revelation of God, and God is so represented in Scripture.[12] This in turn gave rise to the view held by Christian theosophists in connection with the doctrine of the Trinity, that God, who is not quiescent being but an eternally becoming life, not only inwardly moves from darkness to light, from nature to spirit, but also outwardly surrounds himself with some kind of nature, corporeality, glory, or heaven, in which he assumes form and glorifies himself. This is the picture we get in the work of Böhme, Oetinger, Baader, Delitzsch, Auberlen, Hamberger,[13] and others.

7. Tertullian, *Against Marcion,* II, 16.

8. Cf. Steib, "Melito von Sardes," *PRE²,* IX, 539.

9. The Racovian Catechism, qu. 53.

10. J. Crell, *Liber deo ejusque attributis,* I, ch. 15.

11. Cf. I. Dorner, *Gesammelte Schriften aus dem Gebiet der systematischen Theologie* (Berlin: W. Hertz, 1883), 279.

12. A. Franck, *The Kabbalah* (Paris: L. Hatchette, 1843), 179. Ed. note: ET: *The Kabbalah* (New York: Arno Press, 1973).

13. Jakob Böhme and Johannes Claassen, *Jakob Böhme: Sein Leben und seine theosophischen Werke,* 3 vols. (Stuttgart: J. F. Steinkopf, 1885), I, 32, 157; II, 61; F. C. Oetinger, *Die Theologie aus der Idee des Lebens abgeleitet* (Stuttgart: J. F. Steinkopf, 1852), 109ff.; Franz von Baader and Johannes Claassen, *Franz von Baaders Leben und theosophischen Werke als Inbegriff christlicher Philosophie,* 2 vols. (Stuttgart: J. F. Steinkopf, 1886–87), II, 110, 112; Franz Delitzsch, *A System of Biblical Psychology,* trans. Robert E. Wallis (Edinburgh: T. & T. Clark, 1899), 58ff.; K. A. Auberlen, *Die Theosophie Friedrich Oetingers* (Tübingen: L. F. Fues, 1847), 147ff.; Hamberger, in *Jahrbücher für deutsche Theologie* 8 (1863): 448.

Finally, even modern pantheism fails to do justice to the spiritual nature of God. Spinoza ascribed to substance the property of "extension."[14] And in the philosophy of Hegel, Schleiermacher, von Hartmann (et al.) the world is an essential component of the infinite. "Without the world God is not God."[15] God and the world are correlates; they give expression to the same being, first as unity, then as totality.[16] This pantheism, to be sure, continues to speak—even with a certain predilection—of God as Spirit. But what this may mean is hard to tell. Hegel uses the term "spirit" (or "mind") especially to denote the final and highest stage which the idea in its development through nature reaches in humanity, especially in philosophy. "The logical becomes nature and nature becomes Spirit (Mind)."[17] Hegel still seeks the essence of Spirit (Mind) in ideality, in "simple being-in-itself," in "I-ness,"[18] but God becomes Spirit (Mind) only through a lengthy process in and through humans. Others have begun to use the word "spirit" for the final immanent cause of things without the connotation of a distinct existence of its own, or a conscious personal life.[19] Von Hartmann describes the unconscious as pure, unconscious, impersonal, absolute spirit and therefore calls his philosophy "spiritualistic monism" and "panpneumatism."[20]

Over against all these schools of thought the Christian church and Christian theology have steadfastly maintained the spirituality of God.[21] Rather than being treated separately, it was often included under God's simplicity,[22] but has been upheld and defended equally by Roman Catholic, Lutheran, and Reformed theologians.[23] The term was used to mean that God is a unique substance, distinct from the universe, immaterial, imperceptible to the human senses, without composition or extension. Humans can form a faint

14. B. Spinoza, *Ethics*, II, prop. 1–2.

15. G. W. F. Hegel, *Lectures on the Philosophy of Religion,* trans. R. F. Brown, P. C. Hodgson, and J. M. Stewart, with the assistance of J. P. Fitzer and H. S. Harris (Berkeley, Los Angeles, and London: University of Califiornia Press, 1984), 323 (*Philosophie der Religion [Lectures of 1827]*, in *Sämtliche Werke*, 26 vols. [Stuttgart: F. Fromann, 1949–59], XV, 138; *Werke*, XI, 122). Ed. note: When possible, references to Hegel's writings will be cited from the modern Stuttgart edition or a published English edition. The title of Hegel's work and Bavinck's original citation from Hegel's *Werke* will be given in parentheses.

16. F. Schleiermacher, *Dialektik* (Berlin: G. Reimer, 1839), 162.

17. G. F. Hegel, *System der Philosophie,* part 3: *Die Philosophie des Geistes,* in *Sämtliche Werke,* X (1958), 474 (*Werke* VII/2, 468).

18. Idem, *Werke,* 14ff., 18ff.

19. Cf. R. Eisler, *Wörterbuch der philosophischen Begriffe,* s.v. "Geist."

20. E. von Hartmann, *Philosophie des Unbewussten,* 11th ed., 3 vols. (Leipzig: H. Haacke, 1904), II, 457; idem, *Philosophische Fragen der Gegenwart* (Leipzig and Berlin: W. Friedrich, 1885).

21. Irenaeus, *Against Heresies,* II, ch. 13; Origen, *On First Principles,* I, 1, 6; idem, *Against Celsus,* VII, 33ff.; Augustine, *The Trinity,* XV, 5; idem, *City of God,* VIII, 5; idem, *Confessions,* VI, 3; John of Damascus, *The Orthodox Faith,* I, 11; II, 3.

22. P. Lombard, *Sent.,* I, dist. 8, 4ff.; T. Aquinas, *Summa theol.* I, qu. 3, art. 1–2; idem, *Summa contra gentiles,* I, ch. 20; D. Petavius, "De Deo," in *Theol. dogm.,* II, ch. 1.

23. *Theologia Wirceburgensi,* III, 27–34; C. Pesch, *Prael. dogm.,* II, 68; J. Gerhard, *Loci theol.,* II, c. 8, sect. 1; John Forbes, *Intructiones historico-theologicae de doctrina Christiana,* 1, ch. 36; P. van Mastricht, *Theologia,* II, 6.

impression of such an immaterial substance from the analogy of the spiritual nature they find within themselves. But the nature of their own souls is not directly known to them. Observing all sorts of psychical phenomena within themselves, they infer from them an underlying spiritual substance, but the soul's essence as such eludes their observation. And even then the spirituality of God is of a very different nature and unique in its kind. The term "spirit," when applied to God, angels, and souls, must not be understood univocally and synonymously but analogically. This is already evident from the fact that the spirit of angelic and human beings is composite in character, not, to be sure, in the sense that it is composed of elements of matter but in the sense that it is composed of "substance" and "accidents," of "potentiality" and "act," and is therefore subject to change. In God, however, this type of composition is no more present than that of bodily parts. He is pure being. It is further evident from the fact that as "spirit" God is not only "the Father of spirits" (Heb. 12:9) but equally the Creator and Father of all visible things. Also these visible things have not been made out of things that appear (Heb. 11:3) but have their origin in God as Spirit. God as spiritual being is the author not only of all that is called "spirit" (πνευμα) and "soul" (ψυχη) but also of everything that is called "body" (σωμα) and "flesh" (σαρξ) in the category of creatures. Thus the spirituality of God refers to that perfection of God that describes him, negatively, as being immaterial and invisible, analogously to the spirit of angels and the soul of humans; and positively, as the hidden, simple (uncompounded), absolute ground of all creatural, somatic, and pneumatic being.

This utterly distinct spirituality of God was also understood in the past; and for this reason some theologians proposed that we call the spirits of angels and the souls of humans "bodies," and that the term "spirit" be reserved as a distinct characterization of the unique being of God,[24] or otherwise to ascribe neither corporeality nor incorporeality to God, since he is above and beyond both descriptions.[25] But these suggestions do not merit support, because they foster misunderstanding and, second, those who make them forget that, although all knowledge of God is analogical, this analogy is more clearly evident in one class of creatures than in another and more obviously applicable in the realm of invisible things than in that of visible things. It is equally mistaken, on the other hand, to say with Descartes that the spirit's essence is "thought,"[26] and to join Cartesian theologians in describing God as a "thinking thing"[27] or as "purest and most perfect intellection."[28] For in so doing we would immediately equate God's spiritual nature with his personality, as this was in fact done in the

24. Cf. Augustine, *Epist.* 28.

25. D. Petavius, "De Deo," in *Theol. dogm.*, II, ch. 1, §§14–16.

26. Descartes, *Discourse on the Method of Rightly Conducting the Reason*, ch. 4 in *The Philosophical Works of Descartes*, I, 79–130.

27. Chr. Wittichius, *Theologia pacifica*, ch. 15, §218.

28. F. Burmann, *Syn. theol.*, I, 17, 4.

work of Reinhard, Wegscheider, and others.[29] Pantheism, accordingly, did not know what to do with God's spiritual nature and made it a sound conveying no sense, a word without a corresponding reality. For that reason it is important to maintain God's spirituality as a term for his *incorporeal substance.* The term as such falls short of implying personality, self-consciousness, and self-determination. In God they are, of course, implied, because he is a simple being, but not in the term as such. Animal consciousness and unconscious images in humans sufficiently prove that "spirituality" and "personality" are not identical. That which is implied in the word "personality" can only be discussed later in the doctrine of the Trinity, while self-consciousness and self-determination will be dealt with under the properties of the intellect and will. Here, under the rubric of spirituality, our aim is to maintain the spiritual nature of God. And the right understanding of this nature is of such great significance precisely because on it rests the whole character of our worship and service of God. Worship in spirit and in truth is based on the spirituality of God. It alone—in principle and forever—spells the elimination of all image worship.

Invisibility

[199] Directly implied in the spirituality of God is his invisibility, an attribute expressly taught by Scripture.[30] In the Christian church, accordingly, there was little disagreement over the question whether God can be seen by human eyes, a possibility that was generally denied both for this dispensation and the next. Only a few—the Audians, Socinians, Vorstius, as well as a number of Lutherans such as Quenstedt, Hollaz, Hulsemann, Maius, Jaeger (et al.)—accepted the possibility[31] and appealed to Reformed theologians such as Alsted and Bucanus.[32] But Gerhard left the issue undecided; and Baier and Buddeus confined themselves to "intellectual knowledge."[33] For the rest all held that God, being a spirit, cannot be perceived by the senses.[34] If we are at all justified in speaking of "seeing God," this must be restricted to the possibility of seeing him with the eye of the soul or the spirit.

Against this background, however, the question could come up whether an immediate, face-to-face vision of God is possible. Can God, as scholasticism said he could, be seen "as he is in himself, in substance or essence" *(ut est in se per essentiam, in substantia ve essentia)?* The consensus was that such a "vision

---

29. F. V. Reinhard, *Grundriss der Dogmatik* (Munich: Seidel, 1802), 111; J. A. L. Wegscheider, *Institutiones theologiae christianae dogmaticae* (Halle: Gebauer, 1819), §64.

30. Cf. above, pp. 182–83 (#198).

31. J. A. Quenstedt, *Theologia,* I, 554ff., 566; D. Hollaz, *Examen theologicum acroamaticum,* 458.

32. J. H. Alsted, *Theologia scholastica didactica exhibens locos communes theologicos,* 849; G. Bucanus, *Inst. theologicae* (1648), 443.

33. J. Gerhard, *Loci theol.,* loc. 31, §144; J. W. Baier, *Compendium theologiae positivae,* I, ch. 6; J. F. Buddeus, *Institutiones theologiae moralis,* II, ch. 3, §4.

34. Irenaeus, *Against Heresies,* II, 6; IV, 20; Origen, *Against Celsus,* VII, 33ff.; Augustine, *City of God,* XXII, 29; T. Aquinas, *Summa theol.,* I, qu. 12, art. 3, ad. 3; P. Vermigli, *Loci comm.,* 8–9; J. Zanchi(us), *Op. theol.,* I, 225.

of God with respect to his essence" *(visio Dei per essentiam)* was in any case possible only in the state of glory. On earth such a vision of God was not attainable by anyone. At most by a special act of God's grace, and then only for a moment, this privilege was granted to Moses (Exod. 34), Isaiah (Isa. 6), and Paul (2 Cor. 12).[35] By far the majority, however, held that also the vision of God imparted to patriarchs, prophets, and apostles always occurred mediately, say by a cloud, or some sign, or a physical manifestation.[36]

The real issue, therefore, was the question whether in the state of glory there is such a thing as seeing God "with respect to his essence." Now, to be sure, the church fathers often speak of a vision of God reserved for believers in heaven,[37] but they never mention a vision of God "with respect to his essence." They only say, with Scripture, that the blessed will see God, "not in a mirror but face to face." They further add that, though God is invisible, he can make himself visible and reveal himself to humans. "It is not in our power to see him, but it is in his power to appear to us."[38] Others, such as Chrysostom, Gregory of Nyssa, Cyril of Jerusalem, Theodoret, Jerome, Isidore (et al.), accordingly, denied that in the hereafter we would see God "with respect to his essence." Roman Catholic theologians do not know what to do with the statements of these church fathers. Vasquez squarely admits that "if we want to be honest, we are scarcely able to interpret these fathers in a favorable sense." Others, however, weakening these statements, try to explain them by saying that they deal with the physical contemplation of God, or the vision of God in this life, or with the absolute knowledge of God, which is and remains unattainable even in heaven.[39]

Gradually, however, under the influence of the Neoplatonic mysticism, which profoundly influenced Pseudo-Dionysius, a different view of the vision of God made its debut. It was now conceived as a contemplation of God in his essence, "as he is in himself." In this view God no longer comes down to humans; instead, by a supernatural gift, humans are lifted up to God and divinized. Gregory the Great already commented that God will be seen not only in his glory but also in his nature, "for his nature is its own perspicuity; perspicuity itself is his nature."[40] Prosper spoke of the blessed in heaven "contemplating within their hearts the substance of their own creator."[41] Bernard says that God will be seen in all his creatures, but that the Trinity will also be

---

35. Augustine, *Epist.* 112; idem, *Literal Meaning of Genesis*, XII, 27; Basil of Caesarea, *On the Hexaëmeron*, hom. 1; Hilary of Poitiers, *On the Trinity*, V.

36. D. Petavius, "De Deo," in *Theol. dogm.*, VII, ch. 12.

37. According to Irenaeus, *Against Heresies*, IV, 20; Clement of Alexandria, *Stromateis*, V, ch. 1; Gregory of Nazianzus, *Oration* 34; Augustine, *City of God*, XXII, 29; idem, *Literal Meaning of Genesis*, XII, 26.

38. Ambrose, in D. Petavius, "De Deo," in *Theol. dogm.*, VII, ch. 7.

39. T. Aquinas, *Summa theol.*, I, qu. 12, art. 1, ad. 1; idem, *Sent.*, IV, dist. 49, qu. 1, art. 1, ad. 1; D. Petavius, "De Deo," in *Theol. dogm.*, VII, ch. 5; *Theologia Wirceburgensi*, III, 82–86.

40. Gregory the Great, *Moralia in Iobum*, 1.18, ch. 28. Ed. note: ET: *Morals in the Book of Job*, 3 vols. in 4 (Oxford: J. H. Parker, 1844–50).

41. Prosper of Aquitaine, *De vita contemplativa* (Speyer: Peter Drach, 1486), ch. 4.

seen in itself.[42] And the Council of Florence declared that souls, "immediately upon their entrance into heaven, would obtain a clear vision of the one and triune God as he really is—nevertheless in proportion to the diversity of their merits, the one more perfectly than the other."[43] Scholasticism, in this connection, found abundant room for speculation and made generous use of it. In connection with the doctrine of "superadded gifts," it taught that humans, with their natural gifts alone, are unable to attain to this vision of God, and that they needed "divine aid," which augmented, elevated, and completed the natural gifts. As a rule this supernatural aid was described with the term "light of glory." Much disagreement arose, however, about the nature of this light, whether it was objective or subjective, whether it was the Word or the Spirit himself, although it was also generally assumed to be "something created, given to the intellect in the manner of disposition." For the rest it became common doctrine that God in his essence is the object of contemplation, and therefore that the blessed in heaven see in God everything that is inseparable from his essence, hence the attributes as well as the persons. Thomists asserted that God's essence cannot be contemplated apart from the persons, nor the one attribute apart from the others, while nominalists and Scotists held to the opposite view. Everyone agreed, moreover, that God himself and all that is (formally) in him, that is, belongs to his essence, is the object of this contemplation; but again there was disagreement over the question whether this included that which is (eminently) in him, that is, whether that which God called into being in accordance with his decrees is included in this object. As a rule this question was answered affirmatively in order thus to justify the invocation of angels and the blessed in heaven, who according to this view behold in God everything that is going to happen and hence know the needs of believers on earth. Even though the caution was added that the vision of God does not amount to comprehension and differs in believers in proportion to their merits, this doctrine nevertheless resulted in the deification of humans. The human creature, having received a supernatural gift, by his own merits raises himself to a higher level and becomes like God.[44]

42. Bernardus Zane, *Sermon 4*, in *Oratio in festo omnium sanctorum* (Rome: Johann Besicken, 1500–1599?).

43. Cf. H. Denzinger, *Enchiridion*, ##430, 456, 588, 870, 875.

44. P. Lombard, *Sent.*, IV, dist. 49; T. Aquinas, *Summa theol.*, I, qu. 12.; I, 2, qu. 3, esp. art. 12; I, qu. 4, art. 2; idem, *Summa contra gentiles*, III, chs. 38–63; idem, *Sent.*, IV, dist. 49, qu. 1–2; Bonaventure, *Breviloquium*, VII, ch. 7; Hugo of St. Victor, *De sacramentis christianae fidei*, bk. 2, pt. 18, ch. 16; D. Petavius, "De Deo," in *Theol. dogm.*, VII, chs. 1–14; M. Becanus, *Summa theologiae scholasticae*, I, ch. 9; *Theologia Wirceburgensi*, III, 67–90; G. Perrone, *Prael. theol.*, III, 266–76; G. Jansen, *Prael. theol.*, III, 913–35; C. Pesch, *Prael. dogm.*, III, 23–44; J. Kleutgen, *Die Theologie der Vorzeit vertheidigt*, 2d ed., 5 vols. (Münster: Theissing, 1867–74), II, 122–34; M. J. Scheeben, *Handbuch der katholischen Dogmatik*, 4 vols. (1873–1903; reprinted, Freiburg i.B.: Herder, 1933), I, 562ff.; II, 294ff. Ed. note: ET: *A Manual of Catholic Theology: Based on Scheeben's "Dogmatik,"* by Joseph Wilhelm and Thomas B. Scannell, 4th ed., 2 vols. (London: Kegan Paul, Trench, Trübner & Co.; New York: Benziger Brothers, 1909).

With respect to this vision of God the theologians of the Reformation took differing positions. The Lutherans were inclined to accept not just a mental but even a corporeal vision of God in his essence. In their opinion God is so great in power that he can illumine the blessed in heaven so as to enable them to see him in his essence, also with their corporeal eyes.[45] Even some Reformed thinkers considered such an essential vision of God not impossible.[46] But most of them, clinging to [the promise of] a glory that passes all understanding prepared for believers, either brushed aside the "thorny questions" of scholasticism or totally rejected the vision of God in his essence.[47]

This modesty is certainly in keeping with Scripture. The Bible indeed teaches that the blessed in heaven behold God, but does not go into any detail, and elsewhere expressly calls God invisible. The vision awaiting believers is described by Paul as "knowing as we are known." If God, as all accept, cannot be known perfectly, that is, in his essence, but is incomprehensible, he is also invisible in his essence. After all, "vision as to essence" and "comprehension" are completely synonymous. God, moreover, is infinite, and humans beings are finite and remain so also in the state of glory. Humans, therefore, can never have more than a finite human vision of God. Hence, whereas the object may be infinite, its representation in the human consciousness is and remains finite. But in that case the vision of God cannot be "with respect to his essence" either. Every vision of God, then, always requires an act of divine condescension (συγκαταβασις), a revelation by which God on his part comes down to us and makes himself knowable. Matthew 11:27 ["All things have been handed over to me by my Father; and no one knows the Son except the Father, and no one knows the Father except the Son and anyone to whom the Son chooses to reveal him"] remains in force in heaven. A corollary of vision of God in his essence would be the deification of humanity and the erasure of the boundary between the Creator and the creature. That would be in keeping with the Neoplatonic mysticism adopted by Rome but not with the

45. Cf. above, pp. 187–88 (#199).

46. Heinrich Bullinger, on John 1:18, *In divinum Jesu Christi . . . Evangelium secundum Ioannem* (Tigvri: Froschouer, 1561); A. Polanus, *Syn. theol.*, 9, 518; *Synopsis purioris theologiae*, LII, 11–24; John Forbes, *De visione beatifica*, in *Opera omni*, 2 vols. (Amsterdam: H. Wetstenium & R. & G. Wetstenios, 1702–3), I, 282–89.

47. J. Calvin, *Institutes*, III.xxv.11; David Pareus, on 1 Cor. 13:12, *In divinam Ad Corintios Priorem S. Pauli apostoli epistolam commentarius* (Heidelberg: Rhodius, 1613–14); André Rivet, on Ps. 16:11, *Commentarius in Psalmorum propheticorum: De misterijs evangelicis decadem selectam* (Rotterdam: A. Leers, 1645), II, 68; Lambert Danaeu, on 1 Tim. 6:16, *Epistolam ad Timotheum commentarius* (Geneva: E. Vignon, 1577); Franciscus Gomarus, on John 1:18, *Opera theologica omnia* (Amsterdam: Joannis Janssonii, 1664), 249–52; Johannes Maccovius, *Theologia polemica*, in *Maccovius redivivus* (Franeker: Typis Idzardi Alberti & Sumptibus Ludovici Elzevirii, 1654), 162. Ed. note: For a complete bibliography of Maccovius's works, see A. Kuyper Jr., *Johannes Maccovius* (Leiden: D. Donner, 1899), appendix B, pp. 405–7; J. Hoornbeek, *Inst. theol.*, XVI, 20; F. Turretin, *Institutes of Elenctic Theology*, XX, qu. 8; J. H. Heidegger, *Corpus theologiae*, III, 37; XXVIII, 138; B. de Moor, *Comm. in Marckii Comp.*, VI, 720; C. Vitringa, *Doct. christ.*, IV, 18–25; especially G. Voetius, *Select. disp.*, II, 1193–1217; cf. also S. Episcopius, *Institutiones theologicae*, IV, sect. 2, ch. 4; Phillip van Limborch, *Theol. christ.*, VI, 13, 6.

mysticism of the Reformation, at least not with that of the Reformed church and theology. For in Catholic theology human beings are raised above their own nature by a supernatural gift *(donum supernaturale)*, thus actually making them different beings, divine and supernatural humans *(homo divinus et supernaturalis)*.[48] But regardless of how high and glorious Reformed theologians conceived the state of glory to be, human beings remained human even there, indeed raised above "their natural position" but never "above their own kind" and "that which is analogous to that."[49] Humanity's blessedness indeed lies in the "beatific vision of God," but this vision will always be such that finite and limited human nature is capable of it. A divinization (θεωσις), such as Rome teaches, indeed fits into the system of the Pseudo-Dionysian hierarchy but has no support in Scripture.[50]

INTELLECTUAL ATTRIBUTES

[200] All of Scripture presupposes God's consciousness and knowledge. He is light and in him is no darkness (1 John 1:5). He dwells in unapproachable light (1 Tim. 6:16) and is the source of all light in nature and grace (Ps. 4:6; 27:1; 36:9; 43:3; John 1:4, 9; 8:12; James 1:17; etc.). Implied in the designation "light" is that God is perfectly conscious of himself, that he knows his entire being to perfection, and that nothing in that being is hidden from his consciousness.

Light in Scripture, to be sure, also stands for purity, chastity, holiness, and further, for joy, delight, and blessedness (Ps. 27:1; 36:9; 97:11; Isa. 60:19; John 1:4; Eph. 5:8), just as "darkness" is a picture not just of ignorance and error but also of impurity and moral corruption, of sorrow and misery (Ps. 82:5; Eccles. 2:13–14; Isa. 8:22; Matt. 4:16; 8:12; Luke 22:53; John 3:19; Rom. 13:12; Eph. 5:8ff.; 1 Pet. 2:9; etc.).

Still, what stands out in the figurative use of the word "light" is its intellectual meaning. For in the first place, light's main function is to make manifest that which is hidden and wrapped in darkness. Light is anything that becomes visible (Eph. 5:13). Corresponding to it in the world of the mind is consciousness (Prov. 27:19; 1 Cor. 2:11; Matt. 6:22–23). But this intellectual meaning leads naturally as it were to the moral one. For when sin pollutes our very being, we hide ourselves, love the darkness, do not dare to show ourselves, and no longer see ourselves as we truly are (Gen. 3:8; John 1:5; 3:19; etc.). Conversely, when through Christ, who is the light (John 1:4–5; 8:12; 9:5; 12:35; 2 Cor. 4:4), God shines in our hearts and gives the light of the knowledge of the glory of God in the face of Jesus Christ (2 Cor. 4:6), we regain the courage to look at ourselves, learn to love the light, and again walk

48. R. Bellarmine, "De justitia," *Controversiis,* V, 12.

49. F. Turretin, *Institutes of Elenctic Theology,* XX, qu. 8, 12.

50. Cf. below, pp. 511–88 (##279–300), the locus on the image of God; also Stuckert, "Vom Schauen Gottes," *Zeitschrift für Theologie und Kirche* 6/6 (1896): 492–544.

in it (Matt. 5:14, 16; John 3:21; Rom. 13:12; Eph. 5:8; Phil. 2:15; 1 Thess. 5:5; 1 John 1:7; etc.). Thus the term "light," when applied to God, first of all denotes that God completely understands and knows himself, the reason being that sin can never pollute him. There is and can be in him no darkness at all. He is light through and through. He lives in the light and is himself the source of all light. Also, the trinitarian life of God is a completely conscious one (Matt. 11:27; John 1:17–18; 10:15; 1 Cor. 2:10).

Knowledge

In addition God is conscious of and knows all that exists outside his being. Scripture nowhere even hints that anything could be unknown to him. True, the manner in which he obtains knowledge is sometimes stated in striking anthropomorphic language (Gen. 3:9ff.; 11:5; 18:21; etc.), but he nevertheless knows everything. The notion that something should be unknown to him is dismissed as absurd. Would he who plants the ear not hear, and would he who forms the eye not see? (Ps. 94:9). Over and over mention is made of his wisdom, might, counsel, understanding, and knowledge: חָכְמָה, גְּבוּרָה, עֵצָה, תְּבוּנָה, γνωσις, σοφια (Job 12:13; 28:12–27; Prov. 8:12ff.; Ps. 147:5; Rom. 11:33; 16:27; Eph. 3:10; etc.). All creatures fall within the compass of his knowledge. It extends to everything and is therefore omniscience in the strict sense. His eyes run to and fro throughout the whole earth (2 Chron. 16:9). Before him no creature is hidden, but all are open and laid bare to his eyes (Heb. 4:13). The most minor and insignificant details (Matt. 6:8, 32; 10:30); the most deeply concealed things: the human heart and mind (Jer. 11:20; 17:9–10; 20:12; Ps. 7:10; 1 Kings 8:39; Luke 16:15; Acts 1:24; Rom. 8:27); thoughts and reflections (Ps. 139:2; Ezek. 11:5; 1 Cor. 3:20; 1 Thess. 2:4; Rev. 2:23); human origin, nature, and all human action (Ps. 139); night and darkness (Ps. 139:11–12); hell and perdition (Prov. 15:11); wickedness and sin (Ps. 69:5; Jer. 16:17; 18:23; 32:19); the conditional (1 Sam. 23:10–13; 2 Sam. 12:8; 2 Kings 13:19; Ps. 81:14–15; Jer. 26:2–3; 38:17–20; Ezek. 3:6; Matt. 11:21); and the things of the future (Isa. 41:22f.; 42:9; 43:9–12; 44:7; 46:10), particularly the end of a person's life (Ps. 31:16; 39:6; 139:6, 16; Job 14:5; Acts 17:26; etc.)—all are known to God. He knows everything (1 John 3:20). This knowledge is not a posteriori, obtained by observation, but a priori, present from eternity (1 Cor. 2:7; Rom. 8:29; Eph. 1:4–5; 2 Tim. 1:9). His knowledge is not susceptible of increase (Isa. 40:13f.; Rom. 11:34); it is certain and specific (Ps. 139:1–3; Heb. 4:13), so that God's revelations are all true (John 8:26; 17:17; Titus 1:2). All his works make known to us his wisdom (Ps. 104:24; 136:5; Eph. 3:10; Rom. 11:33) and prompt us to worship and adore him (Ps. 139:17ff.; Isa. 40:28; John 11:7ff.; Rom. 11:33; 1 Cor. 2:11).

God's knowledge both of himself and of the universe is so decisively and clearly taught in Scripture that it has at all times been recognized within the Christian church. But pantheism has mounted an attack against it. Since it did not attribute to God an existence of his own distinct from the world, it was unable to ascribe a distinct consciousness to him. Spinoza in fact still spoke of thought as an attribute of God and called God "a thinking thing *(res cogitans)*."[51] However, distinguishing between thought and intellect, he called the latter "a certain mode of thinking" that occurs not in "nature begetting *(natura naturans)*" but only in "nature begotten *(natura naturata)*,"[52] and all these modes of thinking together constitute God's eternal and infinite intellect.[53] By way of Fichte, Schelling, Hegel, and Schopenhauer, this pantheism led to Eduard von Hartmann's *Philosophy of the Unconscious*. In the first volume of his work von Hartmann sets forth at length the universal meaning of the unconscious and then states that this Unconscious is one in all things.[54] And although the author would prefer not to call this Unconscious "God,"[55] in his work it takes the place of God. At times he views this Unconscious not as blind and alogical (like the will in Schopenhauer), but rather as clairvoyant, like instinct in humans and animals, and as possessing an all-knowing, all-wise, superconscious intelligence.[56] But he denies that consciousness is part of the Unconscious. For consciousness implies a distinction between subject and object; accordingly, it always involves limitation and presupposes individualization, even a body.[57] The moment consciousness is viewed absolutely it loses its form and becomes unconscious.[58] If the Absolute still had a consciousness of its own apart from individual consciousness, it would immediately swallow up the latter. Monism, he states, is incompatible with a conscious divine being. Such a being would not be immanent in, but separate from, the world. The Absolute, though the cause of all consciousness, is not itself conscious.[59] It is especially wrong to attribute self-consciousness to the Absolute, for this presupposes a distinction between subject and object, a self-reflection that cannot occur in the Absolute.[60] Pantheism, therefore, denies to God both knowledge of the world ("world-consciousness"), innerworldly self-consciousness, *and* knowledge of himself ("self-consciousness"), extramundane or intradivine self-consciousness. Even where the Absolute comes to consciousness in individuals, it knows the world but not itself.[61]

Now, we can assent to nearly everything von Hartmann says about the power and significance of the unconscious in creatures. The unconscious indeed plays a large role in the life of animals and humans. It is noteworthy, however, that von Hartmann does not even pose the question whether this extensive power of

---

51. B. Spinoza, *Ethics*, II, prop. 1.
52. Ibid., I, prop. 31.
53. Ibid., V, prop. 40 schol.
54. E. von Hartmann, *Philosophie des Unbewussten,* 11th ed., II, 155ff.
55. Ibid., II, 201.
56. Ibid., II, 176ff.
57. Ibid., II, 177ff.
58. Ibid., II, 179.
59. Ibid., II, 178ff.
60. Ibid., II, 187ff.
61. Ibid., II, 176.

the unconscious does not precisely presuppose and demand the intelligence of God. For it is most certainly true that there are many instances of unconscious actions that are nevertheless purposeful. But in those cases the unconscious in humans and animals does not itself act with a purpose. The case is rather that the conscious human mind sees a purpose in that act, a purpose to which it is directed precisely by a superior consciousness.[62]

From ancient times, therefore, the observation of purpose in the world led to the acknowledgment of a divine being. Anaxagoras already assumed the existence of a "mind" (νους) that possesses infinite knowledge with a view to arranging all things in the best possible order. Socrates describes the deity as seeing and hearing all things and being present everywhere. Plato's god is the World-shaper who creates all things on the model of the "ideas." Aristotle reasons that the deity is the "prime mover," absolute essence, "pure act," and absolutely incorporeal. Hence, the deity is thought, mind (νους), and has itself as its content. God cannot derive the content of his thought from outside himself. He can only think what is best, which is himself. God, accordingly, thinks himself; he is the thinking of thought. Thinking and its object coincide in him. God is the thinking of thought (νοησις νοησεως).[63] Even the Stoics, reasoning teleologically, inferred the existence of an intelligent cause from the manifestations of purpose in the universe. Zeno reasons as follows: "No part of that which is without sensation can be sentient; but parts of the universe are sentient: therefore the universe is not without sensation."[64] "That which possesses the capacity to reason is more excellent than that which does not possess the capacity to reason; but nothing is more excellent than the universe; therefore the universe possesses the rational faculty."[65]

One who does not acknowledge a purpose in the universe does not need a self-conscious God but is satisfied with materialism. But one who with von Hartmann argues for a teleological worldview must assume consciousness in God, for that person cannot explain the rise of consciousness from that which is unconscious. Surely the effect cannot have in it more than the cause. "Would he who plants the ear not hear, and would he who forms the eye not see?" A perfection in a creature points to a perfection in God. If a rational being exceeds all other beings in value, if the human ability to think raises humans above all other creatures—though in other respects they are as frail as a reed—it is impossible to conceive God as unconscious. Not only religion—which always and everywhere presupposes a personal, self-conscious God—but also philosophy registers a protest against the theory of an unconscious God. Pantheism may be able to appeal to Spinoza and Hegel; but theism has all the philosophers of antiquity on its side and finds support even in modern philosophers like Descartes, Leibniz, Kant, Schelling (second period), I. H. Fichte, Herbart, Lotze,

62. T. Aquinas, *Summa contra gentiles*, I, 44, 5.
63. Aristotle, *Metaphysics*, XII, 9.
64. Cicero, *On the Nature of the Gods*, II, 8, 22. Cf. III, 9, 22.
65. Cf. T. Aquinas, *Summa contra gentiles*, I, 28, 44.

Ulrici, Carrière, and others. Certainly, the idea that divine self-consciousness differs in kind from that of humans, the latter being but a weak analogue of the former, cannot be doubted. In that sense there would be no objection to calling God "superconscious." But precisely for that reason one cannot argue from the limitations of human self-consciousness to the nature of divine knowledge. Despite all pantheistic argumentation concerning the limitations, individuality, and sense-related basis necessarily inherent in self-consciousness, it is not at all clear why the self-knowledge of God should be considered a limitation of his nature. In our case, self-consciousness is finite and limited because we ourselves are finite and because it is never commensurate to our being. Our being is vastly richer than our self-consciousness. But God is eternal, pure being. And the content of his self-knowledge is no less than this full, eternal, divine being itself. Being and knowing coincide in God. He knows himself through his being. In him consciousness is not the product of a gradual process of development, nor does this consciousness fluctuate from moment to moment, for in him there is no becoming, no process, no development. He is pure being: light without any admixture of darkness.[66]

To be distinguished from God's self-consciousness is his world-consciousness. An earlier theology, accordingly, divided "the knowledge of God" into a natural or necessary knowledge (the knowledge of simple intelligence) and free or contingent knowledge (the knowledge of vision).[67] The two are not identical, as pantheism would have it, for if the Absolute is only to be conceived as being logically and potentially prior to the world, it is totally insufficient to explain the existence of the world. God does not need the world to become personal and self-conscious. God neither has to run through a logical course (Hegel) nor through a historical course (Schelling) to attain his full actuality (von Baader). Still, God's self-consciousness and his world consciousness cannot be so sharply separated as was sometimes done in the dogmatics of the past. The case is rather that the two are organically connected. Out of the infinite fullness of ideas present in his absolute self-consciousness, God did not arbitrarily select a few for the purpose of realizing them outwardly. In this selection he was guided, rather, by the purpose of revealing himself, all his attributes and perfections, in the universe. Hence the "free knowledge of God" encompasses precisely those ideas that in their realization are suited to unfolding God's nature on the level of creaturehood. The "natural knowledge of God" is by its very nature unsuited to being revealed to creatures. God can never be known by creatures as God knows himself, either as it concerns content and scope or as it concerns its mode. God's "free knowledge," however, encompasses all that is capable of realization and suitable, with a view to making known God's perfections in and for creatures. "Free" knowledge relates to "natural" knowl-

---

66. Augustine, *The Trinity*, XV, 14; T. Aquinas, *Summa contra gentiles*, I, chs. 57–48.

67. Ed. note: The Latin formulation of this distinction is *scientia naturalis (necessaria, simplicis intelligentiae)* and *scientia libera (contingens, visionis).*

edge as ectype relates to archetype. Also, with respect to this "free" knowledge of God, however, it must be borne in mind that it is something very different from what it is in creatures. Even though it is communicable, there is a vast difference, not only in scope but also in character and depth, between God's knowledge and that of rational creatures.

Scripture very clearly teaches, first of all, that this knowledge of God is comprehensive: nothing escapes it; nothing is hidden from his all-seeing eye. Past, present, and future; even the minutest detail and the most hidden things—everything is "open and laid bare in the eyes of him with whom we have to do" (Heb. 4:13). This has also at all times been acknowledged in Christian theology, with the exception of Jerome. In his commentary on Habakkuk 1:13 he says it is absurd to lower God's majesty by asserting "that God knows each moment how many mosquitoes are born and how many die; how many bugs, fleas, and flies there are in the world; how many fishes swim in the water and which of the smaller ones should serve as a meal for the bigger ones." But this limitation of God's omniscience finds no support in Scripture and was unanimously rejected by Christian theology.

Furthermore, God knows things not by observation, but from and of himself. Our knowledge is posterior: it presupposes their existence and is derived from it. Exactly the opposite is true of God's knowledge: he knows everything before it exists. Scripture expresses this very clearly when it states that God knows all that happens before it happens (Isa. 46:10; Amos 3:7; Dan. 2:22; Ps. 139:6; Matt. 6:8; etc.). God is the Creator of all things: he thought them before they existed. "This world could not be known to us unless it existed; it could not have existed, however, unless it had been known to God."[68] He is self-existent and cannot depend in his consciousness and knowledge on, or be determined by, anything outside of himself. The utter independence of his knowledge is a corollary of his aseity. His knowledge of all things is not based on things after they came into existence, for then they would have emerged, as in Schopenhauer and von Hartmann, from the unconscious.[69] Rather, he knows all things in and of and by himself. For that reason his knowledge is undivided, simple, unchangeable, eternal. He knows all things instantaneously, simultaneously, from eternity; all things are eternally present to his mind's eye.[70]

Foreknowledge

[201] Consequently—strictly speaking—one cannot speak of foreknowledge in the case of God: with him there are no "distinctions of time."[71] He calls the things that are not as if they were and sees what is not as if it already existed.

---

68. Augustine, *City of God*, XI, 10; idem, *Literal Meaning of Genesis*, V, 18.

69. Augustine, *City of God*, XI, 10; idem, *Confessions*, XIII, 6; idem, *Literal Meaning of Genesis*, V, 15.

70. Irenaeus, *Against Heresies*, I, 12; Augustine, *The Trinity*, XI, 10; XII, 18; XV, 7, 13–14; P. Lombard, *Sent.*, I, dist. 35–36; T. Aquinas, *Summa theol.*, I, qu. 14; idem, *Summa contra gentiles*, I, chs. 44ff.; J. Zanchi(us), *Op. theol.*, II, 195ff.; A. Polanus, *Syn. theol.*, II, ch. 18.

71. Tertullian, *Against Marcion*, III, 5.

"For what is foreknowledge if not knowledge of future events? But can anything be future to God, who surpasses all times? For if God's knowledge includes these very things themselves, they are not future to him but present; and for this reason we should no longer speak of God's foreknowledge but simply of God's knowledge."[72] "Whatever is past and future to us is immediately present in his sight."[73] "However the times roll on, with him it is always present."[74] The division of God's omniscience into foreknowledge, the knowledge of sight (the present), and reminiscence is a human conception through and through.[75] Scripture, however, often conveys the idea that God's omniscience temporally precedes the existence of things. And without this auxiliary image we cannot even speak of God's omniscience. In theology, as a result, the question arose: How can this divine omniscience be squared with human freedom? If God indeed knows all things in advance, everything is set in concrete from eternity, and there is no longer any room for free and contingent acts. Hence, Cicero already denied God's omniscience, since he could not harmonize it with free will.[76] Along with omnipotence and goodness Marcion also denied omniscience to God on the ground that he allowed humanity to fall into sin.[77] In a later period the Socinians taught the same thing. God knows all things, they said, but all things according to their nature. Hence, he knows future contingent (accidental) events, not with absolute certainty (for then they would cease to be accidental), but as contingent and accidental; that is, he knows what the future holds insofar as it depends on humans, but not with infallible foreknowledge. If that were the case, the freedom of the will would be lost, God would become the author of sin, and he himself would be subject to necessity.[78]

But such a limitation of God's omniscience is so far from being consistent with Scripture that all but a few theologians rejected it. Christian theology as a rule sought a solution in another direction. Two approaches presented themselves. On the one hand, there is Origen, who made a distinction between foreknowledge and predestination. God indeed knows all things in advance, but this foreknowledge is not the cause and foundation for their happening; on the contrary, God only knows them with certainty beforehand because in time they are bound to happen as a result of the free decisions of human beings: "For they do not happen because they were known, but they were known because they were going to happen."[79] On the other hand, there is Augustine,

---

72. Augustine, *Ad simplicianum*, II, 2.

73. Gregory the Great, *Moralia in Iobum*, 1, 20, ch. 23. Ed. note: See above, p. 188 n. 40.

74. Marius Victor, in D. Petavius, "De Deo," in *Theol. dogm.*, IV, ch. 4.

75. F. A. Philippi, *Kirchliche Glaubenslehre*, 3d ed., 7 vols. in 10 (Gütersloh: C. Bertelsmann, 1870–90), II, 67.

76. Marcus Tullius Cicero, *De fato liber* (Paris: Andream Wechelum, 1565), ch. 14; *De divinatione*, II, 5–7.

77. According to Tertullian, *Against Marcion*, II, 5.

78. O. Fock, *Der Socinianismus nach seiner Stellung in der Gesammtentwicklung des christlichen Geistes, nach seinem historischen Verlauf und nach seinem Lehrbegriff* (Kiel: C. Schröder, 1847), 337–466.

79. Origen, in *Homilies on Genesis*, I, 14; idem, *Contra Celsus*, II, 20.

who also wants to maintain both divine foreknowledge and human freedom of will. "The religious mind chooses both, confesses both, and confirms both by the faith of piety."[80] But he understands that if God knows something in advance, it is certain to happen as a matter of necessity, or else the whole doctrine of foreknowledge would collapse. "If foreknowledge does not foreknow things that are certain to happen, it is nothing at all."[81] He therefore states that the human will along with human nature and all its decisions, rather than being destroyed by God's foreknowledge, is included in it and posited and maintained by it. "For since he foreknows our will, he foreknows whose will it is going to be. There is therefore going to be a will because he has foreknown it."[82] "Our wills, accordingly, have as much power as God wanted them to have and fore-knew they had; and so, whatever power they have, they have most certainly. And whatever they are to do, they most certainly do those very things, for he whose foreknowledge is infallible foreknew that they would have the power to do it and would do it."[83] Scholasticism, however many distinctions it spun out, aligned itself in principle with Augustine.[84]

The Problem of Middle Knowledge

But the Jesuits, entering the discussion, brought change.[85] With a view to squaring God's omniscience with human freedom, following the semi-Pelagian line, they introduced the so-called middle knowledge *(media scientia)* between God's "necessary" and his "free" knowledge. By this "middle" knowledge they meant a divine knowledge of contingent events that is logically antecedent to his decrees. The object of this knowledge is not the merely possible that will never be realized, nor that which by virtue of a divine decree is certain to happen, but the possibilities that depend for their realization on one condition or another. In governing the world, that is, God makes many possible outcomes depend on conditions, and knows in advance what he will do, in case these conditions are, or are not, fulfilled by humans. In all cases, therefore, God is ready. He foresees and knows all possibilities and makes his decisions and provisions with a view to all those possibilities. He knew in advance what he would do if Adam fell and also if he did not fall; if David did or did not go to Keilah; if Tyre and Sidon did or did not repent. Hence, God's knowledge of contingent events precedes his decree concerning "absolute" future events. Though humans at every moment make their free and independent deci-sions, they can never surprise God with the decisions they make or undo his plans, for in his foreknowledge God has taken account of all possibilities.

80. Augustine, *City of God*, V, 9, 10.

81. Augustine, *De libero arbitrio*, III, 4.

82. Ibid., III, 3.

83. Augustine, *City of God*, V, 9.

84. Anselm, *De concordia praescientiae et praedestinationes et gratiae Dei cum libero arbitrio*; P. Lombard, *Sent.*, I, dist. 38; Bonaventure, *Sent.*, I, dist. 38; T. Aquinas, *Summa theol.*, I, qu. 14; Hugo of St. Victor, *De sacramentis christianae fidei*, I, 9.

85. Cf. H. Bavinck, *Reformed Dogmatics*, I, 152 (#48).

This theory of mediate knowledge was supported with numerous Scripture texts that ascribe to God knowledge of what would happen in a given case if some condition was or was not fulfilled (e.g., Gen. 11:6; Exod. 3:19; 34:16; Deut. 7:3–4; 1 Sam. 23:10–13; 25:29ff.; 2 Sam. 12:8; 1 Kings 11:2; 2 Kings 2:10; 13:19; Ps. 81:14–16; Jer. 26:2–3; 38:17–20; Ezek. 2:5–7; 3:4–6; Matt. 11:21, 23; 24:22; 26:53; Luke 22:66–68; John 4:10; 6:15; Acts 22:18; Rom. 9:29; 1 Cor. 2:8).

Though in fact opposed by the Thomists and Augustinians (e.g., by Bannez, the Salmanticenses [Carmelites of Salamanca, Spain], and Billuart), this theory of middle knowledge was also hotly defended by Molinists and Congruists (Suárez, Bellarmine, Lessius, et al.). Fear of Calvinism and Jansenism favored the theory in the Catholic church and in a more or less pronounced form gained acceptance with almost all Roman Catholic theologians.[86] Thus, the line of thought set forth by Augustine was abandoned and that of Origen resumed. While Greek theology had taken this position from the beginning,[87] Roman Catholic theology now followed. Nor were the Lutherans[88] and the Remonstrants[89] ill-disposed to the theory. In modern times many theologians assert, approximately in the same way, that for God, too, the world is a medium of knowledge. He indeed foreknew future contingent events as possible, but learns from the world whether or not they are actually realized. For all cases, however, he knows "an action that will precisely fit the action of the creature, whatever that may chance to be." He established an outline of the world plan but leaves the fleshing out of the outline to creatures.[90] In contrast to this line of thought, following Augustine's example, the Reformed rejected the theory of a "bare foreknowledge" *(nuda praescientia)* and "middle knowledge" *(media scientia).*[91]

86. Ibid.; also Karl Werner, *Der heilige Thomas von Aquino*, 3 vols. (Regensburg: G. J. Manz, 1858–59), III, 389–442; idem, *Geschichte der katholischen Theologie seit dem Trienter Concil bis zur Gegenwart* (Munich: Cotta, 1866), 98ff.; G. Schneemann, *Die Entstehung der thomistisch-molinistischen Controverse*, Supplement 9 to *Stimmen aus Maria Laach* (Freiburg i.B. and St. Louis: Herder, 1880), 9, 13–14; J. Schwane, *Dogmengeschichte*, 4 vols. (Freiburg i.B.: Herder, 1882–95), IV, 37–59; D. Petavius, "De Deo," in *Theol. dogm.*, IV, chs. 6–7.

87. John of Damascus, *The Orthodox Faith*, II, ch. 30.

88. J. Gerhard, *Loci theol.*, II, c. 8, sect. 13; J. A. Quenstedt, *Theologica*, I, 316; J. F. Buddeus, *Institutiones theologiae moralis*, I, 217; F. Reinhard, *Grundriss der Dogmatik*, 116.

89. S. Episcopius, *Institutiones theologicae*, IV, sect. 2, ch. 19; Phillip van Limborch, *Theol. christ.*, II, ch. 8, §20.

90. I. A. Dorner, *A System of Christian Doctrine*, trans. Alfred Cave and J. S. Banks, rev. ed., 4 vols. (Edinburgh: T. & T. Clark, 1888), I, 332–37; R. Rothe, *Theologische Ethik*, 2d rev. ed., 5 vols. (Wittenberg: Zimmerman, 1867–71), §42; H. L. Martensen, *Christian Dogmatics: A Compendium of the Doctrines of Chrisitianity*, trans. William Urwick (Edinburgh: T. & T. Clark, 1871), §16; K. F. A. Kahnis, *Die lutherische Dogmatik, historisch-genetisch dargestellt*, 3 vols. (Leipzig: Dörffling & Franke, 1861–68), I, 343; A. Gretillat, *Exposé de théologie systématique*, 4 vol. (Paris: Fischbacher, 1885–92), III, 237ff.; C. Secrétan, *La civilization et la croyance* (Paris: Alcan, 1887), 260ff.

91. G. Voetius, *Select. disp.*, I, 254–58; W. Twisse, *Dissertatio de scientia media tribus libris absoluta* (Arnhemii: Jacobum à Biesium, 1639), III, 1ff.; F. Turretin, *Institutes of Elenctic Theology*, III, qu. 13; B. de Moor, *Comm. in Marckii Comp.*, I, 659ff.; A. Comrie and N. Holtius, *Examen van het ontwerp van tolerantie*, 10 vols. (Amsterdam: Nicholaas Byl, 1753), IV, 281ff.

Now with respect to this middle knowledge the question is not whether things [or events] are not frequently related to each other by some such conditional connection, one that is known and willed by God himself. If this is all it meant, it could be accepted without any difficulty, just as Gomarus and Waldeus understood and recognized it in this sense.[92] But the theory of middle knowledge is aimed at something different: its purpose is to harmonize the Pelagian notion of the freedom of the will with God's omniscience. In that view, the human will is by its nature indifferent. It can do one thing as well as another. It is determined neither by its own nature nor by the various circumstances in which it has been placed. Although circumstances may influence the will, ultimately the will remains free and chooses as it wills. Of course, freedom of the will thus conceived cannot be harmonized with a decree of God; it essentially consists in independence from the decree of God. So far from determining that will, God left it free; he could not determine that will without destroying it. Over against that will of his rational creatures God has to adopt a posture of watchful waiting. He watches to see what they are going to do. He, however, is omniscient. Hence, he knows all the possibilities, all contingencies, and also foreknows all actual future events. In this context and in keeping with it, God has made all his decisions and decrees. If a person in certain circumstances will accept God's grace, he has chosen that person to eternal life; if that person does not believe, he or she has been rejected.

Now it is clear that this theory diverges in principle from the teaching of Augustine and Thomas Aquinas. Certainly, to their minds God's foreknowledge precedes events, and nothing can happen except by the will of God. "Nothing, therefore, happens but by the will of the Omnipotent."[93] Not the world but the decrees are the medium from which God knows all things.[94] Hence, contingent events and free actions can be infallibly known in their context and order. Scholasticism, admittedly, sometimes already expressed itself on this point in a way that was different from Augustine. Anselm, for example, stated that foreknowledge did not imply an "internal and antecedent necessity" but only an "external and consequent necessity."[95] And Thomas judged that God indeed knows contingent future events eternally and certainly according to the state in which they are actually, that is, according to their own immediacy, but that in their "proximate causes" they are nevertheless contingent and undetermined.[96] This, however, does not alter the fact that with a view to their "primary cause" these contingent future events are absolutely certain and can therefore not be called contingent. And elsewhere he again states that

92. F. Gomarus, *Disputationum theologicarum*, X, 30ff.; A. Walaeus, *Loci communes s. theologiae*, in *Opera omnia*, I, 174–76; cf. H. Heppe, *Die Dogmatik der evangelisch-reformierten Kirche* (Elberseld: R. L. Friedrich, 1861), 64.

93. Augustine, *Enchiridion*, 95; T. Aquinas, *Summa theol.*, I, qu. 14, art. 9, ad. 3.

94. T. Aquinas, *Summa theol.*, I, qu. 14, art. 8; Bonaventure, *Sent.*, II, dist. 37, art. 1, qu. 1.

95. Anselm, *Cur Deus homo*, 16.

96. T. Aquinas, *Summa theol.*, I, qu. 14, art. 13.

"whatever is was destined to be before it came into being, because it existed in its own cause in order that it might come into being."[97]

The doctrine of middle knowledge, however, represents contingent future events as contingent and free also in relation to God. This is with reference not only to God's predestination but also his foreknowledge, for just as in Origen, things do not happen because God knows them, but God foreknows them because they are going to happen. Hence, the sequence is not necessary knowledge, the knowledge of vision, the decree to create (etc.); instead, it is necessary knowledge, middle knowledge, decree to create (etc.), and the knowledge of vision.[98] God does not derive his knowledge of the free actions of human beings from his own being, his own decrees, but from the will of creatures.[99] God, accordingly, becomes dependent on the world, derives knowledge from the world that he did not have and could not obtain from himself, and hence, in his knowledge, ceases to be one, simple, and independent—that is, God. Conversely, the creature in large part becomes independent vis-à-vis God. It did indeed at one time receive "being" *(esse)* and "being able" *(posse)* from God but now it has the "volition" *(velle)* completely in its own hand. It sovereignly makes it own decisions and either accomplishes something or does not accomplish something apart from any preceding divine decree. Something can therefore come into being quite apart from God's will. The creature is now creator, autonomous, sovereign; the entire history of the world is taken out of God's controlling hands and placed into human hands. First, humans decide; then God responds with a plan that corresponds to that decision. Now if such a decision occurred once—as in the case of Adam—we might be able to conceive it. But such decisions of greater or less importance occur thousands of times in every human life. What are we to think, then, of a God who forever awaits all those decisions and keeps in readiness a store of all possible plans for all possibilities? What then remains of even a sketch of the world plan when left to humans to flesh out? And of what value is a government whose chief executive is the slave of his own subordinates?

In the theory of middle knowledge, that is precisely the case with God. God looks on, while humans decide. It is not God who makes distinctions among people, but people distinguish themselves. Grace is dispensed, according to merit; predestination depends on good works. The ideas that Scripture everywhere opposes and Augustine rejected in his polemic against Pelagius are made standard Roman Catholic doctrine by the teaching of the Jesuits.[100] The proponents of middle knowledge indeed appeal to many texts of Scripture but entirely without warrant. There is no doubt that Scripture acknowledges the fact that God has put things (events, etc.) in a varied web of connections to each other, and that these connections are frequently of a conditional nature, so that

97. Cf. C. R. Billuart, *Cursus theologiae*, 9 vols. (Maastricht: Jacobi Lekens, 1769–70), I, 440ff.

98. G. Jansen, *Prael.theol.*, II, 110ff.

99. J. Schwane, *Dogmengeschichte*, IV, 52.

100. C. R. Billuart, *Cursus theologiae*, I, 479.

one thing cannot happen unless something else happens first. [For examples],
apart from faith there is no salvation; without work there is no food (etc.).
But the texts cited by Jesuits to undergird the theory of middle knowledge
do not prove what needs to be proved. Admittedly, they speak of condition
and fulfillment, of obedience and promise, of assumption and consequences,
of what will happen if one path is chosen or another. But none of these texts
denies that in all cases God—though he speaks to and deals with humans in
human terms—knew and determined what would surely happen. Between that
which is merely possible and will never be realized—present in God only as
an idea—and that which is certain and has been decreed by God, there is no
longer any area left that can be controlled by the will of humans. Something
always belongs either to the one or to the other. If it is only a possibility and
will never be realized, it is the object of God's "necessary" knowledge; and if it
will indeed one day be realized, it is the content of his "free" knowledge. There
is no middle ground between the two, no "middle" knowledge.

The theorists of middle knowledge, furthermore, fail to achieve what they
aim to achieve. They want to bring human freedom of the will—in the sense
of indifference—into harmony with divine foreknowledge. Now, they claim
that this foreknowledge conceived as middle knowledge leaves human conduct
totally free, nonnecessary. And this is indeed correct, except that in that case it
ceases to be foreknowledge. If God infallibly knows in advance what a person
will do in a given case, he can foreknow this only if the person's motives determine his or her will in one specific direction, and this will therefore does not
consist in indifference. Conversely, *if* that will were indifferent, foreknowledge
would be impossible, and only post-factum knowledge would exist. God's
foreknowledge and the will conceived as arbitrariness are mutually exclusive.
For, as Cicero already phrased it, "if he knows it, it will certainly take place,
but if it is bound to take place, no such thing as chance exists." Therefore,
along with Augustine, we must seek the solution of the problem in another
direction. The freedom of the will does not, as we will discover later, consist
in indifference, arbitrariness, or chance, but in "rational delight." This rational
delight, rather than being in conflict with the foreknowledge of God, is implied in and upheld by it. The human will, along with its nature, antecedents
and motives, its decisions and consequences, is integrated into "the order of
causes that is certain to God and embraced by his foreknowledge."[101] In the
knowledge of God things are interrelated in the same web of connections in
which they occur in reality. It is not foreknowledge, nor is it predestination,
that now and then intervenes from above with compelling force; every human
decision and act is motivated, rather, by that which precedes it, and in that
web of connections it is included in the knowledge of God. In keeping with
their own divinely known and ordained nature, contingent events and free

---

101. Augustine, *City of God*, V, 9.

actions are links in the order of causes that, little by little, is revealed to us in the history of the world.

Wisdom

[202] The knowledge of God, viewed from another angle, is called "wisdom." The distinction between the two is known universally. Nearly all languages also have different words for these two concepts. Everyone knows that erudition, knowledge, and wisdom are far from being synonymous and are certainly not always found together in the same person. A simple person often excels a learned one in wisdom. Knowledge and wisdom are rooted in different human capacities. We acquire knowledge by study, wisdom by insight. The former is achieved discursively; the latter, intuitively. Knowledge is theoretical; wisdom is practical and goal-oriented. Knowledge is a matter of the mind apart from the will; wisdom, though a matter of the mind, is made subservient to the will. Knowledge, accordingly, is often totally unrelated to life, but wisdom is oriented to, and closely tied in with, life. It is ethical in nature; it is "the art of living well"; it characterizes the conduct of those who make the right use of their greater store of knowledge and match the best means to the best ends. Even the etymology of the two words points to this distinction. *Sapiens* comes from *sapere*, to taste; it therefore points in the direction of experience, indicating that guided by personal experience a person has arrived at his or her own independent judgment. The Greek word for wise (σοφος) is probably also linked with σαφης (clear, plain, distinct) and in that case has the same basic meaning. Also, among Oriental people we encounter this distinction but with a notable difference. While in Western countries *knowledge* is in the foreground, in the East it is *wisdom*. Orientals tend to live more by contemplation than by abstract thought; they operate with images of the things themselves rather than with concepts. Subjectively, their life is more an expression of the heart than of the mind; and objectively, they are more in touch with the immediate realities of life. Not in the mind but in the heart, the radical center of the personality, subject and object meet each other, and either repel each other most violently or attract each other most tenderly. It is as if the substances of things fuse into each other by a sense of vital congeniality.

We also find this oriental characteristic to a high degree in Israel. Naturally here too, and in due time, wisdom (חכמה from חכם: to be firm, closed, solid; substantive: solidity) emerged. Here, however, it became the handmaiden of revelation. Genuine wisdom is not the product of the human intellect but rooted in the fear of the Lord and consists in the moral discipline that conforms to the law of the Lord and manifests itself in a moral life (Deut. 4:6–8; Ps. 19:7; 111:10; Job 28:28; Prov. 1:7; 9:10). When in the course of history people began to penetrate more deeply into God's revelation in nature and in the law, wisdom achieved a place of its own, developed a literature of its own, and conveyed its thoughts in a form of its own, the form of proverbs (מְשָׁלִים). Not only intellect and knowledge are now ascribed to God in Scripture but also wisdom. Speaking through the word, God created the world (Gen. 1:3; Ps. 33:6; 107:20; 119:105; 147:15; 148:5; Isa. 40:8; 48:13). At first Israel especially notes God's power and majesty in creation. Gradually, however, the Israelite mind, nurtured and led by the fear of the Lord, began to penetrate more deeply into the work of God in nature and in the law, and marveled at his adorable wisdom. Both the constitution of the world and God's revelation in Israel are attributed to God's wisdom (Job 9:4; 12:13, 17; 37:24–38:38; Isa. 40:28; Ps. 104:24; Deut. 4:6–8; Jer. 10:12; Ps. 19:7), and in Proverbs 8:22ff. and Job 28:23ff. this wisdom by which and with which God brought forth all things is personified. The New Testament continues this line of thought; it not only ascribes wisdom to God (Rom. 16:27; 1 Tim. 1:17; Jude 25, Rev. 5:12; 7:12), but also declares that the world was created by the word of God (John 1:3; Heb. 11:3) and sees God's wisdom especially revealed in the foolishness of the cross (1 Cor. 1:18), in Christ (1 Cor. 1:24), in the church (Eph. 3:10), in all of God's providential guidance of Israel and the Gentiles (Rom. 11:33).[102]

It was especially Philo who linked this doctrine of Scripture concerning the word and the wisdom of God with [Plato's] "ideas." Thus the foundation was laid for the doctrine of the Logos, which will be discussed more fully in the locus on the Trinity. In a later period Plato's theory of the ideas once again exerted a powerful influence on Christian theology, now by way of Neoplatonism. In this form it came to Augustine, who assigned to it a place in theology. For this purpose he of course had to modify it at important points. In the first place, the "ideas" [in Augustine's thinking] do not constitute a world by themselves, an "intelligible cosmos" (κοσμος νοητος), next to and outside of God, but now they exist in God and form the contents of his thinking: "These ideas [rationes: active creative principles], however, must be judged to exist only in the mind of the Creator."[103] They are God's thoughts concerning all created beings, both before and after creation; hence, these thoughts are eternal and immutable, for in God there can be nothing that is not eternal and immutable.[104] "For to claim that God has a new plan is absurd, not to say wicked."[105] Yet these ideas in God's

102. Cf. I. Hooykaas, *Wijsheid onder Hebreën* (Leiden: P. Engels, 1862); J. F. Bruch, *Die Weisheitslehre der Hebräer* (Strassburg: Treuttel und Würtz, 1851); Karl Burger, "Weisheit, " *PRE²*, XVI, 715–20; G. F. Oehler, *Die Grundzüge der alttestamentlichen Weisheit* (Tübingen: L. F. Fues, 1854); idem, *Theology of the Old Testament*, §235ff.; H. Schultz, *Alttestamentliche Theologie*, 4th ed., 548ff.; Franz Delitzsch, "Commentar über das solomonische Spruchbuch," in *Biblischer Commentar über die poetischen Bücher des Alten Testaments* (Leipzig: Dörffling & Franke, 1873); H. Cremer, *Biblico-Theological Lexicon of New Testament Greek*, s.v. "σοφος"; Eduard König, *Der Offenbarungsbegriff des Alten Testaments*, 2 vols. (Leipzig: J. C. Hinrichs, 1882), I, 194ff.; R. Smend, *Lehrbuch der alttestamentlichen Religionsgeschichte* (Freiburg: J. C. B. Mohr, 1893), 508ff.; F. Schleiermacher, *The Christian Faith* (Edinburgh: T. & T. Clark, 1989), §§168–69; F. H. R. Frank, *System der christlichen Wahrheit*, 2 vols. (Erlangen: A. Deichert, 1878–80), I, 254ff.

103. Augustine, *Eighty-three Different Questions*, trans. D. L. Mosher, Fathers of the Church 70 (Washington, D.C.: Catholic University of America Press, 1982), qu. 46; idem, *Literal Meaning of Genesis*, IV, 6, 24, 29; V, 13.

104. Augustine, in *The Trinity*, IV, 1; idem, *City of God*, XI, 5.

105. Augustine, *De ordine*, II, 17; ET: *Divine Providence and the Problem of Evil*, trans. Robert P. Russell, Fathers of the Church: Writings of Saint Augustine 1 (New York: CIMA, 1948).

mind are not identical with his self-knowledge, nor with the Logos or the Son, as had sometimes been said by earlier church fathers. Augustine maintains the essential distinction between God and the world and shuns pantheism. "For in one sense those things are present in him, which were made by him; in another sense those things are present in him, which is he himself."[106] On the other hand, Augustine can only believe that God created all things on the model of "ideas," a fact that manifests his wisdom. "Thus the wisdom of God, by which all things have been made, contains all things according to a design before it makes them."[107] "All things were created by reason, for he made nothing unwittingly. Knowing them, he made them; he did not learn to know them after they had been made."[108] The creation is a realization of the ideas of God. Hence, there is a close connection between the ideas and creation. The ideas are the patterns and forms of things, primary forms, the reasons for things, stable and immutable,"[109] and therefore the forms not only of species but of individual objects. "Inasmuch as the creation of all things rests on a rational cause, . . . the creation of individual objects must rest upon particular rational causes."[110]

Still, Augustine does not always strictly adhere to this view. At times the ideas also again occur in Augustine as types and patterns that emerge gradually and are only fully realized in the new heaven and the new earth.[111] Furthermore, the connection which, in Augustine's view, exists between the ideas and created objects is not clear. The ideas do not only exist in God as archetypes but are also active forces and immanent principles in things. In translating the Greek word ἰδέαι, he preferred the word *rationes* (formative rational principles) over Cicero's translation by "forms" or "species."[112] The ideas are, as it were, embodied in the things themselves. Ideas and created things are not dualistically related to each other as original models (παραδειγματα) and likenesses (ὁμοιωματα), as "true" and "untrue," as "immutable" and "mutable"; the ideas are the soul and principle of things. Movement pertains to creatures by virtue of these "innate rational causes."[113] Furthermore, the causality inherent in the ideas is still always mediated by the will of God. That will is the real and final cause of the existence of things.[114]

106. Augustine, *Literal Meaning of Genesis*, II, 6.

107. Augustine, *Lectures on the Gospel of John*, tract. 1, *NPNF (1)*, VII, 131–37.

108. Augustine, *Eighty-three Different Questions*, qu. 46, n. 2; idem, *Literal Meaning of Genesis*, V, 8; idem, *The Trinity*, XV, 13; idem, *City of God*, XI, 10.

109. Augustine, *Eighty-three Different Questions*, qu. 46, n. 2.

110. Ibid.; idem, *City of God*, XI, 10; idem, *Literal Meaning of Genesis*, III, 12, 14; V, 14, 15.

111. Augustine, *Literal Meaning of Genesis*, V, 11.

112. Augustine, *Eighty-three Different Questions*, qu. 46; idem, *Literal Meaning of Genesis*, I, 18; II, 16; IX, 18.

113. Augustine, *Literal Meaning of Genesis*, IV, 33.

114. Augustine, *City of God*, XXI, 8; cf. T. Gangauf, *Metaphysische Psychologie des heiligen Augustinus* (Augsburg: K. Kollmann, 1852), 77ff.; H. Ritter, *Geschichte der christlichen Philosophie*, 4 vols. (Hamburg: F. Perthes, 1841–45), II, 310ff.; E. Melzer, *Die augustinische Lehre vom Kausalitätsverhältnis Gottes zur Welt* (Neisse: Graveur, 1892).

Aside from Augustine, we find this doctrine of the ideas in numerous other authors,[115] also in some Reformed theologians.[116] Later this doctrine of the ideas almost completely disappeared from the field of dogmatics. In modern philosophy the meaning of the word "idea" changed as well. In earlier centuries the word "idea" denoted the model or pattern of things in the mind of the Creator, while a "concept" was the imprint of things in the knowing mind. But in modern philosophy "idea" has become the word for those concepts that are obtained, not by sense perception, but by pure thought (Descartes); of these concepts we have no experience and concerning them, therefore, we have no scientific certainty (Kant); they can only be immediately discerned in feeling or reason (Jacobi).[117] Usage, however, at least in the Dutch and the German language, still frequently carries a reminder of the old meaning. The word still denotes—especially in the realm of art—an objective pattern, a paradigm, a form of ideal perfection. Accordingly, we speak of an idea of God, of freedom, of art, of science, of the true, the good, and the beautiful (etc.). Applied to God, the idea means that God has made all things with wisdom, that wisdom is "the firstborn of his ways" (Prov. 8:22; Col. 1:15; Rev. 3:14). God is the supreme artist. Just as a human artist realizes his idea in a work of art, so God creates all things in accordance with the ideas he has formed. The world is God's work of art. He is the architect and builder of the entire universe. God does not work without thinking, but is guided in all his works by wisdom, by his ideas.

But there is also a difference between God and an earthly artist. God's ideas are absolutely original; they arise from his own being; they are eternal and immutable. Indeed, they are one with his own being. The ideas in God are the very being of God insofar as this being is the pattern of created things and can be expressed and modeled in finite creatures. Every creature is a revelation of God and participates in God's being. The nature of this participation is not such that creatures are modifications of the divine being or that they have in some realistic sense received this divine being into themselves. But every creature has its own distinct being because in its existence it is an exemplification of the divine being. On account of the multiplicity and wealth of the ideas of God realized in the created world God's wisdom is properly called "many-sided"

115. Clement of Alexander, *Stromateis*, IV, ch. 25; V, ch. 3; Tertullian, *De testimonio animae*, 18; Eusebius, *Praeparatio evangelica*, 1, 14, ch. 44; Origen, on John 1:1; Pseudo-Dionysius, *On the Divine Names*, ch. 5; Anselm, *Monologion*, chs. 8ff.; P. Lombard, *Sent.*, I, dist. 35; T. Aquinas, *Summa theol.*, I, qu. 15, qu. 44, art. 3; idem, *Summa contra gentiles*, 54; idem, *Sent.*, I, dist. 36; Bonaventure, *Sent.*, I, dist. 35; D. Petavius, *De theologicis dogmatibus*, IV, chs. 9–11; M. J. Scheeben, *Handbuch der katholischen Dogmatik*, I, 657ff.; Joseph Willhelm and Thomas Bartholomew Scannell, *A Manual of Catholic Theology: Based on Scheeben's "Dogmatik,"* 4th ed., 2 vols. (London: Kegan Paul, Trench, Trubner & Co.; New York: Benziger Brothers, 1909); J. B. Heinrich and C. Gutberlet, *Dogmatische Theologie*, 2d ed., 10 vols. (Mainz: Kirchheim, 1881–90), III, 653; H. Th. Simar, *Lehrbuch der Dogmatik*, 3d ed. (Freiburg i.B.: Herder, 1893), 147ff.

116. A. Polanus, *Syn. theol.*, 267–68; J. Zanchi(us), *Op. theol.*, II, 201; G. Voetius, *Select. disp.*, 258ff.; W. Twisse, *Dissertatio de scientia media tribus libris absoluta* (Arnhemii: Jacobum à Biesium, 1639), 312ff.

117. Cf. R. Eisler, *Wörterbuch der philosophischen Begriffe*, s.v. "Idee."

(Eph. 3:10). Still, God's wisdom is of one piece, and his idea of the world is one, gradually unfolding as it is over the centuries and guiding reality toward the preestablished goal. On account of this paradigmatic character of the ideas in God, there is actually no "idea" of sin as such. For sin has no being of its own. It is rather a diminution of being, a deformation. Although it is an object of God's knowledge and is made subservient to his glory by his wisdom, yet in itself it is not an idea of his wisdom, nor a ray of his light. Evil is known in light of the idea of the good of which it is the privation.[118] The wisdom of God is, however, manifest in the creation, ordering, guidance, and government of all things. Wisdom is and remains the "master worker" (Prov. 8:30), the "fashioner of all things" (Wis. 7:22), which creates and governs all things, leading them onward to their destination, which is the glorification of God's name.

Trustworthiness

[203] Among God's intellectual attributes, finally, is his trustworthiness. The Hebrew word אֱמֶת (adj.: אָמֵן) derives from the verb אָמַן (to make firm, to build, to undergird; intransitive: to be firm; Hiphil: to hang onto, to trust in, to be sure of). It denotes, subjectively, the act of hanging onto something, faith (Greek: πιστις), and, objectively, the firmness, trustworthiness, and truth of the person or cause in which a person has put his or her trust. In line with this twofold meaning of the Hebrew, the Septuagint sometimes renders these words by ἀληθεια, ἐν ἀληθεια, and at other times by πιστευω, πιστις, and πιστος. English translations, accordingly, have "true," "faithful," and "faithfulness." In ordinary Greek, hence also in the Septuagint and the New Testament, the term ἀληθεια had a meaning too specific to adequately convey the Hebrew words and therefore had to be augmented by the word πιστος, and so forth. That is the reason why the trustworthiness of God is not only an attribute of the intellect but also of the will and therefore should, in strict accuracy, have to be treated again later. Veracity and truth, trustworthiness and faithfulness, are too closely associated, however, for us to split them apart. The name YHWH as such already expresses that he remains who he is. He is a God of faithfulness and without deceit (Deut. 32:4; Jer. 10:10; Ps. 31:6; 2 Chron. 15:3). It implies (1) that he is the real, the true God in contrast to false gods, the idols, which are "vanities" (Deut. 32:21; etc.); and (2) that as such he will always stand by his words and promises and prove them true, so that he will be seen as completely trustworthy. He is not a human that he should lie or change his mind (Num. 23:19; 1 Sam. 15:29). All that proceeds from him bears the stamp of truthfulness.

Over and over there is mention of God's kindness (חֶסֶד) and faithfulness (cf. Gen. 24:49; 47:29; Josh. 2:14; 2 Sam. 2:6; 15:20; Ps. 40:11), of his steadfast love (חֶסֶד) and truth (Gen. 24:27; Exod. 34:6; Ps. 57:3; 61:7; 89:14; etc.).[119] All

---

118. T. Aquinas, *Summa theol.*, I, qu. 15, art. 3.

119. Ed. note: The English translation of חֶסֶד as "kindness" and "steadfast love" reflects the Dutch distinction between *weldadigheid* and *goedertierenheid*.

his words, ordinances, paths, works, commandments, and laws are pure truth (2 Sam. 7:28; Ps. 19:9; 25:10; 33:4; 111:7; 119:86, 142, 151; Dan. 4:37). His truth and faithfulness are so abundantly and gloriously manifest on earth that they reach up into the clouds (Ps. 36:5; Exod. 34:6). He repeatedly confirms his word by swearing an oath by himself (Gen. 22:16; etc.; Heb. 6:13). He is therefore frequently called "the Rock," who by his unshakable firmness offers support to his people (Deut. 32:4, 15, 18, 30–31, 37); this word occurs also in many proper names [rock = *zur*] (Num. 1:5–6, 10; 2:12; 3:35; 7:36, 41; 10:19; further in 2 Sam. 22:3, 32; Ps. 18:2, 31; 19:14; 28:1; 31:2–3; 71:3; 144:1–2; Isa. 26:4). As such a God of truth and faithfulness, he keeps covenant (Deut. 4:31; 7:9; Ps. 40:11; Hos. 11:1; etc.) and is a completely trustworthy refuge for all his people (Ps. 31:5–6; 36:5ff.; 43:2; 54:7; 57:3; 71:22; 96:13; 143:1; 146:6; etc.).

Similarly, in the New Testament he is called the true God; that is, only he is the real and true God who revealed himself in Christ (John 17:3; 1 John 5:20). All he reveals is pure truth. He is a true God (θεος ἀληθης), in contrast to all human beings (John 3:33; Rom. 3:4). His word is the truth, his gospel is truth, Christ is the truth (John 14:6; 17:17; Eph. 1:13). Even now he is what he has always been. The New Testament is the fulfillment and confirmation of the promises he made in the days of the Old Testament. He has remembered his holy covenant and the oath he swore to Abraham (Luke 1:68–73). His faithfulness comes out in that he is and remains the God of the covenant and completely grants salvation (1 Cor. 1:9; 10:13; 1 Thess. 5:24; 2 Thess. 3:3; Heb. 10:23; 11:11; 1 John 1:9). He cannot deny himself (2 Tim. 2:13). In Christ all his promises are "Yes" and "Amen" (2 Cor. 1:18, 20). Christ is the "faithful witness" (ὁ μαρτυς ὁ πιστος) (Rev. 1:5; 3:14; 19:11); for that reason he is and can be the unchanging object of our faith (πιστις).[120]

Scripture, accordingly, uses the word "truth" in more than one sense. And philosophy, too, as a rule distinguishes between three concepts of truth: truth or veracity in essence (in things); truth or veracity in expression (in words); truth or veracity in knowing (in the intellect); in other words, metaphysical, ethical, and logical truth or veracity.[121] Metaphysical or ontological truth consists in an object, person, or cause being all that belongs to its nature. In that sense gold that is gold not only in appearance but also in reality is true gold. The antonyms of truth in that sense are falsehood, spuriousness, vanity, nonbeing. In this sense truth is a property of all being; it is identical with substance. Especially Augustine often spoke of truth in that sense. All being or essence as such is true and beautiful and good. Granted, there is immense diversity

---

120. H. H. Wendt, "Der Gebrauch der Wörter ἀληθεια, ἀληθης, und ἀληθινος im Neuen Testamente," *Theologische Studien und Kritiken* 56/3 (1883): 511–47; H. Cremer, *Biblico-Theological Lexicon of New Testament Greek*, 109–26.

121. M. Liberatore, *Institutiones philosophicae*, 8th ed. (1855), I, 70ff.; F. Schmid, "Der Begriff des 'Wahren,'" *Philosophisches Jahrbuch* 6 (1893): 35–48, 140–50; P. van Mastricht, *Theologia*, II, 14, 5; B. de Moor, *Comm. in Marckii Comp.*, I, 676.

in degrees of creaturely being; yet all things have received from God a unique being of their own and as such participate in the divine being.[122] From the consideration of this creaturely being Augustine moves to the consideration of God. In Scripture God is called the true God in distinction from idols, which are vanities. Thus, in Augustine, God is the true, unique, simple, immutable, and eternal being. By comparison to his being, creatural being is to be considered nonbeing. God is the "supreme being, the supreme truth, and the supreme good." He is pure being. He does not possess but is the truth. "O Truth, which you truly are!"[123]

In addition, God is also the truth in the second sense, that is, the ethical sense. By ethical truth we mean the correspondence between a person's being and a person's self-revelation in word or deed. Those who say one thing but think another are untrue; they are liars. The antonym of truth in this sense is the lie. Now in the case of God, there is complete correspondence between his being and his revelation (Num. 23:19; 1 Sam. 15:29; Titus 1:2; Heb. 6:18). It is impossible for God to lie or deny himself.

Finally, God is also the truth in a logical sense. This truth consists in correspondence between thought and reality, the conformity or adequation of the intellect to the [real] thing. Our concepts are true when they bear the exact imprint of reality. In this sense truth is opposed to error. Now God is the truth also in that he knows all things as they really are. His knowing is correct, unchangeable, fully adequate. Indeed, in his knowing he is the truth itself, just as in his being he is the ontological truth. God's knowledge is dynamic, absolute, fully correspondent truth. It is not acquired by research and reflection but is inherent in the divine being (essential) and precedes the existence of things. It is of one piece with God's very nature and, therefore, substantial truth. God's word, law, and gospel, accordingly, are pure truth. They are all as they should be.

Now though these three meanings of the term "truth" are distinct, they are also one. This unity arises from the fact that truth in all three senses consists in correspondence between thought and being, between the ideal and the real. God is truth in a metaphysical sense, for he is the unity of thought and being. He is completely self-conscious. He is truly God, fully answering to the idea of God that is present within himself. God is truth in an ethical sense, for he reveals himself, speaks, acts, and appears as he truly is and thinks. And he is the truth in a logical sense, for he conceives things as they are; rather, things are as he conceives them to be. He is the truth in its absolute fullness. He, therefore, is the primary, the original truth, the source of all truth, the truth in all truth. He is the ground of the truth—of the true being—of all things, of their knowability and conceivability, the ideal and archetype of all truth,

---

122. Cf., e.g., Augustine, *City of God,* XI, 23; idem, *Concerning the Nature of the Good, against the Manichaeans,* ch. 19.

123. Augustine, *Confessions,* X, 41; VII, 10; XII, 25.

of all ethical being, of all the rules and laws, in light of which the nature and manifestation of all things should be judged and on which they should be modeled. God is the source and origin of the knowledge of truth in all areas of life; the light in which alone we can see light, the sun of all spirits. "You I invoke, O God, the truth in, by, and through whom all truths are true."[124]

MORAL ATTRIBUTES

Goodness

[204] Among God's ethical attributes first place is due to God's goodness. This attribute is even known from nature. Plato equated the idea of the good with the deity. But the term "good" is used in a variety of ways. Its original and primary meaning seems to denote a relation of one thing to another rather than an inner quality. In Socrates, for example, the good is identical with the useful, with that which is good and useful for another.[125] Hence, there is no absolute good, only a relative good. Utility and inutility (damage) are the criteria of good and evil. Greek ethics in general stuck with this position; the question concerning the highest good coincides with that concerning human happiness. Good is that which all desire.[126] Hence, the common definition: "Good is that which all things long for."[127] A utilitarian and eudaemonistic morality holds onto this meaning of the word and identifies the standard of the good with the advancement of the well-being of the individual and society.[128] Nietzsche, in writing *The [Will to Power: An Attempted] Transvaluation of All Values,* also proceeded from this meaning of the term. "Good," says he, originally meant something like "distinguished," "strong," "powerful," "beautiful"; and "bad" was the word for the "plain, ordinary person."[129] Indeed, the word "good" often has this meaning, as when we speak of a "good" house, a "good" friend, and so forth, and mean by it that a person or thing has certain good qualities and is useful for some purpose. Used in that sense, the word "good" has no independent concrete meaning of its own but depends for its meaning on the purpose that the person or thing must serve and hence varies in meaning with

124. Augustine, *Soliloquies,* I, 1; cf., T. Aquinas, *Summa theol.,* I, qu. 16, 17; I, 2, qu. 3, art. 7; idem, *Summa contra gentiles,* I, chs. 59–62; III, ch. 51; Bonaventure, *Sent.,* I, dist. 8, art. 1; M. J. Scheeben, *Handbuch der katholischen Dogmatik,* I, 578ff., 663ff. Ed. note: For ET, see p. 206 n. 115. J. Gerhard, *Loci theol.,* II, c. 8, sect. 16; A. Polanus, *Syn. theol.,* II, ch. 27; J. Zanchi(us), *Op. theol.,* II, cols. 226–42; L. Meijer, *Verhandelingen over de goddelyke eigenschappen,* 4 vols. (Groningen: Jacob Bolt, 1783), IV, 1–88.

125. Xenophon, *Memorabilia and Oeconomicus,* IV, 6, 8ff.

126. Plato, *Symposium,* 204E; Aristotle, *Nicomachean Ethics,* I, 2.

127. E.g., in Pseudo-Dionysius, *On the Divine Names,* ch. 4; T. Aquinas, *Summa theol.,* I, qu. 5, art. 1; I, qu. 16, art. 1, 3; idem, *Summa contra gentiles,* I, 38, 40; idem, *Sent.,* I, dist. 8, art. 3.

128. F. Paulsen, *System der Ethik mit einem Umriss der Staats- und Gesellschaftslehre,* 2 vols. (Berlin: Hertz, 1889), 171ff.; W. M. Wundt, *Ethik* (Stuttgart: F. Enke, 1886), 18ff.; cf. also R. Eisler, *Wörterbuch der philosophischen Begriffe,* s.v. "Ethik"; idem, *Kritische Einführung in die Philosophie* (Berlin: E. S. Mittler, 1905), 285ff.

129. F. Nietzsche, *On the Genealogy of Morals,* trans. Douglas Smith (New York and Oxford: Oxford University Press, 1998), 12ff.

different peoples. Greeks associate it with beauty, Romans with high birth and wealth, Germans with what is appropriate and productive; and in each of these contexts also the meaning of ἀρετή, *virtus*, and virtue differs. The category of the good in general includes goods that are useful, delightful, aesthetic, and ethically sound.[130] In all these different senses the good is still a relative concept and denotes "that which all things long for." Still, this does not exhaust the meaning of the word. We also speak of a "good" as such. A transition to that meaning is the good as moral or respectable good. That which is good in a moral sense is good in and by itself regardless of its advantageous or harmful consequences; it has absolute value.

According to Scripture God is the sum total of all perfections (metaphysical goodness). All virtues are present in him in an absolute sense. Scripture only a few times calls God good in an absolute sense. "No one is good but God alone" (Mark 10:18; Luke 18:19). He is perfect (τέλειος, Matt. 5:48). But whatever virtue Scripture ascribes to God, it always presupposes that that virtue is his in an absolute sense. Knowledge, wisdom, power, love, and righteousness are uniquely his, that is, in a divine manner. His goodness, accordingly, is one with his absolute perfection. In him "idea" and "reality" are one. He is "pure form," "utterly pure act." He does not have to become anything, but is what he is eternally. He has no goal outside himself but is self-sufficient, all-sufficient (Ps. 50:8ff.; Isa. 40:28ff.; Hab. 2:20). He receives nothing, but only gives. All things need him; he needs nothing or nobody. He always aims at himself because he cannot rest in anything other than himself. Inasmuch as he himself is the absolutely good and perfect one, he may not love anything else except with a view to himself. He may not and cannot be content with less than absolute perfection. When he loves others, he loves himself in them: his own virtues, works, and gifts.[131] For the same reason he is also blessed in himself as the sum of all goodness, of all perfection.

Aristotle already affirmed that God was the Blessed One, because he was the unity of thinking and thought and completely above all craving, striving, and willing.[132] At all times those who believed in the primacy of the intellect have aligned themselves with Aristotle and aspired to blessedness in thinking, knowing, and contemplation.[133] And this was correct to the extent that absolute blessedness is a condition of rest, incompatible with striving toward a goal, and to the extent that it presupposes consciousness. Blessedness is unique to rational beings. The Unconscious in von Hartmann, like the will in Schopenhauer,

130. T. Aquinas *Summa theol.*, I, qu. 5, art. 6; I, 2, qu. 99, art. 5.

131. On the goodness of God in the sense of perfection: Augustine, *Concerning the Nature of the Good, against the Manichaeans*, 1; idem, *The Trinity*, VIII, 3; Pseudo-Dionysius, *The Divine Names and Mystical Theology*, ch. 13; T. Aquinas, *Summa theol.*, I, qu. 4–6; idem, *Summa contra gentiles*, I, 28; D. Petavius, "De Deo," in *Theol. dogm.*, VI, chs. 1ff.; J. Gerhard, *Loci theol.*, II, c. 8, sects. 10, 17; J. Zanchi(us), *Op. theol.*, II, 138ff.; 326ff.; A. Polanus, *Syn. theol.*, II, ch. 9.

132. E. Zeller, *Die Philosophie der Griechen*, III, 367ff.

133. T. Aquinas, *Summa theologiae*, I, 2, qu. 3, art. 4.

is defined by absolute *un*blessedness, which itself requires redemption.[134] For that reason Drews states that the property of perfection cannot be attributed to God. A perfect God would be a total abstraction and render the existence of the world inexplicable: a God who had everything, who was perfectly blessed and self-sufficient, would need no change, no world.[135] But precisely this theory of the absolute unblessedness of God cautions us against ascribing—in the case both of God and of humans—primacy to the will, as did Duns Scotus and many others after him. Much sounder, therefore, is the position of Bonaventure, who saw the intellect and the will as being conjointly the seat of blessedness.[136] Just as in the case of humans, beatitude will embrace body and soul and all their faculties, so in the case of God it consists not only in perfect knowledge but equally in perfect power, goodness, holiness, and so on. "Beatitude is the perfect state of all goods in their aggregation."[137]

But that which is good in itself is also good for others. And God, as the perfect and blessed One, is the supreme good for his creatures, "the supreme good all things strive for, the fount of all good things, the good of every good, the one necessary and all-sufficient good, the end of all goods" (Ps. 4:6–7; 73:25–26). He alone is the good to be enjoyed, while creatures are goods that are to be used.[138] Especially Augustine frequently described God as "the supreme good."[139] In him alone is everything creatures seek and need. He is the supreme good for all creatures, though in varying degrees, depending on the extent to which each creature shares in the divine goodness and is able to enjoy him. It is he toward whom all creatures, consciously or unconsciously, willingly or unwillingly, strive, the object of every creature's desire. A creature finds no rest except in God alone. Thus Christian theologians have at all times located the supreme good in God, and it did not enter their minds to locate it in some moral deed or virtue of creatures, in duty (Kant), in the kingdom of God (Ritschl), in love (Drummond), or in any other creature. Furthermore, as the supreme good, God is also the overflowing fountain of all goods.[140] "Since God is perfectly good, he is unceasingly beneficent."[141] No good exists in any creature except that which comes from and through him. He is the efficient, exemplary, and final cause of all good, however diverse it may be in creatures.

134. E. von Hartmann, *Philosophie des Unbewussten,* 9th ed., 2 vols. (Berlin: C. Duncker, 1882), II, 434; idem, *Religionsphilosophie,* 2d ed., 2 vols. (Bad Sachsa im Harz: Hermann Haacke, 1907), II, 152ff.

135. A. Drews, *Die deutsche Spekulation seit Kant,* 2d ed. (Leipzig: G. Fock, 1895), II, 593ff.

136. Bonaventure, *Sent.,* IV, dist. 49, pt. 1, art. 1, qu. 4–5.

137. Boethius, *The Consolation of Philosophy,* 4. On the blessedness of God: Augustine, *City of God,* XII, 1; T. Aquinas, *Summa theol.,* I, qu. 26; J. Gerhard, *Loci theol.,* II, c. 8, sect. 19; J. Zanchi(us), *Op. theol.,* II, 155ff.; A. Polanus, *Syn. theol.,* II, ch. 17.

138. Augustine, *On Christian Doctrine,* I, ch. 3; idem, *The Trinity,* X, 10; P. Lombard, *Sent.,* I, dist. 1; Bonaventure, *Sent.,* I, dist. 1.

139. Augustine, *The Trinity,* VIII, 3; idem, *Expositions on the Psalms, NPNF (2),* VIII, 63–64, on Ps. 26; idem, *On Christian Doctrine,* I, 7; cf. Anselm, *Proslogion,* chs. 23–25.

140. Belgic Confession, art. 1.

141. Athenagoras, *A Plea for the Christians,* ch. 26 (in *ANF,* II, 143).

All natural, moral, and spiritual good finds its source in him. Holy Scripture is a hymn of praise to the goodness of the Lord; from it Scripture derives the work of creation, as well as all life and blessing for humans and animals (Ps. 8; 19; 36:5–7; 65:11; 147:9; Matt. 5:45; Acts 14:17; James 1:17). It is extended over all his works (Ps. 145:9) and endures forever (Ps. 136). Over and over the whole creation is summoned to praise the goodness of God (1 Chron. 16:34; 2 Chron. 5:13; Ps. 34:8; 106:1; 107:1; 118:1; 136:1; Jer. 33:11; etc.).[142]

This goodness of God manifests itself in various forms depending on the objects toward which it is directed. Closely related to it is his *steadfast love* (חֶסֶד), from a verb meaning to bind; and kindness (χρηστοτης), akin to meekness (πραΰτης) (2 Cor. 10:1). Sometimes it is used in a general sense (1 Chron. 16:34), but usually it denotes God's special favor to his people, his attachment to those who share in his favor, to Joseph (Gen. 39:21), Israel (Num. 14:19), David (2 Sam. 7:15; 22:50; Ps. 18:51; 1 Chron. 17:13), the pious (Ps. 5:7). It is connected with God's covenant (Neh. 1:5); it is the principle of forgiveness (Ps. 6:4; 31:16; 44:26; 109:26; Lam. 3:22), of grace (Ps. 51:1), of comfort (Ps. 119:76); it endures forever (Isa. 54:8, 10) and is better than life (Ps. 63:3). It has revealed itself in the fullness of its riches in Christ (Rom. 2:4; 2 Cor. 10:1; Eph. 2:7; Col. 3:12; Titus 3:4), and in the present manifests itself to believers, leading them to repentance (Rom. 2:4; 11:22; Gal. 5:22).[143]

The goodness of God, when shown to those in misery, is called *mercy* (רַחֲמִים, σπλαγχνα, *viscera, misericordia*; NT: ἐλεος, οἰκτιρμος). Time and again Scripture refers to this mercy of God (Exod. 34:6; Deut. 4:31; 2 Chron. 30:9; Ps. 86:15; 103:8; 111:3; 112:4; 145:8; etc.), as it contrasts with the attitude of humans (2 Sam. 24:14; Prov. 12:10; Dan. 9:9, 18). His mercy is great (2 Sam. 24:14; Ps. 119:156; Neh. 9:19; Ps. 51:12), without end (Lam. 3:22), tender like that of a father (Ps. 103:13), is shown to thousands (Exod. 20:6), and after periods of chastisement returns (Isa. 14:1; 49:13ff.; 54:8; 55:7; 60:10; Jer. 12:15; 30:18; 31:20; Hos. 2:22; Mic. 7:19; etc.). In the New Testament God, the father of mercies (2 Cor. 1:3), has revealed his mercy in Christ (Luke 1:50ff.), who is a merciful high priest (Matt. 18:27; 20:34; etc.; Heb. 2:17) and further shows the riches of his mercy (Eph. 2:4) in the salvation of believers (Rom. 9:23; 11:30; 1 Cor. 7:25; 2 Cor. 4:1; 1 Tim. 1:13; Heb. 4:16; etc.).[144]

The goodness of God, which spares those who are deserving of punishment, is called *forbearance* or *patience* (רוּחַ or אֶרֶךְ אַפַּיִם, μακροθυμια, ἀνοχη, χρηστοτης). Scripture frequently mentions this attribute as well (Exod. 34:6; Num.

142. H. Schultz, *Alttestamentliche Theologie*, 545ff.; cf. also Pseudo-Dionysius, *On the Divine Names and Mystical Theology*, ch. 4, who portrays the divine goodness in various ways and compares it to the sun that lightens everything; T. Aquinas, *Summa theol.*, I, qu. 6, esp. art. 4; idem, *Summa contra gentiles*, I, c. 40–41; D. Petavius, "De Deo," in *Theol. dogm.*, VI, ch. 3; J. Gerhard, *Loci theol.*, II, c. 8, sect. 10; A. Polanus, *Syn. theol.*, II, c. 20; J. Zanchi(us), *Op. theol.*, II, cols. 326–42.

143. Cf. F. Delitzsch on Ps. 4:4; H. Cremer, *Lexicon*, s.v. "ἐλεος."

144. T. Aquinas, *Summa theol.*, I, qu. 21, art. 3; J. Zanchi(us), *Op. theol.*, II, 370; A. Polanus, *Syn. theol.*, II, ch. 23; J. Gerhard, *Loci theol.*, II, c. 8, sect. 11.

14:18; Neh. 9:17; Ps. 86:15; 103:8; 145:8; Jon. 4:2; Joel 2:13; Nah. 1:3). It was made manifest throughout the time before Christ (Rom. 3:25) and even now, in accordance with the example of Christ (1 Tim. 1:16; 2 Pet. 3:15), is still frequently displayed to sinners (Rom. 2:4; 9:22; 1 Pet. 3:20).[145]

God's goodness is much more glorious when it is shown to those who only deserve evil. It then bears the name *grace* (חֵן, חֲנִינָה, derived from חָנַן, to bow, incline toward; χάρις, from χαρίζομαι). This word also denotes the favor that one person either receives from or bestows on another (Gen. 30:27; 33:8, 10; 47:29; 50:4; etc.; Luke 2:52). Used with reference to God, however, its object is never creatures in general, nor the Gentiles, but only his people. It is shown to Noah (Gen. 6:8), to Moses (Exod. 33:12, 17; 34:9), to Job (8:5; 9:15), to Daniel (1:9), to the meek and miserable (Prov. 3:34; Dan. 4:27), and particularly to Israel as a people. His election and guidance, his rescue and redemption, and all the benefits that Israel received in distinction from other peoples, can only be attributed to God's grace (Exod. 15:13, 16; 19:4; 33:19; 34:6–7; Deut. 4:37; 7:8; 8:14, 17–18; 9:5, 27; 10:14ff.; 33:3; Isa. 35:10; 42:21; 43:1, 15, 21; 54:5; 63:9; Jer. 3:4, 19; 31:9, 20; Ezek. 16; Hos. 8:14; 11:1; etc.). Whether in history or law, in psalmody or prophecy, the basic note is always: "Not to us, O LORD, but to your name give glory" (Ps. 115:1). He does all things for his name's sake (Num. 14:13ff.; Isa. 43:21, 25ff.; 48:9, 11; Ezek. 36:22; etc.). That grace, accordingly, is continually being praised and glorified (Exod. 34:6; 2 Chron. 30:9; Neh. 9:17; Ps. 86:15; 103:8; 111:4; 116:5; Jon. 4:2; Joel 2:13; Zech. 12:10). In the New Testament that grace proves to be even richer and deeper in content. Objectively, χάρις means beauty, charm, favor (Luke 4:22; Col. 4:6; Eph. 4:29); and, subjectively, it means favor, a positive disposition on the part of the giver, and gratitude and devotion on the part of the recipient. Ascribed to God, grace is the voluntary, unrestrained, and unmerited favor that he shows to sinners and that, instead of the verdict of death, brings them righteousness and life. As such it is a virtue and attribute of God (Rom. 5:15; 1 Pet. 5:10), demonstrated in the sending of his Son, who is full of grace (John 1:14ff.; 1 Pet. 1:13), and additionally in the bestowal of all sorts of spiritual and material benefits, all of which are the gifts of grace and are themselves called "grace" (Rom. 5:20; 6:1; Eph. 1:7; 2:5, 8; Phil. 1:2; Col. 1:2; Titus 3:7; etc.), thus radically excluding all merit on the part of humans (John 1:17; Rom. 4:4, 16; 6:14, 23; 11:5ff.; Eph. 2:8; Gal. 5:3–4).[146]

In the Christian church the doctrine of grace was first developed by Augustine. In that connection, however, grace was usually not thought of as a divine virtue but in terms of the benefits that God, out of grace, grants to the church in Christ. Hence, it was usually not treated as one of the attributes of God. Yet this concept of grace, namely, as a divine virtue, is not lacking either. Thomas, for example, writes: "Sometimes, however, by the grace of God is

---

145. A. Polanus, *Syn. theol.*, II, ch. 24.
146. Cf., H. Schultz, *Alttestamentliche Theologie*, 425ff.; H. Cremer, *Lexicon*, s.v. "Χάρις."

meant God's own eternal love, in the same sense as the expression 'the grace of predestination,' meaning that God has predestined or chosen some people gratuitously, not on account of their merits";[147] but immediately thereafter Thomas again reverts to the broader sense in which it will have to be discussed later, in the locus on salvation.[148]

In addition, the goodness of God appears as *love* when it not only conveys certain benefits but God himself. In the Old Testament reference to this love as an attribute of God is still relatively infrequent, but neither is it totally lacking (Deut. 4:37; 7:8, 13; 10:15; 23:5; 2 Chron. 2:11; Isa. 43:4; 48:14; 63:9; Jer. 31:3; Hos. 11:1, 4; 14:4; Zeph. 3:17; Mal. 1:2). Furthermore, in God's election of, in his covenant with, in his entire relationship to, Israel—which is like that of a husband to a wife, a father to his son, and a mother to her baby—this love is pictured concretely and graphically (Ps. 103:13; Isa. 49:15; Hos. 2). And the objects of this love are not only virtues and attributes, such as justice and righteousness (Ps. 11:7; 33:5; 37:28; 45:7), but also persons (Ps. 78:68; 146:8; Prov. 3:12; Deut. 4:37; 7:8, 13; 23:5; 2 Chron. 2:11; Jer. 31:3; Mal. 1:2).

This love of God stands out much more vividly in the New Testament, now that God has given himself in the Son of his love. The Hebrew word אַהֲבָה is not translated by ἔρως, the usual term for sensual love, nor by φιλια, the word for love between relatives, but by ἀγάπη, a word that is not found in the writings of Philo and Josephus, but which is eminently suited to convey the divine love in its fullness and purity (like the Latin *caritas [dilectio]* in distinction from *amor*). The relation between Father and Son is portrayed as a life of love (John 3:35; 5:20; 10:17; 14:31; 15:19; 17:24, 26). But in Christ, who himself loves and proved his love in his self-offering (John 15:13), that love is bestowed not only on the world and the church in general (John 3:16; Rom. 5:8; 8:37; 1 John 4:9), but also individually and personally (John 14:23; 16:27; 17:23; Rom. 9:13; Gal. 2:20). Indeed, God not only loves but is himself love (1 John 4:8), and his love is the foundation, source, and model of our love (1 John 4:10–11). Now it is indeed possible to speak of God's love to creatures or people in general (the love of benevolence), but for this the Scripture mostly uses the word "goodness," and as a rule speaks of God's love, like his grace, only in relation to his chosen people or church (the love of friendship).[149] Granted, this love is not the essence of God in the sense that it is the center

147. T. Aquinas, *Summa theol.*, II, 1, qu. 110, art. 1; cf. J. Schwetz, *Theologia dogmatica catholica*, 3 vols. (Vienna: Congregationis Mechitharisticae, 1851–54), I, 193; J. Gerhard, *Loci theol.*, II, c. 8, sect. 11, qu. 4; W. Musculus, *Loci communes theologiae sacrae*, 317ff.; A. Polanus, *Syn. theol.*, II, ch. 21; J. Zanchi(us), *Op. theol.*, II, 342–58.

148. Cf. D. Kirn, "Gnade," *PRE³*, VI, 717–23; J. P. Lange, *Christliche Dogmatik*, II, §18.

149. G. F. Oehler, *Theology of the Old Testament*, §81; H. Schultz, *Alttestamentliche Theologie*, 545ff.; R. Smend, *Lehrbuch der alttestamentlichen Religionsgeschichte*, 197ff.; H. Cremer, *Lexicon*, s.v. "Φιλια"; Geerhardus Vos, "The Scriptural Doctrine of the Love of God," *Presbyterian and Reformed Review* 13 (Jan. 1902): 1–37.

and core of God's being and the other attributes are its modes,[150] for all the attributes are equally God's being. In him there is no higher and lower, no greater and smaller.[151] Still, love is most certainly identical with God's being. It is independent, eternal, and unchangeable, like God himself. It has its origin in him and also—by way of his creatures—returns to him. Pseudo-Dionysius, accordingly, spoke of God's love as "an endless circle [traveling] through the Good, from the Good, in the Good, and to the Good, unerringly turning, ever on the same center, ever in the same direction, always proceeding, always remaining, always being restored to itself."[152]

Holiness

[205] Very closely related to God's goodness is his *holiness*. In the past it was described as "freedom from all defilement; . . . a purity that is total and utterly untainted."[153] Often it is not treated as a distinct attribute alongside the goodness, perfection, and beauty of God. Neither Lombard nor Thomas discusses it. Protestant theologians defined the holiness of God in essentially the same terms: it consists in "moral perfection" or "purity,"[154] and it was sometimes more closely associated with God's righteousness, his goodness, trustworthiness, or wisdom.[155] Research into the biblical term "holy," however, has gradually given prominence to another view. At present everyone acknowledges that the concept of holiness in the Old and the New Testament expresses a relation of God to the world. There is disagreement, however, about the precise character of that relation. With a view to texts like Hosea 11:9; Isaiah 57:15; and Ezekiel 20:9ff., Menken associated holiness with God's condescending goodness and grace.[156] Baudissin, however, believed it was rather God's utter transcendence and power over all creatures that was expressed in God's holiness,[157] and was

150. F. Schleiermacher, *The Christian Faith*, §167; L. Schoeberlein, *Prinzip und System der Dogmatik* (Heidelberg: C. Winter, 1881), 129; I. A. Dorner, *A System of Christian Doctrine*, I, 454; J. J. van Oosterzee, *Christian Dogmatics*, trans. J. Watson and M. Evans, 2 vols. (New York: Scribner, Armstrong, 1874), §50.

151. J. P. Lange, *Christliche Dogmatik*, II, 203; G. Thomasius, *Christi Person und Werk*, 3d ed., 2 vols. (Erlangen: Theodor Bläsing, 1853–61), I, 105; J. I. Doedes, *Inleiding tot de leer van God* (Utrecht: Kemink, 1876), 231.

152. Pseudo-Dionysius, *The Divine Names and Mystical Theology*, ch. 4, §14; cf. Augustine, *The Trinity*, VIII, 6–12; IX, 6; X, 1; idem, *Confessions*, IV, 12; idem, *Soliloquies*, I, 2; idem, *On True Religion*, ch. 46; P. Lombard, *Sent.*, III, dist. 32, 1; T. Aquinas, *Summa theol.*, I, qu. 20; idem, *Summa contra gentiles*, I, ch. 91; M. J. Scheeben, *Handbuch der katholischen Dogmatik*, I, 692ff.; J. Gerhard, *Loci theol.*, II, c. 8, sect. 11, qu. 2; J. Zanchi(us), *Op. theol.*, II, 359ff.; A. Polanus, *Syn. theol.*, II, ch. 22.

153. Pseudo-Dionysius, *The Divine Names and Mystical Theology*, ch. 12, §2; cf. J. C. Suicerus, *Thesaurus ecclesiasticus*, 2 vols. (Amsterdam: J. H. Wetstein, 1682), s.v. "ἅγιος."

154. A. Polanus, *Syn. theol.*, II, ch. 28; *Synopsis purioris theologiae*, VI, 40; P. van Mastricht, *Theologia*, II, ch. 19; L. Meijer, *Verhandelingen over de goddelyke wigenschappen*, III, 115ff.

155. H. Heppe, *Dogmatik der evangelisch-reformierten Kirche*, 73; cf. K. G. Bretschneider, *Systematische Entwicklung*, 382ff.; Karl A. von Hase, *Hutterus redivivus*, §63.

156. G. Menken, *Versuch einer Anleitung zum eignen Unterricht in den Wahrheiten der heiligen Schrift*, 3d ed. (Bremen: Wilhelm Kaiser, 1833), ch. 1, §9.

157. W. W. Baudissin, *Studien zur semitischen Religionsgeschichte*, 2 vols. (Leipzig: F. W. Grunow, 1876–78), 3–142.

supported in this view by Ritschl and others,[158] who appealed to Numbers 20:13; Isaiah 5:16; Ezekiel 20:41; 28:25; and 36:20–24, and to the linkage between glory and holiness in texts like Isaiah 63:15; 64:11; Jeremiah 17:12; Ezekiel 20:40; and so forth. Closely related to this is the view of Schultz, who, based on Exodus 15:11; 1 Samuel 2:2; 6:20; Isaiah 6:3; 8:13; and 10:17, associates God's holiness with his flaming majesty, his inapproachability, the infinite distance that separates him from all creatures.[159] Inasmuch as the greatest disagreement concerned the question of which divine attribute was in fact meant by God's holiness, others believed that this term, so far from denoting an essential inner quality, only describes a relation and is therefore no more than a relational term. Especially Diestel[160] argued for this view and persuaded many others to accept it as well. Also, those who do not believe that holiness can be completely described as a relation usually proceed from this idea in their definition of the concept.[161]

The stem קָדַשׁ, related to חָדַשׁ, is usually traced to the root קַד, meaning "to cut, separate," and hence it expresses the idea of being cut off and isolated. The verb occurs in Niphal, Piel, Hiphil, and Hithpael stem forms; the adjective is קָדוֹשׁ, the substantive קֹדֶשׁ, and its antonym is חֹל (κοινος), from חָלַל, to make common (Lev. 10:10; 1 Sam. 21:5–6; Ezek. 48:14–15). It is related to, yet also clearly distinguished from, טָהוֹר (pure), whose antonym is טָמֵא (Lev. 10:10). Now the word "holy" is used first of all with reference to an array of persons and things that have been set apart from general use and placed in a special relation to God and his service. So we read of "holy ground" (Exod. 3:5), a "holy assembly" (Exod. 12:16), a "holy sabbath" (Exod. 16:23), a "holy people" (Exod. 19:6), a "holy place" (Exod. 29:31), "sacred anointing oil" (Exod. 30:25), a "holy linen coat" (Lev. 16:4), a "holy year of jubilee" (Lev.

---

158. A. Ritschl, *Die christliche Lehre von der Rechfertigung und Versöhnung*, 4th ed., 3 vols. (Bonn: A. Marcus, 1895–1903), II, 89ff.; E. B. Coe, "The Biblical Meaning of Holiness," *Presbyterian and Reformed Review* 1 (January 1890): 42–68. H. P. Smith, "The Root *qdsh* in the Old Testament," *Presbyterian Review* 2 (July 1881): 588–92.

159. H. Schultz, *Alttestamentliche Theologie*, 554ff.; cf. A. Kuenen, *De Godsdienst van Israël tot den Ondergang van den Joodschen Staat*, 2 vols., De Voornaamste Godsdiensten (Haarlem: Kruseman, 1869–70), I, 47ff.; ET: *The Religion of Israel to the Fall of the Jewish State*, trans. Alfred Heath May, 3 vols. (London: Williams and Norgate, 1882–83); Johann Christian Konrad von Hoffmann, *Der Schriftbeweis*, 3 vols. (Nördlingen: Beck, 1857–60), I, 83; R. Smend, *Lehrbuch der alttestamentlichen Religionsgeschichte*, 333ff.

160. L. Diestel, "Über die Heiligkeit Gottes," *Jahrbuch für deutsche Theologie* 4 (1859): 3–62.

161. Otto Schmoller, "The meaning of קָדַשׁ in the Old Testament," in *Festgruss an Rudolf von Roth* (Stuttgart: W. Kohlhammer, 1893), 39–43; F. Delitzsch, "Heiligkeit," *PRE²*, V, 714–18; R. Kittel, "Heiligkeit Gottes im A.T.," *PRE³*, VII, 566–73; H. Cremer, *Lexicon*, s.v. "Ἅγιος"; Ernst Issel, *Der Begriff der Heiligkeit im Neuen Testament* (Leiden: H. J. Brill, 1887); R. Schröter, *Der Begriff der Heiligkeit im Alten und Neuen Testaments* (Leipzig: Fock, 1892); J. Gloel, *Der heiligen Geist in der Heilsverkündigung des Paulus* (Halle: M. Niemeyer, 1888), 226ff.; J. Köberle, *Natur und Geist nach der Auffassung des Alten Testaments* (Munich: Beck, 1901), 157ff.; W. Robertson Smith, *Die Religion der Semiten* (Freiburg: Mohr, 1899), 64ff., 102ff.; Marie-Joseph Lagrange, *Études sur les religions sémitiques* (Paris: V. Lecoffre, 1903), 140ff.; K. Marti, *Geschichte der israelitischen Religion*, 3d ed. (Strassburg: F. Bull, 1897), 136ff.; A. B. Davidson, *Theology of the Old Testament*, 144ff.; S. Hoekstra, *Wijsgerige Godsdienstleer*, 2 vols. (Amsterdam: Van Kampen, 1894–95), II, 260–80.

25:12), a "holy house" (Lev. 27:14), a "holy field" (Lev. 27:21), a "holy tithe" (Lev. 27:30), "holy water" (Num. 5:17), "holy vessels" (Num. 16:37), a "holy calf" (Num. 18:17), a "holy camp" (Deut. 23:14), "holy gold" (Josh. 6:19), "holy bread" (1 Sam. 21:4), a "holy ark" (2 Chron. 35:3), a "holy race" (Ezra 9:2), the "holy city" (Neh. 11:1), the "holy covenant" (Dan. 11:28), a "holy promise" (Ps. 105:42), and of the temple as "sanctuary" (Exod. 15:17), with its "holy place" and "holy of holies," "holy ones [the angels and the children of Israel]" (Deut. 33:2–3; Job 5:1; 15:15; Ps. 16:3, 10 KJV; 32:6; 89:6–8, 20; Prov. 9:10; 30:3; Dan. 4:17; 7:18, 21–22, 25, 27; Hos. 11:12; Zech. 14:5). In all these instances the term "holy" does not yet refer to an internal moral quality but only indicates that the person or objects so described have been consecrated to the Lord, have been placed in a special relation to his service, and are therefore set apart from the common domain. The persons and things called "holy," however, do not derive this special relation to God from themselves. By nature God and his creatures are dissociated, estranged, distinguished from, and opposed to, each other. By itself the entire world is חֹל, profane, not in communion with God, and unfit for his service, and even that which is pure is as such not yet holy. Nor can these persons and things sanctify themselves and assume for themselves that special relation to God that is conveyed by the word "holy." Sanctification proceeds from God alone. It is he who sanctifies Israel, the priesthood, the temple, the altar, certain special places, persons, and objects, who brings them into his service and communion, and sets them apart from that which is unholy. "I am the Lord, who sanctifies you" (Exod. 31:13; Lev. 20:8; 21:8, 15, 23; 22:9, 16, 32; Ezek. 20:12; 37:28).

Now this sanctification of persons and things by the Lord occurs in two ways: negatively, by choosing a people, person, place, day, or object and setting it apart from all others; and positively, by consecrating these persons or things and causing them to live in accordance with specific rules. God sanctifies the Sabbath, not only by setting it apart from the other days of the week, but also by resting on that day and blessing it (Gen. 2:2–3; Exod. 20:11; Deut. 5:12). He sanctified the whole people of Israel by choosing it from among all the peoples of the earth, by incorporating it in his covenant, and making his laws known to it (Exod. 19:4–6). The holiness of God is the principle marking the whole body of laws, the moral and ceremonial commandments, the entire revelation of salvation given to Israel, for the purpose of this revelation is nothing other than the sanctification of Israel (Exod. 19:4–6; Lev. 11:44–45; 19:2; 20:26). Israel is holy because God makes Israel his own possession, comes to this people, dwells among them, and is their God (Exod. 19:4–6; 29:43–46). And within this circle he again especially sanctifies the firstborn by appropriating them for himself (Exod. 13:2); the people, by having them wash their garments and thus to prepare themselves to meet God (Exod. 19:10, 14); the mountain, by setting bounds about it (Exod. 19:23); the priesthood, by anointing them, sprinkling them with blood, and putting on them the garments of the priesthood (Exod. 28:3, 41; 29:1ff., 21); the tabernacle and the altar, by anointing (Exod. 29:37;

40:9ff.; Lev. 8:10–11; Num. 7:1); the anointing oil, by having it prepared in a special way (Exod. 30:22ff.); the Nazirites, by having them live in accordance with certain specific ordinances (Num. 6:2ff.); and so on.

That which has thus been made holy lives a life of its own, has a character of its own, and is set apart from the common life and laws of the other people. For example, it may not be touched (Exod. 19:23–24); it may not be eaten (Exod. 29:33) or used (Exod. 30:32ff.); it renders holy whatever it touches (Exod. 30:29; Lev. 10:2ff.; Num. 1:51, 53; 3:10, 38; Isa. 8:14). The positive action by which a thing becomes holy is not always identified; sometimes sanctification seems to consist in nothing other than separation (Lev. 25:10; 27:14; Josh. 7:13; 20:7; Judg. 17:3; 1 Sam. 7:1; 2 Sam. 8:11; 1 Chron. 18:11; etc.). Yet, sanctification is something more than merely being set apart; it is, by means of washing, anointing, sacrifice, and the sprinkling with blood (etc.), to divest a thing of the character it has in common with all other things, and to impress upon it another stamp, a stamp uniquely its own, which it must bear and display everywhere. Now the ceremonies necessary to sanctification clearly indicate that also the impurity and sinfulness of the creature in question are considered, impurity and sinfulness which must be removed precisely in that manner. The washing, sacrifice, sprinkling with blood, and anointing served the purpose of cleansing from sin and of consecration (Lev. 8:15; 16:15–16; Job 1:5; etc.). The adjectives "holy" and "pure" are therefore synonymous (Exod. 30:35; Lev. 16:19). But the term "holiness" is not exhausted by that of "moral purity." Granted, the latter is not excluded, but neither is it the only meaning, not even the primary one. Holiness in the Old Testament, especially in the Torah, has a much broader meaning. The entire distinction and opposition between external and internal purity (etc.) has been derived from a later position and imposed upon that of the Mosaic legislation. *Holy* is that which has been chosen and set apart by YHWH; divested of its common character by special ceremonies, it has received a character of its own and now lives in this new condition in accordance with the laws prescribed for it. Israel is a *holy* people because God has chosen it and set it apart; it has been incorporated in a covenant and must now live in conformity to all his laws, including the ceremonial. *Holy* is that which in all things conforms to the special laws God has ordained for it. Holiness is perfection, not only in a moral sense, but in the comprehensive sense in which the unique legislation of Israel conceives it: a religious, ethical, ceremonial, internal, and external sense.

This concept of holiness only becomes fully clear, however, when we examine the sense in which it is applied to God. Cremer has correctly pointed out that holiness does not first of all denote a relation from that which is below to that which is above, but vice versa; it applies first of all to God and, subsequently, in a derivative sense, also to creatures. Creatures are not inherently holy, nor can they sanctify themselves. All sanctification and all holiness proceeds from God. Because YHWH is holy, he wants for himself a holy people, a holy priesthood, a holy dwelling (Exod. 19:6; 29:43; Lev. 11:44–45; 19:2; 20:26;

21:8; Deut. 28:9–10). The predicate "holy" is often ascribed to YHWH (Lev. 11:44–45; 19:2; 20:26; 21:8; Josh. 24:19; 1 Sam. 2:2; 6:20; Ps. 22:3; 99:5, 9; Isa. 5:16; 6:3; etc.). Frequently Isaiah speaks of "the Holy One of Israel" (29:23; 40:25; 43:15; 49:7; 62:12; cf. 2 Kings 19:22; Ezek. 39:7; Hab. 1:12; 3:3). In addition, we also read of God's holy name (Lev. 20:3; 22:32; 1 Chron. 16:35; Ps. 99:3; 103:1; 111:9; etc.), his holy arm (Isa. 52:10), and his holy majesty (2 Chron. 20:21). Now, in the first place, YHWH is not called holy because of an immediately conspicuous attribute. He is rather called holy in a comprehensive sense in connection with every revelation that impresses humans with his deity. Holiness alternates with himself (Amos 4:2; 6:2). He is God, not a human, the Holy One in their midst (Hos. 11:9), the God or the Holy One of Israel. God's holiness is revealed in all the relations that he has posited between himself and his people: in election, in the covenant, in his revelation, in his dwelling among them, and so forth (Exod. 29:43–46; Lev. 11:44–45; 20:26; Ps. 114:1–2). This relation, however, far from being an abstraction, is rich in content. God himself ordered this relation in the laws he gave to Israel. Israel's entire body of legislation is fundamentally stamped by God's holiness and has its purpose in the sanctification of the people. What this sanctification by YHWH implies becomes evident throughout the law, and the people are holy when they conform to it. As the Holy One, he gave himself to Israel and dwells among its people, but now also continues to be faithful to his word and covenant (Ps. 89:35ff.), and over and over delivers Israel. God is the Holy One of Israel, Israel's God, who is what his law shows him to be. For Israel God's holiness means deliverance (Ps. 22:3–4; 89:18; 98:1; 103:1; 105:3; 145:21), answer to prayer (Ps. 3:4; 20:6; 28:2), comfort (Isa. 5:16; Hab. 1:12), trust (Ps. 22:3–5; 33:21; Isa. 10:20). His holiness does not permit him to let Israel perish. As the Holy One, he is the creator, redeemer, and king of Israel (Isa. 43:14–15; 49:7; 54:5; 62:12). Accordingly, his redeemed people thank and praise him as the Holy One (Ps. 30:4; 71:22; 97:12; 1 Chron. 16:10, 35).

At the same time this holiness of God is the principle of punishment and chastisement. When Israel breaks his covenant, desecrates his name, and violates his laws, it is precisely God's holiness that incites him to mete out punishment. His holiness demands that Israel be holy and sanctify him (Lev. 11:44–45; 19:2; 20:7, 26; 21:8). In the event of disobedience he chastises Israel (1 Kings 9:3–7; 2 Chron. 7:16–20). The same holiness that is the principle of deliverance and the object of praise is, for those who violate it, a principle of destruction and the object of dread. "Holy," in the latter case, is synonymous with "zealous" (Josh. 24:19), "majestic" and "terrible" (Exod. 15:11; Ps. 99:3; 111:9), "glorious" and "lofty" (Isa. 6:3; 57:15). Among the gods he is incomparable: the Holy One (Exod. 15:11; 1 Sam. 2:2; Isa. 40:25). To sanctify him is to fear him (Isa. 8:13; 29:23). When people desecrate his name and covenant, he sanctifies himself by justice and righteousness (Isa. 5:16; Ezek. 28:22). But even then he does not forget his people. To Israel his holiness remains the cause of their redemption (Isa. 6:13; 10:20; 27:13; 29:23–24; 43:15; 49:7; 52:10; Jer. 51:5; Hos. 11:8–9;

etc.) and in the end this holiness will vindicate itself by making known to the Gentiles that he is the Lord (Jer. 50:29; Ezek. 36:23; 39:7) and will redeem Israel and cleanse it from all its iniquities (Ezek. 36:25ff.; 39:7).

This view of God's holiness leads directly to holiness in a New Testament sense. Even the choice of the Greek word is significant. Σεμνος, from σεβομαι, denotes that which is venerable (Phil. 4:8; 1 Tim. 3:8, 11; Titus 2:2); ιερος merely expresses a relation to the deity (1 Cor. 9:13; 2 Tim. 3:15; cf. Heb. 8:2; 9:8; etc.); ἁγνος means pure, chaste (2 Cor. 11:2; Titus 2:5; etc.). These words, however, are never used with reference to God. In the New Testament God is only called ὁσιος (Rev. 15:4; 16:5; cf. Heb. 7:26) and particularly ἁγιος (Luke 1:49; John 17:11; 1 John 2:20; 1 Pet. 1:15–16; Rev. 4:8; 6:10). In the Old Testament the holiness of God is not yet clearly distinguished from all the other divine attributes and still denotes the entire relation in which YHWH stands to Israel and Israel to YHWH. For that reason YHWH could be called the Holy One of Israel, who had totally given himself to Israel and by various ways had maintained and preserved it as his own possession. For that reason as well, the people's sanctification is not only religious and ethical in character, but also ceremonial, civil, and political. Just as in God his holiness is not yet defined alongside his other attributes, so also on the side of Israel, holiness embraces the entire people in all of its dimensions. But in the New Testament, when the Holy One of God appears (Mark 1:24; Luke 4:34; Acts 3:14; 4:27), the One who forms the sharpest contrast with the world (John 15:18) and in an absolute sense consecrates himself to God (John 17:19), the holiness of God ceases to be the principle of punishment and chastisement, and the Holy Spirit (rarely so called in the Old Testament [Ps. 51:11; Isa. 63:10–11] but regularly in the New), becomes the principle of the sanctification of the church. From now on the church is the "holy nation" (1 Pet. 2:5, 9; Eph. 2:19; 5:27), composed of the elect, the holy and blameless (Eph. 1:1, 4; Col. 1:2, 22; 3:12; 1 Cor. 7:14), completely freed and cleansed from sin and eternally consecrated with soul and body to God. The holiness by which YHWH put himself in a special relation to Israel and which totally claims Israel for the service of YHWH is finally supremely manifest in that in Christ God gives himself to the church, which he redeems and cleanses from all its iniquities.

Righteousness (Justice)

[206] Closely related to this holiness is the *righteousness* [justice; Dutch, *gerechtigheid*] of God. The words צַדִּיק, צֶדֶק, and צְדָקָה describe the state of a law-abiding person. The first meaning seems to be a forensic one: צַדִּיק is one who is proved right before a trial judge and therefore has to be acquitted (הִצְדִּיק versus the הִרְשִׁיעַ; Deut. 25:1). It is also the word for a person who is right in a dispute or debate (Job 11:2; 33:12, 32; Isa. 41:26), and the substantive, accordingly, can denote the correctness or truth of an assertion (Ps. 52:3; Prov. 16:13; Isa. 45:23). Further, it means in general that a person is right, even aside from a trial or court, and hence that a person has the right on his or her side, is righteous and good, and in step with the law (Gen. 30:33; 38:26; 1 Sam. 24:18;

Ps. 15:2). From here the word crosses into the sphere of religion and is applied to God. God is only twice called צַדִּיק in the Pentateuch (Exod. 9:27; Deut. 32:4). God's righteousness is first of all manifested in history, in his government of the world, and in his providential guidance of Israel, and is therefore especially developed by psalmists and prophets. It is revealed everywhere and extends even to wild animals (Ps. 36:7). God is the Judge of all the earth (Gen. 18:25). It consists in that God repays everyone according to his or her works, treating the righteous one way and the wicked another (Gen. 18:25). It is noteworthy, however, that God's remunerative justice is far more prominent in Scripture than his retributive justice. Diestel rightly called attention to this fact,[162] and the idea has been endorsed by many, including especially Ritschl.[163]

The matter itself, later known in dogmatics as vindictive or retributive justice, is not lacking. On the contrary, God by no means holds the guilty to be innocent (Exod. 20:7; Neh. 1:3ff.); he does not spare the wicked (Ezek. 7:4, 9, 27; 8:18; 9:10). He does not regard persons or take bribes (Deut. 10:17), his judgment is impartial (Job 13:6–12; 22:2–4; 34:10–12; 35:6–7). He is righteous and all his judgments are righteous (Ps. 119:137; 129:4); the punishment of the wicked is often ascribed to God's righteousness (Exod. 6:5; 7:4; Ps. 7:11; 9:4–8; 28:4; 62:12; 73; 96:10, 13; 2 Chron. 12:5–7; Neh. 9:33; Lam. 1:18; Isa. 5:16; 10:22; Dan. 9:14; Rom. 2:5; 2 Thess. 1:5–10). It is also true, however, that the punishment of the wicked is usually inferred from God's wrath, and that the righteousness of God especially comes to the fore in Scripture as the principle of salvation for God's people. In Hebrew there are many words for the wrath of God: אַף, חָרוֹן, כַּעַס, זַעַם, רֹגֶז, קֶצֶף, usually translated by wrath and anger; חֵמָה is usually rendered as fury; עֶבְרָה is usually translated by wrath; in the Septuagint and New Testament θυμος means internal wrath, and ὀργη extraverted wrath; the two are combined in Romans 2:8 (wrath and fury). This wrath—the basic words for which relate in part to the verb "to burn," in part express a vehement, uncontrollable emotion—is often compared to a burning (Lev. 10:6; Deut. 32:22; Ps. 21:9), a fire (Deut. 32:22; 2 Kings 23:26; Ps. 2:11; Isa. 30:27; Jer. 15:14; 17:4), and is therefore called "hot" (Ps. 58:9; Deut. 13:17; 2 Chron. 28:11; Job 20:23; Isa. 13:9, 13) and "smoking" (Deut. 29:27–28; Ps. 74:1). It is kindled by Israel's sins against the theocratic covenant of God: breach of oath (Josh. 9:20), the desecration of God's service (Lev. 10:6; Num. 1:53; 16:46; 18:5), idolatry (Deut. 9:8), the sins of Manasseh (2 Kings 23:26) and David (1 Chron. 27:24), and especially the sins committed by the people, which deserve a range of punishments (Isa. 42:24–25; Jer. 7:20; 21:5; 32:31; etc.; Lam. 2:2ff.; 3:43; Ezek. 5:13ff.; 7:3; 13:1; etc.; Zech. 7:12ff.).

This wrath is terrible (Ps. 76:7), inspires dread (Ps. 2:5; 90:7), brings pain (Job 21:17; Ps. 102:10), punishment (Ps. 6:1; 38:1; Jer. 10:24), and destruc-

162. L. Diestel, "Die Idee der Gerechtigkeit, vorzüglich im Alten Testament," *Jahrbücher für deutsche Theologie* 5 (1860): 173–253.

163. A. Ritschl, *Die christliche Lehre von der Rechtfertigung und Versöhnung*, II, 102–10.

tion (Jer. 42:18; 2 Chron. 29:8; etc.; cf. Job 9:5; Ps. 21:9; 56:7; 85:3–5).[164] As is clear from Deuteronomy 6:15; 29:20; 32:21ff.; Job 16:9; Nahum 1:2, YHWH's hatred, vengeance jealousy, and wrath are closely related. YHWH's hatred almost always has sinful deeds for its object (Deut. 16:22; Ps. 45:7; Prov. 6:16; Jer. 44:4; Hos. 9:15; Amos 5:12; Zech. 8:17; Rev. 2:6), only rarely sinful persons (Ps. 5:6; Mal. 1:3; Rom. 9:13). The vengeance (נְקָמָה, ἐκδίκησις) ascribed to God (Nah. 1:2; 1 Thess. 4:6) and expressly reserved to God (Deut. 32:35; Rom. 12:19; Heb. 10:30) sometimes also manifests itself in judgment (Num. 31:2–3; Judg. 5:2 KJV; 11:36; 16:28; 2 Sam. 4:8; 22:48; Ps. 18:47; 99:8) but will only fully reveal itself in all its power in the future, in the day of wrath (Deut. 32:41–42; Ps. 94:1; 149:7; Isa. 34:8; 35:4; 59:17; 61:2, 4; Jer. 46:10; 50:15, 28; 51:11; Ezek. 25:14ff.; Mic. 5:14). God's jealousy (קִנְאָה, ζῆλος), mentioned repeatedly (Exod. 20:5; 34:14; Deut. 4:24; 5:9; 6:15; Josh. 24:19; Nah. 1:2), is provoked when Israel, YHWH's bride, violates his rights as groom and husband by following after other gods (Deut. 32:16, 21; 1 Kings 14:22; Ps. 78:58; Ezek. 8:3, 5), and manifests itself when YHWH on his part provokes Israel to jealousy by choosing another people (Deut. 32:21; Ps. 79:5; Ezek. 5:13; 16:38; 23:25; Rom. 10:19).

Now, in the context of all these attributes, God's righteousness is most often conceived in a favorable sense and described as the attribute by virtue of which God vindicates the righteous and raises them to a position of honor and well-being. One can in fact to some extent trace the route by which the term "righteousness" developed in this sense in the Old Testament. Already in the law the judge and every Israelite in general is repeatedly urged to demonstrate a sense of justice by not perverting the justice due to the poor, not slaying the innocent and righteous, not accepting bribes, and not oppressing the alien, the widow, and the orphan (Exod. 23:6–9). Justice consists in not regarding the person, in hearing the small and the great alike, in not fearing a person's face, for judgment is for the Lord (Deut. 1:16–17; 16:19; Lev. 19:15). The righteous must be acquitted and the wicked condemned (Deut. 25:1)—that was the rule for kings, judges, and every Israelite.

The actual situation, however, was not at all in keeping with this law. Prophets, psalmists, and the writers of proverbs incessantly complain about the dreadful reality that there was no justice for the poor, widows, orphans, aliens, and the needy, even though the right was completely on their side and they were righteous and pious. Hence, frequently there was no justice for the truly faithful; in the courts and in daily life they were routinely judged wrongly, ignored, oppressed, and persecuted. Accordingly, they hope eagerly for the future, the Messiah, who

164. Cf. on the wrath of God: L. Lactantius, *De ira Dei*; Tertullian, *De ira Dei*; R. Bartholomai, "Vom Zorne Gottes," *Jahrbücher für deutsche Theologie* 6 (1861): 256–77; F. W. Weber, *Vom Zorne Gottes* (Erlangen: Andreas Deichert, 1862); A. Ritschl, *Die christliche Lehre von der Rechtfertigung und Versöhnung*, II, 119–56; L. Diestel, "Gerechtigkeit," 193ff.; Lange, "Zorn Gottes," *PRE¹*, XVIII, 657–71; R. Kübel, "Zorn Gottes," *PRE²*, XVIII, 556–68; G. F. Oehler, *Theology of the Old Testament*, §48; H. Schultz, *Alttestamentliche Theologie*, 560ff.; R. Smend, *Lehrbuch der alttestamentlichen Religionsgeschichte*, 99ff.; H. Cremer, *Lexicon*, s.v. "Ὀργή."

will be the righteous Branch (Jer. 23:5ff.), the righteous One (Zech. 9:9), who will not judge by what his eyes see but with righteousness (Isa. 11:3–5). His judgment above all will consist in helping and saving the needy, who are now being ignored and oppressed and call in vain for justice; in having pity on the poor; and in redeeming their life (Ps. 72:12–14). Hence, the exercise of justice would especially be apparent in the redemption of the wretched. Thus, doing justice with an eye to the needy becomes an act of grace and mercy.

All this is now applied to God; rather, it is fundamentally and originally true of him. YHWH is the true judge. He only judges justly and does not regard the person of the defendant, and therefore, the judges must judge similarly (Exod. 23:7; Deut. 1:17), and the Messiah will one day also judge in this manner. God is completely righteous and acts in accordance with justice. His righteousness (צדקה) consists especially in recognizing and bringing to light the righteousness of the just and causing it to triumph. He is righteous because he bestows salvation on the faithful. He saves them (Ps. 7:10), delivers them (31:1), answers them (65:5), hears them (143:1), rescues them (143:11), gives them life (119:40), acquits them (34:22), vindicates them (35:24), and so on, while the wicked miss being enrolled among the righteous (69:27–28).

YHWH's righteousness therefore is not, like his anger (69:24ff.), opposed to his steadfast love but is closely akin and synonymous with it (Ps. 22:31; 33:5; 35:26–27; 40:10–11; 51:14; 89:14; 145:7; Isa. 45:21; Jer. 9:24; Hos. 2:18–20; Zech. 9:9). The manifestation of God's righteousness is simultaneously the manifestation of his grace (Ps. 97:11–12; 112:3–6; 116:5; 118:15–19). Even the forgiveness of sins is due to God's righteousness (Ps. 51:14; 103:8–12, 17; 1 John 1:9). Hence, the revelations of that righteousness are acts of salvation, rescue, and deliverance (Judg. 5:11; 1 Sam. 12:7; Ps. 103:6; Isa. 45:24, 25; Mic. 6:5). This soteriological character of God's righteousness strikingly stands out especially in Isaiah. Though Israel is a sinful people and has therefore been severely punished (Isa. 43:26; 48:1; 53:11; 57:12; 59:4; 64:5), yet over against the Gentiles, Israel is in the right. Despite all its transgressions Israel's cause is righteous; ultimately, the right is on its side. Accordingly, when Israel has been sufficiently chastised, God's righteousness will reawaken and recognize that right, and deliver his people from all their misery (Isa. 40:1ff.; 54:5, 7ff.; 57:15ff.; 61:1ff.). And this is how things stand with all the faithful. Personally, they are sinners; they are guilty of a whole array of unrighteous things; and as a people they are poor and miserable. But they stand for a righteous cause; they trust in the Lord and expect that he will give them justice, argue their case, and crown them with his salvation (Ps. 17:1ff.; 18:19–21; 34:15; 103:6; 140:12).

This salvation will not consist merely in the outward blessings of prosperity and peace, but above all in the forgiveness God gives to his people, in the Spirit he pours out upon them, in the new heart he gives them, and in the law he inscribes on their heart, so that they will walk before his face in perfection. In a word, salvation consists in God's being fully their God and in their being completely his people (Isa. 43:25; Jer. 31:33, 34; 32:39–40; 33:8; Ezek. 11:19;

36:25; Joel 2:28ff.). Yet this people—which now confesses the name of the Lord and is righteous in his cause—is still sinful and impure (Isa. 43:26ff.; 53:4–6; 59:2ff., 12ff.) and can only be redeemed from that sin by the Lord. In him alone are righteousness and strength (Isa. 45:24), not only for Israel but for Gentile peoples as well (Isa. 2:2ff.; 45:22). The Lord will give *his* justice to his people by the Messiah, who will bring forth justice to the Gentiles (Isa. 42:1), and the Lord will create a new heaven and a new earth, in which righteousness dwells (Isa. 65:17ff.). The righteousness of the Lord vis-à-vis his people consists, finally, in giving them *his* righteousness. Although righteousness and salvation are thus closely interconnected, it is wrong to use them interchangeably. Righteousness is not the same as favor, mercy, or grace; neither is it something like covenant faithfulness (Diestel, Ritschl, Kautzsch, et al.); nor does it signify the positive as opposed to salvation as the negative (Davidson). Righteousness is and remains a forensic term; but in the Old Testament it was viewed as the most important task of people and the strongest proof of righteousness for them to protect the oppressed and to save the wretched from the injustice and persecution to which they are exposed. This is that in which the righteousness of God consisted, and therefore this defense of the rights of the oppressed also had to be the primary task of the judges and kings of the earth.

Now, the concept of righteousness, thus defined, also passes from the Old to the New Testament. The righteousness of God (δικαιοσυνη θεου) consists in the fact that through and by the Messiah it proceeds to bring righteousness to his people: in Christ it offers a means of atonement, which proves God to be righteous; is able to justify the believer; and also grants forgiveness to (1 John 1:9), and bestows salvation on, his own (John 17:25; 2 Tim. 4:8). Finally, even God's anger and jealousy, his hatred and vengeance, are made subservient to the salvation and redemption of his people. His anger is but for a moment (Ps. 30:5; 78:38; 85:5; 103:9; Isa. 10:25; 48:9; 51:22; 54:8; Jer. 3:12ff.; 32:37; Ezek. 43:7–9; Dan. 9:16; Hos. 14:4; Mic. 5:15), and his jealousy will depart from Israel (Ezek. 16:42; 36:6ff.; Zech. 8:2ff.). Then his wrath, jealousy, and vengeance will turn against the enemies of his people in the great day of anger and vengeance (Deut. 32:41–42; Isa. 13:2ff.; 26:11; 30:27ff.; 34:8; 35:4; 41:11; 59:17; 61:2, 4; 63:3ff.; Jer. 10:25; 46:10; 50:15, 28; 51:11; Lam. 3:66; Ezek. 25:14ff.; 38:19; 39:25; Mic. 5:15; Nah. 1:2; Hab. 3:12; Zeph. 1:14ff.; 2:2), and thereby provide blessing and redemption to his people (2 Kings 19:31; Isa. 9:6; 37:32; Joel 2:18; Zech. 1:14; 8:2). In the same vein the New Testament says that, though God's wrath rests on the wicked now already (John 3:36; Eph. 2:3; 1 Thess. 2:16), the manifestation of that wrath in all its terror is reserved for the future (Matt. 3:7; Luke 3:7; 21:23; Rom. 5:9; 1 Thess. 1:10; 5:9; Eph. 5:6; Col. 3:6; Rev. 6:16–17; 11:18; 14:10; 16:19; 19:15).[165]

165. On the righteousness of God in Scripture, in addition to L. Diestel ("Gerechtigkeit") and A. Ritschl (*Rechtfertigung und Versöhnung*), see *Ortloph, "Gerechtigkeit Gottes," *Zeitschrift für lutherische Theologie und Kirche* (1860); E. Kautzsch, *Über die Derivate des Stammes* צדק *im alttestamentlichen Sprachgebrauch* (Tübingen: L. F. Fues, 1881); E. König, *De vi vocis* צדקה *in libris prophetarum* (Paris, 1894); H. Cremer,

In dogmatics, as a rule, the term "righteousness" was given a much broader meaning than it has in Scripture. Sometimes its meaning was extended to include God's perfection and holiness. Righteousness was then equated with virtue and became the sum of all virtues, existing in God as perfect harmony with himself (divine righteousness). Usually, however, theology took it in a more restricted sense, following Aristotle. The latter defined it in his *Nicomachean Ethics* as "the virtue by virtue of which each possesses what belongs to him or herself."[166] Justice is possible only in a society of beings who can possess a greater or lesser quantity of goods. It does not exist among the gods because there is no standard determining how much they may possess, nor among irrational creatures because they cannot be said to possess goods. Justice, therefore, first of all presupposes that there are certain rights established by a lawgiver. So we speak of "legislative justice." Justice next presupposes that by means of treaties and contracts these rights will be respected on both sides reciprocally. This is called "commutative justice." And finally, justice presupposes that the existing rights are maintained, which produces "distributive justice." They are maintained either by rewarding conformity (remunerative justice) or by punishing nonconformity (retributive justice). In all cases justice is "the constant and perpetual desire to grant every person his or her due."

All this was applied to God. Thus the term "righteousness" in dogmatics acquired a much broader meaning than it has in Scripture. Now there is no overriding objection to this, provided the difference in use is kept in mind, for the issues treated in dogmatics under the heading of "the justice of God" all clearly occur in Scripture. There is even an advantage in our discussing the term in the broader sense, because it affords us an opportunity to defend God's justice in its full scope against its assailants. The Gnostics in general and Marcion in particular drew a sharp contrast between law and gospel, works and faith, flesh and spirit, and similarly between the God of wrath, vengeance, and justice who revealed himself in the Old Testament, and the God of love

Lexicon, s.v. "Δικαιοσυνη"; J. Köstlin, "Gott," *PRE*², V, 311; idem, "Die Idee Reiches Gottes und ihre Anwendung in Dogmatik und Ethik," *Theologische Studien und Kritiken* 64/3 (1892): 423–25; G. F. Oehler, *Theology of the Old Testament*, §47; H. Schultz, *Alttestamentliche Theologie*, 540ff.; R. Smend, *Lehrbuch der alttestamentlichen Religionsgeschichte*, 363ff., 410ff.; A. B. Davidson, *Theology of the Old Testament*, 129ff.; A. Kuenen, *Godsdienst van Israël*, I, 65ff.; G. A. Fricke, *Der paulinische Grundbegriff der* δικαιοσυνη Θεου, *erörtert auf Grund von Röm. 3,21–26* (Leipzig: Böhme, 1888); H. Beck, "Die δικαιοσυνη Θεου bei Paulus," *Neue Jahrbuch für deutsche Theologie* 4 (1895): 249–61; G. Dalman, *Die richterliche gerechtigkeit im Alten Testament* (Berlin: Kartell-zeitung; Comissionsverlag, 1897); H. Bouwman, *Het begrip gerechtigheid in het Oude Testament* (Kampen: J. H. Bos, 1899). Also see the literature in the later section on justification, H. Bavinck, *Reformed Dogmatics*, IV, ##467–76.

166. Ed. note: Bavinck gives no specific reference here. A close parallel is found in *Nicomachean Ethics*, 1134a (bk. V, ch. 5, §17): "Justice is the virtue in accord with which the just person is said to do what is just in accord with his decision, distributing good things and bad, between himself and others and between others" (*Nicomachean Ethics/Aristotle; Translated with Introduction, Notes, and Glossary by Terence Irwin*, 2d ed. [Indianapolis: Hackett Publishing, 1999], 76).

and grace who revealed himself in Christ in the New Testament.[167] Later, in essentially the same sense, God's justice, specifically God's punitive justice, was denied to him by many theologians as being in conflict with his love. Now, associated with God's justice there are many difficulties: in the case of God one cannot conceive of a law that is above him and to which he would have to conform, for his will is the supreme law. Before God creatures do not have rights or claims, for they have received all things from his hands and have not given him anything in return; they cannot claim a reward, for even "when [they] have done everything [they] were told to do," they are still "unworthy servants" [Luke 17:10 NIV]. Also, there seems to be nothing in God's nature that would compel him to mete out punishment. Why should he who is omnipotent not be able to forgive without demanding satisfaction or exacting punishment? However, in order not to digress too far from the biblical concept of justice (or righteousness), it is better to discuss these questions later, in connection with God's will and freedom.

[The order of] justice, in the Bible, is not a property of God's "absolute dominion" but rests on a moral foundation.[168] Though one must grant that in the nature of the case creatures can have no rights before God (Rom. 11:35; 1 Cor. 4:7), nor put him under obligation (*justitia commutativa*),[169] yet it is God himself who gives his creatures "rights" (so to speak). By virtue of creation every creature has received a distinct nature of its own. Laws and ordinances exist for all created things; there are "rights" structured into the very existence and nature of all existing beings. Such rights have above all been accorded to rational creatures and among them again for all the areas of life in which they function, for the intellect and the heart, soul and body, art and science, family and society, religion and morality. And when those rights have been forfeited by human sin, God makes a "covenant of nature" with Noah and a "covenant of grace" with Abraham, acts by which he again, out of sheer grace, grants to his creatures an array of rights and binds himself by an oath to maintain these rights. Thus, by the grace of God, a complete order of justice was established, in the realm both of nature and of grace, an order encompassing an array of ordinances and laws that he himself maintains and makes effective. In Scripture, however, these ordinances and laws are not derived from God's justice—what kind of justice after all would obligate him to do that?—but from his holiness and grace. And this way of putting it is certainly better than to describe them as "legislative justice" (*justitia legislativa*). Still, this is not wrong provided the idea is not that by virtue of some kind of justice God was morally bound to grant all these rights to his creatures. The element of truth present here, however, is that God is the supreme Lawgiver, and that the entire order of justice undergirding every domain of life is rooted in him. All laws

167. Adolf von Harnack, *History of Dogma*, trans. N. Buchanan et al., ed. A. Bruce, 7 vols. (London: Williams & Norgate, 1896–99), I, 239ff.

168. A. B. Davidson, *Theology of the Old Testament*, 131ff.

169. T. Aquinas, *Summa theol.*, I, qu. 21, art. 1.

and rights, whatever they may be, have their ultimate ground, not in a social contract, nor in self-existent natural law or in history, but in the will of God, viewed not as "absolute dominion" but as a will of goodness and grace. God's grace is the fountainhead of all laws and rights.

God maintains that order of justice, moreover, in every domain of life. He who is justice in person and the author of all law is also the arbiter and vindicator of justice. His legislative justice includes his judicial justice. Law is not law unless it is enforced, if necessary, by coercion and punishment. This order of justice, of course, does not automatically include the means of maintaining it. This order would have existed even apart from sin, but it would be obeyed voluntarily and out of love by all creatures without any coercion. It is sin that forces the order of justice, in keeping with its nature, to compel respect by means of violence and coercion. Not justice as such, but the coercive character it is now forced to assume, is due to sin. This coercive character, however, far from being arbitrary or accidental, is so necessary now that apart from it we cannot even conceive of justice, a fact attested by our own conscience. The moral order, rather than being in conflict with the order of justice, upholds, demands, and supports it. Justice is an important component of morality. Justice above all is the way in which the grace and love of God are maintained and made to triumph. Those who, with Marcion, assume that justice and grace are antithetical to each other deny the connection between the moral order and the order of justice and do not understand the majesty and glory of the law. Accordingly, God's justice by its very nature has to be judicial and hence be "remunerative," on the one hand, and "retributive," on the other. It is not that a creature could ever have an inherent claim to any reward or be intrinsically unable to receive forgiveness apart from punishment. But God owes it to his covenant, to the order of justice that he himself at one time established, to his name and honor, to lead his people to salvation and to punish the wicked. Thus alone can justice rule and triumph. There is truth in the saying, "Let justice prevail though the world perish." Scripture, however, more beautifully highlights the idea that justice must prevail that the world may be saved.[170]

ATTRIBUTES OF SOVEREIGNTY

[207] Next to be considered are the attributes that belong to God as Sovereign. God is the creator and therefore the owner, possessor, and Lord of all things. Apart from him there is no existence or ownership. He alone has

---

170. Irenaeus, *Against Heresies*, III, 25; IV, 39ff.; Tertullian, *Against Marcion*, passim; Origen, *On First Principles*, II, 5, 3; Pseudo-Dionysius, *The Divine Names and Mystical Theology*, 8, §7; Anselm, *Proslogion*, chs. 9ff.; P. Lombard, *Sent.*, IV, 46 and the commentary from Thomas and Bonaventure; T. Aquinas, *Summa theol.* I, qu. 21; J. Gerhard, *Loci theol.*, II, c. 8, sect. 12; G. Voetius, *Select. disp.*, I, 339–402; John Owen, "On Divine Justice," in *The Works of John Owen* (Edinburgh: T. & T. Clark, 1862), X, 481–624; A. Comrie and N. Holtius, *Examen van het ontwerp van tolerantie*, V; B. de Moor, *Comm. in Marckii Comp.*, I, 674ff., 996ff.; L. Meijer, *Verhandelingen over de goddelyke wigenschappen*, IV, 89ff.

absolute authority. Always and everywhere his will decides. Again and again, accordingly, there is mention in Scripture of God's sovereign will (צְבוּ, חֵפֶץ, רָצוֹן; Dan. 4:35 [32 MT]; 6:16 [17 MT]; Greek: θελημα). That will is the final ground of all things, of their being, and of their being as they are.

God's Will as Ultimate

Everything derives from God's will: creation and preservation (Rev. 4:11), government (Prov. 21:1; Dan. 4:35; Eph. 1:11), Christ's suffering (Luke 22:42), election and reprobation (Rom. 9:15ff.), regeneration (James 1:18), sanctification (Phil. 2:13), the suffering of believers (1 Pet. 3:17), our life and lot (James 4:15; Acts 18:21; Rom. 15:32), even the most minute details of life (Matt. 10:29; etc.). In keeping with all this, Christian theology similarly honored the will of God as the final cause of all that exists and as the end of all contradiction. "The will of the Creator," said Augustine, "is the nature of every created thing."[171] Philosophy, however, has never been satisfied with this position and never stopped looking for another and deeper explanation of things. Plato attempted to trace the visible world to the "ideas" that constituted true being, but did not succeed.[172] Aristotle conceived the deity as pure "form" (εἶδος), as "the thinking of thought" (νοησις νοησεως), which excludes all volition, all creation and action (ποιησις and πραξις). And although he also viewed the deity as the "prime mover," in his work the nature of the movement and God's relation to the world remains totally in the dark.[173] In Stoicism this led to pantheism: God is the rationality, mind, or soul of the world, and the world is his body, garment, or appearance.[174]

Modern philosophy returned to this rationalism. Descartes regarded thought as the essence of spirit and the guarantee of existence. This led, by legitimate inference, to Hegel's philosophy of identity. The absolute is pure thought, but not, as in Plato, a world of ideas, not as true reality. It is thought as such, without any content; not being but becoming; *actually*, it is nothing; *potentially*, it is everything. From this principle, a mere logical abstraction, the world had to be explained. It soon became evident that this was impossible. Hegel left the problem as unsolved as did Plato and Aristotle. This abstract oneness could not possibly produce the multiplicity of the world, nor could thought as such produce being. The fact that Hegel's philosophizing contained even a semblance of truth was due to his [skillful] playing with concepts. Another word Hegel used to describe this absolute kind of thinking was "pure possibility." This logical possibility, however, was dialectically transmuted into "real and absolute power" (δυναμις), and so it seemed in fact to be able to produce the universe. But this was a dialectical game that in the long run could not carry conviction. Opposition to Hegel's philosophy arose from several directions.

171. Augustine, *City of God*, XXI, 8; idem, *The Trinity*, III, 6–9.
172. E. Zeller, *Die Philosophie der Griechen*, II⁴, 744–69.
173. E. Zeller, *Die Philosophie der Griechen*, III³, 357–84.
174. Ibid., IV³, 133–49.

Rationalism had outlived its usefulness; idealism failed to explain the existence of the world; the primacy of the intellect had suffered bankruptcy. No existence or world could be derived from absolute thought without a will. So this time philosophers gave the primacy of the will a try!

This attempt was made by Schelling in his second period. He returned to the theosophy of Böhme and through him to Kabbalah and Neoplatonism. In it Plotinus had already taught that God was "his own cause," the product of his own will and power, and therefore that the will was ultimate being and anterior to the intellect. In the same vein Schelling now made the will the final principle both of the existence of infinite and of finite being. In his philosophical investigations about the nature of human freedom (1809), he already took this position. "Ultimately," he said, "there is no other being than volition. Volition is archetypal being, and to it alone all the predicates of such being apply: groundlessness, eternity, freedom from dependence on time, self-affirmation. All philosophy is solely aimed at finding this supreme expression."[175] With respect to God and created beings, one must distinguish between being insofar as it exists, and being insofar as it is only the ground of existence. God has the ground of his existence within himself, that is, in a nature distinct from God himself. This nature is, so to speak, "the longing experienced by the eternal one to generate itself." It is will, "but a will devoid of intellect, and for that very reason it is not an independent and complete will, since the intellect of the will is in the willing. Still, it is a willing of the intellect, that is, the longing and desire of the intellect, not a conscious but an intuitive will, whose intuition is of the intellect." But this is true of all things: they are something other than God and yet cannot be without him. This contradiction has only one solution: "Things have their ground in that which in God is not God himself, that is, in that which is the ground of his existence." Things have their ground in this dark nature, in the unconscious will of God. The world as we now know it, to be sure, exhibits order, regularity, and form, just as in God the light of the mind and of the personality rose out of the darkness of this nature. "But the chaotic is always there in the depths as if once more it might break through to the surface, and nowhere does it appear as if order and form were original, but rather as if an originally chaotic state had been brought to order."[176] The entire cosmic process is inferred by Schelling from

175. F. W. J. Schelling, "Philosophische Untersuchungen über das Wesen der menschlichen Freiheit und die damit zusammenhängenden Gegenstände," in *Ausgewählte Werke*, 4 vols. (Darmstadt: Wissenschaftlichle Buchgesellschaft, 1968), IV, 294 [*Werke*, I/7, 350; cf. *Werke*, I/1, 401ff.]; ET: *Schelling: Of Human Freedom*, trans. James Gutmann (Chicago: Open Court, 1936). Ed. note: Bavinck's references to Schelling's writings that have been incorporated in the new unrevised but abridged and repaginated *Ausgewählte Werke* (1968) will be cited with the full title of the work as well as Bavinck's original reference. Since this is not a complete republication of Schelling's original *Sämmtliche Werke* (Stuttgart & Augsburg: J. G. Cotta'scher, 1856–61), writings not included in the new edition will be cited simply as *Werke*, using Bavinck's original reference. Where possible, an English version of the work will also be indicated.

176. F. W. J. Schelling, "Freiheit," *Ausgewählte Werke*, IV, 301–4 [*Werke*, I/7, 357–59].

the antithesis between nature and spirit, darkness and light, the real and the ideal, which have been coexistent in God himself from all eternity.

By taking this position Schelling managed to overcome Hegel's rationalism and became of great significance for later philosophy. True, in his later writings,[177] he further developed in a theistic sense the ideas that he had already expressed in his study of human freedom, but remained true to his theory of the primacy of the will and was followed in that respect by Schopenhauer and von Hartmann. Granted, in these philosophers the will is not a will in the true sense of the word, but simply an unconscious desire, a blind urge, a dark force of nature. In part, however, these philosophers themselves admitted this. Schelling expressly states that the will that is without intellect is not independent and complete, inasmuch as "the intellect of the will is in the willing."[178] Schopenhauer, for his part, did attribute consciousness to the manifestation of the will, considering it bound to individuality and brains, but interposed between the will and the phenomenal world the ideas that constitute the eternal norms and patterns of things.[179] And von Hartmann also speaks of the Unconscious as subject as the "transconscious."[180] The will, he says, determines the existence of things, but the intellect their essential character.[181]

But even aside from this admission, their philosophy is of the greatest significance for theism. It has demonstrated the untenability of rationalistic and idealistic pantheism. God cannot be conceived without will, freedom, and power. Against this position it has been advanced that all willing is desiring and striving and therefore proof of imperfection, dissatisfaction, and unrest, things that cannot occur in God. Mysticism, accordingly, sang: "We pray, my Lord and God, your will be done; and look: he has no will; he is eternal silence" (Angelus Silesius). But this objection rests on a mistaken conception of the will. Certainly, willing is often a striving for something one does not possess; but once the will has gotten that which it desired, and now finds rest and enjoyment in it, that rest and enjoyment is also an activity of the will, indeed the highest and most powerful activity of the will.[182] Now, such a will that finds rest and enjoyment in what it has acquired is present also in creatures. It is simply the love that embraces its object and is blessed in so doing. Now, if such rest and enjoyment is not attributed to the will, either it is unattainable by creatures, that is, there is no possibility of creaturely blessedness; or if blessedness will in

---

177. F. W. J. Schelling, "Stuttgarter Privatvorlesungen (1812)," *Ausgewählte Werke*, IV, 361–428 [*Werke*, I/7, 417–84]; idem, "Denkmal der Schrift von den göttlichen Dingen des Herrn F. H. Jacobi (1812)," *Ausgewählte Werke*, IV, 539–656 [*Werke*, I/8, 19–136]; and especially in his *Philosophie der Offenbarung*, 2 vols. (Darmstadt: Wissenshaftliche Buchgesellschaft, 1959) [*Werke*, II³, 4th vol.].

178. F. W. J. Schelling, *Ausgewählte Werke*, IV, 301 [*Werke*, I/7, 359].

179. A. Schopenhauer, *Die Welt als Wille und Vorstellung*, 6th ed. (Leipzig: Brockhaus, 1887), I, 370; I, 154. Ed. note: ET: *The World as Will and Representation*, trans. E. F. J. Payne (New York: Dover Publications, 1966).

180. E. von Hartmann, *Philosophie des Unbewussten*, II, 186.

181. Ibid., I, 100ff.; II, 435ff.; 446ff.; F. W. J. Schelling, *Werke*, II/3, 57–62.

182. Cf. H. Bavinck, *Beginselen der Psychologie* (Kampen: Bos, 1897), 156ff.

fact one day be given to creatures, it can only consist in the annihilation of the will, the stupefaction of consciousness, and the total suppression of personality. True blessedness can therefore be conceived by pantheistic mysticism only as the soul is being lost in, and swallowed up by, the divine, that is, in a nirvana.

This, however, is not what Scripture and Christian theology teach. True blessedness, far from destroying the will, in fact raises it to its highest level of activity, for love is the most abundantly powerful energy of the will. Now, in that sense there is also a will in God. His willing is not a striving for a good but an actual possession without which he would lack something and not be truly blessed. For he is the all-sufficient and fully blessed One himself. He is himself the supreme good, both for his creatures and for himself. He can rest in nothing other than himself. Because he is God he cannot be blessed except in and through himself. His love is self-love and therefore absolute divine love. And that absolute self-love is nothing other than a willing of himself: the supreme and absolute divine energy of his will. Hence the object of God's will is God himself. Not, however, in the sense that he is the product of his own will, as if he had produced himself and were his own cause,[183] for this would again introduce into the divine being the process of becoming and striving and, therefore, the element of imperfection. It does, however, mean that God eternally wills himself with the will of delight, that he eternally loves himself with divine love and is completely blessed within himself. His will is the "superlatively wise propensity toward his own self as the supreme good." It is not a capacity or force in God. It is the case rather that the subject, action, and object of that will coincide with God's very being.[184]

Scripture, however, also speaks of God's will with reference to the created world. Just as God's knowledge is twofold (necessary and free—see section on knowledge), so also his will must be distinguished as being in part his "propensity toward himself" and in part his "propensity toward his creatures." But just as God's "free" knowledge does not make him dependent of his creatures but is known to him from within himself, so also the will of God that is aimed at his creatures must not be dualistically set side by side to the will whose object is his own being. Scripture expressly teaches that God wills "things other than himself" and constantly speaks of his will in relation to creatures, but adds in the same breath that God wills them, not because he needs them, but only for his own sake or name (Prov. 16:4). The creation, accordingly, is not to be conceived as an object existing outside of or over against him, which he lacks and strives to possess, or as something he hopes to gain, which he does not possess. For "from him and through him and to him are all things" (Rom. 11:36). It is not God who finds his destiny in his creatures; rather, they find their destiny in him. "The things outside of himself that he wills are the very

---

183. Cf. above, pp. 156–58 (#193).

184. P. Lombard, *Sent.*, I, dist. 45; T. Aquinas, *Summa theol.*, I, qu. 19, art. 1; idem, *Summa contra gentiles*, I, 72ff.; J. Zanchi(us), *Op. theol.*, II, 246; A. Polanus, *Syn. theol.*, II, ch. 19. Ed. note: Bavinck adds: θέλημα θελητικον, θέλησις, and θέλημα θελητον are identical with God's essence.

things that in a sense already exist in him in whom all things exist."[185] He wills creatures, not for something they are or that is in them, but for his own sake. He remains his own goal. He never focuses on his creatures as such, but through them he focuses on himself. Proceeding from himself, he returns to himself. It is one single propensity that drives him to himself as the ultimate end and to his creatures as the means to that end. His love for himself incorporates into itself the love he has for his creatures and through them returns to himself. Therefore, his willing, also in relation to creatures, is never a striving for some as yet unpossessed good and hence no sign of imperfection and infelicity. On the contrary: his willing is always—also in and through his creatures—absolute self-enjoyment, perfect blessedness, divine rest. In God rest and labor are one; his self-sufficiency coincides with absolute actuality.

Free and Necessary Will of God

[208] Although God wills himself and his creatures with one and the same simple act, still, with a view to the different objects of that will, we must make certain distinctions. In pantheism such differentiation is impossible because in this worldview the world is identical with God himself. Scripture, however, ascribes to creatures an existence of their own, which, while distinct from, is not independent of, God's being. For that reason his creatures cannot be the objects of his will in the same sense and way he himself is. God's will in relation to himself is his "propensity toward himself as *goal*"; his will with respect to his creatures is his "propensity toward his creatures as *means*." The former is necessary, like the knowledge of simple intelligence; God cannot but love himself. He eternally, and with divine necessity, delights in himself. Hence, this will is free from all arbitrariness, yet not bound or subject to coercion. Freedom and necessity coincide here. Things are very different, however, with respect to the will of God, whose object is his creatures. Scripture speaks of this will in the most absolute terms possible. God does whatever he pleases (Ps. 115:3; Prov. 21:1; Dan. 4:35). He owes no one an accounting and justifies none of his deeds (Job 33:13). Humans are in his hands like clay in the hands of a potter (Job 10:9; 33:6; Isa. 29:16; 30:14; 64:8; Jer. 18:1ff.). "Even the nations are like a drop from a bucket, and are accounted as the dust on the scales" (Isa. 40:15ff.). It is as foolish for humans to magnify themselves against God as it would be for an axe to magnify itself against him who hews with it or for a saw to boast against him who wields it (Isa. 10:15)! Before God no human can assert such rights. No one can ask him: "What are you doing?" (Job 9:2ff., 12; 11:10). "Does the clay say to him who fashions it: what are you making?" (Isa. 45:9). Therefore, let humans be silent and lay their hand on their mouth (Job 40:4). And so also the New Testament teaches. Can God not do what he wants to do with what belongs to him (Matt. 20:15)? All things depend solely on God's will for their being—*that* they are and *what* they are (Rev. 4:11). God's

---

185. J. Zanchi(us), *Op. theol.*, II, 246.

will is the ultimate ground of all things. Both mercy and hardening originate there (Rom. 9:15–18). In the church the Holy Spirit apportions to each one individually as he wills (1 Cor. 12:11). Humans have no right whatever to object to God's free dispositions (Matt. 20:13ff.; Rom. 9:20–21).

In Christian theology—for the reasons stated above—the will of God as it relates to his creatures (like the knowledge of vision) was always called "free." Augustine asserted that the will of God is the final ground of all things;[186] there is nothing deeper. To the question: Why did God create the world? the answer is: Because he so willed. Those who then proceed to ask about the cause of that will "demand something that is greater than the will of God; but none such thing can be found."[187] And that, too, was the position of the Christian church and Christian theology.[188] They all taught, indeed, not that God could have done "more" and "better" than he did, for he always acts in a divine and perfect manner, but that he could have made things "greater in number, greater, and better" than he did.[189] Some indeed called the moral law "eternal" and "natural" and viewed it as the expression of God's very being; still, a distinction was made in it between the "essential" and the "accidental," and under special circumstances people could receive an exemption from the requirements of many of the commandments.[190] According to many people, the incarnation and atonement were not strictly necessary. If God had so willed, he could also have forgiven sin apart from any atonement and was under no compulsion to punish sin.[191] God's freedom was even more clearly evident in election and reprobation, for which no ground whatever can be cited, and which rests in the sovereign good pleasure of God alone. We cannot speak of any creature having a claim upon God; there is here no such thing as "commutative" *(quid pro quo)* justice.[192] Nor—since a creature can have no merits before God—is there "remunerative" justice in the true sense of the word.[193] Some even went

186. Augustine, *City of God*, XXI, 8; idem, *The Trinity*, III, 7, 19.

187. Augustine, *De Genesi contra Manichaeos*, I, 2; idem, *City of God*, V, 9.

188. E.g., T. Aquinas, *Summa theol.*, I, qu. 19, art. 5; J. Calvin, *Institutes*, III.xxiii.2.

189. P. Lombard, *Sent.*, I, dist. 44; T. Aquinas, *Summa theol.*, I, qu. 25, arts. 5–6; J. Zanchi(us), *Op. theol.*, II, 184–87; G. Voetius, *Select. disp.*, I, 426, 564; V, 151; F. Burmann, *Syn. theol.*, I, 41, §41.

190. G. Voetius, *Select. disp.*, I, 347ff.; B. de Moor, *Comm. in Marckii Comp.*, II, 614ff.

191. Athanasius, *Against the Arians*, III; Gregory of Nazianzus, *Oration 9*; John of Damascus, *The Orthodox Faith*, III, 18; Augustine, *The Trinity*, XIII, 10; P. Lombard, *Sent.*, III, dist. 20; T. Aquinas, *Summa theol.*, III, qu. 1, art. 2; D. Petavius, "De incarnatione," in *Theol. dogm.*, II, ch. 13; J. Calvin, *Institutes*, II.xii.1; idem, *Commentary*, on John 15:13; J. Zanchi(us), *Op. theol.*, VIII, 144–46; P. M. Vermigli, *Loci communes*, cl. 2, ch. 17; D. Pareus on Rom. 5, in *In divinam ad Romanos S. Pauli Apostoli epistolam commentarius* (Frankfurt: Rhodes, 1608); W. Twisse, *Vindiciae gratiae, potestatis ac providentiae Dei*, 3 vols. (Amsterdami: Guilielmum Blaeu, 1632), I, 153; and others, such as G. J. Vossius, Roell, Vogelsang, B. S. Cremer; cf. C. Vitringa, *Doctr. christ.*, I, 170; *Jan Jacob Schultens, *Waarschuuwing op den kategismus-Verklaaringe . . . van . . . Comrie* (Leiden: A. Kallewier & H. van der Deyster, 1755), 198–222.

192. T. Aquinas, *Summa theol.*, I, qu. 21, art. 1; A. Polanus, *Syn. theol.*, II, ch. 26; G. Voetius, *Select. disp.*, II, 358.

193. T. Aquinas, *Summa theol.*, I, qu. 21, art. 1; Belgic Confession, art. 24; Westminster Confession, ch. 16; A. Comrie and N. Holtius, *Examen van het ontwerp van tolerantie*, X, 288.

so far as to say that, if he so desired, God could punish the innocent either for time or eternity, though he never used that right.[194]

Nominalism

Thus, proceeding from God's absolute freedom, many theologians found themselves thinking along the lines of medieval nominalism. It was Duns Scotus who consistently applied to God the Pelagian notion of the freedom of the will as absolute indifference. In his commentary on Lombard's *Sentences* he argues against Aristotle and Avicenna that, aside from God, nothing is necessary. The world as a whole and in its parts is contingent: to God it is unnecessary. He answers the question why God has willed this world and why he willed one thing rather than another by saying:

> To demand the reasons and proof for all things is to be intellectually undisciplined. For proof is not identical with the principles of proof. That the will wills this thing is an immediate principle, because there is no intermediate cause. Just as it is an immediate [self-evident] fact that heat is heat-producing, so also for this fact, namely, why the will willed this thing, there is no reason other than that the will is will. Granted, the former is an illustration taken from the realm of nature and the latter an illustration from the realm of freedom. The case is similar with respect to the question why heat is heat-producing; there is no reason other than that heat is heat, for there is no prior reason.

One must focus on this statement: "The will of God wills this"; nothing takes precedence over the antecedent reason of the will.[195]

Scotus remains true to this principle with respect to all that is temporal and occurs in time. If the whole world is contingent, this characteristic can only be maintained by saying that God, the first cause, caused it "accidentally." Now God brings the world into being by intellect and will. The accidental character of the world, however, cannot be due to God's intellect insofar as it precedes the will, for the intellect "understands things in a purely natural manner and by natural necessity." Hence, it must be due to the will. This divine will "regards nothing else as being necessarily antecedent to the object, apart from its own being. It therefore considers itself contingently related to everything else with the result that it can be in opposition."[196] Now, Scotus indeed acknowledges that God's knowledge is anterior to his will, and that the ideas in God, though distinct from his essence, exist prior to his decree.[197] But it nevertheless is the will that makes a selection from all those possible ideas and determines which of them will be realized. The will, accordingly, is the cause of all reality. And only

---

194. W. Perkins, *The workes of that famous and worthy minister of Christ*, 3 vols. (London: John Legatt, 1612–18), I, 772; W. Twisse, *Vindiciae gratiae, potestatis ac providentiae Dei*, I, 165, 179, 324ff.; M. Amyraut, *Syntagma thesium theologicorum* (Salmurii, 1664), I, 237.

195. Duns Scotus, *Sent.*, I, dist. 8, qu. 5, n. 24.

196. Ibid., dist. 39, qu. 5, nn. 14, 22.

197. Ibid., dist. 35, qu. unica, nn. 7ff.

as a result of the decision of the will does the intellect know what will become reality.[198] God, therefore, created the world in absolute freedom, granted that the decree to do so was made from eternity.[199]

Scotus naturally also conceived human freedom of will as absolutely as possible. The will is free, he says, "with respect to opposite actions and opposite objects."[200] Nothing determines it; it may just as easily choose a lower good as a higher good. It is itself alone the complete cause of all its actions. "Nor is it any goodness of the object that necessarily prompts the assent of the will, but the will assents freely to any good whatever and thus assents freely to a greater or to a lesser good."[201] "Nothing other than the will is the complete cause of volition in the will."[202] The will is even antecedent to the intellect, for though it is the case that the intellect offers to the will the object of its striving, it nevertheless is the will that fixes the intellect's attention upon the object. And, formally, the will, not the intellect, is the seat of blessedness.[203] Moreover, while Scotus admits that the love for God prescribed in the first table of the law is necessary and natural, he holds that the commandments of the second table are positive [articulated in concrete form] and could have been different.[204] With respect to the incarnation Scotus teaches that the Logos could also have assumed a nature other than human, say that of stone, had he so desired.[205] The incarnation would probably also have occurred apart from sin and was not strictly necessary in the state of sin: God could also have redeemed humanity in some other way.[206] The merits of Christ were not sufficient in themselves, but God accepted them as such.[207] In the abstract, as far as God's absolute power is concerned, God could also have saved the sinner apart from Christ's merits, and sinners themselves could have made atonement had God only been willing to count their works as sufficient.[208] Transubstantiation is possible "because one substance can wholly begin to exist and another can wholly cease to exist."[209] God can even cause a person or thing to cease to exist for an "intermediate period of time" without thereby destroying his, her, or its identity.[210]

Still, Scotus did not go as far as certain Muslim theologians, who asserted that by the will of God all things are created anew from moment to moment apart from any connection with each other, from any laws of nature, without

198. Ibid., dist. 39, qu. 5, nn. 23ff.
199. Ibid., II, dist. 1, qu. 2, n. 5.
200. Ibid., I, dist. 39, qu. 5, nn. 15ff.
201. Ibid., I, dist. 1, qu. 4, n. 16.
202. Ibid., II, dist. 25, qu. 1, n. 22.
203. Ibid., IV, dist. 49, qu. 4.
204. Ibid., III, dist. 37, qu. unica.
205. Ibid., III, dist. 2, qu. 1, nn. 5ff.
206. Ibid., III, dist. 7, qu. 3, n. 3; III, dist. 20, qu. unica.
207. Ibid., III, dist. 19, qu. unica.
208. Ibid., IV, dist. 15, qu. 1, nn. 4ff.; IV, dist. 1, qu. 6, nn. 4ff.
209. Ibid., IV, dist. 11, qu. 1, n. 4.
210. Ibid., IV, dist. 43, qu. 1, n. 4.

substances or qualities.[211] He recognizes the presence in God of ideas that precede the will, considers love for God necessary and natural, believes in a natural knowledge of God, in a world order and natural law, and even says that the incarnation and atonement were necessary in terms of God's "ordained power." Still, Scotus raises God's freedom and omnipotence to such a height that at least the means that must lead to the goal become completely arbitrary.[212] Others even further elaborated this theory of divine freedom and omnipotence. Entirely along Scotist lines, Occam, for example, asserted that according to his absolute power God can grant salvation apart from regeneration and can damn the regenerate; that he can forgive without atonement and count the works of sinful persons as sufficient [for salvation]; that instead of the Son, the Father could have become incarnate, and that the Son could have assumed the nature of a stone or donkey; that by an act of dispensation God can grant people exemption from all the commandments of the moral law.[213] Later this nominalist position was adopted first of all by the Jesuits, further by the Socinians, the Remonstrants, Descartes, by Cartesian theologians such as Burmann,[214] and in the nineteenth century by Charles Secrétan.[215] Given this position, the will in God is completely severed from his nature and all his perfections. It consists in nothing but formal arbitrariness. Creation, incarnation, atonement, good and evil, truth and untruth, punishment and reward—it could all have been different from what it actually was. Nothing is any longer natural; everything has become positive [concrete].

But precisely this nominalism put Christian theology on its guard. Even though, with Augustine, it said that the will of God was the ground of all things, it took care not to divest this will of all its natural specificity and to let it degenerate into pure arbitrariness.

First of all, in its doctrine of God it took its point of departure not in his will but in his nature. The "knowledge of simple intelligence" preceded the

211. H. Ritter, *Geschichte der christlichen Philosophie*, 4 vols. (Hamburg: F. Perthes, 1841–45), III, 732ff.

212. Cf. ibid., IV, 388ff.; A. Stöckl, *Geschichte der Philosophie des Mittelalters*, 3 vols. (Mainz: Kirchheim, 1864–66), II, 832ff.; F. C. Baur, *Die christliche Lehre von der Dreieinigkeit und Menschwerdung Gottes* (Tübingen: C. F. Oslander, 1841–43), II, 642ff.; A. Ritschl, "Geschichtliche studien zur christliche Lehre von Gott," *Jahrbücher für deutsche Theologie* 10 (1865): 298ff.; I. A. Dorner, "Duns," *PRE²*, III, 735–54; R. Seeberg, "Duns Scotus," *PRE³*, V, 62–75; idem, *Die Theologie des Johannes Duns Scotus* (Leipzig: Dieterich, J. Weicher, 1900); F. Loofs, *Leitfaden zum studium der Dogmengeschichte*, 4th ed. (Halle a.S.: M. Niemeyer, 1906), 590.

213. A. Stöckl, *Philosophie des Mittelalters*, II, 1018ff.

214. O. Fock, *Der Socinianismus nach ceiner Stellung in der Gesammtentwicklung des christlichen Geistes, nach seinem historischen Verlauf und nach seinem Lehrbegriff* (Kiel: C. Schröder, 1847), 416ff.; *The Confession or Declaration of the ministers or pastors which in the United Provinces are called Remonstrants, concerning the chief parts of Christian Religion* (London: Francis Smith, 1676), ch. 24; S. Episcopius, *Institutiones theologicae*, V, sect. 5, c. 3; René Descartes, *The Meditations*, trans. John Veitch (Chicago: Open Court, 1908), 84ff. (the sixth meditation). Ed. note: Bavinck's exact reference reads: *Resp. sextae.* (Amsterdam, 1654), 160ff.; F. Burmann, *Synopsis Theologiae*, I, ch. 20, §6; I, ch. 21, §19ff.

215. C. Secrétan, *La philosophie de la liberté*, 3d ed. (Paris: G. Balliere, 1879), I, 305ff.; cf., F. Smitt, *De wereldbeschouwing van Charles Secrétan* (Nijmegen: H. ten Hoet, 1906).

"knowledge of vision," just as the "necessary" will preceded God's "free" will. Self-knowledge and self-love were absolutely necessary in God; and the divine knowledge and will whose object is the creature are not dualistically divorced from, but very closely connected with, the former. The "knowledge of vision" is bound to the "knowledge of simple intelligence" and the "free" will to the "necessary" will. Consistent nominalism claims that not only the existence but also the essential character of things is exclusively determined by the formal will of God. Actually, therefore, there is in God no "knowledge of simple intelligence" in which all possibilities are comprehended, but only a "knowledge of vision" that follows the will. But according to Christian theology, all possibilities exist in the knowledge of simple intelligence; while the knowledge of vision selects them from that source, the will actualizes them. The *existence* of things, accordingly, depends on God's will, but their *essence* depends on his mind.

Leibniz, though building his theory on this foundation, gave it a new twist when he said that God was indeed free to create or not to create the world, humanity, the animals, and plants, but if he created them, he had no choice but to create them according to the idea that his consciousness had conceived prior to and apart from the will. Given God's will to create, the world must be exactly what it is. It therefore is the best of all possible worlds and is so harmoniously put together in all its parts that "to know one part well is to know them all."[216] Scripture, furthermore, everywhere teaches that God created and preserved the world by the word (Logos). It therefore rested on God's thoughts. God did not act arbitrarily and "accidentally" but with supreme wisdom. Hence, even if we could not track down the reasons for his action, they were nevertheless present to him. Christian theology, therefore, attempted to uncover them. Creation was said to have been prompted by his goodness or love. For the permission of sin all sorts of reasons were cited. The incarnation and atonement were perhaps not absolutely necessary, still this way of salvation was the most fitting and excellent.[217] And though many theologians hesitated to restrict God's absolute power, everyone nevertheless recognized that God did not use this absolute right, and so on the point of "ordained power" they were again in total agreement. Finally, on a number of concrete points nominalism was firmly rejected: the moral law cannot have any other content than it has;[218] the punishment of sin is necessary;[219] the incarnation

216. G. W. Leibniz and Johann Christoph Gottsched, *Theodicee*, I, 7, 52; II, 169ff.; A. Pichler, *Die Theologie des Leibniz: Aus sämmtlichen gedruckten . . . Quellen*, 2 vols. (Munich: J. G. Cotta, 1869–70), I, 239ff.; cf. also Schelling, *Werke*, II, 3, 57–62; E. von Hartmann, *Philosophie des Unbewussten*, I, 100ff.; II, 435ff., 446ff.; C. H. Weisse, *Philosophische Dogmatik oder Philosophie des Christentums*, I, §§460ff.

217. D. Petavius, "De incarnatione verbi," in *Theol. dogm.*, II, chs. 5ff.

218. T. Aquinas, *Summa theol.*, I, 2 qu. 100, art. 8; Martinus Becanus, *De triplici sacrificio naturae, legi, gratiae* (Mainz: Joannis Albini, 1610), III, ch. 3, qu. 4; F. Suárez, *Tractatus de legibus*, I, ch. 15; G. Voetius, *Select. disp.*, I, 364–402; S. Maresius, *Systema theologicum*, VII, 4; F. Turretin, *Institutes of Elenctic Theology*, III, qu. 18; XI, qu. 2; J. H. Heidegger, *Corpus theologiae christianae*, III, 89–90.

219. Canons of Dort, II, 1; G. Voetius, *Select. disp.*, I, 358ff.; II, 240ff.; B. de Moor, *Comm. in Marckii Comp.*, I, 683ff., 996–1034.

and atonement are based on God's justice;[220] and God's power was defined so as to exclude the idea that God can effect contradictory outcomes.[221]

In this way nominalism, if not completely overcome, was forced back and checked in Christian theology. When "the free will" [of God] was described as "God's propensity toward creatures as means to his own ends," there was implied in this position fundamental opposition to the idea of the will of God as absolute arbitrariness, for the character of the means is determined by the nature of the end. This is why theology, though giving priority to the will of God and constantly returning to it, also consistently looked for the motives guiding that will. Realism strove to understand the world as a harmonious whole, in which nothing was arbitrary and everything, even including sin, had its proper place, and which in its entirety was subservient to the glorification of God's name. If the nature of a scientific discipline consists in "learning the causes of things," theology cannot opt out of such an investigation. Only, the first duty of every practitioner of science, and particularly of any theologian, is to be humble and modest. A scientist must not think himself or herself to be wiser than he or she ought to think. Every scientific discipline is bound to its object; it may not—for the sake of some preconceived theory—falsify or deny the phenomena it observes.

So also theology is strictly tethered to the facts and evidences that God discloses in nature and Scripture. It must let these facts and evidences stand unimpaired and unmutilated. When it cannot explain them, it must acknowledge its ignorance. For theology, the will of God expressed in the facts is the end of all discussion. In the end theology rests in divine sovereignty. In that sense Augustine's statement remains true: "The will of God is the fundamental nature of every creature." Theology refuses to be seduced by pantheism, which makes the world necessary, for God and the world, the "necessary" and the "free" will, are distinct; nor by Deism, which makes the world a product of chance, for that whole world is a revelation of God's wisdom. And against both it stoutly maintains that the world was brought into being by an act of God's free and sovereign will, and that God had his own wise reasons for that will. To us a thing is good for the sole reason that God wills it. God himself can never have willed anything unless it is either good in itself or for some other reason.[222] We can almost never tell why God willed one thing rather than another, and are therefore compelled to believe that he could just as well have willed one thing as another. But in God there is actually no such thing as choice inasmuch as it always presupposes uncertainty, doubt, and deliberation. He, however, knows

---

220. Irenaeus, *Against Heresies*, III, 20; Anselm, *Cur Deus homo*; Heidelberg Catechism, 11, 40; Lord's Supper liturgy of the Dutch Reformed Churches; J. Trigland, *Antapologia*, ch. 4; G. Voetius, *Select. disp.*, II, 238ff.; F. Turretin, *De satisfactione Christi disputationis* (Trajecti ad Rhenum: A. Schouten & Th. Appels, etc., 1701), II, §16ff.; J. Owen, "On Divine Justice," in *The Works of John Owen*, X, 481–624; A. Comrie and N. Holtius, *Examen van het ontwerp van tolerantie*, V.

221. Cf. below, pp. 245–49 (#210), on divine omnipotence.

222. G. Voetius, *Select. disp.*, I, 387.

what he wills—eternally, firmly, and immutably. Every hint of arbitrariness, contingency, or uncertainty is alien to his will, which is eternally determinate and unchanging. Contingency characterizes creatures and—let it be said in all reverence—not even God can deprive the creature of this characteristic. In God alone existence and essence are of one piece; by virtue of its very nature, a creature is such that it could also not have existed.

But God, by his own eternal and unchanging will, willed all creatures to be contingent. For that reason it is not possible, nor even permissible, for us to look for some ground higher than the will of God. For all such efforts end up seeking a ground for a creature in the very nature of God, thus making it necessary, eternal, and divine, and divesting it of its creaturely, that is, contingent, character. In that sense it is true that the will of God, which has created things as its object, is free. But this freedom does not exclude other divine attributes such as wisdom, goodness, righteousness, and so on. After all, even among creatures true freedom of will is not the kind that needs a long period of doubt, deliberation, and decision; the greatest freedom, rather, is that which establishes all at once, by a single intuition, both the end and the means of an enterprise, and knows nothing of hesitation. Such freedom exists also in God. It is a freedom that must not be conceived as bound to the other perfections of God or, in nominalist fashion, made independent of them, but a freedom that is free in an absolute sense because it is the freedom of a wise, just, holy, merciful, and almighty God. Accordingly, when Augustine, Thomas, Calvin, and others said that there was no "reason *(causa)*" for the divine will, they meant that the will of God, as being one with his essence, has no "causa" behind or above it on which that will would be dependent. But they by no means meant that the will is without reason *(ratio)*, that, in the sense of Schopenhauer's theory, it is blind and irrational. On the contrary, God's will is one with his being, his wisdom, goodness, and all his other perfections.[223] For that reason the human heart and head can rest in that will, for it is the will of an almighty God and a gracious father, not that of a blind fate, incalculable chance, or dark force of nature. His sovereignty is one of unlimited power, but also of wisdom and grace. He is both king and father at one and the same time.[224]

The Problem of Evil

[209] Still other difficulties for the doctrine of the will of God arise from the fact of creation as well. Just as God and the world are distinct and we

223. T. Aquinas, *Summa theol.*, I, qu. 19, art. 5.

224. Cf. J. Kleutgen, *Die Theologie der Vorzeit vertheidigt*, I, 452–585; M. J. Scheeben, *Handbuch*, I, 681ff.; I. A. Dorner, *System of Christian Doctrine*, I, 410ff.; idem, *Gesammelte Schriften*, 341ff.; J. Müller, *The Christian Doctrine of Sin*, trans. Wm. Urwick, 5th ed., 2 vols. (Edinburgh: T. & T. Clark, 1868), II, 180ff.; J. H. A. Ebrard, *Christliche Dogmatik*, 2d ed., 2 vols. (Königsberg: A. W. Unzer, 1862–63), §§71ff.; F. H. R. Frank, *System der christlichen Wahrheit*, 2 vols. (Erlangen: A. Deichert, 1878–80), I, 283ff.; C. Hodge, *Systematic Theology*, 3 vols. (New York: Charles Scribner's Sons, 1888), I, 402.

must therefore distinguish between his "propensity toward himself" and his "propensity toward his creatures," so also in the world among his creatures there is all sorts of diversity. And that diversity is based on the different relations God establishes—with his being, knowledge, and will—with his creatures. God does not will all things in the same fashion and sense, with the same energies of his being. For were that so, no diversity would be possible among his creatures, and the whole world would be one of monotonous uniformity.

But though he wills all creatures as means and for his own sake, he wills some more than others to the degree they are more direct and suitable means for his glorification. God is a Father to all his creatures, but he is that especially to his children. His affection for everything he created is not as deep as his affection for his church, and that in turn is not as great as his love for Christ, the Son of his good pleasure. We speak of a general, a special, and a very special providence; in the same way we make as many distinctions in the will of God (as it relates to his creatures) as there are creatures. For the free will of God is as richly variegated as that whole world is. Hence, it must not be conceived as an indifferent power, a blind force, but as a rich and powerful divine energy, the wellspring of the abundant life that creation spreads out before our eyes. In that world, however, there is one thing that creates a special difficulty for the doctrine of the will of God, and that is the fact of evil, both evil as guilt and evil as punishment, in an ethical as well as a physical sense. Though evil is ever so much under God's control, it cannot in the same sense and in the same way be the object of his will as the good. Hence, with a view to these two very different, in fact diametrically opposed, objects we must again make a distinction in that will of God, as Scripture itself shows. There is a big difference between the will of God that prescribes what we must do (Matt. 7:21; 12:50; John 4:34; 7:17; Rom. 12:2), and the will of God that tells us what he does and will do (Ps. 115:3; Dan. 4:17, 25, 32, 35; Rom. 9:18–19; Eph. 1:5, 9, 11; Rev. 4:11). The petition that God's will may be done (Matt. 6:10) is very different in tenor from the childlike and resigned prayer: "Your will be done" (Matt. 26:42; Acts 21:14). Over and over in history we see the will of God assert itself in two ways. God commands Abraham to sacrifice his son, yet he does not let it happen (Gen. 22). He wants Pharaoh to let his people Israel go, yet hardens his heart so that he does not do it (Exod. 4:21). He has the prophet tell Hezekiah that he will die; still he adds fifteen years to his life (Isa. 38:1, 5). He prohibits us from condemning the innocent, yet Jesus is delivered up according to the definite plan and foreknowledge of God (Acts 2:23; 3:18; 4:28). God does not will sin; he is far from iniquity. He forbids it and punishes it severely, yet it exists and is subject to his rule (Exod. 4:21; Josh. 11:20; 1 Sam. 2:25; 2 Sam. 16:10; Acts 2:23; 4:28; Rom. 1:24, 26; 2 Thess. 2:11; etc.). He wills the salvation of all (Ezek. 18:23, 32; 33:11; 1 Tim. 2:4; 2 Pet. 3:9), yet has mercy on whom he wills and hardens whom he wills (Rom. 9:18).

Revealed and Hidden Will

At an early stage a distinction was made in theology between these two sides of the divine will. Tertullian already speaks of a hidden and higher will on the one hand, and a lower or lesser will on the other.[225] Augustine points out that God often fulfills his good will through the malicious will of humans.[226] Later this twofold will was described, on the one hand, as "the will of God's good pleasure," "God's secret will," and "the decretive will"; and on the other as "the expressed" or "signified" will, "the revealed" or "preceptive" will.[227] The term "signified" or "revealed" will *(voluntas signi)* derives from the fact that this will makes known to us "what is pleasing to God and our duty"; it is known to us from five "signs": precept, prohibition, counsel, permission, and operation. Developed in great detail by scholasticism,[228] this view of the divine will was adopted by Catholic theologians in general,[229] and especially treated with predilection in Reformed theology.[230] Still other distinctions cropped up with respect to the will of God, especially the distinction between the "antecedent" and the "consequent" will of God, which already occurs in Tertullian and John of Damascus;[231] and between "the absolute and the conditioned, the efficacious and inefficacious will of God," found already in Augustine.[232] These distinctions, too, can be readily understood in the sense, namely, that God antecedently and conditionally wills many things (such as the salvation of all humans) that "consequently" and "absolutely" he does not will and therefore does not permit to happen. Zanchius, accordingly, says that all these distinctions come down to the same thing; and this is also the opinion of Hyperius, Walaeus, Voetius,[233] and others.

Although in his book *The Bondage of the Will* Luther had made a very sharp distinction between the "hidden" and the "revealed" God, the Lutherans rejected this distinction between "the will of God's good pleasure" and the "revealed" or "signified" will; at least they did not accept it in the Reformed

225. Tertullian, *Exhortation to Chastity,* 2ff. (*ANF,* IV, 50–58).

226. Augustine, *Enchiridion,* ch. 101.

227. The technical terms Bavinck cites are *voluntas* εὐδοκίας, *beneplaciti, arcana, decernens, decretiva* and *voluntas* εὐαρεστιας, *signi, revelata, praecipiens.*

228. P. Lombard, *Sent.,* I, dist. 45; Hugo of St. Victor, *De sacramentis christianae fidei,* I, pt. 4; idem, *Summa sententiarum septem tractatibus distincta,* tract. 1, ch. 13; T. Aquinas, *Summa theol.,* I, qu. 19, art. 11–12.

229. D. Petavius, "De Deo," in *Theol. dogm.,* V, chs. 4, 6; *Theologia Wirceburgensi,* III, 160; G. Perrone, *Prael. theol.,* II, 199; C. Pesch, *Prael. dogm.,* II, 156ff.

230. J. Calvin, *Institutes,* I.xvii.3–4; W. Musculus, *Loci communes theologiae sacrae,* 978ff.; P. M. Vermigli, *Loci comm.,* 63ff.; Z. Ursinus, *Volumen tractationum theologicarum,* 237ff.; J. Zanchi(us), *Op. theol.,* II, 251ff.; A. Polanus, *Syn. theol.,* II, ch. 19; cf. A. Schweizer, *Die Glaubenslehre der evangelisch-reformirten Kirche,* I, 359–68; H. Heppe, *Dogmatik der evangelisch-reformierten Kirche,* 68ff.

231. Tertullian, *Against Marcion,* II, 11; Chrysostom, on Eph. 1:5 in *Homilies on the Epistles of St. Paul the Apostle to the Galatians and Ephesians, NPNF (1),* XIII, 52; John of Damascus, *The Orthodox Faith,* II, 29.

232. Augustine, *Enchiridion,* chs. 102ff.; idem, *City of God,* XXII, chs. 1–2.

233. A. Hyperius, *Methodi theologiae,* 155–59; A. Walaeus, *Opera omnia,* I, 180; G. Voetius, *Select. disp.,* V, 88.

sense.[234] The Arminians followed that example.[235] Roman Catholic theologians, though formally retaining the distinction, explained it in the sense that the will of God was always "the will of his good pleasure," distinguished in terms of an "antecedent" and a "consequent" will, and that the "signified" or "revealed" will was nothing but a partial revelation of that will.[236] Thus it happened that Roman Catholics and others only retained the distinction between the "antecedent" and "consequent," the "absolute" and "conditional" will, while the Reformed only kept the distinction between "the will of God's good pleasure" and the "expressed" or "revealed" will, that is, between the "decretive" and the "preceptive," the "hidden" and the "revealed" will, while rejecting the "antecedent" and "consequent" will.[237] The difference comes down to this: Roman Catholics, Lutherans, Remonstrants, and others proceed from the "revealed" or "signified" will. This is then the "true" will, which consists in that God does not will sin but only wills to permit it; that he wills the salvation of all humans and offers his grace to all, and so on. Then, after humans have decided, God adjusts himself to that decision and determines what he wants, salvation for those who believe and perdition for those who do no believe. The "consequent" will follows the human decision and is not the actual and essential will of God, but the will of God occasioned by the conduct of humans. The Reformed, by contrast, proceeded from the will of God's good pleasure, viewing this as the actual and essential will of God. That will is always carried out, always effects its purpose; it is eternal and immutable. The "expressed" or "signified" will, on the other hand, is God's precept, concretely stated in law and gospel, the precept that serves as the rule for our conduct.

Now, both in the Old and New Testament, Scripture consistently teaches that the will of God is eternal, immutable, independent, and efficacious. This truth is not just expressed from time to time (e.g., Ps. 33:11; 115:3; Dan. 4:25, 35; Isa. 46:10; Matt. 11:26; Rom. 9:18; Eph. 1:4; Rev. 4:11; etc.), but is pervasively taught throughout Scripture. All God's perfections demand it, and the entire history of the church and the world furnish proof for it. Accordingly, Christian theology taught, especially from Augustine on, that the will of God is simple, eternal, and immutable, that is, identical with his being.[238] God's antecedent will is not really a will in God: "It is a wishing rather than

---

234. J. Gerhard, *Loci theol.*, II, c. 8, sect. 15; J. W. Baier, *Compendium theologiae positivae*, I, ch. 1, §22; J. F. Buddeus, *Institutiones theologiae dogmaticae*, II, ch. 1, §29.

235. S. Episcopius, *Institutiones theologicae*, IV, sect. 2, ch. 21; P. van Limborch, *Theol. christ.*, II, ch. 9, §9.

236. *Theologia Wirceburgensi*, III, 160; C. Pesch, *Prael. dogm.*, II, 156; J. Kleutgen, *Die Theologie der Vorzeit vertheidigt*, I, 564ff.

237. J. Maccovius, *Collegia theol.*, in *Loci communes theologici*, disp. 1–8; N. Gürtler, *Nicolai Gürtleri institutiones theologicae* (Marburgi Cattorum: Sumtibus Philippi Casimiri Mülleri, 1732), ch. 3, §105; B. de Moor, *Comm. in Marckii Comp.*, I, 576; P. van Mastricht, *Theologia*, II, ch. 15, §§24, 27ff.; F. Turretin, *Institutes of Elenctic Theology*, III, qu. 15–16.

238. Augustine, *Confessions*, XIII, 15.

a sheer willing."[239] God's expressed will is called God's will in a metaphorical sense; "just as when someone issues a command, it is a sign that he wills it to be done."[240] The actual will in God is the will of his good pleasure, identical with his being, and efficacious.[241] Pelagianism, mistakenly abandoning this line of thought, raised a powerless desire, an unfulfilled wish in God, to the dignity of will. In so doing it failed to do justice to God's entire being and all his perfections. For if this "wishing" (velleity) were the actual and true will of God, he is robbed of his omnipotence, wisdom, goodness, immutability, independence (etc.); the government of the world is divorced from his providence; an insoluble dualism is created between God's intent and the actual result of the history of the world. This outcome then will be an eternal disappointment for God: his plan for the world has failed, and in the end Satan triumphs. Granted, Pelagianism maintains that it takes this position in defense of God's holiness, and that it honors this holiness more than Paul and Augustine, Thomas and Calvin, seeing that in their system God becomes the author of sin. But this supposed superiority is no more than appearance. On Pelagius's position sin remains just as inexplicable as on that of Augustine. In fact, Augustine's position does more justice to God's holiness, for it is more in accordance with Scripture and Christian faith as a whole to believe that for good and wise reasons, though these reasons are unknown to us, God has in a certain sense willed sin than to believe that, not willing it in any sense, he tolerates and permits it. It is the latter position that fails to do justice to God's holiness and omnipotence.

To this we must add that Scripture, though theologically giving prominence to the will of God's good pleasure, by its teaching of the revealed will of God underscores how and in what sense God does not will sin. In the "signs" of prohibition, admonition, warning, chastisement, and punishment (etc.), God comes down to us and tells us what he desires of us. Because humans are rational, moral beings, God does not deal mechanically with them but speaks and acts in keeping with their nature. Just as a father forbids a child to use a sharp knife, though he himself uses it without any ill results, so God forbids us rational creatures to commit the sin that he himself can and does use as a means of glorifying his name. Hence, God's hidden will and his revealed will are not really incompatible, as the usual objection has it. For in the first place, God's revealed (preceptive) will is not really his (ultimate) will but only the command he issues as the rule for our conduct. In his preceptive will he does not say what *he* will do; it is not the rule for *his* conduct; it does not prescribe what *God* must do, but tells us what *we* must do. It is the rule for *our* conduct (Deut. 29:29). It is only in a metaphorical sense, therefore, that it is called the will of God. Against this view it is objected that the revealed will bears

239. T. Aquinas, *Summa theol.*, I, qu. 19, art. 6.
240. Ibid., art. 11.
241. Ibid., art. 6–7; idem, *Summa contra gentiles*, I, 72ff.; cf. P. Lombard, *Sent.*, I, dist. 45–48.

that name because it reveals what he really wills and hence that it must be in harmony with his secret will. And this—second—is indeed the case: the revealed will is an indication of what God wills that we will do. God's secret will and his revealed will are not diametrically opposed to each other, as though according to the former God willed sin, but according to the latter he did not; as though according to the former he does not will the salvation of all, but according to the latter he does. Also, according to his secret will God takes no pleasure in sin; it is never the object of his delight. He does not afflict any person for the pleasure of afflicting that person. Conversely, even according to his preceptive will God does not will the salvation of everyone individually. With a view to history no one can seriously entertain the notion that he does. Actually the "all" in 1 Timothy 2:4 is restricted to a larger or smaller circle by every interpreter. The two wills, the secret and the revealed, are so far from being opposed to each other that the revealed will is precisely the way in which the secret will is brought to realization. It is in the way of admonitions and warnings, prohibitions and threats, conditions and demands that God carries out his counsel, while God's secret will only insures that human beings violating God's commandment do not for a moment become independent of God, but in the very moment of violating it serve the counsel of God and become, however unwillingly, instruments of his glory. Not only the revealed will but also the secret will of God is holy, wise, and good, and will, precisely in the way of the law and of righteousness, become manifest as such in the end.

Finally, therefore, the distinction between the two needs to be maintained. Facing us at this point is the problem of what ought to be and what is, idea and history, the moral and the actual, what ought to happen and what actually happens. Those who reject God's revealed will fail to do justice to God's holiness, the majesty of the moral law, the seriousness of sin. Those, on the other hand, who deny God's secret will come into conflict with his omnipotence, wisdom, independence, and sovereignty. In both cases, however, there is a danger: either, in an attitude of shallow optimism, people close their eyes to reality and call all that is real rational; or, in an attitude of utter cynicism, they curse life on earth and despair of the world and human destiny. Theism, however, will not seek a solution by canceling one of the terms of the problem, but recognizes and maintains both: at all times, in history, it sees the lines of the rational and the real cross each other. It traces both to the sovereignty of God, viewing it with the high idea that also through the irrational and sinful it will fulfill its holy and wise counsel to the glory of his name. Certainly, it cannot be denied that we witness God's sovereignty at its most brilliant when he magnifies his wisdom in human folly, his strength in human weakness, and his grace and righteousness in human sin.

Omnipotence

[210] God's sovereignty, finally, reveals itself in his omnipotence, a topic that in view of the above hardly calls for extensive treatment. Scripture

nowhere sets bounds to God's power. Already in the names El, Elohim, El Shaddai, and Adonai the idea of power comes to the fore. He is further called "great and terrible" (אֵל גָּדוֹל וְנוֹרָא; Deut. 7:21ff.), whose face no human can see and live [Exod. 33:20], "the Mighty One of Israel" (אֲבִיר יִשְׂרָאֵל, Isa. 1:24), "the great and mighty God (הָאֵל הַגָּדוֹל הַגִּבּוֹר) whose name is YHWH of hosts" (Jer. 32:18); he is "mighty in strength" (אַמִּיץ כֹּחַ, Job 9:4; כַּבִּיר, Job 36:5), "strong and mighty" (עִזּוּז וְגִבּוֹר, Ps. 24:8), "the Lord" (אָדוֹן, κυριος, Matt. 11:25; Rev. 1:8; 22:5), that is, the owner and ruler who possesses authority and "overlordship," the king who eternally rules over all things (Exod. 15:18; Ps. 29:10; 93–99; 2 Kings 19:15; Jer. 10:7, 10; etc.) but especially exercises kingship over Israel, protecting and saving it (Num. 23:21; Deut. 33:5; Judg. 8:23; 1 Sam. 8:7; Ps. 10:16; 24:7; 48:2; 74:12; Isa. 33:22; 41:21; 43:15; etc.). Similarly, in the New Testament he is called "the great king" (μεγας βασιλευς, Matt. 5:35; 1 Tim. 1:17), "the King of kings and Lord of lords" (βασιλευς των βασιλευοντων και κυριος των κυριευοντων, 1 Tim. 6:15; cf. Rev. 19:16); "the Lord Almighty" (παντοκρατωρ, 2 Cor. 6:18; Rev. 1:8; 4:8; 11:17); "the only Sovereign" (μονος δυναστης, 1 Tim. 6:15), who possesses both the power (εξουσια, αρχη) and the authority (δυναμις, κρατος) to act (Matt. 28:18; Rom. 9:21) and the ability, fitness, and power to act (Matt. 6:13; Rom. 1:20).

God's omnipotence is further evident from all his works. Creation, providence, Israel's deliverance from Egypt, nature with its laws, the history of Israel with its marvels—all loudly and clearly proclaim the omnipotence of God. Psalmists and prophets alike constantly revisit these mighty acts to humble the proud and to comfort believers. He is "mighty in power" (Isa. 40:26), creates heaven and earth (Gen. 1; Isa. 42:5; 44:24; 45:12, 18; 48:13; 51:13; Zech. 12:1), maintains their ordinances (Jer. 5:22; 10:10; 14:22; 27:5; 31:35), forms rain and wind, light and darkness, good and evil (Amos 3:6; 4:13; 5:8; Isa. 45:5–7; 54:16). He renders people speechless and enables them to speak, he kills and makes alive, saves and destroys (Exod. 4:11; 15; Deut. 26:8; 29:2; 32:12; 39; 1 Sam. 2:6; 14:6; 2 Kings 5:7; Hos. 13:14; Matt. 10:28; Luke 12:20). He has absolute power over all things so that nothing can resist him (Ps. 8, 18–19, 24, 29, 33, 104, etc.; Job 5:9–27; 9:4ff.; 12:14–21; 34:12–15; 36–37). Nothing is too hard for God; for him all things are possible (Gen. 18:14; Zech. 8:6; Jer. 32:27; Matt. 19:26; Luke 1:37; 18:27). Out of stones he can raise up children to Abraham (Matt. 3:9). He does whatever he pleases (Ps. 115:3; Isa. 14:24, 27; 46:10; 55:10–11) and no one can call him to account (Jer. 49:19; 50:44). His power is, above all, evident in the works of redemption: in the resurrection of Christ (Rom. 1:4; Eph. 1:20), in bringing about and strengthening faith (Rom. 16:25; Eph. 1:18–19), in the dispensing of grace above all we ask or think (Eph. 3:20; 2 Cor. 9:8; 2 Pet. 1:3), in the resurrection of the last day (John 5:25ff.), and so on. This power of God, finally, is also the source of all power and authority, ability and strength, in creatures. From him derives the dominion of humankind (Gen. 1:26; Ps. 8), the authority of governments (Prov. 8:15; Rom. 13:1–6), the strength of his people (Deut. 8:17–18; Ps. 68:35; Isa. 40:26ff.), the might of a horse (Job 39:19ff.), the mighty voice of thunder (Ps. 29:3; 68:33; etc.). In a word, power belongs to God (Ps. 62:11), and his is the glory and the strength (Ps. 96:7; Rev. 4:11; 5:12; 7:12; 19:1).

Entirely in keeping with their doctrine of the will and freedom of God, the nominalists defined the omnipotence of God not only as his power to do whatever he wills, but also as his power to will anything. Differentiating between God's "absolute" and his "ordained" power, they judged that in accordance with the former God could also sin, err, suffer, die, become a stone or an animal, change bread into the body of Christ, do contradictory things, undo the past, make false what was true and true what was false, and so forth. According to his absolute power, therefore, God is pure arbitrariness, absolute potency without any content, which *is* nothing but can *become* anything.[242] In principle this is the position of all who subscribe to the primacy of the will. Hence, this view later surfaced again and again and occurs not only in Christianity but also in other religions, especially in Islam. On the other side are those who say that God can do only what he wills and nothing that he does not will. The "possible" coincides with the "real." That which does not become real is not possible either. God has fully exhausted his power in the existing world. Plato and Plotinus already held this view,[243] as did a number of church fathers,[244] but it was especially advocated in the Middle Ages by Abelard: "God cannot do anything beyond that which he does."[245] This was also the opinion of the Cartesian theologians Burmann, Braun, Wittichius,[246] as well as of Spinoza, Schleiermacher, Strauss, Schweizer, Nitzsch, and others.[247]

Scripture, we believe, condemns the one position as well as the other. On the one hand, it expressly states that there are many things that God cannot do. He cannot lie, he cannot repent, he cannot change, he cannot be tempted (Num. 23:19; 1 Sam. 15:29; Heb. 6:18; James 1:13, 17), and he cannot deny himself (2 Tim. 2:13). For his will is identical with his being, and the theory of absolute power, which separates God's power from his other perfections, is nothing but an empty and impermissible abstraction.

242. Cf. above, pp. 235–39 (#208); also D. Chamier, *Panstratiae catholicae*, II, 1, 2, ch. 3, §5; G. Voetius, *Select. disp.*, I, 411, 427.

243. E. Zeller, *Die Philosophie der Griechen*, II, 928; V, 496ff.

244. D. Petavius, "De Deo," in *Theol. dogm.*, V, ch. 6.

245. P. Abelard, *Introductio ad theologiam*, III, ch. 5.

246. F. Burmann, *Synopsis theologiae*, I, ch. 21, §§24, 26; ch. 25, §§10–11; J. Braun, *Doctrina foederum*, I, 2, ch. 3, §§7ff.; Chr. Wittichius, *Theologia pacifica*, §§199ff.

247. B. Spinoza, *Cogitata metaphysica*, II, ch. 9. Ed. note: ET: appendix in B. Spinoza, *The Principles of Descartes' Philosophy*, trans. Halbert Hains Britan (Chicago: Open Court, 1974), 113–71; idem, *Ethics*, I, prop. 16–17; F. Schleiermacher, *The Christian Faith*, §54; D. F. Strauss, *Die christliche Glaubenslehre*, 2 vols. (Tübingen: C. F. Osiander, 1840–41), I, 582ff.; A. Schweizer, *Die christliche Glaubenslehre nach protestantischen Grundsätzen dargestellt*, I, 246ff.; F. Nitzsch, *Lehrbuch der evangelischen Dogmatik*, 3d ed. (Tübingen: J. C. B. Mohr, 1902), 403–6; S. Hoekstra, *Wijsgerige Godsdienstleer*, II, 112ff.

On the other hand, Scripture states in language that is equally firm that what is possible extends much farther than what is real (Gen. 18:14; Jer. 32:27; Zech. 8:6; Matt. 3:9; 19:26; Luke 1:37; 18:27). And to this [scriptural] position Christian theology has held firm. Augustine states, on the one hand, that God's will and power are not distinct from his being: "With a human it is one thing *to be,* another *to be able. . . .* With God, however, it is not the case that his substance is one thing so that he *is,* and his power another so that he *is able,* but whatever is his and whatever he is, is consubstantial with him because he is God. It is not the case that in one way he *is* and in another way he *is able:* he has being *(esse)* and ability *(posse)* because he holds the willing and the doing together."[248] God's omnipotence consists in that he can do whatever he wants to do, "for certainly he is called omnipotent for no other reason than that he is able to do whatever he wills."[249] But God cannot will anything and everything. He cannot deny himself. "Since he does not will it, he cannot do it, because he is unable even to will it. For justice cannot will what is unjust nor wisdom what is foolish, or truth what is false. Whence we are reminded that the omnipotent God not only cannot deny himself, as the apostle says, but that there are many things that he cannot do: . . . the omnipotent God cannot die, he cannot be changed, he cannot be deceived, he cannot be created, he cannot be overcome."[250] Augustine further asserts that this is not a lack of power but, on the contrary, true, absolute power. If God could err or sin (etc.), that would indeed be a sign of powerlessness.[251] Augustine especially makes this clear in connection with the thesis, often advanced against the omnipotence of God, that God cannot undo what has been done. This statement, he says, can be interpreted two ways. On the one hand it may be interpreted to mean that God undoes the event that has occurred, but this makes no sense because an event that has occurred does not exist anymore; hence, it cannot and need not be undone. On the other hand, it can be construed to mean that God undoes the event in the human consciousness so that it now believes it did not happen. But this does not make sense either, for in that case God, who is truth, would have to make untrue that which is true. Other theologians, only repeating Augustine, have spoken about God's omnipotence in the same vein.[252]

248. Augustine, *Lectures on the Gospel of John,* tract. 20.4, *NPNF (1),* VII, 131–37; idem, *Confessions,* XI, 10; XII, 15.

249. Augustine, *City of God,* XXI, 7.

250. Augustine, *Sermon* 214.

251. Augustine, *Sermon* 213–14; idem, *City of God,* V, 10.

252. P. Lombard, *Sent.,* I, dist. 42–44; T. Aquinas, *Summa theol.,* I, qu. 25; idem, *Summa contra gentiles,* II, chs. 6–10; Bonaventure, *Breviloquium,* I, ch. 7; D. Petavius, "De Deo," in *Theol. dogm.,* V, ch. 7; J. Gerhard, *Loci. theol.,* II, c. 8, sect. 9; J. F. Buddeus, *Institutiones theologiae dogmaticae,* II, ch. 1, §30; W. Musculus, *Loci communes theologiae sacrae,* 952ff.; A. Polanus, *Syn. theol.,* II, ch. 29; J. Zanchi(us), *Op. theol.* II, 159ff.; G. Voetius, *Select. disp.,* I, 403ff.; V, 113ff.; J. H. Alsted, *Theologia scholastica didactica,* 93–96; P. van Mastricht, *Theologia,* II, ch. 20; D. Chamier, *Panstratiae catholicae,* II, 1, 2, chs. 1–3; M. Leydecker, *Fax veritatis,* 163ff., 233ff.

It was especially Reformed theologians who qualified their acceptance of the distinction between God's "absolute" power and his "ordained" power. Nominalists had misused this distinction when they argued that according to the former God is able to do anything, even that which is incompatible with his nature, thereby supporting especially the doctrine of transubstantiation. Calvin, fighting back, rejected as profane this "fiction of absolute power."[253] Roman Catholic scholars, accordingly, accused Calvin of limiting and thus denying God's omnipotence.[254] But Calvin did not deny that God can do more than he actually did, but only opposed a concept of "absolute power" that was not bound to his nature and therefore could do all sorts of contradictory things. Conceived along the lines of Augustine and Thomas, this distinction was generally accepted by Reformed theologians,[255] and so understood, it is worthy of endorsement. Pantheism, indeed, says that God and the world are correlates, and that God has no being, life, consciousness, and will of his own in distinction from the world. But this theory hopelessly jumbles things together and produces endless intellectual confusion. God and the world, eternity and time, infinity and finiteness, being and becoming, the possible and the real, the necessary and the contingent (etc.)—these are not terms with the same content and meaning. The world is such that our thinking cannot deprive it of its contingent character. The notion of its nonexistence does not entail even the least self-contradiction. There *can be* reasons why God called the world into being. It *is* possible that the cosmos, in its entirety and each of its parts, is the embodiment of divine ideas. But it is *impossible* to give a logical explanation of the existence of the world apart from the will of an omnipotent God. The actual, therefore, does not completely cover the possible. God's existence is not exhausted by the existence of the world; eternity does not fully empty itself in time; infinity is not identical with the sum total of finite beings; omniscience does not coincide with the intellectual content embodied in creatures. So also, God's omnipotence infinitely transcends even the boundless power manifested in the world.[256]

PERFECTION, BLESSEDNESS, AND GLORY

[211] All the attributes of God discussed above are summed up in his perfection.[257] Accordingly, in speaking of God's perfection here, we are not referring

253. J. Calvin, *Institutes*, III.xxiii.1, 5; cf. I.xvi.3; II.vii.5; IV.xvii.24; idem, *Commentary*, on Isa. 23:9 and Luke 1:18.

254. R. Bellarmine, "De gratia primi hominis," *Controversiis*, III, 15.

255. A. Polanus, *Syn. theol.*, II, ch. 29; J. H. Alsted, *Theologia scholastica didactica*, 96; J. H. Heidegger, *Corpus theologiae christianae*, III, 109; *Synopsis purioris theologiae*, VI, 36; P. van Mastricht, *Theologia*, II, 20, 13.

256. Cf. C. H. Weisse, *Philosophische Dogmatik oder Philosophie des Christentums*, §§499ff.; I. A. Dorner, *A System of Christian Doctrine*, I, 458ff.; J. H. A. Ebrard, *Christliche Dogmatik*, §§179ff.; F. A. Philippi, *Kirchliche Glaubenslehre*, II, 59ff.; F. Nitzsch, *Lehrbuch der evangelischen Dogmatik*, 503–6; F. H. R. Frank, *System der Christlichen Wahrheit*, I, 249; A. Gretillat, *Exposé de théologie systématique*, III, 256ff.; C. Hodge, *Systematic Theology*, I, 406ff.; W. G. T. Shedd, *Dogmatic Theology*, I, 358ff.

257. Cf. above, p. 211 (#204).

exclusively to his moral perfection (i.e., his goodness or holiness), but mean that God is the sum total of all his perfections, the One than whom no greater, higher, or better can exist either in thought or reality.

In other words, God fully answers to the idea of God. A creature is perfect, that is, perfect in its kind and in its creaturely finite way, when the idea that is its norm is fully realized in it. Similarly, God is perfect inasmuch as the idea of God fully corresponds to his being and nature. To put it this way, however, is to put it in human language and must not be misunderstood. In the case of creatures the idea to which they must answer is posited by God and hence stands over them as the governing norm. In that sense we cannot speak of an "idea" of and for God. There is no idea of God that is normative for God and to which he must answer. But the idea of God is derived from God himself. In him "being" and "self-consciousness" are coextensive; he is as he knows himself to be, and he knows himself to be as he is. Not only does God have perfect knowledge of himself, however; he has also instilled an impression of himself in our hearts. We all have an idea of God and fill it with all the perfections we can conceive and think possible. Granted, that our sense or idea of God has been darkened, and so our ideas of God are widely divergent. But when humans allow themselves to be instructed by Scripture, that sense of God is also clarified; they again learn to know God as he truly is, and say Amen! to all his perfections.

Every attribute of God is precious to believers. They cannot do without any of them. They desire no other God than the only true God, who has revealed himself in Christ, and they glory in all his perfections in truth. Their adoration, their love, their thanksgiving, and praise are aroused not only by God's grace and love but also by his holiness and righteousness, not only by God's goodness but also by his omnipotence, not only by his communicable but also his incommunicable attributes. Now, when we attribute supreme perfection to God, we thereby acknowledge that all the perfections we discover either positively or negatively in observing God's creatures belong absolutely and preeminently, that is, to the highest degree, to God. This implies, however, that they cannot all be attributed to him in the same sense. Some attributes belong to him characteristically, such as eternity, simplicity, and so on, which after all are not found in creatures. Others, such as intellect and will, belong to him preeminently, and because a faint reflection of these can also be discerned in creatures. Still others are ascribed to him only figuratively, such as physical sight and hearing, because these attributes are present in him in a divine way, not in a literal creaturely sense. But whatever difference this may make in the way in which we must ascribe this or that attribute to God, he nevertheless remains the sum of all conceivable perfections, the highest perfection in person, infinitely far removed from all defects and limitations.

And because God is absolutely perfect, he is, and is also called in Scripture, the "blessed" God. In the Old Testament a person's condition of blessedness is affirmed with the exclamation אַשְׁרֵי, a construct plural, meaning "O the

blessedness of, how great the happiness of," and is derived from the verb אשׁר,
which means "to go straight," "to lead in the right direction" (Hiphil), and from
there "to call blessed," "to congratulate." In the New Testament this Hebrew
word is rendered by μακάριος (according to Cremer, more emphatic and ideal
than εὐδαίμων) and is in turn translated *beatus* in Latin, *blessed* in English, and
zalig in Dutch. The [Dutch] word *zalig* is derived from the Gothic word *sêls*,
which means "good, virtuous." *Zalig* is the person of solid virtue, who is what
he or she ought to be. In Scripture the words אַשְׁרֵי and μακάριος, "blessed,"
usually have a religious meaning. They refer to the person who lives in communion with God and is the recipient of God's special benefits, above all the
benefit of the forgiveness of sins (Ps. 32:1; Rom. 4:8). In the New Testament,
God himself is twice called "blessed" (1 Tim. 1:11; 6:15).

Now, when ascribed to God blessedness has three components. In the first
place it expresses that God is absolute perfection, for blessedness is the mark of
every being that is, and to that extent it is complete; in other words, blessedness
is the mark of every being that lives and in living is not hampered or disturbed
by anything from within or without. Now, because God is absolute perfection,
the sum total of all virtues, the supreme being, the supreme good, the supreme
truth (etc.); in other words, because God is absolute life, the fountainhead of all
life, he is also the absolutely blessed God. In Scripture "life" and "blessedness"
are very closely related: life without blessedness is not worthy of the name, and
in the case of God's children eternal life coincides with blessedness. Second,
implied in the words "the blessed God" is that God knows and delights in
his absolute perfection. Scholasticism was divided over the question whether
blessedness in God and humans consisted primarily in knowledge or in love.
Now, apart from knowledge or consciousness there can be no blessedness.
In pantheistic philosophy, accordingly, God is in fact needy, unblessed, pure
potentiality, which *is* nothing and has to *become* everything, and if he is to
become blessed, creatures must make him so. But even given this knowledge,
it is never conceivable without love. God knows himself absolutely and loves
himself absolutely. Knowledge without love and love without knowledge are
both inconceivable, and neither has priority over the other. Hence, the term
"the blessed God" also implies, in the third place, that God absolutely delights
in himself, absolutely rests in himself, and is absolutely self-sufficient. His life
is not a process of becoming, not an evolution, not a process of desiring and
striving, as in the pantheistic life, but an uninterrupted rest, eternal peace.
God's delight in his creatures is part and parcel of his delight in himself. "God
is his own blessedness. Blessedness and God are the same. Through his intellect
God is fully aware of his own perfection, and through his will he supremely
loves it, that is, reposes peacefully in it, and from this repose springs joy, the
joy with which God delights in himself as the supreme good."[258]

---

258. Pseudo-Dionysius, *The Divine Names and Mystical Theology*, ch. 11; T. Aquinas, *Summa theol.*, I,
qu. 26; idem, *Summa contra gentiles*, I, chs. 100–102; M. J. Scheeben, *Handbuch der katholischen Dogmatik*,

The Glory of God

[212] The perfection of God, which is inwardly the ground of his blessedness, outwardly as it were carries his glory with it. The biblical words for glory are כָּבוֹד and δοξα; the Old Testament word כָּבוֹד, from the verb כָּבֵד, to be heavy, weighty, significant, refers to the person who is weighty, important. Also in use is the word הוֹד, which denotes the splendid appearance of one whose name is known far and wide, while הָדָר describes the splendor and beauty of that appearance.[259] The Greek equivalent used in the Septuagint and the New Testament is the word δοξα, subjectively the recognition a person receives or is entitled to receive, the fame or honor that person enjoys (synonyms: τιμη and εὐλογια, Rev. 5:12; antonym: ἀτιμια, 2 Cor. 6:8). Objectively, δοξα is the appearance, form, prestige, splendor, luster, or glory of a person or matter manifest in the public domain, or these themselves in their splendor, and in that case related to εἰδος (appearance), εἰκων (image), μορφη (form) (Isa. 53:2; 1 Cor. 11:7). The "glory of the Lord" is the splendor and brilliance that is inseparably associated with all of God's attributes and his self-revelation in nature and grace, the glorious form in which he everywhere appears to his creatures. This glory and majesty in which God is clothed and which characterizes all his activities (1 Chron. 16:27; Ps. 29:4; 96:6; 104:1; 111:3; 113:4; etc.), though manifest throughout his creation (Ps. 8; Isa. 6:3), is nevertheless especially visible in the realm of grace. It appeared to Israel (Exod. 16:7, 10; 24:16; 33:18ff.; Lev. 9:6, 23; Num. 14:10; 16:19; Deut. 5:24; etc.). It filled the tabernacle and the temple (Exod. 40:34; 1 Kings 8:11), and was communicated to all the people (Exod. 29:43; Ezek. 16:14; etc.). This glory is above all manifested in Christ, the only-begotten Son (John 1:14) and through him in the church (Rom. 15:7; 2 Cor. 3:18), which is looking for "the blessed hope and the manifestation of the glory of our great God and Savior, Jesus Christ" (Titus 2:13). God's glory is often associated with his holiness (Exod. 29:43; Isa. 6:3) and hence also described as a fire (Exod. 24:17; Lev. 9:24) and as a cloud (1 Kings 8:10–11; Isa. 6:4).

Undoubtedly, in referring to that fire and that cloud, Scripture had in mind the visible creaturely forms through which God manifested his presence.[260] The case is different with the light with which the glory of God is often compared and in terms of which it is often represented. Light in Scripture is the image of truth, holiness, and blessedness (Ps. 43:3; Isa. 10:17; Ps. 97:11).

I, §5; J. Heinrich and C. Gutberlet, *Dogmatische Theologie*, III, 856; J. Gerhard, *Loci theologici*, II, §306; D. Hollaz, *Examen theologicum acroamaticum*, I, 1, 37; K. G. Bretschneider, *Systematische Entwicklung*, §37; B. de Moor, *Comm. in Marckii Comp.*, I, 583; H. L. Martensen, *Christian Dogmatics*, §51; F. A. Philippi, *Kirchliche Glaubenslehre*, II, 109; A. von Oettingen, *Lutherische Dogmatik*, II, 185; M. Kähler, "Seligkeit," *PRE³*, XVIII, 179–84.

259. Franz Delitzsch, *Biblical Commentary on the Psalms*, trans. F. Bolton, 3 vols. (Edinburgh: T. & T. Clark, 1871), on Ps. 8:6; cf. also A. Freiherr von Gall, *Die Herrlichkeit Gottes* (Giessen: J. Ricker [A. Töpelmann], 1900).

260. Cf. H. Bavinck, *Reformed Dogmatics*, I, 341 (#94).

This analogy is so simple and natural that it truly does not require the assumption that YHWH was originally a sun god,[261] any more than the term "Rock" has to refer to an earlier period of stone worship.[262] The light of the sun and the lightning of heaven serve the Israelites as metaphors for the description of YHWH's attributes, but they are clearly aware of speaking in images. Just as thunder is the voice of the Lord (Ps. 104:7; Amos 1:2; Isa. 30:30), so the light of nature is his garment (Ps. 104:2). What light is in the natural world—the source of knowledge, purity, and joy—God is in the world of the spirit. He is the "light" of believers (Ps. 27:1); his face and his word shed light (Ps. 44:3; 89:15; 119:105); in his light they see light (Ps. 36:9). He himself is pure light, and in him is no darkness; he is the father of lights (1 John 1:5; 1 Tim. 6:16; James 1:17), and according to the promise (Isa. 9:1; 60:1, 19–20; Mic. 7:8), appeared in Christ as light (Matt. 4:16; Luke 2:32; John 1:4; 3:19; 8:12; 1 John 2:8–11), so that now his church is light in him (Matt. 5:14; Eph. 5:8; 1 Thess. 5:5) and goes out to meet the fullness of light (Rev. 21:23ff.; 22:5; Col. 1:12). In considering "the glory of the Lord" (כְּבוֹד יהוה), the Jews later thought of a created and visible radiance, a body of luminosity, by which he made known his presence in creation, and in the concept of the Shekinah even conceived of it as a personal agent.[263] From Jewish theology this view passed into theosophy. Böhme, for example, describes "the glory of the Lord" as a "body of the Spirit," a "kingdom of the glory of God, the eternal kingdom of heaven, in which the power of God is fundamental, tinctured by the brilliance and energy of fire and light," as an "uncreated heaven," a "paradise."[264] Already at an early stage Lutheran theologians debated the question whether God is called "light" in a literal sense (Dannhauer, Chemnitz) or in a figurative sense (Musaeus, et al.).[265] In the Eastern Orthodox church, the Council of Constantinople (1431) even approved the doctrine of an uncreated divine light that is distinct from the divine being.[266]

This view, however, cannot be endorsed. Scripture clearly teaches the spirituality and invisibility of God. The assumption that the glory of God is a place (מָקוֹם), a figure (תְּמוּנָה, εἶδος, μορφή), a face (פָּנִים), a body, a kingdom, a heaven, which though uncreated is distinct from God's being—this assump-

---

261. A. Kuenen, *De Godsdienst van Israël tot den Ondergang van den Joodschen Staat*, I, 48ff., 240ff., 249, 267.

262. Ibid., I, 392–95.

263. F. W. Weber, *System der altsynagogalen palästinischen Theologie: Aus Targum, Midrasch und Talmud* (Leipzig: Dörffling & Franke, 1880), 160, 179–84.

264. Johannes Claassen, *Jakob Böhme: Sein Leben und seine theosophischen Werke*, I, 157; II, 61; also according to Franz von Baader, *Franz von Baaders Leben und theosophischen Werke als Inbegriff christlicher Philosophie*, II, 90ff.; F. C. Oetinger, *Die Theologie aus der Idee des Lebens abgeleitet und auf sechs Hauptstücke zurückgeführt*, 113ff., 117ff.; Franz Delitzsch, *A System of Biblical Psychology*, 59ff.; P. F. Keerl, *Der Gottmensch, das Ebenbild des unsichtbaren Gottes* (Basel: Bahnmaier, 1866), II, 17ff., 113; idem, *Die Lehre des Neuen Testaments von der Herrlichkeit Gottes* (Basel: Bahnmaier, 1863).

265. C. Vitringa, *Doctrina christianae religionis*, I, 139.

266. J. H. Kurtz, *Lehrbuch der Kirchengeschichte* (Mitau [Jelgava]: Aug. Neumann, 1849), §69, 2.

tion is inconsistent with the above attributes as well as with his simplicity. Also, when Scripture speaks of God's face, glory, and majesty, it uses figurative language. Like all God's perfections, so also that of God's glory is reflected in his creatures. It is communicable. In the created world there is a faint reflection of the inexpressible glory and majesty that God possesses. Just as the contemplation of God's creatures directs our attention upward and prompts us to speak of God's eternity and omnipresence, his righteousness and grace, so it also gives us a glimpse of God's glory. What we have here, however, is analogy, not identity. This already comes out in our language. Speaking of creatures, we call them pretty, beautiful, or splendid; but for the beauty of God Scripture has a special word: glory. For that reason it is not advisable to speak—with the church fathers, scholastics, and Catholic theologians—of God's beauty. Augustine already spoke in this vein, proceeding from the basic premise that "whatever is, insofar as it has being, is true, good, and beautiful." He reasons as follows: in the realm of being and therefore in the realm of the true, the good, and the beautiful, there are distinctions, rankings, and ascendance. To the degree that a thing has more being, to that extent it also has more truth, goodness, and beauty. Everything is beautiful in its kind. "Discernible in the individual works of God are laudable measures and numbers and arrangements in each according to its kind."[267] For all things have a natural beauty peculiarly their own."[268] All creatures, accordingly, contribute to the beauty of the whole. But all creaturely beauty is transitory and changeable; it is not beautiful by itself but by participation in a higher, absolute beauty. Ask all creatures and "they will answer: 'look and see, we are beautiful!' Their beauty is their confession."[269] The pinnacle of beauty, the beauty toward which all creatures point, is God. He is supreme being, supreme truth, supreme goodness, and also the apex of unchanging beauty. "Who is it that made these changeable things beautiful if not the unchangeably beautiful One?" God is the highest beauty, because in his being is absolute oneness, measure, and order. He is lacking in nothing, nor is there anything superfluous in him.[270] Also, in this view of Augustine we encounter the undeniable influence of Neoplatonism, [a philosophy] which similarly viewed the deity as the highest beauty and the cause of all that is beautiful.[271] In this way, nevertheless, this idea of Augustine was accepted by numerous scholastic and Catholic theologians.[272] Protestant theologians, by contrast, preferred to speak of God's majesty and

267. Augustine, *De Genesi contra Manichaeos*, I, 21.

268. Augustine, *Literal Meaning of Genesis*, III, 14.

269. Augustine, *Sermon* 241.

270. Augustine, *De ordine*, I, 26; II, 51. Ed. note: See p. 204 n. 105 above; idem, *De beata vita*, 34; idem, *Against the Academics*, II, 9; cf., H. Ritter, *Geschichte der christlichen Philosophie*, II, 289ff.

271. E. Zeller, *Die Philosophie der Griechen*, V, 483ff.

272. Pseudo-Dionysius, *The Divine Names and Mystical Theology*, ch. 4, §7; Bonaventure, *Breviloquium*, I, ch. 6; D. Petavius, *Theol. dogm.*, VI, ch. 8; M. J. Scheeben, *Handbuch der katholischen Dogmatik*, I, 589ff.; J. B. Heinrich and C. Gutberlet, *Dogmatische Theologie*, III, 852; cf. also Heinrich Krug, *De pulchritudine divina libri tres* (Freiburg: Herder, 1902).

glory.[273] Manifest in God's glory is his sublime greatness, as it is frequently portrayed in the Book of Psalms and in the Prophets (Ps. 104; Isa. 40; Hab. 3). It is called "greatness" and "sublimeness" insofar as it elicits in creatures their worshipful admiration and adoration. It is called "glorious" insofar as it elicits gratitude, praise, and honor. It is called "majesty" insofar as it is bound up with his absolute dignity and demands submission from all creatures.

273. J. Gerhard, *Loci theologici*, I, c. 8, sect. 18; A. Polanus, *Syn. theol.*, II, ch. 31; P. van Mastricht, *Theologia*, II, ch. 22; *Synopsis purioris theologiae*, VI, 43.

6

THE HOLY TRINITY

The seeds that developed into the full flower of New Testament trinitarian revelation are already planted in the Old Testament. Elohim, the living God, creates by speaking his word and sending his spirit. The world comes into being by a threefold cause. Similarly, YHWH, the covenant God, makes himself known to, saves, and preserves his people by his word and spirit. In the angel of the Lord, whether created angel or the Logos, God, specifically his word, was uniquely and powerfully present. Similarly, the spirit of God is the principle of all life and well-being as well as of holiness and renewal. A threefold divine principle underlies creation as well as re-creation and sustains the entire economy of Old Testament revelation.

These Old Testament ideas were further developed in intertestamental Judaism. Divine Wisdom is hypostatized and, under Greek philosophical influence, Philo fused Plato's doctrine of the ideas, Stoic logos-doctrine, and the Old Testament doctrine of wisdom into a single system. However, based on metaphysical dualism keeping God and world separate, Philo regards the Logos as a necessary intermediary being, a mediator between God and the world. In Jewish theology this developed into a complex angelology that increasingly diverged from the Old Testament, which is not dualistic and does not consider logos as immanent reason. In addition, the intermediate beings in Philo and Jewish theologies have no soteriological significance, no connection with the Messiah; the significance of the spirit of the Lord is virtually neglected. While this development shares language with the New Testament, its world of ideas is quite different.

The true development of the trinitarian ideas of the Old Testament is found in the New Testament. In the incarnation of the Son and the outpouring of the Holy Spirit, the one true God is revealed as Father, Son, and Holy Spirit. These three are identical with those who revealed themselves to the Old Testament saints in word and deed, prophecy and miracle. The threefold principle in operation in creation and salvation is, however, made more clear in the New Testament. All salvation, every blessing, and blessedness have their threefold cause in God—the Father, the Son, and the Holy Spirit. The New Testament revelation is trinitarian through and through.

Scripture also gives us insight into the relations between the three persons of the Trinity. God the Father is the Creator, the father of his people, Israel, and supremely the father of his Son, the "Father of our Lord Jesus Christ." The Father is preeminent in creation and redemption, the first in the divine economy. From this the Arians wrongly infer that the Father alone is God; a claim found nowhere in Scripture. On the contrary, the names given to Christ reveal the immanent relations of the triune God. Thus, Logos points to the one who is able to fully reveal God because from all eternity God communicated himself in all his fullness to him. He is also the Son of God in a metaphysical sense; by nature and from eternity he is elevated above angels and prophets. He is the "firstborn" and "only begotten" as the full image of God, who from all eternity bears a unique relation to the Father. He is not a creature, but is and was and remains God, who is over all, blessed forever. The Spirit is God as the immanent principle of life throughout creation; he is holy because he is God. He is both divine and personal. Finally, as Christ is related to the Father, so the Spirit is related to Christ. As the Son witnesses to and glorifies the Father, so the Spirit witnesses to and glorifies the Son. By the Spirit we have communion with no one less than the Son and the Father themselves.

Scripture does not provide a fully developed trinitarian dogma but gives us its essential ingredients. The Apostolic Fathers do little more than cite Scripture though they exalt the Son and avoid both the Docetic and Ebionite heresy. Faced with the challenge of Gnosticism, apologists such as Justin Martyr clearly teach the divinity of the Son, though he does not clearly express the immanent relations between Father and Son. Certain influences of Greek philosophic thought find their way into Justin's formulations and were later rejected by the church. Opposition to Greek philosophic influences is particularly strong in Irenaeus, the great opponent of Gnosticism, with its idea of God as "depth" and its notion of the logos as the immanent principle of the cosmos. It is Tertullian who more clearly distinguished the persons of the Trinity while maintaining the unity of God. He was the first to deduce the Trinity of persons from the very being of God rather than from the person of the Father. Origen took it the next step by conceiving the immanent Trinity totally as an eternal process within the divine being itself, though he subordinates the Son to the Father by deriving the Trinity from the person of the Father.

At Nicaea, the church did not follow Origen but repudiated subordinationism and affirmed the full deity of the Son. The challenge was now to maintain the true unity of the Godhead. Elaborating and developing the doctrine of the Trinity to completion fell to Athanasius, the three Cappadocians, and Augustine. For Athanasius the Trinity is eternal; Father, Son and Holy Spirit are three from eternity. At the same time all three persons are of one essence and have the same attributes. In the main this teaching of Athanasius is affirmed by Basil and the two Gregories and clarified with more names, illustrations, and analogies. In the West, it was Hilary and especially Augustine in their respective treatises De trinitate *who vigorously defended the doctrine. Augustine does not consider the Father but instead the one, simple, uncompounded essence of God as the source of the Trinity. This essence dwells equally and fully in each person. By noting many analogies of the Trinity in creation, Augustine connected the doctrine of God with the cosmos.*

Opposition to the dogma of the Trinity comes from outside (Jews and Muslims) and from within Christianity itself. The confession of the Trinity is the heartbeat of the Christian religion. All error is traceable to a departure from this doctrine: to a denial of the unity in order to preserve threeness (Arianism) or to a formulation of unity that fails to maintain threeness (Sabellianism). Arianism was subordinationist and adoptionist; the Logos was created but a perfect creature who became, as it were, a God. The opposite view, that Father, Son, and Holy Spirit are only different names or modes of the one God came to expression as monarchianism, patripassionism, and modalism. Both errors appealed to Scripture and made use of Greek philosophy to advance their arguments; both positions continued to have influence in the church and theology.

Arianism has appeared in various forms of subordinationism, in Socinianism and in full-blown Unitarianism. Jesus, though exemplary, is an ordinary person, though a great one. Neither the Holy Spirit nor grace is necessary for salvation. Sabellianism retains the divinity of the Son and Spirit but absorbs them into the one divine being so that proper distinctions between them disappear. Father, Son, and Holy Spirit are one and the same person or being, three modes of activity or revelation of the one divine being. The work of the triune God was seen, as in Joachim of Fiore and David Joris, as taking place in three successive periods, each one associated with one person of the Trinity. It was, however, especially Michael Servetus who devoted all his intellectual powers to repudiate the church's doctrine of the Trinity. Gnostic and theosophical speculations can be found in the trinitarian thought of Jakob Böhme, Zinzendorf, and Swedenborg. Such theosophical thinking paved the way for radically philosophical interpretations of the Trinity in Kant, Spinoza, Schelling, Hegel, and Strauss.

Properly to defend Scripture's teaching, the church found it necessary to use language that went beyond Scripture. This affirms the Christian's right of independent reflection and theology's right to exist. Confusion between Greek-speaking and Latin-speaking churches on various terms for the being (unity) of God and the diversity of persons (threeness) accompanied differences in challenges faced by orthodox Christianity in East and West. Terminological disputes have been frequent in the church, particularly concerning the notion of "person." Boethius provided the influential definition of person as an individual rational being, potentially leading to tritheism and a loss of divine unity. In the modern era "personality" is attributed to heroic human qualities and often denied to God. We must not lose sight of the important point: In the dogma of the Trinity the word "person" simply means that the three persons in the divine being are not "modes" but have a distinct existence of their own. The divine being is tripersonal. Thus, settled Christian dogma teaches that in the one being of God there exist three persons, Father, Son, and Holy Spirit, who each fully share the divine essence yet differ in personal attributes. The Father is unbegotten, the Son is begotten or generated, and the Spirit proceeds from the Father (and the Son).

The name "Father" is the preferred description of the first person. "Father" is not a metaphor derived from the earth and attributed to God; "unbegotten" is not to be taken in contrast to creatures but as an inner trinitarian relation. The Father is eternally Father; the Son was generated out of the being of the Father from eternity. It is God's nature to be generative and fruitful. To deny this is to leave one with an abstract, deistic view of God. The generation of the Son is spiritual; it does not create division and separation. Therefore, the most striking human analogy is thought and speech. Just as the human mind objectivizes itself in words, so God expresses his entire being in the Logos. For God to beget is to speak, and his speaking is eternal. The Son is begotten out of the very being of the Father; from eternity the Son is "very God of very God." The personal property of the Holy Spirit is "procession." Both the deity and personality of the Spirit have been contested. It is true that these do not confront us as forcefully in Scripture as do the deity and personality of the Father and the Son. Yet the profound religious significance of making the same confession about the Spirit did become increasingly clear to the church. There is no salvation or communion with God apart from the Holy Spirit. Only if the Holy Spirit is truly God can he impart to us the Father and the Son. He who gives us God himself must himself be truly God. Those who deny the deity of the Holy Spirit cannot maintain that of the Son. The Trinity completes itself in the divine person of the Holy Spirit.

Gradually, however, an important difference developed between the East and the West in the doctrine of the Trinity. The East teaches that the Spirit proceeds from the Father through the Son, but not that the Spirit is also from the Son and receives his existence from him. Unlike Augustine, who posited the unity of the Trinity in the divine nature, the East did not go beyond the church fathers who sought the unity in the person of the Father. Eastern objection to the term filioque is a last lingering remnant of subordinationism and tends to a dualistic separation of orthodoxy and mysticism.

The immanent relations of the three persons in the divine being also manifest themselves outwardly. All God's outward works are common to the three persons and indivisible. There is, however, an appropriation of properties and works to each person. The Father works of himself, through the Son, in the Spirit. All the works of God ad extra have a single author. Yet, all things proceed from the Father, are accomplished by the Son, and completed in the Spirit. In an economic sense, the work of creation is more specifically assigned to the Father, redemption to the Son, and sanctification to the Holy Spirit. In the history of revelation, the economy of the Father was especially that of the

Old Testament, that of the Son began with the incarnation, and that of the Holy Spirit began on the day of Pentecost.

From the beginning of the church's reflection on the Trinity, attempts have been made to elucidate it by illustrations and prove it by arguments. The number three plays an important role in Scripture and in the polytheistic lore of nonbiblical peoples. Numerous trinitarian analogies have been found in the natural world and on a higher level. Augustine and especially medieval thinkers also developed logical analogies. In modern philosophy triplicity even achieved formal dominance in the work of Kant and the dialectical method of Fichte, Schelling, and Hegel. Some sought to go beyond analogy to positive arguments for the Trinity from the nature of thought or of love. Augustine found clear imprints of the Trinity in human consciousness and reason and especially in the self-knowledge of the human soul as memory, intelligence, and will, but he still considered these only a posteriori evidence not a priori proof. Augustine's favorite analogy comes from love itself: Lover, Beloved, and Love. Theosophy in the person of Jakob Böhme and the philosophy of Schelling posited a plural All-Oneness that unites the oneness of Deism and the allness of pantheism. God is subject (will), object (idea), and the identity of both subject and object. Here theogony and cosmogony join: in God's self-revelation to his creatures he at the same time becomes manifest to himself.

Though modern philosophy with its speculation again brought the trinitarian dogma into favor, the church and theology generally assumed a reserved attitude toward these philosophical construals of the Trinity. Analogies at best are a posteriori evidences, and even then the mystery of the Trinity must be honored. Scripture alone is the final ground for the doctrine of the Trinity. Analogies have some value since they remind us that the creation itself shows imprints of the triune God. The arguments also have some value in demonstrating that belief in the Trinity is not irrational. Though grace is superior to nature, it is not in conflict with it. The thinking mind situates the doctrine of the Trinity squarely in the full-orbed life of nature and humanity.

The doctrine of the Trinity makes God known to us as the truly living God, over against the cold abstractions of Deism and the confusions of pantheism. A doctrine of creation—God related to but not identified with the cosmos—can only be maintained on a trinitarian basis. In fact, the entire Christian belief system stands or falls with the confession of God's Trinity. It is the core of the Christian faith, the root of all its dogmas, the basic content of the new covenant. The development of trinitarian dogma was never primarily a metaphysical question but a religious one. It is in the doctrine of the Trinity that we feel the heartbeat of God's entire revelation for the redemption of humanity. We are baptized in the name of the triune God, and in that name we find rest for our soul and peace for our conscience. Our God is above us, before us, and within us.

OLD TESTAMENT SEEDS

[213] God's revelation in the personal names rises to an even higher level than in the attributes, for in the former it makes known to us the distinctions existing within the unity of the divine being. This revelation already begins in the Old Testament. In the Old Testament, to be sure, this [trinitarian] revelation is not yet complete, as it was claimed to be by the church fathers and later theologians who disregarded the historical character of revelation.[1] Nor is it true that this revelation is totally absent from the Old Testament, as was taught first by the Socinians and Remonstrants and later by Semler, Herder, Doederlein, Bretschneider, Hofmann (et al.).[2] The Old Testament conveys only an inexplicit indication of God's trinitarian existence: it is [the first part of] the record of the gradually unfolding doctrine of the Trinity.[3] Still, the Old Testament contains—not just in a few isolated texts but especially in the organism of its revelation as a whole—components that are of the highest significance for the doctrine of the Trinity.

First to be considered is the name "Elohim." Earlier already we commented that the plural form of this name is no proof for the Trinity. Yet it is remarkable that among the proponents of monotheism this name never encountered objection on account of its form. This can only be explained on the assumption that it does not contain any reminiscence of polytheism but refers to the deity in the fullness and richness of its life. The God of revelation is not an abstract "monad" but the true and living God, who in the infinite fullness of his life contains the highest diversity. This is already evident at the time of creation. Elohim creates by speaking his word and by sending out his spirit. The word God speaks is not a mere sound but a force so great that by it he creates and upholds the world. He speaks and it is there (Gen. 1:3; Ps. 33:6, 9; 147:18; 148:8; Joel 2:11). That word, spoken by God, proceeding from him and hence distinct from him, was later hypostatized as wisdom in Job 28:20–28; Prov. 8:22ff.; cf. Prov. 3:19; Jer. 10:12; 51:15). From everlasting, God possessed, prepared, appointed, and searched this wisdom as his foster child and master craftsperson, by whom he created and maintains all things.

The work of creation and providence is established not only by the word and the wisdom of God, however, but also by his spirit (Gen. 1:2 NIV; Ps. 33:6;

1. Cf. the literature on the Trinity in the Old Testament in C. Vitringa, *Doctr. christ.*, I, 213ff., 218.

2. K. G. Bretschneider, *Dogmatik*, 4th ed., 565ff.; ed note: Bavinck's reference is to one of two works by Bretschneider: *Handbuch der Dogmatik der evangelisch-lutherischen Kirche, oder Versuch einer beurtheilenden Darstellung der Grundsätze, welche diese Kirche in ihren symbolischen Schriften über die christliche Glaubenslehre ausgesprochen hat, mit Vergleichung der Glaubenslehre in der Bekenntnisschriften der reformirten Kirche*, 4th ed., 2 vols. (Leipzig: J. A. Barth, 1838); or *Systematische Entwicklung aller in der Dogmatik verkommenden Begriffe nach den symbolischen Schriften der evangelisch-lutherischen und reformirten Kirche und den wichtigsten dogmatischen Lehrbüchern ihrer Theologen*, 4th ed. (Leipzig: J. A. Barth, 1841); J. C. K. von Hofmann, *Der Schriftbeweis*, 2d ed., 2 vols. (Nördlingen: Beck, 1857–60), I, 90ff.; cf. further, J. G. Walch, *Bibliotheca theologica selecta, litterariis adnotationibus instructa*, II, 687.

3. D. Petavius, "De trinitate," in *Theol. dogm.*, II, ch. 7; J. P. Lange, *Christliche Dogmatik*, 3 vols. (Heidelberg: K. Winter, 1852), II, 124ff., 148ff.

104:30; 139:7; Job 26:13; 27:3; 32:8; 33:4; Isa. 40:7, 13; 59:19). Whereas God calls all things into being by his word as mediating agent, it is through his Spirit that he is immanent in the creation and vivifies and beautifies it all. Thus, according to the Old Testament, it is already evident in the creation that all things owe their existence and preservation to a threefold cause. Elohim and the cosmos are not juxtaposed in dualistic fashion; on the contrary, the objective principle of the world created by God is his word, and its subjective principle is his spirit. The world was first conceived by God and thereupon came into being by his omnipotent speech; after receiving its existence, it does not exist apart from him or in opposition to him, but continues to rest in his spirit.

In the Old Testament this threefold cause is even more clearly evident in the domain of special revelation, in the work of re-creation. Then it is no longer only Elohim, but YHWH who reveals him and makes himself known as the God of the covenant and the [covenant] oath, of revelation and history. But even as YHWH he does not reveal himself directly and immediately (Exod. 33:20). It is again by his word that he makes himself known, and saves and preserves his people (Ps. 107:20). And the bearer of that word of redemptive revelation is the angel of YHWH, the messenger of the covenant. The expression "angel of God" or "angel of YHWH," when it occurs in the Old Testament, does not always (as Hengstenberg believed) refer to the "uncreated messenger." In the following verses we encounter an ordinary angel: 2 Samuel 24:16ff.; 1 Kings 19:5–7; 2 Kings 19:35; Daniel 3:25, 28; 6:22; 10:13; also in Matthew 1:20, 24; Luke 1:11; 2:9; Acts 5:19; 8:26; 10:3; 12:7, 23; 27:23; Jude 9; and Revelation 12:7. Other verses, such as Numbers 22:22ff.; Joshua 5:13–14; Judges 2:1–14; 6:11–24; and 13:2–23, leave room for doubt. But in Genesis 16:6–13; 18; 21:17–20; 22:11–19; 24:7, 40; 28:13–17; 31:11–13; 32:24–30 (cf. Hos. 12:4); 48:15–16; Exodus 3:2ff.; 13:21; 14:19; 23:20–23; 32:34; and 33:2ff. (cf. Num. 20:16; Isa. 63:8–9; Zech. 1:8–12; ch. 3; Mal. 3:1), the agent who speaks and acts in "the angel of the Lord" far surpasses a created angel.[4] The church fathers before Augustine were unanimous in explaining this angel of the Lord as a theophany of the Logos.[5] Often, however, this view was linked with the opinion that, while the Father is really invisible, unapproachable, and ineffable, the Son can reveal himself and is the principle of all revelation (Justin Martyr, Theophilus, Irenaeus, Tertullian). But this separation and contrast between the Father and the Son was rightly opposed by the later church fathers (Athanasius, the three Cappadocians, et al.). The Son was truly God and hence equally as invisible as the Father.

This paved the way for the view of Augustine, who also believed that the theophanies in the Old Testament were always mediated by created angels.[6] Scholastic and Roman Catholic theologians as a rule adopted Augustine's ex-

4. Cf. H. Bavinck, *Reformed Dogmatics*, I, 329 (#91).
5. Cf. the references in Chr. J. Trip, *Die Theophanien in den Geschichtsbüchern des Alten Testaments* (Leiden: D. Noothoven van Goor, 1858), 20–41.
6. Augustine, *The Trinity*, III, 11; idem, *City of God*, XVI, ch. 29.

egesis.[7] Luther and Calvin interpreted the angel of YHWH in some verses as a created angel, in others as the uncreated angel.[8] Later Protestant interpreters, however, understood these verses to refer mostly to the Logos, especially to define their position over against the Socinians, Remonstrants, and Rationalists, who read them only as referring to angelophanies. While Hofmann, Baumgarten, Delitzsch, and Cremer[9] aligned themselves with the latter position, the former was again defended by Stier, Hengestenberg, Keil, Kurtz, Ebrard, Philippi (et al.).[10] The difference between the two interpretations is not as big as it seems. On the one hand, the proponents of the view of the ancient church have to admit that the Logos assumed a human form. On the other hand, Augustine and his followers have to grant that in that created angel the Logos revealed himself in an utterly unique way.[11] Add to this that the verses mentioning the angel of YHWH cannot all be construed in the same sense. This much is clear: in the angel of YHWH, who is the preeminent bearer of that name, God, specifically his word, was uniquely present. This is evident from the fact that, though distinct from YHWH, this angel bears the same name, exercises the same power, brings about the same deliverance, dispenses the same blessings, and receives the same adoration and honor as he.[12] This exegesis is supported, moreover, throughout the Old and New Testaments (Job 33:23; Ps. 34:7; 35:5; Prov. 8:22ff., 30:3–4; Isa. 9:6; Hos. 12:4–5; Mic. 5:7; Zech. 1:8–14; 3:1ff.; 12:8; Mal. 3:1; John 8:56, 58; cf. John 1:1–5; 1 Cor. 10:4, 9; while Acts 7:30, 35, 38; Gal. 3:19; and Heb. 2:2 are not inconsistent with this view).

And now, just as YHWH in his work of re-creation reveals himself objectively by his Word, in the angel of YHWH, he does this subjectively in and by his spirit. The spirit of God is the principle of all life and well-being, of all the gifts and powers in the sphere of revelation: of courage (Judg. 3:10; 6:34; 11:29; 13:25; 1 Sam. 11:6), of physical strength (Judg. 14:6; 15:14), of artistic skill (Exod. 28:3; 31:3–5; 35:31–35; 1 Chron. 28:12–19), of the ability to govern (Num. 11:17, 25; 1 Sam. 16:13), of intellect and wisdom (Job 32:8; Isa. 11:2), of holiness and renewal (Ps. 51:12; Isa. 63:10; cf. Gen. 6:3; Neh. 9:20; 1 Sam. 10:6, 9), and of prophecy and prediction (Num. 11:25, 29; 24:2–3; Mic. 3:8; etc.). The Spirit will rest in an unusual measure on the Messiah (Isa. 11:2;

7. T. Aquinas, *Summa theol.*, I, qu. 51, art. 2, 3–5; I 2, qu. 98, art. 3; idem, *Sent.*, II, dist. 8, qu.1, art. 6; D. Petavius, "De trinitate," in *Theol. dogm.*, VIII, ch. 2; M. J. Scheeben, *Handbuch der katholischen Dogmatik*, 4 vols. (1873–1903; reprinted, Freiburg i.B.: Herder, 1933), I, 784ff.; ed. note: ET: *A Manual of Catholic Theology: Based on Scheeben's "Dogmatik,"* trans. Joseph Willhelm and Thomas Bartholomew Scannell, 4th ed., 2 vols. (London: Kegan Paul, Trench, Trübner & Co.; New York: Benziger Brothers, 1909); C. Pesch, *Prael. dogm.*, II, 245.

8. Chr. J. Trip, *Theophanien*, 49–58.

9. H. Cremer, "Engel," *PRE³*, V, 366–67.

10. F. A. Philippi, *Kirchliche Glaubenslehre*, 3d ed., 7 vols. in 10 (Gütersloh: Bertelsmann, 1870–90), II, 191–96.

11. A. Rivetus according to Chr. J. Trip, *Theophanien*, 65.

12. Cf. H. Bavinck, *Reformed Dogmatics*, I, 329 (#91); Chr. J. Trip, *Theophanien*, 100ff.; A. Kuyper, *De Engelen Gods* (Amsterdam: Höveker and Wormser, 1902), 189.

42:1; 61:1), but afterward be poured out on all flesh (Joel 2:28–29; Isa. 32:15; 44:3; Ezek. 36:26–27; 39:29; Zech. 12:10) and give to all a new heart and a new spirit (Ezek. 36:26–27).[13]

This threefold divine principle, which underlies creation as well as re-creation and sustains the entire economy of Old Testament revelation, sometimes occurs in a single passage. Not to be considered here are the threefold repetitions of Daniel 9:19; Zechariah 1:3; and Isaiah 6:3; 33:22; only the high priestly benediction (Num. 6:24–26) in its threefold blessing refers back to a threefold revelation of God and as such is the Old Testament example of the apostolic benediction (2 Cor. 13:13). The plural forms that occur in Genesis 1:26–27; 3:22; and Isaiah 6:8 (etc.) lack cogency in this connection, since they can be explained in the same way as the plural in the name Elohim.[14] Of greater importance are verses like Genesis 19:24; Psalm 45:7; 110:1; and Hosea 1:7, which point to self-differentiation in the divine being. A threefold self-differentiation in the divine being is most clearly expressed in Psalm 33:6; Isaiah 61:1; 63:9–12; and Haggai 2:5–6. In the past many commentators also found a revelation of the Trinity in the three men who appeared to Abraham (Gen. 18).[15] Others believed that one of the three was the Logos and that the other two were ordinary angels (for example, Calvin; the authors of the marginal comments in the [Dutch] Authorized Version).[16] Much more plausible is the exegesis of Augustine, according to whom the three men were created angels in whom YHWH revealed himself and was present in a very special way.[17]

INTERTESTAMENTAL JUDAISM

[214] These Old Testament thoughts have borne fruit in many directions. They were first of all taken over and developed in the Jewish apocryphal literature. Wisdom occupies a large place in Ecclesiasticus, the Wisdom of Jesus Son of Sirach. This wisdom is from God, has been created by him before all things, and remains with him forever. He poured out wisdom upon all his works, but she has her resting place especially in Zion and can be found in the law (1:1–30; 24; also cf. Baruch 3:9–4:4). But the Book of Wisdom goes farther still (6:12–25). Here wisdom is hypostatized to the extent that divine attributes and works are ascribed to her. She is clearly distinguished from God, for she is "a breath of his power," "an emanation of his glory," and "a reflec-

13. Cf. on the Holy Spirit in the Old Testament also: P. Kleinert, "Zur alttestamentlichen Lehre vom Geiste Gottes," *Jahrbücher für deutsche Theologie* 12 (1867): 3–59; B. B. Warfield, "The Spirit of God in the Old Testament," *Presbyterian and Reformed Review* 6 (Oct. 1895): 665–87; H. Cremer, "Geist," *PRE*³, VI, 450; K. Lechler, *Die biblische Lehre vom heiligen Geiste*, vol. I: *Exegetische Darstellung*, 3 vols. (Gütersloh: C. Bertelsmann, 1899–1904).

14. Cf. above, pp. 138–39 (#188).

15. H. Witsius, *The Oeconomy of the Covenants between God and Man: Comprehending a Complete Body of Divinity*, 4 vols. in 3 (New York: Lee & Stokes, 1798), IV, 3, §§3–8.

16. B. de Moor, *Comm. in Marckii Comp.*, I, 807.

17. Augustine, *City of God*, XVI, 29; cf. A. Kuyper, *De engelen Gods*, 194.

tion of his light" (7:25–26). But she is also most intimately bound up with God, lives with him, has been initiated into his knowledge, and selects the ideas that will be carried out (8:3–4). She sits with God on his throne, knows all his works, and was present at the creation of the world (9:4, 9). Indeed, it is she herself who creates, governs, and renews all things (7:27; 8:1, 5). She is identical with God's word (9:1–2; 16:12; 18:15–16) and with his Spirit (1:4–7; 9:17; 12:1).

In this book the influence of Greek philosophy is already perceptible, especially in 7:22ff. But this is even much more strongly the case in Philo. The relation between God and the world had already been examined by Plato. From the distinction and contrast between opinion (δοξα) and knowledge (ἐπιστημη), Plato inferred that, just as the former had to have an empirical object in the world about us, so the latter must have for its object an eternal and immutable form of being, that is, an idea. These ideas, though actually nothing other than universal concepts, were elevated by Plato to the status of metaphysical principles, unique substances, a kind of intermediate beings in whose likeness the "demiurge" had shaped the cosmos and that were therefore the "paradigms" and "causes" of things. Although Aristotle subjected this doctrine of ideas to sharp criticism, the belief that an intelligent spiritual principle underlies all things never disappeared from Greek philosophy. Especially the Stoics stressed that basic to all phenomena is a divine rationality. They called this divine principle "the seminal reason" (λογος σπερματικος) because all being and life sprouts from "logos" as from a seed. Sometimes using the plural, they spoke of "seminal reasons" in order not only to refer to the unity but also to the diversity that arises from the all-creating power of nature.[18] Even the pregnant distinction between "immanent reason" and "expressed reason," which later became so important, was borrowed from the Stoics.

Now, even before Philo this Greek doctrine of the idea, the mind (νους), and the word or reason (λογος) had been linked with the Old Testament teaching about "the word" and "wisdom."[19] Yet it was especially Philo who fused all these different elements—Plato's doctrine of the ideas, the Stoic logos doctrine, and the Old Testament doctrine of wisdom—into a single system. In so doing he proceeded from the premise of the metaphysical dualism between God and the world. God is "devoid of all quality" (ἀποιος), hence indescribable; we can merely say *that* he is, not *what* he is. For that reason, too, he cannot be in immediate contact with matter. Before God made the world we know by our senses, he made a plan and pictured in his mind the "intelligible world" (κοσμος νοητος), the "ideas" as the "paradigms" and "powers" of all things. In Philo's thinking these ideas become the forces enabling God to work in the world. He describes them—sometimes more, sometimes less metaphorically

18. E. Zeller, *Die Philosophie der Griechen*, 3d ed., 5 vols. (Leipzig: Fues's Verlag [L. W. Reisland], 1895), IV³, 159–60, cf. 140 n.

19. Ibid., V, 266.

and personally—as servants, vicegerents, emissaries, mediators; as causative ideas (λογοι) and forces; as bonds and pillars, called "angels" by Moses and "demons" by the Greeks; as ideas existing in the divine mind, which are as "uncreated" and "infinite" as God himself. These ideas, though very numerous, find their unity in the "logos": the idea that contains all ideas, the force that contains all forces, the book that contains all thoughts, the "intelligible world" itself. In the same way as the divine ideas, so also this "logos" is sometimes described more as a divine attribute that is identical with his wisdom, and sometimes more as a being distinct from God. Reason, as it were, is a hypostasis located between God and the world and participating in the nature of both. It is not uncreated in the sense in which God is uncreated, nor created in the sense in which finite things are created. It is the vicar, envoy, interpreter, vicegerent, angel, instrument, image and shadow of God, indeed his firstborn son in distinction from the world, which is his youngest son. Philo even calls him "God," that is, a "second God." Zeller makes very clear that reason (λογος) in Philo, like the divine ideas, bears and must bear this double character. It is an intermediate, hence a double being: an attribute of God, yet a person; neither identical with God nor a creature like the world; an idea in the mind of God and a force in the world, oscillating back and forth between an impersonal attribute and a personal hypostasis, and therefore deemed ideally suited as mediator between God and the world.[20]

In Jewish theology this doctrine of intermediate beings has been still further developed. Being completely transcendent, God cannot establish immediate contact with creatures. As a result he *needs* a variety of intermediate beings. When God merely wants to guide the powers present in nature and humanity, he uses angels. But when he wants to work in the world as creator or re-creator, hypostases emerge that, though creatures, possess divine attributes because they are representatives of God. Such hypostases are *metratons,* those who share God's throne; *memra,* the word of God; *shekinah,* the presence of

20. Cf. E. Zeller, *Die Philosophie der Griechen,* V³, 370–86; for literature on Philo, see also Max Heinze, *Die Lehre vom Logos in der griechischen Philosophie* (Oldenburg: F. Schmidt, 1872); E. Schürer, *The History of the Jewish People in the Age of Jesus Christ,* trans. G. Vermes, F. Miller, and M. Goodman, 5 vols. (Edinburgh: T. & T. Clark, 1987), III.1, 535ff.; H. A. W. Meyer, *Kritisch exegetisches Handbuch über das Evangelium des Johannes,* ed. B. Weiss, 6th ed. (Göttingen: Vandenhoeck & Ruprecht, n.d.), 52ff.; ed. note: The 19th edition of this commentary was published by Vandenhoeck & Ruprecht in 1968 under the editorial hand of Rudolf Bultmann. ET: *Critical and Exegetical Handbook to the Gospel of John,* trans. William Urwick, Frederick Crombie, and A. C. Kendrick (New York: Funk & Wagnalls, 1895); Jean Réville, *La doctrine du Logos* (Paris: J. Brochen, 1881); A. Kuenen, *Volksgodsdienst en Wereldgodsdienst* (Leiden: S. C. van Doesburgh, 1882), 163ff.; Karl Heinrich von Weizsäcker, *Das apostolische Zeitalter der christlichen Kirche,* 2d ed. (Freiburg: Mohr, 1890), 549ff.; E. Hatch, *The Influence of the Greek Ideas on Christianity* (New York: Harper and Brothers, 1957), 182–208; H. Schultz, *Alttestamentliche Theologie,* 4th ed., 2 vols. (Gottingen: Vandenhoeck & Ruprecht, 1889), 552ff.; J. Kaftan, "Das Verhältnis des evangelischen Glaubens zur Logoslehre," *Zeitschrift für Theologie und Kirche* 7/1 (1897): 1–27; Anathon Aall, *Der Logos: Geschichte seiner Entwickelung der griechischen Philosophie und der christlichen Litteratur,* 2 vols. (Leipzig: O. R. Reisland, 1896–99); D. C. Thym, "De Logosleer van Philo en hare Betrekking tot het Evangelie van Johannes, inzonderheid wat den Proloog betreft," *Theologische Studiën* 11/2 (1893): 97, 209, 377; D. Kirn, "Logos," *PRE³,* XI, 599.

God's glory; *bath kol,* the oracular voice of God, which grants revelations; and the *ruach hakkodesh,* the spirit that proceeds from God and imparts a higher knowledge.[21]

Although Ecclesiasticus (Sirach) still quite closely aligns itself with the canonical literature, in the Book of Wisdom, in Philo, and in Jewish theology generally one discerns a philosophical influence that is bound to produce increasing divergence from the ideas of the Old Testament.

In the first place, there is a difference in principle. The doctrine of intermediate beings as we find it in Philo and later Jewish theology is born from Platonic opposition between God and the world, a dualism of which no trace can yet be found in the books of the Old Testament. In the Old Testament "the word" and "wisdom" are not intermediaries between God and the world but stand wholly on the side of God; they belong to him and are the first principles of the created world. In Philo, however, these intermediate beings occupy an impossible position: they are neither divine nor creatural, neither persons nor attributes, neither independent substances nor forces, but participate in the nature of both. They erase the boundary that in the Old Testament always separates the creature from the Creator and pave the way for the philosophy of Gnosticism and the Kabbalah.

In the second place, there is an equally great difference between the character of the doctrine of the "word" and "wisdom" in Scripture and that of Philo's doctrine of intermediate beings. In Philo the primary meaning of "logos" is equivalent to reason, thinking, and thought in God and as such is therefore immanent in him; it is no more than an attribute. Only in its secondary meaning does the "logos" become the word that proceeds from God and play a mediating role between God and the world. In the Old Testament, however, the "word" is not first of all the reason and thought of God, even less an ideal world image, "an intelligible world" (κοσμος νοητος), but the spoken word by which God creates and preserves all things. Similarly, in Job and Proverbs "wisdom" is not presented as an attribute of God, but as a person possessed and ordained by God from eternity as well as searched and consulted in connection with the creation of all things.

In the third place, the intermediate beings in Philo and the Jewish theologians have no soteriological significance. While they impart understanding and knowledge, there is no connection between these intermediate beings and the Messiah. They even force into the background the doctrine of the Messiah as the revelation of truth and as the one who secures salvation. Granted, even the Old Testament does not yet clearly reveal the connection between "word" and "wisdom," the servant of God and the Messiah, the angel of YHWH and the Son of David. The lines, though still running parallel, do converge.

21. J. A. Eisenmenger, *Entdecktes Judenthum,* 2 vols. (Königsberg in Preussen, 1711), I, 265ff.; II, 393ff.; F. W. Weber, *System der altsynagogalen palästinischen Theologie: Aus Targum, Midrasch und Talmud,* 172–89.

Elohim and YHWH is the same God. He who as Elohim creates and preserves the world by his word and spirit is the same as he who as YHWH led Israel by his angel, will save his people by the servant of YHWH, rule them eternally by the Messiah from the house of David, and renew and sanctify them all by his spirit. And these [revelatory] lines, which increasingly converge in the Old Testament, culminate in him who is *the* Logos, *the* prophet, priest, and king, in whom God comes to his people and dwells among them forever. To Philo, a human incarnation of the Logos (Reason) would have been an absurdity. But in the New Testament the incarnation of the Word is the supreme revelation of God.

It may be added here, finally, that Philo's doctrine of intermediate beings (etc.) is not rounded off and has no boundary. While he introduces a certain amount of unity into the divine ideas by summing them up in the Logos, he says of the latter what he also repeatedly says of all divine ideas [individually]. Jewish theology offers an ever-increasing array of intermediate beings. It is a series of emanations comparable to the aeons in Gnosticism. There is no end to the consequences of the dualism on which it rests. The intermediate beings fail to bring about any communion between God and the world, for in fact they are neither one nor the other. The world forever remains something separate and opposed to God. The significance of the spirit of God is not understood. In the Old Testament this doctrine of the Spirit plays a large role, whereas in the apocryphal literature, in Philo, and in Jewish theology it is almost completely neglected. At most it is merely a spirit of prediction given to some,[22] but no longer the Spirit of the Old Testament, who rounds out and consummates the work of creation and re-creation. For all these reasons there is a fundamental difference between the way the trinitarian ideas of the Old Testament have developed in the apocryphal literature, in Philo, and the Jews, and the way they have been shaped in the New Testament. While the New Testament may have some words in common with Philo (et al.) and speak also of Christ as word (λογος), image (εἰκων), effulgence (ἀπαυγασμα), son (υἱος), and God (θεος), this is as far as the agreement goes. The New Testament was written in the people's vernacular Greek, the language which existed at the time and was spoken everywhere. It created no new language. The ideas of God assumed the "flesh" (σαρξ) of ordinary human language. But God invested those words with new meaning. There is agreement in form but the content differs. Philo and John only have the word "logos" in common. This is increasingly being understood and recognized by scholars.[23]

22. E. Zeller, *Philosophie der Griechen*, V³, 384; F. W. Weber, *System der altsynogogalen palästinischen Theologie*, 184ff.

23. A. von Harnack, *History of Dogma*, trans. N. Buchanan, J. Millar, E. B. Speirs, and W. McGilchrist, and ed. A. B. Bruce, 7 vols. (London: Williams & Norgate, 1896–99), I, 97, 109ff.; Chr. J. Trip, *Theophanien*, 126–29; I. A. Dorner, *History of the Development of the Doctrine of the Person of Christ*, trans. Patrick Fairbairn, 3 vols. (Edinburgh: T. & T. Clark, 1868), I, 22ff.; F. L. Godet, *Commentary on John's Gospel* (Grand Rapids: Kregel, 1978), 286ff.; H. Meyer, *Commentar über das Evangelium des Johannes*, 50ff.; B. Weiss,

THE NEW TESTAMENT

[215] The true development of the trinitarian ideas of the Old Testament is found in the New Testament. But now these ideas come to the fore much more clearly, not as a result of abstract reasonings about the divine being but by God's self-revelation in appearance, word, and deed. In the New Testament the oneness of God is as strongly affirmed as in the Old. There is but one being who can be called God, Elohim, θεός (John 17:3; 1 Cor. 8:4), but in the economy of the New Testament, more specifically in the events of the incarnation of the Son and the outpouring of the Spirit, this one true God reveals himself as Father, Son, and Spirit. The principles we encounter in these events are not absolutely new. They are the same principles that were operative also in the event of creation and the entire economy of the Old Testament. The Father, who bears this name mostly in relation to the Son and to his children, is the same as he who can be called Father, and also the same as the Creator of all things (Matt. 7:11; Luke 3:38; John 4:21; Acts 17:28; 1 Cor. 8:6; Heb. 12:9). All things derive their existence from him (1 Cor. 8:6). The Son, who bears this name especially because of his utterly unique relation to God, is identical with the Logos, through whom the Father created all things (John 1:3; 1 Cor. 8:6; Col. 1:15–17; Heb. 1:3). And the Holy Spirit, who received his name especially with a view to his work in the church, is the same Spirit who jointly with the Father and the Son beautifies and completes all things in the creation (Matt. 1:18; 4:1; Mark 1:12; Luke 1:35; 4:1, 14; Rom. 1:4). It is, moreover, the universal teaching of the New Testament writers that these three, Father, Son, and Spirit, are identical with those who also revealed themselves to the fathers—in word and deed, prophecy and miracle—in the economy of the Old Testament. The Old Testament name YHWH, inadequately translated by the word κυριος (Lord), fully unfolds its meaning in the New Testament name "Father" (πατηρ). In the incarnate Son of God we see the fulfillment of every prophecy and shadow of the Old Testament, of prophet and king, of priest and sacrifice, of Servant of the Lord and Son of David, of the angel of the Lord and wisdom. And in the outpouring of the Holy Spirit we witness the realization of what the Old Testament had promised (Acts 2:16ff.; Joel 2:28–29).

But the New Testament, though following up on the Old, does not stop there; it far surpasses it. Much more clearly than in the Old Testament we now discover that the God of the covenant is and has to be a triune God, that is,

Lehrbuch der biblischen Theologie des Neuen Testaments, 3d ed. (Berlin: W. Hertz, 1880), 624; ET: *Biblical Theology of the New Testament*, trans. David Eaton and James E. Duguid, 2 vols. (Edinburgh: T. & T. Clark, 1883); J. Orr, *The Christian View of God and the World as Centering in the Incarnation*, 510–12; H. Cremer, *Biblico-Theological Lexicon of New Testament Greek*, s.v. "Λογος"; E. Sachsse, "Die Logoslehre bei Philo und Johannes," *Neue kirchliche Zeitschrift* 15 (1904): 747–67; J. von Grill, *Untersuchungen über die entstehung des vierten evangeliums* (Tübingen: J. C. B. Mohr, 1902); Kirn, "Logos," *PRE³*, XI, 599–605; O. Bertling, *Der johanneische Logos und seine Bedeutung für das Christliche Leben* (Leipzig: J. C. Heinrichs, 1907); cf. also Max Müller, *Theosophie oder Psychologische Religion* (Leipzig: Engelmann, 1895); ET: *Theosophy, or Psychological Religion* (London; New York: Longmans; Green, 1895).

that there is a threefold principle in operation in the work of salvation. Not merely a few isolated texts but the whole New Testament is trinitarian in that sense. All salvation, every blessing, and blessedness have their threefold cause in God, the Father, Son, and Holy Spirit. We see these three act immediately at the birth of Jesus (Matt. 1:18ff.; Luke 1:35) and at his baptism (Matt. 3:16–17; Mark 1:10–11; Luke 3:21–22). Jesus' instruction is entirely trinitarian in character. In explaining the Father to us, he describes him as Spirit, who has life in himself (John 4:24; 5:26) and is, in an utterly unique sense, his Father (Matt. 11:27; John 2:16; 5:17). While distinguishing himself from the Father, he is nevertheless his only begotten and much-beloved Son (Matt. 11:27; 21:37–39; John 3:16; etc.), one who is with him in life, glory, and power (John 1:14; 5:26; 10:30). And he speaks of the Holy Spirit, who himself leads and enables him (Mark 1:12; Luke 4:1, 14; John 3:34), as of another Paraclete [Helper], whom he will send from the Father (John 15:26) and who will convict, teach, and lead into all truth, and will comfort and remain forever (John 14:16). And before his departure Jesus sums up all this teaching in the baptismal formula "in the name of the Father and of the Son and of the Holy Spirit" (Matt. 28:19), that is, in the one divine name (το ὄνομα, in singular) in which three distinct subjects (*the* Father, *the* Son, and *the* Spirit: notice the purposeful repetition of the article!)[24] all reveal themselves. This instruction is continued and expanded by the apostles. They all know and glory in the threefold divine cause of salvation. The "good pleasure," the foreknowledge, the election, the power, the love, and the kingdom all belong to the Father (Matt. 6:13; 11:26; John 3:16; Rom. 8:29; Eph. 1:9; 1 Pet. 1:2; etc.). Mediatorship, the atonement, salvation, grace, wisdom, and righteousness pertain to the Son (Matt. 1:21; 1 Cor. 1:30; Eph. 1:10ff.; 1 Tim. 2:5; 1 Pet. 1:2; 1 John 2:2; etc.). And regeneration, renewal, sanctification, and communion is from the Holy Spirit (John 3:5; 14–16; Rom. 5:5; 8:15; 14:17; 2 Cor. 1:21–22; 1 Pet. 1:2; 1 John 5:6; etc.). And just as Jesus finally sums up his instruction in the name of the Father, of the Son, and of the Holy Spirit, so also the apostles again and again put these names side by side and on the same level (1 Cor. 8:6; 12:4–6; 2 Cor. 13:13;[25] 2 Thess. 2:13–14; Eph. 4:4–6; 1 Pet. 1:2; 1 John 5:4–6; Rev. 1:4–6).[26]

24. E. Riggenbach, *Der trinitarische Taufbefehl: Matt. 28,19 nach seiner ursprünglichen Textgestalt und seiner Authentie* (Gütersloh: C. Bertelsmann, 1903).

25. On these texts, cf. Rob. Müllensiefen, "Wie sind 2 Kor. 13,13 die drei Teile des Segenswunsches inhaltich auseinandershalten und miteinander zu verbinden?" *Theologische Studien und Kritiken* 72 (1899): 254–66.

26. On the doctrine of the Trinity in the New Testament one can also consult, inter alia: F. C. Baur, *Die christliche Lehre von der Dreieinigkeit und Menschwerdung Gottes in ihrer geschichtlichen Entwicklung*, I, 80ff.; G. L. Hahn, *Die Theologie des Neuen Testaments* (Leipzig: Dörffling & Franke, 1854), I, 106ff.; F. A. Philippi, *Kirchliche Glaubenslehre*, II, 200ff.; I. A. Dorner, *A System of Christian Doctrine*, trans. A. Cave and J. S. Banks, rev. ed., 4 vols. (Edinburgh: T. & T. Clark, 1888), I, 344ff.; E. W. C. Sartorius, *Die Lehre von Christi Person und Werk*, 3d ed. (Hamburg: F. Perthes, 1837), I, 44ff.; J. T. Beck, *Vorlesungen über christliche Glaubenslehre*, 2 vols. (Gütersloh: C. Bertelsmann, 1886–87), II, 40ff. Even A. E. Biedermann

The authenticity of 1 John 5:7 continues to be doubtful. It is absent from all Greek codices (except a couple dating from the sixteenth century), from all Latin codices from the time before the eighth century, and from almost all translations. Furthermore, it was never quoted by the Greek fathers, not even during the Arian controversy, nor by the Latin fathers: Hilary, Ambrose, Jerome, Augustine, and others. *If* it was quoted or assumed by Tertullian, it must have been extant as early as 190; and *if* Cyprian cited it, it must have been known about 220. If the African version contained the text, as attested by a manuscript from the fifth century and one from the seventh century, one can go back even farther, for the African version dates from around 160 and came to Italy around 250. The text certainly occurs in the work of Vigilius toward the end of the fifth century. In the sixteenth century it was included in the Complutensian edition of the Greek New Testament, by Erasmus in his third edition, by Stephanus and Beza, and in the Textus Receptus. It is not definitely required by the context, and its omission and disappearance is very hard to explain. There are still some scholars who defined the passage as genuine,[27] and in 1897 the question whether 1 John 5:7 could be safely rejected or at least omitted as being doubtful was answered in the negative by the Congregation of the Holy Office at Rome, a decision later ratified by the pope. It seems, however, that this verdict of the Holy Office did not really settle the question of the authenticity of 1 John 5:7 or was later tacitly repealed. At any rate, numerous Catholic scholars after that time still upheld the inauthenticity of 1 John 5:7 with a plethora of arguments. Künstle, for example, opposing the authenticity of the text states that it derived from a sentence in an apology of Priscillian dating from the year 380.[28]

Father

[216] Scripture, however, does not stop here; it also gives us insight into the relations existing among these three distinct subjects, Father, Son, and Holy

---

(*Christliche Dogmatik* [Zurich: Crell & Fussli, 1869], II, 37), acknowledges that the doctrine of the Trinity is rooted in Holy Scripture. Cf. also D. F Strauss, *Speculative Betrachtungen über die Dogmatik* as an appendix to *Die Religion in ihrem Begriff, ihrer weltgeschichtlichen Entwicklung und Vollendung* (Weilburg: Lanz, 1841), 409–25; R. A. Lipsius, *Lehrbuch der evangelisch-protestantischen Dogmatik* (Braunschweig: C. A. Schwetschke, 1893), §241; F. Nitzsch, *Lehrbuch der evangelischen Dogmatik*, 3d ed. (Tübingen: J. C. B. Mohr, 1902), 426; H. J. Holtzmann, *Lehrbuch der neutestamentlichen Theologie* (Freiburg and Leipzig: Mohr, 1897); G. Krüger, *Das Dogma von der Dreieinigkeit und Gottmenschheit in seiner geschichtlichen Entwicklung* (Tübingen: J. C. B. Mohr, 1905), 97; Adolf Jülicher, "Die Religion Jesu und die Anfänge des Christentums bis zum Nicaenum," pp. 41–128 of *Die christliche Religion mit Einschluss der israelitisch-jüdischen Religion*, by J. Wellhausen et al., vol. I/4 of *Die Kultur der Gegenwart*, ed. P. Hinneberg (Berlin and Leipzig: B. G. Teubner, 1906), saying on p. 96: "John is the real creator of trinitarian thinking. From [John] 14:16 on, next to the Father and the Son-Logos, he presents the Paraclete as the full replacement for the Son, who is returning to the Father. This Spirit of truth, who proceeds from the Father, in an unseen way furthers the work of the Son in the World. [In this way] the threeness of persons is complete, portraying our knowledge and anticipation of the divine."

27. W. Kölling, *Die Echtheit von 1. Joh. 5:7* (Breslau: C. Dülfer, 1893); cf. the opposing view, Endemann, *Neue kirchliche Zeitschrift* 10 (July 1899): 574–81.

28. K. Künstle, *Das Comma Joanneum, auf seine Herkunft untersucht* (Freiburg: Herder, 1905).

Spirit. To that end we must first of all consider the name "Father." In its most general sense, this name refers to God as the creator of all his works, especially of humankind (Num. 16:22; Matt. 7:11; Luke 3:38; John 4:21; Acts 17:28; 1 Cor. 8:6; Eph. 3:15; Heb. 12:9). In the Old Testament this name has theocratic significance.[29] God is Israel's father inasmuch as he created and preserved his people by his marvelous power (Deut. 32:6; Isa. 63:16; 64:8; Mal. 1:6; 2:10; Jer. 3:19; 31:9; Ps. 103:13; Rom. 9:4). In the New Testament this meaning changes into the ethical one in which God is the father of his children (Matt. 6:4, 8–9; Rom. 8:15; etc.). But in a unique metaphysical sense God is the father of his Son. Jesus consistently makes an essential distinction between the relation in which he himself, and that in which others—the Jews, the disciples—stand to the Father (Matt. 11:25–27; Luke 22:29; John 2:16; 5:17; 20:17; etc.). He called God "his own Father" (John 5:18). Scripture clearly points out that the name "Father" does not in the first place apply to God's relation to Israel and to believers; on the contrary, in its original sense it applies to the Father's relation to the Son (John 14:6–13; 17:25–26). In the true original sense God is the Father of the Son; he loves the Son (John 5:19ff.; 10:17; 17:24, 26), and this love passes from the Father through the Son to others (John 16:27; 17:26). This relation of the Father to the Son was not born in time but exists from eternity (John 1:14; 8:38; 17:5, 24). Hence, repeatedly and in a unique sense, God is called "the Father of our Lord Jesus Christ" in the New Testament (Rom. 15:6; 1 Cor. 15:24; 2 Cor. 1:3; Gal. 1:1; Eph. 1:3; etc.). God's fatherhood of the Son is his particular personal attribute. He alone is of himself, the first in the order of existence (John 5:26) and hence the Father both in creation and re-creation, from whom all things exist (1 Cor. 8:6).

Thus, both in the Old and in the New Testament, God is the Father who occupies first place. His is the purpose (Acts 4:28; Eph. 1:11), the good pleasure (Matt. 11:26; Eph. 1:9), the initiative in creation and re-creation (Ps. 33:6; John 3:16), the kingdom and the power (ἐξουσια, δυναμις, Matt. 6:13 KJV; Rom. 1:20; Eph. 1:19), the righteousness (Gen. 18:25; Deut. 32:4; John 17:25; Rom. 3:26; 2 Tim. 4:8), the goodness, wisdom, immortality, unapproachable light (Matt. 19:17; Rom. 16:27; 1 Tim. 6:16). He, accordingly, regularly bears the name "God" in a special sense. He is Elohim, YHWH Elohim, El Elyon, El Shaddai, the one true God (μονος αληθινος θεος, John 17:3), the one God (εἰς θεος, 1 Cor. 8:6; 1 Tim. 2:5), who is mentioned as God and Father alongside the Lord Jesus Christ and the Holy Spirit (1 Cor. 12:6; 2 Cor. 13:13; 1 Thess. 1:3; Rev. 1:6). Even Christ not only calls him his Father but also his God (Matt. 27:46; John 20:17; Heb. 1:9; 2:17; 5:1; 10:7, 9) and is himself called "the Christ of God" (Luke 9:20; 1 Cor. 3:23; Rev. 12:10).

From these data, however, the Arians of earlier and later times have drawn the unwarranted conclusion that only the Father is God and that the Son and

---

29. P. Baur, "Gott als Vater im Alten Testaments," *Theologische Studien und Kritiken* 72 (1899): 483–507.

the Spirit, though closely related to God, are not part of the divine being. For in the first place—as will be shown in greater detail later—Scripture equally ascribes divine names, attributes, works, and honor to the Son and the Spirit as to the Father. It is also noteworthy that Scripture nowhere says that the *Father alone* is the true God but rather that the Father is the only true God, a fact that is fully recognized in the church's doctrine of the Trinity. Furthermore, it is not that all these verses posit an antithesis between the Father on the one hand and the Son and the Spirit on the other, but instead between the Father as the one true God and the gods of the Gentiles. Then, from the statements that the Father is the one true God, who alone is wise, good, and immortal, it by no means follows that the Son and the Spirit are not divine beings of the same kind, and participants in the same oneness, wisdom, goodness, and immortality, any more than one can argue on the basis of 1 Corinthians 8:6 that only Christ and not God is our Lord, through whom all things exist and we through him. Finally, the Father can be called "the only wise and good God" because he possesses all things of himself and is "the fountain of deity" (πηγη θεοτητος), while the Son and the Spirit possess the same being and the same attributes by communication. The name "God," ascribed to the Father in particular, means that in the divine economy he is first. It is an official title, as it were, a designation of his rank and position, just as among humans, all of whom participate in the same nature, there are nevertheless distinctions of social standing and honor.[30]

Son

We are, moreover, also informed about the immanent relations of the [triune] God by the names that the Son bears in Scripture. There are a great number of these names. They apply mostly to Christ's historical appearance and will therefore be discussed in the locus concerning Christ. But among them there are also those that belong to him prior to and apart from his incarnation.

There is, first of all, the name "Logos." Various reasons have been cited as to why Christ bears this name. The word "logos" has been translated by "reason," "speech," "word," the last again viewed as either "interior" or "exterior."[31] Undoubtedly, however, the premise underlying this name is the consistent teaching of Scripture that both in creation and re-creation God reveals himself by the word. By the word God creates, preserves, and governs all things, and by the word he also renews and re-creates the world. For that reason, too, the gospel is called "the word of God" (λογος του θεου). John calls Christ the Logos because it is he in whom and by whom God reveals himself both in the work of creation and that of re-creation (John 1:3, 14). In the Old Testament, however, the word by which God reveals himself first comes into view at the creation. The hypostasis and eternal existence of that Word is left unexpressed.

30. Augustine, *The Trinity*, I, ch. 6; VI, ch. 9; D. Petavius, "De trinitate," in *Theol. dogm.*, II, ch. 4; III, chs. 1–2; P. van Mastricht, *Theologia*, II, ch. 25.

31. D. Petavius, "De trinitate," in *Theol. dogm.*, VI, ch. 1.

In Proverbs 8, while Wisdom is indeed pictured as personal and everlasting, it is also closely connected with the work of creation. It is with a view to creation that it is was formed, established, and searched by God (Prov. 8:22–23). From the word קָנָנִי (created me, v. 22; LXX: ἐκτισεν με; Syr. Targum.: בְּרָאַנִי; cf. Sir. 1:4, 9; 24:8), the Arians inferred that the Son had not been generated from eternity but was created before all things. Over against this the church fathers claimed that קָנָנִי had to be translated by ἐκτησατο: "he possessed me" (Greek versions of Aquila Symmachus), or "possessed it" (Jerome), or that this word, rather than referring to the Son's essence, applied to his office and dignity in the work of creation and re-creation. The latter is undoubtedly true. There is no mention here of eternal generation. We are only told that God formed (קָנָנִי) and established (נִסַּכְתִּי) wisdom; that it was brought forth (חוֹלָלְתִּי) before and with a view to creation (Prov. 8:22–24).[32]

But the New Testament goes far beyond this. John not only tells us that he through whom God reveals himself is a person, but expressly states that this Logos *was* in the beginning (ἐν ἀρχῇ ἦν ὁ Λογος, John 1:1). He did not *become* Logos; he was not first formed and established at the time of creation. Both as person and by nature he *was* from all eternity the Logos. In addition, he himself was God (θεος), was in regular contact with God, was "in the beginning with God" (ἦν ἐν ἀρχῇ προς τον θεον, 1:2), is "in the bosom of the Father" (εἰς τον κολπον του πατρος, 1:18), and is the object of his eternal love and self-communication (5:27; 17:24). He was fully able to reveal the Father because from all eternity he participated in his divine nature, his divine life, his divine love, and so on, and was by nature Logos. Since God communicated himself to the Logos, the Logos could communicate himself to us. The Logos is the absolute revelation of God, for from all eternity God communicated himself in all his fullness to him.

Another name of Christ is "Son of God." In the Old Testament this name as a rule has a theocratic meaning. Israel is called God's son because the nation was chosen, called, and accepted by God (Exod. 4:22; 19:5–6; Deut. 1:31; 8:5; 14:1; 32:6, 18; Isa. 63:8; Jer. 31:9, 20; Hos. 11:1; Mal. 1:6; 2:10). In the New Testament the church takes the place of Israel and consists of "sons of God" (υἱοι θεου) by adoption or "children of God" (τεκνα θεου) by birth. Specifically, the title "son of God" is often an official name used with reference to judges (Ps. 82:6), to angels (Job 38:7), and especially to the king (2 Sam. 7:11–14; Ps. 89:27–28). In Psalm 2:7 YHWH says to Zion's anointed king: "You are my son; today I have begotten you." On the day the Lord anointed and appointed him as king, he "generated" (LXX: γεγεννηκα σε) him as Son and gave him the right to rule the world. With a view to David this refers back to God's decree in 2 Samuel 7; and with a view to the Messiah whom David foreshadowed, it is interpreted as referring to the eternity (in Heb. 1:5; 5:5; cf. 1:2–3) in which Christ as the Son is generated by the Father, that is, in which

---

32. D. Petavius, "De trinitate," in *Theol. dogm.*, II, ch. 1.

he is brought forth as the effulgence of God's glory and the express image of his nature. Further, according to Acts 13:33 and Romans 1:4, he was proved to be God's Son with power by the resurrection from the dead. In Micah 5:2 we encounter a related idea. The ruler over Israel who will one day come forth from the little town of Bethlehem already existed "from of old." His goings forth as ruler from God have been from the days of old (eternity). He was a ruler from eternity. He has demonstrated this in the history of Israel, and so he will one day visibly emerge in Bethlehem. The name "Son of God" applied to the Messiah, undoubtedly assumes the theocratic significance of this expression in the Old Testament. It is not likely that the demon-possessed (Matt. 8:29; cf. 4:3), the Jews (Matt. 27:40), the high priest (Matt. 26:63), or even the disciples, at least in the early period of their apprenticeship (John 1:49; 11:27; Matt. 16:16), grasped the full content of the name.

But in the case of Christ, the name certainly acquires a much deeper meaning. True, as mediator and king he is sometimes called "the Son of God" in a theocratic sense (Luke 1:35); even then, however, the Adoptionist idea that according to his divine nature Christ is son by generation and according to his human nature by adoption (as it was later held by Socinians and Remonstrants)[33] has no support in Scripture. But Christ was not first adopted in time—as a king in Israel—to be the Son of God. Neither is he called God's Son on account of his supernatural birth, as the Socinians taught and Hofmann[34] still attempts to argue. Neither does he bear that name in an ethical sense, as still others believe.[35] Nor did he first become the Son as a result of his mediatorship and resurrection, an interpretation in support of which John 10:34–36; Acts 13:32–33; and Romans 1:4 are cited. But he is the Son of God in a metaphysical sense: by nature and from eternity. He is elevated far above angels and prophets (Matt. 13:32; 21:27; 22:2) and sustains a unique relation to God (Matt. 11:27). He is the beloved Son in whom the Father is well-pleased (Matt. 3:17; 17:5; Mark 1:11; 9:7; Luke 3:22; 9:35), the only begotten Son (John 1:18; 3:16; 1 John 4:9ff.), God's own Son (Rom. 8:32), the eternal Son (John 17:5, 24; Heb. 1:5ff.; 5:5–6) whom the Father gave to have life in himself ($\zeta\omega\eta\nu$ $\dot{\epsilon}\chi\epsilon\iota\nu$ $\dot{\epsilon}\nu$ $\dot{\epsilon}\alpha\upsilon\tau\omega$, John 5:26); he is equal to the Father in knowledge (Matt. 11:27), honor (John 5:23), creative and re-creative power (John 1:3; 5:21, 27), activity (John 10:28–30), and dominion (Matt. 11:27; Luke 10:22; 22:29; John 16:15; 17:10); and he was condemned to death precisely on account of his Sonship (John 10:33; Matt. 26:63ff.).

33. Cf. Möller, "Adoptianismus," in *PRE³*, I, 180–86; Racovian Catechism; Remonstrant Confession, art. 3; *Apol. Conf., art. 3; P. van Limborch, *Theol. christ.*, II, 17, 10; *B. S. Cremer, cf. *Archief voor nederlandsche Kerkgeschiedenis*, VIII, 419–28.

34. J. C. K. von Hofmann, *Der Schriftbeweis*, I, 116ff.

35. B. Weiss, *Lehrbuch der biblischen Theologie des Neuen Testaments*, §17; A. Ritschl, *The Christian Doctrine of Justification and Reconciliation* (Clifton, N.J.: Reference Book Publishers, 1966), II, 59; J. H. Scholten, *De Leer der Hervormde Kerk in Hare Grondbeginselen*, 2d ed., 2 vols. (Leyden: P. Engels, 1850–51), II, 206.

In the third place, we must consider the name "image of God." By way of analogy it can be applied to humans but in an absolute sense it belongs to Christ. Before his incarnation as Logos and Son (Rom. 1:3–4; 8:3; Gal. 4:4), he existed in the form of God (ἐν μορφῃ θεου, Phil. 2:6), was rich (2 Cor. 8:9), clothed with glory (John 17:5), and has now returned to that state by his resurrection and ascension. Thus he was then and is now "the image of the invisible God" (εἰκων του θεου του ἀορατου, Col. 1:15; 2 Cor. 4:4), the reflection of his glory and the "very stamp of his nature" (ἀπαυγασμα της δοξης και χαρακτηρ της ὑποστασεως αὐτου, Heb. 1:3; note: the original here does not read ἀπαυγασμος, effulgence, but ἀπαυγασμα, the reflection or image of God's glory and the exact imprint of the Father's nature). As such he is the firstborn of all creation (πρωτοτοκος πασης κτισεως, Col. 1:15; Rev. 1:16–18), in whom all things were created (ἐκτισθη, Col. 1:16). "Firstborn" is in comparison with every creature but must be understood as existing before every creature; in other words, as firstborn (πρωτοτοκος) and not just created first (πρωτοκτιστος) or made first (πρωτοπλαστος). He is also "the beginning (ἀρχη), the firstborn from the dead (πρωτοτοκος ἐκ των νεκρων), preeminent in all things (ἐν πασιν πρωτευων)" (Col. 1:18 [cf. Rev. 1:5–6]), "the first-born among many brothers" (Rom. 8:29 NIV), into whose "image" believers "are being transformed" (2 Cor. 3:18; Phil. 3:21). The expression "firstborn" (πρωτοτοκος) does not include Christ in the category of creatures but excludes him from it. Being the "firstborn" and "only begotten," as Son and as Logos, and as the full image of God, he from all eternity sustained an utterly unique relation to the Father. And although as mediator Christ is represented as being dependent on, and subject to, the Father, so that he is a servant sent to effect the work of the Father, obedient even to death and one day delivering up his kingdom to the Father, these expressions are never meant to detract from his essential unity with the Father. In John 14:28 Jesus asserts that for his disciples his going to the Father is an occasion for rejoicing, "because the Father is greater than I." Jesus is not saying that the Father is greater than he in power, something specifically denied in John 10:28–30, but refers to his relation to the Father in the state of humiliation. *Now* the Father is greater. But this lesser greatness of Jesus will end precisely when he goes to the Father, and so his disciples can rejoice over his going away. The case is this: in his essence and nature he is equal to the Father, though in his position and office he is presently less than the Father. He is not a creature, but is and was and remains God, who is over all, blessed forever (John 1:1; 20:28; Rom. 9:5; Heb. 1:8–9; 2 Pet. 3:18; 1 John 5:20; Rev. 1:8, 17–18; also perhaps 2 Thess. 1:2; Titus 2:13; 2 Pet. 1:1). Later, under the heading of Christology, we will have to discuss the attempt made earlier by the Socinians and currently by Ritschl, Schultz, Kaftan, Pfleiderer (et al.) to construe the word "God," when applied to Jesus, as referring, not to his being, but to his office. Here we only wish to comment that this title "God" cannot be properly ascribed to Christ if he does not really coparticipate in the divine nature.[36]

36. *R. A. Lipsius, *Theologische Jahresbericht* 10 (1891): 378.

Holy Spirit

[217] Scripture—finally—also sheds light on the immanent relations of God by the name of "the Holy Spirit." At the very outset it is worth saying that the doctrine of the Holy Spirit is the same throughout the Scriptures of the Old and New Covenant. Though much more clearly revealed in the New than in the Old Testament, in principle it is also present in the Old. The New Testament is aware of not furnishing any other doctrine of the Spirit than that which is found in the Old. It is the same Spirit who at one time spoke through the prophets (Matt. 22:43; Mark 12:36; Acts 1:16; 28:25; Heb. 3:7; 10:15; 1 Pet. 1:10–11; 2 Pet. 1:21), testified in the days of Noah (1 Pet. 3:19–20), was resisted by Israel (Acts 7:51), and produced faith (2 Cor. 4:13), who would descend on the Messiah and dwell in the church (Matt. 12:18; Luke 4:18–19; Acts 2:16–18). And although the divine being we call God is "Spirit" (John 4:24) and "holy" (Isa. 6:3), in Scripture the term "Holy Spirit" is still a reference to a special person in the divine being distinct from the Father and the Son. He owes this name to his special mode of subsistence: "spirit" actually means "wind," "breath." The Holy Spirit is the breath of the Almighty (Job 33:4), the breath of his mouth (Ps. 33:6). Jesus compares him to the wind (John 3:8) and "breathes" him upon his disciples (John 20:22; cf. 2 Thess. 2:8). The Spirit is God as the immanent principle of life throughout creation. And he is called "holy" because he himself exists in a special relation to God and because he puts all things in a special relation to God. He is not the spirit of humans or of creatures but the Spirit of God, the Holy Spirit (Ps. 51:11–12; Isa. 63:10–11). Just as breath comes out of our mouth, so the Spirit proceeds from God and keeps all creatures alive. For that reason he is called the Spirit of God, the Spirit of the Lord, the Spirit of the Father (Gen. 1:2; Isa. 11:2; Matt. 10:20), as well as the Spirit of Christ, the Spirit of the Son (Rom. 8:2, 9; 1 Cor. 2:4–16; 2 Cor. 3:17–18; Phil. 1:19; Gal. 3:2; 4:6; 1 Pet. 1:11), standing before the throne of God and of the Lamb (Rev. 1:4; 3:1; 4:5; 5:6). In Scripture this procession of the Spirit is described by various terms. Usually we are told that the Spirit is *given* by God or by Christ (Num. 11:29; Neh. 9:20; Isa. 42:1; Ezek. 36:27; John 3:34; 1 John 3:24; 4:13), *sent* or *sent forth* (Ps. 104:30; John 14:26; 15:26; 16:7; Gal. 4:6; Rev. 5:6), *poured out* (Isa. 32:15; 44:3; Joel 2:28–29; Zech. 12:10; Acts 2:17–18), *came down* from God (Matt. 3:16), *was put* in the midst of Israel (Isa. 63:11; Hag. 2:5), or *put* on someone (Matt. 12:18), or *breathed upon* persons (John 20:22), and so on. But we are also told that the Spirit proceeds from the Father (ἐκπορευεται παρα του πατρος, John 15:26). This occurred in a special sense on the day of Pentecost. Here for the first time the personal existence, or personality, of the Holy Spirit comes vividly to the fore. In the Old Testament there is indeed a distinction between God and his Spirit, but the nature of that distinction is still obscure. "As yet the Spirit had not been given, because Jesus was not yet glorified" (John 7:39 NRSV marg.). But now he is spoken of as a person. The

personal [demonstrative] pronoun "he" (ἐκεῖνος) is used with reference to him (John 15:26; 16:13–14); he is called "Paraclete" (παράκλητος, John 15:26; cf. 1 John 2:1); "another Paraclete" (John 14:16), who speaks of himself in the first person (Acts 13:2). All kinds of personal capacities and activities are attributed to him: searching (1 Cor. 2:10–11), judging (Acts 15:28), hearing (John 16:13), speaking (Acts 13:2; Rev. 2:7, 11, 17, 29; 3:6, 13, 22; 14:13; 22:17), willing (1 Cor. 12:11), teaching (John 14:26), interceding (Rom. 8:27), witnessing (John 15:26), and so on. He is coordinated with the Father and the Son (Matt. 28:19; 1 Cor. 12:4–6; 2 Cor. 13:13; Rev. 1:4). None of this is possible, we think, unless the Spirit, too, is truly God.

Like his personality, so also his deity first becomes clear in the New Testament. It is evident, first of all, from the fact that, despite the distinction that exists between God and the Spirit, it amounts to the same thing whether God or the Spirit says something, dwells in us, or is despised by us (Isa. 6:9 and Acts 28:25; Jer. 31:31 and Heb. 10:15; Ps. 95:7–11 and Heb. 3:7–11; Acts 5:3–4; Rom. 8:9–10; 1 Cor. 3:16; 6:19; Eph. 2:22). This fact only comes fully into its own if personal distinction and essential oneness go together. Further, an array of divine attributes are ascribed equally to God's Spirit and to God himself—eternity (Heb. 9:14), omnipresence (Ps. 139:7), omniscience (1 Cor. 2:10–11), and omnipotence (1 Cor. 12:4–6)—a fact that again presupposes the essential unity of the Spirit with God himself. The same is true of the divine works of creation (Gen. 1:2; Ps. 33:6; Job 33:4; Ps. 104:30) and of re-creation. Indeed, the Spirit's deity is especially manifest in the latter. The Spirit is the one who by his anointing equipped Christ for his office (Isa. 11:2; 61:1 and Luke 4:18; Isa. 42:1 and Matt. 12:18; Luke 1:35; Matt. 3:16; 4:1; John 3:34; Matt. 12:28; Heb. 9:14; Rom. 1:4), equips the apostles for their special task (Matt. 10:20; Luke 12:12; 21:15; 24:49; John 14:16ff.; 15:26; 16:13ff.; etc.), distributes a wide assortment of gifts and powers to believers (1 Cor. 12:4–11), and above all causes the fullness of Christ to dwell in the church.

As Christ is related to the Father, so the Holy Spirit is related to Christ. Just as the Son has nothing, does nothing, and says nothing of himself but receives everything from the Father (John 5:26; 16:15), so the Spirit takes everything from Christ (John 16:13–14). Just as the Son witnesses to and glorifies the Father (John 1:18; 17:4, 6), so the Spirit in turn witnesses to and glorifies the Son (John 15:26; 16:14). Just as no one can come to the Father but by the Son (Matt. 11:27; John 14:6), so no one can say "Jesus is Lord" except by the Spirit (1 Cor. 12:3). No communion with God is possible except by the Spirit. But that Spirit, accordingly, also grants all the benefits acquired by Christ: regeneration (John 3:3), conviction of sin (John 16:8–11), the gift of child status (Rom. 8:15), renewal (Titus 3:5), the love of God (Rom. 5:5), a wide assortment of spiritual fruits (Gal. 5:22–23), the sealing (Rom. 8:23; 2 Cor. 1:22; 5:5; Eph. 1:13; 4:30), resurrection (Rom. 8:10–11). Indeed, by the Spirit we have communion—direct and immediate communion—with no one less than the Son and the Father themselves. The Holy Spirit is God himself [or Christ] living in us (John 14:23ff.; 1 Cor. 3:16; 6:19; 2 Cor. 6:16; Gal. 2:20; Col. 3:11; Eph. 3:17; Phil. 1:8, 21). Who can grant us all these blessings? Who can cause God himself to dwell in our hearts? Who can do all these things but one [the Spirit] who is himself God? To him, accordingly, divine honor is due. The Spirit exists alongside the Father and the Son as the cause of all blessing and well-being (Matt. 28:19; 1 Cor. 12:4–6; 2 Cor. 13:13; Rev. 1:4). In his name we are baptized (Matt. 28:19). All life and power comes from him. He is the author of our prayers (Zech. 12:10; Rom. 8:15–16). In the face of all these things the church is warned not to grieve him (Isa. 63:10; Eph. 4:30). To blaspheme him, says Christ, is unpardonable (Matt. 12:31–32).[37]

DEVELOPMENT OF TRINITARIAN DOGMA

[218] In all of these elements of revelation, of course, Scripture has not yet provided us with a fully developed trinitarian dogma. But it does teach us that the one name of God is only fully unfolded in that of the Father, the Son, and the Spirit. It very clearly and plainly declares that all God's outgoing works *(ad extra)*, both in creation and re-creation, have a threefold divine cause. It leaves no doubt whatever that this threefold cause constitutes three distinct subjects who relate to each other as persons. And so Scripture contains all the data from which theology has constructed the dogma of the Trinity. Philosophy did not need to add anything essential to that dogma: even the Logos doctrine is part of the New Testament. It all only had to wait for a time when the power of

37. Earlier literature on the Holy Spirit is given by J. G. Walch, *Bibliotheca theologica selecta, litterariis adnotationibus instructa*, I, 75ff., 241, in which especially J. Owen, *Pneumatologia, or, A Discourse concerning the Holy Spirit* (London: J. Darby, 1674), translated into Dutch (Rotterdam: Nicolaas en Paulus Topyn, 1746), deserves attention; literature on the Spirit is also given by A. Kuyper, *The Work of the Holy Spirit*, trans. H. De Vries (New York: Funk & Wagnalls, 1905). More recent literature can be found in M. Beversluis, *De heilige Geest en zijne werkingens volgens de Schriften des Nieuwen Verbonds* (Utrecht: C. H. E. Breijer, 1896), VII, in which the following especially are noteworthy: J. Gloël, *Der heiligen Geist in der Heilsverkündigung des Paulus* (Halle: M. Niemeyer, 1888); H. Gunkel, *Die Wirkungen des heiligen Geistes* (Göttingen: Vandenhoeck & Ruprecht, 1888); in addition, also, J. E. Pruner, *Synopsis der dogmatisch-moraltheologischen Lehre von der Wirksamkeit des heiligen Geistes zunächst nach dem hl. Thomas von Aquin* (Eichstätt: Brönner'sche, 1891); W. Kölling, *Pneumatologie, oder, Die Lehre von der Person des heiligen Geistes* (Gütersloh: C. Bertelsmann, 1894); G. Smeaton, *The Doctrine of the Holy Spirit* (Edinburgh: T. & T. Clark, 1882); K. Lechler, *Die biblische Lehre vom heiligen Geiste*, 3 vols. (Gütersloh: C. Bertelsmann, 1899–1904); K. F. Nösgen, *Geschichte der Lehre vom heiligen Geiste* (Gütersloh: C. Bertelsmann, 1899); idem, *Der heilige Geist: Sein Wesen und die Art seines Wirkens* (Berlin: Trowitzch & Sohn, 1905); W. Lütgert, *Gottes Sohn und Gottes Geist: Vorträge zur Christologie und zur Lehre vom Geiste Gottes* (Leipzig: A. Deichert [G. Böhme], 1905); H. Cremer, "Geist, heiliger," *PRE³*, VI, 450; E. Sokolowski, *Die Begriffe Geist und Leben bei Paulus in ihren Beziehungen zu einander* (Göttingen: Vandenhoeck & Ruprecht, 1903); H. Weinel, *Die Wirkungen des Geistes und der Geister im nachapostolischen Zeitalter bis auf Irenäus* (Freiburg: Mohr, 1899); Th. Schermann, *Die Gottheit des heiligen Geistes nach den griechischen Vätern des vierten Jahrhunderts* (Freiburg i.B.: Herder, 1901); G. Tophel, *The Work of the Holy Spirit in Man: Discourses Delivered at Geneva*, trans. Geo. E. Shipman, 2d ed. rev. (Chicago: Chicago Foundlings' Home, 1883 [c. 1880]); J. H. Garrison, *The Holy Spirit* (St. Louis: Christian Pub. Co., 1905); J. H. B. Mastermann, *"I Believe in the Holy Ghost": A Study of the Doctrine of the Holy Spirit in Light of the Modern Thought* (London: Wells Gardner, 1906).

Christian reason would be sufficiently developed to enter into the holy mystery that presents itself here.

Apostolic Fathers and Apologists

In the period of the Apostolic Fathers that moment had clearly not yet arrived. They parrot Scripture without comprehending the profound meaning and interrelatedness of the truths in question and use expressions that would at a later time prove indefensible. Yet their writings are supremely important also for the doctrine of the Trinity insofar as they polemicize against both the Ebionite and Docetic schools of theology and, in phrases of varying strength, declared the sublime supra-angelic nature of the Christ.

From the very outset it is clear that the dogma of the Trinity was not born from philosophical reasoning about the nature of God, but from reflection on the facts of revelation, specifically on the person and work of Christ. From the beginning it revolved around the deity of Christ, the absolute character of Christianity, the truth of the revelation of God, the true atonement from sin, and the absolute certainty of salvation. Now the writings of the Apostolic Fathers in which Christ occupies an utterly unique position credit him with the possession of attributes that cannot be assigned to creatures. He is called the Son, the only-begotten Son of God (*1 Clement* 36; Ignatius, *Rom.* 1; *Eph.* 20; *Smyrn.* 1; *Diognetus* 9–10; *Barnabas* 7:12); the effulgence and scepter of God's majesty (*1 Clement* 16, 36); the Lord of earth, to whom all things are subject, the creator of all things, the judge of the living and the dead (*Barnabas* 7:12; *Diognetus* 7; *Didache* 16; Polycarp, *Phil.* 1, 2, 6, 12); the holy and incomprehensible Logos, who was sent to earth "as God" (*Diogn.* 7) and may properly be called "God" (*2 Clement* 1; Ignatius, *Rom.* 3; *Smyrn.* 1, 10; *Eph.* 1:18–19). The Father (God), Son (Christ), and the Spirit are mentioned side by side in a single breath (*1 Clement* 46; Ignatius, *Eph.* 9; *Magn.* 13). The Apostolic Fathers rarely mention the Holy Spirit, but when they do, they distinguish him from, and put him on a level with, the Father and the Son. Only with respect to the Pastor (Shepherd) of Hermas (III, *Sim.* 5.5–6) is there disagreement over whether he equates the Holy Spirit with the Son or distinguishes him from the Son.[38]

In the second century, with the rise of Gnosticism, Christian thought awakens. The deity of Christ becomes dogmatically significant and is therefore expressed in much clearer terms. Justin Martyr repeatedly calls Christ "God," even "God" with the definite article, "*the* God" (*Dialogue with Trypho*, 34, 56, 58, 113, 126, etc.), and ascribes to him an array of sublime characteristics. He is the firstborn of creation, the beginning of another race, equipped not with a charisma or two but with all the powers of the Spirit, possessing not just the "seed" (σπερμα) of the Logos but the entire Logos (λογικου το ὁλον), able to

---

38. F. C. Baur, *Die christliche Lehre von der Dreieinigkeit und Menschwerdung Gottes in ihrer geschichtlichen Entwicklung*, I, 134; and in opposition; I. A. Dorner, *History of the Development of the Doctrine of the Person of Christ*, I, 124–34.

divinize the human race, and hence himself God (*Trypho,* 87, 138; *2 Apol.,* 10, 12). Further, he clearly teaches Christ's preexistence, not only as a force but as a person (*Trypho,* 128).

Since the Father is hidden, inexpressible, transcending time and space (*Trypho,* 127; *2 Apol.,* 6), all revelations under the Old Testament dispensation as well as in the Gentile world are revelations of the Logos (*Trypho,* 127; *1 Apol.,* 46, 61, 63; *2 Apol.,* 10, 13). He even existed at the creation; the words of Genesis 1:26 are addressed to him (*Trypho,* 62). But in Justin the immanent relation between the Father and the Son is not yet clear. It seems that the Logos, who is different from the Father "in number but not in thought," was first generated by the Father with a view to the creation and, though not produced by abscission, he was generated by "the power and will (δυναμει και βουλη) of the Father," just as one light is lit from another and as the word proceeds from our mouth (*2 Apol.,* 6; *Trypho,* 61, 100, 128). For that reason he is called the "first-begotten, the firstborn of God" (πρωτογονος, πρωτοτοκος του θεου, *1 Apol.,* 46, 58). This generation is sometimes called a "bringing forth" (προβαλλειν), but more often a "begetting" (γενναν) (*Trypho,* 62, 76, 129; *1 Apol.,* 23; *2 Apol.,* 6), which is why the Logos is called an "offspring" (γεννημα), or "function" (ἐργασια) (*Trypho,* 62, 114, 129). Justin seeks to maintain the unity of God by saying that the Son is indeed another than the Father "in number but not in thought" (ἀριθμῳ ἀλλ᾽ οὐ γνωμη, *Trypho,* 56) and subordinate to the Father. The Son is "the first power after the Father" (ἡ πρωτη δυναμος μετα τον πατερα, *1 Apol.,* 32); he occupies "second place" (δευτερα χωρα, *1 Apol.,* 13). He has received all things from the Father (*Trypho,* 86), is God and Lord, because the Father willed it so (*Trypho,* 127), and is "subordinate to the Father and Lord" (ὑπο τῳ πατρι και κυριῳ τεταγμενος, *Trypho,* 126).

At several points, therefore, Justin still has a defective understanding of the Trinity. Some of the views he held—the hiddenness of the Father by contrast to the Son; the generation of the Son by the will of the Father with a view to creation; the Son's subordination to the Father—were later rejected by the church. Because of these errors some theologians have called Justin an Arian but they are wrong. For (1) this issue did not yet exist in Justin's time, and (2) his writings contain several elements that are diametrically opposed to the views of Arius. Justin firmly and distinctly teaches the deity of the Son; he says that the Son was not created but generated and illustrates this with the—later very common—images of light and the word (see above); he clearly understands the importance of the deity of Christ for the entire work of salvation and for the truth of the Christian religion. For that reason, too, he repeatedly refers to the Father, the Son, and the Spirit together as the object of our worship (*1 Apol.,* 6, 13, 60, 61, 65, 67). Though it is true that he assigns "second place" (δευτερα χωρα) to the Son and "third ranking" (τρειτη ταξις) to the Spirit, Justin in these passages clearly articulates the personality of the Holy Spirit and his distinctiveness from the Son. Some, indeed, have marshalled *1 Apol.,* 33, against this interpretation, but this passage only teaches that Justin interprets the expression "the Spirit" (το πνευμα) in Luke 1:35 as referring not to the Spirit but to the Logos, an exegesis found also in other expositors. We know with certainty, furthermore, that Justin did not rank the Spirit among the angels or among creatures in general. But about the divine nature of the Holy Spirit and his ontological relation to the Father and the Son, we find virtually nothing in Justin. He did not yet appreciate the religious importance of the doctrine of the Holy Spirit. He still viewed the Spirit as the Spirit of prophecy, who inspired the prophets and apostles and equipped Christ for his task, but did not as yet have any idea of the necessity of the ongoing work of the Holy Spirit in the church. To him the objective revelation of God in the Logos seems sufficient, and he does not understand the necessity of the Spirit's subjective illumination.[39]

Finally, the works of Justin Martyr clearly exhibit the nature of the influence that Greek philosophy exerted upon Christian theology. No one denies the reality of it, not the least in the thinking of Justin Martyr. But that influence is most noticeable in those elements of Justin's teaching that were later rejected by the church, namely, in his distinction between the "immanent" and the "revealed" Word (λογος ἐνδιαθετος, προσοεικος), his representation of the Son as "second God" (δευτερος θεος), and his positing the Son as external to the divine essence. All the other elements—the Logos-nature of Christ, his preexistence and generation, the creation of all things by the Logos, his Sonship and deity—were all consciously derived and demonstrated by Justin from Scripture.[40] The succeeding apologists, Theophilus, Tatian, and Athenagoras, still follow the same errors that mark Justin's doctrine of the Trinity. Tatian (*Or. c. Gr.,* 5) does indeed hold that insofar as all things have their ground in God, all things exist in him ideally, that is, as Logos; but this Logos is begotten by the will of God and is the "first begotten work of the Father by participation, not by abscission" (*Or. c. Gr.,* 5). In Theophilus the Logos does exist before creation as "the immanent Word," seeing that he is "the mind and purpose of God," but he (the Logos) is nevertheless generated by the Father to be the revealed Word with a view to creation (*ad Autol.,* II, 10, 22). Athenagoras (*Leg. pro chr.,* ch. 10) similarly teaches that though the Logos existed from eternity inasmuch as God is the eternal "mind" (νους), he is nevertheless also the first "offspring" (γεννημα) of the Father because as the idea and energy of all things he proceeds from the Father. Just as Theophilus was the first to speak of a "triad" in God (*Ad Autol.,* II, 26), so also Athenagoras unites God the Father, God the Son, and the Holy Spirit, who was active in the prophets and an "effluence" of God, proceeds from and returns to God as a sunbeam proceeds from and returns to the sun—and calls them the object of Christian worship (ibid., ch. 10, 12). Though the distinctiveness of the three persons is evident here, their

39. K. G. Semisch, *Justin der Märtyrer,* 2 vols. (Breslau: August Schulz, 1840–42), II, 305–33; ET: *Justin Martyr: His Life, Writings, and Opinions,* 2 vols. (Edinburgh: T. & T. Clark, 1843); J. Schwane, *Dogmengeschichte,* 2d ed. of vols. 1–2, 1st ed. of vols. 3–4 (Freiburg i.B.: Herder, 1882–95), I, 79ff.

40. K. G. Semisch, *Justin der Märtyrer,* II, 295ff.

unity is not sufficiently maintained. Though the Father is represented as the one, unbegotten, eternal and invisible God, the Son and the Spirit are one with him, not in being, but in spirit and in power (ibid., ch. 24).

Irenaeus, Tertullian, Origen

We owe the immediately following development of the doctrine of the Trinity—a development that consisted mainly in the exclusion of the philosophical elements—to three men, each of whom made a specific contribution to the Christian dogma. Irenaeus is the vigorous opponent of the gnostic idea of God and of the theory that makes the Logos the rational principle of the universe. Even he, however, from time to time shows that he had not completely overcome the old schema: he still calls the Father the invisible, hidden God in contrast to the Son (*Adv. haer.*, IV, 20, 10). Nevertheless, he opposes as vigorously as he can the notion of God as "cosmic depth" (βυθος) and the emanation of the aeons, and maintains the scriptural distinction between the Creator and the creature. The Logos is, as it were, divested of his dual nature and definitively put on the side of God. The Logos is not a creature but a hypostatic word (III, 8), preexistent (II, 6; IV, 12), true God (IV, 10, 14; etc.). Also the distinction between the "immanent word" and the "imparted word" is to be rejected (II, 17, 18). For aside from the fact that this distinction fails to do justice to the personality of the Logos and links his generation to creation, the Logos may not be presented as the intellect and reason of God. For God is simple—all spirit, all intellect, all thought, all logos (II, 16, 48)—so that both the Son and the Father are true God. Irenaeus very clearly enunciates the unity of the Father, the Son, and the Spirit. He emphatically maintains their divine nature and repeatedly mentions them in the same breath (IV, 6, 20, 33). The generation of the Son did not occur in time; the Son had no beginning, but existed eternally with God (II, 18; III, 22; IV, 37).

But Irenaeus falls short in showing how the Trinity exists in that unity; that is, how the Father, Son, and Spirit, though partaking in one and the same divine nature, are still personally distinct. At this point Tertullian complements and corrects Irenaeus. It must be granted, however, that Irenaeus surpasses Tertullian in overcoming gnostic dualism. Tertullian distinguishes between the Father and the Son as between an invisible and unseen God and a visible and seen God (*Adv. Prax.*, 14–15). In all sorts of ways and with a panoply of arguments, he stands by that distinction through utilizing the name Logos, the incarnation, and the theophanies, and so on. In fact, in Tertullian the Logos attains the full realization of his sonship and independent personality only as a result of God's speaking, generation, and incarnation (*Adv. Prax.*, 6.7), so that there was a time when the Son did not exist (*Adv. Hermog.*, 3). Although it is true that in his polemic against patripassionism he went too far in articulating the distinctions between the persons, it is also true that precisely for that reason he tries all the harder to maintain the unity in the Trinity and the Trinity in the unity. The three persons are "of one substance, of one condition, and of one power: together they constitute one God." They are distinct as to their order and economy. "The mystery of the economy arranges the unity into a Trinity." They are three, "not in status, but in degree"; yet one God, "from whom these degrees and forms and aspects are defined under the name of the Father, the Son, and the Holy Spirit." As a sun ray is also sun, so there are various aspects, forms, images, and units in the one undivided substance. The three persons, accordingly, are one but not identical. The Son is distinct from the Father and the Spirit is distinct from both, but they have the name "God" and "Lord" in common. Together they are one God and inseparable. Just as the trunk and the branch, the spring and the stream, the sun and the sunray are inseparable, so also are the Father and the Son. Trinity, therefore, does not cancel out the one rule *(monarchia)*. Though the Son differs from the Father, the two are not divided or separate. There is "distinction" and "distribution" but no "contradiction" or "division" between them. It is "a unity that derives the Trinity from within its own self" (*Adv. Prax.*, 2ff.). So Tertullian molds the unyielding Latin language to simultaneously maintain the unity and Trinity in God. Both formally and materially he has been of incalculable significance for the dogma of the Trinity. Despite his failure always to surmount subordinationism and to adequately distinguish the ontological, the cosmological, and the soteriological dimensions of the doctrine of the Trinity, it is nevertheless Tertullian who furnished the concepts and terms that the dogma of the Trinity needed to articulate its true meaning. He replaced Logos speculation with the doctrine of filiation and thereby permanently disentangled the ontological Trinity from cosmological speculation. And he was the first theologian who attempted to deduce the Trinity of persons, not from the person of the Father, but from the very being of God.[41]

But while Tertullian did not yet succeed in freeing the ontological Trinity from the notion of a cosmological and soteriological process, it was Origen who conceived it totally as an eternal process within the divine being itself. The generation [of the Son] is eternal generation (αἰωνιος γεννησις, *De princ.*, I, 2, 4). Just as it is the very nature of light to shine so that it cannot exist without shining, so the Father cannot exist without the Son (*De princ.*, I, 2, 2, 4, 7, 10). There was no time when the Son did not exist (*De princ.*, I, 2, 2, 4; *Contra Celsus*, VIII, 12). The Father is not Father before the existence of the Son but through the existence of the Son (*De princ.*, I, 2, 10). There is no separation: the Father does not exist apart from the Son (*Contra Celsus*, IV, 14, 16). The Father and the Son have all the divine attributes in common: the Son and the Father are one. It is not alongside but in God that we worship the Son (*Contra Celsus*, VIII, 12, 13). The Son has the same wisdom, truth, and reason as the Father (αὐτοσοφια, αὐτοαληθεια, αὐτολογος, *Contra Celsus*, V, 41). But now,

41. J. Stier, *Die Gottes- und Logos-Lehre Tertullians* (Göttingen: Vandenhoeck & Ruprecht, 1899); B. B. Warfield, "Tertullian and the Beginnings of the Doctrine of the Trinity," *Princeton Theological Review* 16 (Oct. 1905, Jan. 1906, April 1906); J. J. Jansen, *De Leer van den Person en het Werk van Christus bij Tertullianus* (Kampen: Kok, 1906).

in order to maintain the distinction of persons while affirming this unity and equality, Origen calls into play the aid of subordinationism, and reaching back behind Tertullian, he again derives the Trinity from the person of the Father, not from the being of God. And that is how Origen came to represent the Father as *the* God (ὁ θεος), as being of himself God (αὐτοθεος), the fountain or root of deity (ριζα θεοτητος), the greatest God over all things (μεγιστος ἐπι πασι θεος), superior (κρειττων) to the Son, the one complete Godhead, exalted above all being, invisible, incomprehensible, and the Son as God (θεος, without the article), as "other than the Father in substance" (ἑτερος του πατρος κατ᾽ οὐσιαν), by so much inferior to the Father as the world is inferior to the Son.[42]

From Nicaea to Augustine

[219] The church, however, did not follow Origen. It rejected his subordinationism and at Nicaea enunciated the true and full deity of the Son. This confession was thoroughly religious in character. It maintained the soteriological principle of Christianity. From this moment onward, the significance of the doctrine of the Trinity changed. Nicaea proclaimed the existence of distinctions in God and taught that the Father and the Son (and the Spirit) together were God. From now on, the challenge was to uphold the unity underlying the distinctions. *Before* Nicaea the main difficulty was to derive a threesome from the oneness of God; *after* Nicaea the reverse is true. From this point on the trinitarian dogma has an independent value and theological significance of its own.

Athanasius, the three Cappadocians, and Augustine now elaborate and complete the doctrine of the Trinity [on the basis of the Nicene Confession]. Athanasius understood better than any of his contemporaries that Christianity stands or falls with the confession of the deity of Christ and the Trinity. He devoted his entire life and all his energies to the defense of this truth. He was not fighting for a philosophical problem, but for the Christian religion itself, for the revelation of God, the teaching of the apostles, the faith of the church. The Trinity is the heart and center of Christianity, differentiating it in principle from Judaism, which denies the distinctions within the divine being, and from paganism, which rejects the oneness of God (*Ad Serap.*, I, 28). Athanasius, accordingly, completely avoids the philosophical intermingling of ontology and cosmology. He rejects the gnostic and Arian dualism between God and the world together with its array of intermediate beings (*C. Arian.*, II, 26). The Trinity, he says, is devoid of any admixture of foreign elements; it does not consist in

---

42. I. A. Dorner, *History of the Development of the Doctrine of the Person of Christ*, II, 118ff. On the doctrine of the Trinity before Nicaea, in addition to the works already cited above, see also D. Petavius, "De trinitate," in *Theol. dogm.*, appendix 1; John Forbes, *Intructiones historico-theologicae de doctrina christiana*, lib. I, chs. 1–5; G. Bull, *Defensio fidei Nicaenae*, vol. 1 in *Opera Omnia*, 6 vols. (London: Typis Samuelis Bridge, Impensis M. Smith, 1703); M. J. Scheeben, *Handbuch der katholischen Dogmatik*, I, 796ff.; ed. note: For ET, see above, p. 263 n. 7; J. B. Heinrich and C. Gutberlich, *Dogmatische Theologie*, 2d ed., 10 vols. (Mainz: Kirchheim, 1881–1900), IV, 250ff.

a combination of the Creator with something that has come into being, but is fully and perfectly divine in character (ibid.). The Trinity, therefore, is eternal. In God there are no nonessential features; God does not *become* anything; he is what he is eternally. As it [the Trinity] always was, so it is and remains; and in it the Father, the Son, and the Spirit (*Ad Serap.,* III 7; *C. Arian.,* I, 18).

The Father was always Father. Unlike human fathers, it belongs to his very nature to be Father (*De decr. nic. syn.,* 12). Just as one cannot conceive of the sun apart from its light, nor of a spring apart from its water, so one cannot conceive of the Father apart from the Son. God is not "without offspring" (ἄγονος); on the contrary, he is always speaking (*C. Arian.,* II, 2; *Ad Serap.,* II, 2). Those who deny the Trinity reduce God to a lifeless principle or end up with the doctrine of the eternal existence of the world (*C. Arian.,* I, 14). Since God is not a lifeless principle, the generation and existence of the Son is also eternal. Neither for the Father, nor for the Son was there a time when he did not exist (*C. Arian.,* I). This Son cannot be a creature and was not begotten by the will of God but is generated from within his being (*C. Arian.,* I, 25). And although Athanasius speaks less often and more sparingly of the Spirit, the same thing is true of the Holy Spirit (*Ad. Serap.,* I, 20–21; etc.). These three persons are truly distinct; they are not three parts of a single whole, or three names for one and the same being. The Father alone is Father; the Son alone is Son; the Spirit alone is Spirit (*C. Arian.,* III, 4; IV, 1; *Ad Serap.,* IV, 4, 6–7). In this connection Athanasius maintains the unity by affirming (1) that all three are the same in essence (ὁμοούσιοι) and one substance (ὑπόστασις) (ὑπόστασις and οὐσία are still synonymous in the work of Athanasius) and have the same attributes (*C. Arian.,* III, 3–4; *De decr. nic. syn.,* 19–25); (2) that the Father is the first principle and fountainhead of the Trinity (*C. Arian.,* IV, 1); and (3) that the three persons exist in each other (*Ad Serap.,* I, 14; III, 6; *C. Arian.,* III, 6) and are united in their working (*Ad Serap.,* I, 28).[43]

In the main we find this trinitarian teaching of Athanasius—only further clarified with more names, illustrations, and analogies—in Basil's *Libri* V against Eunomius, in his book on the Holy Spirit and in many of his letters and homilies; in Gregory of Nyssa in his 12 books *Contra Eunomium* and in his *Oratio catechetica;* and in Gregory of Nazianzus in his 5 *Orationes theologicae.* John of Damascus summarizes the results and takes his cue especially from Gregory Nazianzus. The entire Greek [Orthodox] church accepted this doctrine as defined by the ecumenical councils (of which it recognizes the first seven), diverging from the West only with reference to *filioque* (the phrase "and of the Son").

In the West, after Tertullian and Cyprian, it was especially Hilary who vigorously defended the doctrine of the Trinity, proving it from Scripture in his 12 books *De trinitate.* These books, however, say very little about the Holy Spirit

43. Cf. Fr. Lauchert, *Die Lehre des heiligen Athanasius des Grossen* (Leipzig, 1895), 10–65; J. Schwane, *Dogmengeschichte,* II², 83–108; F. Loofs, *Leitfaden zum Studium der Dogmengeschichte,* 4th ed., (Halle a.S.: M. Niemeyer, 1906), 237ff.

and therefore lend support to the idea that the original title was *De fide contra Arianos*. Next to take up the exposition and defense of this doctrine, but now more speculatively and profoundly, was Augustine of Hippo. His 15 books *De trinitate* contain the most profound exposition of this dogma ever written. He not only sums up what earlier fathers had said on the subject but also treats it independently and introduces important modifications. In the first place, Augustine's starting point is not the person of the Father but the one, simple, uncompounded essence of God, thus enunciating the absolute unity of the three persons more vigorously than was ever done before him. Every person is as great as the entire Trinity (*De trin.*, VIII, 1, 2). Present in each person is the entire self-same divine being, so that there are not three Gods, three Almighties, and so forth, but only one God, one Almighty, and so on (ibid., V, 8). Hence the distinction between the persons cannot arise from attributes or accidents that one person has in distinction from another but stems from the interpersonal relations of the members of the Trinity.

The first person is, and is called, the Father because he stands in a unique relation to the Son and the Spirit, etc. (ibid., V, 5), just as the appellatives "Lord," "Creator," etc., denote God's relation to his creatures but do not introduce any change in his being (ibid., 16, 17). Secondly and consequently, Augustine had to reject the dualism construed earlier between the Father and the Son. The Son, being himself true God, is no less hidden and invisible than the Father and is perfectly equal to the Father. All subordinationism is banished. Augustine goes even further than Athanasius. The latter still allowed for some subordination (*C. Arian.* I, 59) but Augustine has abandoned all trace of the idea that the Father is the real, the original God. He bases himself on the essence of God, which is present equally in all three persons. Although he still calls the Father the fountainhead or first principle of the deity (*De trin.*, IV, 20), in his mind it has another meaning. It does not mean that deity logically exists first in the Father and is then imparted by him to the Son and the Spirit. The Father can only be called Father because it is as person, not as God, that he is the Father of the Son. In that sense Augustine also reads the Nicaean phrase "very God of very God (*De trin.*, VII, 2, 3). For the same reason he arrived at a different view of the Old Testament theophanies as well. Formerly they had always been interpreted as revelations of the Logos inasmuch as the Father was hidden, but Augustine also ascribes them to the Father and to the Spirit, who are also able to manifest themselves and whose manifestations, needless to say, cannot be separated from those of the Son (*De trin.*, II–III). Finally, more than any church father before him, Augustine looked for images, analogies, and vestiges of the Trinity and so brought out the connections between the doctrine of God and that of the cosmos as a whole (*De trin.*, IX–XV).[44]

44. J. Schwane, *Dogmengeschichte*, II², 173–94; T. Gangauf, *Des heiligen Augustinus speculative Lehre von Gott dem Dreieinigen* (Augsburg: Schmidt, 1883), 209ff.; Wilhelm Münscher, *Lehrbuch des christlichen Dogmengeschichte*, ed. Daniel von Coelln, I, 245ff.

Thus Augustine completed what Tertullian had begun. In the West there is, despite all the agreement between them, another view of the doctrine of the Trinity than that which prevails in the East. The Eastern church confessed that, though both the Son and the Spirit proceed from the Father, they otherwise have no relation to one another. But it was felt in the West that the consubstantiality of the three persons and their interrelations only fully come to expression in the *"filioque"* (and of the Son). The West aligned itself with Augustine and, while it developed his trinitarian views on some points, did not introduce any changes in them nor add anything new to them. The Athanasian Creed, which is mistakenly attributed to Athanasius and certainly did not originate before A.D. 400, breathes the spirit of Augustine and was therefore welcomed in the West but not in the East.[45] The Reformers, too, attested their agreement with it. The Lutheran and Reformed confessions openly align themselves with the three ecumenical symbols. In the Belgic Confession (art. 9) the Athanasian Creed is mentioned by name, and in the Anglican church it even received a place in the liturgy. Yet of late strong opposition to this use has surfaced. And generally speaking, there is a substantial difference between the attitude assumed toward the Athanasian creed by Catholics and that of Protestants. The Reformation insisted that no historical belief in the doctrine of the Trinity, however pure, can save people, but only a true and heartfelt faith in God himself, the God who in Christ has revealed himself as the triune God.

[220] The dogma of the Trinity, however, has at all times encountered serious opposition. It not only came from without, from the side of Jews[46] and Muslims,[47] against whose attacks Christians would then defend the doctrine.[48] Both before and after its official adoption, within the boundaries of Christendom, this dogma was also disputed by many. Now in the confession of the Trinity we hear the heartbeat of the Christian religion: every error results from, or upon deeper reflection is traceable to, a departure in the doctrine of the Trinity. It is such an integral component of the Christian faith that it still reverberates even in the confession of the Unitarians. All who value being called Christians continue to speak of the Father, Son, and Spirit.[49] All the greater, however, has been the opposition to the ecclesiastical formulation of the doctrine of the Trinity and the more frequent its restatement. At the same time the history of this dogma clearly demonstrates that only the ecclesiastical formulation of it is capable of preserving inviolate the matter with which we are here concerned. Now the great challenge facing us with this dogma is to see to it that the unity of the

45. A. von Harnack, *History of Dogma*, IV, 129ff.; Ernst Friedrich Karl Müller, *Symbolik* (Erlangen and Leipzig: A. Deichert, 1896), 51ff.

46. F. W. Weber, *System der altsynagogalen palästinischen Theologie* (Leipzig: Dörffling & Franke, 1880), 147ff.

47. See, e.g., Averroes, according to A. Stöckl, *Geschichte der Philosophie des Mittelalters*, 3 vols. (Mainz: Kirchheim, 1864–66), II, 89.

48. Literature in J. G. Walch, *Bibliotheca theologica selecta*, I, 881ff., 896ff.

49. F. Nitzsch, *Lehrbuch der evangelischen Dogmatik*, 425.

divine essence does not cancel out the Trinity of the persons or, conversely, that the Trinity of persons does not abolish the unity of the divine essence. There is always the threat of deviation either to the right or to the left and of falling either into the error of Sabellius or that of Arius.

The precursors of the Arians in the second and third centuries A.D. were the Ebionites, the Alogi, Theodotus, Artemon, and Paul of Samosota. Though regarding Christ as a human being whose birth was supernatural, who was anointed at his baptism with the Holy Spirit, qualified for his task, and exalted as Lord, they firmly denied his preexistence and deity. These were the adherents of an adoptionist Christology.[50] In the fourth century this adoptionist Christology was advocated by Lucian and his pupil Arius, and further by Aetius and Eunomius. According to a work entitled *The Banquet,* a few fragments of which have been preserved for us by Athanasius (*C. Arian.* I), Arius taught that inasmuch as God is "unbegotten" (ἀγεννητος) and without beginning, he is absolutely unique. He is inexpressible, incomprehensible, unable to have direct communion with that which is finite and to communicate his nature, the essence of which is "unbegottenness" (ἀγεννησια). Hence, all that exists outside of him is created, or came into being, by his will. He is not the Father from eternity but Father by creation, the Father of his creatures. But before God proceeded to create the world, he brought into being, as a kind of intermediary, an independent entity (ὑποστασις, οὐσια) through whom or through which he created all things. In Scripture this entity is called "Wisdom," "Son," "Logos," "image of God," and so on. God similarly further called into being a third and lower ὑποστασις, namely, the Holy Spirit. This Logos is not generated from within God's own being, nor is he consubstantial with the Father, for then there would be two Gods. Instead, he was born or created "out of nonbeing" (ἐξ οὐκ ὀντων) and is "a creature" (κτισμα) or "work" (ποιημα) of God brought into being "by his will and counsel" (ἠν ποτε, ὁτε οὐκ ἠν). Accordingly, "there was a time when he did not exist" even though he was created "before the times and ages," that is, before the existence of the world. This Logos, therefore, is not consubstantial (ὁμο οὐσιος) with the Father but totally separate from him, mutable, able to choose evil as well as the good. Yet he was "a perfect creature." He chose the good, thereby became immutable, and as it were became a God. This Logos also became human, preached the truth, and effected our redemption. He is now worthy of our honor but not of our worship.[51]

Arianism was strong and gained many adherents, not least among those who after the conversion of Constantine had for various reasons joined the Christian church. From the writings of Athanasius, moreover, we learn about the formidable weapons they carried into the battle. They appealed first of all to an array of Scripture passages that enunciated the unity of God (Deut.

50. A. von Harnack, *History of Dogma*, I, 191; III, 14–50.
51. Idem, *History of Dogma*, I, 253–62; F. Loofs, *Leitfaden zum Studium der Dogmengeschichte*, 4th ed., 233ff.; F. Loofs, "Arianismus," *PRE³*, II, 6–45.

6:4; 32:39; John 17:3; 1 Cor. 8:6), the birth or genesis of the Son (Prov. 8:22; Col. 1:15), his subordination to the Father (John 14:28; 1 Cor. 15:28; Heb. 3:2), the limited character of his knowledge (Mark 13:32; John 11:34), his limited power (Matt. 28:18) and goodness (Luke 18:19), his increase in wisdom (Luke 2:52), his suffering (John 12:27; 13:21; Matt. 26:39; 27:46), his elevation to the position of Lord and Christ (Acts 2:36; Phil. 2:9; Heb. 1:3–4; etc.). They further argued, with the aid of numerous quotations, that they had many earlier church fathers on their side. Also, they derived various arguments from Aristotelian philosophy, nominalistically construed, and by this means set about proving the uniqueness and ἀγεννησια of God. Finally, they pointed out the weaknesses and contradictions inherent in Nicene Christology, using especially the argument that, if the Son had been begotten, he would by that very fact be essentially different from God, the unbegotten One, and hence had originated in time.

The precursors of Sabellianism in the second and third century A.D. were Noetius, Praxeus, Epigonus, and Celomenes, who taught that in Christ the Father himself had been born and had suffered and died; hence, that the "Father" and the "Son" were names for the same person in different relations, namely, before and during his incarnation, both for the same person as such as well as in his historical manifestation; or also that the *divine* nature in Christ was the Father and the *human* nature, the flesh (σαρξ), the Son. Now, in the third century this monarchianism, patripassianism, or modalism was promulgated and further developed by Sabellius. The Father, Son, and Spirit are the same God; they are three names for one and the same being. Calling this being *Huiopatōr* (υἱοπατωρ), he applied the name to its three successive energies or stages. God consisted first of all in the person (προσωπον), the appearance or mode of the Father, namely, as Creator and Lawgiver; next, in the προσωπον of the Son as Redeemer from the time of his incarnation to the moment of his ascension, and finally in the προσωπον of the Holy Spirit as the Vivifier. In this connection Sabellius appealed especially to Deuteronomy 6:4; Exodus 20:3; Isaiah 44:6; John 10:38. Sabellius, accordingly, included the Holy Spirit in the divine being and positioned the Son and the Spirit on the same level as the Father. He further posited a process of becoming in God: a historical succession in the revelation of his being.[52]

THE OPPOSITION: ARIANISM AND SABELLIANISM

[221] Both schools of thought, Arianism and Sabellianism, the one to the right and the other to the left of the church's dogma of the Trinity, have persisted in the Christian church throughout the centuries. The essence of Arianism is its denial of the Son's consubstantiality with the Father; in other

---

52. A. von Harnack, *History of Dogma*, III, 51–73; A. von Harnack, "Monarchianismus," *PRE³*, XIII, 303; F. Loofs, *Leitfaden zum Studium der Dogmengeschichte*, 4th ed., 181ff.; cf. also the economic trinitarian monotheism of Marcellus of Ancyra in F. Loofs, ibid., 244ff.

words, its assertion that the Father alone and in an absolute sense is the one true God. It follows, of course, that the Son is a being of inferior rank; that he does not share in the divine nature. Arianism places the Son somewhere between God and the created universe and allows a wide margin of interpretation with respect to the exact place he occupies. The distance between God and the world is infinite, and at any point on this span a place may be assigned to the Son, from a place on the throne next to God down to a position alongside creatures, angels or humans. This accounts for the fact that Arianism has appeared in various forms.

It appeared, first of all, in the form of *subordinationism*. According to this view, the Son is indeed eternal, begotten from the essence of the Father, not a creature and not brought into being out of nothing, yet inferior and subordinate to the Father. The Father alone is God (ὁ θεος); he alone is the fountain of deity. The Son is God (θεος) having received his nature from the Father by communication. This was the teaching of Justin, Tertullian, Clement, Origen, and others. It was also the teaching of the semi-Arians, Eusebius of Caesarea and Eusebius of Nicomedia, who gave the Son a place "outside of the Father" and called him "like the Father in essence" (ὁμοιουσιος).[53] In later times this was the position of the Remonstrants,[54] the supranaturalists,[55] and many theologians in modern times.[56]

Second, it reappeared in its ancient form, the form it had in Arius himself, in numerous post-Reformation theologians, especially in England. Milton, for example, held that the Son and the Spirit were created by the free will of the Father before the creation of the world, and were only called "God" by virtue of their office, like the judges and magistrates in the Old Testament.[57] With minor modifications this was also the view of W. Whiston, whose Arianism triggered a spate of polemical counterwritings,[58] of S. Clarke, P. Maty, Dan

53. F. Loofs, *Leitfaden zum Studium der Dogmengeschichte*, 4th ed., 243ff.

54. Remonstrant Confession, art. 3; J. Arminius, *Opera theologica* (Leiden: Godefridum Basson, 1629), 232ff.; S. Episcopius, *Institutiones theologicae*, IV, sect. 2, ch. 32; P. van Limborch, *Theol. christ.*, II, 17, 25.

55. K. G. Bretschneider, *Dogmatik*, I, 612ff.; ed. note: see above, p. 261 n. 2; G. C. Knapp, *Vorlesungen über die christliche Glaubenslehre nach dem Lehrbegriff der evangelischen Kirche*, 2d ed., 2 vols. (Halle: Buchhandlung des Waisenhauses, 1836), I, 260; H. Muntinghe, *Pars theologiae christianae theoretica* (Hardervici: I. van Kasteel, 1800), §§134ff.

56. F. H. R. Frank, *System der christlichen Wahrheit*, 2d ed., 2 vols. (Erlangen: A. Deichert, 1884), I, 207ff.; J. T. Beck, *Vorlesungen über christliche Glaubenslehre*, 2 vols. (Gütersloh: C. Bertelsmann, 1886–87), II, 123ff., 134ff.; A. D. C. Twesten, *Vorlesungen über die Dogmatik der evangelisch-lutherischen Kirche*, 2 vols. (Hamburg: F. Perthes, 1837–38), II, 254; K. F. A. Kahnis, *Die lutherische Dogmatik, historisch-genetisch dargestellt*, 3 vols. (Leipzig: Dörffling & Franke, 1861–68), I, 353, 398; J. J. van Oosterzee, *Christian Dogmatics*, trans. J. Watson and M. Evans, 2 vols. (New York: Scribner, Armstrong, 1874), II, §52; J. I. Doedes, *De Nederlandsche Geloofsbelijdenis en de Heidelbergsche Catechismus* (Utrecht: Kemink & Zoon, 1880–81), 71ff.

57. J. Milton, *De doctrina christiana*, ed. Charles Sumner (Brunsvigae: F. Vieweg, 1827), I, chs. 5–6; ET: *A Treatise on Christian Doctrine: Compiled from Scripture Alone*, trans. Charles R. Sumner (Cambridge: J. Smith for Charles Knight, 1825).

58. J. G. Walch, *Bibliotheca theologica selecta*, I, 957ff.

Whitby, Harwood, of many Remonstrants in the Netherlands, and in a later period, of the Groningen theologians.[59]

A third form in which Arianism reappeared is *Socinianism*. Its position was that the Father is the one true God. The Son is a holy human being, created by God through an immediate supernatural conception, and did not exist before that conception. He was created for no other purpose than to proclaim a new law to humankind. After completing this task, he was elevated to a position in heaven, where he became a partaker of divine grace. The Spirit is no more than a divine power.[60] This Socinianism spread from Poland to Germany, The Netherlands, England, and America. In the last-mentioned two countries its representatives were John Biddle, Nathanael Lardner, Theophilus Lindsey, and Joseph Priestley, the founder of the Unitarian Society, and others. Thus Socinianism passed into Unitarianism.

Socinianism in time proved incapable of maintaining the supernaturalism that it initially still accepted. Jesus, though exemplary in piety and morality, became an ordinary person. In time Christianity became completely detached from his person. The same thing occurred in rationalism[61] and in modern theology. There was no longer any room here for the Trinity, the threesome of Father, Son, and Spirit. God is one and Jesus is an ordinary—though a great—human being.[62] Basically, even Ritschl offered no more than a new form of Socinianism. Jesus was a human being enabled by God to found the kingdom of heaven on earth and was afterward raised to the position of God and Lord of the church.[63] In this entire rationalistic view of the doctrine of the Trinity, there is of course much less need of divine grace, and so the Holy Spirit is hardly even mentioned. His deity and as a rule also his personal nature is denied.

Sabellianism, too, may appear in different forms. Like Arianism it denies the "threeness" present in the divine being but, unlike Arianism, it now seeks to secure the oneness, not by placing the Son and the Spirit outside the divine being, but by so absorbing them into it that all distinctions among the three persons melt away. According to the church's doctrine of the Trinity, it is the personal properties of the Father, Son, and Holy Spirit, specifically eternal generation and spiration, that explain the distinctions we are able to discern. When these personal properties are denied, the three persons are separated from one another, and tritheism makes its appearance.

59. P. Hofstede de Groot, *De Groninger Godgeleerdheid in Hunne Eigenaardigheid* (Groningen: Scholtens, 1855), 160ff.

60. Racovian Catechism, qu. 94–190; cf. F. Socinus, *Bibliotheca fratrum Polonorum quos unitarios vocant*, 10 vols. (Irenopolis [Amsterdam]: Philalethes, 1656–92), I, 789ff.; J. Crell, *De uno Deo Patre libri duo* (Irenopolis [Amsterdam]: C. Fronerus, 1688); according to F. Trechsel, *Die protestantischen Antitrinitarier vor Faustus Socin*, 2 vols. (Heidelberg: K. Winter, 1839–44), II, 221ff., 233ff.

61. J. A. L. Wegscheider, *Institutiones theologiae christianae dogmaticae* (Halle: Gebauer, 1819), §91.

62. Cf., e.g., T. J. Kielstra, *Het Godsdienstig Leven*, 2d ed. (Amsterdam: Van Kampen & Zoon, 1890), 39, 47.

63. A. Ritschl, *The Christian Doctrine of Justification and Reconciliation*, 378.

In antiquity the monophysites John of Ascusnages and John Philopon[64] were charged with this error, and in the Middle Ages so was Roscelin.[65] Later a similar complaint was lodged against Th. Sherlock, who assumed the presence in the divine being of three infinite spirits;[66] against Roëll, because he opposed the doctrine of the generation of the Son;[67] and against Lampe and Sibelius, because they objected to the formula "through the communication of essence."[68] When in addition the divine being is viewed in a Platonic-realistic sense, tritheism turns into tetratheism, an error with which Damian of Alexandria was charged.[69] However, since it is impossible to reconcile such a Trinity of individual separate beings with the unity of God, this unity may also be preserved by saying that Father, Son, and Holy Spirit are one and the same person or being. This [so-called] patripassianism was taught in the second century by Praxeas. Or with Marcellus of Ancyra and Photinus of Sirmium one can also view the Son and the Spirit as divine properties, which, solely for the purpose of accomplishing the work of creation and re-creation, proceeded from God and became self-existent and personal. The Logos was indeed eternal as "reason immanent in God" (λογος ἐνδιαθετος). The Father was never without Logos, in fact he was the "Logos Father" (λογοπατωρ). But this Logos first became Son, the expressed Logos (προφορικος), only in time. As Son and Spirit, God extends himself in time and then again returns to himself.[70] From this cyclical movement arises modalistic monarchianism, which views the three persons only as the three modes of self-revelation of the one divine being.

This, actually, was the teaching of Sabellius, a view of the dogma of the Trinity that keeps coming back in later times. Although the trinitarian speculations of Erigena[71] and Abelard[72] were not untouched by this modalism, it is more clearly evident in the pantheistic sects of the Middle Ages, in Joachim of Floris [Fiore], Amalrik of Bena, and David of Dinant, who distinguished a period of the Father, a period of the Son, and a period of the Spirit, and considered the last period as being near.[73] In the age of the Reformation it was [some from] Anabaptism that rose up in opposition to the church's doctrine of the Trinity. The true God is the

64. F. C. Baur, *Die christliche Lehre von der Dreieinigkeit und Menschwerdung Gottes in ihrer geschichtlichen Entwicklung*, II, 13ff.

65. Cf. Anselm, *Epistola de incarnatione verbi*, in *Complete Philosophical and Theological Treatises of Anselm of Canterbury*, trans. J. Hopkins and H. Richardson (Minneapolis: Banning, 2000), 265–94.

66. J. G. Walch, *Bibliotheca theologica selecta*, I, 972.

67. A. Comrie and N. Holtius, *Examen van het Ontwerp van Tolerantie*, VIII, sam., 10ff.; B. de Moor, *Comm. in Marckii Comp.*, I, 735, 761–71.

68. B. de Moor, *Comm. in Marckii Comp.*, I, 744–55; A. Ypey, *Geschiedenis der Nederlandsche Herformde Kerk*, 4 vols. (Breda: W. Van Bergen, 1819–27), III, 202 nn. 84ff.; *Nederlandsch. Archief voor Kerkelijke Geschiedenis* 8 (1848): 419ff.

69. F. C. Baur, *Dreieinigkeit und Menschwerdung Gottes*, II, 29ff.

70. J. Schwane, *Dogmengeschichte*, II², 135–50.

71. J. S. Erigena, *On the Division of Nature*, trans. Myra L. Uhlfelder (Indianapolis: Bobbs-Merrill, 1976), book I, 19ff.

72. P. Abelard, *Introductio ad theologiam*, I, 7.

73. H. Reuter, *Geschichte der religiösen Aufklärung im Mittelalter*, II, 183–249.

God within; he is the true Christ; and the Word, the Spirit in us, is the true God.[74]
David Joris taught that God is one and reveals himself successively as Father, Son,
and Spirit over the three periods of faith, hope, and love, the first beginning with
Moses, the second with Christ, and the third with himself.[75] But it was above all
Michael Servetus who spent all the power of his intellect on this dogma. In three
writings[76] he subjected the ecclesiastical form of it to a sharp critique but also tried
to rebuild it on positive lines. Servetus could not find words cutting enough to
condemn the church's doctrine of the Trinity. To his mind it is tritheistic, atheistic,
"a three-headed monster," "a three-headed Cerberus," "a tripartite God." In opposing it he proceeds from the premise that the divine being is indivisible and,
therefore, that in order to maintain the deity of Christ and the Holy Spirit one
may not speak in terms of persons but only of dispositions, manifestations, divine
modes. The Father is the divine being in toto, the only God. But he employed
the Logos, who existed already before Christ—not, however, as a person but as
word, reason, thought—to reveal himself in creation and in the Old Testament,
and to become human in Christ. The Logos, who did *not* assume human nature
in Christ, in him became flesh. Accordingly, the human Christ is the true Son of
God: God dwells fully in him. In the same way the Holy Spirit, who is not self-
existent and distinct from the Logos but comprehended in him, is the mode of
divine self-communication. Through him God dwells in all creatures, imparting
his life to them. At the end of this process the "Trinity" ceases to exist.[77]

The gnostic and theosophical elements that reappear here in the doctrine of
the Trinity soon reappeared full-blown in Böhme, Zinzendorf, and Swedenborg.
In Böhme, the Trinity is the result of a process, whose foundations and causative
factors are the mysterious forces of nature, the torch of reason, and the will in
the Godhead.[78] Although Zinzendorf called himself an utterly devoted believer
in the Trinity *(trinitariissimus),* he in fact proceeded from a gnostic concept of
God. God as he is in himself is unattainable, hidden, incomprehensible, but he
reveals himself in Christ. The latter is the true creator of all things, the YHWH
of the Old Testament, who became flesh and is the object of our worship. In
him, too, the Trinity is manifest, not marked by the immanent relations of
generation and spiration (etc.), but as a holy family. The first person is the
Father, the Holy Spirit is the mother, Christ is the Son, and the individual
believer as well as the church as a whole are received into this family as the

---

74. E.g., Camillo, in F. Trechsel, *Die protestantischen Antitrinitarier vor Faustus Socin,* 2 vols. (Heidelberg:
K. Winter, 1839–44), II, 95ff.

75. F. Trechsel, *Die protestantischen Antitrinitarier vor Faustus Socin,* I, 44ff.; A. M. Cramer, *Nederlandsch
Archief voor Kerkelijke Geschiedenis,* 5 (1845): 1–145; 6 (1846): 289–368; idem, *Bijvoegselen tot de levensbeschrijving van David Joris* (Leiden: S. & J. Luchtmans, 1846).

76. M. Servetus, *De trinitatis erroribus libri septem* (Hagenau: Secerius, 1531); idem, *Dialogorum de
trinitate libri duo* (Hagenau: Secerius, 1532); idem, *Christianismi restitutio* (Vienne: Arnoullet, 1553).

77. F. Trechsel, *Die protestantischen Antitrinitarier vor Faustus Socin,* I, 65ff., 103ff., 120ff.; B. Riggenbach,
"Servet, Michael," *PRE³,* XVIII, 228–36.

78. J. Claassen and Jakob Böhme, *Jakob Böhme: Sein Leben und seine theosophischen Werke,* 3 vols.
(Stuttgart: J. F. Steinkopf, 1885), II, 25ff.

Son's bride, who in a thoroughly realistic manner is created from the side and blood of Christ just as Eve was created from the side of Adam.[79]

Swedenborg took an even more radical stand against the doctrine of the Trinity. To him as to Servetus, this doctrine was tritheism pure and simple. God is indeed one, but in Christ he has become manifest as Father, Son, and Spirit, who relate to each other as soul, body, and the activity that proceeds from the two.[80] This theosophy paved the way for the trinitarian theories of modern philosophy. In Spinoza's system with its single unchangeable substance there was as yet no room for it. In Kant's philosophy the three persons are replaced by three qualities: true religion is faith in God as holy legislator, good ruler, and just judge.[81] Schleiermacher subjected the dogma of the Trinity to a severe critique and recognized in it only one true element, namely, that both in the person of Christ and in the communal Spirit of the church God is united with humanity.[82] According to Schelling and Hegel, the dogma contains a profound philosophical truth, one that they interpreted as follows: God is mind, thought, idea. It therefore belongs to his nature to form a conception of himself, to think himself, to objectivize himself.

The content of that thought, however, cannot be an idea as it is with us, but has to be reality. God, accordingly, in thinking himself produces and objectivizes himself, and does so in the form of the world, which is the real Son of God; and from this act of self-objectivization God returns in the Spirit and via the consciousness of humankind to himself.[83] Strauss indeed perceived the great difference between this speculation and the church's doctrine of the Trinity,[84] yet many people still take pleasure in such a philosophical construction.[85] Others are content to distinguish three potencies, moments, or forces in the one personality of God[86] and thus come to the recognition of a divine Trinity of revelation: God in nature (creation), history (Christ), and conscience (church).[87] Averse to metaphysics, which they regard as valueless and even detrimental to the life of

---

79. H. Plitt, *Zinzendorf's Theology,* 3 vols. in 1 (Gotha: F. A. Perthes, 1869–74), I, 211ff.; II, 24, 133ff.; III, 14ff.

80. E. Swedenborg, *The True Christian Religion* (Philadelphia: J. B. Lippincott, 1896), 241ff.

81. I. Kant, *Religion within the Limits of Reason Alone,* trans. Theodore M. Greene and Hoyt Hudson (New York: Harper Torchbooks, 1960), 131.

82. F. Schleiermacher, *The Christian Faith* (Edinburgh: T. & T. Clark, 1989), §§170–72; cf. also R. A. Lipsius, *Lehrbuch der evangelisch-protestantischen Dogmatik,* §368; A. Schweizer, *Die christliche Glaubenslehre nach protestantischen Grundsätzen dargestellt,* §§103ff.; J. H. Scholten, *De Leer der Hervormde Kerk in Hare Grondbeginselen,* II, 238.

83. F. W. J. Schelling, *Ausgewählte Werke,* I, 5, p. 294; I, 6, p. 28; I, 7, pp. 56ff.; G. W. F. Hegel, *Vorlesungen über die Philosophie der Religion* (Lectures of 1831), in *Sämtliche Werke,* XV, 136ff., 145ff. (*Werke,* XI, 120ff., 129ff.); *Sämtliche Werke,* XVI, 181ff. (*Werke,* XII, 181ff.).

84. D. F. Strauss, *Die christliche Glaubenslehre,* 2 vols. (Tübingen: C. F. Osiander, 1840–41), I, 492ff.

85. A. E. Biedermann, *Christliche Dogmatik,* §159; O. Pfleiderer, *Grundriss der christlichen Glaubens und Sittenlehre* (Berlin: G. Reimer, 1888), §122.

86. F. W. J. Schelling in his later period; R. Rothe, *Theologische Ethik,* 2d rev. ed., 5 vols. (Wittenberg: Zimmerman, 1867–71), §§23ff.; F. Nitzsch, *Lehrbuch der evangelischen Dogmatik,* 438–46.

87. K. A. von Hase, *Hutterus redivivus* (Helsingfors: A. W. Gröndahl, 1846), §70; W. M. L. De Wette, *Biblische Dogmatik,* 3d ed. (Berlin: G. Reimer, 1831), 71.

faith, they decline to infer the existence of immanent ontological relations in the divine being from God's self-revelation in Christ and from his self-communication in the Holy Spirit. They refuse to accept the theological elements that are contained not only in the doctrine of the church but also undoubtedly in the teaching of Scripture, and attempt to picture them as useless speculation.[88]

TRINITARIAN TERMINOLOGY

Beyond Scripture's Language?

[222] From the very beginning the Christian church took a different course. To the church the doctrine of the Trinity was the dogma and hence the mystery par excellence. The essence of Christianity—the absolute self-revelation of God in the person of Christ and the absolute self-communication of God in the Holy Spirit—could only be maintained, the church believed, if it had its foundation and first principle in the ontological Trinity. Accordingly, as soon as the data presented to that end by Scripture became the object of theological reflection, a need arose for various terms and expressions that do not occur in Scripture, but are nonetheless indispensable for the twofold purpose of giving expression, however imperfectly, to the truth [of the trinitarian faith] and of maintaining it in the face of misunderstanding and opposition. True, the use of extrabiblical terms was condemned by the Arians as well as by the representatives of many schools of thought in later times, such as the Socinians, the Anabaptists, the Remonstrants, the [so-called] biblical theologians, and others. Christian theology, however, always defended it as proper and valuable.[89] Scripture, after all, has not been given us simply, parrotlike, to repeat it, but to process it in our own minds and to reproduce it in our own words. Jesus and the apostles used it in that way. They not only quoted Scripture verbatim but also by a process of reasoning drew inferences from it. Scripture is neither a book of statutes nor a dogmatic textbook but the foundational source of theology. As the Word of God, not only its exact words but also the inferences legitimately drawn from it have binding authority.[90] Furthermore, reflection on the truth of Scripture and the theological activity related to it is in no way possible without the use of extrabiblical terminology. Not only are such extrabiblical terms and expressions used in the doctrine of the Trinity but also in connection with every other dogma and throughout the entire discipline of theology. Involved in the use of these terms, therefore, is the Christian's right of independent reflection

88. A. von Harnack, *What Is Christendom?* trans. Thomas Bailey Saunders (New York and Evanston: Harper and Row, 1957), 141–57; J. Kaftan, *Dogmatik,* 4th ed. (Tübingen: Mohr, 1902), §21; Th. Häring, *The Christian Faith,* trans. John Dickie and George Ferries, 2 vols. (London: Hodder & Stoughton, 1913), II, 708ff.

89. Augustine, *The Trinity,* VI, 10; T. Aquinas, *Summa theologiae,* I, qu. 29, art. 3; J. Calvin, *Institutes,* I.xiii.5; B. de Moor, *Comm. in Marckii Comp.,* I, 710–12; C. Vitringa, *Doctr. christ.,* I, 191–95; J. Gerhard, *Loci theol.,* III, c. 2; F. A. Philippi, *Kirchliche Glaubenslehre,* II, 149ff.

90. Cf. H. Bavinck, *Reformed Dogmatics,* I, 617–18 (#159).

and theology's right to exist. Finally, the use of these terms is not designed to make possible the introduction of new—extrabiblical or antibiblical—dogmas but, on the contrary, to defend the truth of Scripture against all heresy. Their function is much more negative than positive. They mark the boundary lines within which Christian thought must proceed in order to preserve the truth of revelation. Under the guise of being scriptural, biblical theology has always strayed farther away from Scripture, while ecclesiastical orthodoxy, with its extrabiblical terminology, has been consistently vindicated as scriptural.

Thus also in the doctrine of the Trinity we witness the gradual rise of unusual terms such as ὁμοουσιος, ουσια, ὑπαρξις, ὑποστασις, προσωπον, γενναν, τριας, *unitas, trinitas, substantia, personae, nomina, gradus, species, formae, proprietates,* and so forth. Initially the meaning of these terms was far from precise and clear. The term ουσια (being) was employed as a rule to refer to the one being of God, yet in the works of Origen, Athanasius, and Gregory of Nyssa it still frequently served to describe the three persons in that being. Athanasius in his polemic against Sabellianism expressly defended himself by saying that the Son is not μονοουσιος (one of substance) but ὁμοουσιος (of the same substance) with the Father.[91] So also the term ὑποστασις (subsistence; subsistent) was sometimes used to indicate the one being, then again to denote the three persons. In line with this practice people sometimes spoke of the one "hypostasis" in God and then again of the three "hypostases." But Sabellianism merely regarded the [three] persons as revelatory modes of the one being. To oppose this view the church had to stress that those persons were really existing "subsistences" in the divine being. For that purpose the word ὑποστασις [which thus became the equivalent of "person"] was used. Basil in his letter *Concerning Ousia and Hypostasis* brought about greater uniformity in the use of these terms by employing ουσια for God's being or essence and ὑποστασις or προσωπον for the three persons. Accordingly, every ὑποστασις has its own unique subsistence (ιδια ὑπαρξις) and is distinguished from the other persons by "peculiar traits," "properties," "distinctive features," "signs," "marks," "characteristics," and "forms." This terminology is continued in the language of the two Gregories, John of Damascus, Greek theology, and the Greek church in general.[92]

In the West the confusion was less extensive. Tertullian had established the use of the terms *essentia* and *substantia* for God's being or essence, and the term *persona* or *subsistentia* for the persons.[93] This terminology was later used by the great teachers of the church and in the creeds. Hilary, in his work *De trinitate,* constantly speaks of one *essentia, substantia, natura, genus,* and of three *personae* who are distinguished from each other by their personal *proprietates*

---

91. Athanasius, *Statement of Faith, NPNF (2),* IV, 83–85.

92. D. Petavius, "De trinitate," in *Theol. dogm.,* V, chs. 1ff.; J. Schwane, *Dogmengeschichte,* II², 99, 151ff.; I. A. Dorner, *History of the Development of the Doctrine of the Person of Christ,* II, 313ff.; A. von Harnack, *History of Dogma,* IV, 83; E. Hatch, *The Influence of the Greek Ideas on Christianity* (New York: Harper and Brothers, 1957), 275–82.

93. A. von Harnack in his *History of Dogma,* IV, 89 n. 2, contends that for Tertullian the meaning of *substantia* and *persona* is borrowed from "juristic and political notions," and that *substantia* then had the

(properties). Augustine disapproved of the practice of rendering the Greek word ὑπόστασις by [the Latin] *substantia*. The Latin words *substantia* and *essentia* are not strictly parallel to the Greek words ὑπόστασις and οὐσία. In Latin one cannot speak of the *una essentia* and the *tres substantiae*. *Substantia*, rather than *essentia*, is the Latin equivalent of the Greek word οὐσία, and *essentia* still sounded strange and unusual to Latin ears. As a result the expressions *una substantia* (one substance) and *tres personae* (three persons) were retained in Latin. Augustine, however, sought to avoid *substantia* altogether, both for the divine "being" and for the divine "persons." The reason was that in Latin the word *substantia* denotes that which exists in itself and is the bearer of attributes, the unchanging subject in distinction from its "accidents." Inasmuch as this dichotomy cannot occur in God, since in him the essence and the attributes coincide, Augustine deemed it better to describe the divine being as *essentia*.[94] Furthermore, just as in the East it was necessary, in the face of Sabellianism, to stress the self-existence (ὑπόστασις) of the three persons, so in the West, in the face of Arianism, it was necessary to maintain that the three persons were not three *substantiae* but three *personae*. Scholasticism, expanding this terminology, established a fixed scheme that was later taken over by theologians in general, including those of the Reformation. According to that scheme, there is in God but one being, one essence, one nature *(unitas naturae);* and there are three persons, a Trinity of persons. Within that being these three persons are one, consubstantial, coessential, and they reciprocally exist in each other (ἐμπεριχώρησις, *circumincessio personarum*). But the persons are distinct. For in God there are "two emanations, one through nature and another through the will; three hypostases: Father, Son, and Holy Spirit; four relations: paternity, filiation, active and passive spiration; five notions: innascibility, paternity, filiation, active and passive spiration; and three personal properties, the Father who is unbegotten, the Son who is begotten, the Holy Spirit who is spirated."[95]

Essence and Person

For a true understanding of the doctrine of the Trinity three questions must be answered: What is the meaning of the word "essence"? What is meant by

significance of an economy or ability (*vermögen*), which the three persons share. However, R. Seeberg (*Lehrbuch der Dogmengeschichte*, 2 vols. [Erlangen & Leipzig: A. Deichert (G. Böhme), 1895–98], I, 87) and F. Loofs (*Leitfaden zum Studium der Dogmengeschichte*, 155; and "Christologie, Kirchenlehre," *PRE³*, IV, 40) dispute this. Even Schlossmann (*Persona und προσωπον im Recht und im christlichen Dogmatik* [Kiel: Lipsius & Tischer, 1906]) denies that *persona* and *substantia* in the doctrine of the Trinity have been derived from the science of law. He believes, however, that the use of *persona* originally arose only from a "purely stylistic need" to avoid the overuse of the words Father, Son, and Holy Spirit, and that also the Greek word ὑπόστασις, like, say, the word πραγμα, initially had a very vague and general meaning. Against this, see R. Seeberg (*Theologische L. Blatt*, January 22, 1906), who makes clear that both in the East and in the West there was a *logical* (and not merely a *stylistic*) need to distinguish the "essence" and the "persons."

94. Augustine, *The Trinity*, V, 8; VII, 4.

95. Bonaventure, *Breviloquium*, I, ch. 3, 4; cf. Anselm, *Monologion*, chs. 29ff.; P. Lombard, *Sent.*, I, dist. 22ff.; T. Aquinas, *Summa theol.*, I, qu. 27–32.

the word "person"? And what is the relation between "essence" and "person" and between the persons among themselves? As for the term "being," Aristotle defined οὐσία as "a class of things that are neither present in, nor predicable of, a subject, such as the individual man or the individual horse."[96] Initially, that is how the word was used in theology and applied both to the three persons and to the one divine being. Gradually, however, οὐσία was used in another sense and became the term for the essence or nature of a thing, what Aristotle had called "the being of a thing." And so it became a synonym for nature (φύσις). Since φύσις is a derivative of φῦναι or φύω (to become or be by nature), just as *natura* comes from *nasci* (to be born), some authors considered it less well suited to describe the being or nature of God.[97] Still, the word, like the word "nature," gained currency in theology and was supported by 2 Peter 1:4. So οὐσία, φύσις, *substantia, essentia,* and *natura* became the regular terms for the one divine essence, the Godhead in general, quite apart from its "subsistence" and from its "modes of subsistence," and hence for the divine nature as it is common to all three persons. This one simple divine essence is essentially distinct from all creaturely existence and possesses all the attributes we treated earlier.

The distinction between this divine essence and the three persons in God has its analogy in the life of creatures. Here, too, we make a distinction between the nature of persons and the persons themselves. Paul, John, and Peter all possess the same human nature but, as individual persons they are distinct from that nature and from each other.[98] But a double danger immediately presents itself at this point. According to nominalism, "being"—that which is common or universal in any given category—is no more than a "name," a concept or term. Accordingly, in the doctrine of the Trinity this philosophy leads to tritheism. Excessive realism, on the other hand, associates the word "essence" with some subsistent thing that stands behind or above the persons and so leads to tetratheism or Sabellianism. Even Gregory of Nyssa did not quite succeed in surmounting this exaggerated realism. In support of the argument that God is one and that we may not speak of three Gods, he denied the applicability of number even to finite creatures. According to him, it is wrong to speak in the plural of those who share a single nature and so to speak of many people.[99] This, however, is to overlook the essential difference between God and his creatures. Undoubtedly, there is an analogy between the divine and the human nature. On account of that analogy it is proper for us

96. Aristotle, *Categoriae* 1a, in *The Works of Aristotle,* trans. E. M. Edghill, vol. 1 (Oxford: Oxford University Press, 1928).

97. [Pseudo-]Gregory of Nazianzus, "Ad Evagrium" (ed. note: "Epist. 26," in PG 46:1102–7; recognized there as *"nongenuinus"*); Pseudo-Dionysius, *The Divine Names and Mystical Theology,* ch. 2.

98. Basil, *Epist.* 43, *NPNF (2),* VIII, 146.

99. Gregory of Nyssa, "To Ablabius," *NPNF (2),* V, 529–30; cf. D. Petavius, "De trinitate," in *Theol. dogm.,* IV, ch. 9; J. Schwane, *Dogmengeschichte,* II², 156ff.; I. A. Dorner, *History of the Development of the Doctrine of the Person of Christ,* II, 315ff.; J. Kleutgen, *Die Theologie der Vorzeit vertheidigt,* 2d ed., 2 vols. (Münster: Theissing, 1878), III, 85ff.

to speak of "nature" also with reference to God. At the same time this analogy also presupposes a very important difference. The concept of the nature
of humans is a generic concept. Indeed, human nature exists, not outside of
and above, but *in* people, *in* individual persons. Still it exists in every human
in a unique and finite way. Like the gods in polytheism, humans are of like
substance but not of the same or of one substance. Human nature as it exists
in different people is never totally and quantitatively the same. For that reason
people are not only distinct but also separate. In God all this is different. The
divine nature cannot be conceived as an abstract generic concept, nor does it
exist as a substance outside of, above, and behind the divine persons. It exists
in the divine persons and is totally and quantitatively the same in each person.
The persons, though distinct, are not separate. They are the same in essence,
one in essence, and the same being. They are not separated by time or space
or anything else. They all share in the same divine nature and perfections. It
is one and the same divine nature that exists in each person individually and
in all of them collectively. Consequently, there is in God but one eternal,
omnipotent, and omniscient being, having one mind, one will, and one
power.[100] The term "being" or "nature," accordingly, maintains the truth of
the oneness of God, which is so consistently featured in Scripture, implied
in monotheism, and defended also by unitarianism. Whatever distinctions
may exist in the divine being, they may not and cannot diminish the unity
of the divine nature. For in God that unity is not deficient and limited, but
perfect and absolute. Among creatures diversity in the nature of the case
implies a degree of separation and division. All created beings necessarily
exist in space and time and therefore live side by side or sequentially. But the
attributes of eternity, omnipresence, omnipotence, goodness, and so on, by
their very nature exclude all separation and division. God is absolute unity
and simplicity, without composition or division; and that unity itself is not
ethical or contractual in nature, as it is among humans, but absolute; nor is
it accidental, but it is essential to the divine being.

[223] The glory of the confession of the Trinity consists above all in the
fact that that unity, however absolute, does not exclude but includes diversity.
God's being is not an abstract unity or concept, but a fullness of being, an
infinite abundance of life, whose diversity, so far from diminishing the unity,
unfolds it to its fullest extent. In theology the distinctions within the divine
being—which Scripture refers to by the names of Father, Son, and Spirit—are
called "persons." In the East theologians initially used the word πρόσωπον for
person, a word that corresponded to the Hebrew פָּנִים, meaning face, external appearance, role. But this word was open to misunderstanding. Sabellius
taught that the one divine οὐσία or ὑπόστασις assumed different πρόσωπα or
faces. Challenging this interpretation, the church fathers contended that the
three πρόσωπα in the divine being were not simply appearances or modes of

---

100. Athanasian Creed, 9–18.

revelation, but "enhypostatic προσωπα," that they consisted in *hypostases*. Thus προσωπον was replaced by ὑποστασις, a word that first of all means "basis, substructure, firmness," and second, that which is real and does not merely consist in appearance, or that which exists independently in distinction from "accidents" that inhere in something else.[101]

In the West the Latin word "persona" was used, a word that first of all meant "mask"; then it came to describe the role of an actor; from here it began to refer to the condition, quality, or capacity in which a person acted, and in jurisprudence it meant a person's standing before the law. This term, accordingly, was also fairly woolly; and in Tertullian it even became interchangeable with words such as "name," "species," "form," "degree," "thing." The word was nevertheless kept in Latin even when in the East προσωπον had been replaced by ὑποστασις, the reason being that the word ὑποστασις had no suitable equivalent in Latin. The term "substantia" would not do because it was already in use for "essence." This difference in terminology, however, repeatedly occasioned misunderstanding between the East and the West. The Greeks related the Latin *persona* to their word προσωπον, and the Latins in turn understood ὑποστασις to mean *substantia*. Each party criticized the other for the poverty of their language. Basically, however, both parties taught the same thing, namely, that the three divine persons are not "modes" but "subsistences." Thus, in the language of the church the word προσωπον or *persona* acquired as an essential feature the quality of self-existence, ὑποστασις, subsistence. In Athanasius and the Cappadocians the word ὑποστασις still has that meaning. But later the word *persona* gained still another characteristic. If the word *persona* meant no more than ὑποστασις, self-existence, in distinction from "accident," it could also be used of *things*. In the christological controversy theologians were forced, in the face of Nestorianism and Monophysitism, to devise a more exact definition of the words "nature" and "person." Thus, in *Concerning the Two Natures and One Person of Christ*, a work attributed to Boethius, *persona* was defined as "an individual substance possessing a rational nature." The word "persona" now expresses two things: self-existence and rationality (or self-consciousness). This is its meaning in scholasticism,[102] as well as in the works of the older Roman Catholic, Lutheran, and Reformed dogmaticians.[103]

"Personality" in God

In modern philosophy and psychology, however, a very different conception of personality has surfaced. In the first place, scholars began increasingly

101. Cf. also the use of the word ὑποστασις in the New Testament (2 Cor. 9:4; 11:17; Heb. 1:3; 3:14; 11:1); and see H. Cremer, *Biblico-Theological Lexicon of New Testament Greek*, s.v. "ὑποστασις."

102. P. Lombard, *Sent.*, I, dist. 23 (cf. 25–26); T. Aquinas, *Summa theol.*, I, qu. 29; Bonaventure, *Sent.*, I, dist. 23, qu. I; and dist. 25.

103. D. Petavius, "De trinitate," in *Theol. dogm.*, IV, ch. 9; H. F. F. Schmid, *The Doctrinal Theology of the Evangelical Lutheran Church*, 132ff.; T. Beza, *Tractationum theologicarum*, I, 646; J. Zanchi(us), *Op. theol.*, I, 13; S. Maresius, *Syst. theol.*, III, 7; *Synopsis purioris theologiae*, VII, 8.

to believe that personality can only be the mode of existence of finite beings and, therefore, that in respect to God one cannot speak of personality, nor therefore of self-consciousness and self-determination.

If God exists, he is nothing but the all-powerful, everywhere-present, unconscious force and drive that is present in all things. Second, in psychology the idea arose that even human personality in no way implies independent existence. "I-ness," the soul, is not a substance but merely the nominalistic sum of psychical phenomena, and what is called personality is but the passing mode of existence of the individual being, called a human. Third, from this it was inferred that personality, viewed as the highest stage in the development of a human being, is the final goal a human had to strive for, the greatest good a person can hope to attain. "Personality," wrote Goethe, "and personality alone is the highest happiness attainable by earthlings." Fourth, this naturally led to the hero worship and deification of those individuals who had reached this apex of development and attained personhood. Connected with this view in the minds of some is the hope that such humans who by dint of great effort have reached this pinnacle of development will—either here or in the hereafter—achieve immortality (the doctrine of conditional immortality).

Now even in the case of humans this concept of personality fails to cut ice if for no other reason than that personality, "I-ness," is something other and something more than the sum of psychical phenomena. But it is even much less applicable in the doctrine of the Trinity. Here the term "person" has a meaning of its own. Even Boethius's definition fits much better in the doctrine of Christ than in that of the Trinity. The most solid theologians of the past have always sensed this. Richard of St. Victor rejected this definition because it speaks of "individual substance" and therefore defines "person" as "the incommunicable existence of the divine nature."[104] Calvin defined "person" simply as "subsistence in God's essence."[105] All recognized the truth of Augustine's saying: We speak of persons "not to express what that is but only not to be silent."[106] In the dogma of the Trinity the word "person" simply means that the three persons in the divine being are not "modes" but have a distinct existence of their own. The emphasis here in no way lies on the elements of rationality and self-consciousness, for this follows naturally from the fact that all three persons have the same being and attributes and hence the same knowledge and wisdom. What does come out in the term "person," however, is that the unity of the divine being opens itself up in a threefold existence. It is "a unity that derives the Trinity from within its own self." The persons are not three revelational modes of the one divine personality; the divine being is tripersonal, precisely because it is the absolute divine personality.

104. Richard of St. Victor, *De trinitate*, IV, 21.
105. J. Calvin, *Institutes*, I.xiii.6; cf. H. Alting, *Theologia problematica nova*, III, qu. 31.
106. Augustine, *The Trinity*, V, 9; VI, 10; cf. Anselm, *Monologion*, ch. 37, 38; J. Calvin, *Institutes*, I.xiii.2–4; C. Braun, *Der Begriff "Person" in seiner Anwendung auf die Lehre von der Trinität und Incarnation* (Mainz: F. Kirchheim, 1876).

In humans we witness only a faint analogy of divine personality. Personality in humans arises only because they are subjects who confront themselves as object and unite the two (subject and object) in an act of self-consciousness. Hence, three moments (constituents) constitute the essence of human personality. We use the word "moments" advisedly: in our case they are but moments. In God, however, because he is not subject to space or time, to extension or division, thes0e three are not moments but "hypostases," modes of existence of one and the same being. This comparison between divine and human personality, however, is deficient in still another respect. Human nature is far too rich to be embodied in a single individual. It is therefore present in many persons and comes to its full development only in humanity as a whole. The divine nature similarly develops its fullness in three persons, but in God these three persons are not three individuals alongside each other and separated from each other but a threefold self-differentiation within the divine being. This self-differentiation results from the self-unfolding of the divine nature into personality, thus making it tri-personal. In the case of human nature there is a dual process of unfolding: in the individual, human nature unfolds itself into personality; in the race as a whole, human nature unfolds itself into many individuals, who in turn together constitute a unity or personality, just as Christ and the church together constitute one full-grown person (1 Cor. 12:12; Eph. 4:13). Now this dual unfolding, which in humanity can be no other than it is, is single in God: the unfolding of his being into personality coincides with that of his being unfolding into three persons. The three persons are the one divine personality brought to complete self-unfolding, a self-unfoldment arising out of, by the agency of, and within the divine being.

[224] From this account we may derive an idea of how to answer the question concerning the relation between the being (essence) and the person and between the persons among themselves. In Tertullian the three persons are of one substance, of one condition, of one power, and together they constitute the one God. They are three, "not in status but in degree," yet "one God from whom these degrees and forms and aspects are defined in the name of the Father, the Son, and the Holy Spirit." There is "distinction and distribution, but no contradiction or division." Athanasius and the Cappadocians define the *hypostases* as "modes of subsistence" (τροποι ὑπαρξεως), thereby saying that, though one in being, they each had an existence of their own and therefore differed in the manner of their existence. Hence, the distinction between being (essence) and person and between the persons among themselves played itself out in their reciprocal relations in the fact of their being Father, Son, and Spirit, in the following properties: paternity (ἀγεννησια, unbegottenness), sonship (γεννησις, begottenness), and sanctification (ἐκπορευσις, procession).

All this was worked out in greater detail by Augustine. He does not derive the Trinity from the Father but from the unity of the divine essence, nor does he conceive of it as accidental but rather as an essential characteristic of the divine being. It belongs to God's very essence to be triune. In that regard personhood is identical with God's being itself. "For to God it is not one thing to be and another to be a person, but it is altogether the same thing" (*De trin.*, VII, 6). For if being belonged to God in an absolute sense, and personhood in a relative sense, the three persons could not be one being. Each person, therefore, is identical with the entire being and equal to the other two or all three together. With created beings that is different. One person does not equal three but, says Augustine, "in God that is not so, for the Father, the Son, and the Holy Spirit together are not a greater being than the Father alone or the Son alone; but these three substances or persons, if they must be so called, are at one and the same time equal to each individually" (*De trin.*, VII, 6). "In the full Trinity one is only as much as the three are altogether, nor are two any more than one. They are, moreover, finite in themselves. So each [person] is in each [person], and all are in each, and all are one" (*De trin.*, VI, 10). The Trinity itself is as great as each person in it (*De trin.*, VIII, 1). Accordingly, the distinction between being and person and between the persons among themselves cannot lie in any substance but only in their mutual relations. "Hence, whatever is said concerning God with respect to himself is both said of each person individually, that is, of the Father, the Son, and the Holy Spirit, and at the same time of the Trinity itself, not in the plural but in the singular" (*De trin.*, V, 8). "Moreover, whatever the individual parts are called in the same Trinity, they are in no way so called relative to themselves but relative to one another or to the creature, and therefore it is obvious that these things are said with respect to their relations and not to their essence" (*De trin.*, V, 11). Later theology, accordingly, asserted that "being" and "person" did not differ essentially but "in reason," not, however, in mere reasoning, that is, rationally, or nominally, as Sabellius believed, but in objective rational analysis. The difference did not consist in any substance but only in the relations, but this distinction is grounded in revelation and therefore objective and real. The difference really exists, namely, in the mode of existence. The persons are modes of existence within the being; hence, the persons differ among themselves as one mode of existence differs from another, or—as the illustration has it—as the open palm differs from the closed fist.[107]

DISTINCTIONS AMONG THE THREE PERSONS

If this distinction between "being" and "person," and between the persons among themselves, has to be rendered in a single word or phrase, there is indeed not much more that can be said about it. But the whole distinction becomes clearer when we enter into the relations that produce this differentiation in the divine being. Although Scripture is rigorously monotheistic, it does ascribe a

107. T. Aquinas, *Summa theol.*, I, qu. 28ff.; D. Petavius, "De trinitate," in *Theol. dogm.*, IV, chs. 10–11; J. Kleutgen, *Die Theologie der Vorzeit*, I, 350ff.; J. Calvin, *Institutes*, I.xiii.6, 16–20; J. Zanchi(us), *Op. theol.*, I, 21ff.; B. de Moor, *Comm. in Marckii Comp.*, I, 713ff.; F. Turretin, *Institutes of Elenctic Theology*, III, qu. 27.

divine nature and divine perfections also to the Son and the Spirit and puts them on a par with the Father. The Father, the Son, and the Spirit, accordingly, are distinct subjects in the one divine essence. As such they bear different names, have distinct personal properties, and always appear in a certain order, but in their "inward" and "outward" relations. The distinctness of the individual persons, therefore, arises totally from the so-called "personal properties": (1) paternity ("unbegottenness," active generation, and active spiration); (2) filiation or sonship, passive generation, active spiration; (3) procession or passive spiration. These personal attributes, in the nature of the case, add nothing substantially new to the being. A human person who becomes a father does not fundamentally change, but only acts in a relation that had been foreign to him earlier. So also the divine being is not substantially different from being Father, Son, and Spirit but only relationally. One and the same being is, and is called, "Father" when it is understood in his relation to that same being in the person of the Son. The persons differ individually only in that one is Father, the other Son, and the third Spirit.

A weak analogy, though it may prove helpful, is one that occurs among us humans. Among us fatherhood and sonship, though only a relationship, presuppose a personal individual subject who is the bearer of one or the other relationship but otherwise exists in various ways outside of that fatherhood and sonship. Fatherhood is only an incidental attribute of being human; some men never become fathers; those who do were, for a long time prior to this event, nonfathers and after the event also gradually cease to be fathers. Accordingly, our humanity as men is far from being exhausted by our being fathers or sons. But this is not how it is in the divine being. In him being God and personhood completely coincide. "Just as for him to be is to be God, or to be great or good, and so forth, thus also for him to be is to be personal."[108] In each of the three persons, we might say, the divine being is completely coextensive with being Father, Son, and Spirit. Paternity, filiation, and procession, so far from being accidental properties of the divine being, are the eternal modes of existence of, and the eternal immanent relations within, that being. In humans the unfolding of the one human nature is classifiable in segments. In part it occurs in the individual as he or she becomes a personality; it further occurs in humanity as a whole, as its individual members represent human nature in a particular way; and finally human nature unfolds along the lines of gender and blood relationships, which in each case again reveal a different aspect of human nature.

In the case of humans this triple unfolding of nature is extended in space and over time. It is essentially expansive. In God, however, there is no separation or division. The unfolding of his being into personality immediately, absolutely, and completely coincides with, and includes, the unfolding of his being into persons, as well as that of the immanent relations expressed in the

108. Augustine, *The Trinity*, VII, 6.

names "Father," "Son," and "Spirit." Thus God is archetypically related to humanity. That which in the case of human beings is separate and juxtaposed, extended in space and over time, is eternally and simply present in God. The processions in his being simultaneously bring about in God his absolute personality, his trinitarian character, and his immanent relations. They are the absolute archetypes of all those processions by which human nature achieves its full development in the individual, in the family, and in humanity as a whole. For that reason the three persons, though distinct from each other, are not different. The "threeness" derives from, exists in, and serves the "oneness." The unfolding of the divine being occurs within that being, thus leaving the oneness and simplicity of that being undiminished. Furthermore, although the three persons do not differ in essence, they are distinct subjects, hypostases, or subsistences, which precisely for that reason bring about within the being of God the complete unfolding of that being. Finally, the three persons are, by generation and spiration, related to each other in an absolute manner; their personal distinctness as subjects completely coincides with their immanent interpersonal relationships. The Father is only and eternally Father; the Son is only and eternally Son; the Spirit is only and eternally Spirit. And inasmuch as each person is himself in an eternal, simple, and absolute manner, the Father is God, the Son is God, and the Holy Spirit is God. The Father is God as Father; the Son is God as Son; the Holy Spirit is God as Holy Spirit. And inasmuch as all three are God, they all partake of one single divine nature. Hence, there is but one God, Father, Son, and Holy Spirit. May he be praised forever!

Father: Unbegotten

[225] Having thus set forth the doctrine of the Trinity in general, we must now discuss the three persons separately. The first person is the Father, and his personal attribute is his fatherhood or his "nonbegottenness" (ἀγγενησια). In the Arian controversy this word ἀγγενησια played a prominent role. It was simply taken over from the Greek vernacular. Plato called the ideas "ingenerate" (ἀγεννητους); Aristotle used the word to describe matter; the Gnostics spoke of God as "ingenerate profundity" (βυθος ἀγεννητος).[109]

Paul of Samosata and the Arians Aetius and Eunomius took over this terminology in order by it to combat the doctrine of the "homoousia" (coessentiality) of the Son and the Spirit with the Father. The "unbegottenness," in contrast to all created beings, expressed God's essential nature. The Son, however, is not "unbegotten" (ἀγεννητος): in Scripture he is called the "only begotten" (μονογενης) and orthodoxy calls him "begotten." Hence, he cannot be God and must be a creature. We may not posit the existence of two "ingenerates," that is, two Gods.[110] Note, however, that in Greek there are two words: γεννητος, derived from the verb γεννᾶν, to beget, bring forth; and γενητος, a derivative of

---

109. Irenaeus, *Against Heresies*, I, 1.
110. Athanasius, *Against the Arians*, I, 31ff.; idem, *Defence of the Nicene Definition*, NPNF (2), IV, 149–72; Basil, *Against Eunomius*, II, 25ff.

γινεσθαι, to come into being, be born. Of the two the latter is by far the broader term and denotes all that has been brought forth and has a beginning, whether it is by creation, generation, or procreation. Initially these two words were not always clearly distinguished from each other. It was simply pointed out that the word ἀγέννητος or ἀγένητος could be used in different ways and could be applied to the Son in one sense and not in the other. But gradually it became customary to make a distinction between the two. In contrast to created beings, all three persons could be called ἀγένητος (unbegotten). Not one of them had been brought forth in the manner of creatures; none had a beginning in time. Ἀγένητος is an attribute of the divine being that is common to all three persons. To be distinguished from it, however, is the word ἀγεννησία, an attribute of the Father alone. The Son could be called γεννητός (begotten), not because he had been brought forth as a creature in time, but because he was generated out of the being of the Father from eternity.[111] The church fathers at the same time pointed out that the attribute ἀγεννησία pertains to the person, not the being. God's being is the same in all three persons, but ἀγεννησία is a relation within the being. Just as Adam, Eve, and Abel have the same nature, though each received it in a different way, so also in God the nature is the same, though it exists differently in each of the three persons.[112] Add to this that the word ἀγεννησία is negative and merely states that the Father transcends generation, but tells us nothing positive about God's nature. Actually, therefore, it is not a description of the person of the Father at all, for being ἀγέννητον and being Father is not at all the same thing.[113] The name "Father," accordingly, is to be preferred over the term ἀγέννητος.[114]

The scriptural name "Father" is a much better description of the personal property of the first person. Implied in the word "fatherhood" is a positive relation to the second person. The name "Father" is even more appropriate than the word "God," for the latter is a general name signifying transcendent dignity, but the name "Father," like that of YHWH in the Old Testament, is a proper name, an attribute describing a personal property of God. Those who deny to God the name "Father" dishonor him even more than those who deny his creation. This name of "Father," accordingly, is not a metaphor derived from the earth and attributed to God. Exactly the opposite is true: fatherhood on earth is but a distant and vague reflection of the fatherhood of God (Eph. 3:14–15). God is Father in the true and complete sense of the term. Among humans a father is also someone else's son, and a son in turn becomes a father. Here, too, a father cannot bring forth a son by himself; fatherhood is temporary

111. Cf. Athanasius; Basil, *Against Eunomius*; John of Damascus, *The Orthodox Faith*, I, 8; Augustine, *The Trinity*, V, 3; D. Petavius, "De trinitate," in *Theol. dogm.*, V, chs. 1–3; J. C. Suicerus, *Thesaurus ecclesiasticus*, s.v. "ἀγεννησία."

112. Athanasius, *Defence of the Nicene Definition*, 8; Gregory of Nazianzus, *Theological Orations*, V.

113. Basil, *Against Eunomius*, I, 9, 15; Gregory of Nazianzus, *Theological Orations*, III; Augustine, *The Trinity*, V, 5.

114. Basil, *Against Eunomius*, I, 5.

and accidental, not essentially bound up with being human. It starts relatively late in life; it also ends rather soon, in any case at death. But in God all this is different. He is solely, purely, and totally Father. He is Father alone; he is Father by nature and Father eternally, without beginning or end. For that reason also generation has to be eternal, for if the Son were not eternal, the Father could not be eternal either. The eternity of the Father carries with it the eternity of the Son.[115] Addressing God as Father, one by implication also addresses the Son. In virtue of this relation to the Son and his relation to the Spirit, the Father was often called "self-born" (αὐτογενης), "self-generated" (αὐτογενητος), "uncreated" (αὐτοφυης), "without beginning" (ἀποιητος), "self-originated" (ἀναρχος), "the ground of his own substance," "self-caused"; and further, the beginning (ἀρχη), cause (αἰτια), root (ῥιζα), fount (πηγη), origin or head (etc.) of the Son and of the Spirit or of the Godhead as a whole.[116]

Son: Generation or Filiation

[226] The special qualification of the second person in the Trinity is filiation. In Scripture he bears several names that denote his relation to the Father, such as word, wisdom, logos, son, the firstborn, only-begotten and only son, the image of God, image (εἰκων), substance (ὑποστασις), stamp (χαρακτηρ) [cf. Heb. 1:3]. The doctrine of "eternal generation" (αἰωνος γεννησις), so called for the first time by Origen, was based on these names and a few texts cited above. In using these terms we are of course speaking in a human and hence an imperfect language, a fact that makes us cautious.[117] Yet we have the right to speak this language. For just as the Bible speaks analogically of God's ear, eye, and mouth, so human generation is an analogy and image of the divine deed by which the Father gives the Son "to have life in himself." But when we resort to this imagery, we must be careful to remove all associations with imperfection and sensuality from it. The generation of a human being is imperfect and flawed. A husband needs a wife to bring forth a son. No man can ever fully impart his image, his whole nature, to a child or even to many children. A man becomes a father only in the course of time and then stops being a father, and a child soon becomes wholly independent from and self-reliant vis-à-vis his or her father. But it is not so with God. Generation occurs also in the divine being. God's fecundity is a beautiful theme, one that frequently recurs in the church fathers. God is no abstract, fixed, monadic, solitary substance, but a plenitude of life. It is his nature (οὐσια) to be generative (γεννητικη) and fruitful (καρπογονος). It is capable of expansion, unfolding, and communication. Those who deny this fecund productivity fail to take seriously the fact that God is an infinite fullness of blessed life. All such people have left is an abstract deistic

---

115. Athanasius, *Against the Arians*, I, 23, 28; Gregory of Nazianzus, *Theological Orations*, III, 5, 17; John of Damascus, *The Orthodox Faith*, I, 8; Hilary, *De trinitate contra Arianos*, XII, 24.

116. D. Petavius, "De trinitate," in *Theol. dogm.*, V, ch. 5; J. C. Suicerus, s.v. "ἀγεννησια."

117. Irenaeus, *Against Heresies*, II, 28, 6; Athanasius, *Against the Arians*, II, 36; Basil, *Against Eunomius*, II, 22, 24; Gregory of Nazianzus, *Theological Orations*, XX.

concept of God, or to compensate for this sterility, in pantheistic fashion they include the life of the world in the divine being. Apart from the Trinity even the act of creation becomes inconceivable. For if God cannot communicate himself, he is a darkened light, a dry spring, unable to exert himself outward to communicate himself to creatures.[118]

Still, that generation is to be conceived in divine terms. In the first place, it is *spiritual*. The Arians, in opposing the idea of divine generation, objected that all generation necessarily brings along with it separation (τομη) and division (διαιρεσις), passion (παθος) and emanation (ἀπορροια). And that would be correct if it were physical, sensual, and creaturely. But it is spiritual, divine, and therefore simple, without division (ἀρρευστως) or separation (ἀδιαιρετως). It occurs without flux and division.[119] While giving rise to distinction and distribution in the divine being, it does not create divergence and division. Athanasius writes: "Inasmuch as God is simple, the Father of the Son is indivisible and without passion, for although in the case of humans we speak of outflow and inflow, we cannot predicate these things of anything that is incorporeal."[120] The most striking analogy of divine generation is thought and speech, and Scripture itself suggests this when it calls the Son "Logos" [Speech, Word, Reason]. Just as the human mind objectivizes itself in speech, so God expresses his entire being in the Logos [Christ]. But here, too, we must note the difference. Humans need many words to express their ideas. These words are sounds and therefore material, sense-related. They have no existence by themselves. But when God speaks, he totally expresses himself in the one person of the Logos, whom he also "granted to have life in himself" (John 5:26 NIV).

In the second place, therefore, divine generation implies that the Father begets the Son out of the being of the Father, "God of God, Light of Light, very God of very God; begotten, not made, being of one substance with the Father," as the Nicene symbol has it. The Arians, by contrast, contended that the Son had been brought forth by the will of the Father out of nothing. This, however, is not generation but creation, as John of Damascus points out. Creation is "the bringing into being, from the outside and not from the substance of the Creator, of something created and made entirely dissimilar [in substance]," while "begetting" means "producing of the substance of the begetter an offspring similar in substance to the begetter."[121] The Son is not a creature but he is "God over all, forever praised!" (Rom. 9:5 NIV). Accordingly, he was not brought forth by the will of the Father out of nothing and in time. Rather, he is generated out of the being of the Father in eternity. Hence, instead of viewing "generation" as an actual work, a performance (ἐνεργεια), of the Father, we should ascribe to the Father "a generative nature" (φυσις γεννητικη).

118. Athanasius, *Against the Arians*, II, 2; John of Damascus, *The Orthodox Faith*, I, 8.

119. Athanasius, *Statement of Faith*, 2.

120. Athanasius, *Defence of the Nicene Definition*, 11; idem, *Against the Arians*, I, 16, 28ff.

121. John of Damascus, *The Orthodox Faith*, I, 8; cf. Athanasius, *Defence of the Nicene Definition*, 13–26; idem, *Against the Arians*, I, 5–6.

This is not to say, of course, that the generation is an unconscious and unwilled emanation, occurring apart from the will and power of the Father. It is not an act of an antecedent decreeing will, like creation, but one that is so divinely natural to the Father that his concomitant will takes perfect delight in it. It is a manifestation of what is truly expressive of his nature and essence, and therefore also of his knowledge, will, and power, in fact of all his virtues.[122]

In the third place, therefore, the church confesses its belief in the eternal character of this generation. The Arians said that there was a time when the Son did not exist (ἦν ποτε ὅτε οὐκ ἦν). They appealed especially to the words "he brought me forth," or "created me" in Proverbs 8:22, and pointed out the antinomy between the terms "eternal" (αἰωνος) and "begetting" (γεννησις). But if the "Father" and the "Son" bear their names in a metaphysical sense, as Scripture incontrovertibly teaches, it follows that the generation in question has to be eternal as well. For if the Son is not eternal, then of course God is not the eternal Father either. In that case he was God before he was Father, and only later—in time—became Father. Hence, rejection of the eternal generation of the Son involves not only a failure to do justice to the deity of the Son, but also to that of the Father. It makes him changeable, robs him of his divine nature, deprives him of the eternity of his fatherhood, and leaves unexplained how God can truly and properly be called "Father" in time if the basis for calling him "Father" is not eternally present in his nature.[123] We must, accordingly, conceive that generation as being eternal in the true sense of the word. It is not something that was completed and finished at some point in eternity, but an eternal unchanging act of God, at once always complete and eternally ongoing. Just as it is natural for the sun to shine and for a spring to pour out water, so it is natural for the Father to generate the Son. The Father is not and never was ungenerative; he begets everlastingly. "The Father did not by a single act beget the Son and then release him from his 'genesis,' but generates him perpetually."[124] For God to beget is to speak, and his speaking is eternal.[125] God's offspring is eternal.

122. Athanasius, *Against the Arians*, III, 59–67; Gregory of Nazianzus, *Theological Orations*, III, 6ff.; *Cyril of Alexandria, *De trin.*, II. Ed note: It is not clear if Bavinck is referring to Cyril's treatise *Thesaurus de sancta et consubstantiali Trinitate* (PG 75:9–656) or to *De sancta et consubstantiali Trinitate* (PG 75:657–1124). According to Quasten (*Patrology*, III, 126), the third trinitarian treatise in Migne, *De sancta et vivifica trinitate* (PG 75:1147–90), "is not by Cyril, but by Theodoret of Cyrus." Cf. *Patrology*, III, 546; Hilary, *De trinitate*, III, 4; Augustine, *The Trinity*, XV, 20; P. Lombard, *Sent.*, I, dist. 6–7; T. Aquinas, *Summa theol.*, I, qu. 41, art. 2.

123. Athanasius, *Defence of the Nicene Definition*, 26ff.; idem, *On the Opinion of Dionysius*, 14ff.; idem, *Against the Arians*, I, 12ff.; Basil, *Against Eunomius*, II, 14ff.; idem, *On the Spirit*, 14ff.; Gregory of Nazianzus, *Theological Orations*, III, 3ff.

124. Origen, *S.P.N. Cyrilli archiepiscopi Alexandrini Homiliae XIX. in Ieremiam prophetam*, IX, 4; idem, *On First Principles*, I, 2, 2.

125. Athanasius, *Against the Arians*, I, 14, 20; IV, 12; idem, *On the Opinion of Dionysius*, 15–16; John of Damascus, *The Orthodox Faith*, I, 8; Augustine, *The Trinity*, VI, 1; T. Aquinas, *Summa theol.*, I, qu. 42, art. 2; A. Polanus, *Syn. theol.*, III, ch. 4; G. Voetius, *Select. disp.*, V, 632; *Synopsis purioris theologiae*, VIII, 11; J. H. Scholten, *De Leer der Hervormde Kerk in Hare Grondbeginselen*, 207.

Spirit: Procession

[227] The third person in the Trinity is called the Holy Spirit, and his personal property is "procession" (ἐκπόρευσις) or "spiration" (πνοη). In Christian theology the doctrine of the Holy Spirit has consistently been treated only after that of the Son. While with reference to the second person, the crux of the controversy was almost always his deity—generally speaking, his personhood was not in dispute—in the case of the Holy Spirit it was his personhood that primarily sparked the polemics. If his personality was acknowledged, his deity followed naturally. Along with the Son's deity also that of the Spirit had to be accepted. Pneumatomachians of earlier and later date, however, lodged an assortment of objections against both the personality and deity of the Holy Spirit. They claimed that in Scripture the name "God" was never applied to the Holy Spirit; that there is no mention anywhere of his being worshiped; and that he is repeatedly presented as a power and gift of God. The few instances in which he is represented as a person must be understood as personifications.

Gregory of Nazianzus explained the intense controversy of his day with respect to the Holy Spirit by saying (1) that the Old Testament had clearly revealed the Father but not so clearly the Son, while (2) the New Testament had clearly brought out the divine nature of the Son but had only dimly alluded to the Holy Spirit. Now, however, the Holy Spirit dwells among us and makes himself fully known to us.[126] Contained in this statement, we must admit, is an undeniable element of truth. The personality and deity of the Holy Spirit do not confront us as forcefully and objectively as those of the Father and the Son. The name he bears does not express that personality as plainly as the terms "Father" and "Son." The specific "economy" of the Spirit in the Trinity, namely, that of sanctification, does not stand out in such clear relief to our minds as the work of creation, incarnation, and satisfaction. We ourselves live in that "economy"; the Holy Spirit dwells in and among us, with the result that our prayers are directed more to the Father and to the Mediator than to him. He is much more the author than the object of our prayer. It is for these reasons that the personality or at least the deity of the Holy Spirit was in dispute in the church for such a long time. At first the religious significance of this doctrine was not perceived. As a rule the Spirit's personality was acknowledged, but the Spirit himself was viewed only as the one who had done his work in the past, had illumined the prophets and the apostles, and equipped and qualified Christ for his office. The necessity of interior grace was not yet understood. There was as yet no clearly felt sense of need for an omnipotent divine operation of grace in the human heart, no sense of the depth of the mystical union between God and humans. God's objective revelation in Christ seemed sufficient, and the need for the Spirit's subjective illumination was not yet realized. However, as soon as the church began to probe its own life more deeply and to account for the subjective as well as the objective principles of salvation, it acknowledged

---

126. Gregory of Nazianzus, *Theological Orations*, V.

with joy both the personality and the deity of the Holy Spirit. And so it has always been throughout the centuries. The denial of the personal existence and divine nature of the Holy Spirit always arises, consciously or unconsciously, from a rationalistic, Pelagian, deistic principle: its natural habitat is Arianism, Socinianism, Arminianism, and so on.

This immediately tells us that the confession of the personality and deity of the Holy Spirit is not a product of philosophy but proceeds from the heart of the Christian religion itself, from the faith of the church. Involved in this confession, as also with that of the deity of the Son, is a matter of profound religious importance, in fact the Christian religion itself. Scripture establishes beyond any doubt that the Holy Spirit is the subjective principle of all salvation, of regeneration, faith, conversion, repentance, sanctification, and so on; in other words, that there is no communion with the Father and the Son except in and through the Holy Spirit. The choice is clear: either the Holy Spirit is a creature—whether a power, gift, or person—or he is truly God. If he is a creature he cannot in fact and in truth communicate to us the Father and the Son with all their benefits; he cannot be the principle of the new life either in the individual Christian or in the church as a whole. In that case, there is no genuine communion between God and humans; God remains above and outside of us and does not dwell in humanity as in his temple. But the Holy Spirit is not, nor can he be, a creature. For he is related to the Son as the latter is to the Father and imparts to us both the Son and the Father. He is as closely bound up with the Son as the Son is with the Father. He is coinherent in the Son as the Son is coinherent in him. In substance he is the same as the Son. He is the Spirit of wisdom and truth, of power and of glory; the Spirit by whom Christ sanctifies the church and in whom he communicates himself and all his benefits: the divine nature, the adoption as children, the mystical union. He who gives us God himself must himself be truly God.

Added to this soteriological interest is the theological significance of the personality and deity of the Holy Spirit. Without the personality and deity of the Spirit there can be no true oneness between the Father and the Son. Those who deny the deity of the Holy Spirit cannot maintain that of the Son. The Trinity only completes itself in the divine person of the Holy Spirit. Only through that person does the unity of being in the "threeness" of the persons and the "threeness" of persons in the unity of being, come into being. The entire dogma of the Trinity, the mystery of Christianity, the heart of religion, the true and genuine communion of our souls with God—they all stand or fall with the deity of the Holy Spirit. The church fathers, understanding this interconnectedness, defended the deity of the Spirit along with that of the Son.[127] In the Niceno-Constantinopolitan Creed the church confesses its faith

---

127. Cf. Athanasius in his *Letters to Serapion*; ed. note: ET: *The Letters of Saint Athanasius concerning the Holy Spirit,* trans. C. R. B. Shapland (London: Epworth Press, 1951); Gregory of Nazianzus in his *Theological Orations, On the Holy Spirit*; Basil in his third book *Against Eunomius* and in his *On the Spirit*; Gregory of Nyssa, especially in his writing *Against Ablabius*; Hilary, *De trinitate,* XII.

"in the Holy Spirit, the Lord and giver of life, who proceeds from the Father and the Son; who together with the Father and Son is worshiped and glorified; and who spoke by the prophets." And since that time Christians everywhere confess their faith in "a consubstantial Trinity."[128]

The relation that exists between the Holy Spirit and the Father and the Son is suggested by his name "the Holy Spirit" as well as by many verbal forms, such as "given," "sent," "poured out," "breathed out," "proceeded," "descended." Christian theology in turn described this relation in terms of projection, procession, outgoing, spiration, emission, outpouring. The preferred term was "spiration." The basis for this is that Scripture calls the Holy Spirit רוּחַ (wind, spirit) and πνευμα, and repeatedly associates the Spirit with breath and wind (Ps. 33:6; Job 33:4; John 3:8; 20:22; Acts 2:2; etc.). For the rest, however, theology was modest in describing spiration. Like "generation," it has to be conceived as the eternal communication of the same essence. And although an attempt should be made to differentiate "spiration" from "generation," this was immensely difficult, inasmuch as generation gave to the Son, and spiration gave to the Spirit, the possession of "life in himself."[129] Augustine said: "Speaking of that superlatively excellent nature, who can explain the difference between 'being born' and 'proceeding'? Not everything that proceeds is born, although everything that is born proceeds, just as not every creature with two feet is a human, though every human is a biped. This much I know. But I do not know, nor do I have the skill to say, what the difference is between 'generation' on the one hand and 'procession' on the other."[130] Still, theologians searched for some kind of distinction. What they found was (1) that the Son proceeds only from the Father, but the Holy Spirit from both the Father and the Son;[131] or (2) that the Spirit proceeds from the Father and the Son, as *given* by both, not as *born* from both *(ut datus, non ut natus).*[132]

It was especially noted, however, that the Spirit could not be the Son of the Son because in that case the triad would become a "boundless fullness" and there would be no end to the generative movement of life within the divine being.[133] The Holy Spirit "by himself fully completes the all-praised and blessed Trinity." The Trinity can neither be augmented nor diminished: it is complete (τελεια).[134] Granted, replying to the Arian objection that the Father is more powerful than the Son if only he (the Father) can generate the Son by whom all things are made, Augustine wrote: "May it be far from anyone

128. Basil, in A. Hahn, G. L. Hahn, and A. von Harnack, *Bibliothek der Symbole und Glaubensregeln der alten Kirche*, 3d ed. (Breslau: E. Morgenstern, 1897), 70.

129. Athanasius, *Letter to Serapion*, I, 15ff.; Gregory of Nazianzus, *Theological Orations*, V, 7ff.; Basil, *The Holy Spirit*, 46ff.; John of Damascus, *The Orthodox Faith*, I, 8.

130. Augustine, *Contra Maximinum Arianorum episcopum*, III, 14 (PL 42:743); idem, *The Trinity*, XV, 17, 20; idem, *Lectures on the Gospel of John*, tract. 99, *NPNF (1)*, VII, 131–37.

131. Augustine, *The Trinity*, XV, 26.

132. Ibid., V, 14; D. Petavius, "De trinitate," in *Theol. dogm.*, VIII, ch. 13.

133. Basil, *Against Eunomius*, V.

134. Athanasius, *Against the Arians*, I, 18.

to think, as you do, that the Father is more powerful than the Son because the Father brought forth the creator, unlike the Son who did not. The reason for this is not that he *could not* do this but that it was *not appropriate* for him to do this." The way to understand this last statement becomes immediately clear in the sentence that follows: "Divine generation would be boundless if the generated Son would beget a grandson for the Father, . . . and the generational series would not be completed if each offspring would in turn produce another, for if one were not sufficient, neither would any number ever complete the series."[135] "Within that trinitarian essence there is no way any other person could exist of the same essence."[136] Especially Thomas and his followers, finally, describe the difference between generation and spiration by saying that generation occurred "in the manner of the intellect," while spiration took place "in the manner of the will." This distinction had its background in the tradition of comparing "generation" with thought and utterance and speaking of the Holy Spirit as the love that unites the Father and the Son. In medieval and Catholic theology this distinction became virtually universal.[137] Though Protestant theologians did assume a distinction between "generation" and "spiration"—like the distinction between "Son" and "Spirit"—and also in part acknowledged the correctness of the above distinctions,[138] they were less inclined to speak with this degree of certainty and boldness and considered this distinction insufficiently scriptural and modest.[139]

EAST AND WEST

[228] Gradually, however, an important difference developed between the East and West in the doctrine of the Trinity. In the second century the ontological procession of the Son from the Father was viewed as an eternal generation; and so a similar procession had to be assumed for the Holy Spirit who, after all, could not be pictured as situated loosely next to the Father and the Son. The time had come to determine the relation of the Spirit to the Father and the Son. On this subject Athanasius taught that the Holy Spirit is called both the Spirit of the Father and the Spirit of the Son, and that he possesses the same characteristic relation, order, or nature (ἰδιοτης, ταξις, φυσις) to the Son as the Son does to the Father.[140] He is said to proceed (ἐκπορευεσθαι) from

135. Augustine, *Contra Maximinum;* Athanasius, *Against the Arians*, III, 12.

136. Augustine, *The Trinity*, VII, 6; T. Aquinas, *Summa theol.*, I, qu. 27, art. 5.

137. T. Aquinas, *Summa theol.*, I, qu. 27; idem, *Summa contra gentiles*, IV, 13, 15ff.; Bonaventure, *Breviloquium*, I, ch. 3; T. Aquinas, Bonaventure, et al., in *Sent.*, I, dist. 13; D. Petavius, "De trinitate," in *Theol. dogm.*, VII, ch. 13.

138. P. Melanchthon, *Loci communes*, "De filio"; J. H. Alsted, *Theologia scholastica didactica*, 137, 145; S. Maresius, *Syst. theol.*, III, 28.

139. J. A. Quenstedt, *Theologia*, I, 387ff.; D. Hollaz, *Examen theologicum acroamaticum*, 341ff.; J. Zanchi(us), *Op. theol.*, I, 255; G. Voetius, *Select. disp*, V, 139; *Synopsis purioris theologiae*, IX, 14; B. de Moor, *Comm. in Marckii Comp.*, I, 791.

140. Athanasius, *Letter to Serapion*, I, 21; III, 1.

the Father because he is sent and bestowed by the Logos, who is from the Father.[141] As the One who proceeds from the Father, the Holy Spirit cannot be separated from, and is always in, the hands of the Father, who sends him, and of the Son, who sustains him.[142] He is not the brother or son of the Son but is the Spirit of the Father, just as the Son is Son of the Father.[143] But though the Spirit is not called "Son," he is not separate from the Son (ἐκτὸς τοῦ υἱοῦ), for he is called the Spirit of wisdom and of adoption. If we have the Spirit, we have the Son, and vice versa. Just why the one is called "Son" and the other "Spirit" is incomprehensible, but that is what Scripture teaches.[144] The Spirit, "the image of the Son" (εἰκὼν τοῦ υἱοῦ),[145] is united with the Son, just as the Son is united with the Father. Athanasius, accordingly, very clearly teaches the Spirit's dependence on the Son but not in so many words that he proceeds from the Father *and* the Son.

The three Cappadocians speak in the same vein. They clearly teach that the Holy Spirit is related to the Son as the Son is related to the Father;[146] that in order he follows the Son; that the Spirit gives us the Son and the Father; that he proceeds from the Father and is conceived subsequent to, and along with, the Son; that he is from the Father and through the Son; and that the distinct names given to the three persons arise from their relation to each other.[147] But the Spirit's procession from the Son was neither expressed nor denied. That question simply did not arise at the time. Accordingly, in the works of Gregory of Nyssa, Epiphanius, Didymus, Cyril (et al.) we do find expressions that seem to teach the procession of the Holy Spirit from the Son. They use the prepositions παρά (from the side of) and ἐκ (out of) and say that the Holy Spirit takes everything from Christ and that Christ is the source of the Holy Spirit (John 7:38). They declare that the Spirit derives his being from the being of the Father and the Son and that he is the image, the mouth, and the breath of the Son. They acknowledge that he is the third person, in order following the Son, and receives all things from the Father through the Son (etc.).[148]

Still, in the East the development of the doctrine of the Trinity took a different direction from that of the West. Cyril—opposing Nestorius, who reversed the order of the persons, making Christ dependent on the Spirit—taught, in complete agreement with the Greek fathers, that the Spirit proceeded from the Father through the Son (διὰ τοῦ υἱοῦ).[149] John of Damascus similarly states that the Spirit is also the Spirit of the Son, since he is revealed and communi-

---

141. Ibid., I, 20.
142. Athanasius, *Statement of Faith*, 4; idem, *On the Opinion of Dionysius*, 17.
143. Athanasius, *Letter to Serapion*, I, 16; IV, 3.
144. Ibid., IV, 4–5.
145. Ibid., I, 24, 26; IV, 3.
146. Ibid., I, 31.
147. Gregory of Nazianzus, *Theological Orations*, V, 9; Basil, *Against Eunomius*, III, 1ff.; *On the Spirit*, V.
148. Cf. D. Petavius, "De trinitate," in *Theol. dogm.*, VII, chs. 3–7.
149. J. Schwane, *Dogmengeschichte*, II², 204.

cated by the Son. He goes on to say that the Spirit proceeds from the Father *through the Son*. But he expressly rejects the idea that he is from the Son and receives his existence from him. The Son and the Spirit are traceable to one single cause.[150] And this has remained the doctrine of the Greek Orthodox Church ever since.[151] Whereas the East did not go beyond the theology of the fathers, the West did. Tertullian had already started deriving the Trinity, not from the person of the Father, but from the being of God, and already wrote: "I think the Spirit proceeds from no other source than the Father through the Son."[152] Hilary puts the Spirit in the same relation to the Son as the Son to the Father and states that the Spirit proceeds from the Father and is sent and dispensed by the Son, and indeed, has the Son as Author.[153] But it is especially Augustine who went beyond the thinking of the Greek fathers. He views the three persons as relations in the one simple Godhead and therefore has to put the Spirit in relation not only to the Father but also to the Son. Augustine clearly teaches, accordingly, that the Holy Spirit is related both to the Father and the Son, that he is "a certain ineffable communion between the Father and the Son." Expressed in the names "Father" and "Son," admittedly, is only the mutual relatedness and not the relation to the Spirit. That relation cannot be properly expressed in human language. But the Spirit is nevertheless described as a gift from the Father and the Son. Not only the Father but also the Son is the Spirit's originating cause *(principium)*. But the Father and the Son are not two *principia,* any more than the Father, the Son, and the Spirit are the three *principia* of creation. Indeed not: the Father and the Son are one single *principium* of the Spirit. The Son also received from the Father the role of causing the Spirit to proceed from him along with the Father; for the Son cannot differ in any way from the Father other than in his being the Son.[154]

After Augustine this doctrine of the Holy Spirit's procession is found in the symbol of the Synod of Toledo (circa 400), in the letter of Leo I to Turribius (447), in the Athanasian Creed (no. 23), and in the symbol of the third synod of Toledo (589), which inserted the phrase "and of the Son" *(filioque)* into the text of the Nicene Creed.[155] The church and Christian theology in the West followed Augustine and over and over defended the phrase "and of the Son" against the East,[156] a position that was also adopted by the Reformation. But despite all the efforts to reach an agreement, the East maintained its ancient position right up to 1875, when the Old Catholics held a conference at Bonn,

150. John of Damascus, *The Orthodox Faith*, I, 8, 12.

151. Orthodox Confession, qu. 9, 71; P. Schaff, *The Creeds of Christendom*, 6th ed., 3 vols. (New York: Harper & Row, 1937; reprinted, Grand Rapids: Baker, 1990), II, 282, 350.

152. Tertullian, *Against Praxeas*, 4, 25.

153. Hilary, *De trinitate contra Arianos*, II, 4; VIII, 20.

154. Augustine, *The Trinity*, V, 11–15; XV, 17, 26; idem, *Enchiridion*, II, 9.

155. H. Denzinger, *Enchiridion*, 98, 113, 136.

156. Ibid., 224, 242, 294, 355, 382, 385, 586, 598, 868, 873; *Alcuin, *De processione Spiritus Sancti* (in PL 101:63–84); Anselm, *De processione Spiritus Sancti*; P. Lombard, *Sent.*, I, dist. 11; T. Aquinas, *Summa theol.*, I, qu. 36; D. Petavius, "De trinitate," in *Theol. dogm.*, VII.

Germany.[157] The fruitlessness of all these efforts is all the more remarkable in view of the seeming triviality of the difference. The Eastern church is not subordinationist and acknowledges the full "homoousia" (identity of substance) of the three persons. It also definitely posits a relation between the Spirit and Christ who sends and dispenses him. And they do not object to saying that he proceeds from the Father *through the Son.* The Western church in turn has declared that the Spirit's procession from the Father and the Son should not be understood as a procession from two *principia* and as consisting in two *spirationes,* but as proceeding from one *principium* by a single spiration.[158] Pope Leo acknowledged that the insertion of the phrase "and of the Son" *(filioque)* in the ancient symbol was formally incorrect.[159] Also, the Western church had no problem as such with the formula "from the Father through the Son."[160] Still, no agreement was reached.

The Eastern church never dropped their key objection that if the Spirit also proceeded from the Son, one would have to posit two *principia* or causes (αἰτίαι) for the Spirit's procession. This objection arises from a different doctrine of God and a different type of religious practice. Orthodox opposition to the *filioque* is a last lingering remnant of subordinationism. However much the three persons are considered to be completely one and equal, that unity and equality accrues to the Son and the Spirit from the being of the Father. The Father is the fountain and origin of the Godhead. Accordingly, if the Spirit also proceeds from the Son, the Son is coordinate with the Father, the principle of unity is broken, and a kind of ditheism results. For the Eastern church the unity of the divine essence and the Trinity of persons does not arise from the divine nature as such but from the person of the Father. He is the sole originating principle (αἰτία). The three persons, according to the Orthodox, are not three relations within the one being, not the self-unfolding of the Godhead; rather, it is the Father who communicates himself to the Son and the Spirit. From this it follows, however, that now the Son and the Spirit are coordinated: they both have their originating principle (αἰτία) in the Father. The Father reveals himself in both: the Son imparts the knowledge of God, the Spirit the enjoyment of God. The Son does not reveal the Father in and through the Spirit; the Spirit does not lead [believers] to the Father through the Son. The two are more or less independent of each other: they both open their own way to the Father. Thus orthodoxy and mysticism, the intellect and the will, exist dualistically side by side. And this unique relation between orthodoxy and mysticism is the hallmark of Greek piety. Doctrine and life are separate. Doctrine is for the intellect; it is a suitable object for theological speculation. Alongside it there is another fountain of life: the mysticism of the Spirit. This mysticism does not

---

157. A. von Harnack, *History of Dogma,* IV, 125–37; J. Schwane, *Dogmengeschichte,* II², 198ff.; P. Schaff, *The Creeds of Christendom,* II, 545ff.

158. H. Denzinger, *Enchiridion,* 382, 586.

159. J. Schwane, *Dogmengeschichte,* II², 209.

160. H. Denzinger, *Enchiridion,* 586, 868. P. Schaff, *The Creeds of Christendom,* II, 552.

arise from knowledge but has its own source and nourishes the human heart. The head and the heart are not rightly aligned and related. Ideas and emotions are separate. The ethical linkage that should unite the two is lacking.[161]

THE TRINITARIAN ECONOMY

[229] These immanent relations of the three persons in the divine being also manifest themselves outwardly *(ad extra)* in their revelations and works. Granted, all God's outward works *(opera ad extra)* are common to the three persons. "God's works *ad extra* are indivisible, though the order and distinction of the persons is preserved." It is always one and the same God who acts both in creation and in re-creation. In that unity, however, the order of the three persons is preserved. The "ontological" Trinity is mirrored in the "economic" Trinity. For that reason special properties and works are attributed to each of the three persons—though not exclusively, as Abelard believed[162]—in such a way that the order present between the persons in the ontological Trinity is revealed. These properties, accordingly, are appropriate to the persons, as Scripture itself shows. Hilary, appealing to Matthew 28:19 and 1 Corinthians 8:6, states that the Father is the author from whom all things exist; the Son the only begotten through whom all things exist; and the Spirit a gift in all. Accordingly, there is *one* power, *one* Son, *one* gift. In this perfect divine state nothing is lacking. Eternity is in the Father; the "form" is in the image who is the Son; the "practical use" is in the gift who is the Spirit.[163] Hilary assigns these properties to the three persons because the Father is the originating cause (ἀρχή) and himself without an originating principle *(principium)*; the Son the image of the Father, who reveals the Father in his glory; the Holy Spirit a gift from the Father and the Son, who makes us partakers in communion with God.

Augustine registers some objections to this view, construing the distinctions between the persons somewhat differently: "In the Father is unity, in the Son equality, in the Holy Spirit the harmony of unity and equality; these three attributes are all one on account of the Father, all equal on account of the Son, all connected on account of the Spirit."[164] In his work on the Trinity he further develops the distinction. Here he attributes power to the Father, wisdom to the Son, goodness or love to the Holy Spirit. This does not mean, mind you, that the Father only becomes wise and good as a result of the wisdom of the Son and the goodness of the Holy Spirit. For the Father, Son, and Spirit all share the same divine nature and the same divine attributes. Still, it is permissible

161. Cf. Harnack, *History of Dogma*, IV, 125–37; F. Kattenbusch, *Confessionskunde*, I, 318ff.; *Schmid, *Symbolik*, 30ff.; E. F. K. Müller, *Symbolik* (Erlangen and Leipzig: A. Deichert, 1896), 220; A. Kuyper, *Om de Oude Wereldzee*, 2 vols. (Amsterdam: Van Holkema and Warendorf, 1907–8), I, 125ff.

162. P. Abelard, *Introductio ad theologiam*, I, chs. 7–14.

163. Hilary, *De trinitate*, II, 1.

164. Augustine, *The Trinity*, VI, 10; idem, *On Christian Doctrine*, I, 5.

to ascribe the above properties to the three persons in an "economic" sense.[165] Later theologians adopted this distinction as well.[166]

Corresponding to these distinctions, we also find "economic" distinctions in the works *ad extra*. All of these works are accomplished by the one God, yet in them each of the three persons fulfills the role that corresponds to the order of his existence in the divine being. The Father works *of* himself *through* the Son *in* the Spirit. Scripture marks these distinctions very clearly in the so-called "differentiating prepositions" ἐκ (out of), διά (through), and ἐν (in) (1 Cor. 8:6; John 1:3, 14). Romans 11:36, often advanced in support of these distinctions, is not divisible in trinitarian terms; and Colossians 1:16 is only seemingly at odds with this use of the prepositions. At an early date students of Scripture already noted, and emphatically pointed out, the distinctions Scripture makes between the three persons.[167] Athanasius repeatedly appeals to Ephesians 4:6, saying that as Father God is *above* us all, as Son he is *through* all, and as Spirit he is *in* all, and that the Father creates and re-creates all things *through* the Son *in* the Spirit.[168] Basil was charged with error because in his prayers he would sometimes give thanks to the Father "in common with (μετά) the Son along with (σύν) the Holy Spirit" and at other times "through the Son in the Holy Spirit." In his work on the Holy Spirit Basil defends the first expression because the Son and the Spirit are of one substance with the Father and therefore deserve the same honor, and he speaks at length about the distinctions between the prepositions.[169] Against the Arians he argues that the "inequality" of the prepositions does not prove the inequality of the persons but that it points to a specific order in their existence and activity. The Father is "the initiating cause"; the Son "the operating cause"; the Spirit "the perfecting cause."[170] Later theologians repeat the same distinctions.[171]

All the works of God *ad extra* have one single Author *(principium)*, namely, God. But they come into being through the cooperation of the three persons, each of whom plays a special role and fulfills a special task, both in the works of creation and in those of redemption and sanctification. All things proceed from the Father, are accomplished by the Son, and are completed in the Holy Spirit. Indeed, to some extent also the works *ad extra* are divided

165. Augustine, *The Trinity*, IV, 1ff.; XV, 7.

166. J. S. Erigena, *The Division of Nature*, I, 13; T. Aquinas, *Summa theol.*, I, qu. 39, art. 7–8; Bonaventure, *Breviloquium*, I, ch. 6; Bonaventure, *Sent.*, I, dist. 31, art. 1, qu. 3; art. 2, qu. 3; Hugh of St. Victor, *De sacramentis christianae fidei*, I, pt. 3, ch. 27.

167. Irenaeus, *Against Heresies*, V, 18.

168. Athanasius, *Letter to Serapion*, 14, 28; II, 6, 7.

169. Basil, *On the Spirit*, 3ff.

170. Ibid., 21, 22, 38.

171. Cf. also Schelling, *Werke*, II/3, 341ff. Ed. note: The Schelling citations here and later in notes 181, 197–206, are to his *Philosophie der Offenbarung*. A more recent two-volume edition of this work was published in 1954 by the Wissenschaftliche Buchgesellschaft (Darmstadt). ET: *Schelling's Philosophy of Mythology and Revelation*, trans. Victor C. Hayes (Armindale, N.S.W.: Australian Association for the Study of Religions, 1995).

among the three persons. As stated earlier, Gregory of Nazianzus explained the great controversy of his day about the Holy Spirit in light of the fact that the Spirit had not clearly registered his presence until his indwelling in the church.[172] Pantheism, in its many forms, has often misused the truth enunciated by Gregory. Over and over, from Montanus to Hegel, the notion arose that the three persons represented three successive periods in the history of the church. In that way the "economic" Trinity was detached from its metaphysical foundation; God's being was dragged down into a stream of becoming, and cosmogony was converted into a theogony. It was precisely the struggle of the church fathers to banish this paganistic, pantheistic element from Christian theology, to separate God as *the One who is* from the evolution of becoming, and accordingly, to conceive the Trinity as an eternal movement of life in the divine being itself.

As cited above, Gregory of Nazianzus is not saying that the deity of the Son and of the Holy Spirit only materialized later. In fact, he tries to prove the deity of both as decisively as he can from Scripture. But in his self-revelation God certainly had to reckon with the human capacity for receiving truth. It was dangerous, says Gregory (in the same work), to teach the deity of the Son as long as the deity of the Father was not yet acknowledged, and to "impose" the deity of the Spirit as long as the deity of the Son had not yet been confessed. He did not wish to overload our dinner plates with food or blind us by all at once exposing us to the full light of the sun. All the works *ad extra*: creation, providence, rule, incarnation, satisfaction (atonement), renewal, sanctification, and so on, are works of the Trinity as a whole. Yet, in an "economic" sense, the work of creation is more specifically assigned to the Father, the work of redemption to the Son, the work of sanctification to the Holy Spirit. Just as in the ontological Trinity the Father is first in the order of subsistence, the Son second, the Spirit third, so also in the history of revelation the Father preceded the Son, and the Son in turn preceded the Holy Spirit. The "economy" of the Father was especially that of the Old Testament (Heb. 1:1); the "economy" of the Son started with the incarnation; and the "economy" of the Holy Spirit began on the Day of Pentecost (John 7:39; 14:16–17). The Father came without having been sent, the Son came after being sent by the Father (Matt. 10:40; Mark 9:37; Luke 9:48; John 3:16; 5:23, 30, 37; 6:28ff.; etc.), and the Holy Spirit only came because he was sent both by the Father and the Son (John 14:26; 16:7).[173]

But this "being sent" in time is a reflection of the immanent relations of the three persons in the divine being and is grounded in generation and spiration. The incarnation of the Word has its eternal archetype in the generation of the Son, and the outpouring of the Holy Spirit is a weak analogy of the procession

---

172. Gregory of Nazianzus, *Theological Orations*, V, 26.

173. Augustine, *Lectures on the Gospel of John*, tract. 6; idem, *The Trinity*, II, 5; IV, 20; P. Lombard, *Sent.*, I, dist. 14–17; T. Aquinas, *Summa theol.*, I, qu. 43; D. Petavius, "De trinitate," in *Theol. dogm.*, VIII, ch. 1.

from the Father and the Son. The church fathers, accordingly, derived the eternal and immanent relations existing between the persons from the relations that were manifest before the human eye in time. And rightly so. For, writes Augustine, "the Son cannot be said to have been 'sent' because he became flesh, but he was and is said to be 'sent' *in order* that he would become flesh." The Father never said a word in time to the effect that the eternal Son would be sent.

> Though it is true that in the Word of God, which was in the beginning with God and was God, that is to say, in the Wisdom of God, there was timelessly contained the time in which that Wisdom was to appear in the flesh. So, without any beginning of time, "in the beginning was the Word, and the Word was with God, and the Word was God" (John 1:1); and without any beginning of time, there was in the Word the time at which the Word would become flesh and dwell among us (John 1:14). And when this "fullness of time had come, God sent his Son, born of a woman" (Gal. 4:4), that is, made in time, in order that the Word might be shown to people incarnate; and the time at which this should happen was timelessly contained within the Word. The whole series of all times is timelessly contained in God's eternal Wisdom. Since then it was a work of the Father and the Son that the Son should appear in the flesh, the one who so appeared in the flesh is appropriately said to have been sent, and the one who did not so appear is said to have done the sending. Thus, events that are put on outwardly in the sight of our bodily eyes are aptly called *missa* because they stem from the inner designs of our spiritual nature.[174]

The same thing applies to the "sending" of the Spirit.

> This action, visibly expressed and presented to mortal eyes, is called the sending of the Holy Spirit. Its object was not that his very substance might be seen, since he himself remains invisible and unchanging like the Father and the Son; but that outward sights might in this way stir the minds of men, and draw them on from the public manifestations of his coming in time to the still and hidden presence of his eternity sublime.[175]

The Holy Spirit was a gift before he had been given to anyone. "Because he so proceeds as to be giveable, he was a gift even before there was anyone to give him to. There is a difference between calling something a gift and calling it a donation; it can be a gift even before it is given, but it cannot be called in any way a donation unless it has been given."[176] The sending in time, accordingly, is most intimately bound up with the eternal procession in the divine being. Now while the Son and the Spirit have visibly appeared in the incarnation and the outpouring, their mission is completed in their invisible coming into the hearts of all believers, in the church of the Son, in the temple of the Holy

---

174. Augustine, *The Trinity*, II, 5.
175. Ibid.; cf. D. Petavius, "De trinitate," in *Theol. dogm.*, VIII, ch. 1, §§7–12.
176. Augustine, *The Trinity*, V, 15.

Spirit. There has been an eternal procession of the Son and the Spirit from the Father in order that, through and in them, he himself should come to his people and finally be "all in all."

TRINITARIAN ANALOGIES AND ARGUMENTS

[230] The doctrine of the Trinity is so far above human understanding that from the time it was first formulated attempts have been made to elucidate it by illustrations and prove it by argumentation. Remarkable, in the first place, is that the number three had such rich and deep significance in Scripture. There we read of the three parts of creation: heaven, earth, and what is under the earth; three ethnic groupings originating from the three sons of Noah; three dispensations of the covenant of grace: before, under, and after the law; the three patriarchs; the three divisions of the tabernacle; the three great feasts; the three parts of the Old Testament; the three years of Christ's public ministry; the three offices of Christ [prophet, priest, and king]; his three days in the grave before the resurrection; the three crosses on Golgotha; the three languages in the superscription over the cross; the three beloved disciples; the three witnesses (1 John 5:8); the three prime Christian virtues [faith, hope, and love]; the three kinds of lust (1 John 2:16); the three woes (Rev. 8:13; etc.); a threefold benediction; a threefold action in greetings and blessings; three days of fasting, three daily periods of prayer, and so on.[177]

While the number three is prominent in Scripture, it is also of great importance outside of Scripture. Analogies for the Christian doctrine of the Trinity were discovered not only in the intermediate beings that gradually emerged in Jewish theology,[178] and in the three Sephiroth ("Crown," "Wisdom," and "Understanding") mentioned in the Kabbalah,[179] but traces of the Trinity were also found in the Trimurti of the Southeast Asian Indians: Brahman, Vishnu, and Siva; in the three forms of the Chinese Tao; in the chief Germanic [Norse] gods: Odin, Thor, and Loki; and in various Chaldean, Egyptian, and Greek conceptions of the gods.[180] Favorites were a certain pronouncement of Hermes Trismegistus and Plato's three cosmological principles: the supreme mind (νους), identified with being and goodness; the world of ideas; and matter (ὕλη).[181] But

177. O. Zöckler, *Geschichte der Beziehungen zwischen Theologie und Naturwissenschaft*, 2 vols. (Gütersloh: C. Bertelsmann, 1877–79), 682ff., 696ff.; K. C. W. F. Bähr, *Symbolik des mosaischen Cultus*, 2d ed. (Heidelberg: J. C. B. Mohr, 1874); F. Kaubtsch, "Zahlen bei den Hebräern," *PRE²*, XVII, 410ff.

178. F. W. Weber, *System der altsynagogalen palästinischen Theologie*, 172ff.

179. A. Franck, *The Kabbalah* (New York: Arno Press, 1973); Agrippa of Nettesheim, according to A. Stöckl, *Philosophie des Mittelalters*, III, 413; II, 236.

180. Cf. Also H. Zimmern, *Vater, Sohn und Fürsprecher in der babylonischen Gottesvorstellung* (Leipzig: J. C. Hinrichs, 1896).

181. T. Pfanner, *Systema theologiae gentilis purioris*, ch. 3; B. de Moor, *Comm. in Marckii Comp.*, I, 885–90; A. Tholuck, *Die speculative Trinitätslehre des späteren Orients* (Berlin: F. Dümmler, 1826); J. P. Lange, *Christliche Dogmatik*, II, 143ff.; K. F. A. Kahnis, *Die lutherische Dogmatik, historisch-genetisch dargestellt*, I, 352; F. C. Baur, *Dreieinigkeit und Menschwerdung Gottes*, I, 10ff., 18ff., 33ff.; F. Delitzsch, *System der christlichen*

inasmuch as all these analogies are polytheistic, they can hardly be compared with the Christian doctrine of the Trinity.

Of comparatively greater value are the analogies found in the natural world. Justin Martyr, following Philo, employed the image of a flame that, though igniting another, nevertheless remains the same. Tertullian said that God produced the Logos as a root produces a fruit and a spring produces a river and the sun produces sun rays; he also spoke of a spring, a flood, and a stream; a root, a trunk, and a crown (etc.). These images recur over and over in the later church fathers and theologians and were then elaborated or increased. The more thinkers pondered these things, the more evident it became to them that all things are tripartite: space with its three dimensions; time with its three components; nature with its three kingdoms; the world of matter and spirit and the union of the two in humans; bodies in their solid, fluid, and gaseous state; the forces of attraction and repulsion and of equilibrium between the two; the three functions of the human soul: reasoning, feeling, desiring; the three human capacities: head, heart, and hand; the three constituents that make up a family: man, woman, child;[182] the three classes in society: the educators, the military, and the peasantry (German: *Lehr-*, *Wehr-*, und *Nahrstand*); the three ideal properties of the true, the good, and the beautiful; triadic harmony in music: the key tone, the third tone, and the fifth tone; the rainbow and its many colors; the sun with its invigorating, illuminating, and heat-generating powers (Latin: *vigor, splendor, calor*); the three basic colors: yellow, red, and blue; and so forth—all of these have been used, in earlier or later times, as analogies of the Christian Trinity.[183]

Thought and Love

On a higher level are the logical analogies. Augustine repeatedly points out that everything must first of all have being, unity, and measure; second, a certain form, "species," something specific that distinguishes it from other things; and finally, a certain relation, correspondence, or order between its general and specific qualities. Matter, form (or beauty), and harmony or love between the two are the fundamental components of all existence.[184] "All that is, requires a threefold cause: that by which it exists, that by which it is this particular thing, and that by which it is internally consistent."[185]

Medieval theology, working out these ideas in multiple ways, looked for triads everywhere. It found an analogy of the Trinity in the trivium of grammar, dialectic, and rhetoric; in the three branches of philosophy: logic, physics, and ethics; in the first, second, and third persons of grammar; in the active, passive,

---

Apologetik (Leipzig: Dörffling & Franke, 1870), 286; O. Zöckler, *Theologia naturalis* (Frankfurt am Main: Heyder & Zimmer, 1860), 689, cf. also, Schelling, *Werke*, II/2, 78; II/3, 312ff.

182. Cf. especially Augustine, *The Trinity*, XI, 5ff.

183. F. Delitzsch, *System der christlichen Apologetik*, 282ff.; O. Zöckler, *Theologia naturalis*, 672ff.

184. Augustine, *The Trinity*, VI, 10; idem, *On True Religion*, ch. 7; idem, *De vita beata*, 34; cf. T. Gangauf, *Des heiligen Augustinus speculative Lehre von Gott dem Dreieinigen* (Augsburg: Schmidt, 1883), 209ff.

185. Augustine, *Eighty-three Different Questions*, qu. 18.

and middle voices; in the singular, dual, and plural numbers; in the three basic vowels and the triliteral roots of Hebrew; in the disposition, style, and delivery of rhetoric; in the definition, division, and argumentation of dialectic; in the three forms of poetry: epic, lyric, and dramatic; in the three stages of mysticism: cogitation, meditation, and contemplation; or faith, reason, and contemplation; or the way of purification, illumination, and union; and so forth. Pseudo-Dionysius the Areopagite divided his *Celestial Hierarchies,* and Dante his *Divine Comedy,* into three parts. In modern philosophy triplicity even achieved formal dominance. Kant, said Hegel,[186] as if by instinct rediscovered triplicity and, based on it, produced a threefold scheme for the organs of knowledge: the faculties of the soul, the categories, and the ideas. But this triplicity became a dialectical method only in the Kant-based idealistic philosophies of Fichte, Schelling, and Hegel. It is the nature of idealism to understand things as products of human consciousness, as the development of an idea. That idea must therefore be conceived as living, moving, and generative. This is possible only when it always exists in a state of contradiction between what it is and what it does, and then resolves and reconciles the two in a third something. In the idealistic view this law of contradiction is at the heart of human thought. Thus the idea, unfolding and developing, proceeds through affirmation and negation to limitation, through thesis and antithesis to synthesis. Its phases are "in itself, for itself, in-and-for itself." The whole world develops in terms of this "order of trinities." Logic, with its theory of being, essence, and concept, considers the mind-in-itself; natural philosophy in the three forms of mechanics, physics, and organics has to do with the mind-for-itself, the mind-in-its-otherness, the mind in its self-estrangement; intellectual philosophy, with its subjective, objective, and absolute mind, treats the thinking mind in-and-for itself, in its returning to itself, and its becoming conscious of itself.[187] As a result of this philosophy's influence, triplicity became foundational for countless philosophical and theological systems.

Not satisfied with this array of attempts to find illustrative analogies for the Trinity, some tried to furnish positive proof for the doctrine, deriving it either as a necessary corollary from the nature of thought or from the nature of love. The Logos doctrine, both in Scripture and in Greek philosophy, quite naturally brought out in human thought and speech an image of the trinitarian process in the divine being. Justin Martyr, Tatian, Tertullian, Lacantius, and others already employed this analogy.[188] Athanasius and the Cappadocians

186. G. W. F. Hegel, *The Phenomenology of Mind,* trans. J. B. Bailles, 2d ed. (London: George Allen; New York: MacMillan, 1931), 107; in *Sämtliche Werke,* II, 46 (*Werke* II, 38) (ed. note: Bavinck erroneously cites this as p. 37).

187. Wilhelm Windelband, *A History of Philosophy,* trans. James H. Tufts, 2 vols. (New York: Harper & Row, 1958 [1901]), II, 529–623, esp. 540–96 (ed. note: Bavinck cites from the second German edition of *Geschichte der Philosophie* [Freiburg i.B.: J. C. B. Mohr, 1892], 464ff., 481); G. Rümelin, *Reden und Aufsätze,* vol. I (Tübingen: H. Laupe, 1875), 47ff. (ed. note: Bavinck cites an edition from 1888).

188. Justin Martyr, *Dialogue with Trypho,* ch. 61; Tatian, *Oratio ad Graecos,* ch. 5; Tertullian, *Against Praxeas,* ch. 5ff.; L. C. Lactantius, *The Divine Institutes,* IV, 29.

regularly pictured generation as God's recognition of himself in his image, as the eternal utterance of a Word. The Father and the Son are related, they said, as mind (νους) is to word (λογος).[189] It was especially Augustine, however, who in various ways and perspectives found the clear imprints of the Trinity in human consciousness and reason. In the first place, he found them in the trinity of being, knowing, and willing; essence, knowledge, and love; mind, knowledge, and love.[190] Next he discovered traces of it in the faculties of the soul, specifically in (1) sense perception, which arises in response to an object; (2) the thing itself; (3) through an image of it in the eye and the intention of the will, which directs the sense toward the object.[191] This trinity remains even when the object disappears, for in that case an image of it is preserved in memory, external sight makes way for internal vision, and the will remains to link the two. But Augustine finds the closest analogy to the Trinity in the self-knowledge of the human soul.[192] He usually refers to the trinity he finds here by the names of mind, knowledge, and love (delectation); or memory, intelligence, and will. The mind is first memory, that is, the awareness both of other things and of itself, for there is an awareness that is not yet true knowledge. Hidden in the mind as memory are many items of knowledge, also of itself. A person can know something even without thinking of it at the moment (*De trin.*, XIV, chs. 6–7). But from that mind as memory, from the knowledge that is stored in the memory, knowledge, intelligence is produced by the action of thinking. In that intelligence the mind forms an accurate image of itself, comprehends, knows, and sees itself. "Accordingly, when, the mind beholds itself in thought, it knows and recognizes itself." And this self-knowledge and self-contemplation is generative by nature: "It begets this understanding and knowledge of itself." Now these two are united by the will or by love: "These two, begetter and begotten, are coupled together by love as the third, and this is nothing but the will seeking or holding something to be enjoyed" (*De trin.*, XIV, 6).[193] Thus, Augustine is deeply convinced that all creatures, being works of God, to some extent exhibit "vestiges or evidences of the Trinity" (*De trin.*, VI, 10; XV, 2). Above all, however, he looks for an image of the Trinity in human beings, created as they are in the image of the triune God (ibid.; *De civ.*, XI, 26). To Augustine the entire creation is a mirror of God. In every possible way, therefore, he seeks to show the similarity between the trinity that he discovers in creation, especially in humans, and the Trinity in the divine being. In both cases the triad consists in the fact that all three are one and equal, that each of

189. Athanasius, *Against the Arians*, II, 35ff.; Gregory of Nazianzus, *Fourth Theological Oration*, 20 (*NPNF [2]*, VII, 309–18); and especially Gregory of Nyssa, *The Great Catechism*, chs. 1–3 (*NPNF [2]*, V, 474–77).

190. Augustine, *Confessions*, XIII, 1; idem, *City of God*, XI, 26–28; idem, *The Trinity*, IX, 4–5.

191. Augustine, *The Trinity*, XI, 1–2.

192. Ibid., IX, 4ff.; X, 9ff.; XIV, 6ff.; XV, 6ff.

193. Ed. note: Translation taken from St. Augustine, *The Trinity*, trans. Edmund Hill (Brooklyn, N.Y.: New City Press, 1990), 374–75.

the three is present in the two others, and that these two in turn are present in the one and thus "all are in all" (*De trin.,* IX, 5; X, 11).

In this connection, however, he frankly admits that all these comparisons are but analogies and images, and that in addition to similarity there is also great difference. For example, in human beings the trinity is not the persons themselves but something in or about the persons, whereas in God the Trinity is God himself, and the three persons are the one God. In humans, memory, intelligence, and love are merely human capacities, but in the divine being the three persons are three subjects. In humans these three capacities are frequently unequal and are designed to complement each other, but in the divine being there is complete unity and equality of persons (*De trin.,* XV, 7, 17, 20ff.). Augustine, accordingly, did not intend by these analogies and images to offer a priori proof for the Trinity. On the contrary, he proceeds from faith in the Trinity; he accepts the teaching on the basis of the Word of God. Now on that basis he attempts a posteriori to show its presence throughout nature and by thinking to clarify the doctrine (*De vera relig.,* 7; *De trin.,* I, 1; V 1; IX, 1). Hence, the first seven books of *De trinitate* are mainly devoted to establishing the doctrine from Scripture; only in the last eight books does the author try to further substantiate it from the domain of nature and that of humanity. Finally, he adds that, though everyone can discern the imprint of the Trinity in the human spirit, only believers can recognize it as the imprint of the threefold being of God. Though it is integral to the human spirit and has not been eradicated by sin, it has been obscured and is renewed when humans again learn to "remember, understand, and love" God. And we again become fully his image only when we see him face to face (*De trin.,* XIV, 12ff.). "There our being will know no death; our knowing will be untouched by error, our loving will be free from stumbling blocks" (*De civ.,* XI, 28).

Many theologians, philosophers, and thinkers took over this type of argumentation for the Trinity.[194]

194. E.g., Erigena, *The Division of Nature,* II, 113ff.; Anselm, *Monologion,* chs. 29–67; P. Lombard, *Sent.,* I, dist. 3, 6–23; T. Aquinas, *Summa theol.,* I, qu. 45, art. 7; idem, *Summa contra gentiles,* IV, 26; idem, *Sent.,* I, dist. 3, qu. 2, art. 3; Bonaventure, *Breviloquium,* II, ch. 12; idem, *The Journey of the Mind to God,* chs. 2–4; idem, *Sent.,* I, dist. 3, art. 1–2; Duns Scotus, *Sent.,* I, dist. 3, qu. 9; Hugh of St. Victor, *De sacramentis christianae fidei,* I, pt. 3, chs. 21ff.; Luther, according to J. Köstlin, *Theology of Luther,* trans. C. E. Hay, 2 vols. (Philadelphia: Lutheran Publication Society, 1897), I, 99ff.; P. Melanchthon, *Loci communes,* loc. 3; idem, *Enarratio symboli Niceni, Corpus Reformatorum,* XXIII, col. 235; idem, *Explicatio symboli Niceni, Corpus Reformatorum,* XXIII, col. 359ff.; idem, *Examen ordinandorum, Corpus Reformatorum,* XXIII, col. 3; J. Schegk, *Contra antitrinitarios,* according to F. Trechsel, *Die protestantischen Antitrinitarier,* II, 380ff.; A. Polanus, *Syn. theol.,* 202; J. Zanchi(us), *Op. theol.,* I, col. 356ff.; B. Keckermann, *Systema s. s. theologiae* (Hanoviae: Apud Antonium, 1603), 20ff.; P. Poiret, *Cogitationum rationalium de Deo, anima et malo, libri quatuor* (Amsterdam: Daniel Elsevir, 1677); according to F. C. Baur, *Dreieinigkeit und Menschwerdung Gottes,* III, 315ff.; P. de Mornay, *De veritate religionis Christianae* (Leiden: Andries Cloucq, 1605), ch. 5; G. W. Leibniz, *System der Theologie,* 3d ed. (Mainz: S. Müller, 1825), 30; Ed. note: ET: *A System of Theology,* trans. Charles William Russell (London: Burns and Lambert, 1850); G. E. Lessing, *Erziehung des Menschengeschlechts und andere Schriften,* §73; Schelling, *Werke,* II/3, 315; A. D. C. Twesten, *Vorlesungen über die Dogmatik der evangelisch-lutherischen Kirche,* II, 194–216; J. P. Lange, *Christliche Dogmatik,* II, 141; W. Bilderdijk, *Opstel-*

Combined with this type of argumentation from the mind, however, Augustine also employed another, one that proceeds from the realm of love. Starting from the scriptural assertion that "God is love," he demonstrates that there is always a trinity present in love: "one who loves, that which is loved, and love itself." In love there is always a subject, an object, and a bond between the two. "Oh, but you do see a trinity if you see charity" (*De trin.*, VIII, 8; IX 1, 2). This speculation, too, has been followed by many, especially by Richard of St. Victor.[195] The fullness of divine love, like that of divine goodness, blessedness, and glory, require a plurality of divine persons in the divine being, for love desires an object and one that is equal to the one who loves. But this love is not complete until both the one who loves and the one who is loved welcome into their love a third by whom they are reciprocally loved. We find the same reasoning in Bonaventure[196] and in many moderns.[197]

Theosophy

In addition to these more general speculations derived from the mind and will of God, still other construals of the Trinity have been attempted. The most remarkable one is that of theosophy which, under the combined influences of Neoplatonism, Gnosticism, and the Kabbalah, resurfaced, shortly before the Reformation, in the persons of Pico Mirandola, Reuchlin, Nettesheim, and Paracelsus. It found its true philosopher in the person of Jakob Böhme and was championed again in the nineteenth century by Schelling and Baader. Schelling's premise is that true being cannot be explained from pure thought. The "whatness" of things may be derived from reason; the "thatness" of things cannot possibly be explained in that way. The *essence* and *existence* of things point back to different principles.[198] For that reason both Deism and pantheism must be rejected. God may not be understood as an abstract unity in the manner of the Eleatic school. He is an All-oneness, a plurality that unites the oneness of Deism and the allness of pantheism. The very concept "God" encompasses three elements: (1) the subject, the will, that which has the capacity to exist; (2) the object, the idea, the element of pure being; (3) the identity of both, the subject-object.[199] In these three components the concept of the

len van Godgeleerden en Zedekundigen Inhoud, 2 vols. (Amsterdam: Immerzeel, 1883), I, 24ff.; A. Kuyper, *De Schrift, het Woord Gods* (Tiel: H. C. A. Campagne, 1870); W. G. T. Shedd, *Dogmatic Theology*, 3d ed., 3 vols. (New York: Scribner, 1891–94), I, 183.

195. Richard of St. Victor, *De trinitate*, III, chs. 2ff.

196. Bonaventure, *Sent.*, I, dist. 2, art. 1, qu. 2.

197. E.g., J. Müller, *The Christian Doctrine of Sin*, trans. Wm. Urwick, 5th ed., 2 vols. (Edinburgh: T. & T. Clark, 1868), II, 181ff.; E. W. C. Sartorius, *Die Lehre von der heiligen Liebe* (Stuttgart: S. G. Liesching, 1861), I, 11ff.; C. T. A. Liebner, *Die christliche Dogmatik aus dem christologischen Princip dargestellt* (Göttingen: Vandenhoeck & Ruprecht, 1849–), I, 69ff.; L. Schoeberlein, *Die Grundlehren des Heils entwickelt aus dem Princip der Liebe* (Stuttgart; Berlin: G. Schlawitz, 1848), 22ff.; A. Peip, "Trinität," *PRE¹*, XVI, 465ff. (ed. note: Bavinck erroneously cites *PRE²*); I. A. Dorner, *A System of Christian Doctrine*, I, 432ff.; idem, *Gesammelte Schriften*, 345ff.

198. F. W. J. Schelling, *Philosophie der Offenbarung*, in *Werke*, II/3, 57ff.

199. Ibid., *Werke*, II/2, 24ff., 68ff.; II/3, 205ff.

absolute has been completed. This is what makes it a spirit (mind), perfect spirit (mind), personal and self-conscious, an individual being.[200] But though in our thinking these three moments are the stepping-stones by which we arrive at the perfection of spirit, that spirit is not for that reason the product of these three. On the contrary, the spirit is primordial and contains within himself these three moments as "immanent destinies." Thus, the perfect, the absolute Spirit is the Spirit as he exists in himself, for himself, and with himself. But concealed within that Spirit is all that will be. He is a free Spirit and able to reveal himself outwardly. The three destinies that the Spirit carries within himself are the potencies of extradivine being.[201]

Schelling derives the entire created world, mythology, and revelation from the separation and union of these three potencies; they are the forms of all potentialities, the principles (ἀρχαί) of all existence.[202] In Schelling, however, this cosmogony is simultaneously a theogony. As the world develops, these potencies in the divine being ascend to ever higher levels; in God's self-revelation to his creatures he at the same time becomes manifest to himself. These three destinies inherent in the absolute spirit, the three potencies in the creation of the world and in mythology, pave the way for understanding of the one self-same God as three persons.[203] In the historical course of revelation the absolute Spirit becomes Father, Son, and Spirit. God—the entire Deity, the absolute personality, not a special figure in the Godhead—can be called Father, not only as the Originator of all things, but also to the extent that he can force the first potency of his being from himself in order to realize himself. He is not the real Father at the beginning and during the process but only at the end.[204] The second figure is the Son, whose generation is not eternal but relates to the Son's existence outside of the Father and therefore begins at the moment of creation. The Son is not fully the Son until the end of the process.[205] The same is true of the third potency.[206] At the end the entire deity was realized in three distinct persons who are neither three distinct gods nor merely three different names.[207]

By this speculation modern philosophy again brought the trinitarian dogma into favor. All sorts of attempts were made to construct a Trinity rationally, especially from the essence of the spirit, of self-consciousness, of personality.[208] [Anton] Gunther, like Raymond of Sabunde, Raymond Lull, and other

200. Ibid., *Werke*, II/2, 73ff.; II/3, 174, 238ff.
201. Ibid., *Werke*, II/3, 240ff., 251ff., 261, 272.
202. Ibid., *Werke*, II/2, 61, 112; II/3, 267ff.
203. Ibid., *Werke*, II/3, 316.
204. Ibid., *Werke*, II/3, 311, 322, 335ff., 339.
205. Ibid., *Werke*, II/3, 312, 318, 321ff., 330ff.
206. Ibid., *Werke*, II/3, 333ff.
207. Ibid., *Werke*, II/3, 335, 337.
208. E.g., C. H. Weisse, *Philosophische Dogmatik oder Philosophie des Christentums*, 3 vols. (Leipzig: Hirzel, 1855–62), I, 444ff.; I. A. Dorner, *A System of Christian Doctrine*, I, 422 (ed. note: Bavinck inserts here an elliptical note that appears to refer to I. H. Fichte as author and the title of the work as *Deutinger*,

rationalists, even went so far as to abandon the distinction between "pure" and "mixed" articles, viewing the Trinity as belonging to the category of rational truths and demonstrable from the nature of self-consciousness.[209]

[231] The church and theology as a rule assumed a very reserved attitude toward these philosophical construals of the doctrine of the Trinity. At most they would allow for a posteriori consideration of proofs for the Trinity for the purpose of clarifying the dogma, but even then many warned against the attempt to seek support for this doctrine in reason. More than any other dogma, that of the Trinity was considered a mystery that far surpassed the reach of nature and reason and could only be known from special revelation. Like Augustine, Thomas also accepted the existence of vestiges of the Trinity in creation and attempted to illumine it by reasoning. But he expressly stated that the Trinity was not knowable by reason, for the creation is a work of the Trinity as a whole and therefore displays the unity of the being, not the distinction of persons. "Furthermore, those who try to prove the Trinity of the persons by natural reason derogate from faith in two ways": first, by derogating from the dignity of faith, which consists in its focus only on invisible things; and second, by keeping others from the faith when the latter receive the impression that faith rests on weak grounds.[210] Calvin saw little use in analogies and proofs advanced for the Trinity from nature and human reason.[211] And many Reformed and Lutheran theologians concurred.[212]

THE IMPORTANCE OF TRINITARIAN DOGMA

Now, over against all those who want to base the doctrine of the Trinity on rational grounds, we must undoubtedly maintain that we owe our knowledge of this doctrine solely to God's special revelation. Scripture alone is the final ground for the doctrine of the Trinity. Reason can at most somewhat clarify this doctrine a posteriori. Nevertheless, the arguments advanced to shed light on the dogma of the Trinity are not devoid of all value. In the first place, Scripture itself gives us the freedom to use them when it says that the entire creation and especially humankind is a work of the triune God. Certainly, all God's

---

Rosenkrantz e. a. Martin Deutinger [1815–64] was an influential philosopher/theologian of subjectivity; see Franz Wiedmann, *Martin Deutinger: Leben und Werk,* Wegbereiter heutiger Theologie 6 [Graz: Styria, 1971]; and Stephan Berger, *Zur Grundlegung einer Theologie der Subjectivität* [Frankfurt a.M. and New York: Peter Lang, 1985]). Cf. A. Drews, *Die deutsche Spekulation seit Kant* (Leipzig: G. Fock, 1895), I, 285–531.

209. A. Drews, *Die deutsche Spekulation seit Kant,* I, 447ff.; J. Kleutgen, *Die Theologie der Vorzeit vertheidigt,* I, 399–451.

210. T. Aquinas, *Summa theol.,* I, qu. 32, art. 1; cf. also P. Lombard, *Sent.,* I, dist. 3, n. 6 and the commentaries there.

211. J. Calvin, *Institutes,* I.xiii.8; I.xv.4; *Commentary,* on Gen. 1:26.

212. A. Hyperius, *Methodi theologiae,* 111; J. Zanchi(us), *Op. theol.,* I, 356ff.; A. Waleus, *Opera omnia,* I, 236; *Synopsis purioris theologiae,* VII, 14; P. van Mastricht, *Theologia,* II, 24, 21; J. Gerhard, *Loci theol.,* III, §§23–32; J. A. Quenstedt, *Theologia,* I, 265ff.; D. Hollaz, *Examen theologicum acroamaticum,* 344; cf. in recent times, E. Böhl, *Dogmatik* (Amsterdam: Scheffer, 1887), 80; J. T. Beck, *Vorlesungen über christliche Glaubenslehre,* II, 129.

works *ad extra* are undivided and common to all three persons. Prominent in these works, therefore, is the oneness of God rather than the distinction of the persons. In this unity, however, the diversity cannot be lacking. For Scripture itself points to this truth by saying that all created beings will show these imprints and human beings will exhibit the image of the triune God. Hence, however much the revelation of God in his works has been shrouded and our mind's eye has been darkened by sin, it cannot a priori be denied that the mind, illumined by revelation, can discover in nature the imprints of the God whom it has come to know from Scripture as triune in his mode of existence and actions. Furthermore, though none of these arguments is capable of proving the dogma of the Trinity, and none can or may be the basis for our faith (we would be abandoning the truth to the ridicule of our opponents if we accepted it on such feeble grounds as reason can produce),[213] yet these arguments can serve to refute various objections that have been lodged against the dogma.[214] They can show that what Scripture teaches us is neither impossible nor absurd[215] and demonstrate that the belief of our opponents is ill-grounded and contrary to reason itself.[216]

The doctrine of the Trinity is by no means as absurd as it has seemed to be to a shallow rationalism in earlier or modern times. It cannot be scuttled by the simple calculation that one cannot be three and three cannot be one.[217] Philosophy again and again—and also again in the nineteenth century—returned to the doctrine of the Trinity and has at least to some extent recognized its rich meaning and profound significance. To this, finally, we must add that these arguments uncover and preserve the connectedness between nature and grace, between creation and re-creation. The God who created and sustained us is also he who re-creates us in his image. Grace, though superior to nature, is not in conflict with it. While restoring what has been corrupted in it by sin, it also clarifies and perfects what is still left in it of God's revelation. The thinking mind situates the doctrine of the Trinity squarely amid the full-orbed life of nature and humanity. A Christian's confession is not an island in the ocean but a high mountaintop from which the whole creation can be surveyed. And it is the task of Christian theologians to present clearly the connectedness of God's revelation with, and its significance for, all of life. The Christian mind remains unsatisfied until all of existence is referred back to the triune God, and until the confession of God's Trinity functions at the center of our thought and life. Accordingly, though the analogies and proofs advanced for the Trinity do not demonstrate the truth of the dogma, they serve mainly to make clear the many-sided usefulness and rich significance of this confession for the life

213. T. Aquinas, *Summa theol.*, I, qu. 32, art. 1; I, qu. 46, art. 2; idem, *Summa contra gentiles*, I, 9.

214. T. Aquinas, *Summa contra gentiles*, I, 9.

215. T. Aquinas, *Summa theol.*, II, 2 qu. 1, art. 5, ad 2.

216. Ibid., I, qu. 1, art. 8; G. Voetius, *Select. disp.*, I, 1ff.

217. Cf. E. von Hartmann, *Religionsphilosophie*, 2d ed., 2 vols. (Bad Sachsa im Harz: Hermann Haacke, 1907), I, 599.

and thought of God's [rational] creatures. In the final analysis they owe their existence to a profound religious need, not to a craving for empty speculation or to immodest curiosity. If God is indeed triune, this has to be supremely important, for all things, according to the apostle, are from him and through him and to him (Rom. 11:36).

In the first place, the doctrine of the Trinity makes God known to us as the truly living God. The church fathers already observed that this doctrine rejects the errors of, while absorbing the elements of truth inherent in, Deism and pantheism, monism and polytheism. Deism creates a vast gulf between God and his creatures, cancels out their mutual relatedness, and reduces God to an abstract entity, a pure being, to mere monotonous and uniform existence. It satisfies neither the mind nor the heart and is therefore the death of religion. Pantheism, though it brings God nearer to us, equates him with the created world, erases the boundary line between the Creator and the creature, robs God of any being or life of his own, thus totally undermining religion. But the Christian doctrine of the Trinity makes God known as essentially distinct from the world, yet having a blessed life of his own. God is a plenitude of life, an "ocean of being." He is not "without offspring" (ἀγονος). He is the absolute Being, the eternal One, who is and was and is to come, and in that way the ever-living and ever-productive One.

Attempts have been made to infer the Trinity from God's thinking and willing, from his love, goodness, and perfection, and so forth. Intended as philosophical construals of the doctrine of the Trinity, these attempts have been anything but satisfactory. The derivation of the Trinity from God's thought in no way leads to his tri-personality; instead, it fails to make clear the procession of the third person, and with a view to the Spirit has to pass over into, and augment itself with, a construction from the will of God. The derivation of the Trinity from love is open to the same objections and cannot make clear the procession of the Holy Spirit. The fact is that these attributes [of love and knowledge] as well as all the other attributes only come alive and become real as a result of the Trinity. Apart from it, they are mere names, sounds, empty terms. As attributes of the triune God they come alive both to our mind and to our heart. Only by the Trinity do we begin to understand that God as he is in himself—hence also, apart from the world—is the independent, eternal, omniscient, and all-benevolent One, love, holiness, and glory.

The Trinity reveals God to us as the fullness of being, the true life, eternal beauty. In God, too, there is unity in diversity, diversity in unity. Indeed, this order and this harmony is present in him absolutely. In the case of creatures we see only a faint analogy of it. Either the unity or the diversity does not come into its own. Creatures exist in time and space, exist side by side, and do not interpenetrate each other [like the persons in the Trinity]. Among us unity exists only by attraction, by the will and the disposition of the will; it is a moral unity that is fragile and unstable. And where there is a more profound physical unity as, say, between the capacities of a single substance, there is no independence, and the unity swallows up the diversity. But in God both are present: absolute unity as well as absolute diversity. It is one selfsame being sustained by three hypostases. This results in the most perfect kind of community, a community of the same beings; at the same time it results in the most perfect diversity, a diversity of divine persons. Therefore, if God is triune, the three persons can only be conceived as being "consubstantial" (ὁμοούσιοι). Inasmuch as Arianism in its many different forms does not think consistently about God's being, it cannot satisfy the mind. If there are distinctions within the divine being, these distinctions, that is, these persons, have to be the same in essence. In God there cannot be anything that is something other or less than God. There is nothing intermediate or transitional between the Creator and the creature. Either Father, Son, and Spirit all possess the same being and are truly God, or else they sink to the level of creatures. From a Christian perspective there is no third possibility. The same line of reasoning implies the condemnation of Sabellianism's modal Trinity. For the *homoousia* of the three persons has meaning and significance only if they are truly and really distinct from one another, as distinct bearers of the same substance. The diversity of the subjects who act side by side in divine revelation, in creation and in re-creation, arises from the diversity that exists among the three persons in the divine being. There could be no distinction *ad extra* in the unity of the divine being, if there were no distinction *ad intra*.

Second, the doctrine of the Trinity is of the greatest importance for the doctrine of creation. The latter can be maintained only on the basis of a confession of a triune God. It alone makes possible—against Deism on the one hand—the connection between God and the world, and—against pantheism on the other—the difference between God and the world. [The] creation cannot be conceived as mere happenstance, nor as the outcome of divine self-development. It must have its foundation in God, yet not be a phase in the process of his inner life. How can these two concerns be satisfied if not by the confession of a triune God? The life of God is divinely rich: it is fecund; it implies action, productivity. The doctrine of the Trinity, accordingly, speaks of the generation of the Son and the procession of the Spirit. Both of these acts are essentially distinct from the work of creation: the former are immanent relations, while the latter is work *ad extra*. The former are sufficient in themselves: God does not need the creation. He is life, blessedness, glory in himself. Still, the creation is most closely connected with this fecundity. For in the first place, as Athanasius correctly noted, if the divine being were not productive and could not communicate himself inwardly *(ad intra)*, then neither could there be any revelation of God *ad extra*, that is, any communication of God in and to his creatures. The doctrine of God's incommunicability, with its implicit denial of the Son's generation and the Spirit's procession, carries within itself the corollary of the existence of a world separate from, outside of, and opposed to God. In that case God is absolutely hidden, "cosmic depths," "absolute silence," "the unconscious," "the groundless." The world does not reveal him; there is no possibility of knowing him.

The dogma of the Trinity, by contrast, tells us that God *can* reveal himself in an absolute sense to the Son and the Spirit, and hence, in a relative sense also to the world. For, as Augustine teaches us, the self-communication that takes place within the divine being is archetypal for God's work in creation. Scripture repeatedly points to the close connection between the Son and Spirit on the one hand, and the creation on the other. The names Father, Son (Word, Wisdom), and Spirit most certainly denote immanent relationships, but they are also mirrored in the interpersonal relations present in the works of God *ad extra*. All things come from the Father; the "ideas" of all existent things are present in the Son; the first principles of all life are in the Spirit. Generation and procession in the divine being are the immanent acts of God, which make possible the outward works of creation and revelation. Finally, this also explains why all the works of God *ad extra* are only adequately known when their trinitarian existence is recognized. Of the examples cited earlier, some are extremely contrived and in any case no more than analogies. Still, consciously or unconsciously, philosophy from Plato to von Hartmann has always again returned to three first principles (ἀρχαι) on the basis of which the creation as a whole and in its various parts could be explained. There is much truth in the belief that creation everywhere displays to us vestiges of the Trinity. And because these vestiges are most clearly evident in "humanity," so that "human beings" may even be called "the image of the Trinity," "humanity" is driven from within to search out these vestiges. The perfection of a creature, the completeness of a system, the harmony of beauty—these are finally manifest only in a triad. The higher a thing's place in the order of creation, the more it aspires to the triad. One senses this effect even in the religious aberrations of humankind. Schelling's attempt to interpret mythology along trinitarian lines, for example, is more than a genial fantasy.

Third, the doctrine of the Trinity is of incalculable importance for the Christian religion. The entire Christian belief system, all of special revelation, stands or falls with the confession of God's Trinity. It is the core of the Christian faith, the root of all its dogmas, the basic content of the new covenant. It was this religious Christian interest, accordingly, that sparked the development of the church's doctrine of the Trinity. At stake in this development—let it be said emphatically—was not a metaphysical theory or a philosophical speculation but the essence of the Christian religion itself. This is so strongly felt that all who value being called a Christian recognize and believe in a kind of Trinity. The profoundest question implicit in every Christian creed and system of theology is how God can be both one and yet three. Christian truth in all its parts comes into its own to a lesser or greater extent depending on how that question is answered. In the doctrine of the Trinity we feel the heartbeat of God's entire revelation for the redemption of humanity. Though foreshadowed in the Old Testament, it only comes to light fully in Christ. Religion can be satisfied with nothing less than God himself. Now in Christ God himself comes out to us, and in the Holy Spirit he communicates himself to us. The work of re-creation is trinitarian through and through. From God, through God, and in God are all things. Re-creation is one divine work from beginning to end, yet it can be described in terms of three agents: it is fully accomplished by the love of the Father, the grace of the Son, and the communion of the Holy Spirit. A Christian's faith life, accordingly, points back to three generative principles. "We know all these things," says article 9 of the Belgic Confession, "from the testimonies of holy Scripture, as well as from the operations of the persons, especially from those we feel within ourselves." We know ourselves to be children of the Father, redeemed by the Son, and in communion with both through the Holy Spirit. Every blessing, both spiritual and material, comes to us from the triune God. In that name we are baptized; that name sums up our confession; that name is the source of all the blessings that come down to us; to that name we will forever bring thanksgiving and honor; in that name we find rest for our souls and peace for our conscience. Christians have a God above them, before them, and within them. Our salvation, both in this life and in the life to come, is bound up with the doctrine of the Trinity; yet we grant that we cannot determine the measure of knowledge—also of this mystery—needed for a true and sincere faith.

PART III

GOD'S WILL ON EARTH AS IT IS IN HEAVEN

7

THE DIVINE COUNSEL

God's works with respect to his creatures are classified into two groups: works ad intra or the decrees that are part of his counsel, and works ad extra such as creation and redemption. God's decrees and works do not exhaust the possibilities of his wisdom and knowledge; they are an exercise of his free and absolute will and will be realized in God's own time. All God's decrees, even election and reprobation, are made visible to us in the progress of history. They are, however, rooted in God's eternal foreknowledge and foreordination, which stands forever and will come to pass. God's purpose of election is antecedent to the facts of history; history serves to affirm that preexisting purpose. While Romans 9 most certainly speaks of God's action in time, the ground for the action lies outside of time, in the will and good pleasure of God alone. In all this it must be remembered that the ground of election is found exclusively in God's grace, love, and good pleasure.

When affirming the determining counsel of God, the major theological issue facing Christian theologians concerns human freedom. Against all deterministic thinking, the church maintained the moral free will and responsibility of human beings. It was the teaching and influence of Pelagius that led the church under Augustine's leadership to clarify the doctrine of predestination. For the Pelagians and semi-Pelagians, human nature is not absolutely corrupted after the fall. Fallen human nature can and must cooperate with the grace of God; predestination is only a matter of foreknowledge.

By contrast, Augustine insisted that the elect "are not chosen because they believed but in order that they might believe." God's absolutely sovereign will is the only ground of predestination, which includes both election and reprobation. Augustine did insist that God does not foreordain to destruction and the means that lead to it—namely, sins—in the same sense in which he foreordains to salvation and to the means that lead to it. Reprobation is an act of divine justice, as election is an act of grace.

Pelagianism was condemned at the Council of Ephesus (431) and later at the Synod of Orange (529). The latter, however, was indecisive on the full extent of human corruption and thus opened the door to semi-Pelagianism. As it was influenced by nominalism and hardened its stance at the Council of

Trent, the Roman Catholic church increasingly distanced itself from Paul and Augustine. Through a number of new distinctions, the absolutely gratuitous predestinating activity of God is reduced to, and made dependent upon, a form of foreknowledge. This trend reaches its climax in the thought of Molina, who believed that God, by a mediate knowledge, saw in advance that some humans would make good use of preparatory grace and for that reason decided to bestow it. Reprobation is then only a decree of God to punish eternally those whose sin and unbelief he has foreseen.

The Reformation returned to Augustine and Paul. Still, Luther's anthropological orientation and Melanchthon's synergism meant that predestination was set aside in Lutheranism, and eventually seventeenth-century Lutheran theologians approximated the Remonstrant confession. Here, with the departure of the Lutheran tradition itself from Luther, it parts ways with the Reformed tradition, which maintained the positions of Zwingli and Calvin. It is especially through Calvin's influence that the doctrine of predestination was included in the confessions of all the Reformed churches.

Confessional and theological differences, nonetheless, remained, including where and how the doctrine of predestination was to be treated in the body of Christian doctrine. The synthetic method, beginning with the source and foundation of all blessings, eventually prevailed over the analytic method, which considered the effects first. Systematic order and theological interest demanded that predestination be treated under the doctrine of God, and this became the regular order for all Reformed theologians. The reason for the difference with non-Reformed theologians is not that the latter seek only to reproduce Scripture while Reformed theology speculatively deduces predestination from an a priori, *philosophically deterministic concept of God. The most rigorous Calvinist seeks only to reproduce the teaching of Scripture; the real difference is that for the Reformed the primary concern in predestination is not anthropological or even soteriological but* theological— the glory of God.

The major difference within the Reformed theological camp itself had to do with the logical order of the divine decrees, the debate between supra- and infralapsarianism. The key issue here is whether to consider the decree to elect and to reprobate logically before (supra-) or after (infra-) the decree to create and to permit the fall. The differences must not be exaggerated. All followers of Augustine, including many Thomists, teach a form of double predestination that in some sense considers the fall into sin and reprobation within the counsel of God and not merely subject to his permission or foreknowledge. God's sovereignty is at stake here. While sin may be the proximate cause of reprobation, it is not the ultimate cause. Even if unknown to us, there has to be a higher plan of God, which existed before the fall. At the same time, though it did not condemn supralapsarianism, the Synod of Dort's judgments were infralapsarian in character, emphasizing the fall of the human race "by its own fault." Both views have a right to be called Reformed.

Even the milder predestinarianism of infralapsarianism encountered resistance. Socinians rejected it altogether, and the Arminians' emphasis on the universal of saving grace made human beings the final arbiters of their own destiny. In the Reformed churches this Arminian trend gained ground in the eighteenth and nineteenth centuries. When, in the nineteenth century, a deeper study of nature, history, and humanity demonstrated the untenability of deistic Pelagianism, a pantheistic or materialistic determinism came in its place. Though there is a fundamental difference between such determinism and the biblical doctrine of predestination, many interpret the ecclesiastical doctrine in this deterministic sense. Others reduce predestination to God's immanent action in time and identify the decree with the facts of history. In this way, the distinction between eternity and time, God and the world, is erased and theism is exchanged for pantheism. Most modern theology has no doctrine of election.

The counsel of God is to be understood as his eternal plan for all that exists or will happen in time. This decree must be distinguished from its execution in time as well as from God himself. God is not identical with his decree; his self-knowledge is not exhausted in creation, providence, and redemption. God's counsel is both the "efficient" and "exemplary" cause of all that is. God's counsel is also a single and simple decree, the world plan of a single "artistic" vision, though creatures can only see it unfolding in space and time as a multiplicity.

God's counsel in reference to the physical world is called "providence" and includes preservation and governance. That things exist and the way they exist, are grounded solely in God's good pleasure. If this is granted, then it must be acknowledged that the counsel of God also extends to the moral world and to human conduct. Dualistically splitting the natural and moral world and limiting God's governance to the former is impossible; such a split banishes God from his world, leaving it to chance and caprice. This position is firmly contradicted by Scripture, religious experience, and theological reflection. Scripture teaches that faith is a gift of God's grace, a work of God. Though in theory a person may be Pelagian, in the practice of the Christian life, above all in prayer, every Christian is an Augustinian. Self-glorying is excluded, and God alone is given the honor. Even foreknowledge, by definition, includes predestination. Either God knows the elect with certainty or not at all. If he does, foreknowledge is redundant. If not, even foreknowledge has to go. The doctrine of predestination, therefore, is a dogma of the entire Christian church.

Though proved untenable in general, Pelagianism repeatedly comes back to resume its attack at every special point in the doctrine of predestination. It begins by asserting the existence of an antecedent conditional decree of God to offer to all fallen humanity a grace that is sufficient for salvation. The reality of history, in which grace is particular and not universal, is impossible to square with this assertion. Even in the beginning, opportunity is not equal; being born in a Christian home or later becoming acquainted with the gospel, is undeserved and unconditional, a gift. Furthermore, not all who hear the gospel believe it. Here the Pelagian position becomes confused and introduces notions of merit, a view with no support in Scripture. Finally, Pelagianism's notion of "predestination to glory," a third decree granting salvation to those who persevere (as God foresaw) makes God's decree completely conditional. There is no real decree; only a wish whose fulfillment is uncertain. God does not know his own. Even where churches hold the doctrine of predestination impurely, with semi-Pelagian admixtures, they still confess it. Essentially and materially, predestination is a dogma accepted throughout Christianity.

Both the supralapsarian and infralapsarian position seek to be true to Scripture, and the difference between them cannot be resolved by an appeal to Scripture. Neither party denies that the fall into sin is included in God's plan and decree; both insist that God is not the author of sin. Both parties ultimately rest their case in the sovereign good pleasure of God. The only difference is that infralapsarians adhere to a historical, causal order of the decrees, while supralapsarians prefer the ideal, teleological order. Both positions have strengths and are also one-sided. Infralapsarianism seems more modest, less harsh, but does not finally satisfy the mind. Supralapsarianism has in its favor that it refrains from all useless attempts at justifying God and simply attributes both election and reprobation to God's sovereign good pleasure. Yet it risks making the objects of election and reprobation "possible" human beings rather than actual ones and making sin a means of reprobation in the same manner that Christ's redemptive work is the means of election. Supralapsarians, too, need to introduce notions such as "permission" and "preterition" with respect to sin.

Neither the supralapsarian view nor the infralapsarian view of predestination is capable of incorporating within its perspective the fullness and riches of the truth of Scripture and of satisfying our theological thinking. The truth inherent in supralapsarianism is that all the decrees together form a unity; that there is an ultimate goal to which all things are subordinated and serviceable; that the entrance of sin into the world did not take God by surprise but was willed by him; that creation was designed to make re-creation possible; and that in the creation of Adam, things were structured with a view to Christ. The truth of infralapsarianism is that the decrees can be differentiated with a view to their teleological and causal order; that creation and fall were not merely means to an end; that sin is a catastrophe which of and by itself could never have been willed by God. Full unity of conception here is only known to God and is a teleologically and causally interconnected pattern so rich that it cannot be reproduced in a single word such as "supralapsarian" or "infralapsarian." Just as in any organism all the parts are interconnected and reciprocally determine each other, so the world as a whole is a masterpiece of divine art, in which all the parts are organically connected. And of that world, in all its dimensions, the counsel of God is the eternal design.

The term "double predestination" encompasses both reprobation and election. While Scripture seldom speaks of reprobation as an eternal decree, it does see even in the negative events of history—suffering, hardening, inexplicable disasters—the active sovereign will of God. Believers do not claim

*to comprehend all this; they do believe that the alternative—pessimism as
the fruit of acknowledging the blind will of a chaotic deity—is impossible.
Believers are willing to look at the disturbing reality of life; they do not scatter
flowers over graves, turn death into an angel, regard sin as mere weakness, or
consider this the best of possible worlds. Calvinism has no use for such drivel.
It refuses to be hoodwinked. It takes full account of the seriousness of life,
champions the rights of the Lord of lords, and humbly bows in adoration before
the inexplicable sovereign will of God. This almighty God is also, we believe,
our merciful Father. This is not a "solution" but an invitation to rest in God.*

*Reprobation is, however, not a part of predestination in the same sense and
manner as election. We may not consider God's power as "absolute" in the sense
of capricious, separated from his justice. Though sin is not outside the scope of
God's will, it is definitely against it. The decree of reprobation, grounded in
God's will, must be distinguished from its execution, which is realized through
human culpability. It is a mistake to consider the decree of reprobation by
itself, alongside other decrees; God's decree is as broad as reality itself and in a
single conception encompasses the goal of his glory and the means to reach it.
In real life, sin and grace, punishment and blessing, justice and mercy, do not
exist side by side but are the common experience of all people. Thus, whereas
election and reprobation may culminate in final and total separation, on earth
they continually crisscross each other. Neither is the final goal or cause; both are
means to the attainment of God's glory. But whereas God is removed from all
wickedness and does not will sin and punishment as such and for its own sake,
he does delight in the election and redemption of his own.*

*Predestination finally culminates, therefore, in election. Chosenness exists
everywhere in life; the world is not ordered according to the Pharisaic law
of work and reward. While Scripture and Reformed theology recognize the
significance of secondary causes, these are not the final and most fundamental
causes. The many "why?" questions cannot be answered by mortals; we can
only rest in God's sovereign good pleasure. Even in election, it is not correct,
strictly speaking, to speak of Christ as its "cause." With his church Christ is
better seen as the object of the Father's electing love. The salvation of human
beings is firmly established in the gracious and omnipotent good pleasure of
God. To be elect "in Christ" is to be organically united to his body, the church.
Christ was foreordained to be head of the church. Election is the divine "idea,"
the blueprint of the temple that God builds in the course of the ages and of
which he is the supreme builder and architect. Creation and fall, preservation
and governance, sin and grace, Adam and Christ—all contribute to the
construction of this divine edifice, and this building itself is built to the honor
and glorification of God.*

[232] Until now we have discussed God's being as such—not, of course, in the
sense that we thought and spoke about God apart from his revelation in nature
and Scripture. The truth is, we cannot speak of God except on the basis of his

self-revelation. When we venture to take his names upon our tongue, we need to speak of him as Christians, people who have been taught by God himself and instructed by his Word. Still, in the preceding chapters we considered God as—according to his self-revelation—he exists in himself. We learned to know him as the eternal Being who is at once Supreme Existence and Supreme Life, pure essence and at the same time pure and total activity. Throughout Scripture God is presented as the living, working God. Included in the works of God are creation, preservation, and governance (Gen. 2:3; Deut. 11:7; Job 34:19; Ps. 102:26; Isa. 64:8; John 9:3–4; Heb. 1:10). All those works are perfect (Deut. 32:4), faithful (Ps. 33:4), just and kind (Ps. 111:7; 145:17; Dan. 9:14), great and awesome and marvelous (Ps. 66:3; 92:5; 104:24; 111:2; 139:14; Rev. 15:3), so that the Lord himself delights in them (Ps. 104:31). He neither sleeps nor slumbers (Ps. 121:3–4), does not faint or grow weary (Isa. 40:28). Working is integral to his being; the drive and the need to work is ever present in him. "My Father," said Jesus, "is always at his work" (John 5:17 NIV).

For that reason, too, he did not just begin to work at the time of creation, for his works are from everlasting to everlasting. God's personal attributes, which we studied in the previous chapter, are the immanent and eternal works of God. The Father eternally gives to the Son, and with him to the Spirit, to have life in himself (John 5:26). And the community of being that exists among the three persons is a life of absolute activity. The Father knows and loves the Son eternally—from before the foundation of the world (Matt. 11:27; John 17:24)—and the Spirit searches the deep things of God (1 Cor. 2:10). All these works of God are immanent. They bear no relation to anything that exists or will exist outside of God, but occur within the divine being and concern the relations existing among the three persons. However, they are also very important to us inasmuch as they make God known to us as the all-sufficient and blessed Being, who is "not served by human hands as though he needed anything" (Acts 17:25). God does not need the world for his own perfection. He does not need the work of creation and preservation in order not to be unemployed. He is absolute activity within himself.

Distinguished from these purely immanent works of God are those that relate to the creatures who will exist outside of his being. These works can again be classified in two groups: the works of God *ad intra* (inward) and the works of God *ad extra* (outward). The former are usually designated as "decrees" and are all included in the one, eternal "counsel of God." These decrees establish a connection between the immanent works of the divine being and the external works of creation and re-creation. As such they possess the following three characteristics.

In the first place, all the ideas that are included in the divine decrees and hence designed for realization outside of the divine being are derived from the fullness of knowledge that is eternally present in God. Possibility and actuality do not coincide. The creation of the world does not exhaust the riches of God's knowledge and wisdom. The infinite being of God is infinitely more abundant than the whole world in all its dimensions could ever present to our view. What is included in the decrees is no more than a sketch, a summary, of the depths of the riches of both God's wisdom and knowledge. With God all things are possible (Matt. 19:26), but they are not all actualized.

In the second place, all the decrees of God are based on his absolute sovereignty. God is self-sufficient: in him there is no need or compulsion to actualize any of his ideas in a world of creatures. He is perfectly free in his choices; it is only by his will that all things exist and were created (Rev. 4:11). Accordingly, even though the decrees are eternal (since in God there can be no before or after), and to that extent the decrees coincide with the decreeing God, we must still make a logical distinction between the content of God's self-knowledge and that of his knowledge of the world, between the infinite being of God and the object of his decrees.

In the third place, implied in the idea of the decrees is that in due time they will be realized. Although God as all-sufficient Being does not need a world, it is his decree that makes the creation and preservation of the world necessary. In the counsel of God the theism of Scripture posits a connection between God and the world, simultaneously maintains the absolute sovereignty of God and the complete dependence of his creatures, thus avoiding both the error of pantheism and that of Deism. The things we see are not made out of the things that appear (Heb. 11:3), but owe their causation to God's thought, his will, that is, to his decrees.

THE TEACHING OF SCRIPTURE

Scripture as such does not offer us an abstract description of these decrees; instead, they are made visible to us in the progression of history itself. God is Lord of the entire earth and demonstrates his lordship from day to day in the creation, preservation, and governance of all things. The same is true of election and reprobation. In the Old Testament these two realities are not described as eternal decrees but face us on every page as facts in history. From the beginning the human race was split into two groupings: the God-fearing, holy line of Seth (Gen. 4:25–26; 5:1–32) and the line of Cain, which increasingly alienated itself from God (Gen. 4:17–24). When the two intermarry and wickedness increases, Noah alone finds favor in the eyes of the Lord (Gen. 6). After the flood a blessing is pronounced upon Shem and Japheth, but a curse upon Canaan (Gen. 9:25–27). From among Shem's descendants Abraham is chosen (Gen. 12). Of his sons, Isaac, not Ishmael, is the child of promise (Gen. 17:19–21; 21:12–13). Of Isaac's sons, Jacob was loved and Esau hated (Gen. 25:23; Mal. 1:2; Rom. 9:11–12). When the sons of Jacob are each given a rank and task of their own, Judah is given primacy (Gen. 49). While other nations are passed by for a time and walk in their own ways, Israel alone is chosen by the Lord to be a people for his own possession. This election (Hos. 13:5; Amos 3:2) is not based on Israel's worthiness but arises solely from God's

compassion (Deut. 4:37; 7:6–8; 8:17–18; 9:4–6; 10:15; Ezek. 16:1ff.; Amos
9:7), which is from everlasting (Jer. 31:3). The object of this compassion and
love is Israel as a people and nation, though thousands of its citizens broke
the covenant and thus occasioned the distinction between Israel "according to
the flesh" and Israel "according to the promise" (Rom. 2:28–29; 9–11). The
purpose of this love was that Israel should belong to the Lord, be a people for
his own possession, and walk before him in holiness of life (Exod. 19:5; Deut.
7:6; 14:2; 26:18; Ps. 135:4; Mal. 3:17). Again, within Israel there is repeated
reference to a special election, an election to a special position or ministry.
Examples are the election of Jerusalem and Zion to be the dwelling place of
the Lord (Deut. 12:5; 14:23; 1 Kings 11:32; 2 Kings 21:7; Ps. 78:68, 70); the
election of Moses to be the mediator of the Old Covenant (Exod. 3); of Levi
to the priesthood (Deut. 18:5; 21:5); of Saul and David to kingship (1 Sam.
10:24; 2 Sam. 6:21); of prophets to their office (1 Sam. 3; Isa. 6; Jer. 1; Ezek.
1–3; Amos 3:7–8; 7:15); above all, the election of the Messiah as the redeemer
of his people, who in a unique sense is Israel, the servant of YHWH (Isa. 41:8;
42:1; 44:1; 45:4; etc.).

Now, although this election in the Old Testament usually occurs as a fact
in history and coincides with the "calling" itself, it is rooted in God's foreknowledge and foreordination. Generally speaking, the Old Testament teaches
that God creates, preserves, and rules all things by his word and wisdom (Ps.
33:6; 104:24; Job 38; Prov. 8; etc.), so that everything has its foundation in
the mind of God. But it is also expressly stated that God knows the future
and declares it in advance (Isa. 41:21–23; 42:9; 43:9–12; 44:7; 46:10; 48:3ff.;
Amos 3:7). In prophecy he makes things known beforehand, both the events
that will occur, and the manner in which they will occur (Gen. 3:14ff.; 6:13;
9:25ff.; 12:2ff.; 15:13ff.; 25:23; 49:8ff.; etc.). A person's days are numbered
in advance and recorded in God's book "when none of them as yet existed"
(Ps. 139:16; 31:15; 39:5; Job 14:5). The names of the righteous are recorded
in the Book of Life, just as the names of the inhabitants of a city or of the
citizens of a nation are registered. On that basis they have the assurance that
they will share life in communion with God in Israel's theocracy (Exod. 32:32;
Ps. 87:6; Ezek. 13:9; Jer. 17:13; Ps. 69:28). According to Isaiah 4:3 and Daniel
12:1, those whose names are recorded in the book of life will take part in the
theocratic salvation ordained for the future. Foreshadowed here is the New
Testament idea that the book of life contains the names of those who will inherit
eternal life. All things, furthermore, happen in accordance with the counsel of
God. With him is wisdom and power, counsel and understanding (Job 12:13;
Prov. 8:14; Isa. 9:6; 11:2; 28:29; Jer. 32:19). As a result he ever chooses the
means best suited to the attainment of his goal, needs no one's advice, and
is awesome, elevated far above the counsel of the saints and of all those who
surround him (Isa. 40:13; Jer. 23:18, 22; Ps. 89:7–8). God's counsel is his
determinate thought and fixed decree pertaining to all things (Isa. 14:24–27;
Dan. 4:24). That counsel, though secret (Job 15:8), is realized in history. All

things happen in accordance with that counsel; it stands forever, and no one can withstand it (Isa. 14:24–27; 46:10; Ps. 33:11; Prov. 19:21), while on the other hand the counsel of the enemies will be nullified (Neh. 4:15; Ps. 33:10; Prov. 21:30; Jer. 19:7).

[233] The New Testament speaks in even much clearer language about the counsel of God. Not only are all God's works known to him from eternity (Acts 15:18; cf. the various readings), but all things happen according to "the determinate counsel and foreknowledge of God" [Acts 2:23 KJV]. The New Testament word βουλη denotes the will of God as based on counsel and deliberation, and differs in that respect from θελημα, which is the divine will per se (cf. Eph. 1:11: "the counsel of his will," βουλη του θεληματος αὐτου). This counsel of God antecedes all things. It is all encompassing (Eph. 1:11), including the sinful deeds of humans (Acts 2:23; 4:28; cf. Luke 22:22). God has determined in advance the areas to be inhabited by the peoples as well as the allotted times of their existence (Acts 17:26). God's will is made known also in the perdition of Judas (John 17:12), in the abandonment of the Gentiles (Rom. 1:24), in the rejection of Esau (Rom. 9:13), in the hardening of the hearts of the wicked (Rom. 9:18), in raising up Pharaoh (Rom. 9:17), in "endur[ing] with much patience the objects of wrath that are made for destruction" (Rom. 9:22), in Christ's being set not only for the rising but also for the falling of many (Luke 2:34), for judgment (John 3:19–21), for a stone of stumbling and a rock of offense (1 Pet. 2:7–8; cf. 1 Thess. 5:9; Jude 4).

But the counsel of God (βουλη του θεου) has reference mainly to the work of redemption (Luke 7:30; Acts 13:36; 20:27; Heb. 6:17). And the New Testament possesses a wealth of words to further describe the counsel of God. It speaks of God's good pleasure (εὐδοκια: Matt. 11:26; Luke 2:14; 10:21; Eph. 1:5, 9; Phil. 2:13; 2 Thess. 1:11); his purpose (προθεσις: Rom. 8:28; 9:11; Eph. 1:11; 3:11; 2 Tim. 1:9); his foreknowledge (προγνωσις: Rom. 8:29; 11:2; 1 Pet. 1:2); his election (ἐκλογη: Mark 13:20; Acts 9:15; 13:17; 15:7; Rom. 9:11; 11:5, 28; 1 Cor. 1:27–28; Eph. 1:4; 1 Thess. 1:4; 2 Pet. 1:10; James 2:5); his predestination (προορισμος: Rom. 8:29; 1 Cor. 2:7; Eph. 1:5, 11). Consider also Acts 13:48 [cf. KJV], where we read that "as many as were ordained (τεταγμενοι) to eternal life became believers," that is, not as many as had prepared themselves or were subjectively predisposed, but as many as were ordained to eternal life; also, Ephesians 2:10 says that God had "prepared" (προητοιμασεν) believers for good works.

The different meanings here are as follows: "Purpose" (προθεσις) indicates that in the work of salvation God does not act arbitrarily but according to a fixed plan, an unalterable purpose. "Election" (ἐκλογη) makes clear that this purpose of salvation is not all-inclusive but that "God's purpose of election" (Rom. 9:11) is elective, so that not all but many are saved. "Foreknowledge" (προγνωσις) pertains to the persons who in this elective purpose of God are the object, not of God's bare foreknowledge, but of his active delight. "Foreordination" (προορισμος), finally, refers more to the means God uses to bring his "known ones" to their appointed destiny. "*Prothesis* refers to the end; *prognosis* refers to the objects; *proorismos* to the means; *prothesis* to the certainty of the event; *prognosis* and *eklogē* to the singleness and distinction of persons; *proorismos* to the order of means. This election is certain and immutable by *prothesin;* determinate and definite by *prognosin;* and ordinate by *proorismon.*"[1] Although the eternity of this purpose is not automatically included in the preposition *"pro,"* used in the composition of these words, it is clearly articulated in Ephesians 3:11 and 2 Timothy 1:9 (cf. Matt. 25:34; 1 Cor. 2:7; Eph. 1:4).

It has indeed been asserted that in Romans 9 Paul is not dealing with God's absolute sovereignty and eternal decree but only with "divine conduct whose causes as well as whose operations occur in time, that is, in history."[2] But this assertion is refuted by Romans 9. Here the "purpose of election" is clearly antecedent to the facts of history. History, accordingly, serves to affirm that preexisting purpose (Rom. 9:11). Long before the event itself, Sarah had been promised a "child of promise" (v. 9). And before the birth of Isaac's children God had already said that the elder would serve the younger (vv. 11–12). The verses 15–18 teach us that election has its grounds, not in works, but solely in the will of him who calls. Romans 9 most certainly speaks of God's action in time, but the ground for the action lies outside of time, in the will and good pleasure of God alone. Add to this that the ground of election is found exclusively in God's grace, love, and good pleasure in other places as well (Matt. 11:25; Luke 12:32; Eph. 1:5, 9, 11; 2 Tim. 1:9–10). Nor is it correct to associate Romans 9:21 exclusively with the "incorrupt mass" of supralapsarianism or exclusively with the "corrupt mass" of Augustine and infralapsarianism. Paul does not have this distinction in mind at all. He only wants to say that God has the absolute right to give his creatures the destiny that seems good to him (cf. Isa. 10:15; Jer. 18; Matt. 20:15). From the perspective of absolute right a creature cannot quarrel with its Creator. Paul makes no attempt to demonstrate the fairness or justice of election but simply silences the objectors with an appeal to the absolute sovereignty of God.

1. F. Turretin, *Institutes of Elenctic Theology*, IV, qu. 7.

2. W. Beyschlag, *Die paulinische Theodicee Römer IX–XI: Ein Beitrag zur biblischen Theologie*, 2d ed. (Halle: Strien, 1896); ed. note: Bavinck cites the 2d edition with the date 1905. Also see I. van Dijk, "De Leer der Verkiezing volgens het Nieuwe Testament," *Studiën: Theologisch Tijdschrift* 4 (1878): part 3 (= pages 275–339 in *Gezamenlijke Geschriften van Dr. Isaak van Dikj*, vol. 1 [Groningen: Noordhoff, 1917]), discussion among Saussaye, Valeton, and van Dijk; Buhl, "Der Gedankengang von Röm. 9–11," *Theologische Studien und Kritiken* 59 (1887): 295–320; Robert Kübel, "Prädestination," *PRE²*, XII, 145–62; E. Kühl, *Zur Paulinischen Theodicee, Römer 9–11* (Göttingen: Vandenhoeck & Ruprecht, 1897); Kühl, while accepting an absolutely free foreordination of the redemptive order, rejects that of persons. Others, by contrast, acknowledge that Romans 9:11–21 undoubtedly teaches the election of some and the rejection of others: J. Kaftan, *Dogmatik* (Tübingen: Mohr, 1901), 467; T. Häring, *Der christliche Glaube*, 2d ed. (Calw and Stuttgart: Verlag der Vereinsbuchhandlung, 1912), 516; ed. note: ET: *The Christian Faith*, trans. John Dickie and George Ferries, 2 vols. (London: Hodder & Stoughton, 1913). Likewise, H. J. Holtzmann, *Lehrbuch der neutestamentlichen Theologie*, II, 171; K. Müller, *Die göttliche Zuvorersehung und Erwählung in ihrer Bedeutung für den Heilsstand des einzelnen Gläubigen nach dem Evangelium des Paulus* (Halle a.S.: Max Niemeyer, 1892).

Just as the New Testament more clearly affirms the eternal character of divine election than the Old, so it also views election more in individual and personal terms. Whereas in the Old Testament the object of election is the people of Israel, in the New Testament the objects are certain specific persons. These persons are chosen in Christ, together they form his body, and they are called "the elect" (Matt. 24:31; Luke 18:7; Acts 13:48; Rom. 8:33; Eph. 1:4; Titus 1:1–2; 2 Tim. 2:10; 1 Pet. 1:1, 2, 9; etc.). The same thing is evident from the Book of Life, in which are recorded the names of the heirs of eternal life (Luke 10:20; Heb. 12:23; Phil. 4:3; Rev. 3:5; 13:8; 20:12; 21:27; 22:19). Finally, it is the clear teaching of the New Testament that the goal of election is not an earthly life in Canaan, nor a prominent place in the kingdom of God, but especially the blessedness of heaven. Granted, within the church there exists also an election to some office or ministry, for example, that of the apostles (Luke 6:13; John 6:70; etc.), but election proper has as its purpose holiness (Eph. 1:4), adoption as children (Eph. 1:5), salvation (2 Thess. 2:13), eternal life (Acts 13:48), conformity to Christ (Rom. 8:29; John 17:24), the glorification of God (Eph. 1:6, 12). In Romans 9, too, Paul is not speaking of a superior or inferior place in the kingdom of heaven. Rather, he is making a distinction within Israel itself between "the children of the flesh" and "the children of the promise." He speaks specifically of "vessels of honor" and "vessels of dishonor fitted for destruction." Paul contrasts God's mercy with God's hardening, and in verses 14 and 19 gives voice to objections whose seriousness presupposes precisely the doctrine of such a sovereign election.

AUGUSTINE AND THE PELAGIAN CHALLENGE

[234] Outside the Christian religion there has also been much controversy about predestination and freedom of the will. Philosophy has shifted back and forth between a pantheistic determinism and a deistic theory of freedom. Jewish thought ascribes freedom of the will to humans even in the state of sin.[3] Within Islam there has been controversy about predestination and freedom of the will, which was in many respects analogous to that in the Christian church. In Islam God is the personification of absolute omnipotence and arbitrariness, before whom humans are passive. Opposition to this view arose in the second century of the hegira, when the Motazelites defended free will, argued against predestination, and regarded justice, not omnipotence, as the characteristic essence of God.[4]

3. F. W. Weber, *System der altsynagogalen palästinischen Theologie: Aus Targum, Midrasch und Talmud* (Leipzig: Dörffling & Franke, 1880), 223.

4. M. Th. Houtsma, *De Strijd over het Dogma in den Islam tot op el-Ash'ari* (Leiden: S. C. van Doesburgh, 1875); A. Kuenen, *Volksgodsdienst en Wereldgodsdienst* (Leiden: S. C. van Doesburgh, 1882), 40ff. Cf. also the debate in the school of Ramanuja in Indonesia that is frequently compared with that between Gomarius and the Arminians: P. D. Chantepie de la Saussaye, *Lehrbuch der Religionsgeschichte*, 3d ed., 2 vols. (Tübingen: J. C. B. Mohr [Paul Siebeck], 1905), I, 448; H. Th. Obbink, "Nieuwe Gegevens ter Beoordeeling der Mohammedaansche Praedestinatieleer," *Theologische Studiën* 21 (1903): 350–78.

In the early church, at a time when it had to contend with pagan fatalism and gnostic naturalism, its representatives focused exclusively on the moral nature, freedom, and responsibility of humans and could not do justice, therefore, to the teaching of Scripture concerning the counsel of God. Though humans had been more or less corrupted by sin, they remained free and were able to accept the proffered grace of God. The church's teaching did not include a doctrine of absolute predestination and irresistible grace. The counsel of God consisted in foreknowledge and the determination of reward or punishment that depended on that foreknowledge. God abandons to their unbelief those whom he knows in advance will not believe and elects those whose merits he has foreseen.[5] In essence this has remained the position of the orthodox church. Humanity has been weakened by sin and become mortal. Humans, nevertheless, can still choose the naturally good and accept or reject the grace offered in the gospel (prevenient grace). If humans accept it, they are supported by that grace (cooperative grace) and must persevere to the end, for they can still always fall away. Those who accept that grace and persevere have been foreknown and predestined for salvation. The others—though by an antecedent will God wills the salvation of all—are left in their fallen condition and predestined to perdition.[6]

In his manner of expression Pelagius aligned himself with the older theologians, but his rationalism and ascetic moralism prompted him nevertheless to neglect parts of the doctrine that were generally accepted and recognized earlier, such as original sin, death as the punishment of sin, and so forth.[7] Thus he arrived at a set of ideas that, though incompatible with Christian doctrine, were even more consistently developed and systematized by his followers, Coelestius and Julian of Eclanum. Pelagius proceeded from the premise that God is good and just, and that therefore every creature God has called into being must by nature be good. If this is the case, then that nature can never be changed into an evil and corrupt nature. This is especially true of free will, God's greatest gift to humankind, the real image of God. By virtue of this will humans possess the glorious and inamissible freedom to do both good and evil. While the possibility of doing good or evil is God-given, the willing and doing are totally within their own power. And even when they do evil, they do not thereby lose the nature of the will, which is the possibility and power

5. Justin Martyr, *Dialogue with Trypho*, §141; Irenaeus, *Against Heresies*, IV, 29; Tertullian, *Against Marcion*, II, 23; Wilhelm Münscher, *Lehrbuch des christlichen Dogmengeschichte*, ed. Daniel von Coelln, 3d ed. (Cassel: J. C. Krieger, 1832–38), I, 356ff.; K. R. Hagenbach, *A Text-Book of the History of Doctrines*, trans. C. W. Buch, rev. Henry B. Smith, 2 vols. (New York: Sheldon, 1867), §§48, 57; J. Calvin, *Institutes*, II.ii.4, 9.

6. John of Damascus, *Exposition of the Orthodox Faith*, II, 29–30; The Orthodox Confession, qu. 26–30.

7. A. von Harnack, *History of Dogma*, trans. N. Buchanan, J. Millar, E. B. Speirs, and W. McGilchrist, and ed. A. B. Bruce, 7 vols. (London: Williams & Norgate, 1896–99), V, 172ff.; H. Reuter, *Augustinische Studien* (Gotha: F. A. Perthes, 1887), 37; F. Loofs, *Leitfaden zum studium der dogmengeschichte*, 4th ed. (Halle a.S.: M. Niemeyer, 1906), 422.

to do good. The free will, in the sense of the possibility of doing both good and evil, is an inamissible good of nature. Sin is always a free act of the will; it can never become a natural disposition or condition, and it leaves human nature with its free will unimpaired.

From these ideas it follows, first of all, that Adam's fall has no significance for his posterity. All humans are born in the same moral condition as that in which Adam was created. There is no such thing as original sin; death is not the penalty for sin but common and natural. The enormous spread of sin has to be explained in terms of people following a bad example. Nor is sin, absolutely speaking, universal; not only can we point to Old Testament examples of a sinless life, but it is also possible for Christians to abstain from all sins. Second, given this view, grace can only consist in the fact that in creation God first gave humans "natural power" (to do good), and then in the moral law and in the doctrine and example of Christ, he offers them "divine assistance" according to their merits, that is, to such people who use their free will properly. Finally, on this basis there was nothing left for predestination but divine foreknowledge (prevision) of the free acts and merits of humans, and a corresponding predetermination of reward and punishment. Actually, therefore, there is no predestination on the part of God, neither to grace nor to salvation; it depends completely on the prevision of good deeds accomplished by humans. Only in the case of infant baptism did Pelagius face a real difficulty, since it is conferred apart from any merit; nor could he escape from it except by subterfuges and non sequiturs of every kind.

Pelagius's doctrine was somewhat softened in the semi-Pelagianism—as it was called in the Middle Ages—of John Cassian [ca. 360–432 A.D.], abbot in Marseilles, a pupil of Chrysostom, and well-versed in the Greek fathers. According to John Cassian, sin did in fact corrupt human nature. Fallen humans are not dead, however, but sick. They are now like sick persons who, though they cannot cure themselves, can take medicine and yearn for healing; or they are like a person who has fallen into a well and cannot get out but is able to seize the rope thrown out to rescue him or her. Sinful humans, accordingly, though they cannot merit grace, can accept it and, assisted by it, persevere. God grants that grace, moreover, to those persons—including children and nations—whose acceptance of it and perseverance in it he has foreseen. On the other hand, he withholds it from those of whom he has foreseen the contrary. Predestination and reprobation therefore hinge on the foreknowledge of God concerning the attitude of people toward the grace offered. "[Salvation] is for us to will, for God to complete."[8]

8. G. J. Vossius, *Historiae de controversiis, quas Pelagius eiusque religuiae moverunt* (Leiden: Patius, 1618 (2d, emended ed., Amsterdam: Elzevir, 1655); G. F. Wiggers, *Versuch einer pragmatischen darstellung des Augustinismus und Pelagianismus*, 2 vols. (Hamburg: F. A. Perthes, 1830–31); F. Wörter, *Der Pelagianismus nach seinem Ursprunge und seiner Lehre* (Freiburg: Wagner, 1866); idem, *Beiträge zur Dogmengeschichte des Semipelagianismus* (Paderborn: F. Schöningh, 1898); J. Jüngst, *Kultus- und Geschichtsreligion (Pelagianismus und Augustinismus)* (Giessen: J. Ricker, 1901); A. E. Bruckner, *Julian von Eclanum: Sein Leben und seine Lehre*

Even long before the Pelagian controversy Augustine already taught the doctrine of predestination. He came to his position by his study of the Letter to the Romans[9] and meant only to pass on the teaching of Scripture (*De dono pers.*, ch. 19). He first presented it in his *Quaestiones ad Simplicianum* (397) and further developed it in his works *De correptione et gratia* (427), *De praedestione sanctorum*, and *De dono perseverantiae* (428 or 429). Augustine distinguishes between "foreknowledge" and "predestination," the former being broader in scope than the latter. "To have predestined is to have foreknown what he was going to do" (*De dono pers.*, 18; *De praed. sanct.*, 10, 19). This predestination of the saints is simply "the foreknowledge and the preparation of God's favors by which those who are delivered are most certainly delivered" (*De dono pers.*, 14). This predestination is not according to merit or worth but purely out of grace, not on account of faith but to faith. "They are not chosen because they believed but in order that they may believe" (*De praed. sanct.*, 17). Are not all humans the same—members of a condemned mass? (*De civ.*, XIV, 26; *De praed. sanct.*, 8; *De nat. et gr.*, 4, 8; etc.). This is especially apparent in the predestination of young children, some of whom perish without having been baptized while others are saved by baptism (*De praed. sanct.*, 12; *Enchir.*, 98). Predestination's only ground is the absolutely sovereign will of God. He owes no one anything and can justly condemn all humans, but in his good pleasure he makes of one "a vessel of honor" and of another "a vessel of dishonor" (*De praed. sanct.*, 8 [Rom. 9:21 KJV]).

To speak of predestination, therefore, is also to speak of reprobation. Augustine repeatedly subsumes it under the heading of predestination. He speaks of a "predestination to eternal death" (*De anima et eius orig.*, IV, 10; *De civ.*, XXII, 24), of "those predestined to eternal destruction" (*in Joh. Ev.*, *tract.* 48), of a "world predestined to condemnation" (ibid., 111), of Judas as "predestined to perdition" (ibid., 107), and so forth. Augustine, therefore, interpreted 1 Timothy 2:4 ["who desires everyone to be saved"] in a restricted sense and in various ways (*Enchir.*, 103; *De corr. et. grat.*, 14). Usually, however, he views predestination as foreordination to salvation. In connection with goodness predestination is necessary; in the case of evil, foreknowledge—which he views not merely as passive but also as active—is sufficient. For God does not foreordain to destruction and to the means that lead to it—namely, sins—in the same sense in which he foreordains to salvation and to the means that lead to it. In Augustine, predestination is always fully completed, that is, to salvation and, by implication, also to grace. Included among the predestined are

(Leipzig: J. C. Hinrichs, 1897); H. Zimmer, *Pelagius in Irland* (Berlin: Weidmann, 1901); A. von Harnack, *History of Dogma*, V, 172ff.; F. Loofs, *Leitfaden zum Studium der Dogmengeschichte*, 4th ed. (Halle a.S.: M. Niemeyer, 1906), 422; F. Loofs, "Pelagius," *PRE³*, XV, 747–74; A. Souter, *The Commentary of Pelagius on the Epistles of Paul: The Problem of Its Restoration* (London: Oxford University Press, 1907); A. Jülicher, review of *The Commentary of Pelagius on the Epistles of Paul*, by A. Souter, *Theologische Litteraturzeitung* (February 15, 1907): 203ff.
    9. H. Reuter, *Augustinische Studien*, 5ff.

also those who do not yet believe or have not yet even been born. Still, their number is fixed and unchangeable. In time, they all come to Christ, receive baptism and faith and above all the gift of perseverance. This gift is given only to the predestined. People can only know whether they are predestined from their having persevered to the end. God has included in the membership of the church some people who are not elect and do not persevere, in order that the predestined should not be proud and seek out a false peace (*De corr. et gr.*, 13). Why God should save only some and let others perish is a mystery. It is not unjust, for he owes no one anything. Reprobation is an act of justice, as predestination is an act of grace. God manifests his virtues in both (*De civ.*, XIV, 26).[10]

[235] Pelagianism was condemned, along with Nestorianism, at the council of Ephesus (431). The controversy between the followers of Augustine, Prosper, Hilary, the anonymous author of *De vocatione omnium gentium*, Lucidus, Fulgentius, and others, on the one hand; and the semi-Pelagians Cassian, Faustus of Reji, the anonymous author of the much-discussed book *Praedestinatus*[11] (which originated in the fifth century and was published in 1643 by the Jesuit Sirmond), Gennadius, Vincent of Lerins, and others, on the other—this controversy was not decided until the Synod of Orange (529). This Synod clearly stated, on the one hand, that the whole person is corrupted by the sin of Adam (can. 1–2); that of themselves humans have nothing but falsehood and sin (can. 22); and that we owe both the beginning and increase of our faith, not to our natural powers, that is, to our free will, but to grace, to the infusion, operation, inspiration, and illumination of the Holy Spirit within us, who turns our will from unbelief to faith (can. 3–8). On the other hand, the synod declared concerning free will that it is only weakened and rendered infirm by sin (can. 8, 13, 25); also, by the grace received in baptism, along with Christ's assistance and cooperation, all the baptized are able—if they will only labor faithfully—and under obligation to perform what is necessary for salvation (can. 13, 25).

Furthermore, not a word is said about absolute predestination, irresistible grace, and the particularity of grace. This indecisiveness had a harmful effect, as became clear in the predestinarian controversy surrounding Gottschalk. By that time the semi-Pelagian or Pelagian position had already been adopted by many, such as Hincmar, Rabanus, Erigena, whose positions gained a victory

10. G. F. Wiggers, *Versuch einer pragmatischen darstellung des Augustinismus und Pelagianismus*, I, 290ff.; J. P. Baltzer, *Des heiligen Augustinus Lehre über Prädestination und Reprobation* (Vienna: Braumüller, 1871); O. Rottmanner, *Der Augustinismus, eine dogmengeschichtliche Studie* (Munich: J. J. Lentner'schen Buchhandlung, 1892); J. Schwane, *Dogmengeschichte*, 4 vols. (Freiburg i.B.: Herder, 1882–95), II², 557; F. Loofs, *Leitfaden zum Studium der Dogmengeschichte*, 377ff.; B. B. Warfield, *Two Studies in the History of Doctrine: Augustine and the Pelagian Controversy* (New York: Christian Literature Co., 1897), 1–139.

11. Preuschen, "Prädestinatus," *PRE³*, XV, 602–4; H. von Schubert, *Der sogenannte Prädestinatus: Ein Beitrag zur Geschichte des Pelagianismus* (Leipzig: J. C. Hinrichs, 1903); A. Faure, *Die Widerlegung der Häretiker im ersten Buche des Praedestinatus* (Göttingen: Dieterich, 1903).

at the Synod of Quierzy (853). Nevertheless, there were also numerous erudite men who absolutely disagreed with the condemnation of Gottschalk and the pronouncements of Quierzy. Among them were Prudentius, Remigius, Ratramnus, Lupus, and others, who defended a double predestination: (1) a predestination to glory—not dependent on foreseen faith or merits—which is the cause of predestination to grace, faith, merits, and so forth; and (2) a predestination to damnation that does not in the same manner include a predestination to sins but is, at least as positive reprobation, dependent on the foreknowledge and permission of sin. For that reason 1 Timothy 2:4 was still viewed as restrictive, not as including all humans individually, but all sorts of people; and for that reason, too, it was considered absurd to think that Christ had made satisfaction for all humans, hence also for pagans who had never heard of him, and even of the man of sin, the Antichrist.[12] In addition, there was the position of the Synod of Valence (855) and, later, of scholasticism generally. "Predestination to death" was preferably not called by that name because it might easily be construed to imply, as the means of realization, a predestination to sins. It is usually treated under the name of reprobation. The latter is sometimes differentiated in terms of negative and positive reprobation. The former occurs prior to foreseen merits and is an act of sovereignty; the latter, however, is dependent on and follows foreknowledge and the decree to permit sin. For that reason 1 Timothy 2:4 is still read in a restrictive sense and interpreters still refrain from teaching a universal divine benevolence and universal atonement.[13]

But nominalism, the rejection of the Reformation, and Jesuitism succeeded in distancing the Roman Catholic church and its theology ever farther from Augustine and Paul. Rome, realizing that it could not with impunity dismiss the call to reformation, at Trent established the following dogma:

1. "Although free will, attenuated as it was in its powers and bent down, was by no means lost and extinguished" (*Trent,* session VI, ch. 1 and can. 5); before justification human beings can still perform many natural things that are not at all sinful but truly good (ibid., can. 7).

2. Deprived of "superadded gifts" because of original sin, "the natural man" is incapable of doing good in a supernatural sense, incapable of faith, hope, and love, of justification, of attaining to eternal life. To that end "he" needs more than the powers of nature and the teaching of the law, namely, divine grace, the prevenient inspiration of the Holy Spirit (ibid., can. 1–3).

---

12. J. Weizsäcker, "Das Dogma von der göttlichen Vorherbestimmung im neunten Jahrhundert," *Jahrbücher für deutsche Theologie* 4 (1859): 527–76; H. Schrörs, *Die Streit über die Prädestination im 9. Jahrhundert* (Freiburg i.B.: Herdersche Verlagshandlung, 1884); C. J. Niemeijer, *De Strijd over de Leer der Praedestinatie in de IXde Eeuw* (Groningen: Gebroeders Hoitsema, 1889); J. Schwane, *Dogmengeschichte,* III, 428ff.; H. Denzinger, *The Sources of Catholic Dogma* (*Enchiridion Symbolorum*), translated from the 30th ed. by Roy J. Deferrari (London and St. Louis: Herder, 1955); 283ff.

13. P. Lombard, *Sententiae in IV liberis distinctae,* I, dist. 40–41; in the commentaries of Thomas, Bonaventure, and Duns Scotus; T. Aquinas, *Summa theol.,* I, qu. 19, 23; *Summa contra gentiles,* III, 163.

3. In the case of the children of believers this divine grace is bestowed in baptism, and in the case of adults it consists, objectively, in God's calling them through the gospel and, subjectively, in their being touched by the illumination of the Holy Spirit. This grace is unmerited, prevenient; it is grace bestowed gratuitously (ibid., ch. 5).

4. This grace, however, is not irresistible. It does excite, assist, and move humans and enables them to turn themselves to justification and to assent freely to that grace, but they remain able both to accept and to reject the inspiration of the Holy Spirit (ibid., ch. 5). If they accept this grace and, moved and excited by it, cooperate with God and, by way of seven "preparations," dispose and prepare themselves for justification, they receive it in baptism, by grace, and only in accordance with what scholastics called "a merit of congruity" (ibid., chs. 6, 8; and can. 4).

5. The "infused grace" of justification remains resistible and amissible, but accepted and preserved, it enables humans to do good works and, by a merit of condignity, to earn eternal life (ibid., can. 9–16).

6. In keeping with this position Rome has firmly rejected Augustine's doctrine of absolute predestination. However, in so doing it has always avoided mentioning Augustine by name; it has caricatured his teaching among his followers and condemned it. The book *Predestinatus*, mentioned above, pictures the supposed existence of a sect of ultrapredestinationists in fifth-century Gaul, and reproduces Augustinianism in the form of paradoxical propositions that no follower of Augustine has ever taught.[14] Similarly, the true Augustinianism of Gottschalk, Bradwardine, Wycliffe, Hus, Baius, Jansen, and Quesnel has been condemned under a false name.[15]

The Council of Trent is very cautious in what it says about predestination. On the one hand, it seems to teach a kind of election, inasmuch as it says that nobody has the right to determine in this life that he or she is "surely included among the number of the predestinate." For apart from a special revelation it cannot be known "whom God has chosen for himself" (VI, 12; and can. 15–16). On the other hand, it expressly states that Christ was sent in order that all human beings might receive the adoption of children, that is, that he made atonement for all (VI, chs. 2–3); and that humans are able to accept or reject, to retain or lose God's grace. Trent also condemns the teaching that "the grace of justification is only attained by those who are predestined to life, but that all others who are called are indeed called but do not receive grace as being, by the divine power, predestined to evil" (ibid., can. 17)—as if anyone really taught what is contained in this canon! Although the church has left these two series of statements stand side by side unreconciled, theology has consistently tried in various ways to harmonize them. In the first place, almost

14. A. von Harnack, *History of Dogma*, V, 251.

15. Ibid., VII, 86–101; H. Denzinger, *The Sources of Catholic Dogma* (*Enchiridion symbolorum*), §§477ff., 881ff., 966ff., 1216.

all Roman Catholic theologians teach that by an antecedent will God desires the salvation of all humans, and therefore that Christ has made atonement for all; this antecedent will even includes pagans and unbaptized children who have died in infancy. But according to his consequent grace, which takes account of the good or bad use that people have made of their freedom or of the grace of God, God does not will the salvation of all. Here predestination from the very beginning is made dependent on foreknowledge. In the second place, there has gradually arisen among them a distinction—one that is now generally accepted—between "predestination in the full sense" and "predestination in a limited sense." The former is understood as predestination both to grace and to glory; the latter as that which relates either to one or to the other. The reason for this distinction is that predestination to grace and predestination to glory are not inseparable. A person may be the object of the predestination to grace, have received the grace of faith and of justification yet still lose it, and so have no part in the predestination to glory. This split was unknown to the medieval theologians Anselm, Lombard, Thomas, and others, and is still opposed by some, but is now increasingly gaining ground.

Now, as it concerns predestination to initial grace, everyone agrees, in opposition to Pelagianism, that it is unmerited (Rom. 9:16; John 6:44). It does not occur on account of foreseen merit; also, in contrast to semi-Pelagianism, it precedes the human will; it is "prevenient grace." Now, inasmuch as predestination to initial grace is the beginning of complete predestination, it can be said that predestination in its entirety is grace and unmerited, because it is "gratuitous in its cause," or as the Thomists say, it is "gratuitous in itself." This is not to say, however, that this predestination to initial grace and to every subsequent grace does not follow a certain order. According to Molina, God by a mediate knowledge saw in advance that some humans would make a good use of this—repeatedly offered—grace, and consequently decided to bestow it. Also, having foreseen that the saints by their prayers or by merits of congruity would acquire grace for others, God decided to grant it to them. People cannot earn predestination to initial grace for themselves, but the saints can do this for others; and Christ above all is the cause of our predestination. According to Augustinians and Thomists such as Sylvius, Thoma, the Salmanticenses, Gonet, Gotti, Billuart, Alvarez, Lemos, Goudin, and others, and also according to Bellarmine and Suárez, predestination to glory is indeed absolute. God first decreed to grant salvation to some before and apart from all merits, and then decreed to so shape their hearts by grace that they would be able to merit salvation by their works. But the Molinists (Molina, Valentia, Vasquez, Tanner, Lessius, Becanus, Petavius, Lapide, and others) defended predestination to glory on a basis of foreseen merits.

Finally, as it concerns reprobation, Augustinians and Thomists are divided. Some align themselves completely with Augustine, are infralapsarian, and make the decree of reprobation follow original sin, and that alone, so that reprobation is "a just abandonment in the same mass" (Gonet, Gotti, Gazzaniga). Others make a distinction between a negative (but absolute) decree not to grant salvation to some, and another decree to withhold grace, to permit and to punish sin (Alvarez, Estius Sylvius, the Salmanticenses). Still others view the decree of reprobation as nothing other than the will of God to allow some to perish through their own fault (Billuart, Goudin).[16] Opposing them, however, are the Molinists, who completely reject the so-called "negative reprobation," that is, an absolute sovereign decree preceding sin, and teach that by an antecedent decree God desires the salvation of all; furthermore, they only accept a positive reprobation, that is, a decree of God to punish eternally those whose sin and unbelief he has foreseen. Reprobation, accordingly, is in every respect "based on foreseen merits"; and even then, according to some such as Hincmar of Reims, it is only a foreordination of punishment for the wicked, not the wicked for punishment.[17]

THE REFORMATION RETURN TO PAUL AND AUGUSTINE

[236] The Reformation returned to Paul and Augustine and found, in the confession of God's sovereign election, the strength to counter the Pelagianism of the Roman Catholic church. All the Reformers were united in this position. In the early period Luther taught and defended the doctrine of predestination as vigorously as Zwingli and Calvin, and although in his polemics against the Anabaptists he increasingly stressed God's revelation in the Word and sacraments, he never reversed his position on predestination.[18] Initially Melanchthon taught exactly the same thing (cf. the first edition of the *Loci communes* of 1521, the chapter "On the Powers of Man, especially Free will," and his commentary

16. C. Pesch, *Praelectiones dogmaticae*, II, 217ff.; Johann Baptist Heinrich and Constantin Gutberlet, *Dogmatische Theologie*, 2d ed., 10 vols. (Mainz: Kirchheim, 1881–1900), VIII, 466ff.; G. Jansen, *Prael. theol.*, III, 171ff.; P. Mannens, *Theologiae dogmaticae institutiones*, 3 vols. (Roermand: Romen, 1901–3), II, 123ff.

17. M. Becanus, *Summa theologiae scholasticae* (Rouen: I. Behovrt, 1651), I, tract. 1, chs.14–16; C. R. Billuart, *Summa theologiae* (Thomas Aquinas), 6 vols. (Turin: Typographia Pontificia et Archiepiscopalis, 1893), II; C. G. Daelman, *Theologia seu observationes theologicae in Summam D. Thomae*, 9 vols. in 8 (Antwerp: Jacob Bernard Jouret, 1734), I, 199–316; J. Schwetz, *Theologia dogmatica catholica*, 3 vols. (Vienna: Congregationis Mechitharisticae, 1851–54), II, §121; G. Jansen, *Prael. theol.*, II, 135–77; H. Th. Simar, *Lehrbuch der Dogmatik*, 3d ed. (Freiburg i.B.: Herder, 1893), 556–76. Ed. note: Bavinck also refers to the following Roman Catholic theologians listed at the head of this section in the Dutch edition: R. Bellarmine, "De gratia et lib. arbitrio," *Controversiis*, esp. chs. 9–17; D. Petavius, "De Deo," in *Theol. dogm.*, bk. X; C. Pesch, *Prael. theol.*, II, 165–226; M. Scheeben, *Dogmatik*, III, 734ff.; Heinrich and Gutberlet, *Dogmatische Theologie*, VIII, 329ff.

18. J. Müller, *Lutheri de praedest. et lib. arb. doctrina* (1852); A. Schweizer, *Die protestantischen Centraldogmen in ihrer Entwicklung innerhalb der reformirten Kirche*, 2 vols. (Zürich: Orell & Fuessli, 1854–56), I, 57–94; J. Köstlin, *The Theology of Luther in Its Historical Development and Inner Harmony*, trans. Charles E. Hay, 2 vols. (Philadelphia: Lutheran Publication Society, 1897), I, 196ff., 287ff.; II, 43ff.; Th. Weber, "Luthers Streitschrift 'de Servo arbitrio,'" *Jahrbücher für deutsche Theologie* 23 (1878): 229–48; M. Staub, *(Das) Verhältnis der menschlichen Willensfreiheit zur Gotteslehre bei Martin Luther u. Huldreich Zwingli* (Zürich: Leemann, 1894).

on Rom. 9), but from 1527 on he moved ever further away from the doctrine of predestination and openly espoused synergism (cf. the later editions of the *Loci* from 1535 on and the *Conf. Aug. variata* of 1540).[19] This synergism, like the universalism of Sam Huber, was firmly rejected by the "true" Lutherans; Flacius, Wigand, Amsdorf, Heshusius, and others.[20] The Formula of Concord, moreover, declared in very clear terms that humans are by nature incapable of doing any spiritual good, and that faith is, in the strictest sense, a gift of God. This confession should also have led to the acceptance of the doctrine of absolute predestination. But from the very beginning, Luther's outlook differed somewhat from that of Zwingli and Calvin. In his thinking the confession of predestination was based solely on anthropological grounds, on the profound corruption of sin and human powerlessness to do good. To him it seemed enough to teach that humans have no merit of their own and are solely dependent on grace. Luther, accordingly, increasingly avoided the speculative doctrine of predestination, the will of divine good pleasure, the hidden God, preferring to focus on the ministry of Word and sacraments, to which grace is bound, and giving increasing prominence to God's universal redemptive will, his expressed will. He silently watched Melanchthon's change with respect to this doctrine and confined himself to defending the doctrine of justification by faith. Predestination had no independent theological significance and was of secondary importance. Opposing the synthetic method in this doctrine, theologians favored the analytic method, deriving predestination from the human condition, not from the idea of God.[21]

Therefore, though Melanchthon's synergism was still combated, the doctrine of predestination itself was gradually set aside. At an early date already (1560–1561) Heshusius objected that the teaching of Calvin and Beza introduced a kind of fatalism and made God the author of sin. At Strasbourg, in 1561, Marbach publicly spoke out against Zanchius. Andreae, while still teaching an election rooted solely in divine grace, confined himself to the preaching of the gospel and did not go beyond faith and unbelief as secondary causes.[22] The Formula of Concord unreservedly teaches the bondage of the human will but is silent about an absolute and particular predestination and confines itself to speaking about the universal and serious will of God expressed in the Gospel.

19. A. Schweizer, *Centraldogmen*, I, 381ff.

20. F. H. R. Frank, *Theologie der Concordienformel*, 4 vols. in 2 (Erlangen: T. Blaesing, 1858–65), IV, 152; Kawerau, "Synergismus," *PRE³*, XIX, 229–35. Ed. note: Samuel Huber (1547–1624) opposed Calvin's doctrine of predestination and taught universal election; Matthias Flacius (Illyricus; 1520–75) and Nicholas von Amsdorf (1483–1565) both opposed the Augsburg Interim (the doctrinal formulas accepted as a provisional agreement between Catholics and Protestants at the Diet of Augsburg, 1548) and fiercely defended the doctrine of justification; John Wigand (1523–87) was a staunch defender of Luther in various sixteenth century controversies; Tilemann Heshusius (1527–88) strongly opposed Zwingli's doctrine of communion and Calvin's doctrine of predestination. See *Lutheran Cyclopedia,* ed. Erwin L. Lueker (St. Louis: Concordia, 1954), s.v.

21. A. Schweizer, *Centraldogmen,* I, 398, 445, 466.

22. Ibid., I, 477ff.

It does not deny election nor invoke the assistance of foreknowledge, and it still agrees with the Augsburg Confession that "the Holy Spirit works faith where and when it pleases God" (art. 5); election is unconditional, its sole cause being the will of God. However, it equates election with predestination and makes reprobation dependent on foreknowledge. After teaching the doctrine of election, the Formula immediately adds—from fear of possible danger or misuse—that one must not attempt to speculate about that hidden decree but must view the counsel of God in Christ in the light of the gospel, whose preaching is universal and serious, and that the sole cause of perdition is human unbelief. God wills all humans to be saved: he seeks no person's sin and no person's death. After the Formula of Concord, particularly during the struggle against Huber's universalism, some Lutherans such as Gerlach, Hunnius, and Lyser favored the theory that God by his antecedent will desires the salvation of all, but by his consequent will only the salvation of those whose faith and salvation he had foreseen. Toward the end of the century, theologians began with increasing decisiveness to make a distinction between foreknowledge and predestination. Predestination, which is the same as election, is dependent on Christ's merits, whereas the sole cause of reprobation is human sin. This is clearly taught in the Saxon Visitation Articles of 1592, composed by Aegidius Hunnius, and other writings by the same author, namely, *De providentia Dei et aeterna praedestinatione* (1597) and *De libero arbitrio* (1598). An intermediate solution was sought in the earnestness with which the "natural man" can make use of the means of grace.[23]

The Lutherans, however, could not stop at this point, and when the Remonstrants were condemned at the Synod of Dort, Lutherans felt increasingly drawn to them. Although the Reformed were always careful to distinguish between Lutherans and Remonstrants, the former felt that with the rejection of the Remonstrants their own doctrine had been condemned as well.[24] Seventeenth-century Lutheran theologians in fact approximated the Remonstrant confession. First they taught an antecedent will of God, by virtue of which Christ died for all. God wills the salvation of all, and the Gospel is offered to all. Second, they taught a consequent will, by virtue of which God decides to effectively grant salvation to "those whose ultimate faith in Christ he has foreseen" and to prepare perdition for those who in the end resist grace.[25] In 1724 Mosheim declared that the Five Articles of the

23. Ibid., I, 526–85; H. Heppe, *Dogmatik des deutschen Protestantismus im sechzehnten Jahrhundert*, 3 vols. (Gotha: F. A. Perthes, 1857), II, 1–79.

24. Schweitzer, *Centraldogmen*, II, 206ff.

25. H. F. F. Schmid, *The Doctrinal Theology of the Evangelical Lutheran Church*, trans. Charles A. Hay and Henry Jacobs, 5th ed. (Philadelphia: United Lutheran Publication House, 1899), 279–92. Ed. note: Bavinck also refers to the following Lutheran theologians listed at the head of this section in the Dutch edition: Luther, *Bondage of the Will*; Melanchthon, *Loci communes*, chapter "De hominis viribus adeoque de libeto arbitrio"; Quenstedt, *Theol. did. polem.*, III, 1–74; D. Hollaz, *Examen theol.*, 585–649; Gerhard, *Loci theol.*, loc. VII.

Remonstrants contain the pure Lutheran doctrine.[26] Pietism, rationalism, supernaturalism, and the whole religious mind-set of the eighteenth century were all ill-disposed to the doctrine of predestination. The antecedent will of God totally crowded the consequent will from the scene, and predestination was understood solely as referring to the universal decree of God to save all human beings by faith in Christ.[27] Herder viewed it as a blessing that the controversy over grace had been buried in "the river of oblivion" and exclaimed: "May the hand wither that ever retrieves it from there."[28] Leibniz still made an attempt to reconcile the freedom of the will with predestination.[29] But Kant openly announced that humans still possessed a moral disposition and were able to do what they had to do.[30]

[237] Whereas Lutherans increasingly abandoned Luther's original position as well as that of the entire Reformation, the Reformed remained faithful to it. The origin of the split, therefore, is not to be attributed to the Reformed. Zwingli firmly upheld the doctrine of predestination, not only on anthropological but especially on theological grounds, the grounds derived from God's being.[31] In the first edition of the *Institutes* Calvin expressed himself gently and with great moderation, but his study of the Letter to the Romans in Strasbourg (April 1538–1541) led him to speak with increasing confidence about human bondage and divine election.[32] Although avoiding the paradoxes of Luther and Zwingli and at times assuming predestination rather than outright teaching it (e.g., in the Genevan Catechism with its preface to the "Coetus" of Ostfriesland),[33] Calvin nevertheless forcefully advocated it wherever it was denied or opposed. He defended it against Alb. Pighuis of Kampen, The Netherlands, in writing *A Defense of the Sound and Orthodox Doctrine of the Bondage and Liberation of the Human Will* (1543). Against Bolsee he wrote *De aeterna Dei praedestionatione* (1552), and against Rome his *Acta Synodi Tridentinae cum antidoto* (1547). And he did not rest until his doctrine had been accepted in every part of Reformed Switzerland, specifically in Zürich,

26. A. Schweizer, *Centraldogmen*, II, 210.

27. J. A. L. Wegscheider, *Institutiones theologiae christianae dogmaticae* (Halle: Gebauer, 1819), §147; K. G. Bretschneider, *Systematische Entwicklung aller in der Dogmatik verkommenden Begriffe nach den symbolischen Schriften der evangelisch-lutherischen und reformirten Kirche und den wichtigsten dogmatischen Lehrbüchern ihrer Theologen*, 4th ed. (Leipzig: J. A. Barth, 1841), III, 127ff.; F. V. Reinhard, *Grundriss der Dogmatik* (Munich: Seidel, 1802), 439ff.

28. J. G. Herder, *Vom Geist des Christenthums* (Leipzig: J. F. Hartkroch, 1798), 154.

29. A. Pichler, *Die Theologie des Leibniz aus sämmtlichen Gedruckten*, 2 vols. (Munich: J. G. Cotta, 1869–70), I, 357ff.

30. I. Kant, *Religion within the Limits of Reason Alone*, trans. Theodore Green and Hoyt H. Hudson (1934; reprinted, New York: Harper & Brothers, 1960), 55–72.

31. U. Zwingli, *On Providence and Other Essays*, trans. Samuel Macauley Jackson, ed. William John Hinks (Durham: Labyrinth Press, 1983), *Opera*, IV, 79ff.

32. J. Calvin, *Institutes*, II.ii; III.xxiff.

33. In H. A. Niemeyer, *Collectio confessionum in ecclesiis reformatis publicatarum*, 2 vols. (Leipzig: Iulii Klinkhardti, 1840), 123ff.; in E. F. Karl Müller, *Die Bekenntnisschriften der reformierten Kirche* (Leipzig: A. Deichert, 1903), 117ff.

where Bullinger advocated a moderate infralapsarian view.[34] Through Calvin's influence the doctrine of predestination was included in the confession of all the Reformed churches.

Yet from the start there was substantial difference in the way this doctrine was viewed, both in the confessions and in the writings of the theologians. Aside from the Anhalt Repetition[35] of 1579, the Confession of Sigismund[36] of 1614, the Leipzig Colloquium[37] of 1631—all of which fall short of faithfully reproducing the Reformed doctrine of predestination—there are undeniable differences among the Reformed confessions. Calvin's own Genevan Catechism does not even mention election. The Heidelberg Catechism only refers to it in passing (answers 52 and 54). The Anglican Articles only speak of a predestination to life and states as its object "those whom God has chosen in Christ" (art. 7). The Second Helvetic Confession drawn up by Bullinger (art. 10) and the first Scotch Confession (art. 8) speak of it along approximately the same lines. The Gallic Confession (art. 12), the Belgic Confession (art. 18), and the Helvetic Consensus Formula (4–6) are firm but sober and infralapsarian. The most rigorously Calvinistic statements on the subject are found in the Consensus of Geneva, the Canons of Dort, the Lambeth Articles[38] drawn up by Dr. Whitgift (1595),[39] the Irish Articles of 1615, and the Westminster Confession.[40]

Similar substantial differences occurred among the theologians. There were always those who, fearing misuse of the doctrine, treated it a posteriori, from the effect to the cause, from the fruit to the root.[41] Rather than deriving the doctrine of predestination and election from the idea of God a priori, they followed the reverse order: given faith and conversion, they reasoned back to election and used this doctrine as a means of comfort and assurance. To this group belonged especially Bullinger, Ursinus, Olevianus, Boquinis, Hyperius, Sohnius (et al.).[42] But this does not mean a difference in principle. Without exception the above theologians repeatedly, clearly, and candidly expressed their

34. A. Schweizer, *Centraldogmen*, I, 255–92.

35. H. A. Niemeyer, *Collectio confessionum in ecclesiis reformatis publicatarum*, 638.

36. Ibid., 650; E. F. Karl Müller, *Die Bekenntnisschriften der reformierten Kirche*, 835.

37. H. A. Niemeyer, *Collectio confessionum in ecclesiis reformatis publicatarum*, 661ff., 664ff.

38. In P. Schaff, *The Creeds of Christendom*, 6th ed., 3 vols. (New York: Harper & Row, 1931; reprinted, Grand Rapids: Baker, 1983), III, 523; E. F. Karl Müller, *Die Bekenntnisschriften der reformierten Kirche*, 525.

39. In P. Schaff, *Creeds of Christendom*, III, 526; E. F. K. Müller, *Die Bekenntnisschriften der reformierten Kirche*, 526. Ed. note: John Whitgift (1532–1604), Archbishop of Canterbury under Elizabeth I, was a determined advocate of episcopacy (antipresbyterian) and a strong Calvinist in doctrine. Bavinck erroneously refers to him as "Dr. Whitmaker."

40. In E. F. K. Müller, *Die Bekenntnisschriften der reformierten Kirche*, 542.

41. J. Trigland, *Kerckelycke Geschiedenissen* (Leyden: Andriae Wyngaerden, 1650), 79, 84, 85ff., 92ff., 99.

42. H. Heppe, *Dogmatik des deutschen Protestantismus im sechzehnten Jahrhundert*, 3 vols. (Gotha: F. A. Perthes, 1857), II, 1–79; M. A. Gooszen, *De Heidelbergsche Catechismus en het Boekje van de Breking des Broods* (Leiden: Brill, 1892); A. J. van't Hooft, *De Theologie van Heinrich Bullinger in betrekking tot de Nederlandsche Reformatie* (Amsterdam: Is. de Hoogh, 1888); cf. H. Bavinck, *Reformed Dogmatics*, I, 180 (#54).

agreement with the Calvinistic doctrine of predestination.[43] Conversely, also Calvinists have at all times insisted on sobriety and caution in the treatment of this doctrine. Calvin did not even mention it in the Genevan Catechism. The Canons of Dort (I, 12, 14) and the Westminster Confession (ch. 4, §8) both warn against vain and curious investigations into this doctrine. In the early years many theologians treated the doctrine of election, not under the heading of the doctrine of God, but with the doctrine of salvation.[44] In this regard they followed the order of the apostle Paul, who in Romans 9–11 begins with the doctrine of sin and grace and proceeds to election, and also in Ephesians 1:3 makes the blessings of Christ his starting point. But just as Paul, having arrived at that point, also a priori derives all the saving benefits from election (Rom. 8:29f.; Eph. 1:4ff.), so also in the case of the Reformed the analytic method gradually yielded to the synthetic. Indeed, the life of faith was the condition that gave rise to the confession of election, but the fact of election nevertheless was the source of all saving benefits, "the foundation and principal cause of all blessings." This was not only Calvin's conviction but also that of Melanchthon, Hamming, Bucer, Olevianus, and others.[45] Musculus expressly states: "We treat election after faith, not because we think it follows faith, but in order that from this vantage point (namely, faith) we would look up from the stream to the source itself."[46]

Systematic order and theological interest demanded that predestination be treated under the doctrine of God. This was the order already followed by scholasticism[47] and still followed also by the Lutherans.[48] This also became the regular order for all Reformed theologians,[49] some of whom treated election as part of the doctrine of the divine attributes, while others discussed it in a separate locus following that of the Trinity. This difference in order is not and need not be fundamental. Still, it is not accidental that the a priori order was usually followed by the Reformed, while the a posteriori order, which treats predestination at the beginning or in the middle of the locus of salvation, gradually became customary among Lutheran, Remonstrant, Roman Catholic, and most modern theologians. Even in view of this fact the reason for the difference is not that Reformed theologians speculatively deduce predestination from an a priori, philosophical, deterministic concept of God, while the others

43. J. Trigland, *Kerckelycke Geschiedenissen*, 59–79; A. Schweizer, *Centraldogmen*, I, passim; II, 110.

44. J. Calvin, *Institutes*, III.xxi–xxiv; P. M. Vermigli, *Loci communes* (1580), 229; G. Sohn, *Opera sacrae theologiae*, 2 vols. (Herborn: C. Corvin, 1598), I, 256; II, 42; W. Musculus, *Loci communes theologiae sacrae* (Basileae: Ex officina Heruagiana, 1567), c. 24; Heidelberg Catechism, Q. 54; Belgic Confession, art. 16; Gallican Confession, art. 12.

45. Cf. H. Heppe, *Dogmatik des deutschen Protestantismus*, II, 12, 20, 27, 70.

46. W. Musculus, *Loci communes theologiae sacrae*, 534.

47. P. Lombard, *Sent.*, I, dist. 40; T. Aquinas, *Summa theol.*, I, qu. 23.

48. J. Gerhard, *Loci theol.*, loc. VII.

49. A. Hyperius, *Andreae Hyperii methodi theologiae* (Basil: Oporiniana, 1574), 182; T. Beza, *Tractationum theologicarum* (Geneva: Jean Crispin, 1570), I, 171; III, 402; A. Polanus, *Syn. theol.*, IV, 6–10; J. Zanchi(us), *Op. theol.*, II, 476.

focus consistently on the revelation of God in Christ. Even the most rigorous Calvinists, when teaching the doctrine of God or that of his counsel, seek only to reproduce the doctrine of Scripture, the content of God's revelation. No: the real reason for the difference is that for the Reformed predestination not only has anthropological and soteriological but also and especially theological importance. In Reformed theology the primary interest is not the salvation of humankind but the honor of God. Also the synthetic, a priori, order involves a deeply religious motive. For this reason alone, therefore, the assertion that this order presupposes a nominalistic concept of God and yields an arid, lifeless dogma, as some believe,[50] is totally groundless. The doctrine of predestination can be treated in an arid and abstract fashion either way: in the middle or at the beginning of one's dogmatic system. A true, saving faith is needed to confess not only divine election but all other dogmas as well, also those that concern God, the Trinity, and humanity. If this consideration were decisive, all Christian dogmas should be transferred to the locus of salvation. Dogmatics, however, describes the truth, not as it comes subjectively to the consciousness of believers, but as God presents it objectively in his Word. The synthetic method alone sufficiently safeguards the religious interest of the honor of God.[51]

SUPRA- AND INFRALAPSARIANISM

[238] Soon another disagreement arose among the Reformed: that of supra- versus infralapsarianism. Basically, this difference is already present in Augustine's struggle against the Pelagians. Among the latter the order of the decrees is as follows: (1) the decree to create humankind; (2) the decree—based on the foreseen but nondetermined fall of humankind—to send Christ, to have him make satisfaction for all humankind, to have him preached to all members of the human race, and to grant to them all a grace sufficient [to receive salvation]; and (3) a decree—based on the one hand on foreseen faith and perseverance and on the other on foreseen unbelief—to elect some to eternal life and to destine others for eternal punishment.

For Augustine the order of the decrees was very different. Sometimes, indeed, he includes reprobation in predestination, but even when he does not, he construes foreknowledge, not as being negative and passive but as active. The will of God, after all, is "the necessary ground of things."[52] What is done against his will is not done apart from his will. Permission must be considered positive: "And he of course permits it not against his will but with it."[53] Already implied

---

50. Cf. M. Schneckenburger and E. Güder, *Vergleichende Darstellung des lutherischen und reformirten Lehrbegriffs*, 2 vols. (Stuttgart: J. B. Metzler, 1855), I, 55; J. I. Doedes, *De Nederlandsche Geloofsbelijdenis en de Heidelbergsche Catechismus* (Utrecht: Kemink & Zoon, 1880–81), 185, 203ff.; H. de Cock, *Is de Leer der Absolute Praedest. uitgangspunt of resultaat van Gereformeerde Kerkregeering* (Kampen: Van Velzen, 1868).

51. Cf. H. Bavinck, *Reformed Dogmatics*, I, 93 (#26).

52. Augustine, *The Literal Meaning of Genesis*, trans. and annotated by John Hammond Taylor, Ancient Christian Writers 41 (New York: Newman, 1982), VI, 15.

53. Augustine, *Enchiridion*, 95, 100.

here is the supralapsarian idea that reprobation is an act of God's sovereignty. Usually, however, Augustine speaks of God's "foreknowledge" and "permission" in connection with the fall.[54] First in the order of the decree in that case is the decree to create [humankind] and to permit the fall; then follows the decree of election and reprobation. Both of them, election and reprobation, presuppose a fallen human race, or as Augustine calls it, a "corrupt mass."[55] Hence, in his understanding of the order of the decrees Augustine is usually "infralapsarian": that is, in his thinking he does not go back behind the fall, and he views reprobation as an act of divine justice. "God is good; God is just. He can deliver some humans who do not merit the good, because he is good. He cannot condemn any person not deserving of evil, because he is just."[56] But neither does he position the decree of election and reprobation farther ahead. Only original sin is anterior to it, a sin that is sufficient warrant for reprobation. Actual sins are not taken into account in the decree of reprobation, though they are factored in when determining the measure of punishment. Augustine arrived at this order from what Paul says about Jacob and Esau (Rom. 9:11), and from the fate of unbaptized children who die in infancy.[57]

Nevertheless, though original sin is sufficient ground for reprobation, in the thought of Augustine it is not the final and deepest ground. To the question why God rejected some and chose others, particularly why he rejected this specific person and chose another, there is no answer other than the will and sovereign good pleasure of God. He has mercy on whom he wills and hardens the heart of whom he wills.[58] Finally follows a third decree with respect to the *means* by which the end will be realized. In the case of reprobation, Augustine refrains from drawing a straight line from the decree itself to the means employed. He does say, however, that also in sin God acts in a positive and active manner. God is "the regulator of sins." He thought it right that sin should exist, punishing sin with sin.[59] Generally, however, Augustine views reprobation negatively, that is, as a passing by (preterition) or abandonment (dereliction), and usually does not consider it a part of predestination, but equates the latter with election and subsumes both, election and reprobation, under the rubric of providence. By contrast he does speak of a predestination to the means of salvation. For in Augustine, predestination or election is always predestination to glory, and the latter by implication entails a predestination to grace.

54. Augustine, *City of God*, XIV, 11; idem, *The Trinity*, trans. Stephen McKenna, Fathers of the Church 45 (Washington, D.C.: Catholic University of America Press, 1963), XIII, 12.

55. Augustine, *Enchiridion*, 98ff.; idem, *On Rebuke and Grace*, 7ff.

56. Augustine, *Against Julian*, III, 18.

57. Augustine, *Enchiridion*, 92–99; idem, *City of God*, XIV, 11; idem, *On the Gift of Perseverance*, 8ff.; idem, *Against Julian*, IV, 8.

58. Augustine, *Enchiridion*, 95; idem, *On the Predestination of the Saints*, 8–9; idem, *On Rebuke and Grace*, IV, 8.

59. Augustine, *Confessions*, I, 10; idem, *Enchiridion*, 27, 96; idem, *City of God*, XXII, 1; idem, *Against Julian*, V, 3; idem, *De libero arbitrio (libri tres): The Free Choice of the Will (Three Books)*, trans. Francis Edward Tourscher (Philadelphia: Peter Reilly, 1937), 21.

Election, accordingly, does not occur on the basis of foreseen faith or foreseen good works, or for Christ's sake. But it is election to the ultimate goal and therefore to the means, that is, to Christ, who himself was predestined as well, and so to calling, baptism, faith, and the gift of perseverance. Predestination is a preparatory step toward grace. Accordingly, those who are elect infallibly obtain heavenly salvation in the way of grace in Christ.[60]

In later years many followers of Augustine, therefore, arrived at a doctrine of double predestination: a predestination to death came to be coordinated with a predestination to glory. The former, however, cannot be understood in the same sense as the latter, and so a distinction was made between a negative and a positive reprobation. The negative decree of reprobation was viewed as anterior to the fall and as an act of sovereignty. It is no more based on demerits than election is based on merits.[61] It implies the will to permit certain persons to plunge into guilt, and is the cause of abandonment.[62] Thus many Thomists (Alvarez, the Salmanticenses, Estius, Sylvius, and others) taught that negative reprobation occurs prior to the fall and is purely an act of divine sovereignty and good pleasure.[63] Only this supralapsarian reprobation was viewed as completely negative, as the decree of God not to elect certain people, to allow them to fall, and after that (positive reprobation) to destine them to eternal punishment. Essentially and materially Luther, Zwingli, Calvin, and all supralapsarian Reformed theologians taught exactly the same thing. Roman Catholic theologians sometimes paint a different picture. They accuse the predestinationists of the fifth century—as well as Gottschalk, Bradwardine, Wycliffe, and especially the Reformers of the sixteenth century—of teaching a "predestination to sins" and of making God the author of sin.[64] But the sole motive for doing this is to maintain their own semi-Pelagian position and to align it with the teaching of Augustine and Thomas.

The changes that the Reformers introduced in the teaching of Augustine and Thomas are—aside from the doctrine of the assurance of salvation—secondary and do not touch the heart of the matter. Like them, the Reformers taught that election was not dependent on foreseen merits but was itself the source of faith and good works; that predestination to glory unfailingly carried with it a predestination to grace; that negative reprobation could not be interpreted as an act of justice, but should be viewed as an act of sovereignty occurring prior

---

60. Augustine, *On Rebuke and Grace*, 7, 9, 13; idem, *On the Predestination of the Saints*, 10, 19; idem, *On the Gift of Perseverance*, 18.

61. P. Lombard, *Sent.*, IV, dist. 41, 1.

62. T. Aquinas, *Summa theol.*, I, qu. 23, art. 3; cf. C. G. Daelman, *Theologia seu observationes theologicae in Summam D. Thomae*, 9 vols. in 8 (Antwerp: Jacob Bernard Jouret, 1734), I, 296–303; C. R. Billuart, *Summa theologiae (Thomas Aquinas)*, 6 vols. (Turin: Typographia Pontificia et Archiepiscopalis, 1893), II, 459ff.

63. C. Pesch, *Prael. dogm.*, II, 217ff.

64. R. Bellarmine, *De amiss. gr. et stat. pecc.*, *controversiis*, II, chs. 2ff.; D. Petavius, "De Deo Deique proprietabus," in *Theol. dogm.*, bk. X, chs. 6ff.; J. A. Möhler, *Symbolik: Oder Darstellung der dogmatischen Gegensätze der Katholiken und Protestanten nach ihren öffentlichen Bekenntnisschriften* (Mainz: F. Kupferberg, 1838), §12.

to the commission of sin; that this negative reprobation resulted in a decree to permit sin and to allow some to remain in their fallen state; and that positive reprobation took sin into account. But to this the Reformers frequently added that the concepts of "foreknowledge" and "permission," though not inherently wrong, could not or should not be viewed in a purely passive sense, and even if this was done, it would still not yield a solution to the problem [of God's complicity in sin], and that the distinction between negative and positive reprobation had but little value. Consequently, all three Reformers arrived at the so-called supralapsarian view of predestination, according to which the two decrees of election and reprobation are to be viewed as acts of divine sovereignty prior to those concerning the fall, sin, and redemption in Christ.

Calvin in particular often intentionally confines himself to the immediate causes of salvation and perdition, thus reasoning in an infralapsarian mode. Let not a reprobate look for the cause of his punishment in God's decree but in the corruption of his own nature, for which he himself is responsible. The elect and the reprobate are equally guilty, but God is merciful toward the former and just toward the latter.[65] In Romans 9:21 the word "clay" refers to all fallen humans, of whom God elects some while abandoning others to "their own destruction, to which by nature all are subject." The fall in Adam is "the proximate cause of reprobation." God hates in us only the sin that clings to us.[66] And concerning this idea "that out of the condemned race of Adam, God was pleased to elect some and willed to reject others," Calvin says that "just as it is much more apt to move people to the exercise of faith, so it is also treated with greater profit, . . . so it is not only more conducive to piety but, it seems to me, more theological, more agreeable to Christian faith and practice, more edifying."[67] Still, this does not fully satisfy Calvin. While sin may be the proximate cause of reprobation, it is not the ultimate cause. For the imagined scenario is untenable: that God decided to create humankind without any preexisting plan, then waited and watched to see what humans would do, and then—knowing beforehand what the human response would be—proceeded to the action of election and reprobation. The ideas of "foreknowledge" and "permission" do not yield a solution, for God, foreseeing the fall, could have prevented it. He freely permitted it to happen, since doing so seemed good to him.[68]

Accordingly, Adam's fall, sin in general, and all the evil in the world cannot just have been foreseen by God but must also in a sense have been willed and

---

65. J. Calvin, *Institutes*, III.xxiii.9, 11.

66. J. Calvin, *Commentary,* on Rom. 9:11, 21; idem, "De aeterna praedest.," in *Corpus Reformatorum* (*CR*), XXXVI, 287, 295, 315; Ed. note: ET: *Concerning the Eternal Predestination of God,* trans. J. K. S. Reid (London: James Clarke & Co., 1961). For scholarly convenience the pages in this edition will be listed in parentheses after the *CR* reference as (Reid, 90, 98–99, 121–22).

67. J. Calvin, "De aeterna praedest.," *CR*, XXXVI, 317 (Reid, 125).

68. J. Calvin, *Institutes*, I.xviii.1; II.iv.3; III.xxiii.68; idem, "De aeterna praedest.," *CR*, XXXVI, 359 (Reid, 176). Ed. note: Bavinck also adds the reference *CR*, XXXVII, 291, 294, which may be in error (*CR*, XXXVI, 291, 294, would be Reid, 95, 98).

determined by him (ibid.). Hence, there must have been a reason (unknown to us) why God willed the fall: there has to be a higher plan of God that existed prior to the fall.[69] Hence, when Pighius replies to Calvin by objecting that on his position there must have been in God's mind a difference between the elect and the reprobate prior to the fall of the human race, Calvin indeed initially answers that Pighius fails to distinguish between proximate and remote causes, that every reprobate must look for the proximate cause in his own sin, and that the alternative is burdened by the same objections; but he does not deny the validity of Pighius's conclusion: there is a "secret divine plan" that exists prior to the fall.[70] The ultimate cause of reprobation and election is God's will.[71] Hence, in Calvin's works the supralapsarian approach alternates with the infralapsarian.[72] This is also almost always the case with later theologians who embraced supralapsarianism. They regard the supralapsarian position as permissible but do not for a moment dream of condemning the infralapsarian view or of insisting that their view be marked in the confession as the only valid one. All they plead for is the right of their position to exist alongside, not in the place of, the infralapsarian position.[73]

According to the supralapsarian position, there is a divine knowledge of all

69. J. Calvin, "De aeterna praedest.," *CR*, XXXVI, 288 (Reid, 75).

70. Ibid., *CR*, XXXVI, 296ff. (Reid, 99ff.).

71. J. Calvin, *Institutes*, I.xviii.2; III.xx.11; III.xxiii.1–2, 7–8; idem, "De aeterna praedest.," *CR*, XXXVI, 278, 317 (Reid, 78, 121).

72. Cf. A. Rivetus, *De praed. et elect. nomine et objecto,* in *Operum theologicorum*, II; W. Twisse, *Vindiciae gratiae, potestatis ac providentiae Dei*, 3 vols. (Amsterdam: Guilielmum Blaeu, 1632), I, 105ff.; D. Petavius, "De Deo," in *Theol. dogm.*, bk. X, chs. 6ff.; J. Kreyher, "Die Erwähungslehre von Zwingli und Calvin," *Theologische Studien und Kritiken* 42/3 (1870): 491–524; M. Scheibe, *Calvins Prädestinationslehre* (Halle a.S.: Ehrnhardt Karras, 1897); according to A. Lang, *Der Evangelienkommentar Martin Butzers und die Grundzüge seiner Theologie* (Leipzig: Dietrich, 1900); G. Nathanael Bonwetsch and Reinhold Seeberg, *Studien sur Geschichte der Theologie und der Kirche*, 10 vols. (Leipzig: Dietrich, 1898–1903), II, 2. It was especially Bucer who among the Reformers emphasized the doctrine of predestination and had a great influence on Calvin.

73. Among the great defenders of supralapsarianism are T. Beza, *Tractationum theologicarum*, I, 171–205, 360ff.; III, 402–7; J. Piscator, *Johan, Piscatoris tractatus de gratia Dei* (Herbornae Nassoviorum, 1614); A. Polanus, *Syn. theol.*, IV, chs. 7–10; Paulus Ferrius, *Scholastici orthodoxi specimen* (Gotstadii: J. Lambertin, 1616), ch. 26; W. Whitaker, *Opera theologica*, 2 vols. in 1 (Geneva: S. Crispen, 1610), I, 692; W. Perkins, *The workes of that famous and worthy minister of Christ*, 3 vols. (London: John Legatt, 1612–18), I, 761–806; W. Twisse, *Opera theologica polemico-anti-Arminiana* (Amsterdam, 1699), I, 35ff.; J. H. Alsted, *Encyclopaedia septum tomis distincta* (Herborn: G. Corvini, 1630), 1588; F. Gomarus, *Opera theologica omnia* (Amsterdam: J. Jansson, 1664), I, 428ff.; II, 24ff.; J. Maccovius, *Loci communes theologici* (Amsterdam: n.p., 1658), ch. 25; G. Voetius, *Select. disp.*, I, 354ff.; A. Heidanus, *Corpus theologiae christianae in quindecim locos digestum*, 2 vols. (Leiden, 1686), I, loc. 3; F. Burmann, *Synopsis theologiae et speciatim oeconomiae foederum Dei: Ab initio saeculorum usque ad consummationem eorum*, 2 vols. in 1 (Amsterdam: Joannem Wolters, 1699), 13ff.; Chr. Wittichius, *Theologia pacifica* (Leiden, 1671), §§255ff.; A. Comrie and N. Holtius, *Examen van het Ontwerp van Tolerantie*, 10 vols. (Amsterdam: Nicolaas Byl, 1753), VI, VII, especially 376ff.; cf. also W. Cunningham, *Historical Theology*, 2d ed., 2 vols. (Edinburgh: T. & T. Clark, 1864), I, 416ff.; James Walker, *The Theology and Theologians of Scotland, 1560–1750* (reprinted from the 2d [1888] ed., Edinburgh: Knox Press, 1982), 36ff.; cf. on Ursinus: H. Lang, with Leo Juda, Martin Macronius, and Zacharius Ursinus, *Der Heidelberger Katechismus und vier verwandte Katechismen* (Leipzig: A. Deichert, 1907), XCIX.

possibilities, "a knowledge of simple intelligence," that exists prior to all the decrees. According to the rule "What is last in execution is first in intention," God in his *first* decree established the purpose for which he would create and govern all things. That would be to manifest his virtues, especially his mercy and his justice, in the eternal blessedness and eternal punishment of certain possible human beings to be created and capable of falling. In order that these virtues could be revealed, a *second* decree would determine the existence of human beings so pitiable and wretched that they could be the object of that mercy and justice. In order for such humans to come into being, a *third* decree was needed to establish the creation of one human who, adorned with divine likeness and made head of the whole human race, would "by an efficacious permission" fall and take all his descendants with him in his fall. Finally, in a *fourth* decree, God had to indicate how his mercy would be demonstrated to the elect in the provision of a mediator, in the gift of faith, and in their preservation to the end; and on the other hand how his justice becomes manifest in reprobates by freely withholding from them the saving grace of God and giving them up to their sins.

In this sequence election and reprobation not only occurred prior to faith and unbelief, renewal and hardening, but also before the fall and creation. At this point, however, one problem immediately asserted itself. It was an established Reformed doctrine that the election of Christ and of the church occurred in connection with each other in one single decree, whose object, therefore, was the "mystical Christ." But in the supralapsarian scheme the election of the church was separated from that of Christ by the (two) decrees of creation and fall. Comrie, however, tried to obviate this objection by teaching that the elect are chosen to union with Christ before the decree of creation and fall.[74] This union is so close and unbreakable that when the chosen ones fall—as is determined immediately afterward in a subsequent decree—Christ, who had been elected as head of the church, is now chosen also as the mediator of reconciliation. Comrie, therefore, saw that the election of the church as the body of Christ could not be separated from that of Christ as the head of the church. And so he placed the election of both prior to the decree of creation and fall. Election, accordingly, acquired at its object not only a body of possible people but also a possible Christ.

REMONSTRANCE AND RESISTANCE

The churches, however, consistently opposed this supralapsarian scenario. As a result there is not a single Reformed confession that contains it. At the Synod of Dort [at Dordrecht, 1618–19], to be sure, there were a few who held this position, especially Gemarus and Maccovius;[75] moreover, the delegates of

74. A. Comrie and N. Holtius, *Examen van het Ontwerp van Tolerantie*, VII, 346ff.

75. Acts of Synod of Dort, session 107; G. Voetius, *Select. disp.*, V, 603; H. Edema van der Tuuk, *Johannes Bogerman* (Groningen: Wolters, 1868), 224ff.; N. C. Kist, *Kerkhistorisch Archief*, ed. Willem Moll, 4 vols. (Amsterdam: P. N. van Kampen, 1857–66), III, 505ff. (ed. note: Bavinck cites as date here 1831); A. Kuyper Jr., *Johannes Maccovius* (Leiden: D. Donner, 1899), 31, 92ff., 135.

South Holland, Overijsel, and Friesland preferred to leave the issue unresolved and to find a formulation with which both parties could agree.[76] Yet all the "judgments" of the Dutch as well as the foreign delegates, also those of Geneva, though definitely Reformed, were infralapsarian in character and clothed in mild and moderate language. And in the end the Synod described election as the decree of God "by which . . . he has chosen from the whole human race which had fallen by its own fault from its original innocence into sin and ruin. . . ."[77] Still it—intentionally—did not condemn supralapsarianism, for various theologians (Calvin, Beza, Piscator, Perkins, Hommius, Bogerman, and others) had at times used very strong and hard expressions; for example that: "some humans are created to the end that they may be damned; that innocent persons are reprobated or damned; that God hates people without regard to sin; that certain people are predestined to sin; that it is essential for God to have humans as sinners; that God wants people to sin and makes people sin; that God acts insincerely in calling certain persons"; and so forth.[78] The Remonstrants at the Hague conference had already made convenient use of these harsh expressions and of the difference between infra- and supralapsarianism so that the members of the Synod of Dort were generally inclined to avoid such harsh phrases.[79] But when the delegates from England, Bremen, and Hesse urged the Synod to condemn such harsh language, the Synod balked. It noted that Scripture also at times uses very strong language, that the expressions at issue sometimes have a milder meaning in their original context than when considered by themselves, and further, that responsibility for them rests with the individual authors. The Synod, furthermore, confined itself to warning against the use of harsh expressions (without, however, mentioning any of them specifically) and "many other things of the same kind,"[80] and at a later session warned against administering a strong reprimand to Maccovius for the way he had conducted himself.[81] Accordingly, while supralapsarianism was not incorporated in the confession, neither was it condemned. The Westminster Assembly deliberately left this issue undecided and made no choice

76. Canons of Dort, I, 7.

77. Acts of Synod of Dort, session 130ff.; cf. Gooszen, "Het 'Besluit' dat achter de Dordsche Leerregelen is geplaatst en de Theologie en de Religie van onzen Tijd," *Geloof en Vrijheid* 35 (1901): 530–61; also, several objections against Maccovius, according to A. Kuyper Jr., *Maccovius,* appendix C.

78. A. Kuyper Jr., *Maccovius,* appendix C.

79. Cf. also, Uytenbogaert, *Verdediging van de Resolutie tot den Vrede der Kerken* (1615); and later also S. Episcopius in his *Antidotum continens pressiorem declarationem propriæ et genuinæ sententiæ quæ in Synodo Nationali Dordracena asserta est et stabilita* (Herder-vviici: Ex Officina Typographi Synodalis, 1620); and in his *Eere Gods verdedigd tegen den laster Jac. Triglandii* (Netherlands, 1627).

80. This expression "quae ejus generis sunt alia plurima" was added for the benefit of the delegates from England, Bremen, and Hesse, so that now they could all endorse this decision; Acts of Synod of Dort, session 134.

81. Cf. the literature cited in previous notes. The Synod did warn Maccovius not to use phrases that are offensive to the young and in his teaching to use the kind of language that conforms to Scripture and is clear, plain, and acceptable in orthodox academies.

between infra- and supralapsarianism.[82] As a result many people continued to favor supralapsarianism,[83] but as a rule they coupled this preference with a recognition of the right of infralapsarianism. This view, after all, was officially embodied in the confession of the churches, was warmly advocated and ably defended by many theologians,[84] and was featured as a rule also in the preaching of the gospel.

[239] Still, even this milder form of the doctrine of predestination soon encountered resistance. In the era of the Reformation it was already disputed by Erasmus, Bibliander, Pighius, Bolsec, Trolliet, Castellio, Ochinus (et al.). The Socinians rejected the doctrine of predestination altogether, accepted only a decree of God to grant eternal life to those who keep his commandments and to punish the others, and even offered up God's omniscience to the freedom of the human will.[85] In The Netherlands this doctrine was criticized by numerous theologians,[86] such as Anastasius, Gellius, Coolhaes, Duifhuis, Coornhert, Sybrants, Herberts, Wiggers, and above all by Arminius. Arminius defended predestination as the eternal decree of God to save—in, on account of, and by Christ—those who he foresaw would by a prevenient grace believe and by a subsequent grace persevere; and to punish the others who would not believe or persevere.[87] Arminius still meant to maintain the necessity of grace and the belief that faith is a gift, while his followers tried to do the same in their Remonstrance of the year 1610, articles 3 and 4.[88] Yet this grace was still always considered resistible (art. 4–5). The residual objection to the still as yet certain foreknowledge of God with regard to those who would or would not believe, plus the universal will of God to save all humans, Christ's universal atonement, and the universal offer of the *sufficient* means of grace—these gradually but necessarily resulted in making human beings the final arbiters of their own destiny.[89] This result is clearly evidenced in the later Remonstrant writings, the

---

82. Westminster Confession, ch. 3.

83. In 1640, in Groningen, Gomarius sought to have someone defend a set of supralapsarian theses, but the Curators forebade it, and the provincial Synod did not support his complaint: Wumkes, *De Gereformeerde Kerken in de Ommelanden* (Groningen, 1905), 112.

84. E.g., P. M. Vermigli, *Loci communes*, 232; J. Zanchi(us), *Op. theol.*, II, 485, who therefore cannot be considered—as C. Vitringa (*Doctr. christ.*, II, 41) does—one-sidedly among the supralapsarians; and also Bogerman (according to H. van der Tuuk, *Johannes Bogerman*, 226, 349), J. Polyander, A. Rivetus, A. Walaeus, H. Alting, Molina, Wendelinus, F. Turretin, J. Heidegger, S. Maresius, J. Marck, B. de Moor, and many others. Cf. Walch, *Bibliotheca theologica selecta*, II, 1024ff.

85. F. Socinus, *Praelectiones theologicae*, ch. XIII; J. Crell, *De uno Deo Patre libri duo* (Irenopolis [Amsterdam]: C. Fronerus, 1688), ch. 32; cf. O. Fock, *Der Socinianismus nach seiner Stellung in der Gesammtentwicklung des christlichen Geistes, nach seinem historischen Verlauf und nach seinem Lehrbegriff* (Kiel: C. Schröder, 1847), 653ff.

86. Cf. also Th. van Oppenraaij, *La doctrine de la prédestination dans l'eglise réformée des Pays-Bas depuis l'origine jusqu'au Synode National de Dordrecht en 1618 et 1619* (Louvain: J. van Linthout, 1906).

87. J. Arminius, *Opera* (1629), 119, 283, 389, etc.

88. J. H. Scholten, *Leer der Hervormde Kerk in hare Grondbeginselen*, 2d ed., 2 vols. (Leyden: P. Engels, 1850–51), II, 458.

89. Ibid., II, 472ff.

letter of Episcopius to Reformed believers abroad, the second Remonstrance of the year 1617,[90] the apology and confession published by Episcopius,[91] and the dogmatic works of Uytenbogaert, Episcopius, and Limborch.[92] Remonstrantism [clearly] paved the way for rationalism. Though condemned by the Synod of Dort, as a spiritual disposition, it found increasing acceptance in all countries and churches in the seventeenth and eighteenth centuries. From the side of the Reformed it even received support in the school at Saumur in France. At this school Moyse Amyraut taught a double decree. God first decreed in general that all who believed in Christ would be saved; but knowing in advance that no one can believe of himself or herself, he added to the first (universal and conditional) decree a second (particular and absolute) decree to give to some the gift of faith and to save them.[93] Of course, if the first (universal) decree meant anything at all, it would completely overshadow the second. Despite its condemnation in the Formula Consensus (1675; can. 4–6), this theory exerted much influence and in the case of Pajon led to the rejection of "efficacious grace." In all the Reformed churches an Arminian trend gained ground. All the modalities and sects that surfaced in the seventeenth and eighteenth century (neonomianism, Deism, Quakerism, Methodism, and so forth) to a greater or lesser degree displayed kinship with Arminius. Only a few scattered theologians managed to stand firm, such as Comrie, Holtius, and Brahé in The Netherlands; Boston and the Erskines in Scotland; and especially Jonathan Edwards (1703–58) in North America.[94]

In this [nineteenth] century a deeper study of nature, history, and humanity has demonstrated the untenability of deistic Pelagianism. In its place has come a pantheistic or materialistic, a more ethically or more physically conditioned determinism. Of course, between this determinism and the doctrine of predestination, despite some surface resemblance, there is a fundamental difference. Neither pantheism nor materialism leaves any room for a counsel of God; they only leave room for an unconscious fate, a blind nature, an irrational will. Still, many philosophers and thinkers have understood and interpreted the ecclesiastical doctrine of predestination in this deterministic sense.[95] From

90. Schweizer, *Centraldogmen*, II, 89ff., 106ff.

91. Episcopius, *Opera*, II, 69ff., 95ff.

92. J. Uytenbogaert, *Onderwijzing in de Christelyke Religie*, 2d ed. (Amsterdam: Ian Fred. Sam, 1640); Episcopius, *Opera*, 410ff.; P. van Limborch, *Theologia christiana* (Amsterdam: Wetstein, 1735), II, 18ff.; IV.

93. M. Amyrald [Amyraut], *Traité de la prédestination* (Saumur: Lesnier & Desbordes, 1634); *Synt. Thesium in acad. Salmur.*, 2d ed., 4 parts (Saumur: J. Lesner, 1665), pt. II, 107ff.; cf. Rivetus, *Opera*, III, 828–52; F. Spanheim, *Exercitationes de gratia universali* (Leyden: Maire, 1646), 18, 40; A. Comrie and N. Holtius, *Examen van het Ontwerp van Tolerantie*, VI, 195ff.; VII, 314ff., 450ff.; Schweizer, *Centraldogmen*, II, 225ff.; J. H. Scholten, *Leer der Hervormde Kerk*, II, 612ff.; J. G. Walch, *Bibliotheca theologica selecta*, II, 1028.

94. Cf. J. Ridderbos, *De Theologie van Jonathan Edwards* (The Hague: J. A. Nederbragt, 1907).

95. A. E. Biedermann, *Christliche Dogmatik* (Zürich: Crell & Füssli, 1869), §§847ff.; D. F. Strauss, *Die christliche Glaubenslehre*, 2 vols. (Tübingen: C. F. Osiander, 1840–41), II, 362ff., 462ff.; J. H. Scholten, *Leer der Hervormde Kerk*, especially II, 453–605; idem, *De Vrije Wil, Kritisch Onderzoek* (Leiden: P. Engels, 1859), 385ff.; E. von Hartmann, *Religionsphilosophie*, 2d ed., 2 vols. (Bad Sachsa im Harz: Hermann Haacke, 1907), II, 174ff., 216ff., 271ff.

this viewpoint it is said: "Just as certain as it is that every human is not only predisposed but also predetermined toward evil, so certain is it that every human is not only predisposed but also predetermined toward the good. . . . Just as certain as it is that no purely reprobate persons exist, so certain is it that no purely elect persons exist, for also the most reprobate carry within themselves a degree of grace, and also the most highly favored persons are not exempt from actual evil."[96] In principle, Schleiermacher also agrees with this viewpoint, for though he proceeds from the doctrine of the church and continues to hold onto the revelation in Christ, he only distinguishes election and reprobation in relation to time. In the strict sense of the word there are no reprobates. Under different circumstances everyone would already have been converted in this life or come to conversion later.[97]

All ideas dating from earlier or later times recur in modern theology. In the first place, many theologians try to escape the entire doctrine of predestination by saying that eternity is not a pretemporal span of time, that therefore the divine decrees cannot be conceived as lying ready-made for countless ages, but that, on the contrary, predestination including both election and reprobation is nothing other than the eternal immanent action and government of God becoming manifest in time. In other words, the decrees are identical with the facts of history.[98] In this way, however, the whole distinction between eternity and time, between God and the world, is erased, and theism is exchanged for pantheism. For that reason others do assume the existence of an eternal divine decree, but one that consists only in God's antecedent will, in accordance with which God genuinely desires and wills the salvation of all humans. In history, however, this universal decree becomes particular, at least for the time being. For in carrying out this decree God proceeds to work historically. The object of election is not individual persons but the church as a whole. God calls nations to himself and does this successively as in the course of history and under his providential guidance they become receptive to, and ready for, the higher religion of Christianity. And within the circle of those nations he also again calls special persons. He does this successively and in the context of their people, their natural disposition, and their upbringing.

THE SCOPE OF GOD'S DECREE

Hence, the election of one people and of a single individual occurs, not at the expense but for the benefit of others. Not everyone, not every nation, can be first. Those who have been temporarily bypassed, that is, the rejected

---

96. E. von Hartmann, *Religionsphilosophie*, II, 217.

97. F. Schleiermacher, *The Christian Faith* (Edinburgh: T. & T. Clark, 1989), §§117–20.

98. A. Schweizer, *Die christliche Glaubenslehre nach protestantischen Grundsätzen dargestellt*, 2 vols. in 3 (Leipzig: S. Hirzel, 1863–72), II, 254ff.; R. A. Lipsius, *Lehrbuch der evangelisch-protestantischen Dogmatik* (Braunschweig: C. A. Schwetschke, 1893), §540; cf. also W. Hastie, *The Theology of the Reformed Church in Its Fundamental Principles* (Edinburgh: T. & T. Clark, 1904), 259ff.

peoples and persons, come to conversion later, either in this life or, probably, in the life to come. In any case there is no decree of reprobation from the side of God that would exclude certain persons from salvation; at most there is a possibility of continuing resistance and positive hardening on the part of humans such that it would result in eternal ruin.[99] Still others, going one step farther, teach that in addition to that universal decree there is another special decree by which God has determined to save those whose faith and perseverance he has foreseen and foreknown, and to punish the others eternally. But all agree in according the decision for eternity to the power of the human will. Yet all do not attribute this power to the same source. According to some, the power to accept or to reject grace belongs to humans by virtue of creation or of the pedagogical guidance of God's universal providence.[100] According to others, this power arises from the preparatory and antecedent grace granted to humans in baptism or in the preaching of the law and the gospel.[101] A third group attempts to reconcile the two positions by teaching that grace is granted to those who make good use of the natural powers of the will and earnestly study the Word of God.[102] Kaftan, accordingly, was not altogether wrong when he wrote: "Modern German theology does not have a doctrine of election."[103] Yet it still often resonates with believers and is defended not only in the church but also in theology.[104] It is remarkable that in America the Missouri Synod of the Lutheran church took a position that approximates Calvinism,[105] whereas

99. H. L. Martensen, *Christian Dogmatics*, trans. W. Urwick (Edinburgh: T. & T. Clark, 1871), §§206ff.; R. A. Lipsius, *Dogmatik*, §§541–48; A. Ritschl, *Die christliche Lehre von der Rechtfertigung und Versöhnung*, 4th ed., 3 vols. (Bonn: A. Marcus, 1895–1903), II, 112ff.; C. E. Luthardt, *Compendium der Dogmatik* (Leipzig: Dörffling & Franke, 1865), §§32ff.; F. Nitzsch, *Lehrbuch der evangelischen Dogmatik*, 3d ed. (Tübingen: J. C. B. Mohr, 1902), 607.

100. J. Müller, *Dogmatische Abhandlungen* (Bremer: C. E. Müller, 1870), 243ff.; idem, *The Christian Doctrine of Sin*, trans. W. Urwick, 5th ed., 2 vols. (Edinburgh: T. & T. Clark, 1868), 253ff.; C. I. Nitzsch, *System der christlichen Lehre*, 5th ed. (Bonn: Adolph Marcus, 1844), §144; ed. note: ET: *System of Christian Doctrine* (Edinburgh: T. & T. Clark, 1849); R. Kübel, "Prädestination," *PRE²*, XII, 145–62; cf. Frank, "Synergismus," *PRE²*, XV, 103–13; J. H. A. Ebrard, *Christliche Dogmatik*, 2d ed., 2 vols. (Königsberg: A. W. Unzer, 1862–63), §§325, 344; H. Bavinck, *De Theologie van Prof. Daniel Chantepie de la Saussaye* (Leiden: Donner, 1884), 64ff.

101. T. F. D. Kliefoth, *Acht Bücher von der Kirche* (Schwerin: Stiller, 1854); cf. J. Müller, *Dogmatische Abhandlungen*, 247ff.; E. W. C. Sartorius, *Die Lehre von der heiligen Liebe*, 174ff.; G. Thomasius, *Christi Person und Werk*, 3d ed., 2 vols. (Erlangen: Theodor Bläsing, 1853–61), II, 278, 286; F. H. R. Frank, *System der christlichen Wahrheit*, 2d ed., 2 vols. (Erlangen: A. Deichert, 1884), §§40–41; I. A. Dorner, *A System of Christian Doctrine*, trans. A. Cave and J. S. Banks, rev. ed., 4 vols. (Edinburgh: T. & T. Clark, 1888–91), III, 703–24; R. A. Lipsius, *Dogmatik*, §541; Th. Häring, *Der christliche Glaube*, 507. A. von Oettingen, *Lutherische Dogmatik*, 2 vols. (Munich: C. H. Beck, 1897–1902), II. 2, 543ff.; A. F. C. Vilmar, *Dogmatik*, 2 vols. (Gütersloh: C. Bertelsmann, 1874), II, 138ff.

102. F. A. Philippi, *Kirchliche Glaubenslehre*, 3d ed., 7 vols. in 10 (Gütersloh: C. Bertelsmann, 1870–90), IV, 72ff.; cf. W. G. T. Shedd, *Dogmatic Theology*, 3d ed., 3 vols. (New York: Scribner, 1891–94), II, 511.

103. J. Kaftan, *Dogmatik*, 475.

104. Cf., e.g., E. Böhl, *Dogmatik*, 124ff., 527ff.; C. Hodge, *Systematic Theology*, I, 535ff.; Shedd, *Dogmatic Theology*, I, 393ff.

105. A. W. Dieckhoff, *Der missourische Prädestianismus und die Concordienformel* (Rostock: E. Kahl, 1885); Späth, "Lutherische Kirche in America," *PRE³*, XIV, 184–213.

the Cumberland Presbyterian Church modified the Westminster Confession along Arminian lines.[106] When the revision of the Westminster Confession was in process in Scotland and America, many churches also raised objections to the doctrine of election and reprobation, against the belief in the perdition of pagans and of children who die in infancy, and in general against the Confession's tendency to proceed one-sidedly from the sovereignty of God while disregarding his universal love.[107]

[240] The counsel of God is to be understood as his eternal plan for all that exists or will happen in time. Scripture everywhere assumes that all that is and comes to pass is the realization of God's thought and will and has its model and foundation in God's eternal counsel (Gen. 1; Job 28:27; Prov. 8:22; Ps. 104:24; Prov. 3:19; Jer. 10:12; 51:15; Heb. 11:3; Ps. 33:11; Isa. 14:24–27; 46:10; Prov. 19:21; Acts 2:23; 4:28; Eph. 1:11; etc.). It is even a human privilege to act on the basis of deliberation and planning. In the case of rational creatures idea and purpose precede action. In a far more sublime sense this is true for the Lord our God, apart from whose knowledge and will nothing comes into being. Among Christians, accordingly, there can be no disagreement over the existence of a divine counsel. Only pantheism, which does not acknowledge that God has a life and consciousness of his own that is distinct from the world, can raise objections to that idea. As a result pantheism has to choose between denying or accepting the existence of the Logos in the world. If it opts for denial, it has to attribute the existence of the world to a blind will; if it chooses to accept it, it will have to assume the existence in God of a consciousness that contains the ideas of all things. Rationality in the world presupposes rationality in God. There could be no rationality in creation if it had not been created with intelligence and wisdom. Furthermore, this rationality of the Lord as embodied in creation must not be conceived as an uncertain idea, the realization of which remains doubtful. It is not mere foreknowledge that derives its content from creatures, nor a plan, project, or purpose whose realization can be frustrated. It is at one and the same time both an act of God's intelligence and an act of his will.

Scripture, accordingly, speaks of God's counsel, the thoughts of his heart (Ps. 33:11), of the counsel of this will (Eph. 1:11), of predestination and foreordination (Acts 2:23; 4:28; Rom. 8:29), of purpose (Jer. 4:28; 51:12; Rom. 8:28; Eph. 1:9, 11), will (Ps. 51:18; Isa. 53:10; 60:10; 61:2; Matt. 11:26; Eph. 1:5, 9), decree (Gen. 41:32; 2 Chron. 25:16; Job 38:10; Ps. 2:7). God speaks and it comes to be; he commands and it stands firm (Ps. 33:9). The counsel of God is such that in due time it is realized by its own inner necessity. It is efficacious (Isa. 14:27; Ps. 115:3; 135:6), unchanging (Isa. 46:10; Ps. 33:11; Heb. 6:17; James 1:17), independent (Matt. 11:26; Eph. 1:9; Rom. 9:11, 20–21).

106. P. Schaff, *The Creeds of Christendom*, 6th ed., 3 vols. (New York: Harper & Row, 1931; reprinted, Grand Rapids: Baker, 1990), III, 771.

107. E. F. K. Müller, *Bekenntnisschriften*, 941ff.

Still, we must differentiate between God's decree and its execution, just as we must distinguish between God's being and his works *ad extra*. God's decree is a work *ad intra*, immanent in the divine being, eternal, and extratemporal. Against this view it has indeed been said that eternity cannot and may not be conceived as a time before time, and that the counsel of God and election must not be understood as a decree made ages ago. By itself this comment is correct. Eternity is essentially different from time. God's counsel is no more an act in the past than the generation of the Son. It is an eternal act of God, eternally completed and eternally ongoing outside of and above time.[108] As Scaliger correctly noted, God's decree is not the outcome of wide-ranging reasoning and reflection, following a long period of indecision;[109] nor must it be pictured as a plan lying ready and simply awaiting execution. On the contrary, the counsel of God is the eternally active will of God, the willing and deciding God himself, not something accidental in God, but one with his being, as his eternally active will. God cannot be conceived as being indecisive, devoid of purpose and will.[110] Yet this does not alter the fact that God's counsel remains a work *ad intra,* determined only by God himself, distinct from his works in time (Acts 15:18; Eph. 1:4).

Included in this counsel of God are all the things that exist and will occur in time, in short, the whole plan, [the blueprint of] "the intelligible universe." This world plan, though closely connected with God's being, may not be equated with that being, nor therefore with the Son, that is, the Logos. It relates to God's being in the same way world-consciousness is related to God's self-consciousness. God's self-knowledge is not exhausted in the creation of the world any more than his power or any of his virtues is. Yet the world is a suitable theatre for the display, on a creaturely level, of all God's attributes. The world plan is so conceived by God that it can radiantly exhibit his glory and perfections in a manner and measure suited to each creature. It is a mirror in which God displays his image. It is the creaturely reflection of his adorable being: a finite, limited, nonexhaustive, yet true and faithful reproduction of his self-knowledge. In relation to the world itself, therefore, this counsel of God is both the "efficient" and the "exemplary" cause. It is the efficient cause, for all creaturely beings can in the nature of the case come into existence only by the decree and will of God. The decree is the "womb" of all reality (Zeph. 2:2 MT, KJV). All that exists is ultimately grounded in God's good pleasure (εὐδοκια του θεου). Beyond that we cannot go. The final answer to the question why things exist and are as they are is that "God willed it"; it lies in his absolute sovereignty. But God's counsel is also the "exemplary" cause of all

---

108. P. M. Vermigli, *Loci communes,* 230.

109. B. de Moor, *Comm. in Marckii Comp.,* I, 900; C. Vitringa, *Doct. christ.,* II, 13; H. Heppe, *Dogmatik der evangelisch-reformierten Kirche,* 101–2.

110. J. Maccovius, *Loci communes theologici,* 129; P. van Mastricht, *Theologia,* III, 1, 28; F. Turretin, *Institutes of Elenctic Theology,* IV, 1.7; A. Comrie and N. Holtius, *Examen van het Ontwerp van Tolerantie,* VI, 164–66.

that is and comes to pass. We can form a concept of a thing only after it has come into being and as it is. With God, however, the idea of a thing is first; then it comes into being as he has conceived it. Just as Moses had to make the tabernacle according to the pattern which was shown him on the mountain (Heb. 8:5), just as all fatherhood (πατρια) in heaven and earth is named after the Father (Eph. 3:15), so all things temporal are an image of the eternal, all existing things are a reproduction of the plan of God, and ultimately all that is and comes to pass is a reflection of the divine being. Although Thomas's statement has been criticized because God's world plan does not coincide with God's being, rightly interpreted, it is not untrue: "God in his essence is the likeness of all things."[111]

The counsel of God, accordingly, must be considered a single and simple decree. At the Westminster Assembly (1643–46) the delegates discussed whether to speak of the "decree" in the singular or in the plural. The Westminster Confession only uses the word in the singular. And indeed the world plan is one simple conception in the mind of God. Just as Minerva emerges full-grown from the head of Jupiter, and just as a genius all at once completely grasps the idea of a work of art, so the world plan is eternally complete in the divine consciousness. But just as an artist can only execute his vision in stages, so God unveils before the eyes of his creatures the one vision of his counsel in a series of temporal phases. The world plan of God is one single plan; but as it is being realized, it unfolds itself in all its abundance in the forms of space and time. In creatures and in a creaturely mode, that is, outside of himself, God can only reveal his love and all his other perfections in the [spatial and temporal] dimensions of length, breadth, depth, and height (Eph. 3:18–19). In this way alone do we learn something of God's many-sided wisdom and unsearchable riches. Similarly, the one simple and eternal decree of God unfolds itself before our eyes in time in a vast multiplicity of things and events, a multiplicity that at one and the same time points back to the one decree of God and leads us, humanly speaking, to think of many divine decrees. This kind of language must not be condemned as long as the unity of the decree in God and the inseparable connectedness of all the special decrees is maintained and recognized.

PROVIDENCE

[241] In the counsel of God we must first of all distinguish the decree that in the past was generally denoted by the word "providence." Originally the word "providence" (προνοια; *providentia*) simply meant foreseeing, providing, giving consideration to in advance. This is how the word was initially understood

---

111. T. Aquinas, *Summa theol.*, I, qu. 15, art. 1; I, qu. 44, art. 3; cf. P. Lombard, *Sent.*, I, dist. 36; A. Polanus, *Syn. theol.*, 268; F. Gomarus, *Disputationum theologicarum*, IX, §§28–30; W. Ames, *Marrow of Theology*, I, 7, 13ff.; J. H. Heidegger, *Corpus theologiae christianae*, V, 12; F. Turretin, *Institutes of Elenctic Theology*, IV, 1.7; P. van Mastricht, *Theologia*, III, 1, 28; B. de Moor, *Comm. in Marckii Comp.*, I, 903.

in theology as well. For that reason the providence of God was discussed in connection with the decrees and the will of God. It was then described as the "plan of ordering things to an end," that is, as that act of God's intellect and will by which from eternity he ordered all things to an end ordained by him. As such a plan of ordering it must of course be distinguished from its execution in time, which is more specifically called "governance."[112] Thus many Roman Catholic theologians[113] and initially also several of the early Reformed theologians[114] viewed providence as a divine decree. In this sense providence is a plan or decree or pattern of God in terms of which he maintains and governs all things in time. Later, however, the word "providence" most frequently referred to the divine activity of preservation and governance itself. Zwingli, Calvin, Polanus, and the Leiden *Synopsis*[115] already treated it—after the creation—in that sense. While the name does not matter so much, what is important is that the decree of God encompasses all things, not just the determination of the eternal state of rational creatures (predestination), but the ordering and ranking of all things without exception. Predestination, accordingly, was not something considered in isolation, but was a part of God's decree for all things and only a particular application of it. As Zwingli put it: "Providence is as it were the parent of predestination." Predestination is providence insofar as it concerns the eternal destiny of humans and angels. The Reformed, more nearly following the language of Scripture (which does not use the word προνοια [with God as actor]), called this the counsel of God. This counsel, which is all-inclusive, relates first of all to the universe as a whole. All things, also in the inanimate world, exist and happen in accordance with the counsel of God. All things are grounded in God's ordinances. Heaven and earth, light and darkness, day and night, summer and winter, seedtime and harvest, are ordered, both in their unity and in their diversity, by God, who is "wonderful in counsel, and excellent in wisdom" (Isa. 28:29; Gen. 1:14, 26, 28; 8:22; Ps. 104:5, 9; 119:90–91; 148:6; Job 38:10ff.; Jer. 5:24; 31:25ff.; 33:20, 25).

Now, insofar as God's counsel covers the physical world, it is almost universally recognized, the exception being the Manichaeans (et al.). Even when such a counsel and order of God is more specifically assumed for rational creatures, there is still great unanimity. Almost all acknowledge that the will of God is the most basic reason for the creation of the human race (Gen. 1:26); the scattering of the peoples (Gen. 11); the determination of times and boundaries of places where they would live (Acts 17:26); the differentiation in gifts, talents, ranks, social position, degrees of wealth, and so forth (Deut. 32:8; Prov. 22:2; Matt.

112. Boethius, *The Consolation of Philosophy*, IV, pr. 6; P. Lombard, *Sent.*, I, dist. 35, I; T. Aquinas, *Summa theol.*, I, qu. 22, art. 1; idem, *Summa contra gentiles*, III, 77.

113. D. Petavius, "De Deo," in *Theol. dogm.*, VIII; *Theologia Wirceburgensi*, III, 175ff.; G. Perrone, *Prael. theol.*, II, 233; C. Pesch, *Prael. dogm.*, II, 158.

114. Z. Ursinus, *Catechismus major*, qu. 27; J. Zanchi(us), *Op. theol.*, II, 324, 436; S. Maresius, *Syst. theol.*, IV, §19; Helvetic Confession, II, art. 6; cf. later, on the rule of God.

115. Ed. note: H. Bavinck, *Synopsis purioris theologiae* (Leiden: D. Donner, 1881).

25:15); and even the inequality and diversity of gifts in the church (1 Cor. 4:7; 12:7–11; Rom. 12:4ff.). God's good pleasure alone explains all being and all diversity of being. *That* things are and that they are as they are, is grounded solely in God. The existence of a thing and the specificity of a thing, the multiplicity of life and being, the infinite diversity among creatures in kind, gender, longevity, rank, social position, wealth (etc.)—they all are attributable to God's good pleasure and God's good pleasure alone.

This divine good pleasure, moreover, does not presuppose but creates its object. If animals could talk and argue with their Creator because they are not like us humans, says Augustine, everyone would consider that absurd.[116] And indeed the only appropriate reaction of a creature is to acquiesce in God's good pleasure. A creature really has a choice between only two options: either it chooses to be its own creator and thereby ceases to be a creature, or it must be and remain a creature from beginning to end, and therefore owes its existence and the specific nature of its existence only to God.

However, the moment the counsel of God was also extended to include the moral world, opposition arose on all sides. Here the counsel of God ended, it was said. This, after all, is the special domain of humans, a domain in which they act as the shapers of their own destiny.

With a view to safeguarding human freedom, responsibility, guilt (etc.), Pelagius drew a line of distinction between the natural and the moral world, between the "capacity to" and the "will to," and in each case withdrew the latter from the counsel and the providence of God. All forms of Pelagianism aim to make the moral world, in part or in whole, independent of God. Both on its own merits and quite generally, however, this attempt must be rejected.

In the first place, it is incompatible with Scripture. Granted, Scripture at all times and in no uncertain terms insists on the moral nature of human beings, but it never tries to do this by effecting a dualistic split between the natural and the moral world and by withdrawing the latter from God's governance. God's counsel extends to all things, also to those that belong to the moral world, the evil as well as the good.

Furthermore, such a split is in fact impossible. The world, by its very design, is one organic whole. The two spheres, nature (φύσις) and morality (ἔθος), are most closely interconnected and interpenetrate each other at all times. The two, though certainly distinct, are never separated. One cannot designate a point in creation where the counsel and governance of God and the independent will and action of humans begin. Especially in this century the historic and organic view of things has at every point driven out and condemned this Pelagian split. This dualism, moreover, would withdraw the largest and most important part of the world from God's counsel and slip it into the hands of chance and caprice. Indeed, in that case the world would in large part be taken away not only from God's counsel and will, but even from his knowledge. If

---

116. Augustine, *De verbis apost. sermo*, 11; cf. Calvin, *Institutes*, III.xx.1.

God and his human creatures can only be conceived as competitors, and if the one can only retain his freedom and independence at the expense of the other, then God has to be increasingly restricted both in knowledge and in will. Pelagianism, accordingly, banishes God from his world. It leads both to Deism and atheism and enthrones human arbitrariness and folly. Therefore, the solution of the problem must be sought in another direction. It must be sought in the fact that God—because he is God and the universe is his creation—by the infinitely majestic activity of his knowing and willing, does not destroy but instead creates and maintains the freedom and independence of his creatures.

[242] Pelagianism, however, does not yet marshal its full strength when it opposes the general and special providence of God. To some extent it even recognizes this doctrine. But it comes out fighting especially when the eternal state of rational creatures, the particular decree of predestination, is at issue. Now, predestination is only a particular application of the counsel or providence of God. Just as we cannot separate the natural from the moral world, so neither can we point to a boundary line between the temporal condition of human creatures and their eternal state. With respect to the latter, however, Pelagianism has traded predestination for foreknowledge and described foreordination as the decree of God in which he determined either eternal blessedness or eternal punishment for people, depending on whether he foresaw their persevering faith or their undying unbelief. Now, however generally this view has been adopted in the Christian church (is it not the confession of all Eastern Orthodox, Roman Catholic, Lutheran, Remonstrant, Anabaptist, and Methodist Christians?), it is nevertheless firmly contradicted by Scripture, religious experience, and theological reflection.

In the first place, Scripture clearly teaches that faith and unbelief, salvation and perdition, are not just the objects of God's "bare foreknowledge" but especially also of his will and decree. God's foreknowledge (προγνωσις: Rom. 8:29; 11:2; 1 Pet. 1:2; cf. Acts 2:23) is not a passive form of precognition, not a state of consciousness, but—like the Hebrew ידע (Hos. 13:5 MT, NRSV note; Amos 3:2; etc.)—a self-determination of God, prior to its realization in history, to assume a certain specific relation to the objects of his foreknowledge. It is most closely related to God's purpose (προθεσις), foreordination (προορισμος), and election (ἐκλογη), and is an act of his good pleasure (εὐδοκια).

Second, it is the teaching of Scripture that faith cannot arise from within the heart of an unspiritual person (1 Cor. 2:14), that it is a gift of God (Eph. 2:8; Phil. 1:29; 1 Cor. 4:7) and therefore does not precede election but is its fruit and effect (Rom. 8:29; Eph. 1:4–5; Acts 13:48). Third, it is the unanimous witness of all religious Christian experience that salvation, both in an objective and a subjective sense, is solely the work of God. Though in theory a person may be Pelagian, in the practice of the Christian life, above all in prayer, every Christian is an Augustinian. In that connection all glorying in self is excluded, and God alone is given the honor. Augustine, accordingly, was right when he said that the ancient church's faith in God's grace expressed itself in prayers rather than in its "little works."[117]

Fourth, divine foreknowledge is certainly of such a kind that its object is known in advance as absolutely certain, and then it is identical with predestination. However, if its object is totally accidental and arbitrary, it cannot have been foreknown either. According to the teaching of Eastern Orthodox, Roman Catholic, and Lutheran churches and even according to the Remonstrants—all of whom attempt to substitute foreknowledge for predestination—the number of those who believe and will be saved is just as fixed and certain as it is according to Augustine and Reformed theologians. Said Augustine: "The number of the elect is certain; it can neither be increased nor diminished."[118] This is also the teaching of Lombard, Thomas Aquinas, and all Catholic theologians, although they differ among themselves in that some derive the certainty of the outcome from the will, while others, such as Molina (et al.), derive it from the knowledge of God.[119] In later years Lutheran theologians indeed made predestination depend on foreknowledge, yet they never questioned the certainty and immutability of the outcome.[120] In numerous passages (Dan. 12:1; Matt. 24:24; 25:34; John 10:28; Rom. 8:29–30; 1 Pet. 1:2–4) Scripture speaks in language so clear and strong, after all, that they can hardly deny this immutability.

Formally as well as materially, both in terms of quantity and quality, the number of the saved is unalterably fixed, according to the confession of all Christian churches. But when theologians recognize this fact and think it through, they have to equate foreknowledge with providence and predestination. In advance, with a knowledge that is eternal and immutable, God has known those who would believe. Given this foreknowledge, these people will also most certainly and infallibly come to faith and salvation in time. On this position there nowhere remains any room for "freedom" in the sense of chance and caprice. Foreknowledge, then, by definition includes predestination. If, like Castellio,[121] one says that God foreknew the fortuitous precisely in its fortuitous character, one has reverted to Augustine's line of thought and consequently has no problem harmonizing freedom with predestination. The central question is this: Can these free and fortuitous events be known from eternity with absolute certainty?

If the answer is yes, Augustine is right and the entire doctrine of foreknowledge is redundant. If the answer is no, one has to go on and also reject foreknowledge. In that case the outcome of world history is strictly fortuitous and as such remains incalculable and unknowable. Cicero, seeing this, denied

117. Augustine, *On the Gift of Perseverance*, 23; cf. C. Hodge, *Systematic Theology*, I, 16.

118. Augustine, *On Rebuke and Grace*, 13.

119. P. Lombard, *Sent.*, I, dist. 40; T. Aquinas, *Summa theol.*, I, qu. 23, art. 6, 7; cf. ibid., qu. 24; G. Perrone, *Prael. theol.*, II, 249; C. Pesch, *Prael. dogm.*, II, 205; G. Jansen, *Prael. theol.*, III, 143.

120. J. Gerhard, *Loci theol.*, VII, §§212ff.; J. A. Quenstedt, *Theologia*, III, 20; D. Hollaz, *Examen theologicum acroamaticum*, 641.

121. According to A. Schweizer, *Centraldogmen*, II, 278.

foreknowledge as well. In later years he was followed by the Socinians,[122] Remonstrants,[123] Vorstius,[124] and numerous modern theologians, who in the interest of maintaining the freedom of the human creature, adopted a kind of divine self-limitation in knowledge, will, and power.[125]

Christian churches, however, shrank from this conclusion. All of them confess God's providence and foreknowledge. All things happen in time as God eternally knew they would. The final result and the ways and means leading to it are established in God's providence. Thus considered, the doctrine of predestination is neither just a confession of the Reformed churches, nor a private opinion of Augustine and Calvin, but a dogma of the entire Christian church. Though there are differences in the name by which it is called and the manner in which it is presented, materially there is agreement: all Christian churches and theologians confess that all things exist, happen, and reach their destiny in accordance with God's eternal knowledge. In that sense Augustine could rightly say: "There was never a time when the church of Christ did not hold the truth of this belief in predestination, which is now being defended with fresh concern against new heretics."[126] Although the confessions differ in the degree of attention paid to this doctrine, they all have it. In fact, it can be said that, whether one thinks along Pelagian or Augustinian lines, the matter about which one thinks remains the same. History does not change. The facts and their interconnectedness in world history are as they are regardless of the true or false notions we entertain concerning them.[127] The sole difference is this: Reformed Christians, with Scripture in their hands and Augustine as their leader, did not stop at the consideration of secondary causes but ventured to push on to faith in the primary cause, that is, the will of God, in which alone they experienced rest for their mind and life. The doctrine of predestination finds its invincible power and severity in the facts of world history interpreted by God's Word as the implementation of his eternal counsel. Although the doctrine itself is not harsh and severe, awesomely serious are the *facts* on which it is built.[128] Pelagianism fails to satisfy the human mind for one reason alone: at every point of life and of the history of humankind it conflicts with real-

122. O. Fock, *Der Socinianismus*, 437ff.

123. S. Episcopius, *Institutiones theologicae*, IV, sect. 2, ch. 18.

124. According to J. Scholten, *Leer der Hervormde Kerk*, II, 492.

125. C. H. Weisse, *Philosophische Dogmatik oder Philosophie des Christentums*, 3 vols. (Leipzig: Hirzel, 1855–62), §509; H. L. Martensen, *Christian Dogmatics*, §§115–16; R. Rothe, *Theologische Ethik*, 2d rev. ed., 5 vols. (Wittenberg: Zimmermann, 1867–71), §42; I. A. Dorner, *A System of Christian Doctrine*, I, 332ff.; A. von Oettingen, *Lutherische Dogmatik*, II. 1, 251–59; P. Hofstede de Groot, *Institutiones theologiae naturalis*, 3d ed. (Groningen: W. Zuidema, 1845), 183; cf. J. H. Scholten, *Leer der Hervormde Kerk*, II, 490. In England, some theologians deny God's sovereignty and even creation itself as incompatible with his goodness: cf. John McTaggart and Ellis McTaggart, *Some Dogmas of Religion* (London: E. Arnold, 1906), 221ff.

126. Augustine, *On the Gift of Perseverance*, ch. 23; cf. Prosper of Aquitaine, *Praedestinationem Dei nullus catholicus negat;* in G. Perrone, *Prael. theol.*, II, 249.

127. A. Schweizer, *Glaubenslehre der evangelisch-reformirten Kirche*, I, 73.

128. C. Hodge, *Systematic Theology*, II, 349.

ity—a reality that is awesome indeed. Pelagianism is a veneer that, though highly deceptive, in no way changes reality.

RESPONSE TO PELAGIANISM

[243] Pelagianism, though it has been proved untenable in general, repeatedly comes back to resume its attack at every special point in the doctrine of predestination. In the first place, it assumes the existence of an antecedent conditional decree of God to offer to all fallen humanity a grace that is sufficient for salvation. With this in mind it appeals to a variety of texts in Scripture: Isaiah 5:3; Jeremiah 51:9; Ezekiel 18:23, 32; 33:11; Matthew 23:37; John 3:16; Romans 11:32; and especially 1 Timothy 2:4 and 2 Peter 3:9. Pelagians, semi-Pelagians, Roman Catholics, Lutherans, Remonstrants, Amyraldists among the Reformed, and all universalists of earlier and later times accept such a first, universal decree. This decree, however, immediately clashes with reality. Throughout human history only a small segment of humanity has been familiar with the gospel. In fact, in the history of humankind, grace is not universal but particular. Admittedly, various attempts have been made to reconcile this particularity with the universal decree of God. Pelagians made this attempt by erasing the difference between nature and grace and by identifying the law of nature *(lex naturae)* as a way of salvation. Numerous Roman Catholic theologians believed that grace is or will be granted to all who make a proper use of the light and power of nature. Early Lutherans held that in the time of Adam, Noah, and the apostles (Rom. 10:18), grace had been universal but had again been restricted solely by human sin. Modern theologians have come up with the doctrine that the gospel of grace will be preached after death to all "negative" unbelievers (i.e., those who have never heard the gospel). But all these hypotheses are extrascriptural and cannot undo the fact of the particularity of grace. Now, if this fact is certain, the question arises why the gospel is preached to one and not to another. Why is one person born in a Christian and another in a pagan home? Pelagians and semi-Pelagians attempt to justify this state of affairs by the consideration that also in connection with this predestination to initial grace, God took note of the natural merits of people and the use they made of their natural powers. But Augustine properly refuted this "predestination to initial grace on the basis of foreseen merits that arise from the natural will," by pointing to infants who had no such merits and of whom some had been baptized, while others died unbaptized. The Roman Catholic church, accordingly, consistently opposed this point in Pelagianism, retained the doctrine of "prevenient grace," and called this first grace "unmerited."[129]

In the case of these young children Pelagianism faces an insurmountable difficulty. Predestination to initial grace, that is, being born in a Christian country or only becoming acquainted with the gospel later on, is absolutely

---

129. H. Denzinger, *Enchiridion*, 171, 679.

undeserved and unconditional. Here at the beginning, at the first decree, predestination can only be viewed as absolute and unconditional. The question why one person learns of the gospel and another is denied the message, hence why one is given the opportunity to receive eternal salvation and another is not, is not one that can be answered from within the human situation. Here everyone, whether he or she wants to or not, must acquiesce in the will and good pleasure of God.

Second, Pelagianism seeks to vindicate itself at the point of "predestination to an efficacious grace." Reality teaches us that not everyone who hears the gospel receives it with a true faith. Why this difference? Pelagianism tells us that the grace that is granted to all is sufficient by itself; and that now the human will decides whether that grace will be and remain efficacious or not. In the Pelagian scheme of things, therefore, there is really no decree anymore after that of the universal offer of grace. From this point on, everything is left to humans to decide. God has done his part. He gave the opportunity *(posse)*, and humans possess the power of decision *(velle)*. But not a single Christian confession has ventured to adopt this Pelagian position. To some extent they have all taught an efficacious decree, a gift of faith, and hence have distinguished a second decree in the counsel of predestination. The question still remained, however: To whom is this "efficacious," "habitual," "infused" grace, that is, true faith, actually given?

At this point there is a great deal of confusion. Among Roman Catholic, Lutheran, and Remonstrant theologians there gradually arose the theory that the grace of faith is granted to those who make the proper use of initial grace, that is, of the gospel preached to them, the illumination of the Holy Spirit, and so forth, and do what is within their capacity to do. Granted, this is not "a merit of condignity" ["a full merit inasmuch as the work of the Spirit is absolutely good and is the ground of a truly deserved salvation"], but "a merit of congruity" ["a half-merit inasmuch as no human act can justly deserve the reward of salvation"].[130] In the distribution of the gift of faith God binds himself to the earnestness of the human effort. "Predestination to further graces" is a decree, not of God's sovereignty but of his justice or fairness. It is fair for God to grant faith and forgiveness to those who do their best. Nevertheless, this view also is in conflict with Scripture and reality. Humans, to be sure, are obliged to faith and repentance and are admonished to that end by the preaching of the gospel. But from this obligation one cannot infer the possession of the power; nor does the "you shall" by any means yield the "you can." The question is: Whence does a sinful and corrupt human ever derive the power to accept the gospel and to make the right use of initial grace? Whence would one derive that power—from oneself, from the operation of the Logos within, from baptismal grace? Even the proponents of the "sufficient" grace

---

130. Ed. note: The parenthetical explanations of the terms are from R. Muller, *Dictionary of Latin and Greek Theological Terms* (Grand Rapids: Baker, 1985), s.v. "meritum."

that is offered to all are themselves embarrassed by the question. Scripture, we know, clearly teaches that humans are utterly unwilling and powerless, that faith is an undeserved gift of grace, and that salvation is also a subjective work of God. While nature and grace may be interconnected, there is still an essential difference between them, no gradual transition. Neither Scripture nor reality lend any support to the theory of a "merit of congruity." On the contrary, children have an advantage over the wise and understanding, and publicans and sinners enter the kingdom of heaven before the Pharisees and scribes (cf. Luke 10:21; Matt. 21:31).

Third and finally, Pelagianism seeks to maintain its position at the point of "the predestination to glory." It reasons as follows: even though a person believes in the truth and in consequence receives forgiveness and life, it is not at all certain that he or she will continue in that faith and thus obtain salvation. For that reason a third divine decree is needed. It is the decree to grant salvation to those whose perseverance in the faith to the very end God has foreseen from eternity. So far the Pelagian position. But now all the objections stated above come back with even greater force. God's decree has become completely conditional and has lost its character as will and decree. It is nothing more than a wish whose fulfillment is totally uncertain. God looks on passively and adopts an attitude of waiting; humans decide. Caprice and chance sit on the throne. Even in the case of believers the final outcome is still completely uncertain. At every moment the apostasy of the saints remains a possibility. Furthermore, the separation of predestination to grace from predestination to glory is completely at variance with Scripture. It implies that the chain of salvation (Rom. 8:29) can snap at any point. It dissolves the one great work of re-creation into a series of human acts and actions that occur one after the other, without connection or continuity. Finally, given this doctrine, God's entire work in saving sinners is misconstrued and denied. Scripture always and everywhere powerfully emphasizes God's faithfulness and immutability, the eternity of his covenant, the certainty of his promises. All this has been lost in Pelagianism. In Pelagianism God does not know his own. His covenant and steadfast love are forever infirm from moment to moment. Sheep are constantly being snatched from Jesus' hand. It is not true that God glorifies those whom he has foreknown, called, and justified. Pure and consistent Pelagianism is the total subversion of Christianity and religion. That, too, is the reason why not a single Christian church has accepted it. However much the doctrine of predestination has been rendered impure by semi-Pelagian admixtures in the Roman Catholic and Lutheran churches, it is still confessed by them all. Essentially and materially, predestination is a dogma accepted throughout Christianity.

PREDESTINATION

[244] In Christian theology, however, the word "predestination" (προορισμος) has been used in very different senses. Meanings varied from broad to narrow. On the Pelagian position it is nothing other than the decree to grant

eternal salvation to those whose faith and perseverance God had foreseen, and to consign others, whose sins and unbelief he had foreseen, to eternal punishment. The creation, the fall, Christ, the preaching of the gospel and the offer of grace to all, a persevering faith or unbelief—they all precede predestination, are not included in it but excluded from it. This decree is restricted to the decision to predestine some to eternal life and others to eternal punishment. Here predestination is understood in the most restricted sense and is totally dependent on the bare foreknowledge of God. It is uncertain and undeserving of the name "predestination." Not God but humans make history and determine the outcome of it. This view has been sufficiently rebutted above and needs no further discussion here.[131]

What does need further consideration is the important difference between infralapsarianism and supralapsarianism. This, in fact, consists in nothing other than a more restricted or broader definition of the concept of predestination. Augustine, to cite a major figure in this discussion, restricted the word in two ways. In the first place, in the order of the decrees he had the decree of predestination follow that of creation and the fall; second, he usually construed the word in a favorable sense, equated foreordination with election, and favored describing the decree of reprobation with the word "foreknowledge." Predestination tells us what God does, that is, the good; but foreknowledge refers to what humans do, that is, evil.[132] Generally speaking, scholasticism,[133] Roman Catholicism,[134] and Lutheranism[135] followed this latter usage. The infralapsarians among Reformed theologians similarly had the decree of creation and fall precede that of election and reprobation. But while the majority of them were willing to include reprobation in the decree of predestination—provided it follows that of the fall—and hence spoke of "double predestination,"[136] others preferred to restrict predestination to election and to treat reprobation separately under a different name.[137] Now if the word "predestination" is not construed in a Pelagian sense and reprobation is not withdrawn from the jurisdiction of the divine will, as was done in the thinking of later Catholic and Lutheran theologians, this difference is not material but merely verbal.[138] Still,

---

131. Cf. also, W. Perkins, *Works*, I, 788ff.; W. Twisse, *Op.*, I, 669ff.

132. Augustine, *On the Gift of Perseverance*, chs. 17–19; idem, *On the Predestination of the Saints*, ch. 10.

133. P. Lombard, *Sent.*, I, dist. 40; T. Aquinas, *Summa theol.*, I, qu. 23.

134. H. Denzinger, *Enchiridion*, 279, 285, 296; *Council of Trent*, VI, can. 6.

135. J. T. Müller, *Die symbolischen Bücher der evangelisch-lutherischen Kirche*, 8th ed. (Gütersloh: C. Bertelsmann, 1898), 554.

136. F. Turretin, *Institutes of Elenctic Theology*, IV, 9.6.

137. Hyperius, *Methodi theologiae*, III, 2, 24; P. M. Vermigli, *Loci communes*, 231–33; J. Zanchi(us), *Op. theol.*, II, 479; B. Keckermann, *Systema theologiae*, 296; D. Pareus, *In divinam ad Romanos S. Pauli Apostoli epistolam commentarius*, 562 (on Rom. 8:29–30).

138. P. van Mastricht, *Theologia*, III, 2, 24; F. Turretin, *Institutes of Elenctic Theology*, IV, 7.4; J. F. Stapfer, *Onderwys in de gantsche Wederleggende Godsgeleertheit*, 5 vols. in 6 (Utrecht: Gisb. Tieme van Paddenburg and Abraham van Paddenburg, 1757–63), V, 466ff.

it is characteristic for the infralapsarian position that the decree of creation and fall precedes that of election and reprobation. Supralapsarianism, by contrast, so expanded predestination that it includes the decree of creation and the fall, which are then considered as means leading to an ultimate end: the eternal state of rational creatures.

In Reformed churches and theology both views of predestination, the supra- as well as the infralapsarian, have always been accorded equal recognition. While the Dutch confessional standards are infralapsarian in outlook, no ecclesiastical assembly, not even the Synod of Dort, ever made things difficult for a supralapsarian. The Lambeth articles of 1595, which were included in the Irish Confession of 1615 (ch. 3) as well as the Westminster Confession, intentionally leave the issue undecided. Reformed theologians have always extended equal rights to both views.[139] Spanheim used to say that when he lectured in a theological classroom, he was a supralapsarian, but when speaking to his congregation he was an infralapsarian.[140] And indeed, both are fundamentally Reformed. On the one hand, supralapsarians teach as decisively as infralapsarians that God is not the author of sin but that the cause of sin lies in the human will. Although as the Omnipotent One God may have predestined the fall and exercised his government also in and through sin, he remains holy and righteous. Humans fall and sin voluntarily through their own fault. "Man falls as God's providence ordains, but he falls by his own fault."[141] Also, supralapsarians did not arrive at their view by philosophical speculation, but presented this view because they deemed it to be more in harmony with Holy Scripture. Just as Augustine arrived at his doctrine of predestination by studying Paul, so the scriptural doctrine of sin led Calvin to his supralapsarianism. According to his own testimony, in passing on this perspective he was not giving his readers philosophy but the truth that is according to the Word of God.[142] On the other hand, Reformed theologians of the infralapsarian persuasion fully recognize that God did not, by foreknowledge, merely foresee the fall and sin and eternal punishment, but included and foreordained them in his decree.[143]

On the decrees themselves and on their content, accordingly, there is no disagreement. Both parties reject free will, and deny that faith is the cause of election and that sin is the cause of reprobation, and thus combat Pelagianism. Both parties ultimately rest their case in the sovereign good pleasure of God. The difference only concerns the order of the decrees. Infralapsarians adhere to the historical, causal order; supralapsarians prefer the ideal, teleological

139. G. Voetius, *Select. disp.*, V, 602–7; W. Twisse, *Op.*, I, 50; F. Spanheim, *Friderici Spanhemmi F. Disputatio inauguralis habita in academia Leidensi* (Amsterdam: J. Hinrici, 1658), §§8–9; A. Comrie and N. Holtius, *Examen van het Ontwerp van Tolerantie*, VII, 296, 383ff.

140. A. Comrie and N. Holtius, *Examen van het Ontwerp van Tolerantie*, VII, 296.

141. J. Calvin, *Institutes*, III.xxiii.8.

142. J. Calvin, *Institutes*, I.xviii; III.xxi–xxiii.

143. F. Turretin, *Institutes of Elenctic Theology*, IV, 9.6; A. Kuyper, *De Gemeene Gratie*, 3 vols. (Amsterdam: Hoveker & Wormser, 1905), II, 607.

order. The former construe the term "predestination" in a restricted sense and have the decree of creation, fall, and providence precede it. The latter subsume all the other decrees under the term "predestination." In the thinking of the infralapsarians, the emphasis lies on the plurality of the decrees; in that of the supralapsarians, on the unity of the decrees. In the former, all the decrees to some degree have a significance of their own; in the latter, the preceding decrees are all subordinate to the final decree.

This difference is not resolved by an appeal to Scripture. For while infralapsarianism is supported by all the passages in which election and reprobation have reference to a fallen world and are represented as acts of mercy and of justice (Deut. 7:6–9; Matt. 12:25–26; John 15:19; Rom. 9:15–16; Eph. 1:4–12; 2 Tim. 1:9), supralapsarianism finds support in all the texts that declare God's absolute sovereignty, especially in relation to sin (Ps. 115:3; Prov. 16:4; Isa. 10:15; 45:9; Jer. 18:6; Matt. 20:15; Rom. 9:17, 19–21). The simple fact that each of these views rests on a specific group of texts and fails to do full justice to the other group already suggests the one-sidedness of both groups. Infralapsarianism deserves praise for its modesty inasmuch as it does not offer a solution and abides by the historical causal order. Also, it seems less harsh and shows greater consideration for the demands of [pastoral] practice. However, it does not satisfy the mind, because reprobation can no more be understood as an act of divine justice than election. Faith and good works, we know, are not the cause of election; but neither is sin the cause of reprobation, which lies solely in God's sovereign good pleasure. The decree of reprobation, accordingly, always in a sense precedes the decree to permit sin. Moreover, if in the divine consciousness the decree of reprobation did not occur until after the decree to permit sin, the question inevitably arises: then why did he permit sin? Did that permission consist in an act of bare foreknowledge, and was the fall actually a frustration of God's plan? But no Reformed believers, even if they are infralapsarians, can or may ever say such a thing. Reformed believers must in a sense include the fall in God's decree and conceive of it as having been foreordained. But why did God, by an act of efficacious permission, foreordain the fall? Infralapsarianism has no answer to this question other than God's good pleasure, but in that case it says the same thing as supralapsarianism. Reprobation cannot be explained as an act of divine justice, for the first sinful act at any rate was permitted by God's sovereignty. Infralapsarianism, reasoning backward, still ends up with a supralapsarian position. If it refused to end up there, it would have to resort to "foreknowledge."

Add to this, finally, that it puts the decree of reprobation after that of the fall, but where? Was original sin, the sin committed by our first ancestor, the point at which God decided to reject the "many," and in making this dreadful decree did God leave *actual* sins totally out of consideration? But if reprobation must be traced to God's justice, as infralapsarianism insists, why not rather place it, not only after the entrance of original sin, but after the completed commission of all actual sins and so reject every reprobate individually? This was in fact the teaching of Arminius, who also included the sin of foreseen unbelief in this decree. But that, of course, would not do for a Reformed theologian. For then reprobation would depend on bare foreknowledge, that is, on the conduct of human beings. In that case the sinful deeds of humans would be the ultimate cause of reprobation. For that reason theologians rather arbitrarily placed the decree of reprobation immediately after the fall and stopped there. In reality, therefore, with reference to all actual sins infralapsarianism taught exactly the same thing as supralapsarianism. Reprobation, here, may not precede original sin, but it certainly precedes all other sins. Infralapsarianism may seem more gentle and fair, but upon deeper reflection this proves to be little more than appearance.

Accordingly, supralapsarianism undoubtedly has in its favor that it refrains from all useless attempts at justifying God. In the cases of both reprobation and election, it grounds itself in God's sovereign, incomprehensible, yet always wise and holy good pleasure. Yet it is, if not more unsatisfactory, at least as unsatisfactory as infralapsarianism. While it assumes the appearance of a solution, in fact at no point and in no respect does it offer a solution.

In the first place, while it is true that the revelation of all God's perfections is undoubtedly the ultimate goal of all God's ways, supralapsarianism is mistaken when it immediately includes in this ultimate end the *manner* in which this glory of God will in the hereafter manifest itself in the eternal state of his rational creatures. For that eternal state, both of blessedness and of perdition, is not itself the ultimate goal, but a means designed to reveal all God's perfections on a creaturely level. After all, one cannot say that God could not have manifested his glory in the salvation of all, had he so desired. Nor is it correct to say that in the eternal state of the lost, God *exclusively* reveals his justice, and in that of the elect he *exclusively* reveals his mercy. Also, in the church, purchased as it was by the blood of his Son, God's justice becomes manifest; and also, in the place of perdition there are degrees of punishment and hence glimmerings of his mercy. The ultimate goal of all God's works indeed is, and has to be, his glory; but having said this we have not yet said a word about the *manner* in which his glory will shine forth. This manner has been determined by his will, and although God also had his wise and holy reasons for it, we cannot say why he chose precisely this means and not another, why he planned the destruction of many and not the salvation of all. A further objection to supralapsarianism is that according to it the objects of the decree of election and reprobation are possible humans and, as Comrie added, a possible Christ. Granted, this last component has been eliminated from the supralapsarian position by others,[144] but this does not remove the principle from which this error arose in the first place. Logically speaking, if the object of election is the salvation of possible persons, the decree must include the incarnation of a possible Christ, for the church and its head cannot be separated.

But aside from this, God's decree of election and reprobation, whose sole object is "humans capable of being created and of falling," is not yet actual but

144. A. Kuyper, *De Vleeschwording des Woords* (Amsterdam: Wormser, 1887), 202ff.

only provisional. Before very long supralapsarianism must again proceed to the infralapsarian order. For following the first decree concerning the election and reprobation of possible humans, comes the decree actually to create these possible humans and to let them fall. This decree must then be succeeded by still another with respect to these humans—now no longer regarded as possible but as actually existing entities—to elect some and to reject others. The logical order in supralapsarianism, therefore, leaves a lot to be desired. Actually it differs from infralapsarianism only in that, like Amyraldism, it prefaces the infralapsarian series of decrees with a decree concerning possibilities. But just what is a decree concerning possible human entities whose actual future existence is still absolutely uncertain? In the consciousness of God there is an infinite number of possible humans who will never really exist. The objects of the decree of election and reprobation, therefore, are "nonbeings," not specific persons known to God by name. A final problem associated with supralapsarianism is that it makes the eternal punishment of reprobates an object of the divine will in the same manner and in the same sense as the eternal salvation of the elect; and further, that it makes sin, which leads to eternal punishment, a means in the same manner and in the same sense as redemption in Christ is a means toward eternal salvation.

Now, Reformed theologians all agree that sin and its punishment are willed and determined by God. It is also perfectly true that words like "permission" and "foreknowledge" in fact in no way contribute to the solution of difficulties. The questions, after all, remain precisely the same: Why did God, knowing everything in advance, create humans with the capacity to fall, and why did he not prevent the fall? Why did he allow all humans to fall in the fall of one person? Why does he not have the gospel preached to all humans, and why does he not bestow faith on all? In short, if God foreknows a thing and permits it, he does that either willingly or unwillingly. The latter is impossible. Accordingly, only the former is a real option: God's permission is efficacious, an act of his will. Nor should it be supposed that the notion of permission is of any value or force against the charge that God is the author of sin, for one who permits someone to sin and hence to perish, although he is in a position to prevent it from happening, is as guilty as he who incites someone to sin. On the other hand, all agree also that sin, though not outside of the power of God's will, is and remains nevertheless contrary to his will, that it is not a means to the ultimate goal but a serious disruption of God's creation, and therefore that Adam's fall [into sin] was not a forward step but most certainly a fall. It also has to be granted that, though we can with good reason take exception to such terms as "permission," "foreknowledge," "preterition," and "dereliction," no one is able to come up with better ones. Even the most rigorous supralapsarian cannot dispense with these words, either from the pulpit or from behind an academic theological lectern.[145] For though one may assume that there is a

---

145. F. H. R. Frank, *Theologie der Concordienformel*, IV, 148–272.

"predestination to death," no Reformed theologian has ventured to speak of a "predestination to sin." Every one of them (Zwingli, Calvin, Beza, Zanchius, Gomarus, Comrie, et al.) has maintained that God is not the author of sin, that humans were not created for perdition, that in reprobation also the severity of God's justice is manifested, that reprobation is not the "primary cause" but only the "accidental cause" of sin, that sin is not the "efficient" but the "sufficient" cause of reprobation, and so forth.

Accordingly—and fortunately!—supralapsarianism is consistently inconsistent. It starts out with a bold leap forward but soon afterward it shrinks back and relapses into the infralapsarianism it had previously abandoned. Among the proponents of supralapsarianism this phenomenon is very clear. Almost all of them were reluctant to place the decree of reprobation (in its entirety and without any restriction) before the decree to permit sin. The Thomists differentiated between a negative and a positive reprobation, the former preceding creation and fall, and the latter following them. This distinction, though in a more or less modified form, regularly returns in the works of Reformed theologians. All of them acknowledge that the decree of reprobation must be distinguished from condemnation (which is the implementation of that decree), occurs in time, and is prompted by sin.[146] But in the decree of reprobation itself many of them again differentiate between a preceding, more general decree of God to reveal his perfections, notably his mercy and justice, in certain humans "capable of being created and falling"—and a subsequent specific decree to create these "possible humans," to permit them to fall and to sin, and to punish them for their sins.[147]

INADEQUACY OF SUPRA- AND INFRALAPSARIANISM

[245] Thus neither supralapsarianism nor infralapsarianism succeeded in solving this problem and in doing justice to the many-sidedness of Scripture. In part this failure is due to the one-sidedness that characterizes both views.[148]

---

146. T. Beza, *Tractationum theologicarum*, I, 176; A. Polanus, *Syn. theol.*, 251, 254.

147. T. Beza, *Tract. theol.*, I, 173, 176–77; cf. I, 403; J. Piscator, in W. Twisse, *Op.*, I, 51–52, 71; W. Perkins, *Works*, I, 763; J. Maccovius, *Loci comm.*, 222, 237; G. Voetius, *Select. disp.*, V, 602ff.; P. van Mastricht, *Theologia*, III, 2, 12; A. Comrie and N. Holtius, *Examen van het Ontwerp van Tolerantie*, VII, 375ff.; B. de Moor, *Comm. in Marckii Comp.*, II, 66–67.

148. A. Kuyper, *De Gemeene Gratie*, II, 95: "It is an extremely important issue but one which—in the way it was posed—would neither advance our understanding nor be solved. For everyone who considered the issue from a human perspective simply *had to* join Walaeus in interpreting election as an election from the mass of fallen sinners; and conversely, everyone who thought about it from God's perspective simply *had to* join Gomarus in interpreting election, grounded in a decree made before the foundation of the world, as also governing the ordinance of creation. Accordingly, all the polemics conducted by the two parties over this issue have not helped the church to take a single step forward, for the simple reason that both parties started out from opposing positions. The one stood squarely on the level ground below; the other loftily looked at the issue from a mountain summit. No wonder the two failed to understand each other. For that reason as well, it is absurd to say that a theologian of our time would be called a 'supralapsarian,' or to take the opposite point of view as the self-styled 'infralapsarian.' This is simply inconceivable, if for no other

In the first place, it is incorrect, as we stated above, to describe the ultimate end of all things as the revelation of God's mercy in the elect and of his justice in the lost. Most certainly, the glory of God with the manifestation of his perfections is the ultimate goal of all things; yet the double state of human blessedness and human wretchedness is not included in that ultimate goal but is related to it as a means. It is strictly indemonstrable that this double state has to be an integral part of the ultimate goal of God's glory. When God accomplishes his works *ad extra,* he can never have in view anything other than the honor of his name. But that he seeks to establish his honor in this and in no other way, is to be ascribed to his sovereignty and nothing else. Even aside from this, however, it is not true that God's justice can only be manifested in the wretched state of the lost and his mercy only in the blessedness of the elect, for in heaven, too, his justice and holiness are radiantly present, and even in hell there is still some evidence of his mercy and goodness.

In the second place, it is incorrect to represent the wretched state of the lost as the goal of predestination. Admittedly, sin cannot be traced to a bare foreknowledge and permission of God. The fall, sin, and eternal punishment are included in the divine decree and in a sense willed by God, but then always only in a certain sense and not in the same manner as grace and blessedness. God takes delight in the latter, but sin and punishment are not occasions of pleasure or joy to God. When he makes sin subservient to his honor, he does it by his omnipotence, but this is contrary to the nature of sin. And when he punishes the wicked, he does not delight in their suffering as such; rather, in this punishment he celebrates the triumph of his perfections (Deut. 28:63; Ps. 2:4; Prov. 1:26; Lam. 3:33). And though on the one hand, with a view to the comprehensive and immutable character of God's counsel, there is no objection to speaking of a "double predestination," on the other hand we must bear in mind that in the one case predestination is of a different nature than in the other. "Predestination is the disposition, end, and ordering of a means to an end. Since eternal damnation is not the goal but only the termination of human life, reprobation cannot properly be classified under predestination. For these two things—to order to a goal and to order to damnation—are at variance with each other. For by its very nature, every goal is the optimal end and perfection of a thing. Damnation, however, is the ultimate evil and the ultimate imperfection, so that it cannot properly be said that God predestined some humans to damnation."[149] Hence, no matter how emphatically and often Scripture says that sin and punishment have been determined by God, the words "purpose," "foreknowledge," and "predestination" are used almost exclusively with reference to "predestination to glory."

---

reason than that in our time this profound issue has assumed a very different form." Also cf. the decision taken by the Synod of the GKN [Gereformeerde Kerken in Nederland] at Utrecht, 1905, regarding the doctrinal issue of infra- and supralapsarianism.

149. B. Keckermann, *Systema theologiae,* 296; W. Twisse, *Op.,* I, 53.

In the third place, there is still another reason why it is less proper to coordinate "predestination to eternal death" with "predestination to eternal life" and to treat the former as the ultimate goal in the same sense as the latter. The object of election is not just an aggregate of certain individuals, as in the case of reprobation, but the human race reconstituted under a new head: Christ. Hence, by the grace of God not just some individuals are saved, but the human race itself in conjunction with the entire cosmos. Moreover, in this salvation of the human race and the world as a whole, it is not just some of God's perfections that are manifested, so that in addition a realm of eternal perdition would be needed to manifest his justice, but in the consummated kingdom of God all his virtues and perfections are fully unfolded: his justice as well as his grace, his holiness as well as his love, his sovereignty as well as his mercy. Hence, this state of glory is the real and direct end—although also subordinated to his honor—that God has in view with his creation.

In the fourth place, both supralapsarianism and infralapsarianism erred in that they placed all the things that are antecedent to the ultimate goal as means in subordinate relations also to each other. It is true, of course, that the means are all subordinate to the ultimate goal, but they are not for that reason subordinate to each other. Creation is not just a means for the attainment of the fall, nor is the fall only a means for the attainment of grace and perseverance, and these components in turn are not just a means for the attainment of blessedness and eternal wretchedness. We must never lose sight of the fact that the decrees are as abundantly rich in content as the entire history of the world, for the latter is the total unfolding of the former. Who could possibly sum up world history in a logical outline of just a few terms? Creation, fall, sin, Christ, faith, unbelief, and so forth, are certainly not just related to each other as means, so that a preceding one can fall away the moment the next one has been reached. As Twisse already noted: "These elements are not just subordinated to each other, but are also related coordinately."[150] Certainly the creation of the world did not just occur to make room for the event of the fall, but resulted in something that will continue even in the state of glory. The fall did not just take place to produce creatures existing in a state of misery, but retains its meaning as a fact with all the consequences that have arisen from it. Christ did not only become a mediator—a position that would have been sufficient for the expiation of sin—but God also ordained him to be head of the church. The history of the world is not a means that can be dispensed with once the end has come; instead, it has continuing impact and leaves its fruits in eternity.[151] And election and

---

150. W. Twisse, *Op.*, I, 71.

151. In the work cited above (*De Gemeene Gratie*, II, 91–93) Abraham Kuyper raises the question whether our Reformed dogmatics has not—somewhat contrary to Scripture—viewed preordination almost exclusively as a decree of God concerning the eternal weal or woe of his rational creatures. He answers it by saying that earlier theologians, though rightly putting humanity in the foreground, focused too exclusively on angels and humans, lost sight of the rest of God's creation, and neglected the use of common grace in constructing the doctrine of predestination.

reprobation themselves do not follow two straight parallel lines, for in unbelievers there is much that does not arise from reprobation, and in believers there
is much that cannot be attributed to election. On the one hand, both election
and reprobation presuppose sin and are acts of mercy and justice (Rom. 9:15;
Eph. 1:4); on the other, both are also acts of divine sovereignty (Rom. 9:11, 17,
21). Similarly, even before the fall Adam was already a type of Christ (1 Cor.
15:47ff.), yet in Scripture the incarnation is always based on the fall of the
human race (Heb. 2:14ff.). Sometimes Scripture uses language so strong that
reprobation is completely coordinated with election, and eternal punishment
is as much God's goal as eternal blessedness (Luke 2:34; John 3:19–21; 1 Pet.
2:7–8; Rom. 9:17–18, 22; etc.). At other times eternal death is entirely absent
from the biblical portrayal of the future: the end will be the triumphal consummation of the kingdom of God, the new heaven and the new earth, and the
new Jerusalem, where God will be all in all (1 Cor. 15; Rev. 21–22). All things
will be subordinate to the church as the church is to Christ (1 Cor. 3:21–23),
and reprobation is totally subordinated to election.

Accordingly, neither the supralapsarian nor the infralapsarian view of
predestination is capable of incorporating within its perspective the fullness
and riches of the truth of Scripture and of satisfying our theological thinking.
The truth inherent in supralapsarianism is that all the decrees together form a
unity; that there is an ultimate goal to which all things are subordinated and
serviceable; that the entrance of sin into the world was not something that
took God by surprise, but in a sense willed and determined by him; that from
the very beginning the creation was designed to make re-creation possible; and
that even before the fall, in the creation of Adam, things were structured with a
view to Christ.[152] But the truth inherent in infralapsarianism is that the decrees,
though they form a unity, are nevertheless differentiated with a view to their
objects; that in these decrees one can discern not only a teleological but also
a causal order; that the purpose of the creation and the fall is not exhausted
by their being means to a final end; and that sin was above all and primarily
a catastrophic disturbance of creation, one which of and by itself could never
have been willed by God.

Generally speaking, the formulation of the ultimate goal of all things as
God's will to reveal his justice in the case of the reprobate and his mercy in
the case of the elect, is overly simple and austere. The state of glory, Scripture
tells us, will be rich and splendid beyond all description. We look for a new
heaven, a new earth, a new humanity, a restored creation, an ever-progress-
ing development never again disturbed by sin. To that end the creation and
the fall, Adam and Christ, nature and grace, faith and unbelief, election and
reprobation—all work together, each in its own way, not only consecutively
but in concert. Indeed, even the present world, along with its history, is as

152. "Even creation is built up on redemption lines" (J. Orr, *The Christian View of God and the World
as Centering on the Incarnation* [New York: Randolph, 1893], 323).

such already an ongoing revelation of God's perfections. It is not only a means toward the higher and richer revelation that is coming but has an inherent value of its own. It will continue to exert its influence in depth and in breadth also in the coming dispensation, and to furnish a new humanity with ever new reasons for the worship and glorification of God. Accordingly, inherent in the decrees reciprocally, as in the facts of world history, there is not only a causal and teleological but also an organic order. Given our limitations, we can only put ourselves in one or the other position, so that the proponents of a causal and the proponents of a teleological world-and-life view may at any time clash with each other. But for God the situation is very different. He surveys the whole world-historical scene. All things are eternally present to his consciousness. His counsel is one single conception, one in which all the particular decrees are arranged in the same interconnected pattern in which, a posteriori, the facts of history in part appear to us to be arranged now and will one day appear to be fully arranged.

This interconnected pattern is so enormously rich and complex that it cannot be reproduced in a single word such as "infralapsarian" or "supralapsarian." It is both causally and teleologically connected. Preceding components impact subsequent components, but even future events already condition the past and the present. The whole picture is marked by immensely varied omnilateral interaction. Accordingly, predestination in the ordinary sense of the word as the foreordination of the eternal state of rational creatures and of the steps leading to that state, is *not* the one all-encompassing decree of God. While it is an utterly significant part of the counsel of God, it does not coincide with it. The *counsel of God* is the master concept because it is comprehensive. It covers all things without exception: heaven and earth, spirit and matter, things visible and invisible, creatures animate and inanimate. It is the one will of God governing the whole cosmos, past, present, and future. *Predestination,* however, concerns the eternal state of rational creatures and the steps or means leading to it, but it cannot include among those means everything that exists and occurs in the world. That is why in a previous section we discussed "providence" separately as a decree of God, though not as one that is separate from predestination. Much more than was the case in the past, the subject of common grace must be given its due also in the doctrine of the counsel of God. In short, the counsel of God and the cosmic history that corresponds to it must not be pictured exclusively—as infra- and supralapsarianism did—as a single straight line describing relations only of before and after, cause and effect, means and end; instead, it should also be viewed as a systemic whole in which things occur side by side in coordinate relations and cooperate in the furthering of what always was, is, and will be the deepest ground of all existence: the glorification of God. Just as in any organism all the parts are interconnected and reciprocally determine each other, so the world as a whole is a masterpiece of divine art, in which all the parts are organically interconnected. And of that world, in all its dimensions, the counsel of God is the eternal design.

REPROBATION

[246] From the foregoing it has become evident in what sense reprobation must be considered a part of predestination. From the perspective of the comprehensive character of the counsel of God, we have every right to speak of a "double predestination." Also sin, unbelief, death, and eternal punishment are subject to God's governance. Not only is there no benefit in preferring the terms "foreknowledge" and "permission" over the term "predestination," but Scripture, in fact, speaks very decisively and positively in this connection. It is true that Scripture seldom speaks of reprobation as an eternal decree. All the more, however, does it represent reprobation as an act of God in history. He rejects Cain (Gen. 4:5), curses Canaan (Gen. 9:25), expels Ishmael (Gen. 21:12; Rom. 9:7; Gal. 4:30), hates Esau (Gen. 25:23–26; Mal. 1:2–3; Rom. 9:13; Heb. 12:17), and permits the Gentiles to walk in their own ways (Acts 14:16). Even within the circle of revelation there is frequent mention of a rejection by the Lord of his people and of particular persons (Deut. 29:28; 1 Sam. 15:23, 26; 16:1; 2 Kings 17:20; 23:27; Ps. 53:5; 78:67; 89:38; Jer. 6:30; 14:19; 31:37; Hos. 4:6; 9:17). But also in that negative event of rejection there is frequently present a positive action of God, consisting in hatred (Mal. 1:2–3; Rom. 9:13), cursing (Gen. 9:25), hardening (Exod. 4:21; 7:3; 9:12; 10:20, 27; 11:10; 14:4; Deut. 2:30; Josh. 11:20; 1 Sam. 2:25; Ps. 105:25; John 12:40; Rom. 9:18), infatuation (1 Kings 12:15; 2 Sam. 17:14; Ps. 107:40; Job 12:24; Isa. 44:25; 1 Cor. 1:19), blinding and stupefaction (Isa. 6:9; Matt. 13:13; Mark 4:12; Luke 8:10; John 12:40; Acts 28:26; Rom. 11:8). God's reign covers all things, and he even has a hand in people's sins. He sends a lying spirit (1 Kings 22:23; 2 Chron. 18:22), through Satan stirs up David (2 Sam. 24:1; 1 Chron. 21:1), tests Job (ch. 1), calls Nebuchadnezzar and Cyrus his servants (2 Chron. 36:22; Ezra 1:1; Isa. 44:28; 45:1; Jer. 27:6; 28:14; etc.) and Assyria the rod of his anger (Isa. 10:5ff.). He delivers up Christ into the hands of his enemies (Acts 2:23; 4:28), sets him for the fall of many, and makes him a fragrance from death to death, a stone of stumbling, and a rock of offense (Luke 2:34; John 3:19; John 9:39; 2 Cor. 2:16; 1 Pet. 2:8). He abandons people to their sins (Rom. 1:24), sends a spirit of delusion (2 Thess. 2:11), raises up Shimei to curse David (2 Sam. 16:10; cf. Ps. 39:9), uses Pharaoh to show his power (Rom. 9:17), and heals the man blind from birth to manifest his glory (John 9:3). Certainly in all these works of God one must not overlook people's own sinfulness. In the process of divine hardening humans harden themselves (Exod. 7:13, 22; 8:15; 9:35; 13:15; 2 Chron. 36:13; Job 9:4; Ps. 95:8; Prov. 28:14; Heb. 3:8; 4:7). Jesus speaks in parables not only *in order that* people will fail to understand but also *because* people refuse to see or hear (Matt. 13:13). God gives people up to sin and delusion because they have made themselves deserving of it (Rom. 1:32; 2 Thess. 2:11). And it is ex posteriori that believers see God's governing hand in the wicked deeds of enemies (2 Sam. 16:10; Ps. 39:9–10). Nevertheless, in all these things also the will and power of God

become manifest, and his absolute sovereignty is revealed. He makes weal and creates woe; he forms the light and creates the darkness (Isa. 45:7; Amos 3:6); he creates the wicked for the day of evil (Prov. 16:4), does whatever he pleases (Ps. 115:3), does according to his will among the inhabitants of the earth (Dan. 4:35), inclines the heart of all humans as he wills (Prov. 16:9; 21:1), and orders their steps (Prov. 20:24; Jer. 10:23). Out of the same lump of clay he makes one vessel for beauty and another for menial use (Jer. 18; Rom. 9:20–24), has compassion upon whomever he wills and hardens the heart of whomever he wills (Rom. 9:18). He destines some people to disobedience (1 Pet. 2:8), designates some for condemnation (Jude 4), and refrains from recording the names of some in the Book of Life (Rev. 13:8; 17:8).

These numerous strong pronouncements of Scripture are daily confirmed in the history of humankind. The defenders of reprobation, accordingly, have always appealed to these appalling facts, of which history is full.[153] Present in this world there is so much that is irrational, so much undeserved suffering, so many inexplicable disasters, such unequal and incomprehensible apportionment of good and bad fortune, such a heartbreaking contrast between joy and sorrow, that any thinking person has to choose between interpreting it—as pessimism does—in terms of the blind will of some misbegotten deity, or on the basis of Scripture believingly trusting in the absolute, sovereign, and yet—however incomprehensible—wise and holy will of him who will some day cause the full light of heaven to shine on those riddles of our existence. The acceptance or rejection of a decree of reprobation, therefore, should not be explained in terms of a person's capacity for love and compassion. The difference between Augustine and Pelagius, Calvin or Castellio, Gomarus and Arminius is not that the latter were that much more gentle, loving, and tenderhearted than the former. On the contrary, it arises from the fact that the former accepted Scripture in its entirety, also including this doctrine; that they were and always wanted to be theistic and recognize the will and hand of the Lord also in these disturbing facts of life; that they were not afraid to look reality in the eye even when it was appalling. Pelagianism scatters flowers over graves, turns death into an angel, regards sin as mere weakness, lectures on the uses of adversity, and considers this the best possible world. Calvinism has no use for such drivel. It refuses to be hoodwinked. It tolerates no such delusion, takes full account of the seriousness of life, champions the rights of the Lord of lords, and humbly bows in adoration before the inexplicable sovereign will of God Almighty. As a result it proves to be fundamentally more merciful than Pelagianism. How deeply Calvin felt the gravity of what he said is evident from his use of the expression "dreadful decree."[154] Totally without warrant, this expression has been held against him. In fact, it is to his credit, not to his discredit. The decree, as Calvin's teaching, is not dreadful, but dreadful indeed is the reality

153. J. Calvin, *CR*, XXXVII, 289ff.
154. J. Calvin, *Institutes*, III.xxiii.7.

that is the revelation of that decree of God, a reality that comes through both in Scripture and in history. To all thinking humans, whether they are followers of Pelagius or Augustine, that reality remains completely the same. It is not something that can in any way be undone by illusory notions of it.

Now, in the context of this dreadful reality, far from coming up with a solution, Calvinism comforts us by saying that in everything that happens, it recognizes the will and hand of an almighty God, who is also a merciful Father. While Calvinism does not offer a solution, it invites us humans to rest in him who lives in unapproachable light, whose judgments are unsearchable, and whose paths are beyond tracing out. There lay Calvin's comfort: "The Lord to whom my conscience is subject will be my witness that the daily meditation on his judgments leaves me so speechless that no curiosity tempts me to know anything more, no sneaking suspicion concerning his incomparable justice creeps over me, and in short, no desire to complain seduces me."[155] And in that peaceful state of mind he awaited the day when he would see [God] face to face and be shown the solution of these riddles.[156]

[247] Though, on the one hand, there is every reason to consider reprobation as a part of predestination, it is not in the same sense and manner a component of God's decree as election, as the defenders of a double predestination have also at all times acknowledged. When the sovereignty of God, the positive and unambiguous witness of his Word, or the undeniable facts of history were at issue, these defenders were as intransigent as the apostle Paul and had no interest in compromise or mediation. In such situations they sometimes uttered harsh words, which could trouble the Pelagianistic human heart. Augustine, for example, once commented that God could not even be accused of wrongdoing if he had wanted to damn some people who were innocent. Said he: "If the human race, which exists as originally created out of nothing, had not been born under the guilt of death and with original sin, and the omnipotent Creator had wanted to condemn some to eternal perdition, who could say to the omnipotent Creator: Why have you done this?"[157] Other theologians as well, also among the Reformed, have expressed themselves with a similar harshness. Anyone who realizes something of the incomparable greatness of God and the insignificance of humans, and considers how we frequently contemplate with complete indifference the most severe suffering of humans and animals—especially when such suffering is in our own interest or for the benefit of art or science—will think twice before condemning Augustine or others for such a statement, not to mention calling God to account. If the question here is only one of rights, what rights can we claim over against him

155. J. Calvin, "De aeterna praedest.," *CR*, XXXVI, 316 (Reid, 124).

156. J. Calvin, *Institutes*, III.xxiii.2; idem, *CR*, XXXVI, 366 (Reid, 184).

157. *Admonitio de libro de Praedestione et Gratia, et subsequente epistola Ferrandi ad Egyppium*, PL 65, col. 843A. Ed note: Bavinck cites this as Augustine, *De praed. et gratia*, 16. Migne indicates that the author is uncertain but places it in the oeuvre of Fulgentius, North African bishop (462–527) and devotee of Augustine's theology.

who formed us out of nothing and to whom we owe everything we have and are? Still, though one may for a moment speak in this fashion to someone who believes he or she has a right to accuse God of injustice, Calvin and almost all later Reformed theologians have in the end firmly, and with indignation, rejected such "absolute rule."[158] Although the reason why God willed one thing and not another, chose some and rejected others, may be totally unknown to us, we do know his will is always wise and holy and good, and that he has his righteous reasons for everything he does. His power, we must insist, cannot be separated from his justice.[159] If only God's honor and sovereignty were first recognized, all Reformed theologians recommended the most cautious and tender treatment of the doctrine of predestination and warned against all vain and curious approaches to the subject. "Hence it is not appropriate for us to be too severe. If only we do not in the meantime either deny the truth of what Scripture clearly teaches and experience confirms, or venture to carp at it as if it were unbecoming to God."[160] Although God knows those who are his and the number of the elect is said to be small, "nevertheless, we should cherish a good hope for everyone and not rashly count anyone among the reprobate."[161]

All of them maintained, furthermore, that, though sin is not outside the scope of the will of God, it is definitely against it. Sin, admittedly, could not have been the efficient and impelling cause of the decree of reprobation, for sin itself followed the eternal decree in time, and would, if it had been the cause, have resulted in the reprobation of all humans. However, it was the sufficient cause and definitely the meriting cause of eternal punishment. There is a distinction, after all, between the decree of reprobation and reprobation itself. The former, namely, the decree, has its ultimate ground in the will of God alone, but the act of reprobation itself takes account of sin. The decree of reprobation is realized through human culpability.[162] This decree, therefore, is neither a blind fate impelling humans against their will, nor a sword of Damocles hanging threateningly over their head. It is nothing other than God's idea of reality itself. In the decree cause and effect, condition and fulfillment, and the whole web of things are linked together in precisely the way it is in reality. In the decree sin, guilt, misery, and punishment have the same character and relate to each other in the same way as in the empirical world we daily

158. See above, pp. 237–40 (#208).

159. J. Calvin, *CR*, XXXVI, 310, 361 (Reid, 117, 179).

160. J. Calvin, ibid., 366 (Reid, 184); U. Zwingli, *Op.*, VIII, 21; T. Beza, *Tractationum theologicarum*, I, 197; P. M. Vermigli, *Loci communes*, c. 1; Westminster Confession, according to E. F. Karl Müller, *Die Bekenntnisschriften der reformierten Kirche*, 552; Canons of Dort, I, 12, 14.

161. Helvetic Confession, according to E. F. K. Müller, *Bekenntnisschriften*, 181; J. Piscator, *Aphorismi doctrinae christianae maximam partem ex Institutione Calvini excerpti* (Oxoniae: Ioh. Lichfield and Hen. Curteine, 1630), 223; J. Zanchi(us), *Op. theol.*, II, 497ff.

162. A. Polanus, *Syn. theol.*, 251; W. Twisse, *Vindiciae gratiae*, I, 273ff.; W. Perkins, *Works*, I, 769; F. Turretin, *Institutes of Elenctic Theology*, IV, 14; *Synopsis purioris theologiae*, XXIV, 50; A. Comrie, and N. Holtius, *Examen van het Ontwerp van Tolerantie*, VII, 445; H. Heppe, *Dogmatik der evangelisch-reformierten Kirche*, 132.

observe. With our own eyes we see that decree—which was not revealed to us beforehand—gradually unfold in all its fullness in history. As we on our part think about it, that decree is and has to be an exact reflection of reality. We see and think about things after they occur. But on God's part the decree is the eternal idea of reality as it gradually unfolds in time. His ideas of things precedes their actual existence. What the decree of reprobation finally comes down to is that this entire sinful reality, all of world history as an interconnected series of events, is ultimately caused, not by factors inherent in itself—how indeed could it?—but by something extramundane: the mind and will of God. The decree does not in the least change reality. Reality is and remains identical, whether one follows Augustine or Pelagius. But the decree prompts the believer to confess that also this dreadful world—which Manichaeism attributes to an antigod, pessimism to a blind malevolent will, and many others to fate or chance—exists in accordance with the will of him who presently would have us walk by faith, but who will at sometime in the future, on the day of days, vindicate himself before all creatures.

Entirely mistaken, therefore, is the notion that the counsel of God in general and the decree of reprobation in particular is a single naked decision of the divine will concerning someone's eternal destiny. It is wrong to conceive the decree as if it determined only a person's end and coerced him or her in that direction regardless of what they did. The decree is as inconceivably rich as reality itself. It is, in fact, the fountainhead of all reality. It encompasses in a single conception the end as well as the ways leading to it, the goal along with the means of reaching it. It is not a transcendent power randomly intervening now and then from above and impelling things toward their appointed end. On the contrary, it is the divinely immanent eternal idea that displays its fullness in the forms of space and time and successively—in its several dimensions—unfolds before our limited field of vision that which is one in the mind of God. The decree of reprobation, accordingly, does not exist separately alongside other decrees, not even alongside that of election. In real life sin and grace, punishment and blessing, and justice and mercy do not occur dualistically side by side as though the reprobate were visited only with sin and punishment and the elect only with grace and blessing. Believers, after all, still sin daily and stumble in many ways. Are the sins of believers the consequence of election? No one will say this is so. True, these sins are again made subservient by God to their salvation, and all things work together for good to those who are called (Rom. 8:28). But this is not the natural outcome of those sins themselves; it is the result only of the gracious omnipotence of God, who is able to bring good out of evil. Sins, therefore, are not means of salvation, as regeneration and faith are. They are not "a preparation for grace" but, inherently, the "negation of grace."[163] Hence, the law is still important also for believers. For that reason they are still admonished to be zealous to confirm their election (2 Pet. 1:10), and

---

163. M. Becanus, *Theologiae scholasticae*, I, tr. 1, c. 14, qu. 3, nn. 12–20.

among them, too, we sometimes witness a temporary hardening and rejection. Conversely, the reprobates also receive many blessings, blessings that do not as such arise from the decree of reprobation but from the goodness and grace of God. They receive many natural gifts—life, health, strength, food, drink, good cheer, and so forth (Matt. 5:45; Acts 14:17; 17:27; Rom.1:19; James 1:17)—for God does not leave himself without a witness. He endures them with much patience (Rom. 9:22). He has the gospel of his grace proclaimed to them and takes no pleasure in their death (Ezek. 18:23; 33:11; Matt. 23:27; Luke 19:41; 24:47; John 3:16; Acts 17:30; Rom. 11:32; 1 Thess. 5:9; 1 Tim. 2:4; 2 Pet. 3:9). Pelagians infer from these verses that God's actual intention is to save all people individually, and therefore that there is no preceding decree of reprobation. But that is not what these verses teach. They do say, however, that it is the will of God that all the means of grace be used for the salvation of the reprobates. Now, these means of grace do not as such flow from the decree of reprobation. They can be abused to that end; they may serve to render humans inexcusable, to harden them, and to make their condemnation all the heavier—like the sun, which may warm but also scorch a person. Yet in and by themselves they are not means of reprobation but means of grace with a view to salvation.[164]

So, whereas election and reprobation may culminate in a final and total separation, on earth they continually crisscross each other. This indicates that in and by itself neither of the two is a final goal, and that in the mind of God they were never a final cause. Both are means toward the attainment of the glory of God, which is the ultimate goal and, therefore, the fundamental ground of all things. Accordingly, the beginning and the end, the reason and purpose of all that is, is something good. Sin and its punishment can never as such, and for their own sake, have been willed by God. They are contrary to his nature. He is far removed from wickedness and does not willingly afflict anyone. When he does it, it is not because, deep down, he wants to. They can therefore have been willed by God only as a means to a different, better, and greater good. There is even a big difference between election and reprobation. Whatever God does, he does for his own sake. The cause and purpose of election, accordingly, also lies in God. The truth is that in the work he accomplishes as a result of election, he takes great delight. In that work his own perfections are brilliantly reflected back to him. The new creation is the mirror of his perfections. But what he does in keeping with the decree of reprobation is not directly and as such the object of his delight. Sin is not itself a good. It only becomes a good inasmuch as, contrary to its own nature, it is compelled by God's omnipotence to advance his honor. It is a good indirectly because, being subdued, constrained, and overcome, it brings out God's greatness, power, and justice. God's sovereignty is never more brilliantly manifested than when he

164. *Synopsis purioris theologiae*, XXIV, 54ff.; H. Heppe, *Dogmatik der evangelisch-reformierten Kirche*, 134–35.

manages to overrule evil for good (Gen. 50:20) and makes evil subservient to the salvation of the church (Rom. 8:28; 1 Cor. 3:21–23), the glory of Christ (1 Cor. 15:24ff.; Eph. 1:21–22; Phil. 2:9; Col. 1:16), and the glory of God's name (Prov. 16:4; Ps. 51:4; Job 1:21; John 9:3; Rom. 9:17, 22–23; 11:36; 1 Cor. 15:28).

ELECTION

[248] Predestination finally culminates, therefore, in election. In this activity it reaches its pinnacle and comes to its full realization. In its consummate form it is the decree of God concerning the revelation of his perfection in the eternal glorious state of his rational creatures and the disposition of the means leading to that end. Even at that, reprobation may not be forgotten. It is only by contrast to this dark counterpart that election itself shines most brilliantly. It is a matter of the utmost seriousness that also on this superlatively high level, where the issue is the eternal weal and woe of rational creatures, the day comes up out of the blackness of the night, and light is born out of darkness. It seems that the rule "many are called but few are chosen" is valid everywhere. There's a deep truth in the saying that one person's death is another person's breath. Darwin's doctrine of the survival of the fittest has universal validity and is in force throughout God's creation. Thousands of blossoms fall to the ground so that a few may ripen and bear fruit. Millions of living beings are born, yet only a few remain alive.[165] Thousands of people labor in the sweat of their face in order that a few persons may swim in wealth. Riches, art, science, all that is high and noble, are built on a foundation of poverty, deprivation, and ignorance. The equal distribution envisioned in socialist theory has never been seen anywhere in the world. Equality exists in no area of life. Election exists everywhere alongside, and on the basis of, reprobation. The world is not ordered according to the Pharisaic law of work and reward. Merit and riches are totally unrelated.[166] And even on the highest level, it is only God's grace that makes the difference. Like all the decrees, so also that of election is ultimately rooted in God's good pleasure. Pelagians of all stripes have consistently wanted to view these decrees as acts of divine justice based on human merit. In his decrees God allowed himself to be conditioned by the foreseen behaviors of his creatures. He offers salvation to all. He grants faith to those who by their natural or God-given supernatural power made good use of this offer. He saves those who persevere in faith to the very end. Now, it is true that there is a certain order among the decrees: they include both the goal and the steps leading to it. In God's decree the prayer of his children is linked to his hearing that prayer. When God decreed to give rain in a period of drought, he at the

---

165. *Cf. H. Schmidt, "De vruchtbaarheid in de dierenwereld," *Wetenschappelijke Bladen* (March 1903): 447.

166. A. Schopenhauer, *Die beiden Grundprobleme der Ethik*, 3d ed. (Leipzig: F. A. Brockhaus, 1881), 188.

same time decreed that his people would pray for it, and that he would give rain in answer to their prayer. In his decree he made a connection between sunshine and warmth, sowing and harvesting, indolence and poverty, knowledge and power (etc.); and similarly between sin and punishment, unbelief and perdition, faith and salvation. The harmony existing between phenomena and events in the real world is a complete and exact duplicate of the harmony existing in the world of God's thoughts and decrees.[167]

Scripture often confines itself to these secondary causes, and Reformed theologians, too, have fully recognized their significance. But by implication these secondary causes are not the final and most fundamental causes. And one cannot escape inquiring into the latter. From all directions questions crowd in upon us. What is the interconnection between the phenomena and the events we keep seeing in the world? An appeal to the nature of these things is not conclusive, for that nature also has been created and determined by God. Science can register the *that* of things but not the *why.* Why is there causality between creatures? Why is every creature what it is? Why is there such endless diversity among creatures in kind, nature, gender, species, power, intelligence, riches, honor, and so forth? Within the realm of creation no reason can be found. The same thing is true of rational creatures. Why are some angels destined for eternal glory, while the fall and perdition of others are both foreseen and preordained? Why was the human nature that Christ assumed dignified to this honor? Why is one person born within, and another outside, the precincts of Christianity?

Why does one person have so many advantages over another in character, talent, disposition, and upbringing? Why does the one child die in infancy and as a child of the covenant is taken into heaven, while another dies outside of the covenant and without grace? Why does the one become a believer and another not? All of these are questions that no mortal can answer. God's decrees cannot be understood as acts of a justice that operates according to works performed and merit achieved. Especially in the case of angels it is clear that the ultimate reason for their election and rejection has to lie in the will of God. For even if one resorts to foreknowledge and answers that God foresaw the perseverance of some and the fall of other angels, the fact remains that this foreknowledge preceded their creation. Why then did God create the angels whose fall he foresaw? Why did he not give them sufficient grace to remain obedient like the others? We have here a clear instance of a reprobation based solely on God's sovereignty.[168] On the other hand, election as such is not always an act of mercy or explicable as such. In the election of Christ and of the good angels, there was no sin and hence no mercy either. And the election of humans, though an act of mercy, is not explicable in terms of mercy alone. For then God would have had to be merciful to all, since all [had sinned and] were wretched. Similarly,

167. J. Edwards, *Works*, II, 514.
168. R. Bellarmine, "De gr. et lib. arb.," II, c. 17; W. Twisse, *Vindiciae gratiae*, I, 76.

reprobation, though an act of justice, cannot be explained in terms of justice alone, for then all would have been rejected.[169]

Accordingly, though the decrees are interconnected, as acts of God they are not conditional but absolute: acts of pure sovereignty. Similarly, though God established a causal connection between sin and punishment, and though he maintains that connection in everyone's conscience, the decree of reprobation has its ultimate ground, not in sin and unbelief, but in the will of God (Prov. 16:4; Matt. 11:25–26; Rom. 9:11–22; 1 Pet. 2:8; Rev. 13:8). Similarly, there is a causal connection between faith and salvation, but the decree of election is not prompted by foreseen faith; on the contrary, election is the cause of faith (Acts 13:48; 1 Cor. 4:7; Eph. 1:4–5; 2:8; Phil. 1:29). Even Christ cannot be viewed as "the cause of election," though a good interpretation can be given to this phrase. Thomas correctly states that Christ is the cause of our predestination, not when it is considered as an act or decree, but with a view to its purpose and goal. "For God preordained our salvation by an act of predestination from eternity in order to fulfill it through Jesus Christ."[170] Similarly, some Reformed theologians also spoke of Christ as the "cause" or "foundation of election," or of election through and on account of Christ.[171] Now, Christ is indeed the cause or foundation of election inasmuch as election is realized in and through him. He is also the meritorious cause of salvation, which is the purpose of election, as well as the mediator and head of the elect. The decree of election was made also with a view to the Son—out of love for him.[172] The church and Christ are jointly chosen, in one and the same decree, in fellowship with and for each other (Eph. 1:4). But this does not yet mean that as mediator Christ is the "actual, moving, and meritorious cause" of the decree of election. In that sense Christ has indeed been called the cause of election by many Roman Catholic, Remonstrant,[173] Lutheran,[174] and modern theologians.[175] But Reformed theologians have rightly opposed this view.[176] For Christ, who is himself the object of predestination, cannot at the same time be its cause. He is a gift of the Father's love, which precedes the sending of the Son (John 3:16; Rom. 5:8; 8:29; 2 Tim. 1:9; 1 John 4:9). The Son did not move the Father to love; electing love arose from the Father himself. Scripture,

169. W. Twisse, *Vindiciae gratiae*, IV, 111ff.

170. T. Aquinas, *Summa theol.*, I, qu. 24, art. 4.

171. A. Hyperius, *Methodi theologiae*, 193; Belgic Confession, art. 16; Helvetic Confession, II, art. 10; Martinius, session 65, 67, at the Synod of Dort; Maresius, *Syst. theol.*, IV, §41.

172. J. Heidegger, *Corpus theologiae*, V, 31.

173. In their declaration circa art. 1 de praed., according to C. Vitringa, *Commentarius*, II, 55.

174. Formula of Concord, according to J. T. Müller, *Die symbolischen Bücher der evangelisch-lutherischen Kirche*, 705, 720, 723; J. A. Quenstedt, *Theologia didactico-polemica*, III, 17, 31ff.

175. J. C. K. von Hofmann, *Der Schriftbeweis*, I, 299; H. Meyer, *Critical and Exegetical Commentary to the Ephesians*, on Eph. 1:5; R. Kübel, "Prädestination," *PRE²*, XII, 145–62.

176. P. M. Vermigli, *Loci communes*, 236; A. Polanus, *Syn. theol.*, VI, 27; G. Voetius, *Select disp.*, II, 267; W. Twisse, *Vindiciae gratiae*, I, 139ff.; F. Turretin, *Institutes of Elenctic Theology*, IV, qu. 10; B. de Moor, *Comm. in Marckii Comp.*, II, 18ff.

accordingly, everywhere teaches that the cause of all the decrees does not lie
in any creature but only in God himself, in his will and good pleasure (Matt.
11:26; Rom. 9:11ff.; Eph. 1:4ff.). For that very reason, both for unbelievers
and believers, the doctrine of election is a source of inexpressibly great comfort.
If it were based on justice and merit, all would be lost. But now that election
operates according to grace, there is hope even for the most wretched. If work
and reward were the standard of admission into the kingdom of heaven, its
gates would be opened for no one. Or if Pelagius's doctrine were the standard,
and the virtuous were chosen because of their virtue, and Pharisees because of
their righteousness, wretched publicans would be shut out. Pelagianism has
no pity. But to believe in and to confess election is to recognize even the most
unworthy and degraded human being as a creature of God and an object of his
eternal love. The purpose of election is not—as it is so often proclaimed—to
turn off the many but to invite all to participate in the riches of God's grace in
Christ. No one has *a right* to believe that he or she is a reprobate, for everyone
is sincerely and urgently called to believe in Christ with a view to salvation.
No one *can* actually believe it, for one's own life and all that makes it enjoyable
is proof that God takes no delight in his death. No one *really* believes it, for
that would be hell on earth. But election is a source of comfort and strength,
of submissiveness and humility, of confidence and resolution. The salvation
of human beings is firmly established in the gracious and omnipotent good
pleasure of God.

[249] The glory of election is even more splendidly evident, finally, when
we consider its object and goal. In the past, that object was usually particular-
ized and discussed in three categories: angels, humans, and Christ. On the
subject of humans there is no disagreement. All agree that the real objects of
predestination and election are humans, whether viewed as fallible or fallen,
as actual or potential believers. This is not to be understood in the sense that
humanity, peoples, generations, or even the church in general—without any
further specification and as opposed to individuals and special persons—are
the objects of election, as Schleiermacher, Lipsius, Ritschl, and others claim.[177]
This view is a pure abstraction since humanity, people, family, and church
solely consist of particular persons. It is also contrary to Scripture, for Scripture
teaches a personal election (Mal. 1:2; Rom. 9:10–12 [Jacob]; Acts 13:48 [as
many as]; Rom. 8:29 [whom]; Eph. 1:4 [us]; Gal. 1:15 [Paul]) and speaks of
the names of the elect that are written in the Book of Life (Isa. 4:3; Dan. 12:1;
Luke 10:20; Phil. 4:3; Rev. 3:5; etc.)

It is also true, however, that in Scripture the elect are not viewed separately,
that is, atomistically, but as a single organism. They constitute the people of
God, the body of Christ, the temple of the Holy Spirit. They are, accordingly,
elect *in Christ* (Eph. 1:4), to be members of his body. Hence, both Christ

177. F. Schleiermacher, *Christian Faith*, §119; R. A. Lipsius, *Lehrbuch der evangelisch-protestantischen
Dogmatik*, §§525ff.; A. Ritschl, *Die christliche Lehre von der Rechtfertigung und Versöhnung*, III, 112–30.

and the church are included in the decree of predestination. For that reason Augustine already wrote: "Therefore, just as that one man was predestined to be our head, so we being many, are predestined to be his members."[178] The Synod of Toledo (675) expressed itself along similar lines,[179] and scholasticism treated the predestination of Christ at great length, especially on the basis of Romans 1:5.[180] Lutheran theologians demurred, however, because they viewed predestination as election from sin to salvation through the mercy of God.[181] This prompted the Reformed all the more vigorously to bring out that Christ was also preordained and together with the church was the object of God's election. There was even some debate over whether Christ was the object of predestination alone or also of election. Some, such as Calvin, Gomarus, Marck, and de Moor, said that Christ was destined to be mediator to bring about the salvation of his own. Consequently, the election of his people logically preceded the foreordination of Christ as mediator.[182] But others, such as Zanchius, Polanus, and the [Leiden] *Synopsis* [1625], view Christ also as the object of election, since he was foreordained to be not only the mediator but also the head of the church. In this perspective the election of Christ logically precedes that of the church.[183]

Now it is undoubtedly true that Christ was ordained to be mediator to accomplish everything necessary for the salvation of humans; and it is equally certain that Christ was not elected by God's mercy from sin and misery to glory and blessedness. Yet also in connection with the Messiah Scripture frequently speaks of God's election (Isa. 42:1; 43:10; Ps. 89:3, 19; Matt. 12:18; Luke 23:35; 24:26; Acts 2:23; 4:28; 1 Pet. 1:20; 2:4). This act was rightly called "election" because from all eternity the Father designated the Son to be mediator, and above all because Christ's human nature was foreordained—by grace alone and aside from any merit—to union with the Logos and to the office of mediator. Strictly speaking, however, this still makes Christ only an object of predestination, inasmuch as predestination, in distinction from election, by definition includes the arrangement of means to an end. On the other hand, Scripture states with equal emphasis that the church is elect in and for Christ, to be conformed to his image, and to see his glory (John 17:22–24; Rom. 8:29). Christ was foreordained not only to be the mediator but also to be head

178. Augustine, *On the Predestination of the Saints*, c. 15; idem, *On Rebuke and Grace*, c. 11; idem, *On the Gift of Perseverance*, c. 14.

179. According to H. Denzinger, *Enchiridion*, #232.

180. T. Aquinas, *Sent.*, I, dist. 40, qu. 11; III, qu. 10; idem, *Summa theol.*, III, qu. 24; idem, *Summa contra gentiles*, IV, c. 9; D. Petavius, "De incarn. verbi," in *Theol. dogm.*, bk. XI, chs. 13–14.

181. J. A. Quenstedt, *Theologia*, III, 18, 43.

182. J. Calvin, *CR*, XXXVII, 714; F. Gomarus, *Op.*, I, 430; J. Marck, *Compendium theologiae*, VII, 5; B. de Moor, *Comm. in Marckii Comp.*, II, 55; cf. A. Kuyper, *De Heraut*, 286–87.

183. J. Zanchi(us), *Op. theol.*, II, 535ff.; A. Polanus, *Syn. theol.*, IV, 8; *Synopsis purioris theologiae*, 24; A. Comrie and N. Holtius, *Examen van het Ontwerp van Tolerantie*, VII, 344–53; H. Heppe, *Dogmatik der evangelisch-reformierten Kirche*, 125ff.; cf. A. Kuyper, *Uit het Woord*, 2d ed. (Amsterdam: Wormser, 1896), II, 314.

of the church. All things were created through him and for him (1 Cor. 3:23; Eph. 1:22; Col. 1:16ff.). It is not that Christ was thereby made the ground and foundation of our election; but the election of the church is the very first benefit bestowed on the church; and even this benefit already occurred in union with Christ, and above all it has as its goal, not as its foundation, that all other benefits—rebirth, faith, and so forth—will be imparted to the church by Christ. In this sense, then, the election of Christ logically precedes our own.

But no matter how this logical order was construed, all Reformed theologians agreed that Christ together with his church, that is, the mystical Christ, was the real object of election. "By one indivisible decree we are all elect, both Christ and we."[184] But they did not stop there. In line with Augustine[185] and other scholastics,[186] but contrary to the Lutherans,[187] they also included angels in the decree of predestination. This was occasioned in part by Scripture (1 Tim. 5:21; 2 Pet. 2:4; Jude 6; Matt. 25:41), while the example of Christ was proof that election does not always presuppose a state of sin and misery. Accordingly, although in Scripture election (ἐκλογή) is viewed as separation from the peoples of the world (Gen. 12:1; Deut. 7:6; 30:3; Jer. 29:14; 51:45; Ezek. 11:17; Hos. 11:1; Acts 2:40; Phil. 2:15; 1 Pet. 2:9), and the number of the elect is often represented as being very small (Matt. 7:14; 22:14; Luke 12:32; 13:23–24), still in that elect assembly (ἐκκλησία) the world is being saved. Not just a few people from the world but the world itself is the object of God's love (John 3:16–17; 4:42; 6:33; 12:47; 2 Cor. 5:19). In Christ all things, both in heaven and on earth, are reconciled to God, and in him they are all gathered into one (Eph. 1:10; Col. 1:20). The world, which was created by the Son, is also predestined for the Son as its heir (Col. 1:16; 2 Pet. 3:13; Rev. 11:15). So it is not a random aggregate of things but an organic whole that is known by God in election and saved by Christ's redemption. "A reconciled world will be delivered from a hostile world. The church without spot and wrinkle, gathered from all the nations and destined to reign forever with Christ, is itself the country of the blessed, the land of the living."[188] Precisely because the object of election is a perfect organism, election itself can only be conceived as a fixed and specific decree of God. In an aggregate the number of its parts is totally immaterial. But an organism must by its very nature be based on measure and number. God chose Christ to be the head, and the church as his body; together they must grow into a fully mature "person," in whom every member has his or her own place and fulfills his or her own role. Election is the divine "idea," the eternal blueprint of the temple that he builds in the course of the ages and of which he is the supreme builder and architect. All

---

184. P. van Mastricht, *Theologia*, III, 3, 8; J. Heidegger, *Corpus theologiae*, V, 30.

185. Augustine, *Enchiridion*, 100.

186. T. Aquinas, *Summa theol.*, I, qu. 23, art. 1, ad. 3.

187. J. A. Quenstedt, *Theologia*, III, 18, 43.

188. Augustine, *On Christian Doctrine*, III, 34; W. Perkins, *Works*, I, 770; W. Twisse, *Vindiciae gratiae*, I, 312.

things are subordinate and subservient to the construction of that temple. Just as all the decrees of God culminate in that of the glorification of God, so the entire history of the world and humankind works together for the coming of the kingdom of God. "Even those who are not citizens of that kingdom," says Calvin, "are born with a view to the salvation of the elect."[189] Creation and fall, preservation and governance, sin and grace, Adam and Christ—all contribute, each in his or her own way, to the construction of this divine edifice, and this building itself is built to the honor and glorification of God. "All [things] are yours, and you are Christ's, and Christ is God's" (1 Cor. 3:21–23 KJV).

189. J. Calvin, *CR*, XXXVI, 360 (Reid, 177); A. Polanus, *Syn. theol.*, 252.

8

CREATION

The doctrine of creation, affirming the distinction between the Creator and his creature, is the starting point of true religion. There is no existence apart from God, and the Creator can only be known truly through revelation. Biblical religion rejects both pantheistic emanationism as well as Manichaean dualism, though each have had Christian and philosophical proponents. Along with materialist explanations of the universe, these are not scientific in character but rather are religious worldviews masquerading as science. The sophisticated philosophical systems of Schelling, Hegel, Schopenhauer, and others fail to satisfy human religious need and are riddled with internal contradictions. To them all the Christian church confesses simply "I Believe in God the Father, Almighty, Creator of heaven and earth." This creation is properly said to be ex nihilo, *"out of nothing," thus preserving the distinction in essence between the Creator and the world and the contingency of the world in its dependence on God. The triune God is the author of creation rather than any intermediary. The outgoing works of God are indivisible, though it is appropriate to distinguish an economy of tasks in the Godhead so that the Father is spoken of as the first cause, the Son as the one by whom all things are created, and the Holy Spirit as the immanent cause of life and movement in the universe. Scripture does relate the creation in a special way to the Son through the categories of Wisdom and Logos. The Son is the Logos by whom the Father creates all things; the whole world is the realization of an idea of God. The creation proceeds* from *the Father* through *the Son and* in *the Spirit so that, in the Spirit and through the Son it may return to the Father. Creation also means that time has a beginning; only God is eternal. As creatures we are necessarily* in *time, and speculation about pretemporal or extratemporal reality is useless speculation. The purpose and goal of creation is to be found solely in God's will and glory. It is especially in the Reformed tradition that the honor and glory of God was made the fundamental principle of all doctrine and conduct. A doctrine of creation is one of the foundational building blocks of a biblical and Christian worldview. Creation is neither to be deified nor despoiled, but as the "theater of God's glory" it is to be delighted in and used in a stewardly manner. It is God's good creation.*

[250] The realization of the counsel of God begins with creation. Creation is the initial act and foundation of all divine revelation and therefore the foundation of all religious and ethical life as well. The Old Testament creation story is of a beauty so sublime that it not only has no equal, but all thinkers, including such natural scientists as [Georges] Cuvier and [Alexander] von Humboldt, vie with each other in extolling it. "The first page of the Mosaic document is of greater consequence than all the volumes written by natural scientists and philosophers" (Jean Paul).[1] Subsequently, that [act of] creation comes to the fore again and again throughout the history of revelation.

From the very first moment, true religion distinguishes itself from all other religions by the fact that it construes the relation between God and the world, including man, as that between the Creator and his creature. The idea of an existence apart from and independent of God occurs nowhere in Scripture. God is the sole, unique, and absolute cause of all that exists. He has created all things by his word and Spirit (Gen. 1:2–3; Ps. 33:6; 104:29–30; 148:5; Job 26:13; 33:4; Isa. 40:13; 48:13; Zech. 12:1; John 1:3; Col. 1:16; Heb. 1:2; etc.). There was no substance or principle of any kind to oppose him; no material to tie him down; no force to circumscribe his freedom. He speaks and things spring into being (Gen. 1:3; Ps. 33:9; Rom. 4:17). He is the unrestricted owner of heaven and earth (Gen. 14:19, 22; Ps. 24:1–2; 89:11; 95:4–5). There are no limits to his power; he does all he sees fit to do (Isa. 14:24, 27; 46:10; 55:10–11; Ps. 115:3; 135:6). "From him and through him and to him are all things" (Rom. 11:36; 1 Cor. 8:6; Heb. 11:3). The world is the product of his will (Ps. 33:6; Rev. 4:11); it is the revelation of his perfections (Prov. 8:22f.; Job 28:23f.; Ps. 104:1; 136:5f.; Jer. 10:12) and finds its goal in his glory (Isa. 43:16ff.; Prov. 16:4; Rom. 11:36; 1 Cor. 8:6).

This teaching of creation, which occupies a preeminent and pivotal place in Scripture, is not, however, presented as a philosophical explanation of the problem of existence. Most certainly it also offers an answer to the question of the origin of all things. Yet its significance is first and foremost religious and ethical. No right relation to God is conceivable apart from this basis; it positions us in the proper relation to God (Exod. 20:11; Deut. 10:12–14; 2 Kings 19:15; Neh. 9:6). It is therefore of eminent practical value, serving to bring out the greatness, the omnipotence, the majesty, and the goodness, wisdom, and love of God (Ps. 19; Job 37; Isa. 40). The teaching of creation therefore strengthens people's faith, confirms their trust in God, and is a source of consolation in their suffering (Ps. 33:6f.; 65:5ff.; 89:11; 121:2; 134:3; Isa. 37:16; 40:28f.; 42:5; etc.); it inspires praise and thanksgiving (Ps. 136:3ff.;

---

1. Ed. note: Jean Paul Friedrich Richter (1763–1825), more commonly known simply as Jean Paul after his hero Jean-Jacques Rousseau, was a popular German novelist who significantly influenced the German Romantic movement as well as the Scottish historian and writer Thomas Carlyle (1795–1881). In view of Jean Paul's tendency toward nature pantheism, it is rather remarkable that Bavinck cites him here at the beginning of his section on creation. For a discussion of Jean Paul as a (pre)Romantic novelist, see Alan Menhennet, *The Romantic Movement* (London: Croon Helm; Totowa, N.J.: Barnes & Noble, 1981), 172–85.

148:5; Rev. 14:7); it induces humility and meekness and makes people sense their smallness and insignificance before God (Job 38:4f.; Isa. 29:16; 45:9; Jer. 18:6; Rom. 9:20).

CREATION AND ITS RELIGIOUS ALTERNATIVES: PANTHEISM AND MATERIALISM

[251] The doctrine of creation is known only from revelation and is understood by faith (Heb. 11:3). As we know, Catholic teaching contends that it can also be discovered from nature by reason,[2] and the Vatican Council even elevated this doctrine to the status of a dogma.[3] But the history of religions and philosophy does not support this claim. Islam, indeed, teaches a creation from nothing but borrowed this doctrine from Judaism and Christianity.[4] Pagan cosmogonies, which are at the same time theogonies, are all polytheistic. They all assume the existence of a primordial stuff, whether it is construed as chaos, a personal principle, a cosmic egg, or something like it. Finally, they tend to be either emanationistic, so that the world is an emanation from God; or evolutionistic, so that the world becomes ever more divine; or dualistic, so that the world is a product of two antagonistic principles.[5] Nor is the Chaldean Genesis *[Enuma Elish]*, which for that matter offers striking parallels to that of the Old Testament, an exception to this rule. It is also a theogony and has Bel fashion the world from Tiamat, who chaotically stores all things within herself.[6] Greek philosophy either materialistically seeks the origin of things in a material element (Ionian school; Atomists), or pantheistically in the one eternal immutable being (Eleatic school), or in eternal becoming (Heraclitus, Stoa). Even Anaxagoras, Plato, and Aristotle never rose above a dualism of spirit and matter. God, to them, is not a creator but at best a fashioner of the world *(dēmiourgos)*. Though the Scholastics sometimes asserted that Plato and Aristotle taught a creation out of nothing, this view was rightly rejected by others—Bonaventure, for example.[7] The Greeks knew of a *physis* (nature), *kosmos* (world), but not of a *ktisis* (creation). Christianity gained a victory over this pagan theogony and cosmogony in its controversy with Gnosticism, which to explain sin predicated the existence of an inferior god alongside the

2. T. Aquinas, *Sent.*, II, dist. 1, qu. 1, art. 2; idem, *Contra gentiles*, II, 15; J. Kleutgen, *Philosophie der Vorzeit vertheidigt* (Münster: Theissing, 1863), II, 795f.; M. J. Scheeben, *Handbuch der katholischen Dogmatik* (Freiburg i.B.: Herder, 1933), II, 5–6; J. B. Heinrich and C. Gutberlet, *Dogmatische Theologie*, 2d ed. (Mainz: Kirchheim, 1881–1900), V, 64f.

3. "Dogmatic Constitution, *Dei filius*, on the Catholic Faith," ch. 2, can. 2, in *Documents of Vatican Council I, 1869–1870*, selected and trans. John F. Broderich (Collegeville, Minn.: Liturgical Press, 1971).

4. O. Zöckler, *Geschichte der Beziehungen zwischen Theologie und Naturwissenschaft* (Gütersloh: C. Bertelsmann, 1877–79), I, 426f.

5. O. Zöckler, "Schöpfung und Erhaltung der Welt," *PRE³*, XVII, 681–704.

6. H. H. Kuyper, *Evolutie of Revelatie* (Amsterdam: Höveker & Wormser, 1903), 37–38, 117f.; cf. also ch. 10 (below): "Earth: The Material World," including discussion of the *Enuma Elish*.

7. Bonaventure, *Sent.*, II, dist. 1, p. 1, art. 1, qu. 1; cf. J. Heinrich and C. Gutberlet, *Dogmatische Theologie*, V, 29–30.

supreme deity, or an eternal *hylē* (matter). Pagan explanations of the origin of things, however, have kept surfacing also in Christian centuries. It is already stated in Wisdom of Solomon 11:17 that God's all-powerful hand "created the world out of formless matter" *(amorphos hylē),* and the same expression occurs in Justin Martyr.[8] But in this connection Justin has in mind the later so-called *creatio secunda,* and in another place he expressly also teaches the creation of matter.[9] Just as Gnosticism emerged in the second century, so also, after the Council of Nicaea, Manichaeism arose, which explained sin similarly by assuming the existence of an original evil being in addition to the true God.[10] This dualism was widely disseminated in Christianity, reaching even the Priscillians in Spain, and again surfacing in the Middle Ages among the Bogomils and Cathari.

Not only dualism but also pantheism acquired its interpreters. Under the influence of Neoplatonism, Pseudo-Dionysius taught that the ideas and archetypes of all things existed eternally in God, whose superabundant goodness moved him to confer reality on these ideas and to impart himself to his creatures.[11] In his creatures God as it were emerged from his oneness, multiplying himself and pouring himself out in them,[12] so that God is universal being,[13] the very being of all things.[14] But he adds that God nevertheless maintains his unity[15] and is all in all inasmuch as he is the cause of all.[16]

The same ideas recur in Erigena. Though he repeatedly and expressly teaches a creation out of nothing,[17] what makes his system pantheistic is the way he relates the four natures to each other. The first nature, which creates and is not created, that is, God, by thinking brings forth out of nothing, that is, from within himself, the ideas and forms of all things in the divine Word.[18] This Word is the second nature, which is created and creates. This second nature is created nature *(natura creata)* insofar as it is brought forth by God, and it is creative *(creatrix)* insofar as it is itself the cause and potency of the real world. For this second nature is not really and substantially distinct from the third nature—the phenomenal world, which is created and does not create: the former is the cause, the latter the effect; but it is the same world viewed one moment in the eternity of the Word of God and the next in the temporality

8. Justin Martyr, *Apology,* I, 10 and 59.

9. Justin Martyr, *Dialogue with Trypho,* 5; idem, *Hortatory Address to the Greeks,* 23; K. G. Semisch, *Justin Martyr: His Life, Writings, and Opinions* (Edinburgh: T. & T. Clark, 1843), II, 336.

10. See Augustine, *The Writings against the Manichaeans,* vol. 4 of *NPNF (1);* cf. K. Kessler, "Mani, Manichaer," *PRE³,* XII, 193–228.

11. Pseudo-Dionysius, *The Divine Names,* ch. 4, 10.

12. Ibid., ch. 2, 10.

13. Ibid., ch. 5, 4.

14. Ibid., *The Celestial Hierarchy,* ch. 4, 1.

15. Ibid., *The Divine Names,* ch. 2, 11.

16. Ibid., *The Celestial Hierarchy,* ch. 5, 8.

17. John Scotus Erigena, *On the Division of Nature,* bk. III, V, 24, 33.

18. Ibid., III, 14, 17.

of the world.[19] It is God himself who first, in the ideas, creates himself, then flows down into his creatures and becomes all in all in order finally to return to himself in the fourth nature, which does not create and is not created.[20] And the cause of this process is the goodness of God,[21] his drive to become all things.[22]

Outside of the Christian world pantheism was propagated by the philosophers Avicenna (1036) and Averroes (1198); [among Muslims] by Sufism, which viewed the universe as an emanation of God; and among Jews by the Kabbalah.[23] Toward the end of the Middle Ages and at the dawn of the modern era, all these pantheistic, dualistic, emanationistic ideas freely crisscrossed among mystics, theosophists, and Anabaptists, such as [Joichim of] Fiore, Amalric of Bena, the Brethren of the Free Spirit, the Libertines, [Meister] Eckhart, Tauler, Servetus, Frank, Schwenkfeld, Bruno, Paracelsus, Fludd, Weigel, and Böhme. Even Socinianism only taught a creation from formless matter (*amorphos hylē*),[24] thus abstractly positing the finite and the infinite alongside and over against each other, such that the former could not possibly be the effect of the latter.

Pantheism was nevertheless again restored to a position of honor in modern philosophy by Spinoza. In his view, the one substance is the eternal and necessary efficient and immanent cause of the world; the world is the explication of the divine being, and particulars are the modes by which the divine attributes of thought and extension are determined in a particular way.[25]

Toward the end of the eighteenth century this philosophy found increasing acceptance and was elevated by Schelling and Hegel to *the* system of the nineteenth century. The biblical doctrine of creation was rejected in toto. Fichte wrote: "The assumption of a creation is the basic error of all false metaphysics and religious teaching and particularly the archprinciple of Judaism and paganism."[26] Schelling called creation out of nothing a "cross to the intellect" and firmly opposed it.[27] In his first period he taught an absolute identity between God and the world. The two are related to each other as

19. Ibid., III, 8.

20. Ibid., III, 4, 20.

21. Ibid., III, 2, 4, 9.

22. Ibid., I, 12.

23. A. Stöckl, *Geschichte der Philosophie des Mittelalters* (Mainz: Kirchheim, 1864–66), II, 28, 92, 181, 237.

24. O. Fock, *Der Socinianismus nach seiner Stellung in der Gesammtentwicklung des christlichen Geistes* (Kiel: C. Schröder, 1847), 482.

25. B. Spinoza, *Ethics,* part I.

26. J. G. Fichte, *Die Anweisung zum seligen Leben* (London: Trübner, 1873), 160. Ed. note: A new German edition of this work was published in 1970 by Meiner in Hamburg. The essay is also found in J. G. Fichte, *Characteristics of the Present Age: The Way towards the Blessed Life: Or, the Doctrine of Religion* (Washington, D.C.: University Publications of America, 1977). For a discussion of Fichte's essay, see H. Berkhof, *Two Hundred Years of Theology* (Grand Rapids: Eerdmans, 1989), 26–28.

27. F. W. J. Schelling, *Werke,* I/2, 44f.; I/8, 62f. Ed. note: Bavinck's references to Schelling that are to works incorporated into the new unrevised but abridged and repaginated *Ausgewählte Werke* (Darmstadt: Wissenschaftliche Buchgesellschaft, 1968) will be cited with the full title of the work as well as Bavinck's

essence and form; they are the same, but viewed from different perspectives. God is not the cause of the All, but the All itself, and the All, accordingly, is not in process of becoming but something eternally existing, *en kai pan.*[28] But in his later period, thanks to Baader, he came under the influence of Böhme and thus under that of the Kabbalah and Neoplatonism, and began to look for the world's ground in the dark nature of God. Theogony and cosmogony are most intimately connected. Just as God raises himself from his undifferentiated state—by the opposition of the *principia,* nature (*Urgrund, Ungrund,* darkness) and intellect (word, light),—to the level of Spirit, love, and personality, so these three are simultaneously the potencies of the world. The dark nature in God is the principle of blind confusion, the matter and ground of the created world insofar as it is chaos and has a chaotic character. But also at work in that world is the potency of the divine intellect, which introduces light, order, and regularity into it. God meanwhile manifests himself as Spirit in the spirit of mankind and achieves full personality in the spirit of mankind.[29]

Hegel, too, openly acknowledged his adherence to pantheism, not in the pantheism that regards finite things themselves as God but in the pantheism that in the finite and accidental sees the appearance of the absolute, the fossilized idea, frozen intelligence.[30] This pantheism passed from philosophy into theology. Schleiermacher rejected the distinction between creation and providence and considered the question concerning whether the world was temporal or eternal a matter of indifference, provided the absolute dependence of all things on God was upheld.[31] Similarly, in Strauss, Biedermann, Schweizer, and others, God is no more than the eternal immanent cause and ground of the world.[32]

---

original reference. Since this is not a complete edition of Schelling's original *Sämmtliche Werke* (Stuttgart & Augsburg: J. G. Cotta'scher, 1856–61), writings not included in the new edition will be cited as *Werke,* using Bavinck's original reference.

28. F. W. J. Schelling, *Ausgewählte Werke,* III, 13f. ("Darstellung meines Systems der Philosophie," *Werke* I/4, 117f.); idem, *Werke,* I/5, 24f., 365f., 373f.; idem, *Ausgewählte Werke,* III, 698f. ("System der gesammten Philosophie und der Naturphilosophie insbesondere," *Werke,* I/6, 174).

29. F. W. J. Schelling, *Ausgewählte Werke,* IV, 303f. ("Philosophische Untersuchungen über das Wesen der menslichen Freiheit und die damit zusammenhängenden Gegenstände," *Werke,* I/7, 359f.); idem, *Werke,* II/2, 103f.; II/3, 262f.

30. G. W. F. Hegel, *Sämtliche Werke,* vol. 9 (Stuttgart: F. Frommann, 1958), 49–54 (*System der Philosophie,* part 2: *Die Naturphilosophie,* §§247–51: "Begriff der Natur," *Werke,* VII, 23f.). Ed. note: When possible, references to Hegel's writings will be cited from the modern Stuttgart edition or a published English translation. The title of Hegel's work and Bavinck's original citation from Hegel's *Werke* will be given in parentheses.

31. F. Schleiermacher, *The Christian Faith,* ed. H. R. MacIntosh and J. S. Steward (Edinburgh: T. & T. Clark, 1928), §§36, 41.

32. D. F. Strauss, *Die christliche Glaubenslehre,* 2 vols. (Tübingen: C. F. Osiander, 1840–41), I, 656f.; A. E. Biedermann, *Christliche Dogmatik* (Zürich: Füssli, 1869), §§649f.; A. Schweizer, *Die christliche Glaubenslehre* (Leipzig: Hirzel, 1877), §71; O. Pfleiderer, *Grundriss der christlichen Glaubens und Sittenlehre* (Berlin: G. Reimer, 1888), §84; J. H. Scholten, *Dogmatices christianae initia,* 2d ed. (Lyons: P. Engels, 1858), 111; S. Hoekstra, *Wijsgerige Godsdienstleer,* 2 vols. (Amsterdam: van Kampen, 1894–95), II, 174.

Alongside this pantheism there also emerged a materialism that seeks the final elements of all being in eternal (without beginning) and indestructible material atoms, and attempts to explain all phenomena of the entire universe in light of atomic processes of mechanical and chemical separation and union in accordance with fixed laws. This materialism had its roots in Greek philosophy, was reintroduced in modern times by Gassendi and Descartes, and was advocated by the British and French philosophy of the eighteenth century. It appeared in the nineteenth century, not as the fruit of scientific study, but as the product of philosophical reflection in Feuerbach, who can be called the father of materialism in Germany. After 1850, as a result of a variety of incidental causes, it found acceptance at least for a time among such natural scientists as Vogt, Büchner, Moleschott, Czolbe, and Haeckel.[33]

[252] It needs to be said, first of all, that neither pantheism nor materialism is the result of exact science but of philosophy, of a worldview, of systems of belief. Neither of them is "knowledge" in the strict sense of the word. Granted, materialism loves to pass itself off as an exact science, but it can be easily demonstrated that, both historically and logically, it is the fruit of human thought, a matter of both the human heart and the human head. For the origin and end of things lie outside the boundaries of human observation and research. Science presupposes existence and rests on the foundation of what has been created. In that regard pantheism and materialism are in the same position as theism, which acknowledges the mysterious origin of things. The only question, therefore, is whether pantheism and materialism can replace this mystery with an intelligible explanation. This demand may well be made of both since they both reject the doctrine of creation on account of its incomprehensibility and view it as a "cross to the intellect." Is it indeed the case that pantheism and materialism do a better job of satisfying the intellect than theism and therefore deserve preference? Actually, in the history of humankind both systems have repeatedly made their appearance and again and again have been abandoned; they have so often been subjected to serious and effective criticism that no one can now accept them solely because they are so satisfying to the intellect. Other motives play the decisive role here. If the world did not originate by an act of creation, then certainly there must be some other explanation. And in that case—excluding dualism—there are only two options available here: either one explains matter from mind, or mind from matter. Pantheism and materialism are not pure opposites; rather, they are two sides of the same coin; they constantly merge into each other and only differ in that they address the same problem from opposite directions. Thus, both run into the same objections.

Pantheism, in confronting the transition from thought to being, from idea to reality, from substance to modes, has produced nothing resembling a solution. Indeed, it has assumed various forms and described that transition by different names. It conceives the relation of God to the world as that of *en kai pan* ("one

---

33. F. A. Lange, *Geschichte des Materialismus,* 8th ed. (Leipzig: Baedekker, 1908).

and many"), of nature bringing forth and nature already born (*natura naturans* and *naturata*), of substance and modes, of existence and appearance, of the universal and the particular, of the species and specimens, of the whole and its parts, of idea and objectification, of the ocean and its waves, and so forth; but for all these words it has said nothing about the relation. From the pantheistic perspective it is incomprehensible how "being" emerged from "thought," how multiplicity came from unity, how matter proceeded from mind. This has become abundantly clear from the systems of Schelling and Hegel. There was certainly no lack of words in these systems [as the following characteristic phrases illustrate]: The idea assumes form, incarnates itself, objectivizes itself, passes into another mode of being; it splits off and differentiates itself; it freely decides to release and to realize itself, to turn into its opposite.[34]

This solution, however, proved so unsatisfying to both Schelling and Hegel that they frequently spoke of a "breakaway" or "defection" from the absolute by which the world originated.[35] No wonder, therefore, that Schelling in his second period and so also Schopenhauer, von Hartmann, and others, gave primacy to the will and primarily conceived the Absolute as nature, will, and drive. The pantheistic identity of thought and being proved to be in error, all the more because "Substance," the "Idea," the "All," or however pantheism may designate the Absolute, is not a fullness of being but pure potentiality, an abstraction without content, a mere nothing. And this is supposed to be the explanation of the riches of the world, the multiplicity of the existent! Let those believe it who can! Kleutgen, accordingly, is right on target when he writes: "The difference between pantheistic speculation and that of the theist . . . is this: whereas the former, starting with assumptions—as obscure as they are unprovable—about the divine being, ends in open contradictions; the latter, proceeding from a sure knowledge of finite things, gains ever-higher kinds of insights, until it encounters the Incomprehensible, not losing its grip on the fact that the One whom it recognizes as the eternal and immutable Author of all things is far above our thought processes in his essence and works."[36]

In the case of materialism the origin of things remains similarly unexplained. While pantheism pictures the universe as proceeding from one ultimate principle

34. F. W. J. Schelling, *Ausgewählte Werke*, I, 386f. ("Ideen zu einer Philosophie der Natur, Einleitung," *Werke*, I/2, 62f.); idem, *Ausgewählte Werke*, III, 119f., 153f. ("Bruno oder über das göttliche und natürliche Princip der Dinge," *Werke*, I/4, 223f., 257f.); G. W. F. Hegel, *The Encyclopaedia of Logic (with the Zusätze)*, trans. T. F. Geraets et al. (Indianapolis and Cambridge: Hackett, 1991), 306–7; idem, *Hegel's Philosophy of Nature*, trans. M. J. Petry (London and New York: Allen Unwin, Humanities Press, 1970). Ed. note: Bavinck's references are to Hegel, *Werke*, VI, 413ff.; VII, 23ff., which comprises §§243ff. (likely through §252) of Hegel's *System der Philosophie*, found in vols. 8–10 of Hegel's *Sämtliche Werke* (Stuttgart: F. Frommann, 1958).

35. F. W. J. Schelling, *Ausgewählte Werke*, III, 614ff. ("Philosophie und Religion," *Werke*, I/6, 38f.); G. W. F. Hegel, *Lectures on the Philosophy of Religion*, trans. E. B. Speirs and J. Burdon Sanderson (London: Kegan Paul, Trench, & Trübner, 1895), II, 311–12 (*Werke*, XII, 177).

36. J. Kleutgen, *Philosophie der Vorzeit*, II, 884.

and therefore preferably presents itself today as monism,[37] materialism assumes a multiplicity of "principles." But according to materialism, these ultimate "principles" of all things are nothing other than indivisible particles of matter. Now, if the proponents of this worldview remained true to this fundamental thesis of theirs, they would have no warrant for attributing to these atoms a single metaphysical and transcendent predicate. On the materialist position, rightly considered, it is not permissible to speak of "eternity," "uncreatedness," "the indestructibility of atoms," or even of "matter" and "energy." If one says that the world originated from material atoms, one should remain true to that position. Atoms, after all, since they are elements of the empirical world, can only have empirical and not metaphysical properties. The concept of atom, by definition and as such, in no way implies that it is eternal and indestructible. Those who regard atoms as the ultimate "principles" of all being cut themselves off from the road to speculation and metaphysics and must empirically explain the world solely from those empirical atoms. The materialist can only say that experience teaches that atoms do not come into being or cease to exist; he has no warrant, however, for speaking of the atoms' metaphysical nature and metaphysical properties. Natural science, to which the materialist always makes his appeal, has to do as such with the finite, the relative, with nature and its phenomena; it always starts out from nature, assumes it as a given, and cannot penetrate to what lies behind it. The moment it does this it ceases to be physics and becomes metaphysics. But materialism is not true to itself when it immediately ascribes to atoms all sorts of properties that are not part of the concept itself and are not taught by experience. Materialism, accordingly, is not an exact science nor the fruit of rigorous scientific research, but a philosophy that is built up on the denial of all philosophy; it is inherently self-contradictory; it rejects all absolutes and makes atoms absolute; it denies God's existence and deifies matter.

One can state this in even stronger terms: if materialism wants to explain all things from matter, it lacks all warrant for speaking of atoms. Atoms have never been observed; no one has ever seen them; empirical research has never brought them to light. They are originally of a metaphysical nature and for that reason alone should be contraband to materialism. Further, as metaphysical substances they are caught up in an antinomy that has not yet been resolved

37. On pantheism, see H. Ulrici, "Pantheismus," *PRE¹*, 64–77; M. Heinze, "Pantheismus," *PRE³*, XIV, 627–41; J. I. Doedes, *Inleiding tot de Leer van God* (Utrecht: Kemink, 1870), 61f.; C. W. Opzoomer, *Wetenschap en Wijsbegeerte* (Amsterdam: Gebhard, 1857), ch. 1; A. Pierson, *Bespiegeling, Gezag, en Ervaring* (Utrecht: Kemink, 1885), ch. 1; L. W. E. Rauwenhoff, *Wijsbegeerte van den Godsdienst* (Leiden: Brill & van Doesburgh, 1887), 205f.; S. Hoekstra, *Wijsgerige Godsdienstleer*, II, 73ff.; A. Kuyper, "Pantheism's Destruction of Boundaries," *Methodist Review* 52 (1893): 520–35, 762–78; I. van Dijk, *Aesthetische en ethische Godsdienst*, in vol. 1 of *Gesammelten Schriften* (Groningen, 1895); P. H. Hugenholtz, *Ethische Pantheisme* (Amsterdam: van Holkema & Warendorff, 1903); A. Bruining, "Pantheïsme of Theisme," *Teylers Theologische Tijdschrift* (1904): 433–57. Ed. note: Bavinck adds that this last article was "opposed by De Graaf, op. cit., 165–210," which is likely a reference to the same journal, *Teylers Theologische Tijdschrift*.

by anybody. They are material and (we are told) at the same time indivisible, immutable, infinite in number, eternal, and indestructible. And in addition to all this, if matter itself—the matter assumed as the principle that explains the entire universe—were only known and comprehensible! But exactly the essence and nature of matter is the most mysterious thing of all. It totally eludes our cognitive grasp. It is easier for us to conceive and imagine the nature of spirit than the nature of matter. Matter is a word, a name, but we do not know what we mean by it. We face here a mystery as great in its kind as the existence of spirit, which on account of its incomprehensibility is rejected by materialism. However, if we assume that atoms exist and that they are eternal and immutable, we have not yet done anything to explain the world by that assumption. *How* did the world originate from those atoms? If the now-existing or a preceding world had a beginning, there must be a cause by which the atoms were set in motion, and in the kind of motion that resulted in the present world. But this motion cannot be explained from matter, for all matter is by nature inert and only starts moving as the result of an impulse from without. Materialism, however, cannot accept a prime mover existing independently of matter. So the materialist has no choice but to also declare motion, change, or with [Heinrich] Czolbe, even this existing world to be absolute and eternal (like the atom).

Materialism wraps itself in ever greater contradictions: it confuses the physical with the metaphysical, becoming with being, mutability with immutability, time with eternity, and speaks of infinite space, infinite time, and an infinite world as though it were not the most absurd self-contradiction. Finally, it has been shown, repeatedly and by various parties, that materialism remains utterly unable to explain how purely material, and therefore unconscious, inanimate, unfree, aimless atoms could produce that spiritual world of life, consciousness, purpose, religion, morality, and so on, which surely thrusts itself upon our inner consciousness with no less force than the physical world upon our senses. And it seems that little by little this criticism is beginning to have some kind of impact on the materialists themselves. The materialism that arose from pantheism in the previous century is increasingly reverting to pantheism and even incorporating a variety of mystical elements into itself. The "life force," which for a long time was rejected, once again has its defenders. Atoms are now pictured as being alive and animated. Haeckel again speaks of a "spirit in all things," of a "divine force," a "moving spirit," a "world soul" that indwells all things. In this pantheistic monism he is looking for the connection between religion and science. But in so doing, materialism is itself openly admitting its powerlessness to explain the world: in its impoverishment the mechanism of the atoms again cried out for help from the dynamic principle.[38]

38. On materialism, in addition to M. Heinze, "Materialismus," *PRE³*, XII, 414–24, and the literature cited there, see C. Gutberlet, *Der mechanische Monismus: Eine Kritik der modernen Weltanschauung* (Paderborn: F. Schöningh, 1893); W. Ostwald, *Die Überwindung des wissenschaftliche Materialismus* (Leipzig:

CREATIO EX NIHILO

[253] Against all these movements the Christian church unitedly held fast to the confession: "I believe in God the Father, Almighty, Creator of heaven and earth." And by creation it meant that act of God through which, by his sovereign will, he brought the entire world out of nonbeing into a being that is distinct from his own being. And this is, in fact, the teaching of Holy Scripture. The word *bārā'* originally means to split, divide, or cut (used in the Piel for the clearing away of forests, Josh. 17:15, 18), and then to fashion, bring forth, create. Like the Dutch word *scheppen,* which originally means "to form" (cf. the English "to shape"), the Hebrew word by itself does not imply that something was brought into existence out of nothing, for it is frequently also used for the works of providence (Isa. 40:28; 45:7; Jer. 31:22; Amos 4:13). As used in Psalm 104:30 *bārā'* is a synonym for and alternates with *hāraš, yāṣar, and ʿāśāh.* But it differs from them in that *bārā'* is always used to denote divine "making" and never with reference to human activity, is never accompanied by an accusative of the matter from which something is made, and therefore everywhere expresses the greatness and power of the works of God.[39] The same is true of the New Testament words *ktizein* (Mark 13:19), *poiein* (Matt. 19:4), *phemelioun* (Heb. 1:10), *katartizein* (Rom. 9:22), *kataskeuazein* (Heb. 3:3–4), and *plassein* (Rom. 9:20), and of the Latin word *creare.* These words also do not by themselves express creating out of nothing. The expression "to create out of nothing," accordingly, is not literally derived from Scripture but first occurs in 2 Maccabees 7:28, where it is stated that God made heaven and earth and everything in them out of nonbeing (*ouk ex ontōn epoiēsen;* Vulg.: *fecit ex nihilo*). Some scholars dispute that this expression may be understood in the strict sense and have given it a Platonic interpretation. It is nevertheless worth noting that the author does not speak of *mē on,* that is, a nothing that could not exist *(nihilum privativum),* a matter devoid of quality and form, but of *ouk on,* a nothing that does not exist *(nihilum negativum).* It is not even certain, moreover, that the author of the Wisdom of Solomon (11:17) taught the eternity of a formless matter; the passage can very well be understood to refer to the "secondary creation,"[40] just as is the case in Justin Martyr.

However this may be, Scripture leaves no doubt about the matter in question. Though it does not use the term "creation out of nothing," it clearly teaches the matter. Some scholars certainly do believe that Genesis 1:1–3, too, actually

---

Veit, 1895); J. Reinke, *Die Welt als That,* 4 vols. (Berlin: Paetel, 1905); M. Verworn, *Naturwissenschaft und Weltanschauung: Eine Rede,* 2d ed. (Leipzig: Barth, 1904); T. Lipps, *Naturwissenschaft und Weltanschauung* (Heidelberg: C. Winter, 1906); R. Otto, *Naturalistische und religiöse Weltansicht* (Tübingen: H. Laupp, 1905); A. Kuyper, "Evolution," *Calvin Theological Journal* 31 (1996): 11–50; H. Bavinck, "Evolutie," in *Verzamelde Opstellen* (Kampen: Kok, 1921), 105–20. Ed. note: An English version of Bavinck's views on evolution can be found in his "Creation or Development," *Methodist Review* 61 (1901): 849–74.

39. Franz Delitzsch, *A New Commentary on Genesis,* trans. Sophia Taylor (Edinburgh: T. & T. Clark, 1899), 74.

40. Augustine et al., in J. Heinrich and C. Gutberlet, *Dogmatische Theologie,* V, 44.

proceeded from an original, uncreated chaos. They argue that because *br'št* (in the beginning) is in the construct state, they can translate verses 1–3 as follows: "In the beginning when God created heaven and earth—now the earth was a formless void . . .—then God spoke and said: 'Let there be light.'" Therefore, according to this view, verse 2 presupposes the existence of a formless and vacuous earth in God's act of creating.[41] But this translation is not acceptable.[42] In the first case, the sentence thus acquires the length of a period, which is rare in Hebrew; it is not expected immediately at the beginning and in the style of Genesis 1; and it puts much too strong an accent on the creation of light.[43] Furthermore, the construct state of *bĕrē'šît* ["in the beginning," Gen. 1:1] does not require this translation because it also occurs in the same form without suffix or genitive in Isaiah 46:10 (cf. Lev. 2:12; Deut. 33:21). In the third place, it would be strange if, while the initial clause would say that God still had to create heaven and earth, the intermediate clause already dubbed chaos with the name "earth" and made no mention whatever of the state of heaven. To this we must add that this translation, even if it were correct, in no way teaches the eternity of this desolate earth but at most leaves this issue open.

This overall view militates against the whole spirit of the creation narrative. Elohim is not presented in Genesis 1 as a cosmic sculptor who, in human fashion, with preexisting material, produces a work of art, but as One who merely by speaking, by uttering a word of power, calls all things into being.[44] And with that view the whole of Scripture chimes in. God is the Almighty, who is infinitely higher than all creatures, and who deals with his creatures in accordance with his sovereign good pleasure. He is the absolute owner, the *qōnēh* of heaven and earth (Gen. 14:19, 22), who does whatever he pleases, and to whose power there is no limit. He speaks and it comes to be, he commands and it stands forth (Gen. 1:3; Ps. 33:9; Isa. 48:13; Rom. 4:17). Further, all things in Scripture are described over and over as having been made by God and as being absolutely dependent on him. He has created all things, heaven, earth, the sea, and all that is on them and in them (Exod. 20:11; Neh. 9:6; etc.). Everything has been created by him (Col. 1:16–17), exists only by his will (Rev. 4:11), and is of him, through him, and unto him (Rom. 11:36). Moreover, at no time or place is there even the slightest reference to an eternal formless matter. God alone is the Eternal and Imperishable One. He alone towers above processes of becoming and change. Things, by contrast, have a beginning and an end and are subject to change. [In Scripture] this is expressed in anthropomorphic

41. According to Ewald, Bunsen, Schrader, Gunkel, and others; see H. Schultz, *Alttestamentliche Theologie*, 5th ed. (Göttingen: Vandenhoeck & Ruprecht, 1896), 570f.

42. Ed. note: This is the translation adopted by the NRSV, but see its note.

43. R. Smend, *Lehrbuch der alttestamentlichen Religionsgeschichte* (Freiburg: J. C. B. Mohr, 1893), 456; J. Wellhausen, *Prolegomena to the History of Israel* (Atlanta: Scholars, 1994 [1885]), 387 n. 1.

44. Reinke, *Die Welt als That*, 481ff., mistakenly asserts that Moses has no knowledge of a creation out of nothing, and that such a creation out of nothing would in any case be at variance with the law of the constancy of energy.

language. God was there before the mountains were brought forth, and his years never come to an end (Ps. 90:2; Prov. 8:25–26); he chose and loved [his own] from the foundation of the world (Eph. 1:4; John 17:24; cf. Matt. 13:35; 25:34; Luke 11:50; John 17:5; Heb. 4:3; 9:26; 1 Pet. 1:20; Rev. 13:8; 17:8). And though in Romans 4:17 there is no express mention of creation, it does teach that God calls and summons *ta mē onta,* the things that possibly do not yet exist, as if they did exist, *hōs onta.* Existence or nonexistence are alike to him. Hebrews 11:3 announces even more clearly that God has made the world so that what is seen is not made *ek phainomenōn,* from that which appears before our eyes. By this revelation a "formless matter" is totally ruled out; the visible world did not proceed from what is visible but rests in God, who called all things into existence by his word.

[254] This teaching of Scripture was most pointedly expressed in the words *ex nihilo* (out of nothing) and was thus understood and passed on by Christian theology from the beginning.[45] But among Gnostics and Manichaeans, theosophists and naturalists, pantheists and materialists, this teaching has at all times been disputed. Especially Aristotle's dictum, *"Ex nihilo nihil fit"* (nothing is made from nothing), has been advanced against it. But this polemic is entirely groundless. In the first place, this rule of Aristotle is not at all as simple as it looks. Every moment of the day we confront phenomena that are not reducible to present factors: history is not a simple problem of arithmetic; life is not the product solely of chemical combinations; the genius is something other and more than the child of his time; and every personality is an original. But aside from these things and taken with a grain of salt, this rule of Aristotle is not unacceptable. Theology has never taught that nonbeing is the father, source, and principle of being. Perhaps redundantly, it has repeatedly added that the expression *ex nihilo* was not the description of a preexisting matter from which the world was made, but it only meant that what exists, once did not exist, and that it was only called into existence by God's almighty power. Hence, the expression *ex nihilo* is on a level with the term *post nihilum:* the preposition *ex* does not designate [the cause] but only excludes a material cause; the world has its cause, not in itself, but only in God.[46]

The expression *ex nihilo* was eagerly preserved in Christian theology only because it was admirably suited for cutting off all sorts of errors at the root. In the first place, it served as a defense against the paganistic notion of a formless stuff *(amorphos hylē),* from which not even Plato and Aristotle were able to extricate themselves. In paganism a human being is bound by matter, subject to sensuality and nature worship; he cannot grasp the idea that the mind is free and above matter, and even much less that God is absolutely sovereign, defined by nothing other than his own essence. Over against this view, the

45. Pastor (Shepherd) of Hermas, I, *Vision* 1.1; *Theophilus to Autolycus,* II, 4; Tertullian, *The Prescription against Heretics,* 13; Irenaeus, *Against Heresies,* II, 10.

46. Irenaeus, *Against Heresies,* II, 14; Augustine, *Confessions,* XI, 5; XII, 7; idem, *Literal Meaning of Genesis,* I, 1; Anselm, *Monologion,* ch. 8; T. Aquinas, *Summa theol.,* I, qu. 45., art. 1, and so forth.

doctrine of creation out of nothing teaches the absolute sovereignty of God and man's absolute dependence; if only a single particle were not created out of nothing, God would not be God. In the second place, this expression rules out all emanation, every hint of an essential identity between God and the world. Granted, the Scholastics wrote repeatedly about an emanation or procession of all existence from a universal cause and also occasionally of the creature's participation in the being and life of God. But in saying this they did not mean "emanation" in the strict sense, as if God's own being flowed out into his creatures and so unfolded in them, like the genus in its species. They only meant to say that God is a self-subsistent necessary being *(ens per essentiam)*, but the creature is existent by participation *(ens per participationem)*. Creatures indeed have a being of their own, but this being has its efficient and exemplary cause in the being of God.[47]

The teaching of creation out of nothing maintains that there is a distinction in essence between God and the world. The creation does not exist as a result of a passage of the world from being in God to being outside of God, nor from being without God to being by God, but from nonexistence into existence. The world is certainly no anti-God; it has no independent existence, and remains in God as its ongoing immanent cause, as will have to be demonstrated later in the teaching of preservation, against Manichaeism and Deism. But according to the teaching of Scripture the world is not a part of, or emanation from, the being of God. It has a being and existence of its own, one that is different and distinct from the essence of God. And that is what is expressed by the term *ex nihilo*. Nevertheless this term too has been misused by philosophy. Just as Plato understood *mē on* (nonbeing) as an eternal unformed substance, so Erigena even described God as *nihilum* insofar as he transcends all categories and limitations, all existence and being; "since, then, he is understood to be incomprehensible, he is not undeservedly called 'nihilum' on account of [his] surpassing excellence" *(dum ergo incomprehensibilis intelligitur, per excellentiam nihilum non immerito vocitatur)*. And if he brings forth everything out of nothing, that then means that he "produces essence from his own—as it were—'superessentiality,' [and] lives from his own 'supervitality.'"[48] Even odder was the way Hegel in his *Wissenschaft der Logik* dealt with this concept when he defined "nothingness" as "nonbeing that is simultaneously a kind of being, and a being that is simultaneously nonbeing," a nothingness that is at the same time everything, namely, in potentiality, and nothing specific concretely.[49]

Christian theology is diametrically opposed to this conceptual confusion in philosophy. It understands "nothingness" to be purely negative and rejects all emanation. Still, even in emanation there is an element of truth that,

---

47. T. Aquinas, *Summa theol.*, I, qu. 45, art. 1; J. Kleutgen, *Philosophie der Vorzeit*, II, 828ff., 899f.

48. Erigena, *On the Division of Nature*, III, 19–20.

49. G. W. F. Hegel, *The Encyclopedia of Logic*, 139–45 (*Wissenschaft der Logik*, in *Sämtliche Werke*, IV, 87–118; ed. note: Bavinck's own pagination in his note is to *Werke*, III, 64, 73f., when it should be *Werke*, III, 77–108).

without violating the essence of God, is especially maintained by the biblical doctrine of creation far better than in philosophy. The doctrine of creation out of nothing, in fact, gives to Christian theology a place between Gnosticism and Arianism, that is, between pantheism and Deism. Gnosticism knows no creation but only emanation and therefore makes the world into the Son, wisdom, the image of God in an antiquated sense. Arianism, on the other hand, knows nothing of emanation but only of creation and therefore makes the Son into a creature. In the former the world is deified; in the latter God is made mundane. But Scripture, and therefore Christian theology, knows both emanation and creation, a twofold communication of God—one within and the other outside the divine being; one to the Son who was in the beginning with God and was himself God, and another to creatures who originated in time; one from the being and another by the will of God. The former is called generation; the latter, creation. By generation, from all eternity, the full image of God is communicated to the Son; by creation only a weak and pale image of God is communicated to the creature. Still, the two are connected. Without generation, creation would not be possible. If, in an absolute sense, God could not communicate himself to the Son, he would be even less able, in a relative sense, to communicate himself to his creature. If God were not triune, creation would not be possible.[50]

THE CREATOR IS THE TRIUNE GOD

[255] Holy Scripture, accordingly, teaches that the Triune God is the author of creation. Scripture knows no intermediate beings. In the case of the plural in Genesis 1:26, the Jews thought of angels. The Gnostics saw proceeding from God a series of aeons that played a creative role. The Arians made the Son an intermediate being between Creator and creature who, though created, nevertheless himself created as well. In the Middle Ages many [scholars] were prepared to accept a cooperative role for the creature in the act of creation. They arrived at this thesis because in the church the forgiveness of sins and the dispensing of grace were inherent in [ecclesiastical] office so that a priest performing the Mass could change the bread into the body of Christ and so become "a creator of his own creator" *(creator sui creatoris)* (Biel). It is for this reason that Peter Lombard says in his doctrine of the sacraments that God could also "create some things through some person, not through him as 'author' but as minister with whom and in whom he worked."[51] Some, such as Durand, Suárez, and Bellarmine, followed him, but others, like Thomas, Scotus, Bonaventure, Richard, and so on, dissented.[52] Reformed theologians, who more than Catholic and Lutheran scholars resisted every tendency to

50. Athanasius, *Against the Arians*, I, 12; II, 56, 78.
51. P. Lombard, *Sent.*, IV, dist. 5, n. 3.
52. T. Aquinas, *Summa theol.*, I, qu. 45, art. 3; J. Kleutgen, *Philosophie der Vorzeit*, II, 849f.; J. Heinrich and C. Gutberlet, *Dogmatische Theologie*, V, 89f.

commingle the Creator and the creature, agreed with the latter.[53] Scripture exclusively attributes the act of creation to God (Gen. 1:11; Isa. 40:12f.; 44:24; 45:12; Job 9:5–10; 38:2f.). It is what distinguishes him from false gods (Ps. 96:5; Isa. 37:16; Jer. 10:11–12).

Creating is a divine work, an act of infinite power and therefore is incommunicable in either nature or grace to any creature, whatever it may be. But Christian theology all the more unanimously attributed the work of creation to all three persons in the Trinity. Scripture left no doubt on this point. God created all things through the Son (Ps. 33:6; Prov. 8:22; John 1:3; 5:17; 1 Cor. 8:6; Col. 1:15–17; Heb. 1:3) and through the Spirit (Gen. 1:2; Ps. 33:6; Job 26:13; 33:4; Ps. 104:30; Isa. 40:13; Luke 1:35). In this context the Son and the Spirit are not viewed as secondary forces but as independent agents or "principles" *(principia)*, as authors *(auctores)* who with the Father carry out the work of creation, as with him they also constitute the one true God.

This doctrine of Scripture did not immediately come into its own in the Christian church. Initially the Logos was too frequently viewed as an intermediate being who effected the linkage between God and the world while the person and work of the Holy Spirit initially fell completely into the background. But Irenaeus already pointed out that in the act of creating God needed no alien instruments, nor did he use the angels for that purpose, but had his own hands: the Logos and the Holy Spirit, by whom and in whom he created all things.[54] The doctrine of creation as the work of the whole Trinity was clearly developed by Athanasius and the three Cappadocians in the East, and by Augustine in the West. No creature, says Athanasius, can be the efficient cause *(poiētikon aition)* of creation. So then, if the Son with the Father creates the world, he cannot be an extradivine created demiurge, as Arius thinks, but has to be the very own Son of the Father, the "proper offspring of his own being" *(idion gennēma tēs ousias autou)*.[55] But where the Logos is, there the Spirit is also, and so "the Father through the Word and in the Spirit creates all things" *(ho patēr dia tou logou en tō pneumati ktizei ta panta)*.[56] Augustine puts it even more strongly: "By this supremely, equally, and immutably good Trinity all things are created" *(ab hac summe et aequaliter et immutabiliter bona trinitate creata sunt omnia)* so that the entire creation bears "the stamp of the Trinity" *(vestigium trinitatis)*.[57] This teaching has thus become the common property of Christian theology as a whole[58] and of the

53. G. Voetius, *Select disp.*, I, 556f.; *Synopsis purioris theologiae*, X, 14; F. Turretin, *Institutes of Elenctic Theology*, V, qu. 2; J. H. Heidegger, *Corpus theologiae*, VI, 14; P. van Mastricht, *Theologia*, III, 5, 20; C. Vitringa, *Doct. christ.*, II, 81–82.

54. Irenaeus, *Against Heresies*, IV, 20.

55. Athanasius, *Against the Arians*, II, 21f.

56. Athanasius, *Ad Serap.*, III, 5.

57. Augustine, *Enchiridion*, 10; *On the Trinity*, VI, 10; *City of God*, XI, 24; *Confessions*, XIII, 11.

58. John of Damascus, *Exposition of the Orthodox Faith*, I, 8; T. Aquinas, *Summa theol.*, I, qu. 45, art. 6; M. Luther, *The Smalcald Articles*, I.1; J. Calvin, *Institutes*, I.xiv, xx.

various confessions as well.[59] It was contradicted only among those who also rejected the church's dogma of the Trinity, at best believed in a creation by the Father through the Son, but in no way recognized in that creation the common work of the three divine persons. Among the dissenters were the Arians, Socinians, Remonstrants, Rationalists, and, in more recent times, Martensen, van Oosterzee, and particularly Doedes.[60]

The two dogmas stand and fall together. The confession of the essential oneness of the three persons has as its corollary that all the outward works of God *(opera ad extra)* are common and indivisible *(communia et indivisa)*. Conversely, all opposition to the trinitarian work of creation is proof of deviation in the doctrine of the Trinity. The crucial point here is that, with Scripture and church fathers, like Athanasius, we make a sharp distinction between the Creator and the creature and avoid all gnostic mingling. If in Scripture the Son and the Spirit act as independent agents *(principia)* and "authors" *(auctores)* of creation, then they are partakers of the divine being. Furthermore, if they are truly God, then they truly take part in the work of creation as well. The Arian doctrine, on the other hand, wraps itself in insoluble difficulties. It cannot be denied that Scripture teaches that creation is a work of the Father through the Son. Now, if the Son is viewed as a person outside the divine being, there is validity to the objection that no meaning can be attached to creation by the Father through the Son. Scripture says it, but what can it mean? Did the Father charge the Son to create? But then the Son is the real Creator. Did the Father and Son jointly create all things? But then it is not creation by the Son.[61]

The doctrine of the Trinity provides true light here. Just as God is one in essence and distinct in persons, so also the work of creation is one and undivided, while in its unity it is still rich in diversity. It is one God who creates all things, and for that reason the world is a unity, just as the unity of the world demonstrates the unity of God. But in that one divine being there are three persons, each of whom performs a task of his own in that one work of creation. Not in the sense that the creation is mainly attributable to the Father and less so to the Son and Spirit, nor in the sense that the three persons work independently side by side, supplementing each other's work and constituting three separate efficient causes of creation. The practice of speaking of three associated causes *(tres causae sociae)* therefore encountered

59. Cf. Denzinger, *Enchiridion*, nos. 202, 227, 231–32, 355, 367, 598; H. A. Niemeyer, *Collectio confessionum in ecclesiis reformatis publicatorum* (Leipzig: Iulii Klinkhardti, 1840), 87, 331, 341. Ed. note: In addition, Bavinck here cites J. T. Müller, *Die symbolischen Bücher der evangelisch-lutherischen Kirche*, 5th ed., 38, 299. Likely he is referring to the Augsburg Confession, art. III, and the Smalcald Articles, art. IV, found in *The Book of Concord: or The Symbolical Books of the Evangelical Lutheran Church*, trans. Henry Jacobs (Philadelphia: United Lutheran Publication House, 1908), I, 38, 311.

60. H. Martensen, *Christian Dogmatics*, trans. W. Urwick (Edinburgh: T. & T. Clark, 1871), §61; J. J. van Oosterzee, *Christian Dogmatics*, trans. J. Watson and M. Evans (New York: Scribner, Armstrong, 1874), §56; J. I. Doedes, *De Nederlandsche Geloofsbelijdenis* (Utrecht: Kemink & Zoon, 1880–81), 121ff.

61. J. I. Doedes, *Nederlandsche Geloofsbelijdenis*, 128.

widespread resistance.[62] While there is cooperation, there is no division of labor. All things originate simultaneously from the Father through the Son in the Spirit. The Father is the first cause; the initiative for creation proceeds from him. Accordingly, in an administrative sense, creation is specifically attributed to him. The Son is not an instrument but the personal wisdom, the Logos, by whom everything is created; everything rests and coheres in him (Col. 1:17) and is created for him (Col. 1:16), not as its final goal but as the head and master of all creatures (Eph. 1:10). And the Holy Spirit is the personal immanent cause by which all things live and move and have their being, receive their own form and configuration, and are led to their destination, in God.[63]

[256] Still, while the creation is a work of the whole Trinity, it cannot be denied that in Scripture it also stands in a peculiar relation to the Son, one that deserves independent discussion. The Old Testament repeatedly states that God created all things by his Word (Gen. 1:3; Ps. 33:6; 148:5; Isa. 48:13), that he established the earth by Wisdom and by his understanding spread out the heavens (Ps. 104:24; Prov. 3:19; Jer. 10:12; 51:15). But that Wisdom is also represented personally as the advisor and master worker of creation. God acquired and possessed Wisdom, arranged and searched it out, in order that by it as the beginning of his way, as the first principle of his work, he might create and organize the world. And in that way it was with him even before the creation, worked along with him in the process of creating, and delighted in the works of God's hands, especially in the children of men (Prov. 8:22–31; Job 28:23–27). This teaching is further elaborated in the New Testament. There we read not only that God created all things by the Son (John 1:3; 1 Cor. 8:6; Col. 1:15–17), but there Christ is called "the firstborn of all creation" (*prōtotokos pasēs ktiseōs,* Col. 1:15), "the origin of God's creation" (*archē tēs ktiseōs tou Theou,* Rev. 3:14), the Alpha and Omega, the beginning and end of all things (Rev. 1:17; 21:6; 22:6), for whom all things have been created (Col. 1:16), in order to be again gathered up into him as the head (Eph. 1:10). In all these passages Christ has both soteriological and cosmological significance. He is not only the mediator of re-creation but also of creation.

The Apologists as yet did not know what to do with these ideas of Scripture. Subject as they were to Platonic influence, they frequently saw little more in the Logos than the "intelligible world" *(kosmos noētos).* They associated the Logos most intimately with the world, saw his generation as being motivated by creation, and inadequately distinguished the birth of the Son from the creation of the world. They still wrestled with the gnostic idea that the Father is actually the secret and invisible Deity who is made manifest only by the Logos. Now,

62. O. Zöckler, *Geschichte der Beziehungen zwischen Theologie und Naturwissenschaft,* 2 vols. (Gütersloh: C. Bertelsmann, 1877–79), I, 621f., 679f.

63. F. H. R. Frank, *System der christlichen Wahrheit,* 3d rev. ed. (Erlangen and Leipzig: A. Deichert, 1894), I, 328f.; A. Kuyper, *The Work of the Holy Spirit,* trans. H. De Vries (Grand Rapids: Eerdmans, 1941 [1900]), 21; see above, pp. 318–22 (#229).

while this gnostic element was banished from theology by the ancient church fathers, notably Athanasius and Augustine, it kept creeping back in. The root from which this idea springs is always a certain dualism, a more or less sharp opposition between spirit and matter, between God and the world. God is invisible, inaccessible, hidden; the world, if not anti-God, is nevertheless "ungodly," "God-less," devoid of deity. What is needed to reconcile this basic opposition is an intermediate being, and that being is the Logos. In relation to God he is the cosmic idea, the image of the world, the intelligible world *(kosmos noētos);* and in relation to the world he is the actual Creator, the principle of the possibility that a world is in the making. Among the Hernhutters [Moravians] this notion resulted in the eclipse of the Father and the idea of Christ as the real Creator. Re-creation swallows up creation and grace nullifies nature. Various mediating theologians teach that the Logos is the world in its basic idea, and that it "belongs to the very being of the Son to have his life not only in the Father but also in the world; as the heart of the Father he is simultaneously the eternal heart of the world, the eternal World-logos."[64]

This notion then automatically leads to a doctrine of incarnation apart from sin. The world as such is profane; creation is not really a divine work. For God to be able to create and for the world and mankind to be pleasing to him, he must view them in Christ. God could only have willed the world in Christ and for Christ. It is only in Christ as the head and central individual of the human race that we can be pleasing to God. In this view, the incarnation is necessary for the revelation and communication of God, and the God-man is the supreme goal of creation.[65] Ultimately, this train of thought culminates in the theory that the creation is necessary for God himself. Indeed, God as such is nature, the Ur-ground, the depth-dimension and primal silence of the world *(bythos* and *sigē),* but for him to become personality and spirit, he needs the creation. Creation is God's own history; cosmogony is theogony.[66]

This Gnosticism can only be fundamentally overcome when all dualism between God and the world is cut off at the root. Creation as a work of God is not inferior to re-creation; nature is not of a lower order than grace; the world is not profane of itself. Consequently, there was no need for an inferior divine being to enable the Father to create the world. The Christian church believes in God the Father, Almighty, Creator of heaven and earth. The creation is absolutely no more the work of the Son than of the Father. All things are from God.

---

64. H. Martensen, *Christian Dogmatics,* §125; H. A. W. Meyer, *Critical and Exegetical Handbook to the Epistles to the Philippians and Colossians,* trans. John C. Moore and rev. and ed. William P. Dickson (Edinburgh: T. & T. Clark, 1875), 281–87 (on Col. 1:16).

65. I. A. Dorner, *History of the Development of the Doctrine of the Person of Christ* (Edinburgh: T. & T. Clark, 1868), III, 229–48; C. I. Nitzsch, *System der christlichen Lehre,* 5th ed. (Bonn: Adolph Marcus, 1844), 195; J. P. Lange, *Christliche Dogmatik,* 3 vols. (Heidelberg: K. Winter, 1852), II, 215; and especially P. F. Keerl, *Der Gottmensch, das Ebenbild Gottes,* vol. 2 of *Die Mensch, das Ebenbild Gottes* (Basel: Bahnmeier, 1866), 1ff. Ed. note: Bavinck cites only the series title and volume number in his reference.

66. F. W. J. Schelling, *Werke,* II, 2, 109.

And concerning the Son the Christian church confesses that he is not inferior to the Father, nor closer to creatures, but of one substance with the Father and the Spirit, and that together they are one true and eternal God, Creator of heaven and earth. But it is true that the Son plays a role of his own in the work of creation, something especially Augustine highlighted. Although he did not equate the ideas of things with the Logos as the Apologists had done, he did feel obligated to relate them to the Logos. Truly, the world was not eternal but the idea of the world nevertheless was eternally in the mind of God. The Father expresses all his thoughts and his entire being in the one personal Word, and the idea of the world consequently is contained in the Logos. Accordingly, the Logos can be called "a certain kind of form, a form which is not itself formed but the form of all things that have been formed" *(forma quaedam, forma non formata sed forma omnium formatorum).*[67] By this line of thought the significance of the Son for the creation can be established. First, there is the Father, from whom the initiative for creation proceeds, who thinks the idea of the world; but all that the Father is and has and thinks he imparts to, and expresses in, the Son. In him the Father contemplates the idea of the world itself, not as though it were identical with the Son, but so that he envisions and meets it in the Son in whom his fullness dwells. Contained in the divine wisdom, as a part and in sum, lies also the wisdom that will be realized in the creatures [to come]. He is the Logos by whom the Father creates all things.

The whole world is thus the realization of an idea of God; a book containing letters, large and small, from which his wisdom can be known. He is, however, not merely the "exemplary cause"; he is also the "creating agent" *(archē dēmiourgikē).* The word that God speaks is not a sound without content; it is forceful and living [performative]. The idea of the world that the Father pronounces in the Son is a seminal word *(ratio seminalis),* a fundamental form *(forma principalis)* of the world itself. For that reason the Son is called the beginning *(archē),* the firstborn *(prōtotokos),* the origin of the creation *(archē tēs ktiseōs),* the firstborn who sustains the creation, from whom it arises as its cause and example, and in whom it rests. Therefore, the word that the Father utters at the creation and by which he calls the things out of nothingness into being, is also effective, for it is spoken in and through the Son. And finally, the Son in a sense is also the final cause *(causa finalis)* of the world. Because in him it has its foundation and model, it is also created for him, not as its ultimate goal, but still as the head, the Lord and heir of all things (Col. 1:16; Heb. 1:2). Summed up in the Son, gathered under him as head, all creatures again return to the Father, from whom all things originate. Thus the world finds its idea, its principle *(archē),* and its final goal *(telos)* in the triune being of God. The word that the Father pronounces in the Son is the full expression of the divine being and therefore also of all that will exist by that word as creature outside the divine being. And

---

67. Augustine, *Sermon* 117; *Freedom of the Will,* III, 16–17; *On the Trinity,* XI, 10; XV, 14; cf. Anselm, *Monologion,* 34; T. Aquinas, *Summa theol.,* I, qu. 34, art. 3; I, qu. 44, art. 3.

the procession *(spiratio)* by which the Father and the Son are the "active basis" *(principium)* of the Spirit also contains within itself the willing of that world, the idea of which is comprehended within the divine wisdom.[68] The creation thus proceeds from the Father through the Son in the Spirit in order that, in the Spirit and through the Son, it may return to the Father.

CREATION AND TIME

[257] From this perspective we may also derive some insight into the difficult problem of creation and time. Scripture tells us in simple human language that all things had a beginning. It speaks of a time before the birth of mountains, before the foundation of the world, before the aeons began (Gen. 1:1; Ps. 90:2; Prov. 8:22; Matt. 13:35; 25:34; John 1:1; 17:24; Eph. 1:4; 2 Tim. 1:9; Heb. 4:3; 1 Pet. 1:20; Rev. 13:8). In our own thinking and speaking we also cannot avoid the temporal form. From this human limitation, in fact, spring all the objections that arise over and over against a creation in time. Going back in our thinking, we finally come to the first moment in which all things have a beginning. Before that moment there is nothing but the deep silence of eternity. But immediately a multitude of questions arise in our mind. With what images will we fill up that eternity, and what kind of activity can there be if all the work of creation and providence is eliminated from consideration? The doctrines of the Trinity and the decrees offer us some hint of an answer, but detached from the world they no longer furnish content to our ideas. What did God do before the act of creation—he who cannot be conceived as an idle God *(Deus otiosus)* and is always working (John 5:17)? Did he change? Did he pass from idleness to activity, from rest to labor? How can creation, the transition to the act of creating, be squared with the immutability of God? And why did he only proceed to the work of creation after an eternity had already rushed by? How is there to be found, in all that time-transcending eternity, a moment in which God passed from not-creating to creating? And why did he choose precisely that moment? Why did he not begin creating the world aeons earlier?

All these questions have provoked a variety of answers. Pantheism attempted to furnish a solution by teaching that in God being and acting are one; that God did not become a Creator, but that creation itself is eternal. The world had no beginning; it is the eternal self-revelation of God. Furthermore, God did not precede the world in duration, but only in a logical sense, inasmuch as he is the cause of all things. Nature bringing forth *(natura naturans)* cannot be conceived apart from nature having been brought forth *(natura naturata)*, nor substance apart from modes and attributes, or idea apart from manifestation.[69] Related to this view is Origen's solution: rejecting the eternity of matter, he taught that all things

---

68. J. Kleutgen, *Philosophie der Vorzeit*, II, 870.

69. J. Erigena, *The Divine Nature*, I, 73–74; III, 8–9, 17; B. Spinoza, *The Principles of Descartes' Philosophy (Cogitata Metaphysica)*, trans. Halbert Haine Briton (Chicago: Open Court, 1905), II, ch. 10; G. W. F. Hegel, *Werke*, VII, 25.

were created out of nothing by the Logos, but that God cannot be conceived as being idle. His omnipotence is as eternal as he is, and so he also began to create from all eternity. Not that the present world is eternal, but preceding it there were countless worlds, just as following it there will also be many.[70] This view, which actually comes from the Stoa,[71] was condemned by the church at the Council of Nicaea but has made numerous comebacks.[72] In this connection we must also mention the question—one frequently dealt with in scholasticism—whether the world could have been eternal. In defense of Aristotle, who taught the eternity of the world,[73] some answered this question in the affirmative.[74] But others like Bonaventure, Albertus Magnus, Henry of Ghent, Richard, Valentia, Toletus,[75] the Lutherans,[76] and the Reformed[77] firmly rejected this thesis. Only a very few considered an eternal creation a possibility.[78]

All these answers, however, fail to satisfy the mind. There is, of course, no difference over whether at this moment the world may have existed for millions of centuries instead of thousands of years. Nobody denies this in the abstract. But a very different question is whether the world could have existed eternally in the same sense as God is eternal. This, we have to say, is impossible, for eternity and time differ essentially. Kant saw an insoluble antinomy in the fact that on the one hand the world must have had a beginning because an infinitely past time is inconceivable, and on the other could not have a beginning because an empty time is similarly inconceivable.[79] The second part of the antinomy, however, is invalid: in the absence of the world there is no time, and therefore no empty time.[80] The

70. Origen, *On First Principles*, I, 2; II, 1; III, 5.

71. E. Zeller, *Outlines of the History of Greek Philosophy*, rev. Wilhelm Nestle and trans. L. R. Palmer, 13th ed. (London: Routledge & Kegan Paul, 1969), §61, pp. 215–17.

72. R. Rothe, *Theologische Ethik*, 2d rev. ed. (Wittenberg: Zimmerman, 1867–71), §§61f.; H. Ulrici, *Gott und die Natur* (Leipzig: T. O. Weigel, 1862), 671f.; H. Martensen, *Christian Dogmatics*, §§65–66; J. A. Dorner, *History of the Development of the Doctrine of the Person of Christ* (Edinburgh: T. & T. Clark, 1868), III, 229–48; G. Wetzel, "Die Zeit der Weltschöpfung," *Jahrbücher für protestantische Theologie* 1 (1875): 582f.

73. E. Zeller, *Aristotle and the Earlier Peripatetics (Being a Translation from Zeller's Philosophy of the Greeks)*, trans. B. F. C. Costello and J. H. Muirhead (London, New York, and Bombay, 1897), I, 469–77.

74. By Durandus, Occam, Biel, Cajetan, and also by Thomas Aquinas, *Summa theol.* I, qu. 46, art. 1–2; idem, *Contra gentiles*, II, 31–37; according to T. Esser, *Die Lehre des heiligen Thomas von Aquino über die Möglichkeit einer anfanglosen Schöpfung* (Münster: Aschendorff, 1895). Eugen Rolfes, "Die Controverse über die Möglichkeit einer anfangslosen Schöpfung," *Philosophisches Jahrbuch* 10 (1897): 1–22; J. Heinrich and C. Gutberlet, *Dogmatische Theologie*, V, 134f.

75. Bonaventure, *Sent.*, I, dist. 44, art. 1, qu. 4; cf. D. Petavius, "De Deo," in *Theol. dogm.*, III, chs. 5–6.

76. J. Quenstedt, *Theologia*, I, 421; D. Hollaz, *Examen theol.*, 358.

77. J. Zanchi(us), *Op. theol.*, III, 22; G. Voetius, *Select. disp.*, I, 568; M. Leydecker, *Fax. verit.*, 140; J. Coccejus, *Summa theol.*, ch. 15; B. de Moor, *Comm. in Marckii Comp.*, II, 179; C. Vitringa, *Doctr. christ.*, II, 83; F. Turretin, *Institutes of Elenctic Theology*, V, qu. 3.

78. F. Burmann, *Syn. theol.*, I, 24, 41.

79. I. Kant, *Critique of Pure Reason*, trans. Norman Kemp Smith (1929; reprinted, New York: St. Martin's, 1965), 396–402.

80. Irenaeus, *Against Heresies*, III, 8; Athanasius, *Against the Arians*, I, 29, 58; Tertullian, *Against Marcion*, II, 3; idem, *Against Hermogenes*, 4; Augustine, *City of God*, XI, 6.

fact that we cannot imagine this and will always need such an auxiliary notion as
a time before time is irrelevant and only derives from the necessity of our thinking in a temporal form. To eliminate time from our thinking is to eliminate our
thinking and hence is impossible.

This leaves us with only the first part of Kant's antinomy: namely, that
the world must have had a beginning. However endlessly it is extended, time
remains time and never becomes eternity. There is an essential difference
between the two. The world cannot be conceived apart from time; existence
in time is the necessary form of all that is finite and created. The predicate
of eternity can never, strictly speaking, be attributable to things that exist in
the form of time. Similarly, the question whether God could not have created
from all eternity is based on the identification of eternity and time. In eternity
there is no "earlier" or "later." God *did* eternally create the world: that is, in
the moment in which the world came into existence, God was and remained
the Eternal One, and as the Eternal One he created the world. Even if the
world *had* existed for an endless succession of centuries, and though millions
of worlds *had* preceded the present one, it remains temporal, finite, limited,
and therefore had a beginning. Origen's hypothesis in no way begins to solve
the problem: the question remains absolutely the same; it is only shifted back
a few million [or billion] years.

Even more baseless is the question of what God did before he created. Augustine, Luther, and Calvin answered it in the spirit of Proverbs 26:5 ["Answer
fools according to their folly"].[81] It proceeds from the assumption that God
exists in time, and that creation and providence are for him the strenuous labor
of every day. But God dwells in eternity. He is pure actuality *(actus purissimus),*
an infinite fullness of life, blessed in himself. Without the creation he is not idle,
and involvement in it does not exhaust him. "In [God's] leisure, therefore, is
no laziness, indolence, inactivity; as in His work is no labour, effort, industry.
He can act while He reposes, and repose while He acts."[82]

The case is the same with pantheism. It is not, to be sure, as superficial as
the Socinianism and the materialism that simply transmute eternity into a
time endlessly extended forward and backward, and that are ignorant of the
distinction between endless and infinite. Pantheism does not maintain that
God is all things and that all things are God. It makes a distinction between
"being" and "becoming," the nature that is bringing forth and the nature
that has been brought forth (*natura naturans* and *natura naturata*), between
substance and its modes, the All and all things, the idea and its manifestation,
that is, between eternity and time. But pantheism has no answers to the questions "Wherein then does the difference exist?" "What connection is there
between the two?" "How does eternity pass into time?" It certainly supplies
enough words and images, but they do not permit any real thought. Theism,

81. Augustine, *Confessions,* XI, 2; J. Calvin, *Institutes,* I.xiv.1.
82. Augustine, *City of God,* XII, 17, trans. Marcus Dods (New York: Modern Library, 1950), 400.

however, views eternity and time as two incommensurable magnitudes. We neither may nor can neglect either one of them; both of them urge themselves on our consciousness and powers of reflection. But we cannot clearly understand their interconnectedness. As living, thinking beings in time, we stand before the mystery of eternal uncreated being and marvel. On the one hand, it is certain that God is the Eternal One: in him there is neither past or future, neither becoming or change. All that he is is eternal: his thought, his will, his decree. Eternal in him is the idea of the world that he thinks and utters in the Son; eternal in him is also the decision to create the world; eternal in him is the will that created the world in time; eternal is also the act of creating as an act of God, an action both internal and immanent.[83] For God did not *become* Creator, so that first for a long time he did not create and then afterward he did create. Rather, he is the eternal Creator, and as Creator he was the Eternal One, and as the Eternal One he created. The creation therefore brought about no change in God; it did not emanate from him and is no part of his being. He is unchangeably the same eternal God.

On the other hand, it is certain, also to human thought, that the world had a beginning and was created in time. Augustine correctly stated that the world was not made in time but along with time,[84] as Plato and Philo and Tertullian[85] had already said before him, and as all theologians since have repeated. A time of idleness is inconceivable, nor was there a time before the world existed. Time is the necessary form of the existence of the finite. It is not a separate creation but something automatically given with the world, cocreated with it like space. In a sense, therefore, the world has always existed, for as long as time has existed. All change, then, occurs in it, not in God. The world is subject to time, that is, to change. It is constantly becoming, in contrast with God, who is an eternal and unchangeable being. Now these two, God and the world, eternity and time, are related in such a way that the world is sustained in all its parts by God's omnipresent power, and time in all its moments is pervaded by the eternal being of our God. Eternity and time are not two lines, the shorter of which for a time runs parallel to the infinitely extended one; the truth is that eternity is the immutable center that sends out its rays to the entire circumference of time. To the limited eye of the creature it successively unfolds its infinite content in the breadth of space and the length of time, so that creature might understand something of the unsearchable greatness of God. But for all that, eternity and time remain distinct. All we wish to confess is that God's eternal willing can and does, without ceasing to be eternal, produce effects in time, just as his eternal thought can have temporal objects as its content.[86]

83. Augustine, *City of God*, XII, 17; P. Lombard, *Sent.*, II, dist. 1, n. 2; Bonaventure, *Sent.*, II, dist. 1, art. 1, qu. 2; T. Aquinas, *Contra gentiles*, I, 82; D. Petavius, "De Deo," in *Theol. dogm.*, V, ch. 9, §9; V, ch. 13, §5; G. Voetius, *Select. disp.*, I, 565; F. Turretin, *Institutes of Elenctic Theology*, V, qu. 3, 16.

84. Augustine, *Confessions*, XI, 10–13; idem, *City of God*, VII, 30; XI, 4–6; XII, 15–17.

85. Tertullian, *Against Marcion*, II, 3.

86. Thomas Aquinas, in J. Kleutgen, *Philosophie der Vorzeit*, II, 871.

The power of God's will, which is eternally one, caused things to come into being that did not exist before, yet without bringing about any change in him. God eternally wills things that will only take place after centuries or took place centuries before. And the moment it takes place there is change in things but not in him. [As Augustine has said:]

> But when one speaks of [God's] former repose and subsequent operation (and I know not how men can understand these things), this "former" and "subsequent" are applied only to the things created, which formerly did not exist and subsequently came into existence. But in God the former purpose is not altered and obliterated by the subsequent and different purpose; but [he continues] by one and the same eternal and unchangeable will he effected regarding the things he created, both that formerly, so long as they were not, they should not be, and that subsequently, when they began to be, they should come into existence. And thus, perhaps, he would show in a very striking way, to those who have eyes for such things, how independent he is of what he makes, and how it is of his own gratuitous goodness that he creates, since from eternity he dwelt without creatures in no less perfect a blessedness.[87]

CREATION'S GOAL

[258] Now if this world, which originated and exists in time, is distinct in essence from the eternal and unchangeable being of God, one is all the more insistently confronted by the question as to what moved God to call this world into existence. The Scriptures continually trace all the "isness" and "suchness" of God's creatures back to his will (Ps. 33:6; 115:3; 135:6; Isa. 46:10; Dan. 4:35; Matt. 11:25; Rom. 9:15ff.; Eph. 1:4, 9, 11; Rev. 4:11).[88] For us that is the ultimate ground, the end of all contradiction. "The will of God is the supreme law. The 'nature' of any particular created thing is precisely what the supreme Creator of the thing willed it to be."[89] To the question of why things exist and are as they are, there is no other and deeper answer than that God willed it. If someone should then ask Why did God will it? "he is asking for something that is greater than the will of God, but nothing greater can be found."[90] And this has been the position of the whole Christian church and of Christian theology.

Pantheism, however, is not satisfied with this answer and looks for a deeper ground. It then attempts especially in two ways to explain the world from the being of God. Either it presents that being as so superabundantly rich that the

---

87. Augustine, *City of God*, XII, 17, trans. Marcus Dods (New York: Modern Library), 400; ed. note: The citation adapted here is longer than Bavinck's original.

88. In Rev. 4:11, the preposition *dia* is followed by the accusative and hence actually means "on account of." But here and elsewhere (Rev. 12:11; John 6:57; Rom. 8:10, 20; 2 Pet. 3:12) this meaning passes into that of "through" [an efficient cause] or of a dative.

89. Augustine, *City of God*, XXI, 8.

90. Augustine, *De Gen. contra Manich.*, I, 2.

world automatically flows from it and, to the degree that the world distances itself from that being, approaches nonbeing (the *mē on*) and solidifies into sensible matter. This is the theory of emanation that originated in the East, spread especially in Persia and India, and then, in the systems of Gnosticism and Neoplatonism, also penetrated the West. Or it attempts to explain the world from God's poverty *(penia tou Theou)*, not from his wealth *(ploutos)*. God is so needy and unblessed that he needs the world for his own development. In himself he is pure potentiality who *is* nothing but can *become* anything. He has to objectivize himself and, by contrasting himself with the world, become "spirit" or "personality" in man. In himself God is not yet the Absolute; he only achieves this status through the world process. Being initially the implicit God *(Deus implicitus)*, he gradually becomes explicit *(Deus explicitus)*. The world, accordingly, is necessary for God; it is a necessary developmental component in his being. "Without the world God is not God." Over against this pantheism, which abolishes the personality of God and deifies the world, theism maintains the teaching that creation is an act of God's will. But that will is not to be construed as arbitrary volition. The will of God has indeed been so viewed in Islamic theology and in the thinking of Nominalists, Socinians, and Cartesians. There the world is a product of pure caprice. It exists, but it might just as well not have existed or have been very different. As a rule, however, Christian theology has avoided this extreme position and taught that, though the will of God in creation was totally free and all coercion and necessity is excluded, that divine will had its motives and God, in performing his external works, had his high and holy purposes.[91]

So there remains room for the question of what moved God to create the world; in other words: what goal did he have in mind for the creation? The answers to this question have varied. Many theologians have seen an adequate explanation for the world in God's goodness and love. Scripture, too, often speaks of the fact that God is good, that his goodness is manifest in all his works, that he loves all his creatures and wills their salvation. Furthermore, God could not be conceived as needing anything; he could not have created the world to receive something from it but only to give and communicate himself. His goodness, therefore, was the reason for creation. Plato, Philo, and Seneca already spoke along that line,[92] and Christian theologians often said as well that God did not create the world out of need but out of goodness, not for himself but for human beings. "God made the world not for himself but for man."[93] "If he were not able to make good things, he would possess no power at all; if, however, he were able but did not, there would be great blame."[94] But the God of all is good and excellent by nature. For a good being would be

---

91. Cf. above, pp. 237–45 (##208–9) [= H. Bavinck, *The Doctrine of God*, 232–41].
92. Plato, *Timaeus*, 29D; Seneca, *Letters*, 95; for Philo, see O. Zöckler's article, *PRE³*, XI, 643.
93. Tertullian, *Against Marcion*, I, 43; *Against Praxeas*, 5.
94. Augustine, *Literal Meaning of Genesis*, IV, 16.

envious of no one, so he envies nobody's existence but rather wishes everyone to exist in order to exercise his kindness.[95]

These pronouncements repeatedly alternated, however, with other statements in which God himself and his honor were designated as the cause and purpose of the creation. But humanism placed man in the foreground. Socinianism did not look for man's essence in communion with God but in his dominion over the earth. The doctrine of natural law, natural morality, and natural religion made man autonomous and independent from God. Leibniz taught that by his goodness, wisdom, and power God was morally bound to choose the best of the many possible worlds and to bring that into being. Kant, on grounds of practical reason, only appealed to God for help in supplying to man in the hereafter the eternal life to which his virtue entitled him. And thus, in the rationalism of the eighteenth century, man became the most interesting of creatures: everything else existed for him and was subservient to his perfection. Man was his own end *(Selbstzweck)* and all else, God included, only a means.[96] And even today many thinkers teach that God must impart reality to the idea of the world, which he deems necessary, for otherwise he would be selfish and not the highest love. Because he is good, he does not want to be blessed by himself alone, but establishes a kingdom of love and pursues the blessedness of his creatures, which for him is the ultimate goal.[97]

From a Christian viewpoint, however, this doctrine of man as *Selbstzweck* is unacceptable. Of course God's goodness also becomes manifest in creation, as Scripture repeatedly asserts. Still it is not correct to say that God's goodness requires the creation or else God would be selfish. Remember, God is the all-good Being, perfect love, total blessedness within himself, and therefore does not need the world to bring his goodness or love to maturity, any more than he needs it to achieve self-consciousness and personality. It is in the nature of the case, moreover, that God does not exist for the sake of man, and that man exists for the sake of God. For although man may in a sense be called *Selbstzweck* insofar as he, as a rational, moral being, may never be degraded

95. Athanasius, *Contra gentes,* 41; John of Damascus, *Exposition of the Orthodox Faith,* II, 2; T. Aquinas, *Summa theol.,* I, qu. 19, art. 2; G. Voetius, *Select. disp.,* I, 558.

96. K. G. Bretschneider, *Systematische Entwicklung aller in der Dogmatik* (Leipzig: J. A. Barth, 1841), 442f.; idem, *Handbuch der Dogmatik* (Leipzig: J. A. Barth, 1838), I, 669; J. A. L. Wegschneider, *Institutiones theologiae christianae dogmaticae* (Halle: Gebauer, 1819), §95.

97. R. Rothe, *Theologische Ethik,* §49; I. Dorner, *System of Christian Doctrine,* II, 9–21 (§33); H. Martensen, *Christian Dogmatics,* §59; J. C. K. von Hofmann, *Der Schriftbeweis,* 2d ed., I, 205f.; K. F. A. Kahnis, *Die lutherische Dogmatik* (Leipzig: Dörffling & Franke, 1861–68), I, 428; J. Müller, *Die christliche Lehre von der Sünde* (Bremen: C. Ed. Muller, 1889), II, 187f.; L. Schoeberlein, *Prinzip und System der Dogmatik* (Heidelberg: C. Winter, 1881), 628; G. Thomasius, *Christi Person und Werk* (Erlangen: A. Deichert, 1888), I, 44; James Orr, *The Christian View of God and the World,* 7th ed. (Edinburgh: A. Elliot, 1904), 155; A. Ritschl, *The Christian Doctrine of Justification and Reconciliation,* trans. and ed. H. R. MacIntosh and A. B. MacCaulay (Edinburgh: T. & T. Clark, 1900), 290–96; also Hermes and Günther, according to Kleutgen, *Theologie der Vorzeit,* I, 642.

into a "will-less" instrument, he is nevertheless fundamentally dependent on God and possesses nothing he has not received. God alone is Creator; man is a created being, and for that reason alone he cannot be the goal of creation. Inasmuch as he has his origin in God, he can also have his destiny only in God. And, finally, the theory that creation is grounded in God's goodness and has for its final end the salvation of man, is also at variance with reality. The universe is not, certainly, exhausted by its service to humanity and must therefore have some goal other than utility to man. The pedestrian utilitarianism and the self-centered teleology of the eighteenth century have been sufficiently refuted. The suffering and pain that is the daily lot of humanity cannot be explained in terms only of God's goodness. And the final outcome of world history, which speaks to us not only of the salvation of the elect but also of an eternal triumph over the ungodly, reveals attributes of God entirely different from his goodness and love.

Scripture, accordingly, takes another position and points to a higher goal. It says that all of nature is a revelation of God's attributes and a proclaimer of his praise (Ps. 19:1; Rom. 1:19). God created man after his image and for his glory (Gen. 1:26; Isa. 43:7). He glorified himself in the Pharaoh of the Exodus (Exod. 14:17) and in the man born blind (John 9:3), and made the wicked for the day of trouble (Prov. 16:4; Rom. 9:22). Christ came to glorify God (John 17:4), and he bestows all the benefits of grace for his name's sake: redemption, forgiveness, sanctification, and so forth (Ps. 105:8; 78:9ff.; Isa. 43:25; 48:11; 60:21; 61:3; Rom. 9:23; Eph. 1:6ff.). God gives his glory to no other (Isa. 42:8). The final goal is that all kingdoms will be subjected to him and every creature will yield to him (Dan. 7:27; Isa. 2:2–22; Mal. 1:11; 1 Cor. 15:24f.). Even on earth already he is given glory by all his people (Ps. 115:1; Matt. 6:13 KJV). Someday God alone will be great (Isa. 2:2–22) and receive glory from all his creatures (Rev. 4:11; 19:6). He is the First and the Last, the Alpha and the Omega (Isa. 44:6; 48:12; Rev. 1:8; 22:13). Of him, through him, and to him are all things (Rom. 11:36). On this basis Christian theology almost unanimously teaches that the glory of God is the final goal of all God's works. Although in its early years theologians especially featured the goodness of God as the motive for creation, still the honor of God as the final end of all things is not lacking. Athenagoras, for example, writes that it was "for his own sake and for the purpose of showing that his goodness and wisdom had been advanced in all his works, that God made man."[98] Tertullian says that God created the world "for the embellishment of his majesty."[99] This [emphasis on the] "glory of God" increasingly came into its own, especially in the medieval theology of Anselm, who made the honor of God the fundamental principle of his doctrine of the incarnation and the atonement,[100] but also in Lombard,

98. Athenagoras, *Resurrection of the Dead*, 12.
99. Tertullian, *Apology*, 17.
100. Anselm, *Cur Deus homo*, 11.

Thomas, Bonaventure, and others.[101] And we find the same teaching in the thought of later Roman Catholic theologians,[102] in that of the Lutherans,[103] and finally and particularly in the theology of the Reformed.[104] The difference between the Reformed on the one hand and the Lutherans and Roman Catholics on the other, is not that the former posited the honor of God, while the latter chose man as the final end of creation. It is rather that the Reformed tradition made the honor of God the fundamental principle of all doctrine and conduct, of dogmatics and morality, of the family, society, and the state, of science and art. Nowhere was this principle of the glory of God more universally applied than among the confessors of the Reformed religion.

But a twofold objection has been registered against God's glory as the final goal of all creatures. First, on this view God is made self-centered, self-seeking, devaluing his creatures, specifically human beings, into means. We already confronted this objection earlier and demonstrated that as the perfect good, God can rest in nothing other than himself and cannot be satisfied in anything less than himself. He has no alternative but to seek his own honor. Just as a father in his family and a ruler in his kingdom must seek and demand the honor due to him in that capacity, so it is with the Lord our God. Now a human being can only ask for the honor that is due to him in the name of God and for the sake of the office to which God has called him, but God asks for and seeks that honor in his own name and for his own being. Inasmuch as he is the supreme and only good, perfection itself, it is the highest kind of justice that in all creatures he seek his own honor. And so little does this pursuit of his own honor have anything in common with human egotistical self-interest that, where it is wrongfully withheld from him, God will, in the way of law and justice, even more urgently claim that honor. Voluntarily or involuntarily, every creature will someday bow his knee before him. Obedience in love or subjection by force is the final destiny of all creatures.

Another objection is that, in seeking his honor, God does need his creature after all. Since the world serves as an instrument of his glorification, there is something lacking in his perfection and blessedness. Creation meets a need in God and contributes to his perfection.[105] This objection seems irrefutable,

101. P. Lombard, *Sent.*, II, dist. I; T. Aquinas, *Summa theol.*, I, qu. 44, art. 4; I, qu. 66, art. 2; I, qu. 103, art. 2; idem, *Contra gentiles*, III, 17–18; idem, *Sent.*, II, dist. 1, qu. 2, art. 2; Bonaventure, *Sent.*, II, dist. 1, 2.

102. M. J. Scheeben, *Handbuch der katholischen Dogmatik* (Freiburg i.B.: Herder, 1933), II, 31f.; H. Th. Simar, *Lehrbuch der Dogmatik* (Freiburg i.B.: Herder, 1879–80), 234f.; Kleutgen, *Theologie der Vorzeit*, I, 640–92; J. Schwetz, *Theologia dogmatica catholica*, 3 vols. (Vienna: Congregationis Mechitharisticae, 1851–54), I, 396f.; J. B. Heinrich and C. Gutberlet, *Dogmatische Theologie*, V, 151f.; G. Jansen, *Prael. theol.*, II, 319f.

103. J. Gerhard, *Loci. theol.*, V, c. 5; J. Quenstedt, *Theologia*, I, 418; D. Hollaz, *Examen theol.*, 360.

104. For example, Jonathan Edwards, "Dissertation concerning the End for Which God Created the World," in *Ethical Writings*, ed. Paul Ramsey, vol. 8 of *The Works of Jonathan Edwards* (New Haven, Conn.: Yale University Press, 1989), 399–536.

105. D. F. Strauss, *Christian Faith*, I, 633; E. von Hartmann, *Gesammelte Studien und Aufsätze* (Leipzig: Friedrich, 1891), 715.

though in all kinds of human labor there is an analogy that can clarify God's creative activity for us. At a lower level humans labor, because they have to; they are impelled to work by need or force. But the more refined the work becomes, the less room there is for need or coercion. An artist creates his work of art not out of need or coercion but impelled by the free impulses of his genius. "I pour out my heart like a little finch in the poplars; I sing and know no other goal" (Bilderdijk). A devout person serves God, not out of coercion or in hope of reward, but out of free-flowing love. So there is also a delight in God that is infinitely superior to need or force, to poverty or riches, which embodies his artistic ideas in creation and finds intense pleasure in it. Indeed, what in the case of man is merely a weak analogy is present in God in absolute originality. A creature, like the creation of an artist, has no independence apart from, and in opposition to, God. God, therefore, never seeks out a creature as if that creature were able to give him something he lacks or could take from him something he possesses. He does not seek the creature [as an end in itself], but through the creature he seeks himself. He is and always remains his own end. His striving is always—also in and through his creatures—total self-enjoyment, perfect bliss. The world, accordingly, did not arise from a need in God, from his poverty and lack of bliss, for what he seeks in a creature is not that creature but himself. Nor is its origination due to an uncontrollable fullness *(plērōma)* in God, for God uses all creatures for his own glorification and makes them serviceable to the proclamation of his perfections.

A CREATION-BASED WORLDVIEW

[259] From this perspective arises a very particular worldview. The word "creation" can denote either the act or the product of creation. From one's understanding of the act flows one's view of the product. Pantheism attempts to explain the world dynamically; materialism attempts to do so mechanically. But both strive to see the whole as governed by a single principle. In pantheism the world may be a living organism *(zōon)*, of which God is the soul; in materialism it is a mechanism that is brought about by the union and separation of atoms. But in both systems an unconscious blind fate is elevated to the throne of the universe. Both fail to appreciate the richness and diversity of the world; erase the boundaries between heaven and earth, matter and spirit, soul and body, man and animal, intellect and will, time and eternity, Creator and creature, being and nonbeing; and dissolve all distinctions in a bath of deadly uniformity. Both deny the existence of a conscious purpose and cannot point to a cause or a destiny for the existence of the world and its history.

Scripture's worldview is radically different. From the beginning heaven and earth have been distinct. Everything was created with a nature of its own and rests in ordinances established by God. Sun, moon, and stars have their own unique task; plants, animals, and humans are distinct in nature. There is the most profuse diversity and yet, in that diversity, there is also a superlative kind of unity. The foundation of both diversity and unity is in God. It is he who created all things in accordance with his unsearchable wisdom, who continually upholds them in their distinctive natures, who guides and governs them in keeping with their own increated energies and laws, and who, as the supreme good and ultimate goal of all things, is pursued and desired by all things in their measure and manner. Here is a unity that does not destroy but rather maintains diversity, and a diversity that does not come at the expense of unity, but rather unfolds it in its riches. In virtue of this unity the world can, metaphorically, be called an organism, in which all the parts are connected with each other and influence each other reciprocally. Heaven and earth, man and animal, soul and body, truth and life, art and science, religion and morality, state and church, family and society, and so on, though they are all distinct, are not separated. There is a wide range of connections between them; an organic, or if you will, an ethical bond holds them all together.

Scripture clearly points [to this bond] when it not only sums up the universe under the name of heaven and earth but also calls it ʿôlām, that is, a hidden, invisible, indefinite time in the past or future, aeon, eternity, the world (Eccles. 1:4; 3:11); and in the New Testament kosmos (John 1:10); ta panta (1 Cor. 8:6; 15:25f.); ktisis (Mark 10:6); aiōnes (Heb. 1:2), duration, lifetime, age, world (cf. seculum in connection with sexus), a human lifetime, world, and our word "world" [ME weorld, from OE weoruld, worold, human existence, age, or lifetime]. The words ʿôlām and aiōnes assume the idea that the world has duration, or age, that a history takes place in it which culminates in a specific goal. The Greek word kosmos and the Latin mundus, on the other hand, stress the beauty and harmony of the world. And in fact the world is both. Just as Paul simultaneously compares the church to a body and a building and speaks of a growing temple (Eph. 2:21), and Peter calls believers living stones (1 Pet. 2:5), so also the world is both a history and a work of art. It is a body that grows and a building that is erected. It extends itself in the "breadth" of space and perpetuates itself in the "length" of time. Neither the mechanical principle of materialism nor the dynamic principle of pantheism is sufficient to explain it. But whatever is valid in both is recognized in the doctrine of the world as the Scriptures teach it. It is to be regarded both horizontally and vertically. From the lowest forms of life it strives upward to where the light and life of God is, and at the same time it moves forward to a God-glorifying end. In that way it displays the attributes and perfections of God, in principle already at the outset, to an increasing degree as it develops, and perfectly at the end of the ages.

Augustine, the church father who most deeply understood these ideas, also presented the most elaborate account of them. In The City of God (de civitate Dei) he offers a Christian philosophy of history, demonstrates how the Christian worldview finds its truth and proof in history, and sketches the origin and essence of the heavenly city (civitas coelestis), both in its development and relation to the earthly city (civitas terrena), in its end as well as its goal.[106] But at the same time he includes in it an account of the universe as a splendid harmony. In Augustine the world is a unity: the universe derives its name from the word "unity."[107] Nevertheless, that unity is not a uniformity but an infinitely varied diversity.[108] For God is the supreme being: supremely true, supremely good, and supremely beautiful. For that reason he created many creatures who in varying degrees partake of his being, truth, goodness, and beauty. "To some things he gave more of being and to others less and in this way arranged an order of natures in a hierarchy of being."[109] Appealing to the Wisdom of Solomon ("You have arranged all things by measure and number and weight," 11:20), Augustine states that all things are distinct in mode, species, number, degree, and order. And precisely by these qualities they bring about that world, that universe, in which God, in his good pleasure, distributes good things, and which on that account is a manifestation of his perfections.[110] For all that diversity can only be attributed to God, not to the merits of his creatures. "There is no nature even among the least and lowest of beasts that he did not fashion . . . the properties without which nothing can either be or be conceived."[111]

This worldview has been that of Christian theology in its entirety. The world is one body with many members. In the works of the church fathers, the unity, order, and harmony exhibited in the world is a powerful proof for the existence and unity of God.[112] God is the center, and all creatures are grouped in concentric circles and in a hierarchical order around him.[113] Thomas compares the world to perfectly keyed string music, whose harmonies interpret for us the glory and blessedness of the divine life. "Its parts are found to have been arranged just like the parts of a whole animal, which serve each other reciprocally."[114] "There is no spot in the universe," says Calvin, "wherein you cannot discern at least some sparks of his glory."[115] "Nothing in the whole world is more excellent, more noble, more beautiful, more useful, and more divine than the diversity of its many elements, the distinction and that order in which one is more noble than another and one depends on another, one is subject to another, and one receives obedience from another. Hence comes the adornment, beauty, and excellence of the

---

106. J. Biegler, *Die civitas Dei des heiligen Augustinus* (Paderborn: Junfermann, 1894).

107. Augustine, *De Gen. contra Manich.*, I, 21.

108. Augustine, *City of God*, XI, 10.

109. Ibid., XII, 2.

110. Augustine, *De diversis quaestionibus octoginta*, qu. 41; idem, *Divine Providence and the Problem of Evil*, I, 19; idem, *Literal Meaning of Genesis*, I, 9; II, 13; idem, *Confessions*, XII, 9; idem, *City of God*, XI, 33.

111. Augustine, *City of God*, XI, 15; cf. Konrad Scipio, *Des Aurelius Augustinus Metaphysik* (Leipzig: Breitkopf & Härtel, 1886), 31–80.

112. Athanasius, *Against the Arians*, II, 28, 48; idem, *Against the Heathen*, ch. 39.

113. Pseudo-Dionysius, *Celestial Hierarchies*; idem, *Ecclesiastical Hierarchies*.

114. T. Aquinas, *Summa theol.*, I, qu. 25, art. 6; idem, *Sent.*, II, dist. 1, qu. 1, art. 1.

115. J. Calvin, *Institutes*, I.v.1. Ed. note: The translation is that of F. L. Battles, ed. J. T. McNeill, 2 vols. (Philadelphia: Westminster, 1960), I, 52.

whole world. Thence arise its many uses, usefulness, and benefits for us. Hence, the very goodness, glory, wisdom, and power of God shines forth and is revealed more brilliantly."[116] And for all of them the world is a theater, a "splendidly clear mirror of his divine glory."[117]

As a result of this worldview Christianity has overcome both the contempt of nature and its deification. In paganism a human being does not stand in the right relationship to God, and therefore not to the world either.[118] Similarly, in pantheism and materialism the relation of human beings to nature is fundamentally corrupted. One moment man considers himself infinitely superior to nature and believes that it no longer has any secrets for him. The next moment he experiences nature as a dark and mysterious power that he does not understand, whose riddles he cannot solve, and from whose power he cannot free himself. Intellectualism and mysticism alternate. Unbelief makes way for superstition, and materialism turns into occultism. But the Christian looks upward and confesses God as the Creator of heaven and earth. In nature and history he observes the unfathomability of the ways of God and the unsearchability of his judgments, but he does not despair, for all things are subject to the government of an omnipotent God and a gracious Father, and they will therefore work together for good to those who love God. Here, accordingly, there is room for love and admiration of nature, but all deification is excluded. Here a human being is placed in the right relation to the world because he has been put in the right relation to God. For that reason also creation is the fundamental dogma: throughout Scripture it is in the foreground and is the foundation stone on which the Old and New Covenants rest.

Finally, this doctrine rules out an egoistic theology and a false optimism. Certainly, there is an element of truth in the view that all things exist for the sake of man, or rather for the sake of humanity, the church of Christ (1 Cor. 3:21–23; Rom. 8:28). But that humanity has its ultimate purpose, along with all other creatures, in the glorification of God. To that end all things are subordinate. To that end all things, even sin and suffering, work together. And with a view to this end the world is functionally well organized. In scholasticism the question was sometimes asked whether God could make anything better than he actually made it. Abelard said no, because the goodness of God required that he always had to will the best, or else he would be selfish,[119] and Leibniz

---

116. J. Zanchi(us), *Op. theol.*, III, 45.

117. Cf. also Armin Reiche, *Die künstlerichen Element in der Welt-und Lebensanschauung des Gregor von Nyssa* (Jena: A. Kámpte, 1897), 221f.; Otto Gierke, *Johannes Althusius* (Breslau: W. Koebner, 1880), 60f.; T. Pesch, *Die grossen Welträthsel*, 2d ed., 2 vols. (Freiburg i.B.: Herder, 1892), I, 135f.; M. Scheeben, *Dogmatik*, II, 94f.; J. Heinrich and C. Gutberlet, *Dogmatik*, V, 173f.

118. R. Smend, *Lehrbuch der alttestamentlichen Religionsgeschichte*, 458: "The Hebrew man faces the world and nature in sovereign self-awareness. He has no fear of the world. But that posture is wedded to the strongest possible sense of responsibility. As God's deputy, but only as such, he is in charge of the world. He may not follow his own arbitrary impulses but only the revealed will of God. Paganism, on the other hand, oscillates between presumptuous misuse of the world and a childish terror before its powers."

119. P. Abelard, *Introduction to Theology*, III, ch. 5.

later reasoned along the same line. But in God we cannot posit any uncertainty or choice. He did not choose the best out of many possible worlds. His will is fixed from eternity. A creature as such can always be conceived as better, larger, or more beautiful than it actually is, because a creature is contingent and capable of development and improvement. And even the universe as a contingent entity can be conceived differently and better for us human beings. Thomas indeed said: "The universe cannot be better on account of the ideal order attributed to these things by God, in whom the good of the universe consists; if some one of these things were better, the proportion of the order would be ruined, just as when one string is overplayed, the melody of the cither is ruined." But he also added: "God could nevertheless make other things or add other things to the things that have been made, and that other universe would be better."[120] The nature of a creature is such that both in its "isness" and "suchness" it can only be thought as contingent. But to God this question does not exist. This world is good because it answers to the purpose he has set for it. It is neither the best nor the worst, but it is good because God called it so. It is good because it is serviceable, not to the individual human being, but to the revelation of God's perfections. And to the person who regards it so, it is also good, because it makes known to him the God whom to know is eternal life. Lactantius, accordingly, spoke truly when he said: "The world was made for this reason that we should be born. We are born, therefore, that we should know the Maker of the world and our God. We know Him that we may worship Him. We worship Him that we may gain immortality as a reward for our labors, since the worship of God rests on very great labors. Therefore, we are rewarded with immortality that, made like the angels, we may serve the Father and Lord Most High forever and be an everlasting kingdom for God. This is the sum of everything; this the secret of God; this the mystery of the world."[121]

---

120. T. Aquinas, *Summa theol.*, I, qu. 25, art. 6, ad. 3; cf. P. Lombard, *Sent.*, I, dist. 44; Bonaventure, *Sent.*, I, qu. 44, art. 1, qu. 1–3; Hugh of St. Victor, *On the Sacraments*, II, ch. 22; G. Voetius, *Select. disp.*, I, 553; P. van Mastricht, *Theologia*, III, 6, 11; J. H. Heidegger, *Corpus theologiae*, VI, 21.

121. Lactantius, *The Divine Institutes*, VII, 6, trans. Mary Francis McDonald, Fathers of the Church 49 (Washington, D.C.: Catholic University Press, 1964), 488.

PART **IV**

MAKER
OF HEAVEN
AND EARTH

9

HEAVEN:
THE SPIRITUAL WORLD

*The Bible joins all the world's religions in acknowledging a spiritual,
nonmaterial, invisible realm. While some (Sadducees, modernists) deny the
existence of angels, excessive, unhealthy interest in spirits or speculation about
them is a greater problem. Belief in a spiritual world cannot be demonstrated
philosophically; it is rooted in and profoundly expresses the truth of revelation.
Humans cannot bridge the boundary between this world and the one beyond;
only God can make it known to us, and he has done so in Scripture. The world
of angels is as richly varied as is the material world, and they exist in distinct
kinds and classes. Scripture also teaches that among angels there are distinctions
of rank and status, of dignity and ministry, of office and honor. The elaborate
hierarchical classification of Pseudo-Dionysius, however, far exceeds what is
known from revelation. Speculation about the number of angels or the time
of their creation is unhelpful. While we do not know exact details about their
nature, Scripture does indicate that, unlike God himself, angels are not simple,
omnipresent, or eternal. This has led some to conclude that angels—in their
own ethereal way—are corporeal, bounded in time and space. But though
angels always appear to humans in visible corporeal form and are symbolically
represented in this way, it is best not to ascribe corporeality to angels in order to
avoid all forms of pantheistic identity-philosophy that mixes heaven and earth,
matter and spirit, and erases the distinction between them. Though they are
finite creatures, angels do relate more freely to time and space than humans do.
Modern analogies of light and electricity help us here. There is a unity among
the angels: like humans, they are all created, spiritual, rational, moral beings;
but only humans are God's image-bearers, joined in a common humanity, and
constituting the church. The extraordinary ministry of angels is to accompany
the history of redemption at its cardinal points; their ordinary ministry is
to praise God day and night. Though angels are used by God to watch over
believers, there is no ground for believing [generally] in individual or national
guardian angels. Care must be taken to avoid veneration and worship of
angels; only God is to be worshiped.*

[260] According to Holy Scripture, creation is divided into a spiritual and a material realm, into heaven and earth, into "things in heaven and [things] on earth, things visible and [things] invisible" (Col. 1:16). The existence of such a spiritual realm is recognized in all religions. In addition to the actual gods, also a variety of demigods or heroes, demons, genii, spirits, souls, and so on, have been the objects of religious veneration. Especially in Parsism there was a vigorous development in the doctrine of angels. In it a host of good angels, called *Jazada*, surrounds Ahuramazda, the God of light, just as Ahriman, the God of darkness, is surrounded by a number of evil angels, called *Dewas*.[1] According to Kuenen,[2] as well as many other scholars, the Jews derived their view of angels especially from the Persians after the Babylonian exile. But this hypothesis is grossly exaggerated. In the first place, even Kuenen recognizes that belief in the existence and activity of superior beings was present in [preexilic] ancient Israel. In the second place, there is a big difference between the angelology of the canonical writings and that of Jewish folk religion. And finally, there is still so much uncertainty about the interrelationship between Judaism and Parsism that James Darmesteter in his work about the Zendavesta (1893) claimed, in opposition to the prevailing theory, that the Persian doctrine of angels was derived from Judaism.[3]

This opinion, to be sure, did not meet with much acceptance, but only a few years later Schürer was still able to write: "A carefully detailed study, especially of the influence of Parsism, has not yet been furnished up until now. Scholars will probably have to reduce the extent of this influence to a relatively small measure."[4] But according to Acts 23:8, the existence of angels was denied by the Sadducees, who therefore probably considered the angel appearances in the Pentateuch to be momentary theophanies. Josephus leaves several angel appearances unmentioned and attempts to explain others naturally.[5] According

1. According to Lehmann, in P. D. Chantepie de la Saussaye, *Lehrbuch der Religionsgeschichte* (Tübingen: J. C. B. Mohr [Paul Siebeck], 1905), II, 188–99. Ed. note: The section on Persian religion in de la Saussaye's handbook was written by Dr. Edv. Lehmann.

2. Abraham Kuenen, *The Religion of Israel to the Fall of the Jewish State*, trans. Alfred Heath May (Edinburgh: Williams & Norgate, 1883), III, 37–44.

3. Cf. W. Geesink, "De Bijbel en het Avesta," *De Heraut* 830 (November 1893); contrary to Darmesteter, C. P. Tiele, "Iets over de oudheid van het Avesta," *Verslagen en Mededeelingen der Koninklijke Akademie van Wetenschappen* (1895): 364–83; Lehmann, in de la Saussaye, *Lehrbuch*, 190.

4. Ed. note: The sentence cited by Bavinck comes from the 3d German edition of Shürer's *Geschichte des jüdischen Volkes im Zeitalter Jesu Christi*. The revised English edition (1979), incorporating insights from the Qumran discoveries and therefore focusing on the Essene sect's angelology, reads as follows: "In the circumstances, the issue of foreign influences, which so greatly exercised pre-Qumran scholarship, becomes quite secondary. Buddhist and Indian borrowings must now be considered most likely. Persian impact on Essene dualism and angelology is probable but derives no doubt from Iranian influences on Judaism as such, rather than directly on the sect itself" (Emil Schürer, *The History of the Jewish People in the Age of Jesus Christ [175 B.C.–A.D. 135]*, rev. and ed. G. Vermes, F. Millar, and M. Black, 3 vols. [Edinburgh: T. & T. Clark, 1979], II, 589). Bavinck also adds: cf. Erik Stave, *Über den Einfluss des Parsismus auf das Judentum* (Haarlem: F. Bohn, 1898); B. Lindner, "Parsismus," *PRE³*, XIV, 699–705.

5. F. Josephus, *Antiquities*, VIII, 13, 17.

to Justin,[6] the angels were held by some to be temporary emanations from the divine being, who upon completing their task again returned into God. In a later time the existence of the angels was denied by the followers of David Joris,[7] by the Libertines,[8] by Spinoza,[9] and by Hobbes,[10] who simply regarded them as revelations and workings of God. Balthazar Bekker, in his *Enchanted World (Betoverde Werelt)*, did not go that far but did limit the activity of angels, in many cases considering them to be humans. Like Spinoza, he taught that in their doctrine of angels, Christ and his apostles accommodated themselves to the beliefs of their contemporaries.[11] Leibniz, Wolff, Bonnet, Euler, and the supranaturalists attempted to maintain their existence especially on rational grounds, asserting that beginning from human beings there could be no break *(vacuum formarum)* either upward or downward in the ascending scale of creatures.[12] Even Kant did not rule out the existence of thinking beings other than humans.[13] The eighteenth century erased the distinction between angels and humans, as did the nineteenth century between humans and animals. Swedenborg, for example, had learned from the angels themselves that they were really humans; the inner core of a human being is an angel, and man is destined to become angelic.[14]

In modern theology, however, only little is left of angels. Rationalists like Wegschneider, while they do not deny the existence of angels, do deny their manifestation.[15] Marheineke, in the second edition of his dogmatics, omitted the section on angels. Strauss figured that the worldview of modernity had robbed the angels of their dwelling place: they owe their existence solely to folk sagas, to the desire for balancing the mass of matter in the world with a greater quantity of spirit.[16] In the thinking of Lipsius they are merely "graphic illustrations of the vital workings of divine providence" and belong solely to

6. Justin Martyr, *Dialogue with Trypho*, 128.

7. According to J. Hoornbeek, *Summa contr.*, 413.

8. John Calvin, *Treatises against the Anabaptists and against the Libertines*, ed. and trans. Benjamin Wirt Farley (Grand Rapids: Baker, 1982), 230–33.

9. Baruch Spinoza, *Tractatus Theologico-Politicus*, II, 56.

10. Thomas Hobbes, *Leviathan*, ed. A. R. Waller (Cambridge: Cambridge University Press, 1935), 285–96 (III, 34).

11. Balthasar Bekker, *De Betoverde Wereld* (Amsterdam: D. van den Dalen, 1691), II, 6–15.

12. Franz V. Reinhard, *Grundriss der Dogmatik* (Munich: Seidel, 1802), 184; K. G. Bretschneider, *Handbuch der Dogmatik* (Leipzig: J. A. Barth, 1838), I, 746f.

13. Otto Zöckler, *Geschichte der Beziehungen zwischen Theologie und Naturwissenschaft* (Gütersloh: C. Bertelsmann, 1877–79), II, 69, 249.

14. Emanuel Swedenborg, *The True Christian Religion Containing the Universal Theology of the New Church* (New York: Swedenborg Foundation, 1952), 29 n. 20, 176 n. 115, 179 n. 118, 183 n. 121. Ed. note: These are the passages where Swedenborg deals with humans and angels as spiritual beings; Bavinck cites the second German edition (1873), pp. 42, 178.

15. Julius A. L. Wegschneider, *Institutiones theologiae christianae dogmaticae* (Halle: Gebauer, 1819), 102.

16. David F. Strauss, *Die christliche Glaubenslehre*, 2 vols. (Tübingen: C. F. Osiander, 1840–41), I, 671f.

the domain of religious symbolism.[17] Schleiermacher, too, though he did not rule out the possibility of their existence, judged that Christ and his apostles had not taught anything positive about angels, since they had accommodated themselves to the popular imagination and spoke of angels as we do of fairies and elves; and that angels had no theological or religious significance for us.[18] Furthermore, those who upheld the existence of angels frequently altered their nature. Schelling, for example, held the good angels to be potentialities that, on account of the fall, had not become realities and are now no more than the idea or power of an individual or people.[19]

Others transformed angels into inhabitants of the planets. At an early stage—it already occurs in Xenophanes and some of the Stoics—we encounter the opinion that the planets were inhabited. After modern astronomy had abandoned the geocentric position and acquired a vague notion of the staggering spaces of the universe, the idea that planets other than the earth were also inhabited again found acceptance with Descartes, Wittichius, Allinga, Wilkins, Harvey, Leibniz, Wolff, Bonnet, Kant, Reinhard, Bretschneider, Swedenborg,[20] and many others right into our own times.[21] Some theologians also united this view with the idea that the inhabitants of the stars were angels.[22] In addition, in opposition to materialism, around the middle of the nineteenth century there arose a reaction in the form of spiritism, which not only acknowledges the existence of deceased spirits but also admits the possibility of communion

17. Richard A. Lipsius, *Lehrbuch der evangelisch-protestantischen Dogmatik* (Braunschweig: C. A. Schwetschke, 1893), §§518f.; A. E. Biedermann, *Christliche Dogmatik,* 2d ed. (Berlin: Reimer, 1884–85), II, 550f.

18. F. Schleiermacher, *The Christian Faith,* ed. H. R. MacIntosh and J. S. Steward (Edinburgh: T. & T. Clark, 1928), §42; cf. J. Bovon, *Dogmatique chrétienne,* 2 vols. (Lausanne: Georges Bridel, 1895–96), I, 297.

19. F. W. J. Schelling, *Werke,* II, 4, 284; cf. H. L. Martensen, *Christian Dogmatics,* trans. W. Urwick (Edinburgh: T. & T. Clark, 1871), §§68–69.

20. O. Zöckler, *Geschichte der Beziehungen,* II, 55f.; F. A. Lange, *Geschichte des Materialismus und Kritik seiner Bedeutung in der Gegenwart,* 8th ed. (Leipzig: Baedekker, 1908), 431; David F. Strauss, *The Old Faith and the New,* trans. Mathilde Blind (New York: Holt, 1873), 189–92.

21. C. Du Prel, *Die Planetenbewohner und die Nebularhypothese* (Leipzig: Günther, 1880); C. Flammarion, *La Pluralite des mondes habités* (Paris: Didier, 1875); L. Büchner, *Kraft und Stoff* (Leipzig: Theod. Thomas, 1902), 80–88; E. Haeckel, *The Riddle of the Universe,* trans. Joseph McCabe (New York and London: Harper & Brothers, 1900), 368–72; O. Liebmann, *Zur Analysis der Wirklichkeit: Eine Erörterung der Grundprobleme der Philosophie,* 3d ed. (Strassburg: K. J. Trübner, 1900); F. Bettex, *Het Lied der Schepping* (Rotterdam: Wenk & Birkhoff, 1901), 227f.; C. Snijders, "De Bewoonbaarheid der Hemellichamen," *Tijdspiegel* (February 1898): 182–204; Pohle in *Der Katholiek* (1884) and (1886), cited in J. B. Heinrich and C. Gutberlet, *Dogmatische Theologie,* 2d ed., 10 vols. (Mainz: Kirchheim, 1881–1900), V, 236.

22. J. H. Kurtz, *The Bible and Astronomy: An Exposition of the Biblical Cosmology and Its Relations to Natural Science,* trans. Thomas Davis Simonton (Philadelphia: Lindsay & Blakiston, 1857), 222–28, 456–61; K. Keerl, *Der Mensch das Ebenbild Gottes* (Basel: Bahnmeier, 1866), I, 278f.; F. J. Splittgerber, *Tod, Fortleben und Auferstehung,* 5th ed. (Halle: Fricke, 1879), 150; J. P. Lange, *Christliche Dogmatik,* 3 vols. (Heidelberg: K. Winter, 1849–52), II, 362f.; K. Keerl, "Die Fixsterne und die Engel," *Beweis des Glaubens* 32 (June 1896): 230–47.

between them and human beings on earth. By its sensational seances and extensive literature spiritism has won thousands upon thousands of adherents.[23]

REACHING BEYOND THE BOUNDARY

[261] Philosophically, the existence of angels is not demonstrable. The argument of Leibniz that beginning with man, both downward and upward on the scale of existence, there have to be all kinds of creatures, so that there should be no *vacuum formarum* (a vacuum of forms), nor a leap of nature, is not acceptable because it would by implication erase the distinction between the Creator and the creature and lead to gnostic pantheism. Even much less, however, can philosophy advance any argument against the possibility of such an existence. For as long as we ourselves are psychic beings and cannot explain the life of the soul from metabolism, but have to predicate an underlying spiritual substance for that life, a life that even continues after death—so long also the existence of a spiritual world is not inconsistent with any argument of reason or any fact of experience. Not only Leibniz and Wolff but also Schleiermacher and Kant have roundly acknowledged the possibility. The universality of belief in such a spiritual world proves, moreover, that inherent in such an acknowledgment there is something other and something more than caprice and chance. Strauss's observation that the world of angels is a compensation for the quantity of matter in creation, though it implies the admission that a materialistic worldview is not satisfactory to the human mind, is inadequate as an explanation of the belief in angels. Insufficient to that end is also the reasoning of Daub that human beings, situated as they are between good and evil, [imaginatively] created symbolic types in two directions, thus arriving at the idea of angels as well as devils.[24]

Belief in a spiritual world is not philosophical but religious in nature. It is intimately linked with revelation and miracle. Religion is inconceivable apart from revelation, and revelation cannot occur apart from the existence of a spiritual world above and behind this visible world, a spiritual world in communion with the visible world. In all religions, angels are not factors in the life of religion and ethics itself so much as in the revelation on which this life is built. Given with the fact of religion is the very belief that its deepest causes do not lie within the circle of visible things. Good and evil, both in a religious and an ethical sense, are rooted in a world other than that which appears to our senses. Belief in angels gives expression to that other world. While it does not constitute the essence and center of religion, belief in angels is connected with it. The transcendence of God, belief in revelation and miracle, the essence of religion—all this automatically carries with it belief in spiritual beings. The

---

23. H. N. De Fremery, *Handleiding tot de Kennis van het Spiritisme* (Bussum, 1904); idem, *Een Spiritistische Levensbeschouwing* (Bussum, 1907).

24. I. A. Dorner, *A System of Christian Doctrine*, trans. A. Cave and J. S. Banks (Edinburgh: T. & T. Clark, 1891), II, 98.

world that is present to our senses does not satisfy human beings. Ever and again we thirst for another world that is no less rich than this one. By way of a reaction to it, materialism evokes spiritualism. But the spiritism in which this spiritualism today manifests itself in the lives of many people is nothing other than a new form of superstition. It is hard to prove whether there is any reality underlying it. For not only is the history of spiritism rife with all sorts of deceptions and unmaskings, but there is no way to check whether the spirits that are said to appear are really the persons they claim to be. There always remains a huge distinction, therefore, between the strange and marvelous phenomena to which spiritism appeals and the explanations it gives for those phenomena. Many of these phenomena can be adequately explained in terms of psychology; but concerning the remainder it is absolutely not certain whether they must be attributed to the workings of deceased humans, or of demonic spirits, or of the hidden powers of nature.[25]

One thing is certain: in numerous cases spiritism has a very injurious effect on the psychic and physical health of its practitioners,[26] and it follows a path that is prohibited by Scripture (Deut. 18:11ff.). Between this world and the world beyond there is a gap that humans cannot bridge. If they nevertheless attempt to cross it, they lapse into superstition and become prey to the very spirits they have conjured up.

And just as between the world on this side of the grave and that on the other side there is a boundary which humans must respect, so also we humans here on earth have no knowledge of what takes place on other planets. Under the influence of the Copernican worldview, some people, thinking that the earth had lost its central significance for the universe, took pleasure in populating other planets not only with organic, intelligent beings but with superhuman creatures as well. But others are now also pulling back from these fantastic speculations. Some years ago the well-known British scientist Alfred R. Wallace demonstrated that no planet is inhabitable.[27] He based his arguments not on philosophical reasoning but on facts advanced by recent astronomy, physics, chemistry, and biology; and he simply poses the question of what these facts tell us about the inhabitability of the planets and, if they do not yield absolute proof one way or the other, what they suggest is the greatest likelihood. Now, spectral analysis has shown that the visible universe consists of the same chemical components as the earth, that the same laws of nature prevail everywhere, and accordingly, that also the development of animate beings is most probably bound to the same universal laws. Animate beings, though they may differ

25. O. Zöckler, "Spiritismus," *PRE³*, XVIII, 654–66; Traub, "Der Spiritismus," in *Kirchen und Sekten der Gegenwart*, ed. Ernst Kalb, 2d ed. (Stuttgart: Evangelische Gesellschaft, 1907), 485–549.

26. Zeehandelaar, "Het spiritistisch Gevaar," *De Gids* (August 1907): 306–37.

27. Alfred R. Wallace, *Man's Place in the Universe: A Study of the Results of Scientific Research in Relation to the Unity or Plurality of Worlds* (New York: McClure, Phillips, 1903); cf. H. H. Kuyper, *De Heraut* (October 1904), and subsequent issues; idem, "'s Menschen Plaats in het Heelal," *Wetenschappelijke Bladen* (April 1904): 67–78.

in kind among themselves, do nevertheless have many things in common: all need nitrogen, oxygen, hydrogen, and carbon, moderate temperatures, and the alternation of day and night. Countless conditions must therefore be met before the planets can be considered habitable by animate beings.

Now, Wallace demonstrates at great length how these conditions are met only on earth. The moon is not inhabitable since it has neither water nor atmosphere; the sun is not, because it is largely a gaseous body; Jupiter, Saturn, Uranus, and Neptune are not, because they are still in a seething state; Mercury and Venus are not, because they do not rotate and are therefore intolerably hot in one hemisphere and intolerably cold in the other. This leaves only Mars. This planet does indeed have day and night, summer and winter, good weather and bad, fog and snow, but the atmosphere there is as rare as the atmosphere on earth at 12,500 meters above sea level, while water is scarce and seas presumably nonexistent. So while Mars is not exactly uninhabitable, conditions there can hardly be considered favorable for animate beings. Granted, outside our solar system there are additionally numerous dark and light stars, but concerning them it also cannot be proved that they meet the conditions under which organic life is possible. Wallace thus comes to the conclusion that the earth is a highly privileged celestial body. According to him the stellar world in its totality is not infinitely large but has the shape of a sphere and is surrounded by a belt, the Milky Way, which is thickest in the middle, thus in conjunction with the sphere forming a spheroid. In that Milky Way there are still storms and disturbances, but within the sphere things are relatively quiet and conditions prevail that make the earth inhabitable and existence possible for animate beings, specifically also human beings. Even if it is true that the stellar world in its totality does not constitute a unity but that, as Prof. Kapstein contends, there are two distinct "universes of stellar systems,"[28] or that the present uninhabitability of the stars still does not rule out their inhabitability in an earlier or later time,[29] this much nevertheless is certain: belief in the existence of animate rational beings on planets other than the earth belongs totally to the realm of conjecture and is contradicted rather than confirmed by present-day science.

As a result of this pronouncement of science the doctrine of angels as Scripture presents it to us gains in value and significance. Philosophically, there is nothing that can be advanced against it. The idea of the existence of other and higher rational beings than humans has more in its favor than against it. In the religions, belief in such higher beings is a more than accidental component. And revelation involving this belief gains in reality and liveliness. But while in various religions and spiritistic theories this doctrine of angels is distorted, the boundary between God and his creatures erased, and the distinction

---

28. H. H. Turner, "Man's Place in the Universe," *Fortnightly Review* (April 1907): 600–610.

29. Alfred H. Kellogg, "The Incarnation and Other Worlds," *Princeton Theological Review* 3 (April 1905): 177–99.

between revelation and religion denied, yet in Scripture this doctrine again surfaces in a way that does not rob God of his honor and leaves the purity of religion untouched. For the Christian the revelation given in Scripture is the sure foundation also of belief in angels. In an earlier time people sought to prove the existence of good and especially of bad angels historically, that is, from oracles, appearances, ghosts, the demon-possessed, and so on.[30] But these proofs were no more convincing than those based on reason. In Scripture, on the other hand, the existence of angels is taught very clearly. Spinoza and Schleiermacher, to be sure, advanced against the teaching that Christ and the apostles spoke about angels from a stance of accommodation to folk belief and did not themselves teach anything positive about them. But Jesus and the apostles themselves openly and repeatedly expressed their belief in angels (e.g., Matt. 11:10 [*angelos*, messenger]; 13:39; 16:27; 18:10; 24:36; 26:53; Luke 20:36; 1 Cor. 6:3; Heb. 12:22; 1 Pet. 1:12; etc.). When we speak of elves and fairies, everybody knows this is meant figuratively; but in Jesus' time belief in angels was universal. When Jesus and the apostles spoke of angels, everyone within earshot had to think they themselves believed in them. The ultimate ground for our belief in angels, accordingly, lies also in revelation. Christian experience as such does not teach us anything on this subject. The object of true faith is the grace of God in Christ. Angels are not factors in our religious life, neither are they objects of our trust or our worship. Nowhere in Scripture are they such objects, and therefore they may not be that for us either. In the Protestant confessions there is therefore very little mention of angels.[31] Especially the Reformed tended in this connection to sin more by defect than by excess. In Reformed Catholicism, angelology occupies a much larger place, but there too the subject distorts the religion and obscures the glory of God. In short, though angels are not a factor or an object in our religion, in the history of revelation they are nevertheless of great importance, and especially from this fact they derive their value for the religious life.

THE ANGELS IN SCRIPTURE

[262] The name "angel," under which we usually subsume the entire class of higher spiritual beings, is not a name deriving from their nature *(nomen naturae)* but from their office *(nomen officii)*. The Hebrew *mal'āk* simply means "messenger," "envoy," and can also mean a human being sent either by other humans (Job 1:14; 1 Sam. 11:3; etc.) or by God (Hag. 1:13; Mal. 2:7; 3:1). The same thing is true of *angelos*, which is repeatedly used to denote humans

---

30. T. Aquinas, *Summa theol.*, I, qu. 50, art. 1; J. Zanchi(us), *Op. theol.*, II, 2; G. J. Vossius, "De orig. ac prog. idol.," I, ch. 6; G. Voetius, *Select. disp.*, I, 985–1017.

31. Belgic Confession, art. 12; Heidelberg Catechism, Lord's Day 49 (ed. note: Bavinck's own reference is to questions 112 and 117; the former mentions the devil, but the latter mentions no spiritual beings other than God); H. A. Niemeyer, *Collectio confessium in ecclesiis reformatis publicatorum* (Leipzig: Klinkhardt, 1840), 315–16, 476.

(Matt. 11:10; Mark 1:2; Luke 7:24, 27; 9:52; Gal. 4:14; James 2:25). In some translations it is erroneously reproduced by "angel" instead of "messenger" (e.g., Gal. 4:14; Rev. 1:20). In Scripture there is no common distinguishing name for the entire class of spiritual beings, though they are frequently called "sons of God" ([KJV, NRSV note] Job 1:6; 2:1; 38:7; Ps. 29:1; 89:6); "spirits" (1 Kings 22:19ff.; Heb. 1:14); "holy ones" ([Deut. 33:2–3;] Ps. 89:5, 7; Zech. 14:5; Job 5:1; 15:15; Dan. 8:13); "watchers" (Dan. 4:13, 17, 23).

There are distinct kinds and classes of angels, each of which has a name of its own. The world of angels is as richly varied as the material world, and just as in the material world there is a wide assortment of creatures that nevertheless jointly form a single whole, so it is in the world of spirits. First to be mentioned in Scripture are the *cherubim*. In Genesis 3:24 they act as guards to protect the garden. In the tabernacle and temple they are depicted with faces that are turned to the mercy seat and with wings that cover the mercy seat (Exod. 25:18ff.; 37:8–9; 1 Chron. 28:18; 2 Chron. 3:13; Heb. 9:5), between which the Lord sits enthroned (Ps. 80:1; 99:1; Isa. 37:16). When God comes down to earth he is represented as riding the cherubim (2 Sam. 22:11; Ps. 18:10; 104:3; Isa. 66:15; Heb. 1:7). In Ezekiel 1 and 10 they appear under the name of "living creatures," four in number, in the form of humans, each with four wings and four faces, namely, that of a human, a lion, an ox, and an eagle, while in Revelation 4:6f., as the four living creatures *(zōa),* each with one face [plus eyes behind] and six wings, they surround the throne of God and sing the "thrice-holy" night and day. The name *kĕrûbîm* is variously derived: sometimes from כ and רב, meaning "many" (Hengstenberg); then from רכיב, meaning "wagon"; or also from כרב (Arab.), meaning "to frighten," hence "horrible beings"; but mostly from a stem that means "to seize," "to hold onto" (cf. γρυψ [Greek, "griffin"]).[32]

There is similar disagreement about the nature of the cherubim. Some exegetes consider them to be mythical beings, others as symbolic figures, still others as divine forces in creation, or as the original term for thunderclouds or storms.[33] But in Genesis 3:24, Ezekiel 1, and Revelation 4 they are clearly represented as animate personal beings. Even the human form in them is predominant (Ezek. 1:5). But inasmuch as they are beings of extraordinary human strength and glory, Scripture uses symbolic representation to give us some idea of their spiritual nature. They are pictured as "living beings" *(zōa)* in whom God's power and strength come to expression with greater vividness than in a frail human being. They have the power of an ox, the majesty of a lion, the speed of an eagle, and on top of this, the intelligence of a human being. The wings with which they fly and the sword with which they guard

32. F. Delitzsch, *A New Commentary on Genesis,* trans. Sophia Taylor (Edinburgh: T. & T. Clark, 1899), I, 73–76 (on Gen. 3:24); idem, *Biblical Commentary on the Psalms,* trans. Francis Bolton (Edinburgh: T. & T. Clark, 1871), I, 256–57 (on Ps. 18:10).

33. R. Smend, *Lehrbuch der alttestamentlichen Religionsgeschichte* (Freiburg: J. C. B. Mohr, 1893), 21ff.

the garden point to the same attributes. From this representation, which is not a depiction but symbolic, we learn that among the angels the cherubim are also highly positioned beings who more than any other creatures reveal the power, majesty, and glory of God; they are therefore charged with the task of guarding the holiness of God in the garden of Eden, in the tabernacle and temple, and also in God's descent to earth.[34]

Then, in Isaiah 6, there is mention of the *seraphim (śĕrāpîm)*, a word that is probably derived from the Arabic stem *sarufa* (it was noble). In this passage they are also symbolically represented in human form, but with six wings, two of them to cover the face, two to cover the feet, and two for the swift execution of God's commands. In distinction from the cherubim, they stand as servants around the king, who is seated on his throne; they acclaim his glory and await his commands. Among the angels seraphim are the noble ones, cherubim the powerful. The former guard the holiness of God; the latter serve at the altar and effect atonement. Finally, in Daniel we further encounter two angels with proper names: Gabriel (8:16; 9:21 [cf. 10:5–6]) and Michael (10:13, 21; 12:1). Contrary to the opinion of many earlier and later interpreters, like the Van den Honerts, Burman, Witsius, Hengstenberg, Zahn (et al.), they are to be considered created angels and must not be identified with the Son of God.[35]

According to the New Testament, there are various classes of angels. The angel Gabriel appears in Luke 1:19, 26. Michael appears in Jude 9, Revelation 12:7, and 1 Thessalonians 4:16 [unnamed]. Included among the angels there are also principalities and powers (Eph. 3:10; [6:12;] Col. 2:10); dominions (Eph. 1:21; Col. 1:16), thrones (Col. 1:16), powers (Eph. 1:21; [Rom. 8:38–39;] 1 Pet. 3:22)—all of them terms that point to a distinction in rank and dignity among the angels. In John's Apocalypse, finally, seven angels repeatedly and clearly come into the foreground (8:2, 6; 15:1; etc.). Add to this that the number of angels is very high. This is indicated by the words *Sabaoth* [hosts] and *Mahanaim* [camps] (Gen. 32:1–2), legions (Matt. 26:53), host (Luke 2:13), and the numbers of [myriads or] a thousand times a thousand (Deut. 33:2; Ps. 68:17; Dan. 7:10; Jude 14; Rev. 5:11; 19:14).

Such large numbers naturally call for distinction in order and rank—all the more because angels, unlike humans, are not related by family and are therefore much more alike in many respects. Scripture, accordingly, clearly teaches that among angels there are all kinds of distinctions of rank and status, of dignity and ministry, of office and honor, even of class and kind. This splendid idea of diversity in unity may not be abandoned, even though it was elaborated on a fantastic scale by Jews and Catholics. The Jews made all sorts of distinc-

---

34. Johannes Nikel, *Die Lehre des Alten Testamentes über die Cherubim und Seraphim* (theol. diss., Würzburg; Breslau: Grass Barth, 1890).

35. Wilhelm Lueken, *Michael: Eine Darstellung und Vergleichung der jüdischen und der morgenländisch-christlichen Tradition von Erzengel Michael* (Göttingen: Vandenhoeck & Ruprecht, 1898).

tions among the angels.[36] Initially, in the early church, people were content with the data of Scripture.[37] Augustine still maintained that he did not know how the society of angels was organized.[38] But Pseudo-Dionysius, in his *The Celestial Hierarchy* and *The Ecclesiastical Hierarchy*, offered a schematic division. Proceeding from the idea that at the creation God, as it were, left his oneness behind and entered into multiplicity, he teaches that all things proceed from God in an ever-descending series and so again successively return to him. God is the center, and creatures gather peripherally around him. There is a twofold hierarchy of things, one celestial and the other ecclesiastical. The celestial hierarchy is formed by three classes of angels. The first and highest class exclusively serves God; it embraces the seraphim, who unceasingly behold the being of God; the cherubim, who ponder his decrees; and the thrones, who adore his judgments. The second class serves the visible and invisible creation; it embraces the dominions, who order the things that must happen according to God's will; the powers, who execute the things decreed; and the authorities, who complete the task. The third class serves the earth, both individuals and peoples; it embraces the principalities, who foster the general well-being of human beings; the archangels, who guide particular nations; and the angels, who watch over individual persons. Of that celestial hierarchy the ecclesiastical hierarchy is a mirror: in its mysteries (baptism, the Eucharist, ordination), its functionaries (bishop, priest, deacon), and its laity (catechumens, Christians, monks). This hierarchy as a whole has its origin and head in Christ, the incarnate Son of God, and its goal in deification. This classification of Pseudo-Dionysius, who divulges the celestial and earthly hierarchy as an intimate idea of the Roman Catholic system, found fertile soil and was generally accepted.[39]

Now, Scripture also clearly teaches the distinction and ranking of angels. Some scholars erroneously think that, though different names are used, the reference is always to the same angels, only viewed each time from a different angle.[40] It must even be acknowledged that this ranking has not sufficiently come into its own in Protestant theology. There is order and rank among those thousands of beings. God is a God of order in all the churches (1 Cor. 14:33, 40). The realm of spirits is no less rich and splendid than the realm of material beings. But the [celestial] hierarchy of Roman Catholic doctrine far exceeds the revelation of God in his Word. It was therefore unanimously repudiated by the Protestants.[41] Similarly, all calculations concerning the number of the

36. F. W. Weber, *System der altsynagogalen palästinischen Theologie* (Leipzig: Dörffling & Franke, 1880), 161f.

37. Irenaeus, *Against Heresies,* II, 54; Origen, *On First Principles,* I, 5.

38. Augustine, *Enchiridion,* 58.

39. John of Damascus, *Exposition of the Orthodox Faith,* II, 3; P. Lombard, *Sent.,* II, dist. 9; T. Aquinas, *Summa theol.,* I, qu. 108; D. Petavius, "De angelis," in *Theol. dogm.,* bk. II; J. H. Oswald, *Angelologie* (Paderborn: F. Schöningh, 1883), 57f.

40. J. C. K. von Hofmann, *Der Schriftbeweis,* 3 vols. (Nördlingen: Beck, 1857–60), I, 301.

41. J. Calvin, *Commentaries on the Epistles of Paul the Apostle to the Galatians, Ephesians, Philippians, and Colossians,* trans. T. H. L. Parker and ed. David W. Torrance and Thomas F. Torrance (Grand Rapids:

angels were considered futile and unfruitful, as those of Augustine, for example, who supplemented the number of the angels, after the fall of some, with the number of predestined humans;[42] or of Gregory, who believed that the number of people who were saved would be equal to the number of angels who remained faithful;[43] or of William of Paris, who called the number of angels infinite; or of Hilary and many others, who on the basis of Matthew 18:10 thought that the ratio of the number of humans to that of angels was 1 to 99;[44] or of G. Schott, who put the number of the angels at a thousand billion.[45] Nor were they much interested in the question of whether the angels among themselves were differentiated in essence and species. Thomas was very firm on this teaching,[46] but most of the church fathers were of a different mind.[47] However many distinctions there may have been among the angels, Scripture does not discuss them and offers only scant information. In relation to us humans their unity comes to the fore much more than their diversity: they all have a spiritual nature, they are all called "ministering spirits," and they all find their primary activity in the glorification of God.

ANGELIC NATURE: UNITY AND CORPOREALITY

[263] That unity comes out, in the first place, in the fact that they are all created beings. Schelling may say that the good angels, as pure potencies, are uncreated,[48] but the creation of angels is clearly stated in Colossians 1:16 and implied in the creation of all things (Gen. 1:1–2:4; Ps. 33:6; Neh. 9:6; John 1:3; Rom. 11:36; Eph. 3:9; Heb. 1:2). About the *time* of their creation, however, little can be said with certainty. Many church fathers, appealing to Job 38:4–7, believed that the angels were created before all [other] things.[49] The Socinians[50] and the Remonstrants[51] agreed and in this manner weakened the distinction between the Logos and the angels. But this idea has no support in Scripture. Nothing is anterior to the creation of heaven and earth, of which Genesis 1:1 speaks. Job 38:4–7 indeed teaches that, like the stars, they were present at the time of creation, but not that they already existed before the

---

Eerdmans, 1965), 137 (on Eph. 1:21); G. Voetius, *Select. disp.,* I, 882f.; A. Rivetus, *Op. theol.,* III, 248f.; J. Quenstedt, *Theologia,* I, 443, 450; J. Gerhard, *Loci theol.,* V, c. 4, sect. 9.

42. Augustine, *Enchiridion,* 29; idem, *City of God,* XXII, 1; Anselm, *Cur Deus homo,* I, 18.

43. P. Lombard, *Sent.,* II, 9.

44. D. Petavius, "De angelis," in *Theol. dogm.,* I, ch. 14.

45. C. Busken Huet, *Het Land van Rembrandt,* 2d rev. ed., 2 vols. (Haarlem: H. D. Tjeenk Willink, 1886), II, 2, 37.

46. T. Aquinas, *Summa theol.,* I, qu. 50, art. 4.

47. John of Damascus, *Exposition of the Orthodox Faith,* II, 3; Petavius, "De angelis," in *Theol. dogm.,* I, ch. 14; G. Voetius, *Select. disp.,* V, 261.

48. F. W. J. Schelling, *Werke,* II, 4, 284.

49. Origen, *Homily on Genesis I;* Basil, *Hexaemeron,* homily 1; Gregory of Nazianzen, *Orations,* 38; John of Damascus, *Exposition of the Orthodox Faith,* II, 3; Pseudo-Dionysius, *The Divine Names,* 5.

50. J. Crell, "Liber de deo," 1, 18, in *Opera omnia.*

51. S. Episcopius, *Inst. theol.,* IV, 3, 1; P. van Limborch, *Theol. christ.,* II, 210, 4.

beginning of creation. On the other hand, it is certain that the angels were created before the seventh day, when heaven and earth and all the host of them were finished and God rested from his labor (Gen. 1:31; 2:1–2). As for the rest, we are in the dark. It may, however, be considered likely that, just as in Genesis 1:1 the earth was created as such but still had to be further prepared and adorned, so also heaven was not completed at a single stroke. The word "heaven" in verse 1 is proleptic. Only later in the history of revelation does it become evident what is implied in it.[52] Scripture sometimes speaks of heaven as the sky with its clouds (Gen. 1:8, 20; 7:11; Matt. 6:26 [ET: "air"]); then as the stellar heavens (Deut. 4:19; Ps. 8:3; Matt. 24:29); and finally as the abode of God and his angels (Ps. 115:16; 2:4; 1 Kings 8:27; 2 Chron. 6:18; Matt. 6:19–21; Heb. 4:14; 7:26; 8:1–2; 9:2ff.; etc.). Now, just as the heavens of the clouds and of the stars only came into being in the course of six days, it is possible and even likely that also the third heaven with its inhabitants was formed in stages. To the extent that we think of that spiritual realm as being more fully furnished and populated, even far surpassing the material world in diversity, it is all the more plausible to posit a certain interval of time for the preparation of that heaven as well, even though the creation story does not breathe a word about it.

Second, the unity of angels is evident from the fact that they are all spiritual beings. On this subject, however, there was at all times much difference of opinion. The Jews attributed to them bodies that were airy or fiery in nature,[53] and in this respect they were followed by most of the church fathers.[54] At the Second Council of Nicaea (787), the patriarch Tarasius read a dialogue composed by a certain John of Thessalonica, in which the latter asserted that the angels had delicate, refined bodies and might therefore be depicted, adding that they were spatially defined and had appeared in human form and were therefore depictable. The Synod registered its agreement with this view.[55] But gradually, as the line between spirit and matter was drawn more sharply, many authors attributed to angels a purely spiritual nature.[56] The Fourth Lateran Council in 1215 called the nature of angels "spiritual,"[57] and most Catholic and Protestant theologians concurred in this judgment. Nevertheless, later a certain corporeality of angels was also taught from time to time by Catholics, such as Cajetan, Eugubinus, Bannez, as well as by such Reformed theologians as Zanchius and Vossius;[58] and by Episcopius, Vorstius, Poiret, Böhme, Leibniz,

---

52. *Gebhardt, "Der Himmel im N.T.," *Zeitschrift für kirchliche Wissenschaft und kirchliches Leben* 7 (1886); Cremer, "Himmel," *PRE³*, VIII, 80–84.

53. F. W. Weber, *System der altsynagogalen palästinischen Theologie*, 161f.

54. Justin Martyr, *Dialogue with Trypho*, 57; Origen, *On First Principles*, I, 6; Basil, *On the Holy Spirit*, 16; Tertullian, *On the Flesh of Christ*, 6; Augustine, *On the Trinity*, II, 7.

55. J. Schwane, *Dogmengeschichte*, 4 vols. (Freiburg i.B.: Herder, 1882–95), II, 235.

56. John of Damascus, *Exposition of the Orthodox Faith*, II, 3; T. Aquinas, *Summa theol.*, I, qu. 50, art. 1.; I, qu. 51, art. 1.

57. Denzinger, *Enchiridion*, 355.

58. J. Zanchi(us), *Op. theol.*, 69; G. J. Vossius, "De orig. ac prog. idol.," I, 2, 6.

Wolff, Bonnet, Reinhard, and so on; and in modern times by Kurtz, Beck, Lange, Kahnis, Vilmar, and others.[59] The chief reason for this opinion is that the concept of a purely spiritual, incorporeal nature is metaphysically inconceivable as well as incompatible with the concept of "creature." God is purely Spirit, but he is also simple, omnipresent, eternal. But angels are bounded in relation to time and space; if they really move from one place to another, they have to be—in their own way—corporeal. Similarly, angels are not simple like God but composed of matter and form. For that reason also, a certain material—finely ethereal, to be sure—corporeality has to be attributed to them. Added to this line of thought was the exegesis that considered the "sons of God" in Genesis 6 as angels. This exegesis of Philo, Josephus, the Jews, and the Septuagint [LXX, i.e., Greek Old Testament] was taken over by many church fathers:[60] Justin, Irenaeus, Clement, Tertullian, Lactantius, Cyprian, and Ambrose (et al.); it was adopted also by Luther and again defended in modern times by Ewald, Baumgarten, Hofmann, Kurtz, Delitzsch, Hengstenberg, Köhler, and Kübel (et al.). In addition, in arguing for the corporeality of angels, people appeal to their appearances, to certain special texts in Holy Scripture, such as Psalm 104:4; Matthew 22:30; Luke 20:36; and 1 Corinthians 11:10; and sometimes also to the fact that as inhabitants of the stars they certainly have to be corporeal.

Over against all these arguments, however, stands the clear pronouncement of Holy Scripture that the angels are spirits (*pneumata*; Matt. 8:16; 12:45; Luke 7:21; 8:2; 11:26; Acts 19:12; [23:8;] Eph. 6:12; Heb. 1:14), who do not marry (Matt. 22:30), are immortal (Luke 20:35–36) and invisible (Col. 1:16), may be "legion" in a restricted space (Luke 8:30), and like spirits, have no flesh and bones (Luke 24:39). Moreover, the conception that the "sons of God" *(bĕnê-hāĕlōhîm)* in Genesis 6:2 are angels and not men is untenable. Though this designation is used repeatedly for angels (Job 1:6; 2:1; 38:7), it can also very well denote humans (Deut. 32:5–6; Hos. 1:10 [2:1 MT]; Ps. 80:17 [16 MT]; 73:15), and is in any case inapplicable to bad angels, who must have committed their sin on earth. Moreover, the expression "took to wife" *lqḥ ʾšh* in Genesis 6:2 is always used with reference to a lawful marriage and never to fornication. Finally, the punishment of the sin is imposed only on humans, for they are the guilty party, and there is no mention of angels (Gen. 6:3, 5–7). Neither do the other Scripture passages prove the corporeality of angels. Psalm 104:4 (cf. Heb. 1:7) only says that God uses his angels as ministers, just as wind and fire

59. J. H. Kurtz, *The Bible and Astronomy*, 191–207; Johann Tobias Beck, *Die christliche Lehr-Wissenschaft nach biblische Urkunden*, 2d ed. (Stuttgart: Steinkopf, 1875), I, 176; J. P. Lange, *Christliche Dogmatik*, II, 578; K. F. A. Kahnis, *Die lutherische Dogmatik* (Leipzig: Dörffling & Franke, 1861–68), I, 443; A. F. C. Vilmar, *Handbuch der evangelischen Dogmatik* (Gütersloh: Bertelsmann, 1895), I, 306; K. Keerl, "Die Fixstern und die Engel," 235–47; cf. F. Delitzsch, *A System of Biblical Psychology*, 2d ed. (Edinburgh: T. & T. Clark, 1875), 78–87.

60. Justin Martyr, *Second Apology*, 5 (ed. note: Bavinck erroneously cites *Apol.* I, 1 here); Irenaeus, *Against Heresies*, IV, 16, 2; V, 29, 2.

serve to carry out his commands, but absolutely not that the angels are changed into wind or fire. Matthew 22:30 asserts that after the resurrection believers will be like the angels in that they will not marry, but says nothing about the corporeality of angels. And when 1 Corinthians 11:10 says that wives, as a sign of their subordination to their husbands, should cover their heads in church in order not to displease the good angels who are present in the church, there is no reason here to think of bad angels who would otherwise be seduced by the women. As to angel appearances, it is indeed certain that they always occurred in visible corporeal form, just as symbolic representations always show angels in visible forms as well. But this still does not imply anything in favor of their corporeality. God, remember, is spirit and is nevertheless envisioned by Isaiah (ch. 6) as a King sitting on his throne. Christ appeared in the flesh and is still truly God. Both in their appearances and in symbolism, the angels continually assume different forms. The representations of the cherubim in Genesis 3:24, above the ark of the covenant, in Ezekiel, and in the Apocalypse, are all different; and the forms in which they appear are far from identical (Gen. 18; Judg. 6:11–12; 13:6; Dan. 10:5–11; Matt. 28:2–3; Luke 2:9; Rev. 22:8). How these bodies are to be understood is another question. One cannot say with certainty whether they were real bodies or only apparently real.[61]

The strongest proof for the corporeality of angels, as stated above, is derived from philosophy. But in this connection a variety of misunderstandings plays a role. If corporeality only meant that the angels are limited in both time and space, and are not simple like God, in whom all attributes are identical with his essence, then a certain type of corporeality would have to be attributed to the angels. But usually corporeality does entail a certain materiality, even if it were of a more refined nature than in the case of man and animals. And in that sense there can and may be no ascription of a body to angels. Matter and spirit are mutually exclusive (Luke 24:39). It is a form of pantheistic identity philosophy to mix the two and to erase the distinction between them. And Scripture always maintains the distinction between heaven and earth, angels and humans, the spiritual and the material, invisible and visible things (Col. 1:16). If, then, angels are to be conceived as spirits, they relate differently—more freely—to time and space than humans. On the one hand, they do not transcend all space and time as God does, for they are creatures and therefore finite and limited. Theirs is not a space that is completely filled *(ubi repletivum)*; they are not omnipresent or eternal. Nor do they occupy a circumscribed space *(ubi circumscriptivum)* like our bodies, for the angels are spirits and therefore have no dimensions of length and breadth, hence no extension or diffusion through space. It was usually said, therefore, that theirs was a defined or definite space *(ubi definitivum)*. That is, as finite and limited beings, they are always somewhere. They cannot be in two places at once. Their presence is not extensive but punctual; and

61. John of Damascus, *Expositon of the Orthodox Faith,* II, 3; T. Aquinas, *Summa theol.,* I, qu. 51, art. 1–3; F. Turretin, *Institutes of Elenctic Theology,* VII, 6, 5.

they are spatially so free that they can move at lightning speed and cannot be obstructed by material objects; their translocation is immediate. Of course, such speed of movement and such temporal and spatial freedom that nevertheless is not atemporal or nonspatial, is inconceivable to us. But Scripture clearly refers to it; and in the speed of thought and imagination, of light and electricity, we have analogies that are not to be despised.[62]

[264] The unity of angels is further manifest in the fact that they are all rational beings, endowed with intellect and will. Both of these faculties are repeatedly attributed in Scripture to both good and bad angels (Job 1:6f.; Zech. 3:1ff.; Matt. 8:28ff.; 18:10; 24:36; 2 Cor. 11:3; Eph. 6:11; etc.). All sorts of personal attributes and activities occur in their existence, such as self-consciousness and speech (Luke 1:19f.), desiring (1 Pet. 1:12), rejoicing (Luke 15:10), worshiping (Heb. 1:6), believing (James 2:19), lying (John 8:44), sinning (1 John 3:8; etc.). In addition, great power is ascribed to them; the angels are not timid beings but an army of mighty heroes (Ps. 103:20; Luke 11:15ff.; Col. 1:16; Eph. 1:21; 3:10; 2 Thess. 1:7; Acts 5:19; Heb. 1:14). On this ground it is incorrect, with Schelling and others, to view angels as qualities or forces. Still, it is desirable, in our description of the personality of angels, to stick with the simplicity of Holy Scripture. Augustine distinguished two kinds of knowledge in angels: one knowledge they acquired, as it were, at the dawn of creation, a priori, via the vision of God; and another they acquired, as it were, in the evening of creation, a posteriori, from their contemplation of creatures.[63] The Scholastics not only adopted this distinction but tried to define the nature and extent of that knowledge more precisely. That knowledge is not, as in the case of God, identical with their being and substance. Nor is their knowledge acquired by sense perception. The distinction between potential and active understanding does not apply to them. Their power to understand is never purely a faculty, never at rest, but always active. They cannot *be* without knowing: they know themselves, their own being, by themselves, completely and immutably. They know created things, not from their appearance, but via innate ideas; not by abstraction and discursively, but intuitively and intellectually. And while the angels do not know [things] immediately through their natural powers but by having the form stamped upon them *(per speciem impressam)* through and simultaneously with their own being, still, in the supernatural order to which the angels have been elevated, they know God by immediate vision.[64] Some even taught—in the interest of defending prayer addressed to the angels and

---

62. Augustine, *City of God*, XI, 9; John of Damascus, *Exposition of the Orthodox Faith*, II, 3; T. Aquinas, *Summa theol.*, I, qu. 52–53; G. Voetius, *Select. disp.*, V, 252f.: F. A. Phillipi, *Kirchliche Glaubenslehre* (Gütersloh: C. Bertelsmann, 1902), II, 302; J. H. Oswald, *Angelologie*, 23–43.

63. Augustine, *Literal Meaning of Genesis*, V, 18; idem, *City of God*, XI, 29.

64. T. Aquinas, *Summa theol.*, I, qu. 54–58; idem, *Summa contra gentiles*, II, 96–101; II, 49; Bonaventure, *Sent.*, II, dist. 3, art. 4; II, dist. 4, art. 3; D. Petavius, "De angelis," in *Theol. dogm.*, I, chs. 6–9; J. Kleutgen, *Die Philosophie der Vorzeit Verheidigt*, 2d ed., 2 vols. (Münster: Theissing, 1878), I, 196f.; J. Oswald, *Angelologie*, 43–51.

to the saints—that angels, seeing God who sees all things, saw all things in him and therefore knew all our afflictions and needs.[65]

Protestants, on the other hand, were more cautious, warning people to be modest. In the way in which we humans arrive at knowledge there is so much that is mysterious. How much more would that be true of angels![66] One can only say that they are more richly endowed with knowledge than we here on earth (Matt. 18:10; 24:36). They acquire their knowledge from their own nature (John 8:44), from the contemplation of God's works (Eph. 3:10; 1 Tim. 3:16; 1 Pet. 1:12), and from revelations imparted to them by God (Dan. 8:15ff.; Rev. 1:1). Nevertheless, they are bound to objects (Eph. 3:10; 1 Pet. 1:12). They do not know either the secret thoughts of our hearts or those of each other (1 Kings 8:39; Ps. 139:2, 4; Acts 1:24 [yet cf. 2 Sam. 14:20]), so that also among themselves they need a language for communicating their thoughts (1 Cor. 13:1) and in general to be able, in their own way and in accordance with their own nature, to glorify God in speech and song.[67] They do not know the future, nor future contingencies, but can only conjecture (Isa. 41:22–23). They do not know the day of judgment (Mark 13:32). And their knowledge is capable of expansion (Eph. 3:10). To this we may certainly add that the knowledge and power of angels vary greatly among themselves. In this respect there also is variety and order. From the few angelic names that occur in Scripture, we may even infer that angels are not only members of distinct classes but are also distinct as persons. Each angel as such has an individuality of its own, even though we must reject the opinion of some Scholastics that every angel constitutes a particular species.[68]

Finally, the angels are unified by the fact that they are all moral beings. This is evident from the good angels, who serve God night and day, as well as from the bad angels, who did not remain in the truth. About the original state of angels Scripture says very little. It only testifies that at the end of the work of creation "God saw everything . . . and, behold, it was very good" (Gen. 1:31 KJV). In John 8:44, Jude 6, and 2 Peter 2:4, moreover, the original state of integrity of all angels is assumed. The same view is demanded by the theism of Scripture, which utterly rules out all Manichaeism. Imagination and reasoning had ample play, however, precisely because Scripture reveals so little. Augustine believed that at the very moment of their creation some of the angels had fallen and others had remained standing. To the latter, therefore, God granted the grace of perseverance along with their nature, "simultaneously constituting their nature and lavishing grace on them."[69] To this view scholasticism later

---

65. Gregory the Great, *Moralia in Iob.*, 12–13; T. Aquinas, *Summa theol.*, II, 2, qu. 83, art. 4; III, qu. 10, art. 2; R. Bellarmine, "De sanct. beat.," *Controversiis*, 1, 26.

66. J. Zanchi(us), *Op. theol.*, III, 108f.; G. Voetius, *Select. disp.*, V, 267; J. Gerhard, *Loci theol.*, V, c. 4, sect. 5.

67. D. Petavius, "De angelis," in *Theol. dogm.*, I, ch. 12.

68. Bonaventure, *Sent.*, II, dist. 4, art. 2; T. Aquinas, *Summa contra gentiles*, II, 52.

69. Augustine, *City of God*, XII, 9; cf. idem, *On Rebuke and Grace*, 11, 32.

appealed for its doctrine of the superadded gifts, also in the case of angels. According to Bonaventure,[70] Alexander of Hales, Peter Lombard, Duns Scotus (et al.), the angels first existed for a time as pure natures and later received the assistance of actual grace. But Thomas along with others believed that the distinction between nature and grace could only be understood logically, and that the grace to remain standing was granted to the different angels in various measure.[71] Equipped with that grace, the angels could merit the supreme, inadmissible blessedness that consists in the vision of God.[72] In the locus on man the doctrine of the superadded gifts will call for our special attention. Here we have to confine ourselves to pointing out that at least in the case of angels this doctrine lacks all basis in Scripture. Protestant theology, accordingly, rejected it unanimously. It was content to say that the angels who remained standing were confirmed in the good. And along with Augustine and the Scholastics, it maintained this position against Origen[73] and against the Remonstrants, who considered the will of the good angels as still mutable. Indeed, in Holy Scripture the good angels are always presented to us as a faithful company that invariably does the will of the Lord. They are called "angels of the LORD" (Ps. 103:20; 104:4), "elect" (1 Tim. 5:21), "holy ones" (Deut. 33:2–3; Matt. 25:31), "holy" or "of light" (Luke 9:26; Acts 10:22; 2 Cor. 11:14; Rev. 14:10). They daily behold God's face (Matt. 18:10) and are held up to us as examples (Matt. 6:10); someday believers will become like them (Luke 20:36).

ANGELS, HUMANITY, AND CHRIST

[265] In all these qualities of createdness, spirituality, rationality, and morality, angels are similar to humans. Now, precisely because in Scripture the unity of the angels is highlighted and their diversity recedes into the background, there is a danger that we will neglect the difference between angels and humans. The similarity seems far to surpass the difference between them. Both humans and angels are personal, rational, moral beings; both were originally created in knowledge, righteousness, and holiness; both were given dominion, immortality, and blessedness. In Scripture both are called the sons of God (Job 1:6; Luke 3:38). Still, the difference between them is most rigorously maintained in Scripture by the fact that humans *are,* but the angels are *never,* said to be created in the image of God. In theology this distinction is largely neglected. According to Origen the angels and the souls of humans are of the same species; the union of the soul with the body is a punishment for sin and therefore really accidental. Origen arrived at this position because he taught

---

70. Bonaventure, *Sent.,* II, dist. 4, art. 1, qu. 2.

71. T. Aquinas, *Summa theol.,* I, qu. 62, art. 3, 6.

72. D. Petavius, "De angelis," in *Theol. dogm.,* I, ch. 16; M. Becanus, "De angelis," in *Theol. schol.,* 2–3; *Theologia Wirceburgensis* (1880), III, 466f.; C. Pesch, *Praelectiones dogmaticae,* 9 vols. (Freiburg: Herder, 1902–10), III, 204f.; J. Oswald, *Angelologie,* 81f.; G. Jansen, *Prael. theol.,* II, 361f.

73. Origen, *On First Principles,* I, 5, 3, 4.

that all dissimilarity originated with the creature. In the beginning God created all things alike; that is, he only created rational beings, and all of these, angels and souls, the same. Dissimilarity originated among them by free will. Some remained standing and received a reward; others fell and received punishment. Souls were specifically united to bodies. Hence, the entire material world and all the diversity present in it, is due to sin and to the different degrees of sin. It does not exist to display God's goodness but to punish sin.[74] Now, the church rejected this teaching of Origen, and theology maintained the specific difference between humans and angels.[75] Nevertheless, to a degree the idea persists that the angels, since they are exclusively spiritual, are superior to humans and therefore have at least as much or even more right to be called "image-bearers of God."[76] In the hierarchy of creatures the angels, as purely spiritual beings, are the closest to God. "You were, and nothing was there besides out of which you made heaven and earth; things were of two kinds: one near you and the other near to nothing; one to which you alone would be superior; the other to which nothing would be inferior."[77] "Necessarily, then, he [God] brought forth not only the nature that is at the greatest distance from him—the physical—but also the one very close to him, the intellectual and incorporeal."[78] But Lutheran and Reformed theologians also often have lost sight of this distinction between humans and angels, and called the angels "image-bearers of God."[79] Only a handful, such as Theodoret, Macarius, Methodius, Tertullian (et al.), opposed this confusion.[80] Augustine expressly states: "God gave to no other creature than man the privilege of being after his own image."[81]

However great the resemblance between humans and angels may be, the difference is no less great. Indeed, various traits belonging to the image of God do exist in angels, but humanity alone *is* the image of God. That image does not just reside in what humans and angels have in common, but in what distinguishes them. The principal points of difference are these: first, an angel is spirit, and as spirit the angel is complete; man, on the other hand, is a combination of soul and body; the soul without the body is incomplete. Man, accordingly, is a rational but also a sensuous being. By the body man is bound to the earth, is part of the earth, and the earth is part of man. And of

---

74. T. Aquinas, *Summa theol.,* I, qu. 47, art. 2; J. Heinrich and C. Gutberlet, *Dogmatische Theologie,* V, 177.

75. T. Aquinas, *Summa theol.,* I, qu. 75, art. 7.

76. John of Damascus, *Exposition of the Orthodox Faith,* II, 3; T. Aquinas, *Summa theol.,* I, qu. 93, art. 3; idem, *Commentary on Sent.,* II, dist. 16; J. Oswald, *Angelologie,* 25.

77. Augustine, *Confessions,* XII, 7.

78. Bonaventure, *Breviloquiam,* II, 6.

79. Calvin, *Institutes,* I.xiv.3; A. Polanus, *Syn. theol.,* V, 10; *Synopsis purioris theologiae,* XII, 7; XIII, 17; A. Comrie and N. Holtius, *Examen van het Ontwerp van Tolerantie,* vol. 9: *Over de Staat des rechtschapen Mensch* (Amsterdam: Nicolaas Byl, 1757), 187; B. de Moor, *Comm. in Marckii Comp.,* II, 335; J. Gerhard, *Loci theol.,* V, c. 4, sect. 5; F. Delitzsch, *A System of Biblical Psychology,* 78.

80. D. Petavius, "De opificio sex dierum," in *Theol. dogm.,* II, ch. 3, §§4–8.

81. Cited by T. Aquinas, *Summa theol.,* I, qu. 93, art. 3; cf. S. Maresius, *Syst. theol.,* V, 37.

that earth man is head and master. After the angels had already been created, God said that he planned to create humankind and to give them dominion over the earth (Gen. 1:26). Dominion over the earth is integral to being human, a part of the image of God, and is therefore restored by Christ to his own, whom he not only ordains as prophets and priests, but also as kings. But an angel, however strong and mighty he may be, is a servant in God's creation, not a master over the earth (Heb. 1:14).

Second, as purely spiritual beings the angels are not bound to each other by ties of blood. There is among them no father-son relationship, no physical bond, no common blood, no consanguinity. However intimately they may share an ethical bond, they are disconnected beings, so that when many fell, the others could remain standing. In human beings, on the other hand, there is an adumbration of the divine being, in which there are also persons, united not only in will and affection, but also in essence and nature.

Third, there is consequently something called "humanity" but no "angelity" in that sense. In one man all humans fell, but the human race is also saved in one person. In humanity there could be an Adam and therefore also a Christ. The angels are witnesses, but humans are objects, of God's most marvelous deeds, the works of his grace. The earth is the stage of God's miraculous acts: here the war is fought, here the victory of God's kingdom is won, and angels turn their faces to the earth, longing to look into the mysteries of salvation (Eph. 3:10; 1 Pet. 1:12).

Fourth, angels may be the mightier spirits, but humans are the richer of the two. In intellect and power angels far surpass humans. But in virtue of the marvelously rich relationships in which humans stand to God, the world, and humanity, they are psychologically deeper and mentally richer. The relations that sexuality and family life, life in the family and state and society, life devoted to labor and art and science, bring with them make every human a microcosm, which in multifacetedness, in depth, and in richness far surpasses the personality of angels. Consequently also, the richest and most glorious attributes of God are knowable and enjoyable only by humans. Angels experience God's power, wisdom, goodness, holiness, and majesty; but the depths of God's compassions only disclose themselves to humans. The full image of God, therefore, is only unfolded in creaturely fashion in humans—better still, in *humanity.*

Finally, let me add that the angels therefore also stand in a totally different relation to Christ. That there exists a relation between Christ and the angels cannot be doubted. In the first place, various Scripture passages teach that all things (Ps. 33:6; Prov. 8:22ff.; John 1:3; 1 Cor. 8:6; Eph. 3:9–11; Heb. 1:2) and specifically also the angels (Col. 1:16) were created by the Son, and thus he is the "mediator of union" of all that was created. But in the second place, Ephesians 1:10 and Colossians 1:19–20 contain the profound idea that all things also stand in relation to Christ as the mediator of reconciliation. For God reconciled all things to himself by Christ and gathers them all under him as head. Granted—it is not that the relation consists, as many people have thought, in that Christ has acquired grace and glory for the good angels,[82] nor as others judged, that the angels could be called members of the church.[83] But it consists in the fact that all things, which have been disturbed and ripped apart by sin, are again united in Christ, restored in their original relationship, and are gathered up under him as head. Thus, while Christ is indeed the Lord and head, he is not the Reconciler and Savior of the angels. All things have been created by him, and therefore they are also created unto him so that he may return them, reconciled and restored, to the Father. But humans alone constitute the church of Christ; it alone is his bride, the temple of the Holy Spirit, the dwelling place of God.

THE MINISTRY OF ANGELS

[266] Corresponding to this angelic nature is their ministry and activity. In this connection Scripture makes a distinction between the extraordinary ministry and the ordinary ministry of angels. The extraordinary ministry does not begin until after the fall, having been necessitated by sin. It is an important component in special revelation. We first see the angels play a role in guarding Eden (Gen. 3:24); but then they appear to convey revelations, acting to bless or to punish in the history of the patriarchs and prophets and throughout the entire Old Testament. They appear to Abraham (Gen. 18), to Lot (Gen. 19), to Jacob (Gen. 28:12; 32:1); they function in the giving of the law (Heb. 2:2; Gal. 3:19; Acts 7:53); they take part in Israel's war (2 Kings 19:35; Dan. 10:13, 20); they announce the counsel of God to Elijah and Elisha, to Ezekiel, Daniel, and Zechariah. As if to prove that they are not remnants of polytheism and do not belong to a prehistoric age, their extraordinary ministry even broadens in the days of the New Testament. They are present at the birth of Jesus (Luke 1:13, 26–38; 2:10ff.) and at his temptation (Matt. 4:11); they accompany him throughout his entire earthly life (John 1:51) and appear especially at the time of his suffering (Luke 22:43), resurrection (Matt. 28), and ascension (Acts 1:10). Subsequently they reappear from time to time in the history of the apostles (Acts 5:19; 8:26; 12:7ff., 23; 27:23; Rev. 1:1); then they cease their extraordinary ministry and will only resume a public role at the return of Christ (Matt. 16:27; 25:31; Mark 8:38; Luke 9:26; 2 Thess. 1:7; Jude 14; Rev. 5:2; etc.), when they will do battle against God's enemies (Rev. 12:7; 1 Thess. 4:16; [2 Thess. 1:7–8;] Jude 9), gather the elect (Matt. 24:31), and cast the ungodly into the fire (Matt. 13:41, 49).

Accordingly, the extraordinary ministry of the angels consists in accompanying the history of redemption at its cardinal points. They themselves do not bring about salvation, but they do participate in its history. They

---

82. Cf. G. Voetius, *Select. disp.*, II, 262f.; J. Gerhard, *Loci theol.*, XXXI, c. 4, §42; and later in our discussion of the consummation (ed. note: see Herman Bavinck, *The Last Things: Hope for This World and the Next*, ed. John Bolt and trans. John Vriend [Grand Rapids: Baker, 1996], 142; *Reformed Dogmatics*, IV, #574).

83. J. Gerhard, *Loci theol.*, XXII, c. 6, sect. 9.

transmit revelations, protect God's people, oppose his enemies, and perform an array of services in the kingdom of God. Always, in this connection, they are active in the area of the church. Also, where they receive power over the forces of nature (Rev. 14:14–20; 16:4), or intervene in the fortunes of nations, this activity occurs in the interest of the church. In this ministry they never push aside the sovereignty of God, nor are they the mediators of God's fellowship with humans. But they are ministering spirits in the service of those who will inherit salvation. They especially serve God in the realm of grace, even though the realm of nature is not totally excluded in the process. Consequently, this extraordinary ministry automatically ceased with the completion of revelation. Whereas earlier they constantly had to transmit special revelations and descend to earth, now they rather serve as examples to us, and we rise toward them. As long as special revelation was not yet completed, heaven approached the earth and God's Son descended to us. Now Christ has appeared and the Word of God has been fully revealed to us. Consequently, the angels now look to the earth to learn from the church the manifold wisdom of God. What could the angels still give us now that God himself gave us his own Son?

But Scripture also speaks of an ordinary ministry of angels. The primary feature of that ministry is that they praise God day and night (Job 38:7; Isa. 6; Ps. 103:20; 148:2; Rev. 5:11). Scripture conveys the impression that they do this in audible sounds, even though we cannot imagine what their speech and songs are like. But part of this ordinary ministry is also the fact that they rejoice over the conversion of a sinner (Luke 15:10), watch over believers (Ps. 34:7; 91:11), protect the little ones (Matt. 18:10), are present in the church (1 Cor. 11:10; 1 Tim. 5:21), follow it on its journeys through history (Eph. 3:10), allow themselves to be taught by it (Eph. 3:10; 1 Pet. 1:12), and carry believers into Abraham's bosom (Luke 16:22). They are also active "by standing in the presence of God, assisting devout humans, and resisting devils and evil people."[84]

Scripture usually confines itself to this general description of the ordinary ministry of angels and does not go into detail. But theology was not content to stop there. In all kinds of ways it has elaborated this account, especially in the doctrine of guardian angels. The Greeks and Romans had something similar in view when they spoke of *daimones* (semidivine beings) and *genii*. They not only attributed to every human a good or evil genius but also spoke of the *genii* of houses, families, associations, cities, countries, peoples of the earth, sea, world, and so on. The Jews, appealing to Deuteronomy 32:8 and Daniel 10:13, assumed the existence of seventy angels of nations and further assigned a companion angel to every Israelite.[85] Christian theology soon adopted this view. The Pastor (Shepherd) of Hermas assigned to every

---

84. D. Hollaz, *Examen theologicum acroamaticum*, 390.
85. F. W. Weber, *System der altsynagogalen palästinischen Theologie*, 161f.

human two angels, "one for righteousness and the other for evil," and further placed the whole creation and the whole formation of the church under the guardianship of angels.[86] Origen had a special fondness for developing this doctrine of guardian angels. Sometimes—in his writings—every human has a good and a bad angel; sometimes he adds that only the good angels of baptized Christians see the face of God; sometimes he also says that only Christians and virtuous people have a guardian angel and that, depending on their merit, they receive either a lower-ranking or higher-ranking angel as their guardian. But he also assumes that there are special angels for churches, countries, peoples, the arts and sciences, plants, and animals. Raphael, for example, is the angel of healing; Gabriel, the angel of war; Michael, the angel of prayer, and so on.[87]

In substance, all the church fathers taught this, though there were differences of opinion concerning whether all humans or only Christians had a guardian angel; whether every human had only a good angel or also a bad angel; when the guardian angel was given to a human—at birth or at baptism; when the angel was taken from him or her—on attaining perfection or only at death. All were convinced that there were guardian angels not only for humans but also for countries, peoples, churches, dioceses, provinces, and so on.[88] In part this angelic protection was later restricted and in part it was expanded. It was restricted insofar as some of them, following Pseudo-Dionysius,[89] taught that the three top classes of angels (cherubim, seraphim, and thrones) only served God in heaven,[90] and expanded insofar as scholasticism figured that God's entire providence in nature and history, particularly in the movement of the stars, was mediated by angels.[91] Guardian angels for humans were universally accepted by Roman Catholic theologians and also recognized in the *Roman Catechism* (IV, ch. 9, qu. 4 and 5). But for the rest there is much difference of opinion among them on all the above points.[92] We find the same teaching in Luther,[93] but Lutheran theologians were usually more cautious.[94] Calvin rejected the notion of guardian angels,[95] and most Reformed scholars followed him;[96] only a

---

86. Pastor (Shepherd) of Hermas, II, *Commandment* 6.2; I, *Vision* 3.4.

87. Origen, *On First Principles*, I, 8; III, 3; idem, *Against Celsus*, V, 29; VIII, 31.

88. J. Schwane, *Dogmengeschichte*, II, 244.

89. Pseudo-Dionysius, *The Celestial Hierarchies*, 13.

90. T. Aquinas, *Summa theol.*, I, qu. 112.

91. T. Aquinas, *Summa theol.*, I, qu. 70, art. 3; I, qu. 110, art. 1; idem, *Summa contra gentiles*, III, 78f.; Bonaventure, *Sent.*, II, dist. 14, p. 1, art. 3, qu. 2.

92. Cf. D. Petavius, "De angelis," in *Theol. dogm.*, II, chs. 6–8; M. Becanus, "De angelis," in *Theol. schol.*, tr. III, 6; *Theol. Wirceburgensis* (1880), III, 480; C. Pesch, *Prael. dogm.*, III, 210; J. Oswald, *Angelologie*, 120f.

93. J. Köstlin, *The Theology of Luther in Its Historical Development and Inner Harmony*, trans. Charles E. Hay, 2 vols. (Philadelphia: Lutheran Publication Society, 1897), II, 345.

94. J. Gerhard, *Loci theol.*, V, c. 4, sect. 15; J. Quenstedt, *Theologia*, 1450; D. Hollaz, *Examen theol.*, 390.

95. J. Calvin, *Institutes*, I.xiv.7; *Commentary*, on Ps. 91 and Matt. 18:10.

96. G. Voetius, *Select. disp.*, I, 897.

few of them assumed the existence of guardian angels for humans.[97] In modern times the doctrine of guardian angels again found support in Hahn, Weiss, Ebrard, Vilmar, Martensen, and others.[98] The ordinary ministry of angels was further refined in the view that with their intercession on behalf of believers on earth, they were active for good in heaven. This, too, had already been taught by the Jews as well as by Philo, taken over by Origen[99] and the church fathers, and laid down in the Roman Catholic symbols.[100] The Lutheran confessional writings,[101] as well as Lutheran dogmaticians, still speak of this intercession as well.[102] In contrast, it is unanimously rejected by the Reformed.

For this special ministry of angelic protection and intercession an appeal is made to a number of Scripture passages, especially Deuteronomy 32:8; Daniel 10:13, 20; Matthew 18:10; Acts 12:15; Hebrews 1:14; Revelation 1:20; 2:1 and so on; Job 33:23; Zechariah 1:12; Luke 15:7; Revelation 18:1ff.; and especially to Tobit 12:12–15. By itself this doctrine of the protection and intercession of angels is not objectionable. That God often and even regularly employs angels, in special as well as in general revelation, is not impossible. Nor is it absurd to think that angels send up prayers to God on behalf of humans, inasmuch as they are interested in their fate and the progress of the kingdom of God in the history of humankind. But however unobjectionable these teachings may be as such, in relation to the protection and intercession of angels Scripture observes a sobriety that must also be normative for us. In Deuteronomy 32:8–9 (MT) we read that God, in apportioning the nations and dividing humankind, already thought of his people Israel and determined their dwelling "according to the number of the children of Israel" *(lĕmisppar bĕnê yiśrāʾēl),* so that Israel would receive an inheritance sufficient to accommodate its numbers. The Septuagint (LXX), however, translated these words by "according to the number of angels" *(kata arithmon angelōn)* and thereby occasioned the doctrine of "the angels of nations." The original text, meanwhile, does not say a word about this and therefore totally loses its function as proof text. The case is somewhat different with Daniel 10:13, 20. There we read that the figure who appeared

---

97. J. Zanchi(us), *Op. theol.,* III, 142; G. Bucanus, *Inst. theol.,* VI, 28; Maccovius, *Loci. comm.,* 394; A. Rivetus, *Op. theol.,* II, 250; cf. H. Heppe, *Reformed Dogmatics,* rev. and ed. Ernst Bizer, trans. G. T. Thomson (London: George Allen & Unwin, 1950; reprinted, Grand Rapids: Baker, 1978), 212–13; C. Vitringa, *Doctr. christ.,* II, 117.

98. B. Weiss, *Lehrbuch der biblischen Theologie des Neuen Testaments,* 594 (ed. note: Bavinck is likely referring to the 5th ed. [Berlin: W. Hertz, 1888] or 6th ed. [Berlin: Hertz (Besser), 1895]); J. H. A. Ebrard, *Christliche Dogmatik,* 2d ed., 2 vols. (Königsberg: A. W. Unzer, 1862–63), §239; A. F. C. Vilmar, *Handbuch der evangelischen Dogmatik* (Gütersloh: C. Bertelsmann, 1895), I, 310; H. Martensen, *Christian Dogmatics,* trans. W. Urwick (Edinburgh: T. & T. Clark, 1871), §69; Abraham Kuyper, *De Engelen Gods* (Amsterdam: Höveker & Wormser, n.d.), 279; Cremer, "Engel," *PRE³,* V, 364–72.

99. Origen, *Against Celsus,* VIII, 64.

100. Roman Catechism, ch. 12, qu. 5, no. 2.

101. Apology of the Augsburg Confession, art. 21 (ed. note: ET in *The Book of Concord: The Confessions of the Evangelical Lutheran Church,* ed. Robert Kolb and Timothy Wengert [Minneapolis: Fortress Press, 2000], 107–294); Smalcald Articles, II/2.

102. F. Philippi, *Kirchliche Glaubenslehre* (Gütersloh: Bertelsmann, 1902), II, 324.

to Daniel in verse 5 opposed the prince of Persia and—aided by Michael, who is called "one of the chief princes" (v. 13), the "great prince" and "protector" of the children of Israel (12:1; 10:21)—drove away that prince of Persia, then took his place among the kings of Persia. Calvin and Reformed exegetes after him usually identified that prince of Persia with the Persian kings. But it seems that we must interpret that prince to be someone else, namely, the guardian spirit of Persia. For first, there can be no doubt that Israel has such a guardian angel in Michael, who is called "your prince" (10:13, 21; 12:1). Second, the "kings of Persia" [MT, KJV] are clearly distinguished in 10:13 from that prince. And third, the analogy requires that the spiritual power on the one side should fight against a spiritual power on the other. The Book of Daniel, accordingly, really conveys a picture in which the war between the kingdom of God and the kingdoms of the world is not only conducted down here on earth but also in the realm of spirits between angels. And that is all we may infer from it. There is absolutely no claim here that every country and people has its own angel. But in the colossal struggle waged between Israel and Persia, that is, between the kingdom of God and that of Satan, there are on both sides angels who take part in the struggle and support the [opposing] peoples. Even less can we deduce from Revelation 1:20 (etc.) that every church has its angel, for the "angels" [*angeloi*, messengers] of the seven churches are nothing other than their ministers: they are totally viewed as the representatives of the churches. It is their works that are praised or blamed. It is to them the letters are addressed.

Most support for the doctrine of guardian angels comes from Matthew 18:10, a text undoubtedly implying that a certain class of angels is charged with the task of protecting "the little ones." However, there is here not even a hint that every elect person is assigned his or her own angel. This idea is found only in the apocryphal book of Tobit. But by that very fact this doctrine of guardian angels also betrays its origin. The doctrine is essentially of pagan origin and leads to all kinds of clever questions and futile issues. We do not know whether an angel is assigned to every human, and even to the anti-Christ, as Thomas thought,[103] or only to the elect, nor whether only a good or a bad angel accompanies everyone. Nor do we know when such an angel is given to a person or is taken away; or what the angel's precise ministry is. Consequently all we can say is that certain classes of angels are charged with the promotion of certain interests on earth. It is the same with the intercession of angels that is taught in Tobit 12:6–22, but which does not occur in Scripture. In Job 33:23, there is a reference to the "uncreated [intercessor] Angel." Luke 15:7, 10 also teaches that the angels rejoice over the repentance of one sinner, which indeed presupposes that the angels desire that repentance, but does not speak of intercession in the strict sense of the word. And while in Revelation 8:3 an angel indeed receives a censer with incense to make the prayers of the—inherently sinful—saints lovely and pleasing to the Lord, the text does not breathe

---

103. T. Aquinas, *Summa theol.*, I, qu. 113, art. 4.

a word about intercession. The angel is simply a servant; he does not build the altar; he does not himself prepare the incense but receives it and only lets the prayers, along with the fragrance of the incense, rise to God. The ministry he performs is like that of the seraphim in Isaiah 6:6–7.

VENERATION OF ANGELS

[267] This doctrine of guardian angels and their intercession, finally, also had the disadvantage that in practice it soon led to a veneration and worship of angels. Colossians 2:18 tells us that such "worship of angels" *(thrēskeia tōn angelōn)* already occurred in apostolic times. In his commentary on this passage Theodoret comments that in his day such angel worship was still being practiced in Phrygia, and that the Synod of Laodicea had prohibited it, lest God be abandoned.[104] Many church fathers cautioned against the veneration and adoration of angels.[105] At that time the conviction that only God may be worshiped and that angels are only entitled to "civil honor" was still universal. "We honor them with our love, not our servitude."[106] They are "rather to be imitated than called upon."[107] In his commentary on the Song of Solomon 8, Gregory the Great still says that, since Christ has come on earth, "the church is honored even by those very angels." In the Old Testament dispensation, Joshua worshiped the angel (Josh. 5:14), but in the New Testament, the angel rejected John's worship (Rev. 19:10; 22:9) because angels, though higher in rank, are nevertheless "fellow servants." Still, these warnings do serve as proof that in practice the boundaries between the worship of God and the respect due to angels were being wiped out. The invocation of angels was first clearly mentioned by Ambrose: "We to whom the angels have been given for assistance and protection ought to entreat them."[108]

Eusebius already made the distinction between the "veneration" *(timan)* that is fitting for us to offer to angels, and the "worship" *(sebein)* to which only God is entitled.[109] Augustine adopted it as a strategy for preventing the religious veneration of angels.[110] But before long that distinction was used to sanction the invocation of angels. This already occurred at the [Second] Council of Nicaea (787) and then also among the Scholastics.[111] The Council of Trent called such invocation "good and profitable" (Sess. 25). The Roman Catechism (III, ch. 2, qu. 4, no. 3) found warrant for it on the ground that the angels always behold the face of God and have taken upon themselves "the sponsorship of

---

104. J. Schwane, *Dogmengeschichte,* III, 245.

105. Irenaeus, *Against Heresies,* II, 32; Origen, *Against Celsus,* V, 4–5; VIII, 13; Athanasius, *Against the Arians,* II, 23; Augustine, *On True Religion,* 55; idem, *Confessions,* X, 42; idem, *City of God,* VIII, 25.

106. Augustine, *On True Religion,* 55.

107. Augustine, *City of God,* X, 26.

108. Ambrose, *De viduis,* ch. 9, §55.

109. Eusebius, *Praep. ev.*; Origen, *Against Celsus,* VIII, 13, 57.

110. Augustine, *City of God,* V, 15; VII, 32; X, 1.

111. P. Lombard, *Sent.,* III, dist. 9; T. Aquinas, *Summa theol.,* II, qu. 103, art. 3.

our salvation" *(patrocinium salutis nostrae)*. The Roman Breviary incorporated prayers [addressed to angels] in the Feast of the Angels, and Roman Catholic dogmaticians unanimously defend it,[112] although later they usually treat it under the heading of "the veneration of saints" *(cultus sanctorum)*.

Lutheran and Reformed people and virtually all Protestants were on solid ground, however, when they rejected the religious veneration of angels along with that of the saints.[113] For in the first place, there is not a single example of it in Scripture. True, Roman Catholics do base their position on certain Old Testament passages like Genesis 18:2; 32:26; 48:16; Exodus 23:20ff.; Numbers 22:31ff.; Joshua 5:14–15; Judges 13:17ff.; but in all these passages we are dealing, not with a created angel, but with "the angel of the LORD," and in the New Testament there is not even a semblance of proof for venerating angels. But that is not all: the veneration of angels is devoid of precept or example in Scripture; hence, Rome cannot even say with some semblance of reason that the veneration of angels and saints is not prohibited in Scripture and therefore permitted, and therefore that it does not actually impose and require it but only permits it and regards it as profitable.[114] The fact is that Scripture also clearly prohibits it (Deut. 6:13; 10:20; Matt. 4:10; Col. 2:18–19; Rev. 19:10; 22:9). According to Scripture, religious honor may be accorded only to God, and no creature is entitled to it. Roman Catholics have not had the courage to deny this altogether but, by the distinction between worship *(latria)* and homage *(dulia)*, they have nevertheless sought to justify the veneration of angels. Now, in Catholicism this is not a distinction between religious and civil honor, which might be considered reasonable; instead, in Catholicism the veneration of angels and saints definitely has a religious character, though it is relative. The *dulia* is religious worship. But thus understood it is condemned by both Scripture and practice. Scripture knows no twofold religious veneration, one of a lower kind and the other of a higher kind. Roman Catholics, accordingly, admit that worship *(latria)* and homage *(dulia)* are not distinguished in Scripture as they distinguish them, and also that these words furnish no etymological support for the way they are used. The Hebrew word ʿ*abad* is sometimes rendered by *douleia*, sometimes by *latreia* (cf. Deut. 6:13 and 1 Sam. 7:3; 1 Sam. 12:20 and Deut. 10:12); and Israel is commanded to abstain both from *douleuein* and *latreuein* of other gods (Exod. 20:5; Jer. 22:9). Similarly the Hebrew word *šārat* is translated by both Greek words (Ezek. 20:32; Isa. 56:6). Repeatedly *douleuein* is used with reference to God [or Christ] (Matt. 6:24; Rom. 7:6;

---

112. R. Bellarmine, "De sanct. beat.," in *Controversiis*, I, 11–20; D. Petavius, "De angelis," in *Theol. dogm.*, II, chs. 9–10.

113. Luther, according to J. Kösten, *The Theology of Luther*, II, 23ff.; U. Zwingli, *Opera*, I, 268f., 280f.; III, 135; J. Calvin, *Institutes*, I.xiv.10–12; cf. III.xx.20–24; J. Gerhard, *Loci theol.*, XXXVI, §§370–480 (on angels, esp. §427); J. Quenstedt, *Theologia*, I, 486; F. Turretin, *Institutes of Elenctic Theology*, VII, qu. 9; idem, *De Necessaria secessione nostra ab ecclesia Romana* (Geneva, 1692), disp. 2–4: "De idolatria Romana," 33–109.

114. G. Jansen, *Prael. theol.*, III, 1008.

14:18; 16:18; Gal. 4:9; Eph. 6:7; Col. 3:24; 1 Thess. 1:9); and *latreuein* is also used of service rendered to humans. Neither etymologically nor scripturally do the two words carry the distinctions Catholicism teaches. The entire distinction is arbitrary.

In any case, the implication of monotheism is that there is and can only be one kind of religious veneration. All veneration of creatures is either exclusively civil, or it violates monotheism and attributes divine character to creatures. This reality comes through loud and clear in practice. Even though we are regularly told that angels and saints are only intermediaries, that they themselves are not being directly invoked but that God is being invoked in them, and that by our invoking them God's honor is not diminished but increased—all this is immaterial, for experience shows all too clearly that Roman Catholic Christians put their trust in creatures. Moreover, even if the distinction per se were correct, it still could not serve as warrant for the religious veneration of angels. For if this reasoning were a sufficient defense of the practice, no idolatry and no image worship could any longer be condemned. The Gentiles, praying to animals and images, knew very well that these animals and images were not identical with the gods themselves (Rom. 1:23). The Jews did not equate the golden calf with YHWH himself (Exod. 32:4–5; 1 Kings 12:28). When Satan tempted Christ, he certainly did not demand that Christ should regard him as God (Matt. 4:9). And John by no means believed that the angel who appeared to him was God (Rev. 19:10). Nevertheless Jesus still answered: "Worship the Lord your God, and serve only him" (Matt. 4:10). This *only* is exclusive, just as the only mediator Christ Jesus excludes all other angels or humans as mediators. But this is precisely the point that Roman Catholicism denies. Just as Matthew 19:17; 23:8; John 9:5; 1 Timothy 2:5; 6:16; and the like do not rule out that also humans can be called "good," "master," "light," "mediator," and "immortal," so also—says Rome—Matthew 4:10 does not prove that God alone may be worshiped. Angels and saints, according to Roman Catholic teaching, participate in the very nature of God. The supernatural gifts, though given and derived, are of the same nature as the divine being itself. And therein, according to the teaching of Rome, lies the deepest ground for the worship of saints and angels. In supernatural righteousness *(justitia supernaturalis)* God imparts his own essence to creatures; and for that reason they may also be accorded religious veneration. The controlling idea of Catholicism here is clear: "There are as many species of adoration as there are species of excellence."[115]

By the rejection of the religious veneration of angels, Protestantism has acknowledged that the angels are not an indispensable element in the religious life of Christians. They are not the effective agents of our salvation; neither are they the ground of our trust nor the object of our veneration. It is not with

---

115. T. Aquinas, *Summa theol.*, II, 2, qu. 103, art. 3; R. Bellarmine, "De sanct. beat.," in *Controversiis*, I, 12; D. Petavius, "De angelis," in *Theol. dogm.*, II, ch. 10; G. Jansen, *Prael theol.*, III, 1017; J. A. Möhler, *Symbolik* (Regensberg: G. J. Manz, 1871), 52–53.

them but with God that we enter into communion. They do not even appear to us any more today, and all special revelation by means of angels has ceased. In Protestant churches and confessions angels cannot and may not occupy the place assigned to them in Roman Catholic churches and creeds. Still, this is not to deny the significance for religion of the world of angels. This significance is, first of all, anchored in the fact that God, in his working in the sphere of grace, chooses to make use of the ministry of angels. The angels are of extraordinary significance for the kingdom of God and its history. We meet them at all the great turning points in its history: they are the mediators of the resurrection and witnesses of God's mighty deeds. Their significance is much more of an objective than a subjective nature. In our religious experience we know nothing of communion with the world of angels. Neither on our religious nor on our moral life do the angels have an influence that can be clearly verbalized. Influences and operations of angels do, of course, impact us, but since they no longer appear to us visibly, we cannot trace those operations specifically to concrete rules. Their value lies in the history of revelations, as Scripture makes them known to us.

In the second place, therefore, the angels cannot be the object of the respectful homage that we pay to humans. Most certainly there is a civil honor that we are obligated to accord to them. But this is nevertheless again different from the honor we accord to humans whom we know and have met personally. Roman Catholics undergird the veneration of angels especially with the argument that as envoys of the Most High they are entitled to our homage, as in honoring the ambassadors of rulers we honor the rulers themselves. And as such this is perfectly appropriate. If an angel were to appear to us, it would be entirely fitting for us to welcome him with deeply reverent homage. This is precisely what happened when angels appeared to humans in the days of [such] revelation. And yet, such appearances no longer occur. In our case there cannot be the kind of homage that the patriarchs, prophets, and apostles accorded the angels who appeared to them. It is simply not possible to offer them such reverence and homage.

Nevertheless there is, in the third place, a kind of honor that we are obligated to show to angels. However, that honor is in no respect religious but only civil in nature; it is essentially the same kind of honor we accord to humans or other creatures. This civil honor *(honor civilis)* consists in our thinking and speaking of them with respect, in not despising them in our little ones (Matt. 18:10), in being mindful of their presence (1 Cor. 4:9; 11:10), in proclaiming to them the manifold wisdom of God (Eph. 3:10), in giving them insight into the mysteries of salvation (1 Tim. 5:21), in giving them joy by our repentance (Luke 15:10), in imitating them in the observance of God's will (Matt. 6:10), in feeling ourselves to be one with them and living in the expectation of joining them (Heb. 12:22), and in forming with them and all other creatures a choir for the glorification of the name of the Lord (Ps. 103:20–21). In these things lies the true veneration of angels.

And if these things are correctly understood, then, in the fourth place, the doctrine of angels can also serve us as consolation and encouragement. God has revealed also this teaching to us that he may strengthen us in our weakness and lift us up from our despondency. We are not alone in our spiritual struggle. We are connected with a great cloud of witnesses present all around us. There is still another, a better world than this one, one in which God is served in perfection. This world is for us a model, a stimulus, a source of encouragement; at the same time it awakens our nostalgia and arouses our awareness of the final goal. Just as in revelation the world of angels has come down to us, so in Christ the church rises up to greet that world. We shall be like the angels and daily see the face of our Father, who is in heaven.[116]

---

116. P. van Mastricht, *Theologia,* III, 7, 25; C. Love, *Theol. practica,* 205; F. Philippi, *Kirchliche Glaubenslehre,* II, 320f.; F. Frank, *Christliche Wahrheit,* I, 353. J. van Oosterzee, *Christian Dogmatics,* trans. J. Watson and M. Evans, 2 vols. (New York: Scribner, Armstrong, 1874), §57, 10.

10

EARTH:
THE MATERIAL WORLD

A theological perspective on the material world differs from but should not be isolated from a philosophic/scientific one. All religions have creation stories; all scientific systems are rooted in religious beliefs. Every effort to base the biblical story of creation on foreign sources such as Babylonian myths does not stand up under close scrutiny. The creation narrative in Genesis is utterly unique; it is devoid of theogony and is rigorously monotheistic. The interpretation of Genesis 1–2 has a rich and diverse history. To understand the "week" and the "days" of creation, it is important to distinguish the first act of creation—as immediate bringing forth of heaven and earth out of nothing—from the secondary separation and formation of the six days, which begin God's preservation and government of the world. The six-day period is best divided into three parts: creation, separation, adornment. The Christian church is not confessionally tied to a specific worldview, so the shift away from an Aristotelian and Ptolemaic cosmology is not a problem for Christian theology. The Bible does not provide us with a scientific cosmology—using the language of ordinary experience—but spiritually and ethically, the earth (with humanity) is the center of the universe. The data of natural science must be taken seriously by Christians as general revelation, but only special, biblical revelation can describe the true state of the world. The biblical chronology and order of creation seem, on the face of it, at odds with the accounts given by geology and paleontology, and various attempts to harmonize them achieve only modest and not finally satisfying results. It is important, however, to insist on the historical rather than merely mythical or visionary character of the creation story in Genesis. The science of geology is still young and faces many unanswered questions. The reality of a cataclysmic flood bringing immense changes in the world—a story tradition found among virtually all peoples—complicates matters considerably. Theology should neither fear the sure results of science nor, in immoderate anxiety, make premature concessions to opinions of the day. As the science of divine and eternal things, it should uphold its confessional convictions with dignity and honor and in patience.

[268] Besides the spiritual there also exists a material world. But while the existence and being of the angels are known only from revelation and are

hidden from reason and science, the material world is visible to all and comes up for consideration in philosophy as well as in theology, in religion as well as in science. On this score, therefore, differences and clashes are possible at all times. It is true that philosophy and theology speak about the material world in different ways. The former investigates the origin and nature of all things, but the latter starts with God and traces all things back to him. Theology deals with creatures only insofar as they are the works of God and reveal something of his attributes. Hence also, where it deals with creatures it is and always remains theology.[1] Even though there is an important distinction between the two, theology and philosophy nevertheless deal with the same world. To avoid a clash between them, people have often proposed a division of labor. Science, they said, should study the things that are visible, and leave to religion and theology nothing but the world of ethics and religion; or even more rigorously, all that exists should be for science to explore, and only in the matter of value judgments should religion be allowed to speak. But theoretically as well as practically, such a division is impossible. Just as every scientific system is ultimately rooted in religious convictions, so there is not a single religion that does not bring with it a certain view of the created world. All religions have their cosmogonies, cosmogonies that did not arise from intellectual reasoning but are at least in part based on tradition and represent a religious interest. Even the creation story in Genesis 1 does not pretend to be a philosophical worldview but presents itself as a historical narrative that is based on tradition, and in some respects it agrees with the cosmogonies of other religions but in many ways again exhibits remarkable differences from them.

In recent times it is especially the kinship between the biblical and Babylonian creation stories that has attracted attention. This story [Enuma Elish], which had earlier been known from fragments of Berossus,[2] was rediscovered [in 1874, translated in 1875,] and published in 1876 by George Smith.[3] It again broke into prominence when excavations in Assyria and the discovery of the Tell el-Amarna letters placed in bold relief the great cultural-historical significance that Babylonia possessed in antiquity. Considering the high level of civilization found in Babylonia centuries before the emergence of the people of Israel, many scholars wondered whether all that was uniquely Israelite could not be explained in terms of Babylon. For years critics assumed that the cultural impact of Babylon on the Jews occurred shortly before, during, and after the exile. But this picture of the situation could not be maintained: the excavations made it clear as day that all the surrounding peoples in antiquity had been dominated by the culture of Babylonia. In Canaan, thanks to the Canaanites, or even much earlier in the patriarchal age, the Israelites

---

1. T. Aquinas, *Summa contra gentiles,* II, 2ff.; A. Polanus, *Syn. theol.,* V, 7.

2. Ed. note: Berossus (b. 340 B.C.) was author of a three-volume Greek history of Babylon.

3. Ed. note: George Smith, *The Chaldean Account of Genesis* (New York: Scribner, Armstrong, 1876).

also became familiar with it and took over a variety of things from it that they later refashioned along the lines of their own Yahwistic outlook. Many scholars believe that all that is peculiarly Israelite, as for example the name YHWH, monotheism, the stories of creation, fall, flood, building a tower, the seven-day week, the Sabbath, and so on, has its origin in Babylonia. But this is not all. The facts and ideas of Christianity; the preexistence, supernatural birth, miracles, atoning death, and suffering of Christ; the resurrection, ascension, and return of Christ; the idea of Mary as the mother of God; the doctrine of the Holy Spirit as comforter, and of the Trinity—this and much more are all said to be rooted in the astral worldview that from ancient times was the characteristic possession of the Babylonians.[4] According to Jensen, the entire history of the gospel is interwoven with sagas, so that there is no reason to consider anything said about Jesus to be historical; the Jesus-saga is an "Israelite Gilgamesh-saga" and as such "a sister-saga to numerous, that is, the majority of Old Testament sagas."[5]

The derivation of the creation story from the land of the Tigris and Euphrates, therefore, is only a small part of this pan-Babylonianism. What we are dealing with here is not an isolated instance but a general intellectual trend that, after the literary-critical school had displayed its impotence, attempted to explain the problem of the Bible along religious-historical lines. The sorting out and splitting up of the documents is of no advantage if religion itself remains standing behind them as an enigmatic sphinx. It therefore seemed a godsend when the East began to unveil its treasures. From the East light seemed to dawn over Israel's religion and over the whole phenomenon of Christianity. But even now further investigation is showing and will increasingly bring to light the vanity of this attempt at interpretation. In the case of the creation story in Genesis the assertion that it originated in Babylon is primarily based on the traces of mythological origin that, we are told, can still be found in the biblical story despite the editing process: (1) the portrayal of chaos under the ancient terms of *tĕhôm* [the deep] and *tōhû wābōhû* [formless void] and the notion that God formed the present world out of chaos; (2) the reference to the brooding of the Spirit upon the waters, which implies that the world is here, as in many mythologies, conceived as an egg; (3) the hiatus that exists in Genesis 1 between verses 2 and 3 and that was formerly filled with the theogony; (4) the feature that the darkness was not created by God nor called "good," whereas, in the Israelite teaching, God is the creator of light and darkness (Isa. 45:7); (5) the saying that the sun, moon, and stars were set [in the firmament] to "rule" the day and the night; (6) the plural form in which God speaks of himself at the creation of humankind; the idea that humankind is in the image of God

4. P. Biesterveld, *De Jongste Methode voor de Verklaring van het Nieuwe Testament* (Kampen: Bos, 1905); cf. H. Bavinck, *Reformed Dogmatics*, I, 173 (#53).

5. P. C. A. Jensen, *Das Gilgamesch-Epos in der Weltliteratur,* 3 vols. (Strassburg: Trübner, 1906–28 [i.e., 1929]); cf. H. Schmidt, *Theologische Rundschau* (1907): 189ff.

and bears his likeness and that, upon the completion of the creation week, God rests on the Sabbath.[6]

Of all these comments only the first has some significance because the *těhôm* in Genesis 1:2 indeed corresponds to the Babylonian *Tiamat,* and elsewhere in the Old Testament as well we encounter the idea that God from ancient times waged a struggle against a natural power. In some texts there is mention of *Rahab* (Job 9:13; 26:12; Ps. 40:4 [5 MT, *rěhābîm;* ET: "the proud"]; 87:4; 89:10f.; Isa. 30:7; 51:9f.); *Leviathan* (Job 3:8; 41:1ff.; Ps. 74:12ff.; 104:26; Isa. 27:1); the dragon *Tannin* (Job 7:12; Isa. 27:1; 51:9; Ezek. 29:3; 32:2); the serpent *Naḥash* (Job 26:13; Isa. 27:1; Amos 9:3)—all of them powers that were opposed and overcome by God. But upon a careful reading none of these passages yields virtually any ground for the assertion that belief in creation in Israel still in many respects bears a mythological character.

For in the first place, it cannot be denied that these representations serve to describe very different things. In Job 9:13 and 26:12–13, Rahab is indeed a sea monster, but in Psalms 87:4; 89:10; Isaiah 30:7; and 51:9–10, it is undoubtedly a metaphor for Egypt. In Job 7:12 and Isaiah 51:9 Tannin is a sea dragon, but in Isaiah 27:1 it serves as a symbol of a *future* power that will be overcome by God; and in Ezekiel 29:3 and 32:2 it is used as a metaphor for Egypt. In Job 3:8 Leviathan is the celestial dragon that devours the light of the sun and stars, as does Naḥash in Job 26:13, but in Isaiah 27:1 the prophet employs both of these images to depict *future* world powers. All this is proof that the words *Rahab,* and so forth, whatever may have been their original meaning, are used as images for different things.

Second, when these words are used as descriptions of natural powers, they never in Scripture refer to the natural power that the Babylonian creation story introduces as Tiamat, but to various natural powers that either were in the past, especially in the salvation of Israel from Egypt and the passage through the Red Sea (Ps. 74:13–14; 89:10; Isa. 51:9–10), or are still in the present (Job 3:8; 9:13; 26:12–13) opposed and overcome by God. But we are nowhere told that at the creation there was a natural power opposed to God, which he had to overcome. There is absolutely no proof for the identification of Rahab, Leviathan, and so on, with the Babylonian Tiamat.

Third, the notion that God subdues and overcomes the natural powers is a poetic description that can in no way serve as support for the assertion that Israel's poets and prophets gave credence to pagan mythology. It is indeed possible that in some cases the terms "Tannin" and "Leviathan" (Ps. 74:13–14; 104:26; Job 7:12; 40:21–41:34) refer [also] to real sea monsters. But even where this is not the case, and some natural power, as for example, the darkness devouring the light, is represented as a Rahab or Leviathan or Naḥash (Job

6. H. Gunkel, *Die Genesis übersetzt und erklärt* (Göttingen: Vandenhoeck & Ruprecht, 1902), 109 (ed. note: ET: *Genesis,* trans. Mark E. Biddle [Macon, Ga.: Mercer University Press, 1997]); cf. V. Zapletal, *Der Schöpfungsbericht der Genesis,* 2d ed. (Regensburg: G. J. Manz, 1911), 62–63.

3:8; 9:13; 26:12–13), Hebrew poetry is employing an image in the same way in which we in our day still speak of the zodiac, the Great Bear (Ursa Major) and the Little Bear (Ursa Minor), Cancer the Crab (the fourth sign of the zodiac) and Scorpio (the eighth sign of the zodiac), or Minerva and Venus. Such use of mythological images in no way constitutes proof of belief in their reality. This is even more evidently the case because the Old Testament very often pictures the sea as an enormous natural power that is rebuked by God (Job 26:12; 38:8–11; Ps. 18:15; 65:7; 93:3–4; Jer. 5:22; Nah. 1:4).

Finally, the word *těhôm* as such proves nothing. For even if this is identical with the Babylonian Tiamat, one cannot infer anything from it for the identity of the ideas that are associated with these words in the Babylonian creation story and in Scripture. However, these ideas are in fact not the same but, on the contrary, very far removed from each other. For while the Tiamat is the only existing chaos, whose existence precedes the creation of the gods and who subsequently rebels against the gods, the *těhôm* in Genesis 1:2 is simply the designation of the formless state in which the [created] earth originally existed, just as the phrase *tōhû wābōhû* serves this purpose without any mythological associations.

Actually, the creation stories in Genesis and that of Babylon are very different on all points. According to Genesis, the existence of God is anterior to all things; in the Babylonian creation story the gods are born after, and out of, the chaos. In Scripture, heaven and earth are called into being by a divine word of power, and thereafter the Spirit of God moves over the face of the waters; in Babylonian mythology, chaos originally existed by itself, and from it, in an incomprehensible manner, the gods come forth, against whom the chaos then rebels. In the Bible, after the mention of the formless state of the earth, there first follows the creation of light, but the latter is completely lacking in the Babylonian story. In Genesis 1 the preparation of the earth in regular order is completed in six days; in the Babylonian myth such an order is absolutely nonexistent. The only resemblance between them actually consists in this, that in both stories a chaos precedes the formation of heaven and earth. To construe from this parallel a common identity or common origin for the two stories is premature and unfounded. The creation narrative in Genesis is utterly unique; it is devoid of any trace of a theogony, is rigorously monotheistic, teaches a creation out of nothing, and knows nothing of primary matter. It therefore is unbelievable that the Jews, in exile or even earlier in Canaan, borrowed this story from the Babylonians. In the first place, the creation was known to the Israelites even before the exile. This was also true of the seven-day week, which is based on the days of creation. It is unlikely, further, that the Jews should have taken over such an important piece of their doctrine from Babylonians or Canaanites. And finally, the pagan cosmogonies were so thoroughly polytheistic that they had to repel rather than attract the monotheistic people of Israel; they were therefore unsuited to being easily transformed into a beautiful monotheistic narrative like that of Genesis 1. Everything rather argues for the assumption that in Genesis 1 we have a tradition that derives from the most ancient times, was gradually adulterated in the case of the other peoples, and was preserved in its purity by Israel.[7]

THE WEEK OF CREATION

[269] In the narrative of Genesis 1 the first verse needs to be read as the account of an independent fact. In verse 2 the earth already exists, though in a disordered and vacuous state. And verse 1 reports the origin of that earth; from the very start it was created by God as earth. After a brief initial reference to heaven in verse 1, verse 2 immediately starts speaking about the earth: cosmogony becomes geogony. And from the very first moment that earth is *earth*: not *hylē* (matter) in an Aristotelian sense, nor prime matter, nor chaos in the sense of the pagan cosmogonies. "A created chaos is an absurdity" (Dillmann). It is true that the earth is now described to us as *tōhû wābōhû*, as a *tĕhôm*, which the darkness covered. But this means something very different from what is usually understood by chaos. The word *tĕhôm* occurs repeatedly, especially in Isaiah, and consistently prompts us to think of empty space (cf. Isa. 45:18), an area in which everything is trackless and undeveloped. The word *bōhû* is also found in Isaiah 34:11 and Jeremiah 4:23, both times in conjunction with *tōhû*, and expresses the same idea. The state of the earth in Genesis 1:2 is not that of positive destruction but of not-yet-having-been shaped. There is no light, no life, no organic creature, no form and configuration in things. It is further explained by the fact that it was a *tĕhôm*, a seething watery mass that is wrapped in darkness. The earth was formed "out of water and by means of water" (2 Pet. 3:5; Ps. 104:5–9). This unformed and undeveloped state, according to Genesis, certainly lasted for some time, however short. There is no description here of a purely logical assumption but rather of a factual state. Still, in that case arises the question how long this state lasted. And this question is again completely dependent on whether the creation of heaven and earth of which Genesis 1:1 speaks occurred before or within the span of the first day. Genesis leaves no other impression but that the creation of heaven and earth in verse 1 and the unformed state of the earth in verse 2 are anterior to the first day. In verse 2, after all, darkness still prevails, and there is no light. Now, it is the case that the day is not darkness and does not begin with darkness but with light. It is only the creation of light (v. 3) that makes the day possible. God, accordingly, does not call the darkness "day" but the light, and the darkness he called "night" (v. 5). The alternation of light and darkness could only begin with the creation of light. Only after it had been light could it again be evening and the morning, and with this morning the first day ended, for Genesis 1 calculates the day from evening to morning. Hence, the work of the first day did not consist in the creation of heaven and

---

7. F. Delitzsch, *A New Commentary on Genesis*, trans. Sophia Taylor (Edinburgh: T. & T. Clark, 1899), 60–61; H. H. Kuyper, *Evolutie of Revelatie* (Amsterdam: Höveker & Wormser, 1903), esp. 117–23.

earth, nor in the perpetuation of the unformed state, but in the creation of light and the separation of light and darkness.

Now, there would be absolutely no objection to this exegesis if we did not read elsewhere that God created heaven and earth in six days (Exod. 20:11; 31:17). This can only be understood, however, of the second creation *(creatio secunda)*. Indeed, in both of these texts the emphasis does not fall on the fact that God brought forth all things out of nothing but on the fact that he was occupied for six days with the formation of heaven and earth, and this is offered to us as a paradigm. There is clearly a distinction between what God did "in the beginning" (Gen. 1:1; cf. John 1:1) and what he did "by the words of his mouth" in six days (Gen. 1:3ff.). The unformed state of Genesis 1:2 separates the two. The first creation *(creatio prima)* is immediate, an act of bringing forth heaven and earth out of nothing. It absolutely does not presuppose the existence of available material but occurred "with time" *(cum tempore)*. But the second creation, which starts with verse 3, is not direct and immediate; it presupposes the material created in verse 1 and links up with it. It occurs specifically "in time" *(in tempore)* and that in six days. Hence, this second creation already anticipates the works of preservation and government. In part it is already preservation and no longer merely creation. For that matter, the very moment when heaven and earth were created by God, they were also preserved by him. Creation immediately and instantly passes into preservation and government. Nevertheless, the work of the six days (Gen. 1:3ff.) must still be counted as belonging to creation. For according to Genesis, all the creatures that were brought forth in those six days (light, firmament, sun, moon, stars, plants, animals, humankind) did not emerge by immanent forces in accordance with fixed laws from the available matter in the manner of evolution. That matter was in itself powerless to produce all this solely in the way of natural progression, by immanent development. In itself it did not have the capacity for it; it only possessed a capacity for obedience *(potentia obedientialis)*. From the primary matter of Genesis 1:1, God by speaking and creating brought forth the entire cosmos. While in every new act of formation he linked up with what already existed, the higher phase did not solely proceed by an immanent force from the lower. At every stage a creating word of God's omnipotence was needed.

THE SIX DAYS OF CREATION

[270] Herder and others divided the work of creation into two ternaries, so that the works of the second ternary corresponded to those of the first. There is indeed a correspondence between the work of the first and that of the fourth day; but the second and the fifth days, similarly the third and sixth days, do not exactly fit this parallel pattern. On the fifth day, after all, not only the birds in the firmament but also the fish and aquatic animals were created, which rather fits with the work of the third day. In the works of creation we do,

however, observe a clear progression from a lower to a higher level, from the general conditions for organic life to this organic life itself in its various forms. Therefore, the old division of the overall work of creation into three parts is preferable: *creation* (Gen. 1:1–2); *separation* on the first three days between light and darkness, heaven and earth, land and sea; and *adornment* on the fourth to the sixth days, the population of the prepared earth with all kinds of living entities.[8] Still, even this division is not intended as a sharp demarcation either since the plants, created on the third day, also serve as ornamentation.[9] The *separation* and *adornment* mark the cancellation of the *tōhû* condition of the earth. The unformed and undeveloped state of the earth referred to in verse 2 may not for a moment, however, be thought of as passive. For however long or short a period it may have existed, there were powers and energies at work in it. We read, after all, of the Spirit of God moving over the waters. The verb *rāḥap* means "to hover over" (cf. Deut. 32:11), and the use of this word proves that in the case of *rûaḥ ělōhîm* we must not think of the wind but more specifically of the Spirit of God, to whom elsewhere too the work of creation is attributed (Ps. 33:6; 104:30). The Spirit of God, as the principle of creaturely being and life, impacts the watery mass of the earth in a formative, vivifying way and so anticipates the creative words of God that in six days, following up on the already-existent condition of the earth, called into being the various orders of creatures.

The work of the first day consists in the creation of light, in the separation of light and darkness, in the alternation of day and night, and hence also in movement, change, becoming. According to the most widely accepted hypothesis today, light is not a substance, nor enormously rapid undulation, as Huygens and Young and Fresnel assumed, but consists—according to the theory of Maxwell, later confirmed by Hertz, Lorentz, and Zeeman—in electrical vibrations and is therefore an electrical phenomenon.[10] It is to be distinguished, accordingly, from emitters of light, sun, moon, and stars, and according to Genesis precedes them. Light is also the most general prerequisite for all life and development. Whereas the alternation of day and night is only necessary for animals and humans, light also meets a requirement of the world of plants. In addition, it gives form, shape, and color to all things. On the second day a separation is made between the firmament—the sky and the clouds, which in its appearance to our eyes is often presented as a tent (Ps.

---

8. T. Aquinas, *Summa theol.*, I, qu. 74.

9. V. Zapletal (*Der Schöpfungsbericht,* 107ff.), therefore, chooses a different division and bases this on Genesis 2:1. There we read that heaven and earth were completed and all their multitude (hosts). Thus, a distinction is made between heaven and earth, the dwelling place on one hand, and on the other the multitudes that inhabit heaven and earth. Zapletal poses, therefore, a distinction between *productio regionum* and a *productio exercituum.* The former occurs in the first three days, the latter in the second. Sun, moon, and stars are the multitudes (hosts) of heaven; fish and birds are of water and air; animals and man are of the earth. For this reason the creation of plants takes place on the third day—plants belong not to the multitudes (hosts) of the earth but to the earth as dwelling place and are the necessary condition for the life of animals and man.

10. J. D. van der Waals, "Het Zeeman-verschijnsel," *De Gids* 67 (March 1903): 493–512.

104:2), a curtain (Isa. 40:22), a pavement of sapphire stone (Exod. 24:10; Ezek. 1:22), a molten mirror (Job 37:18), a roof or dome extended over the earth (Gen. 7:11; Deut. 11:17; 28:12; Ps. 78:23; [Mal. 3:10;] etc.)[11]—a separation between the firmament and the earth with its waters (Ps. 24:2; 136:6). The work of separation and demarcation begun on the first day is continued on the second. The distinction between light and darkness, of day and night, is now made subservient to the separation of heaven and earth, of the air and the clouds above, and the earth and the water beneath. At the end of the second day we do not read that God saw that it was good. From this omission some readers have concluded that the number two was an ominous number or that hell was created on that day, but the reason is likely that the work of the second day is very intimately bound up with that of the third day and was only completed in the separation of the waters. Divine approval follows at the end of the third day, for on that day the separation between earth and water, land and sea, is completed, and earth becomes a cosmos with continents and seas, mountains and valleys, fields and streams. Undoubtedly, all these formations occurred under the impact of the colossal mechanical and chemical processes inherent in nature. These processes were aroused by the divine word of power and the animation of the Spirit and have given the earth its cosmic shape and appearance. From this point on, also other forces, that is, organic ones, make their appearance. The earth is still naked and featureless. For that reason this day does not end until the earth is clothed in green with vegetation, which is divided into two kinds, herbs and trees, each of them having seed of their own and thus propagating themselves. This world of vegetation could do without the sun but not without light.

But that is not true of the animal and human world. Before they are created, the fourth day must come, and sun and moon and stars have to be readied. This does not imply that the masses of matter of which the planets are composed were only then called into being, but only that all these planets would on this day become what they would henceforth be to the earth. Together they would for the earth assume the role of light and be signs of wind and weather, of events and judgments. They would serve to regulate the seasons for agriculture, the shipping industry, annual feast days, the life of man and animal, and finally provide a basis for the calculation of days, months, and years. The fourth day, therefore, recounts the appearance of the starry skies in relation to the earth. From now on, day and night and so forth are regulated by the sun; the earth becomes an integrated part of the universe; it is positioned in harmony with all other planets. Now the earth has been readied as the abode of animated living beings, of animals and humans.

On the fifth day, by a divine word of power, the waters themselves bring forth all aquatic animals, and the sky is filled with an assortment of bird species. Of both kinds of animals massive numbers of all kinds are created. Next,

---

11. Cf. G. V. Schiaparelli, *Astronomy in the Old Testament* (Oxford: Clarendon, 1905).

on the sixth day, follows the creation of land animals, who at God's command
come forth from the earth—specifically in three kinds: wild animals, cattle,
and creeping things; and finally also the creation of humankind, who after
a specific counsel of God was formed from the earth as to the body, and the
soul was directly created by God. Thus, the whole creation was completed.
"God saw everything that he had made, and indeed, it was very good" (Gen.
1:31). He took great delight in his own work and for that reason rested on
the seventh day. This rest is a consequence of God's satisfaction with, and
delight in, his works, which are now completed as the works of creation. At
the same time it is a positive act of blessing and sanctifying the seventh day so
that the creation, in its continued existence on the seventh day, having been
blessed with all kinds of forces and consecrated by God to his service and
honor, would henceforth develop under the providential care of the Lord and
answer to its destiny.

[271] Christian theology has always treated this six-day period with
special fondness. The literature on the subject is astonishingly rich but has
been almost exhaustively processed in the work of Zöckler on the history
of the relations between theology and natural science.[12] The most ancient
Christian interpretation of the six-day period has been preserved in the
second book of Theophilus's *Ad Autolycum* (chs. 9–38). It is also more or
less extensively treated in the work of Tertullian and Origen, but especially
by Basil, Gregory of Nyssa, and John of Damascus in the East,[13] and in the
West by Lactantius, Ambrose, and Augustine.[14] These works were utilized
by Isodore, Beda, Alcuin, and others and continue to serve as the basis for
the discussion of the six-day period in scholasticism by Lombard, Thomas,
Bonaventure, and others.

The same worldview and the same view of the six-day period, in both Roman
Catholic and Protestant theology, is maintained after the Reformation. From
the side of Catholicism the most important treatments are those of Cajetan in
his commentary on Genesis, Eugubinus in his *Cosmopoeia* (1535), Catharinus
in his commentary on the first five chapters of Genesis, Pererius in his four-
part work on the first book of Moses, Lapide in his well-known commentary,
Molina in his treatise *De opere sex dierum,* Suárez in his commentary on the
first part of the *Summa,* Petavius, Becanus, and others. From the side of Lutheranism the following deserve to be listed: Luther's commentary on Genesis,
Melanchthon's annotations on Genesis 1–6, and the discussions of Chemnitz,

---

12. O. Zöckler, *Geschichte der Beziehungen zwischen Theologie und Naturwissenschaft Mit besondrer
Rücksicht auf Schöpfungsgeschichte,* 2 vols. (Gütersloh: C. Bertelsmann, 1877–79); cf. idem, "Schöpfung
und Erhaltung der Welt," *PRE³,* XVII, 681–704.

13. Tertullian, *Against Hermogenes,* 19ff.; Origen, in his homily about the Hexaemeron at the beginning
of his seventeen homilies on Genesis; Basil, *On the Hexaemeron Hom.,* IX; Gregory of Nyssa, *Apology in
Hexaemeron;* John of Damascus, *Exposition of the Orthodox Faith,* II.

14. Lactantius, *The Divine Institutes,* II, 8–12; Ambrose, *Hexaemeron,* VI; Augustine, *Literal Meaning
of Genesis,* 1, XII; idem, *City of God,* XI, 4; idem, *Confessions,* XI–XII.

Quenstedt, Hollaz, and others in their systematics. Even richer is the literature produced on the subject by Reformed scholars. This material is considered in the commentaries of Calvin, Zwingli, Oecolampad, Musculus, Martyr, Piscator, [Ludovico] de Dieu, Coccejus, and others; in dogmatic works like those of Polanus, Gomarus, Heidegger, Mastricht, Maresius, and de Moor; but, in addition to commentaries and systematic reflections, also numerous separate treatises are devoted to the subject, like those of Capito, Danaeus, Voetius, Rivet, Hottinger, and so forth.[15]

All these works arise from an Aristotelian-Ptolemaic worldview. The earth sits motionless at the center of the universe; all the stars and the whole expanse of the heavens rotate around it. The authors could not conceive of those stars as moving freely in space, but pictured every star as being fixed in a particular sphere. They therefore had to assume the existence of as many celestial spheres as they observed stars of dissimilar movement and rotational time. To them, it was not the stars but the spheres that moved, carrying their stars with them. The vault of the heavens, then, consisted of a system of eight or more tightly telescoped concentric spheres. The outermost sphere is that of the fixed stars, the "first heaven," as Aristotle called it. The earth was pictured as a bullet or a disc surrounded by water. Only a few of the authors assumed that there could be antipodes and that there was land also on the other side of the ocean. As a rule both of these positions were rejected.

Of course, this Ptolemaic worldview also influenced the exegesis of the six-day period. In this respect one can clearly discern two distinct schools of thought. The one rejects the temporal character of the six days, for the most part ascribes visionary significance to them, sees the entire world as being created simultaneously at a single stroke, and frequently arrives at a variety of allegorical interpretations. It was already represented by Philo and later, in the Christian church, by Clement, Origen, Athanasius, Augustine, Erigena, Abelard, Cajetan, Canus, Gonzales, and others, as well as by Moses Maimonides.[16] The other school adheres to the literal sense of the creation narrative, including that of the six days. It was followed by Tertullian, Basil, Gregory of Nyssa, Ephraem, John of Damascus. Later it achieved almost exclusive dominance in scholasticism, in Roman Catholic as well as Protestant theology, although the alternative exegesis of Augustine was consistently discussed with respect and never branded heretical.[17]

Despite this important disagreement in exegesis, however, there was perfect agreement in the matter of worldview. The Ptolemaic system held firm even into modern times, long after Copernicus had come on the scene with his explanation of the movement of heavenly bodies. It was absolutely not the church and orthodoxy as such that opposed the newer worldview, as people

15. In addition to O. Zöckler, see also J. G. Walch, *Bibliotheca theologica selecta*, 4 vols. (Jena: Croecker, 1757–65), I, 242; C. Vitringa, *Doctr. christ.*, II, 93.

16. M. Maimonides, *Moreh Nevukhim* (Warsaw: Goldman, 1872), II, 30.

17. P. Lombard, *Sentences*, II, dist. 15, 5; T. Aquinas, *Summa theol.*, I, qu. 74, art. 2.

love to portray the situation.[18] Instead, it was Aristotelianism, which in every domain, both that of science and that of religion, that of art and that of the church, sought to maintain itself in the face of modernity.[19] That is the reason why the Christian church and Christian theology, although today they have generally exchanged the Ptolemaic for the Copernican hypothesis, have continued to exist to this day and are by no means dead even in this century. This is proof that the church and theology are not so tightly bound up with these worldviews that they must stand or fall with them. Indeed, it is not at all obvious that the Copernican hypothesis, if in fact it adequately explains the astronomical phenomena, would as such have to be rejected by Christian theology. For Scripture indeed always speaks geocentrically and also explains the origin of things from a geocentric viewpoint, but in this matter it uses the same language of ordinary daily experience as that in which we still speak today, even though we have a very different picture of the movement of the heavenly bodies from that which generally prevailed in the time when the Bible books were written. It can even also be roundly admitted that the Bible writers had no other worldview than what was universally assumed in their day. There is a difference, after all, between historical authority (*auctoritas historiae*: "descriptive") and normative authority (*auctoritas normae*: "prescriptive").[20] From the perspective of this language employed by Scripture we can explain how the miracles narrated in Joshua 10:12–13; 2 Kings 20:9–11; and Isaiah 38:8 are described in terms of the sun standing still and its shadow turning back on the dial. It is by no means established by this account that the miracle itself consisted in an objective "standing still" of the sun and a "turning back" of its shadow. The miracle can be, and has in fact been, interpreted in various ways by scholars[21] who did not rationalistically exegete it into oblivion. Even we today would describe the same phenomena in the same manner: Scripture reports the miracle as a fact; it does not tell us how it came about.

But we must state the matter still stronger: even if, in an astronomic sense, the earth is no longer central to us, it is definitely still central in a religious and an ethical sense, and thus it remains central to all people without distinction, and there is not a thing science can do to change that. Human beings, in a sense, are the weakest of all creatures; the power of nature, the power of many an animal, far surpasses them. Still, humankind is king of the earth, the crown of creation. He may be frail as a reed, but he is "a *thinking* reed *(roseau pensant)*"

---

18. Cf., e.g., J. W. Draper, *History of the Conflict between Religion and Science* (New York: D. Appleton, 1897).

19. E. Dennert, *Die Religion der Naturforscher,* 4th ed. (Berlin: Berliner Stadtmission, 1901), 13; R. Schmid, *Das naturwissenschaftliche Glaubensbekenntnis eines Theologen,* 2d ed. (Stuttgart: Kielmann, 1906), 38–42 (ET: *The Scientific Creed of a Theologian,* trans. J. W. Stoughton from the 2d German ed. [New York: A. C. Armstrong, 1906]).

20. Cf. H. Bavinck, *Reformed Dogmatics,* I, 459 (#120).

21. F. W. J. Dilloo, *Das Wunder an den Stufen des Achas* (Amsterdam: Hoveker, 1885); G. F. Wright, *Wetensch. Bijdragen tot Bevest. der Oud-Test. Geschiedenis,* trans. C. Oranje (Rotterdam: D. A. Daamen, 1907), 63ff. (ET: *Scientific Confirmations of Old Testament History* [Oberlin: O. Bibliotheca Sacra, 1906]).

[Pascal]. The earth may be a thousand times smaller than many other planets; in an ethical sense it is and remains the center of the universe. It is the only planet fit to be the dwelling place for higher beings.[22] Here the kingdom of God has been established; here the struggle between light and darkness is being waged; here, in the church, God is preparing for himself an eternal dwelling. From this earth, therefore, we will continue to look up from where, both in a physical and an ethical sense, the rain and the sunshine and the increase will have to come, without imagining that we are thereby determining the place of heaven in an astronomic sense or know its precise location in the universe. To say, however, that scientific investigation has robbed God and the angels of their place of residence is absurdly superficial. For though Lalande presumed to say that he had searched through the entire universe and had not found God, the truth is that, to our limited vision, the universe with its measureless spaces is still one vast mystery; and one who does not find God in his or her immediate presence, in his or her heart and conscience, in the word and the Christian community, will not find him in the universe either, even though he equips himself with the best telescope that money can buy.[23]

THE HYPOTHESES OF THE NATURAL SCIENCES

[272] Christian theology, then, has no objections to the Copernican world-view. The situation is very different, however, with the hypotheses assumed nowadays by science with respect to the genesis of our solar system and the earth. With respect to the first, Kant and Laplace posed the hypothesis that our solar system and actually even the whole universe was originally one vast blob of gaseous chaos, marked by an extremely high temperature and turning on its own axis from west to east. This rotation moved with such force that parts of this gaseous mass broke away and, since they continued to move in the same direction, took on a spherical shape.[24]

Now, we must note first of all that this hypothesis, however deistically conceived, was absolutely not intended by Kant to eliminate God. It was his judgment, however, that this chaotic condition of all matter was the most

22. Cf. Alfred R. Wallace, *Man's Place in the Universe* (New York: McClure, Phillips, 1903).

23. J. H. A. Ebrard, *Der Glaube an die heilige Schrift und die Ergebnisse der Naturforschung* (Königsberg: n.p., 1851); Paul Wigand, *Die Erde, der Mittelpunkt der Welt*, Heft 144 (Band 19, Heft 8) of *Zeitfragen des christlichen Volkslebens* (Stuttgart: Belser, 1894); H. Schell (*Der Gottesglaube und die Naturwissenschaftliche Welterkenntniss*, 2d ed. [Bamberg: Schmidt, 1904]) writes: "As a result of the Copernican worldview the *earth* has become small, but not *man*. For whereas the magnitude of the earth consists in its massive materiality, that of humankind consists in its *spirit*" (p. 12); also cf. R. Schmid, *Das naturwissenschaftliche Glaubensbekenntnis eines Theologen*, 42 [*Scientific Creed*].

24. E. Haeckel, *Naturliche Schöpfungs-Geschichte*, 5th ed. (1874), 285ff. (9th ed. [Berlin: G. Reimer, 1898]); idem, *The Riddle of the Universe at the Close of the Nineteenth Century*, trans. Joseph McCabe (New York: Harper & Brothers, 1900), 239–40; L. Büchner, *Kraft und Stoff*, 17° A (1888), 130ff. (ET: *Force and Matter*, 4th ed., trans. from the 15th German ed. [New York: P. Eckler, 1891]); F. Pfaff, *Schöpfungsgeschichte*, 3d ed. (Heidelberg: C. Winter, 1881), 190ff.; O. Liebmann, *Zur Analysis der Wirklichkeit*, 3d ed. (Strassburg: K. J. Trübner, 1900), 389ff.

elementary state that could follow on nothingness, and that these materials themselves were all so shaped by God as the first cause that by immanent forces and in accordance with fixed laws they could produce the present world system without any miraculous intervention by God. But in our opinion, this hypothesis is insufficient to explain the origin of the universe, of motion, and of organic beings. In general it needs to be said that, however primitive and chaotic that first state of all matter may be thought to be and however many millions of years it may be projected back, it does not provide rest for our thinking. For one will *either* have to recognize with Kant that this original state of the creation depends in its totality immediately on God and follows upon nothingness, *or* one will have to view that chaotic state not only as the beginning of the present world system but also as the end and the destruction of a preceding world, and so on ad infinitum and thus *eternalize* matter and motion.[25] Furthermore, this hypothesis is open to many objections and does not explain the phenomena. These need not all be discussed here: we can, for example, overlook the objection that there are also heavenly bodies that make a retrograde movement and do not turn from west to east but from east to west. The above objections are so weighty, however, that even Haeckel recognizes them. And we do want to point out that, given this gaseous nebula and given the mechanical motion, this hypothesis is by no means capable of explaining this world system. For motion and matter by themselves are not enough to explain it. There has to be direction in that motion, and aside from matter there also has to be still something else to explain the world of spiritual and mental phenomena. Why did our present world system, which everywhere exhibits order and harmony and would implode or collapse at the least deviation from that order, arise from this nebulous mass? How could an unconscious, purposeless movement of atoms result in the formation of the universe? The chance of such an ordered whole originating from such a chaotic state is highly improbable and actually quite impossible. "It is just as simple to regard the creation as a playful vagary of chance as to explain a Beethoven symphony from marks and dots that have accidentally appeared on a piece of paper."[26]

Add yet that this hypothesis, even if it did explain the phenomena, would still be no more than a hypothesis. For what conclusion can be drawn for reality from a possibility? The consequences do not validate the movement from possibility to existence *(a posse ad esse non valet consequentia)*. What proof can be cited that the world system not only *could* but actually *did* originate in that manner? There is a big difference between a logical assumption and an actual state of affairs that may at one time have existed. When natural science investigates the phenomena, it attempts to trace them to their simplest form.

25. F. A. Lange, *Geschichte des Materialismus und Kritik seiner Bedeutung in der Gegenwart*, 8th ed. (Leipzig: Baedekker, 1908), II, 522; D. F. Strauss, *Der alte und der neue Glaube* (Leipzig: Hirzel, 1872), 225; Büchner, *Kraft und Stoff*, 133 [*Force and Matter*]; Haeckel, *Riddle of the Universe*, 249–50.

26. Oswald Heer, according to E. Dennert, *Moses oder Darwin?* 2d ed. (Stuttgart: Kielman, 1907), 50.

Consequently, it finally assumes the existence of extremely primitive and simple elements such as atoms, dynamisms, energies, ether, chaos, and so on. But these are logical assumptions at which it arrives. The idea that such atoms at one time existed as pure atoms in a primordial state, one that followed upon a state of nothingness, is by no means proved by such assumptions. Like the original elements of things (atoms, dynamisms, monads), so also the primordial states that scientists posit as having preceded the process of becoming are nothing but constructs, not reality. Their status is like the areligious state that is currently assumed in research inquiring into the origin of religion, or like Rousseau's state of nature from which, by way of a social contract, the state is supposed to have originated. Perhaps all such hypotheses can be of some use as constructs, like construction lines in mathematics, but this does not yet make them into actual explanations of existing reality.

What no natural science can teach us, finally, is given us by revelation, which is further confirmed by the tradition of all peoples. It teaches us that it has pleased God, in forming the world, to proceed from the imperfect to the perfect, from the simple to the complex, from the lower to the higher. There is an element of truth in the theory of evolution that is recognized in Scripture, as Genesis 1:2 clearly shows. But there the state of creation is real; there is no chaos in the true sense, no *hylē* (matter) in the Aristotelian sense, no primal matter without form, no inconceivable mass of pure atoms, but a state of cosmic formlessness that existed for a time, over which the Spirit of God hovered and upon which that Spirit brooded. It simply will not do, with many Christian apologists, to adopt the Kant-Laplace hypothesis without any form of criticism and then to be grateful that they have so beautifully managed to fit it into Genesis 1:2. The truth is rather that Scripture tells us the story of an actual state, while natural science is offering us assumptions that are not scientifically tenable.[27]

In recent years this hypothesis has, accordingly, been abandoned by many scientists and exchanged for Lockyer's "meteorite" hypothesis. Thus George Howard Darwin, son of the famed naturalist [Charles Darwin], at a meeting of the British Association held at Johannesburg on August 30, 1905, delivered a lecture in which he spoke about the results of his studies concerning the so-called nebular theory of the origin of the world and expressed his grave doubts about the correctness of this theory. The main "evidence" for this theory was

27. F. Pfaff, *Schöpfungsgeschichte* (Frankfurt a.M.: Heyder & Zimmer, 1877), 731ff.; H. Ulrici, *Gott und die Natur* (Leipzig: T. O. Weigel, 1862), 334–49; F. H. Reusch, *Nature and the Bible*, trans. Kathleen Lyttelton from 4th German ed., 2 vols. (Edinburgh: T. & T. Clark, 1886), II, 31; T. Pesch, *Die grossen Welträthsel*, 2d ed., 2 vols. (Freiburg i.B.: Herder, 1892), II, 326–52; G. Braun, "Die Kant-Laplachesche Weltbildungstheorie," *Neue kirchliche Zeitschrift* 3 (September 1892): 672–704; E. G. Steude, *Christentum und Naturwissenschaft* (Gütersloh: C. Bertelsmann, 1895), 142ff.; P. Schanz, *Über neue Versuche der Apologetik gegenüber dem Natural. und Spiritual.* (Regensburg: Nat. Verl-Anst., 1897), 211ff.; C. Gutberlet, *Der mechanische Monismus* (Paderborn: F. Schöningh, 1893), 28ff.; W. Hahn, *Die Entstehung der Weltkörper* (Regensburg: Pustet, 1895), 6ff.; A. Dippe, *Naturphilosophie* (Munich: C. H. Beck, O. Beck, 1907), 238; W. H. Nieuwhuis, *Twee Vragen des Tijds* (Kampen: Kok, 1907), 73.

the observation that all planets, both large and small, moved in the same direction around the sun and its satellites. But in recent years astronomers have discovered a satellite of Jupiter and a new satellite of Saturn whose movement is not congruent with that of their planets. It also seems doubtful whether one of the two recently discovered moons of Jupiter is really moving in the same direction as the other. But even if one accepts the postulates of Laplace, there are mathematical reasons for doubting whether from the postulated primordial state a system of planets and satellites had to arise rather than a swarm of asteroids or even smaller celestial bodies. George Darwin is therefore attempting to replace the Kant-Laplace hypothesis by another. If one pictures a planet spinning around a sun and inserts into this system a series of smaller meteoric bodies, then these meteors (assuming they are so small that their mutual gravitational pull can be neglected) will describe extraordinarily complicated courses. But after a longer or shorter period the majority of them will either have come to rest in the sun or a planet, and only a few, which from the beginning enjoyed the most favorable conditions of speed and direction, would have preserved their original independent existence and increased in size. Hence, if one accepts an already existent sun and a planet, Darwin's theory only assumes a sufficient quantity of meteoric matter to explain the present solar system. But the theory says nothing about the origination of the sun and the first planet.[28]

THE FORMATION OF THE EARTH

[273] A difference similar to the one we encountered in connection with the formation of our solar system occurs also in connection with the history of the development of the earth. Geology, basing itself on the strata of the earth's crust and the fossils of plants, animals, and humans found in those strata, has formed a hypothesis about the different periods of the earth's development. According to that hypothesis the oldest period is the Azoic,[29] or that of the primeval formation, in which especially the eruptive types of rock were formed and not a trace of organic life is found. Next followed the Paleozoic era or that of the primary formation in which, besides various types of rock, especially also coal was formed and even plants of the simplest kind and all classes of animals except birds and mammals are found. In the third, the Mesozoic era or that of the secondary formation, there occurred limestone formation (among other things), and different kinds of plants and animals, including the first oviparous and mammalian animals, are found. The next-following Tertiary, or

28. *Handelsblad*, November 17, 1905. Darwin's lecture entitled "Cosmic Evolution" has been included in *Wetenschappelijke Bladen* (June 1906): 406–34. A similar judgment has been expressed by Fr. Ratzel in E. Dennert, *Glauben und Wissen* (September 1906): 304; and by Riem, *Glauben und Wissen* (1905): 228; cf. also E. Dennert, *Die Weltanschauung des Modernen Naturforschers* (Stuttgart: M. Rielmann, 1907), 64; R. Schmid, *Das naturwissenschaftliche Glaubensbekenntnis*, 49–50 [*Scientific Creed*]; Stölzle, "Newtons Kosmogonie," *Philosophisches Jahrbuch* 20 (1907): 54.

29. Trans. note: The term "Azoic" is no longer current today; it is roughly equivalent to the early Precambrian era. Cf. "Geologic Time" chart in an English dictionary.

Cenozoic, era runs from the formation of limestone to the Ice Age [Pleistocene glacial epoch], and aside from plants, land animals, and freshwater animals, it witnessed especially the rise of predators and many of the now-extinct mammals. According to some scholars,[30] in the Tertiary period humans already lived side by side with these animals as well, but according to the majority, humans did not appear on the scene until the end of this era, after the Ice Age, in the Quaternary period.[31] There is no doubt that this theory of geological periods is much more firmly grounded than the Kantian hypothesis; it is based on data yielded by the study of the strata of the earth's crust. Here, therefore, the conflict between revelation and science has a much more serious character. On many points there is difference and contradiction, first of all, in the *time* and, second, in the *order* [sequence] in which the various creatures originated.

As to the *time*, the difference is very striking. We know that the chronology of the Septuagint (LXX) differs substantially from that of the Hebrew text. The church fathers, who frequently followed the Greek translation, calculated the time between the creation of the world and the capture of Rome by the Goths at 5611 years.[32] In later times, especially after the Reformation, scholars gave preference to the chronology of the Hebrew text and on that basis calculated that the creation of the world took place in 3950 B.C. (Scaliger), 3984 (Kepler, Petavius), 3943 (Bengel), or 4004 (Ussher). The Jews currently count the year 5689.[33] But some sought an even more precise calculation. There was serious controversy over whether the creation took place in the spring or in the fall of the year. Spring was the opinion of Cyril, Basil, Beda, Cajetan, Molina, Lapide, Luther, Melanchthon, Gerhard, Alsted, Polanus, G. J. Vossius, and others; fall was defended by Petavius, Calvisius, Calov, Danaeus, Zanchius, Voetius, Maresius, Heidegger, and Turretin among others. Sometimes the date was even determined more exactly: on March 25 or October 26.[34] In contrast, the geologists and natural scientists of our day posit calculations based on the rotation of the earth in connection with the flattening of its poles, the constant drop in the earth's temperature at the surface, the formation of the deltas of the Nile and the Mississippi, the formation of the earth's strata, the various

---

30. For example, H. Burmeister, *Geschichte der Schöpfung,* 7th ed. (Leipzig: C. G. Giebel, 1872), 612; L. Reinhardt, *Der Mensch zur Eiszeit in Europa und seine Kulturentwicklung bis zum Ende der Steinzeit* (Munich: Ernst Reinhardt, 1913), 1ff.

31. F. Pfaff, *Schöpfungsgeschichte,* 485ff.; Ulrici, *Gott und die Natur,* 353ff.; Reusch, *Nature and Bible,* I, 265ff.; K. A. von Zittel, *Aus der Urzeit,* 2d ed. (Munich: R. Oldenbourg, 1875), 537.

32. Augustine, *City of God,* XII, 10.

33. O. Zöckler, *Die Lehre vom Urstand des Menschen* (Gütersloh: C. Bertelsmann, 1870), 289ff.; P. Schanz, *Das Alter des Menschengeschlechts nach der heiligen Schrift, der Profangeschichte und der Vorgeschichte* (Freiburg i.B.: Herder, 1896), 1ff.

34. G. Voetius, *Select. disp.,* I, 587; K. R. Hagenbach, *Lehrbuch der Dogmengeschichte* (Leipzig: Hirzel, 1888), 630 note. A parallel to such credulity in modern times occurs in Sigmund Wellisch, who in his *Das Alter der Welt und des Menschen* (Vienna: Hartleben, 1899) assures us that the earth is 9,108,300 years old, the moon 8,824,500, man in his animal state 1,028,000, and man as a cultural being 66,000 years; cf. *Der Beweis des Glaubens* (May 1900): 164.

kinds of rock, especially coal, and so forth. The figures assumed for the age of the earth are fabulous—as among some pagan peoples: Cotta speaks of an unlimited space of time, Lyell of 560 million, Klein of 2000 million, Helmholtz of 80 million, and even Pfaff of at least 20 million years.[35]

In the second place, however, there is also a very great difference between the creation story in Genesis and the opinion of many scholars with respect to the *order* in which created beings originated. To mention just a few points: according to Scripture the light was indeed created on the first day, but our solar system did not come into being until the fourth day, after the earth had been readied on the second and third days and covered with luxuriant plant growth. According to geologists, however, the order is precisely the reverse. According to Genesis, the plant kingdom was created on the third day, but animals were not created until the fifth; geology, however, tells us that in the primary or Paleozoic era animals of the lower kind and also fish appeared. Genesis relates that all aquatic animals and all birds were created on the fifth day, and all land animals plus humans on the sixth day; but according to geology, certain mammals appeared already in the secondary, or Mesozoic, era. Hence, on many significant points there are clear differences between Scripture and science.

HARMONIZING SCIENCE WITH SCRIPTURE

[274] Naturally various attempts at reconciliation have been made. There is, first of all, the *ideal* theory, so called because it only adheres to the idea and not to the letter of the creation story. It does not view Genesis 1 as a historical account but as a poetic description of the creating acts of God. The six days are not seen as chronologically ordered periods of longer or shorter duration, but only as different perspectives from which the one created world can be viewed each time in order to give the limited human eye a better overview of the whole. It is therefore completely left to paleontology to determine the time, the manner, and the order of the origination of the different periods. It can be acknowledged that this theory had its forerunner in the allegorical exegesis that from ancient times had been followed in the Christian church with respect to Genesis 1. Following the example of Philo and appealing to Sirach 18:1 ("God created all things *at once*" [*koinē*, "together"; NRSV: "the whole universe"]), Origen, Augustine, and many others taught that God had created all things at once and simultaneously; the six days are not actually successive periods but only refer to the causal connection and logical order of created beings, describing how in successive stages the angels gained knowledge of the whole of creation. And even among those who clung to the literal sense

35. F. Pfaff, *Schöpfungsgeschichte*, 640–66; idem, "Das Alter der Erde," in *Zeitfragen des christlichen Volkslebens*, VII; O. Peschel, *Abhandlungen zur Erd- und Völkerkunde*, 5th ed., 3 vols. (Leipzig: Duncker & Humblot, 1877–79), 42–52; E. Haeckel, *Natürliche Schöpfungsgeschichte* (Berlin: G. Reimer, 1889), 340ff. (ET: *The History of Creation, or, The Development of the Earth and Its Inhabitants by the Action of Natural Causes*, trans. E. Ray Lankester [London: Henry S. King, 1876]).

of the creation story, allegory nevertheless still played a large role. Chaos, light, the term "one day" instead of the first day, the absence of divine approval at the end of the second day, paradise, the creation of Eve, and so forth—all gave rise to ingenious spiritualizations. Similar allegorizing, mythologizing, and rationalizing interpretations of the creation story flourished especially after the awakening of natural science and were applied by Hobbes, Spinoza, Beverland, Burnet, Bekker, Tindal, Edelmann, J. L. Schmidt, Reimarus, and others. Herder regarded Genesis 1 as a splendid poem of the most ancient humanity, which proceeding from the dawning day hymned the praises of the seven-day week.[36] Modern philosophy and theology have gone farther down this road, rejecting even the concept of creation along with the story of creation and regarding Genesis 1 as a myth that at best has a religious core. Christian theologians have not gone as far, but, in the interest of reconciling religion and science, have frequently returned to the ideal conception of Augustine and abandoned the literal and historical interpretation of Genesis 1.[37] Closely related to this ideal theory is the *visionary* theory, which was composed by Kurtz and later—after other attempts at reconciliation (see below) failed to bring about a satisfactory solution—taken over by many others. According to this hypothesis, we are dealing in the creation story with a prophetic historical tableaux that God showed the first human being in a vision, the same way in which the latter was instructed about the creation of woman in a vision, which he later passed down in a regular story. In that case Genesis 1 is not real history but "a backward-looking prophecy in the form of a visionary presentation" that bears a revelatory character insofar as it leads toward the history of salvation.[38]

36. J. G. Herder, *Älteste Urkunde des Menschengeschlechts* (Riga: Hartknoch, 1774–76); Bishop W. Clifford also held Genesis 1 to be a hymn to the seven-day week; V. Zapletal, *Der Schöpfungsbericht*, 88; J. B. Heinrich, and C. Gutberlet, *Dogmatische Theologie*, 2d ed., 10 vols. (Mainz: Kirchheim, 1881–1900), V, 206; cf. the view—which is related to Clifford's theory—of Prof. de Grijse, in P. Mannens, *Theologiae dogmaticae institutiones*, II, 239.

37. F. Michelis, *Entwicklung der beiden ersten Kapitel der Genesis* (Münster: Theissing, 1845) and in various essays in his journal *Natur und Offenbarung*, 1855ff.; F. Reusch, *Nature and Bible*, I, 348–75; P. Schanz, *Apologie des Christenthums*, 3 vols. (Freiburg i.B.: Herder, 1887–88), I, 293ff. (ET: *A Christian Apology*, trans. Michael F. Glancey and Victor J. Schobel, 4th rev. ed. [Ratisbon: F. Pustet, 1891]); M. J. Scheeben, *Handbuch der katholischen Dogmatik*, 4 vols. (Freiburg i.B.: Herder, 1933), II, 105ff.; J. Heinrich and C. Gutberlet, *Dogmatische Theologie*, V, 234ff.; H. Lüken, *Die Stiftungsurkunde des Menschengeschlechts* (Freiburg i.B.: Herder, 1876); C. Güttler, *Naturforschung und Bibel in ihrer Stellung zur Schöpfung* (Freiburg i.B.: Herder, 1877); F. Hettinger, *Apologie des Christenthums*, 7th ed. prepared by Eugen Müller, 4 vols. (Freiburg i.B.: Herder, 1895–98), III, 206. Belonging to this school on the Protestant side are T. Zollmann, *Bibel und Natur in der Harmonie ihrer Offenbarungen* (Hamburg: Agentur des Rauhen Hauses, 1869), 52ff.; G. Riehm, *Christentum und Naturwissenschaft*, 2d ed. (Leipzig: J. C. Hinrichs, 1896); Steude, *Christentum und Naturwissenschaft*; A. Dillmann, *Genesis* (Edinburgh: T. & T. Clark, 1897); Vuilleumier, "La première page de la Bible," *Revue de théologie et de philosophie* (1896): 362ff., 393ff.

38. J. H. Kurtz, *The Bible and Astronomy*, trans. T. D. Simonton, 3d ed. (Philadelphia: Lindsay & Blakiston, 1857), 112–17; O. Zöckler, *Geschichte der Beziehungen zwischen Theologie und Naturwissenschaft: Mit besondrer Rücksicht auf Schöpfungsgeschichte*, 2 vols. (Gütersloh: C. Bertelsmann, 1877–79); Dennert,

A second attempt at reconciliation is the so-called *restitution* theory. It attempts to bring about agreement between revelation and science as follows: This theory makes a separation between Genesis 1:2 and 1:3, and inserts all the events and phenomena that geology has taught us into the period before the chaos mentioned in verse 2. It does not view the *tōhû wābōhû* as the description of a purely negative, still unformed state, but as the term describing a destruction caused by the preceding great catastrophes. The six-day unit that begins with verse 3 then recounts the restoration from that state of destruction and the preparation of the earth as a dwelling place for humanity. The proponents of this theory believe that by it they can resolve every conceivable conflict between the Bible and geology and thus maintain the literal and historical meaning of the work during the six days of creation.

Whereas the first-mentioned theory could appeal to the example of church fathers, the emergence of this second theory only occurred considerably later. The Remonstrants Episcopius and Limborch had already posited a longer time space between Genesis 1:1 and 2 to make room for the fall of the angels.[39] In the eighteenth century the restitution theory was advocated by J. G. Rosenmuller, J. D. Michaelis, and Reinhard; the theosophists Oetinger, Hahn, St. Martin, von Baader, Schelling, Fr. von Meyer, Steffens, Schubert, Keerl, Kurtz, Delitzsch, and others, linked it with the idea that the first earth, created in Genesis 1:1, was actually the abode of the angels and catastrophically ruined by their fall.[40] Outside this theosophic association it was also accepted by Chambers, Buckland, Cardinal Wisemann, and a few others, but found little acceptance.[41]

A third theory, the so-called *concordistic* theory, seeks to achieve harmony between Scripture and science by viewing the days of creation as periods of longer duration. Already early in Christian history, the exegesis of the six days raised problems. The sun, moon, and stars were not created until the fourth day; the three preceding days in any case therefore had to be different from the second set of three days. Basil's explanation was that God effected the first three days by the emission and contraction of the light created on the first day.[42] But this explanation was not satisfactory to everyone—not to Augustine, for example, who at times deviated from his own simultaneity theory.[43] In addition, there was further disagreement over whether each day's work of creation

---

Moses oder Darwin, 9ff.; F. Hümmelauer, *Der biblische Schöpfungsbericht ein exegetischer Versuch* (Freiburg i.B.: Herder, 1877); idem, *Nochmals der biblische Schöpfungsbericht* (Freiburg i.B.: Herder, 1898); B. Schäfer, *Bibel und Wissenschaft* (Münster: Theissing, 1881); M. Gander, *Naturwissenschaft und Glaube,* Benzigers Naturwissenschaftliche Bibliothek (New York: Benziger Bros., 1905), 117.

39. S. Episcopius, *Instit. theol.,* IV, sect. 3, 3; P. van Limborch, *Theol. christ.* (Amsterdam: Wetstein, 1735), II, 19–21.

40. Cf. below in connection with the fall of the angels.

41. N. Wisemann, *Zusammenhang zwischen Wissenschaft und Offenbarung* (Regensberg: Manz, 1866), 263ff.

42. D. F. Strauss, *Chr. Glaubenslehre,* I, 621.

43. Augustine, *Literal Meaning of Genesis,* I, 16.

was completed in a single moment or successively spread out over the entire course of the day. Descartes, after all, had said that the purely natural things *(res pure naturales)* could have emerged from the existing chaos without any act of divine creation. This suggested the idea of natural development. A few Cartesian theologians, such as Wittichius, Allinga, and Braun, therefore theorized that each work of creation took a full day to complete.[44] And Whiston already said that the days had to be viewed as years, a theory also adopted by others. But the father of the concordistic theory is the abbot of Jerusalem. It was taken over by natural scientists such as de Luc, Cuvier, Hugh Miller, Pfaff, and the like; by theologians such as Lange, Delitzsch, Lougemont, Godet, Ebrard, Luthardt, Zöckler, and others,[45] as well as by Catholics like Heinrich, Palmieri, Simar, Pesch, and so forth.[46] Many scholars combined this view with the restitution theory and contented themselves even then with agreement in essentials. Hugh Miller, for example, had the Azoic period coincide with Genesis 1:3, the Paleozoic with Genesis 1:6–13, the Mesozoic with Genesis 1:14–23, and the Cenozoic with Genesis 1:24.[47]

Finally, the fourth theory, the one sometimes called the *antigeological* theory, continues to hold the literal and historical view of Genesis 1, and tries to place the results of geology in part in the six creation days, in part also in the period between Adam and Noah, and especially in the time of the flood. From ancient times already the flood was regarded as very important in this connection. Exegetes argued about a partial versus a universal flood—an issue that has always been in discussion—about the construction of the ark, and about the height of the flood.[48] But the flood acquired geological significance only after Newton. In 1682 Thomas Burnet published his *Theoria sacra telluris* and in it postulated a very large difference between the time before and the time after the flood. To him the flood becomes the end of an old world and the birth of an entirely new world. It was a tremendous catastrophe that altered the entire surface of the earth, created oceans and mountains, and put an end to the prevailing mild spring climate, the luxuriant fecundity, and the extraordinary longevity of the people who lived before that time. The flood especially changed the earth's axis, which was formerly parallel with that of the sun, so that it was now positioned obliquely in relation to the earth's orbit.

44. Cf. C. Vitringa, *Doctr. christ.*, II, 95; B. de Moor, *Comm. in Marckii Comp.*, II, 212.

45. J. Ebrard, *Der Glaube an die heilige Schrift*; C. E. Luthardt, *Apologetische Vorträge über die Grund-wahrheiten des Christenthums*, 8th ed. (Leipzig: Dörffling & Franke, 1878); O. Zöckler, "Schöpfung," *PRE²*, XIII, 647; Brandt, *Der Beweis des Glaubens* (1876): 339ff.; E. W. Hengstenberg, "Biblischen Kosmogenie und kosmogenischen Wissenschaft," *Beweis des Glaubens* 3 (1867): 400–418; cf. G. F. Wright, *Wetenschappelijke Bijdragen*, 304ff. (English original: *Scientific Confirmations of Old Testament History* [Oberlin, Ohio: Bibliotheca Sacra, 1907]).

46. J. Heinrich and C. Gutberlet, *Dogmatische Theologie*, V, 234, 256; H. Th. Simar, *Lehrbuch der Dogmatik*, 2 vols. (Freiburg i.B.: Herder, 1879–80), 249; C. Pesch, *Praelectiones dogmaticae* (Freiburg i.B.: Herder, 1916–25), III, 40; P. Mannens, *Theologiae dogmaticae institutiones*, II, 233.

47. O. Zöckler, *Geschichte der Beziehungen zwischen Theologie und Naturwissenschaft*, II, 544.

48. Ibid., II, 122ff.

This wholly new theory—while it was vehemently opposed, by Spanheim and Leydecker among others—was nevertheless further developed by Whiston, Clüver, and many others.[49] Toward the end of the eighteenth century, this diluvial theory was increasingly abandoned but continued to be held in honor among many orthodox Catholic and Protestant theologians.[50]

The proponents of this attempt at reconciliation continued to equate the biblical flood with the diluvium or the Ice Age of geology and in that connection judged that the flood was universal and therefore extended over the entire earth. In recent times most geologists and theologians, such as Sedgwick, Greenough, Buckland, Hitchcock, Hugh Miller, Barry, Dawson, Diestel, Dillmann, Pfaff, Kurtz, Michelis, Reusch, and Guttler,[51] believe that the biblical flood was very different from the diluvium of geology and therefore also has to be viewed as partial. It can only be called universal insofar as the entire human race perished as a result of it, although this point is again denied by some, such as Cuvier. Others have also expressed doubts about the reality of such an enormous flood, be it universal or partial, but then had to face the question whether in the flood stories they were dealing with sagas or myths, whether the underlying premise was fact or idea. The Viennese geologist Suess assumed that a horrendous inundation of the valleys of the Euphrates and the Tigris constituted the core of the story.[52] Although this hypothesis at first found wide acceptance, it was later strongly opposed, among other things, with the argument that flood stories are found not only in Babylonia and Israel but also in Egypt and throughout the world, among the Eskimos, the various peoples of the South Sea Islands, and so forth. This distribution of evidence seemed not to be explained by memories of a great flood in Babylonia.[53] For that reason others started to collect, compare, order, and sort out the various flood stories[54] and again came to think either of a certain historical fact, such as for example a flood in Mongolia,[55] or of various inundations in different countries,[56] or of a myth in which the birth and ascendancy of a light-god was narrated.[57] As is

49. Ibid., II, 143–92.

50. C. F. Keil and F. Delitzsch, *Commentary on Genesis,* vol. 1 (Edinburgh: T. & T. Clark, 1864–1901); and others by Zöckler, *Geschichte der Beziehungen zwischen Theologie und Naturwissenschaft,* II, 420–82, 288.

51. Cf. also A. Kuyper, *De Heraut* 929 (October 13, 1895): 1; 930 (October 20, 1895): 1; 962 (May 31, 1896): 1.

52. E. Suess, *Die Sintfluth* (Leipzig: G. Freitag, 1883).

53. On the comparison of the biblical account with the Babylonian flood story, one can consult (inter alia) the following: W. H. Kosters, "De Bijbelsche Zondvloedverhalen met de Babyl. vergeleken," *Theol. Tijdschr.* II (1885): 161ff., 321ff.; J. S. Nikel, *Genesis und Keilschriftforschung* (Freiburg i.B.: Herder, 1903), 173ff.; H. H. Kuyper, *Evolutie of Revelatie,* 123ff.

54. R. Andree, *Die Flutsagen, ethnographisch betrachtet* (Braunschweig: F. Vieweg, 1891); F. von Schwarz, *Sintfluth und Völkerwanderungen* (Stuttgart: Enke, 1894); H. Usener, *Die Sintflutsagen,* vol. 3 of *Religionsgeschichtliche Untersuchungen* (Bonn: Cohen, 1899); M. Winternitz, *Die Flutsagen des Alterthums und der Naturvölker* (Vienna, 1901).

55. Thus F. von Schwarz, *Sintfluth und Völkerwanderungen.*

56. M. Winternitz (*Die Flutsagen des Alterthums*) also held this view, as did L. von Ranke.

57. So H. Usener, *Die Sintflutsagen;* Winternitz, *Die Flutsagen des Alterthums.*

clear from this brief survey, the debate on this important and difficult issue is far from over, and the most recent studies seem rather to argue for the old diluvial view of the flood. G. F. Wright considers it a disaster in Central Asia that concluded a series of disasters in the Ice Age and which, except for Noah's family, destroyed the members of the human race still remaining there.[58]

THE SIX-DAY WEEK OF CREATION

[275] These four attempts to harmonize Scripture and science are not in every respect opposed to each other. Even in the ideal theory listed above there is an element of truth. Everyone agrees, after all, that Scripture does not speak the language of science but that of daily experience; that also in telling the story of creation it assumes a geocentric or anthropocentric viewpoint; and that in this connection it is not attempting to give a lesson in geology or any other science but, also in the story of the genesis of all creatures, remains the book of religion, revelation, and the knowledge of God. "We do not read in the Gospel that the Lord said: 'I will send to you a Paraclete who will teach you about the course of the sun and the moon!' For he wanted to make Christians, not mathematicians."[59] "Moses, accommodating himself to uneducated people, followed the things that appear to the senses."[60] "Scripture intentionally does not treat the things we know in philosophy."[61] But when Scripture, from its own perspective precisely as the book of religion, comes in contact with other sciences and also sheds its light on them, it does not all at once cease to be the Word of God but remains that Word. Even when it speaks about the genesis of heaven and earth, it does not present saga or myth or poetic fantasy but offers, in accordance with its own clear intent, history, the history that deserves credence and trust. And for that reason Christian theology, with only a few exceptions, continued to hold onto the literal historical view of the creation story.

It is nevertheless remarkable that not a single confession made a fixed pronouncement about the six-day continuum, and that in theology as well a variety

---

58. Further cf. L. Diestel, *Die Sintflut und die Flutsagen des Alterthums* (Berlin: Lüderitz, 1871), 2d ed. (Berlin: Habel, 1876); F. Reusch, *Bibel und Natur*, 4th ed., I, 289ff. (*Nature and Bible*); P. Schanz, *Apologie des Christentums*, I, 341ff. (*A Christian Apology*); F. G. Vigouroux, *Les livres saints*, 4 vols. (Paris: A. Roger & F. Chernoviz, 1886–90), IV, 239; Jürgens, "War die Sintflut eine Erdbebenwelle?" *Stimmen aus Maria-Laach* (1884); H. H. Howorth, *The Mammoth and the Flood* (London: S. Low, Marston, Searle, & Rivingon, 1887); R. Girard, *Études de géologie biblique*, I (Freiburg: Fragnière, 1893); C. Schmidt, *Das Naturereignis der Sintflut* (Basel: B. Schwabe, 1895); *O. Zöckler, *Neue Jahrbuch für deutsche Theologie* 3–4 (1894–95); M. Gander, *Die Sündflut in ihrer Bedeutung für die Erdgeschichte* (Münster: Aschendorff, 1896); A. Trissl, *Sündflut oder Gletscher?* (Regensburg: G. J. Manz, 1894); Th. Schneider, *Was ist's mit der Sintflut?* (Wiesbaden, 1903); J. Riem, *Die Sintflut in Sage und Wissenschaft* (Hamburg: Rauhe Haus, 1925); G. F. Wright, *Wetensch. Bijdragen*, 164, 287 (*Scientific Confirmations*).

59. Augustine, *Proceedings against Felix the Manichee*, I, 10.

60. T. Aquinas, *Summa theol.*, I, qu. 70, art. 4.

61. J. Alsted, *Theol.*, I–II, 181; cf. G. Voetius, *Select. disp.*, V, 131; Hettinger, *Apologie des Christenthums*, III, 196.

of interpretations were allowed to exist side by side. Augustine already urged believers not too quickly to consider a theory to be in conflict with Scripture, to enter the discussion on these difficult subjects only after serious study, and not to make themselves ridiculous by their ignorance in the eyes of unbelieving science.[62] This warning has not always been faithfully taken to heart by theologians. Geology, it must be said, may render excellent service to us in the interpretation of the creation story. Just as the Copernican worldview has pressed theology to give another and better interpretation of the sun's "standing still" in Joshua 10, as Assyriology and Egyptology form precious sources of information for the interpretation of Scripture, and as history frequently finally enables us to understand a prophecy in its true significance—so also geological and paleontological investigations help us in this century to gain a better understanding of the creation story. We must remember that the creation and preparation of heaven and earth is a divine work par excellence, a miracle in the absolute sense of the word, full of mysteries and secrets. Genesis nevertheless tells the story of this work in such a simple and sober manner that there almost seems to be a contradiction between the fact itself and its description. Behind every feature in the creation story lies a world of marvels and mighty deeds of God, which geology has displayed before our eyes in a virtually endless series of phenomena. Accordingly, Scripture and theology have nothing to fear from the *facts* brought to light by geology and paleontology. The world, too, is a book whose pages have been inscribed by God's almighty hand. Conflict arises only because both the text of the book of Scripture and the text of the book of nature are often so badly read and poorly understood. In this connection the theologians are not without blame since they have frequently condemned science, not in the name of Scripture but of their own incorrect views. Natural scientists have repeatedly interpreted the facts and phenomena they discovered in a manner, and in support of a worldview, that was justified neither by Scripture nor by science. For the time being it would seem advisable for geology—which is a relatively young science and, though it has already accomplished a lot, has still a vast amount of work to do—to restrict itself to the gathering of material and to abstain from forming conclusions and framing hypotheses. It is still utterly incapable of doing the latter and must still practice patience for a long time before it will be competent and equipped to do it.

Now if these provisional remarks have been taken to heart, I would say that it is probable, in the first place, that the creation of heaven and earth in Genesis 1:1 preceded the work of the six days in verses 3ff. by a shorter or longer period. The restitution theory certainly erred when it located the fall of the angels and the devastation of the earth in Genesis 1:2. There is nothing in this verse that supports this position. The text does not say that the earth *became* waste and void, but that it was so and was so created. The trackless void by no means

62. Augustine, *Literal Meaning of Genesis*, I, 18–21; cf. T. Aquinas, *Summa theol.*, I, qu. 68, art. 1.

implies that the earth had been devastated, but only that though it was already earth, it was still unformed, without configuration or form. For the rest, it is true that the creation of heaven and earth and the trackless and vacuous state of the earth cannot be placed within the boundaries of the first day. The latter only began, and could in the nature of the case only begin, with the creation of the light. The first day was not formed by a combination of original darkness and subsequently created light, but it was formed by the first alternation of evening and morning, which was initiated after the creation of the light. The darkness mentioned in Genesis 1:2 was not the first evening; only after the creation of light was there an evening and then a morning. And that morning brought to completion the first day, which had begun with the creation of light. A day in Genesis begins and ends with the morning.[63] Augustine, Lombard, Thomas, Petavius, and many others rightly judged therefore that the creation of heaven and earth, and the *tōhû wābōhû* state of the earth, occurred before any day existed *(ante omnem diem)*.[64] Only in this way can one do justice to the fact that the creation in Genesis 1:1 is simply recounted as a fact without any further description but that the preparation of the earth (Gen. 1:3ff.) is recounted at length. Genesis 1:1 only states that God is the Creator of all things, but it does not tell us that God created them by his Word and Spirit. Of course, this latter point is not denied, but neither is it stated, nor are we told in how much time and in what manner God created heaven and earth, or how long the unformed state of the earth lasted. Only when the six-day work begins are we told that also the unformed earth is maintained and made fruitful by the Spirit of God (Gen. 1:2), and that all things on and in that earth have been brought into being by the Word of God (Gen. 1:3ff.). In the ordering and adornment of the earth during the six days, God's wisdom is manifest.[65] But even if, with a view to Exodus 20:11 and 31:17, one wanted to include the story of Genesis 1:1–2 in the first day, that would only have resulted in the first day's becoming most unusual. It would then have started at the moment of creation and would initially have been dark for a time and have begun with a long night (Gen. 1:2), a situation that is hard to square with Genesis 1:3–5.

[276] Something similar is true of the days in which the earth was formed and made into an abode for humans. At all times people have entertained different opinions on that matter, and Thomas rightly affirms that in things not belonging to the necessity of faith various opinions are permitted.[66] Augustine believed that God created all things simultaneously in a single instant, so that the days of which Genesis 1 speaks make known to us not the temporal but only the causal order in which the parts of the work of creation stand to each

63. Cf. C. F. Keil and F. Delitzsch, *Comm. on Genesis.*

64. Augustine, *Confessions*, XII, 8; P. Lombard, *Sent.*, II, dist. 12, 1, 2; T. Aquinas, *Summa theol.*, I, qu. 74, art. 2; D. Petavius, "De opificio sex dierum," in *Theol. dogm.*, I, ch. 9, n. 2; W. G. T. Shedd, *Dogmatic Theology*, 2 vols. (New York: Charles Scribner's Sons, 1888–89), I, 474.

65. J. Calvin, *Commentary*, on Gen. 1:3.

66. T. Aquinas, *Sent.*, II, dist. 2, qu. 1, art. 3.

other. And in obscure matters, he warned believers against taking such a firm stand in favor of a certain interpretation of Scripture that, when a clearer light should dawn over a passage, we would rather shine in defending our own opinion than fight for the meaning of Holy Scripture.[67] This has happened, for example, when in an earlier time the Copernican worldview was deemed to be in conflict with Joshua 10:12–13 and hence rejected on the basis of an incorrect exegesis. But Augustine's warning applies to the left as well as to the right. A few years ago the concordistic theory mentioned above was widely accepted because it seemed to bring agreement between the biblical creation story and the periods of geology. But very serious objections have been raised against this theory also, two of which deserve attention in particular. In the first place, with regard to their order and duration, the geological periods, as will appear later, are not so invulnerable to objection that in them we are dealing with an established result of science. And even if that were the case, harmony between geology and Scripture is still not achieved by the concordistic theory because various points of difference remain. The main purpose for which it was proposed and recommended, namely, agreement between Scripture and natural science, could not be achieved by it, and consequently this theory increasingly declined in significance and influence.

An additional objection is, namely, that the days in Genesis 1 are not periods in which there occur repeated daily alternations of light and darkness, but days which in each case are formed by one single alternation of darkness and light and defined by [one] evening and morning. And although despite this objection the concordistic theory is still being advocated by many scholars,[68] others have completely abandoned it, not indeed to return to the historical view accepted earlier, but on the contrary to move on to the ideal, visionary, or even mystical theory.[69] Augustine's opinion, which he himself for that matter presented

67. Augustine, *Literal Meaning of Genesis,* bk. 1, ch. 18, Ancient Christian Writers 41 (New York: Newman, 1982), 41: "In matters that are obscure and far beyond our vision, even in such as we may find treated in Holy Scripture, different interpretations are sometimes possible without prejudice to the faith we have received. In such a case, we should not rush in headlong and so firmly take our stand on one side that, if further progress in the search of truth justly undermines this position, we too fall with it. That would be to battle not for the teaching of Holy Scripture but for our own, wishing its teaching to conform to ours, whereas we ought to wish ours to conform to that of Sacred Scripture." Cf. T. Aquinas, *Summa theol.,* I, qu. 68, art. 1.

68. E.g., J. Heinrich and C. Gutberlet, *Dogmatische Theologie,* V, 256; F. P. Kaulen, *Der biblische Schöpfungsbericht* (Freiburg i.B.: Herder, 1902); P. Mannens, *Theologiae dogmaticae institutiones,* II, 233; F. Bettex, in various works; A. Gnandt, *Der mosaische Schöpfungsbericht in seinem Verhältnis zur modernen Wissenschaft* (Graz, 1906); G. F. Wright, *Wetensch. Bijdragen,* 332ff. (*Scientific Confirmations*).

69. E.g., O. Zöckler, "In eigener Sache," *Beweis des Glaubens* 36 (1900): 32–39; and "Schöpfung," *PRE³*; Bachmann, "Der Schöpfungsbericht und die Inspiration," *Neue kirchliche Zeitschrift* 17 (May 1906): 383–405; cf. also idem, "Die Schöpfungsberichte in Unterrichte," *Neue kirchliche Zeitschrift* 18 (October 1907): 743–62; O. Undritz, *Neue kirchliche Zeitschrift* 10 (October 1899): 837–52; R. Schmid, *Das naturwiss. Glaubens.,* 26ff. (*Scientific Creed*); J. Reinke, *Die Welt als That: Umrisse einer Weltansicht auf naturwissenschaftlicher Grundlage,* 4 vols. (Berlin: Gebruder Paetel, 1905), 481ff.; C. Holzhey, *Schöpfung, Bibel und Inspiration* (Mergentheim: Carl Ohlinger, 1902); F. Hümmelauer, *Nochmals der biblische Schöpfungsbegriff;* M. Gander, *Naturwissenschaft und Glaube* (New York: Benziger Bros., 1905), 117.

only as a possible interpretation, not as undoubted,[70] was usually discussed by theologians with appreciation, but nevertheless quite generally rejected because it seemed to do violence to the text of Holy Scripture. And this is even much more the case with respect to the visionary and mythical theory. We granted that revelation can exploit all kinds and genres of literature, even the fable;[71] but whether a given section of Holy Scripture contains a poetic description, a parable, or a fable, is not for us to determine arbitrarily but must be clear from the text itself. The first chapter of Genesis, however, hardly contains any ground for the opinion that we are dealing here with a vision or myth. It clearly bears a historical character and forms the introduction to a book that presents itself from beginning to end as history. Nor is it possible to separate the facts (the religious content) from the manner in which they are expressed. For if with Lagrange, for example, the creation itself is regarded as a fact, but the days of creation as form and mode of expression, then the entire order in which the creation came into being collapses, and we have removed the foundation for the institution of the week and the Sabbath, which according to Exodus 20:11 is most decidedly grounded in the six-day period of creation and the subsequent Sabbath of God.

So, although for the above reasons the days of Genesis 1 are to be considered days and not to be identified with the periods of geology, they nevertheless—like the work of creation as a whole—have an extraordinary character. This is evident from the following. In the first place, it will not do, as already stated earlier, to pack the "first creation" (Gen. 1:1) and the unformed state of the earth (Gen. 1:2) into the first day. For the first evening (Gen. 1:5), which does not coincide with the darkness of Genesis 1:2, began and could only begin after the light was created and had shone for a time. Hence, the first day began with the creation of light; after it had shone for a time, evening fell and the morning came. At that point the first day was over: Genesis calculates the day from morning to morning. In the second place, the first triduum of the "second creation" is formed and calculated in the biblical story in a way that differs from the second triduum. The essence of a day and night does not consist in their duration (shorter or longer) but in the alternation of light and darkness, as Genesis 1:4 and 5a clearly teaches. In the case of the first triduum this alternation was not effected by the sun, which only made its appearance on the fourth day, but came about in a different way: by the emission and contraction of the light created in verse 3. If this is the case, the first three days, however much they may resemble our days, also differ significantly from them and hence were extraordinary cosmic days. In the third place, it is not impossible that the second triduum still shared in this extraordinary character as well. For while it is true that the sun and the moon and the stars were created on the fourth

70. Augustine, *Literal Meaning of Genesis*, IV, 28.
71. Cf. H. Bavinck, *Reformed Dogmatics*, I, 446–48 (#117).

day, and it is conceivable therefore that the second triduum was determined by the rotation of the earth in relation to the sun, yet it does not follow that from the formation of the sun, the moon, and the stars on the fourth day astronomical and terrestrial relations were the same then as they are now. Scripture itself shows us that as a result of the fall and the flood cataclysmic changes occurred, not only in the human and animal world, but also in the earth and its atmosphere;[72] and the period of creation in the nature of the case existed in very different circumstances from those that prevailed after the completion of creation. In the fourth place, it is very difficult for us to find room on the sixth day for everything Genesis 1–2 has occur in it if that day was in all respects like our days. For occurring on that day are the creation of the animals (Gen. 1:24–25), the formation of Adam (Gen. 1:26; 2:7), the planting of the garden (Gen. 2:8–14), the announcement of the probationary command (Gen. 2:16–17), the conducting of the animals to, and their naming by, Adam (Gen. 2:18–20), Adam's deep sleep and the creation of Eve (Gen. 2:21–23).

Now, it may be possible for all these things to have taken place within the span of a few hours, but it is not likely. In the fifth place, much more took place on each day of creation than the sober words of Genesis would lead us to suspect. The creation was a series of awesome miracles that the biblical story, which is both sublime and simple, portrays to us each time with a single brushstroke without giving details. Just as in the Decalogue one single sin represents many other sins, so in the creation story of each day only the most prominent item is featured: that which was most important and necessary for man as lord of the earth and image of God. Natural science, accordingly, reveals to us all sorts of creatures about which nothing is said in Genesis. A wide assortment of components of celestial bodies, numerous minerals, plants, and animal species are left unreported in Genesis. They must have been created, however, and taken their place among the works of creation of the six days. Each day's work of creation must certainly have been much grander and more richly textured than Genesis summarily reports in its sublime narrative. For all these reasons "day," in the first chapter of the Bible, denotes the time in which God was at work creating. With every morning he brought into being a new world; evening began when he finished it. The creation days are the workdays of God. By a labor, resumed and renewed six times, he prepared the whole earth and transformed the chaos into a cosmos. In the Sabbath command this pattern is prescribed to us as well. As they did for God, so also for man six days of labor are followed by a day of rest. In Israel the divisions of the liturgical calendar were all based on that time of creation. And for the whole world it remains a symbol of the eons of this dispensation that will some day culminate in eternal rest, the cosmic Sabbath (Heb. 4).

72. Cf. A. Kuyper, *De Gemeene Gratie in Wetenschap en Kunst* (Amsterdam: Höveker & Wormser, 1905), I, 10ff., 84ff.

FACTS AND INTERPRETATIONS

[277] Now that we have basically come to know the content of the biblical creation story, it is of some importance also to focus our minds for a moment on the facts and phenomena that have been brought to light by geological research. No one has any objection, no one *can* have any objection, to the facts advanced by geology.[73] These facts are just as much words of God as the content of Holy Scripture and must therefore be believingly accepted by everyone. But these facts must be rigorously distinguished from the exegesis of these facts that geologists present. The phenomena that the earth exhibits are one thing; the combinations, hypotheses, and conclusions that the students of earth science connect with these phenomena are quite another. Regardless now of the absolutely nonimaginary possibility that also the observation, identification, and description of the geological facts and phenomena are sometimes decidedly colored by an a priori worldview, contemporary geology agrees that the earth's crust is composed of different layers, all of which clearly show the marks of having been deposited in water; that these layers, wherever and in as far as they are present, always occur in a certain order, so that, say, a lower formation never occurs in between higher ones; and finally, that these earth layers contain a large mass of fossils, which again are not indiscriminately scattered throughout all the layers but occur in the lower sediments to the degree that they are lower in kind. These are the facts, and on that basis geologists have constructed all those protracted geological periods we listed earlier.

But very serious objections exist precisely to these long periods. In the first place, the fact that geology is a young science deserves consideration. It is not yet a hundred years old. In the first half of its existence, in the case of men like von Buch, de Saussure, and so forth, it was absolutely not hostile to Scripture. It was only when Lyell and others harnessed it to the doctrine of evolution that it became a weapon in the war against the biblical creation story. This consideration alone tells us to be cautious; as geological science becomes older and richer, it will probably review itself on this point.

Second, one can call geology the archaeology of the earth. It acquaints us with the conditions in which the earth existed in earlier times. But, of course, it tells us virtually nothing about the cause, the origin, the duration, and so forth, of these conditions. The wish to reconstruct the history of the earth from the phenomena of the earth seems a priori as precarious an undertaking as the wish to compose the history of a people from its archaeological artifacts. As an auxiliary science archaeology can be very useful, but it cannot replace history. Geology offers important data, but in the nature of the case it can never produce a history of creation. Anyone attempting to write such a history must continually resort to conjectures. All birth, said Schelling, is from darkness into light. All origins are wrapped in obscurity. If no one tells us who our parents

73. Thus already Augustine, *Literal Meaning of Genesis,* I, 21.

and grandparents are or were, we do not know it. Absent a creation story, the history of the earth is and remains unknown to us.

Third, geology, therefore, can never rise to the level of the creation story; it operates on the foundation of what has been created and does not come near to the level of Genesis 1. It can identify what it observes but only conjecture about its origins. The geologist Ritter von Holger very correctly and beautifully observes: "We have to contend with the unpleasant fact that we arrived at the theater only after the curtain had already fallen. We must attempt to guess the play that was presented from the decorations, set pieces, weapons, and so forth, that have been left behind on the stage (they are the paleontological discoveries or fossilizations); hence, it is entirely excusable if we make mistakes."[74]

Fourth, although the earth layers, wherever and insofar as they occur in a given location, are situated in a certain order, it is equally true that they nowhere occur all together and completely, since some are found in one place and others elsewhere. "We nowhere possess a complete copy of the book of the earth; what we have, scattered over the face of it, is a huge mass of defective copies of the most diverse size and format and on very different materials."[75] The series and order of the earth layers and hence also of the geological periods based on them are therefore not immediately conveyed to us by the facts, but they rest on a combination of facts that are open to all sorts of conjectures and errors. As the geologists themselves acknowledge, it takes a lot of patience and painstaking effort to establish the true order of the earth layers.[76]

Fifth, only a very small part of the earth's surface has so far been investigated, notably England, Germany, and France. Very little is known about the other parts of Europe, virtually nothing about the greatest percentage of Asia, Africa, and Australia, and so on. Even Haeckel admits that barely a thousandth part of the earth's surface has been paleontologically examined.[77] And this estimate is certainly not too low. Hence, later investigations may still bring to light an assortment of other facts. In any case, the hypotheses and conclusions of geology have been constructed on too slim a factual foundation.

Sixth, it is a fact, one that is increasingly acknowledged from the side of geology itself, that the time of the formation of the earth layers can absolutely not be determined from the nature and quality of those layers. "The composition of the layers," writes Pfaff, "usually does not yield any clue on which to base a conclusion concerning the time of its formation."[78] Under the influence of Darwinism, which has sought to explain everything in terms of infinitely small changes over infinitely long time spans, scientists have spoken of millions of years. But those are not more than mythological figures that lack all

74. In A. Trissl, *Das biblische Sechstagewerk vom Standpunkte der katholischen Exegese und vom Standpunkte der Naturwissenschaften,* 2d ed. (Regensburg: G. J. Manz, 1894), 73.

75. F. Pfaff, *Schöpfungsgeschichte,* 5.

76. A. S. Geikie, *Geology* (New York: D. Appleton, 1880), 74–82; F. Pfaff, *Schöpfungsgeschichte,* 5.

77. E. Haeckel, *Natürliche Schöpfungsgeschichte,* 355.

78. F. Pfaff, *Schöpfungsgeschichte,* 5.

basis in fact.[79] Geologists absolutely do not know whether in earlier time the same, or different, circumstances prevailed. And even when circumstances are identical, everything grows much more rapidly and vigorously in youth than in later years. Furthermore, all the grounds on which geologists have so far based their figures have proved untenable. The delta formations, the risings and fallings of the landmasses, the coal formations, and so forth, have all again been abandoned as a base for calculation. Level-headed natural scientists, accordingly, speak a very different language today. "We lack any precise standard for the calculation of prehistoric events or processes."[80]

Seventh, even the order in which the earth layers occur cannot be a standard for calculating the time and duration of their formation. Naturally, at a given place the lowest layer is older than the top layer, but all warrant is missing for combining the different earth layers of different places and thus forming a patterned series of formations and periods. "Just as in our lakes limestone deposits build up at certain locations today while at the same time, in other locations, layers of sand or clay are deposited, so also in earlier times differing layers simultaneously built up at different locations, and similar layers at different times."[81] The layers dating back to so-called different periods are not consistently different, and those held to be equally old are not always qualitatively identical.[82] In the same time period, in different parts of the earth, similar formations may have occurred, as it still frequently happens today.

Eighth, the time of the formation of earth layers and the order of their position, therefore, is almost exclusively determined in terms of the fossils found in them. Geology has become dependent on paleontology, and the latter is almost completely captive to the theory of evolution today. It is a priori assumed as a proved fact that organic beings have developed from the lower to the higher; and on this basis, then, the order and duration of sediment formations is determined. Conversely, scientists then use the order of the sedimentations as proof for the theory of evolution, thus following a vicious circle. The truth is that paleontology tends to contradict rather than to favor the theory of evolution, inasmuch as in the different layers different fossils of plants and animals occur, not just a few specimens and species, but large numbers. At each layer geology is all at once confronted by an incalculably rich realm of

79. Cf. already F. W. J. Schelling, *Werke*, II, 1, 229.

80. A. Zittel, *Aus der Urzeit: Bilder aus der Schöpfungsgeschichte* (Munich: R. Oldenburg, 1875), 556. Also George H. Darwin, in the lecture cited above, said that we can neither use the nebular nor the meteorite hypothesis to estimate the time needed for the development of the solar system. He does believe that geologists with their calculations suggesting a time between 50 million and a billion years are closer to the truth than the physicists with their shorter time (as a rule) of about 20 million years. But, he continues, in recent times a new element has been added: radioactivity. A small percentage of radium in the sun would be sufficient to explain its present radiation. This branch of science is still young, but we can learn from it how dangerous it is to decide from our lofty positions what is possible and what is not. The duration of the geological periods remains unknown to us (*Wetenschappelijke Bladen* [June 1906]: 425ff.).

81. F. Pfaff, *Schöpfungsgeschichte*, 5.

82. A. Trissl, *Das biblische Sechstagewerk*, 61.

organic life, differentiated in kinds but not augmented by transitional forms. Fossils of plants and animals are found that have since become extinct, yet they surpassed all later formations in size and strength, and apparently reveal nature in its primal creative power and luxuriant fecundity.[83]

Ninth, now it is true that the fossils are not scattered indiscriminately over all layers, and that in certain layers usually also fossils of certain plants and animals occur. But from this state of affairs, too, nothing can be inferred with certainty, either for the theory of evolution or for the geological periods. The different plant and animal species, after all, were and are distributed over the earth's surface in accordance with their nature and the corresponding conditions of life. They lived in different places and zones and therefore also had to petrify in the different sediments that were formed in various places. Accordingly, the fossils are not the representatives of the time in which these organic beings originated, but of the higher or deeper zones in which they lived. Suppose that plants and animals now living throughout the world were suddenly buried in earth layers and had petrified. In that case no decision could be made with respect to the time of their origin either from the various kinds of fossils that emerged or from the different layers in which they occurred. Add to this the factors that make the division and dating of the geological periods virtually impossible. Examples are that in the earliest times the different species of plants and animals were not so widely distributed over the earth as they were later; that of any number of plants and animals no fossils have been preserved in the various layers; that a wide range of causes may have brought certain plants and animals into places and zones in which they were not indigenous; that the same earth layers, indeed as a rule but far from always, contained the same species of fossils; and that therefore, earth layers that are qualitatively the same and were at one time placed in the same period were later identified as belonging to another period because new and different fossils were found in them.

Finally, geologists themselves frequently admit that the geological periods cannot be clearly distinguished. This is especially evident in the case of the Tertiary and Quaternary periods. Here virtually everything is still uncertain. Uncertainty applies to the boundaries, the beginning and the end, of those two periods, as well as to the cause, extent, and duration of the so-called [Pleistocene] Ice Age. There is disagreement over whether we must assume one or more ice ages. Even the occurrence of any ice age at all is still subject to serious doubt. There is uncertainty about the cause by which, as well as the time and manner in which, the large prehistoric animals perished, animals whose fossils

83. F. Pfaff, *Schöpfungsgeschichte*, 667–709. According to *Glauben und Wissen* (March 1906): 104–5, G. H. Darwin in his South African lecture also stated the following: "We can compare the facts on which theories of evolution are based with a mixed and colorful heap of glass beads from which an astute person in search of truth picks out a few that he then arranges on a string, incidentally noticing that these beads look somewhat alike, . . . but the problem of introducing order in that pile of beads will probably always put the astuteness of the researcher to shame. . . . The immeasurable magnitude of the undiscovered will be forever there to humble the pride of humans."

have in some cases been preserved fully intact. There is uncertainty about the debut of man, before or after the Ice Age, in the Tertiary or Quaternary period, simultaneously with or after the mammoth, the mastodon, and rhinoceros. Uncertainty applies to the cause of the diluvial formations and their distribution over the globe. Scientists are uncertain about the cause and the time of the formation of mountains and glaciers. In this connection the fact that the displacement of glaciers from the north to the center of Europe would require a height of 44,000 meters for the mountains of Scandinavia yields a virtually insurmountable objection.

THE FLOOD FACTOR

[278] Added to all this, finally, is the fact that Scripture and the unanimous tradition of virtually all peoples recount the story of a cataclysmic flood that brought about immense changes in the entire state of the earth. According to Scripture, a whole new state of affairs for humanity and the earth set in after the flood. Before the flood, humankind was distinguished by great intellect, a vigorous enterprising spirit, titanic courage, greatly extended life expectancy, strong physiques, and appalling wickedness. And undoubtedly nature, the plant-and-animal kingdom, was as vigorous as that humanity. But in the flood almost all people perished, numerous plant and animal species became extinct, nature was curbed, and a gentler dispensation was inaugurated, the one in which we live. These testimonies of Scripture are currently being confirmed from every direction by geology. No human remains have as yet been found from the Tertiary period, and it is not likely that such remains will ever be found. Before the flood humanity was probably not yet spread out over the earth. The flood itself explains why no fossils remain of humans before that time. Human skulls and bones found here and there all originated in the Quaternary period and do not differ from our own. Geology further teaches clearly that humans were contemporaneous with the mammoths, the Hebrew "behemoth" (Job 40:15), and that the mammoths therefore belong in historic time. The universality of the diluvial formations proves that the flood must have been extended over the whole earth. Mountains, in large part, originated in historic time. The causes of the Ice Age, if it ever existed, are totally unknown and may therefore very well be traced to the flood and the subsequent lowering of the temperature. It is only by and after the diluvium that the earth acquired its present form.[84] There is actually only one serious objection to the identification of the diluvium with the flood, and that is time. Geology usually places the Ice Age and the diluvium several [ca. 8–38] thousands of years before Christ. But against this objection it may be remarked, on the one hand, that the chronology of Scripture has as yet by no means been established either. One need not go as far as de Sacy, who claimed, "There is no biblical chronol-

84. For the literature on the flood, see above, pp. 493–95 nn. 48–58.

ogy," to still argue with Voetius, "No exact computation can be derived from Holy Scripture."[85] It cannot be ruled out that at times some generations have been skipped and that personal names are intended as the collective names of peoples. And on the other hand, as we said above, the calculations of geology are also much too uncertain to derive from them a solid objection against the view stated above.

If we now summarize the above and take everything into account, we can say that from the moment of creation in Genesis 1:1 to the flood, Scripture offers a time span that can readily accommodate all the facts and phenomena that geology and paleontology have brought to light in this century. It is hard to see why they could not all be placed in that time frame. This is all theology has to do at this point. It does not have to involve itself in the issue of what has caused these phenomena. Let geology explain the facts! But in that connection, Scripture can perhaps render more service than the natural sciences usually suspect. It does, after all, point out that the creation is a divine work par excellence. In the origination and formation of things forces have been at work, up until the flood conditions have existed, and in that flood a catastrophe has occurred, such as has never been seen since. The genesis of things is always controlled by other laws than their subsequent development. The laws issued by the creature are not the rule of creation, still less that of the Creator. Further, theology will be well advised to stick only to the indisputable facts that geology has uncovered, and to be on its guard against the hypotheses and conclusions that geology has added to the mix. For that reason theology should refrain from making any attempt to equate the so-called geological periods with the six creation days. It is no more than an undemonstrable opinion, after all, that these periods have unfolded successively and in that order. This is not to deny that, say, the Azoic formations began to occur already from the moment of creation. Everything rather points to the thesis that, in response to the operation of all kinds of mechanical and chemical forces, these formations then began to occur. But geology can in no way know whether these formations did not occur also later in conjunction with the Paleozoic era, and so on; it sees formations and only guesses about the causes and manner of their origination. The same is true of all the other periods. It is very probable that the so-called Tertiary period extends to the flood, and that diluvium and Ice Age coincide with this catastrophe. Further, nothing is settled in the so-called Paleozoic period by the simultaneous occurrence of plant and animal fossils with respect to the order in which these species originated. For geology does not know the first thing about the origination of these organic beings; it finds them but cannot penetrate the mystery of their origin. And it too must assume that the plant kingdom originated before the animal kingdom, for the simple reason that animals live from plants. Insofar as geology can say a word about the origin of things, it is in perfect agreement with Scripture. First,

85. G. Voetius, *Select. disp.,* V, 153; cf. above, p. 489 n. 34.

there was the inorganic creation; then came the organic creation, beginning with the plant kingdom; next followed the animal kingdom, and this again in the same order, first the aquatic, then the land animals, and among them especially the mammals.[86]

So as Christians and as theologians we await with some confidence the *certain* results of the natural sciences. Theology has nothing to fear from thorough, multifaceted research. It only needs to be on its guard against attaching too much value to a study that is still completely new, imprecise, and incomplete; it therefore is constantly being augmented with conjectures and suspicions. It needs to be on its guard against making premature concessions to, and to seek agreement with, the so-called scientific results that can at any time be knocked down and exposed in their untenability by more thorough research. As the science of divine and eternal things, theology must be patient until the science that contradicts it has made a deeper and broader study of its field and, as happens in most cases, corrects itself. In that manner theology upholds its dignity and honor more effectively than by constantly yielding and adapting itself to the opinions of the day.[87]

86. F. Pfaff, *Schöpfungsgeschichte*, 742; G. F. Wright, *Wetensch. Bijdragen*, 304ff., etc. (*Scientific Confirmations*).

87. Cf. Howorth, *The Mammoth and the Flood;* idem, *The Glacial Nightmare and the Flood* (London: S. Low, Marson, 1893).

PART V

THE IMAGE OF GOD

11

HUMAN ORIGINS

Humanity, where the spiritual and material world are joined together, is the crowning culmination of creation. This is affirmed by the two creation accounts in Genesis 1 and 2. Of the many alternative conjectures about human origins that have been ventured outside of scriptural revelation, the hypothesis of Darwinian evolutionism through natural selection is dominant in the contemporary world. The Christian objection is not to the idea of development as such, which goes back to Greek philosophy, but to the naturalism and materialism of the Darwinian hypothesis. This theory has been seriously opposed, not only by Bible-believers but also by natural scientists and philosophers more broadly. As naturalism and materialism demonstrated its spiritual bankruptcy, a new mystical and even pantheistic spirituality attracted many, further discrediting Darwinism. The arguments against Darwinism in general are weighty, with the problem of human origins and transitions from one species to another particularly insoluble. The theory of evolution also clashes with Scripture with regard to the age, the unity, and the original abode of humanity. Above all, it is essential to maintain the fundamental unity of the human race; this conviction is the presupposition of religion and morality. The solidarity of the human race, original sin, the atonement in Christ, the universality of the kingdom of God, the catholicity of the church, and the love of neighbor—these all are grounded in the unity of humankind.

[279] Creation culminates in humanity where the spiritual and material world are joined together. According to the creation story in Genesis 1, "humankind," the man and the woman, was created on the sixth day (Gen. 1:26ff.), following the creation of the land animals. By this arrangement Scripture, too, teaches the existence of close kinship between man and animal. Both were created on the same day; both were formed from the dust of the earth. But along with this kinship there is also a big difference. At God's command the animals were brought forth by the earth (Gen. 1:24); man, however, was created, after divine deliberation, in the image of God, to be master over all things. These brief descriptions are clarified and expanded in the second chapter of Genesis.[1] The first chapter offers

---

1. According to some exegetes, the so-called second creation story begins at Gen. 2:4, according to others, at Gen. 2:4b, and according to still others at Gen. 2:5. H. Gunkel inclines to the view that Gen.

a general history of creation, which has its goal and end in humanity, while the second deals especially with the human creation and with the relation in which other creatures stand to human beings. In the first report, man is the end of nature; in the second, man is the beginning of history. The first account shows how all other creatures prepare the advent of humanity; the second introduces the history of the temptation and the fall and to that end describes especially the human original state. In the first chapter, therefore, the story of the creation of all other things (heaven, earth, firmament, etc.) is told at some length and in a regular order, but the creation of humanity is reported succinctly; the second chapter presupposes the creation of heaven and earth, follows no chronological but only a topical order, and does not say when the plants and animals are created but only describes the relation in which they basically stand to human beings. Genesis 2:4b–9 does not imply that the plants were formed after human creation, but only that the garden of Eden was planted after that event. The author undoubtedly thought of the creation of plants as occurring between verses 6 and 7. Similarly, in Genesis 2:18ff., though the creation of animals is in fact recounted after that of man, the idea is not thereby to describe the objective course of creational events; it is only to show that a helper for man was not to be found among the animals but only in a being like himself. The account of the creation of the woman, finally, is by no means in conflict with that in Genesis 1 but only a further explication of it.[2]

CREATION AND EVOLUTION: DARWINISM

This divine origin of humankind has never been questioned in the Christian church and in Christian theology. But outside special revelation all sorts of conjectures have been ventured with respect to human origins. Many pagan sagas attribute human creation to the gods or the demigods.[3] Philosophy also, especially that of Socrates, Plato, and Aristotle, usually recognized, in its assessment of man as a being made from the dust of the earth, a rational principle

2:4a originally preceded Gen. 1:1 (H. Gunkel, *Genesis*, trans. Mark E. Biddle [Macon, Ga.: Mercer University Press, 1997], 103); V. Zapletal (*Der Schöpfungsbericht der Genesis* [Regensburg: G. J. Manz, 1911]) considers Gen. 2:4 an interpolation. In the opinion of many scholars, Gen. 2:4b cannot be a postscript to the preceding story since *tôlĕdōth* refers not to the origin, but to the ancestry and procreation of creatures; and according to others it cannot be the title of the following story inasmuch as the Yahwist never uses this formula. Still, Gen. 2:4b is probably intended as a transition to, and title of, the following in the sense that what follows contains the developmental history of heaven and earth, specifically that of the earth, for in v. 4b it is mentioned before heaven.

2. Cf. E. W. Hengstenberg, *Authenthie des Pentateuchs*, in *Beiträge zur Einleitung in Alte Testament*, 2 vols. (Berlin: Oehmigke, 1836–39), I, 306ff. (Ed. note: ET: *Dissertations on the Genuineness of the Pentateuch*, trans. J. E. Ryland, 2 vols. [Edinburgh: John D. Lowe, 1847]); G. F. Oehler, *Theology of the Old Testament*, trans. Ellen D. Smith and Sophia Taylor (Edinburgh: T. & T. Clark, 1892–93), §18; August Köhler, *Lehrbuch der biblischen Geschichte Alten Testamentes*, 2 vols. in 3 (Erlangen: Deichert, 1875–93), I, 24; Chr. E. Baumstark, *Christliche Apologetik*, II (Frankfurt a.M., 1872), 458ff.; H. van Eyck van Heslinga, *De Eenheid van het Scheppingsverhaal* (Leiden, 1896).

3. Hesiod, *Works and Days*, I, 23–25; Ovid, *Metamorphoses*, I, 82ff., 363ff.

that derived from the gods. In both religion and philosophy, however, very different ideas about human origins have frequently been entertained as well. Sometimes man is viewed as having emerged autochthonously from the earth; then again as having evolved from some other animal, or as the fruit of some tree, and so forth.[4] The idea of development or evolution, accordingly, is not a product of modernity but occurred already among the Greek philosophers. We find it among the Ionian philosophers of nature, especially in Anaximenes, elaborated in a pantheistic sense by Heraclitus, and presented in materialistic form by the Atomists. Aristotle, too, incorporated it in his system but attributed an organic and teleological character to it: in the way of development, potentiality turns into actuality. From the Christian position there is not the least objection to the notion of evolution or development as conceived by Aristotle; on the contrary, it is creation alone that makes such evolution possible.[5] But in the eighteenth century evolution was torn from its basis in theism and creation and made serviceable to a pantheistic or materialistic system. Some French Encyclopedists attempted to explain humanity completely—also psychologically—in terms of matter. Bodin, Hobbes, Montesquieu, Rousseau, Voltaire, Kant, Schiller, Goethe, and Hegel all promoted this trend insofar as they reversed the order generally accepted earlier and thought of humanity as starting in an animal state. Nevertheless, man was still viewed as being in a class by himself, produced not by a gradual evolution from an animal but by the creative omnipotence of nature. Evolution was still conceived as organic and teleological. But step by step this evolutionary theory was so refashioned that it led to the descent of humanity from animal ancestry. Lamarck (1744–1829), Saint Hilaire (1772–1844), Oken (1779–1851), Von Baer (1836), H. Spencer (1852), Schaafhausen (1855), Huxley (1859), and Nägeli (1859) had already taken this position before Charles Darwin appeared on the world stage. It was his claim to fame, however, that he made an enormous number of observations that related to the life of humanity and animals and brought to light the kinship between them. He managed to combine them in an unusual way and to make them serviceable to a hypothesis that was already dominant, and showed a way in which human descent from animal ancestors seemed to have been made possible.[6] A legion of scholars—including Lyell, [Richard] Owen, Lubbock, Tylor, Hooker, Tyndall, Huxley, Moleschott, Haeckel, Hellwald, Büchner, Vogt, Bölsche, and others—believed that the earlier hypothesis was virtually proved by Darwin's research, and passed it off as the incontrovertible result of natural science.[7]

4. Cf. A. Lang, *Onderzoek naar de Ontwikkeling van Godsdienst, Kultus en Mythologie,* trans. L. Knappert (Haarlem: F. Bohn, 1893), I, 143, 275.

5. Cf. M. Heinze, "Evolutionismus," *PRE³,* V, 672–81; and H. Bavinck, "Creation or Development," *The Methodist Review* 60 (1901): 849–74; idem, "Evolutie," in *Pro en contra* (Baarn: Hollandia, 1907).

6. C. Darwin, *On the Origin of Species by Means of Natural Selection* (London: J. Murray, 1859); idem, *The Descent of Man* (New York: D. Appleton, 1871).

7. E. Haeckel, for example, writes: "The monophyletic or single-stock origin of the entire class of mammals is therefore now considered a firmly established fact by all well-formed scholars in the field" (*Der Kampf um den Entwickelungs-Gedanken* [Berlin: G. Reimer, 1905], 56, 70).

Now then, by Darwinism we must understand the theory that the various species into which organic entities used to be divided possess no constant properties, but are mutable; that the higher organic beings have evolved from the lower, and that man in particular has gradually evolved, in the course of centuries, from an extinct genus of ape; that the organic, in turn, emerged from the inorganic; and that evolution is therefore the way in which, under the sway of purely mechanical and chemical laws, the present world has come into being. That's the thesis, or rather, the hypothesis. Darwin tries to render this theory of evolution plausible by the following considerations: first, nature everywhere evinces a struggle for life, in which every being participates and by which it is forced to develop and to perfect itself or else to perish; second, from countless plants, animals, and people, nature selects those for survival and reproduction ("natural selection") that are best organized; this natural selection is reinforced by sexual selection, a process in which every female gives preference to the best-organized male; third, the favorable properties acquired in the way of struggle and selection pass from parents to children or even to grandchildren (atavism) and by incremental mutations increasingly perfect the organism. These are not proofs, of course, but assumptions and interpretations of how, according to Darwin, evolution is possible. Proofs for the hypothesis are actually derived exclusively from the kinship that can be observed between organic entities and which, both physically and psychologically, exist also between animal and man; from the mutation and transmission of properties that we observe over and over in the world of humans and animals; from the rudimentary organs that remain in humans from their earlier animal state; from embryology, according to which the higher organisms recapitulate, as embryos, the degrees of development of the lower organisms; from paleontology, which studies fossilized bones and skulls and seeks to infer from them the big difference between the earlier and present-day humans; from mimicry, according to which some animals assume the form, the build, or the color of some other object in nature in order thereby to protect themselves from their enemies; from the blood relationship, which according to transfusion tests, especially those of H. Friedenthal, is alleged to have existed between humans and the higher apes.[8]

[280] Now then, with however much authority this theory of descent has suddenly come upon us, from the beginning it encountered very serious contradiction, not only among theologians and philosophers,[9] but also among natural

8. G. J. Romanes, *The Scientific Evidences of Organic Evolution* (London: Macmillan, 1882). On the mimicry, cf. C. Gutberlet, *Der Mensch* (Paderborn: F. Schöningh, 1903), 106ff. On the blood relationship of man and ape, see E. Wasmann, *Biology and the Theory of Evolution*, trans. A. M. Buchanan, 3d ed. (St. Louis: B. Herder, 1923), 456–61; E. Dennert, *Die Weltanschauung des modernen Naturforschers* (Stuttgart: M. Rielmann, 1907), 21ff.

9. In addition to the titles by the following, listed in the bibliography—H. Lüken, J. S. Nikel, H. Lotze, A. R. Gordon, B. Platz, O. Zöckler, E. de Pressensé, J. Guibert, C. Hodge, D. G. Whitley, J. Orr, W. Geesink—see also the Genesis commentaries of F. Delitzsch, H. Gunkel et al.; cf. H. Ulrici, *Gott und die Natur* (Leipzig: T. O. Weigel, 1862); idem, *Gott und der Mensch* (Leipzig: T. O. Weigel, 1874); E. von

scientists;[10] and that contradiction, so far from having been muted over the years, has made itself heard with increasing volume and vigor. At almost every annual conference of natural scientists, Virchov repeated his protest against those who passed off Darwinism as established dogma. DuBois-Reymond spoke in 1880 of seven world mysteries that could not be solved by natural science, and a few years before his death in December of 1896 he wrote: "The only option left, it seems, is to cast oneself into the arms of supernaturalism."[11] In 1890 Renan reconsidered the great expectations that he had cherished for science in his earlier years.[12] In 1895 Brunetière spoke of science's bankruptcy and, though he was not thereby denying its discoveries, attempted to show that it was not the only means by which humanity could improve its lot.[13] Romanes, who was a resolute Darwinist, died in 1895, having reconciled himself with the faith of the Anglican Church.[14] At the end of the nineteenth century the intellectual life of people underwent a remarkable change. Although an array of brilliant results had been achieved in the natural sciences, in culture, and in technology, the human heart had been left unsatisfied, and so people turned from intellectualism to mysticism, from exact science to philosophy, from mechanicism to dynamism, from dead matter to the vital force, from atheism back to pantheism. Materialism, upon continued scrutiny, proved completely

Hartmann, *Wahrheit und Irrthum im Darwinismus* (Berlin: C. Duncker, 1875; reprinted in idem, *Philosophie des Unbewussten,* 11th ed. [1904], III); B. Carneri, *Sittlichkeit und Darwinismus* (Vienna: W. Braumüller, 1903); G. P. Weygoldt, *Darwinismus, Religion, Sittlichkeit* (Leiden: E. J. Brill, 1878); E. G. Steude, *Christentum und Naturwissenschaft* (Gütersloh: C. Bertelsmann, 1895), 148ff. (Ed. note: Cf. E. Gustav Steude, *Der Beweis für die Wahrheit des Christentums* [Gütersloh: C. Bertelsmann, 1899]); T. Pesch, *Die grossen Welträthsel,* 2d ed., 2 vols. (Freiburg i.B.: Herder, 1892), II, 147–71ff.; F. H. Reusch, *Nature and the Bible: Lectures on the Mosaic History of Creation in Its Relation to Natural Science,* trans. Kathleen Lyttelton, 4th ed., 2 vols. (Edinburgh: T. & T. Clark: 1886), II, 32–120; R. Otto, *Naturalistische und Religiose Weltansicht* (Tübingen: H. Laupp, 1905).

10. L. Agassiz, *Essay on Classification,* ed. Edward Lurie (Cambridge, Mass.: Harvard University Press, Belknap Press, 1962); J. W. Dawson, *Nature and the Bible* (New York: Wilbur B. Ketcham, 1875); Dana [ed. note: The reference here is likely to American geologist James Dwight Dana (1813–95). Dana regarded continental evolution as divinely directed.] (cf. G. F. Wright, *Wetenschappelijke Bijdragen tot Bevestiging der Oud-Testamentische Geschiedenis,* 306 [*Scientific Confirmations of Old Testament History* (Oberlin, Ohio: Bibliotheca Sacra, 1906)]); C. Nägeli, *Entstehung und Begriff der naturhistorischen Art,* 2d ed. (Munich: Köningliche Akademie, 1865); idem, *A Mechanico-Physiological Theory of Organic Evolution* (Chicago: Open Court, 1898); A. Wigand, *Der Darwinismus und die Naturforschung Newtons und Cuviers,* 3 vols. (Braunschweig: F. Vieweg & Sohn, 1874–77); J. Ranke, *Der Mensch,* 2d ed. (Leipzig: Bibliographisches Institut, 1894); G. Beck, *Der Urmensch* (Basel: A. Geering, 1899); F. Bettex, *Naturstudie en Christendom,* 4th ed. (Kampen: J. H. Kok, 1908); J. Reinke, *Die Welt als That,* 4 vols., 3d ed. (Berlin: Gebruder Paetel, 1905); idem, *Die Natur und Wir* (Berlin: Gebruder Paetel, 1908); E. Dennert, *At the Deathbed of Darwinism,* trans. E. V. O'Harra and John H. Peschges (Burlington, Iowa: German Literary Board, 1904); E. Dennert, *Die Weltanschauung des modernen Naturforschers* (Stuttgart: M. Rielmann, 1907); A. Dippe, *Naturphilosophie* (Munich: C. H. Beck, O. Beck, 1907); E. Wasmann, *Modern Biology.*

11. Cf. E. H. DuBois-Reymond, quoted by O. Zöckler in *Beweis des Glaubens* 31 (February 1895): 77–78.

12. E. Renan, *L'avenir de la science* (Paris: Calmann-Levy, 1890).

13. F. Brunetière, *La Science et la Religion* (Paris: Firmin-Didot, 1895).

14. G. J. Romanes, *Thoughts on Religion,* ed. Charles Gore, 6th ed. (Chicago: Open Court, 1911).

untenable. The concept of atom, which was its premise, could not withstand the test of a logical critique. Physics was compelled to abandon the concept of action-at-a-distance and to conceive all of space as being filled with a cosmic ether. The discovery of X-rays led to a heretofore unsuspected divisibility of matter. Monistic thought came to acknowledge that even materialism with its matter and force had not overcome dualism, and philosophical idealism yielded the insight that matter and all of nature are only given us in the form of an idea. All these considerations paved the way for the pantheism of Spinoza or Hegel and exerted such influence that even Haeckel could not escape it, prompting him to elevate his materialistic monism to the level of a new religion.[15]

This change of mood also undermined belief in the truth of Darwinism. In this connection a distinction has to be made, however, between Darwinism in a more restricted sense and Darwinism in a broader sense. Darwinism in a broader sense, that is, the opinion that the higher organisms evolved from the lower organisms and that the human species therefore gradually evolved from animal ancestry, still enjoys as much agreement as it did earlier. Darwinism in the more restricted sense, that is, the peculiar explanation that Darwin, with his theory of natural selection, offered for the origin of species, fell into disrepute with many people or was even completely abandoned. Nevertheless, the Darwinism of the one sense is bound up with the Darwinism of the other. For Darwin himself the truth of his theory of descent depended on the possibility of explaining it;[16] when the explanation attempted proves not to be sound, the theory also begins to totter and sinks to the level of an assumption that has as much or as little right to exist as any other. In fact, then, also the arguments that can be advanced against the theory of human descent are of no less force and weight than those that are directed against Darwin's explanation.

Critique of Darwinism

Those arguments in the main are the following: In the first place, until now the theory of descent has proved completely unable to make the origin of life somewhat understandable.[17] Initially scientists resorted to the notion of an "ambiguous generation" *(generatio aequivoca),* that is, the idea of the

15. E. Haeckel, *Der Monismus als Band zwischen Religion und Wissenschaft,* 6th ed. (Leipzig: A. Kroner, 1908); idem, *The Riddle of the Universe at the Close of the Nineteenth Century,* trans. Joseph McCabe (New York: Harper & Brothers, 1900), 331–46.

16. Cf. J. Orr, *God's Image in Man and Its Defacement in the Light of Modern Denials* (London: Hodder & Stoughton, 1906), 99.

17. O. Hertwig, *Die Entwicklung der Biologie im neunzehnten Jahrhundert,* 2d ed. (Jena: G. Fischer, 1908); E. von Hartmann, "Mechanismus und Vitalismus in der modernen Biologie," *Archiv für Systematische Philosophie* (1903): 139–78, 331–77; R. Otto, "Die mechanistische Lebenstheorie und die Theologie," *Zeitschrift für Theologie und Kirche* (1903): 179–213; idem, *Naturalistische und religiöse Weltansicht,* 2d ed. (Tübingen: J. C. B. Mohr [Paul Siebeck], 1909), 145ff.; ET, *Naturalism and Religion,* trans. J. Arthur Thomson and Margaret R. Thomson (London: Williams & Norgate; New York: Putnam, 1907); R. P. Mees, *De Mechanische Verklaring der Levensverschijnselen* (The Hague, 1899); J. Grasset, *Les limites de la biologie* (Paris: Alcan, 1902).

origination of organic entities by an accidental combination of inorganic materials. When Pasteur's researches had proved its untenability, they latched onto the assumption that the protoplasms or life germs had been brought to the earth by meteorites from other planets (Helmholtz, Thomson).[18] When this hypothesis too proved to be little more than a brain wave, they announced the theory that the cells and life germs had always existed alongside the inorganic and therefore—like matter, force, and movement—were eternal. But by saying this the proponents of evolutionary theory themselves acknowledged the inadequacy of it: those who make "matter," "movement," and "life" eternal do not solve the riddle but despair of a solution.[19] Many natural scientists—including Rindfleisch, Bunge, Neumeister, Merkel, and others—have therefore returned to vitalism.

In the second place, Darwinism has also proved incapable of explaining the further development of organic entities. Scripture, on the one hand, recognizes the truth that inheres in evolution when it has plants and animals come forth from the earth at God's command (Gen. 1:11, 20, 24). On the other hand, however, it says that the earth could only bring forth these organic entities by a word of divine omnipotence, and that these organic entities existed side by side from the beginning as distinct species, each with its own nature (Gen. 1:11, 21). It cannot be ruled out, therefore, that within the distinct species all sorts of changes could occur, nor has the freedom of science to further define the boundaries of these species been curtailed. It is not even absolutely necessary to view all the species now listed by botany and zoology as original creations. The notion of species is far from being sharply and clearly defined.[20] But it is equally certain that the essential diversity and dissimilarity of creatures is rooted in God's creative omnipotence. It is he who makes the difference between light and darkness, day and night, heaven and earth, plant and animal, angel and human.[21] And in Darwinism this diversity and dissimilarity of creatures, specifically of organic entities, remains a riddle. If humans descended from the animals, precisely the huge difference that exists between them and that is manifest in the entire organism would remain an insoluble riddle. Today it is almost universally recognized that the numerous species of plants and animals cannot be inferred from one single organism or even from four or five original organisms.[22] Both morphologically and physiologically the species are much too divergent. Natural and sexual selection are insufficient to make possible

18. Cf. also Th. H. MacGillavry, *De Continuïteit van het Doode en het Levend* (Leiden: Brill, 1898).

19. In an essay ("Geist oder Instinkt," *Neue kirchliche Zeitschrift* [1907]: 39) Edmund Hoppe correctly comments: "Darwinism has ceased to produce an explanation of the theory of evolution; in its place has come the spiritualization of matter and voila! evolution has been rescued."

20. Cf. E. Wasmann, *Modern Biology*, 296–305, 427–29.

21. T. Aquinas, *Summa theol.*, I, qu. 47.

22. "There is no evidence at all in support of a monophyletic phylogeny" (E. Wasmann, *Modern Biology*, 291).

such changes in the species and have accordingly already been significantly limited and modified by Darwin himself.[23]

In addition to this, transitions from one species into another have never been observed, either in the past or in the present. The same species of plants and animals we now know also existed thousands of years ago and appeared suddenly in large numbers. Transitional forms that would bring now-existing species closer together have nowhere been found. Paleontology does not demonstrate a slow, gradual, rectilinear ascent of organic entities from the lower to the higher, but shows that all kinds of species existed side by side from the beginning. Such transitional forms should be available in large numbers, however, because the morphological changes occurred so slowly over thousands of years and were each time only of minute significance. It is inconceivable that all of them were accidentally destroyed by catastrophes; even more so, because right up to the present all the lower organisms have continued to exist alongside the higher ones despite their imperfection and unfitness for the struggle to survive. Add to this that especially August Weismann, but also others, have on good grounds defended the thesis that precisely the acquired properties are not transmitted by heredity, so that on this subject and on heredity in general there are enormous differences of opinion.[24] Totally contrary to Darwin's theory, morphological properties are the most variable. If morphological changes proceeded at such a slow rate and were each time of so little significance, they would be absolutely of no advantage in the struggle for life. In the time of transition they would be more a handicap than a help. For as long as breathing through gills changed into breathing by lungs, the process was more a hindrance than an advantage in the struggle for existence. For all these reasons the natural scientist, whose science must rest on facts, would do well to refrain from making judgments in this matter. Materialism and Darwinism [we should note] are both historically and logically the result of philosophy, not of experimental science. Darwin himself, in any case, states that many of the views he presented were highly speculative.[25] According to Haeckel, Darwin did not discover any new facts; what he did was combine and utilize the facts in a unique way.[26] The profound kinship between humans and animals has always been recognized, a fact that comes through in the concept of "rational animal."[27] But in earlier times this fact was not yet combined with the monistic philosophy that says

23. Darwin's theory that the species originated as a result of minute incremental changes over an endless series of years has yielded, in the work of Hugo de Vries, to the theory of abrupt salutatory mutations: *Species and Varieties: Their Origin by Mutation,* ed. Daniel Trembly MacDougal, 2d ed., corrected and rev. (Chicago: Open Court; London: Kegan Paul, Trench, Trübner & Co., 1906). But in this connection the question whether the resulting new organisms are species or varieties remains unanswered.

24. O. Hertwig, *Biological Problems of Today: Preformation or Epigenesis?* (New York: Macmillan, 1900); H. H. Kuyper, *Evolutie of Revelatie* (Amsterdam: Höveker & Wormser, 1903).

25. C. Darwin, *The Descent of Man,* 620.

26. E. Haeckel, *Naturliche Schöpfungs-Geschichte* (1874), 25 (9th ed., [Berlin: G. Reimer], 1898).

27. E. Wasmann, *Instinkt und Intelligenz im Thierreich,* 8th ed. (Freiburg i.B.: Herder, 1905); W. M. Wundt, *Vorlesungen über die Menschen- und Thierseele,* 2 vols. (Leipzig: L. Voss, 1863).

that from a pure potency, which *is* nothing—like such things as atoms, chaos, or cells—everything can nevertheless evolve.

In the third place, in Darwinism the origin of humanity is an insoluble problem. Positive proofs of human descent from animal ancestry do not really exist. Haeckel's ontogeny can no longer be considered as proof after the refutation by Bischoff and others.[28] Arguments based on a variety of human bones and skulls found in caves, most recently in the Dutch East Indies, have been abandoned in turn in case after case.[29] Study, on the one hand, of anthropoid species of apes and, on the other, of an assortment of bones, skulls, abnormal humans, microcephalics, dwarfs, and so forth, ended in the observation that the difference between animals and humans is essential and has always existed.[30] It is generally recognized, accordingly, that no species of ape, as it exists today or has existed in the past, can be the ancestral stock of the human race.[31] The most ardent defenders of Darwinism admit that some sort of transitional species has to be assumed, a species of which up until now not a trace has been found. At a conference of natural scientists in 1894, Virchov commented: "Until now no ape has as yet been found which can be considered the true ancestor of humans, nor any semiape. This question is no longer on the forefront of research."[32]

In the fourth place, Darwinism above all fails to provide an explanation of humanness in terms of its psychic dimension. Darwin began with the attempt to derive all the mental phenomena to be found in humans (consciousness, language, religion, morality, etc.) from phenomena occurring in animals,[33] and many others have followed him in this regard. But up until now these attempts have not been successful either. Like the essence of energy and matter, the origin of movement, the origination of life, and teleology, so also human consciousness, language, freedom of the will, religion, and morality still belong to the enigmas of the world that await resolution. Ideas, which are entirely mental, relate to the brain in a very different way from the way bile relates to

28. Also cf. O. Hertwig, "Das biogenetische Grundgesetz nach dem heutigen Stande der Biologie," *Internationale Wochenschrift* 1 (1907), nn. 2–3.

29. Hubrecht, *De Gids* 60 (June 1896). As Virchov did earlier, so Dr. Bumuller of Augsburg, at the congress of anthropologists held in September 1899 at Lindau, asserted that the *Pithecanthropus erectus* of Dubois was a gibbon (in *Beweis des Glaubens* [1900]: 80); cf. E. Wasmann, *Modern Biology,* 465–80.

30. F. Pfaff, *Schöpfungsgeschichte,* 3d ed. (Heidelberg: C. Winter, 1881), 721; cf. E. Wasmann, *Modern Biology.*

31. E. Haeckel, *Der Kampf um den Entwickelungsgedanken,* 58.

32. In F. Hettinger, *Apologie des Christenthums,* 7th ed., 5 vols. (Freiburg i.B.: Herder, 1895–98), III, 297 (ed. note: Selections from Hettinger's *Apologie* were translated in a one-volume edition by Henry Sebastian Bowden, *Natural Religion,* 2d ed. [London: Burns & Oates, 1892]); J. Reinke (*Die Entwicklung der Naturwissenschaften insbesondere der Biologie im neunzehnten Jahrhundert* [Kiel: Universitäts-Buchhandlung (P. Toeche), 1900], 19–20) therefore wrote: "We must unreservedly acknowledge that there is not a single completely unobjectionable proof for its [man's animal ancestry's] correctness." Also cf. Branco, in E. Wasmann, *Modern Biology,* 407–79, and Wasmann himself, 456–83.

33. C. Darwin, *Descent of Man,* chs. 3–4; and *The Expression of Emotions in Man and Animals* (London: John Murray, 1872).

the liver and urine to the kidneys. In the words of Max Müller, language is and remains the Rubicon between us and the animal world. The psychological explanation of religion is untenable. And the derivation of morality from human social instincts fails to do justice to the authority of the moral law, to the categorical character of the moral imperative, to the "imperatives" of the good, to conscience, responsibility, the sense of sin, repentance, remorse, and punishment. Indeed, although Darwinism as such is not wholly identical with materialism, it nevertheless tends in that direction, finds there its most significant support, and thus also paves the way for the subversion of religion and morality and the destruction of our humanness. There is no advantage for people to say that it is better to be a highly developed animal than a fallen human. The theory of the animal ancestry of humans violates the image of God in man and degrades the human into an image of the orangutan and chimpanzee. From the standpoint of evolution humanity as the image of God cannot be maintained. The theory of evolution forces us to return to creation as Scripture presents it to us.

THE AGE OF HUMANITY

[281] In connection with the theory of the origin of man the doctrine of evolution also tends to conflict with Scripture in regard to the age, the unity, and the original abode of the human race. Great age was attributed to the human race by many peoples, including the Japanese, the East Indians, the Babylonians, the Egyptians, the Greeks, and the Romans, who spoke of several world ages and of myriads and hundreds of thousands of years. Modern anthropology has from time to time returned to these fabulous figures but is no more consistent than pagan mythology; it ranges between 10,000 and 500,000 years and more.[34]

In recent years there is a general tendency to observe greater moderation in calculating the age of the earth and humanity. Darwin, of course, demanded an incalculable number of years to allow for the origination of species by minute changes, for if evolution never proceeded faster than it does now, the origin of life and of every type of organism required an extraordinarily long time. When scientists began to compute, consistently with this theory of evolution, how long it would take for the human eye to develop from a tiny spot of pigment and for the brains of mammals to develop from an original ganglion, they automatically arrived at immensely long times, which had to be multiplied a number of times for the duration of all of life on earth. Some of them, along with Darwin himself in the first edition of his *Origin of Species,* therefore came to a figure of 300 million years for the age of life on earth, and the majority used even higher figures.[35]

34. A. R. Wallace, for example, speaks of a half million years, according to J. Orr, *God's Image in Man,* 166.

35. H. de Vries, *Species and Varieties,* 14; G. F. Wright, *Wetenschappelijke Bijdragen,* 176 (*Scientific Confirmations*); J. Orr, *God's Image in Man,* 176.

But gradually physicists and geologists began to register objections to these figures. They themselves began to calculate, attempting in various ways and by various methods to estimate the age of the earth, the ocean, the moon, and the sun. And although they differed among themselves over millions of years, still the time they assumed for that age was generally much shorter than that demanded by biologists. They spoke at most of 80 or 100 million, and sometimes went down as low as 10 or 20 million years. Now if the age of the earth requires no more than a figure between 10 to 100 million years—and, as is clear from this difference, the calculation is again highly uncertain and subject to modification at a moment's notice[36]—it is self-evident that the origin of life and of humanity is again much less remote. On this question, accordingly, there is a wide spread of opinion. Some scientists, such as Bourgeois, Delaunay, de Mortillet, Quatrefages, and others, assume that man already occurs in the Tertiary period. Others, on the other hand, such as Virchov, Mor. Wagner, Oskar Schmidt, Zittel, Cathaillac, John Evans, Joseph Prestwich, Hughes, Branco, Wasmann, Dawson, Haynes, and so forth, are of the opinion that humanity did not make a debut until the Quaternary period.[37] The decision is also difficult because the boundaries between the two periods cannot be clearly drawn, and these periods may very well have existed side by side in different regions of the earth. But even if the human species existed in the Tertiary period and man was a contemporary of the mammoth, it does not follow that this establishes the age of humanity; one can equally well infer from this that this period is much more recent than was initially believed. As a matter of fact, in calculating the dates of the Ice Age, scientists have returned to a more modest number. In recent years there is even considerable agreement on this point. Most experts, such as G. F. Wright, Salisbury, Winchell, and others, have arrived at the conclusion that the Ice Age in America, and therefore roughly also that in Europe, is no more than eight or ten thousand years behind us.[38] In this connection one must always bear in mind that the calculations based on the pile dwellings found in Switzerland and elsewhere; on bones and skulls that have been encountered in caves near Liège, Amiens, Dusseldorf, and in many other places; on the delta formations of the Nile and Mississippi; on the formation of the falls at Niagara and of St. Anthony near Minneapolis; on the duration of the Stone, Bronze, and Iron Ages, and so on—that all these calculations rest on a hypothetical foundation and are far from being absolutely certain. In this connection, even more than

36. J. Orr, *God's Image in Man*, 168.

37. Ibid., 174, 306; J. Guibert, *In the Beginning*, trans. G. S. Whitmarsh (London: Kegan Paul, Trench, & Trübner, 1900), 264–97; C. Gutberlet, *Der Mensch*, 265ff.; E. Wasmann, *Modern Biology*, 477. According to Wasmann, no traces of tertiary humans have as yet been found, and the signs of human activity that are thought to have been found in the Tertiary period are extremely doubtful. In contrast, there are many diluvial human remains left, all of which prove that at that time man was already a "complete *Homo sapiens*."

38. J. Orr, *God's Image in Man*, 306; G. F. Wright, *Wetenschappelijke Bijdragen*, 201–7 (*Scientific Confirmations*); Upham ("Die Zeitdauer der geologischen Epochen," *Gaea* 30 [1894]: 621ff.) cites various scholars who situate the Ice Age approximately seven or eight thousand years before Christ.

in that of the age of the earth, it is the case that though scientists can mention numbers, they do not have the material for a history over so long a period.

Of more value for the determination of the age of the human race are the chronological data that are furnished us by the history and monuments of different peoples. The history of India and China does not provide a firm basis for a chronology, arising as it does only a few centuries before Christ. But the situation is somewhat different with the history of Egypt and Babylonia. Here we undoubtedly have an ancient civilization; it already existed as far as we can go back in history. Scripture itself also clearly teaches this. But the chronology is nevertheless still so uncertain that one cannot base much on it. This uncertainty is illustrated by the fact that Champollion has the rule of the Egyptian king Menes start in 5867 B.C., Boeckh in 5702, Unger in 5613, Brugsch in 4455, Lauth in 4157, Lepsius in 3892, Bunsen in 3623, Edward Meyer in 3180, Wilkinson in 2320—a spread of more than 3500 years; and also by the fact that Bunsen has Babylon's historical period begin in 3784, Von Gutschmid in 2447, Brandis in 2458, Oppert in 3540, and so on.[39]

Every student of ancient history has his own chronology. It is a labyrinth without a thread to guide the inquirer. Only in the case of the people of Israel can we actually speak of a history and a chronology. Fritz Hommel is therefore right in saying that the chronology for the first thousand years before Christ is fairly well established, sometimes down to the details; that in the second thousand years before Christ we seem to have been given only a few fixed reference points; and that in the third thousand years, that is, before 2000 B.C., everything is uncertain.[40] As a matter of fact, there are other reasons as well why the human race cannot have existed many thousands of years before Christ. If it had, the world's population at the time of Christ would have been much larger and much more widely distributed. A thousand years before Christ, after all, the largest part of the globe was still uninhabited; this applies to what we now call Northern Asia, Central and Northern Europe, Africa south of the Sahara, Australia, the South Sea Islands, America. Even at the time of Christ—aside from Asia—humanity lived primarily around the Mediterranean Sea. If humanity were as old as it is claimed, many more ruins of cities and human remnants would have been found; as it is, they are now very scarce and limited to a part of the earth. The most reliable figures, accordingly, do not rise beyond from five to seven thousand years before Christ.[41] If in this connection we remember

39. F. Hettinger, *Apologie des Christenthums*, III, 258ff.; A. Baumgartner, *Geschichte der Weltliteratur* (Freiburg i.B.: Herder, 1897), I, 89; H. H. Kuyper, *Evolutie of Revelatie*, 76, 90. The most recent excavations in Egypt have led to the thesis that there a prehistoric civilization preceded historical time. The bearer of that prehistoric civilization was an ancient indigenous race; cf. the article: "Egypte voor den tijd der Piramiden," *Wetensch. Bladen* (August 1907): 274–93; (September 1907): 436–53; J. Orr, *God's Image in Man*, 179, 306.

40. F. Hommel, *Geschichte des alten Morgenlandes* (Leipzig: Göschen, 1895), 38.

41. F. Pfaff, *Schöpfungsgeschichte*, 710–28; M. Gander, *Die Sündflut in ihrer Bedeutung für die Erdgeschichte* (Münster: Aschendorff, 1896), 78–90; P. Schanz, *Das Alter des Menschengeschlechts nach der heiligen Schrift der Prophangeschichte und der Vorgeschichte* (Freiburg i.B.: Herder, 1896).

that scholars are far from having reached agreement about the chronology of the Bible,[42] then on this point too there is no significant disagreement between Scripture and science. But even if according to the usual calculation the flood occurred in 2348 B.C., there was a period of 450 years to the calling of Abraham in 1900 B.C.; this period is sufficiently long to allow for quite powerful empires to develop along the Euphrates and the Nile. In fourteen generations of 33 years each, that is in 462 years, Noah and his three sons (at 6 children per marriage) could have more than 12 million descendants.[43]

THE UNITY OF THE HUMAN RACE

[282] The unity of the human race is a certainty in Holy Scripture (Gen. 1:26; 6:3; 7:21; 10:32; Matt. 19:4; Acts 17:26; Rom. 5:12ff.; 1 Cor. 15:21f., 45f.) but has almost never been acknowledged by the peoples who lived outside the circle of revelation. The Greeks considered themselves autochthonous and proudly looked down on "barbarians." This contrast is found in virtually all nations. In India there gradually came into being even a sharp division between four castes of people, for each of which a distinct origin was assumed. The Stoa was the first school of thought to assert that all human beings formed one single body *(systēma politikon)* of which everyone was a member, and hence proclaimed universal justice and love of men.[44] Following the Renaissance the idea of various origins of the human race again surfaced. This idea sometimes occurred in the form of true polygeneticism, as in Caesalpinus, Blount, and other Deists; in part as coadamitism, that is, the descent of different races from

42. Various attempts have been made to extend the chronology of the Bible and so to bring it into harmony with that of natural science and history. The chronology of the Hebrew text of the Old Testament is different from that of the Greek translation. The genealogies of Genesis 5 and 10 perhaps skip generations, and while they establish the family line, they do not fix the duration of the generations. So, for example, W. H. Green and G. F. Wright, *Wetenschappelijke Bijdragen,* 37 (*Scientific Confirmations*). J. Urquhart (*How Old Is Man? Some Misunderstood Chapters in Scripture Chronology* [London: Nisbet, 1904]) is of the same opinion and calculates the time from Adam to Christ at 8,167 years. Also cf. N. Howard, *Neue Berechnungen über die Chronologie des Alten Testaments und ihr Verhältnis zu der Altertumskunde,* foreword by V. E. Rupprecht (Bonn, 1904); D. R. Fotheringham, *The Chronology of the Old Testament* (Cambridge: Deighton Bell, 1906); A. Bosse, *Untersuchungen zum chronologischen Schema des Alten Testament* (Cöthen: Schettler, 1906); "Bibl. Chronologie," *Herders Kirchenlexicon* (ed. note: Bavinck is likely referring to *Wetzer und Welte's Kirchenlexicon,* ed. Joseph Hergenröther [Freiburg i.B.: Herder, 1903]); J. B. Heinrich and C. Gutberlet, *Dogmatische Theologie,* 2d ed. (Mainz: Kirchheim, 1881–1900), VI, 272; cf. above, pp. 489–90 (#273), 505–7 (#278).

43. For further material on the age of the earth, cf. O. Zöckler, *Geschichte der Beziehungen zwischen Theologie und Naturwissenschaft* (Gütersloh: C. Bertelsmann, 1877–79), II, 755ff.; idem, *Die Lehre vom Urstand des Menschen* (Gütersloh: C. Bertelsmann, 1879), 87ff.; idem, "Mensch," *PRE³,* XII, 624; P. Schanz, *Apologie des Christentums,* 3 vols. (Freiburg i.B.: Herder, 1887–88), I, 333ff. (*A Christian Apology,* trans. Michael F. Glancey and Victor J. Schobel, 4th rev. ed. [Ratisbon: F. Pustet, 1891]); F. Hettinger, *Apologie des Christenthums,* III, 281–310; F. G. Vigouroux, *Les livres saints,* 4 vols. (Paris: A. Roger & F. Chernoviz, 1886–90), III, 452ff.; B. Platz, *Der Mensch* (Würzburg and Leipzig: Woerl, 1898), 385ff.

44. E. Zeller, *Die Philosophie der Greichen,* 3 vols. (Leipzig: Fues [O. R. Reisland], 1879–1920), IV, 287ff.

different ancestors, in Paracelsus and others; in part (in Zanini and especially in Isaac de la Peyrère) as preadamitism, that is, the descent of savage peoples who were dark in color from an ancestor before Adam, while in that case Adam was only the ancestor of the Jews or also of white humanity.

In 1655 de la Peyrère published (without indicating the name of the author, the printer, or the place) a small work entitled *Praeadamitae,* subtitled *Systema theologiae ex praeadamitarum hypothesi.* In this booklet the assertion is made (with an appeal to Gen. 4:14, 16–17; 6:2–4) that people had existed long before Adam. These people descended from the first pair, whose creation is reported in Genesis 1. In Genesis 2, however, we find the story of the creation of Adam and Eve, who are the ancestors of the Jews. These two broke the law given them in paradise and fell into even greater sins than the peoples descended from the first man, for the latter did not, as Paul puts it (Rom. 5:12–14), sin in the likeness of Adam's sin. They did not violate a positive law; they committed natural sins but no sins against law. For a time this theory gained wide acceptance and also provoked opposition from all sides.[45] But it soon fell into oblivion. Only a few authors, such as Bayle, Arnold, and Swedenborg, thought it had some merit. Especially when in the eighteenth century knowledge of the peoples of the world gained more currency and people began to realize the great diversity in color, hair, build, customs (etc.) among them, many scholars again came up with the idea of different ancestors: Sullivan (1795), Crüger (1784), Ballenstedt (1818), Stanhope Smith (1790), Cordonnière (1814), Gobineau (1853–55), and others. By some it was made serviceable to the defense of slavery, as was the case with Dobbs in Ireland against Wilberforce, by Morton Nott, Glidon, Knox, Agassiz, and others. Another kind of polygenesis was taught by Schelling.[46] He too assumed the existence of many races of people before Adam, but these had so elevated and developed themselves from their inferior animal status that finally they brought forth *him* in whom humanness first manifested itself and could therefore bear the name of *the human* ("ha-adam") with good warrant. Similarly, a certain preadamitism was propagated by Oken, Carus, Baumgartner, Perty, and Bunsen.[47] After 1860 there was added to these views Darwinism, which on account of its theory of variability could very well be monogenetic, but among many of its adherents nevertheless became polygenetic. The development from animal to man took place at various times and places and gave rise to different races, according to

45. F. Spanheim, *Opera,* III, 1249ff.; F. Turretin, *Institutes of Elenctic Theology,* V, qu. 8; J. Marckius, *Historia paradisi* (Amsterdam: Gerardus Borstius, 1705), II, 2, §§3ff.; B. de Moor, *Comm. in Marckii Comp.,* II, 1001–5; C. Vitringa, *Doctr. christ.,* II, 127; cf. J. I. Doedes, "Nieuwe Merkwaardigheden uit den Oude-boeken-schat," in *Studien en Bijdragen,* ed. W. Moll and J. G. De Hoop Scheffer (Amsterdam: G. L. Funke, 1880), IV, 238–42; O. Zöckler, *Geschichte der Beziehungen,* I, 545ff.; II, 768ff.; idem, *Die Lehre vom Urstand,* 231ff.

46. F. W. Schelling, *Werke,* II, 1, 500–515.

47. Also cf. W. Bilderdijk, *Opstellen van Godgeleerden en Zedekundigen Inhoud* (Amsterdam: Immerzeel, 1883), II, 75; D. F. Strauss, *Die christliche Glaubenslehre,* 2 vols. (Tübingen: C. F. Osiander, 1840–41), I, 680; G. A. Schwalbe, *Studien zur Vorgeschichte des Menschen* (Stuttgart: Schweizerbart, 1906).

Haeckel, Schaafhausen, Caspari, Vogt, Büchner, and others.[48] On the position of Darwinism, however, the question concerning the origin and age of humanity cannot be answered; the transition from animal to man occurred so slowly that there really was no first man. Against this polygeneticism, monogeneticism was again defended by von Humboldt, Blumenbach, St. Hilaire, von Baer, von Meyer, Wagner, Quatrefages, Darwin, Peschel, Ranke; Virchov, too, allowed for the possibility.[49]

Now the existence of various peoples and races within humanity is most certainly an important issue, whose solution we are not even close to finding. The differences in color, hair, skull, language, ideas, religion, mores, customs, and so on are so great and the expansion of the one human race over the globe—for example, to the South Sea Islands and America—so unknown that the idea of the different origins of peoples can hardly surprise us. In Genesis 11, Scripture accordingly traces the origination of languages and of peoples to a single act of God, by which he intervened in the development of humanity.[50] The origination of distinct peoples has a deep religious-ethical meaning and speaks of intellectual and spiritual decline. The more savage and rough humanity becomes, the more languages, ideas, and so forth, will take different tracks. The more people live in isolation, the more language differences increase. The confusion of languages is the result of confusion in ideas, in the mind, and in life.

Still, in all that division and brokenness unity has been preserved. The science of linguistics has discovered kinship and unity of origin even where in the past it was not even remotely suspected. While the existence of races and peoples is a fact, the determination of their boundaries is nevertheless so difficult that it generates immense disputes. Kant assumed there were four different races, Blumenbach five, Buffon six, Peschel seven, Agassiz eight, Haeckel twelve, Morton even twenty-two.[51] Within and between all races there are again transitional forms that seem to mock all attempts at classification. Genesis 10, accordingly, maintains the unity of the race in the face of all diversity and Johann von Müller with good reason said, "All history must start with this chapter."

Now, against this unity Darwinism cannot really raise any objections. The difference between man and animal is in any case always much greater than

48. Cf. L. Gumplovicz, *Grundriss der Sociologie*, 2d ed. (Vienna: Manzsche Buchhandlung, 1905), who ardently promotes polygeneticism and bases his sociology on it (138ff.).

49. Cf. C. Darwin himself, *Descent*, ch. 7; and further, F. Hettinger, *Apologie des Christenthums*, III, 224.

50. F. W. Schelling, *Werke*, II, 1, 94–118; H. Lüken, *Die Traditionen des Menschengeschlechts* (Münster: Aschendorff, 1869), 278ff.; C. A. Auberlen, *The Divine Revelation*, I (Edinburgh: T. & T. Clark, 1867); F. Kaulen, *Die Sprachenverwirrung zu Babel* (Mainz: F. Kirchheim, 1861); M. Strodl, *Die Entstehung der Völker* (Schaffhausen: Hurter, 1868).

51. O. Peschel, *Abhandlungen zur Erd- und Völkerkunde*, 5th ed. (Leipzig: Duncker & Humboldt, 1878), 316ff.; H. Schurtz, *Katechismus der Völkerkunde* (Leipzig: J. J. Weber, 1893); J. Guibert, *In the Beginning*, 212–53.

that between humans. If man could evolve from an animal, it is hard to see why the idea of a common origin of mankind should as such encounter objection. Darwinism indeed furnishes the conceptual means of explaining the possibility of a wide assortment of changes within a given species as a result of various climatic and lifestyle influences. To that extent, it renders excellent service to the defense of truth. For, however great the difference between the races may be, upon deeper investigation the unity and kinship of all people nevertheless emerges all the more clearly.[52] It is also evident from the facts that parents of the most diverse races can mate and produce fertile children, that every class of humans can inhabit every zone on earth and live there, and that peoples who have never been in contact nevertheless have various attributes and practices in common, such as gestures, the decimal system, skin painting, tattooing, circumcision, couvade, and so forth. Furthermore, numerous physiological phenomena are the same in all races, such as the erect posture, the shape of the skull, the average weight of the brain, the number and length of teeth, the duration of pregnancy, the average number of pulse beats, the interior structure of the organism, the hand, the foot (etc.), average age, body temperature, monthly periods, susceptibility to diseases, and so forth. Finally, in intellectual, religious, moral, social, and political respects, human beings have a wide range of things in common: language, intellect, reason, memory, knowledge of God, conscience, sense of sin, repentance, sacrifice, fasting, prayer, traditions about a golden age, a flood, and so forth. The unity of the human race, as Scripture teaches, is powerfully confirmed by all this. It is, finally, not a matter of indifference, as is sometimes claimed, but on the contrary of the utmost importance: it is the presupposition of religion and morality. The solidarity of the human race, original sin, the atonement in Christ, the universality of the kingdom of God, the catholicity of the church, and the love of neighbor—these all are grounded in the unity of humankind.[53]

52. The significance of the races is alternately exaggerated (as it is by Ammon, Driesmann, H. St. Chamberlain, Dühring, Gumplovicz, Nietzsche, Marx, and so on) and underestimated (as it is by Jentsch, Hertz, Colajanni, esp. Finot); cf. C. Snijders, "Het Ontstaan en de Verbreiding der Menschenrassen," *Tijdspiegel* (April 1897); S. R. Steinmetz, "De Rassenkwestie," *De Gids* 71 (January 1907): 104–39; H. Kern, *Rassen, Volken, Staten* (Haarlem: Bohn, 1904); idem, "Oud en Nieuw over de Menschenrassen," *Wetenschappelijke Bladen* (June 1904): 337–57.

53. On the unity of the human race, cf. further: O. Zöckler, "Die einheitliche Abstammung des Menschengeschlechts," *Jahrbücher für deutsche Theologie* 8 (1863): 51–90; idem, *Geschichte der Beziehungen*, II, 768ff.; idem, *Die Lehre vom Urstand*, 231ff.; idem, in *PRE³*, XII, 621; M. Rauch, *Die Einheit des Menschengeschlechts* (Augsburg: F. Butsch Sohn, 1873); Th. Waitz, *Über die Einheit des Menschengeschlechts und den Naturzustand des Menschen* (Leipzig: Fleischer, 1859); H. Ulrici, *Gott und der Mensch*, I, 2, 146ff.; H. Lotze, *Mircrocosmus*, trans. Elizabeth Hamilton and E. E. Constance Jones (New York: Scribner & Welford, 1866), 173–92; O. Peschel, *Abhandlungen zur Erd- und Völkerkunde*, 14ff.; F. H. Reusch, *Nature and Bible*, II, 181–245; P. Schanz, *Apologie des Christenthums*, I, 318–33 (*A Christian Apology*); F. G. Vigouroux, *Les livres saints*, IV, 1–120; F. Delitzsch, *A New Commentary on Genesis*, trans. Sophia Taylor (Edinburgh: T. & T. Clark, 1899), 190; F. Hettinger, *Apologie des Christenthums*, III, 223–80; J. H. A. Ebrard, *Apologetics*, trans. William Stuart and John Macpherson, 2d ed., 3 vols. (Edinburgh: T. & T. Clark, 1886–87), I, 262–302.

THE ORIGINAL ABODE OF HUMANITY

[283] Finally, there is the difference over the original abode of humankind. Genesis 2 relates that God, after he had created Adam, planted a garden in Eden (2:8). This *ᶜēden* (delight, land of delight) is therefore not identical with paradise but a region in which the garden (LXX *paradeisos*; according to Spiegel from the Persian word *pairi-daēza,* enclosure) was planted. This paradise is then called "the garden of Eden" (Gen. 2:15; 3:23), "the garden of God" (Ezek. 31:8–9), "the garden of the LORD" (Isa. 51:3), and is sometimes equated with Eden (Isa. 51:3; Ezek. 28:13; 31:9). God, further, planted that garden in Eden "eastward," "away to the east," that is, from the point of view of the author. A river flowed out of Eden to water the garden; and from there, that is, from that garden, as it flowed from the garden, it divided itself in four heads or branches, which are named Pishon, Gihon, Hiddekel, and Phrath. The last two rivers are the Tigris and the Euphrates; but about the first two there has always been disagreement. The church fathers, like Josephus, usually associated the Pishon with the Ganges and the Gihon with the Nile. But they never undertook a careful study of the location of paradise. For them, paradise on earth often flowed together with the heavenly paradise and was interpreted allegorically. Augustine says there were three views on paradise.[54] Some viewed it as an earthly paradise, others as a heavenly one, and still others combined the two. Those who regarded it as an earthly paradise believed it was situated on a very high level between heaven and earth, that it even extended to the moon, or that at one time the entire earth had been paradise, or that it was situated on the other side of the ocean. According to some exegetes, paradise was completely destroyed after the fall, especially by the flood; according to others, it still existed but had been rendered inaccessible by mountains and seas; and still others thought it had been incorporated in heaven. The first person who attempted to pin down the geographic location of paradise was Augustine Steuchus of Gubbio, called Eugubinus (d. 1550). In his work *Kosmopoiia,* which was published in Lyons in 1535, he developed the so-called Pasitigris hypothesis, according to which the four rivers are the estuaries of one vast river, the so-called Tigris-Euphrates, and paradise is therefore situated near the present city of Corna. This hypothesis was warmly accepted by Catholics like Pererius, Jansen, Lapide, Petavius, Mersenna; and by Reformed scholars such as Calvin and Marck; also by several Lutherans; it was adopted, in modified form, by Pressel.[55]

In addition, around the middle of the seventeenth century, there arose the so-called Armenia hypothesis, the groundwork for which had already been laid by Rupert of Deutz, Pellican, and Fournier, and which had been developed especially by Reland, professor at Utrecht (d. 1706). Its thesis is that Pishon is the Phasis, Gihon the Araxes, Havilah the Colchis, Cush the land of the *Kossioi*

---

54. Augustine, *Literal Meaning of Genesis,* VIII, 1.
55. J. J. Herzog, "Paradise," *Schaff-Herzog,* VII, 348–49; "Eden," *PRE*², IV, 34–38.

between Media and Susiana, and hence it looked for paradise in a much more northernly area, namely, way up in Armenia, approximately between Erzerum and Tiflis. It found more acceptance than the Pasitigris hypothesis and was still defended in our own time by von Raumer, Kurtz, Baumgarten, Keil, Lange, [Franz] Delitzsch, Rougement, and others. In contrast, Friedrich Delitzsch in his work, *Wo lag das Paradies?* (Leipzig: Hinrichs, 1881), looked for the location of paradise in a more southern direction: in the landscape of Babylon, which on account of its beauty was called "the garden of the God Dunias" by Babylonians and Assyrians. Hence, the river from Eden was the Euphrates in its upper reaches; Pishon and Gihon were two auxiliary canals. Other scholars, however, have gone much further and view the paradise story as a saga that has gradually traveled from east to west and in which Pishon and Gihon originally denote the Indus and the Oxus (J. D. Michaelis, Knobel, Bunsen, Ewald, and others). Others regard it as a myth in which Havilah represents the golden land of the saga, and the Gihon is the Ganges or the Nile (Paulus, Eichhorn, Gesenius, Tuch, Bertheau, Schrader, and others).[56]

Most anthropologists and linguists no longer take any account of Genesis 2 at all and mention very different countries as the original abode of humanity. But they are far from unanimous and have bestowed this honor practically on all countries. Romanes, Klaproth, de Gobineau, and George Browne refer to America; Spiller thought of Greenland, because after the cooling down of the earth the polar regions were the first to be inhabitable. Wagner considered Europe the continent where the ape had first evolved into a human. Unger specified Styria [province of Austria], L. Geiger Germany, Cuno and Spiegel southern Russia, Poesche the region between the Dnieper and the Njemen [Neman], Benfey and Whitney central Europe, Warren the North Pole. Darwin, Huxley, Peschel, and others favored Africa because they deemed the gorilla and the chimpanzee to be man's closest relatives. And Link, Häckel, Hellwald, and Schmidt invented a certain country called "Lemuria," where the apes had first become humans, and which was situated between Africa and Australia, but at the end of the Tertiary period had accidentally sunk into the depths of the sea. In this connection many scholars assume not just one single original abode of man, but believe that the evolution from animal to man occurred in various parts of the earth, thus combining Darwinism with polygeneticism (Haeckel, Vogt, Schaafhausen, Caspari, Fr. Müller, and others).

Even this spectacular disagreement among anthropologists illustrates that up until now natural science has not been able to say anything with certainty on this point. It loses itself in conjectures but knows nothing about the origin and abode of the first humans. There is not a single fact, therefore, that compels us to abandon the stipulation of Holy Scripture concerning Eden.

56. Cf. also H. Zimmern, *Biblische und babylonische Urgeschichte*, 2d ed., 2 vols. (Leipzig: J. C. Hinrichs, 1901); ed. note: Bavinck erroneously cites this as *Bibl. und parad. Urgeschichte*; H. Gunkel and H. Zimmern, *Schöpfung und Chaos,* 2d ed. (Göttingen: Vandenhoeck & Ruprecht, 1921); and his commentary on Genesis.

Ethnology, linguistics, history, and the natural sciences furnish us data that make plausible the choice of Asia as the original abode of man. Neither Africa, nor Europe, nor America, and much less a country like "Lemuria," can match the claim of Asia to this distinction. Here we find the most ancient peoples, the most ancient civilization, the most ancient languages; all of ancient history points us to this continent. From within this part of the earth Europe, Africa, Australia, and also America have been populated. Granted, in this connection many questions arise to which we do not yet know the answers. It is especially uncertain how and when America was populated.[57] But these objections by no means overthrow the teaching of Scripture that Asia is the cradle of humanity. About the location of paradise and Eden there may be different opinions, so that it is alternately placed in the center, east, or south of Asia; the geography may no longer lie within our capacity to determine, but Scripture and science unite in the witness that it is in Asia that we must look for the original abode of man.[58]

57. O. Zöckler, *Geschichte der Beziehungen*, I, 542ff.; O. Peschel, *Abhandlungen zur Erd- und Völkerkunde*, 402ff.; F. G. Vigouroux, *Les livres saints*, IV, 98ff.; E. Schmidt, *Die ältesten Spuren des Menschen in Nord-amerika*, Sammlung gemeinverständlicher wissenschaftlicher Vorträge, n.F., Serie 2, Heft 38–39 (Hamburg: J. F. Richter, 1887), 521–78.

58. O. Peschel, *Abhandlungen zur Erd- und Völkerkunde*, 35–41; O. Zöckler, *Geschichte der Beziehungen*, passim, esp. I, 128ff., 170ff., 395ff., 654ff.; II, 779ff.; idem, *Die Lehre vom Urstand*, 216ff.; idem, *Biblische und kirchenhistorische Studien* (Munich: C. H. Beck, 1893), part V, 1–38; F. H. Reusch, *Nature and Bible*, II, 181–245; F. Delitzsch, *A New Commentary on Genesis*, 114–46; Volck, "Eden," *PRE³*, V, 158–62; W. Engelkemper, *Die Paradiesesflüsse* (Münster, 1901); B. Poertner, *Das biblische Paradies* (Mainz: Kirchheim, 1901); Fr. Coelestinus [H. Vorst], *Het Aardsche Paradijs: Hoe het was en waar het lag* (Tilburg: Bergmans, 1903); and so forth.

12

HUMAN NATURE

To be human is to be an image-bearer of God, created in his likeness and originally righteous and holy. The whole person is the image of the whole deity. There has been extensive debate in the Christian church about the image of God in humanity. Some sought it essentially in human rationality, others in dominion over creation, others in freedom of the will or moral qualities such as love or justice. Pelagian and Socinian rationalist naturalism identified the image with a formal human freedom of moral choice, opening the door to an evolutionary view that sees the essence of humanity in an endless process of self-willed improvement. This view is diametrically contrary to Scripture, which does not consider a primitive animal state as an early stage in human history. Science provides no evidence for this hypothesis either, and it faces numerous philosophical and theological objections. Over against the naturalist view of human nature the Roman Catholic tradition posits a supernatural one that sees infused grace as the means by which human beings achieve and merit their true and supernatural end, the vision of God. Grace elevates nature. Protestant theology rejected key elements of this dualistic understanding, especially the meritorious character of natural elevation. The Reformers judged that the Roman Catholic position also weakened the view of original sin. But among the Protestants too there were differences. Lutherans tended to identify the image with the original gifts of righteousness, while the Reformed incorporated the whole human essence in the image, though they do speak of a narrow and broad sense of the image. Yet it is important to insist that the whole person is the image of the whole, that is, the triune, God. The human soul, all the human faculties, the virtues of knowledge, righteousness, and holiness, and even the human body images God. The incarnation of our Lord is definitive proof that humans, not angels, are created in the image of God, and that the human body is an essential component of that image. From the beginning creation was arranged, and human nature was immediately so created that it was amenable to, and fit for, the highest degree of conformity to God and for the most intimate indwelling of God.

[284] The essence of human nature is its being [created in] the image of God. The entire world is a revelation of God, a mirror of his attributes and perfec-

tions. Every creature in its own way and degree is the embodiment of a divine thought. But among creatures, only man is the image of God, God's highest and richest self-revelation and consequently the head and crown of the whole creation, the *imago Dei* and the epitome of nature, both *mikrotheos* (microgod) and *mikrokosmos* (microcosm). Even pagans have recognized this reality and called man the image of God. Pythagoras, Plato, Ovid, Cicero, Seneca, and others distinctly state that man, or at least the soul of man, was created as God's image, that he is God's kin and offspring.[1]

Not only that, but virtually all peoples have traditions of a golden age. Among the Chinese, the people of India, Iranians, Egyptians, Babylonians, Greeks, Romans, and others, one finds stories of an earlier time when humans lived in innocence and bliss and in communion with the gods. These stories were celebrated in song by the poets Hesiod, Ovid, and Virgil, and acknowledged by the philosophers in their truth.[2] Only Scripture, however, sheds a full and true light on this doctrine of man's divine likeness. The first creation narrative has it that, after intentional deliberation, God created man in God's image and likeness (MT: *bĕṣalmēnû kidmûtēnû*; LXX: *kat' eikona hēmeteran kai kath' homoiōsin*; Vulg.: *ad imaginem et similitudinem nostram*, Gen. 1:26–27). In Genesis 5:1 and 9:6 it is further repeated that God created man in the likeness of God *(bidmût ĕlōhîm)* and in the image of God *(bĕṣelem ĕlōhîm)*. Psalm 8 sings of man as the master of all creation, and Ecclesiastes 7:29 reminds us that God made man upright *(yāšār)*. For the rest, the Old Testament says little of the original state of integrity *(status integritis)*. More than any other people, Israel was a people of hope; she focused on the future, not on the past. Even the New Testament says relatively little about the image of God in which humanity was originally created. There is direct mention of it only in 1 Corinthians 11:7, where the man is called "the image and glory of God," and in James 3:9, where it is said of humans that they "are made in the likeness of God." Luke 3:38 also calls Adam "the son of God," and Paul quotes a pagan poet to the effect that "we are indeed his offspring" (Acts 17:28). Indirectly, however, also Ephesians 4:24 and Colossians 3:10 are of great importance here. In these verses we read of the "new man [self]" that believers must "put on," and of this new man it is said that it was created "according to the likeness of God in true righteousness and holiness," and "renewed in knowledge according to the image of its creator." Here it is implied that the new man, which believers put on, was created by God,

---

1. T. Pfanner, *Syst. theol. gent.*, 189ff.

2. J. G. Friderici, *De aurea aetate quam poëtae finxerunt* (Leipzig, 1736); H. Lüken, *Die Traditionen des Menschengeschlechts* (Münster: Aschendorff, 1869); O. Zöckler, *Die Lehre vom Urstand des Menschen* (Gütersloh: C. Bertelsmann, 1879), 84ff.; J. H. Oswald, *Religiöse Urgeschichte der Menschheit* (Paderborn: F. Schöningh, 1881), 37ff.; E. L. Fischer, *Heidenthum und Offenbarung* (Mainz: Kirchheim, 1878); O. Zöckler, *Biblische und kirchenhistorische Studien* (Munich: C. H. Beck, 1893), part V, 1ff.; O. Willmann, *Geschichte des Idealismus*, 3 vols. (Braunschweig: F. Vieweg, 1894–97), I, 1–136; C. P. Tiele, *Inleiding tot de Godsdienstwetenschap* (Amsterdam: P. N. van Kampen, 1897–99), II, 93ff., 197.

in conformity with God and his image, and that this conformity specifically emerges in righteousness and holiness, which is the fruit of appropriated truth. This, however, refers to the original creation since the words that Paul employs are clearly derived from the [Genesis] creation account; and since the second creation [of redemption]—as the whole of Scripture teaches—is not a "creation from nothing," but a renewal of all that existed; and since the *anakainousthai* (Col. 3:10) of the believer clearly describes this creation as a renewal. Underlying Ephesians 4:24 and Colossians 3:10, therefore, is the idea that humankind was originally created in God's image and in the re-creation is renewed on that model.

Scripture, however, not only recounts the fact of humankind's creation in God's image but also explains its meaning. While the two words "image" and "likeness" (*selem* and *dĕmût, eikōn* and *homoiōsis*) are certainly not identical, there is no essential material distinction to be made between them either. They are used interchangeably, and alternate for no specific reason. Both occur in Genesis 1:26 (cf. 5:3); but in 1:27 and 9:6 (cf. Col. 3:10) only the image is referred to, and in Genesis 5:1 and James 3:9 only the likeness. The distinction between them comes down to this: *selem* means "image," both archetype *(Urbild)* and ectype *(Abbild)*; *dĕmût* means "likeness, both example *(Vorbild)* and copy *(Nachbild)*. The concept of "image" is more rigid, that of "likeness" more fluid and more "spiritual," so to speak; in the former the idea of a prototype predominates, in the latter the notion of an ideal.[3] The likeness is a further qualification, an intensification and complement of the image. "Likeness" as such is weaker and broader than "image"; an animal has some features in common with man (likeness) but is not the image of man. "Image" tells us that God is the archetype, man the ectype; "likeness" adds the notion that the image corresponds in all parts to the original.[4] Just as there is little distinction between these two concepts, so there is little difference between the prepositions "in" *(b)* and "after" *(k)* used in this connection. These two are also used alternatively: in Genesis 5:1 and 3 we have *b* with *dĕmût* and in 5:3 also *k* with *selem*; the New Testament has *kata* with *eikōn* (Col. 3:10) but also with *homoiōsis* (James 3:9). Hence, nothing can be constructed on this basis; all we can say, with Delitzsch, is that in the case of *b* one thinks of the prototype as a cast metal mold, and in the case of *k* as a model held before us. There is therefore no reason, with Böhl, to derive from the preposition *b* the conclusion that the image of God is an atmosphere and element in which man was created.[5]

---

3. F. Delitzsch, *A New Commentary on Genesis,* trans. Sophia Taylor (Edinburgh: T. & T. Clark, 1899), 98–100, on Gen. 1:26; cf. also W. Riedel, *Alttestamentliche Untersuchungen* (Leipzig: A. Deichert [George Böhme], 1902), 42–47.

4. Augustine, *De diversis quaestionibus octoginta tribus liber,* qu. 74; T. Aquinas, *Summa theol.,* I, qu. 93, art. 9; J. Gerhard, *Loci theol.,* VIII, §18; A. Polanus, *Syn. theol.,* V, 10; etc.

5. E. Böhl, *Dogmatik* (Amsterdam: Scheffer, 1887), 154ff.; cf. in opposition, A. Kuyper, *De Vleeschwording des Woords* (Amsterdam: Wormser, 1887), viiiff.; F. E. Daubanton, *Theologische Studiën* 5 (1887): 429–44.

In addition to these words, Scripture offers the following data for the image of God. First, it is clear that the words "image" and "likeness" do not refer to anything in God but to something in humankind, not to the uncreated archetype but to the created ectype. The idea is not that man has been created after something in God that is called "image" or "likeness," so that it could, for example, be a reference to the Son; but that man has been created after God in such a way that humankind is his image and likeness. Further, this creation in God's image is in no way restricted, either on the side of the archetype or on the side of the ectype. It is not stated that man was created only in terms of some attributes, or in terms of only one person in the divine being, nor that man bears God's image and likeness only in part, say, only in the soul, or the intellect, or in holiness. The case is rather that the whole human person is the image of the whole Deity. Third, the meaning of the image of God is further explicated to us by the Son, who in an entirely unique sense is called the Word *(logos)*; the Son *(huios)*; the image *(eikōn)*, or imprint *(charaktēr)*, of God (John 1:1, 14; 2 Cor. 4:4; Col. 1:15; Heb. 1:3); and the one to whom we must be conformed (Rom. 8:29; 1 Cor. 15:49; Phil. 3:21; Eph. 4:23f.; 1 John 3:2). The Son already bears these names now because he is "God of God" and "Light of Light" [Nicene Creed], having the same attributes as the Father. He is not called thus on account of some part of his being but because his nature absolutely conforms to that of God. This, in turn, applies also to man. Like the Son, so also man as such is altogether the image of God. He does not just bear but *is* the image of God. There is this difference, of course, that what the Son is in an absolute sense, man is in only a relative sense. The former is the eternal only begotten Son; the latter is the created son of God. The former is the image of God *within* the divine being, the latter *outside* of it. The one is the image of God in a divine manner, the other is that in a creaturely manner. But thus, then, and within his limits, man is the image and likeness of God. Finally, Scripture here and there tells us in what ways that image reveals and manifests itself openly. The full content of that image of God is nowhere unfolded. But Genesis 1:26 clearly indicates that the image of God manifests itself in man's dominion over all of the created world (cf. Ps. 8; 1 Cor. 11:7). The portrayal of the paradisal state in Genesis 1–2 demonstrates that the image of God includes conformity to the will of God (cf. Eccles. 7:29). And re-creation in conformity to the image of God or Christ primarily consists in putting on the new man, which among other things consists in righteousness and holiness of truth.

DEFINING THE IMAGE

[285] On the content of the image of God there was initially a wide range of opinion in the Christian church. At times it was located in the human body, then in rationality, or in the freedom of the will, then again in dominion over the created world, or also in other moral qualities such as love, justice, and the

like.[6] But gradually two views came to the fore side by side or as opposites, both of them appealing to the distinction between image *(ṣelem)* and likeness *(dĕmût)*. Some, like Clement of Alexandria, Origen, and others, noted that Genesis 1:26 indeed says that God planned to create man after his image and likeness, but that, according to verse 27, he only created him in his image, that is, as a rational being, in order that man himself would acquire likeness with God in the way of obedience and receive it in the end as his reward from God's hand.[7] Others, on the other hand, believed that along with the image, that is, a rational nature, man also immediately received the likeness as a gift and that, having lost that gift by sin, he would regain it through Christ.[8] The first view, which one might call the naturalistic one, found support in the doctrine of the freedom of the will. Consequently, its adherents could not conceive holiness as a divine gift bestowed on humanity at the outset, but only as a good that he had to achieve by his own moral efforts.[9] Many theologians, accordingly, taught that humanity was created in a state, not of positive holiness, but of childlike innocence.[10]

Naturalism

It was to such pronouncements that Pelagius later appealed when he identified the essence and original state of man with moral indifference, with nothing but a formal freedom of moral choice. The image of God, Pelagius taught, consists only in a natural God-given possibility of perfection, which cannot be lost and is therefore still a part of every human being. God bestows the ability *(posse),* but the will *(velle)* is up to us.[11] Later, this view found acceptance among the Socinians, who located the image of God solely in human dominion over nature;[12] among the Anabaptists, who said that as a finite earthly creature man was not yet the image of God but could only realize that status by a rebirth;[13]

6. Cf. J. C. Suicerus, s.v. "εἰκων," *Thesaurus ecclesiasticus* (Amsterdam: J. H. Wetsten, 1682); D. Petavius, "De opifico sex dierum," in *Theol. dogm.*, II, ch. 2; W. Münscher, *Lehrbuch des christlichen Dogmengeschichte,* ed. Daniel von Coelln, 3d ed. (Cassel: J. C. Krieger, 1832–38), I, 339ff.; K. R. Hagenbach, *Lehrbuch der Dogmengeschichte* (Leipzig: Hirzel, 1888), §56.

7. Clement of Alexandria, *Stromateis,* II, 22; Origen, *On First Principles,* III, 6.

8. Irenaeus, *Against Heresies,* V, 16, 2; Athanasius, *Against the Arians,* II, 59; idem, *Against the Heathens,* 2; idem, *On the Incarnation,* 3.

9. A. Harnack, *History of Dogma,* trans. N. Buchanan, J. Millar, E. B. Speirs, and W. McGilchrist, ed. A. B. Bruce, 7 vols. (London: Williams & Norgate, 1896–99), II, 128–48.

10. Tertullian, *Treatise on the Soul,* 38; Theophilus, *To Autolycus,* II, 24, 27; Irenaeus, *Against Heresies,* IV, 38.

11. Augustine, *On the Grace of Christ,* I, 3ff.

12. O. Fock, *Der Socinianismus* (Kiel: C. Schröder, 1847), 484.

13. Ed. note: Bavinck here lists Menno Simons, *Werken,* 125, 126, 180. He is likely referring to Menno's *Foundation of Christian Doctrine* (1539, rev. 1554, 1556) or to *The True Christian Faith* (ca. 1541, rev. 1556), both of which deal with the "new birth" and can be found in *The Complete Works of Menno Simons* (Elkhart: John F. Funk & Brother, 1871), I, 165–78, 103–63; or in *The Complete Writings of Menno Simons,* trans. Leonard Verduin, ed. J. C. Wenger (Scottdale, Pa.: Herald Press, 1956), 103–226, 321–405; cf. H. W. Erbkam, *Geschichte der protestantischen Sekten* (Hamburg and Gotha: F. & A. Perthes, 1848), 461; J. Cloppenburg, *Op. theol.,* II, 144ff.

among the Remonstrants,[14] the Rationalists, and Supernaturalists,[15] and numerous modern theologians,[16] all of whom saw the state of integrity as a state of childlike innocence. As a rule these theologians still hold to the historical reality of such an original state. But in their view of the image of God in the first humans they materially agree totally with those who, detaching the idea from the fact, deny the reality of a state of integrity and locate the image of God solely in man's free personality, his rational or moral nature, in a religious-ethical bent, in man's vocation to enter communion with God.[17] This view then unwittingly prompts them to accept the theory of evolution, according to which the essence of man is situated not in what he was or is but in what he, in an endless process of development and by his own exertions, may become. Paradise lies ahead, not behind us. An evolved ape deserves preference over a fallen human. Originally bearing the image of an orangutan and chimpanzee, man gradually pulled himself up from a state of raw brutishness to that of a noble humanity.

14. *Conf. Remonstr.*, V, 5; S. Episcopius, *Apologia pro confessiones*; idem, *Instit. theol.*, IV, 3, 7; P. van Limborch, *Theol. christ.*, II, 24, 5.

15. J. A. L. Wegscheider, *Institutiones theologiae christianae dogmaticae* (Halle: Gebauer, 1819), §99; K. G. Bretschneider, *Handbuch der Dogmatik* (Leipzig: J. A. Barth, 1838), §§115–16; F. V. Reinhard, *Grundriss der Dogmatik* (Munich: Seidel, 1802), §70.

16. I. A. Dorner, *A System of Christian Doctrine*, trans. Alfred Cave and J. S. Banks, rev. ed., 4 vols. (Edinburgh: T. & T. Clark, 1888), II, 77–84; J. P. Lange, *Christliche Dogmatik*, 3 vols. (Heidelberg: K. Winter, 1849–52), II, 298ff.; J. Müller, *Die christliche Lehre von der Sünde*, 2 vols. (Breslau: J. Mar, 1844), II, 457ff. (ET: *The Christian Doctrine of Sin*, trans. Wm. Urwick, 5th ed. [Edinburgh: T. & T. Clark, 1868]); J. T. Beck, *Die christliche Lehr-Wissenshaft nach den biblischen Urkunden*, 2d ed. (Stuttgart: Steinkopf, 1875), I, 186ff.; idem, *Vorlesungen über christliche Glaubenslehre*, 2 vols. (Gütersloh: C. Bertelsmann, 1886–87), II, 328; H. Martensen, *Die christliche Dogmatik*, trans. from Danish (Leipzig: Hinrichs, 1897), 139 (ET: *Christian Dogmatics*, trans. William Urwick [Edinburgh: T. & T. Clark, 1871]); K. F. A. Kahnis, *Die lutherische Dogmatik* (Leipzig: Dörffling & Franke, 1861–68), I, 432; O. Zöckler, *Die Lehre vom Urstand*, 40ff., 333; Gretillat, *Théol. syst.*, III, 464ff.; P. Hofstede de Groot, *De Groninger Godgeleerdheid in Hunne Eigenaardigheid* (Groningen: Scholtens, 1855), 89ff.; J. I. Doedes, *De Leer der Zaligheid Volgens het Evangelie in de Schriften des Nieuwen Verbonds Voorgesteld* (Utrecht: Kemink, 1876), §24; J. I. Doedes, *De Nederlandsche Geloofsbelijdenis* (Utrecht: Kemink & Zoon, 1880–81), 145; J. I. Doedes, *De Heidelbergsche Catechismus* (Utrecht: Kemink & Zoon, 1881), 69.

17. I. Kant, *Religion within the Limits of Reason Alone*, trans. Theodore M. Greene and Hoyt H. Hudson (New York: Harper & Brothers, 1934), 21–23; J. G. Fichte, *The Vocation of Man*, trans. William Smith, 2d ed. (Chicago: Open Court, 1910); G. W. F. Hegel, *Sämtliche Werke* (Stuttgart: Fr. Frommann, 1959), vol. 15, 199ff. ("Vorlesung über die Philosophie der Religion, Erster Band," *Werke*, XI, 183ff.); F. Schleiermacher, *The Christian Faith*, ed. H. R. MacIntosh and J. S. Steward (Edinburgh: T. & T. Clark, 1928); D. F. Strauss, *Der alte und der neue Glaube* (Leipzig: Hirzel, 1872), II, 72; A. E. Biedermann, *Christliche Dogmatik* (Zürich: Füssli, 1869), II, 562; R. Lipsius, *Dogm.*, §§420, 440; A. Ritschl, *Die christliche Lehre von der Rechtfertigung und Versöhnung*, 4th ed. (Bonn: A. Marcus, 1895–1903), III, 314; F. A. B. Nitzsch, *Lehrbuch der evangelische Dogmatik*, 3d ed. prepared by Horst Stephan (Tübingen: J. C. B. Mohr, 1902), 306ff.; J. Kaftan, *Dogmatik* (Tübingen: J. C. B. Mohr, 1901), §39; Th. Häring, *Der christliche Glaube*, 2d ed. (Calw: Vereinsbuchhandlung, 1912), 248ff. (ET: *The Christian Faith: A System of Dogmatics*, trans. John Dickie and George Ferries, 2 vols. [London & New York: Hodder & Stoughton, 1913]); J. Bovon, *Dogmatique chrétienne*, 2 vols. (Lausanne: Georges Bridel, 1895–96), I, 132, 139; J. H. Scholten, *De Leer der Hervormde Kerk*, 2d ed., 2 vols. (Leyden: P. Engels, 1850–51), I, 304ff.; II, 67ff.

[286] It hardly needs saying that Holy Scripture is diametrically opposed to this theory of evolution. Christian churches, accordingly, almost unanimously rejected the naturalistic Pelagian view of the image of God and man's original state. Aside from the arguments for the Darwinian hypothesis, which we already rebutted earlier, there are actually no direct historical proofs for the animal state of man as pictured by evolutionary theorists. The bones and skulls that have been found all prove, on closer scrutiny, to derive from beings wholly like ourselves. As far as we can go back into history we find a condition of relatively high levels of civilization in China, India, Babylonia, and Egypt. All proof that the peoples of those areas evolved from an animal state is lacking. The appeal to so-called primitive people, who for that matter are not completely devoid of culture either, has no cogency, for it cannot be proved that they are closer than the civilized peoples to the original state of humanity. There is greater reason to believe that, being isolated from humanity, they gradually declined into a state of barbarism. They all bear the character of degenerates who, like branches off a tree, were torn from the main stock and, not receiving fresh vitalities from without, died away and disappeared.[18]

The question pertaining to the primitive state of humans, accordingly, is not really historical but philosophical, since that state by definition precedes all historical evidence. The answer given to that question is determined by the idea one has of human nature. The more one thinks about this being, the more impossible it becomes to imagine human history as starting with a barbaric or animal state. Life, consciousness, language, religion, the difference between truth and untruth, and so forth, cannot be explained from the perspective of evolution but presuppose an origin of their own, a creation ex nihilo. Even in the theology of modernists this is evident. They indeed deny the creation of man in God's image and hence the state of integrity, but the idea of creation suddenly appears again at the most critical point. Either consciousness is something specifically human; or at least religion has its own original principle in humans. Or if evolution has been accepted as interpretive principle also at this point, a halt is called in the case of the ethical dimension, and this theology insists on its independence; the moral life and the moral disposition is unique *(sui generis)* and has its own origin *(sui originis)*.[19] But this intermediate position between creation and evolution is untenable. It was repeatedly held by a variety of Pelagian schools of thought because their adherents objected to

---

18. Th. Waitz, *Über die Einheit des Menschengeschlechts und den Naturzustand des Menschen* (Leipzig: Fleischer, 1859), 334ff.; O. Peschel, *Abhandlungen zur Erd- und Völkerkunde*, 5th ed. (Leipzig: Duncker & Humboldt, 1878), 135ff.; F. Ratzel, *Völkerkunde* (Leipzig: Bibliographisches Institut, 1885–90), I, 4ff.; S. Steinmetz, *De Studie der Völkenkunde* (1907); W. Schneider, *Die Naturvölker* (Paderborn: F. Schöningh, 1885); C. Gutberlet, *Der Mensch* (Paderborn: F. Schöningh, 1903), 475ff.; J. Froberger, *Die Schöpfungsgeschichte der Menschheit in der "voraussetzungslosen" Völkerpsychologie* (Trier: Paulinus, 1903); O. Zöckler, *Geschichte der Beziehungen zwischen Theologie und Naturwissenschaft* (Gütersloh: C. Bertelsmann, 1877–79), II, 744ff.; F. G. Vigouroux, *Les livres saints*, 4 vols. (Paris: A. Roger & F. Chernoviz, 1886–90), IV, 171ff.; J. Guibert, *In the Beginning*, trans. G. S. Whitmarsh (London: Kegan Paul, Trench, & Trübner, 1900), 366–79.

19. S. Hoekstra, *Wijsgerige Godsdienstwetenschap*, I, 1ff., 213ff.

both creation and evolution and hence looked for a mediating theory. The first human was neither an animal nor a perfect holy human being but an innocent child. He was neither positively good, nor positively evil, but stood somewhere in between; he was morally indifferent and could do one thing as well as another. In actual fact he was nothing; potentially he was everything, pious and wicked, holy and unholy, good and evil. The disposition and ability *(posse)* originated by creation, but everything constructed on that foundation of potentiality was developed by man's own work and volition. Now, as we will note in the following section, there is an element of truth in this picture insofar as the first humans had not yet attained the highest good and hence still had to develop. But aside from this point, and for many reasons, this view is totally unacceptable.

In the first place, Scripture clearly teaches that both physically and psychically humans were created as adults at "an age of vigor."[20] The Genesis account of the first humans is very simple, but their state was that of full-grown, aware, freely acting agents. Creation in the image of God (Gen. 1:27; Eccles. 7:29; Eph. 4:24; Col. 3:10), the blessing of procreation and multiplication (Gen. 1:28), divine approval (Gen. 1:31), the probationary command (Gen. 2:16–17), the naming of the animals (Gen. 2:19–20), the pronouncement about Eve (Gen. 2:23–24), the manner of the temptation (Gen. 3:1ff.), and the attitude of Adam and Eve after the fall (Gen. 3:7ff.)—all attest to the truth that the first humans were created positively good, not morally indifferent. The only counterargument could perhaps be based on the fact that the first humans knew no shame. This, accordingly, has always been brought up by the opposition as a very strong argument.[21] It does not hold water, however, because before the fall the sex life was very well known to the first humans (Gen. 1:27–28; 2:23–24), and because shame is derived specifically from the fall and not from the awakening of sexuality.

Second, this view suffers from irresolution and makes the problem before us even more complicated. It is irresolute insofar as, on the one hand, it favors evolution but, having arrived at a certain point, it again pays tribute to creation. It wants no part of a creation of the act but does assume a creation of potentiality. It speaks of an ability *(Fähigkeit)* without readiness *(Fertigkeit)*; and it considers the creation of a child, both in a physical and a psychic sense, simpler and more reasonable than that of an adult. This is as such inherently absurd, for one who believes in the creation rather than the evolution of potentiality can no longer in principle object to the doctrine of original justice and the state of integrity. But on top of that, it makes the issue even harder to imagine. Potentiality does not automatically develop into actuality. Max Müller correctly stated: "If we would attempt to picture the first man created as a child

---

20. Augustine, *Literal Meaning of Genesis,* VI, 13–14; P. Lombard, *Sent.,* II, dist. 17.

21. H. Ellis, *Geschlechtstrieb und Schamgefühl* (Leipzig: Wigand, 1900); W. Francken, *Ethische Studiën* (Haarlem, 1903), 110–28.

and as gradually developing his physical and psychic powers, we cannot grasp how he managed even for a day without supernatural assistance."[22] Along the same lines is Schelling's comment: "I definitely consider the state of culture as being original for the human race."[23] And also J. G. Fichte wrote: "One wonders—if indeed it is necessary to assume an origin of the entire human race—who brought up the first human couple? They had to be brought up—a human being could not have educated them. Hence, they had to be brought up by another rational being, one who was not a human. This naturally holds true only up to the time when they could educate each other. A spirit adopted them, quite in the manner pictured in a venerable ancient document, which generally speaking contains the profoundest and most sublime wisdom and posits results to which in the end all philosophy has to return."[24] To avoid one miracle, many miracles have to be assumed.

Third, underlying this view is the error that innate holiness cannot possibly exist. Holiness, we are told, is always the product of struggle and effort. If Adam had been created a positively holy being, he was necessarily good and without freedom to be otherwise.[25] As a result, these theologians have to dream up a state between good and evil, holiness and unholiness, an undifferentiated state that is anterior to the moral dimension either in a good or a bad sense, and from which humans then have to evolve by an act of free will in one direction or another. In that case man is robbed of all intellectual and ethical substance, and the image of God is located in a purely naked, merely formal personality.[26] Such a concept of personality, however, is a mere abstraction, to which nothing in reality corresponds. No human being can be conceived without certain qualities of intellect and will. A completely undifferentiated state of the will, without any inclination in one direction or another, is simply an impossibility. Just as in nature only a good tree can produce good fruit, so also in ethical life a good nature precedes good works. To act one must first *be (Operari sequitur esse)*. Scripture, accordingly, teaches that both in creation and re-creation holiness is a gift from God. One who has this gift can further develop it in word and deed; but one who lacks it can never acquire it.

Finally, this view does less than justice to the justice of God, who has then allowed his creature to be tempted beyond his power to resist. It also fails to

22. M. Müller, *Vorlesungen über die Wissenschaft der Sprache*, 3d ed. (Leipzig: Mayer, 1866), 410.

23. F. W. Schelling, *Ausgewählte Werke* (Darmstadt: Wissenschaftliche Buchgesellschaft, 1968), III, 520–29 ("Vorlesungen über die Methode des Akademischen Studiums," [1803], *Werke* I/5, 286–95); III, 643–45 ("Philosophie und Religion," [1804], *Werke* I/6, 57–59).

24. J. G. Fichte, *Grundlage des Naturrechts nach Principien der Wissenschaftslehre* (Jena: Gabler, 1796). ET: *The Science of Rights*, trans. A. E. Kroeger (New York: Harper & Row, 1970 [1889]).

25. R. Rothe, *Theologische Ethik*, 2d rev. ed., 5 vols. (Wittenberg: Zimmerman, 1867–71), §§480ff.

26. C. I. Nitzsch, *System der christlichen Lehre*, 5th ed. (Bonn: Adolph Marcus, 1844), 211; J. Müller, *Die christliche Lehre von der Sünde*, I, 154ff., 493ff. (*The Christian Doctrine of Sin*); K. F. A. Kahnis, *Die lutherische Dogm.*, I, 432; G. Thomasius, *Die christliche Dogmengeschichte als Entwicklungs-Geschichte des kirchlichen Lehrbegriffs*, 2 vols. (Erlangen: A. Deichert, 1886–89), I, 110ff.; J. T. Beck, *Christliche Glaube*, II, 333; J. I. Doedes, *De Leer der Zaligheid*, 55ff.

do justice to the seriousness of the temptation, which then becomes a crafty piece of trickery, and to the character of the fall, which ceases to be an appalling sin and changes into a nonculpable misfortune, an almost unavoidable lot. It erases the boundaries that exist between the state of integrity and the state of corruption, and allows man to keep intact the image of God, which exists in something purely formal, even after the fall. It conceives the relation between the formal (personality, free will) and the material (the religious and ethical life) to be as loose and dualistic as Rome pictures it between purely natural things and the superadded gift, with the sole difference that in the case of Rome holiness is the fruit of grace, and in the case of Pelagius and his followers it is a product of caprice.

Roman Catholic Supernaturalism

[287] Alongside and over against this naturalistic view of the image of God there arose another view that we may call supernaturalistic. It did not arise from the distinction between "image" and "likeness," although it was later associated with this distinction as well. Nor is it based on the interpretation of Genesis 1–2, inasmuch as many theologians acknowledge that it does not occur there, at least not literally. It was derived from the idea—one that gradually appeared in the Christian church—of the state of glory *(status gloriae)* to which believers are elevated by Christ and his Spirit (John 1:12; Rom. 8:14–17; 1 Cor. 2:7ff.; Eph. 1:15ff.; 2 Pet. 1:2ff.; 1 John 3:1–2, etc.).[27] Gradually, under Neoplatonic influence, this state of glory was viewed as a condition that far transcended the state of nature, not only in an ethical but also in a corporeal sense. In christological disputes after the fourth century this idea became so prominent that the deity of Christ and of the Spirit was affirmed particularly with the argument that they were the authors of deification for humans. The essence of the state of glory increasingly came to be the vision of God according to his essence *(per essentiam)*, deiformity or deification, a participation in the divine nature that was not only moral but corporeal, a "melting union" with God.[28] Added to this doctrine of "the state of glory" was that of the meritorious nature of good works. Infused grace, granted in baptism, was definitely necessary, but also enabled a person to do such good works as could *ex condigno* (by a full merit)[29] earn eternal blessedness, the vision of God *per essentiam*.

From these two ideas, the mystical view of man's final destiny and the meritoriousness of good works, was born the Catholic doctrine of the "superadded gift" *(donum superadditum)*. The first to formulate it was Alexander of Hales. The heavenly blessedness and the vision of God, which is man's final destiny—and was so for Adam—can be merited *ex condigno* only by

27. M. J. Scheeben, *Handbuch der katholischen Dogmatik*, 4 vols. (Freiburg i.B.: Herder, 1933), II, 272–81.

28. See above, pp. 187–91 (#199).

29. Ed. note: Cf. Richard A. Muller, *Dictionary of Latin and Greek Theological Terms* (Grand Rapids: Baker, 1985), s.v. "*meritum*," 190–92.

such good works as are in accord with that final destiny. In other words, like that destiny, they have a supernatural character and hence proceed from a supernatural principle: infused grace. The righteousness that Adam possessed as a human, earthly being by virtue of creation was not, of course, sufficient to that end. So for Adam to reach his final destiny he too needed to be given a supernatural grace, that is, the *gratia gratum faciens* ("the grace that renders one engraced or pleasing to God"), the image of God. "But this elevation of the rational creature is a supernatural complement; and therefore neither consecration nor adoption nor any elevation *(assumptio)* of this kind happens through any property of nature but only through a gift superadded to nature. This consecrates nature so that it may be a temple, assimilating it to God so that it may be a son or a daughter, allying it to God or making it one with God through a conformity to the will so that it may be a bride. This, however, comes about by God's mediation as grace renders it pleasing to him."[30]

This doctrine of supernaturalism found general acceptance among the Scholastics.[31] It was incorporated in the Roman Catechism[32] and later defended and maintained against the Reformers, Baius, Jansen, and Quesnel.[33] Now it constitutes one of the most important and characteristic loci in Roman Catholic theology.[34] But although in substance there was consensus, at subordinate points there was a variety of differences. Some, such as Hales, Bonaventure, Albert the Great, Duns Scotus, Biel, and others, asserted that the supernatural gift of *gratia gratum faciens* was distinct from the original righteousness that man immediately possessed by nature at the moment of his creation, and was bestowed later in time than this original righteousness.[35] According to them, man was first created with "original righteousness" *(iustitia originalis)*, which enabled him to earn the grace which makes acceptable by a merit of congruity *(gratia gratum faciens ex congruo)*; and having received the latter, he could by it

---

30. Alexander of Hales, *Summa theol.,* II, qu. 91, membr. 1, art. 3.

31. T. Aquinas, *Summa theol.,* I, qu. 95; Bonaventure, *The Breviloquium,* II, c. 11–12; V, c. 1; Commentaries of T. Aquinas, Bonaventure, Duns Scotus, e.a., on *Sentences,* II, dist. 29.

32. Roman Catechism, I, 2, qu. 18, 3.

33. R. Bellarmine, *De gratia primi hominis* (Heidelberg: Rosa, 1612); H. Denzinger, *The Sources of Catholic Dogma (Enchiridion symbolorum),* trans. Roy J. Deferrari, 30th ed. (London and St. Louis: Herder, 1955), n. 881ff.

34. Cf. in addition to the above-mentioned works, M. Becanus, *Summa theologiae scholasticae* (Rouen: I. Behovrt, 1651), I, tract. 5; A. Casini, *Controv. de statu purae naturae,* printed as an appendix to book II of "De opificio sex dierum," in vol. IV, 587–653, of *De theologicis dogmatibus,* by D. Petavius (Paris: Vivès, 1868); *Theologia Wirceburgensi (Theologia dogmatica: Polemica, scholastica et moralis),* VII, 145ff.; G. Perrone, *Prael. theol.,* 1838–43), III, 166–82; M. J. Scheeben, *Handbuch der katholischen Dogmatik,* II, 239–514; idem, *Nature and Grace,* trans. Cyril Vollert (St. Louis: B. Herder, 1954); C. Schäzler, *Natur und Übernatur* (Mainz: Kirchheim, 1865) (ed. note: Bavinck's citation reads simply *Natur u. Gnade*); H. Th. Simar, *Lehrbuch der Dogmatik,* 3d ed., 2 vols. (Freiburg i.B.: Herder, 1879–80), 326ff.; C. Pesch, *Praelectiones dogmaticae,* III: *De Deo creante et elevante* (Freiburg i.B.: Herder, 1916–25), 76–111, etc.

35. Alexander of Hales, *Summa theol.,* II, qu. 96, m. 1; Bonaventure, *Sent.,* II, dist. 29, art. 2, qu. 2; etc.

gain heavenly blessedness *ex condigno,* a condigned or full merit. But Thomas objected to this idea, because in that case the *gratia gratum faciens* was also grounded on merits if a personal gift to Adam could not have been lost or acquired for all his descendants and could not then be bestowed without merit on small children in baptism. Thomas, therefore, taught that at the moment of his creation Adam had received the *gratia gratum faciens* along with original righteousness.[36] The Council of Trent avoided taking sides in this dispute between Franciscans and Dominicans and only declared (session V, 1) that Adam had "lost the holiness and justice in which he had been constituted." Although later theologians usually followed Thomas and let original justice coincide *in fact and in time* with the *gratia gratum faciens,* ideally and logically the position remained the same.

Roman Catholic theology has a dual conception of humanity: humankind in the purely natural sense, without supernatural grace, is indeed sinless but only possesses natural religion and virtue and has his destiny on earth; humankind endowed with the superadded gift of the image of God has a supernatural religion and virtue and a destiny in heaven. But with this dual notion of man the search was not over. As soon as one attempted to imagine what belonged to the former idea of man and what belonged to the latter, one ran into trouble with the various gifts granted to the first human being. Immortality and impassibility could not strictly be called natural, for they are not qualities belonging to Adam's earthly body as such and could be lost. On the other hand, they could not be the consequence of the *gratia gratum faciens* either, for then man in his purely natural state without the superadded gift would have been susceptible to death and suffering, and in that case death would not be the penalty for sin. The same is true for inordinate lust (concupiscence). According to Rome, the conflict between flesh and spirit is natural. The subjection of the flesh to the spirit, therefore, is something supernatural, not something given with creation as such. At the same time, it can also not be attributed only to the *gratia gratum faciens,* for in that case a sinless human being without the superadded gift would not be possible. Consequently, between the two ideas described above, Rome had to insert a third notion—preternatural.

Human beings are, therefore, conceived as endowed with natural, preternatural, and supernatural gifts. There are three kinds of justice: natural, preternatural, and supernatural. It is not surprising that some theologians—such as Berti, Norisius, and others—could not imagine a human being endowed only with natural and preternatural gifts. In terms of God's absolute power *(potentia absoluta)* such a human was indeed possible, but not in terms of his ordained power *(potentia ordinata)* (i.e., power exerted in and through the natural order). The beatific vision actually properly belongs to man by nature "at least as far as inclination and appetite are concerned" *(saltem quoad inclinationem et ap-*

36. T. Aquinas, *Summa theol.,* I, qu. 100, art. 1; *Sent.,* II, dist. 20, qu. 2, art. 3; II, dist. 29, qu. 1, art. 1.

petitum).[37] But even if the conceivability and possibility of a human being in his or her purely natural state is upheld, all sorts of differences in the doctrine of the image of God remain. Some theologies make a distinction between the "image" and the "likeness" such that the former embraces the natural gifts and the latter the supernatural. Others, like the Roman Catechism, apply both concepts to the supernatural gifts. Hales, Bonaventure, Thomas, and others, in considering original justice, thought of natural righteousness, but the Roman Catechism and most later theologians refer especially to the superadded gifts as original justice. Immortality, impassibility, free will, and the restraint of concupiscence were sometimes derived from a divine gift and at other times from the "image" or the "likeness," and also at times attributed to original righteousness.[38] The Roman Catechism simply lists all these things and does not achieve a consistent view of the whole: thanks to a divine gift, Adam was not susceptible to death and suffering; his soul was created in God's image and likeness; furthermore, his concupiscence was restrained and made subject to reason; then to all this God added original righteousness and dominion.[39] On top of all this, then, comes the disagreement over the nature of the *gratia gratum faciens,* its relation to the Spirit of God, to the soul and its faculties, to the theological virtues, to good works, and so forth. All this is enough to show that the Roman Catholic doctrine of the image of God is inherently incomplete and in part for that reason fails to satisfy the theological mind.

Critique of Supernaturalism

[288] This doctrine is inadequate, in the first place, because it is based on a mistaken view of man's final destiny. The state of grace and of glory, in which the church of Christ is a participant both here and in the hereafter, is most splendidly described in Holy Scripture as the state of the children of God, as participation in the divine nature, as the vision of God, as eternal life, as heavenly bliss, and so forth. On this issue there is no disagreement between Rome and us: What no eye has seen, nor ear heard, nor the heart of man conceived, that is what God, in the New Testament dispensation of the covenant of grace, has prepared for those who love him (1 Cor. 2:9). But Rome views this final human destiny, which has been realized by Christ, as a Neoplatonic vision of God and a mystical fusion of the soul with God.[40] And that is not what Scripture teaches. All the benefits that Christ has acquired for his own are not just bestowed in the state of glory but are in principle already granted here on earth (1 Cor. 2:9) and do not, even according to Rome, include the

37. G. Perrone, *Prael. theol.,* III, 167; J. H. Oswald, *Religiöse Urgeschichte der Menschheit,* 52ff. (ed. note: cf. idem, *Die Schöpfungslehre im allgemeinen und in besonderer Beziehung auf den Menschen* [Paderborn: F. Schöningh, 1885]); C. Pesch, *Prael. dogm.,* III, 109.

38. T. Aquinas, *Summa theol.,* I, qu. 95, art. 1; *Sent.,* II, dist. 19, qu. 1, art. 4; C. Pesch, *Prael. dogm.,* III, 89ff.

39. Roman Catechism, I, 2, qu. 18, 3. For the doctrine of the Greek Orthodox Church, see Georgius B. Matulewicz, *Doctrina Russorum de statu justitiae originalis* (Freiburg i.B.: Herder, 1904).

40. See above, pp. 187–91 (#199).

vision of God *per essentiam*. Becoming a child of God is the fruit of faith (John 1:12; Rom. 8:14ff.; Gal. 4:6; 1 John 3:1–2). Eternal life is our portion here already and consists in knowing God in the face of Christ (John 3:16, 36; 17:3). Christ is and remains the way to the Father, to the knowledge and vision of God (Matt. 11:27; John 1:18; 14:6; 1 John 3:2b). The vision of God can only be achieved in the way of ethical Christian living (Matt. 5:8; 1 John 3:6). Even participation in the divine nature is not something for the future alone but a goal envisaged already by the granting of God's promises here on earth (2 Pet. 1:4) and again ethically mediated (Heb. 12:10).

Second, Scripture nowhere teaches that this state of glory, which is already initiated in the state of grace on earth, is "supernatural" and "superadded" in the Roman Catholic sense. Certainly this state of grace and glory far surpasses the reach of human thought and imagination (1 Cor. 2:9; 13:12; 1 John 3:2). It must be remembered, however, that according to 1 Corinthians 2 it is the wisdom of this age and the spirit of this world and the unspiritual person (vv. 6, 8, 12, 14) from whom these divine benefits remain hidden; and this "unspiritual" person is the one who is guided only by animal instinct, devoid of the Spirit of God, and hence darkened in mind. Add to this that what God bestows and will bestow on believers will also remain to them an unmerited gift of grace, a gift that will always and ever arouse them to amazement and worship. Remember further that Christ not only acquired what Adam lost but also what Adam, in the way of obedience, would have gained. The salvific benefits of the covenant of grace, therefore, far surpass the reach of all our thoughts; but nothing in Scripture even hints at the notion that it is all a "superadditive" that originally did not belong to our human nature.

Third, the conclusion for Adam's state before the fall drawn by Rome from these benefits of grace in Christ is incorrect. Rome reasons as follows: If the state of glory for restored human beings consists in conformity to God, it must have consisted in that state also in the case of the first human. And if that state of glory is now attained by believers only by way of the state of grace, the same must be true of Adam before the fall. The connection between the state of grace and that of glory, according to Rome, consists in the fact that in justification man receives infused grace, and by virtue of this grace performs good works which *ex condigno* merit eternal life. This entire scheme is then transferred to the first human. His final destiny, too, was the state of glory, a state he could only attain by way of the state of grace by which he could *ex condigno* merit eternal life. Like the state of glory, so also the grace in question is by its very nature supernatural, on a level above the natural man, and therefore a superadded gift. In the case of the restored human this reasoning on the part of Rome is correct insofar as from the image of God it infers that of the first human. There is, in fact, only one image of God. It is also correct insofar as it assumes that Adam's final destiny was no other than that which the believer now receives through Christ: eternal life. There is, in fact, but one ideal for man. But this reasoning is also incorrect.

It is incorrect because between "grace" and "glory" it constructs a bridge of meritoriousness and proceeds by applying it also to Adam. The meritorious value of good works can only be treated later. At this point, however, it must be pointed out that, even if the Roman Catholic view of man's final destiny were correct, Rome still has no right to conceive of grace in an "adequated" supernatural sense. It is also possible, after all, to posit a connection forged by God between certain promises of reward and certain works such that the rewards are not in a strict sense merited *ex condigno* by those works. The promise of eternal life made to Adam in case of obedience was of such a nature as Reformed theologians taught in their doctrine of the covenant of works.[41] There was a merit *ex pacto* (arising from a covenant), not *ex condigno*. The good works of man never merit the glory of heaven; they are never of the same weight and worth *(condignity)*. Rome, however, by introducing the idea of the meritoriousness of good works both in the case of the believer and that of Adam, fails to do full justice to grace. Grace, in Roman Catholic thought, entirely changes its character. It stands in physical, not in ethical, contrast to nature. It does not presuppose sin and guilt, only a lower nature. On the one hand, it transforms everything into grace and so ensures that there is no longer any grace at all. Grace in the case of Adam and the believer, though it is indeed grace, is grace only in the sense in which also life, intellect, wisdom, power, and so forth, are grace. There is here no reason to call only the superadded gift by the name "grace." The fact that Adam was created and received an intellect and will was also and equally grace, even though there are quantitative differences among the various gifts of grace. In that way, really everything that God initially grants to man in creation or in re-creation becomes grace. But that is true only in that initial moment. For the moment man has received those initial gifts, says Rome, he himself is moved by that grace to go to work, and everything he receives from here on he receives as a reward for his merits. Even eternal life is no longer a truly gracious gift of God but a fitting, worthy, proportionate reward for work done. It could still be called a gift of grace only because the power that enabled humans to perform meritorious works was a gift of grace. It is just as the Pelagians put it in ancient times: the enablement *(posse)* is from God, the will *(velle)* from man.[42]

Fourth, we have indicated above that the Roman Catholic doctrine of the superadded gift has led, and had to lead, to a threefold understanding of human nature. To Rome there is not just one idea and one moral law and one destiny for humanity. Just as in other creaturely realms, so in the human world, hierarchy and rankings persist as well. In the abstract there conceivably is one human with natural justice, another with preternatural justice, and a third with supernatural justice. The first of these three humans is only slightly above an

---

41. See ch. 13, below.

42. The value of Bensdorp's statement needs to be judged in this light: "Catholic doctrine splendidly maintains the absolute gratuity of grace. It is not only *factually* but by its very nature entirely gratuitous" (*De Katholiek* 114 [1898]: 81).

animal, subject to inordinate lust, to the natural contrast between flesh and spirit, as well as to physical suffering and temporal death. But in his will there still remains the power to do good, not to let inordinate lust issue into sinful deeds, and thus indeed to live a natural but still sinless life. The human being after the fall virtually still corresponds to that image. Although original sin is still frequently construed not only in a negative but also in a positive sense, it is nevertheless consistently conceived as weakened to the degree that the physical contrast between nature and grace replaces the ethical antithesis between sin and grace. According to many Catholic thinkers, it consists only negatively in a loss of the superadded gift that God in his good pleasure bestowed on the first human.[43] The human being lacking that gift therefore remains a complete and perfect human person in his kind; and however hard it might be for him, especially over time, to remain so, nevertheless, if he so desires, he can remain a sinless one. This explains Rome's mellow judgment concerning unbaptized dying children and the pagans who have made good use of the light and powers of nature. They have no guilt and will therefore not be punished; they receive a penalty of loss *(poena damni)*, not of the senses *(poena sensus)*.

God, however, did not create the first human as such a natural man. He immediately gave him a preternatural righteousness as well. Hence, Adam was not subject to inordinate lust, suffering, and death, even physical death, apart from the actual superadded gift (i.e., *gratia gratum faciens*). This is a second idea of man that is conceivable and possible. Such a person could have kept God's commandments without resistance from the flesh (the gift of integrity), but his righteousness would nevertheless have remained natural and not have merited the vision of God *per essentiam*. This second conception of man is then once more taken a step further by the addition of the superadded gift that results in a human being complete with supernatural righteousness. As is the case throughout the Roman Catholic system, so also here in the doctrine of the image of God we encounter the contrast between the natural and the supernatural, between the human and the divine, between the terrestrial and the celestial, and within each of these categories a host of gradations. In the ethical and religious life there is a wide range of ranks and classes and standings. Not all people are on—or aspire to—the same level. If God is at the center, his creatures gather round him in ever widening circles. Most distant from him is the natural man, then comes the preternatural man, and finally the supernatural man. And in the last class there again are all kinds of distinctions and degrees. There are clergy and laypersons, monks and ordinary people, precepts and counsels, a lower and a higher morality. On the highest level stands the mystic, who by meditation, ascesis, and prayer already here on earth achieves contemplation. And above the humans stand the angels, in turn organized in all sorts of rankings. Everything tends to rise upward toward God in ever increasing proximity to him. The soul's fusion with God is the highest bliss. So

43. Cf., e.g., J. Oswald, *Religiöse Urgeschichte*, 59, 137ff.

in Catholicism there is a place for everyone. It takes account of each person's capacity and fitness. It has varying ideals for different people. It does not make the same moral and religious demands on everybody. Pierson correctly highlighted this fact; only he regarded as the principle and essence what is no more than a consequence and appearance.[44] It was against this Neoplatonic Areopagite philosophy that the Reformation, taking its stand in Scripture, took action. Scripture knows of no such contrast between the natural and the supernatural. It knows only one idea of humanness, one moral law, one final destiny, and one priesthood, which is the portion of all believers.

Fifth, it is clear from this that the reason why Rome teaches a preternatural and supernatural justice is not that otherwise the amissibility of original justice cannot be explained. It is true that Roman Catholic theologians keep advancing this objection against the teaching of the Reformation: original righteousness belongs to man's essence or it does not; if the former is true, it is amissible, or if it is nevertheless lost, then man by that token loses a part of his essence and ceases to be a complete human being. But however often this objection is repeated, Rome did not come to the doctrine of the superadded gift in order to escape this objection. The very same difficulty still adheres to the Roman Catholic view, since Adam also had natural, original righteousness. This natural righteousness, though it is natural and flows from the basic principles and powers of the natural man without supernatural assistance (albeit not without the universal help of divine preservation), can nevertheless still be lost and is in fact lost by many persons. Yet, even the most degenerate sinner, one devoid of all natural justice, is still a human being. The possibility of losing and the actual loss of original righteousness, therefore, can absolutely not serve as an argument against its natural character. If that were the case, the natural justice that Rome also teaches would have to be called supernatural. The question between Rome and us is a very different one.

Original righteousness can be lost because it is an incidental property (accident) of human nature, not part of its substance. But among the "accidents," which as such can be lost, Rome again makes a distinction between that which is naturally an "accident" and that which is supernaturally an "accident."[45] In our view, however, all natural righteousness is a natural "accident"; according to Rome, the *gratia gratum faciens* is a supernatural "accident." Why is that? Not to make possible or clear the possibility of its being lost, but because without it man would be a defective creature. Rome expressly teaches that, given the fact that God wanted to make a being consisting of soul and body, spirit and matter, he could no more fashion these two, soul and body, in complete harmony than he could make a square circle. Flesh and spirit by their very nature fight each other, and without supernatural grace God cannot prevent conflict

44. A. Pierson, *Geschiedenis van het Roomsch-katholicisme tot op het Concilie van Trente*, 4 vols. (Haarlem: A. C. Kruseman, 1868–72), I, 24ff.

45. Bensdorp, *De Katholiek* 110 (1894): 56.

between these two elements. Bellarmine clearly states that man is composed of flesh and spirit and therefore in part tends to a corporal good and in part to a spiritual good; and that "from these diverse or contrary propensities there exists a certain conflict in one and the same human being." He further taught that "from the beginning of creation divine providence, in order to apply a remedy *to this sickness or weakness of human nature that arises from its material condition,* added to man a certain noteworthy gift, namely, original righteousness, so as to hold, as though by a kind of golden bridle, the inferior part to the superior, and [to hold] the superior part, which is easily subjected, to God."[46] Here it is clearly stated that the flesh by its very nature is opposed to the spirit. Matter is a power that stands over against God, one that is not per se sinful, as in Manichaeism, but nevertheless of a very low order; it moves totally in a direction of its own and automatically tempts man to engage in struggle and sin. That power is even of such a magnitude that reason alone cannot, at least not without great difficulty, control the motion of the soul. Needed to that end is a special supernatural grace. As in the philosophy of Plotinus, matter here is a creation that is very far removed from God, by nature hostile to all that is spiritual, and therefore has to be forcibly restrained.

Finally, in the sixth place, Rome's doctrine of the superadded gift implies a peculiar view of Christianity. In Rome's view, the Christian religion indeed also serves to save [us] from sin; but primarily and most importantly its purpose is to restore to man the grace that had been granted to Adam as a superadded gift but was lost to him. This grace was as necessary to man before the fall as it is necessary to us now, and was as supernatural then as it is now after the fall. Hence, according to Rome, grace is a supernatural gift as such and not incidentally *(per accidens),* not only because of sin.[47] Sin has not in any way changed the nature of grace. Perhaps grace has been increased by sin; but both before and after the fall it was identically the same, namely, an *elevation* [of man] *above nature.* That is its character and essence. Christianity, accordingly, may also still be a religion of redemption; but preeminently it is not a *reparation* but an *elevation* of nature; it serves to elevate nature above itself, that is, to divinize humanity. In the case of Adam the *gratia gratum faciens* served that goal; now Christianity serves that goal. Hence, then and now his grace is the same; that is, the essential element in Christianity was not necessitated by the fall; it was already necessary before the fall. As the elevation of nature, Christianity was already present to Adam prior to the fall. The reception of infused grace is now bound—aside from the preparations—specifically to belief in two dogmas: the Trinity and the incarnation.[48] Now then, the same was true in the case of Adam. Even before the fall he was familiar with both.[49] The incarnation, by

---

46. R. Bellarmine, *De gratia primi hominis,* 5, cf. 7; Bensdorp, *De Katholiek* 114 (1898): 256.

47. R. Bellarmine, *De gratia primi hominis,* 5.

48. Cf. H. Bavinck, *Reformed Dogmatics,* I, 610 (#158).

49. M. Becanus, *Theol. schol.,* I, tr. 5, c. 2; H. Th. Simar, *Lehrbuch der Dogmatik,* 3d ed., 332; C. Pesch, *Prael. dogm.,* II, 89, etc.; T. Aquinas, *Summa theol.,* II, 2, qu. 2, art. 7; II, 2, qu. 5, art. 1.

this logic, was therefore necessary before the fall and apart from sin. In other words, in order that man might become like God, God had to become man. This law was in effect both before and after the fall. Now, solely as a subordinate component, the incarnation brings atonement with it. But for Rome the point of gravity does not lie in satisfaction for, and the forgiveness of, sin but in the humanization of God and the divinization of man.[50]

THE REFORMATION VIEW OF THE IMAGE

[289] The Reformers unanimously rejected this teaching, especially because it led to a weakening of [the doctrine of] original sin. Their opposition was primarily directed against the Scholastic thesis: "While the supernatural qualities are lost, the natural ones still remain whole." And from there they reasoned back to the image of God. If by sin, by the loss of the image of God, man had become totally corrupt, it must also have belonged to his nature. Thus, Luther maintained "that righteousness was not a gift which came from without, separate from man's nature, but . . . was truly part of his nature, so that it was Adam's nature to love God, to believe God, to know God, etc."[51] But even the Reformers had to maintain a distinction between what was left and what was lost of the image of God. To that end they used the words "substance," "essence," "attributes," "gifts," even "supernatural gifts." The Apology of the Augsburg Confession calls the knowledge and fear of God in Adam "gifts," and the Formula of Concord speaks of the "properties concreated in the paradise of nature."[52] The Lutheran dogmaticians indeed called the image of God natural insofar as human nature could not be pure without that image and was immediately concreated with that image. But they denied that the image of God was natural in the sense that it automatically flowed from human nature as such and was therefore an inamissible and essential component of it. Some, such as Gerhard, Quenstedt, and others, also specifically called the supernatural favor of God, the gracious inhabitation of the holy Trinity and the resulting pleasure and enjoyment, supernatural gifts.[53] So also Calvin makes a distinction between the substance of the soul and its attributes, and with Augustine says: "The natural attributes were corrupted in man by sin, but the supernatural ones were removed." He even calls the latter "extraneous, not an intrinsic part of nature."[54] And many Reformed theologians similarly drew a distinction between natural qualities and supernatural gifts.[55] Many of them derived immortality from the grace of God, not from

---

50. Cf. H. Bavinck, *Reformed Dogmatics,* I, 355–59 (#98).

51. M. Luther, *Luther's Works,* vol. 1: *Lectures on Genesis 1–3,* 165.

52. J. T. Müller, *Die symbolischen Bücher der evangelisch-lutherischen Kirche,* 5th ed. (Gütersloh: C. Bertelsmann, 1898), 80–81, 580.

53. J. Gerhard, *Loci theol.,* VIII, c. 1–3; J. Quenstedt, *Theologia,* II, 1–48; D. Hollaz, *Examen theol.,* 461–88.

54. J. Calvin, *Institutes,* I.xv.2; II.ii.12.

55. J. Maccovius, *Loci comm.,* 105ff.

Adam's nature.[56] Even the ancient distinction between "image" and "likeness" was taken over by many and also applied in that sense.[57] It soon became clear, however, that even where Protestants retained the expression "supernatural gifts," they meant something else by it. The idea among Roman Catholics is that one can very well conceive a human being without these supernatural gifts. Indeed, as a rational and moral being, man would also have some knowledge of God, the moral law, and righteousness. But [according to Rome] there is an essential difference among knowledge, love, and righteousness in a natural sense and these qualities in a supernatural sense, between the natural and the supernatural man, between a human being and a Christian, between the world and the church, between nature and grace. Grace is not merely restorative, but an elevation and completion of nature. It was this position that the Reformation opposed as a matter of fundamental principle. And so it had to come around, and in fact did come around, to the doctrine that the image of God essentially belonged to man by nature, and that without it man could only exist in an "impure nature," as a sinner.

But the scholars of the Reformation, too, held differing views of the image of God. In the early period some Lutherans still equated the image of God with the essence of man and the substance of the soul,[58] but Lutheran theology as such was grounded in another idea. Its subjective soteriological character necessarily led to an exclusive identification of the image of God with the moral qualities that the first man received and whose loss made man, religiously and ethically, a "block of wood." Luther already frequently put all the emphasis on the gifts, and completely equated the image of God with them.[59] The confessional writings followed the same lines,[60] and so did the theologians Heerbrand, Hunnius, Gerhard, Quenstedt, Hollaz, and others.[61] The Lutherans did not indeed deny that the essence of man also expresses something divine, but [held that] the actual image of God consists only in "original righteousness," with the associated qualities of "immortality, impassibility, dominion," and a "most blissful condition." Only the Son, after all, is essentially and substantially the image of God (Heb. 1:3); in man the image is an "accidental perfection," capable of being lost and in fact lost (Rom. 3:23) and only renewed and restored in the believer (Rom. 8:29; 2 Cor. 3:18; 5:17; Eph. 4:24; Col. 3:10).

56. J. Zanchi(us), *Op. theol.*, III, 497; A. Polanus, *Syn. theol.*, V, 29; F. Junius, *Op. theol. select.*, I, 211; G. Bucanus, *Theol.*, XI, 12; J. Maccovius, *Loci*, 409.

57. J. Zanchi(us), *Op. theol.*, III, 486; Justin Martyr on Gen. 1:26; J. Alsted, *Theol.*, 281.

58. M. Luther, in J. Köstlin, *The Theology of Luther in Its Historical Development and Inner Harmony*, trans. Charles E. Hay, 2 vols. (Philadelphia: Lutheran Publication Society, 1897), I, 144–55; Melancthon, Hemming, and Selnecker, in H. Heppe, *Dogmatik des deutschen Protestantismus im sechzehnten Jahrhundert*, 3 vols. (Gotha: F. A. Perthes, 1857), I, 338ff.

59. M. Luther, in J. Köstlin, *Theology of Luther*, II, 339–61; Heppe, *Dogmatik des deutschen Protestantismus*, I, 345.

60. J. T. Müller, *Die symbolischen Bücher der evangelisch-lutherischen Kirche*, 80, 576.

61. E.g., J. Gerhard, *Loci theol.*, VIII, c. 1; J. Quenstedt, *Theologia*, II, 3–10, 17–23; D. Hollaz, *Examen theol.*, 464ff.

From the beginning, however, Reformed theologians, incorporated also the essence of man in the image of God. Heppe is wrong when he asserts that Calvin and Zanchius did not teach this.[62] While Calvin does make a distinction between the soul's substance and its gifts, he expressly states that the image of God consisted in "those marks of excellence with which God had distinguished Adam over all other living creatures," and that consequently it also consists in integrity.[63] All the Reformed theologians agreed with this;[64] only Coccejus,[65] presenting an alternative view, taught that while the soul and its properties were presupposed by the image of God, they were not its content but only the canvas, so to speak, on which God painted his image. The image itself, according to Coccejus, consisted only in the gifts, as taught by 2 Corinthians 3:18, Ephesians 4:24, and Colossians 3:10. Others put it this way: the image of God consists antecedently in man's spiritual nature, formally in sanctity, and consequently in dominion.[66] As a rule, however, Reformed theologians continued to speak of the image of God in a broader and a narrower sense. In Holy Scripture they read that man, on the one hand, is still called the image of God after the fall and should be respected as such (Gen. 5:1; 9:6; Acts 17:28; 1 Cor. 11:7; James 3:9); and that, on the other hand, he had nevertheless lost the primary content of the image of God (i.e., knowledge, righteousness, and holiness) and only regains these qualities in Christ (Eph. 4:24; Col. 3:10). By observing this distinction in Scripture and incorporating it in their theology, Reformed theologians have maintained the bond between the physical and the ethical nature of man, and thereby also at this point (the relation between nature and grace) kept themselves from falling into various errors. Soon an additional distinction arose that was especially worked out in the doctrine of the covenant of works. This distinction answered the question what Adam had to become, not what Adam was. It is only in these three areas, the image of God in the broad sense, the image of God in the narrow sense, and the development or destination of the image of God—that is, in the doctrine of the covenant of works—that the locus of the image of God can be treated to the full extent.

62. H. Heppe, *Reformed Dogmatics,* rev. and ed. E. Bizer, trans. G. T. Thomson (London: Allen & Unwin, 1950; reprinted, Grand Rapids: Baker, 1978), 232–33.

63. J. Calvin, *Institutes,* I.xv.2; II.xii.6; *Commentary,* on Gen. 1:26 and 9:6; *Commentary,* on James 3:9.

64. J. Zanchi(us), *Op. theol.,* III, 486, 477ff.; Z. Ursinus, *Commentary on the Heidelberg Catechism,* trans. G. W. Willard (Grand Rapids: Eerdmans, 1954), qu. 7; Justin Martyr, *Loci,* c. 46ff.; A. Polanus, *Syn. theol.,* V, 34; *Synopsis purioris theologiae,* XIII, 36; M. Leydekker, *Fax veritatis,* 395; etc.

65. J. Coccejus, *Summa theologiae ex Scripturis repetita,* XVII, §§12–24; cf. also J. H. Heidegger, *Corpus theologiae,* VI, 119; J. Braun, *Doctrina foederum,* I, 2, 15, 5ff.

66. F. Turretin, *Institutes of Elenctic Theology,* V, qu. 10, §6; L. Ryssen, *Summa theol.,* 178; H. Witsius, *The Oeconomy of the Covenants between God and Man,* 4 vols. in 3 (London: Edward Dilly, 1763), I.2, §11; W. Brakel, *The Christian's Reasonable Service,* trans. Bartel Elshout, 4 vols. (Ligonier, Pa.: Soli Deo Gloria, 1992), I, 323–26.

Rome and the Reformation

[290] Between the Roman Catholic doctrine of the image of God and that of the Reformation there is a profound difference that makes itself felt over the whole field of theology. This difference is not located in the expression "original justice or righteousness." For though Roman Catholic theologians use this term in a variety of senses, later ones sometimes also describe the supernatural righteousness by means of it. The righteousness of the first human being can be called "original" since from his origin he was characterized by his positive correspondence to the law of God, and since original righteousness can be distinguished as such from habitual or actual righteousness. Also, in the case of Adam, the original righteousness was the beginning and root of his actual righteousness. After Thomas there was not even disagreement over the question of whether this original righteousness would, for all humanity, have been the source of its actual righteousness if Adam had remained standing, since Adam received it not as a private but as a public person. The dispute concerned the question of whether that original righteousness was *natural* or, at least in part, *supernatural.* Reformed theologians asserted the former. By that they did not mean to say that this original righteousness arose automatically from human nature understood in the sense of a union of spirit and matter, nor that it could not be called a gift—even of God's grace in a broad sense. Rather, they used this term to maintain the conviction that the image of God, that is, original righteousness, was inseparable from the idea of man as such and that it referred to the normal state, the harmony, the health of a human being; that without it a human cannot be true, complete, or normal. When man loses that image of God, he does not simply lose a substance while still remaining fully human. Rather, he becomes an abnormal, a sick, a spiritually dead human being, a sinner. He then lacks something that belonged to his nature, just as a blind man loses his sight, a deaf man his hearing, and a sick man his health. In Rome's view a human being can lose the "supernatural righteousness" and still be a good, true, complete, sinless human, with a natural justice that in its kind is without any defect. But according to Protestant theologians, a human being cannot. There is no intermediate state between man as image of God and man as sinner. He is either a son of God, his offspring, his image, or he is a child of wrath, dead in sins and trespasses. When that human being again by faith receives that perfect righteousness in Christ, that benefit is indeed a supernatural gift, but it is supernatural "as an accident," "incidentally"; he regains that which belongs to his being, like the blind man who again receives his sight.

Now this doctrine is grounded in Holy Scripture, which nowhere speaks of "supernatural gifts" in connection with the creation of man. Rome, accordingly, does not appeal to Genesis 1:26–31, Ecclesiastes 7:29, and so forth, but to the New Testament representation of the state of grace and the state of glory, an appeal that can in no way serve as proof. Scripture everywhere proceeds from the assumption that humanity is akin to God and his offspring. The service of God, the love for God, and fellowship with God are not superadded gifts but originally and integrally human. God claims all of man—mind, heart, soul, body, and all his or her energies—for his service and his love. The moral law is one for all humans in all times, and the moral ideal is the same for all people. There is no "lower" or "higher" righteousness, no double morality, no twofold set of duties. Original righteousness is so natural that, even according to most Catholic theologians, it would have been inherited by Adam's descendants in the event of his obedience, and that even now the pagans still do what the law requires (Rom. 2:15). Accordingly, the objection that the Reformed position is caught in an antinomy since on the one hand it calls original righteousness "natural," and on the other "amissible" and "accidental"[67]—this objection is based solely on misunderstanding.[68] Original righteousness is called natural, not because it consists in a certain substance or essence, but because it is a natural attribute or quality. Just as good health belongs to the nature of man, but is still "amissible," that is, can still be lost, so it is with the image of God. Rome and the Reformation both agree that original righteousness is neither a material nor a spiritual substance, as the Manichaeans taught, but an "accident," a quality. And the sole difference concerns the question whether it is naturally "accidental" or, at least in part, supernaturally "accidental."[69] Rome only says

67. Bensdorp, De Katholiek 110 (1894): 43; cf. also D. F. Strauss, Der alte und der neue Glaube (Leipzig: Hirzel, 1872), I, 708; R. Lipsius, Dogm., §434.

68. Cf. F. A. Philippi, Kirchliche Glaubenslehre (Gütersloh: C. Bertelsmann, 1902), III, 408.

69. Bensdorp, De Katholiek 110 (1894): 56–60. Bensdorp later provides a yet more elaborate defense of the Roman Catholic teaching concerning original righteousness in De Katholiek 112 (September 1896); 114 (July–August); 114 (October–November 1898); 115 (1899): 23–46; 116 (1900): 22–42. However, Bensdorp cannot escape the objections brought against this view except by making all sorts of distinctions that serve no other purpose than to rescue the notion out of the difficulty. He not only distinguishes substance and essence on the one hand from attributes (accidens) and on the other from qualities (qualitas); but also when it is pointed out to him that attributes (accidentia) that are essential to human nature such as health, unity of body and soul, mind, original righteousness (justitia originalis) are still amissible, he makes further distinctions between essential qualities (qualitates essentialis) that are in the essence (essentia) (such as rationality), and essential attributes (accidentia essentialia) that are outside the essence (essentia) but still necessarily flow forth from them. He also distinguishes qualities (accidens) over against essence (substantia) from qualities (accidens) over against properties (proprium); between attributes of kind (accidens speciei) and individual attributes (accidens individui); between natural righteousness (justitia naturalis) as potentia, which as an attribute of kind (accidens speciei) is not amissible, and a natural righteousness (justitia naturalis) as act (actus), which as an individual attribute (accidens individui) flows forth from a contingent free will and is therefore amissible. He thus comes to the conclusion finally that the original supernatural righteousness (justitia supernaturalis [originalis]) was indeed an attribute of kind (accidens speciei) but "not a natural attribute of kind (accidens speciei naturale) (in other words, not an essential attribute [accidens essentiale], not an attribute of kind [accidens speciei], therefore, in a strict sense)" (De Katholiek 114 [October–November 1898]: 251, cf. 261). He then proceeds to argue that the original righteousness (justitia originalis) was an attribute of kind (accidens speciei), and that the human nature notwithstanding, the fact that it was lost remains undamaged. This demonstrates thus "that the original righteousness (justitia originalis) was not an attribute of kind (accidens speciei) in the ordinary sense of the term." In other words, at the end of all this argumentation, the thesis from which Bensdorp proceeded was simply reiterated, and the one and only proof

of natural justice that it is naturally accidental, while the Reformation makes this claim for the whole of original righteousness.

But for that reason, as stated above, Rome's entire case against the teaching that the image of God is natural collapses, for Rome itself acknowledges that natural justice is natural and still amissible, and thus it is no longer in a position to lodge this objection against the teaching of the Protestants. Its doctrine, accordingly, did not arise from the objection that the naturalness of original righteousness cannot be squared with its amissibility, but it owes its origin to an entirely different rationale, namely, the Neoplatonic view of the ideal for the Christian life. It is *that* Neoplatonism that the Reformation, basing itself on Scripture, rejected. In that connection it took care not to fall into the trap of any form of Manichaeism. Man lost none of his substance as a result of sin. In that sense humans are fully human even after the fall. But when man lost his original righteousness, he lost the harmony and health of his nature and became a sinner through and through. His nature in the sense of substance or essence remained, but the moral qualities naturally belonging to his nature were lost.[70]

Lutheran or Reformed

Now this splendid view of the image of God and of original righteousness has come more clearly into its own in the Reformed church and Reformed theology than in the Lutheran. In Lutheran theology the image of God is restricted to original righteousness and was therefore totally lost when the latter was lost. In this theology the lines of demarcation between the spiritual and the worldly, between the heavenly and the earthly, are so sharply drawn that

---

given was borrowed from Rome's teaching concerning the *donum superadditum*. It is this that is a priori infallible and the reason why the distinction *must* be made. The objections brought against it therefore remain as strong as before: Just as health, unity of body and soul, reason, and natural righteousness (not substantial being in Manichaean sense, but still) belong to the essence of humanity and are nonetheless still losable, so too the original righteousness is naturally and essentially proper to humans. When this is lost, one does not cease to be human but becomes an abnormal, fallen person.

70. Cf. J. H. Scholten, *De Leer der Hervormde Kerk,* I, 304–26; T. Cannegieter, "De Godsdienst in den Mensch en de Mensch in den Godsdienst," *Teylers Theologische Tijdschrift* (1904): 178–211, esp. 199f.; A. Bruining, "De Roomsche Leer van het donum superadditum," *Teylers Theologische Tijdschrift* (1907): 564–97. The last-mentioned correctly contends that the natural man *(homo naturalis)* as understood by Rome is indeed a religious being and that, therefore, religion (as natural religion) is not extrinsic to human nature or added to it as a *donum superadditum*. But he weakens the significance of the distinction that Rome makes between natural religion *(religio naturalis)* and supernatural religion *(religio supernaturalis)* when he says that the image of a rein "is merely an image and nothing more," that the *donum superadditum* in the Roman Catholic view in fact merges with the pure nature *(natura pura)*. From this Bruining also comes to the notion that the Roman Catholic viewpoint is more reasonable than the old Protestant view, and that the Roman Catholic Church has advantage of strength over her opposition. One could only come to this conclusion if one substantially misunderstood Roman teaching concerning the image of God in man and its significance for the Roman system, and saw nothing in it but a peculiar, supernaturalistic form of the religious notion that it is not *my* work but a work of *God* in me that brings me to my highest goal. The Roman Catholic teaching was far better portrayed by De Bussy, "Katholicisme en Protestantisme," *Theol. Tijdschrift* (1888): 253–313.

the result is two hemispheres, and the connection between nature and grace, between creation and re-creation is totally denied.[71] The supernaturalist view is still at work here; the image of God stands alongside nature, is detached from it, and is above it. The loss of the image, which renders man totally deaf and blind in spiritual matters, still enables him in earthly matters to do much good and in a sense renders him independent from the grace of God in Christ. Reformed theology, on the other hand, by its distinction between the image of God in a broader and a narrower sense, has most soundly maintained the connection between substance and quality, nature and grace, creation and re-creation. It must be granted that this distinction has often been conceived too mechanically and needs to be further developed organically. Nevertheless, Reformed theology has most vividly brought out the fact that the image of God in the narrower sense is most intimately bound up with that image in the broader sense, and that the two components together make up the full image of God. The whole being, therefore, and not *something in man* but *man himself,* is the image of God. Further, sin, which precipitated the loss of the image of God in the narrower sense and spoiled and ruined the image of God in the broader sense, has profoundly affected the whole person, so that, consequently, also the grace of God in Christ restores the whole person, and is of the greatest significance for his or her whole life and labor, also in the family, society, the state, art, science, and so forth.

THE WHOLE PERSON AS THE IMAGE OF GOD

[291] In our treatment of the doctrine of the image of God, then, we must highlight, in accordance with Scripture and the Reformed confession, the idea that a human being does not *bear* or *have* the image of God but that he or she *is* the image of God. As a human being a man is the son, the likeness, or offspring of God (Gen. 1:26; 9:6; Luke 3:38; Acts 17:28; 1 Cor. 11:7; James 3:9).

Two things are implied in this doctrine. The first is that not something in God—one virtue or perfection or another to the exclusion of still others, nor one person—say, the Son to the exclusion of the Father and the Spirit—but that God himself, the entire deity, is the archetype of man. Granted, it has frequently been taught that man has specifically been made in the image of the Son or of the incarnate Christ,[72] but there is nothing in Scripture that supports this notion. Scripture repeatedly tells us that humankind was made in the image of God, not that we have been modeled on Christ, but that he was made [human] in our likeness (Rom. 8:3; Phil. 2:7–8; Heb. 2:14), and that we, having been

---

71. Cf. H. Bavinck, *Reformed Dogmatics,* I, 305–6 (#85).

72. Clement of Alexandria, *Stromateis,* V, 14; Tertullian, *On the Resurrection of the Flesh,* c. 6; A. Osiander, according to J. Calvin, *Institutes,* I.xv.2; II.xii.6; J. C. K. von Hofmann, *Der Schriftbeweis,* 3 vols. (Nördlingen: Beck, 1857–60), I, 290; G. Thomasius, *Christi Person und Werk,* 3d ed. (Erlangen: Theodor Bläsing, 1853–61), I, 126; J. T. Beck, *Christliche Glaubenslehre,* II, 329; L. F. Schoeberlein, "Ebenbild Gottes," *PRE*[2], IV, 4–8; H. Martensen, *Christian Dogmatics,* trans. William Urwick (Edinburgh: T. & T. Clark, 1871), §§72, 136–37; F. Delitzsch, *A System of Biblical Psychology,* trans. Robert E. Wallis, 2d ed. (Edinburgh: T. & T. Clark, 1875), 86–87; etc.

conformed to the image of Christ, are now again becoming like God (Rom. 8:29; 1 Cor. 15:49; 2 Cor. 3:18; Phil. 3:21; Eph. 4:24; Col. 3:10; 1 John 3:2). It is therefore much better for us to say that the triune being, God, is the archetype of man,[73] while at the same time exercising the greatest caution in the psychological exploration of the trinitarian components of man's being.[74]

On the other hand, it follows from the doctrine of human creation in the image of God that this image extends to the whole person. Nothing in a human being is excluded from the image of God. While all creatures display *vestiges* of God, only a human being is the *image* of God. And he is such totally, in soul and body, in all his faculties and powers, in all conditions and relations. Man is the image of God because and insofar as he is truly human, and he is truly and essentially human because, and to the extent that, he is the image of God. Naturally, just as the cosmos is an organism and reveals God's attributes more clearly in some than in other creatures, so also in man as an organism the image of God comes out more clearly in one part than another, more in the soul than in the body, more in the ethical virtues than in the physical powers. None of this, however, detracts in the least from the truth that the whole person is the image of God. Scripture could not and should not speak of God in a human manner and transfer all human attributes to God, as if God had not first made man totally in his own image. And it is the task of Christian theology to point out this image of God in man's being in its entirety.

God is, first of all, demonstrable in the human soul. According to Genesis 2:7, man was formed from the dust of the earth by having the breath of life *(nišmat ḥayyîm)* breathed into his nostrils and so becoming a living soul *(nepeš ḥayyâ, psychē zōsa)*. The breath of life is the principle of life; the living soul is the essence of man. By means of this combination Scripture accords to man a unique and independent place of his own and avoids both pantheism and materialism. The names *rûaḥ* and *nepeš (pneuma* and *psychē)*, which in Scripture denote the invisible component of man, make this very clear. Trichotomism, which is fundamentally rooted in Plato's dualism and repeatedly found acceptance in gnostic and theosophical schools of thought, sees here two distinct substances.[75] But

---

73. Augustine, *The Trinity*, XII, 6; P. Lombard, *Sent.*, II, dist. 16; T. Aquinas, *Summa theol.*, I, qu. 13, art. 5.

74. J. Calvin, *Institutes*, I.xv.4; idem, *Commentary*, on Gen. 1:26; J. Polyander, *Synopsis purioris theologiae*, XIII, 7; J. Quenstedt, *Theologia*, II, 4; D. Hollaz, *Examen theol.*, 466.

75. Trichotomism, in its first phase, passed from Platonic philosophy to certain Christian authors, but later, especially because of Apollinaris, fell into disrepute. Not until modern times did it again find acceptance in the work of Olshausen, Beck, Delitzsch, Auberlen, and others. In England it was particularly defended—in connection with conditional immortality—by J. B. Heard (*The Tripartite Nature of Man*, 2d ed. [Edinburgh: T. & T. Clark, 1866]) but refuted inter alia by J. Laidlaw (*The Bible Doctrine of Man* [Edinburgh: T. & T. Clark, 1895], 66ff.) and in the article "Psychology," *Dictionary of the Bible*, ed. J. Hastings, rev. F. C. Grant and H. H. Rowley, rev. ed. (New York: Charles Scribner's Sons, 1963), IV, 166. Cf. also H. Bavinck, *Beginselen der Psychologie* (Kampen: Kok, 1923), §3; W. Geesink, *Van 's Heeren Ordinantiën*, 3 vols. (Amsterdam: W. Kirchener, 1907–8), 310ff.; J. Köberle, *Natur und Geist nach der Auffassung des Alten Testaments* (Munich: Beck, 1900).

this is wrong. Hebrews 4:12 and 1 Thessalonians 5:23 no more contain a list of all the essential constituents of man than, say, Luke 10:27, and therefore do not prove anything. Soul and spirit in Scripture repeatedly occur in parallelism and interchangeably. One moment "body and soul" constitute the nature of man, the next it is "body and spirit" (Matt. 10:28; 1 Cor. 7:34; James 2:26). Psychic activities are in turn attributed to the spirit and to the soul (Ps. 139:13ff.; Prov. 19:2 and 17:27; Ps. 77:6; 1 Cor. 2:11; Num. 21:4 and Job 21:4; 1 Sam. 1:10 and Isa. 54:6; Luke 1:46–47; etc.). Dying is called both the surrender of the soul (Gen. 35:18; 1 Kings 17:21; Matt. 20:28; Acts 15:26; 20:10) and the surrender of the spirit (Ps. 31:5; Matt. 27:50; Luke 8:55; 23:46; Acts 7:59). Sometimes the spirit and sometimes the soul is called immortal (Eccles. 12:7; Matt. 10:28); the dead are called "souls" (Rev. 6:9; 20:4) as well as "spirits" (Heb. 12:23; 1 Pet. 3:19). Still, though not essentially different, they are by no means identical. Man is "spirit" because he did not, like the animals, come forth from the earth, but had the breath of life breathed into him by God (Gen. 2:7); because he received his life-principle from God (Eccles. 12:7); because he has a spirit of his own, distinct from the Spirit of God (Gen. 41:8; 45:27; Exod. 35:21; Deut. 2:30; Judg. 15:19; Ezek. 3:14; Zech. 12:1; Matt. 26:41; Mark 2:8; Luke 1:47; 23:46; John 11:33; Acts 7:59; 17:16; Rom. 8:16; 1 Cor. 2:11; 5:3–5; 1 Thess. 5:23; Heb. 4:12; 12:23; etc.); and because as such he is akin to the angels, can also think spiritual or heavenly things, and if necessary also exist without a body. But man is "soul," because from the very beginning the spiritual component in him (unlike that of the angels) is adapted to and organized for a body and is bound, also for his intellectual and spiritual life, to the sensory and external faculties; because he can rise to the higher faculties only from a substratum of the lower ones; and hence, because he is a sentient and material being and as such is related to the animals. Man is a rational animal, a thinking reed, a being existing between angels and animals, related to but distinct from both. He unites and reconciles within himself both heaven and earth, things both invisible and visible. And precisely as such he is the image and likeness of God. God is most certainly "spirit," and in this respect also the angels are related to him. But sometimes there is reference also to his soul, and throughout Scripture all the peculiar psychic feelings and activities that are essentially human are also attributed to God. In Christ, God assumed the nature of humanity, not that of angels. And precisely on that account man, rather than the angels, is the image, son, and offspring of God. The spirituality, invisibility, unity, simplicity, and immortality of the human soul are all features of the image of God. This image itself emerges in the fact that he has a spirit (*pneuma*), which was from the beginning organized into a soul (*psychē*).

Belonging to the image of God, in the second place, are the human faculties. While the spirit is the principle and the soul the subject of life in man, the heart, according to Scripture, is the *organ* of man's life. It is, first, the center of physical life but then also, in a metaphorical sense, the seat and fountain of man's entire psychic life, of emotions and passions, of desire and will, even of thinking and knowing. From the heart flow "the springs of life" (Prov. 4:23). This life, which originates in the heart, then splits into two streams. On the one hand, we must distinguish the life that embraces all impressions, awarenesses, perceptions, observations, thoughts, knowledge, and wisdom. Especially in its higher forms, the central organ of this life is the *mind (nous)*. This life further embodies itself in words and language. On the other hand, the heart is the seat of all the emotions, passions, urges, inclinations, attachments, desires, and decisions of the will, which have to be led by the mind *(nous)* and express themselves in action.

In all these psychic capacities and activities of human beings we can see features of the image of God as well. The very diversity and abundance of these forces reflect God. To the degree that a given creature is on a lower level, it is also less intricately organized and hence less related to, and less susceptible of, the highest good, which is God. In this regard even angels are of a lower rank than humans. Precisely because man is so wonderfully and richly endowed and organized, he can be conformed to and enjoy God in the fullest manner—from all sides, as it were, in all God's virtues and perfections. In the heart, mind, and will *(memoria, intellectus, voluntas)* Augustine even saw an analogy of the triune being of God. Just as the Father gives life to the Son and the Spirit, and the Spirit proceeds from the Father through the Son, so in human beings it is the heart *(memoria)*, the deep, hidden life of the psyche, which gives birth and being to the intellect and the will, and specifically places the will second in order to the intellect. Rationalism and Pelagianism detach the intellect and the will from the heart and equate the total being of man with intellect and will. Mysticism, despising the conscious, active life of the will, retreats into the depths of the mind. The Greek Orthodox Church and Greek Orthodox theology place head and heart immediately side by side. But thanks to the leadership of Augustine, Western theology has avoided all these errors. It discovered that the doctrine of God and the doctrine of man are most intimately related. In the doctrine of the Trinity, therefore, it held onto the unity of the being, the distinctiveness of the three Persons, and the *filioque*; and in psychology, accordingly, it taught that the deep, hidden life of the soul comes to expression through the cognitive and the conative capacities, and that between these two the latter was led and guided by the former.[76]

[292] In the third place, the image of God manifests itself in the virtues of knowledge, righteousness, and holiness with which humanity was created from the start. For a well-ordered arrangement we had to deal first with the nature and faculties of the soul, but this analysis was only meant to furnish certain logical distinctions. Man was not created as a neutral being with morally indifferent powers and potentialities, but immediately made

---

76. In the interest of space, for further discussion on human psychology, the reader is referred to H. Bavinck, *Beginselen der Psychologie* and the literature cited there. See also W. Geesink, *Van 's Heeren Ordinantiën,* I, 310ff.

physically and ethically mature, with knowledge in the mind, righteousness in the will, holiness in the heart. Goodness, for a human being, consists in moral perfection, in complete harmony with the law of God, in holy and perfect being, like God himself (Lev. 19:2; Deut. 6:5; Matt. 5:48; 22:37; Eph. 5:1; 1 Pet. 1:15–16). That law is one and the same rule for all persons. Scripture knows of no two sorts of human beings, no double moral law, no two kinds of moral perfection and destiny. If man was created good, he must have been created with original justice. On the one hand, this is not to be conceived as childlike innocence, but it must not be exaggerated either, as though the original state of integrity *(status integratis)* were already equal to the state of glory *(status gloriae)*. Adam's knowledge, though pure, was limited and capable of growth; he walked by faith, not by sight; he not only possessed intuitive knowledge but also discursive knowledge; he knew the future only by special revelation.[77] The same was true of his righteousness and holiness; they were his from the beginning, for otherwise he could have never done any good work. Good fruits presuppose a good tree; one must first *be* before he can *do (operari sequitur esse)*. But that increated righteousness and holiness must nevertheless still be kept, developed, and converted into action.

This does not mean that Adam, equipped as he was with the necessary gifts, now had to go to work apart from God. Original righteousness *(justitia originalis)* was a free gift of God, and it was also from moment to moment maintained in man by the providence of God. It is not for a second conceivable without communion with God. Just as the Son was already the mediator of union before the fall, so also the Holy Spirit was even then already the craftsman of all knowledge, righteousness, and holiness in humanity. Some church fathers argued this point with the aid of Genesis 2:7, saying that man was first formed by the Logos, and that afterward he had the breath of life, that is, the Holy Spirit, breathed into him.[78] While this exegesis was incorrect, it is perfectly true that man in the state of integrity only possessed the virtues of knowledge and righteousness by and in the Holy Spirit. Granted, between the indwelling of the Holy Spirit in man before sin and in the state of sin, there is a big difference. Now that indwelling, after all, is "above nature" *(supra naturam)* because the Holy Spirit has to come to humans as it were from without and is diametrically opposed to sinful nature. In the case of Adam that entire contrast did not exist; his nature was holy and did not, as in the case of believers, have to be made holy; it was from the very beginning fit for the indwelling of the Holy Spirit. In the case of Adam, therefore, this indwelling was entirely natural. No truly good and perfect human being is even conceivable apart from the fellowship of the Holy Spirit. There is no such

77. T. Aquinas, *Summa theol.,* I, qu. 94, arts. 1–3.

78. Cf. J. Kleutgen, *Die Theologie und Philosophie der Vorzeit,* 2 vols. (Münster: Theissing, 1868), II, 541ff.; G. Thomasius, *Christi Person und Werk,* I³, 155.

entity as the natural man, in the Roman Catholic sense, between the sinful man after the fall and the perfect human being created after God's image. A human being, that is, a human being in a full and true sense, is and must be an image of God, a child of God, God's own offspring, living in communion with him by the Holy Spirit. Thus, also before the fall, a human being was the dwelling place of the entire holy Trinity, a most splendid temple of the Holy Spirit.

In the fourth place, also the human body belongs integrally to the image of God. A philosophy that either does not know or rejects divine revelation always lapses into empiricism or rationalism, materialism or spiritualism. But Scripture reconciles the two. Man has a "spirit" *(pneuma)*, but that "spirit" is psychically organized and must, by virtue of its nature, inhabit a body. It is of the essence of humanity to be corporeal and sentient. Hence, man's body is first (if not temporally, then logically) formed from the dust of the earth and then the breath of life is breathed into him. He is called "Adam" after the ground from which he was formed. He is dust and is called dust (Gen. 2:7; Ps. 103:14; Job 10:9; 33:6; Isa. 2:22; 29:16; 45:9; 64:8; "from the earth, a man of dust," 1 Cor. 15:47). The body is not a prison, but a marvelous piece of art from the hand of God Almighty, and just as constitutive for the essence of humanity as the soul (Job 10:8–12; Ps. 8; 139:13–17; Eccles. 12:2–7; Isa. 64:8). It is our earthly dwelling (2 Cor. 5:1), our organ or instrument of service, our apparatus (1 Cor. 12:18–26; 2 Cor. 4:7; 1 Thess. 4:4); and the "members" of the body are the weapons with which we fight in the cause of righteousness or unrighteousness (Rom. 6:13). It is so integrally and essentially a part of our humanity that, though violently torn from the soul by sin, it will be reunited with it in the resurrection of the dead. The nature of the union of the soul with the body, though incomprehensible, is much closer than the theories of "occasionalism" or "preestablished harmony" *(harmonia praestabilitia)* or "a system of influence" *(systema influxus)* imagine. It is not ethical but physical. It is so intimate that one nature, one person, one self is the subject of both and of all their activities. It is always the same soul that peers through the eyes, thinks through the brain, grasps with the hands, and walks with the feet. Although not always present in every part of the body in its full strength *(secundum totalitem virtutis)*, it is nevertheless present in all parts in its whole essence *(secundum totalitatem essentiae)*. It is one and the same life that flows throughout the body but operates and manifests itself in every organ in a manner peculiar to that organ. Now, this body, which is so intimately bound up with the soul, also belongs to the image of God. Granted, this fact must not be construed to mean that God himself also has a material body, as the Audians thought; nor that God in creating man also assumed a body, as Eugubinus taught; nor that God created man in the image of the still-to-be-incarnated Christ, as Osiander believed. God, after all, is "spirit" *(pneuma,* John 4:24) and has no body. The human body is a part of the image of God in its organization as instrument of the soul, in its formal perfection, not in its material substance as flesh *(sarx)*.[79]

Just as God, though he is spirit *(pneuma)*, is nevertheless the Creator of a material world that may be termed his revelation and manifestation, with this revelation coming to its climax in the incarnation, so also the spirit of man is designed for the body as its manifestation. The incarnation of God is proof that human beings and not angels are created in the image of God, and that the human body is an essential component of that image. From the beginning creation was so arranged and human nature was immediately so created that it was amenable to and fit for the highest degree of conformity to God and for the most intimate indwelling of God. God could not have been able to become man if he had not first made man in his own image. And precisely because the body, being the organ of the soul, belongs to the essence of man and to the image of God, it originally also participated in immortality. God is not a God of the dead, but of the living (Matt. 22:32). Death is a consequence of sin (Gen. 2:7; 3:19; Rom. 5:12; 6:23; 1 Cor. 15:21, 56). In the case of Adam, however, this immortality did not consist in a state of not being able to die *(non posse mori)*, or in eternal and imperishable life, but only in the condition of being able not to die *(posse non mori)*, the condition of not going to die in case of obedience. This state was not absolute but conditional; it depended on an ethical precondition. It is not correct, therefore, to say with Pelagians, Socinians, Remonstrants (etc.) that man was created mortal and that death is a given with the material organism, and therefore the normal and natural state of man. On the other hand, there is nevertheless an essential difference between Adam's not-going-to-die as long as he remained obedient and the not-being-able-to-die, which he was to receive as the reward for his obedience. Just as in Adam's case knowledge, righteousness, and holiness are still devoid of the gift of perseverance *(donum perseverantiae)*, so immortality was not yet totally integrated into inamissible eternal life. Adam's human nature was created so that, in case of his violation of God's commandment, it could and had to die. Adam was still a man of dust from the earth; only Christ is the Lord from heaven; the natural is first, then the spiritual (1 Cor. 15:45f.). Now through his body man was bound to earth but could also exercise dominion over the earth. Dominion over the earth, like immortality, is a part of the image of God. True, the Socinians went much too far when they located the entire being of man and the entire content of the image of God in dominion. Nonetheless, Genesis 1:26, 28; 2:19–20; 9:2–3; and Psalm 8:7–9 clearly teach that this dominion is most closely tied in with the creation in God's image and given with it. It is not an external appendix to the image; it is not based

---

79. Augustine, *Literal Meaning of Genesis*, VI, 12; Gregory of Nyssa, *On the Making of Man*, c. 8; T. Aquinas, *Summa theol.*, I, qu. 93, art. 6; idem, *Summa contra gentiles*, IV, 26; D. Petavius, "De opificio sex dierum," in *Theol. dogm.*, II, chs. 4, 7ff.; J. Gerhard, *Loci theol.*, VIII, 3; J. Calvin, *Institutes*, I.xv.3; A. Polanus, *Syn. theol.*, 328; J. Zanchi(us), *Op. theol.*, III, 677ff.; M. Becanus, *Inst. theol.*, VIII, 13; *Synopsis purioris theologiae*, XIII, 13; P. Mastricht, *Theologia*, III, 9, 30.

on a supplementary special dispensation; but being the image of God, man is thereby at the same time elevated above all other creatures and appointed lord and king over them all.

Finally, also belonging to this image is man's habitation in paradise (Gen. 2:8–15). Holiness and blessedness belong together; every human conscience witnesses to the fact that there is a connection between virtue and happiness; the ethical dimension and the physical dimension, the moral and the natural order in the world, being and appearance, spirit and matter—these may not be opposites. Congruent with a fallen humanity, therefore, is an earth that lies under a curse; a place of darkness therefore awaits the wicked in the hereafter; the righteous will one day walk in the light of God's countenance; the not-yet-fallen but still earthy man makes his home in a paradise.

[293] So the whole human being is image and likeness of God, in soul and body, in all human faculties, powers, and gifts. Nothing in humanity is excluded from God's image; it stretches as far as our humanity does and constitutes our humanness. The human is not the divine self but is nevertheless a finite creaturely impression of the divine. All that is in God—his spiritual essence, his virtues and perfections, his immanent self-distinctions, his self-communication and self-revelation in creation—finds its admittedly finite and limited analogy and likeness in humanity. There is a profound truth in the Kabbalah's idea that God, who is the Infinite in himself, manifests himself in the ten *sefiroth,* or attributes, and that these together make up the Adam Cadmon [human being].[80] Among creatures human nature is the supreme and most perfect revelation of God. And it is that [revelation] not just in terms of its pneumatic side, but equally in terms of its somatic side; it is that precisely as human, that is, as psychic, nature. In the teaching of Scripture God and the world, spirit and matter, are not opposites. There is nothing despicable or sinful in matter. The visible world is as much a beautiful and lush revelation of God as the spiritual. He displays his virtues as much in the former as in the latter. All creatures are embodiments of divine thoughts, and all of them display the footsteps or vestiges of God. But all these vestiges, distributed side by side in the spiritual as well as the material world, are recapitulated in man and so organically connected and highly enhanced that they clearly constitute the image and likeness of God. The whole world raises itself upward, culminates and completes itself, and achieves its unity, its goal, and its crown in humanity. In order to be the image of God, therefore, man had to be a recapitulation of the whole of nature. The Jews used to say that God had collected the dust for the human body from all the lands of the earth.[81] Though the image is strange, a true and beautiful thought is expressed in it. As spirit, man is akin to

80. A. Franck, *The Kabbalah* (New York: Arno, 1973), 148.

81. F. W. Weber, *System der altsynagogalen palästinischen Theologie* (Leipzig: Dörffling & Franke, 1880), 202ff.; cf. J. te Winkel, "Eene Friesche Mythe" ["A Frisian Myth"], in *Geschiedenis der Nederlandsche Letterkunde van Middeleeuwen en Rederijkerstijd,* in *De Ontwikkelingsgang der Nederlandsche Letterkunde,* 2d ed., 7 vols. (Haarlem: F. Bohn, 1922–27), I, 28.

the angels and soars to the invisible world; but he is at the same time a citizen of the visible world and connected with all physical creatures. There is not a single element in the human body that does not also occur in nature around him. Thus man forms a unity of the material and spiritual world, a mirror of the universe, a connecting link, compendium, the epitome of all of nature, a microcosm, and, precisely on that account, also the image and likeness of God, his son and heir, a micro-divine-being *(mikrotheos)*. He is the prophet who explains God and proclaims his excellencies; he is the priest who consecrates himself with all that is created to God as a holy offering; he is the king who guides and governs all things in justice and rectitude. And in all this he points to One who in a still higher and richer sense is the revelation and image of God, to him who is the only begotten of the Father, and the firstborn of all creatures. Adam, the son of God, was a type of Christ.

13

HUMAN DESTINY

The ultimate destiny of humanity, individually as well as corporately, was Adam's goal and not yet a given of his creation. Christ, not Adam, is the first full, true, spiritual man. Even in the state of integrity, Adam was only the beginning; Christ is the "end" of humanity, the one who gives us the possibility of imperishable eternal life. The parallel between Christ and Adam prompted theologians to conceive the original state of integrity in terms of a covenant, a covenant of works. This doctrine is based on Scripture and is eminently valuable. Covenant is of the essence of true religion, making possible a relation between the Creator and the creature and underscoring the dependence of rational, moral human beings on God. The Roman Catholic doctrine of the donum superadditum, *though it seeks to honor the conviction that eternal life is a gift of grace, in fact reintroduces meritorious good works. By contrast, Lutheran views exalt the original state of Adam as already a possession of highest possible blessing and thus tend to antinomianism—Adam was* exlex, *outside the law. But, before the fall, our first parents did not yet enjoy the eternal heavenly Sabbath; the state of integrity was not yet the state of glory. Full and complete humanity is found in community; humanity as a whole is the image of God—in creation and in redemption. This underscores the notion of federal headship: Adam's over creation, Christ's over redeemed humanity. This emphasis on the organic unity of the human race also sheds light on its origins and propagation. The theory of the preexistence of human souls is rooted in a pagan dualism between spirit and matter, destroys the unity of humanity, and erases the distinction between human beings and angels. The debate between creationism and traducianism is less fixed. Although both face insoluble difficulties, Reformed along with Orthodox and Roman Catholic theologians, almost unanimously embraced creationism, while traducianism found acceptance mainly among Lutherans. Creationism alone sufficiently maintains the specific uniqueness of humanity since it fends off both pantheism and materialism, and respects both the organic unity of the human race in its entirety and at the same time the independent value, worth, and mysterious individual personality of every single human being. The state of integrity is a preparation for eternal glory, when God will be all in all.*

563

[294] Although Adam was created in God's image, he was not that image immediately in the full sense, nor was he that image by himself alone. The image of God will only present itself to us in all of its many-splendored richness when man's destiny, both for this life and the life to come, is included in it. In 1 Corinthians 15:45–49 Paul contrasts the two covenant heads, Adam and Christ, with each other and compares them, not so much (as in Rom. 5:12–21 and 1 Cor. 15:22) in terms of what they did as in terms of their nature and person. The comparison here reaches its greatest depth and penetrates to the root of the distinction between them. The whole Adam, both before and after the fall, is contrasted to the whole Christ, after as well as before the resurrection. In virtue of creation the first man became a "living being" *(psychē zōsa),* "natural" *(psychikos),* "of the dust of the earth" *(ek gēs choikos);* but by his resurrection the second man became a "life-giving spirit" *(pneuma zōopoioun),* "spiritual" *(pneumatikos),* "from heaven" *(ex ouranou).*[1] Although Adam was created after God's image, since he was "from the earth, earthy," he was dependent on the earth. He, after all, needed food and drink, light and air, day and night, hence did not yet have a glorified spiritual body on a level transcending all those needs. His natural body had not yet fully become an instrument of the spirit. As such, Adam, by comparison to Christ, stood on a lower level. Adam was the first; Christ the second and the last. Christ presupposes Adam and succeeds him. Adam is the lesser and inferior entity; Christ the greater and higher being. Hence, Adam pointed to Christ; already before the fall he was the type of Christ. In Adam's creation Christ was already in view. The whole creation, including the creation of man, was infralapsarian. The natural came first, the spiritual second.

What Paul is here setting forth in great depth and breadth is grounded in Genesis 1–2 itself. Man, though spirit *(pneuma)* and bearing a breath of life within him, became a living being (soul) like the animals. He was given the fruit of herbs and trees for food (Gen. 1:29), a paradise as his dwelling place (Gen. 2:8ff.), a woman as helper (Gen. 2:18ff.), a command for guidance (Gen. 2:16–17), and a threat of punishment in case of transgression (Gen. 2:17). It is evident from this scenario that the first man, however highly placed, did not yet possess the highest humanity. There is a very great difference between the natural and the pneumatic, between the state of integrity and the state of glory. After the resurrection both the stomach and food will be destroyed (1 Cor. 6:13), but both were realities to Adam. In heaven God's children will no longer marry, but be like the angels (Matt. 22:30); Adam, however, needed the help of a wife.

COVENANT WITH ADAM: ONLY THE BEGINNING

Adam, accordingly, stood at the beginning of his "career" not at the end. His condition was provisional and temporary and could not remain as it was. It either had to pass on to higher glory or to sin and death. The penalty for

---

1. Cf. W. Lütgert, "Der Mensch aus dem Himmel," in *Greifswalder Studien,* ed. Samuel Oettli (Gütersloh: C. Bertelsmann, 1895), 207–28.

transgressing the command was death; the reward for keeping it, by contrast, was life, eternal life. Our common conscience already testifies that in keeping God's commands there is great reward, and that the violation of these commands brings punishment, and Holy Scripture also expresses this truth over and over. It sums up all the blessedness associated with the doing of God's commandments in the word "life," eternal life. Both in the covenant of works and that of grace, Scripture knows but one ideal for a human being, and that is eternal life (Lev. 18:5; Ezek. 20:11; Ps. 9:13; Matt. 19:17; Luke 10:28; Gal. 3:12). Hence, Adam still stood at the beginning. As yet he did not have this reward of eternal life but still had to acquire it; he could still err, sin, fall, and die. His relation to God was such that he could gradually increase in fellowship with God but could also still fall from it. In Scripture this unique relation is perhaps compared to a covenant in *one* verse. In Hosea 6:7 the Lord says of Israel and Judah that, despite all the labor spent on them, they, like Adam, transgressed the covenant (MT: *kĕʾādām ʿābĕrû bĕrît*; LXX: *hōs anthrōpos*; Vulg.: *sicut Adam*). The translation "like a man" is burdened by the objection that in that case it is said of people in general that they transgressed the covenant. Furthermore, the translation "like [the covenant of] a man" would in any case require that the word *kĕʾādām* be placed after the word *bĕrît*, not after the subject *hēmmâ*. So, unless the word is corrupt or refers to a place name ["at Adam"], there remains the translation "like Adam." Implied, then, is that the command given to Adam was at bottom a covenant because it was intended, like God's covenant with Israel, to convey eternal life to Adam in the way of [covenantal] obedience. This is further reinforced by the parallel that Paul draws in Romans 5:12–21 between Adam and Christ. As the obedience of one man, that is, Christ, and the grace granted to humanity in him, brought acquittal, righteousness, and life, so the one transgression and misdeed of the one man is the cause of condemnation, sin, and death for humanity as a whole. The relation between us and Adam is like that between us and Christ. We in fact stand to Adam in the same relation. He is a type of Christ, our head, from whom guilt and death accrue to us because of his transgression. He is the cause of the death of us all; we all die in Adam (1 Cor. 15:22). Here, too, Adam's relation to God is a covenant relation, described now not so much in the direction of God as in the direction of those who are included in that covenant under Adam as head.

[295] This richly valuable idea of Scripture has not always come into its own in Christian theology. A naturalistic view located the image of God solely in aptitude, naked potential, the freedom of the will, formal personhood, and even considered death natural. The image or at least the likeness of God consisted much more in what human beings had to acquire by their own exertions than in what they were given immediately at the creation. The supranaturalistic view, by contrast, struck out toward another extreme, attributing a totally supernatural character to the state of integrity. Not only was original righteousness considered a supernatural gift; immortality was viewed as a special

benefaction of the Creator, and all susceptibility to suffering and pain was denied to Adam.[2] Some, like Gregory of Nyssa, John of Damascus, Böhme, and others, however, judged that before the fall man had no need of food because he was immortal.[3] In any case excretion would have occurred without any taint of unseemliness.[4] According to most church fathers, Scholastics, Roman Catholic, Lutheran, Remonstrant, and also certain Reformed theologians like Zwingli, Musculus, Martyr, Zanchius, Junius, Piscator, and so forth, human food consisted only in plants and not in meat. Procreation occurred without any sensual pleasure, and children were born able to speak, though needy, but very swiftly grew up to adulthood.[5] Many, going even further, believed that procreation occurred entirely apart from coitus,[6] that humans were first created androgynous, and that the creation of the woman as such was proof of the fall.[7] Hence, women did not really participate in the divine image and in human nature.[8] Origen even derived corporeality and all inequality among men from a fall of preexistent souls; others attributed to man before the fall a body totally different from ours.[9] In connection with all this, paradise was often construed in very idealistic terms and even interpreted allegorically: animals did not die there; no wild or unclean animals existed there; roses blossomed but had no thorns; the air was much cleaner, the water much softer, and the light much brighter.[10]

Still, everyone acknowledges that Adam did not yet possess the highest humanity, a truth implicit in the probationary command, the freedom of choice, the possibility of sin and death. Especially Augustine made a clear distinction between the ability not to sin *(posse non peccare)* and not to die *(posse non mori)*, which Adam possessed, and the inability to sin *(non posse peccare)* and

2. Augustine, *City of God*, XIV, 26; T. Aquinas, *Summa theol.*, I, qu. 97, art. 2.

3. D. Petavius, "De opificio sex dierum," in *Theol. dogm.*, II, ch. 7.

4. T. Aquinas, *Summa theol.*, I, qu. 97, art. 3.

5. Augustine, *On the Merits and Remission of Sins*, I, 37–38; P. Lombard, *Sent.*, II, dist. 20; T. Aquinas, *Summa theol.*, I, qu. 98, art. 1.

6. Augustine, *The Retractions*, I, 10; Gregory of Nyssa, *On the Making of Man*, 16–17; John of Damascus, *Exposition of the Orthodox Faith*, II, 30.

7. So, already, the Jews thought; cf. F. W. Weber, *System der altsynagogalen palästinischen Theologie* (Leipzig: Dörffling & Franke, 1880), 202ff.; and then also J. S. Erigena, *The Division of Nature*, II, 6, 10, 23; IV, 12; and many philosophers such as Böhme, Oetinger, Baader, and Schelling; J. P. Lange, *Christliche Dogmatik*, 3 vols. (Heidelberg: K. Winter, 1852), II, 324ff.; F. Delitzsch, *A System of Biblical Psychology* (Edinburgh: T. & T. Clark, 1899), 102ff.; J. C. K. von Hofmann, *Weissagung und Erfüllung im Alten und im Neuen Testamente*, 2 vols. (Nördlingen: C. H. Beck, 1841–44), I, 65ff.; idem, *Der Schriftbeweis*, 2d ed., 3 vols. (Nördlingen: Beck, 1857–60), I, 403ff.; etc.

8. Cf. Augustine, *The Trinity*, XII, 7; T. Aquinas, *Summa theol.*, I, qu. 93, art. 4; I, qu. 99, art. 2; Bonaventure, *Sent.*, II, dist. 16, art. 2, qu. 2; II, dist. 20, art. 1, qu. 6; J. Gerhard, *Loci theol.*, VIII, c. 6; J. Quenstedt, *Theologia*, II, 15; J. Janssen, *Geschichte des deutschen Volkes seit dem Ausgang des Mittelalters*, 8 vols. (Paris: Librairie Plon, 1887–1911), VI, 395–97.

9. Origen, *Against Celsus*, I, 32, 33; idem, *On First Principles*, II, 9; cf. R. Liechtenhan, "Ophiten," *PRE*[3], XIV, 404–13; and also Böhme, Ant. Bourignon, Baader, et al.

10. Luther, on Gen. 3; cf. D. F. Strauss, *Die christliche Glaubenslehre*, 2 vols. (Tübingen: C. F. Osiander, 1840–41), I, 700ff.

the inability to die *(non posse mori)*, gifts that were to be bestowed along with the glorification of the first man in case of obedience and now granted to the elect out of grace.[11] The relation in which Adam originally stood vis-à-vis God was even described by Augustine as a covenant, a testament, a pact;[12] and the translation of the words *kĕʾādām* by "like Adam" led many to a similar view.[13] Materially, therefore, the doctrine of what was later called "the covenant of works" also already occurs in the church fathers. Included in Adam's situation, as it was construed by the Scholastics, Roman Catholic, and Lutheran theologians, lay all the elements that were later summed up especially by Reformed theologians in the doctrine of the covenant of works.[14] The relation in which believers have come to stand to God by Christ is repeatedly described in Scripture with the term "covenant." Zwingli and Bucer already seized upon these scriptural thoughts to defend the unity of the Old and New Testaments against the Anabaptists. Now when, following the example of Scripture, the Christian religion was portrayed as a covenant, Paul's parallel between Adam and Christ prompted theologians also to conceive the state of integrity as a covenant.

In distinction from the covenant of grace this was then called the covenant of nature or of works *(foedus naturae* or *operum)*. It was called "covenant of nature," not because it was deemed to flow automatically and naturally from the nature of God or the nature of man, but because the foundation on which the covenant rested, that is, the moral law, was known to man by nature, and because it was made with man in his original state and could be kept by man with the powers bestowed on him in the creation, without the assistance of supernatural grace. Later, when the term occasioned misunderstanding, it was preferentially replaced by that of "covenant of works"; and it bore this name inasmuch as in this covenant eternal life could only be obtained in the way of works, that is, in the way of keeping God's commandments. Now this covenant, as parallel to the covenant of grace, was taught and developed with special predilection by Reformed theologians.[15] The Reformed Confessions do not mention it in so many words. Materially, however, it is nevertheless embodied in articles 14 and 15 of the Belgic Confession, where we read that man's entire nature was corrupted by Adam's transgression of the command of life;[16] in Lord's Day 3 and 4 of the Heidelberg Catechism (Q. & A. 6–11)

11. Augustine, *City of God,* XXII, 30; idem, *Admonition and Grace*; idem, *Enchiridion,* 104–7; idem, *Literal Meaning of Genesis,* III, 2; VI, 25; idem, *Against Julian,* V, 58; VI, 5; etc.

12. Augustine, *City of God,* XVI, 27.

13. J. Marck, *Historia Paradisi* (Amsterdam: Gerardus Borstius, 1705), II, 6–7.

14. Cf. P. Lombard, *Sent.,* II, dist. 19–20.

15. Ed. note: Bavinck here refers to the literature at the head of the chapter section in the Dutch edition. Check the following authors in the bibliography: Boston, Brahé, Cloppenburg, Coccejus, Comrie, de Moor, Gomarus, van den Honert, Junius, Marck, Mastricht, Olevianus, Polanus, Trelcatius, Trelcatius Jr., Ursinus, Vitringa, Walker, Wollebius.

16. In its original version, art. 14 of the Belgic Confession read that God formed man "after his own image and likeness, good, righteous, and holy, *entirely perfect in all things (et tout parfait en toutes choses)*." Later these words were omitted and replaced by "capable in all things to will agreeably to the will of God."

it is said that man was created in God's image, so that he might live with God in eternal happiness, but humankind is also described as totally corrupted by Adam's fall; and in chapter III/IV of the Canons of Dort it is stated that Adam's corruption spread to all his descendants "by God's just judgment." Formally, the covenant of works is incorporated in the Irish Articles (1615), the Westminster Confession (1647), the Helvetic Consensus Formula (1675), and the Walcheren Articles (1693).[17] Although the doctrine of the covenant of works also found acceptance with some Roman Catholic[18] and Lutheran theologians,[19] it was vigorously opposed by Remonstrants and Rationalists.[20] Only in modern times was the doctrine of the covenant of works again understood and explained by a number of theologians in its true significance.[21]

[296] One can certainly raise the objection against the doctrine of the covenant as it has been developed in Reformed theology, that it was overly detailed and treated too scholastically. Although later theologians still defended the doctrine, they no longer felt its significance and its theological and religious importance. Since it had lost its vitality, it was easy to combat it. But the doctrine of the covenant of works is based on Scripture and is eminently valuable. Among rational and moral creatures all higher life takes the form of a covenant. Generally, a covenant is an agreement between persons who voluntarily obligate and bind themselves to each other for the purpose of fending off an evil or obtaining a good. Such an agreement, whether it is made tacitly or defined in explicit detail, is the usual form in terms of which humans live and work together. Love, friendship, marriage, as well as all social cooperation in business, industry, science, art, and so forth, is ultimately grounded

17. Ed. note: For a description of the Helvetic Consensus Formula (1675), see P. Schaff, *The Creeds of Christendom*, 6th ed., 3 vols. (New York: Harper, 1919), I, 477–89. The five Walcheren Articles (1693) were adopted by the Dutch Reformed Classes of Walcheren against the liberal-rationalist views of Herman Alexander Roëll, Balthasar Bekker, and Johannes Vlak. Discussion of the articles and the rejected views of these three can be found in the respective essays of the *Christelijke Encyclopedie*, ed. F. W. Grosheide and G. P. Van Itterzon (Kampen: Kok, 1961). The full text of the Walcheren Articles is found in *Documenta Reformatoria*, ed. J. N. Bakhuizen van den Brink et al. (Kampen: Kok, 1960), I, 460–70.

18. M. J. Scheeben, *Handbuch der katholischen Dogmatik*, 4 vols. (Freiburg i.B.: Herder, 1933), II, 500; C. Pesch, *Praelectiones dogmaticae* (Freiburg i.B.: Herder, 1916–25), III, 136.

19. J. F. Buddeus, *Institutiones theologiae moralis* (Leipzig: T. Fritsch, 1715), 527; and others, cf. C. Vitringa, *Doctr. christ.*, II, 242.

20. S. Episcopius, *Inst. theol.*, II, c. 2; P. van Limborch, *Theol. christ.*, III, c. 2; J. Alting, on Heb. 8:6; and *Opera omnia theologica* (Amsterdam: Borst, n.d.), V, 392; H. Venema, *Korte Verdediging van zijn Eere en Leere* (Leeuwarden: van Desiel, 1735); N. Schiere, *Doctrina testamentorum et foederum divinorum omnium* (Leovardiae: M. Injema, 1718); J. Vlak, *Eeuwig evangelie* (1684) (ed. note: The title was not given by Bavinck), who is disputed by H. Brink, *Toet-Steen der waarheid en der dwalingen* (Amsterdam, 1685). Even J. J. Van Oosterzee (*Christian Dogmatics,* trans. J. Watson and M. Evans, 2 vols. [New York: Scribner, Armstrong, 1874], §75) saw it as a Jewish work of art.

21. A. Kuyper, *De Heraut*, 161ff.; C. Hodge, *Systematic Theology,* 3 vols. (New York: Charles Scribner's Sons, 1888), II, 117; G. Vos, "The Doctrine of the Covenant in Reformed Theology," in *Redemptive History and Biblical Interpretation,* ed. Richard B. Gaffin Jr. (Phillipsburg: Presbyterian & Reformed, 1980), 234–70.

in a covenant, that is, in reciprocal fidelity and an assortment of generally recognized moral obligations. It should not surprise us, therefore, that also the highest and most richly textured life of human beings, namely, religion, bears this character. In Scripture "covenant" is the fixed form in which the relation of God to his people is depicted and presented. And even where the word does not occur, we nevertheless always see the two parties, as it were, in dialogue with each other, dealing with each other, with God calling people to conversion, reminding them of their obligations, and obligating himself to provide all that is good. Later, when we discuss the covenant of grace, we will spotlight the biblical concept of *běrît*. Here we will confine ourselves to reminding the reader of the general idea of covenant. Even if the term "covenant" never occurred in Scripture for the religious relation between Adam and God, not even in Hosea 6:7, still the religious life of man before the fall bears the character of a covenant. Reformed scholars were never so narrow as to insist on the word "covenant" since the matter itself was certain: one may doubt the word, provided the matter is safe *(de vocabulo dubitetur, re salva)*. But hidden behind the opposition to the word was opposition to the matter itself. And this must never be surrendered inasmuch as covenant is the essence of true religion.

Why should this be? First of all, because God is the Creator, man a creature; and with that statement an infinite distance between the two is a given. No fellowship, no religion between the two seems possible; there is only difference, distance, endless distinctness. If God remains elevated above humanity in his sovereign exaltedness and majesty, then no religion is possible, at least no religion in the sense of fellowship. Then the relation between the two is exhaustively described in the terms "master" and "servant." Then the image of the potter and the clay is still much too weak to describe that relation because clay has existence—and hence rights—independently of, and over against, the potter, but human beings have nothing and are nothing apart from God. Accordingly, if there is truly to be religion, if there is to be fellowship between God and man, if the relation between the two is to be also (but not exclusively) that of a master to his servant, of a potter to clay, as well as that of a king to his people, of a father to his son, of a mother to her child, of an eagle to her young, of a hen to her chicks, and so forth; that is, if not just one relation but all relations and all sorts of relations of dependence, submission, obedience, friendship, love, and so forth among humans find their model and achieve their fulfillment in religion, then religion must be the character of a covenant. For then God has to come down from his lofty position, condescend to his creatures, impart, reveal, and give himself away to human beings; then he who inhabits eternity and dwells in a high and holy place must also dwell with those who are of a humble spirit (Isa. 57:15). But this set of conditions is nothing other than the description of a covenant. If religion is called a covenant, it is thereby described as the true and genuine religion. This is what no religion has ever understood; all peoples either pantheistically pull God down into what is creaturely, or deistically elevate him endlessly above it. In neither case does one arrive at true fellowship, at covenant, at genuine religion. But Scripture insists on both: God is infinitely great and condescendingly good; he is Sovereign but also Father; he is Creator but also Prototype. In a word, he is the God of the covenant.

It is clear, in the second place, that a creature cannot bring along or possess any rights before God. That is implicitly—in the nature of the case—impossible. A creature as such owes its very existence, all that it is and has, to God; it cannot make any claims before God, and it cannot boast of anything; it has no rights and can make no demands of any kind. There is no such thing as merit in the existence of a creature before God, nor can there be since the relation between the Creator and a creature radically and once-and-for-all eliminates any notion of merit. This is true after the fall but no less before the fall. Then too, human beings were creatures, without entitlements, without rights, without merit. When we have done everything we have been instructed to do, we are still unworthy servants (*douloi achreioi,* Luke 17:10). Now, however, the religion of Holy Scripture is such that in it human beings can nevertheless, as it were, assert certain rights before God. For they have the freedom to come to him with prayer and thanksgiving, to address him as "Father," to take refuge in him in all circumstances of distress and death, to desire all good things from him, even to expect salvation and eternal life from him. All this is possible solely because God in his condescending goodness gives rights to his creature. Every creaturely right is a given benefit, a gift of grace, undeserved and nonobligatory. All reward from the side of God originates in grace; no merit, either of condignity or of congruity,[22] is possible. True religion, accordingly, cannot be anything other than a covenant: it has its origin in the condescending goodness and grace of God. It has that character before as well as after the fall. For religion, like the moral law and the destiny of man, is one. The covenant of works and the covenant of grace do not differ in their final goal but only in the way that leads to it. In both there is one mediator: then, a mediator of union; now, a mediator of reconciliation. In both there is one faith: then, faith in God; now, faith in God through Christ; and in both covenants there is one hope, one love, and so forth. Religion is always the same in essence; it differs only in form.

In the third place, men and women are rational and moral beings. That is how God created them, and that therefore is how he treats them. He maintains what he created. God, accordingly, does not coerce human beings, for coercion is inconsistent with the nature of rational creatures. He deals with them, not as irrational creatures, as plants or animals, as blocks of wood, but goes to work with them as rational, moral, self-determining beings. He wants human beings to be free and to serve him in love, freely and willingly (Ps. 100:3f.). Religion is freedom; it is love that does not permit itself to be coerced. For that reason

22. Ed. note: See p. 539 n. 29, above.

it must by its very nature take the shape of a covenant in which God acts, not coercively, but with counsel, admonition, warning, invitation, petition, and in which humans serve God, not under duress or violence, but willingly, by their own free consent, moved by love to love in return. At bottom religion is a duty but also a privilege. It is not work by which we bring advantage to God, make a contribution to him, and have a right to reward. It is grace for us to be allowed to serve him. God is never indebted to us, but we are always indebted to him for the good works we do (Belgic Confession, art. 24). On his part there is always the gift; on our part there is always and alone the gratitude. For that reason religion is conceivable only in the form of a covenant and comes to its full realization only in that form. God, accordingly, made such a covenant with the first human beings. We must completely set aside the fragmentary development of this doctrine. The matter itself is certain. After creating men and women after his own image, God showed them their destiny and the only way in which they could reach it. Human beings could know the moral law without special revelation since it was written in their hearts. But the probationary command is positive; it is not a given of human nature as such but could only be made known to human beings if God communicated it to them. Nor was it self-evident that keeping that command would yield eternal life. In that sense the "covenant of works" is not a "covenant of nature." Initially, the church did not yet clearly understand this,[23] but gradually it became obvious—and was taught as such—that God was in no way obligated to grant heavenly blessedness and eternal life to those who kept his law and thereby did not do anything other than what they were obligated to do. There *is* no natural connection here between work and reward.[24]

REFORMED AND OTHER VIEWS OF HUMAN DESTINY

And *that* is the truth that inheres in Rome's doctrine of the added gift *(donum superadditum)*. Eternal life is and remains an unmerited gift of God's grace. But because Rome does not know the doctrine of the covenant of works, it infers from this gracious gift of eternal life that also the image of God in man has to be supernatural and, by virtue of the supernatural power granted with the image of God, has humans again meriting eternal life *ex condigno*. Under the guise of honoring grace, Rome therefore again introduces the meritoriousness of good works. But Reformed theologians maintained, on the one hand, that the image of God in man was natural and that man,

23. F. Gomarus, *De foedere.*

24. J. Coccejus, *Summa doctrinae de foedere et testamento Dei* (Frankfurt: J. M. a Sande, 1704), II, 23ff.; F. Burmann, *Syn. theol.,* II, 8, 2, 4; J. Marck, *Hist. parad.,* 479; J. Cloppenburg, *Exerc. theol.,* VI, disp. 5; idem, *De foedere,* I, 8ff.; H. Witsius, *The Oeconomy of the Covenants between God and Man,* 4 vols. in 3 (London: Edward Dilly, 1763), I, 4, §§10–23; M. Leydekker, *Fax veritatis* (Leiden: Daniel Gaesbeeck & Felicem Lopez, 1677), 399ff.; A. Comrie and N. Holtius, *Examen van het Ontwerp van Tolerantie,* 10 vols. (Amsterdam: Nicolaas Byl, 1753), IX, 227ff.; X, 288ff., 318ff.; J. Brahé, *Aanmerkingen over de Vijf Walchersche Artikelen* (Vlissingen, 1758; reprinted, Rotterdam: De Banier, 1937), 125ff., 261ff.

who was this image of God, could know as well as keep the moral law without supernatural power, and, on the other hand, they firmly asserted that a higher state of blessedness than that which prevailed in paradise on earth could never, in the nature of the case, be merited but could only be granted by a free dispensation of God. And they combined these two ideas in their theory of the covenant of works. This covenant is rooted in a free, special, and gracious dispensation of God. It proceeds from God and he decrees all the parts of it: condition and fulfillment, compliance and reward, transgression and punishment. It is monopleuric (unilateral) in origin, and it is added to the creation in God's image. On their part, the first human beings, being created in God's image, rested in it and saw in this covenant a revelation of a way to a higher blessedness. The covenant of works, accordingly, does justice to both the sovereignty of God—which implies the dependency of creatures and the nonmeritoriousness of all their works—and to the grace and generosity of God, who nevertheless wants to give the creature a higher-than-earthly blessedness. It maintains both the dependence as well as the freedom of mankind. It combines Schleiermacher [dependence] and Kant [freedom]. The probationary command relates to the moral law as the covenant of works relates to man's creation in God's image. The moral law stands or falls in its entirety with the probationary command, and the image of God in mankind in its entirety stands or falls with the covenant of works. The covenant of works is the road to heavenly blessedness for the [first] human beings, who were created in God's image and had not yet fallen.

[297] The covenant of works, accordingly, includes still another beautiful thought. It not only realizes the true and full idea of religion; it also gives expression to the fact that humanity before the fall, though created in God's image, did not yet possess the highest possible blessing. On this point Reformed theology has a primary difference with Lutheran theologians. In their view, creation in God's image was the realization of the highest idea of man. In Adam that ideal was fully attained, and a higher state was not possible. Adam did not have to become anything; he only had to remain what he was, namely, a participant in the full gracious indwelling of the holy Trinity. Accordingly, he was not subject to a law that commanded him to do anything positive. The law that applied to him had only a negative thrust, and not until sin appeared was he brought under the dominion of the law. That is why in the works of Lutheran theologians, as in those of the church fathers, the original state of man was frequently pictured in a very exaggerated manner. It is also why the state to which believers in Christ are elevated is essentially equated with that of Adam before the fall. In reference to the believer, everything is focused for the Lutheran on justification. Once the believer is justified, he or she has enough and is completely satisfied and blessed. Salvation completely coincides with forgiveness. No need is felt to connect it backward with eternal election and forward with the whole of the Christian life, good works, and eternal life. Neither predestination nor perseverance is needed here. The Lutheran believer enjoys the new life in the present

and feels no need for more.[25] For the Reformed, who walked in the footsteps of Augustine, things were different. According to them, Adam did not possess the highest kind of life. The highest kind of life is the material freedom consisting of not being able to err, sin, or die. It consists in being elevated absolutely above all fear and dread, above all possibility of falling. This highest life is immediately bestowed by grace through Christ upon believers. They can no longer sin (1 John 3:9) and they can no longer die (John 3:16) since by faith they immediately receive eternal, inamissible life. Theirs is the perseverance of the saints; they can no longer be lost. Hence, Christ does not [merely] restore his own to the state of Adam before the fall. He acquired and bestows much more, namely, that which Adam would have received had he not fallen. He positions us not at the beginning but at the end of the journey that Adam had to complete. He accomplished not only the passive but also the active obedience required; he not only delivers us from guilt and punishment, but out of grace immediately grants us the right to eternal life.

Adam, however, did not yet have this high state of blessedness; he did not yet have eternal life. He received the possibility to remain standing *(posse stare)* but not the will *(velle stare)*. He could have it if he willed it *(posse si vellet)* but did not have the will to want what he was able to have *(velle, quod posset)*. He had the possibility of not erring, sinning, and dying *(posse non errare, peccare, mori)*, but not yet the impossibility of erring, sinning, and dying *(non posse errare, peccare, mori)*. He still lived in the state of one who could sin and die, and was therefore still in some fear and dread. His was not yet the invariable perfect love that casts out all fear. Reformed theologians rightly pointed out, therefore, that this possibility, this being changeably good, this still being able to sin and die, was no part or component of the image of God, but was its boundary, its limitation, its circumference.[26] The image of God therefore had to be fully developed—thereby overcoming and nullifying this possibility of sin and death—and glitter in imperishable glory. In virtue of this view of the state of integrity Reformed theologians, in distinction from others, were able to observe a commendable sobriety in their account of the paradisal state. Adam was not Christ. The natural was not the spiritual. Paradise was not heaven. However careful we must be to resist the naturalism that denies the power of sin and considers death natural, no less to be avoided is the supranaturalism that defines the image of God as a supernatural addition to nature. Sin, according to Reformed theologians, spoiled and destroyed everything, but because it is not a substance it could not alter the essence

25. Luther, in J. Köstlin, *The Theology of Luther in Its Historical Development and Inner Harmony*, trans. Charles E. Hay (Philadelphia: Lutheran Publication Society, 1897), II, 361; M. Schneckenburger and E. Güder, *Vergleichende Darstellung des lutherischen und reformirten Lehrbegriffs*, 2 vols. (Stuttgart: J. B. Metzler, 1855), I, 90ff., 120ff.; II, 185ff.; A. F. C. Vilmar, *Handbuch der evangelishen Dogmatik* (Gütersloh: C. Bertelsmann, 1895), I, 340; F. H. R. Frank, *System der christlichen Wahrheit* (Erlangen: A. Deichert, 1878–80), I, 375.

26. H. Heppe, *Reformed Dogmatics*, rev. and ed. Ernst Bizer, trans. G. T. Thomson (London: Allen & Unwin, 1950; reprinted, Grand Rapids: Baker, 1978), 249–50; W. G. T. Shedd, *Dogmatic Theology* (New York: Charles Scribner's Sons, 1888–89), II, 104, 150.

or substance of the creation. The human being as sinner is still a human being. Similarly, all other creations (earth, heaven, nature, plant, animal), despite the curse of sin and the rule of corruption, essentially and substantially remained the same. As we noted above in the case of religion, so it is also in the case of all the other things: sin did not take away the substance of things, and grace therefore does not restore that substance either. The stuff *(materia)* of all things is and remains the same. However, the form *(forma)*, given in creation, was *de*formed by sin in order to be entirely *re*formed again in the sphere of grace.[27]

This serious and yet most wholesome view of the paradisal state held by the Reformed comes to expression at countless points. Against the Lutherans and Remonstrants they defended the thesis that, aside from the probationary command, Adam was also thoroughly bound to the moral law. He was not "law-less" *(exlex,* bound by no law), even though he fulfilled it without any coercion, willingly and out of love. Adam knew the moral law by nature. Hence, it did not, like the probationary command, have to be revealed to him in a special way. It is essentially the same as the Ten Commandments but differed in form, for the law given on Sinai presupposes a catalog of sins and therefore almost always speaks in the negative ("Thou shalt not . . ."), and the moral law before the fall was much more positive. But precisely because in the prefall life of Adam the moral law was in the nature of the case entirely positive, it did not make clear to Adam's mind the possibility of sin. Hence, in addition to the *pre*scriptions there had to come a *pro*scription, and in addition to the commandments a positive law. In addition to the commandments, whose naturalness and reasonableness were obvious to Adam, this command was in a sense arbitrary and incidental. In the probationary command the entire moral law came to Adam at a single throw, confronting him with the dilemma: either God or man, God's authority or one's own insight, unconditional obedience or independent research, faith or skepticism. It was a momentous test that opened the way either to eternal blessedness or eternal ruin. Against the Cocceians, Reformed theologians maintained that the Sabbath command also belonged to that moral law. Before the fall our first parents did not yet enjoy the eternal heavenly Sabbath. Just as they were subject to the alternation of day and night, they were also bound to the rule of six days of labor and one of rest. A day of rest and days of labor were therefore also distinct before the fall. Then, too, the religious life required a form and service of its own alongside the life of culture. Reformed theologians, with increasing unanimity and decisiveness, rejected the magical, theosophic notion that the two trees in the garden of Eden possessed the power to kill or to make alive of themselves, either by nature (Thomas, Suárez, Pererius), or in a supernatural manner (Augustine, Bonaventure), either upon onetime use[28] or upon repeated use.[29] A few, however,

27. G. Voetius, *Select. disp.,* I, 776.
28. R. Bellarmine, *De gratia primi hominis* (Heidelberg: Rosa, 1612), c. 14.
29. T. Aquinas, *Summa theol.,* I, qu. 97, art. 4; cf. also A. Kuyper, *De Heraut* 941 (January 5, 1896): 1.

such as Pareus, Rivet, and Zanchius,[30] initially still assumed that the eating of the fruit had an effect on the physical life of man.[31] This view, though it is consistent with the Roman Catholic doctrine of the sacraments, is in part for that reason unacceptable to the Reformed tradition since it makes life and death independent of the ethical condition, that is, of the act of obeying or disobeying God's command. Rather, it assumes that human beings would continue to live even after the fall if only they had *ex opere operato* eaten of the tree of life. It thus implies that eternal life could be effected in humanity either at one stroke or gradually by the eating of a physical fruit, and thus denies the distinction between the natural and the spiritual. Reformed theologians, accordingly, preferred to view the tree of life as sign and seal of the covenant of works, which bestowed life in a sacramental manner.

Similarly, Reformed theologians unanimously rejected,[32] as contrary to Scripture, all theosophic speculations concerning an androgynous maiden, the absence of the sex drive, and magical generation. The creation of the woman does not presuppose a kind of fall in Adam's life, nor did any new species emerge in the plant or animal kingdom after the entry of sin. According to Voetius, wild animals and creeping things were already created on the sixth day and predate the fall.[33] And finally, Calvin and most Reformed theologians were of the opinion that eating meat was permitted to humans even before the flood and the fall.[34] The fact that Genesis 1:29 does not expressly mention it cannot, as an argument from silence, be of service here. In Genesis 1:30 only the plant world is divided between man and animal; nothing is said about man's dominion over and claims upon the animal world. The animal world had already been placed under human dominion in Genesis 1:28, an act that certainly includes, especially with respect to the fish of the sea, the right to kill and use animals. Immediately after the fall God himself made garments of animal skins (3:21), and Abel made a sacrifice that was surely followed by a sacrificial meal. The practice of eating meat, moreover, was certainly in use before the flood, and if God did not authorize it before Genesis 9:3, it would have been unlawful and sinful before that time. Genesis 9:1–5 does not present a new commandment, but renews the blessing of creation; a new feature is only the prohibition against eating meat with its life, that is, its blood. The ground for the injunction against killing human beings (Gen. 9:5–7) is not present in the case of animals, for they were not made in God's image. Incomprehensible,

---

30. J. Zanchi(us), *Op. theol.*, III, 501.

31. J. Calvin, *Institutes,* IV.xiv.12, 18; idem, *Commentary on Genesis,* trans. John King (Grand Rapids: Baker, 1979), 115–18, 182–84 (on Gen. 2:9; 3:22); J. Marck, *Historia paradisi,* I, c. 17; cf. further literature in C. Vitringa, *Doctr. christ.,* II, 220ff.

32. J. Marck, *Historia paradisi,* 279ff.

33. G. Voetius, *Select. disp.,* V, 191.

34. J. Calvin, *Commentary on Genesis,* 98–100, 291–93 (on Gen. 1:29; 9:3); J. Heidegger, *De libertate christianorum a re cibaria* (1662); G. Voetius, *Select. disp.,* IV, 387; V, 194; J. Coccejus, *Summa theol.,* XX, 17; J. Marck, *Historia paradisi,* 341; B. de Moor, *Comm. in Marckii Comp.,* III, 35–38; etc.

finally, is why of all times God should permit mankind to eat meat *after* the fall and *after* the flood; one would expect the contrary, namely, that the rights and rule of man would be restricted after the fall. One would expect that, to counter lawlessness and degradation, the use of meat would be abolished, and that vegetarianism would be considered much more in accord with the postfall and postflood state of mankind than the practice of eating meat.[35]

In all these issues Reformed theology was able to make such sound judg- ments because it was deeply imbued with the idea that Adam did not yet enjoy the highest level of blessedness. Sin undoubtedly has cosmic significance. As is evident from the phenomenon of death, sin also impacts our physical existence and has brought the entire earth under the curse. Without sin the development of humanity and the history of the earth would have been very different—though still unimaginable. Still, on the other hand, the state of integrity cannot be equated with the state of glory. We may not draw conclu- sions from the former for the conditions of the latter. Isaiah 11:6 and 65:25 can no more be applied to the state of human life before the fall than Mark 12:25; Luke 20:36; and 1 Corinthians 6:13 (etc.). Though the form *(forma)* has changed, the matter *(materia)* of humankind, plant, animal, nature, and earth is the same before and after the fall. All the essential components exist- ing today were present also before the fall. The distinctions and dissimilarities between men and women, parents and children, brothers and sisters, relatives and friends; the numerous institutions and relations in the life of society such as marriage, family, child rearing, and so forth; the alternation of day and night, workdays and the day of rest, labor and leisure, months and years; man's dominion over the earth through science and art, and so forth—while all these things have undoubtedly been modified by sin and changed in appearance, they nevertheless have their active principle and foundation in creation, in the ordinances of God, and not in sin. Socialism and communism, also the socialism and communism of many Christian sects, are right in combating the appalling consequences of sin, especially also in the sphere of society. But these systems do not stop there; they also come into conflict with the nature of things, the creation ordinances, and therefore consistently take on, not a reformational, but a revolutionary character.

HUMAN DESTINY IN COMMUNITY

[298] The doctrine of the covenant of works, finally, contains a third idea, an idea of the richest religious and ethical significance. Adam was not created *alone*. As a man and by himself he was incomplete. He lacked something that no lower creature could make up (Gen. 2:20). As a man by himself, accordingly,

35. O. Zöckler, *Die Lehre vom Urstand des Menschen* (Gütersloh: C. Bertelsmann, 1870), 273ff.; M. Köhler, *Biblische Geschichte des Alten und Neuen Testaments* (Potsdam: Rentel, n.d.), I, 33ff.; R. Kraetzschmar, *Die Bundesvorstellung im Alten Testament in ihrer geschichtlichen Entwickelung* (Marburg: N. G. Elwert, 1896), 193ff.; V. Zapletal, *Der Schöpfungsbericht der Genesis* (Regensburg: G. J. Manz, 1911), 65.

neither was he yet the fully unfolded image of God. The creation of humankind in God's image was only completed on the sixth day, when God created both man and woman in union with each other (cf. *ʾōtām*, Gen. 1:27), in his image. Still, even this creation in God's image of man and woman in conjunction is not the end but the beginning of God's journey with mankind. It is not good that the man should be alone (Gen. 2:18); nor is it good that the man and woman should be alone. Upon the two of them God immediately pronounced the blessing of multiplication (Gen. 1:28). Not the man alone, nor the man and woman together, but only the whole of humanity is the fully developed image of God, his children, his offspring. The image of God is much too rich for it to be fully realized in a single human being, however richly gifted that human being may be. It can only be somewhat unfolded in its depth and riches in a humanity counting billions of members. Just as the traces of God *(vestigia Dei)* are spread over many, many works, in both space and time, so also the image of God can only be displayed in all its dimensions and characteristic features in a humanity whose members exist both successively one after the other and contemporaneously side by side. But just as the cosmos is a unity and receives its head and master in humankind; and just as the traces of God *(vestigia Dei)* scattered throughout the entire world are bundled and raised up into the image of God of humankind; so also that humanity in turn is to be conceived as an organism that, precisely as such, is finally the only fully developed image of God. Not as a heap of souls on a tract of land, not as a loose aggregate of individuals, but as having been created out of one blood; as one household and one family, humanity is the image and likeness of God. Belonging to that humanity is also its development, its history, its ever-expanding dominion over the earth, its progress in science and art, its subjugation of all creatures. All these things as well constitute the unfolding of the image and likeness of God in keeping with which humanity was created. Just as God did not reveal himself all at once at the creation, but continues and expands that revelation from day to day and from age to age, so also the image of God is not a static entity but extends and unfolds itself in the forms of space and time. It is both a gift *(Gabe)* and a mandate *(Aufgabe)*. It is an undeserved gift of grace that was given to the first human being immediately at the creation but at the same time is the grounding principle and germ of an altogether rich and glorious development. Only humanity in its entirety—as one complete organism, summed up under a single head, spread out over the whole earth, as prophet proclaiming the truth of God, as priest dedicating itself to God, as ruler controlling the earth and the whole of creation—only it is the fully finished image, the most telling and striking likeness of God.

Scripture clearly teaches all this when it says that the church is the bride of Christ, the temple of the Holy Spirit, the dwelling of God, the new Jerusalem to which all the glory of the nations will be brought. This is a picture, to be sure, of the state of glory that will now be attained through the thickets of sin; but religion, the moral law, and man's final destiny are essentially the same in both the covenant of works and the covenant of grace. In both the goal and end is a kingdom of God, a holy humanity, in which God is all in all.

Only one point in this presentation requires further discussion. Humanity cannot be conceived as a completed organism unless it is united and epitomized in one head. In the covenant of grace Christ has that position, and he is the head of the church; in the covenant of works that position is occupied by Adam. Eve was created from Adam so that he could be the first principle of the whole race *(principium totius speciei),* and so that the unity of the human race would be rooted in the unity of its origin. The woman, accordingly, is very much a partaker of human nature and of the image of God, and she represents that nature and image in accordance with her own nature and in a manner uniquely her own; but she is a partaker of both human nature and the image, not over against others, but alongside them, and in solidarity with the man. She is "from man," "for the man," and "the glory of man," and not independent of man; but also the man, though head of his wife and "the image and glory of God" because he in the first place is the bearer of dominion, is nevertheless incomplete without the woman, for she is the mother of all living (1 Cor. 11:7–12; Eph. 5:22ff.). Paul above all points out to us this unity of humanity when he opposes Adam to Christ (Rom. 5:12–21; 1 Cor. 15:22, 45–49). The human race is not only physically of one blood (Acts 17:26), for that would not be enough for humanity. The same thing is true, after all, of all the animal species created in the beginning. Furthermore, Christ, the antitype of Adam, is not our ancestor; we did not physically descend from him. He himself is a descendant of Adam according to the flesh. In this respect Adam and Christ are not alike. But the similarity consists in the fact that in a juridical and ethical sense humanity stands in the same relation to Adam as to Christ. Just as Christ is the cause of our righteousness and our life, so Adam is the cause of our sin and our death. God considers and judges the whole human race in one person.

Now, Reformed theologians have expressed this idea in their doctrine of the covenant of works. Only in this covenant does the ethical—not the physical—unity of mankind come into its own. And this ethical unity is requisite for humanity as an organism. Generally speaking, the law of architectonics everywhere requires the monarchical system. A work of art must be controlled by a single thought; a sermon must have a single theme; a church comes to completeness in a steeple; the man is the head of the family; in a kingdom the king [or queen] is the bearer of authority; as an organic whole, an ethical community, the human race is not conceivable without a head. In the covenant of works Adam had that position. The probationary command is proof that he occupied an entirely exceptional post. He was not only the ancestor but also the head and representative of the entire human race, and his conduct was decisive for all. Just as the fate of the whole body rests with the head, which thinks and judges and decides for all the organs; just as the well-being of a family depends on the husband and father; just as a sovereign ruler can be a blessing or a curse for thousands and millions of his subjects—so also the fate of humanity was put in the hands of Adam. His transgression became the fall of all his descendants, but his obedience would also have been the life of all his descendants, as Christ, his antitype, proves. If we could not be subjected to condemnation in Adam without our knowledge, neither could we have been accepted unto grace in Christ without our participation. The covenant of works and the covenant of grace stand and fall together. The same law applies to both. On the basis of a common physical descent an ethical unity has been built that causes humanity—in keeping with its nature—to manifest itself as one organism and to unite its members in the closest possible way, not only by ties of blood but also by common participation in blessing and curse, sin and righteousness, death and life.

[299] From this vantage point fresh light falls on the question of the propagation of the human race. At all times opinions have been divided on this issue. The preexistence theory of Pythagoras, Plato, Plotinus, Philo, and the later Jews found little acceptance among Christians,[36] but it was revived in a more or less modified form in modern times,[37] and today, under the influence of Buddhism and the doctrine of evolution, it even has many strong advocates.[38] If there exists no personal God and no Creator, if evolution can only develop what is and cannot produce anything absolutely new, and if for some reason one nevertheless wants to maintain the immortality of the soul—then it is natural to think that the souls continuing to exist forever in the future also existed eternally in the past. Just as Haeckel, for want of an explanation via the theory of evolution, made matter and energy, movement and life, consciousness and feeling eternal, so in the same way others draw the conclusion that the souls of humans at no time originated but have always existed in the cosmos. But since the Christian religion arises from very different premises and is based on the confession of God's personal existence and creative activity, it has no room for this doctrine of the eternal preexistence of souls. Nor is our soul in any way conscious of such preexistence, and rather than viewing the body as a prison and place of punishment, it shrinks from the event of death. The theory of the preexistence of the soul, moreover, is rooted

36. Origen, *On First Principles*, I, 6, 2; I, 8, 3; II, 9, 2; idem, *Against Celsus*, I, 32–33; H. More, *Mysterium pietatis* (1660).

37. G. E. Lessing, *Erziehung des Menschengeschlechts und andere Schriften* (Stuttgart: Reclam, 1997), §§91–95; I. Kant, *Religion within the Limits of Reason Alone*, trans. T. M. Greene and H. H. Hudson (New York: Harper and Brothers, 1934), 145–51 (ed. note: For a fuller bibliographic note on Kant's views of preexistence and immortality, see R. Eisler, "Unsterblichkeit," *Kant-Lexikon* [Berlin: Mittler & Sohn, 1930], 555–57); F. W. Schelling, *Ausgewählte Werke* (Darmstadt: Wissenschaftliche Buchgesellschaft, 1968), IV, 329ff. ("Philosophische Untersuchungen über das Wesen der menschlichen Freiheit und die damit zusammenhängenden Gegenstände," *Werke*, I/7, 385ff.); I. H. von Fichte, *Anthropologie* (Leipzig: Brockhaus, 1860), 494; J. Müller, *The Christian Doctrine of Sin*, trans. Wm. Urwick, 5th ed., 2 vols. (Edinburgh: T. & T. Clark, 1868), ch. 3, pt. 3; C. Secrétan, *La philosophie de la liberté*, 2 vols. (Paris: G. Balliere, 1849), II, 204; cf. also F. E. Daubanton, *Het Voortbestaan van het Menschelijk Geslacht* (Utrecht: Kemink, 1902), 4–54.

38. Cf. esp. John McTaggart and Ellis McTaggart, *Some Dogmas of Religion* (London: E. Arnold, 1906), 112ff.

in a pagan dualism between spirit and matter, destroys the unity of the human race, and erases the distinction between human beings and angels.[39]

CREATION AND TRADUCIANISM

By contrast, the argument between traducianism and creationism remained undecided in Christian theology.[40] In the ancient period the former had many advocates, such as Tertullian, Rufinus, Makarios, Eunomius, Apollinaris, Gregory of Nyssa, and according to a probably highly exaggerated statement by Jerome, even "by the majority of the Westerners." Later, however, with a few exceptions, it was only embraced by the Lutherans: by Luther himself (though he was initially a creationist),[41] then by Melanchthon, Gerhard, Quenstedt (et al.).[42] Creationism already appeared in Aristotle, and in the Christian church it received the early endorsement of Clement of Alexandria, Lactantius, Hilary, Pelagius, Cassian, Gennadius, Theodoret, Athanasius, Gregory of Nazianzus, Cyril, Alexandrinus, Ambrose, and others; thus Jerome could already speak of it as a church doctrine. Greek scholastic and Roman Catholic theologians, accordingly, have all adopted creationism,[43] and only a few, such as Klee, show some sympathy for traducianism.[44] The Reformed theologians, with few exceptions,[45] also opted for creationism.[46] Some theologians, such as especially Augustine and Gregory the Great, prefer to leave the question undecided,[47] and others look for a compromise.[48]

39. F. E. Daubanton, *Het Voortbestaan*, 55–78.

40. Ed. note: Traducianism holds that the soul is derived from the parents; creationism holds that God creates the soul at conception.

41. J. Köstlin, *Theology of Luther*, II, 348.

42. J. Gerhard, *Loci theol.*, VIII, c. 8; J. Quenstedt, *Theologia*, I, 519; D. Hollaz, *Examen theol.*, 414; F. A. Philippi, *Kirchliche Glaubenslehre* (Gütersloh: C. Bertelsmann, 1902), III, 103; A. F. C. Vilmar, *Handbuch der evangelischen Dogmatik* (Gütersloh: C. Bertelsmann, 1895), I, 348; F. Frank, *System der christliche Wahrheit*, I, 400; F. Delitzsch, *A System of Biblical Psychology*, 106ff.; H. Cremer, "Seele," *PRE³*, XIV, 27; A. von Oettingen, *Lutherische Dogmatik*, 2 vols. (Munich: C. H. Beck, 1897–1902), II, 370, 390ff.; W. Schmidt, *Christliche Dogmatik*, 4 vols. (Bonn: E. Weber, 1895–98), II, 260.

43. P. Lombard, *Sent.*, II, 17, 18; T. Aquinas, *Summa theol.*, qu. 90 and 118; idem, *Summa contra gentiles*, II, 86–89; R. Bellarmine, *De amiss. gr. et statu pecc.*, IV, 2; M. J. Scheeben, *Dogmatik*, II, 172ff.; J. Kleutgen, *Philosophie der Vorzeit*, 2d ed. (Münster: Theissing, 1860), II, 583ff.; J. B. Heinrich and C. Gutberlet, *Dogmatische Theologie*, 2d ed., 10 vols. (Mainz: Kirchheim, 1881–1900), VI, 265–315.

44. H. Klee, *Katholische Dogmatik*, 2d ed., 3 vols. (Mainz: Kirchheim, 1861), II, 313ff.

45. G. Sohn, *Opera sacrae theologiae* (Herborn: C. Corvin, 1593), II, 563; Justin Martyr, *Loci*, 81; W. G. T. Shedd, *Dogmatic Theology* (New York: Charles Scribner's Sons, 1888–89), II, 22, 75; III, 250.

46. J. Calvin, *Commentary on Hebrews*, trans. John Owen (Grand Rapids: Baker, 1979), 163–65 (on Heb. 12:9); J. Zanchi(us), *Op. theol.*, III, 609; A. Polanus, *Syn. theol.*, V, 31; G. Voetius, *Select. disp.*, I, 798; B. de Moor, *Comm. in Marckii Comp.*, II, 1064; III, 289; J. Marck, *Historia paradisi*, II, 4, §§7–9; etc.

47. Augustine repeatedly revisited the issue of the origin of the soul (*Literal Meaning of Genesis*, I, 10; *The Retractions*, II, 45) but always ended with the statement that he did not know. Also, Leo the Great, Isodore, Chemnitz, Buddeus, Musculus, Piscator, Maresius, van Oosterzee, Böhl, et al., refrained from taking a position.

48. G. W. Leibniz and J. C. Gottsched, *Theodicee* (Leipzig: Foerster, 1744), I, 91; R. Rothe, *Theologische Ethik*, 2d rev. ed., 5 vols. (Wittenberg: Zimmerman, 1867–71), §136; J. H. A. Ebrard, *Christliche Dogmatik,*

Indeed, in the strength of their arguments traducianism and creationism are almost equal. Traducianism appeals to the creation of Eve, of whose soul there is no special mention and who is therefore called "from" or "out of man" (*ex andros*; 1 Cor. 11:8; Gen. 2:23); to the language of Holy Scripture, which says that descendants were included in, and sprang from the loins of, their fathers (Gen. 46:26; Heb. 7:9–10); to the word *yāda*ʿ, to know, which is said to include a spiritual act; to the completion of creation on the seventh day (Gen. 2:2); to the fact that also animals can reproduce their own kind (Gen. 1:28; 5:3; 9:4; John 3:6); and especially to the hereditary transmission of sin and all sorts of psychological attributes.[49] Creationism, on the other hand, derives its support from the creation of Adam's soul (Gen. 2:7); many texts such as Ecclesiastes 12:7, Zechariah 12:1, and especially Hebrews 12:9 (cf. Num. 16:22), of which even Franz Delitzsch says: "There can hardly be a more classical proof text for creationism";[50] and above all from the simple, indivisible, immortal, spiritual nature of the soul.

And just as both traducianism and creationism advance weighty arguments for their respective positions, so both are incapable of solving the difficulties present in this area. Traducianism neither explains the origin of the soul nor the hereditary transmission of sin. As for the first difficulty, there are two possibilities: the first is to end with the theory that the soul of the child already existed in the parents and their ancestors—hence to a kind of belief in preexistence—or that the soul was potentially present in the seed of the man or the woman or in both (i.e., to come up with a materialist view). The second is that the parents themselves somehow produced it (i.e., to a creationist view), with the human agent in the place of God. As for the second difficulty, traducianism cannot help resolve it because sin is not material, not a substance, but a moral quality, moral guilt, and moral corruption.[51] To obviate these difficulties Daubanton pictures the new body originating as a result of material contact between the procreative products, and the new spiritual soul similarly originating as a result of spiritual (metaphysical) contact between the psychic potencies inherent in the procreative products. Both the ovum and the sperm are "ensouled" prior to this contact, and both are bearers of psychic life. Now, when the two touch and penetrate each other both physically and psychically (metaphysically) in the mother's body, they have the capacity not only to produce a material fetus

---

2d ed., 2 vols. (Konigsberg: A. W. Unser, 1862–63), I, 327ff.; H. Martensen, *Christian Dogmatics*, trans. William Urwick (Edinburgh: T. & T. Clark, 1871), 164–70; F. E. Daubanton, *Het Voortbestaan*, 195ff.

49. All these arguments are set forth at length by Daubanton, *Het voortbestaan*, 125ff. His main objection to creationism is that it is bound up with the doctrine of the covenant of works, which to him is an ingenious juridical invention (132, 141). He all too easily dismisses creationism when he writes that "the theologian of our day who does not practice his discipline in isolation from its sister disciplines as though in a cloister . . . has finished with this theory. He bequeaths to it a place of honor in the archives of the history of dogma" (150). Cf. Bierens de Haan, in ibid., 187.

50. F. Delitzsch, *System of Biblical Psychology*, 137–38.

51. The objections to traducianism and the grounds for creationism are unfolded at length by A. G. Honig, *Creationisme of Traducianisme?* (Kampen: J. H. Bos, 1906).

but also to produce in that fetus a new and newly become pneumatic human soul.[52] This scenario is of course [partially] correct.

[It is true that] insofar as both the ovum and the sperm, for as long as they are part of the living body, are "animated" [Ed.: *bezieled,* lit. "ensouled"]. But the crucial question here is what the nature of that "animated" life is. One can hardly imagine that in each of the two components, the ovum and the sperm, there is a "spiritual immortal" soul, as Daubanton himself describes the essence of the soul, for then the souls would be preexistent [cf. Wisd. 8:19–20; 2 Esd. 8:4ff.], every human being would possess countless souls, and each time the sperm and ovum would decompose, a soul would be lost. Daubanton, accordingly, does not speak of souls but of psychic potencies inherent in the sperm and ovum. But it is hard to tell what this expression—"psychic potencies"—means; capacities and powers can be potential as long as they do not begin to act, but a psychic potency is an impossible notion. A soul, as Daubanton himself defines it, either exists or doesn't exist. Presumably the idea is that the sperm and the ovum, both of them alive and "animated," possess the capacity to produce a fetus, which is itself alive and "animated." But then the same question recurs, namely, what is the nature of the life that the fetus possesses in its initial stages? If one answers that that life is already present, thanks to the individual immortal spiritual soul that indwells the fetus, one faces the question of where such a soul came from. It was present neither in the sperm nor in the ovum, nor can the union of the two produce it. If one answers that God gave to the sperm and the ovum the *capacity,* on being united, to produce a soul that neither of them had prior to the union but that is still spiritual and immortal, then we are actually dealing with another form of creationism. For then both sperm and ovum possess the actual *creative* power to impart existence to an immortal spiritual soul from within a life that, though "animated," is devoid of such a soul. And if one's answer to the question posed above is that sperm and ovum possess the capacity, upon being united, to produce a fetus which, though animated and alive, doesn't yet possess an immortal spiritual soul, but which is so organized that, after a period of development, it can attain the possession of an immortal spiritual soul, then one has only managed to shift the locus of the difficulty. For then one immediately faces the further questions of *when* and *how* the fetus becomes a human being, *when* and *how* psychic life becomes pneumatic life. And then one can only answer *either* in one of two ways. The first is that this occurs gradually in keeping with the laws of evolution. In that case, however, something vanishes—the *essential* difference between the psychic and the pneumatic life, between the vital soul and the immortal spiritual soul, between animal and man. The alternative is that the fetus itself has the capacity at a given moment to raise the psychic life into a spiritual soul. What we have then is another form of creationism, with this modification that now it is not God but a human (or better still a fetus) who becomes the creator.

52. F. E. Daubanton, *Het Voortbestaan,* 194, 205–7, 211, 240.

When traducianism pursues its own logic, it either lapses into materialism or again smuggles creationism into its tent under another label.

Another objection must be added. The moment an immortal spiritual soul dwells in an organism, there exists a human being, an individual, a personality, be it only germinally. Now somebody will say that either the sperm as such, or the ovum as such, or the fetus that originated from the union of the two in the first days of its life, is a human being who has a self of his or her own and will always exist. So there has to be a moment in which the fetus becomes a human being who will have his or her own independent and continuing existence. *When* this happens or *how* this happens is a mystery. Science has no idea when or how this happens, and theology with its conjecture of the fortieth or sixtieth day is only guessing. Creationism can no more explain this mystery than traducianism. But it has the advantage over the latter theory in that it is prepared respectfully to leave this mystery alone and not to subject it to a spurious explanation. The latter is the danger to which traducianism exposes itself. For if—as was stated above—it does not again smuggle in creationism under another name, it may nevertheless equip the sperm and ovum jointly or the fetus alone with a creative power, and so lapse into an evolutionary theory implying that animal life can gradually and of itself develop into human life. But evolutionary theory here, as in many other cases, is totally unable to explain the phenomena. This already applies in a chemical sense. A union of different atoms or substances exhibits properties that are very different from those that are unique to those of each of the components. For that reason—to cite an example—Oliver Lodge states: "There is no necessary justification for assuming that a phenomenon exhibited by an aggregate of particles must be possessed by the ingredients of which it is composed; on the contrary, wholly new properties may make their appearance simply by aggregation."[53]

Even in inanimate creatures the process of combining, uniting, or mixing elements already produces something new and, as it were, raises creation to a higher level. That is even much more powerfully true in the case of animate and rational beings. No person and particularly no person like, say, Goethe can be explained purely by genetics from his parents or ancestors. "Neither the physical stature of Goethe's father, nor his mother's happy disposition, give us any indication for understanding how this extraordinary personality came about. And just as genius suddenly makes its appearance, so also its marks soon disappear."[54] Granted, for years now an intense study has been made of the laws of heredity, but until now the result only consists in the knowledge that heredity is a complex question. The theories and hypotheses that have been posited in recent years have shed little or no light on the extent and manner

53. O. J. Lodge, *Life and Matter,* 4th ed. (London: Williams & Norgate, 1907), 49–50, and cf. further chs. 5 and 10.

54. W. Lexis, "Das Wesen der Kultur," in *Die allgemeinen Grundlagen der Kultur der Gegenwart,* by W. Lexis et al., Die Kultur der Gegenwart, I/1 (Berlin: Teubner, 1906), 16.

of hereditary transmission.[55] No one taking account of the uniqueness of the human soul and its frequently unique and outstanding gifts will therefore be able to avoid acknowledging—in addition to and in connection with the truth of traducianism—an important creationist component in the formation of the soul. This creative activity of God which, although we do not know it, undoubtedly makes its power felt in various other areas of nature and history as well, surely ties in as intimately as possible with what is given in the tradition: *by creating*, said Lombard already, God influenced them and by influencing creates them.[56] He does not first create a soul apart from the body in order then to introduce it into the body from without, but at the proper time[57] and in a manner incomprehensible to us[58] he elevates the existing psychic life to the level of a higher human spiritual life.[59] In keeping with this, accordingly, the hereditary transmission of sin cannot be explained by saying that the soul, though first created pure by God, is polluted by the body,[60] for in that case sin would be materialized. It is rather to be understood by the idea that the soul, though called into being as a rational spiritual entity by a creative activity of God, was nevertheless preformed in the psychic life of the fetus, that is, in the life of parents and ancestors, and thus receives its being, not from above or outside but under the conditions of, and amid, the sin-nexus that oppresses the human race.[61]

[300] Although creationism and traducianism both face insoluble difficulties, it is nevertheless remarkable that Eastern Orthodox, Roman Catholic, and Reformed theologians almost unanimously embraced the former view, while the latter found acceptance only among the Lutherans. This cannot be an accident; there has to be a reason for it. That reason lies in a different view of the nature and destiny of man. For in the first place, Lutheran theology locates the image of God solely in a number of moral qualities, in original righteousness. As always, so here as well, it limits its focus to the ethical-religious life of humanity and feels no need to relate this life to the whole of cosmic existence and to view it as a link in the whole counsel of God. As a result, human nature comes into its own neither vis-à-vis the angels nor vis-à-vis the animals. For if human beings possess this image of God, we are virtually equal to the angels. The difference between us and them, by comparison with what we have in common, is negligible. The angels also bear the image of God. And

55. W. H. Nieuwhuis, *Twee Vragen des Tijds* (Kampen: Kok, 1907), 76ff.

56. P. Lombard, *Sent.*, II, dist. 17.

57. Cf. A. Polanus, *Syn. theol.*, V, 31; Bucanus, *Inst. theol.*, VIII, 26.

58. T. Aquinas, *Summa theol.*, I, qu. 118, art. 2; idem, *Summa contra gentiles*, 59, 68.

59. Also Rabus writes that the "psychic life principle of the sensory organism, originally passed down by generation," can only be raised to a higher and independent human life "by the assumption of a divine act of creation" ("Vom Wirken und Wohnen des göttlichen Geistes in der Menschenseele," *Neue kirchliche Zeitschrift* 15 [November 1904]: 828).

60. P. Lombard, *Sent.*, II, dist. 31.

61. G. Voetius, *Select. disp.*, I, 1097; F. Turretin, *Institutes of Elenctic Theology*, IX, 12; B. de Moor, *Comm. in Marckii Comp.*, III, 289.

if humans lack this image, they fall to the level of the animals and become "blocks and stones."[62] What still distinguishes us from animals has so little theological and religious value that it is almost negligible. The crucial distinction, after all, consisted in possessing the image of God, an image humanity totally lost. Hence, the boundaries between human beings and angels and between human beings and animals are no longer sharply drawn here. Original righteousness is everything; all else in humanity is subordinate and virtually of no theological value. But for that reason it is also a matter of indifference to Lutheran theology *how* the human race originated. Rather, it is more correct to say that what human beings have in common with the angels, namely, the image of God, "original righteousness," can and must come into being only by an act of creation. *That,* in an absolute sense, is a gift. But everything else a human being possesses is passed down from one generation to the next in the same way as in the animal world. But Roman Catholic and Reformed theologians, even if they sometimes still denominated the angels as "image of God," from the beginning sought the image of God in the total and entirely unique nature of human beings. It certainly consisted in the virtues of knowledge, righteousness, and holiness, but these qualities, even in human beings, nevertheless bore a different character from those in the angels, and it not only consisted in those virtues but extended to all of our humanness. Hence, it also consisted in the fact that the human spirit *(pneuma)* was from the beginning adapted to union with a human body *(sōma),* and that the body *(sōma)* was from the beginning designed for the spirit *(pneuma).* Before and after the fall, in the state of integrity and that of corruption, in the state of grace and that of glory—human beings always are and always remain essentially distinct from the angels and the animals.

If human beings have the image of God, they do not become angels, and if they lose it, they do not become animals. Always and forever they remain human and to that extent are always and forever the image of God. This reality is sufficiently preserved only in creationism. Because human beings *exist* as wholly unique beings, they also *originate* in an entirely special way. Though related to angels and animals, they are nevertheless essentially different from them. Differing from them in their nature, they consequently differ from them also in their origin. Adam's creation was different from that of the animals and also different from that of the angels. Creationism alone sufficiently maintains the specific uniqueness of humanity since it fends off both pantheism and materialism and respects the boundaries between humanity and animals.

In the second place, a consequence of the Lutheran view of the image of God is that the moral unity of the human race has to take a backseat to physical descent. As a result of the fall human beings lost all spiritual and moral unity when they

---

62. Ed. note: Bavinck's phrase here is taken from Canons of Dort, III/IV, 16, which insists that "regeneration does not act in people as if they were blocks and stones; nor does it abolish the will and its properties or coerce a reluctant will by force, but spiritually revives, heals, reforms and—in a manner at once pleasing and powerful—bends it back."

lost the entire image of God. Natural religion and natural morality, and the like, are of almost no importance. Only physical descent holds them together and is at the same time the cause of their moral depravity. The sin, which has robbed humanity of all religion and morality and of the entire image of God, for that very reason cannot be passed on to all human beings by ethical means but only by physical descent. Granted, it is not a substance (though Luther and others, especially Flacius, used very strong language in this connection). It is still primarily a stain, a form of decay that affects the whole of a human being and above all kills the religious and ethical human faculties. In response and by contrast, Roman Catholic and Reformed theology, each in its own way, posited that the unity of mankind was not only of a physical but also of an ethical nature. Physical descent, certainly, is not enough; if it were, animal species would also constitute a unity. Similarity in moral virtues by itself is also insufficient; if it were sufficient, the angels among themselves and angels collectively with humanity would also constitute a unity. Animal species, though they are physically of one blood, are not a moral body *(corpus morale)*; and angels, though they form a unity, are not related by blood. Human uniqueness, therefore, requires that the unity of humankind be both physical and ethical. And because original sin is not physical in nature but only ethical, it can only be rooted in the ethical and federal unity of the human race. Physical descent is not sufficient to explain it and runs the danger of materializing it. The so-called realism, say of Shedd,[63] is inadequate both as an explanation of Adam's sin and as an explanation of righteousness by faith in Christ. Needed among human beings is another kind of unity, one that causes them to act unitedly as a moral body, organically connected as well as ethically united. And that is a federal unity. Now on the basis of a physical unity an ethical unity has to be constructed. Adam as our ancestor is not enough: he must also be the covenant head of the human race, just as Christ, though he is not our common ancestor in a physical sense, is still able, as covenant head, to bestow righteousness and blessedness upon his church. Now this moral unity of the human race can only be maintained on the basis of creationism, for it has a character of its own, is distinct from that of animals as well as that of the angels, and therefore also comes into being in its own way, both by physical descent and by a creative act of God, the two of them in conjunction with each other.

Finally, in the third place, in virtue of its view of the image of God Lutheran theology does not trouble itself much about human destiny. Adam had everything he needed; he only had to remain what he was. The distinction between the "able not to sin" *(posse non peccare)* and the "not able to sin" *(non posse peccare)* carries little weight. Perseverance is not a higher good granted in Christ to his own. Thus Adam did not have to gain anything higher for his descendants. For that purpose traducianism is sufficient; there is no room for a covenant of works or creationism.

63. Ed. note: See W. G. T. Shedd, *Dogmatic Theology,* 3d ed., 3 vols. (New York: Scribner, 1891–94), II, ch. 1: "Anthropology."

Again, Roman Catholic and Reformed theology thought otherwise, arguing as they did from another perspective. The destiny of man consists in heavenly blessedness, eternal life, the contemplation of God. But he can only reach this destiny in the way of obedience. There is no proportion between this obedience and that prospect. How then can that heavenly blessedness nevertheless be granted to a human being as a reward for his or her works? Rome says: Because in the image of God he or she is supplied with a supernatural grace that enables him or her to merit eternal life *ex condigno*. The Reformed theologian says: Because God has established a covenant with humanity and desires to give it eternal life, not in proportion to the value of works, but in accordance with his own gracious dispensation. Both parties, however, agree that the destiny of man lies in eternal blessedness, that this blessedness can only be reached in the way of moral obedience, and that on behalf of the whole human race God put the decision in this matter in the hands of Adam. And for that reason these two parties also arrived at creationism. Needed to this end was (1) that all human beings should be included under the covenant head, Adam; and (2) that at the same time they themselves should remain persons, individuals, having their own independence and responsibility. Physical descent alone would have resulted in a situation where the sin we received from Adam would be a deterministic fate, a process of nature, a sickness that had nothing to do with our will and hence did not imply any guilt on our part. That is not what sin is. Nor is the righteousness that Christ as the last Adam confers on us of that nature. Both the *sin* and the *righteousness* presuppose a federal relation between humanity as a whole and its heads.

Thus creationism maintains that every human person is an organic member of humanity as a whole, and at the same time that, in that whole, he or she occupies an independent place of his or her own. It upholds the unity of the human race in its entirety and at the same time the independent significance of every individual. Human beings are not specimens, not numbers of a kind, nor are they detached individuals like the angels. They are both parts of a whole and individuals: *living stones* of the *temple* of God. Creationism preserves the organic—both physical and moral—unity of humanity and at the same time it respects the mystery of the individual personality. Every human being, while a member of the body of humanity as a whole, is at the same time a unique idea of God, with a significance and destiny that is eternal! Every human being is himself or herself an image of God, yet that image is only fully unfolded in humanity as a whole! Whereas in virtue of that unity humanity as a whole fell in Adam, its progenitor and its head, that fall is nevertheless not a fate, a natural process, but on the contrary it is based on a free and sovereign dispensation of God. And this dispensation, however free and sovereign, is nevertheless so far removed from being arbitrary that it rather presupposes the physical connectedness of humankind, brings about and maintains its ethical unity, and is able to reveal and manifest in all its splendor not only the severity of God but also the riches of his grace. For when Adam falls Christ stands ready to take his place. The covenant of grace can replace the covenant of works because both are based on the same ordinances. If we could not have been condemned in Adam, neither could we have been acquitted in Christ. Hence, however the first human being should choose, creation could not miss its destiny. In Genesis cosmogony immediately passes over into geogony and geogony into anthropogony. The world, the earth, humanity are one organic whole. They stand, they fall, they are raised up together. The traces of God *(vestigia Dei)* in creation and the image of God in humanity may be mangled and mutilated by the sin of the first Adam; but by the last Adam and his re-creating grace they are all the more resplendently restored to their destiny. The state of integrity—either through the fall or apart from the fall—is a preparation for the state of glory in which God will impart his glory to all his creatures and be "all in all" [1 Cor. 15:28].

PART VI

GOD'S
FATHERLY
CARE

14

PROVIDENCE

God's work of preserving needs to be distinguished from that of creation,
though they are inseparable. Preservation is a great and glorious divine work
no less than creating new things out of nothing. Creation brings forth existence;
preservation is persistence in existence. Providence in some form is known
to all people, though not as the gracious care of a loving heavenly Father.
Providence is not merely foreknowledge but involves God's active will ruling all
things and includes preservation, concurrence, and government. The notion of
concurrence was developed to ward off pantheism on the one side and Deism
on the other. In the former providence coincides with the course of nature as
blind necessity; in the latter providence is replaced by pure chance, and God is
removed from the world. In this manner an attempt was made to exalt human
autonomy; for humanity to have freedom God must be absent or powerless.
God's sovereignty is viewed as a threat to humanity. Though the doctrine of
God's providence logically covers the entire scope of all God's decrees, extending
to all topics covered in dogmatics, it is preferable to restrict the discussion to
God's relation to his creation and creatures. Providence includes God's care
through the secondary causality of the created order of law as he maintains it.
A miracle is thus not a violation of natural law since God is no less involved
with maintaining the ordinary order of the natural created world. It is the
high respect Christianity has for the natural order of creation that encouraged
science and made it possible. The Christian posture toward creation's order is
never fatalism; astrology is appalling superstition. The providence of God does
not cancel out secondary causes or human responsibility. Governance points
to the final goal of providence: the perfection of God's kingly rule. While it is
correct on occasion to speak of divine "permission," this must not be construed
in such a way as to deny God's active sovereignty over sin and judgment. While
riddles remain for human understanding of providence, this doctrine affords
the believer with consolation and hope. God is Almighty Father: able and
desirous of turning everything to our good.

[301] When on the seventh day God completed his work that he had done, he
rested on the seventh day from all his work (Gen. 2:2; Exod. 20:11; 31:17).
Thus, Scripture describes the transition from the work of creation to that of

preservation. As Scripture also makes very clear (Isa. 40:28), this resting was not occasioned by fatigue, nor did it consist in God standing idly by. Creating, for God, is not work, and preserving is not rest. God's "resting" only indicates that he stopped producing new kinds of things (Eccles. 1:9–10); that the work of creation, in the true and narrow sense as producing things out of nothing *(productio rerum ex nihilo),* was over; and that he delighted in this completed work with divine pleasure (Gen. 1:31; Exod. 31:17; Ps. 104:31).[1] Creation now passes into preservation.

The two are so fundamentally distinct that they can be contrasted as labor and rest. At the same time they are so intimately related and bound up with each other that preservation itself can be called "creating" (Ps. 104:30; 148:5; Isa. 45:7; Amos 4:13). Preservation itself, after all, is also a divine work, no less great and glorious than creation. God is no indolent God *(deus otiosus).* He works always (John 5:17), and the world has no existence in itself. From the moment it came into being, it has existed only in and through and unto God (Neh. 9:6; Ps. 104:30; Acts 17:28; Rom. 11:36; Col. 1:15ff.; Heb. 1:3; Rev. 4:11). Although distinct from his being, it has no independent existence; independence is tantamount to nonexistence. The whole world with everything that is and occurs in it is subject to divine government. Summer and winter, day and night, fruitful and unfruitful years, light and darkness—it is all his work and formed by him (Gen. 8:22; 9:14; Lev. 26:3ff.; Deut. 11:12ff.; Job 38; Ps. 8, 29, 65, 104, 107, 147; Jer. 3:3; 5:24; Matt. 5:45; etc.). Scripture knows no independent creatures; this would be an oxymoron. God cares for all his creatures: for animals (Gen. 1:30; 6:19ff.; 7:2ff.; 9:9–17; Job 38:41; Ps. 36:7; 104:27; 147:9; Joel 1:20; Matt. 6:26; etc.), and particularly for humans. He sees them all (Job 34:21; Ps. 33:13–14; Prov. 15:3), fashions the hearts of them all, and observes all their deeds (Ps. 33:15; Prov. 5:21); they are all the works of his hands (Job 34:19), the rich as well as the poor (Prov. 22:2). God determines the boundaries of their habitation (Deut. 32:8; Acts 17:26), turns the hearts of all (Prov. 21:1), directs the steps of all (Prov. 5:21; 16:9; 19:21; Jer. 10:23; etc.), and deals according to his will with the host of heaven and the inhabitants of the earth (Dan. 4:35). They are in his hands as clay in the hands of a potter, and as a saw in the hand of one who pulls it (Isa. 29:16; 45:9; Jer. 18:5; Rom. 9:20–21).

God's providential government extends very particularly to his people. The entire history of the patriarchs, of Israel, of the church, and of every believer, is proof of this. What other people meant for evil against them, God turned to their good (Gen. 50:20); no weapon fashioned against them will succeed (Isa. 54:17); even the hairs on their head are all numbered (Matt. 10:30); all things work together for their good (Rom. 8:28). Thus all created things exist in the

---

1. Augustine, *City of God,* XI, 8; XII, 17; idem, *Literal Meaning of Genesis,* IV, 8ff.; P. Lombard, *Sent.,* II, dist. 15; T. Aquinas, *Summa theol.,* I, qu. 73; J. Calvin, *Commentary on Genesis,* trans. J. King (Grand Rapids: Baker, 1979), 103–5 (on Gen. 2:2); J. Zanchi(us), *Op. theol.,* III, 537.

power and under the government of God; neither chance nor fate is known to Scripture (Exod. 21:13; Prov. 16:33). It is God who works all things according to the counsel of his will (Eph. 1:11) and makes all things serviceable to the revelation of his attributes, to the honor of his name (Prov. 16:4; Rom. 11:36). Scripture beautifully sums up all this in repeatedly speaking of God as a king who governs all things (Ps. 10:16; 24:7–8; 29:10; 44:4; 47:6–7; 74:12; 115:3; Isa. 33:22; etc.). God is King: the King of kings and the Lord of lords; a King who in Christ is a Father to his subjects, and a Father who is at the same time a King over his children. Among creatures, in the world of animals, humans, and angels, all that is found in the way of care for, love toward, and protection of one by the other is a faint adumbration of God's providential order over all the works of his hands. His absolute power and perfect love, accordingly, are the true object of the faith in providence reflected in Holy Scripture.

Added to this witness of Scripture is the testimony of all peoples. The doctrine of divine providence is a "mixed article," known in part to all humans from God's revelation in nature. It is an article of faith in every—even in the most corrupt—religion. One who denies it undermines religion. Without it, there is no longer any room for prayer and sacrifice, faith and hope, trust and love. Why serve God, asks Cicero,[2] if he does not at all care about us? For that reason all religions agree with the statement of Sophocles:[3] "Still great above is Zeus, who oversees all things in sovereign power." Philosophy has also frequently recognized and defended this providence of God.[4] Nevertheless, the doctrine of providence as it comes to expression in pagan religion and philosophy was not identical with that doctrine in Christianity. Among pagans belief in providence was more theory than practice, more a matter of philosophical opinion than of religious dogma. It proved inadequate in time of distress and death and always swung back and forth between chance and fate. Since in Plato, for example, God was not the creator but only the shaper of the world, his power found its limit in finite matter.[5] Although Aristotle repeatedly mentions his belief in divine providence, for him it nevertheless totally coincides with the working of natural causes; the deity as "thought thinking itself" *(noēsis noēseōs)* exists in solitary self-contemplation outside the world, devoid of both will and action; a creature must expect neither help nor love from it.[6] In the teaching of the Stoa *foreknowledge (pronoia)* was identical with *destiny (heimarmenē)* and

---

2. M. T. Cicero, *On the Nature of the Gods,* I, 2.

3. Sophocles, *Electra,* 173 (trans. D. Grene [Chicago: University of Chicago Press, 1957]).

4. E.g., Socrates, in Xenophon, *Memorabilia,* I, 4; IV, 3; idem, *Oeconomicus;* Plato, *Leg.,* X, 901; idem, *Rep.,* X, 613A; Aristotle, *Eth. nic.,* X, 9; M. T. Cicero, "De Stoa," in *On the Nature of the Gods,* II; also see I, 2; III, 26; L. A. Seneca, *De providentia;* idem, *De beneficiis;* Plutarch, *De fortuna;* Plotinus, "On Fate" *(Enneads,* III, 1) and "On Providence" *(Enneads,* III, 2); Philo, *On Providence;* cf. E. Schürer, *The History of the Jewish People in the Age of Jesus Christ (175 B.C.–A.D. 135),* rev. and ed. Geza Vermes, Fergus Miller, and Matthew Black (Edinburgh: T. & T. Clark, 1979 [orig. ed., 1885]), III, 531ff.

5. E. Zeller, *Outlines of the History of Greek Philosophy,* 13th ed., trans. L. R. Palmer (New York: Humanities, 1969), 139, 147–48.

6. Ibid., 180, 198.

nature (physis), and according to Epicurus providence was inconsistent with the blessedness of the gods.[7] While some, like Plutarch and Plotinus, did their best to escape both chance and fate, in actual fact fate always again took a position behind and above the deity, whereas chance crept into the lower creatures and minor events from below. "The big things the gods take care of; the little ones they ignore" *(magna Dei curant, parva negligunt)*.[8]

[302] Christian belief in God's providence, however, is not of that kind. On the contrary, it is a source of consolation and hope, of trust and courage, of humility and resignation (Ps. 23; 33:10ff.; 44:4ff.; 127:1–2; 146:2ff.; etc.). In Scripture belief in God's providence is absolutely not based solely on God's revelation in nature but much more on his covenant and promises. It rests not only on God's justice but above all on his compassion and grace, and it presupposes the knowledge of sin (much more profoundly than is the case in paganism) but also the experience of God's forgiving love. It is not a cosmological speculation but a glorious confession of faith. Ritschl, accordingly, was right in again closely linking faith in providence to faith in redemption. In the case of the Christian, belief in God's providence is not a tenet of natural theology to which saving faith is later mechanically added. Instead, it is saving faith that for the first time prompts us to believe wholeheartedly in God's providence in the world, to see its significance, and to experience its consoling power. Belief in God's providence, therefore, is an article of the *Christian* faith. For the "natural" human being, so many objections can be raised against God's cosmic government that one can only adhere to it with difficulty. But the Christian has witnessed God's special providence at work in the cross of Christ and experienced it in the forgiving and regenerating grace of God, which has come to one's own heart. And from the vantage point of this new and certain experience in one's own life, the Christian believer now surveys the whole of existence and the entire world and discovers in all things, not chance or fate, but the leading of God's fatherly hand. Still, though all this has been unfolded by Ritschl with complete accuracy, saving faith may not be equated with, or dissolved in, faith in providence. Special revelation is distinct from general revelation, and a saving faith in the person of Christ is different from a general belief in God's government in the world. It is above all by faith in Christ that believers are enabled—in spite of all the riddles that perplex them—to cling to the conviction that the God who rules the world is the same loving and compassionate Father who in Christ forgave them all their sins, accepted them as his children, and will bequeath to them eternal blessedness. In that case faith in God's providence is no illusion, but secure and certain; it rests on the revelation of God in Christ and carries within it the

---

7. Ibid., 217, 237.

8. M. T. Cicero, *On the Nature of the Gods*, II, 167; cf. T. Pfanner, *Syst. theol. gentilis purioris* (Basel: Joh. Hermann Widerhold, 1679), c. 8; F. Creutzer, *Philosophorum veterum loci de providentia divina ac de fato* (Heidelberg: Gutmann, 1806); R. Schneider, *Christliche Klänge aus den griechischen und römischen Klassikern* (Gotha: F. A. Perthes, 1865), 231ff.

conviction that nature is subordinate and serviceable to grace, and the world [is likewise subject] to the kingdom of God. Thus, through all its tears and suffering, it looks forward with joy to the future. Although the riddles are not resolved, faith in God's fatherly hand always again arises from the depths and even enables us to boast in afflictions.[9]

THE LANGUAGE OF PROVIDENCE

In this connection it is noteworthy that Scripture does not use the abstract word "providence." Attempts have indeed been made to give to this word a scriptural character by appealing to Genesis 22:8; 1 Samuel 16:1; Ezekiel 20:6; and Hebrews 11:40. A few times the word [pronoia, pronoein] also occurs with reference to human forethought (Rom. 12:17; 13:14; 1 Tim. 5:8). But all this does not alter the fact that Scripture, speaking of God's providence, uses very different words. It does not compress the activity of God expressed by this word into an abstract concept and does not discuss its theological implications. Instead, it depicts the activity itself in a most splendid and vital way and exhibits it to us in history. Scripture in its totality is itself the book of God's providence. Thus depicting this providence, it refers to creating (Ps. 104:30; 148:5); making alive (Job 33:4; Neh. 9:6); renewing (Ps. 104:30); seeing, observing, letting (Job 28:24; Ps. 33:14ff.); saving, protecting, preserving (Num. 6:24ff.; Ps. 36:6; 121:7–8); leading, teaching, ruling (Ps. 9:19–20; 25:5, 9; etc.); working (John 5:17); upholding (Heb. 1:3); caring (1 Pet. 5:7). The word "providence" is derived from philosophy. According to Laertius, Plato was the first person to use the word *pronoia* in this sense.[10] The Apocrypha already uses the word (Wisd. 14:3; 17:2; 3 Macc. 4:21; 5:30; 4 Macc. 9:24; 13:19; 17:22) alongside *diatērein* (Wisd. 11:25), *diakybernan* (3 Macc. 6:2), and *dioikein* (Wisd. 8:1; etc.). The church fathers took it over and gave it legitimacy in Christian theology.[11]

In the process, however, the word underwent a significant change in meaning. Originally "providence" meant the act of foreseeing *(providentia)* or foreknowing *(pronoia)* what was to happen in the future. "Providence is that through which some future event is seen."[12] Thus conceived, the word was absolutely not fit to encompass everything the Christian faith confesses in the doctrine of God's providence. As advance knowledge of the future, the providence of God would of course solely belong under the heading of "the knowledge of God" and be fully treated in the locus on the attributes of God.

9. Cf. J. Ulrich, "Heilsglaube und Vorsehungsglauben," *Neue kirchliche Zeitschrift* 12 (1901): 478–93; F. Winter, "Wesen und Charakter des christliche Vorsehungsglaubens," *Neue kirchliche Zeitschrift* 18 (1907): 609–31.

10. E. Zeller, *Outlines of the History of Greek Philosophy*, 148.

11. J. C. Suicerus, "Pronoia," *Thesaurus ecclesiasticus, e patribus graecis ordine alphabetico* (Amsterdam: J. H. Wetsten, 1682).

12. "Povidentia est, per quam futurum aliquid videtur" (M. T. Cicero, *De inventione rhetorica*, II, 53).

But the Christian faith does not understand the providence of God to mean a mere foreknowledge *(nuda praescientia)*; it confesses that all things are not only known by God in advance but also determined and ordained in advance. For that reason providence was not only at an early stage attributed to the intellect but also to the will of God and described by John of Damascus as "that will of God by which all existing things receive suitable guidance through to their end."[13] Understood in that sense, the providence of God would belong to the doctrine of the decrees of God and have to be treated there. But again, the Christian faith confesses more than is indicated by the word in that sense. For the decrees of God are carried out, and the creatures who thereby come into being do not for a moment exist on their own but are only sustained from moment to moment by God's almighty hand. The origination and existence of all creatures have their origin, not in foreknowledge, nor even in a decree, but specifically in an omnipotent act of God. Hence, according to Scripture and the church's confession, providence is that act of God by which from moment to moment he preserves and governs all things. It is not only to "see for" *(Fürsehung)* but also to "foresee" *(Vorsehung)*.[14]

These different meanings attributed to the word "providence," however, were the reason why the place and content of this doctrine kept shifting in Christian dogmatics and were subjected to all kinds of changes. Sometimes it was counted among the attributes, then again among the decrees *(opera Dei ad intra)*, then to the outgoing works of God *(opera ad extra)*.[15] John of Damascus defines it as "the solicitude that God has for existing things," and though he treats it after the doctrine of creation, he does so in close connection with "foreknowledge" and "predestination."[16] Lombard discusses it in the chapter on predestination, but before creation.[17] Thomas offers a very clear exposition. First, he describes the doctrine in general as "the exemplar of the order of things foreordained toward an end" and considers it the primary part of prudence, whose precise task it is to order other things to an end. He then further adds that "two things pertain to the work of providence, namely the *exemplar* of the order, which is called 'providence' and 'disposition,' and the *execution* of the order, which is called 'government.'"[18] In line with these and other examples the doctrine of providence was either treated in Roman Catholic theology along with predestination

---

13. John of Damascus, *Exposition of the Orthodox Faith*, II, 29.

14. Ed. note: The two German words are functionally equivalent. *Fürsehung* was replaced by *Vorsehung* in the nineteenth century as the conventional term for "providence." *Fürsehung* is found in the semantic field that suggests "precaution," and our translation is an attempt to capture the idea that God's providence not only accompanies us in a caring way but is active in our behalf. The help of Dr. Barbara Carvill of Calvin College is gratefully acknowledged in helping sort out this linguistic puzzle.

15. See above, pp. 374–77 (#241).

16. John of Damascus, *Exposition of the Orthodox Faith*, II, 29–30.

17. P. Lombard, *Sent.*, I, dist. 35.

18. T. Aquinas, *Summa theol.*, I, qu. 22, art. 1; cf. Bonaventure, *Sent.*, I, dist. 35; and Hugo of St. Victor, *Sent.*, tr. 1, c. 12.

under the will of God,[19] or only as "preservation" *(conservatio)* or "govern-ment" *(gubernatio)*, each by itself, subsequent to the creation,[20] or in its entire scope and in its broadest sense after the locus of creation.[21]

Similarly, in the theology of the Reformation providence was sometimes viewed as a "counsel" *(consilium)* according to which God governs all things,[22] then again as an external work of God.[23] The difference, as Alsted and Baier correctly remarked,[24] pertained more to the term than to the matter itself. If God really maintains and governs the world, he must have foreknowledge of it *(providentia)*, will it, and be able to care for it *(prudentia)*, and also actu-ally so preserve and govern it in time that the end he had in mind would be attained. Taken in this broad sense, providence embraces (1) an internal act *(actus internus)*, which can further again be differentiated as "foreknowledge" *(prognōsis)*, a purpose or proposed end *(prothesis)*, and a plan *(dioikēsis)*;[25] and (2) an external act *(actus externus)*, which as the execution of the order *(executio ordinis)* was described as preservation *(conservatio)*, concurrence *(concursus)*, and government *(gubernatio)*. However, the internal act of this providence has already been completely treated earlier in the doctrine of the attributes and decrees of God. Hence here—after the doctrine of creation—providence can only be discussed as an external act, an act of God *ad extra*. Although providence in this sense can never be conceived in isolation from the internal act (the foreknowledge, purpose, and plan), it *is* distinct from it, just as the execution of a plan is distinct from that plan.

With that the word "providence" underwent a major modification. One may well therefore ask whether the word can still serve to describe the mat-ter itself. In the past, when providence was still treated in the doctrine of the attributes or decrees of God, it retained its original meaning; but since it has increasingly been understood as preservation and government and was dis-

19. D. Petavius, "De deo," in *Theol. dogm.*, VIII, chs. 1–5; M. Becanus, *Summa theologiae scholasticae* (Rouen: I. Behovrt, 1651), I, c. 13; *Theologia Wirceburgensi (Theologia dogmatica: Polemica, scholastica et moralis)*, 5 vols. (Wirceburgensi, 1852–53), III, 175; G. Perrone, *Prael. theol.*, II, 233; C. Pesch, *Praelectiones dogmaticae* (Freiburg i.B.: Herder, 1916–25), II, 158; P. Mannens, *Theologiae dogmaticae institutiones*, 3 vols. (Roermand: Romen, 1901–3), II, 105ff.

20. T. Aquinas, *Summa theol.*, I, qu. 103–5; idem, *Summa contra gentiles*, III, 65; idem, *Commentatores op sent.*, II, dist. 37; J. B. Heinrich and C. Gutberlet, *Dogmatische Theologie*, 2d ed., 10 vols. (Mainz: Kirch-heim, 1881–1900), V, 279.

21. J. Schwetz, *Theologia dogmatica catholica*, 3 vols. (Vienna: Congregationis Mechitharisticae, n.d.), I, 405; G. Jansen, *Prael. theol.*, II, 329; H. Th. Simar, *Lehrbuch der Dogmatik*, 2 vols. (Freiburg i.B.: Herder, 1879–80), 252; M. J. Scheeben, *Handbuch der katholischen Dogmatik*, 4 vols. (Freiburg i.B.: Herder, 1933), II, 12; F. Dieringer, *Lehrbuch der katholischen Dogmatik*, 4th ed. (Mainz: Kirchheim, 1858), 266ff.

22. Second Helvetic Confession, art. 6; Z. Ursinus, *Commentary on the Heidelberg Catechism*, trans. G. W. Willard (Grand Rapids: Eerdmans, 1954), qu. 27; J. Zanchi(us), *Op. theol.*, II, 425; S. Maresius, *Syst. theol.*, IV, §19; J. Alsted, *Theol.*, 174.

23. J. Calvin, *Institutes*, I.xvi.3–4; A. Polanus, *Syn. Theol.*, VI, 1; F. Junius, *Theses theologiae*, in *Opuscula theol. select.*, XVII, 1–2; *Synopsis purioris theologiae*, XI, 3; J. H. Heidegger, *Corpus theologiae*, VII, 3; etc.

24. J. Alsted, *Theol.*, 175; J. W. Baier, *Comp. theol.* (St. Louis: Concordia, 1879), I, 5, 2.

25. J. Gerhard, *Loci. theol.*, VI, c. 2.

cussed subsequent to creation, that original meaning has almost been totally lost. Providence in this latter, narrow sense is no longer a true *providentia*, no "exemplar of the order of things foreordained toward an end," for this precedes it and is assumed by it. It is itself the execution of the order. This execution, accordingly, was further defined in dogmatics as preservation *(conservatio)* or as government *(gubernatio)* or as a combination of the two.[26]

Later, to ward off pantheism and Deism, concurrence or cooperation was inserted between the two. Materially, this doctrine has always been treated as part of the doctrine of providence[27] but later also formally acquired a place of its own between preservation and government.[28] This shows that the word "providence" as a term for the execution of the order was not adequate and was further defined as "preservation" and "government." These terms are undoubtedly more precise, more graphic, and more in keeping with scriptural usage as well. Especially when the word "providence" is used abstractly and put in the place of God, as Plutarch already started doing,[29] with the rationalism of the eighteenth century following suit, it is open to objection. Still the word, which gained legitimacy in the language of theology and religion, may be kept, provided only that the matter described by it is understood in the scriptural sense.

NON-CHRISTIAN COMPETITORS

[303] The Christian doctrine of providence as an omnipotent act of God by which he preserves and governs all things must be distinguished not only from pagan "fate" and "chance" but consequently also from pantheism and Deism, which keep cropping up in revived forms over the centuries of Christianity. After all, "there are but three alternatives for the sum of existence: chance, fate,

26. L. C. Lactantius, *De ira Dei* (1543; reprinted, Darmstadt: Gentner, 1957), ch. 10; T. Aquinas, *Summa theol.*, I, qu. 103–4; Bonaventure, *Breviloquium*, pt. II; Belgic Confession, art. 13; Heidelberg Catechism, Lord's Day 10, Q. & A. 27–28; J. Zanchi(us), *Op. theol.*, II, 425; *Synopsis purioris theologiae*, XI, 3.

27. Augustine, *The Trinity*, III, 4; idem, *City of God*, V, 8–11; Theodoret, Bishop of Cyrrhus, *On Divine Providence*, X; Boethius, *The Consolation of Philosophy*, IV–V; John of Damascus, *Exposition of the Orthodox Faith*, II, 29; T. Aquinas, *Summa theol.*, I, qu. 48–49, 104, art. 2; I, qu. 105, art. 5; I, 2, qu. 19, art. 4; idem, Roman Catechism, I, c. 2, qu. 20; U. Zwingli, *On Providence and Other Essays*, trans. S. M. Jackson and ed. W. J. Hinks (Durham, N.C.: Labyrinth, 1983), c. 3; *Op.*, IV, 86; J. Calvin, *Institutes*, I.xvi.2; idem, *Treatises against the Anabaptists and Libertines* (*CR* 186), trans. and ed. B. W. Farley (Grand Rapids: Baker, 1982), 242–49; idem, "Providence," ch. 10 (*CR* 347–66), in *Concerning the Eternal Predestination of God*, trans. J. K. S. Reid (London: James Clarke, 1961); J. Zanchi(us), *Op. theol.*, II, 449; Justin Martyr, *Loci c.*, 56, 59; J. Wollebius, *Compendium theologiae*, c. 30; *Synopsis purioris theologiae*, XI, 13; J. Gerhard, *Loci theol.*, VI, c. 9; etc.

28. P. van Mastricht, *Theologia*, III, 10, 10.29; F. Turretin, *Institutes of Elenctic Theology*, VI, qu. 4; A. Comrie and N. Holthuis, *Examen van het Ontwerp van Tolerantie*, VI, 270; IX, 210; W. Brakel, *The Christian's Reasonable Service*, trans. B. Elshout (Ligonier, Pa.: Soli Deo Gloria, 1992), XI, 6; J. Marck, *Godg.*, X, 9; J. Quenstedt, *Theologia*, I, 531; D. Hollaz, *Examen theologicum acroamaticum* (Rostock and Leipzig: Russworm, 1718), 421; J. F. Buddeus, *Institutiones theologiae moralis* (Leipzig: Lipsiae, 1715), 409.

29. Cf. H. Cremer, *Biblico-Theological Lexicon of New Testament Greek*, trans. D. W. Simon and William Urwick (Edinburgh: T. & T. Clark, 1872), s.v., "pronoia."

or Deity. With chance there would be variety without uniformity, with fate there would be uniformity without variety; but variety in uniformity is the demonstration of primal design and the seal of the creative mind. In the world as it exists, there is infinite variety and amazing uniformity."[30]

The Problem of Pantheism

Pantheism knows of no distinction between the being of God and the being of the world and—idealistically—lets the world be swallowed up in God or—materialistically—lets God be swallowed up in the world. On that position there is no room for the [act of] creation and therefore no room, in the real sense, for preservation and government. Providence, then, coincides with the course of nature. The laws of nature are identical with the decrees of God, and the rule of God is nothing other than "the fixed and immutable order of nature" or "the concatenation of natural things."[31] On that view there is no room for miracle, the self-activity of secondary causes, personality, freedom, prayer, sin, and religion as a whole. While pantheism may present itself in ever so beautiful and seductive a form, it actually takes its adherents back into the embrace of a pagan fate. On its premises there is no existence other than the existence of nature; no higher power than that which operates in the world in accordance with ironclad law; no other and better life than that for which the materials are present in this visible creation. For a time people may flatter themselves with the idealistic hope that the world will perfect itself by an immanent series of developments, but soon this optimism turns into pessimism, this idealism into materialism.

Over against this pantheism it was the task of Christian theology to maintain the distinction between creation and preservation, the self-activity of secondary causes, the freedom of personality, the character of sin, the truth of religion. It did this by rejecting fate and by clearly elucidating the confession of God's providence in distinction from it. The distinguishing feature of the theory of fate is not that all that exists and occurs in time is grounded and determined in God's eternal counsel, but the idea that all existence and occurrence is determined by a power that coincides with the world and that, apart from any consciousness and will, determines all things through blind necessity. According to Cicero, the fate of the Stoa was "an order and series of causes, with one cause producing another from within itself."[32] A further distinction made was that between a *mathematical* or *astral* fate, when events on earth were thought to be determined by the stars, and a *natural* fate, when they were deemed to be determined by the nexus of nature. It is in this latter form that the theory of fate presently appears in pantheism and materialism. It is noteworthy, however,

---

30. James Douglas, in H. B. Smith, *System of Christian Theology* (New York: Armstrong, 1890), 107.

31. B. Spinoza, *Tractatus Theologico-Politicus*, trans. S. Shirley (Leiden: Brill, 1991), c. 3; cf. D. F. Strauss, *Die christliche Glaubenslehre*, 2 vols. (Tübingen: Osiander, 1840–41), II, 384; F. Schleiermacher, *The Christian Faith*, ed. H. R. MacIntosh and J. S. Steward (Edinburgh: T. & T. Clark, 1928), §46; cf. above, pp. 410–11 (#251).

32. M. T. Cicero, *De divinatione*, 1; cf. Seneca, *De beneficiis*, IV, 7; idem, *Nat.*, II, qu. 36.

that in recent times also belief in astral fate has been reinvigorated and has its enthusiastic advocates.[33] Now, Christian theology by no means opposes the idea that all things were known and determined by God from eternity. To that extent it even recognized a "fate," and some theologians believed they could also use the word in a good sense. If we remember, says Augustine, that *fatum* is a derivative of *fari* and then describe by means of it the eternal and unchanging word by which God sustains all things, the name can be justified.[34] Boethius referred to fate as "a disposition inherent in changeable things by which Providence connects all things in their due order."[35] And even Maresius believed he could make Christian sense of the word.[36] But as a rule people were more cautious. Belief in fate, after all, proceeded from the idea that all things happen as a result of an irresistible blind force having neither consciousness nor will, and those events were called *fatalia,* which happen apart from the will of God and men by the necessity of a certain order.[37] In this sense, "fate" was most firmly opposed by all Christian theologians, by Augustine and his followers no less than by those who championed free will. "So far from saying that everything happens by fate, we say that nothing happens by fate."[38] On the Christian position, the only "necessity of order" is the wise, omnipotent, loving will of God. This is not to deny, as will appear later, that in the world of creatures there is a nexus of causes and consequences, and that there are firm ordinances. However, the natural order is not behind and above, nor outside of and opposed to, God's will, but grounded in the will of an omnipotent and loving God and Father, governed by that will and serviceable to that will. Nor does it stand, as a blind coercive power, outside of and in opposition to our will, for "the fact is that our choices fall within the order of the causes, which is known for certain to God and is contained in his foreknowledge."[39]

The Problem of Deism

On the other side of this spectrum stands Deism, which separates God and the world. This position is one that, in total or in part, separates the creatures from God, once they have been created; and then, again in larger or smaller part, it allows them to exist and function on their own power, a power received at the time of creation. Deism thus basically revives the pagan theory of

33. Cf. *Wetenschappelijke Bladen* 4 (1896): 453; *De Holl. Revue* (September 25, 1905).

34. Augustine, *City of God,* V, 9.

35. Boethius, *The Consolation of Philosophy,* bk. IV, 6.

36. S. Maresius, *Syst. theol.,* 149.

37. Augustine, *City of God,* V, 3.

38. Ibid.

39. Ibid., and further comments in Bonaventure, *Sent.,* I, dist. 35; T. Aquinas, *Summa theol.,* I, qu. 116; idem, *Summa contra gentiles,* III, 93; D. Petavius, "De Deo," in *Theol. dogm.,* VIII, ch. 4; J. Gerhard, *Loci theol.,* VI, 13; J. Calvin, *Institutes,* I.xvi.8; T. Beza, *Volumen tractationum theologicarum* (Geneva, 1573–76), I, 313ff.; H. Alting, *Theologia elenctica nova* (Amsterdam, 1654), 290; J. H. Heidegger, *Corpus theologiae,* VII, 2; F. Turretin, *Institutes of Elenctic Theology,* VI, 2; C. Vitringa, *Doctr. christ.,* II, 170, 177–81; K. G. Bretschneider, *Systematische Entwicklung aller in der Dogmatik* (Leipzig: J. A. Barth, 1841), 472.

chance. Jerome once stated—more or less echoing Aristotle, Epicurus, Cicero, the Sadducees,[40] and others whose slogan was that "the gods take care of the big things but ignore the small"—that God's providential care did not cover all small insects.[41] Pelagianism, like Cicero,[42] attributed virtue to people's own will and power, while semi-Pelagianism divided the work, attributing some to both God and man. Later, when this system penetrated Catholic theology, no small dissension arose over God's cooperation in providence. The Thomists conceived it as a "natural predetermination," "an application of energy for the purpose of making it work."[43] The Molinists, on the other hand, understood by it a kind of "simultaneous concourse, a merely formal cooperation, by which God—with the concurrence of the other—exerted influence on the same act and effect."[44]

Socinianism so abstractly and dualistically opposed the infinite to the finite that God could not even create the world out of nothing but only from an eternally existing finite substance. In accordance with this view it also withdrew a large area of the world from God's providence, leaving it to the independent insight and judgment of mankind. By nature the human will is so free that God cannot even beforehand calculate what a person will do in a given case. Only when a decision has been made does God adapt his own action to it. Free causes, accordingly, function in complete independence alongside and outside of God. The relation between God and the world is like that between a mechanical engineer and a machine. After making it and starting it, he leaves it to its own devices and only intervenes if something has to be repaired.[45] The Remonstrants similarly judged that at the creation creatures were endowed with powers enabling them to live independently. Preservation, therefore, was a negative act of God, implying that he did not wish to destroy the essences, powers, and faculties of created things but to leave them to their own vigor to the extent that they were able to flourish and endure by the power with which they had been endowed by creation—at least this view was not judged incorrect. In this connection, concurrence—defined "as a certain natural influence in all things emanating from the perfection of the divine nature"—was rejected. The idea of the predestination of the number of people, of marriages, of the end of life, of the elect, and of the lost, was contested; free will was defended; and all "efficacious providence with respect to sin" was replaced by a negative "permission" or

40. On the Sadducees, see E. Schürer, *History of the Jewish People*, II, 392ff.

41. See above, p. 196 (#200).

42. M. T. Cicero, *On the Nature of the Gods*, III, 36.

43. T. Aquinas, *Summa theol.*, I, 2, qu. 9, art. 6 to 3, qu. 79, 109; idem, *Summa contra gentiles*, III, 67–70, 162.

44. Cf. Daalman, *Summa S. Thomae*, II, 286–314; *Theologia Wirceburgensi*, I, c. 2; P. Dens, *Theologia moralis et dogmatica*, 8 vols. (Dublin: Richard Coyne, 1832), I, 66ff.; M. Liberatore, *Institutiones philosophicae* (Rome, 1861), III, c. 4a, 1–2; M. J. Scheeben, *Handbuch der katholischen Dogmatik*, II, 22ff.; G. Jansen, *Prael. theol.*, II, 334.

45. J. Volkel, *De vera religione libri quinque* (Racoviae, 1630), II, c. 7; J. Crell, *De Deo et ejus attributis*, c. 2–6; O. Fock, *Der Socinianismus* (Kiel: C. Schröder, 1847), 496ff.

"nonobstruction."[46] Although Arminianism was condemned at Dordrecht and expelled from the Reformed domain, as an intellectual trend it found acceptance everywhere and penetrated all Christian countries and churches.

The period beginning in the middle of the seventeenth century was marked by a powerful effort to emancipate nature, world, humanity, science, and so forth from God and to make them self-reliant in relation to him, to Christianity, church, and theology. In this respect latitudinarianism, Deism, rationalism, and the Enlightenment were all in agreement.[47] This is the best of all possible worlds; endowed with intellect and will, humanity is self-sufficient; natural law, the forces of nature, natural religion, and natural morality together comprise a reserve of energies with which God endowed the world at the creation and which are now entirely adequate for its existence and development. Revelation, prophecy, miracles, and grace are totally redundant. Deism did not deny the existence of God, creation, or providence. On the contrary, it loved to refer to the "Supreme Being" and discoursed at length on providence. But there was no longer any vitality in this belief. Deism in principle denied that God worked in creation in any way other than in accordance with and through the laws and forces of nature. Thus it was, from the outset, antisupranaturalistic. Preservation was enough; a kind of cooperation or divine influx operative along with every act of a creature was unnecessary.[48]

In its eighteenth-century form, this Deism indeed belongs to the past. But in substance in both theory and practice it still holds sway in wide circles. Since, especially in the present [nineteenth] century, our knowledge of nature has greatly expanded and the stability of its laws has been recognized, many people are inclined to separate nature in its pitiless and unchanging character from God's government, to let it rest independently in itself, and to restrict the providence of God to the domain of religion and ethics. But here, of course, providence cannot be taken absolutely either and finds its limit in human freedom.[49] It is not surprising that with such a view the old doctrine of "concurrence" was no longer understood and was set aside as superfluous or incorrect.[50]

46. S. Episcopius, *Inst. theol.,* IV, sect. 4; idem, *Apol. conf.; Conf. remonstr.,* in S. Episcopius, *Op. theol.;* P. van Limborch, *Theol. christ.,* II, 25ff.

47. On Deism, cf. G. V. Lechler, *Geschichte des englischen Deismus* (Tübingen, 1814); idem, "Deismus," *PRE²*; E. Troeltsch, "Deismus," *PRE³,* IV, 532–59; B. Pünjer, *Geschichte der christlichen Religionsphilosophie seit der Reformation* (Brussels: Anastaltique Culture et Civilisation, 1880–83), I, 209ff.; J. W. Hanne, *Die Idee der absoluten Personlichkeit,* 2d ed. (Hannover: C. Rumpler, 1865), II, 76ff.; T. Pesch, *Die grossen Welträthsel,* 2d ed., 2 vols. (Freiburg i.B.: Herder, 1892), II, 534ff.; J. I. Doedes, *Inleiding tot de Leer van God* (Utrecht: Kemink, 1870), 80ff.

48. F. V. Reinhard, *Grundriss der Dogmatik* (Munich: Seidel, 1802), §61; J. A. L. Wegscheider, *Institutiones theologiae christianae dogmaticae* (Halle: Gebauer, 1819), §106.

49. Cf. G. Kreibig, *Die Räthsel der göttlichen Vorsehung* (Berlin, 1886); W. Schmidt, *Die göttliche Vorsehung und das Selbstleben der Welt* (1887); idem, *Christliche Dogmatik,* 4 vols. (Bonne: E. Weber, 1895–98), I, 216ff.; W. Beyschlag, *Zur Verständigung über den christlichen Vorsehungsglauben* (Halle: Eugen Strien, 1888).

50. R. Rothe, *Theologische Ethik,* 2d rev. ed., 5 vols. (Wittenberg: Zimmerman, 1867–71), §54; J. Müller, *The Christian Doctrine of Sin,* trans. W. Urwick, 5th ed. (Edinburgh: T. & T. Clark, 1868), I, 318; A. F. C.

On those premises it even follows naturally to do what the "ethical" modernists[51] have done in our country, namely, juxtapose and contrapose natural power and moral power as it were like two deities in the Manichaean manner. This runs the risk that the domain of the latter, like that of the Native Americans, will increasingly shrink and finally be taken over completely by blind irrational forces.[52] This consequence is probably the most serious objection to Deism. By separating God from the world, the infinite from the finite, and placing them dualistically side by side, it turns the two into competing powers that are continually at loggerheads as they vie for sovereignty. Whatever is ascribed to God is taken from the world. The more God's providence is expanded, the more the creature loses its independence and freedom, and conversely, the creature can only maintain its self-activity if it drives God back and deprives him of his sovereignty. Peace between the two is therefore possible only on condition of complete separation.

Deism is essentially irreligious. For the Deist the salvation of humanity consists not in communion with God but in separation from him. The Deist's mind is at ease only in detachment from God, that is, if he can be a practical atheist. And because he realizes he can never free himself from God, he is a fearful creature, always afraid that he will be deprived of a part of his domain. For that reason there are always gradations in Deism; the boundaries between God's activity and that of the world are ever being drawn differently. There are entire, one-half, and three-quarters Pelagians, and so forth, depending on whether the world and humanity are completely or in greater or smaller part withdrawn from God's control. In principle, Deism is always the same: it deactivates God, but one Deist will walk that road further than another. A Deist is a person who in his short life has not found the time to become an atheist.[53] Now, the area that Deism takes out from under God's rule then falls under the sway of another power, be it fate or chance. Also in this regard, Deism constantly gets into conflict with itself. Especially today, now that everyone is so deeply convinced of the stability of the natural order, there is no room in it for chance, and Deism again falls back into the embrace of ancient fate, while chance is mainly reserved for the domain of religious and ethical concerns. But the doctrine of chance is no better than that of fate. "Fate" could, in a pinch, still have a good meaning in the Christian world-and-life view; but

---

Vilmar, *Handbuch der evangelischen Dogmatik* (Gütersloh: C. Bertelsmann, 1895), I, 255; R. A. Lipsius, *Lehrbuch der evangelisch-protestantischen Dogmatik* (Braunschweig: C. A. Schwetschke, 1893), §§397ff.; W. Schmidt, *Christliche Dogmatik*, II, 210ff.; J. J. van Oosterzee, *Christian Dogmatics*, trans. J. Watson and M. Evans, 2 vols. (New York: Scribner, Armstrong, 1874), §59, 5, 7; cf. also F. Philippi, *Kirchliche Dogmatik*, 3d ed., II, 266; and J. Köstlin, "Concursus Divinus," *PRE³*, IV, 262–67.

51. Ed. note: Bavinck's reference here is to a mediating school of Dutch theology known as the *Ethischen*. See H. Bavinck, *Reformed Dogmatics*, I, 127 (#39), 171 (#53), 290–92 (#83), 372 (#102), 436 (#115), 471–72 (#123), 519–20 (#135); idem, *De Theologie van Prof. Daniel Chantepie de la Saussaye* (Leiden: D. Donner, 1884).

52. See H. Bavinck, *Reformed Dogmatics*, I, 540 (#142).

53. H. P. G. Quack, "Port Royal par Sainte-Beuvre," *De gids* 36 (December 1872): 180.

chance *(casus)* and fortune *(fortuna)* are un-Christian through and through. Something is "fortuitous" only in the eyes of people when at that moment they are ignorant of its cause. But nothing is or can be objectively "fortuitous." All things have a cause, and that cause is ultimately a component in the almighty and all-wise will of God.[54]

AN ATTEMPT AT DEFINITION

[304] The providence of God, thus distinguished from God's knowledge and decree and maintained against pantheism and Deism, is—in the beautiful words of the Heidelberg Catechism—"the almighty and ever present power of God by which he upholds, as with his hand, heaven and earth and all creatures and so rules them that . . . all things, in fact, come to us, not by chance but from his fatherly hand" (Lord's Day 10, Q. & A. 27). Even thus defined, the doctrine of providence has enormous scope. It actually encompasses the entire implementation of all the decrees that have bearing on the world after it has been called into being by creation. If the act of creation is excepted from providence, it is as full as the free knowledge of God *(scientia libera)* and the decrees of God, as is everything that exists and occurs in time. It extends to everything that is treated in dogmatics after the doctrine of creation and includes both the works of nature and of grace. All the works of God *ad extra,* which are subsequent to creation, are works of his providence. Only, the locus of providence does not discuss these works themselves but describes in general the nature of the relation in which God stands to the created world, which is always the same, notwithstanding the many different works that he in his providence accomplishes in the world. For that reason it is also not desirable for us to bring up in this locus a vast array of topics such as miracles, prayer, the end of life, the freedom of the will, sin, theodicy, and so forth, for in part these topics have already been treated earlier in the context of the doctrine of the attributes and decrees of God, and in part they will be fully treated in their own place. The task of theodicy is not confined to the locus of providence alone but rests on the whole field of dogmatics. Hence, the doctrine of providence does not include the material to be considered in the following loci but limits itself to a description of the relation—one that remains the same in all the various works—in which God stands toward his creatures. That relation

54. Cf. Augustine, *Eighty-three Different Questions,* trans. D. L. Mosher, Fathers of the Church 70 (Washington, D.C.: Catholic University of America Press, 1982), qu. 24; idem, *Against the Academics,* I, 1; idem, *Divine Providence and the Problem of Evil,* I, 2; idem, *City of God,* V, 3; T. Aquinas, *Summa theol.,* I, qu. 22, art. 2; I, qu. 103, art. 5; *Summa contra gentiles,* III, 72; J. Gerhard, *Loci theol.,* VI, 3; J. Calvin, *Institutes,* I.xvi.2, 9; D. Chamier, *Panstratiae catholicae* (Geneva: Rouer, 1626), II, 2, 4ff.; F. Turretin, *Institutes of Elenctic Theology,* III, qu. 12; P. Mastricht, *Theologia,* III, 10, 30; J. Müller, *Sünde,* II, 34ff.; C. H. Weisse, *Philosophische Dogmatik oder Philosophie des Christentums,* 3 vols. (Leipzig: Hirzel, 1855–62), I, 518; J. Kirchner, *Über den Zufall* (Halle: Pfeffer, 1888); G. Rümelin, "Über den Zufall," *Deutsche Rundschau* (March 1890): 353–64; R. Eisler, "Zufall," *Wörterbuch der philosophischen Begriffe,* 3 vols. (Berlin: E. S. Mittler & Sohn, 1910); E. Dennert, *Natuurwet, Toeval, Voorzienigheid* (Baarn: Hollandia, 1906).

is expressed by the words "preservation," "concurrence," and "government," which over time were viewed as aspects of providence. Whatever God may do in nature and grace, it is always he who preserves all things, who empowers them by the influx of his energy, and who governs them by his wisdom and omnipotence. Preservation, concurrence, and government, accordingly, are not parts or segments in which the work of providence is divided and which, being materially and temporally separate, succeed one another. Nor do they differ from one another in the sense that preservation relates only to the existence of creatures, concurrence only to their activities, and government exclusively to guidance toward the final goal of these creatures. But they are always integrally connected; they intermesh at all times. From the very beginning preservation is also government, and government is concurrence, and concurrence is preservation. Preservation tells us that nothing exists, not only no substance, but also no power, no activity, no idea, unless it exists totally from, through, and to God. Concurrence makes known to us the same preservation as an activity such that, far from suspending the existence of creatures, it above all affirms and maintains it. And government describes the other two as guiding all things in such a way that the final goal determined by God will be reached. And always, from beginning to end, providence is one simple, almighty, and omnipresent power.

Conceived as such a power and act of God, providence is most intimately connected with, while nevertheless being essentially distinct from, the activity of God in creating the world. Pantheism and Deism, in addressing the problem that is present here, seek to solve it by denying either creation [pantheism] or providence [Deism]. But theism maintains both and attempts to elucidate for theoretical as well as practical reasons both the unity and the distinction between the two. Always to be a theist in the full and true sense of the word, that is, to see God's counsel and hand and work in all things and simultaneously, indeed for that very reason, to develop all available energies and gifts to the highest level of activity—*that* is the glory of the Christian faith and the secret of the Christian life.

Scripture itself leads the way in taking this approach. On the one hand, it describes the activity of providence as an activity of creation (Ps. 104:30), of making alive (Neh. 9:6), of speaking (Ps. 33:9; 105:31, 34; 107:25; Job 37:6), of sending out his Word and Spirit (Ps. 104:30; 107:25), of commanding (Ps. 147:15; Lam. 3:37), of working (John 5:17), of upholding (Heb. 1:3), of willing (Rev. 4:11), so that all things without exception exist from, through, and to God (Acts 17:28; Rom. 11:36; Col. 1:17). God is never idle. He never stands by passively looking on. With divine potency he is always active in both nature and grace. Providence, therefore, is a positive act, not a giving permission to exist but a causing to exist and working from moment to moment. If it consisted merely in a posture of nondestruction, it would not be God who upheld things, but things would exist in and by themselves, using power granted at the creation. And this is an absurd notion. A creature is, by definition, of itself a completely dependent being: that which does not exist *of* itself cannot for a moment exist *by* itself either. If God does not do anything, then nothing exists and nothing happens. "For the power and might of the Creator, who rules and embraces all, makes every creature abide, and if this power ever ceased to govern creatures, their essences would pass away and all nature would perish."[55] And just as providence is a power and an act, so it is also an almighty and everywhere present power. God is immanently present with his being in all creatures. His providence extends to all creatures; all things exist in him. Scripture posits with the utmost certainty that nothing, however insignificant, falls outside of God's providence. Not just all things in general (Eph. 1:11; Col. 1:17; Heb. 1:3), but even the hairs of one's head (Matt. 10:30), sparrows (Matt. 10:29), the birds of the air (Matt. 6:26), the lilies of the field (Matt. 6:28), the young ravens (Ps. 147:9)—all are the objects of his care. In any case, what is small or large to him who is only great? In the context of the cosmos that which is small is as important in its setting as that which is large, as indispensable and as necessary, and often of even greater significance and of weightier consequence.[56] While providence may be differentiated as "general" (Ps. 104; 148:1–13), "special" (Ps. 139:15ff.; Job 10:9–12; Matt. 12:12; Luke 12:7), and "most special" (1 Tim. 4:10), as a power of God it nevertheless encompasses every single creature. Though Habakkuk (1:14) complains that God by his chastisements makes people like the fish of the sea that are caught in a net and like crawling things that have no ruler (i.e., to protect them from their enemies), he is not thereby saying that God's providence does not extend to all his creatures. In defense of the limited scope of God's providence, people appeal with greater semblance of veracity to 1 Corinthians 9:9 ("Is it for oxen that God is concerned?"). Still, Paul, who everywhere else takes God's sovereignty to be absolute (Acts 17:28; Rom. 11:36; Col. 1:17), by no means denies here that God's concern also includes oxen; he only indicates that this saying is included in the law of God for humanity's sake, not for the sake of oxen. Also, this saying concerning the oxen is there "for our sake" (*di' hēmas*, 1 Cor. 9:10; cf. Rom. 4:23–24; 15:4; [1 Cor. 10:6;] 2 Tim. 3:16) so that we might learn from it that the gospel worker is worthy of his wages. So then, providence as an activity of God is as great, all-powerful, and omnipresent as creation; it is a continuous or continued creation. The two are one single act and differ only in structure.[57]

55. Augustine, *Literal Meaning of Genesis*, IV, 12; idem, *Confessions*, IV, 17; cf. T. Aquinas, *Summa theol.*, I, qu. 104, arts. 1–4; idem, *Summa contra gentiles*, III, 65ff.; J. Calvin, *Institutes*, I.xvi.4; M. Leydekker, *Fax veritatis* (1677), VIII, 2; J. Alsted, *Theol.*, 304.

56. Cf. Calvin, cited by Paul Henry, *The Life and Times of John Calvin*, trans. Henry Stebbing, 2 vols. (New York: Robert Carter & Brothers, 1853), I, 358.

57. Augustine, *Literal Meaning of Genesis*, IV, 15; idem, *Confessions*, IV, 12; idem, *City of God*, XII, 17; T. Aquinas, *Summa theol.*, I, qu. 104, art. 2; J. Quenstedt, *Theologia*, I, 351; Z. Ursinus, *Commentary on the Heidelberg Catechism*, qu. 27; C. Vitringa, *Doctr. christ.*, II, 183; H. Heppe, *Die Dogmatik der evangelisch-reformierten Kirche* (Elberseld: R. L. Friedrich, 1861), 190.

When earlier theologians used this language, it was by no means their intention to erase the distinction that exists between creation and providence, as Hodge for one fears.[58] Scripture, on the other hand, represents providence as a resting from the work of creation (Gen. 2:2; Exod. 20:11; 31:17), and further as a seeing (Ps. 14:2; 33:13), and observing (Ps. 33:15; 103:3), all of which presuppose the existence, the self-activity, and the freedom of the creature. *These* scriptural givens may not be neglected either. Creation and providence are not identical. If providence meant a creating anew every moment, creatures would also have to be produced out of nothing every moment. In that case, the continuity, connectedness, and "order of causes" would be totally lost, and there would be no development or history. All created beings would then exist in appearance only and be devoid of all independence, freedom, and responsibility. God himself would be the cause of sin. Although many theologians called providence a "continuous creation," they by no means meant to erase the difference between the two. They all regarded providence rather as simultaneously also an act of causing creatures to persist in their existence, as a form of preservation that presupposes creation. Augustine, for example, writes that God rested on the seventh day and no longer created any new species, and continues by describing the work of providence in distinction from that of creation as follows: "God moves his entire creation by a hidden power. . . . It is thus that God unfolds the generations that He laid up in creation when first He founded it; and they would not be sent forth to run their course if He who made creatures ceased to exercise His provident rule over them."[59] Providence may sometimes be called a creation, therefore, but it is always distinguished from the first and actual creation by the fact that it is a "continuous creation."

So the two agree in that it is the same omnipotent and omnipresent power of God that is at work both in creation and in providence. The latter act is not inferior to the former since power, divine power, is required for both. Also, creation and providence are naturally not distinct in God himself either, for in him, the Eternal One, there is no variation or shadow due to change. He did not pass from not-creating to creating, nor from creating to preserving. He is invariably the same.[60] Creation and preservation, accordingly, are not objectively and materially distinct as acts of God in God's being, but only in reason. But that understanding is not to say that the distinction is arbitrary and only exists in our mind. No: that distinction is most definitely grounded in God's revelation and derived from it by our thinking. There is a difference between creation and preservation, but that difference does not lie in God's being as such but in the relation that God assumes toward his creatures. What happens to things as a result of creation is one thing; what happens with them

---

58. Charles Hodge, *Systematic Theology,* 3 vols. (New York: Charles Scribner's Sons, 1888), I, 577ff.

59. Augustine, *Literal Meaning of Genesis,* V, 20.

60. See above, p. 428–29 (#257).

as a result of preservation is another. The relation in which God's creatures are placed vis-à-vis God by these two actions differs in each case. This difference cannot be indicated by saying that creation is "out of nothing" and preservation concerns that which exists. Rather, creation calls into being the things that are not, things that have no other existence than that of ideas and decrees in the being of God. By preservation, with the same power, God summons those things that have received an existence distinct from his being and are nevertheless solely and exclusively from, through, and to God. Creation yields existence, while preservation is persistence in existence. The difficulty for the mind to maintain both creation and preservation always arises from the fact that by creation God's creatures have received their own unique existence, which is distinct from God's being, and that that existence may and can never even for a moment be viewed as an existence of and by itself, independent from God.

We are confronted here by a mystery that far surpasses our understanding, and we are always inclined to do less than justice to either one or the other. It is this inclination that underlies pantheism and Deism. Both of these trends proceed from the same error and oppose God and the world to each other as two competing entities. The former sacrifices the world to God, creation to providence, and believes that God's existence can only be a divinely infinite existence if it denies the existence of the world, dissolves it into mere appearance, and allows it to be swallowed up by divine existence. The latter sacrifices God to the world, providence to creation, and believes that creatures come into their own to the extent that they become less dependent on God and distance themselves from God. The Christian, however, confesses that the world and every creature in it have received their own existence, but increase in reality, freedom, and authenticity to the extent that they are more dependent on God and exist from moment to moment from, through, and to God. A creature is the more perfect to the degree that God indwells it more and permeates it with his being. In that respect preservation is even greater than creation, for the latter only initiated the beginning of existence, but the former is the progressive and ever increasing self-communication of God to his creatures. Providence is "the progressive expression in the universe of his divine perfection, the progressive realization in it of the archetypal ideal of perfect wisdom and love."[61]

CONCURRENCE: SECONDARY CAUSES

[305] With that we have now indicated the manner in which God exercises his providential rule in the world—which in former times was expressed by the doctrine of concurrence. This is as richly diversified as the diversity with which God distinguished his creatures at the time of creation. The variety exhibited in God's manner of government is just as great as that exhibited in his creation.[62]

61. S. Harris, *God the Creator and Lord of All* (Edinburgh: T. & T. Clark, 1897), I, 532.
62. J. Alsted, *Theol.*, 315: "Sicut creationis magna est varietas, ita et gubernationis."

By creation God called into being a world that simultaneously deserves to be called a "cosmos" *(kosmos)* and an "age" *(aiōn),* and which in both space and time is "a most brilliant mirror of the divine glory."[63] Now, providence serves to take the world from its beginning and to lead it to its final goal; it goes into effect immediately after the creation and brings to development all that was given in that creation. Creation, conversely, was aimed at providence; creation conferred on creatures the kind of existence that can be brought to development in and by providence. For the world was not created in a state of pure potency, as chaos or a nebulous cloud, but as an ordered cosmos, and human beings were placed in it not as helpless toddlers but as an adult man and an adult woman. Development could only proceed from such a ready-made world, and that is how creation presented it to providence. In addition, that world was a harmonious whole in which unity was coupled to the most marvelous diversity. Every creature received a nature of its own, and with that nature an existence, a life, and a law of its own. Just as the moral law was increated in the heart of Adam as the rule for his life, so all creatures carried in their own nature the principles and laws for their own development.

All things are created by the word. All things are based on thought. The whole creation is a system grounded in the ordinances of God (Gen. 1:26, 28; 8:22; Ps. 104:5, 9; 119:90–91; Eccles. 1:10; Job 38:10ff.; Jer. 5:24; 31:25ff.; 33:20, 25). On all creatures God conferred an order, a law that they do not violate (Ps. 148:6).[64] In all of its parts it is rooted in the counsel of God, a design that emerges in things great and small. This all comes from the Lord of hosts; he is wonderful in counsel and excellent in wisdom (Isa. 28:23, 29).

This is how Scripture teaches us to understand the world, and this is also how Christian theology has understood it. Augustine said that "hidden seeds" *(semina occulta),* "original principles" *(originales regulae),* and "seminal reasons" *(seminariae rationes)* were implanted in creatures, are concealed in the secret womb of nature, and thus are the principles of all development. "Whatever things, by being born, become visible to our eyes receive the principles of their development from hidden seeds, and take the increases in size appropriate to them, as well as the distinctiveness of their forms as though from these original causes."[65] The world, accordingly, is pregnant with the causes of beings. "For as mothers are pregnant with unborn offspring, so the world itself is pregnant with the causes of unborn beings, which are not created in it except from that highest essence, where nothing is either born or dies, begins to be, or ceases to be."[66]

The world is a tree of things *(arbor rerum),* bringing forth branch and blossom and fruit.[67] God so preserves things and so works in them that they

---

63. See above, pp. 435–39 (#259).
64. Cf. H. Bavinck, *Reformed Dogmatics,* I, 336 (#93).
65. Augustine, *The Trinity,* III, 7; idem, *Literal Meaning of Genesis,* IV, 33.
66. Augustine, *The Trinity,* III, 9.
67. Augustine, *Literal Meaning of Genesis,* VIII, 9.

themselves work along with him as secondary causes. This is not to say that we must stop there. On the contrary, we must always ascend to the cause of all being and movement, and that is the will of God alone. "The 'nature' of any particular created thing is precisely what the supreme Creator of the thing willed it to be."[68] To that extent providence is not only a positive but also an immediate act of God. His will, his power, his being is immediately present in every creature and every event. All things exist and live together in him (Acts 17:28; Col. 1:17; Heb. 1:3). Just as he created the world by himself, so he also preserves and governs it by himself. Although God works through secondary causes, this is not to be interpreted, in the manner of Deism, to mean that they come in between God and the effects with their consequences and separate these from him. "God's immediate provision over everything extends to the exemplar of the order."[69]

For that reason a miracle is not a violation of natural law nor an intervention in the natural order. From God's side it is an act that does not more immediately and directly have God as its cause than any ordinary event, and in the counsel of God and the plan of the world it occupies as much an equally well-ordered and harmonious place as any natural phenomenon. In miracles God only puts into effect a special force that, like any other force, operates in accordance with its own nature and therefore also has an outcome of its own.[70]

But at the creation God built his laws into things, fashioning an order by which the things themselves are interconnected. God is not dependent on causes, but things do depend on one another. That interconnectedness is of many kinds. Although in general it can be called "causal," the word "causal" in this sense must by no means be equated with "mechanical," as materialism would have us do. A mechanical connection is only one mode in which a number of things in the world relate to each other. Just as creatures received a nature of their own in the creation and differ among themselves, so there is also difference in the laws in conformity with which they function and in the relation in which they stand to each other.

These laws and relations differ in every sphere: the physical and the psychological, the intellectual and the ethical, the family and society, science and art, the kingdoms of earth and the kingdom of heaven. It is the providence of God that, interlocking with creation, maintains and brings to full development all these distinct natures, forces, and ordinances. In providence God respects and develops—and does not nullify—the things he called into being in creation. "It does not pertain to divine providence to corrupt the nature of things but to preserve [that nature]."[71] Thus, therefore, God preserves and governs all

---

68. Augustine, *City of God*, XXI, 8; idem, *The Trinity*, III, 6–9.

69. T. Aquinas, *Summa theol.*, I, qu. 22, art. 3; I, qu. 103, art. 6; I, qu. 103, art. 2; *Summa contra gentiles*, III, 76ff.

70. Cf. H. Bavinck, *Reformed Dogmatics*, I, 188–89 (#56); P. Mezger, *Räthsel des christlichen Vorsehungsglaubens* (Basel: Helbing & Lichterbahn, 1904), 20ff.

71. T. Aquinas, *Summa theol.*, II, 1, qu. 10, art. 4.

creatures according to their nature, the angels in one way, humans in another, and the latter again in a way that differs from animals and plants. But insofar as God in his providence maintains things in their mutual relatedness and makes creatures subserve each other's existence and life, that providence can be called mediate. "God immediately provides for all things as it pertains to the exemplar of the order, but as it pertains to the execution of the order he, to be sure, provides through other means."[72] Thus he created all the angels simultaneously but lets humans spring from one blood; thus he preserves some creatures individually and others as species and families. In each case, then, he employs all sorts of creatures as means in his hand to fulfill his counsel and to reach his goal.

Christian theology did not deny these things. On the contrary, following the example of Scripture, it has always emphatically upheld the natural order and the causal nexus of the phenomena. It is not true that Christianity with its supernaturalism was hostile to the natural order and made science impossible, as Draper, for example, and others have sought to demonstrate with such relish.[73] Much more in line with the facts is the judgment of DuBois-Reymond when he wrote: "Modern natural science, however paradoxical this may sound, owes its origin to Christianity."[74] In any case, Christianity made science—specifically natural science—possible and prepared the ground for it. For the more the natural phenomena are deified—as in polytheism—and viewed as the visible images and bearers of deity, the more scientific inquiry is made impossible since it becomes automatically a form of desecration that disturbs the mystery of Deity. But Christianity distinguished God and the world, and by its confession of God as the Creator of all things, separated God from the nexus of nature and lifted him far above it. The study of nature, therefore, is no longer a violation of Deity. At the same time and by this very fact it has made human beings free and given them independent status vis-à-vis nature, as is clearly demonstrated by the splendid view of nature we find in the psalmists and prophets, in Jesus and the apostles. For the believer, nature is no longer an object of worship and dread.[75] Whereas before God he bows down in deep

72. T. Aquinas, *Summa theol.*, I, qu. 22, art. 3.

73. J. W. Draper, *History of the Conflict between Religion and Science* (New York: D. Appleton, 1897).

74. E. H. DuBois-Reymond, *Culturgeschichte und Naturwissenschaft* (Leipzig: Veit, 1878), 28; cf. also F. A. Lange, *Geschichte des Materialismus und Kritik seiner Bedeutung in der Gegenwart* (1882), 129ff. (8th ed. Leipzig: Baedekker, 1908); H. Martensen-Larsen, *Die Naturwissenschaft in ihrem Schuldverhältnis zum Christentum* (Berlin: Reuther & Reichard, 1897); E. Dennert, in W. H. Nieuwhuis, *Twee Vragen des Tijds* (Kampen: Kok, 1907), 9–52; idem, *De Verdiensten der Katholieke Kerk ten opzichte der Natuurwet*, foreword by F. Hendrichs (Amsterdam, 1906).

75. "The Hebrews faced the world and nature with sovereign self-awareness—being without fear of the world—but also with a sense of the utmost responsibility. As God's representative, humanity exercises dominion over the world but only as such. Human beings may not follow their arbitrary impulses but only the revealed will of God. Paganism, in contrast, alternates between presumptuous misuse of the world and childish dread before its powers" (R. Smend, *Lehrbuch der alttestamentlichen Religionsgeschichte* [Freiburg: J. C. B. Mohr, 1893], 453).

humility and is utterly dependent on him, in relation to the earth he has the calling to exercise dominion over it and to subject all things to himself (Gen. 1:26). Dependence on God is something very different from living conformably to nature and adapting oneself to circumstances. Many writers argue either in such a way that they attribute all things and events to the will of God and consider resistance impermissible, or they limit God's providence and place many things in the hands of humans.[76]

Scripture, however, warns us against both this antinomianism and this Pelagianism; it cuts off at the root all false fatalistic resignation on the one hand, and all presumptuous self-confidence on the other. Bowing before the powers of nature is something very different from childlike submission to God, and exercising dominion over the earth is a matter of serving God. The sea captain who went to his cabin to pray and read the Bible during a storm did submit to the power of the elements, but not to God.[77] There is much more real piety in Cromwell's dictum: "Trust God and keep your powder dry." It is, moreover, the confession of God as the Creator of heaven and earth that immediately brings with it the one absolute and never self-contradictory truth, the harmony and beauty of the counsel of God, and hence the unity of the cosmic plan and the order of all of nature. "If in a free and wonderful way, on the basis of the full scope of nature, one attributes to the one God also a unified manner of working, then the connectedness of things in terms of cause and effect not only becomes conceivable but even a necessary consequence of the assumption."[78] Scripture itself models to us this recognition of such a natural order, of a wide range of ordinances and laws for created things. And miracle is so far from making an inroad on that natural order that it rather presupposes and confirms it. At all times the Christian church and theology have generously acknowledged such an order of things. Augustine repeatedly appealed to the saying in Wisdom 11:20: "You have arranged all things by measure and number and weight." At least in the early period they energetically opposed the appalling superstition that crested in the third and fourth centuries, and especially fought against astrology.[79] The controversy that often erupted was not a conflict between Christianity and natural science; the alignments were very different; it was usually a struggle between an earlier and later worldview, with believing Christians on both sides.[80]

76. So, e.g., W. Beyschlag, *Vorstehungsglauben*, 24ff.
77. S. Harris, *God the Creator and Lord of All*, I, 545.
78. F. A. Lange, *Geschichte des Materialismus*, 130.
79. Augustine, *City of God*, V, 1–8; T. Aquinas, *Summa contra gentiles*, III, 84ff.; J. Calvin, "A Warning against Judiciary Astrology and Other Prevalent Curiosities," trans. Mary Potter, *Calvin Theological Journal* 18 (1983): 157–89 (*CR*, XXXV, 509–44); F. Turretin, *Institutes of Elenctic Theology*, VI, qu. 2; B. de Moor, *Comm. in Marckii Comp.*, II, 435; C. Vitringa, *Doctr. christ.*, II, 180, etc.; cf. also A. von Harnack, *The Expansion of Christianity in the First Three Centuries*, trans. James Moffatt, 2 vols. (New York: G. P. Putnam's Sons, 1904), I, 152–80.
80. Cf. above, pp. 483–84 (#271).

This fundamentally correct view of nature, which Christian theology advocated, is nowhere more clearly in evidence than in its doctrine of "concurrence" and "secondary causes." In neither pantheism nor Deism can this doctrine come into its own. In the former there are no longer any *causes,* and in the latter no *secondary* causes. In pantheism the secondary causes, that is, the immediate causes of things within the circle of created things, are identified with the primary cause, which is God. Between the two there is no distinction of substance and effect. Both materially and formally, God is the subject of all that happens, and hence also of sin. At best the so-called secondary causes are opportunities and passive instruments for the workings of God. Whereas this theory only sporadically surfaced in earlier times, in the more modern philosophy of Descartes it came to dominance and so led to the idealism of Berkeley and Malebranche, and to the pantheism of Spinoza, Hegel, Schleiermacher, Strauss, and others. So Malebranche, for example, posits that "there is only one true cause because there is only one true God; that the nature or power of each thing is nothing but the will of God; that all natural causes are not *true* causes but only *occasional* causes." The true cause can only be God because he alone can create and he cannot communicate that power to a creature. If creatures could be the true cause of motions and phenomena, they themselves would be gods. But "all these insignificant pagan divinities and all these particular causes of the philosophers are merely chimeras that the wicked mind tries to establish to undermine worship of the true God."[81] Accordingly, there are only phenomena, representations, and the only reality, power, and substance behind these phenomena is that of God himself.[82]

Conversely, in Deism the secondary causes are separated from the primary cause and made independent. The primary cause is totally restricted to the creation, the communication of the possibility *(posse),* and totally excluded in the case of the "willing" *(velle)* and the doing *(facere),* as in the original Pelagianism. Or the two causes are conceived as associated causes that work with and alongside each other, like two draft horses pulling a wagon, even though one is perhaps stronger than the other, as in semi-Pelagianism and synergism. In this view the creature becomes the creator of his or her own deeds. Scripture, however, tells us both that God works all things so that the creature is only an instrument in his hand (Isa. 44:24; Ps. 29:3; 65:10; 147:15ff.; Matt. 5:45; Acts 17:25; etc.) *and* that providence is distinct from creation and presupposes the existence and self-activity of creatures (Gen. 1:11, 20, 22, 24, 28; etc.). In keeping with this witness, Christian theology teaches that the secondary causes are strictly subordinated to God as the primary cause and in that subordination nevertheless remain true causes. The odd theologian, to be sure, diverged from this position, such as the nominalist Biel in the Middle Ages and Zwingli in the

81. N. Malebranche, *The Search after Truth: Elucidations of the Search after Truth* (Columbus: Ohio State University Press, 1980), 448, 451.

82. Cf. J. Kleutgen, *Die Philosophie der Vorzeit vertheidigt,* 2d ed., 2 vols. (Münster: Theissing, 1878), II, 336–47; C. Hodge, *Systematic Theology,* I, 592.

time of the Reformation, who believed that secondary causes were mistakenly so-called and preferred to call them instruments.[83]

The constant teaching of the Christian church, nevertheless, has been that the two causes, though they are totally dependent on the primary cause, are at the same time also true and essential causes. With his almighty power God makes possible every secondary cause and is present in it with his being at its beginning, progression, and end. It is he who posits it and makes it move into action *(praecursus)* and who further accompanies it in its working and leads it to its effect *(concursus)*. He is "at work" [in us] "both to will and to do for his good pleasure" (Phil. 2:13). But this energizing activity of the primary cause in the secondary causes is so divinely great that precisely by that activity he stirs those secondary causes into an activity of their own. "The providence of God does not cancel out but posits secondary causation."[84] Concurrence is precisely the reason for the self-activity of the secondary causes, and these causes, sustained from beginning to end by God's power, work with a strength that is appropriate and natural to them. So little does the activity of God nullify the activity of the creature that the latter is all the more vigorous to the degree that the former reveals itself the more richly and fully. Hence, the primary cause and the secondary cause remain distinct. The former does not destroy the latter but on the contrary confers reality on it, and the second exists solely as a result of the first. Neither are the secondary causes merely instruments, organs, inanimate automata, but they are genuine causes with a nature, vitality, spontaneity, manner of working, and law of their own. "Satan and evildoers are not so effectively the instruments of God that they do not also act in their own behalf. For we must not suppose that God works in an iniquitous man as if he were a stone or a piece of wood, but He uses him as a thinking creature, according to the quality of his nature, which He has given him. Thus, when we say that God works in evildoers, that does not prevent them from working also in their own behalf."[85]

In relation to God the secondary causes can be compared to instruments (Isa. 10:15; 13:5; Jer. 50:25; Acts 9:15; Rom. 9:20–23); in relation to their effects and products they are causes in the true sense. And precisely because the primary and the secondary cause do not stand and function dualistically on separate tracks, but the primary works through the secondary, the effect that proceeds from the two is one and the product is one. There is no division of labor between God and his creature, but the same effect is totally the effect of the primary cause as well as totally the effect of the proximate cause. The

83. U. Zwingli, *On the Providence and Other Essays,* IV, 95ff.; cf. the American theologian Emmons, in A. H. Strong, *Systematic Theology,* 2d ed. (New York: A. C. Armstrong, 1890), 205; C. Hodge, *Systematic Theology,* I, 594; H. B. Smith, *System of Christian Theology,* 103.

84. J. Wollebius, in H. Heppe, *Reformed Dogmatics,* rev. and ed. Ernst Bizer, trans. G. T. Thomson (London: Allen & Unwin, 1950; reprinted, Grand Rapids: Baker, 1978), 258.

85. J. Calvin, *Treatises against the Anabaptists and Libertines,* trans. B. W. Farley (Grand Rapids: Baker, 1982), 245.

product is also in the same sense totally the product of the primary as well as totally the product of the secondary cause. But because the primary cause and the secondary cause are not identical and differ essentially, the effect and product are *in reality* totally the effect and product of the two causes, to be sure, but *formally* they are only the effect and product of the secondary cause. Wood burns and it is God alone who makes it burn, yet the burning process may not be formally attributed to God but must be attributed to the wood as subject. Human persons speak, act, and believe, and it is God alone who supplies to a sinner all the vitality and strength he or she needs for the commission of a sin. Nevertheless the subject and author of the sin is not God but the human being. In this manner Scripture draws the lines within which the reconciliation of God's sovereignty and human freedom has to be sought.

PROVIDENCE AS GOVERNMENT

[306] Implicitly included in providence conceived as preservation and concurrence is divine government. One who so preserves things that he not only, by his will and being, sustains existent beings but also even their powers and effects, is absolutely sovereign: a true king. Government, therefore, is not a new element added to preservation and concurrence. Rather, it is as such like each of these two, the whole of God's providence, only now considered from the perspective of the final goal toward which God by his providence is guiding the whole created world. It is a beautiful and evocative thought when Scripture over and over calls God "king" and describes his providence as a kind of government. There are many people in our time who reject every idea of sovereignty in the family, the state, and society and want nothing to do with anything other than democracy and anarchy. Under the influence of this view there are also those who in theology find the idea of God as king too reminiscent of the Old Testament and antiquated, and who at most still want to speak of God as Father. But this judgment is shallow and untrue. In the first place, the name "Father" for God is not limited to the New Testament but is used also in the Old Testament and even among the Gentiles. The New Testament may have a deeper and richer understanding of it, but it was not the first to accord this name to God.[86] Conversely, the name "king" is not only repeatedly used for the divine being in the Old but also in the New Testament (Matt. 6:10, 13 [KJV], 33; 1 Tim. 1:17; 6:15; Rev. 19:6; etc.). And in the second place, the name "king" is no less fitting for God than the name Father. All *patria* (lit., "fatherhood") in heaven and on earth derives its name from him who is the Father of our Lord Jesus Christ (Eph. 3:15). All relations that exist among creatures between superiors and inferiors are analogies of that one original relation in which God stands to the works of his hands. What a father is for his family, what an educator is for the young, what a commander

86. See above, p. 147 (#191).

is for the army, what a king is for his people—all that and much more God is in a totally original way for his creatures. Not just one but all his attributes come to expression in the world and therefore need to be honored by us. Now "kingship" for one is a glorious divine institution as well. It not only confers on a people a unity symbolized in a person, but as a hereditary kingship it also assumes the character of originality, loftiness, independence, and constancy. In all this it is a beautiful—albeit a weak—image of the kingship of God.

All sovereignty on earth is derivative, temporary, and limited, and in the case of abuse, more a curse than a blessing. But God is king in the absolute and true sense. The government of the universe is not democratic, nor aristocratic, nor republican, nor constitutional, but monarchical. To God belongs the one undivided legislative, judicial, and executive power. His sovereignty is original, eternal, unlimited, abundant in blessing. He is the King of kings and the Lord of lords (1 Tim. 6:15; Rev. 19:6). His royal realm is the whole of the universe. His are the heavens and the earth (Exod. 19:5; Ps. 8:1; 103:19; 148:13). He possesses all the nations (Ps. 22:28; 47:8–9; 96:10; Jer. 10:7; Mal. 1:14) and is supreme in all the earth (Ps. 47:2, 7; 83:18; 97:9). He is king forever (Ps. 29:10; 1 Tim. 1:17); no opposition stands a chance against him (Ps. 93:3–4). His kingdom will surely come (Matt. 6:10; 1 Cor. 15:24; Rev. 12:10); his glory will be revealed and his name feared from the rising of the sun to its going down (Isa. 40:5; 59:19); he will be king over the entire earth (Zech. 14:9). Also, in this government God deals with each thing according to its kind. "God rules over all things conformably to their nature."[87] Consequently, that rule of God is variously represented in Scripture and described with various names. By his rule he upholds the world and establishes it so that it will not be moved (Ps. 93:1); he ordains the light and the darkness (Ps. 104:19–20), commands the rain and withholds it (Gen. 7:4; 8:2; Job 26:8; 38:22ff.), gives snow and hoarfrost and ice (Ps. 147:16), rebukes and stills the sea (Nah. 1:4; Ps. 65:7; 107:29), sends curses and destruction (Deut. 28:15ff.). All things fulfill his command (Ps. 148:8). With equally sovereign power and majesty he rules in the world of rational creatures. He rules among the Gentiles and possesses all nations (Ps. 22:28; 82:8); he deems the nations as emptiness and less than nothing (Isa. 40:17), deals with the inhabitants of the earth according to his will (Dan. 4:35), and directs the hearts and thoughts of all (Prov. 21:1).

And this government of God over his rational creatures extends not only to the good things of which he is the Giver both in nature and in grace (James 1:17); nor only to the beneficiaries of his favor, whom he chooses, preserves, cares for, and leads to eternal salvation; but also to evil and to those who love evil and do it. Granted, God hates sin with his whole being, as all of Scripture testifies (Deut. 32:4; Ps. 5:4–6; Job 34:10; 1 John 5; etc.), and by the prohibition of sin in law and in the human conscience as well as and by its judgments, God's government gives undeniable witness to this aversion. At the same time

---

87. J. Alsted, *Theol.*, 301.

the whole of Scripture also teaches that sin, from beginning to end, is subject to God's rule.[88] At its inception God sometimes acts to stop it (Gen. 20:6; 31:7), destroys the counsel of the wicked (Ps. 33:10), gives strength to resist temptation (1 Cor. 10:13), and always thwarts sin in that he prohibits it and inhibits the sinner through fear and trembling in his conscience.

But this prevention *(impeditio)* is by far not the only form in which God governs sin. Many times he allows it to happen and does not stop it. He gave Israel up to their stubborn hearts to follow their own counsels (Ps. 81:12), allowed the nations to walk in their own ways (Acts 14:16; 17:30), gave people up to their own lusts (Rom. 1:24, 26, 28). And it can similarly be said that God permitted the fall of Adam, the murder of Abel, the iniquity of the people before the flood (Gen. 6:3), the sale of Joseph (Gen. 37), the condemnation of Jesus, and so on. But this permission *(permissio)* is so little negative in nature that even from its earliest beginning sin is subject to God's governing power and sovereignty. He creates and arranges the opportunities and occasions for sinning to test humans, thereby either to strengthen and to confirm them or to punish and to harden them (Gen. 27; 2 Chron. 32:31; Job 1; Matt. 4:1; 6:13; 1 Cor. 10:13). Although at first a given sin seemed to be nothing but an arbitrary act of humans, it turns out later that God had his hand in it and that it happened according to his counsel (Gen. 45:8; 2 Chron. 11:4; Luke 24:26; Acts 2:23; 3:17–18; 4:28). It is sometimes materially—though not formally and subjectively—even attributed to God in its inception. God is the potter and humans are the clay (Jer. 18:5ff.; Lam. 3:38; Isa. 45:7, 9; 64:7; Amos 3:6). He hardened and blinded certain persons (Exod. 4:21; 7:3; 9:12; 10:20, 27; 11:10; 14:4; Deut. 2:30; Josh. 11:20; Isa. 6:10; 63:17; Matt. 13:13; Mark 4:12; Luke 8:10; John 12:40; Acts 28:26; Rom. 9:18; 11:8); he turned a man's heart so that it was hateful and disobedient (1 Sam. 2:25; 1 Kings 12:15; 2 Chron. 25:20; Ps. 105:24–25; Ezek. 14:9). God sent an evil spirit or a lying spirit (Judg. 9:23; 1 Sam. 16:14; 1 Kings 22:23; 2 Chron. 18:22). Using Satan he incited David to number the people (2 Sam. 24:1; 1 Chron. 21:1), prompted Shimei to curse David (2 Sam. 16:10), gave people over to their sins, allowed them to fill the full measure of their iniquity (Gen. 15:16; Rom. 1:24), sent a strong spirit of delusion (2 Thess. 2:11), and set Christ for the fall and rising of many (Luke 2:34; John 3:19; 9:39; 2 Cor. 2:16; 1 Pet. 2:8; etc.).[89]

Not only at the outset but also upon its continuation God keeps sin under his omnipotent control. Repeatedly he restrains or restricts it, inhibits its momentum and puts a stop to it by his judgment (Gen. 7:11; Exod. 15; Matt. 24:22; 2 Pet. 2:9), but also in cases where he allows it to continue he directs it (Prov. 16:9; 21:1), and whether forgiving or punishing it, he ultimately makes it subservient to the fulfillment of his counsel, the glorification of his

<hr />

88. C. Clemen, *Die christliche Lehre von der Sünde* (Göttingen: Vandenhoeck & Ruprecht, 1897), I, 123–51.

89. See above, pp. 345–46 (#233) and pp. 393–95 (#246); and additional literature about God's activity in relation to the sinful deeds of humans in C. Vitringa, *Doctr. christ.*, II, 196ff., 206ff.

name (Gen. 45:7–8; 50:20; Ps. 51:4; Isa. 10:5–7; Job 1:20–22; Prov. 16:4; Acts 3:13; Rom. 8:28; 11:36).

Like sin (a culpable evil), so also suffering (a punitive evil), is subject to the dominion of God. He is the creator of light and darkness, of good and evil (Amos 3:6; Isa. 45:7; Job 2:10). Death, which was God's punishment and came at his command (Gen. 2:17), and all disasters and adversities, all sorrow and suffering, all afflictions and judgments, are imposed on humanity by God's omnipotent hand (Gen. 3:14ff.; Deut. 28:15ff.; etc.). Already in the days of Israel people observed the dissonance that exists in this life between sin and punishment, holiness and blessedness (Ps. 73; Job; Ecclesiastes). Faith struggled with this momentous problem but also again raised its head in victory over it, not because it saw the solution to it, but because it continued to cling to the royal power and fatherly love of the Lord. The prosperity of the wicked is a mere illusion and in any case temporary, while the righteous, even in their deepest suffering, still enjoy the love and grace of God (Ps. 73; Job). The suffering of the faithful is frequently rooted not in their personal sin but in the sin of humankind, and has its goal in the salvation of humankind and the glory of God. Suffering serves not only as retribution (Rom. 1:18, 27; 2:5–6; 2 Thess. 1–2) but also as testing and chastisement (Deut. 8:5; Job 1:12; Ps. 118:5–18; Prov. 3:12; Jer. 10:24; 30:11; Heb. 12:5ff.; Rev. 3:19), as reinforcement and confirmation (Ps. 119:67, 71; Rom. 5:3–5; Heb. 12:10–11; James 1:2–4), as witness to the truth (Ps. 44:24; Acts 5:41; Phil. 1:29; 2 Tim. 4:6–8), and to glorify God (John 9:2). In Christ, justice and mercy embrace, suffering is the road to glory, the cross points to a crown, and the timber of the cross becomes the tree of life.[90] The end toward which all things are being led by the providence of God is the establishment of his kingdom, the revelation of his attributes, the glory of his name (Rom. 11:32–36; 1 Cor. 15:18; Rev. 11:15; 12:10; etc.).

In this consoling fashion Scripture deals with the providence of God. Plenty of riddles remain, both in the life of individuals and in the history of the world and humankind. From this point on, systematic theology's sole concern is with the mysteries that the providence of God has put on our docket in sin, freedom, responsibility, punishment, suffering, death, grace, atonement, reconciliation, prayer, and so forth, and therefore it does not have to discuss all these topics here.

But God lets the light of his Word shine over all these enigmas and mysteries, not to solve them, but that "by steadfastness and by the encouragement of the Scriptures we might have hope" (Rom. 15:4). The doctrine of providence is not a philosophical system but a confession of faith, the confession that, notwithstanding appearances, neither Satan nor a human being nor any other creature, but God and he alone—by his almighty and everywhere pres-

---

90. We later revisit the problem of suffering in the section on the punishment of sin; see H. Bavinck, *Reformed Dogmatics*, III, ##335–42.

ent power—preserves and governs all things. Such a confession can save us both from a superficial optimism that denies the riddles of life, and from a presumptuous pessimism that despairs of this world and human destiny. For the providence of God encompasses all things, not only the good but also sin and suffering, sorrow and death. For if these realities were removed from God's guidance, then what in the world would there be left for him to rule? God's providence is manifest not only, nor primarily, in the extraordinary events of life and in miracles but equally as much in the stable order of nature and the ordinary occurrences of daily life. What an impoverished faith it would be if it saw God's hand and counsel from afar in a few momentous events but did not discern it in a person's own life and lot? It leads all these things toward their final goal, not against but agreeably to their nature, not apart from but through the regular means; for what power would there be in a faith that recommended stoical indifference or fatalistic acquiescence as true godliness? But so, as the almighty and everywhere present power of God, it makes us grateful when things go well and patient when things go against us, prompts us to rest with childlike submission in the guidance of the Lord and at the same time arouses us from our inertia to the highest levels of activity. In all circumstances of life, it gives us good confidence in our faithful God and Father that he will provide whatever we need for body and soul and that he will turn to our good whatever adversity he sends us in this sad world, since he is able to do this as almighty God and desires to do this as a faithful Father.[91]

91. Ed. note: Cf. Heidelberg Catechism, Lord's Day 9 and 10, Q. & A. 26–28.

BIBLIOGRAPHY

This bibliography includes the items Bavinck listed at the head of sections 26–39 in the *Gereformeerde Dogmatiek,* vol. 2, as well as any additional works cited in his footnotes. Particularly for the footnote references, where Bavinck's own citations were quite incomplete by contemporary standards—titles often appearing significantly abbreviated—this bibliography provides fuller information. In some cases, full bibliographic information was available only for an edition other than the one Bavinck cited. Where English translations of Dutch or German works are available, they have been cited rather than the original. In a few instances where Bavinck cited Dutch translations of English originals, the original work is listed. In cases where multiple versions or editions are available in English (e.g., Calvin's *Institutes*), the most recent, most frequently cited, or most accessible edition was chosen. In spite of best efforts to track down each reference and confirm or complete bibliographic information, some of Bavinck's abbreviated and cryptic notations remain unconfirmed or incomplete. Where information is unconfirmed, incomplete, and/or titles have been reconstructed, the work is marked with an asterisk.

The improvement of this bibliography over Bavinck's own citations in the *Gereformeerde Dogmatiek* is largely thanks to a valuable tool he did not have available to him—the Internet—and its diligent perusal by a number of Calvin Theological Seminary students who labored as the editor's student assistants. Graduate students Raymond Blacketer and Claudette Grinnell worked on the eschatology section in *GD IV,* published separately as *The Last Things* (Baker, 1996). Colin Vander Ploeg, Steven Baarda, and Marcia De Haan-Van Drunen worked on the creation section of *GD II,* published as *In the Beginning* (Baker, 1999). Ph.D. students Steven J. Grabill and Rev. J. Mark Beach worked on volume 1, and Courtney Hoekstra worked full-time during the summer of 2002 to complete the bibliography of volume 1. She also was the major contributor to the completed bibliography of the present volume. Dr. Roger Nicole carefully checked the eschatology and creation bibliographies and helped reduce the errors and asterisks. The assistance of all is gratefully acknowledged here.

ABBREVIATIONS

ANF   *The Ante-Nicene Fathers.* Edited by Alexander Roberts and James Donaldson.
           10 vols. New York: Christian Literature Co., 1885–96. Reprinted, Grand
           Rapids: Eerdmans, 1950–51.
NPNF (1) *A Select Library of Nicene and Post-Nicene Fathers of the Christian Church.*
           Edited by Philip Schaff. 1st series. 14 vols. New York: Christian Literature Co.,
           1887–1900. Reprinted, Grand Rapids: Eerdmans, 1956.
NPNF (2) *A Select Library of Nicene and Post-Nicene Fathers of the Christian Church.*
           Edited by Philip Schaff and Henry Wace. 2d series. 14 vols. New York:
           Christian Literature Co., 1890–1900. Reprinted, Grand Rapids: Eerdmans,
           1952.
PG   Patrologia Graeca. Edited by J.-P. Migne. 162 vols. Paris, 1857–86.
PL   Patrologia Latina. Edited by J.-P. Migne. 217 vols. Paris, 1844–64.
PRE¹   *Realencyklopädie für protestantische Theologie und Kirche.* Edited by J. J. Herzog.
           22 vols. Hamburg: R. Besser, 1854–68.
PRE²   *Realencyklopädie für protestantische Theologie und Kirche.* Edited by J. J. Herzog
           and G. L. Plitt. 2d rev. ed. 18 vols. Leipzig: J. C. Hinrichs, 1877–88.
PRE³   *Realencyklopädie für protestantische Theologie und Kirche.* Edited by Albert
           Hauck. 3d rev. ed. 24 vols. Leipzig: J. C. Hinrichs, 1896–1913.

BOOKS

Aall, Anathon. *Der Logos: Geschichte seiner Entwickelung der griechischen Philosophie und der christlichen Litteratur.* 2 vols. Leipzig: O. R. Reisland, 1896–99.

Abelard, Peter. *Introductio ad theologiam.* PL 178.

Agassiz, Louis. *Essay on Classification.* Edited by Edward Lurie. Cambridge, Mass.: Belknap Press, Harvard University Press, 1962.

Alexander of Hales. *Summa theologica.* 4 vols. Quarracchi: Collegium S. Bonaventurae, 1924–58.

Alsted, Johann Heinrich. *Johannis Henrici Alstedii Encyclopaedia septum tomis distincta.* Herborn: G. Corvini, 1630.

———. *Praecognita theologiae, I–II,* in *Methodus,* as books I and II: *Methodus sacrosanctae theologiae octo libris tradita.* Hanover, C. Eifrid, 1619.

———. *Theologica catechetica: Exibens sacratissimam novitiolorum christianorum scholam, in qua summa fidei et operum . . . exponitur.* Hanover: Eifrid, 1622.

———. *Theologica naturalis: Exibens augustissimam naturae scholam, in qua creaturi Dei communi sermone ad omnes pariter docendos utuntur: adversus Atheos, Epicureos et Sophistas huius temporis.* Hanover: C. Eifrid, 1620.

———. *Theologica polemica: Exibens praecipuas huius aevi in religione negatio controversias.* Hanover: C. Eifrid, 1627.

———. *Theologia scholastica didactica: Exhibens locos communes theologicos.* Hanover: C. Eifrid, 1618.

Alting, Heinrich [and Johann Heinrich Schweitzer]. *Heinrici Alting theologi Palatini Historiae sacrae et profanae compendium: Cum orbis & incolarum descriptione; Accessit Joh. Heinrici Suiceri Historiae ecclesiasticae N. Test. chronologica delineatio ad nostra usque tempora producta.* Tiguri: Typis Davidis Gessneri, 1691.

———. *Scriptorum theologicorum Heidelbergensium.* 2 vols. Freistadii [Amsterdam?]: Typographorum Belgicae Foederatae, 1646. [Contains: *Loci communes cum didactici, tum elenchticos.* 2: *Problemata theologica, tam theorica, quam practica.*]

———. *Theologia elenctica nova.* Amsterdam: J. Jansson, 1654.

———. *Theologia probematica nova: Sive systema problematum theologicorum, in inclyta academia Groningae et Omlandiae publicis praelectionibus propositum.* Amselodami: Joan. Janssonium, 1662.

Alting, Jacob. *Opera omnia theologica.* 5 vols. Amsterdam: Borst, 1687.

Ambrose. *Hexameron, Paradise, and Cain and Abel.* Translated by John J. Savage. Fathers of the Church 42. New York: Fathers of the Church, 1961.

Amyraut [Amyrald], Moyse, Louis Cappel, and Josue La Place. *Syntagma thesium theologicarum in Academia Salmuriensi varriis temporibus disputatarum.* 2d ed. 4 parts. Saumur: Joannes Lesner, 1664; 1665.

————. *Traité de la prédestination.* Saumur: Lesnier & Desbordes, 1634.

Andree, Richard. *Die Flutsagen: Ethnographisch betrachtet.* Braunschweig: F. Vieweg, 1891.

Anselm of Canterbury. *Basic Writings.* LaSalle, Ill.: Open Court, 1962.

————. *Complete Philosophical and Theological Treatises of Anselm of Canterbury.* Tanslated by Jasper Hopkins and Herbert Richardson. Minneapolis: Banning, 2000.

Aquinas. *See* Thomas Aquinas.

Aristotle. *Metaphysics.* Translated by Arthur Madigan. Oxford: Clarendon Press; New York: Oxford University Press, 1999.

————. *Nicomachean Ethics.* Translated by Terence Irwin. Indianapolis: Hackett, 1985.

Arminius, Jacob. *Opera theologica.* Leiden: Godefridum Basson, 1629.

Armstrong, Richard Acland. *Agnosticism and Theism in the Nineteenth Century.* Edited by Philip Henry Wicksteed. London: P. Green, 1905.

Athanasius. *Against the Arians. NPNF (2),* IV, 303–447.

————. *Against the Heathens.* Edited and translated by Robert W. Thomson. Oxford: Clarendon Press, 1971.

————. *Council of Nicaea. NPNF (2),* IV, 76, §11.

————. *Defence of the Nicene Definition. NPNF (2),* IV, 149–72.

————. *Discourses against the Arians. NPNF (2),* IV, 303–442.

————. *Epistles. NPNF (2),* IV, 510–12.

————. *Letter to Serapion. NPNF (2),* IV, 564–66.

————. *The Letters of Saint Athanasius concerning the Holy Spirit.* Translated by C. R. B. Shapland. London: Epworth Press, 1951.

————. *On the Incarnation. NPNF (2),* IV, 31–67.

————. *On the Opinion of Dionysius. NPNF (2),* IV, 173–87.

————. *Statement of Faith. NPNF (2),* IV, 83–85.

Athenagoras. *Apologia, vel legatio, vel potius supplicatio pro christianis: Ad imperatores Antoninum & Commodum.* Cologne, A. Birckmann, 1567.

————. *The Resurrection of the Dead. ANF,* II, 149–62.

Auberlen, Karl August. *The Divine Revelation: An Essay in Defence of the Faith.* Translated by A. B. Paton. Edinburgh: T. & T. Clark, 1867.

————. *Die Theosophie Friedrich Oetinger's nach ihren Grundzügen.* Tübingen: L. F. Fues, 1847.

Augustine, Aurelius. *Acts or Disputation against Fortunatus the Manichaean. NPNF (2),* IV, 113–24.

————. *Admonition and Grace.* Translated by J. C. Murray. In *Selections.* Fathers of the Church 2. Writings of Saint Augustine 4. Washington, D.C.: Catholic University of America Press, 1968.

————. *Against Julian.* Translated by M. A. Schumacher. Fathers of the Church 35. Writings of Saint Augustine 16. Washington, D.C.: Catholic University of America Press, 1984.

————. *Against the Academics.* Translated by John J. O'Meara. Ancient Christian Writers 12. Westminster, Md.: Newman Press, 1950.

————. *The City of God. NPNF (1),* II, 1–511.

————. *Concerning the Nature of the Good, against the Manichaeans.* NPNF (1), IV, 351–65.

————. *Confessions.* NPNF (1), I, 27–207.

————. *De diversis quaestionibus ad simplicianum.* Edited by Almut Mutzenbecher. Turnholti: Typographi Brepols, 1970.

————. *Divine Providence and the Problem of Evil.* Translated by Robert P. Russell. In *Selections.* Fathers of the Church 5. Writings of Saint Augustine 1. New York: Cima, 1948.

————. *Eighty-three Different Questions.* Translated by D. L. Mosher. Fathers of the Church 70. Washington, D.C.: Catholic University of America Press, 1982.

————. *Enchiridion.* NPNF (1), III, 229–76.

————. *Expositions on the Psalms.* NPNF (2), VIII.

————. *De Genesi contra Manichaeos* I.ii, PL 34, 173–220.

————. *De immortalitate animae; The Immortality of the Soul.* Translated by Francis E. Tourscher. Philadelphia: Peter Reilly Co., 1937.

————. *Lectures on the Gospel of John.* NPNF (1), VII, 1–452.

————. *De libero arbitrio (libri tres): The Free Choice of the Will (Three Books).* Translated by Francis Edward Tourscher. Philadelphia: Peter Reilly Co., 1937.

————. *The Literal Meaning of Genesis.* Translated and annotated by John Hammond Taylor. Ancient Christian Writers 41. New York: Newman, 1982.

————. *The Magnitude of the Soul.* New York: Fathers of the Church, 1947.

————. *On Christian Doctrine.* NPNF (1), II, 519–97.

————. *On Free Will.* NPNF (1), V, 436–43.

————. *On the Grace of Christ and Original Sin.* Translated by P. Holmes and edited by Whitney Oates. Vol. 1 of *Basic Writings of Saint Augustine.* New York: Random House, 1948.

————. *On the Merits and Remission of Sins.* NPNF (1), V, 12–79.

————. *On True Religion.* Translated by John H. S. Burleigh. Chicago: Regnery, 1959.

————. *The Retractions.* Translated by Mary Inez Bogan. Fathers of the Church 60. Washington, D.C.: Catholic University of America Press, 1968.

————. *Soliloquies.* NPNF (1), VII, 537–47.

————. *The Trinity.* Translated by Stephen McKenna. Fathers of the Church 45. Washington, D.C.: Catholic University of America Press, 1963.

————. *De vita beata.* Cologne: Iohanne[m] Gymnicum, 1529.

Baader, Franz von, and Johannes Claassen. *Franz von Baaders Leben und theosophischen Werke als Inbegriff christlicher Philosophie.* 2 vols. Stuttgart: J. F. Steinkopf, 1886–87.

Baentsch, Bruno. *Altorientalischer und israelitischer Monotheismus.* Tübingen: J. C. B. Mohr, 1906.

Bähr, Karl Christian Wilhelm Felix. *Symbolik des mosaischen Cultus.* 2d ed. Heidelberg: J. C. B. Mohr, 1874.

Baier, Johann Wilhelm. *Compendium theologiae positivae.* 3 vols. in 4. St. Louis: Concordia, 1879.

Baltzer, Johann Peter. *Des heiligen Augustinus Lehre über Prädestination und Reprobation: Ein dogmengeschichtliche Abhandlung.* Vienna: Braumüller, 1871.

Bardenhewer, Otto. *Patrology: The Lives and Works of the Fathers of the Church.* Translated by T. J. Shahan. St. Louis: Herder, 1908.

Basil of Caesarea. *Epistle 43.* NPNF (2), VIII, 146.

————. *On the Hexaëmeron: Exegetical Homilies.* Translated by Agnes Clare Way. Washington, D.C.: Catholic University of America Press, 1963.

————. *On the Holy Spirit.* NPNF (2), VIII, 1–50.

————. *S. Basilii Caesareae Cappadociae archiepiscopi Liber de spiritu sancto ad*

Amphilochium Iconii episcopum. London: D. Nutt, 1875.

Baudissin, Wolf Wilhelm. *Studien zur semitischen Religionsgeschichte.* 2 vols. Leipzig: F. W. Grunow, 1876–78.

Baumgartner, Alexander. *Geschichte der Weltliteratur.* Freiburg im Breisgau: Herder, 1897.

Baumstark, Christian Eduard. *Christliche Apologetik auf anthropologischen Grundlage.* Frankfurt am Main, 1872.

Baur, F. C. *Die christliche Lehre von der Dreieinigkeit und Menschwerdung Gottes in ihrer geschichtlichen Entwicklung.* 3 vols. Tübingen: C. F. Oslander, 1841–43.

Bavinck, Herman. *De Algemeene Genade.* Kampen: G. Ph. Zalsman, 1894.

———. *Beginselen der Psychologie.* Kampen: Bos, 1897.

———. *Doctrine of God.* Translated by William Hendriksen. Grand Rapids: Eerdmans, 1951.

———. *Gereformeerde Dogmatiek.* 4th ed. 4 vols. Kampen: Kok, 1928.

———. *Schepping of Ontwikkeling.* Kampen: Kok, 1901.

Bavinck, Herman, ed. *Synopsis purioris theologiae.* By Polyander et al. 6th ed. Leiden: D. Donner, 1881.

Becanus, Martin. *Summa theologiae scholasticae.* Rouen: I. Behovrt, 1651.

———. *De triplici sacrificio naturae, legi, gratiae.* Mainz: Joannis Albini, 1610.

Beck, Gottlieb. *Der Urmensch.* Basel: A. Geering, 1899.

Beck, Johann Tobias. *Einleitung in das System der christlichen Lehre.* 2d ed. Stuttgart: J. F. Steinkopf, 1870.

———. *Vorlesungen über christliche Glaubenslehre.* 2 vols. Gütersloh: C. Bertelsmann, 1886–87.

Bekker, Balthasar. *De Betoverde Weereld, Zynde een Grondig Ondersoek van't Gemeen Geloeven Aangaande de Geesten, Deselver Aart en Vermogen, Bewind en Bedrijft: Als Ook't Gene de Menschen door Derselver Kraght en Emeenschap Doen.* 4 vols. Amsterdam: D. van den Dalen, 1691–93.

Bellarmine, Robert. *De controversiis Christanae fidei, adversus huius temporis haereticos.* Cologne: Gualtheri, 1617–20.

———. *De gratia primi hominis.* Heidelberg: J. Lancellot, 1612.

———. *De justitia.* 1607.

———. *Opera omnia.* Edited by J. Fèvre. 12 vols. Paris: Vivès, 1870–74.

Bensow, Oscar. *Über die Möglichkeit eines ontologischen Beweises für das Dasein Gottes.* Rostock: Adler's Erben, 1898.

Bernard de Clairvaux. *De consideratione.* Utrecht: Nicolaus Ketelaer & Gerhardus Leempt, 1473.

Bertling, O. *Der Johanneische Logos und seine Bedeutung für das christliche Leben.* Leipzig: J. C. Heinrichs, 1907.

Bettex, Frederic. *Das Lied der Schöpfung.* 5th ed. Stuttgart: J. F. Steinkopf, 1906.

———. *Naturstudie en Christendom.* 4th ed. Kampen: J. H. Kok, 1908.

Beversluis, Martien. *De heilige Geest en zijne werkingens volgens de Schriften des Nieuwen Verbonds.* Utrecht: C. H. E. Breijer, 1896.

Beyschlag, Willibald. *Die paulinische Theodicee Römer IX–XI: Ein Beitrag zur biblischen Theologie.* 2d ed. Halle: Strien, 1896.

———. *Zur Verständigung über den christlichen Vorsehungsglauben.* Halle: Eugen Strien, 1888.

Beza, Theodore. *Tractationum theologicarum,* vol. 1. Geneva: Jean Crispin, 1570.

Biedermann, Alois Emanuel. *Christliche Dogmatik.* Zürich: Crell & Füssli, 1869.

Biegler, J. *Die civitas Dei des heiligen Augustinus.* Paderborn: Junfermann, 1894.

Biesterveld, Petrus. *De jongste methode voor de verklaring van het Nieuwe Testament.* Kampen: Bos, 1905.

Bilderdijk, Willem. *Opstellen van Godgeleerden en Zedekundigen Inhoud.* 2 vols. Amsterdam: Immerzeel, 1883.

Billuart, Charles René. *Cursus theologiae.* 9 vols. Maastricht: Jacobi Lekens, 1769–70.

————. *Summa S. Thomae hodiernis aca-demiarum moribus accommodata*. Liège, Belgium: E. Kints, 1746–51.

Billuart, Charles René, ed. *Summa theolo-giae*. By Thomas Aquinas. 6 vols. Turin: Typographia Pontificia et Archiepiscopa-lis, 1893.

Boethius. *The Consolation of Philosophy*. Translated by Peter Glassgold. Los Ange-les: Sun and Moon Press, 1994.

Böhl, Eduard. *Dogmatik*. Amsterdam: Schef-fer, 1887.

Böhme, C. F. *Die Lehre von den göttlichen eigenschaften*. Altenburg: C. Hahn, 1821.

Böhme, Jakob, and Johannes Claassen. *Jakob Böhme: Sein Leben und seine the-osophischen Werke*. 3 vols. Stuttgart, J. F. Steinkopf, 1885.

Bonaventure. *The Breviloquium*. Translated by Jose De Vinck. In vol. 2 of *The Works of Bonaventure*. Paterson, N.J.: St. An-thony Guild Press, 1963.

————. *Commentarius in IV libros senten-tarium*. Vols. 1–4 of *Opera omnia*.

————. *The Journey of the Mind to God*. Edited by Stephen F. Brown. Translated by Philotheus Boehner. Indianapolis: Hackett Pub. Co., 1993.

Bonwetsch, G. Nathanael, and Reinhold Seeberg. *Studien sur Geschichte der The-ologie und der Kirche*. 10 vols. Leipzig: Dietrich, 1898–1903.

Bosizio, Athanasius. *Das Hexaemeron und die Geologie*. Mainz: Franz Kirchheim, 1865.

Bosse, Alfred. *Untersuchungen zum chro-nologischen Schema des Alten Testament*. Cöthen: Schettler, 1906.

Boston, Thomas. *A View of the Covenant of Grace from the Sacred Records*. 1677. Re-printed, Edmonton, Alberta: Still Waters Revival Books, 1993.

Bouwman, Harm. *Het begrip gerechtigheid in het Oude Testament*. Kampen: J. H. Bos, 1899.

Bovon, Jules. *Dogmatique chrétienne*. 2 vols. Lausanne: Georges Bridel, 1895–96.

Brahé, Jan Jacob. *Aanmerkingen over de Vijf Walchersche Artikelen*. Vlissingen, 1758.

New edition edited by G. H. Kersten. Rotterdam: De Banier, 1937.

Brakel, Wilhelmus. *The Christian's Reason-able Service*. Translated by Bartel Elshout. Ligonier, Pa.: Soli Deo Gloria Publica-tions, 1992.

Braun, C. *Der Begriff "Person" in seiner An-wendung auf die Lehre von der Trinität und Incarnation*. Mainz: F. Kirchheim, 1876.

Braun, Johannes. *Doctrina foederum: Sive systema theologiae didacticae et elenchticae*. Amsterdam: A. Van Sommeren, 1668.

Bretschneider, Karl Gottlieb. *Handbuch der Dogmatik der evangelisch-lutherischen Kirche, oder Versuch einer beurtheilenden Darstellung der Grundsätze, welche diese Kirche in ihren symbolischen Schriften über die christliche Glaubenslehre ausgesprochen hat, mit Vergleichung der Glaubenslehre in der Bekenntnisschriften der reformirten Kirche*. 4th ed. 2 vols. Leipzig: J. A. Barth, 1838.

————. *Systematische Entwicklung aller in der Dogmatik verkommenden Begriffe nach den symbolischen Schriften der evangelisch-lutherischen und reformirten Kirche und den wichtigsten dogmatischen Lehrbüchern ihrer Theologen*. 4th ed. Leipzig: J. A. Barth, 1841.

Brink, Henricus. *Toet-Steen der Waarheid en der Dwalingen*. Amsterdam, 1685. 2d ed. Utrecht: W. Clerc, 1690.

Bruce, Alexander Balmain. *Apologetics*. Edin-burgh: T. & T. Clark, 1892.

————. *The Moral Order of the World in Ancient and Modern Thought*. London: Hodder & Stoughton, 1899.

Bruch, Johann Friedrich. *Die Lehre von den göttlichen Eigenschaften*. Hamburg: Fried-rich Perthes, 1842.

————. *Weisheits-Lehre der Hebräer: Ein Bei-trag zur Geschichte der Philosophie*. Strass-burg: Treuttel und Würtz, 1851.

Bruckner, Albert Emil. *Julian von Eclanum, sein Leben und seine Lehre*. Leipzig: J. C. Hinrichs, 1897.

Bruining, A. *Het Bestaan van God*. Leiden: S. C. van Doesburgh, 1891.

Brunetière, Ferdinand. *La science et la religion, réponse à quelques objections.* Paris: Firmin-Didot, 1895.

Bucanus, Guillaume. *Institutiones theologicae, seu locorum communium christianae religionis, ex Dei Verbo, et praestantissimorum theologorum orthodoxo consensu expositorum.* Bern: Johannes & Isaias Le Preux, 1605.

Büchner, Ludwig. *Force and Matter; or Principles of the Natural Order of the Universe.* 4th ed. Translated from the 15th German ed. New York: P. Eckler, 1891.

———. *Der Gottes-Begriff und dessen Bedeutung in der Gegenwart.* 2d ed. Leipzig: Th. Thomas, 1874.

Budde, Karl. *Die biblische Urgeschichte.* Giessen: J. Ricker, 1883.

Buddeus, Johann Franz. *Institutiones theologiae dogmaticae variis observationibus illustratae.* Leipzig: T. Fritsch, 1723.

———. *Institutiones theologiae moralis.* Leipzig: T. Fritsch, 1715.

———. *Theses theologicae de atheismo et superstitione: Variis observationibus illustratae et in usum recitationum academicarum editae.* Ienae: Joan. Felic. Bielckium, 1717.

Bull, George. *Opera omnia.* 6 vols. London: Typis Samuelis Bridge, Impensis M. Smith, 1703.

Burmann, Frans. *Synopsis theologiae et speciatim oeconomiae foederum Dei: Ab initio saeculorum usque ad consummationem eorum.* 2 vols. in 1. Amsterdam: Joannem Wolters, 1699.

Burmeister, Hermann. *Geschichte der Schöpfung: Eine Darstellung des Entwickelungsganges der Erde und ihrer Bewöhner.* 7th ed. Leipzig: C. G. Giebel, 1872.

Busken Huet, Conrad. *Het Land van Rembrandt: Studien over de Noordnederlandsche Beschaving in de Zeventiende Eeuw.* 2 vols. Haarlem: H. D. Tjeenk Willink, 1886.

Buxtorf, Johannes II. *Dissertationes philologico-theologicae.* Basel, 1645.

Caird, John. *An Introduction to the Philosophy of Religion.* Glasgow: J. Maclehose, 1880.

Caldecott, Alfred. *The Philosophy of Religion in England and America.* New York: Macmillan, 1901.

Calovius, Abraham. *Isagoges ad ss. theologia.* [Introduction to theology of the saints.] Wittenberg: A. Hartmann, 1652.

Calvin, John. *Commentary on Genesis.* Translated by John King. Grand Rapids: Baker, 1979.

———. *Commentary on Hebrews.* Translated by John Owen. Grand Rapids: Baker, 1979.

———. *Commentary on the Epistle of Saint Paul to the Romans.* Edinburgh: Calvin Translation Society, 1844.

———. *Commentary on the Epistles of Paul the Apostle to the Galatians, Ephesians, Philippians, and Colossians.* Translated by T. H. L. Parker. Grand Rapids: Eerdmans, 1965.

———. *Concerning the Eternal Predestination of God.* Translated by J. K. S. Reid. London: James Clarke & Co., 1961.

———. *Institutes of the Christian Religion* (1559). Edited by John T. McNeill and translated by F. L. Battles. 2 vols. Philadelphia: Westminster, 1960.

———. *Treatises against the Anabaptists and Libertines.* Translated and edited by Benjamin W. Farley. Grand Rapids: Baker, 1982.

Capito, Wolfgang. *Hexaemeron Dei opus explicatum.* Strasbourg: Vendelinus Richel, 1539.

Carneri, Bartholomew. *Der moderne Mensch: Versuche über Lebensführung.* Leipzig: Kröner, 1901.

———. *Sittlichkeit und Darwinismus: Drei Bücher Ethik.* Vienna: W. Braumüller, 1903.

Caro, E. *L'idée de Dieu et ses nouveaux critiques.* Paris: Hachette et cie., 1905.

Carrière, Moriz. *Die sittliche Weltordnung.* Leipzig: F. A. Brockhaus, 1877.

Casini, Antonio. *Controv. de statu purae naturae.* Appendix to book II of "De opificio sex dierum," in vol. IV, 587–653, of *De theologicis dogmatibus,* by D. Petavius. Paris: Vivès, 1868.

Caspari, C. P. *Der Glaube an die Trinität Gottes in der Kirche des ersten christlichen Jahrhunderts.* Leipzig: Akademischen Buchhandlung (W. Faber), 1894.

Cassiodorus, Senator. *Historia ecclesiastica tripartita.* Paris: Franciscus Regnault, 1499.

Catechism of the Council of Trent. Translated by J. Donovan. New York: Catholic Publ. Society, 1829.

Chamier, Daniel. *Panstratiae Catholicae, sive controversiarum de religione adversus Pontificios corpus.* 4 vols. Geneva: Rouer, 1626.

Chantepie de la Saussaye, Pierre Daniel. *Lehrbuch der Religionsgeschichte.* 3d ed. 2 vols. Tübingen: J. C. B. Mohr (Paul Siebeck), 1905.

Charnock, Stephen. *Several Discourses upon the Existence and Attributes of God.* London: D. Newman, 1682.

Chemnitz, M. *Loci theologici.* 3 vols. Frankfurt and Wittenberg: T. Merius and E. Schumacher, 1653.

Christ, Paul. *Die sittliche Weltordnung.* Leiden: E. J. Brill, 1894.

Chrysostom, *Homilies on Ephesians.* In *Homilies on the Epistles of St. Paul the Apostle to the Galatians and Ephesians, NPNF (1),* XIII, 49–172.

Cicero, Marcus Tullius. *De divinatione.* Translated by Wm. A. Falconer. Loeb Classical Library. Cambridge: Harvard University Press, 1923.

———. *De fato liber.* Paris: Andream Wechelum, 1565.

———. *De inventione.* Translated by H. M. Hubbell. 4 vols. Loeb Classical Library. Cambridge: Harvard University Press, 1949.

———. *On the Nature of the Gods.* Translated by H. Rackham. Loeb Classical Library. New York: G. P. Putnam's Sons, 1933.

———. *Tusculan Disputations.* Translated by John Edward King. London: W. Heinemann; New York: G. P. Putnam's Sons, 1927.

Claassen, Johannes, and Jakob Böhme. *Jakob Böhme: Sein Leben und seine the-*

osophischen Werke: In geordnetem Auszuge mit Einleitungen und Erläuterungen. 3 vols. Stuttgart: J. F. Steinkopf, 1885.

Clemen, Carl. *Die christliche Lehre von der Sünde.* Göttingen: Vandenhoeck & Ruprecht, 1897.

Clement of Alexandria. *Paedagogus. ANF,* II, 207–98.

———. *Stromateis.* Translated by John Ferguson. Fathers of the Church 85. Washington, D.C.: Catholic University of America Press, 1991.

Cloppenburg, Johannes. *Disputatio de foedere Dei.* 1643.

———. *Exercitationes super locos communes theologicos.* Franeker: Black, 1653.

———. *Theologica opera omnia.* 2 vols. Amsterdam: Borstius, 1684.

Coccejus, Johannes. *Epistolae ad Hebraeos explicatio et veritatis ejvs demonstratio.* Leiden: J. Elsevir, 1659.

———. *Summa doctrinae de foedere et testamento Dei.* 2d ed. Leiden: Elsevir, 1654.

———. *Summa theologiae ex Scripturis repetita.* Amsterdam: J. Ravenstein, 1665.

Cock, Helenius de. *Gereformeerde kerkregeering.* Kampen: Van Velzen, 1868.

Coelestinus. *See* Vorst.

Coignet, C. *La morale indépendante, dans son principe et dans son objet.* Paris: G. Baillière, 1869.

Comrie, Alexander, and Nicolaus Holtius. *Examen van het Ontwerp van Tolerantie.* 10 vols. Amsterdam: Nicolaas Byl, 1753.

Cramer, A. M. *Bijvoegselen tot de Levensbeschrijving van David Joris.* Leiden: S. & J. Luchtmans, 1846.

Crell, Johann. *De uno Deo Patre libri duo.* Irenopolis: C. Fronerus, 1688.

———. *Liber de deo euisque attributis.* Vol. IV of *Opera omnia.* Amsterdam: Irenicus Philalethes, 1656.

Cremer, Hermann. *Biblico-Theological Lexicon of New Testament Greek.* Translated by D. W. Simon and William Urwick. Edinburgh: T. & T. Clark; New York: Charles Scribner's Sons, 1895.

————. *Die christliche Lehre von den Eigenschaften Gottes.* Gütersloh: C. Bertelsmann, 1897.

Creutzer, Friedrich. *Philosophorum veterum loci de providentia divina ac de fato.* Heidelberg: Gutmann, 1806.

Cunningham, W. *Historical Theology.* 2d ed. 2 vols. Edinburgh: T. & T. Clark, 1864.

Cusanus (Nicholas of Cusa). *Of Learned Ignorance.* Translated by Germain Heron. New Haven: Yale University Press, 1954.

Cyprian. *On the Vanity of Idols. ANF,* V, 465–69.

Daelman, Charles Guislin. *Theologia seu observationes theologicae in Summam D. Thomae.* 9 vols. in 8. Antwerp: Jacob Bernard Jouret, 1734.

Dähne, August Ferdinand. *Geschichtliche Darstellung der jüdisch-alexandrinischen Religions-Philosophie.* 2 vols. Halle: Verlag der Buchhandlung des Waisenhauses, 1834.

Dalman, Gustaf. *Die richterliche Gerechtigkeit im Alten Testament.* Berlin: Kartell-Zeitung, Comissionsverlag, 1897.

Daneau, Lambert. *Epistolam ad Timotheum commentarius.* Geneva: E. Vignon, 1577.

Darwin, Charles. *The Descent of Man.* New York: D. Appleton and Co., 1871.

————. *The Expression of Emotions in Man and Animals.* London: John Murray, 1872.

————. *On the Origin of Species by Means of Natural Selection.* London: J. Murray, 1859.

————. *Het Voortbestaan van het Menschelijk Geslacht.* Utrecht: Kemink, 1902.

Davidson, Andrew Bruce. *The Theology of the Old Testament.* Edited from the author's manuscripts by S. D. F. Salmond. New York: Charles Scribner's, 1904.

Dawson, John William. *Nature and the Bible: A Course of Lectures Delivered in New York on the Morse Foundation of the Union Theological Seminary.* New York: Wilbur B. Ketcham, 1875.

De Fremery, H. N. *Handleiding tot de Kennis van het Spiritisme.* Bussum, 1904.

————. *Het Spiritische Levensbeschouwing.* Bussum, 1904.

Delitzsch, Franz. *Biblical Commentary on the Psalms.* Translated by Francis Bolton. 3 vols. Edinburgh: T. & T. Clark, 1871.

————. *Biblischer Commentar über die poetischen Bücher des Alten Testaments.* Leipzig: Dörffling & Franke, 1873.

————. *Commentary on Job.* Reprinted, Grand Rapids: Eerdmans, 1975.

————. *Neuer Commentar über die Genesis.* Leipzig: Dörffling & Franke, 1887.

————. *A New Commentary on Genesis.* Translated by Sophia Taylor. Edinburgh: T. & T. Clark, 1899.

————. *System der christlichen Apologetik.* Leipzig: Dörffling & Franke, 1870.

————. *A System of Biblical Psychology.* Translated by Robert E. Wallis. Edinburgh: T. & T. Clark, 1899.

Delitzsch, Friedrich. *Babel and Bible.* Translated by T. J. McCormack and W. H. Carruth. Chicago: Open Court, 1903.

————. *Mehr Licht.* Leipzig: J. C. Hinrichs, 1907.

Dennert, Eberhard. *At the Deathbed of Darwinism.* Translated by E. V. O'Harra and John H. Peschges. Burlington, Iowa: German Literary Board, 1904.

————. *Moses oder Darwin?* 2d ed. Stuttgart: Kielmann, 1907.

————. *Natuurwetenschap, Toeval, Voorzienigheid.* Baarn: Hollandia, 1906.

————. *Die Religion der Naturforscher.* 4th ed. Berlin: Buchhandlung der Berliner Stadtmission, 1901.

————. *Die Weltanschauung des modernen Naturforschers.* Stuttgart: M. Rielmann, 1907.

Dens, Pierre. *Theologia moralis et dogmatica.* 8 vols. Dublin: Richard Coyne, 1832.

Denzinger, Heinrich. *The Sources of Catholic Dogma (Enchiridion symbolorum).* Translated from the 30th ed. by Roy J. Deferrari. London and St. Louis: Herder, 1955.

————. *Vier Bücher von der religiösen Erkenntniss.* Frankfurt am Main: Minerva-Verlag, 1856.

Descartes, René. *The Philosophical Works of Descartes.* Translated by Elizabeth S. Haldane and G. R. T. Ross. 2 vols. London: Cambridge University Press, 1931.

De Wette, Wilhelm Martin Leberecht. *Biblische Dogmatik.* 3d ed. Berlin: G. Reimer, 1831.

Dieckhoff, August Wilhelm. *Der missourische Prädestianismus und die Concordienformel.* Rostock: E. Kahl, 1885.

Diekamp, Franz. *Die Gotteslehre des heiligen Gregor von Nyssa.* Münster: Aschendorff, 1896.

Dieringer, Franz. *Lehrbuch der katholischen Dogmatik.* 4th ed. Mainz: Kirchheim, 1858.

Diestel, Ludwig. *Die Sintflut und die Flutsagen des altherthums: Ein Vortrag.* Sammlung gemeinverständlicher wissenschaftlicher Vorträge, Serie 6, Heft 137. Berlin: Lüderitz, 1871.

Dijk, Isaäk van. *Aesthetische en Ethische Godsdienst.* In vol. 1 of *Gesammelte Geschriften.* Groningen, 1895.

Dillmann, August. *Genesis.* Edinburgh: T. & T. Clark, 1897.

Dilloo, F. W. J. *Das Wunder an den Stufen des Achas.* Amsterdam: Hoveker, 1885.

Dippe, Alfred. *Naturphilosophie.* Munich: C. H. Beck and O. Beck, 1907.

Documents of Vatican Council I, 1869–1870. Selected and translated by John F. Broderick. Collegeville, Minn.: Liturgical Press, 1971.

Doedes, Jacobus Izaak. *De Heidelbergsche Catechismus.* Utrecht: Kemink & Zoon, 1881.

———. *Inleiding tot de Leer van God.* Utrecht: Kemink, 1876.

———. *De Leer der Zaligheid Volgens het Evangelie in de Schriften des Nieuwen Verbonds Voorgesteld.* Utrecht: Kemink, 1876.

———. *De Nederlandsche Geloofsbelijdenis en de Heidelbergsche Catechismus.* Utrecht: Kemink & Zoon, 1880–81.

Dorner, Isaak August. *Gesammelte Schriften aus dem Gebiet der systematischen Theologie.* Berlin: W. Hertz, 1883.

———. *History of the Development of the Doctrine of the Person of Christ.* Translated by Patrick Fairbairn. 3 vols. Edinburgh: T. & T. Clark, 1868.

———. *A System of Christian Doctrine.* Translated by Alfred Cave and J. S. Banks. Rev. ed. 4 vols. Edinburgh: T. & T. Clark, 1888–91.

Dozy, Reinhart Pieter Anne. *Het Islamisme.* Haarlem: A. C. Kruseman, 1836.

Draper, John William. *History of the Conflict between Religion and Science.* New York: D. Appleton and Company, 1897.

Drews, Arthur. *Die deutsche Spekulation seit Kant.* 2d ed. 2 vols. Leipzig: G. Fock, 1895.

———. *Die Religion als Selbst-Bewusstsein Gottes.* Jena und Leipzig: E. Diederichs, 1906.

DuBois-Reymond, Emil Heinrich. *Culturgeschichte und Naturwissenschaft.* Leipzig: Veit, 1878.

Duker, A. C. *Gisbertus Voetius.* 4 vols. Leiden: Brill, 1897–1915.

Du Prel, Carl. *Die Planetenbewohner und die Nebularhypothese: Neue Studien zur Entwicklungsgeschichte des Weltalls.* Leipzig: Günther, 1880.

Ebrard, Johannes Heinrich August. *Apologetics: The Scientific Vindication of Christianity.* Translated by William Stuart and John Macpherson. 2d ed. 3 vols. Edinburgh: T. & T. Clark, 1886–87.

———. *Christliche Dogmatik.* 2d ed. 2 vols. Königsberg: A. W. Unzer, 1862–63.

———. *Der Glaube an die heilige Schrift und die Ergebnisse der Naturforschung.* Königsberg: n.p., 1851.

Edwards, Jonathan. *Dissertation concerning the End for Which God Created the World.* In *Ethical Writings,* edited by Paul Ramsey. The Works of Jonathan Edwards, vol. 8. New Haven: Yale University Press, 1989.

Eisenmenger, Johann Andreae. *Entdecktes Judenthum.* 2 vols. Königsberg in Preussen, 1711.

Eisler, Rudolf. *Kant-Lexikon.* Berlin: Mittler & Sohn, 1930.

————. *Kritische Einführung in die Philosophie.* Berlin: E. S. Mittler, 1905.

————. *Wörterbuch der philosophischen Begriffe.* 2 vols. Berlin: E. S. Mittler, 1904.

Ellis, Havelock. *Geschlechtstrieb und Schamgefühl.* Leipzig: Wigand, 1900.

Engelkemper, Wilhelm. *Die Paradiesesflüsse.* Münster: Aschendorff, 1901.

Episcopius, Simon. *Antidotum continens professiorem declarationem propriae et genuinae sententiae quae in Synodo Nationali Dordracena asserta est et stabilita.* Herder-Wici: Officina Typographi Synodalis, 1620.

————. *Apologia pro confessione sive declaratione sententiae eorum, qui in Foederato Belgio vocantur Remonstrantes, super praecipuis articulis religionis christianae contra censuram quatuor professorum Leidensium.* Vol. 2, pp. 95–283 of *Opera.* 1629.

————. *Eere Godts, Verdedight teghen den Laster Jacobi Triglandij.* Netherlands: s.n., 1627.

————. *Institutiones theologicae.* In vol. 1 of *Opera.* Amsterdam: Johan Blaeu, 1650.

————. *Opera theologica.* 2 vols. Amsterdam: Johan Blaeu, 1650–65.

Erbkam, Heinrich Wilhelm. *Geschichte der protestantischen Sekten im Zeitalter der Reformation.* Hamburg und Gotha: F. & A. Perthes, 1848.

Erigena, Johannes Scotus. *The Division of Nature.* Translated by Myra L. Uhlfelder. Indianapolis: Bobbs-Merrill, 1976 [1681].

Esser, Thomas. *Die Lehre des heiligen Thomas von Aquino über die Möglichkeit einer anfanglosen Schöpfung.* Münster: Aschendorff, 1895.

Eunomius. *Eunomius: The Extant Works.* Translated by Richard Paul Vaggione. Oxford: Clarendon Press, 1987.

Eusebius of Caesarea. *Praeparatio evangelica.* PG 21.

Eyck van Heslinga, H. van. *De Eenheid van het Scheppingsverhaal.* Leiden: n.p., 1896.

Falckenberg, Richard. *Geschichte der neueren Philosophie.* 5th ed. Leipzig: Veit, 1908.

Faure, Alexander. *Die Widerlegung der Häretiker im ersten Buche des Praedestinatus.* Göttingen: Dieterich, 1903.

Ferrius, Paulus. *Scholastici orthodoxi specimen.* Gotstadii: J. Lambertin, 1616.

Feuerbach, Ludwig. *Das Wesen des Christenthums.* Leipzig: O. Wigand, 1841.

————. *The Essence of Christianity.* Translated by Marion Evans. London: J. Chapman, 1854. Translated by G. Eliot. Harper Torchbook: Harper & Row, 1957.

Fichte, Immanuel Hermann von. *Anthropologie.* Leipzig: Brockhaus, 1860.

————. *Grundlage der gesammten Wissenschaftslehre.* Leipzig: Bel Christian Ernst Gabler, 1794.

————. *Die idee der Persönlichkeit und der individuellen Fortdauer.* Leipzig: Dyk, 1855.

Fichte, Johann Gottlieb. *Anweisung zum seligen Leben.* Translated by William Smith as "The Doctrine of Religion." In *Popular Works.* London: Trübner & Co., 1873.

————. *Attempt at a Critique of All Revelation.* Translated by Grant Green. Cambridge: Cambridge University Press, 1978.

————. *Gesamtausgabe.* 15 vols. Stuttgart: Bad Cannstatt, 1977.

————. *The Popular Works of Johann Gottlieb Fichte.* Translated by William Smith. 2 vols. Bristol: Thoemmes, 1999.

————. *The Science of Rights.* Translated by A. E. Kroeger. London: Trübner & Co., 1889. Reprinted. New York: Harper and Row, 1970.

————. *Versuch einer Kritik aller Offenbarung.* Königsberg: Hartungschen Buchhandlung, 1792.

————. *The Vocation of Man.* Translated by William Smith. 2d ed. Chicago: Open Court Pub. Co., 1910.

Fischer, Engelbert Lorenz. *Heidenthum und Offenbarung.* Mainz: Kirchheim, 1878.

Fischer, Kuno. *Geschichte der neueren Philosophie im Urteil der Jahrzehnte: 1852–1924.* 11 vols. Heidelberg: Winter, 1924.

Flammarion, Camille. *La Pluralité des Mondes Habités*. Paris: Mallet-Bachelier, 1862.

Flint, Robert. *Anti-theistic Theories*. 3d ed. Edinburgh and London: W. Blackwood and Sons, 1885.

———. *Theism*. Edinburgh: W. Blackwood, 1877.

Flügel, O. *Die Probleme der Philosophie und ihre Lösungen*. Cöthen: O. Schulze, 1888.

———. *Die spekulativ Theologie der Gegenwart*. Cöthen: O. Schulze, 1888.

Fock, Otto. *Der Socinianismus nach seiner Stellung in der Gesammtentwicklung des christlichen Geistes, nach seinem historischen Verlauf und nach seinem Lehrbegriff*. Kiel: C. Schröder, 1847.

Forbes, John. *Instructiones historico-theologicae, de doctrina Christiana*. Amsterdam: Elzevirius, 1645.

———. *Opera omnia*. 2 vols. Amsterdam: H. Wetstenium & R. & G. Wetstenios, 1702–3.

Fortlage, Karl. *Darstellung und Kritik der Beweise fürs Dasein Gottes*. Heidelberg: Karl Groos, 1840.

Fotheringham, David Ross. *The Chronology of the Old Testament*. Cambridge: Deighton Bell, 1906.

Franck, Adolphe. *The Kabbalah*. New York: Arno Press, 1973.

Francken, Wijnaendts. *Ethische Studiën*. Haarlem: n.p., 1903.

Frank, Franz Hermann Reinhold. *System der christlichen Wahrheit*. 2d ed. 2 vols. Erlangen: A. Deichert, 1884.

———. *Theologie der Concordienformel*. 4 vols. in 2. Erlangen: T. Blaesing, 1858–65.

Fraser, Alexander Campbell. *Philosophy of Theism*. New York: Scribner's, 1899.

Fricke, Gustav Adolf. *Ist Gott persönlich?* Leipzig: Georg Wigand, 1896.

———. *Der paulinische Grundbegriff der δικαιοσυνη Θεου, erörtert auf Grund von Röm. 3:21–26*. Leipzig: Böhme, 1888.

Friderici, Johannes Gottlieb. *De aurea aetate quam poëtae finxerunt*. Leipzig: n.p., 1736.

Fritschel, George J. *Die Schriftlehre von der Gnadenwahl*. Leipzig: A. Deichert, 1907.

Froberger, Josef. *Die Schöpfungsgeschichte der Menschheit in der "voraussetzungslosen" Völkerpsychologie*. Trier: Paulinus, 1903.

Gall, August Freiherr von. *Die Herrlichkeit Gottes: Eine biblisch-theologische Untersuchung ausgedehnt über das Alte Testament, die Targume, Apokryphen, Apokalypsen und das Neue Testament*. Giessen: J. Ricker (A. Töpelmann), 1900.

Gander, Martin. *Naturwissenschaft und Glaube*. Benzigers Naturwissenschaftliche Bibliothek. New York: Benziger Bros., 1905.

———. *Die Sündflut in ihrer Bedeutung für die Erdgeschichte*. Münster: Aschendorff, 1896.

Gangauf, Theodor. *Des heiligen Augustinus speculative Lehre von Gott dem Dreieinigen*. Augsburg: Schmidt, 1883.

———. *Metaphysische Psychologie des heiligen Augustinus*. Augsburg: K. Kollmann, 1852.

Garrison, J. H. *The Holy Spirit*. St. Louis: Christian Pub. Co., 1905.

Geesink, Wilhelm. *Van 's Heeren Ordinantiën*. 3 vols. Amsterdam: W. Kirchener, 1907.

Geikie, Archibald S. *Geology*. New York: D. Appleton & Company, 1880.

Genz, Wilhelm. *Der Agnostizismus Herbert Spencers mit Rücksicht auf August Comte und Friedr. Alb. Lange*. Greifswald, 1902.

Gerhard, Johann. *Loci theologici*. Edited by E. Preuss. 9 vols. Berlin: G. Schlawitz, 1863–75.

Gierke, Otto. *Johannes Althusius*. Breslau: W. Koebner, 1880.

Girard, Raymond de. *Études de géologie biblique: Le déluge devant la critique historique*. 3 vols. Fribourg: Fragnière, 1893–95.

Glassius, Salomo(n). *Philologiae sacrae*. 4th ed. Jena: Steinmann, 1668. 6th ed. Francofurti & Lipsiae: Fleischer, 1691.

Gloel, Johannes. *Der heiligen Geist in der Heilsverkündigung des Paulus*. Halle: M. Niemeyer, 1888.

Gnandt, Albert. *Der mosaische Schöpfungs-bericht in seinem Verhältnis zur modernen Wissenschaft.* Graz, 1906.

Godet, Frédéric Louis. *Commentaire sur l'Évangile de Saint Jean.* 2d ed. 3 vols. in 2. Paris: Sandoz & Fischbacher; Neuchatel: Librairie Générale J. Sandoz, 1876–77.

———. *Commentary on John's Gospel.* Grand Rapids: Kregel Publications, 1978.

———. *Études Bibliques: Première série: Ancien Testament.* 2d ed. Paris: Sandoz and Fischbacher, 1873.

———. *Studies on the Old Testament.* Translated by W. H. Lyttelton. 6th ed. London: Hodder & Stoughton, 1892.

Gomarus, Franciscus. *Disputationum theologicarum quarto repetitarum quadragesima-tertia de paedobaptismo.* Leiden: Officina Ioannis Patii, 1606.

———. *Opera theologica omnia.* Amsterdam: J. Jansson, 1664.

Gooszen, M. A. *De Heidelbergsche catechismus en het boekje van de breking des broods.* Leiden: Brill, 1892.

Gordon, Alex. R. *The Early Traditions of Genesis.* Edinburgh: T. & T. Clark, 1907.

Gottschick, Johannes. *Die Kirchlichkeit der soganannte kirchliche Theologie.* Freiburg im Breisgau: J. C. B. Mohr, 1890.

Grasset, Joseph. *Les limites de la biologie.* Paris: Alcan, 1902.

Gregory Nazianzus. *Against Eunomius. NPNF (2),* V, 33ff.

———. *Apologia in Hexaëmeron.* PL 44, 61–124.

———. *Gregorii Nazianzeni Oratio in novam Dominicam.* Leipzig: Typis Elbertianis, 1836.

———. *Theological Orations, NPNF (2),* VII, 309–18.

Gregory of Nyssa. *On the Making of Man. NPNF (2),* V, 387–427.

———. *To Ablabius. NPNF (2),* V, 529–30.

Gregory the Great. *Moralia in Iobum.* In *Corpus Christianorum,* Series Latina, 143. A. Turnholti: Typographi Brepols Editores Pontifici, 1979.

———. *Morals on the Book of Job.* 3 vols. in 4. Oxford: J. H. Parker, 1844–50.

Gretillat, Augustin. *Exposé de théologie systématique.* 4 vols. Paris: Fischbacher, 1885–92.

Grill, Julius von. *Untersuchungen über die Entstehung des vierten Evangeliums.* Tübingen: J. C. B. Mohr, 1902.

Guibert, Jean. *In the Beginning.* Translated by G. S. Whitmarsh. London: Kegan Paul, Trench, & Trübner, 1900.

Gumplovicz, Ludwig. *Grundriss der Sociologie.* 2d ed. Vienna: Manzsche Buchhandlung, 1905.

Gunkel, Hermann. *Genesis.* Translated by Mark E. Biddle. Macon, Ga.: Mercer University Press, 1997.

———. *Die Genesis übersetzt und erklärt.* Göttingen: Vandenhoeck & Ruprecht, 1902.

———. *Die Wirkungen des heiligen Geistes.* Göttingen: Vandenhoeck & Ruprecht, 1888.

Gunkel, Hermann, and Heinrich Zimmern. *Schöpfung und Chaos in Urzeit und Endzeit.* 2d ed. Göttingen: Vandenhoeck & Ruprecht, 1921.

Gürtler, Nicolaus. *Nicolai Gürtleri Institutiones theologicae.* Marburgi Cattorum: Sumtibus Philippi Casimiri Mülleri, 1732.

Gutberlet, Constantin (Konstantin). *Der Mechanische Monismus.* Paderborn: F. Schöningh, 1893.

———. *Der Mensch.* Paderborn: F. Schöningh, 1903.

Güttler, Carl. *Naturforschung und Bibel in ihrer Stellung zur Schöpfung.* Freiburg im Breisgau: Herder, 1877.

Haeckel, Ernst. *The History of Creation, or, The Development of the Earth and Its Inhabitants by the Action of Natural Causes [Natürliche Schöpfungsgeschichte].* Translated and revised by E. R. Lankester. 2 vols. New York: D. Appleton, 1883.

———. *Der Kampf um den Entwickelungs-Gedanken.* Berlin: G. Reimer, 1905.

――――. *Der Monismus als Band zwischen Religion und Wissenschaft.* 6th ed. Leipzig: A. Kroner, 1908.

――――. *The Riddle of the Universe at the Close of the Nineteenth Century.* Translated by Joseph McCabe. New York: Harper & Brothers, 1900.

Hagenbach, Karl Rudolf. *A Text-Book of the History of Doctrines.* Translated by C. W. Buch. Revised by Henry B. Smith. Rev. ed. 2 vols. New York: Sheldon, 1867.

Hahn, August, G. L. Hahn, and Adolph von Harnack. *Bibliothek der Symbole und Glaubensregeln der alten Kirche.* 3d ed. Breslau: E. Morgenstern, 1897.

Hahn, G. L. *Die Theologie des Neuen Testaments.* Leipzig: Dörffling & Franke, 1854.

Hahn, W. *Die Entstehung der Weltkörper.* Regensburg: Pustet, 1895.

Hanne, Johann Wilhelm. *Die Idee der Absoluten Persönlichkeit.* 2d ed. Hannover: C. Rümpler, 1865.

Häring, Theodor. *The Christian Faith.* Translated by John Dickie and George Ferries. 2 vols. London: Hodder & Stoughton, 1913.

Harnack, Adolf von. *History of Dogma.* Translated by N. Buchanan, J. Millar, E. B. Speirs, and W. McGilchrist. Edited by A. B. Bruce. 7 vols. London: Williams & Norgate, 1896–99.

――――. *The Mission and Expansion of Christianity in the First Three Centuries.* New York: Harper, 1962.

――――. *Der Vorwurf des Atheismus in den drei ersten Jahrhunderten.* Leipzig: J. C. Hinrichs, 1905.

――――. *What Is Christendom?* Translated by Thomas Bailey Saunder. New York and Evanston: Harper and Row, 1957.

Harris, Samuel. *God the Creator and Lord of All.* 2 vols. Edinburgh: T. & T. Clark, 1897.

――――. *The Philosophical Basis of Theism.* New York: Charles Scribner's Sons, 1883.

Hartmann, Eduard von. *Gesammelte Studien und Aufsätze.* Leipzig: Friedrich, 1891.

――――. *Philosophie des Unbewussten.* 9th ed. 2 vols. Berlin: C. Duncker, 1882.

――――. *Philosophie des Unbewussten.* 11th ed. 3 vols. Leipzig: H. Haacke, 1904.

――――. *Philosophische Fragen der Gegenwart.* Leipzig and Berlin: W. Friedrich, 1885.

――――. *Religionsphilosophie.* 2d ed. 2 vols. Bad Sachsa im Harz: Hermann Haacke, 1907.

――――. *Das sittliche Bewusstsein.* Leipzig: W. Friedrich, 1886.

――――. *Wahrheit und Irrthum im Darwinismus: Eine kritische Darstellung der organischen Entwickelungstheorie.* Berlin: C. Duncker, 1875.

Hase, Karl A. von. *Hutterus redivivus.* 2 vols. in 1. Helsingfors: A. W. Gröndahl, 1846–47.

Hastie, William. *The Theology of the Reformed Church in Its Fundamental Principles.* Edinburgh: T. & T. Clark, 1904.

Hatch, Edwin. *The Influence of the Greek Ideas on Christianity.* New York: Harper and Brothers, 1957.

Heard, John Bickford. *The Tripartite Nature of Man: Spirit, Soul, and Body.* 2d ed. Edinburgh: T. & T. Clark, 1868.

Hegel, Georg Wilhelm Friedrich. *The Encyclopaedia of Logic (with the Zusätze).* Translated by T. F. Geraets et al. Indianapolis and Cambridge: Hackett, 1991.

――――. *Encyclopedia of the Philosophical Sciences in Outline.* Translated by Steven A. Taubneck. New York: Continuum, 1990.

――――. *Lectures on the Philosophy of Religion.* Translated by E. B. Spiers and J. Burdon Sanderson. 3 vols. London: Kegan Paul, Trench, Trübner & Co., 1895.

――――. *The Phenomenology of Mind.* Translated by J. B. Bailles. 2d ed. London: George Allen; New York: MacMillan, 1931.

――――. *Philosophy of Nature.* Translated by M. J. Petry. London and New York: Allen Unwin, Humanities Press, 1970.

――――. *Sämtliche Werke.* 26 vols. Stuttgart: F. Frommann, 1949–59.

Heidanus, Abraham. *Corpus theologiae christianae in quindecim locos digestum*. 2 vols. Leiden, 1686.

Heidegger, Johann Heinrich. *Corpus theologiae christianae*. 2 vols. Zürich: J. H. Bodmer, 1700.

———. *De libertate christianorum a lege cibaria veteri*. 2d ed. Zürich: Gessner, 1678.

Heine, Ronald E. *The Commentaries of Origen and Jerome on St. Paul's Epistle to the Ephesians*. New York: Oxford University Press, 2002.

Heinrich, Joann Baptist, and Constantin (Konstantin) Gutberlet. *Dogmatische Theologie*. 2d ed. 10 vols. Mainz: Kirchheim, 1881–1900.

Heinze, Max. *Die Lehre vom Logos in der griechischen Philosophie*. Oldenburg: F. Schmidt, 1872.

Hengstenberg, Ernst Wilhelm. *Dissertations on the Genuineness of the Pentateuch*. Translated by John D. Lowe. 2 vols. Edinburgh: Continental Translation Society, 1847.

Henry, Paul Emil. *Life and Times of John Calvin*. Translated by Hans Stebbing. 2 vols. New York: Robert Carta and Brothers, 1853.

Heppe, Heinrich. *Die Dogmatik der evangelisch-reformierten Kirche*. Elberseld: R. L. Friedrich, 1861.

———. *Dogmatik des deutschen Protestantismus im sechzehnten Jahrhundert*. 3 vols. Gotha: F. A. Perthes, 1857.

———. *Reformed Dogmatics: Set Out and Illustrated from the Sources*. Revised and edited by Ernst Bizer and translated by G. T. Thomson. London: Allen & Unwin, 1950. Reprinted, Grand Rapids: Baker, 1978.

Herder, Johann Gottfried. *Älteste Urkunde des Menschengeschlechts*. Riga: Hartknoch, 1774–76.

———. *Vom Geist des Christenthums*. Leipzig: J. F. Hartkroch, 1798.

Herner, S. *Die Anwendung des Wortes κυριος im Neuestestament*. Lund: E. Malström, 1903.

Herrmann, Wilhelm J. *Die Religion im Verhältnis zum Welterkennen und zur Sittlichkeit*. Halle: M. Nieymeyer, 1879.

Hertwig, Oskar. *Biological Problems of Today: Preformation or Epigenesis?* New York: Macmillan Co., 1900.

———. *Die Entwicklung der Biologie im neunzehnten Jahrhundert*. Jena: G. Fischer, 1908.

Hesiod. *Essential Hesiod (Works and Days)*. Translated by C. J. Rowe. Bristol, England: Bristol Classical Press, 1978.

Hettinger, Franz. *Apologie des Christentums*. Edited by Eugen Müller. 9th ed. 5 vols. Freiburg im Breisgau and St. Louis: Herder, 1906–8.

———. *Natural Religion*. Edited by Henry Sebastian Bowden. London: Burns and Oats, 1892.

Hilarius (Hilary), Episcopus Pictaviensis. *De Trinitate contra Arianos*. Venice: Paganinus de Paganinis, 1498.

Hinneberg, Paul, ed. Die Kultür der Gegenwart. 24 vols. Berlin and Leipzig: B. G. Teubner, 1905–23.

Hobbes, Thomas. *De cive; or, The Citizen*. Edited by Sterling Power Lamprecht. New York: Appleton-Century-Crofts, 1949.

———. *Leviathan*. London: J. M. Dent, 1924.

Hodge, Charles. *Systematic Theology*. 3 vols. New York: Charles Scribner's Sons, 1888.

Hoekstra, Sytze. *Bronnen en Grondslagen van het Godsdienstig Geloof*. Amsterdam: P. N. van Kampen, 1864.

———. *Des Christens Godsvrucht*. Amsterdam: Kraay, 1866.

———. *Grondslag, Wezen en Openbaring van het Godsdienstig Geloof*. Rotterdam: Altmann & Roosenburg, 1861.

———. *Wijsgerige Godsdienstleer*. 2 vols. Amsterdam: Van Kampen, 1894–95.

Hofmann, Johann Christian Konrad von. *Der Schriftbeweis*. 2d ed. 2 vols. Nördlingen: Beck, 1857–60.

———. *Weissagung und Erfüllung im Alten und im Neuen Testament*. 2 vols. Nördlingen: C. H. Beck, 1841–44.

Hofstede de Groot, Petrus. *De Groninger Godgeleerdheid in Hunne Eigenaardigheid.* Groningen: Scholtens, 1855.

———. *Institutiones theologiae naturalis.* 3d ed. Groningen: W. Zuidema, 1845.

Hollaz, David. *Examen theologicum acroamaticum.* Rostock and Leipzig: Russworm, 1718.

Holtzmann, H. J. *Lehrbuch der neutestamentlichen Theologie.* 2 vols. Freiburg and Leipzig: Mohr, 1897.

Holzhey, Carl. *Schöpfung, Bibel und Inspiration.* Mergentheim: Carl Ohlinger, 1902.

Hommel, Fritz. *Geschichte des alten Morgenlandes.* Leipzig: Göschen, 1895.

Honert, Johan van den. Voorrede [preface] to *Schatboek der Verklaring over den Nederlandsche Catechismus,* by Zacharius Ursinus. Gorinchem: Nicholas Coetzee, 1736.

Honig, A. G. *Creationisme of Traducianisme?* Kampen: J. H. Bos, 1906.

Hoornbeek, Johannes. *Institiones theologicos.* Utrecht, 1653.

———. *Socianismus Confutatus.* 3 vols. Utrecht, 1650–54.

———. *Summa controversiarum religionis, cum infidelibus, haereticis et schismaticis.* Utrecht: J. à Waersberge, 1658.

Hooykaas, Isaäc. *Geschiedenis der Beoefening van de Wijsheid onder de Hebreën.* Leiden: P. Engels, 1862.

———. *God in de Geschiedenis: Eene Voorlezing.* Schiedam: Van Dijk, 1870.

Hooykaas, Isaäc, J. H. Herderscheê, H. Oort, A. G. van Hamel. *Godsdienst volgens de Beginselen der ethische Richting onder de Modernen.* 's Hertogenbosch: G. H. van der Schuyt, 1876.

Houtsma, M. Th. *De Strijd over het Dogma in den Islam tot op el-Ash'ari.* Leiden: S. C. van Doesburgh, 1875.

Howard, Nikolas. *Neue Berechnungen über die Chronologie des Alten Testaments und ihrer Verhaltnis zu der Altertumskunde.* Bonn, 1904.

Howorth, Sir Henry Hoyle. *The Glacial Nightmare and the Flood: A Second Appeal to Common Sense from the Extravagance of Some Recent Geology.* London: S. Low, Marson and Company Ltd., 1893.

———. *The Mammoth and the Flood.* London: S. Low, Marston, Searle, & Rivington, 1887.

———. *Neue Berechnungen über die Chronologie des Alt. Test. und ihr Verhältnis zu der Altertumskunde.* Foreword by V. E. Rupprecht. Bonn, 1904.

Hugenholtz, P. H. *Ethisch Pantheïsme.* Amsterdam: Van Holkema & Warendorff, 1903.

Hugh (Hugo) of St. Victor. *De sacramentis christianae fidei.* PL 176, cols. 173–618.

———. *Summa sententiarum septem tractatibus distincta.* PL 176, cols. 41–174.

Hümmelauer, Franz. *Der biblische Schöpfungsbericht.* Freiburg im Breisgau: Herder, 1877.

———. *Nochmals der biblischen Schöpfungsbegriff.* Freiburg im Breisgau: Herder, 1898.

Hyperius, Andreas. *Andreae Hyperii methodi theologiae.* Basil: Oporiniana, 1574.

Illingworth, J. R. *Personality, Human and Divine.* London: Macmillan and Co., 1895.

Irenaeus. *Against Heresies. ANF,* I, 309–567.

Issel, Ernst. *Der Begriff der Heiligkeit im Neuen Testament: Eine von der Haager Gesellschaft zur Verteidigung der christlichen Religion gekrönte Preisschrift.* Leiden: E. J. Brill, 1887.

Iverach, James. *Is God Knowable?* London: Hodder & Stoughton, 1884.

Jacobi, F. H. *Werke.* 8 vols. Leipzig: Gerhard Fleischer, 1812–25.

James, William. *The Varieties of Religious Experience.* Modern Library. 1902. Reprinted, New York: Random House, n.d.

Janet, Paul. *Les causes finales.* Paris: G. Balliére et Cie, 1882.

Jansen, G. M. *Praelectiones theologiae fundamentalis.* Utrecht, 1875–77.

———. *Theologia dogmatica specialis.* Utrecht, 1877–79.

Jansen, Johannes J. *Geschichte des deutschen Volkes seit dem Ausgang des Mittelalters.* 8 vols. Paris: Librairie Plon, 1887–1911.

———. *De Leer van den Person en het Werk van Christus bij Tertullianus.* Kampen: Kok, 1906.

Jensen, Peter C. A. *Das Gilgamesch-Epos in der Weltliteratur.* 3 vols. Strassburg: Trübner, 1906–28 (i.e., 1929). Vol. I: *Die Ursprünge der alttestamentlichen Patriarchen-, Propheten- und Befreier-Sage und der neutestamentlichen Jesus-Sage.* Strassburg: Trübner, 1906.

John of Damascus. *Exposition of the Orthodox Faith. NPNF (2),* IX, 259–360.

———. *The Orthodox Faith.* Translated by Frederic H. Chase Jr. In *Writings.* Fathers of the Church 37. Washington, D.C.: Catholic University of America Press, 1958.

Josephus, Flavius. *The Works of Josephus.* Translated by William Whiston. New updated ed. Peabody, Mass.: Hendrickson, 1987.

Jüngst, Johannes. *Kultus- und Geschichtsreligion (Pelagianismus und Augustinismus).* Giessen: J. Ricker, 1901.

Junius, Franciscus. *Opuscula theologica selecta.* Edited by Abraham Kuyper. Amsterdam: F. Muller, 1882.

———. *Theses theologicae.* Vol. 1 of *Opuscula.*

Justin Martyr. *Dialogue with Trypho. ANF,* I, 194–270.

———. *Discourse to the Greeks. ANF,* I, 271–73.

———. *The First Apology.* Edited by John Kaye. Edinburgh: J. Grant, 1912.

———. *Loci aliquot selecti.* Zürich: Schulthess, 1824.

Kaftan, Julius. *Dogmatik.* 2d ed. Tübingen: Mohr, 1897. 4th ed. 1901.

———. *The Truth of the Christian Religion.* Translated by George Ferries. 2 vols. Edinburgh: T. & T. Clark, 1894.

———. *Das Wesen der christlichen Religion.* Basel: C. Detloff, 1888.

———. *Zur Dogmatik: Sieben Abhandlungen aus der "Zeitschrift für Theologie und Kirche."* Tübingen: Mohr (Paul Siebeck), 1904.

Kähler, Martin. *Die Wissenschaft der christlichen Lehre.* 3d ed. Leipzig: A. Deichert, 1905.

Kahnis, Karl Friedrich August. *Die Lutherische Dogmatik, historisch-genetisch dargestellt.* 3 vols. Leipzig: Dörffling & Franke, 1861–68.

Kalb, Ernst. *Kirchen und Sekten der Gegenwart, unter Mitarbeit verschiedener evangelischer Theologen.* 2d ed. Stuttgart: Verlag für Buchhandlung der Evangelische Gesellschaft, 1907.

Kant, Immanuel. *Critique of Judgment.* Translated by J. H. Bernard. 1951. Reprinted, New York and London: Hafner Publishing, 1968.

———. *Critique of Practical Reason.* Translated by Mary Gregor. Cambridge: Cambridge University Press, 1997.

———. *Critique of Pure Reason.* Translated by Norman Kemp Smith. 1929. Reprinted, New York: St. Martin's Press, 1965.

———. *Kritik der Urtheilskraft.* Edited by Julius Hermann von Kirchman. 2d ed. Berlin: L. Heimann, 1872.

———. *Religion within the Limits of Reason Alone.* Translated by Theodore M. Greene and Hoyt H. Hudson. New York: Harper and Brothers, 1934.

Kattenbusch, F. *Confessionskunde.* Freiburg im Breisgau: J. C. B. Mohr, 1892.

Kaufmann, David. *Geschichte der Attributenlehre in der judischen Religionsphilosophie von Saadja bis Maimuni.* Gotha: F. A. Perthes, 1877.

Kaulen, Franz Philipp. *Der biblische Schöpfungsbericht.* Freiburg im Breisgau: Herder, 1902.

———. *Die Sprachenverwirrung zu Babel.* Mainz: F. Kirchheim, 1861.

Kautzsch, E. *Über die Derivate des Stammes* צדק *im altestamentlichen Sprachgebrauch.* Tübingen: L. F. Fues, 1881.

Keckermann, Bartholomäus. *Systema s.s. theologiae.* Hanoviae: Antonium, 1603.

Keerl, P. F. *Der Gottmensch, das Ebenbild des unsichtbaren Gottes.* Vol. 2 of *Der Mensch, das Ebenbild Gottes.* Basel: Bahnmaier, 1866.

————. *Die Lehre des Neuen Testaments von der Herrlichkeit Gottes.* Basel: Bahnmaier, 1863.

Keil, Carl Friedrich, and F. Delitzsch. *Bible Commentary on the Old Testament.* 24 vols. Edinburgh: T. & T. Clark, 1864–1901.

Kennedy, James Houghton. *Gottesglaube und moderne Weltanschauung.* Berlin: H. Reuther's, 1893.

Kern, H. *Rassen, Volken, Staten.* Haarlem: Bohn, 1904.

Kielstra, T. J. *Het godsdienstig leven.* 2d ed. Amsterdam: Van Kampen & Zoon, 1890.

Kirchner, J. *Über den Zufall.* Halle: Pfeffer, 1888.

Kirn, Otto. *Vorsehungsglaube und Naturwissenschaft.* Berlin: Edwin Runge, [n.d.].

Kist, N. C. *Kerkhistorisch Archief.* Edited by Willem Moll. 4 vols. Amsterdam: P. N. van Kampen, 1857–66.

Klee, Heinrich. *Katholische Dogmatik.* 2d ed. 3 vols. Mainz: Kirchheim, 1861.

Kleutgen, Joseph. *Die Philosophie der Vorzeit vertheidigt.* 2 vols. Münster: Theissing, 1863. 2d ed. 1878.

————. *Die Theologie der Vorzeit vertheidigt.* 2d ed. 5 vols. Münster: Theissing, 1867–74.

Kliefoth, Theodor Friedrich Dethlof. *Acht Bücher von der Kirche.* Schwerin: Stiller, 1854.

Kluge, Friedrich. *Etymologisches Wörterbuch der deutsche Sprache.* Strassburg: K. J. Trübner, 1883.

Knapp, Georg Christian. *Vorlesungen über die christliche Glaubenslehre nach dem Lehrbegriff der evangelischen Kirche.* 2d ed. 2 vols. Halle: Buchhandlung des Waisenhauses, 1836.

Knight, William Angus. *Aspects of Theism.* London and New York: Macmillan and Co., 1893.

Köberle, Justus. *Natur und Geist nach der Auffassung des Alten Testaments.* Munich: Beck, 1901.

Köhler, Ludwig. *Old Testament Theology.* Translated by A. S. Todd. Philadelphia: Westminster Press, 1957.

Kölling, Wilhelm. *Die Echtheit von 1. Joh. 5:7.* Breslau: C. Dülfer, 1893.

————. *Pneumatologie, oder, Die Lehre von der Person des heiligen Geistes.* Gütersloh: C. Bertelsmann, 1894.

König, Edmund. *W. Wundt: Seine Philosophie und Psychologie.* Stuttgart: F. Frommann, 1901.

König, Eduard. *Das Hauptproblem der altisraelitischen Religionsgeschichte.* Leipzig: J. C. Hinrichs, 1884.

————. *Der Offenbarungsbegriff des Alten Testaments.* 2 vols. Leipzig: J. C. Hinrichs, 1882.

Köstlin, Julius. *The Theology of Luther in Its Historical Development and Inner Harmony.* Translated by Charles E. Hay. 2 vols. Philadelphia: Lutheran Publication Society, 1897.

Kraetzschmar, Richard. *Die Bundesvorstellung im Alten Testament in ihrer geschichtlichen Entwicklung.* Marburg: N. G. Elwert, 1896.

Kreibig, Gustav. *Die Räthsel der göttlichen Vorsehung.* Berlin, 1886.

Krug, Heinrich. *De pulchritudine divina libri tres.* Freiburg: Herder, 1902.

Krüger, Gustav. *Das Dogma von der Dreieinigkeit und Gottmenschheit in seiner geschichtlichen Entwicklung.* Tübingen: J. C. B. Mohr, 1905.

Kuenen, Abraham. *De Godsdienst van Israël tot den Ondergang van den Joodschen Staat.* 2 vols. De Voornaamste Godsdiensten. Haarlem: Kruseman, 1869–70.

————. *The Religion of Israel to the Fall of the Jewish State.* Translated by Alfred Heath May. 3 vols. London: Williams and Norgate, 1882–83.

————. *Volksgodsdienst en Wereldgodsdienst.* Leiden: S. C. Van Doesburgh, 1882.

Kühl, Ernst. *Zur paulinischen Theodicee, Römer 9–11.* Göttingen: Vandenhoeck & Ruprecht, 1897.

Kuhn, J. *Die christliche Lehre von der göttlichen Gnade.* Tübingen: H. Laupp'sche Buchhandlung, 1868.

Künstle, K. *Das Comma Joanneum, auf seine Herkunft untersucht.* Freiburg: Herder, 1905.

Kurtz, Johann Heinrich. *The Bible and Astronomy: An Exposition of the Biblical Cosmology, and Its Relations to Natural Science.* Translated by T. D. Simonton. 3d ed. Philadelphia: Lindsay & Blakiston, 1857.

———. *Lehrbuch der Kirchengeschichte.* Mitau [Jelgava]: Aug. Neumann, 1849.

Kuyper, Abraham. *De Engelen Gods.* Amsterdam: Höveker and Wormser, 1902.

———. *Ex ungue leonem.* Amsterdam: Kruyt, 1882.

———. *De Gemeene Gratie in Wetenschap en Kunst.* Amsterdam: Höveker & Wormser, 1905.

———. *Om de oude Wereldzee.* 2 vols. Amsterdam: Van Holkema and Warendorf, 1907–8.

———. *De Schrift, het Woord Gods.* Tiel: H. C. A. Campagne, 1870.

———. *Uit het Woord.* 2d ed. Amsterdam: Wormser, 1896.

———. *De Vleeschwording des Woords.* Amsterdam: Wormser, 1887.

———. *The Work of the Holy Spirit.* Translated by J. Hendrik De Vries. 1900. Reprinted, Grand Rapids: Eerdmans, 1941.

Kuyper, Abraham, Jr. *Johannes Maccovius.* Leiden: D. Donner, 1899.

Kuyper, Herman Huber. *Evolutie of Revelatie.* Amsterdam: Höveker & Wormser, 1903.

Lactantius, Lucius C. *The Divine Institutes.* Translated by Sister Mary Francis McDonald. Washington, D.C.: Catholic University of America Press, 1964.

———. *De ira Dei.* 1543. Darmstadt: Gentner, 1957.

———. *De opificio Dei.* Cologne: Quentell, 1506.

Ladd, George Trumbull. *The Philosophy of Religion.* New York: Scribner, 1905.

Lagrange, Marie-Joseph. *Études sur les religions sémitiques.* Paris: V. Lecoffre, 1903.

Laidlaw, John. *The Bible Doctrine of Man.* Edinburgh: T. & T. Clark, 1895.

Lang, Andrew. *Onderzoek naar de Ontwikkeling van Godsdienst, Kultus en Mythologie.* Translated by L. Knappert. Haarlem: F. Bohn, 1893.

Lang, Andrew, with Leo Juda, Martin Macronius, and Zacharius Ursinus. *Der heidelberger Katechismus und vier verwandte Katechismen.* Leipzig: A. Deichert, 1907.

Lange, Friedrich Albert. *Geschichte des Materialismus und Kritik seiner Bedeutung in der Gegenwart.* 8th ed. Leipzig: Baedekker, 1908.

Lange, Johann Peter. *Christliche Dogmatik.* 3 vols. Heidelberg: K. Winter, 1852.

Lauchert, Friedrich. *Die Lehre des heiligen Athanasius des Grossen.* Leipzig, 1895.

Lechler, Gotthard Victor. *Geschichte des englischen Deismus.* Stuttgart: J. G. Cotta, 1841.

Lechler, Karl. *Die biblische Lehre vom heiligen Geiste.* 3 vols. Gütersloh: C. Bertelsmann, 1899–1904.

Leeuwen, Everardus Henricus van. *Bijbelsche Anthropologie.* Utrecht: G. J. A. Ruys, 1906.

———. *De Leer Aangaande God.* Utrecht: C. H. E. Breijer, 1892.

Leibniz, Gottfried Wilhelm. *System der Theologie.* 3d ed. Mainz: S. Müller, 1825.

———. *A System of Theology.* Translated by Charles William Russell. London: Burns and Lambert, 1850.

Leibniz, Gottfried Wilhelm, and Johann Christoph Gottsched. *Theodicee.* Leipzig: Foerster, 1744.

Lessing, Gotthold Ephraim. *Erziehung des Menschengeschlechts und andere Schriften.* Stuttgart: Reclam, 1997.

Lexis, Wilhelm, et al. *Die allgemeinen Grundlagen der Kultur der Gegenwart.* Die Kultur der Gegenwart 11. Berlin: Teubner, 1906.

Leydekker, Melchior. *Fax veritatis, seu exercitationes ad nonnullas controversias quae hodie in Belgio potissium moventur, multa ex parte theologico-philosophicae*. Leiden: Daniel Gaesbeeck & Felicem Lopez, 1677.

Liberatore, Matteo. *Institutiones philosophicae*. 8th ed. 3 vols. Rome: n.p., 1855.

Liebmann, Otto. *Gedanken und Thatsachen*. 2 vols. Strassburg: K. J. Trübner, 1882–99.

———. *Zur Analysis der Wirklichkeit: Eine Erörterung der Grundprobleme der Philosophie*. 3d ed. Strassburg: K. J. Trübner, 1900.

Liebner, Carl Theodor Albert. *Die christliche Dogmatik aus dem christologischen Princip dargestellt*. Göttingen: Vandenhoeck & Ruprecht, 1849–.

Limborch, Phillip van. *Theologia christiana ad praxin pietatis ac promotionem pacis christianae unice directa*. Amsterdam: Wetstein, 1735.

Lipps, Theodor. *Naturwissenschaft und Weltanschauung*. Heidelberg: C. Winter, 1906.

Lipsius, Richard Adelbert. *Lehrbuch der evangelisch-protestantischen Dogmatik*. Braunschweig: C. A. Schwetschke, 1893.

Locke, John. *An Essay concerning Human Understanding*. 8th ed. 2 vols. London: A. Churchill & A. Manship, 1721.

Lodge, Oliver J. *Life and Matter*. 4th ed. London: Williams and Norgate, 1907.

Lombard. *See* Peter Lombard.

Loofs, Friedrich. *Leitfaden zum Studium der Dogmengeschichte*. 4th ed. Halle a.S.: M. Niemeyer, 1906.

Lotz, Wilhelm. *Die biblische Urgeschichte*. Leipzig: A. Deichert, 1907.

Lotze, Hermann. *Mircrocosmus*. Translated by Elizabeth Hamilton and E. E. Constance Jones. New York: Scribner & Welford, 1866.

Love, Christoph. *Theologia Practica*. 4th ed. Amsterdam: J. H. Boom, 1669.

Lucas, G. J. *Agnosticism and Religion*. Baltimore: J. Murphy & Co., 1895.

Lueken, Wilhelm. *Michael: Eine Darstellung und Vergleichung der jüdischen und der morgenländisch-christlichen Tradition*.

Göttingen: Vandenhoeck & Ruprecht, 1898.

Lüken, Heinrich. *Die Stiftungsurkunde des Menschengeschlechts*. Freiburg im Breisgau: Herder, 1876.

———. *Die Traditionen des Menschengeschlechts*. Münster: Aschendorff, 1869.

Lütgert, Wilhelm. *Gottes Sohn und Gottes Geist: Vorträge zur Christologie und zur Lehre vom Geiste Gottes*. Leipzig: A. Deichert (G. Böhme), 1905.

Luthardt, Christoph Ernst. *Apologetic Lectures on the Truths of Christianity*. Edinburgh: T. & T. Clark, 1870.

———. *Apologetische Vorträge über die Grundwahrheiten des Christenthums*. Leipzig: Dörffling und Franke, 1870. 8th ed., 1878.

———. *Compendium der Dogmatik*. Leipzig: Dörffling & Franke, 1865.

Luther, Martin. *The Bondage of the Will*. Translated by J. I. Packer and O. R. Johnson. Old Tappan, N.J.: Revell, 1957.

———. *Lectures on Genesis 1–3*. Vol. 1 of *Luther's Works*. St. Louis: Concordia, 1958.

Maccovius, Johannes. *Loci communes theologici*. Amsterdam: n.p., 1658.

———. *Redivivus*. Franeker: Typis Idzardi Alberti & sumptibus Ludovici Elzevirii, 1654.

MacGillavry, Theodorus Henricus. *De Continuïteit van het Doode en het Levende*. Leiden: Brill, 1898.

Maimonides, Moses. *Moreh Nevukhim*. Warsaw: Goldman, 1872.

Malebranche, Nicholas. *The Search after Truth: Elucidations of The Search after Truth*. Translated by R. Sault. Columbus: Ohio State University Press, 1980.

Mannens, Paulus. *Theologiae dogmaticae institutiones*. 3 vols. Roermand: Romen, 1901–3.

Mansel, Henry Longueville. *The Limits of Religious Thought Examined in Eight Lectures, Preached before the University of Oxford*. Oxford: J. Wright, 1858.

Marck, Johannes à. *Compendium theologiae christianae didactico-elencticum.* Groningen: Fossema, 1686.

————. *Historia Paradisi.* Amsterdam: Gerardus Borstius, 1705.

————. *Het Merch der Christene Gotgeleerheit.* 4th ed. Rotterdam: Nicolaas en Paulus Topyn, 1741.

Maresius, Samuel. *Collegium theologicum sive systema breve universae theologiae comprehensium octodecim disputationibus.* Groningen: Francisci Bronchorstii, 1659.

————. *Systema theologicum.* Groningen: Aemilium Spinneker, 1673.

Martensen, Hans. *Christian Dogmatics: A Compendium of the Doctrines of Christianity.* Translated by William Urwick. Edinburgh: T. & T. Clark, 1871.

————. *Christian Ethics.* Translated by C. Spence, William Affleck, and Sophia Taylor. 3 vols. Edinburgh: T. & T. Clark, 1873–82.

Martensen-Larsen, Hans. *Die Naturwissenschaft in ihrem Schuldverhältnis zum Christentum: Eine religionsgeschichtliche Skizze.* Berlin: Reuther & Reichard, 1897.

Marti, Karl. *Geschichte der israelitischen Religion.* 3d ed. Strassburg: F. Bull, 1897.

Martineau, James. *A Study of Religion, Its Sources and Contents.* Oxford: Clarendon Press; New York: Macmillan and Co., 1888.

Mastricht, Peter van. *Theoretico-practica theologia.* Utrecht: Appels, 1714.

Matulewicz, Georgius B. *Doctrina Russorum de statu justitiae originalis.* Freiburg: Herder, 1904.

Mayer, Emil Walter. *Das christliche Gottvertrauen und der Glaube an Christus.* Göttingen: Vandenhoeck & Ruprecht, 1899.

Mayer, J. *Der teleologische Gottesbeweis und der Darwinismus.* Mainz: F. Kirchheim, 1901.

McCosh, James. *The Intuitions of the Mind Inductively Investigated.* New York: R. Carter, 1860.

————. *The Method of Divine Government, Physical and Moral.* 4th ed. New York: R. Carter, 1860.

McTaggart, John, and Ellis McTaggart. *Some Dogmas of Religion.* London: E. Arnold, 1906.

Mees, Rudof Pieter. *De mechanische Verklaring der Levensverschijnselen.* The Hague, 1899.

Meijer, Laurentius. *Verhandelingen over de Goddelyke Wigenschappen.* 4 vols. Groningen: Jacob Bolt, 1783.

Melanchthon, Philipp. *Corpus doctrinae christianae.* Lipsiae, 1561.

————. *Enarratio symboli Nicaeni.* 8 vols. Wittenberg: Ioannis Lufft, 1550.

————. *Examen ordinandorum.* 4 vols. in 2. Lipsiae: Imprimebat I. Steinman, 1584.

————. *Explicatio symboli Niceni.* 8 vols. Wittenberg: Ioannis Cratonis, Impensis Cunradi Ruelii, 1561.

————. *Loci communes.* Berlin: G. Schlawitz, 1856.

Melzer, Ernst. *Die augustinische Lehre vom Kausalitätsverhältnis Gottes zur Welt.* Neisse: Graveur, 1892.

Menken, Gottfried. *Versuch einer Anleitung zum eignen Unterricht in den Wahrheiten der heiligen Schrift.* 3d ed. Bremen: Wilhelm Kaiser, 1833.

Menno, Simons. *The Complete Works of Menno Simons.* Elkhart: John F. Funk and Brother, 1871.

————. *The Complete Writings of Menno Simons.* Translated by Leonard Verduin. Edited by J. C. Wenger. Scottdale, Pa.: Herald Press, 1956.

Menzel, Wolfgang. *Christliche Symbolik.* 2d ed. 2 vols. Regensburg: Manz, 1855.

Meyer, H. A. W. *Critical and Exegetical Handbook to the Epistle to the Ephesians and the Epistle to Philemon.* Translated by Maurice J. Evans. Edited by William P. Dickson. Edinburgh: T. & T. Clark, 1884.

————. *Critical and Exegetical Handbook to the Epistle to the Galatians.* Translated by G. H. Venables. Edinburgh: T. & T. Clark, 1884.

————. *Critical and Exegetical Handbook to the Epistles to the Philippians and Colossians.* Translated by John C. Moore. Revised and edited by William P. Dickson. Edinburgh: T. & T. Clark, 1875.

————. *Critical and Exegetical Handbook to the Gospel of John.* Translated by William Urwick, Frederick Crombie, and A. C. Kendrick. New York: Funk & Wagnalls, 1895.

————. *Kritisch exegetisches Handbuch über das Evangelium des Johannes.* Edited by B. Weiss. 7th ed. Göttingen: Vandenhoeck & Ruprecht, 1886.

Mezger, Paul. *Räthsel des christlichen Vorsehungsglaubens.* Basel: Helbing & Lichterbahn, 1904.

Michelis, Friedrich. *Entwicklung der beiden ersten Kapitel der Genesis.* Münster: Theissing, 1845.

Milton, John. *De doctrina christiana.* Edited by Charles Sumner. Brunsvigae: F. Vieweg, 1827.

————. *A Treatise on Christian Doctrine.* Translated by Charles R. Sumner. Cambridge: Printed by J. Smith for Charles Knight, 1825.

Minucius Felix, Marcus. *The Octavius of Marcus Minucius Felix.* Translated by G. W. Clarke. New York: Newman Press, 1974.

Möhler, Johann Adam. *Symbolik: Oder Darstellung der Dogmatischen Gegensätze der Katholiken und Protestanten nach Ihren öffentlichen Bekenntnisschriften.* Mainz: F. Kupferberg, 1838.

Möller, Wilhelm. *Die Entwicklung der alttestamentlichen Gottesidee in vorexilischer Zeit.* Gütersloh: C. Bertelsmann, 1903.

Moor, Bernhard de. *Commentarius perpetuus in Johannis Marckii Compendium theologiae christianae didactico-elencticum.* 7 vols. in 6. Leiden: J. Hasebroek, 1761–71.

More, Henry. *Mysterium pietatis, An Explanation of the Grand Mystery.* 3 vols. London: J. Fletcher, 1660.

Mornay, Philippe de. *De veritate religionis Christianae.* Leiden: Andries Cloucq, 1605.

Morris, J. *A New Natural Theology: Based upon the Doctrine of Evolution.* London: Rivington, Percival, 1896.

Müller, Ernst Friedrich Karl. *Die Bekenntnisschriften der reformierten Kirche.* Leipzig: A. Deichert, 1903.

————. *Symbolik.* Erlangen und Leipzig: A. Deichert, 1896.

Müller, Joseph T. *Die symbolischen Bücher der evangelisch-lutherischen Kirche.* 8th ed. Gütersloh: C. Bertelsmann, 1898.

Müller, Julius. *The Christian Doctrine of Sin.* Translated by Wm. Urwick. 5th ed. 2 vols. Edinburgh: T. & T. Clark, 1868.

————. *Dogmatische Abhandlungen.* Bremen: C. E. Müller, 1870.

Müller, Karl. *Die göttliche Zuvorersehung und Erwählung in ihrer Bedeutung für den Heilsstand des einzelnen Gläubigen nach dem Evangelium des Paulus.* Halle a.S.: Max Niemeyer, 1892.

Müller, Max. *Theosophie, oder psychologische Religion.* Leipzig: Engelmann, 1895.

————. *Theosophy, or Psychological Religion.* London; New York: Longmans, Green, 1895.

————. *Vorlesungen über die Wissenschaft der Sprache.* 3d ed. Leipzig: Mayer, 1866.

Münscher, Wilhelm. *Lehrbuch des christlichen Dogmengeschichte.* Edited by Daniel von Coelln. 3d ed. 2 vols. in 3. Cassel: J. C. Krieger, 1832–38.

Muntinghe, Hermann. *Pars theologiae christianae theoretica.* Harderwijk: I. van Kasteel, 1800.

Musculus, Wolfgang. *Loci communes theologiae sacrae.* Basileae: Heruagiana, 1567.

Nägeli, Carl. *Entstehung und Begriff der naturhistorischen Art.* 2d ed. Munich: Köningliche Akademie, 1865.

————. *A Mechanico-Physiological Theory of Organic Evolution.* Chicago: Open Court Pub. Co., 1898.

Neander, August. *Geschichte der Pflanzung und Leitung der christlichen Kirche durch die Apostel.* 5th ed. 2 vols. Gotha: F. A. Perthes, 1890.

————. *History of the Planting and the Training of the Christian Church by the*

Apostles. Translated by J. E. Ryland. 2 vols. London: Bell and Daly, 1864.

Nicholas of Cusa. *Of Learned Ignorance.* 1954. Reprinted, Westport, Conn.: Hyperion Press, 1979.

Niemeijer, Cornelius Johan. *De Strijd over de Leer der Praedestinatie in de IXde Eeuw.* Groningen: Gebroeders Hoitsema, 1889.

Niemeyer, H. A. *Collectio confessionum in ecclesiis reformatis publicatarum.* 2 vols. Leipzig: Sumptibis Iulii Klinkhardti, 1840.

Nietzsche, Friedrich Wilhelm. *On the Genealogy of Morals.* Translated by Douglas Smith. New York and Oxford: Oxford University Press, 1998.

Nieuwhuis, Willem Hillebrand. *Twee Vragen des Tijds.* Kampen: Kok, 1907.

———. *De Verdiensten der Katholieke kerk ten Opzichte der Natuurwet.* Translated from English. Foreword by F. Hendrichs. Amsterdam, 1906.

Nikel, Johannes Simon. *Genesis und Keilschriftforschung.* Freiburg im Breisgau: Herder, 1903.

———. *Die Lehre des Alten Testamentes über die Cherubim und Seraphim.* Theol. diss., Würzburg. Breslau: Grass Barth, 1890.

Nitzsch, Carl Immanuel. *System der christlichen Lehre.* 5th ed. Bonn: Adolph Marcus, 1844.

———. *System of Christian Doctrine.* Edinburgh: T. & T. Clark, 1849.

Nitzsch, Friedrich A. B. *Lehrbuch der evangelischen Dogmatik.* Prepared by Horst Stephan. 3d ed. Tübingen: J. C. B. Mohr, 1902.

Noordtzij, M. *Oostersche Lichtstralen over Westersche Schriftbeschouwing.* Kampen: J. H. Bos, 1897.

Nösgen, K. F. *Geschichte der Lehre vom heiligen Geiste.* Gütersloh: C. Bertelsmann, 1899.

———. *Der heilige Geist: Sein Wesen und die Art seines Wirkens.* Berlin: Trowitzch & Sohn, 1905.

Novatianus. *Novatiani romanae urbis presbyteri De trinitate liber = Novatian's Treatise on the Trinity.* Edited by W. Yorke Faussett. Cambridge: Cambridge University Press, 1909.

Oehler, Gustav Friedrich. *Die Engelwelt.* Stuttgart, 1890.

———. *Die Grundzüge der alttestamentlichen Weisheit.* Tübingen: L. F. Fues, 1854.

———. *Theology of the Old Testament.* Translated by Ellen D. Smith and Sophia Taylor. Edinburgh: T. & T. Clark, 1892–93.

Oetinger, Friedrich Christoph. *Die Theologie aus der Idee des Lebens abgeleitet und auf sechs Hauptstücke zurückgeführt.* Stuttgart: J. F. Steinkopf, 1852.

Oettingen, Alexander von. *Lutherische Dogmatik.* Vol. I: *Principienlehre.* Vol. II: *System der christlichen Heilswahrheit.* II.1: *Die Heilsbedingungen.* II.2: *Die Heilsverwirklichung.* Munich: C. H. Beck, 1897–1902.

Olevianus, Caspar. *De Bediening van het Genade Verbond* [*De substantia foederis gratiae* (1585)]. Rotterdam: Mazijk, 1939. Reprinted in *Geschriften van Caspar Olevianus.* The Hague: Reformatorische Boekhandel, 1963.

Oorthuys, Gerardus. *De Anthropologie van Zwingli.* Leiden: E. J. Brill, 1905.

Oosterzee, J. J. van. *Christian Dogmatics.* Translated by J. Watson and M. Evans. 2 vols. New York: Scribner, Armstrong, 1874.

Oppenraaij, Th. van. *La doctrine de la prédestination dans l'Eglise réformée des Pays-Bas depuis l'origine jusqu'au Synode National de Dordrecht en 1618 et 1619.* Louvain: J. van Linthout, 1906.

Opzoomer, C. W. *Wet en Wijsbegeerte.* Amsterdam: Gebhard, 1857.

Origen. *Against Celsus.* ANF, IV, 395–669.

———. *Homilies on Genesis and Exodus.* Translated by Ronald E. Heine. Washington, D.C.: Catholic University of America Press, 1982.

———. *On First Principles.* ANF, IV, 239–384.

———. *S. P. N. Cyrilli archiepiscopi Alexandrini Homiliae XIX. in Ieremiam prophetam.* 8 vols. Plantiniana Balthasaris Moreti, 1648.

Orr, James. *The Christian View of God and the World as Centering in the Incarnation.* New York: Randolph, 1893.

———. *God's Image in Man and Its Defacement in the Light of Modern Denials.* London: Hodder & Stoughton, 1906.

———. *The Problem of the Old Testament.* London: James Nisbet, 1905.

"Orthodox Confession, The." Vol. II, 275–400, of *Creeds of Christendom,* edited by Philip Schaff. New York: Harper & Row, 1931. Reprinted, Grand Rapids: Baker, 1990.

Ostwald, Wilhelm. *Die Überwindung des wissenschaftlichen Materialismus.* Leipzig: Veit, 1895.

Oswald, Johann Heinrich. *Angelologie.* Paderborn: F. Schöningh, 1883.

———. *Eschatologie.* Paderborn: F. Schöningh, 1868.

———. *Religiöse Urgeschichte der Menschheit.* Paderborn: F. Schöningh, 1881.

———. *Die Schöpfungslehre im allgemeinen und in besonderer Beziehung auf den Menschen.* Paderborn: F. Schöningh, 1885.

Otto, Rudolf. *Naturalism and Religion.* Translated by J. Arthur Thomson and Margaret R. Thomson. Edited by W. D. Morrison. London: Williams & Norgate, 1907.

———. *The Philosophy of Religion.* London: Williams & Norgate, 1931.

Outrein, Johannes d'. *Proef-stukken van heilige Sinne-Beelden.* Amsterdam: G. Borstius, 1700.

Ovid. *The Metamorphoses.* Translated by Henry T. Riley. New York: G. Bell & Sons, 1889.

Owen, John. "On Divine Justice." In *The Works of John Owen.* Edinburgh: T. & T. Clark, 1862.

———. *Pneumatologia, or, A discourse concerning the Holy Spirit.* London: J. Darby, 1674.

Pareus, David. *In divinam ad Corinthios priorem S. Pauli apostoli epistolam commentarius.* Geneva: Petrus Aubertus, 1614.

———. *In divinam ad Romanos S. Pauli apostoli epistolam commentarius.* Frankfurt: Rhodes, 1608.

Pastor [Shepherd] of Hermas. ANF, II, 1–58.

Paulsen, Friedrich. *Einleitung in die Philosophie.* Berlin: Hertz, 1892.

———. *System der Ethik mit einem Umriss der Staat- und Gesellschaftslehre.* 2 vols. Berlin: Hertz, 1889.

Perkins, William. *The workes of that famous and worthy minister of Christ.* 3 vols. London: John Legatt, 1612–18.

Perrone, Giovanni. *Praelectiones theologicae.* 9 vols. Louvain: Vanlinthout & Vandezande, 1838–43.

Pesch, Christian. *Compendium theologiae dogmaticae.* 5th ed. 4 vols. Freiburg im Breisgau: Herder, 1935.

———. *Praelectiones dogmaticae.* 9 vols. Freiburg: Herder, 1902–10.

———. *Theologische Zeitfragen: Alte und neue Apologetik.* Freiburg im Breisgau: Herder, 1900–16.

Pesch, Tillman. *Die grossen Welträthsel.* 2d ed. 2 vols. Freiburg: Herder, 1892.

Peschel, Oscar. *Abhandlungen zur Erd- und Völkerkunde.* 5th ed. 3 vols. Leipzig: Duncker & Humblot, 1877–79.

Petavius, Dionysius [Petau, Denis]. *De theologicis dogmatibus.* 8 vols. Paris: Vivès, 1865–67.

Peter Lombard. *Sententiae in IV liberis distinctae.* 3d ed. 2 vols. Grottaferrata: Colleggi S. Bonaventurae et Claras Aquas, 1971–81.

Pfaff, Friedrich. *Schöpfungsgeschichte.* Frankfurt am Main: Heyder & Zimmer, 1877.

Pfanner, Tobias. *Systema theologiae gentilis purioris.* Basel: Joh. Hermann Widerhold, 1679.

Pfleiderer, O. *Grundriss der christlichen Glaubens und Sittenlehre.* Berlin: G. Reimer, 1888.

———. *Der Paulinismus.* 2d ed. Leipzig: O. R. Reisland, 1890.

Philippi, Friedrich A. *Kirchliche Glaubenslehre.* 3d ed. 7 vols. in 10. Gütersloh: C. Bertelsmann, 1870–90.

Pichler, Aloys. *Die Theologie des Leibniz: Aus sämmtlichen gedruckten und vielen noch ungedruckten Quellen.* 2 vols. Munich: J. G. Cotta, 1869–70.

Pierson, Allard. *Bespiegeling, Gezag, en Ervaring.* Utrecht: Kemink, 1885.

———. *Geschiedenis van het Roomsch-katholicisme tot op het Concilie van Trente.* 4 vols. Haarlem: A. C. Kruseman, 1868–72.

Piscator, Johannes. *Aphorismi doctrinae Christianae maximam partem ex Institutione Calvini excerpti.* Oxoniae: typis Ioh. Lichfield, impensis Hen. Curteine, 1630.

———. *Johan. Piscatoris Tractatus de gratia Dei.* Herbornae Nassoviorum, 1614.

Plato. *The Laws.* Translated by E. B. England. 2 vols. New York: Longmans, Green & Co., 1921.

———. *The Republic.* Translated by Benjamin Jowett. Oxford: Clarendon Press, 1888.

Platz, Bonifacius. *Der Mensch.* Würzburg & Leipzig: Woerl, 1898.

Plitt, Hermann. *Zinzendorf's Theology.* 3 vols. in 1. Gotha: F. A. Perthes, 1869–74.

Plotinus. *Psychic and Physical Treatises: Comprising the Second and Third Enneads.* Translated by Stephen MacKennna. London: Philip Lee Warner, 1921.

Plutarch. *On Fate.* Translated by Phillip H. De Lacy and Benedict Einarson. Vol. VII, 303–60, of *Plutarch's Moralia.* Loeb Classical Library. Cambridge, Mass.: Harvard University Press, 1959.

Poertner, Balthasar. *Das biblische Paradies.* Mainz: Kirchheim, 1901.

Poiret, Pierre. *Cogitationum rationalium de Deo, anima et malo, libri quatuor.* Amsterdam: Daniel Elsevir, 1677.

Polanus, Amandus. *Syntagma theologiae christianae.* 5th ed. Hanover: Aubry, 1624.

Polyander à Kerckhoven, Johannes, André Rivet, Antonius Walaeus, and Antoine Thysius. *Synopsis purioris theologiae.* Edited by H. Bavinck. 6th ed. Leiden: Didericum Donner, 1881.

Pressensé, Edmond de. *Les origines: Le problème de la connaissance, le problème cosmologique, le problème anthropologique, l'origine de la morale et de la religion.* 2d ed. Paris: Libraire Fischbacher, 1883.

Prosper of Aquitaine. *Praedestinationem Dei nullus catholicus negat.*

———. *De vita contemplativa.* Speyer: Peter Drach, 1486.

Pruner, Johann Ev. *Synopsis der dogmatisch-moraltheologischen Lehre von der Wirksamkeit des hl. Geistes zunächst nach dem hl. Thomas von Aquin.* Eichstätt: Brönner'sche, 1891.

Pseudo-Dionysius the Areopagite. *The Divine Names and Mystical Theology.* Translated by John D. Jones. Milwaukee: Marquette University Press, 1980.

———. *Pseudo-Dionysius: The Complete Works.* Translated by Colin Luibheid. Edited by Paul Rorem. New York: Paulist Press, 1987.

———. *S. Thomae Aquinatis in librum beati Dionysi De divinis nominibus expositio.* Turin: Marietti, 1950.

Pünjer, Bernhard. *Geschichte der christlichen Religionsphilosophie seit der Reformation.* Brussels: Impression Anastaltique Culture et Civilisation, 1880–83.

Quenstedt, Johann Andreas. *Theologia didactico-polemica sive systema theologicum.* 1685. ET of chs. 1–3: *The Nature and Character of Theology.* Abridged, edited, and translated by Luther Poellot. St. Louis, Mo.: Concordia, 1986.

Quirmbach, J. *Die Lehre des heiligen Paulus von der natürlichen Gotteserkenntnis und dem natürlichen Sittengesetz.* Freiburg: Herder, 1906.

Racovian Catechism, The. Translated by Thomas Rees. London, 1609. Reprinted, London, 1818.

Ranke, Johannes. *Der Mensch.* 2d ed. Leipzig: Bibliographisches Institut, 1894.

Ratzel, Friedrich. *The History of Mankind.* Translated by A. J. Butler. 3 vols. New York: Macmillan Co., 1896–98.

Rauch, Matthaeus. *Die Einheit des Menschengeschlechts.* Augsburg: F. Butsch Sohn, 1873.

Rauwenhoff, L. W. E. *Wijsbegeerte van den Godsdienst.* Leiden: Brill & van Doesburgh, 1887.

Reiche, Armin. *Die künsterlichen Elemente in der Welt- und Lebensanschauung des Gregor von Nyssa.* Jena: A. Kámpte, 1897.

Reinhard, Franz Volkmar. *Grundriss der Dogmatik.* Munich: Seidel, 1802.

Reinhardt, Ludwig. *Der Mensch zur Eiszeit in Europa und seine Kulturentwicklung bis zum Ende der Steinzeit.* Munich: Ernst Reinhardt, 1913.

Reinke, Johannes. *Die Entwicklung der Naturwissenschaften insbesondere der Biologie im neunzehnten Jahrhundert.* Kiel: Universitäts-Buchhandlung (P. Toeche), 1900.

———. *Die Natur und Wir.* Berlin: Gebruder Paetel, 1908.

———. *Die Welt als That: Umrisse einer Weltansicht auf Naturwissenschaftlicher Grundlage.* 3d ed. 4 vols. Berlin: Gebruder Paetel, 1905.

Renan, Ernest. *L'avenir de la science: Pensées de 1848.* Paris: Calmann-Levy, 1890.

Reusch, Franz Heinrich. *Nature and the Bible: Lectures on the Mosaic History of Creation in Its Relation to Natural Science.* Translated by Kathleen Lyttelton from the 4th German ed. 2 vols. Edinburgh: T. & T. Clark, 1886.

Reuter, Hermann. *Augustinische Studien.* Gotha: F. A. Perthes, 1887.

———. *Geschichte der religiösen Aufklärung im Mittelalter.* 2 vols. in 1. Berlin: W. Hertz, 1875–77.

Réville, Jean. *La doctrine du logos.* Paris: J. Brochen, 1881.

Richard of St. Victor. *De trinitate.* Paris: J. Vrin, 1958.

Ridderbos, Jan. *De Theologie van Jonathan Edwards.* The Hague: J. A. Nederbragt, 1907.

Riedel, Wilhelm. *Alttestamentliche Untersuchungen.* Leipzig: A. Deichert (Georg Böhme), 1902.

Riehm, Eduard. *Handwörterbuch des biblischen Altertums für gebildete Bibelleser.* 2 vols. Bielefeld and Leipzig: Velhagen & Hasms, 1893–94.

Riehm, Gottfried. *Christentum und Naturwissenschaft.* 2d ed. Leipzig: J. C. Hinrichs, 1896.

Riem, Johannes. *Die Sintflut in Sage und Wissenschaft mit 2 Zeichn. und einer Weltkarte.* Hamburg: Rauhe Haus, 1925.

Riggenbach, Eduard. *Der trinitarische Taufbefehl: Matt. 28,19 nach seiner ursprünglichen Textgestalt und seiner Authentie.* Gütersloh: C. Bertelsmann, 1903.

Ritschl, Albrecht. *The Christian Doctrine of Justification and Reconciliation.* Clifton, N.J.: Reference Book Publishers, 1966.

———. *Die christliche Lehre von der Rechfertigung und Versöhnung.* 4th ed. 3 vols. Bonn: A. Marcus, 1895–1903.

———. *Gesammelte Aufsätze, Neue Folge.* Freiburg im Breisgau: J. C. B. Mohr, 1896.

———. *Theologie und Metaphysik.* Bonn: A. Marcus, 1881.

Ritter, Heinrich. *Geschichte der christlichen Philosophie.* 4 vols. Hamburg: F. Perthes, 1841–45.

Ritter, Heinrich, and Ludwig Preller. *Historia philosophiae Graecae.* Gotha: F. A. Perthes, 1888.

Rivetus, Andreas. *Commentarius in Psalmorum propheticorum; de misterijs evangelicis decadem selectam.* Rotterdam: A. Leers, 1645.

———. *Operum theologicorum.* 3 vols. Rotterdam: Leers, 1651–60.

Robertson, James. *The Early Religion of Israel.* 2d ed. New York: Westminster Press [Thomas Whittaker], 1903.

———. *Israel's oude Godsdienst.* Culemborg: Blom en Olivierse, 1896.

Romanes, George John. *The Scientific Evidences of Organic Evolution.* London: Macmillan and Co., 1882.

———. *Thoughts on Religion.* Edited by Charles Gore. 6th ed. Chicago: Open Court Publishing Co., 1911.

Rose, Fritz Otto. *Die Lehre von den eingeborenen Ideen bei Descartes und Locke.* Bern: C. Sturzenegger, 1901.

Roth, Rudolf von, and Ernst Kuhn. *Festgruss an Rudolf von Roth.* Stuttgart: W. Kohlhammer, 1893.

Rothe, Richard. *Theologische Ethik.* 2d, rev. ed. 5 vols. Wittenberg: Zimmermann, 1867–71.

Rottmanner, Odilo. *Der Augustinismus, eine dogmengeschichtliche Studie.* Munich: Verlag der J. J. Lentner'schen Buchhandlung, 1892.

Rümelin, G. *Reden und Aufsätze.* Tübingen: H. Laupe, 1875.

Runze, Georg. *Der ontologische Gottesbeweis: Kritische Darstellung seiner Geschichte seit Anselm bis auf die Gegenwart.* Halle: C. E. M. Pfeffer, 1882.

Ryssen, Leonardus. *De oude Rechtsinnige Waerheyt Verdonkert.* Middleburgh: Benedictus Smidt, 1764.

———. *Summa theologiae elencticae completa, et didacticae quantum sufficit.* Edinburgh: G. Mosman, 1692.

Sabatier, Auguste. *Outlines of a Philosophy of Religion Based on Psychology and History.* Translated by T. A. Seed. New York: James Pott, 1902.

Sanseverino, Gaëtano. *Philosophia christiana com antiqua et nova comparata.* Neapoli: Manfredi, 1861–66.

Sartorius, Ernst Wilhelm Christian. *Die Lehre von Christi Person und Werk.* 3d ed. Hamburg: F. Perthes, 1837.

———. *Die Lehre von der heiligen Liebe.* Stuttgart: S. G. Liesching, 1861.

Schäfer, Bernhard. *Bibel und Wissenschaft.* Münster: Theissing, 1881.

Schaff, Philip. *The Creeds of Christendom.* Revised by D. A. Schaff. 6th ed. 3 vols. New York: Harper & Row, 1931. Reprinted, Grand Rapids: Baker, 1990.

Schanz, Paul. *Das Alter des Menschengeschlechts nach der heiligen Schrift der Profangeschichte und der Vorgeschichte.* Freiburg im Breisgau: Herder, 1896.

———. *A Christian Apology.* Translated by Michael F. Glancey and Victor J. Schobel. 4th rev. ed. Ratisbon: F. Pustet, 1891.

———. *Über neue Versuche der Apologetik gegenüber dem Naturalismus und Spiritualismus.* Regensburg: Nat. Verl-Anst, 1897.

Schäzler, Constantin von. *Natur und Übernatur.* Mainz: Kirchheim, 1865.

Scheeben, Matthias Joseph. *Handbuch der katholischen Dogmatik.* 4 vols. 1873–1903. Reprinted, Freiburg im Breisgau: Herder, 1933.

———. *Natur und Gnade.* Mainz: Kirchheim, 1861.

Scheibe, Max. *Calvins Prädestinationslehre.* Halle a.S.: Ehrnhardt Karras, 1897.

Schell, Herman. *Der Gottesglaube und die Naturwissenschaftliche Welterkenntniss.* 2d ed. Bamberg: Schmidt, 1904.

Schelling, F. W. J. *Ausgewählte Werke.* 4 vols. Darmstadt: Wissenschaftliche Buchgesellschaft, 1968.

———. *Schelling's Philosophy of Mythology and Revelation.* Translated by Victor C. Hayes. Armindale, New South Wales: Australian Association for the Study of Religions, 1995.

Schermann, Theodor. *Die Gottheit des heiligen Geistes nach den griechischen Vätern des vierten Jahrhunderts.* Freiburg im Breisgau: Herder, 1901.

Schiaparelli, G. V. *Astronomy in the Old Testament.* Oxford: Clarendon Press, 1905.

Schiere, Nicolaus. *Doctrina testamentorum et foederum divinorum omnium.* Leovardiae: M. Injema, 1718.

Schleiermacher, Friedrich. *The Christian Faith.* Edinburgh: T. & T. Clark, 1989.

———. *Dialektik.* Berlin: G. Reimer, 1839.

———. *On Religion: Speeches to Its Cultured Despisers.* Cambridge and New York: Cambridge University Press, 1996.

Schlossmann, Siegmund. *Persona und πρόσωπον im recht und im christlichen Dogmatik.* Kiel: Lipsius & Tischer, 1906.

Schmid, C. F. *Biblische theologie des Neuen Testamentes.* 3d ed. Stuttgart: S. G. Liesching, 1864.

Schmid, Heinrich F. F. *The Doctrinal Theology of the Evangelical Lutheran Church.* Translated by Charles A. Hay and Henry Jacobs. 5th ed. Philadelphia: United Lutheran Publication House, 1899.

Schmid, Rudolf. *The Scientific Creed of a Theologian*. Translated by J. W. Stoughton from the 2d German ed. New York: A. C. Armstrong, 1906.

Schmidt, Carl. *Das Naturereignis der Sintflut*. Basel: B. Schwabe, 1895.

Schmidt, Wilhelm. *Christliche Dogmatik*. 4 vols. Bonn: E. Weber, 1895–98.

———. *Die Göttliche Vorsehung und das Selbstleben der Welt*. Berlin: Wiegandt & Grieben, 1887.

Schneckenburger, Matthew, and Eduard Güder. *Vergleichende Dartstellung des lutherischen und reformirten Lehrbegriffs*. 2 vols. Stuttgart: J. B. Metzler, 1855.

Schneemann, G. *Die Entstehung der thomistisch-molinistischen Controverse*. Freiburg im Breisgau and St. Louis: Herder, 1880.

Schneider, Richard. *Christliche Klänge aus den griechischen und römischen Klassikern*. Gotha: F. A. Perthes, 1865. Reprinted, Leipzig: Siegismund & Volkening, 1877.

Schneider, Th. *Was ist's mit der Sintflut?* Wiesbaden, 1903.

Schneider, Wilhelm. *Die Naturvölker*. Paderborn: Schöningh, 1885.

Schoeberlein, Ludwig. *Die Grundlehren des Heils entwickelt aus dem Princip der Liebe*. Stuttgart and Berlin: G. Schlawitz, 1848.

———. *Prinzip und System der Dogmatik*. Heidelberg: C. Winter, 1881.

Scholten, Johannes Henricus. *Dogmatices christianae initia*. 2d ed. Lyons: P. Engels, 1858.

———. *De Leer der Hervormde Kerk in Hare Grondbeginselen*. 2d ed. 2 vols. Leyden: P. Engels, 1850–51.

———. *De Vrije Wil, Kritisch Onderzoek*. Leiden: P. Engels, 1859.

Schopenhauer, Arthur. *Die beiden Grundprobleme der Ethik*. 3d ed. Leipzig: F. A. Brockhaus, 1881.

———. *Parerga and Paralipomena*. Translated by E. F. J. Payne. 2 vols. Oxford: Clarendon Press, 1974.

———. *Die Welt als Wille und Vorstellung*. 6th ed. Leipzig: Brockhaus, 1887.

———. *The World as Will and Representation*. Translated by E. F. J. Payne. New York: Dover Publications, 1966.

Schrörs, H. *Die Streit über die Prädestination im 9. Jahrhundert*. Freiburg im Breisgau: Herdersche Verlagshandlung, 1884.

Schröter, R. *Der Begriff der Heiligkeit im Alten und Neuen Testaments*. Leipzig: Fock, 1892.

Schubert, Hans von. *Der sogenannte Prädestinatus: Ein Beitrag zur Geschichte des Pelagianismus*. Leipzig: J. C. Hinrichs, 1903.

Schultz, Herman. *Alttestamentliche Theologie*. 4th ed. 2 vols. Gottingen: Vandenhoeck & Ruprecht, 1889.

Schürer, Emil. *Geschichte des judischen Volkes im Zeitalter Jesu Christi*. 4th ed. 3 vols. Leipzig: J. C. Hinrichs, 1901–9.

———. *The History of the Jewish People in the Age of Jesus Christ (175 B.C.–A.D. 135)*. Original, 1885. Revised and edited by Geza Vermes, Fergus Miller, and Matthew Black. Vol. 3. Edinburgh: T. & T. Clark, 1979.

Schurtz, Heinrich. *Katechismus der Völkerkunde*. Leipzig: J. J. Weber, 1893.

Schwalbe, Gustav Albert. *Studien zur Vorgeschichte des Menschen*. Stuttgart: Schweizerbart, 1906.

Schwane, Joseph. *Dogmengeschichte*. 2d ed. of vols. I–II. 1st ed. of vols. III–IV. Freiburg im Breisgau: Herder, 1882–95.

Schwarz, Franz von. *Sintfluth und Völkerwanderungen*. Stuttgart: Enke, 1894.

Schweizer, Alexander. *Die christliche Glaubenslehre nach protestantischen Grundsätzen dargestellt*. 2 vols. in 3. Leipzig: Hirzel, 1863–72.

———. *Die Glaubenslehre der evangelisch-reformirten Kirche*. 2 vols. Zürich: Orell, Füssli, 1844–47.

———. *Die protestantischen Centraldogmen in ihrer Entwicklung innerhalb der reformirten Kirche*. 2 vols. Zürich: Orell & Fuessli, 1854–56.

Schwetz, Johann. *Theologia dogmatica ca-tholica.* 3 vols. Vienna: Congregationis Mechitharisticae, 1851–54.

———. *Theologia fundamentalis seu ge-neralis.* 2 vols. Vienna: Congregationis Mechitharisticae, 1867.

Scipio, Konrad. *Des Aurelius Augustinus Metaphysik im Rahmen seiner Lehre vom Übel dargestellt.* Leipzig: Breitkopf and Härtel, 1886.

Secrétan, Charles. *La civilization et la cro-yance.* Paris: Alcan, 1887.

———. *La philosophie de la liberté.* 2 vols. Paris: G. Balliere, 1849. 3d ed. 1879.

Seeberg, Reinhold. *Lehrbuch der Dogmenge-schichte.* 2 vols. Erlangen & Leipzig: A. Deichert (G. Böhme), 1895–98.

———. *Die Theologie des Johannes Duns Scotus.* Leipzig: Dieterich, J. Weicher, 1900.

Semisch, K. G. *Justin Martyr: His Life, Writ-ings, and Opinions.* 2 vols. Edinburgh: T. & T. Clark, 1843.

Seneca, Lucius Annaeus. *De Beneficiis.* Translated by John W. Basore. Loeb Clas-sical Library. Cambridge, Mass.: Harvard University Press, 1928.

———. *Naturales quaestiones.* Translated by Thomas Corcoran. 2 vols. Loeb Classi-cal Library. Cambridge, Mass.: Harvard University Press, 1971–72.

———. *De providentia.* Translated by John W. Basore. In vol. 1 of *Moral Essays.* Loeb Classical Library. New York: G. P. Putnam's Sons, 1928.

Sertillanges, A. G. *Les sources de la croyance en Dieu.* Paris: Perrin, 1906.

Servetus, Michael. *Christianismi restitutio.* Vienne: Arnoullet, 1553.

———. *Dialogorum de trinitate libri duo.* Hagenau: Secerius, 1532.

———. *De trinitatis erroribus libri septem.* Hagenau: Secerius, 1531.

Seth Pringle-Pattison, A. *Hegelianism and Personality.* Edinburgh and London: W. Blackwood and Sons, 1887.

———. *Two Lectures on Theism.* Edinburgh: Blackwood, 1897.

Shedd, William Greenough Thayer. *Dog-matic Theology.* 3d ed. 3 vols. New York: Scribner, 1891–94.

Simar, H. Th. *Lehrbuch der Dogmatik.* 3d ed. Freiburg im Breisgau: Herder, 1893.

Simons. *See* Menno.

Smeaton, George. *The Doctrine of the Holy Spirit.* Edinburgh: T. & T. Clark, 1882.

Smend, Rudolf. *Lehrbuch der alttestamentli-chen Religionsgeschichte.* Freiburg: J. C. B. Mohr, 1893.

Smit, Pieter. *De wereldbeschouwing van Charles Secrétan.* Nijmegen: H. ten Hoet, 1906.

Smith, George. *The Chaldean Account of Genesis.* New York: Scribner's, 1880.

Smith, Henry Boynton. *System of Christian Theology.* Edited by William S. Karr. 4th ed. rev. New York: A. C. Armstrong, 1892 (©1890).

Smith, Norman Kemp. *Descartes' Philosophi-cal Writings.* London: Macmillan & Co., 1952.

Smith, W. Robertson. *Die Religion der Semiten.* Freiburg: Mohr, 1899.

Socinus, Faustus. *Bibliotheca fratrum Po-lonorum quos Unitarios vocant.* 10 vols. Irenopolis [Amsterdam]: Philalethes, 1656–92.

———. *Fausti, et Laelii Socini, item Ernesti Sonneri tractatus aliquot theologici.* Eleu-theropoli [Amsterdam?]: Typis Godfridi Philadelphi, 1654.

———. *Praelectiones theologicae.* Racoviae: Sebastiani Sternacii, 1627.

Sohn(ius), Georg. *Opera sacrae theologiae.* 2 vols. Herborn: C. Corvin, 1598.

Sokolowski, Emil. *Die Begriffe Geist und Leben bei Paulus in ihren Beziehungen zu einander.* Göttingen: Vandenhoeck & Ruprecht, 1903.

Sophocles. *Electra.* Translated by E. A. Heary. Edited and introduced by Wil-liam-Alan Landes. Studio City, Calif.: Players Press, 1995.

Souter, Alexander. *The Commentary of Pela-gius on the Epistles of Paul: The Problem of Its Restoration.* London: Oxford Univer-sity Press, 1907.

Spanheim, Friedrich. *Exercitationes de gratia universali.* Leyde: Maire, 1646.

———. *Friderici Spanhemmi F. Disputatio inauguralis habita in academia Leidensi.* Amsterdam: J. Hinrici, 1658.

———. *Opera.* 3 vols. Leiden: Cornelium Boutestein et al., 1701–3.

Spencer, Herbert. *First Principles.* 5th ed. London: Williams & Norgate, 1887.

Spinoza, Baruch [Benedictus de]. *Ad Benedicti de Spinoza opera quae supersunt omnia.* Amsterdam: F. Muller, 1862.

———. *Ethics.* Edited and translated by James Gutman. New York: Hafner, 1949.

———. *The Letters.* Translated by Samuel Shirley. Indianapolis and Cambridge: Hackett Publication Company, 1995.

———. *The Principles of Descartes' Philosophy.* Chicago: Open Court, 1974.

———. *Tractatus theologico-politicus.* Translated by Samuel Shirley. Leiden: Brill, 1991.

Splittgerber, Franz Joseph. *Tod, Fortleben und Auferstehung.* 3d ed. Halle: Fricke, 1879.

Spruyt, Cornelius Bellaar. *Proeve van eene geschiedenis van de leer der aangeboren begrippen.* Leiden: Brill, 1879.

Stade, Bernhard. *Geschichte des Volkes Israel.* 2 vols. Berlin: Baumgärtel, 1887.

Stapfer, Johann Friedrich. *Onderwys in de Gantsche Wederleggende Godsgeleertheit.* 5 vols. in 6. Utrecht: Gisb. Tieme van Paddenburg and Abraham van Paddenburg, 1757–63.

Staub, Max. *(Das) Verhältnis der menschlichen Willensfreiheit zur Gotteslehre bei Martin Luther und Huldreich Zwingli.* Zürich: Leemann, 1894.

Staudenmaier, Franz Anton. *Die christliche Dogmatik.* Freiburg im Breisgau: Herder, 1844.

Stave, Erik. *Über den Einfluss des Parsismus auf das Judentum.* Haarlem: F. Bohn, 1898.

Steinmetz, S. R. *De Studie der Völkenkunde.* 1907.

Steude, E. Gustav. *Der Beweis für die Wahrheit des Christentums.* Gütersloh: C. Bertelsmann, 1899.

———. *Christentum und Naturwissenschaft.* Gütersloh: C. Bertelsmann, 1895.

Stier, Johann. *Die Gottes- und Logos-Lehre Tertullians.* Göttingen: Vandenhoeck & Ruprecht, 1899.

Stirling, James Hutchison. *Philosophy and Theology.* Edinburgh: T. & T. Clark, 1890.

Stöckl, Albert. *Geschichte der neueren Philosophie von Baco und Cartesius bis zur Gegenwart.* Mainz: F. Kirchheim, 1883.

———. *Geschichte der Philosophie des Mittelalters.* 3 vols. Mainz: Kirchheim, 1864–66.

———. *Die Speculative Lehre vom Menschen und Ihre Geschichte.* Würzburg: Stahel, 1858.

Strauss, David Friedrich. *Die christliche Glaubenslehre in ihrer geschichtlichen Entwicklung und im Kampf mit der moderne Wissenschaft.* 2 vols. Tübingen: C. F. Osiander, 1840–41.

———. *The Old Faith and the New.* Translated by Mathilde Blind. New York: Hold, 1873.

Strodl, Michael Anton. *Die Entstehung der Völker.* Schaffhausen: Hurter, 1868.

Strong, Augustus Hopkins. *Systematic Theology.* 2d ed. New York: A. C. Armstrong, 1889. Rev., enlarged ed. 3 vols. Philadelphia: Griffith & Rowland, 1907–9.

Suárez, Francisco. *Tractatus de legibus.* London: J. Dunmore, T. Dring, B. Tooke, and T. Sawbridge, 1679.

Suess, Eduard. *Die Sintfluth.* Leipzig: G. Freitag, 1883.

Suicerus, J. C. *Thesaurus ecclesiasticus.* 2 vols. Amsterdam: J. H. Wetstein, 1682.

Swedenborg, Emanuel. *The True Christian Religion: Containing the Universal Theology of the New Church, Foretold by the Lord in Daniel VII.13, 14 and in Revelation XXI.1, 2.* Philadelphia: J. B. Lippincott Company, 1896.

Sylvius, Franciscus. *Francisci Sylvii a Brania comitis . . . Commentarii in totam primam partem S. Thomae Aquinatis.* 4 vols. Venetiis: Typographia Balleoniana, 1726.

Talma, A. S. E. *De Anthropologie van Calvijn.* Utrecht: n.p., 1882.

Tatian. *Oratio ad Graecos.* Leipzig: J. C. Heinrichs, 1888.

———. *Oratio contra gentes.* Leiden, 1677.

Tertullian. *Against Marcion. ANF,* III, 269–475.

———. *Against Praxeas. ANF,* III, 597–632.

———. *The Apology. ANF,* III, 17–60.

———. *On the Resurrection of the Flesh. ANF,* III, 545–95.

———. *The Prescription against Heretics. ANF,* III, 243–67.

———. *De testimonio animae.* Leiden: E. J. Brill, 1952.

———. *The Treatise against Hermogenes.* Translated and annotated by J. H. Wiszink. Ancient Christian Writers 24. Westminster, Md.: Newman Press, 1956.

———. *A Treatise on the Soul. ANF,* II, 181–235.

Theodoret. *On Divine Providence.* Translated by Thomas Halton. New York: Newman Press, 1988.

Theologia Wirceburgensi. 3d ed. 10 vols. in 5. Paris: Berche at Tralin, 1880.

Theophilus. *To Autolycus. ANF,* II, 85–121.

Thilo, Christfried Albert. *Kurze pragmatische Geschichte der neueren Philosophie.* Cöthen: O. Schulze, 1874.

———. *Die Wissenschaftlichkeit der modernen speculativen Theologie in ihren Principien.* Leipzig: F. Fleischer, 1851.

Tholuck, August. *Die speculative Trinitätslehre des späteren Orients.* Berlin: F. Dümmler, 1826.

Thomas Aquinas. *Aquinas on Creation: Writings on the Sentences of Peter Lombard, Book II.* Translated by Steven E. Baldner and William E. Carroll. Toronto: Pontifical Institute of Mediaeval Studies, 1997.

———. *Summa contra gentiles.* Translated by the English Dominican Fathers. London: Burns, Oates & Washbourne, 1924.

———. *Summa theologiae.* Translated by Thomas Gilby et al. 61 vols. New York: McGraw-Hill, 1964–81.

Thomasius, Gottfried. *Christi Person und Werk.* 3d ed. 2 vols. Erlangen: Theodor Bläsing, 1853–61.

———. *Die christliche Dogmengeschichte als Entwicklungs-Geschichte des kirchlichen Lehrbegriffs.* 2 vols. Erlangen: A. Deichert, 1886–89.

Tiele, Cornelis Petrus. *Elements of the Science of Religion.* 2 vols. Edinburgh and London: William Blackwood and Sons, 1897–99.

———. *Geschiedenis van den Godsdienst, tot aan de Heerschappij der Wereldgodsdiensten.* Amsterdam: P. N. van Kampen & Zoon, 1876.

———. *Inleiding tot de Godsdienstwetenschap.* Amsterdam: P. N. van Kampen, 1897–99.

———. *Verslag en Mededeelen van de Koninglijke Akademie van Wetenschappelijke Letterkunde.* 1895.

Tophel, G. *The Work of the Holy Spirit in Man: Discourses Delivered at Geneva.* Translated by Geo. E. Shipman. 2d ed. rev. Chicago: Chicago Foundlings' Home, 1883 (©1880).

Traub, Friedrich. *Die sittliche Weltordnung.* Freiburg: Akademische Verlagsbuchhandlung von J. C. B. Mohr (Paul Siebeck), 1892.

Trechsel, Friedrich. *Die protestantischen Antitrinitarier vor Faustus Socin.* 2 vols. Heidelberg: K. Winter, 1839–44.

Trelcatius, Lucas, Jr. *Scholastica et methodica locorum communium s. theologiae institutio.* London, 1604.

Trendelenburg, Friedreich Adolf. *Logische Untersuchungen.* Hindelsheim: Gg. Olms, 1870.

Trigland, Jacob. *Antapologia.* Amsterdam: Joannam Janssonium et al., 1664.

———. *Kerckelycke geschiedenissen.* Leyden: Andriae Wyngaerden, 1650.

Trip, Christian J. *Die Theophanien in den Geschichtsbüchern des Alten Testaments.* Leiden: D. Noothoven van Goor, 1858.

Trissl, Alois. *Das biblische Sechstagewerk vom Standpunkte der katholischen Exegese und vom Standpunkte der Naturwissenschaften.* 2d ed. Regensburg: G. J. Manz, 1894.

———. *Sündflut oder Gletscher?* Regensburg: G. J. Manz, 1894.

Turretin, Francis. *Institutes of Elenctic Theology.* Translated by George Musgrove Giger. Edited by James T. Dennison. 3 vols. Phillipsburg, N.J.: Presbyterian and Reformed, 1992.

———. *De necessaria secissiones nostra ab Ecclesia Romana.* In vol. 4, pp. 1–203 of *Opera.* New York: Carter, 1848.

Tuuk, H. Edema van der. *Johannes Bogerman.* Groningen: Wolters, 1868.

Twesten, August Detlev Christian, and W. M. L. De Wette. *Vorlesungen über die Dogmatik der evangelisch-lutherischen Kirche.* 2 vols. Hamburg: F. Perthes, 1837–38.

Twisse, William. *Dissertatio de scientia media tribus libris absoluta.* Arnhemii: Jacobum à Biesium, 1639.

———. *Guilielmi Twissi Opera theologica polemico-anti-Arminiana.* Amsterdam, 1699.

———. *Vindiciae gratiae, potestatis ac providentiae Dei.* 3 vols. Amsterdam: Guilielmum Blaeu, 1632.

Ueberweg, Friedrich. *Geschichte der Philosophie.* Edited by Max Heinze. 9th ed. 4 vols. Berlin: E. S. Mittler & Sohn, 1901–5.

Uhlmann, Josue. *Die Persönlichkeit Gottes und ihre modernen Gegner.* Freiburg im Breisgau: Herder, 1906.

Ulrici, Hermann. *Gott und der Mensch.* Leipzig: T. O. Weigel, 1874.

———. *Gott und die Natur.* Leipzig: T. O. Weigel, 1862.

Urquhart, John. *How Old Is Man? Some Misunderstood Chapters in Scripture Chronology.* London: Nisbet, 1904.

Ursinus, Zacharias. *Catechismus major.* In *Opera theologica.* Heidelberg: John Lancellot, 1612.

———. *The Commentary of Dr. Zacharius Ursinus on the Heidelberg Catechism.*

Translated by G. W. Willard. Grand Rapids: Eerdmans, 1954.

———. *Volumen tractationum theologicarum.* Neustadii, 1584.

Usener, Hermann. *Die Sintflutsagen.* Vol. 3 of *Religionsgeschichtliche Untersuchungen.* Bonn: Cohen, 1899.

Uytenbogaert, Johannes. *Onderwijzing in de Christelyke Religie.* 2d ed. Amsterdam: Ian Fred. Sam, 1640.

Venema, Herman. *Korte Verdediging van zijn Eere en Leere.* Leeuwarden: van Desiel, 1735.

Vermigli, Pietro Martire. *Petri Martyris Vermilii . . . Loci communes.* London: Kyngston, 1576.

Verworn, Max. *Naturwissenschaft und Weltanschauung.* 2d ed. Leipzig: Barth, 1904.

Vigouroux, Fulcran Grégoire. *Les livres saints et la critique rationaliste, histoire, et réfutation des objections des incrédules contre les saintes Écritures.* 4 vols. Paris: A. Roger & F. Chernoviz, 1886–90.

Vilmar, August Friedrich Christian. *Dogmatik: Akademische Vorlesungen.* 2 vols. Gütersloh: C. Bertelsmann, 1874.

Vitringa, Campegius. *Commentarius in librum prophetiarum Jesaiae.* Leovardiae: Excudit Franciscus Halma et Typographus Ordinum Frisiae, 1714–20.

———. *Doctrina christianae religionis.* 8 vols. Leiden: Joannis le Mair, 1761–86.

Vlak, J. *Eeuwig evangelium.* Amsterdam: G. Borstius, 1684.

Voetius, Gisbert. *Selectae disputationes theologicae.* 5 vols. Utrecht, 1648–69.

Volkel, Johann. *De vera religione libri quinque.* Racoviae, 1630.

Vorst, Henricus Johannes van (Fr. Coelestinus). *Het Aardsche Paradijs: Hoe het Was en Waar het Lag.* Tilberg: Bergmans, [1903].

Vos, Geerhardus. *Redemptive History and Biblical Interpretation.* Edited by Richard B. Gaffin. Phillipsburg, N.J.: Presbyterian and Reformed Publishing Co., 1980.

Vossius, Gerardus Joannes. *Historiae de controversiis, quas Pelagius eiusque religuiae moverunt.* 2d, emended ed. Amsterdam: Elzevir, 1655.

Vries, Hugo de. *Species and Varieties: Their Origin by Mutation.* Edited by Daniel Trembly MacDougal. 2d ed., corrected and rev. Chicago: Open Court Publishing Company, 1906.

Waitz, Theodor. *Über die Einheit des Menschengeschlechts und den Naturzustand des Menschen.* Liepzig: Fleischer, 1859.

Walaeus, Antonius. *Loci communes s. theologiae.* Leiden: F. Hackius, 1640.

———. *Opera omnia.* Leiden: Francisci Hackii, 1643.

Walch, Johann George. *Bibliotheca theologica selecta, litterariis adnotationibus instructa.* 4 vols. Jena: Croeckerianal, 1757–65.

Walker, James. *The Theology and Theologians of Scotland, 1560–1750.* Reprinted from the 1888 2d ed. Edinburgh: Knox Press, 1982.

Wallace, Alfred Russel. *Man's Place in the Universe: A Study of the Results of Scientific Research in Relation to the Unity or Plurality of Worlds.* London: Chapman and Hall, 1903.

Ward, James. *Naturalism and Agnosticism: The Gifford Lectures Delivered before the University of Aberdeen in the Years 1896–1898.* London: A. & C. Black, 1915.

Warfield, Benjamin Breckenridge. *Two Studies in the History of Doctrine: Augustine and the Pelagian Controversy.* New York: Christian Literature Co., 1897.

Wasmann, Erich. *Biology and the Theory of Evolution.* Translated by A. M. Buchanan. 3d ed. St. Louis: B. Herder, 1923.

———. *Instinkt und Intelligenz im Thierreich.* 8th ed. Freiburg im Breisgau: Herder, 1905.

Weber, Ferdinand Wilhelm. *System der altsynagogalen palästinischen Theologie: Aus Targum, Midrasch und Talmud.* Leipzig: Dörffling & Franke, 1880.

Weber, Ferdinand Wilhelm, and Franz Delitzsch. *Vom Zorne Gottes.* Erlangen: Andreas Deichert, 1862.

Weber, Otto. *Die Literatur der Babylonier und Assyrer.* Leipzig: J. C. Hinrichs, 1907.

———. *Theologie und Assyriologie: Im Streite um Babel und Bible.* Leipzig: J. C. Hinrichs, 1904.

Wegscheider, Julius August Ludwig. *Institutiones theologiae christianae dogmaticae.* Halle: Gebauer, 1819.

Weinel, Heinrich. *Die Wirkungen des Geistes und der Geister im nachapostolischen Zeitalter bis auf Irenäus.* Freiburg: Mohr, 1899.

Weiss, Bernhard. *Biblical Theology of the New Testament.* Translated by David Eaton and James E. Duguid. 2 vols. Edinburgh: T. & T. Clark, 1883.

———. *Lehrbuch der biblischen Theologie des Neuen Testaments.* 3d ed. Berlin: W. Hertz, 1880.

Weisse, Christian Herman. *Philosophische Dogmatik oder Philosophie des Christentums.* 3 vols. Leipzig: Hirzel, 1855–62.

Weizsäcker, Karl Heinrich von. *Das apostolische Zeitalter der christlichen Kirche.* 2d ed. Freiburg: Mohr, 1890.

Wellhausen, Julius. *Geschichte Israels.* 2 vols. Berlin: Reimer, 1878.

———. *Prolegomena to the History of Israel.* Translated by J. Sutherland Black and Allan Menzies. Edinburgh: Adam & Charles Black, 1885.

Wellisch, Sigmund. *Das Alter der Welt und des Menschen.* Vienna: Hartleben, 1899.

Werner, Karl. *Geschichte der katholischen Theologie seit dem Trienter Concil bis zur Gegenwart.* Munich: Cotta, 1866.

———. *Der heilige Thomas von Aquino.* 3 vols. Regensburg: G. J. Manz, 1858–59.

Weygoldt, G. P. *Darwinismus, Religion, Sittlichkeit.* Leiden: E. J. Brill, 1878.

Whitaker, William. *Opera Theologica.* 2 vols. in 1. Geneva: S. Crispen, 1610.

Wichelhaus, Johannes. *Die Lehre der heiligen Schrift vom Worte Gottes.* Stuttgart: J. F. Steinkopf, 1892.

Wigand, Albert. *Der Darwinismus und die Naturforschung Newtons und Cuviers: Beiträge zur Methodik der Naturfor-*

schung und zur Speciesfrage. 3 vols. Braunschweig: F. Vieweg und Sohn, 1874–77.

Wiggers, Gustav Friedrich. *Versuch einer
pragmatischen Darstellung des Augustinismus und Pelagianismus.* 2 vols. Hamburg:
F. A. Perthes, 1830–31.

Wilhelm, Joseph, and Thomas Bartholomew
Scannell. *A Manual of Catholic Theology:
Based on Scheeben's "Dogmatik."* 4th ed.
2 vols. London: Kegan Paul, Trench,
Trübner and Co.; New York: Benziger
Brothers, 1909.

Willmann, Otto. *Geschichte des Idealismus.*
1894. Reprinted, Braunschweig: F.
Vieweg und Sohn, 1907.

Winckler, Hugo. *Keilinschriftliches Textbuch
zum Alten Testament.* 2d ed. Leipzig: J. C.
Hinrichs, 1903.

Windelband, Wilhelm. *A History of Philosophy.* Translated by James H. Tufts. 2 vols.
1901. Reprinted, New York: Harper &
Row, 1958.

Winternitz, Moriz. *Die Flutsagen des Alterthums und der Naturvölker.* Offprint
from *Mittheilungen der anthropologischen
Gesellschaft in Wien* 31 (1901): 305–33.
Vienna, 1901.

Wisemann, Nicholas Patrick Stephen.
*Zusammenhang zwischen Wissenschaft und
Offenbarung.* Regensburg: Manz, 1866.

Witsius, Herman. *The Oeconomy of the
Covenants between God and Man: Comprehending a Complete Body of Divinity.*
4 vols. in 3. New York: Lee & Stokes,
1798.

Wittichius, Christophorus. *Theologia pacifica.* Leiden, 1671.

Wobbermin, Georg. *Der christliche Gottesglaube in seinem Verhältnis zur gegen-
wärtigen Philosophie.* Berlin: Alexander
Duncker, 1902.

———. *Theologie und Metaphysik.* Berlin:
Alexander Duncker, 1901.

Wollebius, Johannes. *Compendium theologiae
christianae.* Basel, 1626; Oxford, 1657.

Wollebius, Johannes, G. Voetius, and F. Turretin. *Reformed Dogmatics.* Edited and
translated by John W. Beardslee III. New
York: Oxford University Press, 1965.
Original Latin, 1655.

Wörter, Friedrich. *Beiträge zur Dogmengeschichte des Semipelagianismus.* Paderborn: F. Schöningh, 1898.

———. *Der Pelagianismus nach seinem
Ursprunge und seiner Lehre.* Freiburg:
Wagner, 1866.

Wright, G. F. *Scientific Confirmations of Old
Testament History.* Oberlin, Ohio: Bibliotheca Sacra Co., 1906.

Wundt, Wilhelm Max. *Ethik: Eine Untersuchung der Thatsachen und Gesetze des
sittlichen
Lebens.* Stuttgart: F. Enke, 1886.

———. *Vorlesungen über die Menschen- und
Thierseele.* 2 vols. Leipzig: L. Voss, 1863.

Wurm, Paul. *Handbuch der Religionsgeschichte.* Calwer Verlagsverein; Stuttgart:
Verlag der Vereinsbuchhandlung, 1904.

Xenophon. *Memorabilia* and *Oeconomicus.*
Translated by E. C. Marchant. 7 vols.
Loeb Classical Library. New York: G. P.
Putnam's Sons, 1918–68.

Ypey, Anneaus. *Geschiedenis der Nederlandsche Herformde Kerk.* 4 vols. Breda: W.
Van Bergen, 1819–27.

Zanchi(us), Jerome (Hieronymus). *Operum
theologicorum.* 8 vols. [Geneva]: Samuelis
Crispini, 1617.

———. *De tribus elohim.* Neustadii Palati-
norum: Typis Iosuae & Wilhelmi Harni-
siorum, 1597.

Zane, Bernardus. *Oratio in festo omnium
sanctorum.* [Rome: Johann Besicken?,
1500–1599?].

Zapletal, Vincenz. *Der Schöpfungsbericht der
Genesis.* Regensburg: G. J. Manz, 1911.

Zeller, Eduard. *Outlines of the History of
Greek Philosophy.* Translated by L. R.
Palmer. 13th ed. New York: Humanities
Press, 1969.

———. *Die Philosophie der Griechen in ihrer
geschichtlichen Entwicklung.* 3 vols. in 6.
Leipzig: O. R. Reisland, 1879–1920.

———. *Vorträge und abhandlungen geschichtlichen Inhalts.* 3 vols. Leipzig: Fues
(L. W. Reisland), 1865–84.

Zimmer, Heinrich. *Pelagius in Irland.* Berlin:
Weidmann, 1901.

Zimmermann, Hellmuth. *Elohim: Eine Studie zur israelitischen Religions und Litteraturgeschichte.* Berlin: Mayer & Müller, 1900.

Zimmern, Heinrich. *Biblische und babylonische Urgeschichte.* 2d ed. 2 vols. Leipzig: J. C. Hinrichs, 1901.

———. *Vater, Sohn und Fürsprecher in der babylonischen Gottesvorstellung.* Leipzig: J. C. Hinrichs, 1896.

Zittel, Karl Alfred von. *Aus der Urzeit: Bilder aus der Schöpfungsgeschichte.* 2d ed. Munich: R. Oldenbourg, 1875.

Zöckler, Otto. *Biblische und Kirchenhistorische Studien.* 5 monographs in 1 vol. Munich: C. H. Beck, 1893.

———. *Geschichte der Beziehungen zwischen Theologie und Naturwissenschaft: Mit besondrer Rücksicht auf Schöpfungsgeschichte.* 2 vols. Gütersloh: C. Bertelsmann, 1877–79.

———. *Das Kreuz Christi.* Gütersloh: C. Bertelsmann, 1875.

———. *Die Lehre vom Urstand des Menschen.* Gütersloh: C. Bertelsmann, 1879.

———. *Theologia naturalis.* Frankfurt am Main: Heyder & Zimmer, 1860.

Zollmann, Theodor. *Bibel und Natur in der Harmonie ihrer Offenbarungen.* Hamburg: Agentur des Rauhen Hauses, 1869.

Zwingli, Ulrich. *Ad illustrissimum Cattorum principem Philippum: sermonis de providentia dei anamnema.* Zürich: Froschauer, Christoph, d.Ä., 1530.

———. *De Claritate et certitudine verbi Dei.* In *Opera.* Edited by Schuler and Schulthess. Turici: Officina Schulthessiana, 1842.

———. *On Providence and Other Essays.* Translated by Samuel Macauley Jackson. Edited by William John Hinks. Durham: Labyrinth Press, 1983.

ARTICLES

Adlhoch, Beda. "Zur wissenschaftlichen Erklärung des Atheismus." *Philosophisches Jahrbuch* 18 (1905): 297–311, 377–90.

Bachmann, D. "Der Schöpfungsbericht und die Inspiration." *Neue kirchliche Zeitschrift* 17 (May 1906): 383–405. Second part: "Die Schöpfungsberichte in Unterrichte." *Neue kirchliche Zeitschrift* 18 (October 1907): 743–62.

Bartholomai, R. "Vom Zorne Gottes: Eine biblisch-dogmatische Studie." *Jahrbuch für deutsche Theologie* (1861): 256–77.

Bavinck, H. "Evolutie." *Pro en Contra.* Baarn: Hollandia, 1907. Reprinted in *Verzamelde Opstellen,* pp. 105–20. Kampen: Kok, 1921.

Beck, H. "Die δικαιοσυνη Θεου bei Paulus." *Neue Jahrbuch für deutsche Theologie* 4 (1895): 249–61.

Bensdorp. Articles on grace and justification. *De Katholiek* 110 (1894): 43–60(?); 114 (1898): 81.

Borchert. "Der Gottes Name Jahre Zebaoth." *Theologische Studien und Kritiken* 68 (1896): 619–42.

Braun, Gustav. "Die Kant-Laplachesche Weltbildungstheorie." *Neue kirchliche Zeitschrift* 3 (September 1892): 672–704.

Bruining, A. "Pantheisme of Theisme." *Teylers Theologische Tijdschrift* 5 (1907): 564–97.

———. "De Roomsche Leer van het Donum Superadditum." *Teylers Theologische Tijdschrift* 5 (1907): 564–97.

Buhl, Karl. "Der Gedankengang von Röm. 9–11." *Theologische Studien und Kritiken* 59 (1887): 295–320.

Burger, Karl. "Weisheit." *PRE²,* XVI, 715–20.

Calvin, John. "A Warning against Judiciary Astrology and Other Customs." Translated by Mary Potter. *Calvin Theological Journal* 18 (1983): 157–89. Original appears as "Contre l'astrologie." In *Corpus Reformatorum* 35 [7]: 513–42.

Cannegieter, Tjeerd. "De Godsdienst in den Mensch and de Mensch in den Godsdienst." *Teylers Theologische Tijdschrift* 2 (1904): 178–211.

Coe, Edward B. "The Biblical Meaning of Holiness." *Presbyterian and Reformed Review* 1 (January 1890): 42–47.

Comrie, Alexander. "Verhandeling van het Verbond der Werken." In *Een Beschouwing van het Verbond der Genade,* by

Thomas Boston. Amsterdam: N. Bijl, 1741.

Cremer, Hermann. "Ebenbild Gottes." *PRE³*, V, 113–18.

———. "Engel." *PRE³*, V, 364–72.

———. "Geist, heiligen."*PRE³*, VI, 444–50.

———. "Gerechtigkeit." *PRE³*, VI, 546–53.

———. "Herz." *PRE³*, VII, 773–76.

———. "Himmel." *PRE³*, VIII, 80–84.

———. "Pronoia." In *Biblical-Theological Lexicon of New Testament Greek*. Translated by D. W. Simon and William Urwick. Edinburgh: T. & T. Clark, 1872.

———. "Seele." *PRE³*, XVIII, 128–32; *PRE²*, XIV, 25–30.

Darwin, G. H. "Kosmische Evolutie." *Wetenschappelijke Bladen* 14 (June 1906): 406–34.

———. "Report on a Discourse in South Africa." *Glauben und Wissen* 4 (March 1906): 104–5.

Daubanton, F. E. "Belangrijkheid der Anthropologie: Hare Plaats in het dogmatisch Systeem." *Theologische Studiën* 11 (1893): 1–16.

———. "Eene Nieuwe Dogmatiek op Gereformeerde-Kerkelijken Grondslag?" *Theologische Studiën* 5 (1887): 429–44.

———. "Het Saamgesteld Wezen van den Mensch." *Theologische Studiën* 11 (1893): 326–60.

De Bussy, I. J. "Katholicisme en Protestantisme." *Theologische Tijdschrift* 36 (1888): 253–313.

De Graaf, H. T. "Bezwaren Tegen het Theisme." *Teylers Theologische Tijdschrift* 53/2 (1905): 165–210.

Delitzsch, F. "Heiligkeit." *PRE²*, V, 714–18.

———. "Die neue Mode der Herleitung des Gottesnamens." *Lutherische Zeitschrift* 20 (1877).

Dennert, Eberhard. "Verhandlungen des letzten Anthropologen-Kongress in Lindau (Sept. 3–7, 1899)." *Der Beweis des Glaubens* 36 (1900): 80.

Diestel, [Ludwig]. "Die Idee der Gerechtigkeit, vorzüglich im Alten Testament, bib-lischtheologisch dargestellt." *Jahrbücher für deutsche Theologie* 5 (1860): 173–253.

Dijk, Isaäk van. "De Leer der Verkiezing volgens het Nieuwe Testament." *Studiën: Theologisch Tijdschrift* 4 (1878): part 3 (= pages 275–339 in vol. 1 of *Gezamenlijke Geschriften van Dr. Isaak van Dijk*. Groningen: Noordhoff, 1917). [Discussion among P. D. Chantepie de la Saussaye, J. J. P. Valeton Jr., and Isaäk van Dijk.]

Doederlein, J. "Was fehlt dem ontologischen Beweis?" *Zeitschrift für Philosophie und philosophischen Kritik* 88/1 (1886): 47–63.

Doedes, Jacobus Izaak. "Nieuwe Merkwaardigheden uit den Oude-boeken-schat." Vol. IV, 238–42, of *Studien en Bijdragen*, edited by W. Moll and J. G. De Hoop Scheffer. Amsterdam: G. L. Funke, 1880.

Dorner, I. A. "Duns."*PRE²*, III, 735–54.

DuBois-Reymond, Emil Heinrich. "Rede." *Sitzungsberichte der Berliner Akademie* 32 (1894).

Eisler, Rudolf. "Zufall." *Wörterbuch der philosophischen Begriffe*. 3 vols. Berlin: E. S. Mittler, 1910.

Endemann, K. "D. W. Koeling und I Joh. 5:7–8." *Neue kirchliche Zeitschrift* 10 (July 1899): 574–81.

Frank. "Synergismus." *PRE²*, XV, 103–13.

Gebhardt. "Der Himmel im Neuen Testaments." *Zeitschrift für kirchliche Wissenschaft und kirchliches Leben* 7 (1886).

Geesink, W. "De Bijbel en het Avesta." *De Heraut* 830 (November 1893).

Gooszen, M. A. "Het 'Besluit' dat achter de Dordsche Leerregelen is geplaatst en de Theologie en de Religie van onzen Tijd." *Geloof en Vrijheid* 35 (1901): 530–61.

Gunkel, Hermann. "Die judische und die babylonische Schöpfungeschichte." *Deutsche Rundschau* (May 1903): 267–86.

Hamilton, W. "On the Philosophy of the Unconditioned." *Edinburgh Review* (October 1829).

Hartmann, Eduard von. "Mechanismus und Vitalismus in der modernen Biologie." *Archiv für systematische Philosophie* (1903): 139–78, 331–77.

Haupt, Erich. "Der christliche Vorsehungs- glaube." *Der Beweis des Glaubens* 24 (1888): 201–28.

Heinze, M. "Evolutionismus." *PRE³*, V, 672–81.

———. "Neoplatonismus." *PRE³*, XIII, 772ff.

Hengstenberg, Ernst Wilhelm. "Die Wohl- vereinbarkeit der biblischen Kosmologie mit den feststehenden Resultaten der kosmologenischen Wissenschaft." *Der Beweis des Glaubens* 3 (1867): 400–418.

*Herrmann, W. "Die Lehre von den gött- lichen Vorsehung und Weltregierung." *Christliche Welt* 2 (1887).

Hertwig, Oskar. "Das biogenetische Grund- gesetz nach dem heutigen Stande de Biologie." *Internationale Wochenschrift* 1 (1907).

Herzog, J. J. "Eden." *PRE²*, IV, 34–38.

———. "Paradise." *Schaff-Herzog,* VII, 348–49.

Himpel, F. von. "Biblishe Chronologie. A–F." Vol. III, col. 311–15, of *Herders Kirchenlexikon.* Freiburg im Breisgau: Herder, 1884.

Hobson. "English Theistic Thought at the Close of the 19th Century." *Presbyterian and Reformed Review* 12 (October 1901).

Hodge, A. "The Relation of God to the World." *Presbyterian and Reformed Re- view* (1887).

Hoennicke. "Prädestination, Schriftlehre." *PRE³*, XV, 581–86.

Honert, Johan van den. "Voorrede." In *Schatboek der Vaerlkaringen over den Ne- derlandschen Catechismus,* by Z. Ursinus. Gorinchem: Nic. Goetze, 1736.

Hoppe, Edmund. "Geist oder Instinkt." *Neue kirchliche Zeitschrift* 18 (1907): 36–64, 91–114.

Jülicher, Adolf. Review of *The Commentary of Pelagius on the Epistles of Paul,* by Alex- ander Souter. *Theologische Litteraturzei- tung* (February 15, 1907): 203ff.

Jürgens. "War die Sintflut eine Erdbeben- welle?" *Stimmen aus Maria-Laach,* nos. 85 and 86 (1884).

Kaftan, J. "Das Verhältniss des evangelischen Glaubens zur Logoslehre." *Zeitschrift für Theologie und Kirche* 7/1 (1897): 1–27.

Kähler, M. "Seligkeit." *PRE³*, XVIII, 179–84.

Katzer, Ernest. "Der Moralische Gottesbe- weis nach Kant und Herbert." *Jahrbuch für protestantische Theologie* 4 (1878): 482–532, 635–89.

Kaubtsch, F. "Zahlen bei den Hebräern." *PRE²*, XVII, 407–15.

Kawerau. "Synergismus." *PRE³*, XIX, 229–35.

Keerl, K. "Die Fixsterne und die Engel: Die Fixsterne unde die Spektralanalyse." *Der Beweis des Glaubens* 32 (June 1896): 230–47.

Kellogg, Alfred H. "The Incarnation and Other Worlds." *Princeton Theological Re- view* 3/2 (April 1905): 177–99.

Kern, H. "Oud en Nieuw over de Men- schenrassen." *Wetenschappelijke Bladen* (June 1904): 337–57.

Kessler, K. "Mani, Manichaer." *PRE³*, XII, 193–267.

Kirn, D. "Gnade." *PRE³*, VI, 717–23.

———. "Logos." *PRE³*, XI, 599–605.

Kittel, R. "Heiligkeit Gottes im A.T." *PRE³*, VII, 566–73.

Kleinert, P. "Zur alttestamentlichen Lehre vom Geiste Gottes." *Jahrbücher für deutsche Theologie* 12 (1867): 3–59.

Kosters, W. H. "De Bijbelsche Zond- vloedverhalen met de Babylonischen vergeleken." *Theologische Tijdschrift* 11 (1885): 161–79, 321–46.

Köstlin, Julius. "Die Beweise für das Da- sein Gottes." *Theologische Studien und Kritiken* 48 (1875): 601–55; 49 (1876): 7–80.

———. "Concursus Divinus." *PRE³*, IV, 262–67.

———. "Gott." *PRE²*, V, 289–312.

———. "Gott." *PRE³*, VI, 779ff.

———. "Die Idee des Reiches Gottes und ihre Anwendung in Dogmatik und Ethik." *Theologische Studien und Kritiken* 64/3 (1892): 401–73.

Kreyher, J. "Die Erwähungslehre von Zwingli und Calvin." *Theologische Studien und Kritiken* 43 (1870): 491–524.

Kübel, Robert. "Prädestination." *PRE²*, XII, 145–62.

Kuyper, Abraham. "Evolution." Translated by C. Menninga. *Calvin Theological Journal* 31 (1996): 11–50.

———. "Pantheism's Destruction of Boundaries." *Methodist Review* 52 (1893): 520–35, 762–78. A revised translation appears on pp. 363–402 of *Abraham Kuyper: A Centennial Reader,* edited by James D. Bratt. Grand Rapids: Eerdmans, 1998.

Kuyper, Herman Huber. "Egypte voor den Tijd der Piramiden." *Wetenschappelijke Bladen* (August 1907): 274–93; (September): 436–53.

———. "'s Menschen Plaats in het Heelal." *Wetenschappelijke Bladen* (April 1905): 67–78.

Laidlaw, John. "Psychology." In vol. IV of *Dictionary of the Bible,* edited by James Hastings. Revised edition by Frederick C. Grant and H. H. Rowley. New York: Charles Scribner's Sons, 1963.

Lechler, G. V. "Deismus." *PRE²*, III, 529–35.

Liechtenhan, R. "Ophiten." *PRE³*, XIV, 404–13.

Linder. "Parismus." *PRE³*, 699–703.

Loofs. "Arianismus." *PRE³*, II, 6–45.

———. "Athanasianum." *PRE³*, II, 177–94.

———. "Christologie, Kirchenlehre." *PRE³*, IV, 16–56.

———. "Macedonius." *PRE³*, XII, 41–48.

———. "Monarchianismus." *PRE³*, XIII, 303–36.

———. "Pelagius." *PRE³*, XV, 747–74.

Lütgert, Wilhelm. "Der Mensch aus dem Himmel." Pp. 207–28 of *Greifswalder Studien,* edited by Samuel Oettli et al. Gütersloh: C. Bertelsmann, 1895.

Möller. "Adoptianismus." *PRE³*, I, 180–86.

Nowack, W. "Altorientalischer und israelitischer Monotheismus." *Theologische Rundschau* 10 (December 1906): 449–59.

Obbink, H. Th. "Nieuwe gegevens ter beoordeeling der Mohammedaansche Praedestinatieleer." *Theologische Studiën* 21 (1903): 350–78.

*Ortloph. "Gods." *Zeitschrift für lutherische Theologie und Kirche* 21 (1860).

Otto, Rudolf. "Die mechanistische Lebenstheorie und die Theologie." *Zeitschrift für Theologie und Kirche* 13 (1903): 179–213.

Peip, Albert. "Trinität." *PRE¹*, XVI, 437–68.

Pesch, Chr. "Ist Gott die Ursache seiner Selbst?" *Theologische Zeitfragen* (Freiburg, 1900): 133–67.

Pfaff, F. "Das Alter der Erde." *Zeitschrift für des christliche Volksleben* 7 (1882).

Pressel, Wilhelm. "Paradies." *PRE³*, XV, 332–97.

Preuschen. "Prädestinatus." *PRE³*, XV, 602–4.

Quack, Hendrick Peter Godfried. "Port Royal par Saint-Beuve." *De Gids* [Amsterdam] 36 (December 1872).

Rabus, Leonhard. "Vom Wirken und Wohnen des göttlichen Geistes in der Menschenseele." *Neue kirchliche Zeitschrift* 15 (November 1904): 768–86, 823–59.

Raubsch, E. "Zebaoth." *PRE²*, XVIII, 720.

Riggenbach, B. "Servet, Michael." *PRE³*, XVIII, 228–36.

Ritschl, A. "Geschichtliche studien zur christliche Lehre von Gott." *Jahrbücher für deutsche Theologie* 10 (1865): 277–318; 13 (1868): 78–133, 251–302.

Rümelin, G. "Über den Zufall." *Deutsche Rundschau* 17 (March 1890).

Sachsse, Eugen. "Die Logoslehre bei Philo und Johannes." *Neue kirchliche Zeitschrift* 15 (1904): 747–67.

Schmid, Franz. "Der Begriff des 'Wahren.'" *Philosophisches Jahrbuch* 6 (1893): 35–48, 140–50.

Schmidt, E. *Die ältesten Spuren des Menschen in Nordamerika.* Sammlung gemeinverständlicher wissenschaftlicher Vorträge, n.F., Serie 2, Heft 38–39. Hamburg: J. F. Richter, 1887.

Schmidt, Hans. "Das Gilgamesepos und die Bible." *Theologische Rundschau* 10 (1907): 189–208.

Schoeberlein, Ludwig F. "Ebenbild Gottes." *PRE²*, IV, 4–8.

Schrader, Eberhard. "Semitismus und Babylonismus." *Jahrbücher für protestantische Theologie* 1 (1875).

Schultze, V. "Sinnbilder." *PRE³*, XVIII, 388–95.

Seeberg, R. "Duns Scotus," *PRE³*, V, 62–75.

Smith, H. P. "The Root *qdsh* in the Old Testament." *Presbyterian Review* 2 (July 1881): 588–92.

Snijders, C. "Het ontstaan en de verbreiding der menschenrassen." *Tijdspiegel* (April 1897).

———. [Article on inhabitants of planets]. *Tijdspiegel* (February 1898): 182–204.

Späth. "Luth. Kirche in Am." *PRE³*, XIV, 184–213.

Steib. "Melito von Sardes." *PRE²*, IX, 537–39.

Steinmann, Th. "Das Bewusstsein von der vollen Wirklichkeit Gottes." *Zeitschrift für Theologie und Kirche* 12 (1902): 429–96.

Steinmetz, S. R. "De Rassenkwestie." *De Gids* 71 (January 1907).

Stölzle, R. "Newtons Kosmogonie." *Philosophisches Jahrbuch* 20 (1907): 54–62.

Straub, J. "Kant und die natürliche Gotteserkenntnis." *Philosophisches Jahrbuch* 12 (1899): 261–70, 393–406.

Thym, D. C. "De Logosleer van Philo en hare Betrekking tot het Evangelie van Johannes, inzonderheid wat den Proloog betreft." *Theologische Studiën* 11/2 (1893).

Troeltsch, E. "Deismus." *PRE³*, IV, 532–59.

Turner, H. H. "Man's Place in the Universe: A Further Note on the Views of Dr. A. R. Wallace." *The Fortnightly Review* (1907): 600–610.

Ulrich, Julius. "Heilsglaube und Vorsehungsglauben." *Neue kirchliche Zeitschrift* 12 (1901): 478–93.

Ulrici, H. "Pantheismus." *PRE³*, XI, 183–93.

Upham. "Die Zeitdauer der geologischen Epochen." *Gaea* 30 (1894).

Undritz, Oskar. "'Ist es als feststehend zu betrachten, dass die Tage im Schöpfungsbericht als Zeitperioden aufzufassen seien und ist darauf in der Konfirmandenlehre einzugehen?'" *Neue kirchliche Zeitschrift* 10 (October 1899): 837–52.

Valeton, J. P. P., Jr. "De Israëlitische Godsnaam." *Theologische Studiën* 7 (1889): 173–221.

Volck. "Eden." *PRE³*, V, 158–62.

Vos, Geerhardus. "The Scriptural Doctrine of the Love of God." *Presbyterian and Reformed Review* 13 (January 1902): 1–37.

Vossius, Gerardus Joannes. "De origine ac progressu idololatriae." In bk. I of *Opera omnia*. Amsterdam: Blaeu, 1641.

Vuilleumier. "La première page de la Bible." *Revue de théologie et de philosophie* 29 (1896): 364–418.

Waals, J. D. van der. "Het Zeemanverschijnsel." *De Gids* 67 (March 1903): 493–512.

Warfield, B. B. "The Spirit of God in the Old Testament." *Presbyterian and Reformed Review* 6 (October 1895): 665–87.

———. "Tertullian and the Beginnings of the Doctrine of the Trinity." *Princeton Theological Review* 3 (October 1905); 4 (January 1906); 4 (April 1906).

Weber, Th. "Luthers Streitschrift 'De servo arbitrio.'" *Jahrbücher für deutsche Theologie* 23 (1878): 229–48.

Weiss, B. "Die Prädestinationslehre des Paulus." *Jahrbücher für deutsche Theologie* 2 (1857): 54–115.

Weizsäcker, Julius. "Das Dogma von der göttlichen Vorherbestimmung im neunten Jahrhundert." *Jahrbücher für deutsche Theologie* 4 (1859): 527–76.

Wendt, H. H. "Der Gebrauch der Wörter ἀλήθεια, ἀληθής, und ἀληθινος im Neuen Testamente." *Theologische Studien und Kritiken* 56/3 (1883): 511–47.

Went. "Ondoelmatigheid in de Levende Natuur." *De Gids* 70 (1906): 77–99.

Wetzel, G. "Die Zeit der Weltschöpfung." *Jahrbücher für protestantische Theologie* 1 (1875).

Whitley, D. Gath. "What Was the Primitive Condition of Man?" *Princeton Theological Review* 4 (October 1906): 513–34.

*Wigand, Paul. "Die Erde der Mittelpunkt der Welt." *Zeitschrift fur der christliche Volksleben*, 144.

Winkel, J. te. "Eene Friesche Mythe." In *Geschiedenis der Nederlandsche Letterkunde*. Haarlem: F. Bohn, 1887–.

Winter, Friedrich. "Wesen und Charakter des christliche Vorsehungsglaubens." *Neue kirchliche Zeitschrift* 18 (1907): 609–31.

Wunsche. "Kabbala." *PRE*[3], IX, 670–89.

Zeehandelaar. "Het Spiritistisch Gevaar." *De Gids* 2 (August 1907): 306–37.

Zöckler, Otto. Comments on E. DuBois-Reymond's address to the Berliner Akademie (1894). *Beweis des Glaubens* 31 (February 1895): 77–80.

———. "Darwinismus und Materialismus beim Begin des 20e Jahrhunderts." *Beweis des Glaubens* 36 (1900): 161–75.

———. "Die einheitliche Abstammung des Menschengeschlechts." *Jahrbuch für die Theologie* 8 (1863): 51–90.

———. "In eigener Sache." *Beweis des Glaubens* 36 (1900): 32–39.

———. "Mensch." *PRE*[3], XII, 624.

———. "Polytheismus." *PRE*[3], XV, 538ff.

———. "Schöpfung." *PRE*[2], XIII, 647.

———. "Schöpfung und Erhaltung der Welt." *PRE*[3], XVII, 681–704.

———. "Spiritismus." *PRE*[3], XVIII, 654–66.

Select Scripture Index

Ed. note: The Scripture index follows the pattern of the Dutch original, indicating only those passages that receive more or less detailed attention. The key Scripture texts for all four volumes of the *Gereformeerde Dogmatiek* appear at the conclusion of volume 4.

NAME INDEX

SUBJECT INDEX